LIABILITY IN MEDICINE AND PUBLIC HEALTH

By

Marcia M. Boumil, MA, MS, JD, LL.M.
Assistant Professor of Family Medicine and Community Health
Tufts University School of Medicine

David J. Sharpe, LL.B, LL.D
Professor Emeritus
George Washington University School of Law

AMERICAN CASEBOOK SERIES®

Mat # 40193765

COPYRIGHT © 2000 By WEST GROUP
© 2004 West, a Thomson business
        610 Opperman Drive
        P.O. Box 64526
        St. Paul, MN 55164–0526
        1–800–328–9352

ISBN 0–314–15077–3

TEXT IS PRINTED ON 10% POST CONSUMER RECYCLED PAPER

Preface

In 1991 the editors, with two colleagues, created a specialized casebook that they called *Medical Liability.* It was designed to support courses on medical malpractice taught by specialists in the field. Many teachers would be practicing lawyers bringing their trial expertise to the academic arena. The casebook supplemented the teachers' practical experience by providing up-to-date cases from every region of the United States. This new casebook, *Liability in Medicine and Public Health,* keeps the foundation and expands the coverage.

Part I, *Liability in Medicine,* retains the format and topics of *Medical Liability,* but more than 80% of the cases represent twenty-first century law. Part I maintains the practice orientation as it looks at medical liability through the eyes of litigators and clients rather than administrators and planners. As educators the editors are not oriented toward plaintiffs or defendants; rather the editors seek to demonstrate the interplay of the primary contenders, as the United States law of medical liability has evolved over the past 50 or more years.

Part II, *Public Health,* adds new materials to support public health law courses, whether in law schools, schools of public health, or other professional degree programs. Part II changes the orientation, from compensation and private law to compliance and public law. In most of the public health cases one antagonist is a city, municipality or governmental official, and the target of litigation is an ordinance, regulation or private nuisance. The cases show the competing concepts of judicial activism and restraint in the development of public health law.

For courses that offer a broad scope of health law, Part I contains traditional medical liability materials, including cases on ERISA and quality control regulation, and Part II contains materials on reproductive health, end-of-life issues, domestic violence, infectious disease, and public safety.

The editors caution users not to quote the casebook in place of actual law reports. Brackets indicate omitted citations. The editors have taken some liberties with editing the cases so as to enhance readability without altering meaning.

MARCIA M. BOUMIL
ANDOVER, MASSACHUSETTS

DAVID J. SHARPE
CLAVERACK, NEW YORK

*

Introduction to Liability in Medicine

In 1994 a landmark research effort, the Harvard Medical Practice Study (Leape, 1994), documented the large number of "adverse medical events" suffered by hospital patients. Error was documented throughout all areas of medical practice, with the largest number of errors resulting from drug complications. The Harvard Study suggested that 2.9% of hospitalizations resulted in an adverse event attributable to erroneous medical management. Nearly a decade later the Institute of Medicine issued its own alarming report, *"To Err is Human,"* which publicized the issue and unsettled the medical community. The IOM report suggested that as many as 98,000 preventable deaths per year are due to medical mishaps. Further, since most health care takes place in outpatient settings, it is reasonable to assume that the problem is substantially larger. Significant progress in eliminating the systemic issues that result in errors has been painfully slow.

Though neither the medical nor legal communities deny the gravity of the problem, they differ dramatically on proposed solutions. Most lawyers believe that the current liability system is necessary to keep physicians accountable for the quality of their practices. Under this theory, a system that divorces error from liability creates a disincentive for physicians to observe the highest standards of practice. Many physicians, on the other hand, believe that the key to resolving the problem of error in medicine is to implement an improved data collection system that documents mishaps and allows physicians to learn from their mistakes. They believe that fear of medical liability has hindered the reporting process and thus the ability to learn from errors. Their solution is to develop ways of unhinging medical liability from the reporting of adverse medical events. Only then can there be meaningful progress in reducing the error rate. They point to the dramatic improvement that other industries—most notably the airlines industry—have managed to achieve by implementing a confidential reporting system for "near misses" to benefit from mistakes.

Part One of this casebook focuses on medical liability. It addresses legal issues and theories, defenses, immunities and harms. It also addresses quality control and efforts toward malpractice reform. For the most part these are matters that few physicians and practicing lawyers will agree upon. Indeed, the terminology itself is a matter of contention: a physician would look at this material and see medical error, while a lawyer would see the same material and consider it medical malpractice. Is this merely a matter of semantics, or do the two professions genuinely disagree on the fundamental nature of medical liability? In medicine, an honest mistake still can be medical malpractice notwithstanding the good intentions of the physician.

Part Two of this casebook focuses on public health. It is noteworthy that these two subjects are contained under the same cover. In 2004, medical error was documented as the 8th leading cause of death in the United States. Clearly the sheer numbers of medical mistakes make it a matter of grave public health concern. Both medical error and medical liability truly result in issues affecting the health of the public, and it is good to see this matter finally cast as a serious public health issue.

A further complicating factor is the escalating medical malpractice insurance crisis, with premiums for some physicians in excess of $200,000 per year. Once again, physicians and lawyers disagree as to the cause of the crisis. Many physicians believe that fear of malpractice lawsuits leads to the practice of so-called defensive medicine, which increases the cost of medical care. Additionally, it is intuitive that large malpractice judgments would increase the cost of medical practice, as physicians pass on the costs of exorbitant insurance premiums. Malpractice lawyers point out, however, that empirical data suggest that less than one per cent of total health care costs are directly attributable to malpractice judgments.

Nevertheless, reports of doctors leaving practice in states where insurance premiums have risen dramatically fill the newspapers. The public is rightfully concerned about access to needed care, as the supply of crucial primary care physicians and specialists dwindles. Although many states have tried to deal with the perceived medical liability crisis by reforming the tort system, the real issue—eliminating the errors that result in liability claims—remains largely untouched. Though several states have mandatory reporting of medical errors, physicians and lawyers agree that fear of provoking claims undermines the reporting of adverse events.

There are no obvious solutions to the problems of medical error in the United States or around the world. The incidence of malpractice and the collateral issues of exorbitant insurance premiums and scarcity of affordable care make medical error a true public health crisis. It is not entirely clear whether a meaningful reduction in errors can be achieved through various proposed tort reform measures, or whether a fault-based system is needed to maintain accountability. Compensation to victims must also be addressed. The purpose of this text is to train students of the law and other graduate disciplines to function within the parameters of the present legal system and at the same time search for strategies to improve the quality of health care delivery.

HARRIS A. BERMAN, M.D., DEAN
PUBLIC HEALTH AND PROFESSIONAL DEGREE PROGRAMS.
TUFTS UNIVERSITY SCHOOL OF MEDICINE, BOSTON

Summary of Contents

Table of Contents

Table of Cases

The principal cases are in bold type. Cases cited or discussed in the text are roman type. References are to pages. Cases cited in principal cases and within other quoted materials are not included.

LIABILITY IN MEDICINE AND PUBLIC HEALTH

*

Part I

LIABILITY IN MEDICINE

———

Chapter 1

THE MEDICAL PROFESSIONAL RELATIONSHIP

INTRODUCTORY NOTE

A fundamental principle of tort law is that a defendant is not responsible for harm to a plaintiff in the absence of a relationship that establishes a duty to the plaintiff. A body of case law has developed challenging the existence and scope of physicians' professional duties to their patients, and sometimes to non-patients. The courts begin that inquiry by determining whether a medical professional relationship existed in law, and if so, whether the physician's action, or inaction, constituted a breach of that duty.

When a physician promises to use best efforts to perform medical services, and when a patient promises to pay for the services, the parties have created a medical professional relationship. When medical error occurs, and the patient elects to sue, usually the theory of claim is not breach of the medical professional relationship, but instead "malpractice," where "mal" means "bad," and "practice" means "work." While damages for breach of a personal service contract ordinarily would not include non-pecuniary elements, such as pain and suffering and loss of enjoyment, malpractice as a tort permits the plaintiff to recover for a long list of non-pecuniary damages. Nevertheless, unless and until the plaintiff establishes that a professional relationship existed, there is no claim.

Even a decade ago, establishment of the physician/patient relationship was a less complex issue. Patients and physicians came together face-to-face, and each had a clear role in the professional relationship. Issues developed concerning the role of attending physicians overseeing the practice of physicians in various stages of training, but each party usually understood who was providing treatment. In the next decade— the age of telecommunication—those roles may be less clear: a physician in New York City may be assisting in the care of a patient in New Zealand. The law is struggling to keep pace with the technology, and the next edition of this casebook expects to tell the tale of a new era in physician/patient relationships.

The sections of this chapter deal with (a) whether and when the professional relationship commenced, (b) if and how emergency circumstances displace the traditional rules of physician/patient obligations, (c) circumstances that create a professional relationship with persons other than the plaintiff and (d) terminating the professional relationship.

SECTION A. COMMENCEMENT OF THE PROFESSIONAL RELATIONSHIP

OLIVER v. BROCK

Supreme Court of Alabama, 1976.
342 So.2d 1.

SHORES, J.

Anita Oliver, through her mother, Cathy Oliver, brought suit against Bryan Whitfield Memorial Hospital of Demopolis, Dr. F. S. Whitfield, Dr. Paul Ketcham and Dr. E. C. Brock, alleging that the plaintiffs had retained Drs. Whitfield, Ketcham and Brock to treat her for injuries received as a result of an automobile accident. The allegations are that " ... the Defendant, Ernest C. Brock, was consulted by the Defendants, F. S. Whitfield, and Paul Ketcham, as to the diagnosis of the Plaintiff's injury, course of care and treatment to the Plaintiff, and the Defendant, Ernest C. Brock, responded by providing technical medical information to the Defendants, F. S. Whitfield and Paul Ketcham, for the diagnosis, care and treatment of the Plaintiff, Anita Oliver."

The trial court granted Dr. Brock's motion for summary judgment and the plaintiffs appealed.

The motion for summary judgment was supported by three affidavits, Dr. Brock's own and that of Drs. Whitfield and Ketcham.

Dr. Brock's affidavit stated:

"I am Ernest C. Brock, one of the Defendants in the above styled cause; I practice medicine in Tuscaloosa County, Alabama, and have been practicing medicine in Tuscaloosa for several years. I have never seen or talked to Anita Oliver or Cathy Oliver; I have never had Anita Oliver and Cathy Oliver as a patient. I have never been engaged or requested to serve as a consultant in the treatment of Anita Oliver, I was not employed or engaged to consult with the doctors treating Anita Oliver concerning her complaints or medical problems.

"I have never had Anita Oliver as a patient of mine; there has never been the doctor-patient relationship between Anita Oliver and myself; I have never been employed by the parents or guardians of Anita Oliver to treat, diagnose, or assist in any way in the care and treatment of Anita Oliver.

"I have never been employed, or associated by Dr. F. S. Whitfield or Dr. Paul Ketcham of Demopolis, Alabama, to consult with, diagnose or treat Anita Oliver.

"I know Dr. F. S. Whitfield of Demopolis and I have talked to him on the telephone on occasions in the past. During the year 1974 and the early part of 1975, Dr. Whitfield did not mention Anita Oliver's name to me on the phone and I was not employed by him to assist in the treatment of Anita Oliver, or to act as a consultant with him in the treatment of Anita Oliver.

"Anita Oliver has never been my patient, she is not now my patient, I have never been employed or requested to care for or treat Anita Oliver and I have not been employed or requested to advise anyone with regard to her medical problems."

Dr. Whitfield stated by affidavit:

"I am F. S. Whitfield, and I am one of the defendants in the above styled cause... I treated the plaintiff following an accident on or about October 1, 1974; that during the period plaintiff, Anita Oliver, was confined to the Bryan Whitfield Memorial Hospital as a patient, Affiant had the occasion to and did call Dr. Ernest C. Brock, a practicing physician in Tuscaloosa, Alabama, with reference to Dr. Brock's recommendations concerning the care and treatment of *another* patient of Affiant; that during the course of such conversation, Affiant did describe generally the injuries of plaintiff and the type of treatment Affiant was then giving plaintiff, and Dr. Brock did indicate to Affiant that under the circumstances described he thought the treatment to be correct; Affiant did not disclose to Dr. Brock the name of the patient; Affiant's discussion with Dr. Brock was gratuitous on his part and for the guidance of Affiant in connection with the treatment of plaintiff; Affiant did not employ Dr. Brock to care for or treat plaintiff and Dr. Brock did not care for or treat plaintiff to the knowledge of Affiant. In the discharge summary dictated by Affiant, Affiant did make note of the telephone conversation with Dr. Brock and of the suggestions made to Affiant by Dr. Brock but did not suggest and does not now suggest that Dr. Brock was in any way employed by him or the plaintiff in connection with the care and treatment of plaintiff or plaintiff's injuries, and the fact is that Dr. Brock was not so employed and was never employed to care for or treat plaintiff's said injuries or to advise anyone with regard thereto."

In opposition to the motion for summary judgment, the following affidavit of Cathy Oliver, mother of Anita, was offered:

"That I am the Plaintiff in the law suit involving Dr. Ernest C. Brock and that I am the Plaintiff who is suing Dr. Ernest Brock as the mother of Anita Oliver * * * While my daughter was a patient at that hospital, I became concerned regarding the care and treatment rendered or done by Dr. Whitfield and Dr. Ketcham. Dr. Whitfield told me that he would call Dr. Brock in Tuscaloosa to get some advise [sic] on how to treat my daughter's injuries. Dr. Whitfield later told me that he had talked with Dr. Brock and that Dr. Brock told him that Dr. Whitfield was treating the injuries correctly and told him to continue the same treatment.

The question before us is whether, based upon the supporting affidavits, Dr. Brock has carried the burden placed upon a movant for summary judgment to demonstrate that there is no genuine issue of material fact and that he is entitled to prevail on the motion as a matter of law * * *.

A physician owes his patient the duty of due care in his treatment of that patient. That is not controverted. The question is whether there is any evidence to suggest that a physician-patient relationship was ever created between Dr. Brock and the plaintiff patient. The general rule is stated in 61 Am.Jur.2d, Physicians, Surgeons, and Other Healers, § 96:

> "A physician is under no obligation to engage in practice or to accept professional employment, . . . the relation of physician and patient is created. The relation is a consensual one wherein the patient knowingly seeks the assistance of a physician and the physician knowingly accepts him as a patient. The relationship between a physician and patient may result from an express or implied contract, either general or special, and the rights and liabilities of the parties thereto are governed by the general law of contract . . . However, the voluntary acceptance of the physician-patient relationship by the affected parties creates a prima facie presumption of a contractual relationship between them. A physician may accept a patient and thereby incur the consequent duties although his services are performed gratuitously or at the solicitation and on the guaranty of a third person. . . . "

In the instant case Dr. Brock says that he has never seen Anita Oliver as a patient, or otherwise. He has never been engaged or requested to serve as a consultant in the treatment of Anita Oliver either by her parents or the doctors treating her. Dr. Ketcham concurs in this statement and Dr. Whitfield says that he called Dr. Brock on the telephone about *another* of his patients and, during the course of conversation, described generally the injuries suffered by Anita and the type treatment he was administering to her. Dr. Whitfield at no time disclosed to Dr. Brock his patient's name, the conversation was completely gratuitous on his part, and he did not attempt to employ Dr. Brock to care for or treat the patient. He did not suggest that Dr. Brock was in any way requested to advise anyone with respect to the treatment being given the plaintiff.

* * *

We fail to see any evidence from which it could be concluded that Dr. Brock has consented to treat the child, or any from which it could be inferred that he consented to act in a consulting capacity * * *.

Mrs. Oliver states in her affidavit that she "sincerely believes" that Dr. Brock took part in the treatment of her daughter. However, it has been held that belief, no matter how sincere, is not equivalent to knowledge that a statement in an affidavit that the affiant verily believes does not satisfy the requirements of Rule 56(e) * * * Apart from her belief that Dr. Brock took part in the treatment of her daughter, Mrs.

Oliver offers only the hearsay statements of Dr. Whitfield, who told her that Dr. Brock told him that he was treating the child correctly * * *

There is nothing in this record to support the allegation that Dr. Brock took any part in the treatment of Anita Oliver, by way of advising her physicians, or otherwise. The judgment of the trial court in granting motion for summary judgment on his behalf is, therefore, affirmed.

AFFIRMED.

PROSISE v. FOSTER

Supreme Court of Virginia, 2001.
261 Va. 417, 544 S.E.2d 331.

ELIZABETH B. LACY, J.

The issue in this case is whether an on-call attending physician for a teaching hospital owed a duty of care to a patient based upon a physician-patient relationship in the absence of direct contact with or consultation concerning the patient.

Dr. Robin L. Foster was the attending physician for the Medical College of Virginia Hospitals Pediatric Emergency Room (MCVPER) from noon on March 27 through 8:00 a.m. on March 28, 1994. She was physically present at the MCVPER until 5:00 p.m., March 27, and was "on call" from then until 8:00 a.m. on March 28. As an on-call attending physician, Dr. Foster was not physically present in the emergency room, but she was available to answer any questions from the treating residents and interns.

Florence A. Prosise took her four-year-old daughter, Crystal, to the MCVPER in the early evening of March 27, 1994. Crystal had chicken pox lesions in her mouth, was lethargic, and was not eating or drinking. The first physician to see Crystal in the emergency room was Dr. Omprakash v. Narang, a first-year resident. Prosise told Dr. Narang that Crystal had been treated for asthma with intravenous corticosteroids as an inpatient at another hospital from March 16 to March 18, 1994. Dr. Narang consulted Dr. Valerie Curry, a third-year resident, regarding Crystal's condition and prior treatment. Dr. Curry examined Crystal but did not read Crystal's chart or otherwise learn that Crystal had been treated with corticosteroids. Neither Dr. Curry nor Dr. Narang called Dr. Foster regarding Crystal's condition or treatment. Crystal was treated for dehydration and released early the next morning, March 28, 1994, with instructions to see her pediatrician the next day.

When Prosise took Crystal to her pediatrician on March 29, Crystal was immediately transported back to the MCVPER because of a grave respiratory condition. At the MCVPER, Crystal was seen for the first time by Dr. Foster. Dr. Foster concluded that Crystal was suffering from "Varicella Infection S/P immunosuppresion asthma R/O Pneumonitis," a condition in which the chicken pox virus affects the body's entire system rather than just the skin. Dr. Foster placed Crystal on an anti-viral medication administered intravenously. The treatment was unsuccessful, and Crystal died as a result of the infection on April 22, 1994.

Prosise, as administrator of the estate of Crystal Nicole Prosise, filed a medical malpractice and wrongful death action against Dr. Foster and MCV Associated Physicians. Prosise alleged that Dr. Foster, as the on-call attending physician for the MCVPER on March 27 and 28, 1994, had a duty to supervise and was responsible for the medical care rendered by the residents working at the MCVPER during that time. The motion for judgment claimed that Dr. Foster and her alleged employer, MCV Associated Physicians, were "vicariously liable and legally responsible for the acts and omissions of, and negligence of" Dr. Narang and Dr. Curry, which resulted in the death of Crystal.

Dr. Foster and MCV Associated Physicians filed a motion for summary judgment asserting that there was no physician-patient relationship between Crystal and the defendants, and, "therefore, the defendants owed no duty of care to" Crystal * * *. Following oral argument, the trial court entered judgment in favor of Dr. Foster and MCV Associated Physicians, finding that there was no "minimum contact" between Dr. Foster and Crystal and, therefore, no physician-patient relationship existed. We awarded Prosise an appeal from this judgment.

In Lee [v. Bourgeois, 477 S.E.2d 495 (1996)], an attending physician in a state university hospital was sued for medical malpractice in the treatment rendered to a patient by residents in the hospital. The issue in the case was whether the attending physician was entitled to sovereign immunity. We concluded that under the circumstances presented, teaching was not the primary function of the attending physician. Rather, the attending physician's primary function was directly related to assuring the proper care of the patient, regardless of whether the care was delivered by the attending physician or through the residents. [citation omitted]. This patient care function involved only a slight degree of state interest and involvement, and, therefore, * * * the attending physician was not entitled to sovereign immunity. [citation omitted].

The liability of an attending physician at a teaching hospital was not at issue in Lee. Thus, we did not consider in Lee whether a duty of care existed between the attending physician and the patient, and, therefore, that case is not applicable to the issue presented here. * * *

We also reject Prosise's suggestion that Code § 54.1–2961(B) imposes a duty of care on an on-call attending physician in a teaching hospital because the statute requires that interns and residents "be responsible and accountable at all times to a licensed member" of the hospital staff. Although we discussed that statutory provision in Lee with regard to the question of sovereign immunity, [ ], we did not consider whether its requirements imposed a duty of care. We engage in that analysis now.

Code § 54.1–2961 is found within a series of provisions defining conditions under which medical students, interns, and residents may work in or be employed by a hospital. Medical students may work in hospitals only under the "direct tutorial supervision of a licensed physician who holds an appointment on the faculty" of a medical school. Code § 54.1–2959. Third and fourth year medical students may be employed by hospitals to perform certain examinations and to take medical histories, but the attending physician retains the responsibility to assure "that a licensed physician [completes] a history and physical examination on each hospitalized patient." Code § 54.1–2960. Finally, interns and residents employed by hospitals while part of an approved internship or residency program are "responsible and accountable" to licensed staff members but are not subject to further restrictions under Code § 54.1–2961(B).

We cannot conclude that the General Assembly, in merely listing the conditions under which medical students, interns, and residents may work in a hospital during the course of their educational programs, intended to create a statutory physician-patient relationship between an on-call attending physician in a teaching hospital and a patient that would give rise to a duty of care. Thus, we reject Prosise's argument that, under Lee and Code § 54.1–2961, a physician-patient relationship existed between Dr. Foster and Crystal because Dr. Foster, as the on-call attending physician, "accepted" Crystal as a patient when she came to the MCVPER the evening of March 27, 1994.

Finally, Prosise urges us to follow the North Carolina Supreme Court and impose a common law duty on Dr. Foster, arguing that such duty is necessary to ensure appropriate supervision of residents and interns by attending physicians. In Mozingo v. Pitt County Memorial Hospital, Inc., 331 N.C. 182, 415 S.E.2d 341 (N.C. 1992), the North Carolina Supreme Court held that an on-call attending physician had a common law duty to supervise residents who provided medical care to patients, even though the relationship "did not fit traditional notions of the doctor-patient relationship," because of the "increasingly complex modern delivery of health care." Mozingo, 415 S.E.2d at 344–45.

Dr. Foster and MCV Associated Physicians ask us to reject the rationale of Mozingo, as they assert that the Maryland Court of Special Appeals did in Rivera v. Prince George's County Health Dept., 102 Md.App. 456, 649 A.2d 1212 (Md. Ct. Spec. App. 1994), cert. denied, 338 Md. 117, 656 A.2d 772 (Md. 1995). The Maryland court stated that it would impose no duty on an on-call attending physician in the absence of proof that the doctor had accepted the patient, had consulted with a physician about the patient, or had been summoned for consultation or treatment, "unless the 'on call' agreement between a hospital and a physician provides otherwise." Rivera, 649 A.2d at 1232. Thus, although the court acknowledged that direct treatment of a patient was not necessary to give rise to a duty of care, the court required that the evidence show that an on-call attending physician in a teaching hospital accepted responsibility for the patient's treatment in some way. We agree with the Maryland court's analysis in Rivera * * *

Accordingly, to resolve this case, we look to the record to determine whether it contains any facts which indicate that Dr. Foster, by virtue of her actions or her status as the on-call attending physician for the MCVPER, agreed to accept responsibility for the care of Crystal. Clearly, Dr. Foster's direct actions do not indicate that she accepted Crystal as a patient prior to March 29. She did not treat Crystal, she did not participate in any treatment decisions regarding Crystal, and she was not consulted by Dr. Curry, Dr. Narang, or any other hospital staff regarding Crystal's condition.

Similarly, the record in this case does not support a finding that, by agreeing to act as an on-call attending physician in a teaching hospital, Dr. Foster accepted responsibility for Crystal's care. The record contains no information about the duties of attending physicians, whether on-call or otherwise, and there is no evidence of the hospital's policy regarding attending physicians. Cf., e.g., Lee v. Bourgeois, 252 Va. at 333, 477 S.E.2d at 498 (hospital policy that all patients be assigned an attending physician). The only evidence the record contains in this regard are statements from Dr. Curry that she assumed attending physicians had to review all patient charts and from Dr. Narang that he understood attending physicians were "ultimately responsible." Furthermore, Dr. Foster's employment contract, which is in the record, makes no reference to her duties as an attending physician. Thus, on this record, there is no basis to support a finding that Dr. Foster, directly, by contract, or by hospital policy, assumed responsibility for the care of Crystal.

Accordingly, for the above reasons, we conclude that the trial court did not err in holding that there was no physician-patient relationship between Dr. Foster and Crystal because the evidence failed to show a consensual relationship in which the patient's care was entrusted to the physician and the physician accepted the case.

Affirmed.

Notes

1) What are the reasonable expectations of a patient who receives treatment in an emergency room concerning supervision of the treating physician?

2) Does it matter if it is a teaching hospital?

3) What is the obligation of the hospital itself to provide oversight for physicians in training programs? See *infra* at Chapter 3, sections A and B for cases and discussion on that issue.

SECTION B.   EMERGENCY CIRCUMSTANCES

BRYANT v. ADVENTIST–REDBUD HOSPITAL, INC.

United States Court of Appeals for the Ninth Circuit, 2002.
289 F.3d 1162.

PAEZ, Circuit Judge:

Plaintiffs, the heirs of minor decedent David Bryant ("David"), brought this wrongful death action against Redbud Community Hospital

("Redbud") for damages and injunctive relief for, among other things, violation of the Emergency Medical Treatment and Active Labor Act ("EMTALA"), 42 U.S.C. § 1395dd, commonly known as the "Patient Anti–Dumping Act." Plaintiffs alleged that when David sought care from Redbud's emergency room, the emergency room staff failed to detect his emergency medical condition and then discharged him without stabilizing his condition, in violation of EMTALA's stabilization requirement. Plaintiffs further alleged that after David returned to the emergency room the next day and was admitted to the hospital for inpatient care, Redbud again violated EMTALA's stabilization requirement by failing to stabilize his condition during the three days after it admitted him for treatment.

I. Factual and Procedural History

David was a 17–year–old boy who was severely disabled and had the mental capacity of a young child. He was unable to communicate with anyone other than close relatives. He had a history of asthma, bronchitis, and pneumonia. On the evening of January 24, 1997, David, accompanied by his mother and other family members, went to Redbud's emergency room because he had been coughing up blood and had a fever. After examining David, a nurse classified his condition as "urgent."

Soon thereafter, Dr. Robert Rosenthal examined David. David's mother told Dr. Rosenthal that her son had suffered from a fever for approximately four days and appeared to be experiencing pain in the right side of his chest. Dr. Rosenthal noticed that David was coughing up yellow phlegm, had a mild fever, and was wheezing. Dr. Rosenthal ordered a chest x-ray and blood tests. He failed to detect on the x-ray a large lung abscess, which Defendants concede constituted an emergency medical condition, and diagnosed David with only pneumonia and asthma. Dr. Rosenthal then treated David with Albuterol, which assists breathing, and prescribed an antibiotic, Rocephrin, for the pneumonia. Because David was agitated, the medical staff was not able to inject the full dosage of Rocephrin. Nonetheless, the medical staff determined that it had injected a sufficient amount of the antibiotic to stabilize his pneumonia. Because David's condition appeared stable and because Dr. Rosenthal and David's family agreed that David would be more relaxed at home, Dr. Rosenthal discharged him. Dr. Rosenthal, however, requested that the family return with David the following day for further diagnosis and treatment. David and his family left the hospital at approximately 2:30 a.m. on January 25.

In the afternoon of January 25, as David and his family were preparing to leave for the hospital, a hospital employee called and told them to return immediately because Dr. Richard Furtado had determined from David's chest x-ray that he had a lung abscess. Dr. Furtado considered the abscess to be a "problem worthy of admission." Shortly after David's arrival at the emergency room, Dr. Furtado admitted David to the hospital, and he was transferred from the emergency room to a medical/surgical room.

By January 28, David's condition had declined rapidly, and the doctor responsible for his care decided to transfer him to the Intensive Care Unit. Because there were no beds available in the Intensive Care Unit, David was transferred to U.C. Davis Medical Center, where he eventually had surgery. Plaintiffs do not contend that this emergency transfer to the Center was improper or a violation of EMTALA. On February 20, David was released from U.C. Davis and returned home. Although David appeared to be improving, he died suddenly and unexpectedly on March 1, 1997.

Plaintiffs filed this action in district court against Redbud Community Healthcare District; Adventist Health System/ West, Inc.; Janzen, Johnston & Rockwell Emergency Medical Group of California; and several of the treating physicians. The amended complaint alleged violations of EMTALA, violation of a similar state law (California Health & Safety Code § 1317), and negligence. * * *

III. DISCUSSION

A. *EMTALA*

Congress enacted EMTALA to ensure that individuals, regardless of their ability to pay, receive adequate emergency medical care. *Jackson v. E. Bay Hosp.*, 246 F.3d 1248, 1254 (9th Cir. 2001). "Congress was concerned that hospitals were 'dumping' patients who were unable to pay, by either refusing to provide emergency medical treatment or transferring patients before their conditions were stabilized." *Eberhardt v. City of Los Angeles*, 62 F.3d 1253, 1255 (9th Cir. 1995). EMTALA protects all individuals, not just those who are uninsured or indigent. *Arrington v. Wong*, 237 F.3d 1066, 1069–70 (9th Cir. 2001).

If an individual seeks emergency care from a hospital with an emergency room and if that hospital participates in the Medicare program, then "the hospital must provide for an appropriate medical screening examination within the capability of the hospital's emergency department ... to determine whether or not an emergency medical condition ... exists." 42 U.S.C. § 1395dd(a); *Eberhardt*, 62 F.3d at 1255–56. If the hospital's medical staff determines that there is an emergency medical condition, then, except under certain circumstances not relevant here, the staff must "stabilize" the patient before transferring or discharging the patient. 42 U.S.C. § 1395dd(b)(1); *Baker v. Adventist Health, Inc.*, 260 F.3d 987, 992 (9th Cir. 2001). The term "to stabilize" means "to provide such medical treatment of the condition as may be necessary to assure, within reasonable medical probability, that no material deterioration of the condition is likely to result from or occur during the transfer of the individual from a facility[.]" 42 U.S.C. § 1395dd(e)(3)(A). Transfer includes both discharge and movement to another facility. *Id.* § 1395dd(e)(4).

B. *The January 24–25 Emergency Room Visit*

Plaintiffs concede that Redbud's staff performed an appropriate medical screening on January 24 but argue that the hospital violated

EMTALA by failing to stabilize David's lung abscess condition. Plaintiffs contend that § 1395dd(b)(1) should be read to include a reasonableness standard in determining whether a hospital has detected an emergency medical condition. Thus, Plaintiffs argue, in effect, that a hospital should be liable under EMTALA if its staff negligently fails to detect an emergency medical condition.

EMTALA, however, was not enacted to establish a federal medical malpractice cause of action nor to establish a national standard of care. *Baker*, 260 F.3d at 993 * * * Thus, we have held that a hospital has a duty to stabilize only those emergency medical conditions that its staff detects. *Jackson*, 246 F.3d at 1254–55 * * * Every circuit to address this issue is in accord. [citations omitted]. To restate our ruling in *Jackson*, we hold that a hospital does not violate EMTALA if it fails to detect or if it misdiagnoses an emergency condition. *Baker*, 260 F.3d at 993–94. An individual who receives substandard medical care may pursue medical malpractice remedies under state law. *Eberhardt*, 62 F.3d at 1258.

* * *

C. The January 25–28 Hospitalization

To determine whether Defendants may be liable under EMTALA during David's three-day hospitalization at Redbud, we must decide when EMTALA's stabilization requirement ends. We hold that the stabilization requirement normally ends when a patient is admitted for inpatient care.

When David and his family returned to the emergency room in the afternoon of January 25, the hospital staff knew that David suffered from an emergency medical condition. EMTALA's stabilization provision requires a hospital, when confronted with an "emergency medical condition," to provide "(A) within the staff and facilities available at the hospital, for such further medical examination and such treatment as may be required to stabilize the medical condition, or (B) for transfer of the individual to another medical facility in accordance with [the statute]." 42 U.S.C. § 1395dd(b)(1). Although the term "stabilize" appears to reach a patient's care after the patient is admitted to a hospital for treatment, the term is defined only in connection with the transfer of an emergency room patient. *Id*. § 1395dd(e)(3)(A) ("The term 'to stabilize' means ... to provide such medical treatment of the condition as may be necessary to assure, within reasonable medical probability, that no material deterioration of the condition is likely *to result from or occur during the transfer* of the individual from a facility.... " (emphasis added)). Thus, the term "stabilize" was not intended to apply to those individuals who are admitted to a hospital for inpatient care. As the Fourth Circuit explained in *Bryan v. Rectors & Visitors of the University of Virginia*:

> The stabilization requirement is ... defined entirely in connection with a possible transfer and without any reference to the patient's long-term care within the system. It seems manifest to us that the

stabilization requirement was intended to regulate the hospital's care of the patient only in the immediate aftermath of the act of admitting her for emergency treatment and while it considered whether it would undertake longer-term full treatment or instead transfer the patient to a hospital that could and would undertake that treatment. It cannot plausibly be interpreted to regulate medical and ethical decisions outside that narrow context.

95 F.3d 349, 352 (4th Cir. 1996) * * *

In contrast to the Fourth Circuit, the Sixth Circuit has suggested that it would not so limit EMTALA's stabilization requirement, stating in dictum that a violation of EMTALA can occur even after a patient has been hospitalized for a number of days. *Thornton v. Southwest Detroit Hosp.*, 895 F.2d 1131, 1135 (6th Cir. 1990). After suffering a stroke, the patient in *Thornton* sought care at a hospital's emergency room and was subsequently admitted to the hospital. The patient spent ten days in the Intensive Care Unit and eleven days in inpatient care. The patient's doctor wanted a rehabilitation facility to admit the patient for post-stroke rehabilitation, but the facility refused because the patient's health insurance would not cover the cost. The patient was discharged from the hospital and her condition deteriorated.

The Sixth Circuit explained that, "once a patient is found to suffer from an emergency medical condition in the emergency room, she cannot be discharged until the condition is stabilized, regardless of whether the patient stays in the emergency room." *Id*. at 1134. The court held that, in the case before it, the hospital had stabilized the patient's condition and, thus, the defendant was not liable under EMTALA. *Id*. at 1135. The court stressed, however, that its conclusion was not based on the fact that the patient had been in the hospital for a "prolonged period" but on the fact that there was no genuine issue of material fact whether her condition was stable when she was released.

* * *

Thus, the Sixth Circuit explained that a violation of EMTALA could be established even after a patient is transferred from the emergency room and admitted into the hospital for treatment.

Although we recognize the concerns raised by the Sixth Circuit, we agree with the Fourth Circuit's approach in determining when EMTALA's stabilization requirement ends. We hold that EMTALA's stabilization requirement ends when an individual is admitted for inpatient care. Congress enacted EMTALA "to create a new cause of action, generally unavailable under state tort law, for what amounts to failure to treat" and not to "duplicate preexisting legal protections." *Gatewood*, 933 F.2d at 1041.

We agree with the Sixth Circuit that a hospital cannot escape liability under EMTALA by ostensibly "admitting" a patient, with no intention of treating the patient, and then discharging or transferring the patient without having met the stabilization requirement. In general, however, a hospital admits a patient to provide inpatient care. We will not assume that hospitals use the admission process as a subterfuge to circumvent the stabilization requirement of EMTALA. If a patient demonstrates in a particular case that inpatient admission was a ruse to avoid EMTALA's requirements, then liability under EMTALA may attach. But this is not such a case.

AFFIRMED

ARRINGTON v. WONG

United States Court of Appeals for the Ninth Circuit, 2001.
237 F.3d 1066.

REINHARDT, Circuit Judge:

We are required on this appeal to construe the language of the Emergency Medical Treatment and Active Labor Act of 1986 (EMTALA), 42 U.S.C. § 1395dd, as implemented by 42 C.F.R. § 489.24. EMTALA prevents transfers, without stabilizing treatment, of patients who "come to" a hospital' emergency room. The complaint alleges that: (1) decedent Harold E. Arrington suffered a heart attack on his way to work; (2) in the ambulance, on the way to the Queen's Medical Center (Queen's hospital), the emergency personnel radioed ahead to advise the hospital's emergency room of their imminent arrival; (3) Dr. Norbert Wong, the emergency room doctor on duty, redirected the ambulance to a different hospital five miles away from Queen's; and (4) Mr. Arrington died soon after arrival at the more distant hospital. The issue before us is whether the plaintiffs have stated a claim under EMTALA on the basis of the defendants' failure to provide emergency treatment to Mr. Arrington.

I. BACKGROUND

On May 5, 1996, at approximately 11:30 p.m., Harold Arrington (Arrington) was driving to his job as a security guard when he experienced difficulty breathing. One of his co-workers called for an ambulance; it arrived shortly after midnight. The ambulance left the scene at 12:24 a.m. to take Arrington to the closest medical facility, the Queen's Medical Center (Queen's hospital).

Dr. Norbert Wong was the emergency room physician on duty at Queen's hospital. While under way, the ambulance personnel contacted the hospital emergency room by radio. They relayed the details of Arrington's medical condition to Dr. Wong. Arrington was "in severe respiratory distress speaking 1–2 words at a time and ... breathing about 50 times a minute." Dr. Wong asked the ambulance personnel who was the patient's doctor. The ambulance personnel replied "patient is a Tripler [Army Medical Center] patient, being that he was in severe respiratory distress we thought we'd come to a close facility." Dr. Wong responded: "I think it would be okay to go to Tripler." The ambulance personnel took this as a directive and changed their route so as to proceed to the more distant hospital. By the time the ambulance arrived at Tripler it was 12:40 a.m. and Arrington's condition had deteriorated. He was pronounced dead at 1:17 a.m.

* * *

III. ANALYSIS

* * * Under EMTALA, for those hospitals with an emergency department: "if any individual . . . comes to the emergency department and a request is made on the individual's behalf for examination or treatment for a medical condition, the hospital must provide for an appropriate medical screening examination within the capability of the hospital's emergency department." 42 U.S.C. § 1395dd(a) (emphasis added). If, after screening, the hospital determines that an emergency medical condition exists, the hospital generally may not transfer the patient without stabilizing his condition. Id. § 1395dd(b)(1)(A). In the case before us, the question we must decide is whether Arrington's attempt to reach the hospital falls within the scope of EMTALA's "comes to" language.

* * *

In the instant case, appellees urge in their briefs that the phrase "comes to the emergency department" in § 1395dd(a) plainly and unambiguously means "arrives at a hospital." At oral argument, they again acknowledged that the provision at issue encompasses the entire hospital and its grounds, not just the "emergency department." Appellants, however, interpret the phrase to include the act of traveling to the hospital. Webster's Third New International Dictionary supports both definitions. It defines "comes to" as, among other things, to "move toward or away from something . . . APPROACH," or "to arrive at a particular place." Webster's Third New International Dictionary of the English Language Unabridged, 453 (Philip Babcock Gove, ed. 1986). Purely as a matter of dictionary definition, comes to the emergency department could mean either physical arrival at the emergency room or the act of traveling from the scene of an emergency to or towards the hospital. Thus, all agree that the statutory provision may not simply be applied: rather it must be construed by an appropriate body.

The Department of Health and Human Services has taken an expansive approach to the scope of the phrase "comes to the emergency department." See 42 C.F.R. § 489.24. The Department interprets that statutory phrase broadly, to include not just the emergency room itself, but all hospital property—sidewalks, outlying facilities, and ambulances—so that once a patient seeking medical treatment presents himself at any facility or vehicle owned or operated by the hospital, he has "come to" the emergency department. See id. Under this provision of the regulation, individuals in non-hospital-owned ambulances have unquestionably "come to the hospital" when that ambulance is itself on hospital property. Id.

The remaining problem—the problem presented by Arrington's case—is whether hospitals must admit emergency patients who are being transported to the hospital in non-hospital owned ambulances. Specifically, may the hospital's emergency room personnel refuse to treat such patients and divert them to other hospitals when the emergency room is called by paramedics or other ambulance attendants and notified that the patient is en route to the hospital. The regulation answers this question as well. It provides that if ambulance personnel contact the hospital to "inform[ ] the hospital that they want to transport the individual to the hospital for examination and treatment," the hospital may not deny the individual access unless it "is in 'diversionary status,' that is, it does not have the staff or facilities to accept any additional emergency patients." Id. In other words, a hospital may not prevent a non-hospital-owned ambulance from coming to the hospital unless it has a valid treatment-related reason for doing so. Moreover, even if the hospital is in diversionary status, where the ambulance continues to the hospital in spite of an instruction to take the patient elsewhere, that ambulance "comes to" the hospital, and emergency treatment of the patient must be provided. Id.

In the instant case, Arrington was in a non-hospital-owned ambulance that was en route to Queen's hospital, and the ambulance personnel contacted the hospital's emergency room on his behalf and requested treatment. By the plain language of the agency's rules, the hospital was obliged to treat Arrington unless the hospital was in "diversionary status," or, in other words, lacked "the staff or facilities to accept any additional emergency patients at the time "it was contacted. 42 C.F.R. § 489.24. Here, Queen's hospital has not contended that it was in "diversionary status" at the time Dr. Wong directed Arrington away from Queen's hospital and to the more distant Tripler facility. To be in compliance with EMTALA regulations, Queen's hospital would have to show that there were insufficient emergency staff available to treat Arrington at the time the ambulance personnel called the emergency room; that appropriate staff would not be available by the time Arrington arrived at the hospital; that the hospital did not have the proper equipment with which to treat Arrington's medical condition; or that the appropriate equipment was unavailable (because in use, out of order, etc.). Finally, Queen's hospital would have to demonstrate that Dr. Wong knew that there were inadequate staff or facilities available, and that he based his decision to redirect Arrington to Tripler on a treatment-related reason, rather than on some other unrelated factor.

REVERSED

HARRY v. MARCHANT

United States Court of Appeals for the Eleventh Circuit, 2002.
291 F.3d 767.

BLACK, Circuit Judge:

This case involves the Emergency Medical Treatment and Active Labor Act (EMTALA), 42 U.S.C. § 1395dd. EMTALA was enacted to prevent "patient dumping," the publicized practice of some hospitals turning away or transferring indigent patients without evaluation or treatment. Under EMTALA, when an individual presents for treatment at the emergency department of a hospital, the hospital must provide an appropriate medical screening to determine whether an emergency medical condition exists. If an emergency medical condition is determined to exist, the hospital ordinarily must provide stabilization treatment before transferring the patient. The issue before this Court is whether EMTALA imposes a federal statutory obligation on a hospital to provide stabilization treatment to a patient with an emergency medical condition who is not transferred. We hold no such duty exists under EMTALA.

I. BACKGROUND

A. Factual Background

* * * At approximately 1:17 a.m. on November 26, 1997, Miami–Dade Fire Rescue brought Lisa Normil to the emergency room at Aventura Hospital and Medical Center (Aventura Hospital) and requested medical treatment on her behalf. Normil was seen first by Dr. Wayne Marchant, an emergency room physician, whose notes indicated a diagnosis of "pneumonia rule out sepsis."

Dr. Marchant contacted Dr. Kevin Coy, who was acting as the on-call attending physician on behalf of Normil's primary care provider, to report his diagnosis and to request permission to admit Normil into the intensive care unit (ICU) of the hospital for concentrated care and management. Dr. Coy refused to authorize admission into the ICU and instead directed Dr. Marchant to obtain a ventilation perfusion scan (VQ Scan). Dr. Marchant advised Dr. Coy a VQ Scan could not be performed because the hospital had insufficient isotopes to conduct the scan. Despite the unavailability of a VQ Scan, Dr. Coy continued to deny authorization for Normil's admittance into the ICU.

Later that morning, Dr. Marchant was able to contact Normil's primary care physician, Dr. Ali Bazzi. Approximately five hours after he was contacted by Dr. Marchant, Dr. Bazzi examined Normil in the emergency room, reviewed her available radiological evidence, and assessed her vital signs. Following Normil's examination by Dr. Bazzi, she was admitted into the ICU at Aventura Hospital. Although Dr. Bazzi prescribed antibiotics, the ICU nurse, Polly Linker, never administered the medication.

After Normil's admittance into the ICU, she lapsed into respiratory and cardiac failure. Dr. Christopher Hanner, a physician working at the hospital, unsuccessfully attempted to resuscitate Normil. She died at approximately 12:45 p.m.

III. DISCUSSION

* * * The sole issue before this Court is the extent to which EMTALA requires a hospital to provide stabilization treatment to a patient with an emergency medical condition who is not transferred.

A. *Language of the Statute*

The stabilization requirement of EMTALA provides in relevant part:

* * * (1) In general.

If any individual (whether or not eligible for benefits under this subchapter) comes to a hospital and the hospital determines that the individual has an emergency medical condition, the hospital must provide either—

(A) within the staff and facilities available at the hospital, for such further medical examination and such treatment as may be required *to stabilize* the medical condition, or

(B) for transfer of the individual to another medical facility in accordance with subsection (c).

42 U.S.C. § 1395dd (b)(1) (1994) (emphasis added).

The term "to stabilize" is specifically defined by the statute. Under EMTALA, the term "to stabilize" means "with respect to an emergency medical condition ... [a hospital must] provide such medical treatment of the condition as may be necessary to assure, within reasonable medical probability, that no material deterioration of the condition is likely to result or occur during the transfer of the individual from a facility." 42 U.S.C. § 1395dd(e)(3)(A).

* * * Reading the statute in its specifically defined context, it is evident EMTALA mandates stabilization of an individual only in the event of a "transfer" as defined in EMTALA.

By limiting application of the stabilization requirement to patient transfers, the statutory structure of § 1395dd(b)(1) makes sense. The statute is logically structured to set forth two options for transferring a patient with an emergency medical condition: a hospital must either provide stabilization treatment prior to transferring a patient pursuant to subsection (A), or, pursuant to subsection (B), provide no treatment and transfer according to one of the statutorily recognized exceptions. Hence, the stabilization requirement *only* sets forth standards for transferring a patient in either a stabilized or unstabilized condition. By its own terms, the statute does not set forth guidelines for the care and treatment of patients who are not transferred.

C. *Cases Discussing EMTALA's Stabilization Requirement*

In the sixteen years since EMTALA's enactment, there have been relatively few cases discussing the stabilization requirement imposed by the statute. The only opportunity we have had to address EMTALA was in *Holcomb v. Monahan*, 30 F.3d 116 (11th Cir. 1994). Although we did not squarely address whether EMTALA's stabilization requirement imposes an obligation on hospitals to provide treatment to individuals outside the context of a transfer, our discussion in *Holcomb* is consistent with our conclusion here.

In *Holcomb*, a patient was discharged after a hospital provided an appropriate medical screening and determined there was no emergency medical condition. *Id.* Subsequently, the patient died and the administratix of the patient's estate brought suit claiming violations of §§ 1395dd(a) and (b). *Id.* In addressing the plaintiff's claims, we set forth the requirements that must be established to succeed on a § 1395dd(b) stabilization requirement claim: (1) the patient had an emergency medical condition; (2) the hospital knew of the condition; (3) the patient was not stabilized before being transferred; and (4) the hospital neither obtained the patient's consent to transfer nor completed a certificate indicating the transfer would be beneficial to the patient. *Id.* * * *

Like this Circuit, no other Circuit has squarely addressed whether EMTALA's stabilization requirement imposes an obligation on hospitals to provide treatment to individuals outside the context of a transfer. To date, cases from other Circuits discussing EMTALA's stabilization requirement have addressed only tangential issues arising out of an alleged failure to provide an appropriate medical screening, an alleged failure to stabilize an emergency medical condition prior to an actual transfer, or a combination thereof. We, therefore, rely solely on the clear language of the statute in reaching our conclusion.

IV. CONCLUSION

There is no duty under EMTALA to provide stabilization treatment to a patient with an emergency medical condition who is not transferred. Because Normil was not transferred, Appellant's § 1395dd(b) stabilization requirement claim fails to state a valid cause of action. In so holding, we recognize Appellant is not without recourse. Remedies provided by state malpractice and tort law remain available to redress negligent patient care by hospitals. Accordingly, the judgment of the district court is affirmed with respect to the dismissal of the EMTALA claims * * *

Notes

1) In *Coleman v. Deno*, 813 So.2d 303 (La. 2002), the Louisiana Supreme Court held it was error for the lower court to find intentional patient dumping where the patient's cause of action against the physician was based solely upon a claim of medical malpractice. The Court found that the gravamen of the plaintiff's claim was that the physician failed to properly diagnose and treat the plaintiff's condition. The court held that while claims of medical malpractice and patient dumping can overlap, here the treatment decision was inseparable from the transfer decision.

2) These cases highlight the relationship between ordinary negligence and duties imposed upon physicians under EMTALA. Why would it be advantageous for a plaintiff to successfully prove that the hospital or physician violated the provisions of EMTALA, in addition to proving ordinary negligence?

3) Hospitals can designate themselves as being on "diversionary status" when they temporarily have reached their treatment capacity and do not have the staff to treat additional patients. In *Arrington v. Wong*, the plaintiff alleged that it was a violation of EMTALA to divert a non-hospital ambulance. Can you think of circumstances in which it would be appropriate to divert an ambulance without violating the spirit of EMTALA? What if the staff were not capable of handling the type of case that was en route, even for purposes of stabilization?

SECTION C.   PROFESSIONAL SERVICES THAT HARM NON–PATIENTS

BRADSHAW v. DANIEL

Supreme Court of Tennessee, at Jackson, 1993.
854 S.W.2d 865.

[See Opinion at Text Page 86] (Chapter 2(c))

REED v. BOJARSKI

Supreme Court of New Jersey, 2001.
166 N.J. 89, 764 A.2d 433.

LONG, J.

The requirement of a physician's examination as a condition of employment, often paid for by the prospective employer, is not uncommon. This case focuses on the responsibility of a physician in such circumstances. More particularly, we are confronted with the question whether a physician, performing a pre-employment screening, who determines that the patient has a potentially serious medical condition, can omit informing the patient and delegate by contract to the referring agency the responsibility of notification * * *

I

The facts of the case are not seriously disputed: Arnold Reed was a heavy-equipment operator for the Woolston Construction Company. In 1991, Woolston entered into a contract with the I.T. Davey Corporation to perform work at a New Jersey landfill. Occupational Safety and Health Administration (OSHA) regulations required Reed to undergo a pre-employment physical. Davey contracted with Environmental Medicine Resources, Inc. (EMR) to perform the examinations for the Woolston workers. EMR, located in Georgia, subcontracted the examinations to Life Care Institute Inc. (Life Care), of Glassboro, New Jersey, an outpatient medical facility that provides various types of medical imaging services, physical therapy, and occupational medicine. Pursuant to the agreement between Davey and EMR, Reed's examination was to include, among other tests, a single, frontal X ray of the chest. The EMR–Life Care contract provided that Life Care's responsibility was to analyze the chest X ray and evaluate it either as "normal" or "abnormal." If Life Care determined that the X ray was abnormal, it was to forward it to

EMR within twenty-four hours. EMR took responsibility for "over-reads and evaluation to obtain a diagnosis."

Dr. Michael H. Bojarski, an employee of Life Care, conducted Reed's physical. Another physician employed by Life Care, D.A. DePersia, M.D., a radiologist, was responsible for reading the chest X rays and reporting to Dr. Bojarski. Upon reviewing Reed's X ray, Dr. DePersia told Dr. Bojarski that Reed had a widened mediastinum, the cavity in the center of the chest. Dr. Bojarski testified that he could not "personally" see the widened mediastinum on the X ray but relied on the expertise of Dr. DePersia. It is an accepted medical fact that, among men in their twenties, a widened mediastinum may be an indicator of lymphoma, including Hodgkin's disease. Dr. DePersia also noted that Reed's heart was unusually large, a medical condition known as cardiomegaly. Reed was apparently aware of that condition.

Dr. Bojarski sent the X ray, along with the rest of Reed's examination package, to EMR. He noted that the X ray was abnormal and wrote "cardiomeg" in the comments section. No reference to the widened mediastinum was made. Although two days later Dr. DePersia gave Dr. Bojarski a written report on Reed's X ray recommending a follow-up CT-scan, Dr. Bojarski never conveyed that suggestion or the report to EMR. Inexplicably, on May 14, 1991, Dr. Michael Barnes of EMR wrote to Reed and informed him that he was in good health. In the letter he made no mention of the widened mediastinum or any potentially dangerous condition.

About six months later, in November 1991, Reed returned to Life Care for another examination. In the interim, he had lost 25 pounds and was suffering from flu-like symptoms. Dr. Bojarski did not ask Reed whether he had ever learned of or followed up on the widened mediastinum. In December 1991, Reed was admitted to the hospital and, after a chest X ray showed a large mass in his mediastinum, he was diagnosed with Stage IIB Hodgkin's disease. Reed died eight months later on October 27, 1992, at the age of 28.

Linda Reed, executor of her husband Arnold's estate, brought suit on behalf of the estate * * *

* * * In answering Reed's counsel's questions about the obligations of a physician in the circumstances of this case, [plaintiff's treating physician] stated:

That X ray has to be pursued. That X ray has to be acted upon. If a * * * certified radiologist who is entrusted with looking at an X ray and making a medical opinion says that the mediastinum is widened, until proven otherwise, the physician who has knowledge of these results must be concerned about the possibility of malignancy, must convey that information on to the patient, and must do further testing.

During the defense case * * * defendants called Dr. George Mellendick as an expert in occupational medicine. Dr. Mellendick testified that, in an examination scheme like the one used by EMR and Life Care, the common approach is for "the data [to] be centrally collated and transmitted in a sensible way." He further testified that he understood that Dr. Barnes had the "responsibility ... to get the information and to communicate directly to the patient-employee what the findings were.... Ideally, we like one physician to collate the information and get it back to the patient."

Dr. Mellendick stated that the EMR–Life Care contract "clearly spelled out that [Life Care] would have certain responsibilities for getting data ... and forwarding anything which was abnormal." He testified that the arrangement between EMR and Life Care was "fairly standard" and that Dr. Bojarski's conduct was "reasonable" in light of the contract and typical practices in occupational medicine.

Both sides proposed jury instructions. Reed's version incorporated the traditional duties that flow from the existence of a doctor-patient relationship. Dr. Bojarski's version focused on the reasonableness of his conduct. Reed's counsel asked the Court to instruct the jury that Dr. Bojarski's duty to advise Reed is non-delegable, and that the duty exists notwithstanding the contract. The trial court agreed to instruct the jury that the contract affected only the relationship between EMR and Life Care.

The trial court properly informed the jury that a physician performing a pre-employment physical owes the examinee a duty of reasonable care in the conduct of the examination and that that duty encompasses taking reasonable steps to inform the examinee of findings that pose a danger to his health. He went on to say:

What plaintiff alleges is that upon the chest X ray having been read by Dr. DePersia, and she having discussed her finding, a possibility of a mediastinal abnormality, and suggesting CT scanning, that Dr. Bojarski breached the duty of reasonable care owed by him to the plaintiff, to inform the plaintiff directly or EMR of those X ray findings.

Dr. Bojarski, on the other hand, contends that he did act reasonably by reading the X ray, advising EMR that it was abnormal and forwarding the original X ray to EMR. Defendant Dr. Bojarski likewise alleges that EMR breached the standard of care by the letter written to Mr. Reed in light of the report of abnormal X ray mailed to EMR by Dr. Bojarski.

Now if you find that Dr. Bojarski satisfied his duty of reasonable care, and the duty to inform, then you may not find him negligent, and your verdict should be for the defendant. On the other hand, if you find Dr. Bojarski breached the duty owed by a reasonable care, including the duty to inform, your verdict should be for the plaintiff.

You must make the determination of whether Dr. Bojarski took reasonable steps to inform the plaintiff, Mr. Reed, of any findings under the facts of this case. In other words, you must determine whether it was reasonable for Dr. Bojarski to forward the materials concerning Mr.

Reed to EMR and rely upon EMR's contractual obligation to review the materials and inform Mr. Reed of any adverse findings.

If you find that it was reasonable for Dr. Bojarski to expect EMR to do that, then you may not find Dr. Bojarski negligent. On the other hand, if you find that Dr. Bojarski acted unreasonably in relying on EMR to inform the patient of findings, and in not informing EMR or the plaintiff of Dr. DePersia's findings, including her letter to him diagnosing a widened mediastinum, you must determine Dr. Bojarski's conduct to have been negligent.

The following day, the jury unanimously determined that Dr. Bojarski had not deviated from accepted standards of medical care. Judgment was entered accordingly. Reed's motion for a new trial on all issues was denied.

Reed appealed. The Appellate Division affirmed the judgment entered upon the jury verdict in an unpublished per curiam opinion. After reviewing the facts and procedural history, the panel addressed the instruction in light of Reed's contention that the trial court erred in explaining Dr. Bojarski's duties and the extent to which those duties were defined by the contract between EMR and Life Care. The Appellate Division agreed with Reed that the contract could not alter Dr. Bojarski's duties, but concluded that it was proper for the trial court to allow the jury to use the contract to determine whether Bojarski's conduct was "reasonable." Because the sole issue of malpractice involved communication of the diagnosis, the panel determined that the charge, the testimony, and the jury's common sense provided a sufficient basis to sustain the verdict.

* * *

II

Courts throughout the nation have been grappling with the question of the obligation owed by a physician to a patient in the pre-employment screening setting * * *

Most jurisdictions adhere to the traditional malpractice model in which the absence of a classic physician-patient relationship results in the physician owing no duty to the examinee to discover and disclose abnormalities or conditions, let alone report them.

* * *

Two cases invoking the traditional model are instructive for their dissenting opinions that reveal movement away from the model. Indeed, in one of those jurisdictions, the dissenting view has subsequently been adopted as the majority rule. Both cases involve doctors who, in accordance with policy guidelines that required intermediary institutions to collate and transmit information, failed to disclose life-threatening abnormalities to examinees.

In Beaman v. Helton, 573 So.2d 776 (Miss. 1990), overruled by Meena v. Wilburn, 603 So.2d 866 (Miss. 1992), plaintiff sought Social Security benefits, and the Disability Determination Service (DDS) of Mississippi ordered an examination. Beaman, 573 So.2d at 777. DDS employed a physician to conduct the examination during which X rays were taken revealing "probable pulmonary malignancy." Ibid. That night, in accordance with DDS guidelines requiring the agency to inform an examinee of a life threatening illness, the doctor sent a report by telephone to DDS, specifically stating his impression that the plaintiff had a malignancy and recommending that the DDS examiner contact the plaintiff about this problem. Ibid. DDS, however, never informed the plaintiff of the abnormality. Ibid.

In resolving the subsequent malpractice suit against the doctor, the Supreme Court of Mississippi held that no physician-patient relationship existed and refused to impose a duty upon an examining physician independent of that relationship. Beaman, 573 So.2d at 778. The court concluded that the doctor discharged his duty to the examinee when the doctor complied with the DDS guidelines in simply notifying the DDS examiner of the life-threatening condition. Ibid.

In a dissenting opinion, three justices fashioned alternative theories of liability. First, the dissent posited that an actual physician-patient relationship, although not coextensive with the traditional model, is created when a physician examines a person at the behest of a third party and that that relationship comes with an attendant duty to the extent of the examination. Beaman, 573 So.2d at 783 (Sullivan, J., dissenting). Second, the dissent determined that the doctor also owes the plaintiff a common-law duty to conduct the examination with reasonable care, even in the absence of a doctor-patient relationship. Ibid. Under either theory, the dissent concluded that the plaintiff could reasonably expect the doctor, in a five-minute phone call, to notify him directly of a life-threatening condition that required immediate treatment. Ibid. "Under such circumstances, what, if any, duty does one human owe to another?" Beaman, 573 So.2d at 779.

Two years later, in Meena v. Wilburn, 603 So.2d 866 (Miss. 1992), the Supreme Court of Mississippi adopted the latter of the two alternative theories of liability posited by the dissent in Beamon. The Meena court held that the absence of a physician-patient relationship will not insulate a physician from liability where the traditional elements of negligence are established. Meena, 603 So.2d at 869–70. The court explained that "the presence or absence of a doctor-patient relationship is simply a factor to consider in determining the type or nature of duty owed, if any, to the injured patient or non-patient." Id. at 870.

* * *

A second line of cases acknowledges that, even in the absence of a traditional physician-patient relationship in the pre-employment physical context, there is a disclosure requirement where the examination reveals a medical abnormality.

For example, in Daly v. United States, supra, 946 F.2d at 1468, plaintiff, as part of a preemployment physical examination for the Veteran's Administration (VA) hospital, submitted to a chest X ray and tuberculosis test. Ibid. The radiologist's review of the X ray indicated an abnormality of the lung. Ibid. The radiologist, however, never informed the plaintiff. Ibid. For the next two years, plaintiff sought treatment several times for lung-related disorders at the VA employee health unit. Ibid. Further chest X rays were ordered, and the VA radiologist noted the lung abnormality but the radiologist again failed to inform Daly of the abnormality. Daly, 946 F.2d at 1469. Four years after the initial X ray, the plaintiff consulted a pulmonary specialist who diagnosed the lung disease sarcoidosis. Ibid. Sarcoidosis is incurable and potentially fatal, but prompt treatment may halt its progress. Daly, 946 F.2d at 1468. The plaintiff in Daly did not receive a diagnosis until the sarcoidosis had reached an irreversible advanced stage, rendering him permanently disabled. Ibid.

Although the Ninth Circuit refused to determine the "exact contours" of the doctor's duty to disclose, it nonetheless found persuasive expert testimony given at trial "that, at a minimum, the radiologist should have notified Daly of the abnormality." Id. at 1470. The court thus held that the VA radiologist had the "hardly burdensome" duty to inform Daly of what he detected in the X ray. Ibid.

It added, "this duty is stronger when the physician has no reason to believe that the examinee is aware of the condition and danger." Ibid.

REVERSED

NOLD v. BINYON

Supreme Court of Kansas, 2001.
272 Kan. 87, 31 P.3d 274.

SIX, J.: This first impression medical malpractice action arises from the pregnancy of Bonnie Nold and the later birth of her daughter Audra Nold. Joseph and Bonnie Nold, Audra's parents, on her behalf, alleged that certain physicians and a hospital were negligent in their care and treatment of Bonnie and Audra. We consider, in a managed care environment, the duty owed by the mother's physicians and the delivery hospital to the baby of a mother who intends to carry the fetus to term. We also consider the reporting responsibilities of physicians whose pregnant patient tests positive for hepatitis B.

Bonnie is not asserting a personal claim for damages. The jury returned a verdict for Audra and awarded damages totaling $800,000, apportioning negligence as follows: Dr. Scott Moser, 90 percent; Dr. James Donnell, 6 percent; Dr. Michael Brown, 2 percent; and Dr. Ernie Binyon, 2 percent.

INTRODUCTION

The focus of all of Audra's claims is on the failure to notify Bonnie of her hepatitis B status and to administer gamma globulin and vaccine treatment to Audra at the time of her birth. While pregnant, Bonnie was treated by numerous physicians. Laboratory test results obtained early in her pregnancy showed she was a carrier of hepatitis B, although she was asymptomatic and experienced no related health problems. A carrier, during pregnancy and delivery, can pass hepatitis B to her child. That happened here. Audra did not receive the necessary preventive treatment and has tested positive for the presence of hepatitis B surface antigens and is a chronic carrier. As of trial, she had none of the identifiable risk factors for more severe stages of hepatitis B and had remained asymptomatic and without physical problems related to her status as a carrier.

FACTS

In February 1990, Bonnie was under the care of Dr. Kernie Binyon, a family practice physician. She became pregnant and was referred by Dr. Binyon to Dr. Michael Brown, a board-certified obstetrician and gynecologist. On February 12, 1990, during Bonnie's first visit, Dr. Brown ordered laboratory tests, including one for hepatitis B. Those orders were given to Bonnie, who took them to Dr. Binyon's office. Dr. Binyon's staff drew blood samples and transmitted them to a laboratory for testing. The laboratory sent the results to Dr. Binyon's office, which then sent them to Dr. Brown. Included in the test results was a report dated February 20, 1990, which showed that Bonnie tested positive for hepatitis B. Neither Dr. Brown nor Dr. Binyon informed Bonnie of the results of this test.

During Bonnie's second visit to Dr. Brown, he requested a sonogram because he believed her growth was a bit abnormal. Due to managed care insurance constraints, Dr. Brown had to have a referral from Dr. Binyon. Dr. Binyon refused to provide the sonogram referral. Dr. Brown elected to terminate his doctor-patient relationship with Bonnie, still in her first trimester of pregnancy, because he said he could not properly treat her without conducting tests he believed necessary to protect her health and the health of the developing fetus.

Bonnie then sought the care of another physician. She first terminated her doctor-patient relationship with Dr. Binyon and requested that he forward her medical records to Dr. James Donnell. On March 30, 1990, Dr. Donnell became Bonnie's primary care physician under her Equicor Health Plan. Sometime between March 30, 1990, and May 22, 1990, Dr. Binyon's office delivered Bonnie's medical records to Dr. Donnell. Included within those records was the laboratory test result on Bonnie's positive hepatitis B status. Shortly after March 30, 1990, Dr. Donnell, a family practice physician who had chosen to limit his practice to nonobstetrical cases, referred Bonnie to Dr. Scott Moser for obstetrical care.

Despite the referral to Dr. Moser, Bonnie visited Dr. Donnell's office five times before giving birth to Audra * * * Dr. Donnell never reviewed the hepatitis B test result nor advised Bonnie or later health care providers of her hepatitis B status.

Dr. Moser, a physician certified in family practice, made obstetrics an active part of his practice. He first saw Bonnie on April 11, 1990, when she was 18 weeks pregnant. On that visit Dr. Moser decided that a sonogram would be helpful and requested her medical records from Dr. Brown. After Dr. Moser received the medical records, he noted and entered the hepatitis B information in Bonnie's chart. Dr. Moser's standard practice in the care of hepatitis B positive pregnant women is to enter the information at a prominent place in the medical record. He does this so that at the time of delivery anyone involved in the mother's care will be aware of her hepatitis B status and ensure that the child receives appropriate treatment. He testified that he believed he entered the information sometime after the initial visit on April 11, 1990 * * *. Dr. Moser testified that he recalled telling Bonnie about her hepatitis B status and advising her of the implications it would have for her fetus, but he was not sure when the conversation took place. Bonnie testified Dr. Moser did not tell her about her positive hepatitis B test or its implications for the fetus.

Dr. Moser testified that a patient's prenatal records are customary sent to [Wesley] the delivering hospital at about 34 to 36 weeks' gestation * * *

* * *

After a baby is born, Wesley's standard practice is to place information in the mother's chart in the medical chart for the baby. Dr. Moser expected the standard practice to occur in Bonnie and Audra's case. He assumed that the hepatitis B information would find its way in a timely manner to the appropriate caregivers for Audra, including her designated pediatrician. The pediatrician could then provide Audra with appropriate care and treatment to prevent hepatitis B transmission.

In 1990, Dr. Eric Pekarski was a resident physician at Wesley training to become a specialist in family medicine * * *. On the night of September 14, 1990, between 9:40 and 10 p.m., Dr. Pekarski was called to the LDR. Dr. Pekarski examined Bonnie, determined she was in active labor, contacted his attending physician, Dr. Katie Mroz, and agreed with Dr. Mroz that Bonnie should be admitted.

* * *

It was Dr. Pekarski's practice to check in with his attending physician when he was providing care to a patient. Dr. Mroz, a physician in Dr. Moser's office, was on weekend call for Dr. Moser on that particular Friday night. Dr. Pekarski's practice of consulting with the attending physician was intended at least in part to find out any information about risk factors, including any information in the prenatal records. Thus, Dr. Mroz played a role in the process of putting together the chart for Bonnie.

Dr. Moser arrived at the hospital at 11:06 p.m. By the time Dr. Moser arrived, Bonnie was already in the delivery room, the baby was having distress, and delivery was imminent. The fetal heart tones were dangerously slow, suggesting that the baby's health might be compromised and that the baby's condition was not improving. Because of the emergency situation, Dr. Moser immediately focused on the distressed baby and did not review Bonnie's prenatal records. Forty-four minutes after Dr. Moser's arrival, Audra was delivered by Cesarean section, and Dr. Moser helped with the efforts to resuscitate her.

In emergencies such as Bonnie's, Dr. Moser and other physicians rely on the records system to make sure that the transfer of information from the mother's prenatal records to the baby's chart takes place. As part of this record transfer system, Dr. Moser relied primarily on Dr. Mroz and Dr. Pekarski. Dr. Mroz remained at the hospital through the delivery despite Dr. Moser's arrival and was actively involved in the delivery.

Dr. Moser testified that typically he is both the mother's doctor and the baby's doctor. As the baby's doctor, he would order the hepatitis B inoculation and vaccination needed by the baby of a hepatitis B positive mother. However, in this instance, Dr. Pekarski was covering for the baby's designated pediatrician, Dr. Phillip James. Thus, Dr. Moser did not order postdelivery treatment for Audra.

Dr. Pekarski handled Bonnie's discharge from the hospital on September 7, 1990. On October 9, 1990, he dictated a discharge summary, reviewing her medical chart in its entirety. Dr. Pekarski's discharge summary did not contain information either that Bonnie is hepatitis B positive, or that Audra was born to a hepatitis B positive mother. At trial, Dr. Pekarski testified that Dr. Moser's prenatal records were not in Bonnie's hospital medical chart at the time she presented to the LDR, when he reviewed it while providing her care, or at the time he dictated her discharge summary.

It is recommended that a gamma globulin injection be given to an infant exposed to hepatitis B within the first 12 hours after birth. However, the gamma globulin treatment is still effective if administered up to and perhaps beyond 2 days after birth. The hepatitis B vaccine is also given to such a baby within the first week of life. When this treatment is administered, there remains a 10 percent chance that the newborn will contract hepatitis B.

* * *

DISCUSSION

Existence and Parameters of Physicians' Duties to a Fetus

Defendants acknowledge that a doctor owes a duty of care, i.e., must meet or exceed the standard of care applicable to a given patient, once he or she establishes a doctor-patient relationship. Dr. Donnell disputes the district court's holding as a matter of law that a physician who establishes a doctor-patient relationship with a pregnant woman who intends to carry to term also establishes a doctor-patient relationship with the fetus, particularly as applied to a referring primary care physician like himself. Drs. Moser and Brown do not deny they had duties to Audra; however, they argue their duties ended when their doctor-patient relationship with Bonnie terminated.

The first portion of the district court's holding does not trouble us in the abstract. To the extent a pregnant woman desires to continue her pregnancy and deliver a healthy baby at its conclusion, her interest in receiving adequate health care is inevitably intertwined with any interest or potential interest of her fetus. In such a situation, the patient cannot be separated from her pregnancy nor her pregnancy from herself. We need not look beyond this incomparable relationship that is the genesis of the human condition. The mother who wishes to carry her pregnancy to term looks to her physician to guide her through her pregnancy, with the ultimate goal of the delivery of a healthy infant. Childbirth involves a universally recognized unique relationship between mother and child.

Other jurisdictions have recognized the relationship between a physician and a pregnant patient and her fetus. See *Hughson v. St. Francis Hosp.*, 92 A.D.2d 131, 132, 459 N.Y.S.2d 814 (1983) (finding "it is now beyond dispute that in the case of negligence resulting in prenatal injuries, both the mother and the child in utero may each be directly injured and are each owed a duty, independent of the other"); *Wheeler v. Yettie Kersting Memorial Hosp.*, 866 S.W.2d 32, 44 n.16 (Tex. Civ. App. 1993) (pointing out that *Burgess v. Superior Court*, 2 Cal.4th 1064, 9 Cal.Rptr.2d 615, 831 P.2d 1197 [1992], noted the scope of duty owed by a treating physician to a pregnant woman extends to the fetus and includes a duty to avoid injury to the fetus). These decisions support our holding that a duty to the fetus exists in the abstract.

The difficulty arises when we leave the abstract for the real world. Does a referring family practice physician such as Dr. Donnell have a doctor-patient relationship with Bonnie—and thus Audra—sufficient for a duty to arise? Do the duties Drs. Brown and Moser admit they have to Audra extend beyond the termination of their relationship to Bonnie? Does their knowledge of Bonnie's communicable disease and ways to minimize the risk of its transmission to Audra affect the answer? What are the parameters of the duty in such a situation?

Where a communicable disease has been diagnosed in a pregnant woman who desires to continue her pregnancy to term and deliver a healthy baby, we agree with the district court that the woman's physician has an obligation as a matter of law to inform the woman of the diagnosis. See Annot., Malpractice: Failure of Physician to Notify Patient of Unfavorable Diagnosis or Test, 49 A.L.R. 3d 501 p. 507–512, and 2001 Supp. p. 43; see also *Jacobs v. Theimer*, 519 S.W.2d 846, 848 (Tex. 1975) (finding that a physician was under the duty to disclose to a pregnant woman that she had contracted rubella and to inform her of the risk of proposed treatment in continuing the pregnancy) * * *.

Because a woman's interest in preventing the spread of a disease is intertwined with any interest or potential interest of her fetus at that point, this holding is consistent with the physician's tandem duty to the fetus. It is also philosophically consistent with decisions from other jurisdictions recognizing a doctor's duty to inform nonpatient third parties of infectious disease to prevent its spread * * *

* * *

The other specific questions posed by this case are questions of fact that require further development of the record on retrial. Whether all or some of the physicians treating Bonnie failed to use the required care and diligence in discharging their duty to inform her of her hepatitis B status is to be decided with the aid of expert medical testimony * * *

Expert witnesses should be permitted to testify on retrial for both sides to assist the jury in determining the contours of the doctor-patient relationship and resulting duty in a referral system.

Dr. Moser's contention that he had no physician-patient relationship with Audra following her delivery, and Dr. Brown's evidence that he ended his doctor-patient relationship with Bonnie during the first trimester of her pregnancy, should also be considered by the trier of fact. The effect of the termination of Dr. Binyon's care by Bonnie also should be considered. Whether a doctor-patient relationship exists is generally a question of fact for the jury * * *

CONCLUSION

We hold, as a matter of law, that a physician who has a doctor-patient relationship with a pregnant woman who intends to carry her fetus to term and deliver a healthy baby also has a doctor-patient relationship with the fetus. We also hold as a matter of law that the pregnant woman is entitled to be informed if test results reveal that she has a communicable disease that can be transmitted to her baby during labor and delivery.

Reversed and remanded for a new trial.

Notes

1) Providing medical treatment to a person creates a physician-patient professional relationship. Where a patient is examined, however, for reasons other than treatment, does the examinee have any legitimate expectations of the physician? Assume the results of the examination are transmitted to the employer (if it is pre-employment screening) or the insurance company (if it is a screening for an insurance policy). Should an examinee who is accepted for employment or obtains the insurance policy be entitled to rely on the examination for any purpose?

2) In *Petrosky v. Brasner*, 718 N.Y.S.2d 340, 279 A.D.2d 75 (2001), a New York appeals court held that an insurer and its agents had no duty

to disclose an applicant's serious medical condition that was discovered during a pre-insurance physical examination. The requested policy was ultimately denied on the basis that the applicant's cholesterol levels in his blood and nicotine levels in the urine indicated that he misrepresented his status as a non-smoker. The applicant died of myocardial infarction and sued the physician for failing to disclose the results of an EKG taken during the examination. The appeals court reasoned that "[f]oreseeability of injury does not determine the existence of a duty."

3) If the plaintiff's claim is that the results of the examination were not communicated to him/her, does it matter whether the examination was performed non-negligently?

4) In *Nold v. Binyon*, the court held that a physician owes a duty of care to a woman's unborn fetus if her intent is to carry the fetus to term. What if she chooses not to carry the fetus to term? What if she changes her mind?

5) Does a physician who treats a patient with a communicable disease have any obligation to family members who might also contract the disease. How far should that obligation extend? *Bradshaw v. Daniel* is distinguishable from cases in which a patient is treated for a communicable disease and thereafter transmits that disease to a family member. Assuming a physician is aware of the so-called clustering effect of certain conditions, how far is he or she obligated to reach in warning others who might have been in the same "cluster" to seek treatment?

SECTION D.   TERMINATING THE PROFESSIONAL RELATIONSHIP

PAYTON v. WEAVER

Court of Appeal of California, First Appellate District, Division One, 1982.
131 Cal.App.3d 38, 182 Cal.Rptr. 225.

GRODIN, J

Occasionally a case will challenge the ability of the law, and society, to cope effectively and sensitively with fundamental problems of human existence. This is such a case. Appellant, Brenda Payton, is a 35–year–old black woman who suffers from a permanent and irreversible loss of kidney function, a condition known as chronic end stage renal disease. To stay alive, she must subject herself two or three times a week to hemodialysis (dialysis), a process in which the patient's circulatory system is connected to a machine through which the blood is passed. Using salts and osmotic membranes, artificial kidneys in the machine drain the blood of excess liquids and accumulated impurities. Without such treatment, the volume of liquids in the patient's system will increase dangerously; liquid will begin to fill the lungs, making breathing difficult and possibly leading to heart failure. The resulting toxic waste buildup and chemical imbalances can also threaten the function of the heart and other organs.

Brenda has other difficulties. Unable to care for her children, she lives alone in a low-income housing project in West Oakland, subsisting on a $356 per month Social Security check. She has no family support; one brother is in prison and another is a mental patient. She confesses that she is a drug addict, having been addicted to heroin and barbiturates for over 15 years. She has alcohol problems, weight problems and, not surprisingly, emotional problems as well.

Despite these difficulties Brenda appears from the record to be a marvelously sympathetic and articulate individual who in her lucid moments possesses a great sense of dignity and is intent upon preserving her independence and her integrity as a human being. At times, however, her behavior is such as to make extremely difficult the provision of medical care which she so desperately requires.

The other principal figure in this case is respondent John C. Weaver, Jr., a physician specializing in kidney problems. He conducts his practice through respondent Biomedical Application of Oakland, Inc. (BMA), which operates an outpatient dialysis treatment unit on the premises of respondent Providence Hospital.

Dr. Weaver began treating Brenda in 1975 when, after the birth of Brenda's twin daughters, her system rejected a transplanted kidney. He has been treating her ever since. To her, "Dr. Weaver is and was and still is the man between me and death . . . other than God, I don't think of nobody higher than I do Dr. Weaver."

On December 12, 1978, Dr. Weaver sent Brenda a letter stating he would no longer permit her to be treated at BMA because of her "persistent uncooperative and antisocial behavior over . . . more than . . . three years . . . her persistent refusal to adhere to reasonable constraints of hemodialysis, the dietary schedules and medical prescriptions . . . the use of barbiturates and other illicit drugs and because all this resulted in disruption of our program at BMA."

In the latter part of 1978, Brenda applied for admission to the regular dialysis treatment programs operated by respondents Alta Bates and Herrick Hospitals, and was refused.

For several months Dr. Weaver continued to provide Brenda with necessary dialysis on an emergency basis, through Providence. On April 23, 1979, he again notified her by letter that he would no longer treat her on an outpatient basis. This letter led to Brenda's filing of a petition for mandate to compel Dr. Weaver, BMA, and Providence to continue to provide her with outpatient dialysis services. That litigation was settled by a stipulated order which called for continued treatment provided Brenda met certain conditions: that she keep all appointments at their scheduled time; that she refrain from use of alcohol and drugs; that she maintain prescribed dietary habits; and that she "in all respects cooperate with those providing her care and abide by her physician's prescribed medical regimen." Later, a sixth stipulation was added: that Brenda would "enter into and participate in good faith in a program of regular psychotherapy and/or counseling."

Dr. Weaver and BMA continued treatment of Brenda as an outpatient pursuant to the stipulation, but on March 3, 1980, Dr. Weaver, contending that Brenda had failed to fulfill any part of the bargain, again notified her that treatment would be terminated. He provided her with a list of dialysis providers in San Francisco and the East Bay, and volunteered to work with her counsel to find alternative care.

Brenda then instituted a second proceeding, again in the form of a petition for writ of mandate, this time naming Herrick and Alta Bates Hospitals as respondents, along with Dr. Weaver, BMA and Providence. As pertinent here, the petition alleges that all respondents have "wrongfully failed and refused and continue to fail and refuse to provide Petitioner with regular hemodialysis treatment and medical supervision as required by her chronic end-stage kidney condition"; and, more specifically, that the refusal by Herrick and Alta Bates to admit her as an outpatient to their dialysis treatment programs violated their obligations under Health and Safety Code section 1317 to provide "emergency" treatment. The petition also contained allegations that Herrick and Alta Bates had discriminated against her on grounds of race and indigency, in violation of the Civil Rights Act of 1968 and the Hill–Burton Act (42 U.S.C. § 291), but the trial court found these allegations to be unsupported, and they are not at issue here.

The trial court, after a lengthy evidentiary hearing, found that Brenda had violated each and every condition which she had accepted as part of the stipulated order providing for continued treatment, and that finding is basically undisputed. There was evidence that Brenda continued, after the stipulated order, to buy barbiturates from pushers on the street at least twice a week; that she failed to restrict her diet, gaining as much as 15 kilograms between dialysis treatments; that she continued to be late and/or miss appointments; that due primarily to missed appointments she had 30 emergencies requiring hospitalization in the 11 months preceding trial; that she would appear for treatment in an intoxicated condition; that she discontinued her program of counseling after a brief period; and, as the trial court found, she displayed in general "gross non-cooperation with her treating physician, BMA of Oakland and Providence Hospital." The trial court found that her behavior in these respects was "knowing and intentional."

Brenda's behavior was found to affect not only Dr. Weaver but the other patients and the treating staff as well. Dialysis treatment is typically provided to several patients at a time, all of them connected to a single dialysis machine. There was evidence that Brenda would frequently appear for treatment late or at unscheduled times in a drugged or alcoholic condition, that she used profane and vulgar language, and that she had on occasion engaged in disruptive behavior, such as bothering other patients, cursing staff members with obscenities, screaming and demanding that the dialysis be turned off and that she be disconnected before her treatment was finished, pulling the dialysis needle from the connecting shunt in her leg causing blood to spew, and exposing her genitals in a lewd manner. The trial court found that during the times she has sought treatment "her conduct has been disruptive, abusive, and unreasonable such as to trespass upon the rights of other patients and to endanger their rights to full and adequate treatment," and that her conduct "has been an imposition on the nursing staff." The court determined that, on balance, the rights and privileges of other patients endangered by Brenda's conduct were superior to the rights or equities which Brenda claimed.

The court also found, contrary to Brenda's contentions, that Dr. Weaver had given sufficient notice to Brenda, and that Dr. Weaver was not responsible for Brenda being refused dialysis by any other respondent. It concluded that Dr. Weaver had "discharged all obligations imposed by the patient-physician relationship" with Brenda.

As to Alta Bates and Herrick Hospitals the court found that they had not refused Brenda "emergency" treatment in violation of Health and Safety Code section 1317. In late 1978, after receiving notification from Dr. Weaver that he would no longer treat her, Brenda made application to the *regular outpatient dialysis programs* at these two hospitals and was refused—for reasons, as the trial court found, that did not include her race, her indigency, or any actions on the part of Dr. Weaver. It concluded, on the basis of reasoning which we shall discuss later in this opinion, that Brenda's chronic kidney disease did not itself constitute an "emergency" within the meaning of that section.

Finally, the trial court found that Brenda "has freedom of several choices available by which she can be kept away from dangerous drugs and alcohol, helped to stay on a proper dietary regimen, and in all other ways caused to cooperate with those attempting to provide her with care," so that she is "not without means to arrange for her own care." It concluded, after a weighing of the equities, that Brenda "has no legal right to compel medical service from any of the Respondents for chronic or regular care of her kidney problems through dialysis," and so denied her petition for writ of mandate. At the same time, however, the court stayed execution of its judgment and continued in effect its temporary order requiring Dr. Weaver, and BMA, to provide hemodialysis to Brenda on a regular basis pending appeal.

Discussion

We begin our analysis by considering the trial court's conclusion that Dr. Weaver and the clinic with which he is associated have no present legal obligation to continue providing Brenda with dialysis treatment. Brenda does not claim that Dr. Weaver has any such obligation on the basis of the stipulated order that was entered in the prior proceeding, nor could she reasonably do so. The trial court found that she was estopped from so claiming by her frequent violations of the conditions contained in that order, and that finding is amply supported by the evidence.

Rather, Brenda relies upon the general proposition that a physician who abandons a patient may do so "only . . . after due notice, and an ample opportunity afforded to secure the presence of other medical attendance." [ ]

The trial court found, however, that Dr. Weaver gave sufficient notice to Brenda, and discharged all his obligations in that regard, and that finding, also, is amply supported. Dr. Weaver supplied Brenda with a list of the names and telephone numbers of all dialysis providers in San Francisco and the East Bay, and it is apparent from the record that nothing would have pleased him more than to find an alternative facility for her, but there is no evidence that there is anything further he could have done to achieve that goal under the circumstances.

During the proceedings, the trial court observed that Dr. Weaver "is one of the most sensitive and honest physicians that I have been exposed to either in a courtroom or out of a courtroom," that he was "in fact sensitive to [Brenda's] needs, that he has attempted to assist her to the best of his medical abilities, that he continues to have concern for her as a person and has continued to serve her medical needs," and that "[the] man has the patience of Job." It appears that Dr. Weaver has behaved according to the highest standards of the medical profession, and that there exists no basis in law or in equity to saddle him with a continuing sole obligation for Brenda's welfare. The same is true of the clinic, the BMA.

We turn now to Brenda's contention that Herrick and Alta Bates Hospitals violated their obligations under Health and Safety Code section 1317, the text of which is set forth in the margin, by denying her admission to their regular outpatient dialysis programs in late 1978. The trial court found that at the time Brenda applied for admission to these programs she was not in an "emergency condition," by which the court obviously meant that she was in no imminent physical danger on the day she applied. Brenda contends, however, that her illness is itself "a chronic/acute emergency which requires that she receive medical treatment every third day to avoid death," and that such a condition qualifies for mandated service under section 1317.

The trial court, in response to Brenda's contention, found that a patient with end stage renal disease "will not become a medical emergency if that person obeys medical orders, avoids drug abuse and appears for and has regularly scheduled hemodialysis treatments," and that regular outpatient dialysis treatment requires expertise and equipment not normally found in emergency rooms. It concluded that a chronic requirement for continued dialysis treatment does not constitute a need for "emergency" services or care within the meaning of section 1317. It declared, in that connection, that should Brenda present herself at any emergency department of any of the respondent health care providers claiming a need for emergency care, "a determination shall be made at that time by qualified physicians to see whether her condition constitutes an emergency" and, if so, she would be entitled to medical services under section 1317. Since that was not the situation at the time of Brenda's application to the two hospitals, the court found no liability.

We agree with the trial court's conclusion. While end stage renal disease is an extremely serious and dangerous disease, which can create imminent danger of loss of life if not properly treated, the need for continuous treatment as such cannot reasonably be said to fall within the scope of section 1317. There are any number of diseases or conditions which could be fatal to the patient if not treated on a continuing basis. If a patient suffering from such a disease or condition were to appear in the emergency room of a hospital in need of immediate life-saving treatment, section 1317 would presumably require that such treatment be provided. But it is unlikely that the Legislature intended to impose upon whatever health care facility such a patient chooses the unqualified obligation to provide continuing preventive care for the patient's lifetime.

It does not necessarily follow that a hospital, or other health care facility, is without obligation to patients in need of continuing medical services for their survival. While it has been said that "[a] private hospital owes the public no duty to accept any patient not desired by it, and it is not necessary to assign any reason for its refusal to accept a patient for hospital service" [ ] * * * And, while disruptive conduct on the part of a patient may constitute good cause for an individual hospital to refuse continued treatment, since it would be unfair to impose serious inconvenience upon a hospital simply because such a patient selected it, it may be that there exists a *collective* responsibility on the part of the providers of scarce health resources in a community, enforceable through equity, to *share* the burden of difficult patients over time, through an appropriately devised contingency plan.

Whatever the merits of such an approach might be in a different factual context, however—and we recognize that it poses difficult problems of administration and of relationship between hospitals and physicians—it cannot serve as a basis for imposition of responsibility upon these respondents under the circumstances present here. Apart from the fact that the record does not demonstrate to what extent respondent hospitals are the sole providers of dialysis treatment in the area accessible to Brenda, her present behavior, as found by the trial court, is of such a nature as to justify their refusal of dialysis treatment on either an individual or collective basis. Whatever collective responsibility may exist, it is clearly not absolute, or independent of the patient's own responsibility.

What we have said to this point is analytically sufficient to dispose of Brenda's legal arguments, and thus to sustain the trial court's ruling, but the circumstances are such that we cannot responsibly avoid confronting the more fundamental question posed by Brenda's challenge, and considered at some length by the parties in their briefs and at oral argument, namely: what alternatives exist for assuring that Brenda does not die from lack of treatment as a result of her uncooperative and disruptive behavior.

One possibility which has been considered is an involuntary conservatorship * * * Such a conservatorship is appropriate in the case of persons "gravely disabled as a result of mental disorder or impairment by chronic alcoholism" [ ]. The County of Alameda has apparently determined, however, that the conditions of that statute cannot be met in Brenda's case.

A second possibility is an involuntary conservatorship under the provisions of Probate Code section 1801 et seq. Under section 1801, subdivision (a), "[a] conservator . . . may be appointed for a person who is unable properly to provide for his or her personal needs for physical health, food, clothing, or shelter." Such a conservator "may consent to medical treatment to be performed upon the conservatee, and may require the conservatee to receive such medical treatment, in any case which the conservator determines in good faith based upon medical advice that the case is an emergency case in which the medical treatment is required. . . . " [ ] This possibility remains a viable alternative.

A third possibility, and the one which appears from recent developments to be the most promising, is a voluntary conservatorship under Probate Code section 1802. While Brenda has heretofore resisted consenting to such a conservatorship, her attorneys advise us in a postargument declaration that they are willing to use their influence to persuade Brenda to consent and that they believe they can arrange for her placement in a private, closed psychiatric facility. They suggest that we remand the matter to the superior court for the institution of appropriate proceedings. Respondents also appear to consider a voluntary conservatorship the best approach.

We have no authority to "remand" for the institution of a voluntary conservatorship, as Brenda's attorneys suggest. The trial court's order requiring Dr. Weaver to provide dialysis treatment to Brenda pending appeal will, however, remain in effect until our decision becomes final. If, during that period, Brenda institutes proceedings for a voluntary conservatorship, and a conservator is appointed, it will be that person's obligation to arrange for continued treatment under statutory authority, and subject to such conditions as the court may impose. The judgment is affirmed.

THOMPSON v. SUN CITY COMMUNITY HOSPITAL

Supreme Court of Arizona, 1984.
141 Ariz. 597, 688 P.2d 605.

* * *

Michael Jessee, plaintiff's son, was injured on the evening of September 4, 1976. Jessee was 13 years old at the time of this accident. He was rushed by ambulance from the place of the accident (Wittman, Arizona) to the Boswell Memorial Hospital operated by Sun City Community Hospital, Inc. (Boswell) in Sun City. Among Jessee's injuries was a transected or partially transected femoral artery. The injury was high in the left thigh and interrupted the flow of blood to the distal portion of the leg. Upon arrival at the emergency room at 8:22 p.m., Jessee was examined and initially treated by Dr. Steven Lipsky, the emergency room physician. Fluids were administered and blood was ordered. The leg injury prompted Dr. Lipsky to summon Dr. Alivina Sabanas, an orthopedic surgeon. She examined Jessee's leg and determined that he needed surgery. Dr. Jon Hillegas, a vascular surgeon, was consulted by phone.

At some time after 9:30 p.m. Jessee's condition "stabilized" and the decision was made to transfer him to County Hospital. There is no clear indication in the record of *who* ordered the transfer. Dr. Lipsky determined that Jessee was "medically transferable" but stated that "Michael Jessee was transferred for economic reasons after we found him to be medically transferable." Dr. Lipsky had no authority to admit patients to Boswell. Dr. Sabanas, who did have such authority and who knew that Jessee needed vascular surgery, claimed that Jessee was transferable from an orthopedic standpoint. Dr. Hillegas told Dr. Lipsky that Jessee could be transferred when "stabilized." A witness for the plaintiff testified that "The doctor at Boswell [apparently Dr. Lipsky] said [to Ada Thompson], 'I have the shitty detail of telling you that Mike will be transferred to County.... ' " A Boswell administrator testified that emergency "charity" patients are transferred from Boswell to County whenever a physician, in his professional judgment, determines that "a transfer could occur."

Thus, at 10:13 Jessee was discharged from the Boswell emergency room, placed in an ambulance, and taken to County. The doctors who attended to him at County began administering fluids and ordered blood. They testified that Jessee's condition worsened but that he was eventually "stabilized" and taken to surgery at about 1:00 a.m. Jessee underwent abdominal surgery and, immediately thereafter, surgery to repair his torn femoral artery. He survived but has residual impairment of his left leg. His mother, as *guardian ad litem*, brought a malpractice action against Boswell and the physicians.

The trial, hard fought and sometimes acrimonious, lasted three weeks. The trial record reveals a confusion of the issues of duty of care and causation. In any case such as this there are two types of causation questions. The first, relating to the question of breach of duty, pertains to the cause for the transfer to another hospital. Was the patient transferred for medical or other reasons? The second question relates to the cause of injury and is concerned with whether the transfer, with its attendant movement and delay, caused a new or additional injury or aggravated any injury which already existed. The first question was answered by defense counsel in chambers, prior to any testimony being taken in the case:

> We admit and stipulate that the plaintiff in this case was transferred from Boswell to County Hospital for financial reasons. There is no question about it.

* * *

Thus, as soon as he became "medically transferable," Jessee was transferred because he lacked the necessary financial standing and not because surgery at County Hospital could be performed more quickly or by a more skilled surgeon. Nevertheless, there was some testimony at trial that other factors involved in "medical transferability" might have had some influence on the decision to transfer—e.g. the claim that County was better prepared to take a patient immediately into emergency surgery.

* * *

In this state, the duty which a hospital owes a patient in need of emergency care is determined by the statutes and regulations interpreted by this court in *Guerrero v. Copper Queen Hospital*, 112 Ariz. 104, 537 P.2d 1329 (1975). Construing the statutory and regulatory scheme governing health care and the licensing of hospitals as of 1972, we held that it was the "public policy of this state" that a general "hospital may not deny emergency care to any patient without cause." [ ]

* * *

As guidelines for minimum requirements, the director was mandated to use the standards of the Joint Commission for Accreditation of Hospitals (JCAH). A.R.S. § 36–405(A). Several of the JCAH requirements are set out at length in the opinion of the court of appeals (142 Ariz. at 6–7, 688 P.2d at 652–653). The emergency services section of the JCAH states that:

> no patient should arbitrarily be transferred if the hospital where he was initially seen has means for adequate care of his problem. [ ]

The "Patient's Rights" section of the JCAH manual makes it clear that the financial resources of a patient are among the "arbitrary" considerations within the contemplation of the above language:

> no person should be denied impartial access to treatment or accommodations that are available and *medically indicated*, on the basis of such considerations as ... the nature of the source of payment for his care. [ ]

Principles governing the functioning of hospitals were not left in the abstract. Specific regulations were adopted and in 1976, A.C.R.R. R9–10–248, concerning "emergency departments," provided that "general hospitals shall provide facilities for emergency care." In addition, such hospitals were required "to have on call one or more physicians licensed to practice medicine and surgery in Arizona or resident physician or intern physician." Our holding in *Guerrero* is reinforced by A.R.S. § 41–1837(A). This statute is of particular relevance in understanding the entire legislative scheme bearing on the issue of emergency care. It reads as follows:

> A. When an indigent emergency medical patient is received by an emergency receiving facility from a [licensed] ambulance ... , the county shall be liable pursuant to § 11–297.01, to the ambulance

service for the cost of transporting the patient and to the facility for the reasonable costs of all medical services rendered to such indigent by the facility until such patient is transferred by the county to the county hospital, or some other facility designated by the county.

The quoted statute was in effect in 1975 when we decided *Guerrero* and is still in effect. It provides the answer to a serious problem. Charging hospitals with a legal duty to render emergency care to indigent patients does not ignore the distinctions between private and public hospitals. Imposition of a duty to render emergency care to indigents simply charges private hospitals with the same duty as public hospitals under a statutory plan which permits reimbursement from public funds for the emergency care charges incurred at the private hospital.

This legislative and regulatory history provides no reason to retreat from or modify *Guerrero*. We therefore affirm its holding that, as a matter of public policy, licensed hospitals in this state are required to accept and render emergency care to all patients who present themselves in need of such care. The patient may not be transferred until all medically indicated emergency care has been completed. This standard of care has, in effect, been set by statute and regulation embodying a public policy which requires private hospitals to provide emergency care that is "medically indicated" without consideration of the economic circumstances of the patient in need of such care. n3 Thus, the word "cause" used in the quoted portion of *Guerrero* refers to something other than economic considerations. [ ]. Interpreting the standard of care in accordance with the public policy defined in *Guerrero*, we hold that reasonable "cause" for transfer before completion of emergency care refers to medical considerations relevant to the welfare of the patient and not economic considerations relevant to the welfare of the hospital. A transfer based on the forbidden criterion of economic considerations may be for the convenience of the hospital but it is hardly "medically indicated."
* * *

Neither of the first two defenses are at issue under the facts of this case. The third is more troublesome. Many people who enter the doors of an emergency room do not truly require "emergency care." The statutes and regulations do not apply to those who go to an "emergency room;" they apply to those in need of "emergency care." * * *

Given the stipulation that Boswell ordered the transfer of Jessee to County Hospital because of financial reasons, the relevant inquiries in the case at bench did not relate to "stabilization" and "transferability," but rather to the nature and duration of the emergency. The question was whether, before transfer, the hospital had rendered the emergency care medically indicated for this patient. The facts of this case indicate that emergency surgery was indicated for Jessee. Dr. Hillegas testified that "once the diagnosis is made, you should move on with definitive treatment," and that "you want to repair the arterial injury just as soon as you can." Dr. Lipsky knew Jessee needed surgery. * * * . The undisputed evidence established that the patient was transferred for financial reasons while emergency care was medically indicated. As a matter of law this was a breach of the hospital's duty. Thus, the only question before the jury on the issue of the hospital's liability was whether its breach of duty was a cause of some compensable damage.

* * *

CAUSATION

Boswell's theory of the case was that the breach of duty, if any, in transferring the patient had caused no damage, since Jessee's serious injuries might have led to precisely the residual injury which he did sustain.

Generally, two different rules have evolved. The first holds that the plaintiff must introduce evidence from which the jury may find a probability that because of the defendant's negligence the ultimate result was different from or greater than that attributable to the original injury or condition. Under this rule the issue of causation is taken from the jury if plaintiff fails to carry this evidentiary burden. * * * Under this rule, plaintiff fails in his burden of proof and a verdict is directed if the evidence does not warrant a finding that the chance of recovery or survival absent defendant's negligence, was over 50%. * * *

Under the second rule, even if the evidence permits only a finding that the defendant's negligence increased the risk of harm or deprived plaintiff of some significant chance of survival or better recovery, it is left for the jury to decide whether there is a probability that defendant's negligence was a cause in fact of the injury. * * *

* * *

We hold, therefore, that because the protection of the chance interest was within the range of the duty breached by defendant and the harm which followed was the type from which the defendant was to have protected the plaintiff, the jury may be allowed to consider the increase in the chance of harm on the issue of causation. If the jury finds that defendant's failure to exercise reasonable care increased the risk of the harm he undertook to prevent, it may from this fact find a "probability" that defendant's negligence was the cause of the damage.

We therefore * * * adopt the rule of *Restatement (Second) of Torts* § 323 in Arizona.

> One who undertakes, ... , to render services to another which he should recognize as necessary for the protection of the other's person or things, is *subject to liability* to the other for physical harm resulting from his failure to exercise reasonable care to perform his undertaking, if (a) his failure to exercise such care increases the risk of such harm,....

* * *

The judgments in favor of defendants Hillegas and Lipsky are affirmed. The judgment in favor of Boswell is reversed and the case remanded for further proceedings.

Notes

1) In *Payton v. Weaver* it appears that Dr. Weaver was sympathetic to Brenda Payton's circumstances and sought guidance from the court as to how best to service her. He was clearly frustrated by her unreliability, but at the same time seemed to want to do well by his patient. If he had come to you for advice, what might you have recommended short of seeking judicial intervention? Consider the various alternatives and their likely outcomes.

2) The standard for transferability looks to whether the patient can safely be moved from one facility to another without compromising his or her medical condition by virtue of the transfer. If it appears at the point of transfer that no compromise in condition is anticipated, what would be the liability of the transferring physician if the patient's condition does deteriorate as a result of the transfer? In matters of indigence, would there usually be a presumption that failure to anticipate the deterioration amounts to negligence?

Chapter 2

NEGLIGENCE OF THE HEALTH CARE PROVIDER

INTRODUCTORY NOTE

Negligence is the failure to use due care under the circumstances. This definition needs no citation, but how does it apply to medical negligence today?

In a bygone fatalistic age, when a trip to the doctor was an intimation of mortality, and when most people left the hospital feet first, a medical "bad result" was usually accepted by patients and next of kin without litigation. Today, patients and next of kin expect health care providers to make people well, and "bad result," to these lay persons, is a euphemism for medical error or negligence. Physicians are aware of the irony that they are the legal victims of scientific medicine's successes.

While medical attendance is a contract for personal services, a bad result accomplished through the physician's "best efforts" is not good enough. There is no such thing as an honest mistake. The tort theory of these claims demands due care under the circumstances. It has displaced breach of contract.

Standards of "due care" involve two components: defining the forms of words in which the standards are expressed, and defining the eligibility of persons to apply the definitions. The courts (and even legislatures), necessarily assisted by medical experts, but not necessarily governed by them, set the form of words, and this chapter deals with the process of formulation. Chapter four treats the need for and the eligibility of experts to apply the definitions in particular cases.

The practical outcome of due care standards is to sort medical negligence cases into three groups, so that the victims of plain medical negligence will be compensated, bad results that happen in spite of due care will not be called medical negligence, and juries will decide doubtful cases with minimum precedential effect.

This chapter's first section deals with establishing due care standards: personal, primary care, specialty, local, regional or national and adjusting due care to medical progress. The second section looks at cases alleging reckless or intentional wrongdoing by a health care provider. Section three examines the claims of third parties who allege that lack of due care toward one person caused harmful consequences to the plaintiff, a different person.

SECTION A.   DEFINING MEDICAL DUE CARE

VELAZQUEZ v. PORTADIN

Supreme Court of New Jersey, 2000.
163 N.J. 677, 751 A.2d 102.

LONG, J., writing for a unanimous Court.

This appeal addresses the propriety of the medical judgment charge
* * *

Barbara and Luis Velazquez instituted a medical malpractice action against Dr. Ronald Portadin, Vineland Obstetrical and Gynecological Professional Association, and Nurses Eileen Cinotti and Ann Spaltore (collectively defendants) alleging that defendants failed to adhere to the accepted standard of medical care in connection with the birth of their daughter, Diana, resulting in Diana's cerebral palsy. According to the Velazquezes, defendants deviated from accepted standards of care while administering the drug Pitocin to Barbara to hasten her contractions during labor, because they negligently monitored Diana's fetal heart rate and, as a result, failed to timely discontinue the use of Pitocin, causing Diana to be deprived of oxygen. Defendants denied the malpractice claims.

At trial, the experts testifying on behalf of the Velazquez family (the Velazquez experts) opined that Diana's cerebral palsy was caused by birth asphyxia. The Velazquez experts concluded that the oxygen deprivation occurred within the last one and one-half hours of birth while Pitocin was being administered. All experts agreed at trial that it was appropriate for Dr. Portadin to give Pitocin to enhance the contractions and that fetal monitoring was necessary. However, the experts strongly disagreed about whether monitoring actually took place and whether the monitoring strips were sufficiently readable to determine Diana's reaction to Pitocin.

According to the Velazquez experts, there is no evidence that the fetal monitor was ever read, that the strips were unreadable and that they showed fetal distress. According to these experts, when the strip became unreadable, the nurses should have discontinued the Pitocin and notified Dr. Portadin so that he could determine the appropriate course of action * * *

Dr. Portadin testified on his own behalf. He stated that the decision to use an internal scalp monitor is a medical judgment that requires the weighing of the risk of infection with the benefits of the monitor readings. Dr. Portadin testified that the monitoring strips did not indicate that Diana was experiencing difficulty; that the options offered by the Velazquez experts would have taken longer than spontaneous delivery; and that other delivery options were foreclosed * * * by the passage of time and the risk-benefit analysis. In addition, Dr. Portadin's obstetrical expert as well as the nurses' expert testified that the strips overall were readable, that any unreadable portions were followed by reassuring tracings, and that the strips did not reveal fetal distress.

At the conclusion of trial, the trial court, over objection of the attorney representing the Velazquezes, gave a charge based on the Model Jury Charge on exercise of judgment. That charge basically states that a physician or nurse cannot be found negligent if exercising judgment so long as he or she bases his or her judgment on accepted standards of medical or nursing practice:

["You should understand that the law recognizes that the practice of medicine and the practice of nursing are not exact sciences. Therefore, the law recognizes that the practice of medicine or nursing according to accepted medical or nursing standards will not always prevent a poor or unanticipated result. If the physician or nurse has applied the required knowledge, skill, and care in the diagnosis and treatment of the plaintiff, he or she is not negligent simply because a bad result has occurred. Likewise, where according to accepted medical or nursing practice the manner in which the diagnosis or treatment is conducted is a matter subject to the judgment of the physician or nurse, the physician or nurse must be allowed to exercise that judgment. Where a judgment must be exercised, the law does not require the doctor or nurse [to be] infallible ... Thus, a physician or nurse cannot be found negligent so long as he or she employs such judgment as is allowed by ... accepted medical or nursing practice. If, in fact, in the exercise of his or her judgment, a doctor or nurse selects one or two or more courses of action each of which in the circumstance has substantial support as proper practice by the medical or nursing profession, the doctor or nurse cannot be found negligent if the course chosen produces a poor result."]

* * *

Given the relationship between medical judgment and the standard of care, our courts have often struggled in determining whether the facts of a particular case call for the application of the judgment charge. We have generally limited the application of the judgment charge to medical malpractice actions concerning misdiagnosis or the selection of one of two or more generally accepted courses of treatment. Aiello, supra, 159 N.J. at 628–29; see Patton v. Amblo, 314 N.J. Super. 1, 9, 713 A.2d 1051 (App. Div. 1998) (finding that doctor was not entitled to "exercise of judgment" charge where alleged malpractice involved making scalpel incision too deep because alleged deviation was in manner doctor performed procedure); Adams v. Cooper Hosp., 295 N.J. Super. 5, 10–11, 684 A.2d 506 (App. Div. 1996) (holding that court did not err by refusing to charge jury with "exercise of judgment" instruction where issue was whether nurse had duty to constantly monitor patient because case did not involve selection between one of two courses of treatment or two schools of thought), certif. denied, 148 N.J. 463, 690 A.2d 610 (1997).

Indeed, the Model Charge itself is facially limited to cases in which the physician exercised judgment in selecting among acceptable courses of action:

If * * * in the exercise of his/her judgment a doctor selects one of two or more courses of action, each of which in the circumstances has substantial support as a proper practice by the medical profession, the doctor cannot be found negligent if the course chosen produces a poor result.

[Model Jury Charge 5.36A (Civil), supra, at 5.]

* * *

It is often difficult to determine what evidence must be presented in order to entitle a defendant to the exercise of judgment charge. However, that is an important determination because "if the exercise of judgment rule is inappropriately or erroneously applied in a case that involves only the exercise of reasonable care, the aspect of the rule that excuses physicians for 'mistakes' would enable the physician to avoid responsibility for ordinary negligence." Aiello, supra, 159 N.J. at 632. In other words, the "mistake" that inheres in negligence, that is, failure to exercise reasonable care, is not the kind of mistake that is excusable. If, therefore, the physician's professional conduct implicates only the exercise of reasonable care in the performance of a medical procedure and not the exercise of medical judgment in selecting among acceptable and medically reasonable courses of treatment, the medical judgment rule should not be invoked.

* * *

Here, the trial court failed to tailor the charge to the theories and facts presented. First, he neglected to explain that it was the jury's duty to determine whether the defendants, in fact, monitored Mrs. Velazquez at all while she was on Pitocin. All experts agreed that monitoring was required and that if it was not done, it was a deviation from the standard of care. There was evidence from which the jury could have concluded that defendants failed to monitor Mrs. Velazquez and that the reason they did not take action when the strips became unreadable was that they were unaware of it. That issue had to be presented to the jury as involving a deviation from the standard of care without reference to the judgment charge.

Second, the issue of whether the strips were readable was not a judgment call. Experts testified on both sides as to the standard for readability. It was for the jury to decide which standard was correct and to determine whether there was a deviation. The judgment charge was thus inapplicable to that aspect of the case.

Third, if the jury found that the strips were not readable, and no other meaningful monitoring technique was in place, all experts agreed that the Pitocin should have been stopped. That was not a judgment issue.

Fourth, if the jury found the strips were, in fact, readable, the issue was whether they revealed fetal distress. If there was no fetal distress, no action was required. If fetal distress was evident, the issue was whether continuing the Pitocin without remedying that distress comported with the standard of care. Again, no judgment was required.

* * *

The only issue of judgment was whether to utilize an internal monitor because that decision apparently involved choosing between two equally acceptable approaches. In short, the bulk of this case implicated the question of deviation from the standard of care, not judgment. The able defense lawyers, knowing the power of the judgment charge, took every opportunity to lead the court and jury into thinking that the entire case revolved around the exercise of judgment. It did not. Although one or possibly a few judgment issues may have been implicated, the heart of the case was about whether there was a deviation from the standard of care. The undifferentiated instruction on medical judgment misled the jury and thus improperly insulated defendants from liability.

We engaged in a rather painstaking factual analysis here to reaffirm for trial judges the nature of the inquiry that is essential when a medical judgment charge is at issue. Court and counsel should analyze the parties' testimony and theories in detail, on the record, to determine whether the charge is applicable at all and, if so, to which specific issues. The charge should then be tailored accordingly. Only such an approach will avoid the error that occurred in this case.

Because the judgment charge was not tailored to the facts of this case, its coverage was overbroad and had the potential to improperly insulate defendants from liability. Accordingly, a new trial is required.

ADVINCULA v. UNITED BLOOD SERVICES

Supreme Court of Illinois, 1996.
176 Ill.2d 1, 223 Ill.Dec. 1, 678 N.E.2d 1009.

JUSTICE FREEMAN delivered the opinion of the court:

This case primarily concerns the standard of care under section 3 of the Blood and Organ Transaction Liability Act (Blood Shield Act) [ ], against which the conduct of a nonprofit blood bank charged with negligence in collecting whole blood contaminated with the human immunodeficiency virus (HIV) must be measured.

Plaintiff, Marietta Advincula, as the special administrator of the estate of her husband, Ronaldo Advincula, deceased, brought wrongful death [ ], family expense [ ] and survival actions * * * against defendant, United Blood Services (UBS). UBS operates nonprofit blood banks which collect donated whole human blood and is an operating division of Blood Systems, Inc., a nonprofit Arizona corporation.

Following trial, the jury returned a verdict of $2.14 million in plaintiff's favor on all claims. * * *

* * *

BACKGROUND

UBS operates 20 blood centers in 19 states, including a center in Chicago. UBS conducts mobile blood drives, collecting whole human blood from volunteer donors at churches, schools, and places of employment throughout the Chicago metropolitan area. UBS belongs to that sector of the blood banking community which receives donations from volunteers as opposed to the commercial sector which depends on paid donors.

UBS is a member of the AABB, an association of blood banks and blood banking professionals engaged in the collection of whole blood from volunteer donors. AABB promulgates, establishes and publishes standards and policies for the collection, processing and distribution of blood, blood components and tissue by its members. AABB also inspects and accredits its members based on compliance with these standards and policies and issues advisory recommendations and guidelines. Federal and state governments generally accept AABB standards as authoritative.

Blood banks in general are regulated, inspected and licensed by the FDA [ ] The Code of Federal Regulations also requires that the suitability of a blood donor shall be determined by or under the supervision of a qualified physician. [ ] * * * Transfusion medicine is a recognized medical specialty with specific board certification.

The initial spread of AIDS, a disease of unknown cause and origin, presented detection challenges to the medical community and, particularly, the blood banking community. . . .

By January 1983, academics, physicians, government public health organizations and members of the blood banking community met as a workgroup to consider opportunities for preventing AIDS, posed by person-to-person contact and by blood. In the absence of a laboratory test that could detect the AIDS virus in blood, the workgroup addressed the public health imperative of balancing the risk of AIDS against the impact screening measures might have on the nation's blood supply.

In the area of AIDS transmission by blood, the workgroup considered the benefits and risks posed by several screening options. Educating volunteer donors to self-defer was considered generally effective because such persons were known to be altruistic. . . Donations by friends and family to specific recipients was not recommended by blood banking physicians because such persons are often pressured and, under such circumstances, might be less likely to admit high-risk behavior. Finally, several laboratory tests, known as surrogate tests, were between 66% and 88% effective in ultimately identifying HIV-infected donors, but they also had a 5% false positive rate, resulting in the rejection of safe blood. The tests also increased the price of collection and distribution of blood products.

The workgroup reached no consensus regarding the best method to effectively exclude high-risk donors. At the time, there were 11 possible reported cases of AIDS related to transmission by blood and blood products. *Kozup [v. Georgetown University, 663 F.Supp. 1048 (D.D.C 1987)]* at 1051.

Shortly thereafter, major blood banking organizations and associations with assistance from the National Gay Task Force, the National Hemophilia Foundation and government public health representatives issued the first in a series of joint statements relating to the transmission of AIDS. [ ]. The statement recommended that blood screening include questioning donors to detect possible AIDS or exposure to persons with AIDS. [ ]

The United States Public Health Service Committee, comprised of federal government public health organizations and the FDA, similarly recommended that blood banks screen by educating donors with information pamphlets describing high-risk groups so that potential at-risk donors might exclude themselves. [ ]. The FDA also individually recommended voluntary self-deferral by potential at-risk donors. The FDA recommended, as well, improved educational programs for blood bank personnel to enable them to better assist donors in recognizing AIDS symptoms.

UBS revised its procedures, taking the course generally recommended by these governmental agencies and blood banking community associations and organizations, which did not include directed donations, surrogate tests or direct questioning of potential donors regarding their sexual preferences and habits.

* * *

On February 11, 1984, UBS collected a unit of HIV-contaminated blood from a donor, anonymously referred to as "John Donor," at a volunteer blood drive held at a Catholic parish on Chicago's southwest side. Later that month, the blood was transfused to the deceased during open-heart bypass surgery at Illinois Masonic Medical Center. Plaintiff alleged that defendant negligently failed to screen the HIV-contaminated blood, resulting in the deceased's contraction of AIDS and his eventual death, some four years following the February 1984 transfusion.

Specifically, plaintiff alleged that UBS inadequately educated donors about high-risk behavior for AIDS exposure; did not conduct the blood drive properly; did not directly question donors about their sexual preferences or sexual practices; and did not implement surrogate tests, before February 1984, although allegedly one test, the hepatitis B core antibody test, was proven effective in screening at-risk donors.

ISSUES

We are asked to decide whether: (1) the trial court properly construed section 3 [of the Blood Shield Act] and applied the proper standard of care; (2) plaintiff proved proximate cause * * *

* * *

SECTION 3 OF BLOOD SHIELD ACT

In order that there may be negligence or actionable negligence, there must be a legal duty to exercise care in favor of the person injured, a breach of such duty, and injury proximately caused by that breach. [citation omitted] Section 3 of the Blood Shield Act, "Imposition of liability," imposes a legal duty upon blood banks and their staffs by stating:

"*Every person, firm or corporation* involved in the rendition of any of the services described in Section 2 *warrants* to the person, firm or corporation receiving the service and to the ultimate recipient *that he has exercised due care and followed professional standards of care in providing the service according to the current state of the medical arts.*" (Emphasis added.) [ ].

ANALYSIS

I

Construction of Section 3—Standard of Care

UBS claims that the trial and appellate courts erroneously interpreted section 3 to allow UBS's conduct to be measured against an ordinary reasonableness negligence standard of care. UBS generally interprets section 3 as imposing an overriding obligation to adhere to "professional standards of care" *and* a secondary obligation to exercise "due care" in the conduct which conforms to those standards. UBS claims that where professional standards of care are duly adhered to, negligence liability does not arise.

Plaintiff, on the other hand, claims that the interpretation of section 3 adopted by the trial court and affirmed by the appellate majority is correct. That is, under the express terms of section 3, compliance with professional standards is not the sole inquiry; if professional "standards" or rules are themselves inadequate to constitute due care, then compliance with them does not satisfy the statutory standard of care. Plaintiff generally interprets section 3 as imposing an overriding obligation to exercise due care *and* a subordinate obligation to follow professional "standards," as in "rules."

Essentially, the controversy concerns whether section 3 of the Blood Shield Act contemplates a professional standard of care or an ordinary, reasonableness standard of care, and whether satisfaction of professional standards of care constitutes the lack of negligence.

* * *

* * * [E]ach party specifically argues that the plain language of section 3 supports its interpretation. UBS claims that the provision's end phrase, "according to the current state of the medical arts," modifies the dual obligation to both "exercise[ ] due care" and "follow[ ] professional standards of care." [ ]. As one *amicus curiae* states it, "the overarching reference to the 'current state of the medical arts' makes clear that the legislature intended negligence actions against blood banks and blood and plasma processors to be governed by a professional standard of care and that blood providers must exercise due care in conforming to that standard."

Like UBS, plaintiff also argues that the express terms of section 3 impose dual obligations, but she interprets the phrase "follow[ ] professional standards of care" as professional *rules*, not legal standards of care. Plaintiff claims that UBS's interpretation renders superfluous the first obligation, "to exercise due care," which result violates a basic statutory construction principle.

A commonly accepted definition of "due care" is:

"just, proper, and sufficient care, so far as the circumstances demand; the absence of negligence. That *degree of care* that a reasonable person can be expected to exercise That care which an ordinarily prudent person would have exercised under the same or similar circumstances." Black's Law Dictionary 499 (6th ed. 1990).

* * *

If one relies only on commonly accepted and understood meanings, section 3 appears ambiguous, seemingly indicating that a blood bank's conduct is to be measured both by a lay, reasonable person standard of care and by professional standards of care. "And" joins "exercised due care" with "followed professional standards of care," indicating that the two phrases are additional to one another and implying that they are also grammatically coordinate. Black's Law Dictionary 86 (6th ed. 1990)[ ].

Further, under section 3, blood banks make both warranties while "providing the service according to the current state of the medical arts." Without any resolution concerning the intended operation of the two warranties, it is impossible to determine exactly what this qualifying phrase means. We conclude that section 3 is therefore ambiguous and requires construction.

* * *

As expressly stated in section 1, the legislature viewed the persons and organizations engaged in "scientific procedures" as exercising "medical judgment" which would be inhibited by the imposition of strict liability. The legislature also expressly stated its belief that the availability of "important scientific knowledge" and "skills" would be restricted by such an imposition. * * *. These clear expressions reveal the legislative view concerning the types of judgments involved in blood banking as well as the level of expertise attendant to these "scientific procedures." Any construction of section 3 must be consistent with these expressions of the Act's purpose. See *People v. Burpo*, 164 Ill.2d 261, 207 Ill.Dec. 503, 647 N.E.2d 996 (1995) (statute should be given construction that is consistent with purposes and policies of the statutes).

Moreover, the legislature apparently deemed it necessary to enact section 3, a provision which imposes a particular form of statutory liability apart from existing common law negligence liability, despite that the Act's express purpose was fully accomplished by section 2. Accepting the express purpose of the Act, there was no need for the legislature to go beyond section 2 in crafting a specific statutory liability for blood service providers; existing common law negligence standards of care would have sufficed.

* * *

In Illinois, the basic [common laws] standard of care in instances of negligence is that of the "ordinarily careful person" or "reasonably prudent" person[ ]. This basic formulation reflects the community's demand for a standard that is external and objective. To be complete, however, a standard of care must also be subjective, in that it makes proper allowance for the actor's capacity to meet the risk apparent to him, and the circumstances under which he must act. [ ].

Accordingly, the basic reasonable person standard allows for and incorporates the physical characteristics of the defendant, himself. * * *

The professional standard of care accomplishes this incorporation of certain subjective qualities and circumstances. Professionals are held to a particularized form of the basic reasonable person standard because in addition to that degree of care, they are expected to possess a higher degree of skill, care, and learning than the average person. The common statement that due care is the degree of care that a reasonable person is bound to exercise is thus only a statement of the general negligence standard of conduct or duty in its most basic terms. Professionals, in general, are required not only to exercise reasonable care (*i.e.*, due care) in what they do, but also to possess and exercise a standard minimum of special knowledge and ability * * *

In Illinois, the established standard of care for all professionals is stated as the use of the same degree of knowledge, skill and ability as an ordinarily careful professional would exercise under similar circumstances.

* * *

Section 3 then represents no more than a classic statement of the general duty to which every professional is answerable, to exercise due care, and the particularized measure of his conduct, by professional standard of care. We therefore conclude that, under section 3, a blood bank's conduct is to be measured against "professional standards of care" while the bank is bound to exercise care which is due.

* * *

CONCLUSION

We hold that section 3 of the Blood Shield Act requires that the allegedly negligent conduct of UBS be measured against the standard of care applied to professional conduct. The trial court erred as a matter of law in allowing judgment of UBS's conduct against a reasonable blood bank standard of care. We therefore reverse the judgments of the appellate and trial courts and remand this cause to the trial court for retrial.

Reversed.

HELLING v. CAREY

Supreme Court of Washington, 1974.
83 Wash.2d 514, 519 P.2d 981.

HUNTER, ASSOCIATE JUSTICE. * * *

The plaintiff, Barbara Helling, suffers from primary open-angle glaucoma. Primary open-angle glaucoma is essentially a condition of the eye in which there is an interference in the ease with which the nourishing fluids can flow out of the eye. Such a condition results in pressure gradually rising above the normal level to such an extent that damage is produced to the optic nerve and its fibers with resultant loss in vision. The first loss usually occurs in the periphery of the field of vision. The disease usually has few symptoms and, in the absence of a pressure test, is often undetected until the damage has become extensive and irreversible.

The defendants (respondents), Dr. Thomas F. Carey and Dr. Robert C. Laughlin, are partners who practice the medical specialty of ophthalmology. Ophthalmology involves the diagnosis and treatment of defects and diseases of the eye.

The plaintiff first consulted the defendants for myopia, nearsightedness, in 1959. At that time she was fitted with contact lenses. She next consulted the defendants in September 1963 concerning irritation caused by the contact lenses. Additional consultations occurred in October 1963, February 1967, September 1967, October 1967, May 1968, July 1968, August 1968, September 1968, and October 1968. Until the October 1968 consultation, the defendants considered the plaintiff's visual problems to be related solely to complications associated with her contact lenses. On that occasion, the defendant, Dr. Carey, tested the plaintiff's eye pressure and field of vision for the first time. This test indicated that the plaintiff had glaucoma. The plaintiff, who was then 32 years of age, had essentially lost her peripheral vision, and her central vision was reduced to approximately 5 degrees vertical by 10 degrees horizontal.

Thereafter, in August of 1969, after consulting other physicians, the plaintiff filed a complaint against the defendants alleging, among other things, that she sustained severe and permanent damage to her eyes as a proximate result of the defendants' negligence. During trial, the testimony of the medical experts for both the plaintiff and the defendants established that the standards of the profession for that specialty in the same or similar circumstances do not require routine pressure tests for glaucoma upon patients under 40 years of age. The reason the pressure test for glaucoma is not given as a regular practice to patients under the age of 40 is that the disease rarely occurs in this age group. Testimony indicated, however, that the standards of the profession do require pressure tests if the patient's complaints and symptoms reveal to the physician that glaucoma should be suspected.

The trial court entered judgment for the defendants following a defense verdict. * * * [The Court of Appeals affirmed without a reported opinion.]

[T]he plaintiff contends, in effect, that she was unable to argue her theory of the case to the jury: that the standard of care for the specialty of ophthalmology was inadequate to protect the plaintiff from the incidence of glaucoma; and that the defendants, by reason of their special ability, knowledge and information, were negligent in failing to give the pressure test to the plaintiff at an earlier point in time which, if given, would have detected her condition and enabled the defendants to have averted the resulting substantial loss in her vision.

We find this to be a unique case. The testimony of the medical experts is undisputed concerning the standards of the profession for the specialty of ophthalmology. * * * The issue is whether the defendants' compliance with the standard of the profession of ophthalmology, which does not require the giving of a routine pressure test to persons under 40 years of age, should insulate them from liability under the facts in this case, where the plaintiff has lost a substantial amount of her vision due to the failure of the defendants to timely give the pressure test to the plaintiff.

* * *

The incidence of glaucoma in one out of 25,000 persons under the age of 40 may appear quite minimal. However, that one person, the plaintiff in this instance, is entitled to the same protection as afforded persons over 40, essential for timely detection of the evidence of glaucoma when it can be arrested to avoid the grave and devastating result of this disease. The test is a simple pressure test, relatively inexpensive. There is no judgment factor involved, and there is no doubt that by giving the test the evidence of glaucoma can be detected. The giving of the test is harmless if the physical condition of the eye permits. The testimony indicates that although the condition of the plaintiff's eyes might have at times prevented the defendants from administering the pressure test, there is an absence of evidence in the record that the test could not have been timely given.

Justice Holmes stated in Texas & P. Ry. v. Behymer, 189 U.S. 468, 470, 23 S.Ct. 622, 47 L.Ed. 905 (1903), "What usually is done may be evidence of what ought to be done, but what ought to be done is fixed by a standard of reasonable prudence, whether it usually is complied with or not."

In The T.J. Hooper, 60 F.2d 737, 740 (2d Cir.1932), Judge Hand stated:

[I]n most cases reasonable prudence is in fact common prudence; but strictly it is never its measure; a whole calling may have unduly lagged in the adoption of new and available devices. It never may set its own tests, however persuasive be its usages. *Courts must in the end say what is required; there are precautions so imperative that even their universal disregard will not excuse their omission.* (Italics ours.)

Under the facts of this case reasonable prudence required the timely giving of the pressure test to this plaintiff. The precaution of giving this test to detect the incidence of glaucoma to patients under 40 years of age is so imperative that irrespective of its disregard by the standards of the ophthalmology profession, it is the duty of the courts to say what is required to protect patients under 40 from the damaging results of glaucoma.

We therefore hold, as a matter of law, that the reasonable standard that should have been followed under the undisputed facts of this case was the timely giving of this simple, harmless pressure test to this plaintiff, and that, in failing to do so, the defendants were negligent, which proximately resulted in the blindness sustained by the plaintiff for which the defendants are liable.

There are no disputed facts to submit to the jury on the issue of the defendants' liability. Hence, a discussion of the plaintiff's proposed instructions would be inconsequential in view of our disposition of the case.

The judgment of the trial court and the decision of the court of appeals is reversed, and the case is remanded for a new trial on the issue of damages only.

* * *

UTTER, ASSOCIATE JUSTICE, concurring.

I concur in the result reached by the majority. I believe a greater duty of care could be imposed on the defendants than was established by their profession. * * *

The difficulty with this approach is that we as judges, by using a negligence analysis, seem to be imposing a stigma of moral blame upon the doctors who, in this case, used all the precautions commonly pre-scribed by their profession in diagnosis and treatment. Lacking their training in this highly sophisticated profession, it seems illogical for this court to say they failed to exercise a reasonable standard of care. It seems to me we are, in reality, imposing liability, because, in choosing between an innocent plaintiff and a doctor, who acted reasonably accord-ing to his specialty but who could have prevented the full effects of this disease by administering a simple, harmless test and treatment, the plaintiff should not have to bear the risk of loss. As such, imposition of liability approaches that of strict liability.

[S]trict liability serves a compensatory function in situations where the defendant is, through the use of insurance, the financially more responsible person. * * *

If the standard of a reasonably prudent specialist is, in fact, inadequate to offer reasonable protection to the plaintiff, then liability can be imposed without fault. To do so under the narrow facts of this case does not offend my sense of justice. The pressure test to measure intraocular pressure with the Schiotz tonometer and the Goldman applanometer takes a short time, involves no damage to the patient, and consists of placing the instrument against the eyeball. An abnormally high pressure requires other tests which would either confirm or deny the existence of glaucoma. It is generally believed that from 5 to 10 years of detectable increased pressure must exist before there is permanent damage to the optic nerves.

* * *

FINLEY and HAMILTON, JJ., concurred.

Note on the Aftermath of Helling v. Carey

Probably the outcome of *Helling v. Carey* could have been explained as well by the physicians' negligent failure to rule out a specific (if unlikely) cause of Mrs. Helling's eye complaints, rather than by their negligent failure to use a test designed for screening large populations for glaucoma. However that may be, the court's strong rule on its capacity to set the standard of medical care threatened the structure of lawmaking. While no reported opinion followed the remand, *Helling* did not fade into the legal literature; the repercussions of the court's declaration of lawmaking freedom were felt throughout the United States.

One might expect the physicians to seek relief from the legislature, and sure enough, the Washington state legislature at its first extraordinary session in 1975 enacted this statute:

In any civil action for damages based on professional negligence against * * * a member of the healing arts * * *, the plaintiff in order to prevail shall be required to prove by a preponderance of the evidence that the defendant or defendants failed to exercise that degree of skill, care, and learning possessed by other persons in the same profession * * *. Wash.Rev.Code § 4.24.290.

In 1979 Gates v. Jensen, another glaucoma case reached the Washington supreme court. A woman 54 years old had tested borderline for glaucoma, but she was not given then either of two further tests, dilation of the pupils for better view of the optic nerve discs, or a visual field examination that, she later alleged, would have showed that she suffered from the disease. The trial judge let the jury have the case without the *Helling* instruction, and the jury found for defendant ophthalmologists. The court of appeals affirmed, holding that § 4.24.290 had overruled

Helling. The supreme court reversed, holding that *Helling* was still in effect:

The original house bill would have established the standard of care as that skill and care *practiced* by others in the same profession and specialty. H.B. 246, 44th Regular Sess. (1975). Respondent contends the clear intent of this bill was to abrogate the *Helling* rule. The original bill was amended, though. The statute as passed requires physicians to exercise the skill, care and learning *possessed* by others in the same profession. This standard is much broader than the one embodied in the original bill, and allows ample scope for the application of the limited *Helling* rule. It is not argued that respondent and other ophthalmologists did not possess the skill, care and learning required to choose and administer the two alternative, simple and risk-free tests. We therefore find no bar to the requested instruction under Wash.Rev.Code § 4.24.290. 595 P.2d at 924.

Wrote a dissenting justice,

The *Helling* decision represented a deviation from the "standard of the profession" test used in medical malpractice actions. It rested on the "reasonably prudent person" standard which is applied in ordinary tort cases. * * *

* * * I do not believe that the change of the word "practiced" to "possessed" frustrated the legislature's purpose in enacting Wash.Rev. Code § 4.24.290. * * *

* * * Plaintiff's proposed supplemental instruction No. 3 says that even if the defendants met "the applicable standard of care followed by practicing ophthalmologists in the diagnosis of glaucoma" the jury could still find defendants negligent. This is absolutely contrary to the mandate of the legislature. [ ].

In 1983 came *Harris v. Groth*, yet another glaucoma case. The trial judge kept the plaintiff's sole expert (who was not a physician) from testifying on the standard of care, and he refused to give the *Helling* instruction, and so the jury found for the defendant. After summarizing the evolution of Washington law and citing law review comment, the court noted that in 1975 the legislature had enacted a second standard-setting statute, West's Rev.Code Wash.Ann. § 7.70.040, applicable only to actions arising after June 25, 1976—which was too late for *Gates.* Section 7.70.040 called for a "reasonably prudent health care provider," while the pre-*Helling* case-law standard had said "average medical or dental practitioner." Affirming the trial court's rejection of the plaintiff's proffered instruction, the court wrote,

The instruction should have been framed in the language of * * * [the two statutes], i.e., whether a reasonably prudent ophthalmologist, possessing the degree of skill, care, and learning possessed by other ophthalmologists in the state of Washington, and acting in the same or similar circumstances as the defendant, would have performed an intraocular pressure test. 663 P.2d at 118.

Judgment for the defendant was affirmed.

Apparently the model jury instructions have settled down in the format of the passage quoted from *Harris*. The Washington legislature did not try to draw together the two code sections, and the muscle that the supreme court showed in *Helling* would not been flexed again.

GRACEY v. EAKER

Supreme Court of Florida, 2002.
837 So.2d 348.

LEWIS, J.

We have for review Gracey v. Eaker, 747 So.2d 475 (Fla. 5th DCA 1999), in which the district court affirmed the dismissal of an action initiated by the petitioners, Donna and Joseph Gracey ("Graceys"), a couple allegedly injured by the counseling activities of a psychotherapist, against Dr. Donald W. Eaker ("Eaker"). The Graceys sought the recovery of emotional distress damages that were allegedly inflicted by Eaker's actions in revealing the most confidential of information disclosed to him by each individual during and only as part of a confidential and fiduciary relationship. In affirming the dismissal of the Graceys' action, the district court held that their complaint sounded in negligence and failed to adhere to the "requirement [of the impact rule] that some physical impact to a claimant . . . be alleged and demonstrated before the claimant can recover [emotional distress] damages." [ ].

WHETHER FLORIDA'S IMPACT RULE IS APPLICABLE IN A CASE IN WHICH IT IS ALLEGED THAT THE INFLICTION OF EMOTIONAL INJURIES HAS RESULTED FROM A PSYCHOTHERAPIST'S BREACH OF A DUTY OF CONFIDENTIALITY TO HIS PATIENT, WHEN THE PSYCHOTHERAPIST HAS CREATED A STATUTORY CONFIDENTIAL RELATIONSHIP.

FACTS

[T]he Graceys averred that Eaker is a licensed psychotherapist who, for profit, provided treatment to them in individual counseling sessions, ostensibly seeking to intervene in the most personal of matters directed to marital difficulties. They also alleged that Eaker, during individual therapy sessions, would inquire about, and each of the [petitioners] would disclose to him, very sensitive and personal information that neither had disclosed to the other spouse at any time during their relationship. [Petitioners] would disclose this information because they were led to believe, by [Eaker], that such information was necessary for treatment purposes.

The petitioners further alleged that a direct violation of Florida law occurred in that despite being under a statutorily imposed duty to keep the disclosed information confidential, Eaker nevertheless unlawfully divulged to each of the petitioners "individual, confidential information which the other spouse had told him in their private sessions." Subsequent to these disclosures, the Graceys set forth that they realized that

Eaker had devised "a plan of action . . . designed to get [them] to divorce each other." The Graceys claimed that such actions by Eaker constituted "breaches . . . of his fiduciary duty of confidentiality [that was] owed [individually] to [them]."

With regard to the damages resulting from Eaker's actions, the Graceys alleged that they have sustained severe mental anguish upon learning of [the] actions of the other spouse, of which they individually were not aware, and that [Eaker's] disclosure [of these actions] has caused irreparable damage to any trust that they would have had for each other. . . . [Moreover, they alleged that Eaker's] actions have caused great mental anguish for them individually in their personal relationships with others due to their inability to trust the others in those personal relationships.

Additionally, the Graceys asserted that they have incurred substantial costs and expenses in undergoing further treatment in an attempt to correct the mental damage inflicted upon them by Eaker's actions.

In upholding the trial court's dismissal of the petitioners' action, the district court expressed that it was "constrained to agree" with Eaker's assertion that a dismissal was proper, "because Florida law does not recognize a cause of action for negligent infliction of emotional distress without an accompanying physical injury." Gracey [ ].

ANALYSIS

We conclude that while the determinations by both the trial court and the district court relied upon general principles of Florida tort law and general application of the "impact rule," such does not accommodate the intent and purpose of section 491.0147 of the Florida Statutes and renders its protection meaningless. Accepting all well-pled allegations as true, which we are required to do because this case is before us on the dismissal of the action at the pleading stage,[3] we determine that the plaintiffs have presented a cognizable claim for recovery of emotional damages under the theory that there has been a breach of fiduciary duty arising from the very special psychotherapist-patient confidential relationship recognized and created under section 491.0147 of the Florida Statutes.

Decades ago, we commented on the nature of the fiduciary relationship:

---

3. "Wrongful birth" claims are generally described as causes of action brought by the parents of a child born with birth defects alleging that due to negligent medical advice or testing they were precluded from making an informed decision about whether to conceive a potentially handicapped child or, in the event of a pregnancy, to terminate it. Cowe v. Forum Group, Inc., 575 N.E.2d 630, 633 (Ind. 1991). A cause of action based upon the same type of negligent conduct that seeks damages on behalf of the child rather than the parents is often referred to as "wrongful life." Id. The phrases "wrongful conception" or "wrongful pregnancy" refer to claims for damages brought by the parents of an unexpected child alleging that the conception of the child resulted from negligent sterilization procedures or a defective contraceptive product. Id.

If a relation of trust and confidence exists between the parties (that is to say, where confidence is reposed by one party and a trust accepted by the other, or where confidence has been acquired and abused), that is sufficient as a predicate for relief. The origin of the confidence is immaterial. Quinn v. Phipps, 93 Fla. 805, 113 So. 419, 421 (Fla. 1927).

We have also accepted the concept that "the purpose of a duty in tort is to protect society's interest in being free from harm." [ ]. Here, the Graceys allege that Eaker advertised himself as a licensed psychologist with special competence as a marital therapist. The relationship between Eaker and the Graceys was not merely of a casual nature, which states typically do not regulate. For profit, Eaker intentionally interjected himself between the Graceys in the role of confidant and counselor, and under a veneer of trust and confidence encouraged each to reveal without hesitation the most private of thoughts, emotions, fears, and hopes. Without justification or authorization, Eaker is alleged to have repaid this repositing of confidence in him by placing the dagger of damage in the very soul of the Graceys' marriage, thereby exacerbating the problem for which the Graceys sought his assistance.

The Florida Legislature has recognized and found that one's emotional stability and survival must be protected to the same extent as physical safety and personal security.

* * * [S]ection 491.0147 of the Florida Statutes * * * states in pertinent part: "Any communication between any person licensed or certified under this chapter and her or his patient or client shall be confidential." If this legislative provision is to have any life or meaning and afford reliable protection to Florida's citizens, our people must have access to the courts without an artificial impact rule limitation, to afford redress if and when the fiduciary duty flowing from the confidential relationship and statutory protection is defiled by the disclosure of the most personal of information.

In addition to our stated public policy and statutory structure of protection for certain confidential relationships, we have recently recognized the fiduciary duty generally arising in counseling relationships in Doe v. Evans, 814 So.2d 370, 373–75 (Fla. 2002). There, one having marital difficulties alleged that a priest intervened in the situation and during counseling activities breached a duty of trust and confidence by becoming sexually involved with her. [ ]. Recognizing the principles suggested in the Restatement (Second) of Torts, we noted that a fiduciary relationship does exist between persons when one is under a duty to act for or give advice for the benefit of another upon matters within the scope of the relationship. [ ]. Further, one in such a fiduciary relationship is subject to legal responsibility for harm flowing from a breach of fiduciary duty imposed by the relationship. [ ].

* * *

The elements of a claim for breach of fiduciary duty are: the existence of a fiduciary duty, and the breach of that duty such that it is the proximate cause of the plaintiff's damages. Florida courts have previously recognized a cause of action for breach of fiduciary duty in different contexts when a fiduciary has allegedly disclosed confidential information to a third party. See Barnett Bank of Marion County, N.A. v. Shirey, 655 So.2d 1156 (Fla. 5th DCA 1995) (plaintiff entitled to damages for breach of fiduciary duty because bank employee disclosed sensitive financial information to a third party). Moreover, courts in other jurisdictions, along with legal commentators, have concluded that a fiduciary relationship exists between a mental health therapist and his patient. See, e.g., Hoopes v. Hammargren, 102 Nev. 425, 725 P.2d 238, 242 (Nev. 1986) (psychiatrists and all physicians have fiduciary relationship with patients)...)

Restatement (Second) of Torts, § 874 cmt. a. ("A fiduciary relation exists between two persons when one of them is under a duty to act for or to give advice for the benefit of another upon matters within the scope of that relation.") [ ].

* * *

We have previously stated that " 'duty' is not sacrosanct in itself, but only an expression of the sum total of those considerations of policy which lead the law to say that the particular plaintiff is entitled to protection [or not]." [ ]. Here, the statute unambiguously indicates the intent of the Legislature to protect from unauthorized disclosure the confidences reposed by a patient in his or her psychotherapist. A breach of this duty not to disclose is therefore actionable under the common law cause of action for breach of fiduciary duty.

* * *

We emphasize that while we determine that a duty of confidentiality exists, it is not absolute. For instance, section 491.0147(1)–(3) of the Florida Statutes delineates three instances in which communications between patient and psychotherapist are not cloaked with confidentiality (none of which applies in the instant case). See also MacDonald v. Clinger, 446 N.Y.S.2d at 805 ("Disclosure of confidential information by a psychiatrist to a spouse [is] justified whenever there is a danger to the patient, the spouse or another person; otherwise information should not be disclosed without authorization."). It is unnecessary for us at this time to define the exact contours of the exceptions to the duty of confidentiality. The Graceys satisfied the "breach" and "causation" elements of their claim by alleging that Eaker disclosed the confidences of one spouse to the other, and that these disclosures were the proximate cause of their emotional distress. The remaining element of their cause of action, for which the district court certified the question of great public importance, concerns the damage element. Specifically, the issue is whether the "impact rule" is applicable when a psychotherapist is alleged to have inflicted emotional distress on the patient as a result of breaching his fiduciary duty of confidentiality.

The "impact rule" requires that a plaintiff seeking to recover emotional distress damages in a negligence action prove that "the emotional distress ... flows from physical injuries the plaintiff sustained in an impact [upon his person]." [ ]. Florida's version of the impact rule has more aptly been described as having a "hybrid" nature, requiring either impact upon one's person or, in certain situations, at a minimum the manifestation of emotional distress in the form of a discernible physical injury or illness. [ ]. We have stated that "the underlying basis for the [impact] rule is that allowing recovery for injuries resulting from purely emotional distress would open the floodgates for fictitious or speculative claims." [ ].

We have, however, in a limited number of instances either recognized an exception to the impact rule or found it to be inapplicable. In Kush v. Lloyd, we noted that the impact rule generally "is inapplicable to recognized torts in which damages often are predominately emotional." [ ]. Also in Kush, we held that the emotional distress damages of parents who had endured the wrongful birth of their deformed child, after having been assured by medical personnel that they were not at risk of conceiving a deformed child, were not subject to proof under the impact rule. [ ] We recognized that if the impact rule was inapplicable to emotional distress damages for torts such as defamation or invasion of privacy, in which the emotional distress of the victim was likely less severe, it should also be inapplicable to the more severe emotional distress of parents who had been assured that they were not at risk of bringing a deformed child into the world. [ ].

The emotional distress that the Graceys allege they have suffered is at least equal to that typically suffered by the victim of a defamation or an invasion of privacy. Indeed, we can envision few occurrences more likely to result in emotional distress than having one's psychotherapist reveal without authorization or justification the most confidential details of one's life. Our reasoning in Kush thus provides ample support for the notion that the impact rule should be inapplicable to the instant case.

"...We reaffirm ... our conclusion that the impact rule continues to serve its purpose of assuring the validity of claims for emotional or psychic damages, and find that the impact rule should remain part of the law of this state.["]

[ ] Today we simply hold that the impact rule is inapplicable under the particular facts of the case before us.

BADER v. JOHNSON
Supreme court of Indiana, 2000.
732 N.E.2d 1212.

RUCKER, Justice

* * *

FACTS AND PROCEDURAL HISTORY

The facts most favorable to the Johnsons as nonmoving parties show they gave birth to their first child in 1979. Born with hydrocephalus and severe mental and motor retardation, the child required extensive medical care until her death at four months of age. When Connie became pregnant again in 1982, the Johnsons were fearful of bearing another child with congenital defects so they sought consultation with Dr. Bader. Testing showed the pregnancy was normal. Apparently the birth proceeded without complication. The Johnsons again sought counseling with Dr. Bader when Connie became pregnant in 1991. An amniocentesis performed at 192 weeks gestation revealed no abnormalities. However, Dr. Bader performed an ultrasound test the same day that revealed a fetus with a larger than expected cavity within the brain and an unusual head shape. Dr. Bader requested her staff to schedule Connie for follow-up testing. Due to an office error however Connie was not scheduled and the ultrasound report was not forwarded to Connie's treating physician.

At 33 weeks gestation Connie's treating physician performed his own ultrasound test and discovered that the unborn child had hydrocephalus. It was too late to terminate the pregnancy and Connie gave birth on September 4, 1991. In addition to hydrocephalus, the child had multiple birth defects and died as a result four months later.

The Johnsons filed against Healthcare Providers a proposed complaint with the Indiana Department of Insurance. The complaint alleged negligence in Healthcare Providers' failure to inform the Johnsons of the result of the ultrasound test conducted at 192 weeks gestation. In due course a medical review panel rendered an opinion concluding that Healthcare Providers failed to meet the applicable standard of care. Thereafter, the Johnsons filed a complaint in the Allen Circuit Court alleging that Healthcare Providers' failure to inform deprived the Johnsons of the opportunity to terminate the pregnancy. As a result the Johnsons sought a variety of damages.

Healthcare Providers responded with a motion for summary judgment contending Indiana does not recognize a claim for wrongful birth, and even if it does recognize such a claim, the trial court needed to determine what if any damages were recoverable. The trial court denied the summary judgment motion and concluded the Johnsons could recover damages for the following: (1) the extraordinary costs necessary to treat the birth defect, (2) any additional medical or educational costs attributable to the birth defect during the child's minority, (3) medical and hospital expenses incurred as a result of the physician's negligence, (4) the physical pain suffered by the mother, (5) loss of consortium, and (6) the mental and emotional anguish suffered by the parents. Healthcare Providers appealed the decision. Except for emotional distress damages, the Court of Appeals affirmed the judgment of the trial court. We grant transfer.

Discussion

* * *

II. Cause of Action

Although not disputing the operative facts in this case, Healthcare Providers contend the trial court erred in denying its motion for summary judgment because as a matter of law Indiana does not recognize a claim in tort for wrongful birth. Although a popular characterization among some commentators and a number of jurisdictions the term "wrongful birth" seems to have its genesis as a play upon the statutory tort of "wrongful death." [ ] However, as the Nevada Supreme Court observed, "we see no reason for compounding or complicating our medical malpractice jurisprudence by according this particular form of professional negligence action some special status apart from presently recognized medical malpractice or by giving it the new name of 'wrongful birth.'" Greco v. United States, 111 Nev. 405, 893 P.2d 345, 348 (Nev. 1995). We agree. It is unnecessary to characterize the cause of action here as "wrongful birth" because the facts alleged in the Johnsons' complaint either state a claim for medical malpractice or they do not. Labeling the Johnsons' cause of action as "wrongful birth" adds nothing to the analysis, inspires confusion, and implies the court has adopted a new tort.

Medical malpractice cases are no different from other kinds of negligence actions regarding that which must be proven. The plaintiff must show: (1) duty owed to plaintiff by defendant, (2) breach of duty by allowing conduct to fall below the applicable standard of care, and (3) compensable injury proximately caused by defendant's breach of duty. [ ]. This jurisdiction has long recognized a physician's duty to disclose to her patient material facts relevant to the patient's decision about treatment. [ ]. Although a discussion of this duty has generally arisen in cases involving informed consent and the doctrine of fraudulent concealment neither of which is alleged here, the underlying premise is still the same. In order for a patient to make an informed decision about her health, she must have the relevant facts at her disposal. If the physician has possession of those facts, then the physician has a duty to disclose them. "This duty arises from the relationship between the doctor and patient, and is imposed as a matter of law as are most legal duties." [ ]

In this case, the Johnsons allege they consulted Healthcare Providers to obtain information having a direct bearing on Connie's health, namely: a decision to terminate the pregnancy. According to the Johnsons the ultrasound test conducted by Healthcare Providers, revealing pre-natal abnormalities, was precisely the kind of information the couple needed to make an informed decision. For purposes of this summary judgment action we accept the Johnsons' assertions as true. [ ]. As a matter of law Healthcare Providers owed a duty to the Johnsons to disclose the result of the test.

As for a breach of duty, expert medical testimony is usually required to determine whether a physician's conduct fell below the applicable standard of care. [ ]. This is generally so because the technical and complicated nature of medical treatment makes it impossible for a trier of fact to apply the standard of care without the benefit of expert opinion on the ultimate question of breach of duty. [ ] Here, however, we doubt whether expert testimony is required to determine whether Healthcare providers breached its duty. See Harris v. Raymond, 715 N.E.2d 388, 394 (Ind. 1999) (stating that "not all medical malpractice cases are so technical that they require expert testimony."), [ ] If Healthcare Providers did not provide the Johnsons with the result of the ultrasound, then Healthcare Providers breached its duty. It does not appear to us that expert testimony is required on this point * * *

Assuming duty and breach of duty, we next address the third element of a medical malpractice cause of action: compensable injury proximately caused by the breach. According to the Johnsons, as a result of Healthcare Providers' conduct they were not informed of the fetus' condition until it was too late to terminate the pregnancy, resulting in Connie carrying to term and giving birth to a severely deformed child.

An indispensable element of a negligence claim is that the act complained of must be the proximate cause of the plaintiff's injuries. [ ]. A negligent act is the proximate cause of an injury if the injury is a natural and probable consequence, which in the light of the circumstances, should have been foreseen or anticipated. [ ]

On the question of causation, Healthcare Providers make two claims: (1) there is an insufficient nexus between the Johnsons' claimed injury and the alleged act of negligence, and (2) Healthcare Providers did not "cause" the Johnsons' injury. At a minimum, proximate cause requires that the injury would not have occurred but for the defendant's conduct. [ ]. The "but for" test presupposes that absent the defendant's conduct, a plaintiff would have been spared suffering the claimed injury. [ ]. The Johnsons' claimed injury is that but for Healthcare Providers' failure to provide them with the result of the ultrasound test, the pregnancy would have been terminated. Whether the Johnsons can carry their burden of proof on this point at trial remains to be seen. However, at this stage of the proceedings the question is whether the Johnsons' carrying to term and giving birth to a severely deformed child can be the natural and probable consequence of Healthcare Providers' breach of duty, which Healthcare Providers should have foreseen or anticipated. This question must be answered affirmatively. Again, for purposes of this summary judgment action only, we accept as true the allegations contained in the Johnsons' complaint and the reasonable inferences to be drawn therefrom. The record shows the Johnsons consulted Healthcare Providers in 1982 when Connie was pregnant with her second child and again in 1991 when she became pregnant with her third child. The consultations were inspired by experiences the Johnsons encountered with their first child who was born with severe defects. The facts most favorable to the Johnsons suggest that Healthcare Providers knew or reasonably should have known that depending on the results of the ultrasound test, the Johnsons would not carry the pregnancy to term. We conclude, therefore that the Johnsons have made a *prima facie* claim of legal causation.

Advancing several public policy arguments, Healthcare Providers contend that even assuming duty, breach, and proximate cause the Johnsons still should not be allowed to pursue their claim. Chief among its arguments is that the court is being called upon "to weigh life (however imperfect) against the non-existence of life as that directly impacts the parents of the child." [ ]. Characterizing the Johnsons' injury as the birth of a child with congenital defects, Healthcare Providers argue "life, even life with severe defects, cannot be an injury in the legal sense." [ ].

We first observe that the injury claimed in this case is not the child's defects themselves. The Johnsons do not claim that the negligence of Healthcare Providers "caused" their child's defects. Instead, they contend that Healthcare Providers' negligence caused them to lose the ability to terminate the pregnancy and thereby avoid the costs associated with carrying and giving birth to a child with severe defects. In the context of this medical malpractice action, the distinction between causing the Johnsons to forego termination of the troubled pregnancy and causing a defective birth is significant. The former is a matter of causation while the latter goes to the question of damages, which we discuss in more detail in the next section of this opinion. This distinction was amplified in Cowe where we were confronted with a claim by a child born to a mentally retarded mother. While in the custody of a nursing home the mother was raped, resulting in the child's birth. The child sued the nursing home contending, among other things, that because of the nursing home's negligence in failing to protect the mother from rape, the child was wrongly born "into a world in which there was no natural parent capable of caring for and supporting him." [ ]. We rejected the child's claim on two interrelated grounds: (1) "a general conceptual unwillingness to recognize any cognizable damages for a child born with a genetic impairment as opposed to not being born at all", and (2) "the impossibility of calculating compensatory damages to restore a birth defective child to the position he would have occupied were it not for the defendant's negligence." [ ]. Both interrelated grounds go to the issue of damages. It was in that context we declared "life, even life with severe defects, cannot be an injury in the legal sense." [ ].

Thus, in Cowe, the injury was life itself. And as with numerous other jurisdictions we were unwilling to allow a child plaintiff to proceed with this cause of action, in part because it involved "a calculation of damages dependant upon the relevant benefits of an impaired life as opposed to no life at all . . . a comparison the law is not equipped to make." [ ]. Here, however, the injury is the lost opportunity and ability to terminate the pregnancy. Failure to allow the Johnsons to proceed with their claim would "immunize those in the medical field from liability for their performance in one particular area of medical practice." Garrison v. Foy, 486 N.E.2d 5, 8 (Ind. Ct. App. 1985) (recognizing the existence of a cause of action for wrongful pregnancy). We decline to carve out an exception in this case, and see no reason to prohibit the Johnsons from pursuing their claim.

III.   Damages

It is a well-established principle that damages are awarded to fairly and adequately compensate an injured party for her loss, and the proper measure of damages must be flexible enough to fit the circumstances. * * *

Viewing this case as asserting a tort of "wrongful birth" the trial court determined that the Johnsons could recover the following damages: (1) the extraordinary costs necessary to treat the birth defect, (2) any additional medical or educational costs attributable to the birth defect during the child's minority, (3) medical and hospital expenses incurred as a result of the physician's negligence, (4) the physical pain suffered by the mother, (5) loss of consortium, and (6) the mental and emotional anguish suffered by the parents. The Court of Appeals also viewed this case as one for "wrongful birth." Thus, following the lead from other jurisdictions, with the exception of mental and emotional distress, the Court of Appeals agreed the Johnsons were entitled to recover the foregoing damages. However, we have determined that this case should be treated no differently than any other medical malpractice case. Consequently, we need not evaluate the type of damages that may be allowed in a claimed "wrongful birth" action. Rather, we look at the damages the Johnsons contend they suffered and determine whether, if proven, they be can said to have been proximately caused by Healthcare Providers' breach of duty. [ ]

Consolidated and rephrased the Johnsons' complaint essentially sets forth the following damages: (1) hospital and related medical expenses associated with the pregnancy and delivery, (2) costs associated with providing the infant with care and treatment, (3) lost income, (4) emotional distress, and (5) loss of consortium. Indiana subscribes to the general principle of tort law that all damages directly attributable to the wrong done are recoverable. [ ]. As we have indicated, the Johnsons' claimed injury in this case is the lost opportunity and ability to terminate the pregnancy. In turn, the loss can be measured by the medical and other costs directly attributable to Connie carrying the child to term. In addition to emotional distress damages [ ] the damages the Johnsons seek are consistent with those naturally flowing from Healthcare Providers' breach of duty.

[Vacated]

Notes

1) If a physician were to ask you what it means to exercise "medical due care", what would you tell him/her that would be useful? Is it realistic to expect physicians never to make a mistake, or face the threat of a malpractice claim should they ever do so?

2) Medical negligence has often been defined as that conduct which falls below that level of care expected of the average or ordinary, qualified physician. Is it really acceptable to be average or ordinary if a higher level of care would make a material difference to the plaintiff's outcome? Do juries think so?

3) Physicians are expected to provide the learning-and-skill, care-and-diligence and best-judgment for which they are capable. Are these time-honored buzz words that have long been used to describe medical due care consistent with "average" and "ordinary"?

4) Finally, who defines "due care"? Often times medical malpractice cases boil down to a battle of the experts: plaintiff's experts opine that there was negligence; defense experts opine that there was not. How does a lay jury assess who is and is not credible? Credentials of the experts? Presentation? Ability to sustain cross-examination? Is there any recourse for an aggrieved party who believes the jury simply could not understand the science?

SECTION B.   INTENTIONAL ACTS

BENAVIDEZ v. UNITED STATES OF AMERICA

United States Court of Appeals for the Tenth Circuit, 1999.
177 F.3d 927.

LUCERO, Circuit Judge.

* * *

I

Appellant Mario G. Benavidez is a member of the Laguna Pueblo Indian Tribe in New Mexico. As a teenager, Benavidez suffered from depression and a drug and alcohol dependency problem that led to frequent arrests by the local police. After attempting suicide, Benavidez was referred by the police and the Indian Health Service ("IHS") to a government-employed psychologist, Dr. David J. Bullis, for counseling. Bullis diagnosed Benavidez, who was then just shy of his sixteenth birthday, as suffering from a variety of psychological disorders, including depression with suicidal intent, polysubstance abuse, and cannabis dependence.

Despite this diagnosis, Bullis allegedly told Benavidez that continued alcohol and drug abuse would be appropriate and even therapeutic. Bullis also allegedly used therapy sessions to convince Benavidez that he was homosexual and that he should have sex with Bullis. During the course of the patient-therapist relationship, Bullis allegedly engaged in sexual contact with Benavidez. Together, the two also allegedly used alcohol, marijuana and other illegal drugs.

The record includes testimony that Bullis had a reputation for using drugs and alcohol with many of his teenage patients, and Bullis himself told one of his supervisors that he had engaged in "some exploratory sexual contact" with Benavidez. The supervisor never notified his superiors of Bullis's conduct, but merely wrote in his notes that he felt comfortable allowing Bullis to continue with his regular duties. The IHS did not relieve Bullis of his clinical responsibilities until January 1995, when Benavidez filed an administrative tort claim against the agency.

In July 1995, Benavidez * * * filed suit in the United States District Court for the District of New Mexico, alleging various injuries as a result of Bullis's conduct and seeking recovery against the United States under the respondeat superior theory of liability. The district court concluded that Benavidez's allegations constituted a claim for assault and battery rather than for professional negligence or malpractice. Applying the intentional tort exception to the FTCA's waiver of sovereign immunity, the court thus granted the government's motion to dismiss for lack of jurisdiction.

II

* * *

The FTCA provides that the United States can be sued for personal injury resulting from:

[The] negligent or wrongful act or omission of any employee of the Government while acting within the scope of his office or employment, under circumstances where the United States, if a private person, would be liable to the claimant in accordance with the law of the place where the act or omission occurred.

[ ]. But this waiver of sovereign immunity does not extend to claims arising out of assault or battery. [ ].

The issue before us, therefore, is whether, Bullis's alleged conduct constituted a "negligent, or wrongful act" rather than an assault or battery for purposes of the FTCA.

* * *

A

A review of relevant federal and state court cases shows that Bullis's conduct has traditionally been understood and commonly defined as negligent malpractice, which does not fall within the intentional tort exception to the FTCA's waiver of sovereign immunity. See, e.g., Simmons v. United States, 805 F.2d 1363, 1368–71 (9th Cir. 1986) * * *

In Simmons, for example, an IHS therapist seduced his patient, a member of the Chehalis Indian Tribe, into a sexual relationship. [ ]. The patient suffered a subsequent deterioration in her mental and emotional health. Another therapist traced her worsening condition to the sexual relations she had with the former therapist. The patient thereupon filed suit against the government under the FTCA, and the district court entered judgment in her favor. Dismissing the government's appeal, the Ninth Circuit ruled that by seducing his patient, the therapist had mismanaged the "transference phenomenon" and thus engaged in negligent malpractice. [ ].

"Courts have uniformly regarded mishandling of transference as malpractice or gross negligence." Id. [citations omitted]. The "transference phenomenon" refers to the tendency of patients to become emotionally dependent upon, and trusting of, their psychologist or psychiatrist. See generally Michael D. McCafferty & Steven M. Meyer, Medical Malpractice: Bases of Liability § 10.18 (1985) (explaining that transference "is one of the most significant concepts in psychoanalytic therapy," and accounts for the "strong dependency of the patient upon the therapist"). Specifically, transference describes a patient's "projection of feelings, thoughts and wishes onto the analyst, who has come to represent some person from the patient's past." [ ]

[ ].

Although it occurs in other professional relationships, "it is only in psychotherapy that the management of this [transference] effect is so critical—legally as well as therapeutically." Joseph T. Smith, Medical Malpractice: Psychiatric Care § 9.10 (1995). No other professional relationship "offers a course of treatment and counseling predicated upon handling the transference phenomenon." [ ]. In order to manage the transference phenomenon properly a therapist must avoid emotional involvement with a patient who transfers feelings of affection to him. [ ].

Despite the wide acceptance of transference in the medical and legal communities, the district court summarily dismissed the Simmons court's reliance on the phenomenon. [ ] But we need not rely exclusively on Simmons and other cases that employ the transference phenomenon. Faced with a case very similar to the one before us, the Fourth Circuit, without relying on transference, concluded that a therapist's sexual relationship with his patient constituted grounds for a negligent malpractice claim. See Andrews [v. United States, 732 F.2d 366,] 370–71.

In Andrews, a government-employed therapist diagnosed the plaintiff as suffering from chronic depression. The therapist soon began using counseling sessions to convince his patient that she needed an affair, and ultimately succeeded in seducing her into a sexual relationship. [ ]. As a result of the therapist's conduct, the plaintiff's emotional health worsened, and she ultimately filed suit under the FTCA. The government argued that the suit stemmed from an assault and battery for which sovereign immunity is not waived. [ ]. The Fourth Circuit disagreed, and simply held that when a therapist seduces his patient while purporting to provide counseling, "the resulting cause of action is described as medical malpractice [and] not assault and battery." Id.

The government attempts to distinguish Andrews by arguing that the patient in that case consented to her therapist's sexual advances because he convinced her that sexual intercourse with him was the best course of treatment for her. The government contends that unlike the plaintiff in Andrews, Benavidez did not consent to Bullis's sexual contacts. Thus, this case involves the intentional tort of assault and battery rather than negligent malpractice. The district court agreed, stating that "there is no doubt that Plaintiff does not allege that the sexual acts were consensual." [ ].

To state a claim for negligence rather than a claim for assault and battery, Benavidez did not have to allege that he engaged in consensual sexual relations with Bullis. One of the key distinctions between claims sounding in negligence and those sounding in intentional tort like assault and battery is that the latter requires an unconsented touching. See Restatement (Second) of Torts § 13 cmt. d (1965) ("The absence of consent . . . is inherent in the very idea of those invasions of interest and of personality which, at common law, were the subject of an action for trespass for battery [or] assault."). By alleging negligence, Benavidez implicitly asserted that he consented to Bullis's sexual advances, and thus pleaded a claim for professional negligence or malpractice rather than for assault and battery.

Of course, a mere allegation of negligence does not turn an intentional tort into negligent conduct * * * In concluding that Benavidez asserted a claim for assault and battery, the district court merely stated that "the complaint avers that Bullis forced himself on the plaintiff by misusing the therapeutic relationship and by encouraging the Plaintiff to use alcohol and drugs." [ ]. Nowhere in the complaint or in the record, however, do we discern any support for the district court's conclusion that Bullis forcibly engaged in sexual relations with Benavidez.

B

The government argues, alternatively, that Benavidez admits to being so incompetent during the course of his therapy as to render meaningless whatever consent he may have given to Bullis's conduct * * *

The district court's finding and Benavidez's testimony merely reveal Benavidez's confusion about how to respond to the unsolicited sexual advances of a therapist upon whom he was so emotionally dependent, and whose suggestions he was unable to resist. The plaintiff in Andrews displayed a similar "confused dependency" and "ambivalence about continuing treatment" in the face of her therapist's sexual advances. Andrews [ ]. Nonetheless, the Fourth Circuit rejected the government's argument that the therapist's sexual relationship with the plaintiff was nonconsensual.

Moreover, the court suggested that in such a case, consent may be irrelevant because the egregious nature of the therapist's conduct constitutes an act of professional negligence separate and apart from the act of intercourse. " 'The injury to the plaintiff [is] not merely caused by the consummation of acts of sexual intercourse. Harm [is] also caused by the [therapist's] failure to treat the patient with professionally acceptable procedures.' " [ ]

III

The gravamen of the complaint in this case is that under the guise of providing counseling, a therapist violated professionally acceptable procedures and induced an emotionally depressed and suicidal teenager, already prone to alcohol and drug abuse, to indulge in the use of such substances and to engage in sexual conduct. Given the settled federal and state law on this issue, we conclude that the allegations in the complaint sufficiently support a claim for professional negligence or malpractice. This sort of claim does not fall within the intentional tort exception to the FTCA's waiver of sovereign immunity.

REVERSED.

MARCUS v. LIEBMAN

Appellate Court of Illinois, First District, First Division, 1978.
59 Ill.App.3d 337, 16 Ill.Dec. 613, 375 N.E.2d 486.

* * *

Plaintiff testified that in July of 1970 she was having difficulty sleeping, was "completely overwrought" and at the recommendation of her psychologist, Dr. Bass, decided to enter a hospital for several days of rest. On July 20, 1970, plaintiff voluntarily admitted herself as a patient at Lutheran General Hospital where she was placed in the psychiatric wing and introduced to the defendant psychiatrist, Dr. Liebman, for the first time. Plaintiff testified that during one of her first sessions with the defendant she began throwing things at him because she did not want him as her doctor; that she was then placed in restraints after which she began screaming and singing in order to annoy people; and that after a drug was administered to calm her down, she was removed from the restraints.

Plaintiff went on to testify that during her fourth day in the hospital she informed Dr. Liebman that she wanted to sign a release paper which made mandatory her release within five days of signing the form. Dr. Liebman gave her the form and she signed it. Several days later, the defendant told her to rescind her request for release. He instructed her to "sign this piece of paper or you will be committed to Elgin State Hospital." Plaintiff testified that although she told the defendant she wanted to be released and that he had no right to force her to sign that piece of paper, she was frightened and, believing the defendant could actually have sent her to Elgin State Hospital, signed the paper thus rescinding her prior request to be released. Plaintiff admitted that while a patient at Lutheran General Hospital she took trips outside the hospital to see movies and to bowl. She also stated that she was eventually released from the hospital on August 19, 1970.

Called pursuant to section 60 of the Civil Practice Act [ ], Dr. Liebman denied threatening the plaintiff or telling her he would have her placed in Elgin State Hospital. Dr. Liebman testified that he did tell the plaintiff that if she persisted in her request to leave, a court order could be sought to keep her in the hospital. Dr. Liebman denied telling the plaintiff he would or could seek such an order.

Also called as a witness by the plaintiff was Dr. Cyrus Bass, who had treated plaintiff since 1968 in the capacity of a clinical psychologist. Dr. Bass testified that in July of 1970 plaintiff was disturbed and had become a bit incoherent at times and that he called plaintiff's brother and recommended hospitalization. Dr. Bass visited plaintiff in the hospital on August 5, 1970, and plaintiff told him she wanted to be released from the hospital and from Dr. Liebman's care.

Plaintiff contends that a question of fact was created concerning the issue of false imprisonment and that the trial court, under the standard in *Pedrick v. Peoria & Eastern R.R. Co.* (1967), 37 Ill.2d 494, 229 N.E.2d 504, erroneously entered a directed verdict in defendant's favor.

False imprisonment consists of an unlawful restraint of individual personal liberty or freedom of locomotion against a person's will. [citations omitted]. This unlawful restraint may be effected by words alone, by acts alone, or both. [ ] Actual force is unnecessary to an action in false imprisonment. [ ] However, the submission must be to a threatened and reasonably apprehended force. [ ] The defendant contends that the trial court correctly granted his motion for a directed verdict because plaintiff's apprehension of force or coercion was not reasonable. Defendant cites plaintiff's testimony that she knew she could be released from the hospital within five days and her statement "you have no right to do that" was made in response to Dr. Liebman's alleged threat to have her committed to Elgin State Hospital. Defendant concludes that even at the moment of the alleged threat plaintiff knew she could leave. We disagree and believe that based upon the record before us the question of whether plaintiff's apprehension of force or coercion was reasonable is a question of fact for the jury. On both direct examination and cross-examination, plaintiff testified that she believed Dr. Liebman could have her committed to Elgin State Hospital if she did not sign the piece of paper rescinding her request to leave. Considering plaintiff's mental condition and the fact that she was behind locked doors in a hospital, the jury could find her belief reasonable. It is true that the plaintiff, since she voluntarily admitted herself, knew that she would be released in five days after so requesting. However, plaintiff signed a piece of paper rescinding that request to leave. Plaintiff never testified that she knew she could leave within five days even though she rescinded her request to leave. In fact, her testimony is to the contrary. We do not say as a matter of law plaintiff's belief was reasonable, but we do believe that this was a question of fact for the jury and afforded no basis for the trial court's entering a directed verdict in defendant's favor.

Defendant also cites the fact that plaintiff received telephone calls, had visitors, and even made trips outside the hospital during her last weeks there in support of the contention that plaintiff's actions were not the result of a reasonably apprehended threat. While the above facts may be relevant to a determination of whether plaintiff's apprehension was reasonable, they are not sufficient to support a directed verdict and are better left to the jury to consider in light of the other evidence.

Defendant further argues that the directed verdict is proper because the threat which gave rise to the alleged false imprisonment was of a future action. Although our research has disclosed no Illinois case involving the threat of a future action the Restatement (Second) of Torts § 40, comment b, at 60 (1965) provides:

> "b. The submission must be made to a threat to apply the physical force immediately upon the other's going or attempting to go beyond the area within which the threat is intended to confine him. Submission to the threat to apply physical force at a time appreciably later than that at which the other attempts to go beyond the given area is not confinement.

> 2. A tells B that if he leaves the room he, A, will shoot him the next time he meets him on the street. B, in submission to the threat, remains in the room. A has not confined B."

Prosser similarly indicates that "threats for the future, as for example, to call the police and have the plaintiff arrested," are insufficient. Prosser, Torts § 11, at 45 (4th ed. 1971). [ ].

* * *

Considering the testimony at trial, we conclude that the trial court incorrectly directed a verdict for the defendant. Plaintiff's testimony, if believed, established a cause of action for false imprisonment. * * *

Reversed.

VASSILIADES v. GARFINCKEL'S

District of Columbia Court of Appeals, 1985.
492 A.2d 580.

* * * [I]n contemplation of undergoing plastic surgery, Mrs. Vassiliades * * * contacted Dr. Magassy to discuss the possibility of having him perform the surgery. [H]e performed the surgery successfully the next month. Before and after the surgical procedure, Dr. Magassy took photographs of Mrs. Vassiliades' face. Mrs. Vassiliades understood the photographs were being taken as part of the doctor's regular routine for use with other patients. Dr. Magassy testified he also took photographs as a protective measure in the event a patient later claimed there had been no improvement in appearance.

Several months after Mrs. Vassiliades' last postoperative visit, Dr. Magassy was invited by the director of public relations for Garfinckel's to participate in a store promotion during the month of March 1979. He agreed to participate without compensation in a program entitled, "Creams versus Plastic Surgery," a topic chosen by Garfinckel's partly as a result of recent publicity about the plastic surgery operations of the wives of Presidents Ford and Carter. In connection with its promotion and prior to the presentation at Garfinckel's, Garfinckel's arranged to have Dr. Magassy and other participants appear on the "Panorama" television program on WTTG, Channel 5, in Washington, D.C

During his television presentation, Dr. Magassy used slide photographs of several of his patients, including two "before" and two "after" of Mrs. Vassiliades. Although Mrs. Vassiliades' face appeared on the television screen for less than one minute and her name was not mentioned, a former coworker, Beatrice Brooks, recognized her. Mrs. Brooks testified she had not previously known about Mrs. Vassiliades' surgery and after seeing Mrs. Vassiliades' photographs during the television program, she immediately called a friend at work to share this information. The coworker whom Mrs. Brooks called told another employee, Elliott Woo, a neighbor of Mrs. Vassiliades * * *

Mrs. Vassiliades learned about the presentations on April 1, 1979. She testified that when she learned of the disclosure she was "devastated," "absolutely shocked" and "felt terrible" that everyone at her former office knew about her face-lift. She "went into a terrible depression," and did not want to go out in public anymore. She claimed she virtually went into hiding and refused to accompany her husband to many places because she knew everyone talked about her cosmetic surgery.

The key issue at trial was whether Mrs. Vassiliades had consented to the use of her photographs by Dr. Magassy. She categorically denied that she had. Dr. Magassy contended that he had obtained her verbal consent: on two occasions she had expressed her willingness to help him in any way she could with other patients who might be contemplating plastic surgery, and on her last visit she had told him that he could use her photographs in his lectures or in any other way to help other patients. Dr. Magassy's former assistant office manager corroborated his testimony about Mrs. Vassiliades' verbal consent.

II

Mrs. Vassiliades alleged that her right to privacy was violated because unreasonable publicity was given to her private life, her photographs were used for commercial gain by the defendants, and she was portrayed in a false light. Her additional claim for breach of a fiduciary duty was also a part of her invasion of privacy claim. RESTATEMENT (SECOND) OF TORTS § 652A, at 377–78 (1977) (although plaintiff may maintain invasion of privacy cause of action on several theories, she is entitled to only one recovery of damages) * * *

* * * [T]he trial court held that the right of privacy is not absolute and that, in balancing the individual's right to be let alone and the public's right to know, there are occasions on which the public right must prevail. We agree. We also agree that the precise boundaries of the public interest may be exceedingly difficult to define, that the subject matter of plastic surgery, as the trial court noted, "at a time when many well-known and highly visible men and women were the objects of news articles about face-lifts and other plastic surgery" was of general public

interest, and that a professional presentation with photographs would enhance the public interest in the subject. We disagree, however, with the trial court's conclusions that "reasonable minds could not differ in finding the publication [of Mrs. Vassiliades' photographs] to be of legitimate public interest," and that "certainly, the subject of face-lifts and plastic surgery was no longer a subject calculated to generate offense to persons of ordinary sensibilities." We hold Mrs. Vassiliades was entitled to expect photographs of her surgery would not be publicized without her consent.

Professor Prosser [W.PROSSER, LAW OF TORTS, s 117 (4th ed. 1971)] categorized four distinct kinds of invasions: (1) intrusion upon one's physical solitude or seclusion; (2) public disclosure of private facts; (3) publicity that places someone in a false light in the public eye; and (4) appropriation of one's name or likeness for another's benefit. *Id.* This formulation has been widely accepted by courts and adopted by the American Law Institute (ALI) as its general statement of the law. [ ].

* * *

A.

The RESTATEMENT, *supra*, § 652D, recognizes that publicity of a private matter may constitute an invasion of privacy.[1] The drafters contemplated that "any broadcast over the radio, or statement made in an address to a large audience, is sufficient to give publicity" to the private life of a person. [ ] The determinative factor is whether the communication is public as opposed to private. Mrs. Vassiliades offered evidence that, after agonizing over losing her youthful appearance and contemplating plastic surgery for many years, she underwent plastic surgery and kept her surgery secret, telling only family and very intimate friends.

In this jurisdiction, a cause of action for the invasion of privacy "represents a vindication of the right of private personality and emotional security." *Afro–American, supra*, 125 U.S.App.D.C. at 74, 366 F.2d at 653. Publication of a photograph of a nonpublic person without his consent is a violation of that right. [ ]. While we recognize that the right is not absolute, we agree with the Supreme Court of Missouri that "certainly if there is any right of privacy at all, it should include the right to obtain medical treatment at home or in a hospital for an individual personal condition (at least if it is not contagious or dangerous to others) without personal publicity." *Barber v. Time, Inc.*, 348 Mo. 1199, 159 S.W.2d 291, 295 (1942).

---

1. The RESTATEMENT, *supra*, § 652D, provides:

One who gives publicity to a matter concerning the private life of another is subject to liability to the other for invasion of his privacy, if the matter publicized is of a kind that

(a) would be highly offensive to a reasonable person, and

(b) is not of legitimate concern to the public.

We find the analysis in *Barber v. Time* persuasive, although the issue in that case differed from the issue before us. The Missouri Supreme Court faced the question of whether the media, which enjoys a broader protection than the average person, had invaded the plaintiff's right to privacy in publishing certain photographs of her. The plaintiff claimed her privacy had been invaded because a magazine had published an article, using her name and picture, about an unusual physical ailment for which she had been hospitalized and was being treated. In upholding the jury's finding that the plaintiff's privacy had been invaded, the Missouri Supreme Court held that "while plaintiff's ailment may have been a matter of some public interest because unusual, certainly the identity of the person who suffered this ailment was not." *Id.* The court's decision, however, did not turn on the identification of plaintiff by name; the court was concerned primarily with the individual patient's right to privacy, recognizing that for a physician effectively to treat a patient, the patient frequently is required to divulge "information which it would be both embarrassing and harmful to have circulated generally throughout the community." *Id.*

This is precisely what happened to Mrs. Vassiliades. Medical information which was embarrassing and emotionally distressing to her was broadcast on television and to a large audience. Publicizing the photographs as part of a presentation on plastic surgery communicated private facts about Mrs. Vassiliades' life. The nature of the publicity ensured that it would reach the public. * * *

The tort of invasion of privacy also requires, however, that the publicity be "highly offensive." RESTATEMENT, *supra*, § 652D comment c. "The claimant [must have] suffered an unreasonable and serious interference with protected interests." [Citations omitted]. The trial court found that the photographs were not highly offensive because there was nothing "uncomplimentary or unsavory" about them. Although the photographs may not have been uncomplimentary or unsavory, the issue is whether the publicity of Mrs. Vassialiades' surgery was highly offensive to a reasonable person, a factual question usually given to a jury to determine. * * *

Appellees also contend, and the trial court found, that the publicity was protected because there was a legitimate public interest in the publication. It is a defense to a claim of invasion of privacy that the matter publicized is of general public interest. [Citations omitted] Moreover, this defense or privilege is not limited to dissemination of news about current events or public affairs, but also protects "information concerning interesting phases of human activity and embraces all issues about which information is needed or appropriate so that that individual may cope with the exigencies of their period." *Campbell v. Seabury Press*, 614 F.2d 395, 397 (5th Cir. 1980) * * *

Nevertheless, the privilege to publicize matters of legitimate public interest is not absolute. *See Gilbert v. Medical Economics Co., supra,* 665 F.2d at 307. Certain private facts about a person should never be publicized, even if the facts concern matters which are, or relate to persons who are, of legitimate public interest. [ ]. We thus find persuasive the distinction Mrs. Vassiliades draws between the private fact of her reconstructive surgery and the fact that plastic surgery is a matter of legitimate public interest.

The conflict between the public's right to information and the individual's right to privacy requires a balancing of the competing interests. In this jurisdiction "the right of privacy stands on a high ground, cognate to the values and concerns protected by constitutional guarantees." *Afro–American Publishing Co. v. Jaffe, supra*, [ ]. Accordingly, upon balancing the two interests, we hold that Mrs. Vassiliades had a higher interest to be protected. Although Dr. Magassy and Garfinckel's may well have performed a public service by making the presentations about plastic surgery, and the public undoubtedly has an interest in plastic surgery, it was unnecessary for Dr. Magassy to publicize Mrs. Vassiliades' photographs. Publication of her photographs neither strengthened the impact nor the credibility of the presentations nor otherwise enhanced the public's general awareness of the issues and facts concerning plastic surgery. * * *

This finding of liability does not compel a like result with respect to Garfinckel's. The undisputed evidence is that Dr. Magassy had unqualifiedly assured Garfinckel's that he had obtained his patients' consent. Clear evidence of consent will insulate a party from liability. [citations omitted]. Thus, the issue is whether Garfinckel's was justified in relying on Dr. Magassy's oral assurance. Garfinckel's decision to ask Dr. Magassy to participate in its program was based on its understanding that he was a reputable professional; Garfinckel's director of public relations testified about Dr. Magassy's prior complimentary public exposure. Before the television program, Garfinckel's director examined each of the slides on a view finder and, upon finding some to be not particularly pleasant, asked Dr. Magassy if he had obtained permission from his patients to use the slides. Based on Dr. Magassy's assurance that he had, the director did not inquire about consent prior to the department store presentation. No evidence was presented to suggest that Garfinckel's had any reason to doubt Dr. Magassy's statement.

Under these circumstances, we hold that Garfinckel's was justified in relying on Dr. Magassy's assurances that he had Mrs. Vassiliades' consent and that Mrs. Vassiliades has failed to meet her burden to prove Garfinckel's liability for invasion of her privacy. * * *

AFFIRMED IN PART AND REVERSED IN PART

K.A.C. v. BENSON

Supreme Court of Minnesota, 1995.
527 N.W.2d 553.

STRINGER, Justice.

Plaintiff-respondent, T.M.W., brought this action against Dr. Philip Benson and the Palen Clinic for emotional damages she allegedly suffered upon learning that Dr. Benson had performed upon her two gynecological procedures while Dr. Benson was infected with the human immunodeficiency virus (HIV) and was suffering from open sores on his hands and forearms. We reject plaintiff's claims and hold that a plaintiff must allege actual exposure to HIV in order to establish a claim for emotional damages resulting from a fear of contracting AIDS.

Over 50 former patients, including T.M.W., filed complaints against defendants asserting various claims. The district court filed a series of orders resulting in summary judgment in favor of defendants because plaintiffs failed to allege actual exposure or direct contact with Dr. Benson's HIV-infected blood or body fluids. In its unpublished opinion, the court of appeals affirmed in part and reversed in part, holding that a genuine issue of material fact existed as to whether Dr. Benson placed his patients in a "zone of danger." [ ]. The court of appeals reversed the district court with respect to all of T.M.W.'s claims, permitting T.M.W.'s claims for negligent and intentional infliction of emotional distress, battery, negligent nondisclosure, and consumer fraud. The court of appeals also limited as a matter of law plaintiff's emotional distress damages to "a reasonable window of anxiety" between the time they learned of Dr. Benson's illness until they received negative HIV test results. This appeal followed.

We reverse the decision of the court of appeals, and reinstate summary judgment in favor of defendants.

Dr. Philip Benson was a family practitioner at the Palen Clinic and the Palen Heights Clinic from 1980 until June 1991. Early in 1989, Dr. Benson began losing weight while following a weight control program. In March 1989, he developed a series of skin conditions on his face, hands, arms, and head. Initially, Dr. Benson self-treated these conditions. In early 1990, Dr. Benson consulted a dermatologist who diagnosed a variety of skin disorders, including vitiligio, alopecia areata, and folliculitis.

In June 1990, Dr. Benson developed nodular lesions on his hands and forearms. In September 1990, Dr. Benson consulted another dermatologist who diagnosed the lesions as exudative dermatitis (Mycobacterium marinum) and ordered an HIV test. Dr. Benson tested HIV seropositive. Dr. Benson's dermatologist reported Dr. Benson's HIV seropositive status to the Minnesota Department of Health, and in October 1990 Dr. Benson met with the Minnesota Board of Medical Examiners (Board) regarding his medical practice. At that time, the Board had no formal guidelines regarding HIV seropositive health-care providers. The Board advised Dr. Benson to wear two pairs of gloves when caring for patients and to refrain from performing surgery. He complied with the Board's requirements, and voluntarily ceased delivering babies.

After meeting with the Board, Dr. Benson performed two gynecological exams on T.M.W. during the time he suffered from dermatitis: the first in late October 1990, the second in early January 1991. By the end of 1990, Dr. Benson's dermatitis condition had significantly healed.

After Dr. Benson performed the second gynecological exam on T.M.W. in January 1991, Dr. Benson again met with the State Board of Medical Examiners. As a result of that meeting Dr. Benson entered into a Stipulation and Order with the Board, restricting him from delivering babies, from performing surgery, or performing invasive procedures using a sharp instrument in a patient's body cavity.

In May 1991 the State Board of Medical Examiners and the Minnesota Department of Health contacted 336 patients on whom Dr. Benson performed one or more invasive procedures while gloved, but at a time when he suffered from exudative dermatitis. The letter, dated June 17, 1991 and signed by Dr. Benson, stated in relevant part as follows:

> Under most conditions there would be no reason to alert you [of Dr. Benson's AIDS diagnosis] since current recommendations suggest that physicians infected with the AIDS virus pose little or no risk to their patients. However, between May 1, 1990 and February 21, 1991, I had a skin rash on my hands and fingers. I am sending you this letter because there is a very minimal possibility that you were exposed to the AIDS virus through body fluids from this rash during certain medical procedures. At the time that I had this rash, I did not realize that there may have been any risk to you because I was wearing gloves. I am now aware that even with gloves, an extremely minimal risk still existed.

> Based on the most current information about AIDS and the opinions of many experts, the likelihood that you have been infected with the AIDS virus from this type of exposure is extremely low. However, for your peace of mind and absolute safety, I am recommending that you be tested for antibody to the AIDS virus. This test will tell us whether or not you are infected with the AIDS virus. Because people generally have no symptoms when they first become infected with the AIDS virus, it is important for you to be tested. * * *

(Letter from Dr. Benson of June 17, 1991) (emphasis in original). Following receipt of Dr. Benson's letter, over 50 former patients commenced individual actions against Dr. Benson and the Palen Clinic for various claims. None of the 325 patients tested HIV seropositive.

Scientists have developed a medically reliable test for the presence of an antibody produced by individuals who have contracted HIV. Blood tests for detection of HIV are extremely accurate. Two antibody tests exist: a screening enzyme-linked immunosorbent assay (ELISA) test (or enzyme immunoassay test (EIA)), and a second confirmatory test called a Western Blot. Used together, these tests are more than 99.0 percent accurate. Ninety-five percent of HIV-infected individuals will test HIV positive within 6 months of the date of viral transmission. After an individual tests positive for HIV, there may be a latency period of several years before physical symptoms of AIDS develop. An AIDS diagnosis is made when an individual tests seropositive for HIV and has a severely compromised immune system as a result of the virus, or contracts one or more opportunistic diseases.

Dr. Benson ceased his medical practice in June 1991. He died of AIDS-related complications in September 1991.

T.M.W.'s Claims

a. *Negligent Infliction of Emotional Distress*

The first issue presented on appeal is whether plaintiff must allege actual exposure to the body fluids of an HIV-infected individual to recover emotional distress damages. To establish a claim for negligent infliction of emotional distress, plaintiff must show she: (1) was within a zone of danger of physical impact; (2) reasonably feared for her own safety; and (3) suffered severe emotional distress with attendant physical manifestations. [Citation omitted]. T.M.W. argues that although she cannot prove actual exposure to HIV occurred, it is possible she was exposed to a body fluid transfer. Thus, T.M.W. in effect alleges her proximity to Dr. Benson's HIV-infected body fluids put her within the "zone of danger" of physical impact. She offers the affidavit of Dr. Sanford Kuvin, who would testify that gloves are inadequate protection against HIV transmission. We are not persuaded by this argument, and hold, as a matter of law, for the reasons stated hereafter, that plaintiff was beyond the "zone of danger" for purposes of a claim of negligent infliction of emotional distress.

In Purcell v. St. Paul City Ry. Co., 48 Minn. 134, 50 N.W. 1034 (1892), this court first ruled that actual physical impact is not necessary to sustain a claim for emotional distress damages. There, plaintiff suffered a miscarriage after the cable car on which she was a passenger narrowly avoided a collision with another cable car. Id. The court adopted the "zone of danger" test, noting the impending cable car collision "seemed so imminent, and was so nearly caused, that the incident and attending confusion of ringing alarm-bells and passengers rushing out of the car caused to plaintiff sudden fright and reasonable fear of immediate death or great bodily injury * * * ." Id. The zone of danger test has remained the law in Minnesota for over 100 years.

We adhered to the "zone of danger" test in Okrina v. Midwestern Corp., 282 Minn. 400, 401, 165 N.W.2d 259, 261(1969), where plaintiff was in a dressing room at a J. C. Penney store when "she heard what sounded like a bomb and witnessed the collapse of the wall." Id. Plaintiff ultimately escaped "without being physically struck by debris other than dust." Id. This court held that plaintiff was within the zone of danger. The court of appeals applied the "zone of danger" test in Quill v. Trans–World Airlines Inc., [ ] where the aircraft on which plaintiff was a passenger suddenly rolled and plunged toward the earth. [ ]. The pilot regained control of the craft only seconds before it would have struck the ground. [ ].

This court has limited the zone of danger analysis to encompass plaintiffs who have been in some actual personal physical danger caused by defendant's negligence. [ ]

Thus, cases permitting recovery for negligent infliction of emotional distress are characterized by a reasonable anxiety arising in the plaintiff, with attendant physical manifestation, from being in a situation where it was abundantly clear that plaintiff was in grave personal peril for some specifically defined period of time. Fortune smiled and the imminent calamity did not occur. Here, the situation is quite different. The facts as alleged by T.M.W. indicate that Dr. Benson's actions never did place T.M.W. in "apparent, imminent peril" of contracting HIV because she was not actually exposed to the AIDS virus. [ ]. Transmission of HIV from Dr. Benson to plaintiff was, fortunately, never more than a very remote possibility.

That T.M.W.'s risk of contracting HIV was no more than a remote possibility is acknowledged by the numerous resource materials referred to by the district court and the parties. HIV is transmitted through direct fluid-to-fluid contact with the blood, semen, vaginal secretions, or breast milk of an HIV-infected individual. n6 While other body fluids may contain HIV, the virus apparently is not transmitted by other fluids.

> Documented modes of HIV transmission include: unprotected sexual intercourse with an HIV-infected person; using contaminated needles; contact with HIV-infected blood, blood components, or blood products by parenteral mucous membrane or nonintact skin; transplants of HIV-infected organs and/or tissues; transfusions of HIV-infected blood; artificial insemination of HIV-infected semen; and perinatal transmission from mother to child around the time of birth.

> Ninety-nine percent of reported AIDS cases are transmitted by sexual intercourse, intravenous drug abuse, or perinatal transmission.

This court has long recognized that a person within the zone of danger of physical impact who reasonably fears for his or her own safety during the time of exposure, and who consequently suffers severe emotional distress with resultant physical injury, may recover emotional distress damages whether or not physical impact results. [ ]. However, a remote possibility of personal peril is insufficient to place plaintiff within a zone of danger for purposes of a claim of negligent infliction of emotional distress. Consequently, we hold that a plaintiff who fails to allege actual exposure to HIV is not, as a matter of law, in personal physical danger of contracting HIV, and thus not within a zone of danger for purposes of establishing a claim for negligent infliction of emotional distress.

The actual exposure requirement we adopt today is consistent with the court's historical caution regarding emotional distress claims. Concerns about unintended and unreasonable results prompted this court to limit negligent infliction of emotional distress claims to persons who experienced personal physical danger as a result of defendant's negligence. We determined the "zone-of-danger rule" would lead to reasonable and consistent results because courts and juries can objectively determine whether plaintiffs were within the zone of danger. [ ]. The standard we adopt today, requiring a plaintiff to allege actual exposure to HIV as a predicate to recovery, retains the objective component this court has long deemed necessary to ensure stability and predictability in the disposition of emotional distress claims.

We also find persuasive several policy considerations articulated by the California Court of Appeals on remand in Kerins v. Hartley (Kerins II), 27 Cal.App.4th 1062, 33 Cal.Rptr.2d 172 (Cal. Ct. App. 1994).

> The magnitude of the potential class of plaintiffs seeking emotional distress damages for negligent exposure to HIV or AIDS cannot be overstated. * * * "the devastating effects of AIDS and the wide-spread fear of contamination at home, work, school, healthcare facilities and elsewhere are, sadly, too well known to require further discussion at this point." Proliferation of fear of AIDS claims in the absence of meaningful restrictions would run an equal risk of compromising the availability and affordability of medical, dental and malpractice insurance, medical and dental care, prescription drugs, and blood products. Juries deliberating in fear of AIDS lawsuits would be just as likely to reach inconsistent results, discouraging early resolution or settlement of such claims. Last but not least, the coffers of defendants and their insurers would risk being emptied to pay for the emotional suffering of the many plaintiffs uninfected by exposure to HIV or AIDS, possibly leaving inadequate compensation for plaintiffs to whom the fatal AIDS virus was actually transmitted.

Although our decision is based upon existing Minnesota case law, we note that it is consistent with the majority of jurisdictions that have addressed the issue of emotional distress damages arising from a plaintiff's fear of contracting HIV. The majority of courts that have decided fear of HIV exposure cases hold the plaintiff must allege actual exposure to HIV to recover emotional distress damages. We concur with the majority of jurisdictions and reject plaintiff's claim in this case. In an action for damages based solely upon plaintiff's fear of acquiring AIDS, without allegation of actual exposure to HIV, no legally cognizable claim exists under Minnesota law. Accordingly, we reverse the court of appeals decision and reinstate summary judgment in favor of defendants, Dr. Philip Benson and the Palen Clinic.

Indeed, Maryland is the only jurisdiction in which the highest court permits recovery when a plaintiff alleges potential exposure to the AIDS virus, absent either a proven channel of exposure or a positive HIV test. [Citations omitted] A few trial courts have also employed this test. [Citations omitted]

b. Intentional Infliction of Emotional Distress

To sustain a claim for intentional infliction of emotional distress, plaintiff must establish: (1) the conduct was extreme and outrageous; (2) the conduct was intentional or reckless; (3) it caused emotional distress; and (4) the distress was severe. [Citation omitted]. The actor must intend to cause severe emotional distress or proceed with the knowledge that it is substantially certain, or at least highly probable, that severe emotional distress will occur. [Citation omitted]. Here, the court of appeals focused on the "extreme and outrageous conduct" element and concluded that a factual dispute existed with regard to Dr. Benson's conduct.

The undisputed facts show that upon learning of his HIV seropositive status Dr. Benson sought guidance from the Minnesota State Board of Medical Examiners regarding his medical practice. When Dr. Benson treated T.M.W. he complied with the restrictions imposed by the Minnesota Board of Medical Examiners pursuant to the October 1990 meeting. There is no evidence Dr. Benson either knew of or recklessly disregarded a known risk to T.M.W., nor in fact did Dr. Benson actually pose any reasonable risk of exposing T.M.W. to the AIDS virus. Consequently, we hold that T.M.W. failed to establish that Dr. Benson's conduct was either intentional or reckless for purposes of meeting the Dornfeld test. [ ].

c. Battery

T.M.W.'s claim for battery is predicated on her assertion that Dr. Benson's nondisclosure of his HIV status vitiated any initial consent to medical care because she would not have consented to treatment by Dr. Benson had she known he was infected with HIV. T.M.W. alleges she asked Dr. Benson about his weight loss and the sores on his hands and arms, and that Dr. Benson told her the sores resulted from a sunburn he received while on vacation. The weight loss was due to a weight control program.

The district court held that plaintiff could not sustain her battery claim absent allegations of actual exposure to HIV. The court of appeals reversed, adopting the reasoning of the California Court of Appeals in Kerins I, which was subsequently vacated and reversed on remand. [Citations omitted].

In medical malpractice claims, battery consists of touching of a substantially different nature and character from that to which the patient consented. [ ] For example, in Mohr v. Williams, 95 Minn. 261, 104 N.W. 12 (1905), plaintiff's consent to surgery on her right ear did not authorize her doctor to operate on the left ear. A claim of battery also lies when a doctor fails to disclose a very material aspect of the nature and character of a procedure to be performed, because any supposed consent is undermined and thus an unpermitted touching occurs. [ ] However, a patient's consent is not rendered void when the patient is touched in exactly the way she consented. [ ]

T.M.W. does not allege that Dr. Benson performed a different procedure from that to which she consented. Moreover, because Dr. Benson's conduct did not significantly increase the risk that T.M.W. would contract HIV, it cannot be said that Dr. Benson failed to disclose a material aspect of the nature and character of the procedure performed. Consequently, plaintiff's battery claim must fail.

d. Negligent Nondisclosure

The court of appeals reversed the summary judgment as to T.M.W.'s claim of negligent nondisclosure, holding that plaintiff had indeed stated a claim for relief.

A claim for negligent nondisclosure focuses on a doctor's duty to inform patients of the risks attendant upon certain medical procedures. [Citation omitted] To prevail on a claim for negligent nondisclosure plaintiff must demonstrate that a reasonable person knowing of the risk would not have consented to treatment, and that the undisclosed risk actually materialized in harm. [ ]

Doctors have a duty to disclose risks of death or serious bodily harm which are a significant probability. [ ] A doctor must also disclose risks which a skilled practitioner of good standing in the community would reveal, and to the extent a doctor is aware that a patient attaches a particular significance to risks not generally considered serious enough to require discussion, these too must be discussed. [Citations omitted] Indeed, "[a] peculiar or unfounded fear of cancer on [plaintiff's] part might, if anything, require [defendant] to devote more time discussing its probability with her * * * " Kinikin, 305 N.W.2d at 595.

This court has not yet addressed the issue of physicians' duty to disclose their HIV status to patients, and we do not reach that issue today. Whether or not Dr. Benson had a legal duty to disclose his HIV status to his patients, the breach of a legal duty without compensable damages recognized by law is not actionable. [ ]. Here, the undisclosed, minuscule "risk" of HIV exposure did not materialize in harm to plaintiff because T.M.W. tested negative for the HIV antibody. Therefore, T.M.W.'s claim for negligent nondisclosure fails.

* * *

For the foregoing reasons we reverse the decision of the court of appeals and reinstate summary judgment in favor of defendants, Dr. Philip Benson and the Palen Clinic.

Notes

1) Matters involving physician or therapist misconduct were previously brought as negligence claims. It was rationalized that therapists misunderstood and thus mishandled the so-called transference phenomenon, resulting in sexual attraction between therapist and patient. As a practical matter, these cases were also brought under a negligence theory because an allegation of "intentional" misconduct would result in malpractice carriers attempting to disclaim coverage for the act. In recent years, however, with the increasing numbers of claims of sexual misconduct, malpractice carriers now routinely disclaim coverage in their policies. Consequently, sexual misconduct cases now often allege intentional tort, and seek punitive damages as well.

In *Mazza v. Huffaker*, 61 N.C.App. 170, 300 S.E.2d 833 (1983), an action was brought against a psychiatrist who engaged in a sexual relationship with his patient's wife while the couple was separated. Though the wife was not a patient, the court held that it should have been clear to the doctor that his conduct would cause foreseeable harm to his patient, violating the trust that was at the heart of the physician/patient relationship. The psychiatrist defended, in part, by claiming that he had reason to believe the plaintiff had terminated their professional relationship. Though that issue was never submitted to the jury, other courts have specifically held that the strict obligation of a mental health professional to avoid sexual misconduct is not overcome by terminating the physician/patient relationship. Punitive damages were awarded.

2) In matters alleging false imprisonment, is there a meaningful distinction between reckless conduct and intentional wrongdoing?

3) The question of whether, and under what circumstances, an HIV-positive physician has an obligation to disclose his HIV status to his patients is uncertain and an ongoing subject of litigation. See, e.g., *Estate of Behringer v. Medical Center*, 249 N.J.Super. 597, 592 A.2d 1251 (Law Div. 1991 at p. 795). The issues arise on several fronts. One is the obligation of a hospital or health care facility that learns that a staff physician is HIV-positive. Another is the obligation of the hospital or other facility that hears a credible rumor that a staff physician may be HIV-positive, and the physician declines voluntary testing. Yet another issue concerns the liability (civil or criminal) of physicians and other staff who engage in procedures that put patients at risk for contracting HIV. There are also cases of "AIDS phobia"—civil suits brought by individuals who are negligently (or recklessly) put at risk for contracting HIV, and sue for the anguish and uncertainty as well as periodic HIV testing. Most never contract the illness.

There is also a wide variation among jurisdictions as to how the local public health department responds once it determines that patients may have been exposed to HIV. Some, as in KAC above, locate and notify patients of their possible exposure. Others are much more protective of the privacy rights of patients and exclude HIV from the list of communicable diseases that require notification following an exposure.

SECTION C. THIRD PARTIES AND MEDICAL NEGLIGENCE

BRADSHAW v. DANIEL

Supreme Court of Tennessee, at Jackson, 1993.
854 S.W.2d 865.

BACKGROUND

On July 19, 1986, Elmer Johns went to the emergency room at Methodist Hospital South in Memphis, Tennessee, complaining of headaches, muscle aches, fever, and chills. He was admitted to the hospital under the care and treatment of the defendant, Dr. Chalmers B. Daniel,

Jr. Dr. Daniel first saw Johns on July 22, 1986, at which time he ordered the drug Chloramphenicol, which is the drug of choice for a person in the latter stages of Rocky Mountain Spotted Fever. Johns' condition rapidly deteriorated, and he died the next day, July 23, 1986. An autopsy was performed, and the Center for Disease Control in Atlanta conclusively confirmed, in late September 1986, that the cause of death was Rocky Mountain Spotted fever. Although Dr. Daniel communicated with Elmer Johns' wife, Genevieve, during Johns' treatment, he never advised her of the risks of exposure to Rocky Mountain Spotted Fever, or that the disease could have been the cause of Johns' death.

A week after her husband's death, on August 1, 1986, Genevieve Johns came to the emergency roam of Baptist Memorial Hospital in Memphis, Tennessee, with similar symptoms of chills, fever, mental disorientation, nausea, lung congestion, myalgia, and swelling of the hands. She was admitted to the hospital and treated for Rocky Mountain Spotted Fever, but she died three days later, on August 4, 1986, of that disease. It is undisputed that no patient-physician relationship existed between Genevieve Johns and Dr. Daniel.

The plaintiff, William Jerome Bradshaw, is Genevieve Johns' son. He filed this suit alleging that the defendant's negligence in failing to advise Genevieve Johns that her husband died of Rocky Mountain Spotted Fever, and in failing to warn her of the risk of exposure, proximately caused her death. * * *

* * *

Legal Duty

The defendant physician argues that he owed his patient's wife no legal duty because first, there was no physician-patient relationship, and second, Rocky Mountain Spotted Fever is not a contagious disease and, therefore, there is no duty to warn of the risk of exposure.

We begin our analysis by examining how we determine when a legal duty may be imposed upon one for the benefit of another. While duty was not part of the early English common law jurisprudence of tort liability, n1 it has since become an essential element in negligence cases. No claim for negligence can succeed in the absence of any one of the following elements: (1) a duty of care owed by the defendant to the plaintiff; (2) conduct falling below the applicable standard of care amounting to a breach of that duty; (3) an injury or loss; (4) causation in fact; and (5) proximate, or legal cause * * *

The existence or nonexistence of a duty owed to the plaintiff by the defendant is entirely a question of law for the court.

* * *

[T]he imposition of a legal duty reflects society's contemporary policies and social requirements concerning the right of individuals and the general public to be protected from another's act or conduct ....

Indeed it has been stated that " 'duty' is not sacrosanct in itself, but is only an expression of the sum total of those considerations of policy which lead the law to say that the plaintiff is entitled to protection." Prosser § 53 at 358...

The defendant contends that the absence of a physician-patient relationship negates the existence of a duty in this case. While it is true that a physician-patient relationship is necessary to the maintenance of a medical malpractice action, it is not necessary for the maintenance of an action based on negligence, and this Court has specifically recognized that a physician may owe a duty to a non-patient third party for injuries caused by the physician's negligence, if the injuries suffered and the manner in which they occurred were reasonably foreseeable. Wharton Transport Corp. v. Bridges, 606 S.W.2d 521, 526 (Tenn. 1980) (physician owed duty to third party injured by disabled truck driver's negligence, where the physician was negligent both in his physical examination and certification of the truck driver for the employer).

Here, we are asked to determine whether a physician has an affirmative duty to warn a patient's family member about the symptoms and risks of exposure to Rocky Mountain Spotted Fever, a non-contagious disease. Insofar as we are able to determine, there is no reported decision from this or any other jurisdiction involving circumstances exactly similar to those presented in this case.

We begin by observing that all persons have a duty to use reasonable care to refrain from conduct that will foreseeably cause injury to others. [citation omitted].

In determining the existence of a duty, courts have distinguished between action and inaction. Professor Prosser has commented that "the reason for the distinction may be said to lie in the fact that by 'misfeasance' the defendant has created a new risk of harm to the plaintiff, while by 'nonfeasance' he has at least made his situation no worse, and has merely failed to benefit him by interfering in his affairs." Prosser, § 56 at 373.

Because of this reluctance to countenance nonfeasance as a basis of liability, as a general rule, under the common law, one person owed no affirmative duty to warn those endangered by the conduct of another. Prosser, § 56 at 374; Tarasoff v. Regents of University of California, 17 Cal.3d 425, 551 P.2d 334, 343, 131 Cal.Rptr. 14 (Cal. 1976).

To mitigate the harshness of this rule, courts have carved out exceptions for cases in which the defendant stands in some special relationship to either the person who is the source of the danger, or to the person who is foreseeably at risk from the danger. [ ] Accordingly,

> while an actor is always bound to prevent his acts from creating an unreasonable risk to others, he is under the affirmative duty to act to prevent another from sustaining harm only when certain socially recognized relations exist which constitute the basis for such legal duty.

Harper & Kime, The Duty to Control the Conduct of Another, 43 Yale L.J. 886, 887 (1934).

One of the most widely known cases applying that principle is Tarasoff, supra, in which the California Supreme Court held that when a psychotherapist determines or, pursuant to the standards of his profession, should determine that his patient presents a serious danger of violence to another, the therapist has an affirmative duty to use reasonable care to protect the intended victim against such danger, and the duty may require the physician to warn the intended victim of the danger. [ ]. The special relationship of the patient to his psychotherapist supported imposition of the affirmative duty to act for the benefit of third persons [ ] * * *.

Decisions of other jurisdictions have employed the same analysis and held that the relationship of a physician to his patient is sufficient to support the duty to exercise reasonable care to protect third persons against foreseeable risks emanating from a patient's physical illness. Specifically, other courts have recognized that physicians may be liable to persons infected by a patient, if the physician negligently fails to diagnose a contagious disease, or having diagnosed the illness, fails to warn family members or others who are foreseeably at risk of exposure to the disease.

* * *

For example, in Hofmann, supra, an action was brought against a physician by a child who had contracted tuberculosis as a result of the physician's negligent failure to diagnose the disease in his patient, the child's father. Reversing a summary judgment for the physician, the Florida District Court of Appeals held

> that a physician owes a duty to a minor child who is a member of the immediate family and living with a patient suffering from a contagious disease to inform those charged with the minor's well being of the nature of the contagious disease and the precautionary steps to be taken to prevent the child from contracting such disease and that the duty is not negated by the physician negligently failing to become aware of the presence of such a contagious disease. [ ]

Likewise, in Shepard, supra, a wrongful death action was filed by the mother of a child who was infected and died of spinal meningitis after the physician failed to diagnose the disease in his patient, the mother. Again, reversing a summary judgment in favor of the defendant on the issue of legal duty, the Michigan Court of Appeals stated that the

> defendant had a physician-patient relationship with plaintiff. This was a special relationship with the one who allegedly infected Eric, leading to his death.... Because defendant had a special relationship with plaintiff we conclude that defendant owed a duty of reasonable care to Eric. As plaintiff's son and a member of her household, Eric was a foreseeable potential victim of defendant's conduct. [ ]

Finally in Wojcik, supra, an action was brought by a woman who was infected with tuberculosis against the physician who discovered her husband had the disease, but did not inform her. The New York court held that the physician owed a duty to warn his patient's wife of the risks associated with contracting the disease and stated that

> one who by reason of his professional relations is placed in a position where it becomes his duty to exercise ordinary care to protect others from injury or danger is liable in damages to those injured by reason of his failure to do so. [ ]

Returning to the facts of this case, first, it is undisputed that there was a physician-patient relationship between Dr. Daniel and Elmer Johns. Second, here, as in the contagious disease context, it is also undisputed that Elmer Johns' wife, who was residing with him, was at risk of contracting the disease. This is so even though the disease is not contagious in the narrow sense that it can be transmitted from one person to another. Both Dr. Daniel and Dr. Prater, the plaintiff's expert, testified that family members of patients suffering from Rocky Mountain Spotted Fever are at risk of contracting the disease due to a phenomenon called clustering, which is related to the activity of infected ticks who transmit the disease to humans Dr. Prater also testified that Dr. Daniel negligently failed to diagnose the disease and negligently failed to warn his patient's wife, Genevieve Johns, of her risk of exposure to the source of disease. Dr. Daniel's expert disputed these conclusions, but Dr. Daniel conceded there is a medical duty to inform the family when there is a diagnosis of the disease. Thus, this case is analogous to the Tarasoff line of cases adopting a duty to warn of danger and the contagious disease cases adopting a comparable duty to warn. Here, as in those cases, there was a foreseeable risk of harm to an identifiable third party, and the reasons supporting the recognition of the duty to warn are equally compelling here.

We, therefore, conclude that the existence of the physician-patient relationship is sufficient to impose upon a physician an affirmative duty to warn identifiable third persons in the patient's immediate family against foreseeable risks emanating from a patient's illness. Accordingly, we hold that under the factual circumstances of this case, viewing the evidence in a light most favorable to the plaintiff, the defendant physician had a duty to warn his patient's wife of the risk to her of contracting Rocky Mountain Spotted Fever, when he knew, or in the exercise of reasonable care, should have known, that his patient was suffering from the disease Our holding here is necessarily limited to the conclusion that the defendant physician owed Genevieve Johns a legal duty. We express no opinion on the other elements which would be required to establish a cause of action for common-law negligence in this case.

Accordingly, the judgment of the Court of Appeals granting the defendant's motion for summary judgment is reversed * * *.

TARASOFF v. THE REGENTS OF THE UNIVERSITY OF CALIFORNIA

Supreme Court of California, 1976.
17 Cal.3d 425, 131 Cal.Rptr. 14, 551 P.2d 334.

TOBRINER, J

On October 27, 1969, Prosenjit Poddar killed Tatiana Tarasoff. Plaintiffs, Tatiana's parents, allege that two months earlier Poddar confided his intention to kill Tatiana to Dr. Lawrence Moore, a psychologist employed by the Cowell Memorial Hospital at the University of California at Berkeley. They allege that on Moore's request, the campus police briefly detained Poddar, but released him when he appeared rational. They further claim that Dr. Harvey Powelson, Moore's superior, then directed that no further action be taken to detain Poddar. No one warned plaintiffs of Tatiana's peril.

Concluding that these facts set forth causes of action against neither therapists and policemen involved, nor against the Regents of the University of California as their employer, the superior court sustained defendants' demurrers to plaintiffs' second amended complaints without leave to amend. This appeal ensued.

Plaintiffs' complaints predicate liability on two grounds: defendants' failure to warn plaintiffs of the impending danger and their failure to bring about Poddar's confinement pursuant to the Lanterman–Petris–Short Act. Defendants, in turn, assert that they owed no duty of reasonable care to Tatiana and that they are immune from suit under the California Tort Claims Act of 1963.

We shall explain that defendant therapists cannot escape liability merely because Tatiana herself was not their patient. (1) When a therapist determines, or pursuant to the standards of his profession should determine, that his patient presents a serious danger of violence to another, he incurs an obligation to use reasonable care to protect the intended victim against such danger. The discharge of this duty may require the therapist to take one or more of various steps, depending upon the nature of the case. Thus it may call for him to warn the intended victim or others likely to apprise the victim of the danger, to notify the police, or to take whatever other steps are reasonably necessary under the circumstances.

In the case at bar, plaintiffs admit that defendant therapists notified the police, but argue on appeal that the therapists failed to exercise reasonable care to protect Tatiana in that they did not confine Poddar and did not warn Tatiana or others likely to apprise her of the danger * * *.

1. *Plaintiffs' complaints*

Plaintiffs, Tatiana's mother and father, filed separate but virtually identical second amended complaints. The issue before us on this appeal is whether those complaints now state, or can be amended to state, causes of action against defendants. We therefore begin by setting forth the pertinent allegations of the complaints.

Plaintiffs' first cause of action, entitled "Failure to Detain a Dangerous Patient," alleges that on August 20, 1969, Poddar was a voluntary outpatient receiving therapy at Cowell Memorial Hospital. Poddar informed Moore, his therapist, that he was going to kill an unnamed girl, readily identifiable as Tatiana, when she returned home from spending the summer in Brazil. Moore, with the concurrence of Dr. Gold, who had initially examined Poddar, and Dr. Yandell, assistant to the director of the department of psychiatry, decided that Poddar should be committed for observation in a mental hospital. Moore orally notified Officers Atkinson and Teel of the campus police that he would request commitment. He then sent a letter to Police Chief William Beall requesting the assistance of the police department in securing Poddar's confinement.

Officers Atkinson, Brownrigg, and Halleran took Poddar into custody, but, satisfied that Poddar was rational, released him on his promise to stay away from Tatiana. Powelson, director of the department of psychiatry at Cowell Memorial Hospital, then asked the police to return Moore's letter, directed that all copies of the letter and notes that Moore had taken as therapist be destroyed, and "ordered no action to place Prosenjit Poddar in 72–hour treatment and evaluation facility."

Plaintiffs' second cause of action, entitled "Failure to Warn On a Dangerous Patient," incorporates the allegations of the first cause of action, but adds the assertion that defendants negligently permitted Poddar to be released from police custody without "notifying the parents of Tatiana Tarasoff that their daughter was in grave danger from Posenjit Poddar." Poddar persuaded Tatiana's brother to share an apartment with him near Tatiana's residence; shortly after her return from Brazil, Poddar went to her residence and killed her.

* * *

Plaintiffs can state a cause of action against defendant therapists for negligent failure to protect Tatiana.

The second cause of action can be amended to allege that Tatiana's death proximately resulted from defendants' negligent failure to warn Tatiana or others likely to apprise her of her danger. Plaintiffs contend that as amended, such allegations of negligence and proximate causation, with resulting damages, establish a cause of action. Defendants, however, contend that in the circumstances of the present case they owed no duty of care to Tatiana or her parents and that, in the absence of such duty, they were free to act in careless disregard of Tatiana's life and safety.

In analyzing this issue, we bear in mind that legal duties are not discoverable facts of nature, but merely conclusory expressions that, in cases of a particular type, liability should be imposed for damage done * * *.

The most important of these considerations in establishing duty is foreseeability. (4) As a general principle, a "defendant owes a duty of care to all persons who are foreseeably endangered by his conduct, with respect to all risks which make the conduct unreasonably dangerous." [Citations omitted] As we shall explain, however, when the avoidance of foreseeable harm requires a defendant to control the conduct of another person, or to warn of such conduct, the common law has traditionally imposed liability only if the defendant bears some special relationship to the dangerous person or to the potential victim. Since the relationship between a therapist and his patient satisfies this requirement, we need not here decide whether foreseeability alone is sufficient to create a duty to exercise reasonable care to protect a potential victim of another's conduct.

Although, as we have stated above, under the common law, as a general rule, one person owed no duty to control the conduct of another [citations omitted], the courts have carved out an exception to this rule in cases in which the defendant stands in some special relationship to either the person whose conduct needs to be controlled or in a relationship to the foreseeable victim of that conduct. Applying this exception to the present case, we note that a relationship of defendant therapists to either Tatiana or Poddar will suffice to establish a duty of care. * * *

Although plaintiffs' pleadings assert no special relation between Tatiana and defendant therapists, they establish as between Poddar and defendant therapists the special relation that arises between a patient and his doctor or psychotherapist. Such a relationship may support affirmative duties for the benefit of third persons. Thus, for example, a hospital must exercise reasonable care to control the behavior of a patient which may endanger other persons. A doctor must also warn a patient if the patient's condition or medication renders certain conduct, such as driving a car, dangerous to others.

Although the California decisions that recognize this duty have involved cases in which the defendant stood in a special relationship *both* to the victim and to the person whose conduct created the danger, we do not think that the duty should logically be constricted to such situations. Decisions of other jurisdictions hold that the single relationship of a doctor to his patient is sufficient to support the duty to exercise reasonable care to protect others against dangers emanating from the patient's illness....

Since it involved a dangerous mental patient, the decision in *Merchants Nat. Bank & Trust Co. of Fargo* v. *United States* (D.N.D. 1967) 272 F.Supp. 409 comes closer to the issue. The Veterans Administration arranged for the patient to work on a local farm, but did not inform the farmer of the man's background. The farmer consequently permitted the patient to come and go freely during nonworking hours; the patient borrowed a car, drove to his wife's residence and killed her. Notwithstanding the lack of any "special relationship" between the Veterans

Administration and the wife, the court found the Veterans Administration liable for the wrongful death of the wife.

* * *

Defendants contend, however, that imposition of a duty to exercise reasonable care to protect third persons is unworkable because therapists cannot accurately predict whether or not a patient will resort to violence. In support of this argument amicus representing the American Psychiatric Association and other professional societies cites numerous articles which indicate that therapists, in the present state of the art, are unable reliably to predict violent acts; their forecasts, amicus claims, tend consistently to overpredict violence, and indeed are more often wrong than right. Since predictions of violence are often erroneous, amicus concludes, the courts should not render rulings that predicate the liability of therapists upon the validity of such predictions.

The role of the psychiatrist, who is indeed a practitioner of medicine, and that of the psychologist who performs an allied function, are like that of the physician who must conform to the standards of the profession and who must often make diagnoses and predictions based upon such evaluations. Thus the judgment of the therapist in diagnosing emotional disorders and in predicting whether a patient presents a serious danger of violence is comparable to the judgment which doctors and professionals must regularly render under accepted rules of responsibility.

We recognize the difficulty that a therapist encounters in attempting to forecast whether a patient presents a serious danger of violence. Obviously, we do not require that the therapist, in making that determination, render a perfect performance; the therapist need only exercise "that reasonable degree of skill, knowledge, and care ordinarily possessed and exercised by members of [that professional specialty] under similar circumstances." [citations omitted].

In the instant case, however, the pleadings do not raise any question as to failure of defendant therapists to predict that Poddar presented a serious danger of violence. On the contrary, the present complaints allege that defendant therapists did in fact predict that Poddar would kill, but were negligent in failing to warn.

Amicus contends, however, that even when a therapist does in fact predict that a patient poses a serious danger of violence to others, the therapist should be absolved of any responsibility for failing to act to protect the potential victim. In our view, however, once a therapist does in fact determine, or under applicable professional standards reasonably should have determined, that a patient poses a serious danger of violence to others, he bears a duty to exercise reasonable care to protect the foreseeable victim of that danger. While the discharge of this duty of due care will necessarily vary with the facts of each case, in each instance the adequacy of the therapist's conduct must be measured against the traditional negligence standard of the rendition of reasonable care under the circumstances.

* * *

The risk that unnecessary warnings may be given is a reasonable price to pay for the lives of possible victims that may be saved. We would hesitate to hold that the therapist who is aware that his patient expects to attempt to assassinate the President of the United States would not be obligated to warn the authorities because the therapist cannot predict with accuracy that his patient will commit the crime.

Defendants further argue that free and open communication is essential to psychotherapy * * *.

We recognize the public interest in supporting effective treatment of mental illness and in protecting the rights of patients to privacy, and the consequent public importance of safeguarding the confidential character of psychotherapeutic communication. Against this interest, however, we must weigh the public interest in safety from violent assault. The Legislature has undertaken the difficult task of balancing the countervailing concerns. In Evidence Code section 1014, it established a broad rule of privilege to protect confidential communications between patient and psychotherapist. In Evidence Code section 1024, the Legislature created a specific and limited exception to the psychotherapist-patient privilege: "There is no privilege ... if the psychotherapist has reasonable cause to believe that the patient is in such mental or emotional condition as to be dangerous to himself or to the person or property of another and that disclosure of the communication is necessary to prevent the threatened danger."

We realize that the open and confidential character of psychotherapeutic dialogue encourages patients to express threats of violence, few of which are ever executed. Certainly a therapist should not be encouraged routinely to reveal such threats; such disclosures could seriously disrupt the patient's relationship with his therapist and with the persons threatened. To the contrary, the therapist's obligations to his patient require that he not disclose a confidence unless such disclosure is necessary to avert danger to others, and even then that he do so discreetly, and in a fashion that would preserve the privacy of his patient to the fullest extent compatible with the prevention of the threatened danger.

The revelation of a communication under the above circumstances is not a breach of trust or a violation of professional ethics; as stated in the Principles of Medical Ethics of the American Medical Association (1957), section 9: "A physician may not reveal the confidence entrusted to him in the course of medical attendance ... *unless he is required to do so by law or unless it becomes necessary in order to protect the welfare of the individual or of the community.*" (Italics added.) We conclude that the public policy favoring protection of the confidential character of patient-psychotherapist communications must yield to the extent to which disclosure is essential to avert danger to others. The protective privilege ends where the public peril begins.

Our current crowded and computerized society compels the interdependence of its members. In this risk-infested society we can hardly tolerate the further exposure to danger that would result from a concealed knowledge of the therapist that his patient was lethal. If the exercise of reasonable care to protect the threatened victim requires the therapist to warn the endangered party or those who can reasonably be expected to notify him, we see no sufficient societal interest that would protect and justify concealment. The containment of such risks lies in the public interest. For the foregoing reasons, we find that plaintiffs' complaints can be amended to state a cause of action against defendants Moore, Powelson, Gold, and Yandell and against the Regents as their employer, for breach of a duty to exercise reasonable care to protect Tatiana.

Finally, we reject the contention of the dissent that the provisions of the Lanterman–Petris–Short Act which govern the release of confidential information prevented defendant therapists from warning Tatiana. The dissent's contention rests on the assertion that Dr. Moore's letter to the campus police constituted an "application in writing" within the meaning of Welfare and Institutions Code section 5150, and thus initiates proceedings under the Lanterman–Petris–Short Act. A closer look at the terms of section 5150, however, will demonstrate that it is inapplicable to the present case.

Section 5150 refers to a written application only by a professional person who is "a member of the attending staff . . . of an evaluation facility designated by the county," or who is himself "designated by the county" as one authorized to take a person into custody and place him in a facility designated by the county and approved by the State Department of Mental Hygiene. The complaint fails specifically to allege that Dr. Moore was so empowered. Dr. Moore and the Regents cannot rely upon any inference to the contrary that might be drawn from plaintiff's allegation that Dr. Moore intended to "assign" a "detention" on Poddar; both Dr. Moore and the Regents have expressly conceded that neither Cowell Memorial Hospital nor any member of its staff has ever been designated by the County of Alameda to institute involuntary commitment proceedings pursuant to section 5150.

* * *

Conclusion

For the reasons stated, we conclude that plaintiffs can amend their complaints to state a cause of action against defendant therapists by asserting that the therapists in fact determined that Poddar presented a serious danger of violence to Tatiana, or pursuant to the standards of their profession should have so determined, but nevertheless failed to exercise reasonable care to protect her from that danger.

McKENZIE v. HAWAI'I PERMANENTE MEDICAL GROUP, INC.

Supreme Court of Hawaii, 2002.
98 Haw. 296, 47 P.3d 1209.

MOON, C.J.

Plaintiffs Carole McKenzie, individually and as Prochein Ami for Kathyrn McKenzie, a minor, and Roger McKenzie [hereinafter, collectively, the McKenzies] filed an action in the United States District Court for the District of Hawai'i (the district court) against defendants Hawai'i Permanente Medical Group, Inc., Kaiser Foundation Health Plan, Inc. [hereinafter, collectively, Kaiser], and Jerry I. Wilson for negligence arising out of an incident in which plaintiff Kathryn McKenzie, a pedestrian, was seriously injured when she was struck by an automobile driven by Wilson. The McKenzies and Wilson claim that the accident was caused by a fainting episode precipitated by the negligent prescription of medication to Wilson by Robert Washecka, M.D. (Dr. Washecka), an employee of Kaiser. Kaiser is being sued under the doctrine of respondeat superior. Recognizing that there is no clear Hawaii precedent concerning whether a physician could be sued for negligence by a third party who is not the physician's patient, the district court certified the following question to this court pursuant to Hawai'i Rules of Appellate Procedure (HRAP) Rule 13 (2000):

> Does a physician owe a legal duty which would create a cause of action legally cognizable in the courts of Hawai'i for personal injury of a third party who was injured in an accident caused by his or her patient's adverse reaction to a medication that the physician negligently prescribed three days prior to the accident?

We answer the certified question with a qualified "yes" as discussed herein.

I. BACKGROUND

This case involves a medical malpractice and personal injury action to recover damages for injuries suffered by Kathryn McKenzie, a minor, who was injured on August 8, 1997 when she was hit by a vehicle driven by Wilson. The McKenzies and Wilson claim the accident occurred because Wilson fainted while driving due to an adverse reaction to a medication negligently prescribed by Wilson's physician, Dr. Washecka.

On August 5, 1997, Dr. Washecka, a Kaiser physician, prescribed prazosin hydrochloride, a generic form of the drug Minipress [hereinafter, prazosin], to treat a medical condition that Wilson had. Wilson was instructed to take a two milligram (mg.) tablet of prazosin at bedtime for three days, starting on August 5, 1997. Wilson was further instructed that, if he did not experience any side effects during the first three days, he was to take a 2 mg. tablet of prazosin twice a day, once in the morning and once at bedtime beginning the fourth day, August 8, 1997. Factual disputes exist as to whether the prescribed dosages were proper.

Wilson was verbally warned by Dr. Washecka (presumably on August 5), and also through the medication's warning labels, of potential side effects and precautions regarding driving while on the medication.

Wilson alleges that he took his first three bedtime-doses of prazosin on August 5, 6, and 7 without incident. Wilson also contends that he took his August 7 bedtime dose at approximately 2:00 a.m., i.e., in the early morning hours of August 8. On August 8, 1997, Wilson alleges that he took his first morning dose of prazosin at approximately 7:45 a.m. and then drove to work.

As Wilson approached Vineyard Boulevard from Pali Highway, heading towards downtown Honolulu, he began to feel nauseated and dizzy and began to hyperventilate. A few blocks later, as he proceeded southbound on Bishop Street, he allegedly fainted and hit the car in front of him. Wilson's car then veered right and entered onto the sidewalk striking Kathryn McKenzie.

Prazosin has several known side effects, including fainting. The McKenzies' expert states that Kaiser doctors were the only physicians in Honolulu who prescribed prazosin. According to the McKenzies' expert, prazosin was not the preferred drug to prescribe in 1997 for the treatment of Wilson's condition; other available medications should have been used to treat Wilson because the use of these other medications would have reduced the risk of an adverse reaction. The McKenzies also state that prazosin is three times cheaper than the other preferred medications. The McKenzies and Wilson argue that Wilson fainted because he took prazosin that morning. Thus, the McKenzies and Wilson allege that Dr. Washecka negligently prescribed prazosin, negligently prescribed an excessive dose of prazosin, and failed to give Wilson sufficient warning of its side effects. Kaiser disputes liability and the contentions of the McKenzies' expert witness and claims that the accident was not in any way caused by the prazosin prescribed to Wilson.

* * *

II. Discussion

A prerequisite to any negligence action is the existence of a duty owed by the defendant to the plaintiff that requires the defendant to conform to a certain standard of conduct for the protection of the plaintiff against unreasonable risks. [ ]. This court ordinarily addresses whether a defendant owes a duty of care to a particular plaintiff as a question of law. [ ]. The existence of a duty concerns "whether such a relation exists between the parties that the community will impose a legal obligation upon one for the benefit of the other—or, more simply, whether the interest of a plaintiff who has suffered invasion is entitled to legal protection at the expense of a defendant[.]" [ ]. Because our task is to ascertain whether Dr. Washecka owes a duty to the McKenzies, it necessarily requires a presumption that Dr. Washecka was negligent in his treatment of Wilson. We, therefore, assume, for the purpose of our analysis, that Dr. Washecka was negligent.

The parties to this case present several arguments. Kaiser essentially argues that: (1) it owes no duty to the McKenzies because they are not patients of Dr. Washecka; (2) Dr. Washecka does not have a "special relationship" with Wilson mandating that Dr. Washecka control Wilson's behavior for the McKenzies' benefit; and (3) public policy concerns further compel the conclusion that physicians do not owe a duty to non-patient third parties. According to Kaiser, the social utility of medication usage far outweighs the risk of harm to unrelated non-patients. Kaiser maintains that exposing physicians to liability for harm to such persons would discourage beneficial medication prescriptions and would create "divided loyalties" between physicians and their patients, requiring physicians to choose between the interests of their patients and those of unknown non-patients. The McKenzies, on the other hand, argue that: (1) where—as here—the defendant's conduct in negligently prescribing prazosin creates the injury, pursuant to Restatement (Second) of Torts (1965) [hereinafter, Restatement (Second)] § 302, foreseeability, rather than the existence of a "special relationship" between the physician and patient, is the major criterion determining whether a duty is owed them by Dr. Washecka; (2) even if a "special relationship" is necessary to create a duty entitling them to protection, a physician-patient relationship is such a relationship; and (3) policy considerations, including deterrence of negligent conduct, the fair allocation of the costs of harm, and fair compensation for victims, mandate that Kaiser owes a duty to them. The McKenzies further contend that Kaiser's policy concerns are exaggerated and that imposition of a duty in this case would impose no more of a duty upon physicians than they presently owe to their own patients. Wilson agrees with the McKenzies and also generally asserts that it is sound public policy to hold physicians accountable to the general public for negligent prescribing practices when it is foreseeable that a member of the public will be harmed by such practices.

* * *

Applicability of the "Special Relationship" Analysis and Restatement (Second) § 302

1. "Special Relationship"

The parties dispute whether Dr. Washecka has a "special relationship" with Wilson that entitles the McKenzies to protection. The Restatement (Second) § 315 (1965) states:

> There is no duty so to control the conduct of a third person as to prevent him from causing physical harm to another unless

> (a) a special relation exists between the actor and the third person which imposes a duty upon the actor to control the third person's conduct, or

> (b) a special relation exists between the actor and the other which gives to the other a right to protection.

Section 315 is a special application of the general rule stated in Restatement (Second) § 314 (1965) that a person does not have a duty to act affirmatively to protect another person from harm * * * Section 314 applies "only where the peril in which the actor knows the other is placed is not due to any active force which is under the actor's control. If a force is within the actor's control, his failure to control it is treated as though he were actively directing it and not as a breach of duty to take affirmative steps[.]" Restatement (Second) § 314 (1965) comment d; see also Touchette v. Ganal, 82 Hawai'i 293, 302, 922 P.2d 347, 356 (1996) (Noting that the considerations pertaining to "special relationships" are "based on the concept that a person should not be liable for 'nonfeasance' in failing to act as a 'good Samaritan.' [Such considerations have] no application where the defendant, through his or her own action (misfeasance) has made the plaintiff's position worse and has created a foreseeable risk of harm from the third person. In such cases the question of duty is governed by the standards of ordinary care.") [ ]. Accordingly, the "special relationship" arguments put forth by the parties are inapplicable to this case because medical malpractice involving the negligent prescription of medication is "misfeasance" that is not analogous to the "nonfeasance" in failing to act as a "Good Samaritan" or failing to take affirmative "action" as the term is used by Restatement (Second) § 314.

2. Applicability of Restatement § 302

Relying upon Touchette and Restatement (Second) § 302, the McKenzies contend that the proper framework for analyzing this case is whether Dr. Washecka's action in negligently prescribing prazosin created a risk of harm to them through the action of a third party—his patient Wilson. The McKenzies are correct, although Touchette and the language of Restatement (Second) § 302 do not necessarily mandate that Dr. Washecka owes a duty to them.

Restatement (Second) § 302 states:

A negligent act or omission may be one which involves an unreasonable risk of harm to another through either

(a) the continuous operation of a force started or continued by the act or omission, or

(b) the foreseeable action of the other, a third person, an animal, or a force of nature.

Ostensibly, Kaiser could be liable to the McKenzies pursuant to subsection (b) because it is foreseeable that Wilson would drive after ingesting a negligently prescribed medication and therefore subject them to harm. When the tortfeasor instigates the act causing harm—such as by prescribing medication—Restatement (Second) § 302 generally applies. [ ]. Consistent with this view, we held in Touchette that, under Restatement (Second) § 302, the defendant might owe a duty to the plaintiffs, family members of her extramarital lover who were harmed by the assaultive behavior of the defendant's husband (the third party), where the husband's behavior was ostensibly caused by the defendant's affirmative "misfeasance" of taunting her husband and causing him to suffer extreme emotional distress leading to the assaults. [ ] cf. Lee, 83 Hawaii at 156–58, 162, 925 P.2d at 326–28, 332 (veterans counselor who did not provide psychiatric or psychological counseling services did not owe a duty, pursuant to Restatement (Second) § 302, for alleged "nonfeasance" in failing to warn a veteran's father of the veteran's threat to commit suicide).

However, Restatement (Second) § 302 by itself does not create or establish a legal duty; it merely describes a type of negligent act. Comment a to this section states in relevant part that:

[Section 302] is concerned only with the negligent character of the actor's conduct, and not with [the actor's] duty to avoid the unreasonable risk. In general, anyone who does an affirmative act is under a duty to others to exercise the care of a reasonable [person] to protect them against an unreasonable risk of harm to them arising out of the act. . . . If the actor is under no duty to the other to act, his failure to do so may be negligent conduct within the rule stated in this Section, but it does not subject him to liability, because of the absence of duty.

(Emphases added). See also Restatement (Second) (1965) table of contents (the structure of which indicates that the conduct described in § 302 is one of several "types of negligent acts"). Accordingly, the fact that Dr. Washecka's negligent conduct falls under the rubric of Restatement § 302 does not establish per se that he owes a duty to the McKenzies; it only describes the manner in which he may be negligent if he owed a duty to the McKenzies. To determine whether the negligent prescription of prazosin created an "unreasonable risk of harm" to the McKenzies—and thus whether Dr. Washecka owed a duty to them—we turn to the usual considerations that constitute an analysis of whether a duty exists.

B. Determining Whether to Impose a Duty

Regarding the imposition of a duty of care, this court has noted generally that:

In considering whether to impose a duty of reasonable care on a defendant, we recognize that duty is not sacrosanct in itself, but only an expression of the sum total of those considerations of policy which lead the law to say that the particular plaintiff is entitled to protection. * * * The question of whether one owes a duty to another must be decided on a case-by-case basis. [ ]. However, we are reluctant to impose a new duty upon members of our society without any logical, sound, and compelling reasons taking into consideration the social and human relationships of our society * * *

Blair, [supra]. We now turn to these policy considerations and the cases from other jurisdictions that the parties call to our attention.

We begin by noting that, although the certified question inquires whether a duty is owed to a third party injured in an accident caused by an adverse effect of negligently prescribed medication, the facts supplied by the district court suggest that the McKenzies' negligence claim appears to rest on three general theories. First, the McKenzies claim that the decision to prescribe prazosin in the first instance constituted negligence. Second, the McKenzies claim that the manner in which Dr. Washecka prescribed the prazosin was negligent, namely, that the dosages were too high. Third, the McKenzies claim that Dr. Washecka was negligent because he did not provide Wilson with adequate warning of the danger associated with driving an automobile while taking the medication. The first two theories involve decisions such as whether to prescribe a medication at all, which particular medication to prescribe, and the particular dosage level or schedule to prescribe [hereinafter, prescribing decisions]; the latter theory involves failure to warn. Although the cases relied upon by the parties do not always expressly delineate this distinction, the distinction is often a key factor in their outcome

* * *

1. Negligent Prescribing Decisions

The McKenzies argue that the fair allocation of the costs of harm and the need for fair compensation to victims mandates that physicians owe a duty to non-patient third parties injured as a result of negligent prescribing decisions. Wilson suggests that physicians owe a duty to the public generally. Indeed, other courts have recognized that imposition of a tort duty upon physicians for the benefit of the general public is not new. See generally Gooden v. Tips, 651 S.W.2d 364, 370–71 (Tex. Ct. App. 1983) (discussing statutory requirement that physicians report the existence of certain sexually transmitted diseases to health authorities); Welke v. Kuzilla, 144 Mich.App. 245, 375 N.W.2d 403, 406 (Mich. Ct. App. 1986) (noting generally in discussion of duty that highway safety is an important public concern). All of the foregoing policy considerations are important.

* * *

* * * [W]e would carve out an exception in a case involving controlled substances, we hold that a physician does not owe a duty to non-patient third parties injured in an automobile accident caused by the patient's adverse reaction to a medication negligently prescribed by the physician three days earlier where the negligence involves prescribing decisions as that term is used in this opinion.

2. Negligent Failure to Warn of Driving Risks

If Dr. Washecka owes any duty to the McKenzies in this case, such a duty arises from negligently failing to warn Wilson about the risk of operating a vehicle while under the influence of the medication. The strongest support for this proposition in the case law can be found in Kaiser v. Suburban Transportation System, 65 Wn.2d 461, 398 P.2d 14,

401 P.2d 350 (Wash. 1965). In Kaiser, the defendant physician prescribed a sedating antihistamine to his patient, whom the physician knew to be a bus driver. [ ]. After taking the first dose of the medication the following morning, the driver went to work and was involved in an accident after falling asleep while driving the bus. [ ] (Hale, J., dissenting). The driver had apparently felt groggy before the accident but continued to drive nonetheless. Id. A passenger on the bus was injured in the accident and sued the doctor and the bus company. [ ] (majority opinion). The trial court dismissed the case against the doctor at the conclusion of the evidence on the grounds that the evidence did not show any standard of care to which the doctor was bound and that, even if the doctor was negligent in not warning the driver that the medication may cause sedation, the driver's negligence in failing to stop when he began to feel drowsy was an intervening cause. Id. The trial court, therefore, directed a verdict against the driver. Id. The Washington Supreme Court reversed.[ ]

In so doing, the supreme court noted that the evidence suggested that the doctor may not have informed his bus driver-patient of "the dangerous side effects of drowsiness or lassitude" from the drug and that expert evidence suggested that it was negligent not to do so. The court also held that the plaintiff was entitled to judgment as a matter of law on the issue of liability against either the bus driver, the doctor, or both, depending upon whether the doctor had informed the driver of the risk of drowsiness and whether the driver was contributorily negligent. [ ]

To summarize, we balance the considerations in favor of imposing a duty to warn for the benefit of third parties against the considerations militating against imposition of a duty. The primary considerations favoring a duty are that: (1) it is evident that a patient who is unaware of the risk of driving while under the influence of a particular prescription medication will probably do so; (2) warning against such activity could prevent substantial harm; (3) imposing a duty would create little additional burden upon physicians because physicians already owe their own patients the same duty; and (4) the majority of jurisdictions appear to recognize a duty under some circumstances. The primary consideration militating against the imposition of a duty is that it may not be worth the marginal benefit, in some circumstances, where the effectiveness of the warning is minimal or where the reasonable patient should be aware of the risk. Such circumstances may include, e.g., situations where patients have previously taken a particular medication and where patients are prescribed medications commonly known to affect driving ability * * * Balancing these considerations, we believe that a logical reason exists to impose upon physicians, for the benefit of third parties, a duty to advise their patients that a medication may affect the patient's driving ability when such a duty would otherwise be owed to the patient.

* * *

III. CONCLUSION

Based on the foregoing, we answer the certified question as follows. A physician does not owe a duty to non-patient third parties injured in an automobile accident caused by the patient's adverse reaction to a medication that is not a controlled substance and negligently prescribed by the physician three days earlier where the alleged negligence involves such "prescribing decisions" as whether to prescribe the medication in the first instance, which medication to prescribe, and the dosage prescribed. A physician owes a duty to non-patient third parties injured in an automobile accident caused by an adverse reaction to the medication prescribed three days earlier where the physician has negligently failed to warn the patient that the medication may impair driving ability and where the circumstances are such that the reasonable patient could not have been expected to be aware of the risk without the physician's warning. Factors to consider in determining whether the reasonable patient could have been expected to be aware of the risk include: (1) the relative knowledge of the risk as between lay persons and physicians; (2) whether the patient has previously used the medication and/or experienced the adverse effect; and (3) whether a warning would otherwise have been futile.

Notes

1) The *Tarasoff* doctrine, imposing a duty to warn a victim about a patient's dangerousness, has evolved a long way since 1976: from warning an *identified* third person, to *identifying* a third person known to exist, to confirming the existence of the third person *so identification could be made*. The progressively attenuated knowledge by the psychiatrist of the victim is the "special relationship" without which there can be no liability. Predicting dangerousness is a capacity that most psychiatrists say is imperfect at best, and therapeutically harmful at its worst. Of course, assessing negligence in the prediction requires that we look at what the psychiatrist knew or should have known at the time of the assessment, without the benefit of hindsight.

2) In *Bragg v. Valdez*, 111 Cal.App.4th 421, 3 Cal.Rptr.3d 804 (2003), a mentally unstable patient was involuntarily committed to a healthcare facility. Lee's mother informed the staff that he was threatening to harm himself and others. The facility certified the patient for fourteen days of additional inpatient care, but discharged him the following day due to lack of health insurance. Nineteen days later he killed the plaintiffs' mother, and he killed himself a few days hence. The trial court allowed defendant's motion to dismiss on the basis that no doctor-patient relationship existed with plaintiff's mother. The Court of Appeals reversed. Here the alleged tort was not failure to warn potential victims, but failure to make a good faith judgment about release of a dangerous patient. The court also rejected defendant's argument that there was no duty to warn unless the patient made a specific threat. Finally, the court held it was an issue of fact as to whether there was a

causal connection between defendant's alleged negligence and the murder of plaintiff's mother.

3) In *McKenzie*, how might the imposition of a duty to warn the patient of the risks of driving, with the attendant threat of liability should he fail to do so, affect the physician/patient relationship? Is it an exercise of concern and compassion for the patient, or adversarial protection for the physician?

4) In *Hoehn v. U.S.*, 217 F.Supp.2d 39 (D.D.C. 2002) a federal district court held that a hospital did not owe a duty to an unidentified third person who was harmed by a 75–year–old cancer patient who drove her automobile after a chemotherapy treatment. The patient, who had been heavily medicated, blacked out while behind the wheel and injured the plaintiff. The court held that the hospital had no duty to control the patient since a "heavily medicated individual is not of a class of persons to whom the tendency to act injuriously is normal." Furthermore, the court held that the hospital did not "take charge" of a voluntary outpatient scheduled for a brief treatment.

Is there a meaningful distinction between *McKenzie* and *Hoehn*?

5) Note the discussion in *McKenzie* as to whether there existed a "special relationship" that requires a duty of care to foreseeable third persons. Is it the duty to a third person that prevails here, or a duty to the patient to avoid the consequences *to himself* that might result if he harmed a third person?

Chapter 3

CLAIMS AGAINST MULTIPLE MEDICAL DEFENDANTS

INTRODUCTORY NOTE

The law has ways of allocating medical liability between defendants who are physicians and defendants who are lay persons.

Making physicians liable for the medical negligence of their allied health care helpers (lay persons in this usage) is no longer an issue. Suppose that a physician employs a nurse, who has assets inadequate to pay a large medical malpractice judgment. If the nurse negligently injures a patient without any involvement of the physician except the employment relation, the patient may be able to recover against the physician under respondeat superior: let the higher-up pay. Legal complications arise when the negligent nurse was employed by one master, such as a hospital, but at the time of the harm was directed by an independent master, such as a surgeon. The first section summarizes these developments.

Making hospitals and other institutional health care providers liable for physicians' negligence is a more recent development. Fifty years ago a hospital was regarded as a hotel where physicians practiced medicine, and because a lay organization could not "control" the medical acts of a physician, respondeat superior could not make the innocent employer liable for the employed physician's negligence. Today the issue is whether a hospital can be liable for the medical negligence of a non-employee physician who has the privilege of practicing within the hospital. The second section brings these matters up to date.

The third section takes up situations in which a plaintiff has a medical liability claim against a managed care organization, usually for failure to approve or provide insurance coverage for a procedure sought by the plaintiff. Unless and until the legislature amends the Employee Retirement Income Security Act of 1974 (ERISA), it will continue to preempt many state law claims against managed care organizations.

In a perfect world of logic in litigation, all of the claims and defendants would be sorted out before the summons and complaint were served, and common law pleading had that objective. But for 65 years now, the Federal Rules of Civil Procedure, and the large number of state pleading systems based on the Federal Rules, have turned to a different logic, the logic of getting everybody involved into court first, and sorting out thereafter who is alleged to be liable to whom for what:

> Rule 20. Permissive Joinder of Parties. (a) * * * All persons * * * may be joined in one action as defendants if there is asserted against them jointly, severally, or in the alternative, any right to relief in respect of or arising out of the same transaction, occurrence, or series of transactions or occurrences and if any question of law or fact common to all defendants will arise in the action.

But what if the plaintiff joins health care defendants who cannot all be liable, yet the plaintiff cannot produce the evidence to show which is which? It occurred to defendants that if they hung together, they could tie up the evidence so that they could not hang separately, but the courts shrewdly made too great the risk that all would be found liable:

> [Otherwise] a patient who received permanent injuries of a serious character, obviously the result of some one's negligence, would be entirely unable to recover unless the doctors and nurses in attendance voluntarily chose to disclose the identity of the negligent person and the facts establishing liability. * * * If this were the state of the law of negligence, the courts, to avoid gross injustice, would be forced to invoke the principles of absolute liability, irrespective of negligence, in actions by persons suffering injuries during the course of treatment under anesthesia. Ybarra v. Spangard, 25 Cal.2d 486, 154 P.2d 687, 689 (1944).

Today the plaintiff's lawyer expects multiple defendants to whipsaw one another, furnishing evidence to the plaintiff that exonerates some and thereby implicates others.

Another aspect of joinder of defendants troubles physicians: why not wait to join them until the plaintiff has done enough discovery to indicate whether they are truly involved? The answer is lawyer-logic. While adding a defendant looks easy under Fed.R. 21, to do so after the proceedings are well under way requires the judge's permission, Fed.R. 15(a), and it can be altogether impossible, Fed.R. 15(c). The opposite practice is quite simple: if as the pre-trial proceedings move along, a previously joined defendant turns out not to be involved, the defendant is "dropped" under Fed.R. 21 or its state-court equivalent.

After it has been established that all the remaining defendants are or may be liable to the plaintiff, substantive liability law, not procedure, governs the ways of sharing and spreading the plaintiff's damages among the defendants. One provider can sue another provider for indemnification (passing all the liability along), and under the laws of most states today, one provider can sue another provider for contribution (sharing the liability equally or in proportion to fault).

This leads to a particularly troublesome legal problem. The plaintiff has the capacity to let some of the defendants out of the case by settling with them, leaving only one or two defendants actively engaged at trial. On the one hand, the law encourages settlements; on the other hand, if a jury doesn't know the contractual arrangements in a "Mary Carter" agreement between the plaintiff and settling defendants for sharing a plaintiff's judgment among parties who are only nominally in the case, the jury verdict may be seriously skewed against the remaining parties. Whether to permit Mary Carter agreements seems to be a dead issue, but how to handle them before juries is a very lively issue.

SECTION A. PHYSICIAN LIABILITY UNDER RESPONDEAT SUPERIOR

LEWIS v. PHYSICIANS INSURANCE COMPANY OF WISCONSIN

Supreme Court of Wisconsin, 2001.
243 Wis.2d 648, 627 N.W.2d 484.

JON P. WILCOX, J.

* * *

I

The parties have stipulated to the relevant facts. Seldera removed Lewis' gallbladder at Lakeland on November 8, 1993. During the surgery, Seldera packed off the gallbladder with laparotomy pads (sponges). Nurses Patricia Vickery (Vickery) and Ellen Chapman (Chapman) were in charge of counting the sponges. Under Lakeland's procedures, the nurses, not Seldera, were responsible for counting the sponges and overseeing the counting of the sponges. Indeed, Chapman, the "circulating nurse" assigned to the operation, had an independent duty delineated in the administrative code to count the sponges. [ ] ([T]he " 'circulating nurse' " is "a registered nurse who is present during an operation . . . who, before the surgical procedure . . . is completed, . . . ensures that the sponge, needle and instrument counts have been done according to hospital policy"). Both Vickery and Chapman were employed by Lakeland, not Seldera. According to the medical records from the surgery, Vickery and Chapman counted the number of sponges used on four occasions and they thought that the correct number of sponges had been collected at the end.

However, Lewis began to have problems and Seldera operated again on January 30, 1994. During this second surgery, a retained sponge was discovered. After this sponge was removed, Lewis recovered. He then brought suit against Lakeland and Seldera.

Prior to trial, Lakeland agreed that it was responsible for the actions of its employees, Vickery and Chapman. Because Lakeland was a county-owned hospital at the time of the surgery, its liability for the negligence of Vickery and Chapman was limited to $50,000. [ ] After settling with Lakeland for the maximum amount allowed under § 893.80(3), Lewis pursued this case against Seldera. In consideration for Seldera's stipulation to the above facts, Lewis dropped all claims except for the allegation that Seldera could be held vicariously liable for Vickery and Chapman's negligence. Both parties moved for summary judgment on the issue of whether Seldera could be so held liable.

The circuit court issued an oral decision, finding "as a matter of law, that [Seldera] is, in fact, responsible and liable for the actions of the parties that were in the operating room with him and working under his supervision." The circuit court maintained that the "doctor is the captain of the ship. That the doctor is responsible for everything." Seldera appealed.

The court of appeals reversed the circuit court's ruling. [ ] Judge Fine, writing for the court, rejected the argument that Seldera could be liable for the negligence of the nurses by distinguishing our decision in Fehrman v. Smirl, 25 Wis.2d 645, 131 N.W.2d 314 (1964) (Fehrman II), which held that two doctors could be held liable for a single injury. Judge Fine further observed that "no appellate court in Wisconsin has used the 'captain of the ship' doctrine to impose liability in a medical malpractice case, and the doctrine has generally lapsed into disuse elsewhere with the passage of time." Lewis [ ]. Therefore, the court of appeals declined to apply that doctrine to the present case. [ ].

Lewis subsequently appealed and this court accepted his petition for review.

II

* * *

At the outset, we note that Lewis is not contending that Vickery and Chapman were employed by Seldera or that Vickery and Chapman were "borrowed servants." Nor is Lewis contending that Seldera was responsible for counting the sponges. Instead, this case turns on whether Seldera is vicariously liable for the negligence of Vickery and Chapman under our holding in Fehrman II or whether we adopt the "captain of the ship" doctrine.

It is a basic principle of law, as well as common sense, that one is typically liable only for his or her own acts, not the acts of others. Nevertheless, the law in certain circumstances will impose "vicarious liability" on a non-negligent party. Vicarious liability is "liability that a supervisory party (such as an employer) bears for the actionable conduct of a subordinate or associate (such as an employee) because of the relationship between the two parties." Black's Law Dictionary 927 (7th ed. 1999). There is a tension, then, between the basic principle of individual responsibility under the law on the one hand and the imposition of vicarious liability on an innocent party for a tortfeasor's acts on the other hand. Because vicarious liability is a severe exception to the basic principle that one is only responsible for his or her own acts, we proceed with caution when asked to impose vicarious liability on an innocent party, doing so only in accordance with well-settled law.

One well-settled doctrine for imposing vicarious liability is respondeat superior, which allows a non-negligent employer to be held liable for an employee's actions. See Shannon v. City of Milwaukee, 94 Wis.2d 364, 370, 289 N.W.2d 564 (1980) ("Under the doctrine of respondeat superior an employer can be held vicariously liable for the negligent acts of his employees while they are acting within the scope of their employment."). Respondeat superior is perhaps the most familiar context in which vicarious liability is imposed. It arises due to the employer's control or right of control over the employee; because of this control or right of control, the negligence of the employee is imputed to the employer in certain circumstances. [ ]. Indeed, in the present case, the hospital admitted that it could be held vicariously liable for the negligence of the two nurses under the doctrine of respondeat superior. Lewis, however, does not argue that Seldera is vicariously liable for the negligence of Vickery and Chapman under the doctrine of respondeat superior; instead, he contends that Seldera is vicariously liable under our holding in Fehrman II or alternatively, under the "captain of the ship" doctrine. We examine each of his theories for imposing vicarious liability on Seldera in turn.

In Fehrman v. Smirl, 20 Wis.2d 1, 6–7, 121 N.W.2d 255 (1963) (Fehrman I), the plaintiff's surgeon, Smirl, asked another surgeon, McDonnell, to assist with treating the defendant after Smirl had removed the defendant's prostate gland. The plaintiff was injured during the course of this treatment and filed an action against Smirl. [ ]. During the jury's deliberations, it raised a question regarding Smirl's responsibility relative to McDonnell's responsibility. Fehrman II [ ]. The circuit court responded that Smirl "would be responsible for any failure upon the part of Dr. McDonnell to exercise such care and skill" and Smirl objected on the ground that this response may have led the jury to impose liability on him for negligence committed by McDonnell. [ ]. Justice Gordon, writing for the majority of this court, but not agreeing with it on this issue, stated the majority's holding as such: "under the circumstances of this case, Dr. Smirl either was in charge of the patient or was acting jointly with Dr. McDonnell." [ ]. Therefore, this court upheld the circuit court's response to the jury's question. Id. Lewis characterizes our holding in Fehrman II as imposing vicarious liability on a doctor whenever the doctor continues to actively care for and participate in the treatment of the patient. His reading is too broad.

We begin our analysis of Fehrman II by recognizing that this court's holding on the issue of vicarious liability was grounded in the particular facts presented. Id. Importantly, we did not assert a new doctrine for imposing vicarious liability. Instead, we merely approved of a response to a question the jury raised during its deliberation regarding Smirl's responsibility relative to McDonnell's responsibility. [ ]. We decline to stretch Fehrman II to hold that this court's refusal to overturn a circuit court's response to a jury question created a new doctrine for imposing vicarious liability.

Moreover, in Fehrman II we allowed the circuit court's response to stand in part because it was unclear whose negligence was the cause of the plaintiff's injury. n6 As noted, Smirl was objecting "to the fact that under the court's instruction he was held responsible for the negligence which may have been chargeable to Dr. McDonnell." Id. (emphasis added). Therefore, as the court of appeals commented, Fehrman II more closely resembles the "alternative liability" case of Summers v. Tice, 33 Cal.2d 80, 199 P.2d 1 (1948). There, two hunters simultaneously and negligently shot in the direction of the plaintiff, but it was unclear which bullet injured the plaintiff. 199 P.2d at 2. Because this extraordinary fact pattern made it impossible for the plaintiff to identify which hunter caused his injury, the court determined that he could hold both defendants liable. [ ] Thus, the "alternative liability" theory was born.

Without adopting the "alternative liability" theory, we discussed the holding of Summers in Collins v. Eli Lilly Co., 116 Wis.2d 166, 342 N.W.2d 37 (1984) where the plaintiff sought to impose liability on 17 drug companies because she was unable to determine what specific drug company had made the particular drug that caused her injuries. [ ]. Although we rejected the imposition of liability upon the 17 drug companies, our discussion of "alternative liability" in Collins is instructive. In discussing the rule of Summers, we wrote that under alternative liability "when all defendants, although acting independently, have breached a duty of care toward the plaintiff but only one of them caused the injury, each defendant must prove that he or she did not cause the plaintiff's injury or be jointly and severally liable with all other defendants." [ ] The direct proof of negligence in Fehrman II, presented to the jury with the res ipsa loquitur instruction, indicates that both Smirl and McDonnell may have violated their respective duties of care to the plaintiff, but only one doctor's actions may have caused his injury. [ ]. Our decision in Fehrman II then, while confined to its facts, is more akin to this theory of alternative liability than creating a "continuing active management" theory for imposing vicarious liability. Consequently, Fehrman II does not support Lewis' new "continuing active management" theory.

Not only does Fehrman II fail to support Lewis' new theory, it is distinguishable from the instant case. In this case, Seldera did not breach a duty to Lewis; instead, he stipulated that Seldera was not negligent. In contrast, both Smirl and McDonnell in Fehrman II may have breached their duties to the plaintiff. [ ]. Although in this case there was clearly a breach of duty owed to Lewis, that duty was breached by Vickery and Chapman, the nurses employed by the hospital. Their duties were defined by hospital policy, not by Seldera. Chapman's duty, as the circulating nurse, was also defined by the administrative code. [ ]. In further contrast to Fehrman II where Smirl selected McDonnell to assist with the surgery, the nurses here were selected by Lakeland, not Seldera. Fehrman II, therefore, is distinguishable from the present case and cannot be relied upon to impose vicarious liability on Seldera under any theory.

Lewis, however, seeks support for his "continuing active management" theory for imposing vicarious liability on Seldera in the two cases cited by this court in Fehrman II, Morrill v. Komasinski, 256 Wis. 417, 41 N.W.2d 620 (1950), and Heimlich v. Harvey, 255 Wis. 471, 39 N.W.2d 394 (1949). In Morrill, this court confronted the issue of whether three doctors could be held jointly and severally liable for failing to diagnose a broken arm properly. 256 Wis. at 426. The family doctor, Dr. Komasinski, objected to being held jointly liable with a more experienced doctor, Dr. Bump, whom he called to assist with the diagnosis and treatment of the plaintiff's broken arm. Id. We held that the "evidence amply supports the findings of the jury." Id. The evidence indicated that three doctors, Dr. Komasinski, Dr. Bump, and a Dr. Wright, who was in charge of taking the X rays, "examined the X rays together and decided upon the treatment to be administered." [ ]. The three doctors then "concluded that the arm should be placed at right angles to the body with the forearm pointing straight upward. . . . " It was this diagnosis and treatment by all three doctors that caused the plaintiff's injury. [ ] Therefore, all three doctors were jointly and severally liable. [ ].

The central fact that distinguishes Morrill from the instant case is that there the jury found negligence on the part of all three doctors who acted in concert whereas here Lewis has stipulated that Seldera was not negligent. There was no imposition of vicarious liability in Morrill. Accordingly, Morrill does not support the theory advanced by Lewis of imposing vicarious liability when the non-negligent doctor "continues active participation" in the patient's case.

* * *

As a result, Lewis has not presented a viable doctrine for imposing vicarious liability on Seldera under existing Wisconsin law.

III

Alternatively, Lewis asks this court to follow the circuit court's lead and adopt the "captain of the ship" doctrine in order to impose vicarious liability on Seldera. Similar to respondeat superior, "captain of the ship" is another theory that allows a party to invoke vicarious liability, but it has never been recognized in Wisconsin and, as the court of appeals acknowledged, has fallen into disfavor in other jurisdictions. [ ]. Because "captain of the ship," which enabled plaintiffs to recover in the face of a hospital's "charitable immunity," is an antiquated doctrine that fails to reflect the emergence of hospitals as modern health care facilities, we decline to adopt it now.

The "captain of the ship" doctrine is an outgrowth of the largely defunct "charitable immunity" doctrine, which granted immunity to most hospitals prior to 1940. [ ]. To provide some form of recovery for plaintiffs in the face of "charitable immunity," the "captain of the ship" doctrine enabled them to hold a doctor liable for the negligence of assisting hospital employees. Courts reasoned that charitable hospitals of the late nineteenth century and early twentieth century lacked the financial wherewithal to survive a negligence action against their employees relative to the doctors who conducted surgery on their premises.

But now, as numerous commentators have observed, modern health care facilities are in a better position to protect patients against negligence from their employees and insure against the corresponding liability. See id. (acknowledging that modern charitable hospitals "are now larger in size, better endowed, and on a more-sound economic basis" and that "insurance covering their liability is available and prudent management would dictate that such protection be purchased"). Over the last 60 years, hospitals have become increasingly vital facilities for the delivery of health care. We recognized this shift in Kashishian v. Port, 167 Wis.2d 24, 38–39, 481 N.W.2d 277 (1992), where we confronted the issue of whether a hospital could be held vicariously liable under the doctrine of apparent authority for the allegedly negligent acts of a doctor working at a hospital as an independent contractor. In so doing, we observed that "modern hospitals have spent billions of dollars marketing themselves, nurturing the image with the consuming public that they are full-care modern health facilities." [ ]. As full-care modern health facilities, hospitals are no longer " 'mere structures where physicians treated and cared for their patients.' " [ ]. We acknowledged the important role hospitals have in our health care system and their advent as full-care modern health care facilities when we stated:

> In essence, hospitals have become big business, competing with each other for health care dollars. As the role of the modern hospital has evolved, and as the image of the modern hospital has evolved (much of it self-induced), so too has the law with respect to the hospital's responsibility and liability towards those it successfully beckons. Hospitals not only employ physicians, surgeons, nurses, and other health care workers, they also appoint physicians and surgeons to their hospital staffs as independent contractors. 167 Wis.2d at 38–39.

We recognize the development of the modern hospital as a health care delivery facility and the attendant responsibilities this transition has entailed. Simply put, "captain of the ship" has lost its vitality across the country as plaintiffs have been able to sustain actions against full-care modern hospitals for the negligence of their employees.

Accordingly, we decline to resurrect the anachronistic "captain of the ship" doctrine or create a new theory to enable Lewis to impose vicarious liability on Seldera. Lewis, under the current negligence law in Wisconsin, had a viable cause of action against Lakeland. We are mindful of the harsh consequence Lewis must endure because Lakeland, at the time of the negligent sponge count, was a county hospital and therefore its liability was capped at $50,000, which was insufficient to cover his damages of $150,000. [ ]. While this is a troubling deficiency, it is the result of a legislative policy decision, which may be supported by broader considerations. These broader considerations include providing full-care modern health care facilities to service citizens who might otherwise not have access to such a facility. If we circumvented this statute in order to impose liability on Seldera, we would discourage doctors from working at government-owned hospitals because they would incur the liability of the hospital's assisting employees, whom they had no hand in selecting. To attach this nondelegable liability to doctors utilizing government-owned health care facilities would create a disturbing dichotomy between government hospitals and private hospitals, which do not attach such nondelegable liability to doctors utilizing their facilities. Thereby we would induce doctors to practice only at private hospitals, which are liable for the full amount of damages a negligent employee may inflict upon a patient.

Of course, patients can hold government-owned health care facilities liable for the negligence of their employees under respondeat superior, but, as noted, the legislature has capped that liability at $50,000 per occurrence. In accordance with principles of judicial restraint, we leave it to the legislature to make any necessary policy adjustments. [ ] Therefore, while recognizing the unfortunate result in this case, we must also remain cognizant of the legislative balancing, which weighs the costs of individual unfairness against the benefits of having government-owned health care facilities where doctors are willing to provide health care to all segments of the population. As a result, we believe it would be shortsighted for this court to engage in judicial lawmaking so that Lewis could impose vicarious liability on Seldera and recover beyond the statutory maximum.

IV

In conclusion, we hold that Seldera cannot be held vicariously liable for the negligence of Vickery and Chapman under either Fehrman II or "captain of the ship."

DIAS v. BRIGHAM MEDICAL ASSOCIATES, INC.

Supreme Judicial Court of Massachusetts, 2002.
438 Mass. 317, 780 N.E.2d 447.

IRELAND, J.

The plaintiffs, Stella and Luis Dias, administrators of the estate of their son, Ethan Dias, claim that defendant Brigham Medical Associates, Inc. (BMA), is vicariously liable under the theory of respondeat superior for the alleged medical malpractice of one of its physician practice group members, Dr. Daniel Schlitzer. Dr. Schlitzer was the on-call obstetrician at St. Luke's Hospital who treated the pregnant Stella Dias (plaintiff), following a motor vehicle accident. A Superior Court judge granted summary judgment for BMA, concluding that to hold BMA vicariously liable for Dr. Schlitzer's negligence, the plaintiffs would have to show that the corporation exercised, or had the right to exercise, direction and control over his treatment decisions. The judge found that BMA did not and could not exercise such control over Dr. Schlitzer. The plaintiffs appealed, and we transferred the case to this court on our own motion.

Because we conclude that traditional respondeat superior liability applies to the employer of a physician, and that to establish such liability it is not necessary that the employer have the right or ability to control the specific treatment decisions of a physician-employee, we vacate the judgment and remand the case for further proceedings consistent with this opinion.

1. Facts. We summarize the facts relevant for disposition of this appeal. On May 19, 1995, the plaintiff, at the time thirty-two weeks pregnant, was involved in a motor vehicle accident that resulted in her emergency treatment at St. Luke's Hospital in New Bedford. After being examined in the emergency room, she was transferred to the labor and delivery department, where she was treated by Dr. Schlitzer. The plaintiffs contend that the care rendered by him was negligent and resulted in the stillbirth of their son.

BMA, a Massachusetts corporation, a so-called "medical practice group," was comprised entirely of physicians specializing in obstetrical medicine. The record is undisputed that Dr. Schlitzer, at the time of the incident, was an employee and officer of BMA. In fact, both Dr. Schlitzer and BMA admitted in their respective interrogatory answers that Dr. Schlitzer was an employee of BMA "during the period in question," and that Dr. Schlitzer was on staff at BMA "all times relevant hereto." The judge found that, "as a member of BMA, [Dr.] Schlitzer had been assigned by BMA to, and was then responsible for 'on-call' coverage at St. Luke's Hospital, and was in fact working a conventional [twenty-four]-hour shift at the hospital." As to this latter point, however, the record contains ambiguities regarding Dr. Schlitzer's on-call coverage obligations on the night in question, as more fully discussed below.

2. Discussion. On a motion for summary judgment, the moving party, here BMA, has the burden to "show that there is no genuine issue as to any material fact and that [it] is entitled to judgment as a matter of law." [ ] Additionally, "a party moving for summary judgment in a case in which the opposing party [here the plaintiffs] will have the burden of proof at trial is entitled to summary judgment if [it] demonstrates ... that the party opposing the motion has no reasonable expectation of proving an essential element of that party's case." [ ] In light of these well-established principles, we consider the plaintiffs' contention that the judge erred in granting summary judgment for BMA.

Broadly speaking, respondeat superior is the proposition that an employer, or master, should be held vicariously liable for the torts of its employee, or servant, committed within the scope of employment. [ ] In one of its earliest cases concerning respondeat superior, the court concluded that an employer could not be held liable on that theory where the employer was unable to give direction and control to the employee regarding the precise actions that resulted in the tort, in that case an employee's method of driving or choice of route while on an errand for his employer. Khoury v. Edison Elec. Illuminating Co., 265 Mass. 236, 238, 164 N.E. 77 (1928) ("the employee must be subject to control by the employer, not only as to the result to be accomplished but also as to the means to be used").

In 1969, however, in circumstances similar to those at issue in the Khoury case, this court broadened the scope of liability under the theory of respondeat superior, and held that an employer need not control the details of an employee's tasks in order to be held liable for the employee's tortious acts. See Konick v. Berke, Moore Co., 355 Mass. 463, 467, 468, 245 N.E.2d 750 (1969). The facts of Konick were similar to those of Khoury: both involved an employee who, it was alleged, was negligently driving an automobile while on an errand for the employer. In the Khoury case the employer was not liable for its employee's actions, while the employer in the Konick case was found to be liable for the employee's automobile accident, even though the employer was unable to control the precise manner and means of the employee's driving. [ ]. The court declared that it "should no longer follow our cases to the extent that they indicate that a master-servant relationship does not exist unless the employer has a right to control the manner and means (the details, in other words)," of the allegedly negligent conduct. [ ] Our Konick decision comported with the view of the vast majority of States. [ ]. The doctrine of respondeat superior in the Commonwealth thus evolved to place the burden of liability on the party better able to bear that burden. See Kansallis Fin. Ltd. v. Fern, 421 Mass. 659, 664, 659 N.E.2d 731 (1996) ("as between two innocent parties—the principal-master and the third party—the principal-master who for his own purposes places another in a position to do harm to a third party should bear the loss").

While acknowledging these general rules, both the judge and BMA rely on Kelley v. Rossi, 395 Mass. 659, 662, 663, 481 N.E.2d 1340 (1985), where we stated that the general rule is that a resident-physician is a servant (employee) of a hospital where she is employed, but also said that, "the very nature of a physician's function tends to suggest that in most instances he will act as an independent contractor." [ ]. The judge understandably pointed to this statement to support his conclusion that, in the absence of evidence that an employer of a physician reserved the right to direct and control a physician's treatment decisions, a physician is presumed to be an independent contractor. However, the Kelley court was required to determine as a preliminary matter whether a physician was a "public employee," as defined by the Massachusetts Torts Claim Act statute, G. L. c. 258, § 1. [ ]. The point was significant because a public employee is not liable in tort for acts of negligence performed within the scope of his or her public employment. [ ]. The critical language in the Kelley case on which the judge relied thus concerned whether a particular physician was a "public employee" as that term was used in a statute, not with the common-law analysis of respondeat superior that governs BMA's liability for the acts or omissions of its admitted "employee."

To prevail against BMA, the plaintiffs need only establish that (1) at the time of the alleged negligence Dr. Schlitzer was an employee of BMA, and (2) the alleged negligent treatment of the plaintiff occurred within the scope of Dr. Schlitzer's employment by BMA. Once employment is established, the only remaining issue is whether he was working for BMA at the time of the alleged negligent treatment, i.e., whether his treatment of the plaintiff was within the scope of his employment by BMA. This comports with traditional agency law that "an employer is liable for torts committed by employees while acting in the scope of their employment." Restatement (Third) of Agency § 2.04 (Tent. Draft No. 2 2001).

In order to determine whether an employer-employee relationship actually exists, a judge may consider a number of factors. [ ]. These factors may include, but are not limited to, the method of payment (e.g., whether the employee receives a W-2 form from the employer), and whether the parties themselves believe they have created an employer-employee relationship. While the point is not of import in this case where both BMA and Dr. Schlitzer admit the existence of the employer-employee relationship, we recognize that the task of determining what constitutes an employer-employee relationship is fact dependent, and that in cases where there is no clear admission of employment, a direction and control analysis may be useful to determine whether the relationship is that of employer-employee as opposed to that of an independent contractor. The right to direct and control the details of an alleged employee's actions "may be very attenuated," but remains an important factor that should be examined when the employer-employee relationship is contested. [ ]. Once an employer-employee relationship is established, however, any further analysis of the employer's right to direct and control is unnecessary. * * *

Applying these principles, corporate liability for the negligence of physician employees is commonly recognized. See 61 Am. Jur. 2d § 277 (2002) ("Clearly, a corporation or an individual employing a physician to act as an agent is liable for the malpractice of the physician, this being held so on the ordinary principles of agency, or respondeat superior"). See also Bing v. Thunig, 2 N.Y.2d 656, 163 N.Y.S.2d 3, 143 N.E.2d 3 (1957), cited in numerous jurisdictions as a turning point in holding hospitals liable for the malpractice of their physicians. The Bing case, and other cases across jurisdictions that have followed it, stand for the proposition that although a corporate entity may not control the precise treatment decisions of physicians, the entity should not be able to escape liability for physician malpractice. [ ]

Because BMA admitted that Dr. Schlitzer is its employee, the judge erred in holding that, as a matter of law, BMA could not be held liable for his alleged negligent acts because of BMA's inability to exert direction and control over his clinical decisions. The judge's rationale, that such control is presumed absent unless there is evidence to the contrary, undercuts the evolved purpose of respondeat superior liability, and would create an exception for physicians not recognized for any other profession.

There remains one point that requires further comment. Dr. Schlitzer was the employee of BMA on the date of the alleged negligent treatment, but the record is ambiguous as to whether he was acting as BMA's employee at the time he treated the plaintiff. Asked at his deposition for which practice group he was covering when he treated her, Dr. Schlitzer was unable to answer. Dr. Schlitzer did testify that he covered the labor and delivery department on behalf of BMA on a rotating basis, and that at least part of his twenty-four hour shift on May 19, was in fulfilment of his obligation as a BMA employee. Dr. Schlitzer also testified, however, that he had been asked to assume coverage for additional practice groups at some point during his twenty-four hour shift. If Dr. Schlitzer was under an obligation to BMA to be present at the hospital at the time he treated the plaintiff, his treatment of her would be within the scope of his employment by BMA, regardless of whether he had agreed to take on additional coverage shifts for other groups. If, however, he was providing coverage for some other group, under an arrangement independent of his relationship with BMA, at the time he treated the plaintiff, that treatment would not have been rendered within the scope of his BMA employment. Thus, while the record conclusively establishes that Dr. Schlitzer was an employee of BMA, the record before us is inadequate for any definitive determination whether Dr. Schlitzer's treatment of the plaintiff was within the scope of his employment by BMA.

We vacate the judgment entered in the Superior Court, and remand this case for further proceedings consistent with this opinion.

So ordered.

COHEN v. ALLIANT ENTERPRISES

Supreme Court of Kentucky, 2001.
60 S.W.3d 536.

JUSTICE STUMBO

The sole issue in this case is whether a principal can be held vicariously liable for the negligence of its agent when the agent has escaped liability by virtue of the statute of limitations. Appellant sustained an injury to his foot and presented for medical treatment at an immediate care center owned by Appellee, Alliant Enterprises, Inc. in May 1996. At the facility, he was treated by a Dr. Ewing. Dr. Ewing, detecting no foreign bodies in the small puncture wound on the bottom of Mr. Cohen's foot, advised that Mr. Cohen soak his foot in Epsom salts, and seek additional treatment if the foot became infected. Over the next eight months, Mr. Cohen continued to suffer with his foot, and in December 1996, he underwent surgery by Dr. Morton Kasdan. Dr.

Kasdan removed a wooden splinter from Mr. Cohen's foot, and opined that Dr. Ewing had been negligent in his treatment of Mr. Cohen, as he should have anesthetized the foot and more fully explored the wound in May of 1996.

Mr. Cohen filed suit against a Dr. Thomas, and, on a theory of vicarious liability, against Alliant Enterprises. Dr. Thomas was named in the suit because his name appeared in type on some of Mr. Cohen's medical reports from the May 6th visit. Dr. Thomas, however, had not treated Mr. Cohen, and the reports were, in fact, signed by Dr. Ewing. When the mistake was discovered, Mr. Cohen filed an Amended Complaint, dismissing Dr. Thomas and leaving Alliant as the only defendant. Mr. Cohen was then unable to add Dr. Ewing as a defendant because the statute of limitations had run as to Dr. Ewing by the time the mistake was discovered.

Alliant then moved for summary judgment, asserting that, because suit was prohibited against the agent/doctor, due to the statute of limitations, the principal/Alliant could not be held liable under a theory of respondeat superior. The Circuit Court granted the motion, relying upon Copeland v. Humana of Kentucky. Inc., Ky. App., 769 S.W.2d 67 (1989) and Floyd v. Humana of Virginia. Inc., Ky. App., 787 S.W.2d 267 (1989). The Court of Appeals affirmed.

In Copeland, supra, a child undergoing corrective eye surgery allegedly suffered brain damage as a result of improperly administered anesthesia. The child's parents entered into a settlement agreement or covenant not to sue with the anesthesiologist. They later brought suit against the surgeon and hospital, on a theory of vicarious liability, based on the actions of the agent/anesthesiologist, and on a theory of independent negligence by the hospital. The hospital moved for, and was granted, partial summary judgment on the vicarious liability claim, with the Court referencing the document executed by the minor child's parents and the anesthesiologist. In affirming the lower court's decision to dismiss the plaintiffs vicarious liability claim, the Court of Appeals stated: "Having agreed not to sue the servant/agent, and made recovery by settlement therefrom, the appellant may not now seek additional recovery from the master/principal based upon the same acts of alleged negligence, whether the document is called a 'release' or 'covenant not to sue'." Copeland, [ ]. The case at bar is clearly distinguishable from Copeland, in that there has been no settlement of any sort here. The Copelands were able to recover for the negligence of the anesthesiologist/agent via the "release" or "covenant not to sue" and therefore, the vicarious liability of the hospital for the negligent actions of its agent could not serve as a second recovery for the same offending conduct. The fact that Mr. Cohen cannot recover from the agent here does not negate the fact that liability may exist, and that it can be imputed to the principal. It is the negligence of the servant that is imputed to the master, not the liability. "The test as to the liability of the master is whether the servant was guilty of negligence ... " Horne v. Hall, Ky. App., 246 S.W.2d 441 (1951).

The preclusion of recovery from an agent based upon a statute of limitations is analogous to prior law in Kentucky that precluded recovery for negligence based upon the theory of interspousal immunity. Even when that doctrine was recognized in Kentucky, such immunity did not enure to the benefit of an employer whose employee negligently injured his or her spouse while in the course and scope of his employment.

[ ]. Likewise, the fact that an employee is able to escape liability for his alleged negligence because the statute of limitations had run as to him does not also insulate the employer from vicarious liability for that negligence.

* * *

In Floyd v. Humana of Virginia, Inc., Ky. App., 787 S.W.2d 267 (1989) a patient again alleged injury caused by the improper administration of anesthesia, and brought medical malpractice actions against the physician and hospital. It was determined that the physician/agent named in the action had not acted negligently, and, on that basis, the plaintiff was precluded from recovering against the hospital under a vicarious liability theory. Again, this case is clearly distinguishable from the case at bar. There has been no finding that Appellee's agent acted without negligence. Clearly, if The agent did not act negligently, there can be no vicarious liability imputed to the principal.

In sum, the case law relied upon by the lower courts in dismissing Appellant's action against Alliant has no applicability here, as the agent's liability has not been released, nor has he been exonerated.

Appellant cites Southeastern Greyhound Lines v. McCafferty, 169 F.2d 1 (6th Cir. 1948), for the proposition that he was not obligated to bring suit against both the principal and agent together to recover under a vicarious liability theory, nor was he required to get a judgment against the negligent agent before the principal could be held vicariously liable. In that case, the Court stated:

> As a matter of procedure appellee was not required to sue both Southeastern [principal] and Masters [agent]. He could have sued them separately; or jointly, as he did here. If he prosecuted his action against Masters as an individual he would be required to show by the weight of the evidence that Masters' negligence was the proximate cause of the accident. If he prosecuted his action jointly he would be required to establish by the weight of the evidence that Masters, as the agent and employee of Southeastern, was negligent and the law would attribute his negligence as an employee to Southeastern. He was not required to obtain a verdict and judgment of liability against Masters individually as a prerequisite to recovery against Southeastern.

[ ] Thus, a plaintiff may bring suit and recover from the principal under a vicarious liability theory without first filing suit and getting a judgment against the agent. The negligence of Dr. Ewing can be estab-

lished at trial in Appellant's suit against Alliant. * * * Accordingly, we reverse the decision of the Kentucky Court of Appeals.

SECTION B.   MEDICAL LIABILITY OF INSTITUTIONS

DARLING v. CHARLESTON COMMUNITY MEMORIAL HOSPITAL

Supreme Court of Illinois, 1965.
33 Ill.2d 326, 211 N.E.2d 253.

OPINION:

This action was brought on behalf of Dorrence Darling II, a minor, (hereafter plaintiff) by his father and next friend, to recover damages for allegedly negligent medical and hospital treatment which necessitated the amputation of his right leg below the knee. The action was commenced against the Charleston Community Memorial Hospital and Dr. John R. Alexander, but prior to trial the action was dismissed as to Dr. Alexander, pursuant to a covenant not to sue. The jury returned a verdict against the hospital in the sum of $150,000. This amount was reduced by $40,000, the amount of the settlement with the doctor. The judgment in favor of the plaintiff in the sum of $110,000 was affirmed on appeal by the Appellate Court for the Fourth District, which granted a certificate of importance. [ ].

On November 5, 1960, the plaintiff, who was 18 years old, broke his leg while playing in a college football game. He was taken to the emergency room at the defendant hospital where Dr. Alexander, who was on emergency call that day, treated him. Dr. Alexander, with the assistance of hospital personnel, applied traction and placed the leg in a plaster cast. A heat cradle was applied to dry the cast. Not long after the application of the cast plaintiff was in great pain and his toes, which protruded from the cast, became swollen and dark in color. They eventually became cold and insensitive. On the evening of November 6, Dr. Alexander "notched" the cast around the toes, and on the afternoon of the next day he cut the cast approximately three inches up from the foot. On November 8 he split the sides of the cast with a Stryker saw; in the course of cutting the cast the plaintiff's leg was cut on both sides. Blood and other seepage were observed by the nurses and others, and there was a stench in the room, which one witness said was the worst he had smelled since World War II. The plaintiff remained in Charleston Hospital until November 19, when he was transferred to Barnes Hospital in St. Louis and placed under the care of Dr. Fred Reynolds, head of orthopedic surgery at Washington University School of Medicine and Barnes Hospital. Dr. Reynolds found that the fractured leg contained a considerable amount of dead tissue which in his opinion resulted from interference with the circulation of blood in the limb caused by swelling or hemorrhaging of the leg against the constriction of the cast. Dr.

Reynolds performed several operations in a futile attempt to save the leg but ultimately it had to be amputated eight inches below the knee.

The evidence before the jury is set forth at length in the opinion of the Appellate Court and need not be stated in detail here. The plaintiff contends that it established that the defendant was negligent in permitting Dr. Alexander to do orthopedic work of the kind required in this case, and not requiring him to review his operative procedures to bring them up to date; in failing, through its medical staff, to exercise adequate supervision over the case, especially since Dr. Alexander had been placed on emergency duty by the hospital, and in not requiring consultation, particularly after complications had developed. Plaintiff contends also that in a case which developed as this one did, it was the duty of the nurses to watch the protruding toes constantly for changes of color, temperature and movement, and to check circulation every ten to twenty minutes, whereas the proof showed that these things were done only a few times a day. Plaintiff argues that it was the duty of the hospital staff to see that these procedures were followed, and that either the nurses were derelict in failing to report developments in the case to the hospital administrator, he was derelict in bringing them to the attention of the medical staff, or the staff was negligent in failing to take action. Defendant is a licensed and accredited hospital, and the plaintiff contends that the licensing regulations, accreditation standards, and its own bylaws define the hospital's duty, and that an infraction of them imposes liability for the resulting injury.

The defendant's position is stated in the following excerpts from its brief: "It is a fundamental rule of law that only an individual properly educated and licensed, and not a corporation, may practice medicine. * * * Accordingly, a hospital is powerless under the law to forbid or command any act by a physician or surgeon in the practice of his profession. * * * A hospital is not an insurer of the patient's recovery, but only owes the patient the duty to exercise such reasonable care as his known condition requires and that degree of care, skill and diligence used by hospitals generally in that community. * * * Where the evidence shows that the hospital care was in accordance with standard practice obtaining in similar hospitals, and Plaintiff produces no evidence to the contrary, the jury cannot conclude that the opposite is true even if they disbelieve the hospital witnesses. * * * A hospital is not liable for the torts of its nurse committed while the nurse was but executing the orders of the patient's physician, unless such order is so obviously negligent as to lead any reasonable person to anticipate that substantial injury would result to the patient from the execution of such order. * * * The extent of the duty of a hospital with respect to actual medical care of a professional nature such as is furnished by a physician is to use reasonable care in selecting medical doctors. When such care in the selection of the staff is accomplished, and nothing indicates that a physician so selected is incompetent or that such incompetence should have been discovered, more cannot be expected from the hospital administration."

The basic dispute, as posed by the parties, centers upon the duty that rested upon the defendant hospital. That dispute involves the effect to be given to evidence concerning the community standard of care and diligence, and also the effect to be given to hospital regulations adopted by the State Department of Public Health under the Hospital Licensing Act [ ] to the Standards for Hospital Accreditation of the American Hospital Association, and to the bylaws of the defendant.

As has been seen, the defendant argues in this court that its duty is to be determined by the care customarily offered by hospitals generally in its community. Strictly speaking, the question is not one of duty, for " * * * in negligence cases, the duty is always the same, to conform to the legal standard of reasonable conduct in the light of the apparent risk. What the defendant must do, or must not do, is a question of the standard of conduct required to satisfy the duty." (Prosser on Torts, 3rd ed. at 331.) "By the great weight of modern American authority a custom either to take or to omit a precaution is generally admissible as bearing on what is proper conduct under the circumstances, but is not conclusive." (2 Harper and James, The Law of Torts, sec. 17.3, at 977–78.) Custom is relevant in determining the standard of care because it illustrates what is feasible, it suggests a body of knowledge of which the defendant should be aware, and it warns of the possibility of far reaching consequences if a higher standard is required. [ ] But custom should never be conclusive. As Judge Learned Hand said, "There are, no doubt, cases where courts seem to make the general practice of the calling the standard of proper diligence; we have indeed given some currency to the notion ourselves. * * * Indeed in most cases reasonable prudent is in fact common prudence; but strictly it is never its measure; a whole calling may have unduly lagged in the adoption of new and available devices. It never may set its own tests, however persuasive be its usages. Courts must in the end say what is required; there are precautions so imperative that even their universal disregard will not excuse their omission." *The T. J. Hooper*, (2d cir. 1932,) 60 Fed.2d 737, 740.

In the present case the regulations, standards, and bylaws which the plaintiff introduced into evidence, performed much the same function as did evidence of custom. This evidence aided the jury in deciding what was feasible and what the defendant knew or should have known. It did not conclusively determine the standard of care and the jury was not instructed that it did.

"The conception that the hospital does not undertake to treat the patient, does not undertake to act through its doctors and nurses, but undertakes instead simply to procure them to act upon their own responsibility, no longer reflects the fact. Present-day hospitals, as their manner of operation plainly demonstrates, do far more than furnish facilities for treatment. They regularly employ on a salary basis a large staff of physicians, nurses and internes, as well as administrative and manual workers, and they charge patients for medical care and treatment, collecting for such services, if necessary, by legal action. Certainly, the person who avails himself of 'hospital facilities' expects that the hospital will attempt to cure him, not that its nurses or other employes will act on their own responsibility." (Fuld J., in *Bing* v. *Thunig*, (1957) 2 N.Y.2d 656, 143 N.E.2d 3, 8.) The Standards for Hospital Accreditation, the state licensing regulations and the defendant's bylaws demonstrate that the medical profession and other responsible authorities regard it as both desirable and feasible that a hospital assume certain responsibilities for the care of the patient.

We now turn to an application of these considerations to this case. The defendant did not object to the instruction on the issues, which followed Illinois Pattern Jury Instruction 20.01. Nor did it move to withdraw any issues from the jury. Under section 68 of the Civil Practice Act, an entire verdict is not to be set aside because one asserted ground of recovery was defective or inadequately proven, if one or more of the grounds is sufficient, unless a motion to withdraw the issue in question was made. [ ] Therefore we need not analyze all of the issues submitted to the jury. Two of them were that the defendant had negligently: "5. Failed to have a sufficient number of trained nurses for bedside care of all patients at all times capable of recognizing the progressive gangrenous condition of the plaintiff's right leg, and of bringing the same to the attention of the hospital administration and to the medical staff so that adequate consultation could have been secured and such conditions rectified; * * * 7. Failed to require consultation with or examination by members of the hospital surgical staff skilled in such treatment; or to review the treatment rendered to the plaintiff and to require consultants to be called in as needed."

We believe that the jury verdict is supportable on either of these grounds. On the basis of the evidence before it the jury could reasonably have concluded that the nurses did not test for circulation in the leg as frequently as necessary, that skilled nurses would have promptly recognized the conditions that signalled a dangerous impairment of circulation in the plaintiff's leg, and would have known that the condition would become irreversible in a matter of hours. At that point it became the nurses' duty to inform the attending physician, and if he failed to act, to advise the hospital authorities so that appropriate action might be taken. As to consultation, there is no dispute that the hospital failed to review Dr. Alexander's work or require a consultation; the only issue is whether its failure to do so was negligence. On the evidence before it the jury could reasonably have found that it was.

* * *

Judgment affirmed.

SIMMONS v. TUOMEY REGIONAL MEDICAL CENTER

Supreme Court of South Carolina, 2000.
341 S.C. 32, 533 S.E.2d 312.

WALLER, A.J.: This case presents the novel issue of whether a hospital owes a common law nondelegable duty to render competent service to its emergency room patients, such that it may not avoid liability for the negligent acts of emergency room physicians hired as independent contractors under a contract between the hospital and a separate corporation.

* * *

FACTS

P.J. McBride received medical care at Tuomey Regional's emergency room for a head injury he suffered in a moped accident. His daughter, Simmons, signed a form consenting to treatment at the emergency room that contained a provision stating, "THE PHYSICIANS PRACTICING IN THIS EMERGENCY ROOM ARE NOT EMPLOYEES OF TUOMEY REGIONAL MEDICAL CENTER. THEY ARE INDEPENDENT PHYSICIANS, AS ARE ALL PHYSICIANS PRACTICING IN THIS HOSPITAL." Simmons said she did not read the form because she was upset about her father's injuries. She believed the physicians were Tuomey Regional employees.

The emergency room physicians examined McBride, but released him without treating a serious head injury that was visible on the back of his head, Simmons alleged. The physicians apparently believed his confused state was a result of intoxication. McBride was returned to Tuomey Regional's emergency room the next day by ambulance after his condition worsened. This time, physicians diagnosed him as suffering from a subdural hematoma and transferred him to a Columbia hospital. McBride died about six weeks later of complications caused by the head injury, Simmons alleged.

Cooper, who had suffered a previous heart attack, experienced chest pains while driving. A friend drove him to Tuomey Regional's emergency room, where Cooper informed the receptionist he was having a heart attack and asked for immediate help. Cooper alleged he sat on a gurney for at least 1 ½ hours before seeing a doctor, causing him serious injury. Unlike Simmons, he did not sign any form containing the "independent physician" statement. He believed the physicians were Tuomey Regional employees. Both Simmons and Cooper stated in affidavits they saw no signs or other indications that the physicians, working in an area that was an integral part of the hospital campus, were not Tuomey Regional employees.

Tuomey Regional signed a contract with Coastal Physicians Services, Inc. (Coastal), in 1987. The contract describes Coastal as an "independent contractor" that provides "independent-contractor physicians" to work in Tuomey Regional's emergency room on an around-the-clock basis. The contract provides that, "except as hereinafter provided and to the extent practice and professional conduct of all Hospital's medical staff members are regulated by the Hospital, the Physicians shall not be under the direction or supervision of the Hospital in performance of their Emergency Department duties."

The contract states the physicians are not Tuomey Regional's employees, and the hospital does not directly pay or provide any benefits to the physicians. Under a 1989 amendment to the original contract, Tuomey Regional bills patients and their insurers for emergency room services provided by both it and Coastal physicians. Tuomey Regional then pays Coastal under a formula based on the "direct cost" plus a specified amount for each hour Coastal physicians work in the emergency room. Coastal physicians must maintain their own liability insurance coverage in minimum amounts.

Coastal physicians must meet many of the same requirements as any physician who seeks staff privileges, i.e., the right to admit patients to Tuomey Regional. Coastal physicians must, for example, apply and qualify for medical staff privileges in accordance with the bylaws and regulations of the medical staff. Their professional conduct is governed by Tuomey Regional and medical staff bylaws and rules, as well as standards set by the Joint Commission on the Accreditation of Hospitals, applicable statutes, and regulations of governmental bodies.

Tuomey Regional, however, maintains much more extensive control over Coastal physicians than physicians who only have staff privileges. For example, Tuomey Regional selects the emergency room medical director from among the physicians, with the consent of Coastal. Coastal physicians must remain on Tuomey Regional's premises during their shift, and must provide services to anyone who desires treatment. Tuomey Regional has the authority to prevent any physician from working in the emergency room when it "deems the clinical performance of any Physician ... to be detrimental to the health or safety of Hospital's patients." Within five days written notice, Coastal "shall reassign that Physician from the Hospital and shall not permit him to provide further services at the Hospital without the Hospital's approval."

Tuomey Regional retains the last word in most disagreements. The contract provides that "all matters relating to the Hospital's policies, rules, regulations, services, and other items of conduct wherein the Physicians may be involved, shall be determined jointly by [Coastal] and the Hospital's Chief Executive Officer, and in the event of a disagreement ... the decision of the Hospital shall be final."

ISSUE

Did the Court of Appeals err in holding that hospitals have a nondelegable duty under the common law to render competent service to the patients of their emergency rooms?

* * *

DISCUSSION

It is uncontroverted that the role that hospitals play in the delivery of health care across America has changed dramatically since the days when the doctrine of charitable immunity shielded hospitals from malpractice liability. * * *

Until the 1940s, hospitals were protected from malpractice liability by the doctrine of charitable immunity. Courts and legislators reasoned that a charitable institution should devote its resources to the endeavor at hand and the greater good, not to reimbursing individuals injured by the institution's negligent acts. * * *

Hospitals and the medical sciences improved dramatically throughout the twentieth century, and with those improvements came a concomitant increase in the importance of hospitals' role in providing medical care. Today, hospitals compete aggressively in providing the latest medical technology and the best facilities, as well as in attracting patients and physicians who will funnel patients to them. * * *

Acknowledging such changes, this Court limited the doctrine of charitable immunity in Brown v. Anderson County Hosp. Ass'n, 268 S.C. 479, 234 S.E.2d 873 (1977), holding that a hospital could be held liable when a plaintiff proved "the injuries occurred because of the hospital's heedlessness and reckless disregard of the plaintiff's rights." Id. [ ]. Four years later, the Court abolished charitable immunity * * *.

It is against this backdrop that we are asked to decide whether the Court of Appeals properly imposed a common law nondelegable duty on hospitals with regard to physicians who work in their emergency rooms. Tuomey Regional presents several arguments explaining why it believes the Court of Appeals erred.

A. NOT SUPPORTED BY LAW IN SOUTH CAROLINA

Tuomey Regional contends that South Carolina law does not support the Court of Appeals' "quantum unsubstantiated leap of logic." We disagree.

The term "nondelegable duty" is somewhat misleading. A person may delegate a duty to an independent contractor, but if the independent contractor breaches that duty by acting negligently or improperly, the delegating person remains liable for that breach. It actually is the liability, not the duty, that is not delegable. The party which owes the nondelegable duty is vicariously liable for negligent acts of the independent contractor. Simmons [ ].

This Court and the Court of Appeals have applied the nondelegable duty doctrine in several situations. An employer has a nondelegable duty to employees to provide a reasonably safe work place and suitable tools, and remains vicariously liable for injuries caused by unsafe activities or tools under the employer's control. A landlord who undertakes repair of his property by use of a contractor has a nondelegable duty to see that the repair is done properly, and remains vicariously liable for injuries caused by improper repairs.

A common carrier has a nondelegable duty to ensure that cargo is properly loaded and secured, and remains vicariously liable for injuries caused by an unsecured load. A bail bondsman has a nondelegable duty to supervise the work of his employees, and remains vicariously liable for injuries caused by those employees. A municipality has a nondelegable duty to provide safe streets even when maintenance is undertaken by the state Highway Department, and remains vicariously liable for injuries caused by defective repairs.

Tuomey Regional mentions some of the above cases and argues they are distinguishable because in this case it is the independent-contractor physician—not the hospital—who controls a patient's medical treatment. Tuomey Regional also contends regulations promulgated by the state Department of Health and Environmental Control do not impose such a duty.

We find Tuomey Regional's arguments unpersuasive. The cited cases clearly illustrate that a person or entity entrusted with important duties in certain circumstances may not assign those duties to someone else and then expect to walk away unscathed when things go wrong. A principle that applies in cases of poorly repaired brick floors and sloppily loaded cargo certainly applies to situations in which people must entrust that most personal of things, their physical well-being, to physicians at an emergency room intimately connected with and closely controlled by a hospital. However, as explained further below, we do not believe it is necessary, as the Court of Appeals did, to impose an absolute nondelegable duty on hospitals.

B. Not Supported by Law in Other Jurisdictions

Tuomey Regional contends that the law of other jurisdictions does not support the Court of Appeals' decision. We disagree.

Alaska, Florida, and New York courts have applied the nondelegable duty doctrine to care provided by a hospital's emergency room physicians. See Jackson v. Power, 743 P.2d 1376, 1385 (Alaska 1987) (holding that a general acute care hospital may not delegate its duty to provide physicians for emergency room care because the law imposes a duty on hospital to provide that health care); superseded in part by Alaska Stat. § 09.65.096 (2000) * * *

In contrast, Texas and Missouri courts have rejected the nondelegable duty doctrine in connection with care provided by emergency room physicians. Baptist Mem'l Hosp. System v. Sampson, 969 S.W.2d 945, 949 (Tex. 1998) (finding it unnecessary to adopt nondelegable duty doctrine for malpractice by emergency room physicians because the patient may sue the negligent physician, and sue the hospital for violation of any duties owed directly to patients) * * *

While few courts have adopted the nondelegable duty doctrine, numerous courts have endorsed the doctrine of apparent authority or apparent agency to hold hospitals liable when an injured patient proves a physician was the hospital's apparent agent. Although it found it unnecessary to address it in the present cases, the Court of Appeals has sanctioned the use of the apparent agency doctrine in this setting. See

Strickland v. Madden, 323 S.C. 63, 70–71, 448 S.E.2d 581, 585 (Ct. App. 1994) (hospital may be vicariously liable for negligent health care rendered by a physician who is not an employee of the hospital under doctrine of apparent agency; but plaintiff failed to show apparent agency where doctor was a private practitioner whose only connection to hospital was that he had staff privileges to admit patients) * * *

Under the apparent agency doctrine, the injured patient must establish that (1) the hospital consciously or impliedly represented the physician to be its agent, (2) the patient relied upon the representation, and (3) the patient changed his position to his detriment in reliance on the representation. * * *

An instructive example of a court grappling with a case like those we are presented with today, and ultimately adopting an expanded theory of apparent agency, is found in three Ohio cases.

In 1987, the Ohio Court of Appeals held that a hospital has a nondelegable duty to its emergency room patients that is not affected by the hospital's contract with an independent-contractor physicians group. [ ]. Three years later, the Ohio Supreme Court held that a hospital does not have a nondelegable duty to assure the absence of negligence in the care provided by private, independent physicians granted staff privileges. Albain v. Flower Hosp., 50 Ohio St.3d 251, 553 N.E.2d 1038 (Ohio 1990). The Albain court found Griffin, which dealt with emergency room physicians, inapplicable. The court did not explicitly overrule Griffin, but questioned its validity by describing it as a "misdirected attempt to circumvent the necessity of proving agency by estoppel." [ ]

A mere four years later, a divided Ohio Supreme Court rejected the narrowly drawn apparent agency theory it had set out in Albain. Clark v. Southview Hosp., 68 Ohio St.3d 435, 628 N.E.2d 46 (Ohio 1994). In Clark, the administrator of the decedent's estate alleged that emergency room physicians committed malpractice in the death of a woman who suffered an asthma attack. The 26–year–old woman, who had suffered previous attacks, chose to drive to the defendant hospital. Apparently impressed by the hospital's advertising, its reputation, and her mother's belief it was the destination of choice in an emergency, the woman (with her 18–month–old daughter) had driven past another hospital's emergency room en route to the defendant hospital.

The Clark court comprehensively explained the shortcomings of its analysis and the narrow view expressed in Albain. The court described how hospitals have changed from places where physicians essentially experimented upon people too poor to summon a physician to their home to places that employ highly trained medical staffs, expensive technology, and public relations experts to parlay public confidence into paying patients. The Clark court adopted a broader theory that we believe ultimately will be followed by the many other courts using the apparent agency approach in this setting:

> A hospital may be held liable under the doctrine of agency by estoppel for the negligence of independent medical practitioners

practicing in the hospital if it holds itself out to the public as a provider of medical services and in the absence of notice or knowledge to the contrary, the patient looks to the hospital, as opposed to the individual practitioner, to provide competent medical care. . . .

As to notice to the plaintiff that care is being provided by independent medical practitioners, we stress that such notice, to be effective, must come at a meaningful time.

Clark [ ]. The court went on to reject suggestions that a hospital could insulate itself from liability by giving notice to patients through consent forms signed upon admission or signs posted in the emergency room. [ ]

In sum, our decision is amply supported by law in other jurisdictions. Courts throughout the nation have struggled with this issue, and nearly all have held hospitals liable under one or more theories. The Ohio cases illustrate what we perceive to be the likely trend among the many courts that have adopted an apparent agency theory in these cases. Under that trend, hospitals will not be allowed to escape liability by giving last-minute notice of independent-contractor practitioners through admission forms or emergency room signs. The result is that hospitals may be held liable for the malpractice of their emergency room physicians, regardless of whether it is through a theory of apparent agency or nondelegable duty.

We also conclude it is appropriate to find a nondelegable duty in this case because apparent agency in its traditional form requires a representation by the principal (the hospital) and proof of reliance on that representation by the patient. * * *

* * *

[W]e conclude it is not necessary, as the Court of Appeals did in the cases at hand, to impose an absolute nondelegable duty on hospitals. Instead, we adopt the approach expressed in Restatement (Second) of Torts: Employers of Contractors § 429 (1965). That section, sometimes described as ostensible agency, provides:

> One who employs an independent contractor to perform services for another which are accepted in the reasonable belief that the services are being rendered by the employer or by his servants, is subject to liability for physical harm caused by the negligence of the contractor in supplying such services, to the same extent as though the employer were supplying them himself or by his servants.

Section 429 applies not only when the injured person accepts services in the belief they are being rendered by the independent contractor's employer, but also when a third person accepts such services on the injured person's behalf and reasonably believes the services are being rendered to the injured person by the independent contractor's employer. * * *

Under section 429, the plaintiff must show that (1) the hospital held itself out to the public by offering to provide services; (2) the plaintiff looked to the hospital, rather than the individual physician, for care; and (3) a person in similar circumstances reasonably would have believed that the physician who treated him or her was a hospital employee. When the plaintiff does so, the hospital will be held vicariously liable for any negligent or wrongful acts committed by the treating physician. The hospital may attempt to avoid liability for the physician's acts by demonstrating the plaintiff failed to prove these factors.

Although the present cases involve emergency room physicians, our decision is not necessarily limited to such physicians. It is limited, however, to those situations in which a patient seeks services at the hospital as an institution, and is treated by a physician who reasonably appears to be a hospital employee. Our holding does not extend to situations in which the patient is treated in an emergency room by the patient's own physician after arranging to meet the physician there. Nor does our holding encompass situations in which a patient is admitted to a hospital by a private, independent physician whose only connection to a particular hospital is that he or she has staff privileges to admit patients to the hospital. Such patients could not reasonably believe his or her physician is a hospital employee. * * *

Viewed in the light most favorable to respondents, the record in the present cases shows that they may allege that they or their relative sought care at Tuomey Regional's emergency room based on the hospital's offering of services to the public, that they looked to the hospital to provide the care, not an individual physician, and that they were treated by physicians who reasonably appeared to be hospital employees. Genuine issues of material fact exist; therefore, summary judgment is not appropriate.

CONCLUSION

For the foregoing reasons, we affirm as modified the Court of Appeals' decision to impose a nondelegable duty on hospitals with regard to the physicians who practice in their emergency rooms. We adopt the Restatement of Torts (Second) § 429 instead of imposing an absolute duty on hospitals. In both respondents' cases, we reverse the grant of summary judgment to Tuomey Regional * * *

JOHNSON v. LeBONHEUR CHILDREN'S MEDICAL CENTER

Supreme Court of Tennessee, Western Section, at Jackson, 2002.
74 S.W.3d 338.

JANICE M. HOLDER, J

BACKGROUND/PROCEDURAL HISTORY

Amman Johnson underwent surgery at LeBonheur Children's Medical Center (LeBonheur) on November 4, 1991, to repair a heart condition. During the surgery, Amman sustained permanent neurological damage resulting from cardiac arrest. Mary Johnson, Amman's mother, filed suit against LeBonheur and other health care providers involved in the surgery seeking damages for the injuries sustained by Amman.

The complaint alleges, *inter alia*, that Dr. Michael Citak and Dr. Michael Martindale were acting as the agents and servants of LeBonheur during Amman's surgery and that LeBonheur is vicariously liable under the doctrine of respondeat superior for their negligence. Dr. Citak and Dr. Martindale were physician residents in the University of Tennessee (UT) training program. They were compensated by UT and thus were state employees pursuant to Tenn. Code Ann. § 8–42–101(3). While in the UT training program, both resident physicians worked on rotation at LeBonheur. During their rotation, they were required to follow LeBonheur's protocols, rules, and regulations in providing treatment or services, or otherwise in attending patients of LeBonheur. Amman Johnson was one of the LeBonheur patients for whom the resident physicians provided services. Dr. Citak assisted in performing Amman's surgery, and Dr. Martindale assisted in providing the anesthesia care during the surgery.

LeBonheur filed a motion for partial summary judgment. LeBonheur asserted that it could not be held vicariously liable based solely upon the actions of Dr. Citak and Dr. Martindale because the physician residents were immune from liability as state employees under Tenn. Code Ann. § 9–8–307. On December 8, 1998, the trial court entered an order overruling the motion. LeBonheur was granted permission to seek an interlocutory appeal pursuant to Tenn. R. App. P. Rule 9. The Court of Appeals affirmed the trial court's overruling of the partial summary judgment motion. We granted appeal.

* * *

Analysis

II. *Tennessee Code Annotated § 9–8–307*

To determine whether LeBonheur may be held vicariously liable under the doctrine of respondeat superior for the actions of physician residents employed by the State, we begin with an examination of the relevant portions of Tenn. Code Ann. § 9–8–307 (1998). The statute provides in pertinent part:

(a)(1) The commission or each commissioner sitting individually has exclusive jurisdiction to determine all monetary claims against the state based on the acts or omissions of "state employees," as defined in § 8–42–101(3), falling within one (1) or more of the following categories:

* * *

(D) Legal or medical malpractice by a state employee; provided, that the state employee has a professional/client relationship with the claimant;

* * *

(b) Claims against the state filed pursuant to subsection (a) shall operate as a waiver of any cause of action, based on the same act or omission, which the claimant has against any state officer or employee. The waiver is void if the commission determines that the act or omission was not within the scope of the officer's or employee's office or employment.

* * *

(h) State officers and employees are absolutely immune from liability for acts or omissions within the scope of the officer's or employee's office or employment, except for willful, malicious, or criminal acts or omissions or for acts or omissions done for personal gain. For purposes of this chapter, "state officer" or "employee" has the meaning set forth in 8–42–101(3).

Tenn. Code Ann. § 9–8–307 (1998) (emphasis added).

When construing statutes, we are required to ascertain and effectuate the legislative intent and purpose of the statutes. [ ]. We should "assume that the legislature used each word in the statute purposely and that the use of [each] word [ ] conveyed some intent." [ ]. Applying these principles, we hold that the legislative purpose and intent of Tenn. Code Ann. § 9–8–307 is to protect state employees from individual liability for acts or omissions that occur in the scope of their employment.

Section 9–8–307 of the Tennessee Code Annotated vests the Tennessee Claims Commission with exclusive jurisdiction for medical malpractice claims against the State of Tennessee based upon the actions of physician residents employed by the State. The filing of a claim against the State in the Claims Commission waives any cause of action against such a physician resident based on the same act or omission occurring within the scope of employment. [ ]. The statute further provides that state employees are absolutely immune from liability unless their acts or omissions are willful, malicious, criminal, or done for personal gain. [ ]. Nothing in the statute, however, immunizes a private hospital from liability for the acts or omissions of physician residents employed by the State who are also acting as agents or servants of the private hospital. Section 9–8–307 of the Tennessee Code Annotated therefore provides LeBonheur no protection against the imposition of vicarious liability based upon the acts or omissions of Dr. Citak and/or Dr. Martindale if the residents are found to have been the agents of the hospital.

III. Traditional Agency Principles

We must now determine whether LeBonheur may be held vicariously liable under traditional agency principles for the acts of state-employed physician residents who are "immune" from individual liability. We begin with a review of relevant agency principles.

The creation of an agency relationship does not require a contract, an explicit agreement, or an understanding between the parties. [ ]. The existence of an agency relationship, however, "is a question of fact under the circumstances of the particular case," id. [ ], and is determined by examination of agreements among the parties or of the parties' actions. Id. The principal's right to control the acts of the agent is a relevant factor when determining the existence of an agency relationship. The amount of actual control exercised by the principal over the agent also may be determinative of whether an agency relationship exists. [ ]

When an agency relationship exists, the principal may be bound by the acts of the agent performed on the principal's behalf and within the actual or apparent scope of the agency. White [v. Revco Disc. Drug Ctrs., Inc., 33 S.W.3d 713, 724 (Tenn. 2000)] at 724. In Tennessee, the doctrine of respondeat superior permits the master/principal to be held liable for the negligent actions of his servant/agent. [ ]. To hold the master/principal vicariously liable, "it is enough that the servant or agent was acting in the business of his superior." White [ ].

Moreover, an agent may serve two masters simultaneously when the objectives of the dual masters are not contrary. "A person may be the servant of two masters, not joint employers, at one time as to one act, if the service does not involve abandonment of the service to the other." [ ]. Two parties "may agree to employ a servant together or to share the services of a servant. If there is one agreement with both of [the parties], the actor is the servant of both [when] the servant is subject to joint control." Restatement of the Law, Second, Agency, § 226. Thus, a person serving two masters may subject both to liability for the same act "if the act is within the scope of employment for both." White [ ]. We hold, therefore, that a physician resident may be the agent of both the State and a private hospital. Whether an agency relationship exists is determined by the trier of fact. [ ]

LeBonheur argues that if physician residents may also be agents of a private hospital, then the absolute immunity granted physician residents would be removed, contrary to legislative intent. LeBonheur contends that the immunity provided by statute to resident physicians could not apply to residents who have dual masters. LeBonheur's argument incorrectly presumes that an agent can act for only one master at a time. When a state-employed physician resident performs a rotation at a private hospital, the same acts or omissions may be within the resident's scope of employment with the State and within the resident's scope of employment with the private hospital. Permitting a finding of dual masters, therefore, does not serve to abolish the absolute immunity granted to a state-employed physician resident pursuant to section 9–8–307(h).

LeBonheur also asserts that a principal/master may not be held vicariously liable under the doctrine of respondeat superior based solely upon the acts of an agent who is immune from liability. In support of this proposition, LeBonheur cites numerous cases. Our analysis of Tennessee case law, however, reveals that this proposition is not without limitation.

Loveman Co. v. Bayless, 128 Tenn. 307, 160 S.W. 841 (Tenn. 1913), represents the first category of cases addressing this issue. In Loveman Co., the employer's liability was predicated solely upon the doctrine of respondeat superior. [ ]. The jury rendered a verdict against the employer but in favor of the employees. The Court held that when an action is filed against an employer based solely upon the tortious actions of its employee under the doctrine of respondeat superior, a verdict in favor of the employee entitles the employer to a discharge from liability. [ ]. The Court reasoned that it is contradictory to find the master liable when the servant by whose act the injury occurred is exonerated on the same evidence. [ ].

Subsequently, the Court, in Raines v. Mercer, addressed the issue of whether a father could be held liable to his son's wife under the doctrine of respondeat superior for his son's negligent conduct. [ ]. The plaintiff, the wife of the defendant's son, filed suit against the defendant for his son's negligent operation of the defendant's vehicle. [ ]. The negligent incident occurred before the marriage of the plaintiff and the defendant's son. The Raines Court held that the rule of marital unity extinguished the plaintiff's right of action against her husband. [ ]. The Court reasoned that since the plaintiff could not maintain a direct action against her husband, she "could not avoid the forbidden frontal attack by an encircling movement against [the principal, her husband's father].... " Raines, 165 Tenn. 415, 420, 55 S.W.2d 263, 264 (1932) [ ]. Thus, by extinguishing the right of action against the son, the marital unity rule precluded an action against the father.

In Stewart v. Craig, 208 Tenn. 212, 344 S.W.2d 761 (1961), this Court established a third category of cases that prohibited a party from maintaining an action against the principal for vicarious liability under the doctrine of respondeat superior based solely upon the acts of an agent. In Stewart, the plaintiffs were injured in an automobile accident in which the driver was an employee of the defendant. [ ]. The plaintiffs executed a covenant not to sue the employee/driver but then filed suit against the employer based on the doctrine of respondeat superior. [ ]. The Stewart Court held that the covenant not to sue prohibited a suit for negligence against the employer based solely on vicarious liability. [ ]

These cases indicate that a principal may not be held vicariously liable under the doctrine of respondeat superior based upon the acts of its agent in three instances: (1) when the agent has been exonerated by an adjudication of non-liability, (2) when the right of action against the agent is extinguished by operation of law, or (3) when the injured party extinguishes the agent's liability by conferring an affirmative, substantive right upon the agent that precludes assessment of liability against the agent. [ ]

The first and third categories above clearly do not apply to the facts of this case. The resident physicians in this case have not been exonerated by an adjudication of non-liability; and Ms. Johnson has not taken any affirmative action to prevent an assessment of liability against the residents. The second category similarly provides no basis for LeBonheur's assertion that the resident physicians' personal immunity should insulate LeBonheur from vicarious liability. The marital unity rule extinguished a spouse's right of action that was based upon the other spouse's tortious conduct. The statute conferring immunity upon the residents, however, does not extinguish a claimant's right of action. Section 9–8–307(h) of the Tennessee Code Annotated simply immunizes physician residents from individual monetary liability. The residents' conduct remains available as a basis for the imposition of liability in the Claims Commission against the State. Thus, Ms. Johnson's right of action against the residents survives. Fault may be assessed for the residents' tortious conduct, but the State has assumed responsibility for the damages assessed as a result of that fault. Accordingly, we hold that a physician resident's personal immunity does not prohibit LeBonheur from being held vicariously liable under the doctrine of respondeat superior based upon the actions of a physician resident.

LeBonheur further maintains that it may not be held vicariously liable for the actions of the resident physicians because to do so would violate common law indemnity principles. Courts in Tennessee have long recognized that a principal is entitled to seek indemnification against a negligent agent. [ ]. LeBonheur asserts, however, that it would be barred from seeking indemnification against the residents. The residents are provided absolute immunity from individual liability. [ ]. Moreover, the State has not consented to suit for indemnity claims based upon the actions of its employees. See Northland Ins. Co. v. State of Tennessee, 33 S.W.3d 727 (Tenn. 2000) (holding that "a waiver of sovereign immunity must be clear and unmistakable"). We decline, however, to hold that the unavailability of an action for indemnity precludes the imposition of vicarious liability against a private hospital for the negligence of physician residents who are found to be agents of the hospital. Section 9–8–307(h) of the Tennessee Code Annotated eliminates the common law right to indemnification by providing absolute immunity to resident physicians who are working within the scope of their employment. It is within the prerogative of the legislature, therefore, to either modify this individual immunity or to waive the State's sovereign immunity to permit private, dual masters of state employees to seek indemnification against the State in the Claims Commission.

* * *

CONCLUSION

We hold that a physician resident may be the agent of both the State and a private hospital. Further, the absolute immunity granted pursuant to Tenn. Code Ann. § 9–8–307(h) to a state-employed physician resident is not removed by the creation of a dual master relationship. A material issue of fact exists as to whether Dr. Citak and/or Dr. Martindale were acting as the agents of LeBonheur at the time of Amman Johnson's

surgery. Accordingly, * * * [t]he case is remanded to the trial court
* * *.

COX v. BOARD OF HOSPITAL MANAGERS

Supreme Court of Michigan, 2002.
467 Mich. 1, 651 N.W.2d 356.

CORRIGAN, C.J.

In this medical malpractice case, we consider * * * whether a court
may instruct a jury that it may find a hospital vicariously liable for the
negligence of a "unit" of the hospital * * *

I

FACTUAL BACKGROUND AND PROCEDURAL POSTURE

On February 8, 1990, Brandon Cox was born at 26 or 27 weeks
gestation, weighing approximately 900 grams. He was placed in the
neonatal intensive care unit (NICU) of defendant hospital, and an
umbilical arterial catheter (UAC) was inserted into his abdomen to
monitor his blood gases, among other uses. At 4:00 p.m. on February 10,
Nurse Martha Plamondon drew blood from the UAC and repositioned
Brandon. At 4:20 p.m., it was discovered that the UAC had become
dislodged, causing Brandon to bleed from his umbilical artery and lose
approximately half his blood supply. No cardiac or respiratory alarm
sounded. The events that followed are in dispute. Nurse Plamondon
testified that she immediately applied pressure to stop the bleeding and
summoned Dr. Robert Villegas, who ordered a push of 20cc of Plasmanate. Dr. Villegas did not recall the event. Nurse Plamondon also
testified that she paged Dr. Amy Sheeder, a resident in the NICU. Dr.
Sheeder ordered another 10cc of Plasmanate and 20cc of packed red
blood cells. On February 11, Brandon was transferred to Children's
Hospital. On February 13, a cranial ultrasound showed that Brandon
had suffered intracranial bleeding. He was subsequently diagnosed with
cerebral palsy as well as mild mental retardation.

In 1992, plaintiffs filed this medical malpractice action against
defendant and one of its doctors, Dr. Edilberto Moreno. Plaintiffs presented expert testimony at trial that Nurse Plamondon and others had
breached the applicable standard of care. Defendant offered expert
testimony supporting a contrary view. Defendants argued that plaintiffs
could not prove that the removal of the UAC caused Brandon's injuries,
as the injuries were not uncommon for infants born at 26 or 27 weeks'
gestation. The judge ruled, over defense objection, that a "national"
standard of care applies to nurses and the other individuals alleged to
have been negligent.

The jury found in favor of plaintiffs and awarded $2,400,000 in
damages. Defendant moved for judgment notwithstanding the verdict, a
new trial, or remittitur. The trial court found that little evidence of
causation existed and ruled that it would grant a new trial unless
plaintiffs accepted remittitur to $475,000. Plaintiffs appealed, and the

Court of Appeals ordered the trial court to produce a detailed opinion indicating the basis for remittitur. On remand, the trial court reversed the prior grant of remittitur and granted a judgment notwithstanding the verdict in favor of defendant, holding that plaintiff had failed to establish negligence on the part of any particular nurse or doctor.

Again plaintiffs appealed, and the Court of Appeals reversed and reinstated the original jury verdict. The Court held that sufficient circumstantial evidence of negligence existed and that defendant had not preserved its arguments by filing a cross-appeal. Defendant then filed a cross-appeal, which was dismissed because defendant had not submitted a copy of the circuit court order. The circuit court then vacated the order granting judgment notwithstanding the verdict and reinstated the jury verdict. Defendant appealed, and the Court of Appeals held, over a dissent, that defendant's appellate issues were not preserved because it had failed to file a cross-appeal from the original circuit court order.

Defendant appealed to this Court. We vacated the decision of the Court of Appeals and remanded for consideration of defendant's issues. On remand, the Court of Appeals again affirmed, over a dissent, in a published decision. Defendant filed an application for leave to appeal to this Court. We denied leave to appeal. We then granted defendant's motion for reconsideration and granted leave to appeal.

II

* * *

B

Discussion

We hold that the trial court improperly modified SJI2d 30.01 by substituting "hospital neonatal intensive care unit" for the specific profession or specialties at issue. Further, we hold that the error requires reversal because failure to do so would be inconsistent with substantial justice.

When the trial judge discussed the jury instructions with the parties, he indicated that he would phrase SJI2d 30.01 "in [his] own way." The judge stated:

Well, I'm going to indicate that with respect to Defendant's conduct, the failure to do something which a hospital with a neonatal intensive care unit would do or would not do. That's the way I'm going to phrase this.

Defendant objected, requesting that the instructions state the standard of care "with regard to a neonatal nurse practitioner of ordinary learning or judgment or skill in this community or similar one." Defense counsel contended that the case had focused on Nurse Plamondon and her responsibility regarding the UAC and was not as broad as the entire unit. The judge overruled defendant's objection.

When he instructed the jury, the judge significantly modified SJI2d 30.01, stating:

When I use the words professional negligence or malpractice with respect to the Defendant's conduct, I mean the failure to do something which a hospital neonatal intensive care unit would do or the doing of something which a hospital neonatal intensive care unit would not do under the same or similar circumstances you find to exist in this case.

It is for you to decide, based upon the evidence, what the hospital neonatal intensive care unit with the learning, judgment or skill of its people would do or would not do under the same or similar circumstances.

In other words, the jury instruction as modified eliminated any reference to any particular profession, person, or specialty, substituting instead the phrase "neonatal intensive care unit." The modified jury instruction also failed to differentiate between the various standards of care applicable to different professions and specialties.

The plaintiff in a medical malpractice action "bears the burden of proving: (1) the applicable standard of care, (2) breach of that standard by defendant, (3) injury, and (4) proximate causation between the alleged breach and the injury. Failure to prove any one of these elements is fatal."[ ]

Crucial to any medical malpractice claim "is whether it is alleged that the negligence occurred within the course of a professional relationship." [ ] A hospital may be 1) directly liable for malpractice, through claims of negligence in supervision of staff physicians as well as selection and retention of medical staff, or 2) vicariously liable for the negligence of its agents. [ ] Here, plaintiffs have not advanced claims of direct negligence on the part of defendant hospital. Therefore, defendant's liability must rest on a theory of vicarious liability.

Vicarious liability is "indirect responsibility imposed by operation of law." [ ]. As this Court stated in 1871:

The master is bound to keep his servants within their proper bounds, and is responsible if he does not. *The law contemplates that their acts are his acts, and that he is constructively present at them all.* [*Smith v. Webster*, 23 Mich. 298, 299; 2 Brown N.P. S 98–300 (1871) (emphasis added).]

In other words, the principal "is only liable because the law creates a practical identity with his [agents], so that he is held to have done what they have done." *Id.* at 300.

Applying this analysis, defendant hospital can be held vicariously liable for the negligence of its employees and agents only. The "neonatal intensive care unit" is neither an employee nor an agent of defendant. At most, it is an organizational subsection of the hospital, a geographic location within the hospital where neonates needing intensive care are treated. No evidence in the record suggests that the neonatal intensive care unit acts independently or shoulders any independent responsibilities. Therefore, because no evidence exists that the neonatal intensive care unit itself is capable of any independent actions, including negligence, it follows that the unit itself could not be the basis for defendant's vicarious liability.

The negligence of the agents working in the unit, however, could provide a basis for vicarious liability, provided plaintiffs met their burden of proving (1) the applicable standard of care, (2) breach of that standard, (3) injury, and (4) proximate causation between the alleged breach and the injury *with respect to each agent alleged to have been negligent.* The phrase "neonatal intensive care unit" is not mere shorthand for the individuals in that unit; rather, plaintiffs must prove the negligence of at least one agent of the hospital to give rise to vicarious liability. Instructing the jury that it must only find the "unit" negligent relieves plaintiffs of their burden of proof. Such an instruction allows the jury to find defendant vicariously liable without specifying which employee or agent had caused the injury by breaching the applicable standard of care.

On this point, we agree with the Court of Appeals decision in *Tobin v. Providence Hosp.*, 244 Mich.App. 626, 624 N.W.2d 548 (2001). In *Tobin*, the trial court refused to modify SJI2d 30.01 to require the jury to determine whether each individual category of specialist who attended the decedent had violated the standard of care applicable to that specialty. Instead, the trial court instructed:

When I use the words "professional negligence" or "malpractice" with respect to the defendant's conduct, I mean the failure to do something which a hospital's agents/servants/employees of ordinary learning, judgment or skill in this community or a similar one would do, or the doing of something which a hospital's agents/servants/employees of ordinary learning, judgment or skill would not do, under the same or similar circumstances you find to exist in this case.

It is for you to decide, based upon the evidence, what the ordinary hospital's agents/servants/employees or [sic, of] ordinary learning, judgment or skill would do or would not do under the same or similar circumstances.

The Court of Appeals found that the refusal to modify was error, stating:

The unmodified standard instruction, under the circumstances of this case, was not specific enough; it permitted the jury to find that, for example, the nurse anesthetist violated the standard of care applicable to a critical care unit physician. The standard instruction is sufficient to inform the jury of the definitions of "professional negligence" and "malpractice" in the ordinary case involving one or two named defendants. However, in this case plaintiff chose to bring suit against the hospital and its (unnamed) agents, servants, or employees. Thus, it was incumbent on the trial court to ensure that the jurors clearly understood how they were to determine whether any of defendant's employees committed professional negligence or malpractice under the particular standard of practice applicable to their specialty. The unmodified standard instruction did not fulfill that function.

Similarly, in this case, plaintiffs did not name any specific agents of the hospital in their lawsuit at the time of trial. Dr. Carolyn S. Crawford, an expert witness for plaintiffs, criticized the care of several agents of defendant, including a neonatologist, a respiratory therapist, a resident, and Nurse Plamondon. The trial court's "unit" instruction did not specify the agents involved, nor did it ensure that the jurors understood the applicable standards of care. The respiratory therapist, for example, may not be held to the standard of care of the neonatologist. The "unit" instruction failed to ensure that the jury clearly understood 1) which agents were involved, and 2) that it could find professional negligence or malpractice only on the basis of the particular standard of care applicable to each employee's profession or specialty.

We hold that, in order to find a hospital liable on a vicarious liability theory, the jury must be instructed regarding the specific agents against whom negligence is alleged and the standard of care applicable to each agent. As stated above, a hospital's vicarious liability arises because the hospital is held to have done what its agents have done. Here, the general "unit" instruction failed to specify which agents were involved or differentiate between the varying standards of care applicable to those agents. The instruction effectively relieved plaintiffs of their burden of proof and was not specific enough to allow the jury to "decide the case intelligently, fairly, and impartially." *Johnson, supra* at 327. Under these circumstances, failure to reverse would be inconsistent with substantial justice.

* * *

IV

CONCLUSION

We conclude that to find a hospital liable on a vicarious liability theory, the jury must be instructed regarding the specific agents against whom negligence is alleged and the standard of care applicable to each agent. An instruction merely naming a unit of the hospital, without more, relieves plaintiffs of their burden of proof and does not comport with substantial justice. * * * Accordingly, we reverse the judgment of the Court of Appeals and remand to the trial court for a new trial.

Notes

1) In *Johnson v. Sisters of Charity of Nazareth Health Systems, Inc.*, 2003 WL 22681562 (Ky Ct. App. 2003), the court held that a hospital was not liable for the death of its patients because the physician who treated him was an independent contractor. The matter was ultimately dismissed against the physician on statute of limitations grounds. As to the defendant hospital, the trial court and the appeals court found that the defendant physician was an independent contractor, based up criteria

such as direct billing by the physician and a highly specialized field that permitted minimal control over the details of his work. Further, there was adequate notice on the hospital admission forms that the physicians were independent contractors. The appeals court rejected plaintiff's allegation that because the hospital was required by regulation to provide pathology services, it could not delegate that duty to an independent contractor.

2) In *St. Joseph Hospital v. Wolff*, 94 S.W.3d 513 (Tex. 2002), the Texas Supreme Court held that a hospital was not vicariously liable for the alleged negligence of one of its residents that was rotating at a different hospital. St. Joseph's Hospital ran an "integrated" general surgery residency program involving more than one institution. According to the affiliation contract, the various institutions would "not control the details of the medical tasks performed by the residents" at each other's institutions. Although the contract labeled the resident as an "independent contractor," the hospital was obligated to determine his "professional duties and standards of medical practice" and it withheld taxes from his paycheck.

The Texas Supreme Court reversed the trial and appeals courts on several grounds, including an improper jury instruction concerning joint enterprises. The Court held that an instruction stating that a joint enterprise can be found if there is a "common business or pecuniary interest" is too broad, subjecting vicarious liability to parties who have business or pecuniary interests but no community of interest. Although St. Joseph's was the sponsoring institution that controlled the academic training and other aspects of the residency program, it was not responsible for overseeing the resident's treatment of patients while he was working at another hospital.

SECTION C. LIABILITY OF MANAGED CARE ORGANIZATIONS

Note on Pegram v. Herdrich

In *Pegram v. Herdrich*, 530 U.S. 211, 120 S.Ct. 2143, 147 L.Ed.2d 164 (2000), the United States Supreme Court issued it's first long-awaited decision concerning the effect of the Employee Retirement Income Security Act of 1974 ("ERISA") preemption on HMO liability. In *Pegram*, plaintiff Cynthia Herdrich was covered under her husband's medical insurance policy issued by a Health Maintenance Organization (HMO). After having suffered a ruptured appendix, allegedly as a result of improper medical care rendered by her physician, Dr. Lori Pegram, plaintiff sued in state court alleging negligence, breach of fiduciary duty and fraud against the HMO operators. In particular, Dr. Pegram required Herdrich to wait eight days before undergoing an ultrasound, allegedly as part of a scheme wherein the HMO rewarded physicians for limiting care. During this eight day period, Herdrich's appendix ruptured, causing peritonitis. Plaintiff claimed the HMO issued incentives to physicians to ration care, and such rationing resulted in injury to her. Defendants removed the case to federal court and defended on the basis that ERISA preempted state law as to the breach of fiduciary duty and fraud counts. The federal district court granted defendants' motion for summary judgment on those counts, and allowed the negligence claims to go to the jury. Plaintiff received a judgment on the negligence counts. She then appealed the denial of Count III-breach of fiduciary obligation.

On appeal, the Seventh Circuit reversed, holding the trial court erred in dismissing the claim based upon breach of fiduciary duty. The Court held that plaintiff properly stated a claim under ERISA as she had alleged that defendants, as HMO fiduciaries, breached their fiduciary obligation to her, resulting in harm. Under ERISA, any state substantive law that relates to employer benefit plans and conflicts with the federal law is preempted. Further, pursuant to the ERISA scheme, a plaintiff who proves that she was denied a benefit is only entitled to receive that benefit, or to recover the value of the benefit denied.

The United States Supreme Court reversed, holding that plaintiff had, indeed, failed to state a claim under ERISA. The Court held the decision concerning Herdrich's treatment was one of "mixed eligibility and treatment" and such decisions by HMO physicians are not fiduciary decisions under ERISA. The Court acknowledged the HMO's rationing scheme might not be "socially desirable" but reasoned that some "inducement to ration care goes to the very point of any HMO scheme." As such, the legislature, in permitting the HMO structure, made the decision that some forms of rationing are acceptable.

As to Herdrich's claim that defendants breached their fiduciary obligation by allowing physician owners of the HMO to profit from treatment decisions that harmed patients, the Court distinguished between "pure eligibility decisions" (which are based upon the plan's coverage of a treatment or condition) and "treatment decisions" (which involve how to diagnose and treat a patient). The Court held that Congress had not intended that HMO's be fiduciaries under ERISA such that physician members make "mixed eligibility and treatment" decisions. The Court determined that to hold otherwise would allow suit against an HMO any time a plaintiff showed a profit incentive to ration care. According to the Court, finding for Herdrich "would be nothing less than elimination of the for-profit HMO." Since, for all intents and purposes, virtually every mixed eligibility and treatment decision that goes awry can be filed as a malpractice claim, a contrary holding in *Pegram* would result in every malpractice claim being turned into a breach of fiduciary obligation.

Given this background, *Rush Prudential HMO, Inc. v. Moran* was granted certiorari by the Supreme Court, and the following decision was handed down two years after *Pegram*.

RUSH PRUDENTIAL HMO, INC. v. MORAN

Supreme Court of the United States, 2002.
536 U.S. 355, 122 S.Ct. 2151, 153 L.Ed.2d 375.

JUSTICE SOUTER delivered the opinion of the Court.

* * *

I

Petitioner, Rush Prudential HMO, Inc., is a health maintenance organization (HMO) that contracts to provide medical services for employee welfare benefit plans covered by ERISA. Respondent Debra Moran is a beneficiary under one such plan, sponsored by her husband's employer. Rush's "Certificate of Group Coverage," issued to employees who participate in employer-sponsored plans, promises that Rush will provide them with "medically necessary" services. The terms of the certificate give Rush the "broadest possible discretion" to determine whether a medical service claimed by a beneficiary is covered under the certificate. The certificate specifies that a service is covered as "medically necessary" if Rush finds:

"(a) [The service] is furnished or authorized by a Participating Doctor for the diagnosis or the treatment of a Sickness or Injury or for the maintenance of a person's good health.

"(b) The prevailing opinion within the appropriate specialty of the United States medical profession is that [the service] is safe and effective for its intended use, and that its omission would adversely affect the person's medical condition.

"(c) It is furnished by a provider with appropriate training, experience, staff and facilities to furnish that particular service or supply." Record, Plaintiff's Exh. A, p. 21.

As the certificate explains, Rush contracts with physicians "to arrange for or provide services and supplies for medical care and treatment" of covered persons. Each covered person selects a primary care physician from those under contract to Rush, while Rush will pay for medical services by an unaffiliated physician only if the services have been "authorized" both by the primary care physician and Rush's medical director. [ ].

In 1996, when Moran began to have pain and numbness in her right shoulder, Dr. Arthur LaMarre, her primary care physician, unsuccessfully administered "conservative" treatments such as physiotherapy. In October 1997, Dr. LaMarre recommended that Rush approve surgery by an unaffiliated specialist, Dr. Julia Terzis, who had developed an unconventional treatment for Moran's condition. Although Dr. LaMarre said that Moran would be "best served" by that procedure, Rush denied the request and, after Moran's internal appeals, affirmed the denial on the ground that the procedure was not "medically necessary." [ ]. Rush instead proposed that Moran undergo standard surgery, performed by a physician affiliated with Rush.

In January 1998, Moran made a written demand for an independent medical review of her claim, as guaranteed by § 4–10 of Illinois's HMO Act [ ] which provides:

"Each Health Maintenance Organization shall provide a mechanism for the timely review by a physician holding the same class of license as the primary care physician, who is unaffiliated with the Health Maintenance Organization, jointly selected by the patient ... , primary care physician and the Health Maintenance Organization in the event of a dispute between the primary care physician and the Health Maintenance Organization regarding the medical necessity of a covered service proposed by a primary care physician. In the event that the reviewing physician determines the covered service to be medically necessary, the Health Maintenance Organization shall provide the covered service."

The Act defines a "Health Maintenance Organization" as

"any organization formed under the laws of this or another state to provide or arrange for one or more health care plans under a system which causes any part of the risk of health care delivery to be borne by the organization or its providers." [ ]

When Rush failed to provide the independent review, Moran sued in an Illinois state court to compel compliance with the state Act. Rush removed the suit to Federal District Court, arguing that the cause of action was "completely preempted" under ERISA. 230 F.3d at 964.

While the suit was pending, Moran had surgery by Dr. Terzis at her own expense and submitted a $94,841.27 reimbursement claim to Rush. Rush treated the claim as a renewed request for benefits and began a new inquiry to determine coverage. The three doctors consulted by Rush said the surgery had been medically unnecessary.

Meanwhile, the federal court remanded the case back to state court on Moran's motion, concluding that because Moran's request for independent review under § 4–10 would not require interpretation of the terms of an ERISA plan, the claim was not "completely preempted" so as to permit removal [ ]. The state court enforced the state statute and ordered Rush to submit to review by an independent physician. The doctor selected was a reconstructive surgeon at Johns Hopkins Medical Center, Dr. A. Lee Dellon. Dr. Dellon decided that Dr. Terzis's treatment had been medically necessary, based on the definition of medical necessity in Rush's Certificate of Group Coverage, as well as his own medical judgment. Rush's medical director, however, refused to concede that the surgery had been medically necessary, and denied Moran's claim in January 1999.

Moran amended her complaint in state court to seek reimbursement for the surgery as "medically necessary" under Illinois's HMO Act, and Rush again removed to federal court, arguing that Moran's amended complaint stated a claim for ERISA benefits and was thus completely preempted by ERISA's civil enforcement provisions, 29 U.S.C. § 1132(a) [ ]. The District Court treated Moran's claim as a suit under ERISA, and denied the claim on the ground that ERISA preempted Illinois's independent review statute.

The Court of Appeals for the Seventh Circuit reversed. [ ]. Although it found Moran's state-law reimbursement claim completely preempted by ERISA so as to place the case in federal court, the Seventh Circuit did not agree that the substantive provisions of Illinois's HMO Act were so preempted. The court noted that although ERISA broadly preempts any state laws that "relate to" employee benefit plans [ ] state laws that "regulate insurance" are saved from preemption [ ]. * * *

II

To "safeguard ... the establishment, operation, and administration" of employee benefit plans, ERISA sets "minimum standards ... assuring the equitable character of such plans and their financial soundness," 29 U.S.C. § 1001(a), and contains an express preemption provision that ERISA "shall supersede any and all State laws insofar as they may now or hereafter relate to any employee benefit plan.... " § 1144(a). A saving clause then reclaims a substantial amount of ground with its provision that "nothing in this subchapter shall be construed to exempt or relieve any person from any law of any State which regulates insurance, banking, or securities." § 1144(b)(2)(A). The "unhelpful" drafting of these antiphonal clauses [ ]. In trying to extrapolate congressional intent in a case like this, when congressional language seems simultaneously to preempt everything and hardly anything, we "have no choice" but to temper the assumption that " 'the ordinary meaning ... accurately expresses the legislative purpose,' " [ ], with the qualification " 'that the historic police powers of the States were not [meant] to be superseded by the Federal Act unless that was the clear and manifest purpose of Congress.' " [ ]

It is beyond serious dispute that under existing precedent § 4–10 of the Illinois HMO Act "relates to" employee benefit plans within the meaning of § 1144(a). The state law bears "indirectly but substantially on all insured benefit plans," [ ] by requiring them to submit to an extra layer of review for certain benefit denials if they purchase medical coverage from any of the common types of health care organizations covered by the state law's definition of HMO. As a law that "relates to" ERISA plans under § 1144(a), § 4–10 is saved from preemption only if it also "regulates insurance" [ ]. Rush insists that the Act is not such a law.

A

In *Metropolitan Life*, we said that in deciding whether a law "regulates insurance" under ERISA's saving clause, we start with a "common-sense view of the matter," [ ] under which "a law must not just have an impact on the insurance industry, but must be specifically directed toward that industry." [ ]. We then test the results of the common-sense enquiry by employing the three factors used to point to insurance laws spared from federal preemption under the McCarran–Ferguson Act, 15 U.S.C. § 1011 *et seq.* * * *

1

The common-sense enquiry focuses on "primary elements of an insurance contract[, which] are the spreading and underwriting of a policyholder's risk." [ ] The Illinois statute addresses these elements by defining "health maintenance organization" by reference to the risk that it bears. [ ]

Rush contends that seeing an HMO as an insurer distorts the nature of an HMO, which is, after all, a health care provider, too. This, Rush argues, should determine its characterization, with the consequence that regulation of an HMO is not insurance regulation within the meaning of ERISA.

The answer to Rush is, of course, that an HMO is both: it provides health care, and it does so as an insurer. Nothing in the saving clause requires an either-or choice between health care and insurance in deciding a preemption question, and as long as providing insurance fairly accounts for the application of state law, the saving clause may apply. There is no serious question about that here, for it would ignore the whole purpose of the HMO-style of organization to conceive of HMOs [ ] without their insurance element.

"The defining feature of an HMO is receipt of a fixed fee for each patient enrolled under the terms of a contract to provide specified health care if needed." *Pegram* v. *Herdrich*, 530 U.S. 211, 218, 147 L.Ed.2d 164, 120 S.Ct. 2143 (2000). "The HMO thus assumes the financial risk of providing the benefits promised: if a participant never gets sick, the HMO keeps the money regardless, and if a participant becomes expensively ill, the HMO is responsible for the treatment.... " * * *

* * *

2

On a second tack, Rush and its *amici* dispute that § 4–10 is aimed specifically at the insurance industry. They say the law sweeps too broadly with definitions capturing organizations that provide no insurance, and by regulating noninsurance activities of HMOs that do. Rush points out that Illinois law defines HMOs to include organizations that cause the risk of health care delivery to be borne by the organization itself, or by "its providers." [ ] In Rush's view, the reference to "its providers" suggests that an organization may be an HMO under state law (and subject to § 4–10) even if it does not bear risk itself, either because it has "devolved" the risk of health care delivery onto others, or because it has contracted only to provide "administrative" or other services for self-funded plans. [ ]

These arguments, however, are built on unsound assumptions. Rush's first contention assumes that an HMO is no longer an insurer when it arranges to limit its exposure, as when an HMO arranges for capitated contracts to compensate its affiliated physicians with a set fee for each HMO patient regardless of the treatment provided. Under such an arrangement, Rush claims, the risk is not borne by the HMO at all. In a similar vein, Rush points out that HMOs may contract with third-party insurers to protect themselves against large claims.

The problem with Rush's argument is simply that a reinsurance contract does not take the primary insurer out of the insurance business [ ] and capitation contracts do not relieve the HMO of its obligations to the beneficiary. The HMO is still bound to provide medical care to its members, and this is so regardless of the ability of physicians or third-party insurers to honor their contracts with the HMO.

Nor do we see anything standing in the way of applying the saving clause if we assume that the general state definition of HMO would include a contractor that provides only administrative services for a self-funded plan.[6] Rush points out that the general definition of HMO under Illinois law includes not only organizations that "provide" health care plans, but those that "arrange for" them to be provided, so long as "any part of the risk of health care delivery" rests upon "the organization or its providers." [ ] Rush hypothesizes a sort of medical matchmaker, bringing together ERISA plans and medical care providers; even if the latter bear all the risks, the matchmaker would be an HMO under the Illinois definition. Rush would conclude from this that § 4–10 covers noninsurers, and so is not directed specifically to the insurance industry. Ergo, ERISA's saving clause would not apply.

It is far from clear, though, that the terms of § 4–10 would even theoretically apply to the matchmaker, for the requirement that the HMO "provide" the covered service if the independent reviewer finds it medically necessary seems to assume that the HMO in question is a provider, not the mere arranger mentioned in the general definition of an HMO. * * *

In sum, prior to ERISA's passage, Congress demonstrated an awareness of HMOs as risk-bearing organizations subject to state insurance regulation, the state Act defines HMOs by reference to risk bearing, HMOs have taken over much business formerly performed by traditional indemnity insurers, and they are almost universally regulated as insurers under state law. That HMOs are not traditional "indemnity" insurers is no matter; "we would not undertake to freeze the concepts of 'insurance' . . . into the mold they fitted when these Federal Acts were passed." [ ]. Thus, the Illinois HMO Act is a law "directed toward" the

---

6. ERISA's "deemer" clause provides an exception to its saving clause that forbids States from regulating self-funded plans as insurers. See 29 U.S.C. § 1144(b)(2)(B); *FMC Corp.* v. *Holliday*, 498 U.S. 52, 61, 112 L.Ed.2d 356, 111 S.Ct. 403 (1990). There- fore, Illinois's Act would not be "saved" as an insurance law to the extent it applied to self-funded plans. This fact, however, does not bear on Rush's challenge to the law as one that is targeted toward non-risk-bearing organizations.

insurance industry, and an "insurance regulation" under a "commonsense" view.

B

The McCarran–Ferguson factors confirm our conclusion. A law regulating insurance for McCarran–Ferguson purposes targets practices or provisions that "have the effect of transferring or spreading a policyholder's risk; ... [that are] an integral part of the policy relationship between the insurer and the insured; and [are] limited to entities within the insurance industry." [ ]. Because the factors are guideposts, a state law is not required to satisfy all three McCarran–Ferguson criteria to survive preemption [ ] and so we follow our precedent and leave open whether the review mandated here may be described as going to a practice that "spreads a policyholder's risk." For in any event, the second and third factors are clearly satisfied by § 4–10.

It is obvious enough that the independent review requirement regulates "an integral part of the policy relationship between the insurer and the insured." Illinois adds an extra layer of review when there is internal disagreement about an HMO's denial of coverage. The reviewer applies both a standard of medical care (medical necessity) and characteristically, as in this case, construes policy terms. [ ]. The review affects the "policy relationship" between HMO and covered persons by translating the relationship under the HMO agreement into concrete terms of specific obligation or freedom from duty. Hence our repeated statements that the interpretation of insurance contracts is at the "core" of the business of insurance. [ ]

* * *

The final factor, that the law be aimed at a "practice ... limited to entities within the insurance industry" [ ] is satisfied for many of the same reasons that the law passes the commonsense test. The law regulates application of HMO contracts and provides for review of claim denials; once it is established that HMO contracts are, in fact, contracts for insurance (and not merely contracts for medical care), it is clear that § 4–10 does not apply to entities outside the insurance industry (although it does not, of course, apply to all entities within it).

* * *

III

Given that § 4–10 regulates insurance, ERISA's mandate that "nothing in this subchapter shall be construed to exempt or relieve any person from any law of any State which regulates insurance," [ ] ostensibly forecloses preemption. See *Metropolitan Life*, 471 U.S. at 746 ("If a state law 'regulates insurance,' ... it is not pre-empted"). Rush, however, does not give up. It argues for preemption anyway, emphasizing that the question is ultimately one of congressional intent, which sometimes is so clear that it overrides a statutory provision designed to save state law from being preempted. * * *

In ERISA law, we have recognized one example of this sort of overpowering federal policy in the civil enforcement provisions [ ] authorizing civil actions for six specific types of relief. In *Massachusetts Mut. Life Ins. Co. v. Russell*, 473 U.S. 134, 87 L.Ed.2d 96, 105 S.Ct. 3085 (1985), we said those provisions amounted to an "interlocking, interrelated, and interdependent remedial scheme," [ ] which *Pilot Life* described as "representing a careful balancing of the need for prompt and fair claims settlement procedures against the public interest in encouraging the formation of employee benefit plans," [ ]. So, we have held, the civil enforcement provisions are of such extraordinarily preemptive power that they override even the "well-pleaded complaint" rule for establishing the conditions under which a cause of action may be removed to a federal forum. *Metropolitan Life Ins. Co. v. Taylor*, 481 U.S. at 63–64.

A

Although we have yet to encounter a forced choice between the congressional policies of exclusively federal remedies and the "reservation of the business of insurance to the States," [ ] we have anticipated such a conflict, with the state insurance regulation losing out if it allows plan participants "to obtain remedies ... that Congress rejected in ERISA" [ ].

In *Pilot Life*, an ERISA plan participant who had been denied benefits sued in a state court on state tort and contract claims. He sought not merely damages for breach of contract, but also damages for emotional distress and punitive damages, both of which we had held unavailable under relevant ERISA provisions. [ ] We not only rejected the notion that these common-law contract claims "regulated insurance," [ ] but went on to say that, regardless, Congress intended a "federal common law of rights and obligations" to develop under ERISA [ ] without embellishment by independent state remedies. * * *

Rush says that the day has come to turn dictum into holding by declaring that the state insurance regulation, § 4–10, is preempted for creating just the kind of "alternative remedy" we disparaged in *Pilot Life*. As Rush sees it, the independent review procedure is a form of binding arbitration that allows an ERISA beneficiary to submit claims to a new decisionmaker to examine Rush's determination *de novo,* supplanting judicial review under the "arbitrary and capricious" standard ordinarily applied when discretionary plan interpretations are challenged. [ ]. Rush says that the beneficiary's option falls within *Pilot Life*'s notion of a remedy that "supplements or supplants" the remedies available under ERISA. [ ].

We think, however, that Rush overstates the rule expressed in *Pilot Life*.

* * *

[T]his case addresses a state regulatory scheme that provides no new cause of action under state law and authorizes no new form of ultimate relief. While independent review under § 4–10 may well settle the fate of a benefit claim under a particular contract, the state statute does not enlarge the claim beyond the benefits available in any action brought under § 1132(a). And although the reviewer's determination would presumably replace that of the HMO as to what is "medically necessary" under this contract the relief ultimately available would still be what ERISA authorizes in a suit for benefits under § 1132(a). * * *

B

Rush still argues for going beyond *Pilot Life*, making the preemption issue here one of degree, whether the state procedural imposition interferes unreasonably with Congress's intention to provide a uniform federal regime of "rights and obligations" under ERISA. However, "such disuniformities . . . are the inevitable result of the congressional decision to 'save' local insurance regulation." [ ] Although we have recognized a limited exception from the saving clause for alternative causes of action and alternative remedies in the sense described above, we have never indicated that there might be additional justifications for qualifying the clause's application. Rush's arguments today convince us that further limits on insurance regulation preserved by ERISA are unlikely to deserve recognition.

To be sure, a State might provide for a type of "review" that would so resemble an adjudication as to fall within *Pilot Life*'s categorical bar. Rush, and the dissent, *post,* at 8, contend that § 4–10 fills that bill by imposing an alternative scheme of arbitral adjudication at odds with the manifest congressional purpose to confine adjudication of disputes to the courts. It does not turn out to be this simple, however, and a closer look at the state law reveals a scheme significantly different from common arbitration as a way of construing and applying contract terms.

In the classic sense, arbitration occurs when "parties in dispute choose a judge to render a final and binding decision on the merits of the controversy and on the basis of proofs presented by the parties." [ ]. Arbitrators typically hold hearings at which parties may submit evidence and conduct cross-examinations [ ] and are often invested with many powers over the dispute and the parties, including the power to subpoena witnesses and administer oaths [ ].

Section 4–10 does resemble an arbitration provision, then, to the extent that the independent reviewer considers disputes about the meaning of the HMO contract and receives "evidence" in the form of medical records, statements from physicians, and the like. But this is as far as the resemblance to arbitration goes, for the other features of review under § 4–10 give the proceeding a different character, one not at all at odds with the policy behind § 1132(a). The Act does not give the independent reviewer a free-ranging power to construe contract terms, but instead, confines review to a single term: the phrase "medical necessity," used to define the services covered under the contract. This limitation, in turn, implicates a feature of HMO benefit determinations that we described in *Pegram* v. *Herdrich* [ ]. We explained that when an HMO guarantees medically necessary care, determinations of coverage "cannot be untangled from physicians' judgments about reasonable medical treatment." [ ]. This is just how the Illinois Act operates; the independent examiner must be a physician with credentials similar to those of the primary care physician [ ] and is expected to exercise independent medical judgment in deciding what medical necessity requires. Accordingly, the reviewer in this case did not hold the kind of conventional evidentiary hearing common in arbitration, but simply received medical records submitted by the parties, and ultimately came to a professional judgment of his own. [ ]

Once this process is set in motion, it does not resemble either contract interpretation or evidentiary litigation before a neutral arbiter, as much as it looks like a practice (having nothing to do with arbitration) of obtaining another medical opinion. The reference to an independent reviewer is similar to the submission to a second physician, which many health insurers are required by law to provide before denying coverage.

The practice of obtaining a second opinion, however, is far removed from any notion of an enforcement scheme, and once § 4–10 is seen as something akin to a mandate for second-opinion practice in order to ensure sound medical judgments, the preemption argument that arbitration under § 4–10 supplants judicial enforcement runs out of steam.

Next, Rush argues that § 4–10 clashes with a substantive rule intended to be preserved by the system of uniform enforcement, stressing a feature of judicial review highly prized by benefit plans: a deferential standard for reviewing benefit denials. Whereas *Firestone Tire & Rubber Co.* v. *Bruch* [ ] recognized that an ERISA plan could be designed to grant "discretion" to a plan fiduciary, deserving deference from a court reviewing a discretionary judgment, § 4–10 provides that when a plan purchases medical services and insurance from an HMO, benefit denials are subject to apparently *de novo* review. If a plan should continue to balk at providing a service the reviewer has found medically necessary, the reviewer's determination could carry great weight in a subsequent suit for benefits under § 1132(a), depriving the plan of the judicial deference a fiduciary's medical judgment might have obtained if judicial review of the plan's decision had been immediate.

Again, however, the significance of § 4–10 is not wholly captured by Rush's argument, which requires some perspective for evaluation. First, in determining whether state procedural requirements deprive plan administrators of any right to a uniform standard of review, it is worth recalling that ERISA itself provides nothing about the standard. It simply requires plans to afford a beneficiary some mechanism for internal review of a benefit denial [ ] and provides a right to a subsequent judicial forum for a claim to recover benefits [ ]. Whatever the standards for reviewing benefit denials may be, they cannot conflict with anything in the text of the statute, which we have read to require a uniform judicial regime of categories of relief and standards of primary conduct, not a uniformly lenient regime of reviewing benefit determinations. [ ]

Not only is there no ERISA provision directly providing a lenient standard for judicial review of benefit denials, but there is no requirement necessarily entailing such an effect even indirectly. When this Court dealt with the review standards on which the statute was silent, we held that a general or default rule of *de novo* review could be replaced by deferential review if the ERISA plan itself provided that the plan's benefit determinations were matters of high or unfettered discretion [ ]. Nothing in ERISA, however, requires that these kinds of decisions be so "discretionary" in the first place; whether they are is simply a matter of plan design or the drafting of an HMO contract. In this respect, then, § 4–10 prohibits designing an insurance contract so as to accord unfettered discretion to the insurer to interpret the contract's terms. As such, it does not implicate ERISA's enforcement scheme at all, and is no different from the types of substantive state regulation of insurance contracts we have in the past permitted to survive preemption, such as mandated-benefit statutes and statutes prohibiting the denial of claims solely on the ground of untimeliness. [ ]

In sum, § 4–10 imposes no new obligation or remedy like the causes of action considered in *Russell*, *Pilot Life*, and *Ingersoll–Rand*. Even in its formal guise, the state Act bears a closer resemblance to second-opinion requirements than to arbitration schemes. Deferential review in the HMO context is not a settled given; § 4–10 operates before the stage of judicial review; the independent reviewer's *de novo* examination of the benefit claim mirrors the general or default rule we have ourselves recognized; and its effect is no greater than that of mandated-benefit regulation.

In deciding what to make of these facts and conclusions, it helps to go back to where we started and recall the ways States regulate insurance in looking out for the welfare of their citizens. Illinois has chosen to regulate insurance as one way to regulate the practice of medicine, which we have previously held to be permissible under ERISA [ ]. While the statute designed to do this undeniably eliminates whatever may have remained of a plan sponsor's option to minimize scrutiny of benefit denials, this effect of eliminating an insurer's autonomy to guarantee terms congenial to its own interests is the stuff of garden variety insurance regulation through the imposition of standard policy terms. [ ]. It is therefore hard to imagine a reservation of state power to regulate insurance that would not be meant to cover restrictions of the insurer's advantage in this kind of way. And any lingering doubt about the reasonableness of § 4–10 in affecting the application of § 1132(a) may be put to rest by recalling that regulating insurance tied to what is medically necessary is probably inseparable from enforcing the quintessentially state-law standards of reasonable medical care. [ ] To the extent that benefits litigation in some federal courts may have to account for the effects of § 4–10, it would be an exaggeration to hold that the objectives of § 1132(a) are undermined. The saving clause is entitled to prevail here, and we affirm the judgment.

It is so ordered.

JUSTICE THOMAS, with whom THE CHIEF JUSTICE, JUSTICE SCALIA, and JUSTICE KENNEDY join, dissenting.

This Court has repeatedly recognized that ERISA's civil enforcement provision [ ] provides the exclusive vehicle for actions asserting a claim for benefits under health plans governed by ERISA, and therefore that state laws that create additional remedies are pre-empted. [ ]. Such exclusivity of remedies is necessary to further Congress' interest in establishing a uniform federal law of employee benefits so that employers are encouraged to provide benefits to their employees * * *

[A]s the Court concedes [ ] even a state law that "regulates insurance" may be pre-empted if it supplements the remedies provided by ERISA, despite ERISA's saving clause [ ] Today, however, the Court takes the unprecedented step of allowing respondent Debra Moran to short circuit ERISA's remedial scheme by allowing her claim for benefits to be determined in the first instance through an arbitral-like procedure provided under Illinois law, and by a decisionmaker other than a court. [ ] This decision not only conflicts with our precedents, it also eviscerates the uniformity of ERISA remedies Congress deemed integral to the "careful balancing of the need for prompt and fair claims settlement procedures against the public interest in encouraging the formation of employee benefit plans." [ ]. I would reverse the Court of Appeals' judgment and remand for a determination of whether Moran was entitled to reimbursement absent the independent review conducted under § 4–10.

I

From the facts of this case one can readily understand why Moran sought recourse under § 4–10. Moran is covered by a medical benefits plan sponsored by her husband's employer and governed by ERISA. Petitioner Rush Prudential HMO, Inc., is the employer's health maintenance organization (HMO) provider for the plan. Petitioner's Member Certificate of Coverage (Certificate) details the scope of coverage under the plan and provides petitioner with "the broadest possible discretion" to interpret the terms of the plan and to determine participants' entitlement to benefits. * * *

In the course of its review, petitioner informed Moran that "there is no prevailing opinion within the appropriate specialty of the United States medical profession that the procedure proposed [by Moran] is safe and effective for its intended use and that the omission of the procedure would adversely affect [her] medical condition." [ ] Petitioner did agree to cover the standard treatment for Moran's ailment [ ] concluding that peer-reviewed literature "demonstrates that [the standard surgery] is effective therapy in the treatment of [Moran's condition]." [ ]

Moran, however, was not satisfied with this option. After exhausting the plan's internal review mechanism, Moran chose to bypass the relief provided by ERISA. She invoked § 4–10 of the Illinois HMO Act, which requires HMOs to provide a mechanism for review by an independent physician when the patient's primary care physician and HMO disagree about the medical necessity of a treatment proposed by the primary care physician.

Dr. A. Lee Dellon, an unaffiliated physician who served as the independent medical reviewer, concluded that the surgery for which petitioner denied coverage "was appropriate," that it was "the same type of surgery" he would have done, and that Moran "had all of the indications and therefore the medical necessity to carry out" the non-standard surgery. * * *

Nevertheless, petitioner again denied benefits, steadfastly maintaining that the unconventional surgery was not medically necessary. While the Court of Appeals recharacterized Moran's claim for reimbursement under § 4–10 as a claim for benefits under ERISA [ ] it reversed the judgment of the District Court based solely on Dr. Dellon's judgment that the surgery was "medically necessary."

II

Section 514(a)'s broad language provides that ERISA "shall supersede any and all State laws insofar as they ... relate to any employee benefit plan," except as provided in § 514(b). [ ]. This language demonstrates "Congress's intent to establish the regulation of employee welfare benefit plans 'as exclusively a federal concern.' " [ ]. It was intended to "ensure that plans and plan sponsors would be subject to a uniform body of benefits law" so as to "minimize the administrative and financial burden of complying with conflicting directives among States or between States and the Federal Government" and to prevent "the potential for conflict in substantive law ... requiring the tailoring of plans and employer conduct to the peculiarities of the law of each jurisdiction. "[ ]

* * *

Consequently, the Court until today had consistently held that state laws that seek to supplant or add to the exclusive remedies in § 502(a) of ERISA [ ] are pre-empted because they conflict with Congress' objective that rights under ERISA plans are to be enforced under a uniform national system. [ ]. The Court has explained that § 502(a) creates an "interlocking, interrelated, and interdependent remedial scheme," and that a beneficiary who claims that he was wrongfully denied benefits has "a panoply of remedial devices" at his disposal. [ ]. It is exactly this enforcement scheme that *Pilot Life* described as "representing a careful balancing of the need for prompt and fair claims settlement procedures against the public interest in encouraging the formation of employee benefit plans," [ ]. Central to that balance is the development of "a federal common law of rights and obligations under ERISA-regulated plans." [ ]

In addressing the relationship between ERISA's remedies under § 502(a) and a state law regulating insurance, the Court has observed that "the policy choices reflected in the inclusion of certain remedies and the exclusion of others under the federal scheme would be completely undermined if ERISA-plan participants and beneficiaries were free to obtain remedies under state law that Congress rejected in ERISA." [ ] Thus, while the preeminent federal interest in the uniform administration of employee benefit plans yields in some instances to varying state regulation of the business of insurance, the exclusivity and uniformity of ERISA's enforcement scheme remains paramount. * * *

III

* * *

Section 4–10 cannot be characterized as anything other than an alternative state-law remedy or vehicle for seeking benefits. In the first place, § 4–10 comes into play only if the HMO and the claimant dispute the claimant's entitlement to benefits; the purpose of the review is to determine whether a claimant is entitled to benefits. Contrary to the majority's characterization of § 4–10 as nothing more than a state law regarding medical standards [ ] it is in fact a binding determination of whether benefits are due: "In the event that the reviewing physician determines the covered service to be medically necessary, the [HMO] *shall provide* the covered service." [ ]. Section 4–10 is thus most precisely characterized as an arbitration-like mechanism to settle benefits disputes. [ ]

There is no question that arbitration constitutes an alternative remedy to litigation. [ ] Consequently, although a contractual agreement to arbitrate—which does not constitute a "State law" relating to "any employee benefit plan"—is outside § 514(a) of ERISA's pre-emptive scope, States may not circumvent ERISA pre-emption by mandating an alternative arbitral-like remedy as a plan term enforceable through an ERISA action.

To be sure, the majority is correct that § 4–10 does not mirror all procedural and evidentiary aspects of "common arbitration." *Ante,* at 25–26. But as a binding decision on the merits of the controversy the § 4–10 review resembles nothing so closely as arbitration.

* * *

IV

For these same reasons, it is troubling that the Court views the review under § 4–10 as nothing more than a practice "of obtaining a second [medical] opinion." [ ]. The independent reviewer may, like most arbitrators, possess special expertise or knowledge in the area subject to arbitration. But while a second medical opinion is nothing more than that—an opinion—a determination under § 4–10 is a conclusive determination with respect to the award of benefits. And the Court's reference to *Pegram* v. *Herdrich* [ ] as support for its Alice in Wonderland-like claim that the § 4–10 proceeding is "far removed from any notion of an enforcement scheme," [ ] is equally perplexing, given that the treatment is long over and the issue presented is purely an eligibility decision with respect to reimbursement.

* * *

Section 4–10 constitutes an arbitral-like state remedy through which plan members may seek to resolve conclusively a disputed right to benefits. Some 40 other States have similar laws, though these vary as to applicability, procedures, standards, deadlines, and consequences of independent review.[ ] Allowing disparate state laws that provide inconsistent external review requirements to govern a participant's or beneficiary's claim to benefits under an employee benefit plan is wholly destructive of Congress' expressly stated goal of uniformity in this area. Moreover, it is inimical to a scheme for furthering and protecting the "careful balancing of the need for prompt and fair claims settlement procedures against the public interest in encouraging the formation of employee benefit plans," given that the development of a federal common law under ERISA-regulated plans has consistently been deemed central to that balance. [ ] While it is true that disuniformity is the inevitable result of the Congressional decision to save local insurance regulation, this does not answer the altogether different question before the Court today, which is whether a state law "regulating insurance" nonetheless provides a separate vehicle to assert a claim for benefits outside of, or in addition to, ERISA's remedial scheme. [ ]. If it does, the exclusivity and uniformity of ERISA's enforcement scheme must remain paramount and the state law is pre-empted in accordance with ordinary principles of conflict pre-emption. * * *

For the reasons noted by the Court, independent review provisions may sound very appealing. Efforts to expand the variety of remedies available to aggrieved beneficiaries beyond those set forth in ERISA are obviously designed to increase the chances that patients will be able to receive treatments they desire, and most of us are naturally sympathetic to those suffering from illness who seek further options. Nevertheless, the Court would do well to remember that no employer is required to provide any health benefit plan under ERISA and that the entire advent of managed care, and the genesis of HMOs, stemmed from spiraling health costs. To the extent that independent review provisions such as § 4–10 make it more likely that HMOs will have to subsidize beneficiaries' treatments of choice, they undermine the ability of HMOs to control costs, which, in turn, undermines the ability of employers to provide health care coverage for employees.

As a consequence, independent review provisions could create a disincentive to the formation of employee health benefit plans, a problem that Congress addressed by making ERISA's remedial scheme exclusive and uniform. While it may well be the case that the advantages of allowing States to implement independent review requirements as a supplement to the remedies currently provided under ERISA outweigh this drawback, this is a judgment that, pursuant to ERISA, must be made by Congress. I respectfully dissent.

CICIO v. JOHN DOES 1–8

United States Court of Appeals for the Second Circuit, 2003.
321 F.3d 83.

SACK, Circuit Judge:

* * *

BACKGROUND

Carmine Cicio's Illness and Treatment

Because this case comes to us on appeal from the grant of a motion to dis[miss], we review the facts as they have been alleged by the plaintiff. [ ]. In March 1997, the plaintiff's spouse, Carmine Cicio, was diagnosed with multiple myeloma.[1] He began chemotherapy the following month. At that time, both he and the plaintiff received health care benefits pursuant to an "Agreement for Comprehensive Health Services" (the "Plan") administered by Vytra, an "Individual Practice Association—Health Maintenance Organization."[2] The plaintiff's employer, North Fork Bank, had purchased the Plan from Vytra. The Plan, it is now undisputed, is an "employee benefit plan," as defined in 29 U.S.C. § 1002 (3) of ERISA.

The Plan's subscriber agreement explains that Vytra provides Plan enrollees with, inter alia, "diagnosis and treatment of disease, injury or other conditions." [ ]. The Plan cautions, however, that "Vytra shall provide only Medically Necessary Vytra Services. [ ]." Vytra also disclaims the obligation to provide "any procedure or service which, in the judgment of Vytra's Medical Director, is experimental or is not generally recognized to be effective for a particular condition, diagnosis, or body area.... " [ ].

On January 28, 1998, some ten months after Carmine Cicio's disease was first diagnosed, his treating oncologist, Dr. Edward Samuel, wrote a detailed letter to Vytra "requesting insurance approval for treatment of Mr. Cicio with high dose chemotherapy supported with peripheral blood

---

1. "Multiple myeloma is the second most prevalent blood cancer and represents approximately 1 of all cancers and 2 of all cancer deaths." Multiple Myeloma Research Foundation, The Statistics, at http://www.multiplemyeloma.org/aboutmyeloma/statistics.html (last visited September 16, 2002).

2. An independent practice association is a "local physician group . . . comprised of physicians who are active on [a] hospital's medical staff" and contract with a health maintenance organization to provide medical services.... "HMOs are not guarantee-

ing to reimburse the insured for medical expenses; rather, their obligation to the insured is more direct—to actually provide medical services to them." [ ]

In an "Individual Practice Association—Health Maintenance Organization," "physicians' services are established with a relatively large number of generally small or medium-sized group practices, with physicians receiving some type of discounted fee-for-service payment from the HMO, rather than ... salaried reimbursement.... " Id. at 81 (internal citation omitted).

stem cell transplantation, in a tandem double transplant, for a diagnosis of multiple myeloma."[4] [ ] Dr. Samuel set forth Carmine Cicio's clinical history and prior treatments, including one type of chemotherapy that had failed, before explaining why "a change in strategy of treatment ... had to be made." [ ] And Dr. Samuel explained why he thought that Mr. Cicio was a good "candidate" for the transplant. [ ]

Almost a month later, in a letter dated February 23, 1998, Vytra's medical director, the defendant Dr. Spears, denied Dr. Samuel's request, stating only that the procedure sought was "not a covered benefit according to this member's plan which states [that] experimental/investigational procedures are not covered." [ ]. On March 4, after unsuccessful attempts to contact Dr. Spears by telephone, Dr. Samuel wrote Dr. Spears "appealing to [him] to reconsider [his] decision." [ ] Dr. Samuel argued that

> The treatment of multiple myeloma by high-dose chemotherapy/autologous stem cell transplantation is a well-established method of treatment with a superior response rate, complete response rate, post therapy disease-free interval, and possibly even a long-term cure in some patients, as compared to standard therapies. These facts are true for single transplant methodologies, and the statistical response rate and CR rates are improved even further with double transplants.

[ ]. He further argued, based on medical literature listed in his letter, that "treatment NOW with high-dose chemotherapy and autologous stem transplant ... offers [Mr. Cicio] better chances of survival than any other available method of treatment." [ ]. While this letter made the one reference to "single transplant methodologies" quoted above, it made clear that Dr. Samuel viewed that procedure as a less appropriate treatment for Mr. Cicio than a double stem cell transplant and was not requesting approval for it. [ ]

Three weeks later, in a letter dated March 25, 1998, Dr. Spears tersely replied that "based on the clinical peer review of the additional material, [ ] a single stem cell transplant has been approved" but "the original request for [a] tandem stem cell transplant remains denied." [ ]. Mr. Cicio, who, according to the complaint, was by March 25 no longer a candidate for a stem cell transplant, died less than two months later, on May 11, 1998. [ ]

The Complaint

Bonnie Cicio filed a complaint, on behalf of herself and the estate of her late husband, in New York Supreme Court, Suffolk County, naming

---

4. A peripheral blood stem cell transplantation is "[a] procedure in which blood containing mobilized stem cells is collected by apheresis [a procedure in which blood is removed from a donor, a blood component, e.g., white blood cells, is separated out, and the remaining blood is reinfused back into the donor], stored, and infused following high-dose chemotherapy or radiation therapy." Multiple Myeloma Research Foundation, Myeloma Dictionary, at http://www.multiplemyeloma.org/ aboutmyeloma/defs.html (last visited September 16, 2002).

Vytra, Dr. Spears, and eight unknown physicians employed by Vytra ("John Does 1–8") as defendants. The complaint contains eighteen counts alleging "medical malpractice, negligence, gross negligence, intentional infliction of emotional distress, negligent infliction of emotional distress, misrepresentation, breach of contract, bad faith breach of insurance contract and violation of New York State law" based on Dr. Spears's denial of treatment to Mr. Cicio.

On May 30, 2000, the defendants removed the proceedings from New York state court to the United States District Court for the Eastern District of New York pursuant to 28 U.S.C. § 1441. On June 21, 2000, they filed a Rule 12(b)(6) motion to dismiss the complaint for failure to state a claim.

The Magistrate Judge's Report and Recommendation and the District Court's Decision

The case was referred by the district court to Magistrate Judge E. Thomas Boyle, who * * * recommended that the defendants' Rule 12(b)(6) motion be granted. [ ] Magistrate Judge Boyle reasoned that the plaintiff's state law claims were preempted under §§ 502(a) and 514(a) of ERISA, 29 U.S.C. §§ 1132 (a)(1)(B) & 1144(a), because the plaintiff sought "to enforce the terms of [an employee welfare benefit] plan" and that her claims were "within the scope of" § 502(a). [ ]. He concluded that both removal and dismissal were therefore required. [ ]. He also recommended that the plaintiff's state law deceptive business practices claim be dismissed because it was "exceedingly vague." [ ]

In so concluding, the magistrate judge rejected several counterarguments proffered by Ms. Cicio. First, he rejected her argument that Vytra's Agreement for Comprehensive Health Services was not a "plan" governed by ERISA. [ ]. Then he declined to endorse the plaintiff's argument that her medical malpractice claims were not preempted because they concerned "mixed eligibility and treatment decisions," as described in Pegram v. Herdrich, 530 U.S. 211, 229, 147 L.Ed.2d 164, 120 S.Ct. 2143 (2000). [ ] While many decisions by health insurance providers "involve[ ] some medical judgment," Magistrate Judge Boyle said, "there is no evidence that Congress intended that these quasi-medical/administrative decisions made by a plan administrator survive ERISA preemption." [ ]. Even if such malpractice claims were not preempted, Magistrate Judge Boyle continued, Ms. Cicio had not challenged "the quality of the care but rather . . . the benefits decision that was made," and hence had alleged the kind of claim that ERISA preempted. [ ]

The plaintiff formally objected to the magistrate judge's report and recommendation. The district court nonetheless adopted it in full. [ ]. The court agreed that Vytra's health plan was a "benefit plan" as defined by ERISA. [ ]. The court also disagreed with the renewed contention that under Pegram, claims for improper medical care are not preempted by ERISA. It concluded instead that because all of the plaintiff's malpractice claims "involved eligibility for coverage," such that the "defendants' roles, including that of Dr. Spears, were administrative," these claims concerned benefits decisions and thus were also preempted. [ ] The plaintiff appeals.

DISCUSSION

* * *

II. The Nature of the Plaintiff's Claims

Because the plaintiff asserts a variety of claims, we must first determine which of them remain on appeal. * * *

The claims [ ] remaining on appeal pertain in substance to (1) the timeliness of Dr. Spears's decisions relating to Mr. Cicio's treatment [ ] (2) the allegedly misleading nature of Vytra's representations about the Plan [ ] (3) the quality of the medical decision, if any, made by the defendants with respect to Mr. Cicio's treatment [ ] Both the magistrate judge, Cicio, [ ] and the district court [ ] determined that the complaint did not challenge the quality of the medical decision because "all of the Plaintiff's state law claims center on Vytra's refusal to approve coverage and thus stem from an adverse benefits determination," [ ]. We disagree.

A Rule 12(b)(6) dismissal "is inappropriate unless it appears beyond doubt, even when the complaint is liberally construed, that the plaintiff can prove no set of facts which would entitle [her] to relief." [ ] Under this broad standard, Ms. Cicio's complaint identifies a medical decision that may be the predicate for a state-law medical malpractice claim.

The complaint alleges that Dr. Spears and other physicians employed by Vytra "failed to exercise the degree of care required of them and were negligent in the provision and delivery of medically necessary care." [ ]. It is possible that in attacking Dr. Spears's determination that a "tandem double stem cell transplant" was an "experimental/ investigational procedure[ ]," Ms. Cicio is questioning only Dr. Spears's assessment of the then-current state of medical science without regard to Mr. Cicio's particular medical affliction. This kind of decision about the scope of generally available benefits lacks a significant application of medical judgment to Mr. Cicio's case and, as the district court correctly noted, would be treated as a decision simply about the scope of benefits. But correspondence between Drs. Samuel and Spears attached to the complaint [ ] strongly suggests that Ms. Cicio is contending additionally or in the alternative that Dr. Spears, in making negligent medical decisions about Mr. Cicio's condition, was engaged in medical malpractice. The liberal construction we are required to give the complaint requires us to consider this understanding of the allegations it contains.

In his request for approval for treatment dated January 28, 1998, Dr. Samuel provided Vytra's Medical Director, Dr. Spears, with a thorough description of the case history of Mr. Cicio's illness. [ ]. This information at least permitted Dr. Spears to make a medical determination regarding Mr. Cicio's treatment on the basis of his aggregate symptoms. And while Dr. Spears stated in reply only that the requested "procedure is not a covered benefit according to this member's plan," [Letter from Spears to Samuels dated February 23, 1998] his decision could have rested either on an analysis of the appropriate treatment for Mr. Cicio's specific condition, or on whether in the abstract a double stem cell transplant to treat multiple myeloma was experimental given the current state of the medical art. Therefore, there is at least a possibility that the [ ] letter reflected a medical decision.

The impression that the February 23rd letter may have embodied a medical decision is strengthened by the subsequent correspondence. Dr. Samuel's response stressed the appropriateness of double stem cell transplants in light of Mr. Cicio's particular symptoms. Dr. Spears's answer, that "based on the clinical peer review of the additional information, a single stem cell transplant has been approved [but] the original request for tandem stem cell transplant remains denied," [ ] appears to reflect a decision about an appropriate level of care. By denying one treatment and authorizing another that Dr. Samuel had not specifically requested, Dr. Spears at least seems to have been engaged in a patient-specific prescription of an appropriate treatment, and, ultimately, a medical decision that a single stem cell transplant was the appropriate treatment for Mr. Cicio.

At this stage of the litigation, reading the plaintiff's complaint and the attachments thereto together, then, we conclude that the plaintiff has alleged that the defendants made a decision that could implicate a state law duty concerning the quality of medical decision-making, in addition to and independent of her claims concerning the administration of benefits with respect to her late husband's course of care.

We do not, however, draw any conclusion about the availability of a malpractice claim in these circumstances under New York law, or whether any of the elements of such a claim, if it exists, would be satisfied by the facts as alleged in this case. We conclude only that, for the purposes of this Rule 12(b)(6) motion, the plaintiff has alleged more than an adverse benefits decision. She has also alleged that the defendants made a negligent medical determination with respect to the treatment of her late husband.

III. Subject Matter Jurisdiction

The district court concluded that defendants' removal of the complaint to federal court was proper. We agree.

* * *

V. Preemption of Medical Malpractice Claims

The question whether a state law medical malpractice claim brought with respect to a medical decision made in the course of prospective utilization review by a managed care organization or health insurer is preempted under ERISA § 514, and therefore beyond the reach of state tort law, is one of first impression in this Circuit. We conclude, largely on the basis of recent Supreme Court decisions, that such a state law claim is not preempted.

A. *The Practice of Utilization Review*

The plaintiff's medical malpractice claims are based on Dr. Spears's denial of coverage for a double stem cell transplant for Mr. Cicio. [ ] Dr. Spears's decision occurred in the course of Dr. Samuel's attempt to obtain authorization for the double stem cell transplant from Vytra. [ ]. The complaint then details a process of utilization review, and it is the nature of this procedure, and its relation to ERISA, upon which we now focus.

Utilization review usually involves "prospective review by a third party of the necessity of medical care." [ ] such as Vytra's Medical Director, Dr. Spears. "Although prospective utilization review involves no traditional face-to-face clinical encounter, it is still quasi-medical in nature. It necessarily involves evaluation of data collected in such an encounter." [ ] Prospective utilization review blurs boundaries between the traditionally "distinct sphere of professional dominance and autonomy" of the medical profession on the one hand [ ] and the managerial domain on the other. As such, it represents a development apparently unforeseen at the time of ERISA's enactment.

Moreover, as other courts have noted, "a system of prospective decisionmaking influences the beneficiary's choice among treatment options to a far greater degree than does the theoretical risk of disallowance of a claim facing a beneficiary in a retrospective system." [ ]. And, "in many instances, a denial of coverage results in the patient forgoing the procedure altogether." [ ] Thus, decisions with a medical component—i.e., involving the exercise of medical judgment in relation to a particular patient's symptoms—are made in the course of utilization review by staff who are independent of and separate from the locus of traditional medical decision-making authority. These medical decisions have possibly dispositive consequences for the course of treatment that a patient ultimately follows.

B. *ERISA's Preemptive Scope*

The Supreme Court, in its early pronouncements on ERISA preemption, suggested that the sweeping reference to "any and all State laws [that] ... relate" to benefits plans in ERISA's preemption provision, 29 U.S.C. § 1144 (a), entailed an expansive preemptive effect that corresponded to the provision's broad wording. [ ] Since then, however, the Court has "tempered the assumption that the ordinary meaning [of § 514] ... accurately expresses the legislative purpose ... with the qualification that the historic police powers of the States were not meant to be superseded by the Federal Act unless that was the clear and manifest purpose of Congress." Rush Prudential HMO, Inc. v. Moran, 536 U.S. 355, 122 S.Ct. 2151, 2159, 153 L.Ed.2d 375 (2002) [ ]. * * *

Specifically, the Supreme Court has rejected the notion that any finely filigreed connection between ERISA and a state law establish

ERISA preemption, and, instead, has held that a court must begin with the presumption that "in the field of health care, a subject of traditional state regulation, there is no ERISA preemption without clear manifestations of congressional purpose." [ ] Moving beyond presumptions, the Supreme Court has also, in its own words, thrown "cold water" on the idea that state regulation of health and safety is necessarily preempted even when it overlaps with rights protected by ERISA. Pegram [ ].

In deciding the preemption question, it is also noteworthy that ERISA's "repeatedly emphasized purpose [is] to protect contractually defined benefits." [ ] Indeed, one of ERISA's stated goals involves increasing "the likelihood that full benefits will be paid to participants and beneficiaries of [covered] plans." [ ]. State medical malpractice law, by contrast, even if implicated by the execution of a benefits decision, involves the application of duties of conduct that are defined independent of ERISA plans. As such, it is not among the "rights and expectations brought into being by [ERISA]," is designed to protect.

We must therefore ask whether the plaintiff's medical malpractice causes of action "relate to" the benefits plan administered by Vytra, keeping in mind both the Supreme Court's warning that state law regulation of medical practice is not to be lightly disturbed, and the observation that ERISA's primary focus is the protection of contractual rights defined by benefits plans.

C. The Preemption of Medical Malpractice Claims Against Utilization Review Decisions

1. Pegram v. Herdrich. At first blush, the defendants' contention that Dr. Spears's decision concerned a benefits determination about what medical treatments Mr. Cicio could receive pursuant to the plan, a decision that can only be challenged in a § 502(a)(1)(B) action, has considerable force. Other courts addressing similar facts have concluded that malpractice claims based on utilization review decisions are indeed preempted by § 514. They have reasoned, first, that utilization review involves "medical decisions as part and parcel of [a plan's] mandate to decide what benefits are available," and then held that, as benefits decisions, utilization review decisions can be challenged only in § 502(a)(1)(B) actions. [ ] These cases rest on the proposition that a decision cannot be the basis of a malpractice claim even if it involves the exercise of medical judgment if at the same time it has a benefits determination component. According to these cases, the performance of contractual interpretation in order to determine benefits triggers preemption without regard to the medical content of a decision.

But Corcoran, Jass, and Tolton were decided before the Supreme Court's recent retrenchment of ERISA preemption's margins, and before the Court, in its unanimous decision in Pegram v. Herdrich, addressed (albeit in dicta) medical malpractice actions against those engaged in medical decision making.

Pegram concerned a defendant physician who "decided (wrongly, as it turned out) that [the plaintiff's] condition did not warrant immediate action; the consequence of that medical determination was that [the defendant HMO] would not cover immediate care, whereas it would have done so if [the defendant physician] had made the proper diagnosis and judgment to treat." [ ]. Pegram, the Court addressed only whether an HMO had, by its method of sharing profits with doctors, breached its fiduciary duty to members, and expressly declined to address the interaction between § 502 and state law claims. [ ]. Pegram is nonetheless relevant to the case at hand because of the reasoning upon which the Court's conclusion was based. The Court decided that no fiduciary breach action could be brought under ERISA because, in part, such an action would be a "mere replication of state malpractice actions with HMO defendants." [ ]. The creation of a fiduciary breach action through "the formulaic addition of an allegation of financial incentive [to a malpractice claim] would do nothing but bring the same claim into a federal court under federal-question jurisdiction." [ ]. We thus infer that the continued availability of some state law malpractice actions based on at least some varieties of utilization review decisions was a predicate of the Court's holding.

But the Pegram opinion has further ramifications for our analysis because of its detailed description and analysis of decision-making in the context of health care provision. The Court categorized the defendant Dr. Pegram's act as a "mixed eligibility and treatment" decision, i.e., an "eligibility decision [that] cannot be untangled from physicians' judgments about reasonable medical treatment." [ ] The Pegram Court then explained:

> What we will call pure "eligibility decisions" turn on the plan's coverage of a particular condition or medical procedure for its treatment. "Treatment decisions," by contrast, are choices about how to go about diagnosing and treating a patient's condition: given a patient's constellation of symptoms, what is the appropriate medical response?

> These decisions are often practically inextricable from one another.... This is so not merely because, under a scheme like [the benefits plan in Pegram], treatment and eligibility decisions are made by the same person, the treating physician. It is so because a great many and possibly most coverage questions are not simple yes-or-no questions, like whether appendicitis is a covered condition (when there is no dispute that a patient has appendicitis), or whether acupuncture is a covered procedure for pain relief (when the claim of pain is unchallenged). The more common coverage question is a when-and-how question. Although coverage for many conditions will be clear and various treatment options will be indisputably compensable, physicians still must decide what to do in particular cases. The issue may be, say, whether one treatment option is so superior to another under the circumstances, and needed so promptly, that a decision to proceed with it would meet the medical necessity requirement that conditions the HMO's obli-

gation to provide or pay for that particular procedure at that time in that case. [ ]

Pegram thus suggests that some decisions involve interpretation of a benefits contract, eligibility decisions, and some involve application of medical judgment to a particular patient's condition, treatment decisions. And these two categories overlap. The resulting third category, described in Pegram, of "mixed eligibility and treatment decisions, is not limited to decisions made by treating physicians, such as Dr. Pegram, who both assess which benefits a plan provides and make treatment decisions. A decision about who will "pay for" a procedure, even when this decision is not made by a "treating physician," is also a "mixed eligibility and treatment decision" if it involves answering the question: "given a patient's constellation of symptoms, what is the appropriate medical response?" [ ] In other words, even if a physician does not directly control, direct, or influence a plaintiff's treatment, and even if the sole consequence of a physician's decision is reimbursement or its denial, that decision may nonetheless be a mixed eligibility and treatment decision like Dr. Pegram's. [ ]

Pegram thus alters the framework used in Corcoran, Jess, and Tolton, in which a decision must be about either "treatment" or "eligibility," and in which any element of benefits determination suffices to make a decision an "eligibility" decision that may only be challenged in a § 502(a) action. The Pegram Court's analysis suggests instead that courts should recognize that "in recent years, the medical profession's monopoly on the authority to define appropriate health care outcomes for society has been severely eroded." [ ] The "separation between professional providers and lay financiers * * * no longer exists." [ ]. Decisions now regularly made by third-party payers, such as "whether one treatment option is so superior to another under the circumstances, and needed so promptly, that a decision to proceed with it would meet the medical necessity requirement" in a health benefits contract, "cannot be untangled from physicians' judgments about reasonable medical treatment." [ ] And such coverage decisions based on medical determinations often have an outcome-determinative effect. [ ]

The defendants' decision in this case, in the current procedural posture of this appeal, must be treated as a mixed decision because it allegedly involved both an exercise of medical judgment and an element of contract interpretation.

2. Applying Pegram's Tripartite Analysis to ERISA Preemption. We conclude that a state law malpractice action, if based on a "mixed eligibility and treatment decision," is not subject to ERISA preemption when that state law cause of action challenges an allegedly flawed medical judgment as applied to a particular patient's symptoms. We reach this conclusion by applying the presumptions previously discussed, our understanding of congressional intent in enacting ERISA, and the analytic framework established in Pegram.

At the threshold, we decline to adopt the categorical distinction between "quality of care" decisions and "benefits administration" questions applied by other courts in the ERISA preemption context [ ]. To frame the issue in that fashion is to ignore the nature of "countless medical administrative decisions every day" in which "the eligibility decision and the treatment decision [are] inextricably mixed." Pegram [ ]. Pegram teaches that this dichotomy is no longer tenable.

Further, Pegram demonstrates that the mere presence of an administrative component in a health care decision no longer has determinative significance for purposes of preemption analysis when the decision also has a medical component. In its brief discussion of the "puzzling issue of preemption," the Pegram Court rejected one of the plaintiff's arguments as "a prescription for preemption of state malpractice law." [ ] The Court said, as we have noted, that previous cases had already thrown "cold water on the preemption theory [with regard to state law malpractice claims]." [ ]. The Court's analysis strongly suggests, without holding, that the plaintiff's malpractice action against Dr. Pegram would not be preempted even though Dr. Pegram simultaneously made a contractual interpretation concerning Herdrich's eligibility for given benefits, and that a defendant can no longer simply point to the overlay of medical decision-making on contractual claims and ask the court to conclude that, because ERISA preempts the contract claims, it also preempts all state tort-law claims based on the same decision.

As we have explained, nothing in ERISA suggests that Congress intended any displacement of "the quintessentially state-law standards of reasonable medical care" as applied to the medical component of a mixed decision. Rush Prudential, 122 S.Ct. at 2171. And ERISA requires that we distinguish between "contractually defined benefits," [ ] and those rights that state law delimits independent of benefits plans, such as medical quality standards, which hinge instead on statutory and common law development of malpractice law unique to each state.

Finally, we note our skepticism of a line of reasoning that would draw from "a comprehensive statute designed to promote the interests of employees and their beneficiaries in employee benefit plans," [ ] the elimination of protective standards of professional conduct. We see no reason then to bar as preempted state law malpractice actions that rest on the application of standards for medical decision-making—which are established by states independent of and prior to health benefits contracts—to "a patient's constellation of symptoms." Pegram, 530 U.S. at 228. [ ]

Focusing on mixed eligibility and treatment decisions, then, we conclude that § 514 preemption does not obtain with regard to those claims predicated on the violation of a state tort law by a failure to meet a state-law defined standard of care in diagnosing or recommending treatment of a plaintiff "patient's constellation of symptoms" Pegram [ ].

3. The Distinction Between Treating Physicians and Utilization Review Agents. The district court appeared to distinguish between a tort action based on a pre-certification decision, such as Dr. Spears's decision here, and one based on a contemporaneous treatment decision, such as Dr. Pegram's. [ ]. In support of this distinction, it might be argued that, in the pre-certification context, the treatment analysis precedes the contract interpretation question such that adjudication of a tort action necessarily involves an interpretation of the ERISA contract, which in turn triggers preemption. And it might be further argued that in contemporaneous treatment questions, the contract interpretation question does not play the same intervening role.

But we are not convinced such a distinction can in fact be drawn. Pegram, as noted, did not distinguish between the decisions of a treating physician empowered to interpret a benefits contract, and medical administrative decisions executed prior to the delivery of care. Its category of mixed eligibility and treatment decisions consisted of "when-and-how questions," including, critically, the question whether "a decision to proceed with [a procedure] would meet the medical necessity requirement that conditions the HMO's obligation to provide or pay for that particular procedure." [ ]. Even when making decisions about whether to pay for particular procedures, "physicians still must decide what to do in particular cases" on the basis of medical assessments. [ ]

And, "in practical terms, . . . eligibility decisions cannot be untangled from physicians' judgments about reasonable medical treatment," or, at least, the untangling will in many instances be no easy task. [ ] For instance, some managed care organizations require that utilization review agents "negotiate with the treating physician to achieve conformity" in levels of care provided. [ ]. That sort of negotiation is reflected in the correspondence between Drs. Spears and Samuel. While Dr. Samuel initiated negotiations with a detailed description of Mr. Cicio's status, Dr. Spears parried with an assertion of the requested treatment's experimental nature. Dr. Samuel then supplemented his argument with support from the medical literature. In response, Dr. Spears apparently made a patient-specific prescription of appropriate treatment by denying one treatment and authorizing another that Dr. Samuel had not requested. At least on the basis of the material on which we review the grant of the Rule 12(b)(6) motion by the district court, we cannot identify distinct moments at which treatment decisions—as distinct from eligibility decisions—were made in the course of this negotiation, let alone the sequence of such decisions.

In the Pegram context of contemporaneous treatment decisions, too, how to distill the moment of the eligibility determination from the facts is far from obvious. Examining the Supreme Court's description of Dr. Pegram's behavior, we cannot determine whether she (1) thought first about how soon Herdrich needed an ultrasound and then considered whether the plan comprised ultrasound tests in a given medical facility, or (2) considered first which benefits were available, and only then analyzed which one was medically warranted within that constrained range. [ ] In other words, it is difficult, at best, to determine whether her violation of the standard of medical care was apart from and independent of a determination of benefits, or whether the benefits determination preceded and controlled the medical determination.

In sum, it would likely often be difficult to delve into physicians' minds to examine their decisions, which are frequently executed in very brief time-periods and under tremendous pressures, to determine what part of them is medical and what part is administrative. Nor do we think it likely that significant contract interpretation issues will arise in an ensuing tort action. Assuming arguendo that Ms. Cicio were to establish that Dr. Spears's decision violated a state law duty of professional care, we are hard pressed to see how the defendants could successfully contend—as a defense to the tort action—that the contract permitted them to violate a state law duty standard of care.

D. Caveats

We underscore the fact that this case comes before us on appeal from the grant of a Rule 12(b)(6) motion to dismiss. We therefore hold only that a set of facts consistent with the allegations contained in the complaint would permit the granting of relief—oddly, in this case, remand to state court for a determination, inter alia, of whether the complaint states a cause of action under the law of New York. If Dr. Spears's actions that are the subject of the complaint indeed constituted a medical decision or a mixed medical and eligibility decision, then Ms. Cicio's remaining medical malpractice claims should not be dismissed, but remanded to state court for resolution. [ ]. It may nonetheless be that, as a matter of fact, Dr. Spears's decision was purely one concerning eligibility, i.e., a determination that, without regard to Mr. Cicio's "constellation of symptoms" but in the abstract, double cell stem transplants were experimental as treatment for multiple myeloma. In that case, the claims would be completely preempted by ERISA and therefore subject to dismissal. We therefore do not rule out the possibility that the defendants can demonstrate, as a matter of fact, that dismissal of the complaint is warranted. We leave it to the district court to determine what proceedings, if any, would be appropriate to that end.

Finally, we reiterate that we do not decide under what circumstances, if any, the decisions made by Vytra or Dr. Spears, or utilization review decisions generally, may be actionable under New York law when they are negligently made. Perhaps they never are. Unless the district court determines that Dr. Spears was in fact making pure eligibility decisions with respect to Mr. Cicio's health care and dismisses the claim on that ground, that will be a question for the New York courts to decide upon remand.

CONCLUSION

We affirm the district court's disposition of the timeliness and misrepresentation claims, but vacate its resolution of the medical malpractice claims and remand for further proceedings consistent with this opinion.

VILLAZON v. PRUDENTIAL HEALTH CARE PLAN, INC.

Supreme Court of Florida, 2003.
843 So.2d 842.

LEWIS, J.

* * *

MATERIAL FACTS AND PROCEEDINGS BELOW

Petitioner Rolando Villazon, personal representative of the estate of his deceased wife, Susan Villazon, seeks review of the decision of the Third District Court of Appeal affirming the trial court's summary judgment in favor of Prudential Health Care Plan, Inc., (PruCare) in Petitioner's action against PruCare for the wrongful death of his wife. Through her employer, Susan Villazon became a member of PruCare, a health maintenance organization. After having a mouth ailment allegedly misdiagnosed or mistreated, Mrs. Villazon died as a result of an untreated cancerous tongue condition.

Villazon filed an action for wrongful death based on negligence against Mrs. Villazon's primary care physician, Dr. Melvyn Sarnow and against her health care provider, respondent PruCare. * * * Villazon alleged the basis for PruCare's vicarious liability and breach of a nondelegable duty to be:

* * *

By statute, rule, and contract, the Defendant, PRUDENTIAL HEALTH CARE PLAN, INC., had the non-delegable duty to provide SUSAN COHEN VILLAZON with quality health care including without limitation, in-patient hospital services, and medical, surgical, diagnostic, x-ray, laboratory, nursing, physical therapy, and pharmaceutical services.

* * *

As set forth in the Third District's opinion:

Villazon argues that Prudential Health care controlled the referral process and required that authorization be obtained prior to the performance of diagnostic and therapeutic procedures. Prudential Health also required that the contracted physicians adhere to rules and seek approval for diagnostic tests. Physicians had to provide and arrange health care services through Prudential Health and refer subscribers to contracted providers. Villazon, however, does not allege that his wife was denied proper medical testing and referrals to specialists. [ ]

PruCare filed a motion for summary judgment, asserting that the claims filed against it were preempted by section 514(a) of the Employee

Retirement Income Security Act (ERISA) and that Villazon could not prevail on those claims as a matter of state law. The trial court entered summary final judgment in favor of PruCare, holding that "ERISA governed the claims filed against [PruCare] because they related to the manner in which [PruCare] administered its health care plans, and further, that there were no issues of fact as to the theory of vicarious liability or any recognizable cause of action for breach of a non-delegable duty against [PruCare] under state law." [ ]. On appeal, the district court agreed. [ ]

In addressing the state law issues, the Third District rejected Villazon's position and reasoned that the medical providers were independent contractors because as an independent practice associated health maintenance organization (IPA HMO), PruCare entered into contracts with physicians who had their own independent practices and who agreed to provide covered services for a contracted rate. The district court highlighted that Dr. Sarnow was an independent contractor who had his own private practice and agreed to render services to PruCare subscribers pursuant to a Primary Care Physician Agreement, continuing his own independent practice after he entered into this agreement.

In rejecting Villazon's argument that PruCare had assumed a non-delegable duty to render medical care to his wife in a nonnegligent manner when she purchased health care coverage from PruCare, the court noted that Villazon had not cited any support for this proposition. The court looked only to the contract between PruCare and the physicians and reasoned that it was the best evidence of the intent of the parties, and its meaning and legal effect were questions of law for determination by the court. It was important to the court below that the contractual provisions designated physicians as independent contractors, and the court found no evidence of control upon which to justify imposing responsibility on PruCare. [ ]. In focusing solely on the one contract that attempted to designate physicians as independent contractors and also limiting its vision to the issue of actual control, the Third District's decision is also in conflict with Nazworth v. Swire Florida, Inc., 486 So.2d 637 (Fla. 1st DCA 1986), which demonstrates that it is the right to control, not the actual control, that may be determinative.

ERISA Preemption

[W]e begin our legal analysis by determining the threshold issue of ERISA preemption. Villazon correctly cites Frappier for the proposition that "if a claim relates to the manner in which the ERISA plan is administered, ERISA preempts the claim." [ ] see also Frappier, 678 So.2d at 887 ("Concerning the direct negligence, corporate liability and implied contract claims, we concur with the lower court's decision that these allegations would be completely preempted because they present issues unequivocally related to the administration of the plan and are within the scope of section 502(a)(1)(B).") .

However, Villazon directly conflicts with Frappier in its determination of whether a state law wrongful death claim by a deceased patient member's estate against a health maintenance organization (HMO) based upon vicarious liability for asserted medical malpractice of its member physicians "relates to" administration of the ERISA plan and is therefore preempted. In Villazon, the district court below incorrectly concluded that it did. [ ] (determining that Villazon's claims "directly relate to the health plan as they arise from the denial of medical care and treatment benefits"). In Frappier, in contrast, the district court correctly determined that ERISA does not preempt such vicarious liability claims.

In Frappier, the decedent's estate filed an action against Health Options, Inc., an HMO, and the two Health Options physicians who had provided medical care to Frappier, asserting that medical malpractice had occurred. The trial court had dismissed Frappier's complaint with prejudice. [ ]

The appellate court remanded the case to the trial court to determine whether an ERISA plan ever existed, agreeing that "this threshold question must be resolved prior to addressing the issue of whether the dismissed counts are preemptable." [ ] Nevertheless, the district court was "compelled to address the merits of the trial court's determination that the estate's claims against Health Options are preempted by the federal ERISA statute." [ ]. Nor was this exercise simply gratuitous, as reflected in the district court's directive to the trial court, in remanding the case: "Upon an appropriate finding, the trial court may dismiss the estate's direct negligence, corporate liability and implied contract claims for a lack of subject matter jurisdiction. However, in no event may the vicarious liability count be dismissed as the same does not 'relate to' an employee benefit plan."[ ].

Because no Florida case had yet addressed whether direct negligence or vicarious liability claims against an entity involved in an ERISA plan are preempted, the Fourth District found guidance from decisions rendered by federal courts. It first framed the inquiry pursuant to section 514(a) of ERISA:

The ERISA regulatory scheme was promulgated to entrench as exclusively a federal matter pension plan legislation. [ ]. The governing provision of ERISA relevant to this discussion is section 514(a) which provides that "this Chapter shall supersede any and all state laws insofar as they may now or hereafter 'relate to' any employee benefit plan." [ ].

Properly phrased, the issue becomes whether Frappier's claims against Health Options * * * are to recover plan benefits due, or to enforce rights, or to clarify rights to benefits under the terms of the plan, as those concepts are detailed in section 502(a)(1)(B) of ERISA [ ]. Although Pilot Life [Ins. Co. v. Dedeaux, 481 U.S. 41, 107 S.Ct. 1549, 95 L.Ed.2d 39 (1987)] suggested an expansive interpretation of the triggering jurisdictional clause of the ERISA federal regulatory scheme, the

United States Supreme Court * * * and several more recent lower federal court decisions caution against a literal reading of section 514(a) in determining whether preemption is appropriate. New York Blue Cross directs that in construing the "relate to" phrase of section 514(a), trial courts must analyze the objectives of the ERISA statute to resolve which state laws Congress contemplated would continue to survive the ambit of federal regulation. [ ]. In other words, statutory or common law claims actionable in state court that are periphery or remotely related to competing laws affecting ERISA should not be preempted to federal court. [ ]

In deciding that ERISA did not preempt Frappier's vicarious liability claim, the district court made a key distinction between causes of action based upon an HMO having administratively withheld benefits from its member patient and those based upon the quality of HMO benefits actually provided:

In its appellate decision, the Dukes court drew the distinction between a lawsuit against an ERISA claiming the withholding of benefits and a claim initiated by Dukes which attacked the quality of benefits provided by the HMO. [ ] As the court explained:

The plaintiff's claims, even when construed as U.S. Healthcare suggests, merely attack the quality of the benefits they received: The plaintiffs here simply do not claim that the plans erroneously withheld benefits due. Nor do they ask the state courts to enforce their rights under the terms of their respective plans or to clarify their rights to future benefits. As a result, the plaintiffs' claims fall outside of the scope of § 502(a)(1)(B) and these cases must be remanded to the state courts from which they were removed. [ ]

Accordingly, Dukes considered and rejected the line of cases cited and relied upon by the lower court in determining that ERISA preempts the instant vicarious liability claim. We agree with the factual dichotomy expressed in Dukes that is critical for this analysis:

> There is no allegation here that the HMOs denied anyone any benefits that were due under the plan. Instead the plaintiffs here are attempting to hold the HMOs liable for their role as the arrangers of their decedents' medical treatment. [ ]

Thus where, as here, an ERISA is implicated by a complaint for failing to provide, arrange for, or supervise qualified doctors to provide the actual medical treatment for plan participants, federal preemption is inappropriate. [ ] Therefore, even if Health Options is an ERISA subject to federal preemption, we must conclude that the trial court erred in dismissing the vicarious liability count of the instant complaint.

[ ] We conclude that this ERISA preemption discussion is a correct interpretation as applied to state law causes of action against HMOs based upon allegations of direct and vicarious liability for negligence in the provision of medical services to member patients. [ ].

A similar analysis was employed by the Pennsylvania Supreme Court in Pappas II upon remand from the United States Supreme Court. In Pappas v. Asbel, 555 Pa. 342, 724 A.2d 889 (Pa. 1998) (Pappas I), the Pennsylvania Supreme Court had originally held that the plaintiff's claim for vicarious liability against the HMO was not preempted by ERISA. [ ]. Upon appeal to the United States Supreme Court, the case was remanded to the Pennsylvania Supreme Court for reconsideration in light of Pegram v. Herdrich, 530 U.S. 211, 147 L.Ed.2d 164, 120 S.Ct. 2143 (2000). In applying the reasoning in Pegram, the Pappas II court again determined that the plaintiff's claim was not subject to conflict preemption under ERISA:

We now turn, as instructed by the Supreme Court, to a reconsideration of our decision in Pappas I in light of Pegram * * *

* * *

The Court [in Pegram] * * * held that Congress did not intend that any HMO be treated as an ERISA fiduciary to the extent that it makes mixed eligibility and treatment decisions acting through its physicians. Id. at 2155. [Note 4] Observing that under the common law of trusts, which is the source of ERISA's fiduciary duties, fiduciary responsibility characteristically attaches to financial decisions about managing assets and property, the Court doubted that Congress would have ever thought of a mixed decision as fiduciary in nature. [ ] Because the defense of any HMO of a mixed decision would be that its physician acted for good medical reasons, the plausibility of which would require reference to traditional standards of reasonable medical practice in like circumstances, the Court was concerned that a decision to view a mixed decision as an act of ERISA fiduciary duty would "federalize malpractice litigation". [ ]. Lastly, the Court touched upon (but declined to resolve) the "puzzling issue of preemption" that would be raised by the imposition of ERISA's fiduciary requirements upon an HMO physician making a pure treatment or mixed decision, in view of its holding in Travelers:

On its face, federal fiduciary law applying a malpractice standard would seem to be a prescription for preemption of state malpractice law, since the new ERISA cause of action would cover the same subject of a state-law malpractice claim.... To be sure, [Travelers] throws some cold water in the preemption theory; there, we held that, in the field of health care, a subject of traditional state regulation, there is no ERISA preemption without clear manifestation of congressional purpose. But in that case the convergence of state and federal law was not so clear as in the situation we are positing; the state-law standard had not been subsumed by the standard to be applied under ERISA. We could struggle with this problem, but first it is well to ask, again, what would be gained by opening the federal courthouse doors to a fiduciary malpractice claim.... Pegram [ ].

* * *

Not surprisingly, U.S. Healthcare argues that its decision about Pappas' referral "constituted a quintessential 'coverage' determination". We, however, disagree. In our view, the undisputed facts in this case, and the inferences drawn from them, establish the sort of mixed eligibility and treatment decision that Pegram discussed. Dr. Leibowitz, U.S. Healthcare's physician, reviewed Pappas' case, and rejected another medical doctor's opinion based on his clinical judgment that Pappas needed to be referred to Jefferson for treatment of a medical emergency. Instead of referring Pappas to Jefferson, a non-HMO hospital, as Dr. Dickter recommended, Dr. Leibowitz referred Pappas to one of three other facilities for medical care. He did not, in the Supreme Court's words, only make a "simple yes or no" decision as to whether Pappas' condition was covered; it clearly was. Rather, Dr. Leibowitz also determined where and, under the circumstances, when Pappas' epidermal abscess would be treated. His was a mixed eligibility and treatment decision, the adverse consequences of which, if any, are properly redressed, as Pegram teaches, through state medical malpractice law. This law as Travelers teaches, is not preempted by ERISA. Pappas II [ ].

The Second Circuit's recent interpretation of the United States Supreme Court's decision in Pegram also has application here. In Cicio v. Does, 321 F.3d 83 (2d Cir. 2003), the circuit court held that "a state law malpractice action, if based on a 'mixed eligibility and treatment decision,' is not subject to ERISA preemption when that state law cause of action challenges an allegedly flawed medical judgment as applied to a specific patient's symptoms." [ ] The court's decision correctly recognizes that HMO plan administration is often inextricably intertwined with treatment decisions, and that ERISA does not preempt viable state law causes of action arising from such decisions. The Cicio decision is consistent with and reflective of the current state of the law in Florida.

Here, Villazon bases his vicarious liability claim against PruCare on allegations that agents or apparent agents of PruCare made negligent treatment decisions in caring for Mrs. Villazon. As the Pappas II court correctly observed, "Travelers instructs that ERISA does not preempt state law that regulates the provision of adequate medical treatment." Pappas II [ ].

Therefore, applying the analysis employed in Frappier and Pappas II, we conclude that Villazon's complaint for vicarious liability—which was clearly based upon allegations of negligent failure to provide adequate medical treatment for his wife's cancer—is not subject to ERISA conflict preemption. [ ] Accordingly, we approve the preemption analysis in Frappier, and quash the decision in Villazon to the extent of inconsistency with our opinion here.

VICARIOUS LIABILITY

Turning now to the state law issue, there are multiple different theories upon which vicarious liability was sought to be imposed: a nondelegable duty under the HMO Act; common law actual agency; and common law apparent agency. We agree with the district court's rejection of Villazon's argument that PruCare "assumed a non-delegable duty to render medical care to his wife in a non-negligent manner when she purchased health care coverage from Prudential Health." [ ]. Villazon argues that such nondelegable duty arises under the "Health Maintenance Organization Act," [ ] (the "Act"). The Act does not specifically provide a private right of action for damages based upon an alleged violation of its requirements.[ ]. There are other regulatory statutes in which the legislature has specifically created a private right of action. * * * Absent such expression of intent, a private right of action is not implied. [ ]

This does not, however, preclude the right to bring a common law negligence claim based upon the same allegations. [ ] Further, contrary to the district court's decision below, we conclude that here, at the summary judgment level, it has not been conclusively established that there are no genuine issues of material fact with regard to the motion for summary judgment concerning Villazon's common law negligence claim based upon allegations that Mrs. Villazon's treating physicians were agents or apparent agents of PruCare. [ ]

The existence of an agency relationship is normally one for the trier of fact to decide. * * *

Here, in affirming the trial court's summary final judgment in favor of PruCare on the issue of agency, the district court concluded that all medical providers were independent contractors simply because as an IPA HMO, PruCare entered into contracts with physicians who had their own independent practices and who agreed to provide covered services for a contracted rate. The district court concluded that because the contractual provisions designated the physicians as independent contractors and that there was no evidence that PruCare exercised actual control over the medical judgments and decisions made in the care and treatment of Villazon's wife, summary judgment was appropriate.[ ] Although the district court's view was that there was no evidence that PruCare exercised actual control over Dr. Sarnow's medical judgments in this case that, alone, is not the proper test.

When one considers an action based on actual agency, it is the right to control, rather than actual control, that may be determinative. [ ]

* * * [I]ndependent contractors may indeed become agents depending on the totality of the circumstances. The degree of control retained or exercised may certainly be determined by a single contract or [ ] by reference to multiple writings, policies, or procedures that may be operative in addition to an underlying contract. [ ] While an evaluation of a single contract may be a question of law to be determined by the court, when there are multiple relationships along with multiple practices and procedures to be evaluated, and the totality of the evidence is susceptible to multiple inferences and interpretations, the existence and scope of an agency relationship are generally questions of fact.

It is not uncommon for parties to include conclusory statements in documents with regard to the independence of the relationship of the parties. This may occur even when other contractual provisions and the totality of the circumstances reflect otherwise. Such a situation has caused this Court to reason:

While the obvious purpose to be accomplished by this document was to evince an independent contractor status, such status depends not on the statements of the parties but upon all the circumstances of their dealings with each other.

Here, the record evidence reflects significant indicia of PruCare's right to control the means by which medical services were rendered by Member Physicians to Member Patients. The facts peculiar to each case must govern the ultimate disposition. While physicians of the past in the traditional pattern of American life may have constituted distinct independent entities and independent centers of occupation and profession, that model has been dramatically altered through the HMO concept in a significant manner which a legal system cannot simply ignore. The thought of visiting a private and independent office of a totally independent physician may now be one more of history and cultural conditioning than current reality. The economic structures alone may so impact the relationships that the prism through which we consider and evaluate issues of control must be honed for this current reality.

On deposition, the PruCare representative, Dominick Messano, testified regarding PruCare's relationship with the HMO network physicians. Consistent with the Certificate of Coverage, Messano indicated that PruCare determines which providers are part of the HMO network, and that HMO patient members are required to use HMO network physicians. Significantly, the Certificate of Coverage contains provisions which demonstrate PruCare's right to control important aspects of patient care provided by the HMO.

In Part I (explaining the scope of Group Health Care Coverage), the Certificate provides that PruCare "will arrange or provide for benefits for the Eligible Services and Supplies" set forth in the Certificate of Coverage. All Eligible Services and Supplies must be furnished by a Primary Care Physician, another Participating Health Care Provider authorized by a Primary Care Physician, or a Non–Participating Health Care Provider authorized by a Primary Care Physician. "In addition, certain services and supplies" (such as infertility services or counseling services upon the death of a terminally ill covered person) "must be authorized by the Medical Director to be eligible."

[The definitions section is omitted]

[W]hile on the one hand, the Certificate of Coverage contains a disclaimer which states that participating hospitals and physicians have an independent contractor relationship with PruCare, on the other hand, it reflects PruCare's recognition of potential liability for its part in "making arrangements for furnishing supplies and services to Covered Persons." This is evidenced by inclusion of a provision that "neither the

Contract Holder nor any Covered Person under the Group Contract will be liable for any acts or omissions of PruCare, its agents or employees, or any Hospital, Physician or other health care provider with which Pru-Care, its agents or employees" makes such arrangements.

These contractual provisions, along with the contractual provisions between the HMO and the physicians, and the totality of the circumstances operating within the current reality of the interaction within the decision-making process, create genuine issues of material fact sufficient to withstand a motion for summary judgment with respect to the question of whether PruCare can be held vicariously liable for the alleged medical negligence of its member physicians when providing service pursuant to the PruCare health plan under theories of actual agency. PruCare has not conclusively demonstrated the absence of genuine issues of material fact.

As for the cause of action based on apparent agency, however, it must be remembered that apparent authority exists "only where the principal creates the appearance of an agency relationship." [ ] Therefore, as to the claim of apparent agency, because this issue has not been fully addressed, on remand the trial court should have the opportunity to reevaluate whether under an apparent agency theory there are genuine issues of material fact.

Accordingly, we quash the decision in Villazon to the extent of inconsistency with this opinion, and remand to the district court for further proceedings in accordance herewith.

It is so ordered.

Note on **Pryzbowski v. US Healthcare**

Following *Pegram*, and prior to *Rush Prudential*, the Third Circuit in *Pryzbowski v. US Healthcare, Inc.*, 245 F.3d 266 (3rd Cir. 2001), considered whether ERISA preempts a plaintiff's claim against an HMO alleging negligent delay of treatment. In *Pryzbowski*, plaintiff consulted her primary care physician seeking treatment for severe back pain. She was referred to a neurosurgeon, but the neurosurgeon referred her to a general surgeon who had previously operated on her because it was he who implanted a neurostimulator. Because the general surgeon was not part of the HMO network, plaintiff was required to seek approval from the plan for the surgery. Although approval was eventually granted, plaintiff alleged that the delay resulted in various permanent injuries. The case was removed from state to federal court, and the federal court granted summary judgment for the defendants based upon ERISA preemption. The court also dismissed the negligence count on the basis that plaintiff had failed to state a claim upon which relief could be granted.

The Third Circuit reversed in part. It held that plaintiff's claims against US Healthcare were preempted by ERISA. Determining that the issue of alleged delay of approval of benefits under ERISA was one of first impression, the court held that the alleged delays constituted "administering of benefits" under ERISA and plaintiff, had she chosen to do so, could have filed for an injunction to accelerate the approval.

The Third Circuit reversed the grant of summary judgment as to other defendants, holding that ERISA did not preempt the claims based on "medical treatment" decisions. Stated the court, "there is a strong suggestion in *Pegram* that claims based upon medical treatment decisions remain outside the preemptive effect of ERISA." The matter was remanded to the trial court to assess the scope of New Jersey malpractice law to determine whether, as plaintiff alleged, the physician had a duty to advocate for treatment on her behalf.

AETNA HEALTH INC. v. DAVILA
CIGNA HEALTHCARE OF TEXAS, INC. v. CALAD

Supreme Court of the United States, 2004.
___ U.S. ___, 124 S.Ct. 2488, 159 L.Ed.2d 312.

JUSTICE THOMAS delivered the opinion of the Court.

* * *

I

A

Respondent Juan Davila is a participant, and respondent Ruby Calad is a beneficiary, in ERISA-regulated employee benefit plans. Their respective plan sponsors had entered into agreements with petitioners, Aetna Health Inc. and CIGNA Healthcare of Texas, Inc., to administer the plans. Under Davila's plan, for instance, Aetna reviews requests for coverage and pays providers, such as doctors, hospitals, and nursing homes, which perform covered services for members; under Calad's plan sponsor's agreement, CIGNA is responsible for plan benefits and coverage decisions.

Respondents both suffered injuries allegedly arising from Aetna's and CIGNA's decisions not to provide coverage for certain treatment and services recommended by respondents' treating physicians. Davila's treating physician prescribed Vioxx to remedy Davila's arthritis pain, but Aetna refused to pay for it. Davila did not appeal or contest this decision, nor did he purchase Vioxx with his own resources and seek reimbursement. Instead, Davila began taking Naprosyn, from which he allegedly suffered a severe reaction that required extensive treatment and hospitalization. Calad underwent surgery, and although her treating physician recommended an extended hospital stay, a CIGNA discharge nurse determined that Calad did not meet the plan's criteria for a continued hospital stay. CIGNA consequently denied coverage for the extended hospital stay. Calad experienced postsurgery complications forcing her to return to the hospital. She alleges that these complications would not have occurred had CIGNA approved coverage for a longer hospital stay.

Respondents brought separate suits in Texas state court against petitioners. Invoking THCLA § 88.002(a), respondents argued that petitioners' refusal to cover the requested services violated their "duty to exercise ordinary care when making health care treatment decisions," and that these refusals "proximately caused" their injuries. *Ibid.* Petitioners removed the cases to Federal District Courts, arguing that respondents' causes of action fit within the scope of, and were therefore completely pre-empted by, ERISA § 502(a). The respective District Courts agreed, and declined to remand the cases to state court. Because respondents refused to amend their complaints to bring explicit ERISA claims, the District Courts dismissed the complaints with prejudice.

B

Both Davila and Calad appealed the refusals to remand to state court. The United States Court of Appeals for the Fifth Circuit consolidated their cases with several others raising similar issues. The Court of Appeals recognized that state causes of action that "duplicate or fall within the scope of an ERISA § 502(a) remedy" are completely pre-empted and hence removable to federal court. *Roark* v. *Humana, Inc.,* 307 F.3d 298, 305 (2002) (internal quotation marks and citations omitted). After examining the causes of action available under § 502(a), the Court of Appeals determined that respondents' claims could possibly fall under only two: § 502(a)(1)(B), which provides a cause of action for the recovery of wrongfully denied benefits, and § 502(a)(2), which allows suit against a plan fiduciary for breaches of fiduciary duty to the plan.

Analyzing § 502(a)(2) first, the Court of Appeals concluded that, under *Pegram* v. *Herdrich,* 530 U.S. 211, 147 L. Ed. 2d 164, 120 S. Ct. 2143 (2000), the decisions for which petitioners were being sued were "mixed eligibility and treatment decisions" and hence were not fiduciary in nature. 307 F.3d at 307–308. The Court of Appeals next determined that respondents' claims did not fall within § 502(a)(1)(B)'s scope. It found significant that respondents "assert tort claims," while § 502(a)(1)(B) "creates a cause of action for breach of contract," *id.,* at 309, and also that respondents "are not seeking reimbursement for benefits denied them," but rather request "tort damages" arising from "an external, statutorily imposed duty of 'ordinary care.'" *Ibid.* From *Rush Prudential HMO, Inc.* v. *Moran,* 536 U.S. 355, 153 L. Ed. 2d 375, 122 S. Ct. 2151 (2002), the Court of Appeals derived the principle that complete pre-emption is limited to situations in which "States ... duplicate the causes of action listed in ERISA § 502(a)," and concluded that "because the THCLA does not provide an action for collecting benefits," it fell outside the scope of § 502(a)(1)(B). [ ].

II

* * *

B

Congress enacted ERISA to "protect ... the interests of participants in employee benefit plans and their beneficiaries" by setting out substantive regulatory [*14] requirements for employee benefit plans and to "provide for appropriate remedies, sanctions, and ready access to the Federal courts." 29 U.S.C. § 1001(b). The purpose of ERISA is to provide a uniform regulatory regime over employee benefit plans. To this end, ERISA includes expansive pre-emption provisions [ ] which are intended to ensure that employee benefit plan regulation would be "exclusively a federal concern." [ ]

ERISA's "comprehensive legislative scheme" includes "an integrated system of procedures for enforcement." [ ]. This integrated enforcement mechanism [ ] is a distinctive feature of ERISA, and essential to accomplish Congress' purpose of creating a comprehensive statute for the regulation of employee benefit plans. * * *

III

A

ERISA § 502(a)(1)(B) provides:

"A civil action may be brought—(1) by a participant or beneficiary— ... (B) to recover benefits due to him under the terms of his plan, to enforce his rights under the terms of the plan, or to clarify his rights to future benefits under the terms of the plan." 29 U.S.C. § 1132(a)(1)(B).

This provision is relatively straightforward. If a participant or beneficiary believes that benefits promised to him under the terms of the plan are not provided, he can bring suit seeking provision of those benefits. A participant or beneficiary can also bring suit generically to "enforce his rights" under the plan, or to clarify any of his rights to future benefits. Any dispute over the precise terms of the plan is resolved by a court under a *de novo* review standard, unless the terms of the plan "give the administrator or fiduciary discretionary authority to determine eligibility for benefits or to construe the terms of the plan." [ ]

It follows that if an individual brings suit complaining of a denial of coverage for medical care, where the individual is entitled to such coverage only because of the terms of an ERISA-regulated employee benefit plan, and where no legal duty (state or federal) independent of ERISA or the plan terms is violated, then the suit falls "within the scope of" ERISA § 502(a)(1)(B).[ ] In other words, if an individual, at some point in time, could have brought his claim under ERISA § 502(a)(1)(B), and where there is no other independent legal duty that is implicated by a defendant's actions, then the individual's cause of action is completely pre-empted by ERISA § 502(a)(1)(B).

To determine whether respondents' causes of action fall "within the scope" of ERISA § 502(a)(1)(B), we must examine respondents' complaints, the statute on which their claims are based (the THCLA), and the various plan documents. Davila alleges that Aetna provides health coverage under his employer's health benefits plan. Davila also alleges that after his primary care physician prescribed Vioxx, Aetna refused to pay for it. The only action complained of was Aetna's refusal to approve payment for Davila's Vioxx prescription. Further, the only relationship Aetna had with Davila was its partial administration of Davila's employer's benefit plan.

Similarly, Calad alleges that she receives, as her husband's beneficiary under an ERISA-regulated benefit plan, health coverage from CIGNA. She alleges that she was informed by CIGNA, upon admittance into a hospital for major surgery, that she would be authorized to stay for only one day. She also alleges that CIGNA, acting through a discharge nurse, refused to authorize more than a single day despite the advice and recommendation of her treating physician. Calad contests only CIGNA's decision to refuse coverage for her hospital stay. And, as in Davila's case, the only connection between Calad and CIGNA is CIGNA's administration of portions of Calad's ERISA-regulated benefit plan.

It is clear, then, that respondents complain only about denials of coverage promised under the terms of ERISA-regulated employee benefit plans. Upon the denial of benefits, respondents could have paid for the treatment themselves and then sought reimbursement through a § 502(a)(1)(B) action, or sought a preliminary injunction * * *

Respondents contend, however, that the complained-of actions violate legal duties that arise independently of ERISA or the terms of the employee benefit plans at issue in these cases. Both respondents brought suit specifically under the THCLA, alleging that petitioners "controlled, influenced, participated in and made decisions which affected the quality of the diagnosis, care, and treatment provided" in a manner that violated "the duty of ordinary care set forth in §§ 88.001 and 88.002." * * *

The duties imposed by the THCLA in the context of these cases, however, do not arise independently of ERISA or the plan terms. The THCLA does impose a duty on managed care entities to "exercise ordinary care when making health care treatment decisions," and makes them liable for damages proximately caused by failures to abide by that duty. § 88.002(a). However, if a managed care entity correctly concluded that, under the terms of the relevant plan, a particular treatment was not covered, the managed care entity's denial of coverage would not be a proximate cause of any injuries arising from the denial. Rather, the failure of the plan itself to cover the requested treatment would be the proximate cause. More significantly, the THCLA clearly states that "the standards in Subsections (a) and (b) create no obligation on the part of the health insurance carrier, health maintenance organization, or other managed care entity to provide to an insured or enrollee treatment which is not covered by the health care plan of the entity." [ ] Hence, a managed care entity could not be subject to liability under the THCLA if it denied coverage for any treatment not covered by the health care plan that it was administering.

Thus, interpretation of the terms of respondents' benefit plans forms an essential part of their THCLA claim, and THCLA liability would exist here only because of petitioners' administration of ERISA-regulated benefit plans. Petitioners' potential liability under the THCLA in these cases, then, derives entirely from the particular rights and obligations established by the benefit plans. So, unlike the state-law claims in *Caterpillar, supra,* respondents' THCLA causes of action are not entirely independent of the federally regulated contract itself. * * *

Hence, respondents bring suit only to rectify a wrongful denial of benefits promised under ERISA-regulated plans, and do not attempt to remedy any violation of a legal duty independent of ERISA. We hold that respondents' state causes of action fall "within the scope of" ERISA § 502(a)(1)(B) [ ] and are therefore completely pre-empted by ERISA § 502 and removable to federal district court.

* * *

C

Respondents also argue—for the first time in their brief to this Court—that the THCLA is a law that regulates insurance, and hence that ERISA § 514(b)(2)(A) saves their causes of action from pre-emption (and thereby from complete pre-emption). This argument is unavailing. The existence of a comprehensive remedial scheme can demonstrate an "overpowering federal policy" that determines the interpretation of a statutory provision designed to save state law from being pre-empted. *Rush Prudential*, 536 U.S., at 375, 153 L. Ed. 2d 375, 122 S. Ct. 2151. ERISA's civil enforcement provision is one such example. See *ibid.*

As this Court stated in *Pilot Life*, "our understanding of [§ 514(b)(2)(A)] must be informed by the legislative intent concerning the civil enforcement provisions provided by ERISA § 502(a), 29 U.S.C. § 1132(a)." 481 U.S., at 52, 95 L. Ed. 2d 39, 107 S. Ct. 1549. The Court concluded that "the policy choices reflected in the inclusion of certain remedies and the exclusion of others under the federal scheme would be completely undermined if ERISA-plan participants and beneficiaries were free to obtain remedies under state law that Congress rejected in ERISA." *Id.*, 481 U.S., at 54, 95 L. Ed. 2d 39, 107 S. Ct. 1549. The Court then held, based on

> "the common-sense understanding of the saving clause, the McCar-ran–Ferguson Act factors defining the business of insurance, and, *most importantly*, the clear expression of congressional intent that ERISA's civil enforcement scheme be exclusive, ... that [the plaintiff's] state law suit asserting improper processing of a claim for benefits under an ERISA-regulated plan is not saved by § 514(b)(2)(A)." *Id.*, 481 U.S., at 57, 95 L. Ed. 2d 39, 107 S. Ct. 1549 (emphasis added).

Pilot Life's reasoning applies here with full force. Allowing respondents to proceed with their state-law suits would "pose an obstacle to the purposes and objectives of Congress." *Id.*, 481 U.S., at 52, 95 L. Ed. 2d 39, 107 S. Ct. 1549. As this Court has recognized in both *Rush Prudential* and *Pilot Life*, ERISA § 514(b)(2)(A) must be interpreted in light of the congressional intent to create an exclusive federal remedy in ERISA § 502(a). Under ordinary principles of conflict pre-emption, then, even a state law that can arguably be characterized as "regulating insurance" will be pre-empted if it provides a separate vehicle to assert a claim for benefits outside of, or in addition to, ERISA's remedial scheme.

IV

Respondents, their *amici*, and some Courts of Appeals have relied heavily upon *Pegram* v. *Herdrich,* 530 U.S. 211, 147 L. Ed. 2d 164, 120 S. Ct. 2143 (2000), in arguing that ERISA does not pre-empt or completely pre-empt state suits such as respondents'. They contend that *Pegram* makes it clear that causes of action such as respondents' do not "relate to [an] employee benefit plan," ERISA § 514(a), 29 U.S.C. § 1144(a), and hence are not pre-empted. [ ]

Pegram cannot be read so broadly. In *Pegram*, the plaintiff sued her physician-owned-and-operated HMO (which provided medical coverage through plaintiff's employer pursuant to an ERISA-regulated benefit plan) and her treating physician, both for medical malpractice and for a breach of an ERISA fiduciary duty. [ ]The plaintiff's treating physician was also the person charged with administering plaintiff's benefits; it was she who decided whether certain treatments were covered. [ ] We reasoned that the physician's "eligibility decision and the treatment decision were inextricably mixed." [ ] We concluded that "Congress did not intend [the defendant HMO] or any other HMO to be treated as a fiduciary to the extent that it makes mixed eligibility decisions acting through its physicians." [ ]

A benefit determination under ERISA, though, is generally a fiduciary act. [ ] "At common law, fiduciary duties characteristically attach to decisions about managing assets and distributing property to beneficiaries." *Pegram, supra* [ ]. Hence, a benefit determination is part and parcel of the ordinary fiduciary responsibilities connected to the administration of a plan. [ ] The fact that a benefits determination is infused with medical judgments does not alter this result.

Pegram itself recognized this principle. *Pegram*, in highlighting its conclusion that "mixed eligibility decisions" were not fiduciary in nature, contrasted the operation of "traditional trustees administering a medical trust" and "physicians through whom HMOs act." [ ] A traditional medical trust is administered by "paying out money to buy medical care, whereas physicians making mixed eligibility decisions consume the money as well." [ ] And, significantly, the Court stated that "private trustees do not make treatment judgments." [ ] But a trustee managing a medical trust undoubtedly must make administrative decisions that require the exercise of medical judgment. Petitioners are not the employers of respondents' treating physicians and are therefore in a somewhat analogous position to that of a trustee for a traditional medical trust.

ERISA itself and its implementing regulations confirm this interpretation. ERISA defines a fiduciary as any person "to the extent . . . he has any discretionary authority or discretionary responsibility in the administration of [an employee benefit] plan." [ ] When administering employee benefit plans, HMOs must make discretionary decisions regarding eligibility for plan benefits, and, in this regard, must be treated as plan fiduciaries. [ ] Also, ERISA § 503, which specifies minimum requirements for a plan's claim procedure, requires plans to "afford a reasonable opportunity to any participant whose claim for benefits has been denied for a full and fair review by the appropriate named fiduciary of the decision denying the claim." [ ] This strongly suggests that the ultimate decisionmaker in a plan regarding an award of benefits must be a fiduciary and must be acting as a fiduciary when determining a participant's or beneficiary's claim. The relevant regulations also establish extensive requirements to ensure full and fair review of benefit denials. [ ] These regulations, on their face, apply equally to health benefit plans and other plans, and do not draw distinctions between medical and nonmedical benefits determinations. Indeed, the regulations strongly imply that benefits determinations involving medical judgments are, just as much as any other benefits determinations, actions by plan fiduciaries. [ ] Classifying any entity with discretionary authority over benefits determinations as anything but a plan fiduciary would thus conflict with ERISA's statutory and regulatory scheme.

Since administrators making benefits determinations, even determinations based extensively on medical judgments, are ordinarily acting as plan fiduciaries, it was essential to *Pegram*'s conclusion that the decisions challenged there were truly "mixed eligibility and treatment decisions," [ ] *i.e.*, medical necessity decisions made by the plaintiff's treating physician *qua* treating physician and *qua* benefits administrator. Put another way, the reasoning of *Pegram* "only makes sense where the underlying negligence also plausibly constitutes medical maltreatment by a party who can be deemed to be a treating physician or such a physician's employer." *Cicio*, 321 F.3d at 109 (Calabresi, J., dissenting in part). Here, however, petitioners are neither respondents' treating physicians nor the employers of respondents' treating physicians. Petitioners' coverage decisions, then, are pure eligibility decisions, and *Pegram* is not implicated.

V

We hold that respondents' causes of action, brought to remedy only the denial of benefits under ERISA-regulated benefit plans, fall within the scope of, and are completely pre-empted by, ERISA § 502(a)(1)(B), and thus removable to federal district court. The judgment of the Court of Appeals is reversed, and the cases are remanded for further proceedings consistent with this opinion.

It is so ordered.

CONCURBY: GINSBURG

CONCUR: JUSTICE GINSBURG, with whom JUSTICE BREYER joins, concurring.

The Court today holds that the claims respondents asserted under Texas law are totally preempted by § 502(a) of the Employee Retirement Income Security Act of 1974 (ERISA or Act), 29 U.S.C. § 1132(a). That decision is consistent with our governing case law on ERISA's preemptive scope. I therefore join the Court's opinion. But, with greater enthusiasm, as indicated by my dissenting opinion in *Great–West Life & Annuity Ins. Co.* v. *Knudson,* 534 U.S. 204, 151 L. Ed. 2d 635, 122 S. Ct. 708 (2002), I also join "the rising judicial chorus urging that Congress and [this] Court revisit what is an unjust and increasingly tangled ERISA regime." *DiFelice* v. *AETNA U.S. Healthcare,* 346 F.3d 442, 453 (CA3 2003) (Becker, J., concurring).

Because the Court has coupled an encompassing interpretation of ERISA's preemptive force with a cramped construction of the "equitable relief" allowable under § 502(a)(3), a "regulatory vacuum" exists: "Virtually all state law remedies are preempted but very few federal substitutes are provided." *Id.,* at 456 (internal quotation marks omitted).

* * *

The Government notes a potential amelioration. Recognizing that "this Court has construed Section 502(a)(3) not to authorize an award of money damages against a *non-fiduciary,*" the Government suggests that the Act, as currently written and interpreted, may "allow at least some forms of 'make-whole' relief against a breaching *fiduciary* in light of the general availability of such relief in equity at the time of the divided bench." [ ] As the Court points out, respondents here declined the opportunity to amend their complaints to state claims for relief under § 502(a); the District Court, therefore, properly dismissed their suits with prejudice. [ ] But the Government's suggestion may indicate an effective remedy others similarly circumstanced might fruitfully pursue.

"Congress ... intended ERISA to replicate the core principles of trust remedy law, including the make-whole standard of relief." [ ] I anticipate that Congress, or this Court, will one day so confirm.

Note on Aetna v. Davila *and* Cigna v. Calad

In this unanimous opinion, the Supreme Court was unambiguous in its ruling that patients cannot use the state courts to bring an action against an ERISA-sponsored health insurance plans for refusal to provide coverage for certain medical treatments. *Davila* held definitively that ERISA pre-empts state law, and the recourse available under ERISA—the cost of the benefits denied—is all that is available to plaintiffs from a managed care organization defendant.

The decision was issued in the wake of a movement by patients' rights advocates to try to utilize state courts to wage a challenge against insurance company coverage decisions much like the routine medical malpractice lawsuits brought against physicians. Indeed, at least ten states have recently passed Patients' Bill of Rights legislation that explicitly provide for lawsuits against insurance companies based upon negligent coverage decisions. Justice Ginsburg (with whom Justice Breyer joined), in her concurring opinion, urged Congress—engaged in an ERISA debate for years—to directly address the issue and bring closure through legislative rulemaking. Opponents of the cause argue that permitting patients to sue HMO's (in addition to their physician) for negligence, including punitive damages, will further escalate the cost of healthcare, and result in fewer people who can afford to obtain coverage. Opponents also point out that the very purpose of the HMO (managed care) cost containment scheme is to allow organizations to make hard coverage decisions in order to keep the cost of health care affordable. Nevertheless, under this ruling physicians remain accountable for the delivery of medical care, while managed care plans have little incentive to approve medically necessary but expensive treatment. The Supreme Court clearly sent a message to Congress that the time has come for it to bring closure to the debate with legislation that strikes a balance between the competing interests.

Chapter 4

EVIDENCE OF MEDICAL
NEGLIGENCE

INTRODUCTORY NOTE

Evidence of medical negligence comes in three kinds: materials (chiefly medical records) that tell what *treatment* was administered before, during, and after the allegedly negligent event; materials external to the particular case that set the *standard of care;* and materials generated after the patient became a plaintiff, for *trial preparation*. Most of these records, like treatment records, are documents, that can either be introduced or used as the foundation for oral testimony; other testimony will be reduced to documentary form (affidavits, answers to interrogatories, and depositions); and items of tangible property may be used as exhibits at trial, whether they were actually involved in the case or merely illustrate what happened.

Another way of looking at medical evidence is to match up hurdles to discovery against the types and times of evidence. Inadmissibility is not an obstacle in federal courts, because modern rules of procedure let the parties engage in fishing expeditions.[1] Privileged communications rules are obstacles, however, because the matter fished for must not be privileged, nor may it consist of "trial preparation materials," that is, the work product of the lawyers, not the doctors. Privileges can be waived, and they usually are waived by putting the plaintiff's condition in controversy. The minuet sketched in Federal Rule 35(b) shows how trial preparation materials can be obtained from an adversary, quite apart from showing substantial need and undue hardship under Federal Rule 26(b)(3). Throughout the chapter, as throughout medical liability practice, lawyers keep asking a pair of questions about each item of medical evidence of negligence: (1) What is it? (2) Can we get it?

Assuming that medical evidence is available for presentation in litigation, another type of hurdle presents itself: How can technical evidence be turned into information that the trier of fact (whether jury

---

1. Federal R.Civ.P. 26(b)(1): "It is not ground for objection that the information sought will be inadmissible at the trial if the information sought appears reasonably calculated to lead to the discovery of admissible evidence."

188

or judge) can assimilate? Medical scientific evidence comes in three classes:

Data: Outputs such as symbols, lines, columns of figures, and electrical impulses, that can be observed and recorded but intrinsically have no communicative value;

Fact: Data expressed within theoretical frameworks to produce linguistic formulations by which experts convey meaning among themselves ("narrowing" shown in an x-ray; "P-wave" in an electrocardiogram); and

Opinion: Interpretations of facts imparting a sense of perspective that can be explained and communicated to intelligent lay persons ("within normal limits"; "unusual electrical activity"). Theoretically, an infinite number of scientists given the same *data* would express the data as the same *facts;* but the scientists' *opinions* on the same facts could legitimately range from agreement to disagreement.

The key to using scientific medical evidence in the courtroom is expert medical opinion, even though using it leads to battles of experts. Most medical liability cases use medical experts, whether they are required or not. Occasionally the medical negligence in a case will be so obvious that the plaintiff need not produce expert opinion testimony on the violation of the standard of care, but expert opinion testimony is still likely to be needed on causation and damages.

As litigation proceeds, the evidence can be tested by motions asserting that the evidence is insufficient to justify going forward with the proceedings: motions for summary judgment (before trial), directed verdict (during trial), and judgment notwithstanding the verdict (after judgment on the verdict); and, likewise after judgment, the weight of the evidence can be challenged, by motion for new trial on the ground that the verdict was against the clear weight of the evidence.

SECTION A. MEDICAL EVIDENCE

COOPER v. EAGLE RIVER MEMORIAL HOSPITAL, INC.

United States Court of Appeals for the Seventh Circuit, 2001.
270 F.3d 456.

Flaum, *Chief Judge.*

* * *

I. Background

On June 6, 1998, Cooper, who was approximately 30 weeks pregnant, was vacationing in Eagle River, Wisconsin. Cooper experienced severe cramping in her lower abdomen and visited Eagle River for treatment. At the hospital, Diego Perez, a nurse practitioner, administered an internal examination and diagnosed Cooper with mild dehydration and mild hypoglycemia. Perez subsequently discharged Cooper.

Cooper's pain worsened following her discharge from Eagle River. Accordingly, she visited the Howard Young Medical Center ("Howard Young"), where treating physicians performed an emergency Cesarian section and delivered Cooper's son, Matthew. Matthew's condition at birth required an emergency transfer from Howard Young to the Marshfield Clinic. Eight days later, Matthew died.

On November 15, 1999, Cooper filed a medical malpractice lawsuit against Eagle River and other defendants. Cooper alleged that Eagle River was negligent for failing to arrange for a physician consultation, failing to conduct standard medical monitoring procedures, and failing to immediately transfer Cooper to Howard Young. The case proceeded to a jury trial. At trial, Cooper offered testimony of several experts on the issues of liability and causation. In defense, Eagle River presented expert testimony from Dr. Nancy Ness, a family physician, regarding the appropriate standard of care for nurse practitioners. Eagle River also relied on expert testimony from Dr. Janice Lage, who examined a pathology slide containing samples of Cooper's placenta tissue and testified as to the cause of Cooper's placental abruption.

After the close of evidence, Cooper asked the court to instruct the jury that Eagle River may be liable under a negligence per se theory because Eagle River allegedly violated two provisions of the Wisconsin administrative code. The first requires nurse practitioners to consult with physicians via telephone; the second requires hospitals to maintain policies and procedures regarding emergency care. The trial court declined to issue the negligence per se instruction and prohibited Cooper from introducing the provisions into evidence.

The jury returned a verdict in favor of Eagle River, and Cooper filed a notice of appeal. * * *

Cooper raises five issues on appeal. First, Cooper argues that the district court should have allowed her to present to the jury a liability theory based upon negligence per se. Second, Cooper maintains the district court should have allowed her to offer into evidence Eagle River's operating procedures and policies regarding emergency obstetrical care * * *

II. Discussion

* * *

B. *Negligence Per Se Instruction*

Cooper first argues that the district court erred in refusing to provide the jury with a negligence per se instruction based upon Eagle River's alleged violation of two provisions of the Wisconsin administrative code. The first is Wisconsin Administrate Code N. 8.10 (2) ("Number 8.10 (2)"), which states:

Advanced practice nurse prescribers shall facilitate collaboration with other health care professionals, at least one of whom shall be a physician, through the use of modern communication techniques.

The second, Wisconsin Code HFS § 124.01 ("Section 124.01") requires hospitals to maintain "written policies for caring for emergency cases, including policies for transferring a patient to an appropriate facility when the patient's medical status indicates the need for emergency care which the hospital cannot provide." Because Nurse Practitioner Perez failed to consult with a physician during Cooper's treatment, and because Eagle River failed to maintain the necessary written policies governing emergency care, Cooper asserts that a negligence per se instruction was appropriate.

Under Wisconsin law, negligence per se instructions are appropriate in a narrowly defined range of circumstances. Specifically, a per se instruction is warranted only when the defendant has violated a "safety statute." To prove that a legislative enactment is a safety statute, a plaintiff seeking a negligence per se instruction must establish three facts:

(1) the harm inflicted was the type the statute was designed to prevent; (2) the person injured was within the class of persons sought to be protected; and (3) there is some expression of legislative intent that the statute become a basis for the imposition of civil liability. [ ].

The Wisconsin courts have interpreted this last requirement narrowly; only when the legislature unambiguously demonstrates an intent to alter the common law standards will a negligence per se instruction be appropriate. [ ]. In distinguishing "safety statutes" from more general regulatory measures, plaintiffs must do more than baldly assert that the statute in question protects a specific class of individuals. All legislation promotes the public welfare to some degree. Instead, the legislation must evince a clear and unambiguous legislative desire to establish civil liability. [ ]

In *Leahy [v. Kenosha Memorial Hospital, 118 Wis 2d 441, 348 N.W. 2d 607 (Wis. Ct. App. 1984)]*, the plaintiff's evidence included a Wisconsin statute that defined the practices of professional nursing and practical nursing. Plaintiff argued that the defendant-hospital violated the statute because the individuals caring for the plaintiff were not registered nurses as defined by the law. Based on this testimony, the trial court included a negligence per se instruction, and the jury found for the defendant liable of medical malpractice. [ ].

In reversing the jury verdict, the Wisconsin Court of Appeals held that a statute regulating the nursing profession and providing for the licensing of nurses was not a safety statute and did not evince a legislative intent to create new standards for civil liability. [ ]. Specifically, the court held that the statute served three clear purposes: regulation of the nursing profession; licensure of nurses; and establishment of penalties for violations. *Id.* While the law ensured public safety generally, nothing in the act revealed "a legislative intent to grant a private right of action for a violation of the statute." *Id.*

The *Leahy* court rejected the appropriateness of the negligence per se instruction because it improperly focused the jury's attention on whether "the nurses' conduct fell within the concept of professional nursing or practical nursing under the statute." [ ] Accordingly, the negligence per se instruction "effectively prohibited consideration of the quality and competency" of the nurses' conduct, which was the proper inquiry in a negligence action. [ ] (emphasis in original).

This case is fundamentally the same as the situation presented in *Leahy*. The administrative code provisions at issue here are clearly regulatory in nature and do not reveal the clear and unambiguous language necessary to impose civil liability. Number 8.10 (2) is part of a larger chapter governing the certification of advanced practice nurses. Similarly, while Section 124.24 requires hospitals to maintain written policies, failure to comply with the provision allows the Wisconsin Department of Health and Family Services to revoke or suspend a hospital's license. [ ] This, too, supports the conclusion that the relevant administrative code provisions do not constitute "safety statutes" as the Wisconsin Supreme Court has defined that term. * * *

The problem associated with issuing a negligence per se instruction based upon alleged statutory violations is easy to identify in this case, just as it was in *Leahy*. A negligence per se instruction would improperly focus the jury's attention on whether Perez complied with the licensure statute governing nurse practitioners. Instead, the appropriate inquiry should have been, as the district court instructed, whether Perez's care for Cooper fell within the appropriate standards of care for nurse practitioners. Because the two code provisions upon which Cooper relies do not reflect the clear and unambiguous language required to warrant a negligence per se instruction, we affirm the district court's refusal to issue one in this case.

B.   *Hospital Policies and Procedures*

Cooper next argues that the district court erred in excluding evidence of Eagle River's written operating procedures and policies. In large measure, Cooper's second argument is inconsistent with her first, in which she claimed that the absence of any hospital procedures constituted negligence as a matter of law.

As a general rule in Wisconsin, the internal procedures of a private organization do not set the standard of care applicable in negligence cases. *See Johnson v. Misericordia Community Hospital,* 97 Wis.2d 521, 294 N.W.2d 501, 510 (Wis. Ct. App. 1980), *citing Marolla v. American Family Mut. Ins. Co.,* 38 Wis.2d 539, 157 N.W.2d 674, 678 (Wis. 1968). However, the *Marolla* court also recognized an exception to this general rule, "if it could be shown that an entire industry or substantially an entire industry had essentially the same safety regulations," or if Wisconsin law required the regulations. [ ].

Even assuming the exception discussed in *Marolla* applied in the present case, Cooper's argument must still fail. Cooper presented no evidence that the policies and procedures were in effect at the time she received medical treatment at Eagle River. Cooper was not entitled to introduce policies that were not in effect during the relevant time period. As a result, the district court's decision to exclude them does not constitute an abuse of discretion.

* * *

[AFFIRMED]

HAWES v. CHUA

District of Columbia Court of Appeals, 2001.
769 A.2d 797.

REID, *Associate Judge*:

In this medical malpractice action relating to the fetal death of twins, the jury returned a verdict for appellees Maureen Chua, M.D., Maureen Chua, M.D., P.C., and Carin Kleiman, M.D. Appellants Trizah Hawes and Derrick Hawes filed a timely appeal, alleging several trial court errors, including the failure of the trial judge to strike the standard of care testimony of defense witness, Dr. Charles F. Hill, Jr. We affirm the judgment of the trial court and conclude, in part, that the trial court did not commit manifest error in admitting Dr. Hill's national standard of care testimony, since that testimony: (a) reflected some evidence that it was based on a national standard, and (b) was grounded on neither the expert's personal opinion, nor mere speculation or conjecture. We emphasize the closeness of this case, however, and reiterate that it is insufficient for a defense expert's standard of care testimony to merely recite the words "national standard of care."

* * *

FACTUAL SUMMARY

The record before us reveals the following pertinent facts. On December 25, 1994, Mrs. Hawes gave birth to stillborn identical twins by emergency C-section. The twins had died *in utero* one to two days earlier. One of appellants' experts, Dr. Janice Marie Lage, Vice Chairman of the Department of Pathology and Professor of Pathology, with expertise in obstetrical and perinatal pathology, at the Georgetown University Medical School, attributed the twins' death to twin-to-twin transfusion syndrome, which in essence, means that one twin was drained of fluid by the other, and the second twin suffered from fluid overload from the first twin.

The case centered on the proper course of care and treatment for identical twins exposed to a risk of twin-to-twin transfusion syndrome, as well as a risk of intrauterine growth retardation. Dr. Chua initially provided care for Mrs. Hawes, who was diagnosed with the twin pregnancy on July 18, 1994. By November 1994, Dr. Chua's associate, Dr. Kleiman had assumed primary responsibility for Mrs. Hawes' care.

On November 29, 1994, when the twins were about 31 weeks into their fetal development, an in-office sonogram suggested that they were not developing properly when compared with a November 16th sonogram. A December 6th sonogram, performed at 32 weeks of growth by the Washington Radiology Associates, continued to show growth problems for the twins; they were getting smaller. No decision was made to hospitalize Mrs. Hawes or to deliver the babies, despite the results of the December 6th sonogram.

A complete biophysical profile, including a sonogram, was ordered on December 13th. However, the complete biophysical profile was never done. Dr. Kleiman became concerned for Mrs. Hawes' pregnancy and arranged for home uterine contraction monitoring. Dr. Kleiman also prescribed a medication, terbutaline, to prevent premature contractions. When the monitoring device showed a lot of contractions, Mrs. Hawes was told to return to Dr. Kleiman's office on December 15th. On that day, she complained of pain, and another in-office sonogram was done. Mrs. Hawes was not hospitalized, and the twins were not delivered. After December 15th, no other sonogram was performed in-office, or by the Washington Radiology Associates.

When Mrs. Hawes arrived at the emergency room of the Washington Hospital Center on December 18th, complaining of continued cramping, pain and irregular contractions, Dr. Kleiman directed Mrs. Hawes to return home and to continue taking the terbutaline to prevent premature contractions. During her December 20th visit to Dr. Kleiman's office, she complained of a reduction in fetal movement, and was placed on a fetal heart monitor. No sonogram was performed, and she was sent home.

On December 25th, Mrs. Hawes called the home fetal monitoring service and informed them that she was experiencing decreased fetal movement. Dr. Chua called Mrs. Hawes back and told her to go to the hospital immediately. A sonogram revealed that both fetuses had died.

In their lawsuit against the appellees, Mr. and Mrs. Hawes maintained that the November and December sonograms showed the early warning signs of trouble for the high-risk twin pregnancy, including a size discrepancy between the twins and a deficit of amniotic fluid around one of the twins; that a sonogram should have been done on December 20th; that the signs of premature labor should have been interpreted as signs that the twins were in distress and were trying to be born; and that the twins should have been delivered sometime earlier since they were past the stage of viability during the period beginning around mid-November.

After the jury returned a verdict in favor of the appellees, Mr. and Mrs. Hawes moved for a new trial, which ultimately was denied. Their appeal followed.

ANALYSIS

We turn first to appellants' argument that the testimony of Dr. Charles F. Hill, Jr., appellees' expert witness regarding the standard of care owed to Mrs. Hawes, should have been struck by the trial court, because he failed "to provide any basis for his opinion as to the national standard of care." Appellees argue that the trial court did not abuse its discretion in deciding not to strike Dr. Hill's testimony, because, "as the [trial] court ... noted, there was no need to recite the mantra of 'national' in each and every question and answer.... "

" 'The trial judge has wide latitude in the admission or exclusion of expert testimony, and his [or her] decision with respect thereto should be sustained unless it is manifestly erroneous.' " *In re Melton*, 597 A.2d 892, 897 (D.C. 1991) [ ] * * *.

* * * During his trial testimony, Dr. Hill revealed that he was licensed in the District of Columbia, Maryland, and Virginia; and had a practice in obstetrics and gynecology * * * Dr. Hill completed his residency in 1978 at Georgetown Hospital. He was board certified at the time of trial, presumably in obstetrics and gynecology, and served as an associate clinical instructor at Georgetown.

* * *

In providing this background information, Dr. Hill did not mention any textbooks, journal articles, or national professional meetings he had attended, pertaining to the specialty areas for which he was qualified to testify.

Before stating his professional opinion, Dr. Hill indicated that he reviewed the medical records of Mrs. Hawes, and the depositions of Doctors Chua and Kleiman; as well as the deposition of Dr. Joel Palmer, appellants' standard of care expert. After revealing this information, Dr. Hill was asked:

Based upon all that you [have] reviewed, Dr. Hill, have you been able to form an opinion, one that you can base and express on a reasonable degree of medical certainty, as to whether or not the overall management of this pregnancy of Drs. Chua and Kleiman did or did not meet appropriate standards of care for a nationally board certified obstetrician in 1994?

He replied: "I think that they did meet the standard, yes." Dr. Hill's responses generally did not reference a specific basis for his opinions when he responded to individual questions * * *

* * *

We now turn to the trial court's ruling on the issue of Dr. Hill's testimony. Prior to his cross-examination, counsel for appellants moved to strike Dr. Hill's testimony on the ground that he failed to:

"establish[ ] a legally sufficient basis for his opinions in this jurisdiction. He must testify to a national standard of care to a reasonable degree of medical certainty, and he—moreover, must state the basis for his opinions...."

In support of his argument, counsel referenced *Travers v. District of Columbia*, 672 A.2d 566 (D.C. 1996). The trial judge disagreed, saying:

> This witness has in fact testified to a national standard of care. There's a more recent case ... It's a '99 or late '98 case that says, as long as you say the words, that it's a national standard of care. You don't have to prove how you know it's a national standard of care. We don't have to state that I know it's a national standard of care because I reviewed enough literature or I worked at enough hospitals. As long as you say there's a national standard of care, that's sufficient, and he has done that.

* * *

Our review of *Travers* and *District of Columbia v. Wilson*, [721 A.2d 591 (D.C.1998)], as well as some of our earlier medical malpractice cases, reveals that, in this jurisdiction, at least seven legal principles are important in assessing the sufficiency of national standard of care proof. First, the standard of care focuses on "the course of action that a reasonably prudent doctor with the defendant's specialty would have taken under the same or similar circumstances." *Meek [v. Shepard, 484 A.2d 579,]* 581. Second, the course of action or treatment must be followed nationally. [ ]. Third, the fact that District physicians follow a national standard of care is insufficient in and of itself to establish a national standard of care. *Travers, supra*, 672 A.2d at 569. Fourth, in demonstrating that a particular course of action or treatment is followed nationally, reference to a published standard is not required, but can be important. [ ]. Fifth, discussion of the course of action or treatment with doctors outside this jurisdiction, at seminars or conventions, who agree with it; or reference to "specific medical literature" may be sufficient. *Id.* at 569. Sixth, an expert's personal opinion does not constitute a statement of the national standard of care; thus a statement only of what the expert "would do under similar circumstances ... " is inadequate. *Meek, supra*[ ]. Seventh, national standard of care testimony may not be based upon mere speculation or conjecture. [ ].

* * * [A] trial judge should be guided by the following factors in assessing the admissibility of national standard of care testimony: (1) it is insufficient for an expert's standard of care testimony to merely recite the words "national standard of care"; (2) such testimony may not be based upon the expert's personal opinion, nor mere speculation or conjecture; and (3) such testimony must reflect some evidence of a national standard, such as attendance at national seminars or meetings or conventions, or reference to published materials, when evaluating a medical course of action or treatment. * * *

* * *

Here, Dr. Hill's testimony was at least minimally sufficient for admission into evidence since he testified as a board certified obstetrician and gynecologist; kept abreast of "the state of the medical art [in] obstetrics and gynecology," attended national meetings; was familiar with, and based his opinions on, the literature of his specialty, as well as the standards of care, including those of the American College, applicable to a reasonable obstetrician and gynecologist who undertakes the management of twin pregnancies. Moreover, we cannot say that Dr. Hill's opinions were based on nothing more than speculation or conjecture, nor merely constituted his personal opinion. Therefore, we conclude that the trial judge's decision not to strike his testimony did not constitute manifest error. However, we stress that while the trial judge retains considerable discretion in determining whether to admit defense national standard of care expert testimony, (1) it is insufficient for the expert to merely recite the words "national standard of care"; (2) the expert's testimony may not be based on his or her personal opinion, nor on mere speculation or conjecture; and (3) the expert's opinion must reflect some evidence of a national standard, such as attendance at national seminars or meetings or conventions, or reference to published materials, when assessing a medical course of action or treatment.

[AFFIRMED]

QUIJANO v. UNITED STATES OF AMERICA

United States Court of Appeals for the Fifth Circuit, 2003.
325 F.3d 564.

HUDSPETH, District Judge:

Cristina Quijano, the civilian spouse of a retired Army service member, underwent coronary artery bypass surgery at the Brooke Army Medical Center ("BAMC") in San Antonio, Texas. Following the surgery, she developed sepsis which was traced to a bacterial infection introduced through a blood transfusion. She died the day after surgery. Her surviving spouse and their adult children ("Quijano family") brought a wrongful death and survival action against the United States under the Federal Tort Claims Act [ ] ("FTCA"). Following a bench trial, the district court found in favor of the Quijano family, and awarded damages of $400,000. The United States appeals.

I. FACTS

On September 18, 1995, Mrs. Cristina Quijano, a 69 year-old woman, came to the BAMC Emergency Room complaining of chest pains. She was admitted to the hospital for tests. Those tests revealed blockage of the coronary arteries. The cardiologists recommended bypass surgery, which was scheduled for September 26, 1995.

On September 22, 1995, Quijano family members met with Dr. Alfred Gorman, one of the attending cardiologists. They requested the opportunity to give directed donations of blood1 in case Mrs. Quijano should require a transfusion during or after surgery. That request was denied by Dr. Gorman. The family did not repeat the request to anyone else.

Mrs. Quijano's surgery was postponed three days, and was actually performed on September 29, 1995. During surgery, she received a transfusion of two units of packed red blood cells. A later investigation revealed that the blood had been donated by voluntary donors at Fort Hood Texas, and stored for 34 days. The standard pre-transfusion inspection of the blood revealed no abnormality. Nevertheless, Mrs. Quijano developed septic shock and died approximately 36 hours after surgery. It was later determined that her death was caused by a blood-borne bacterial infection called Yersinia enterocolitica. This bacteria is so rare it is believed to be present in only one out of one million units of donated blood and causes fatality in one out of nine million cases.

In 1995 there were no known screening tests for the presence of Yersinia in transfused blood other than visual inspection immediately prior to infusion. The district court found no negligence in connection with the inspection performed in this case. However, the district court found that BAMC was negligent in refusing the Quijano family's request for directed donation of blood for the benefit of Mrs. Quijano, and that such negligence was a proximate cause of her death.

* * *

III. DISCUSSION

The FTCA authorizes civil actions for damages against the United States for personal injury or death caused by the negligence of a government employee under circumstances in which a private person would be liable under the law of the state in which the negligent act or omission occurred. [ ]. In this case, we apply Texas law. Texas authorizes civil actions both for wrongful death and for the survival of actions for personal injury when the injured person dies. [ ]. When the negligence alleged is in the nature of medical malpractice, the plaintiff has the burden of proving (1) a duty by the physician or hospital to act according to an applicable standard of care; (2) a breach of that standard of care; (3) an injury, and (4) a causal connection between the breach of care and the injury [citations omitted]. The standard of care is a threshold issue which the plaintiff must establish before the fact finder moves on to consider whether the defendant breached that standard of care to such a degree that it constituted negligence. Mills [v. Angel,] 995 S.W.2d 262, 268; Expert testimony is generally required to prove the applicable standard of care. * * * That testimony must focus on the standard of care in the community in which the treatment took place or in similar communities. [ ].

The district court found that in September 1995, the Food and Drug Administration had not promulgated any specific regulation applicable to directed donations of blood, nor had the American Association of Blood Banks adopted a policy with respect to the use of directed donations. The Plaintiff's expert, Dr. Dawson, testified that directed donations were safer than donations from volunteer donors; that in 1995, directed donations were generally accepted by hospitals around the United

States; that a hospital policy highly discouraging directed donations would have been "unconscionable"; and that BAMC breached the applicable standard of care by failing to accommodate the Quijano family's request for directed donations. The Defendant's expert, Dr. Sandler, testified that directed donations of blood were not safer than volunteer donations; that in 1995, it might have taken up to ten working days to process blood obtained through directed donations in order to verify its safety; that the standard of care with respect to directed donations differed from community to community and hospital to hospital around the country; and that BAMC's policies in 1995 were within the standard of care. The district court noted these conflicting expert opinions, but found that BAMC's own internal policy of highly discouraging, but not prohibiting, directed donations represented the standard of care, and that not allowing the Quijano family to give directed donations in this case violated the standard of care and was negligent. This was an erroneous application of Texas law. In Texas, a hospital's internal policies and bylaws may be evidence of the standard of care, but hospital rules alone do not determine the governing standard of care. [ ]. A hospital might maintain a higher standard of care than the prevailing community standard. Hicks [v. Canessa], 825 S.W.2d 542, 544. Because the district court's finding that BAMC policy established the applicable standard of care was clearly erroneous, we are required to remand the case to the district court. Upon remand, the court should consider whether the expert testimony offered by the parties established a community standard of care and whether the actions of the Defendant's agents and employees breached that standard of care.

REVERSED

PHILLIPS v. COVENANT CLINIC

Supreme Court of Iowa, 2001.
625 N.W.2d 714.

CADY, Justice.

* * *

I. BACKGROUND FACTS AND PROCEEDINGS

Paul Harvey Phillips went to the Covenant Clinic in Waterloo on January 3, 1996, complaining of flu-like symptoms. He was eighty years old. Debra Cortes, a physician's assistant, examined Paul and learned he was experiencing chest pains. Paul had recently suffered congestive heart failure. Dr. Ronald Roth, who was supervising Cortes, ordered an EKG and a chest x-ray.

After the EKG was performed, Paul was permitted to walk on his own to the neighboring hospital for the chest x-ray. He collapsed, however, on his way to the hospital in cardiac arrest. Around the same time, Dr. Thomas Pattee reviewed Paul's EKG strip. When Dr. Pattee learned Paul had collapsed on his way to the hospital, he grabbed Paul's entire medical file from the clinic, which included the EKG results, and hand-delivered the file to the intensive care unit of the hospital, where Paul was being treated. Doctors at the hospital were unable to save Paul's life. He died at the hospital.

In June 1996, Janet sought her father's medical records from the clinic. The clinic subsequently informed Janet that her father's medical file was missing. No one at the hospital or clinic had seen Paul's medical file since it had been hand-delivered to the intensive care unit by Dr. Pattee on January 3, 1996. The only document the clinic was able to produce was Cortes' notes from the January 3 office visit. The clinic asked Janet to check Paul's personal belongings from the January 3 hospitalization to ensure the clinical records had not been inadvertently included with those belongings. The medical records were not found.

Janet filed this wrongful death action on January 2, 1998. She alleged medical malpractice against the Covenant Clinic, Dr. Roth, Dr. Pattee, and Dr. Ronald Flory. Pursuant to Iowa Code section 668.11 (1997), Janet named Dr. R. William Overton, III, as her medical expert. Dr. Overton concluded the clinic doctors breached their duty of care in treating Paul on January 3, 1996, by permitting him to leave the clinic before reviewing the EKG results. However, because Paul's medical file was unavailable for review, Dr. Overton was unable to conclude the breach caused Paul's death. The only document available for Dr. Overton to review was the office notes prepared by Cortes regarding the January 3 office visit. This document consisted of both dictated and handwritten notes. Dr. Overton concluded Cortes added the handwritten notes after her dictation had been transcribed, and found this conduct was potentially indicative of an attempt to conceal the medical records.

The defendants moved for summary judgment. They claimed Janet's failure to establish a causal relationship between the doctors' purported breach of the standard of care and Paul's death was fatal to her claim. Janet resisted the motion. She claimed the defendants' failure to produce relevant records within their control entitled her to an inference that the missing medical records contained evidence unfavorable to the defendants, and that this inference gave rise to a genuine issue of material fact on the causation element.

The district court granted the motion for summary judgment. Janet appeals. She claims the district court erred in holding the spoliation inference could not support a proximate cause finding under the circumstances.

* * *

III. SPOLIATION OF EVIDENCE

To establish a prima facie case of medical malpractice, the plaintiff must demonstrate the applicable standard of care, the violation of this standard of care, and a causal relationship between the violation and the harm allegedly suffered by the plaintiff. [ ] Expert testimony is nearly always required to establish each of these elements. [ ] Moreover, proximate cause, like the other elements, cannot be based upon mere speculation. [ ] No consequential fact in a case can be resolved by pure guesswork.[ ]

Although the expert in this case, Dr. Overton, concluded the defendants breached the duty of care they owed to Paul, he was unable to establish the existence of a causal relationship between this breach and Paul's death. Additionally, Dr. Overton could not even state that there was a possibility that Paul would have survived absent the defendants' breach. [ ]

Notwithstanding, Janet argues that the clinic's failure to produce the medical records gives rise to an inference that the physicians' conduct in treating her father was negligent and the cause of his death. She claims this inference is sufficient to overcome the motion for summary judgment.

It is a well established legal principle that the intentional destruction of or the failure to produce documents or physical evidence relevant to the proof of an issue in a legal proceeding supports an inference that the evidence would have been unfavorable to the party responsible for its destruction or nonproduction. [ ] The nonproduction, alteration, or destruction of evidence is commonly referred to as spoliation. [ ] When established, the inference is regarded as an admission by conduct of the weakness of the party's case. [ ] The inference is imposed both for evidentiary and punitive reasons. [ ]. The evidentiary value of the inference is derived from the common sense observation that a party who destroys a document with knowledge that it is relevant to litigation is likely to have been threatened by the document. *Beil v. Lakewood Eng'g & Mfg. Co.*, 15 F.3d 546, 552 (6th Cir. 1994) (when a party to an action has notice that an item is relevant to the lawsuit and proceeds to destroy the item, "common sense" dictates an inference that the party destroying the item is likely to have been threatened by the evidence) [ ]. Additionally, an inference serves to deter parties from destroying relevant evidence. [ ]

The inference can arise in a variety of circumstances, including medical malpractice actions involving the failure to produce relevant medical records. [ ] However, the inference can only be based upon the intentional destruction of evidence. [ ] It is not warranted if the disappearance of the evidence is due to mere negligence, or if the evidence was destroyed during a routine procedure. [ ]. Furthermore, the missing evidence must be *within the control of a party* whose interests would naturally call for its production." [ ] These elements are essential to both the common sense evidentiary rationale for the inference and its punitive sanction.

Janet argues she is entitled to the inference for purposes of summary judgment because the facts of her case must be considered in a light most favorable to her claim and all reasonable inferences must be drawn in her favor. However, this familiar rule of summary judgment applies to factual inferences, not those grounded in a legal principle.

Janet is not entitled to the spoliation inference without showing the existence of a genuine issue of material fact supporting the inference. Thus, she must show intentional destruction of the records as well as control of the records. In doing this, she is entitled to have all reasonable inferences from the evidence drawn in her favor.

The factual basis to support the intentional nonproduction of the records in this case is based on Dr. Overton's belief that the addition of handwritten notes to the transcribed notes of the physician's assistant was unusual and suspicious, and could indicate a broader attempt by the clinic and its doctors to conceal information. Yet, we think this logic amounts only to bare speculation and conjecture, and cannot be legitimately inferred from the facts. [ ]

The handwritten notes made by the physician's assistant may support a reasonable inference that the information was added to the transcribed notes with a motive to protect against potential litigation. However, it would be rank speculation to infer from that fact, considered in a light most favorable to Janet's claim, that the other records of the clinic were intentionally destroyed because the doctors believed that those records contained adverse information relevant to a potential lawsuit. The motive of the physician's assistant to bolster her notes in anticipation of potential litigation does not show a motive by the clinic or its doctors to intentionally purge themselves of any records to prevent their production during any subsequent litigation. Moreover, Janet has produced no other circumstances in addition to the physician's assistant's notes to support the spoliation inference. There were no circumstances alleged to show the clinic or its physicians believed the records might be harmful to them in any lawsuit, or other circumstances raised by Janet which are compatible with the common sense observation which supports the inference and the imposition of sanctions against the clinic or the physicians. Additionally, Janet has failed to show the existence of a genuine factual issue that the clinic even possessed or controlled the records at any relevant time to support the imposition of the spoliation inference. To the contrary, the facts are unchallenged that the records were delivered to the hospital.

Janet also argues that the failure to grant her the benefit of the spoliation inference violates public policy by punishing the blameless party and rewarding the party who lost the records. To the contrary, we find public policy supports the dismissal of this action. A spoliation inference should be utilized prudently and sparingly. [ ] In cases in which we have permitted the spoliation inference, the party against whom the inference was used was in possession of the evidence and engaged in conduct resulting in the loss of the evidence under circumstances giving rise to a common sense observation that the evidence would have been unfavorable to the party. [ ] In this case, there is no direct or circumstantial evidence to contradict the evidence presented by the clinic and its physicians that the medical records were delivered to the hospital and never returned, and no evidence to raise a genuine issue of fact whether the conduct of the clinic in failing to produce the records justified an inference that the records contained evidence which would have established the elements of negligence. Moreover, there is no evidence to show the motive of the physician who hand-delivered the medical file to the hospital was anything but to help the doctors at the hospital in their fight to save Paul's life. [ ]

We acknowledge that we are slow to grant summary judgment in negligence actions. [ ] Clearly, claims of negligence are fact-based and must normally be resolved by a trial. [ ] We also recognize the frustration faced by litigants, like Janet, when documents and other evidence needed to help prove their claim disappear. Yet, the spoliation inference sought to be utilized by Janet is not grounded on the need or blamelessness of the party seeking the inference, or the mere fact that the evidence has disappeared. It is based on the nature of the conduct of the party who destroyed the evidence and the need to punish such conduct. [ ] This rationale is simply nowhere to be found under the circumstances presented in this case. Thus, without the inference, there is no evidence to support the proximate cause element of the claim and summary judgment is warranted.

The spoliation inference must be carefully applied in a fair and even manner to all parties. This means the party seeking the inference must generate a genuine factual issue whether the party in control of the evidence intentionally altered or destroyed it. If we permit the inference to be used under any lesser standard, the inference will lose its validity and impose unfair sanctions. It may also impose other unwanted burdens on our legal system. [ ]

IV. CONCLUSION

We conclude the district court properly granted summary judgment. Janet was not entitled to a spoliation inference, and thus is unable to establish a sufficient showing of proximate causation to withstand defendant's summary judgment motion.

AFFIRMED.

Notes

1) Is an instruction to the jury as to negligence *per se* unduly prejudicial in a matter grounded primarily in negligence? Can you make a convincing argument that violation of an administrative provision requiring a nurse practitioner to check in with a physician was sufficiently probative to overcome any perceived undue prejudice? Based upon the information known to the nurse-practitioner in *Cooper*, what might the physician have suggested that would have mitigated plaintiff's damages?

2) Even a generation ago, there was good rationale for a local standard of care. A physician in Boise, Idaho did not have access to the information, training and technology available to a physician in Boston, Massachusetts. Over the past decade the so-called locality rule has

yielded to a national standard of care. Can you think of circumstances under which evidence of local practice should still be the norm?

3) Some courts have imposed strict liability for contaminated blood products on the theory that blood is a "product" subject to strict products liability. Other courts have rejected that theory, finding that blood transfusion is a "service" subject to a negligence standard. How should courts determine when the incidence of a rare bacteria infecting a blood product is too small to warrant the extra cost of screening? Is some form of strict liability socially responsible in this type of case, or does it invite courts to redefine medical practice in epidemiological terms?

4) On the issue of spoliation of evidence, compare *Keene v. Brigham and Women's Hospital*, *infra* at page 303.

SECTION B.   EXPERT MEDICAL TESTIMONY

RICHARDSON v. WESLEY HEALTH CENTER

Supreme Court of Mississippi, 2002.
807 So.2d 1244.

WALLER, J.:

FACTS

After complaining of nausea and vomiting blood, Wheeless was admitted to Wesley Health Center where she was originally diagnosed with upper gastrointestinal hemorrhage. Wheeless had a history of poor health, which included a stroke, delirium tremens secondary to alcohol abuse, elevated heart rate, fast breathing, and high blood pressure. During her stay at Wesley, Wheeless suffered a second stroke and subsequently died. The cause of Wheeless's death was recorded on the death certificate as cerebral vascular accident (stroke) secondary to artherosclerotic vascular disease as a consequence of hypertension. Wheeless's physicians concluded the stroke was caused by a totally blocked left carotid artery. Wheeless was a patient at Wesley from December 5, 1996, until her death on January 8, 1997.

Richardson alleges that Wesley caused or contributed to her mother's pain, suffering, and death by providing negligent and sub-standard nursing care. Richardson's expert was Crystal D. Keller, a Registered Nurse and Certified Legal Nurse Consultant, who was designated to testify to the appropriate nursing standards of care and deviations therefrom committed by the hospital staff. In her report, Keller set out in detail areas of failure attributable to the nursing staff at Wesley, which included: failure to monitor adequately; failure to inform physicians of significant changes in the patient's status; failure to follow physician's orders; failure to safeguard adequately; failure to provide adequate care; failure to document properly, accurately, and consistently; failure to assess and reassess adequately; failure to implement an appropriate plan of care; failure to evaluate the patient appropriately; failure to use critical thinking in the nursing process; and failure to assess adequately the patient's risk for injury. Keller's proffered testimony cites there were noted instances during Wheeless's hospitalization where she exhibited signs of gastrointestinal bleeding (black tarry stools), decreased laboratory values, changes in mental status and confusion, decreased blood pressure, increased heart and respiratory rates, restlessness, and agitation, all of which either were not reported to the physician or documented appropriately. Keller opined that the deviations from the requisite standard of nursing care led to Wheeless's suffering and subsequent death.

DISCUSSION

A. Testimony as to Pain and Suffering

Richardson argues that summary judgment should not have been granted because there was a genuine issue of fact concerning Wheeless's pain, suffering, and death, established through the expert testimony of Keller. In support, Richardson offers Keller's education and sixteen years experience as a registered nurse and six years work as a legal consultant. Richardson believes that Keller's expert opinion is admissible as it is "helpful to the trier of fact," which is the relevant inquiry to be made pursuant to Mississippi Rule of Evidence 702.

We set the standard for expert witnesses in medical malpractice cases in *Hall v. Hilbun*, 466 So. 2d 856 (Miss. 1985), where we said expert opinion testimony should be allowed where the witness is qualified and independent, and the testimony will assist the trier of fact. We find the trial court's ruling was overly restrictive in not allowing Keller to testify concerning the appropriate standard of nursing care and the deviations from that standard. There is sufficient proffered evidence from Keller for a jury to consider whether the inadequate nursing care resulted in worsening Wheeless's physical pain and suffering.

In *Drummond v. Buckley*, 627 So. 2d 264 (Miss. 1993), the plaintiff filed a medical malpractice action after suffering pain and swelling in his lower back following surgery for a herniated disc. In *Drummond*, the plaintiff did not have an expert witness to show proximate causation; however, we ruled summary judgment was precluded. The facts of *Drummond* reflect there was a dispute over a conversation between the physician and patient over the doctor's recommendation that the patient enter the hospital for treatment of his back infection. We noted that *Clayton v. Thompson*, 475 So. 2d 439, 445 (Miss. 1985), stated "proximate cause arises when omission of a duty contributes to cause an injury." *Drummond*, 627 So. 2d at 270. Here there is substantial evidence documenting deficient nursing care that may have contributed to Wheeless's suffering.

The fact that Keller is not a physician does not bar her right to testify concerning the standard of care for the nursing staff, but more appropriately may affect the weight of her testimony, which is an issue for the trier of fact. Considering all of the evidence in the light most favorable to Richardson, we find there is a genuine issue of fact concerning whether Wheeless suffered more physically and incurred more expense from the failures of the nursing staff documented by Wheeless's expert and that the circuit court improperly granted summary judgment as to pain and suffering.

* * *

The facts in Richardson's case reflect that the nurses' negligent actions exacerbated Wheeless's condition and caused pain and suffering, even if that negligence was not determined to be the ultimate cause of death. Though the survival statute is not specifically cited in the complaint, the pleadings in this case delineate two specific causes of action and are sufficient under our system of notice pleadings. We hold that Richardson demonstrated a genuine issue of material fact requiring a trial on her separate cause of action for Wheeless's pain and suffering. Therefore, the circuit court erred in granting summary judgment as to that claim.

B.   Testimony as to the Cause of Death

* * * While Keller is qualified to testify concerning deviations in nursing care and resultant pain and suffering, she is not qualified to testify concerning the causal nexus between these deviations and Wheeless's death.

Richardson has cited other cases involving personal injuries where medical testimony was not required for proof of causation, including our decision in *Sonford Prods. Corp. v. Freels*, 495 So. 2d 468 (Miss. 1986), *overruled on other grounds, Bickham v. Department of Mental Health*, 592 So. 2d 96, 98 (Miss. 1991). In *Sonford*, we held that a toxicologist should have been able to render expert testimony that prolonged exposure to toxic chemicals caused injury and death to a workers' compensation claimant. We further held that there need not be expert testimony from a medical doctor to establish causation. [ ]

While we do not require expert testimony by a medical doctor in order to establish the cause of death, the plaintiff must show that there is causation in fact. [ ]. It is not enough to show that there were deviations from the requisite standard of care for nursing. Here, Richardson has failed to make a required showing that the nurses' negligent failure to abide by the standard of care in fact caused or contributed to Wheeless's death.

* * *

The trial court ruled that Richardson's designated expert witness, Keller, was not "qualified by education or experience to render relevant testimony with regard to the mechanism of Ms. Wheeless's death and/or causal connection between these alleged deviations and Ms. Wheeless's multiple severe medical problems," and therefore "would not be allowed to render medical opinions as to the multiple medical diseases and/or conditions suffered by the Plaintiff during this lengthy hospitalization at Wesley or the cause of these conditions and/or the cause of her death."

We agree with the circuit court that Keller lacks the requisite education and experience as an expert to testify concerning the causal link between Wheeless's death and the alleged deviations in nursing care and further that her proffered testimony does not specify such a link. Therefore, the circuit court did not err in granting summary judgment for Wesley on the charge of causing her wrongful death.

AFFIRMED IN PART AND REVERSED IN PART

DREVENAK v. ABENDSCHEIN

District of Columbia Court of Appeals, 2001.
773 A.2d 396.

FACTUAL SUMMARY

The record on appeal shows that, in March 1993, Ms. Drevenak was a 5' 4", 72–year–old senior citizen, weighing around 210 pounds, who suffered from severe degenerative osteoarthritis in her right knee. Twenty years earlier a surgical procedure, known as "a high tibial osteotomy," had been performed on the knee to remove bone and straighten her leg, but the knee continued to degenerate through the years, resulting in pain and instability. Consequently, she was advised to undergo total knee replacement surgery, which Dr. Abendschein performed on March 10, 1993. There were no complications during or after the surgery, and Ms. Drevenak began some physical therapy while she was still in the hospital. However, medical records, at the time of Ms. Drevenak's discharge from the hospital, reflected the presence of "a small area of draining sinus in the distal aspect of the knee."

* * *

Following her hospital discharge, Ms. Drevenak continued with physical therapy. On March 26, 1993, approximately two weeks after surgery, a therapist was assisting Ms. Drevenak in her exercises. After Ms. Drevenak had ascended some steps, she was in the process of descending them when she suddenly sat down and her knee split open. Examination revealed an open patellar tendon rupture, which Dr. Abendschein diagnosed as "a traumatic rupture." That same day, Dr. Abendschein reattached the tendon, and did a "complete debridement of the knee with pulsatile lavage." He saw no sign of infection. After surgery to reattach the tendon, Ms. Drevenak apparently was sent to the Carriage Hill Nursing Center in Silver Spring, Maryland. While she was there, a culture was taken on April 9, 1993 of the fluid draining from her right knee. The laboratory report showed "staphylococcus aureus, heavy growth" and "streptococcus, Beta–Hemolytic, Presumptive Group A . . . moderate growth." When Ms. Drevenak saw Dr. Abendschein on April 9, 1993 for the removal of sutures, he noted that the "incision [from the knee replacement surgery] is angry but not cellulitic. . . . " He concluded that there was no significant infection.

* * *

Dr. Abendschein examined Ms. Drevenak's knee again on April 12, 1993. He detected no sign of cellulitis or deep infection, but there was some drainage from the knee and the incision was "irritated." Because of the April 9th culture, Dr. Abendschein suspected a superficial infection and prescribed the antibiotic, Augmentin, and an antiseptic solution for daily cleaning of the wound. Another examination by Dr. Abendschein took place on April 23, 1993; he noted: "The patient has a serous draining sinus but no evidence of infection in her knee. She is continued on Augmentin for the present time and betadine dressings." Dr. Abendschein saw "no sign of excessive swelling, pain, [or] tenderness."

During the period of her recovery from the patellar tendon rupture, Ms. Drevenak fell on April 29, 1993, hurt her left hip, and "sustained an avulsion of the patella tendon" or a second rupture in her right knee. She was admitted to Sibley Memorial Hospital on the same day. Dr. Abendschein called in an infectious disease consultant who ordered cultures and prescribed intravenous antibiotics.

Ms. Drevenak's second rupture was repaired on May 4, 1993, apparently without incident. * * * With respect to her knee, the following entry appears in the Sibley Memorial Hospital record:

Her knee did well. The incision had closed, and she was placed in a specially constructed double-upright long-leg brace.

She was kept on antibiotics through her course for both the previous knee cultures. * * * All of this was directed by the Infectious Disease specialist.

* * *

The patient is evaluated for her right total knee replacement and her left total hip replacement. X-rays show good position of the left total hip replacement, she is having no problem whatsoever. She has no pain in the right knee, she has a 20 degree flexion lag but is able to perform SLR exercises, she has 90 degrees of flexion. X-rays show good position of the prosthesis and good position of the patella indicating the patellar tendon mechanism is still intact. She is continued in the use of the brace and will be re-evaluated in two months.

After her discharge * * * Ms. Drevenak returned to her home in West Virginia. On July 7, 1993, she was admitted to the City Hospital in Martinsburg, West Virginia, due to fever, redness and tenderness of the right leg. Hospital records stated: "The right leg incision showed a large area of erythema [redness] with warmth and tenderness. There was a small open area draining a small amount of pus." The impressionistic diagnosis was: "Cellulitis and/or infection of right knee prosthesis." Although a culture was taken, it "was lost by a combination of laboratory and nursing error." On July 8, 1993, Ms. Drevenak was transferred to Sibley Memorial Hospital.

Upon examining Ms. Drevenak following her return to Sibley Memorial Hospital, Dr. Abendschein concluded that her right knee was infected. She was given intravenous antibiotics, and Dr. Abendschein performed arthroscopic surgery and irrigation on July 8th and 12th. Moreover, on July 12th, cultures of fluid were taken from Ms. Drevenak's knee. When improvement did not occur, cultures of knee fluid again were taken, and Dr. Abendschein removed the knee prosthesis on July 19th, noting:

> The patient has undergone two arthroscopies with vigorous debridement and still has a recurrent effusion of the knee. The last culture was negative but the fluid was clearly purulent and the components were removed and she was placed in a spacer with an immobilizer.

After her discharge in early September 1993, Ms. Drevenak * * * had a range of medical problems relating to the knee * * * Medical records also show that Ms. Drevenak's problems with right knee infection persisted into 1996.

On March 8, 1996, Ms. Drevenak filed suit against Dr. Abendschein, alleging negligence, medical malpractice, with respect to her total right knee replacement. In essence, Ms. Drevenak maintained that Dr. Abendschein failed to recognize and properly treat the symptoms of deep infection that caused her patellar tendon to rupture twice, and ultimately forced the removal of her right knee prosthesis. * * *

ANALYSIS

Ms. Drevenak's arguments on appeal are directed toward the trial court's assessment of the expert evidence presented, and its findings pertaining to sinus and sinus tract drainage. In particular, she maintains, in essence, that her experts were superior to those of the defense because, consistent with *Frye [v. United States, 54 App.D.C. 46, 293 F. 1013 (1923])* and *Daubert [v. Merrell Dow Pharmaceuticals, Inc., 509 U.S. 579, 125 L.Ed.2d 469, 113 S.Ct. 2786 (1993)]*, her experts supported their opinions with scientific publications. Before addressing Ms. Drevenak's specific contentions, we set forth a summary of the pertinent expert testimony * * *.

In this complex and hard-fought case, five experts testified during trial. Two of the experts rendered opinions relating to infectious diseases and Ms. Drevenak's right knee infection * * * Dr. Abendschein also testified on his own behalf.

* * *

At trial, Dr. Smialowicz stated that Dr. Abendschein failed to "fulfill[ ] the national [standard of] care required in diagnosing and treating ... a possible postoperative infection after he performed the total knee replacement on ... [Ms.] Drevenak on March 10, 1993." Specifically, he failed to recognize "clues" that deep infection was present. Had Dr. Abendschein diagnosed the deep infection during the critical first four weeks in the postoperative period ... [and had a debridement been performed] followed by six weeks of antibiotic therapy, the literature and the experience has been that there is a significant salvage rate of 80 percent or more in saving these prostheses, and that once one ignores these signs and clues, and once one gets past one month, and the farther you get past it, you are now in the chronic stage of a prosthetic knee infection, and now if you try to perform the same procedure with debridement followed only by antibiotics in the attempt to salvage that prosthesis, your success rate drops down to something like 8 percent.

In connection with deep infection, Dr. Smialowicz referenced the work of Dr. Conen in the late 1950s on staphylococcus aureus and its dangers. He discussed group A beta-hemolytic streptococcus, which is "extremely virulent in infecting tissue and in destroying tissue."

* * *

Because Dr. Abendschein failed "to fulfill the national standard of care between March the 10th and the 22nd with respect to his diagnosis and treatment of [Ms.] Drevenak's infection ... ," in Dr. Smialowicz' view, "a sequence of other injuries [resulted,] aside from having to have the prosthesis eventually removed...." To support his opinion, Dr. Smialowicz referenced the TEXTBOOK OF INFECTIOUS DISEASES, edited by Dr. Gorbach, and specifically, Dr. Karchner's chapter on infected prostheses; Campbell's TEXTBOOK OF OPERATIVE ORTHO-PEDIC PROCEDURES; Dr. Lotke's POSTOPERATIVE INFECTIONS; and THE PRINCIPLES AND PRACTICE OF INFECTIOUS DISEASES by Doctors Mandel, Douglas and Bennett.

* * *

On cross-examination, counsel for Dr. Abendschein used Dr. Smia-lowicz' earlier deposition to try to show his lack of familiarity then with some of the medical works on which he relied at trial, or to point out that counsel for Ms. Drevenak had sent him the material. In fact, during his deposition, Dr. Smialowicz apparently referenced only one study, which appeared in the AMERICAN JOURNAL OF KNEE SURGERY IN SPRING 1996, "Diagnosis and Management of the Infected Total Knee Arthroplasty" by Simmons and Stern.

Defense infectious disease expert, Dr. Mayrer, had a different evaluation of Dr. Abendschein's course of action. He opined that: "Dr. Abendschein comported with the [ ] standard of care expected of an orthopedic surgeon following [Ms. Drevenak's] knee procedure, and subsequent events relating to two or three episodes of dehiscence, opening up of the surgical wound that Dr. Abendschein had initially closed." He found Ms. Drevenak's "mild post-operative temperature" to be "fairly typical," based on his experience and involvement with "the dozen of scores and hundreds of orthopedic patients." The "intermittent drainage" from Ms. Drevenak's wound was not unusual and "did not constitute ... any evidence of a serious side effect or infection" at the time of Ms. Drevenak's discharge from the hospital.

* * *

Mayrer acknowledged that an April 9th culture of the fluid drainage from the site of Ms. Drevenak's surgical knee wound contained "Group A Beta, beta strep," and "staph aureus." However, he rejected Dr. Smialowicz' theory of a synergistic infection based on the presence of the two organisms. He opined that a synergistic infection was "not at all likely." Had there been a synergistic infection, the consequences would have been worse than those previously identified by Dr. Mayrer. * * *

* * *

Of the three standard of care experts, Dr. Larry M. Shall testified for Ms. Drevenak * * *

* * *

Dr. Shall became "familiar with the national standard of care required of a board certified orthopedic surgeon in diagnosing and treating an infected knee prosthesis" through his training, his practice and continuing medical education, and attending conferences sponsored by the American Academy of Orthopedic Surgeons. He opined that Dr. Abendschein's diagnosis, care and treatment of Ms. Drevenak "fell below the standard of care," essentially because he ignored warning signs and "no attempt was made to make a definitive diagnosis of a deep space infection until the time had passed where salvage of the prosthesis was no longer possible or no longer probable."

* * *

When Ms. Drevenak's counsel asked whether Dr. Shall was "aware of any treatise which [he] would consider to be authoritative in the diagnosis and treatment of an infected knee prosthesis," he mentioned "several." In terms of the relationship between these articles and his testimony, Dr. Shall stated that his opinions were "formulated", in part, "from the existing literature." [ ]

On cross-examination Dr. Shall estimated that "5 percent" of his experience concerned total knee replacement surgeries. * * * Dr. Shall also rejected the theory that Ms. Drevenak's patellar tendon ruptured because of trauma, but indicated that he has never attended to a "total knee arthropasty" patient with a ruptured tendon.

Dr. Randall Lewis, a Clinical Professor of Orthopedic Surgery at George Washington University and Associate Clinical Professor of Orthopedic Surgery at Georgetown University, with medical privileges at Sibley Memorial Hospital, Georgetown University Hospital, George Washington University Hospital, Suburban Hospital and the National Rehabilitation Hospital, testified for the defense. Dr. Lewis graduated with highest honors from Yale University in 1965 and with honors from Harvard Medical School in 1969 * * * .

* * *

Dr. Lewis estimated that during his career, he has performed between 2,000 and 3,000 total knee replacement surgeries, including approximately 12 to 15 involving the repair of a ruptured tendon. Other doctors have referred cases, manifesting complications of joint replacement, to Dr. Lewis. During a twenty-five year period, Dr. Lewis has "seen probably 125, perhaps 150 infected total knees."

Dr. Lewis opined that Ms. Drevenak did not have a deep knee infection between March 10th and March 22nd * * *

* * *

My opinion is that the clinical judgment is what counts; that it is not required that you put a needle into the knee if there is no sign . . . that there is a deep infection. It is possible to get information from that, but it is possible . . . to introduce infection, although that is infrequent, but also to be misled. There is a recent study from a Dr. Harris at Harvard in which—a prospective study . . . of every patient who came to have a second operation had an aspiration, and what Dr. Harris' group found was that the results of the aspiration were not useful. * * *

* * *

Dr. Richard Grant, who is board certified in orthopedic surgery, and a director and board examiner for the American Board of Orthopedic Surgery, also testified on behalf of Dr. Abendschein. Dr. Grant received his under graduate degree from Stanford University in 1971, and completed his medical degree at the Howard University College of Medicine in 1976.

* * *

Dr. Grant has performed "hundreds" of total knee replacement operations, and participated in "over 600, 700 total joint replacements." * * *

Dr. Grant expressed the opinion to a degree of reasonable medical probability that * * * Abendschein followed an appropriate course of treatment and action, including consulting with an infectious disease specialist, thoroughly evaluating the knee, administering intravenous antibiotics, irrigation and debridement of the knee. * * *

* * *

Sufficiency of the Evidence and the Applicable Legal Standard

The first issues raised by Ms. Drevenak pertain to the trial court's evaluation of the sufficiency of the evidence, particularly its assessment of the testimony presented by the experts. Noting that the trial court characterized the case as "a battle of experts," Ms. Drevenak asserts that: "The trial court admitted that the published scientifically reliable evidence favored [Ms. Drevenak]," but nonetheless gave greater weight to the defense experts whose testimony was not well supported by scientific evidence. * * *

* * *

Expert testimony is not binding on the trier of fact [ ] and the trier of fact is given considerable latitude in determining the weight to be given such evidence. *Id* * * *

* * *

In light of this court's prior approach to sufficiency of the evidence challenges in medical malpractice cases, we first address Ms. Drevenak's argument that the "[*Frye*] standard should be used by a trial court sitting without a jury in evaluating expert testimony." On the record before us, we decline to apply *Frye* to the sufficiency of the evidence issue. *Frye* and *Daubert, supra*, not only apply to the admissibility, instead of the sufficiency, of evidence; but equally important, to "novel scientific evidence" or "a novel scientific test or a unique controversial methodology or technique." *See Ibn–Tamas v. United States*, 455 A.2d 893, 895 (D.C. 1983) (Gallagher, J., concurring) ("*Frye* requires the profferor of the expert on a new scientific theory to show that the evidence is not still in the experimental stage but has gained a scientific acceptance substantial enough to warrant the exercise of judicial discretion in favor of admissibility"); * * *. In contrast to *Frye, supra*, which concerned early consideration of "the systolic blood pressure deception" test, the forerunner of the polygraph test, and which is followed in this jurisdiction, Ms. Drevenak's case does not relate to any novel scientific evidence or test, nor to any unique, controversial methodology or technique. Rather, what is at issue in her case, primarily, is the exercise of clinical judgment based upon specialized medical knowledge. No question is presented here concerning the integrity of the knee prosthesis implanted in Ms. Drevenak's knee; nor is there any indication that the method of aspiration used to obtain cultures of the drainage from her knee was in the experimental stage at the time the aspirations were done. Therefore, we do not regard Ms. Drevenak's case as fitting the mold of one in which novel scientific evidence or a unique controversial methodology or technique is involved.

In arguing for the applicability of the *Frye* principle to the sufficiency of the evidence, Ms. Drevenak's counsel expresses concern about determining the reliability of expert evidence. However, there are indicia of reliability other than sole reliance on the quantity of published scientific articles. Even *Daubert*, [ ], as Ms. Drevenak acknowledges, identifies publication as only one factor in considering the admissibility of expert evidence, and *Daubert* specifically states that: "publication ... does not necessarily correlate with reliability." [ ]. Indeed, the following factors are all relevant to assessing the reliability of an expert's testimony in a medical malpractice action: the expert's training, board certification in the pertinent medical specialty, specialized medical experience, attendance at national seminars and meetings, familiarity with published specialized medical literature, and discussions with medical specialists from other geographical regions. Of these factors, the trial court obviously emphasized training, board certification in the pertinent medical specialty, and specialized medical experience, but did not ignore the expert's familiarity with published specialized medical literature.

The trial judge credited the testimony of the defense experts, generally, because they were "more qualified...." He explained that:

If you look at the collective experience of these experts, it's clear that the defense experts had many more years of practice and experience in the areas that they were talking about than [Ms. Drevenak's] experts. And they also had a lot more experience in the number of cases that they'd seen over the course of their practice compared to [Ms. Drevenak's] experts.

The record on appeal supports the trial court's conclusions regarding the qualifications and experience of the experts. Dr. Smialowicz, Ms. Drevenak's infectious disease expert was not certified in internal medicine nor in infectious diseases. Thus there is a basis in the record for determining that his testimony should not be credited, [ ] or that the testimony of the defense expert should be given greater weight. In contrast to Dr. Smialowicz, Dr. Mayrer, the defense expert in infectious diseases, who holds degrees from Columbia College and Yale Medical School, has taught at Yale, Johns Hopkins, and the University of Maryland, * * * is board certified both in internal medicine and infectious diseases. Furthermore, in comparison with Dr. Smialowicz who consults on at least two cases of prosthetic infection per year; over the past twenty years, Dr. Mayrer has consulted on one case of prosthetic infection per month, including hip (75 to 80 percent) and knee joint infection. * * *. Given the respective training, board certifications, experience, publications, and knowledge of the specialized literature, we see no reason to question the trial judge's decision to credit the testimony of Dr. Mayrer. * * *

[AFFIRMED]

TATE v. DETROIT RECEIVING HOSPITAL

Court of Appeals of Michigan, 2002.
249 Mich.App. 212, 642 N.W.2d 346.

COOPER, P.J.

* * *

Robert Hall was admitted to defendant hospital after suffering a stroke. During Hall's hospitalization a urinary catheter was inserted. Shortly thereafter, defendant's employees made a notation on Hall's charts regarding a possible urinary tract infection. However, Hall was transferred from defendant hospital without any treatment for this possible infection. On the day of transfer Hall suffered a seizure and went into a coma. Thereafter, Hall's condition slowly deteriorated and he died approximately a month after his stay at defendant hospital.

Plaintiff filed a complaint against defendant hospital, raising general allegations against defendant's employees and agents. Dr. David Lavine, who supervised certain medical students and residents, treated Hall. A third-year medical student noted the presence of bacteria in Hall's urine and indicated a concern about urosepsis. When Hall was transferred from defendant hospital, an obstetrics/gynecology resident noted Hall's temperature of 99.2 degrees. Plaintiff argues that these findings indicate that Hall suffered a urinary tract infection that needed medical attention. She asserts that Hall's seizure and ultimate death were the result of this untreated infection.

In August 1997, plaintiff filed a complaint and an affidavit of merit signed by Dr. Jack Kaufman. The affidavit stated that Dr. Kaufman was board certified and a specialist in internal medicine. * * * Defendant argued that Dr. Kaufman was not qualified to render testimony against Dr. Lavine * * *. Dr. Lavine was board certified in internal medicine, critical care medicine, and nephrology. The trial court ultimately granted defendant's motion, concluding that Dr. Kaufman was not board certified in the same specialties as Dr. Lavine and was therefore unqualified to testify.

* * *

III. ANALYSIS

Plaintiff essentially argues that when a health professional is board certified in several specialties, § 2169 should be read so as to allow an expert to testify if that expert is board certified in the same specialty being practiced by the health professional *at the time* of the alleged malpractice. We agree.

Generally, a trial court determines the need for expert witness testimony pursuant to MRE 702, which provides:

If the court determines that recognized scientific, technical, or other specialized knowledge will assist the trier of fact to understand the evidence or to determine a fact in issue a witness qualified as an expert by knowledge, skill, experience, training, or education, may testify thereto in the form of an opinion or otherwise.

In malpractice actions, each party is obligated to provide an expert witness to articulate the applicable standard of care involved. [ ]. Moreover, each party's expert witness must file an affidavit of merit as provided in § 2912d. [ ]. Section 2912d describes the contents of an affidavit of merit and states that an attorney must reasonably believe that the expert witness meets the requirements of MCL 600.2169. Section 2169 provides in pertinent part:

(1) In an action alleging medical malpractice, a person shall not give expert testimony on the appropriate standard of practice or care unless the person is licensed as a health professional in this state or another state and meets the following criteria:

(a) If the party against whom or on whose behalf the testimony is offered is a specialist, *specializes at the time of the occurrence that is the basis for the action* in the same specialty as the party against whom or on whose behalf the testimony is offered. However, if the party against whom or on whose behalf the testimony is offered is a specialist who is board certified, the expert witness must be a specialist who is board certified in that specialty.

(b) Subject to subdivision (c), during the year immediately preceding the date of the occurrence that is the basis for the claim or action, devoted a majority of his or her professional time to either or both of the following:

(i) The active clinical practice of the same health profession in which the party against whom or on whose behalf the testimony is offered is licensed and, if that party is a specialist, the active clinical practice of that specialty.

(ii) The instruction of students in an accredited health professional school or accredited residency or clinical research program in the same health profession in which the party against whom or on whose behalf the testimony is offered is licensed and, if that party is a specialist, an accredited health professional school or accredited residency or clinical research program in the same specialty. [Emphasis supplied.]

Furthermore, to determine the qualifications of an expert witness in a medical malpractice case, subsection 2169(2) requires the court to evaluate (a) the witness' educational and professional training, (b) the witness' area of specialization, (c) the length of time the witness has been engaged in the active clinical practice or instruction of the specialty, and (d) the relevancy of the witness' testimony.

* * *

Subsection 2169(1)(a) specifically states that an expert witness must "specialize[ ] at the time of the occurrence that is the basis for the action" in the same specialty as the defendant physician. The statute further discusses board-certified specialists and requires that experts testifying against or on behalf of such specialists also be "board certified in that specialty." * * *

The trial court in this case failed to correctly interpret and apply the provisions of § 2169. In fact, we find that the trial court's strained reading of the statute actually defeats its true purpose. The Legislature's intent behind the enactment of § 2169 is clear. As pointed out by our Supreme Court in *McDougall [v. Schanz,* 461 Mich. 15,] 25 [ ], the Legislature enacted § 2169 to make sure that expert witnesses actually practice or teach medicine. In other words, to make sure that experts will have firsthand practical expertise in the subject matter about which they are testifying. In particular, with the malpractice crisis facing high-risk specialists, such as neurosurgeons, orthopedic surgeons and ob/gyns, this reform is necessary to insure that in malpractice suits against specialists the expert witnesses actually practice in the same specialty. This will protect the integrity of our judicial system by requiring real experts instead of "hired guns."

* * *

Certainly § 2169 cannot be read or interpreted to require an exact match of every board certification held by a defendant physician. Such a "perfect match" requirement would be an onerous task and in many cases make it virtually impossible to bring a medical malpractice case * * * Thus, where a defendant physician has several board certifications and the alleged malpractice involves only one of these specialties, § 2169 requires an expert witness to possess the same specialty as that engaged in by the defendant physician during the course of the alleged malpractice.

* * *

Reversed and remanded.

Notes

1) Distinguish cause-in-fact and legal cause. The *Richardson* court followed the general rule that one professional (in this case, a nurse) may be qualified to testify on deviations from the standard of care of his/her profession, but not necessarily the cause-in-fact of the decedent's death. Once the expert is qualified to testify, his or her expertise goes to the weight of the testimony.

2) *Frye* and *Daubert* are generally cited to determine whether novel or controversial scientific methods, technique, devices or theories have sufficient reliability or have gained sufficient merit in scientific circles to be admissible in court. Is *Frye* or *Daubert* applicable if the evidence or testimony in question is not a methodology or technique, but the exercise of clinical judgment based upon specialized medical knowledge?

3) *Tate* raised the issue of whether a physician board certified in several specialties should be allowed to testify if he is not board certified in the specialty being practiced at the time of the alleged malpractice. A related question is whether a specialist in one field is qualified to testify on a matter in a related field. The trial court has wide latitude in determining whether a proposed expert has adequate scientific, technical or specialized knowledge, skill, experience or training to offer an opinion that will assist the trier of fact in understanding the evidence. The availability of expert witnesses can be considered. In a jurisdiction where expert medical testimony is readily available, the court may be less willing to allow experts in related fields to offer testimony. In those jurisdictions where willing medical experts are in shorter supply, some courts have allowed greater leeway.

Using *Frye* and *Daubert* principles, how would you address this issue if a plaintiff alleged that her limited resources prevented her from securing a high-priced specialist for testimony?

SECTION C.   PROOF OF MEDICAL NEGLIGENCE WITHOUT EXPERTS

BENSON v. TKACH

Court of Civil Appeals of Oklahoma, Division Two, 2001.
2001 OK CIV APP 100, 30 P.3d 402.

TAYLOR, JUDGE:

* * *

Plaintiff is the daughter of Edd A. Robbins. In October 1994, Mrs. Robbins underwent hip replacement surgery. The surgery was performed by Dr. Tkach (who Plaintiff asserts is an employee of McBride Clinic) at Bone and Joint Hospital. Mrs. Robbins was later transferred to Healthsouth Rehabilitation Hospital for rehabilitation. After the surgery, Mrs. Robbins developed an infection and died on June 11, 1995.

Plaintiff filed a malpractice lawsuit. She asserted Defendants acted negligently, causing Mrs. Robbins pain and suffering and, ultimately, her death. * * *

* * * Defendants sought summary judgment. Defendants asserted they were entitled to summary judgment because Plaintiff had failed to produce any expert testimony in support of her allegations. Defendants submitted affidavits from Dr. Tkach and Healthsouth's director of nursing denying any negligence.

Plaintiff filed a response, attaching two affidavits. One was from an Arizona physician, Dr. Vadee Kroft [who opined that plaintiff's injuries were caused by Defendant's negligence, but provided no basis for the opinion.]

* * *

Plaintiff also attached her own affidavit, in which she states [in part]:

> * * * My mother continued to suffer greatly from her left hip and upon several occasions, I asked Dr. Tkach about replacing the left hip joint, or at least removing it so the infected area could heal. Dr. Tkach refused to do so and stated that "Medicare had his hands tied," which told me he would not remove the source of the infection because there was no money to pay for the surgery.

Defendants filed replies, asserting Dr. Kroft's affidavit failed to include qualifying statements and specific allegations of negligence, and thus was insufficient to avoid summary judgment. Defendants also asserted Plaintiff's affidavit was insufficient to establish malpractice because Plaintiff was not a medical expert.

* * *

Normally, when a patient sues a physician for failure to properly diagnose or treat the patient, the issue of fact is one of science and must be established and determined upon the testimony of skilled, professional witnesses. [ ]. In other words, the rule in medical malpractice cases is that a physician's negligence must ordinarily be established by expert medical testimony. [citation omitted] A plaintiff has the burden of proving through expert testimony: (1) the standard of medical care required of physicians, (2) that a duty existed and was breached, and (3) that this breach of duty resulted in harm to the plaintiff.

Plaintiff essentially asserts she has satisfied this rule by introducing Dr. Kroft's affidavit, in which he generally opines that all the defendants were negligent and all caused Plaintiff's mother's injury. We hold that the affidavit is not sufficient to satisfy the rule.

* * *

Similarly, Plaintiff has failed to produce any evidence showing the required standard of care. The rationale for this rule is that a trier of fact must have sufficient technical and scientific testimony at its disposal to answer a scientific and technical question of fact. [ ] Dr. Kroft's blanket statement opining liability, without providing any information as to the required standard of care, and without offering any reason for his conclusions, is simply not sufficient to satisfy the rule. In regard to the affidavit's failure to offer reasons, the Oklahoma Supreme Court has recognized that:

> The reasons given in support of the opinions rather than the abstract opinions are of importance, and the opinion is of no greater value than the reasons given in its support. If no rational basis for the opinion appears, or if the facts from which the opinion was derived do not justify it, the opinion is of no probative force, and it does not constitute evidence sufficient to authorize submission of the issue to the jury. . . .

Downs v. Longfellow Corp., 1960 OK 107, 351 P.2d 999 (quoting 32 C.J.S. Evidence § 569). We conclude Dr. Kroft's affidavit is insufficient to satisfy the rule.

However, we nonetheless agree with Plaintiff that summary judgment is inappropriate. While expert testimony is *ordinarily* required in cases involving medical negligence . . . "when a physician's lack of care has been such as to require only common knowledge and experience to understand and judge it, expert medical testimony is not required to establish that care."[ ]. The court explained that the need for expert testimony is limited to establishing an appropriate standard of care; however, the court also stated that an expert opinion *may* be necessary to show the proper standard of care. [ ]. The court did not state that expert testimony is *always* necessary to show the appropriate standard of care.

According to Plaintiff's affidavit, Dr. Tkach refused to perform additional surgery to allow her mother's infected area to heal because, " 'Medicare had his hands tied,' which told me he would not remove the source of the infection because there was no money to pay for the surgery." Reasonable persons could infer from this remark and the surrounding circumstances that Dr. Tkach did not provide what he considered proper treatment because of financial considerations.

* * * In her affidavit, Plaintiff attested that prior to the surgery on her mother's hip, she was not suffering from infections or receiving medication for infection, but that, after the surgery and the transfer to Healthsouth, the wound began to drain and the decedent was in great pain.

* * * Plaintiff further stated that, in spite of subsequent corrective surgery, her mother continued to suffer great pain until her death.

Based upon Plaintiff's testimony, reasonable persons could conclude that the failure of [Defendants] to provide proper medical treatment constituted gross negligence. The decedent's injury was so apparent and objective that expert testimony was not necessary for the issue of negligence to reach the jury.

REVERSED AND REMANDED.

MILLER v. JACOBY

Supreme Court of Washington, 2001.
145 Wn.2d 65, 33 P.3d 68.

IRELAND, J.

In this case, we review a Court of Appeals' decision affirming summary dismissal of Petitioner Mary Lou Miller's medical malpractice claims. At issue is whether expert medical testimony is necessary to a determination that health care providers' actions, in placing a Penrose drain in a patient's body during surgery and in not removing the entire drain postoperatively, constitute negligence.

Whether the drain was negligently placed during surgery is not readily observable to laypersons, and thus expert testimony must be presented to establish the standard of care necessary during the procedure. No such testimony was presented. However, inadvertently leaving a foreign object in a patient's body is negligent as a matter of law. There is a genuine issue of material fact as to the health care providers' alleged negligence in failing to remove the entire drain postoperatively.

* * *

FACTS

On January 30, 1997, Mary Lou Miller (Miller) was admitted to Northwest Hospital by her physician, Robert C. Ireton, M.D. (Ireton). Miller underwent surgery to remove kidney stones (pyelolithotomy) and to repair a malformed right kidney (pyeloplasty).

According to Ireton, the surgery was "uneventful and without complications." Before final closure of the incision, Ireton placed a

Penrose drain in the wound to facilitate postoperative healing.[1] Ireton intended that the Penrose drain would be removed some days later.

Dr. Karny Jacoby (Jacoby), the urologist who provided weekend coverage for Ireton, saw Miller in the hospital on February 1 and February 2. On February 1, Jacoby found that the dressing over the Penrose drain was moist. The dressing was changed, and Jacoby ordered that the drain be removed later the same day if the dressing stayed dry.

On the morning of February 2, Leslie Rockom, R.N. (Rockom), an employee of Northwest Hospital, attempted to remove the Penrose drain as Jacoby had ordered. Rockom felt resistance and notified Jacoby, who removed the drain and disposed of it with the soiled dressing.

In her deposition, Rockom estimated that since 1965 she has cared for about 100 patients with Penrose drains. She estimated that in about 5 cases, she encountered resistance that caused her to notify a physician.

Jacoby stated that she "did not note any resistance or difficulty in removing the drain," so she did not "feel that it was necessary to examine the Penrose drain in detail."

Miller stated that when Rockom tried to remove the drain "it resisted her pull and caused me pain." Miller also stated that when Jacoby removed the drain, the doctor said, "I hope I got it all."

Jacoby was not present when the drain was placed, and Ireton was not present when Jacoby removed the drain. Ireton stated that he was not advised that any difficulty or complication had been encountered in removing the drain.

Ireton next saw Miller on February 3, noted that she was doing well, and discharged her from the hospital. In the course of follow-up visits with Ireton, Miller reported pain in her right flank and abdomen. Ireton ordered tests, including an intravenous pyelogram on April 29, 1997, to evaluate her complaints. The diagnostic imaging report included impressions that there were "post-operative changes consistent with a right pyeloplasty" and that there was "radiopaque material in the soft tissues adjacent to the ... right kidney." . It was reported that the material "may represent a retained drain or sponge." *Id.* The findings were communicated to Ireton, and he informed Miller that he suspected a portion of the Penrose drain had been retained in the area of the surgical site.

Miller subsequently sought treatment by Robert Weissman, M.D. (Weissman). On May 23, 1997, Weissman performed surgery to remove the foreign body—a 5.5 centimeter length of collapsed plastic tubing. Weissman's operative record contains the following observation:

After more careful blunt and sharp dissection the drain was identified on the inferior aspect of the incision, several cm anterior to the

---

1. A Penrose drain is a piece of soft tubing that is placed into a wound area to   drain off fluid.

drain scar, and the drain was grasped and removed intact. The proximal portion was noted to be a straight edge and the distal portion an angled, more ragged and irregular edge, possibly representing where the drain broke off.

In granting Jacoby's motion for summary judgment, the trial court considered a declaration by Wayne Weissman, M.D, a board-certified urologist, who reviewed the operative record of Miller's second surgery and stated as follows: Given the fact that one end of the Penrose drain removed by Dr. [Robert] Weissman was ragged and irregular, it is highly likely that the Penrose drain was inadvertently sutured in place, deep within the wound, below the muscle layers. It is the usual and customary practice to lay the Penrose drain in place, deep within the wound, and only secure the drain with a single superficial suture at the skin level. [ ]. He also stated that "it would not be reasonable for Dr. Jacoby to examine in detail the edges of the Penrose drain, as there was no indication of a problem in removing the drain." [ ]. He opined that "Jacoby met the standard of care of a reasonably prudent urologist when removing the Penrose drain." [ ].

* * *

ANALYSIS

* * *

Expert Testimony

Generally, expert testimony is necessary to establish the standard of care for a health care provider in a medical malpractice action. [ ]. Washington courts, however, have long recognized that inadvertently leaving a foreign object in a patient's body is negligent:

[T]he court can say, as a matter of law, that, when a surgeon inadvertently introduces into a wound a foreign substance, closes up the wound, leaving that foreign substance in the body, there being no possibility of any good purpose resulting therefrom, that act constitutes negligence. [ ]

When medical facts are "observable by [a layperson's] senses and describable without medical training," a plaintiff can establish the standard of care for a health care provider without expert testimony. [ ]

In the case before us, the proper use, purpose, and insertion of a Penrose drain are not within the common understanding or experience of a layperson. Therefore, Miller must present expert medical testimony to show that Ireton acted negligently. Such testimony must be presented to establish the standard of care under the circumstances.

We disagree with the Court of Appeals' majority that the same conclusion can be reached regarding the actions of Rockom (Northwest Hospital) and Jacoby.

The facts of the instant case vary somewhat from a straightforward "foreign object" case in that Ireton, the surgeon, did not inadvertently leave the Penrose drain in the patient's body. Rather, the drain was deliberately left in place to facilitate recovery. Rockom and Jacoby attempted to remove the drain in a separate, postoperative procedure.

Nevertheless, as Judge Appelwick notes in his dissent, "The moment of Dr. Jacoby's incomplete removal of the drain resulted in a foreign object that was placed in the body intentionally and temporarily during surgery, then becoming a foreign object inadvertently and permanently left in the patient at the completion of surgery." [ ].

Rockom and Jacoby were the health care providers charged with the removal procedure. Rockom, an experienced nurse, stated that she was concerned enough about the resistance when she tried to remove the drain to request Jacoby's assistance. In addition, when viewed in the light most favorable to Miller, it is reasonable to infer from the statement attributed to Jacoby—"I hope I got it all"—that the doctor was somewhat doubtful about complete removal. A portion of the Penrose drain, a foreign object, inadvertently remained in Miller's body. "Simply put, it is not reasonable prudence to unintentionally leave a foreign substance in a surgical patient." [ ] Expert testimony is not needed to assert negligence under these circumstances.

Res Ipsa Loquitur. Miller argues that the evidence she presented is sufficient to entitle her to the inference of negligence established by the doctrine of res ipsa loquitur.

To prevail on a complaint for negligence, a plaintiff must show duty, a breach of that duty, and injury. [ ]. In addition, a plaintiff must show that the breach of duty was a proximate cause of his or her injury. [ ] In some cases, breach of duty may be proved by circumstantial evidence under the doctrine of res ipsa loquitur. [ ]. Under circumstances proper to its application, res ipsa loquitur can apply to physicians and hospitals. [ ]. For res ipsa loquitur to apply, the following three criteria must be met:

"(1) [T]he occurrence producing the injury must be of a kind which ordinarily does not occur in the absence of negligence; (2) the injury is caused by an agency or instrumentality within the exclusive control of the defendant; and (3) the injury-causing occurrence must not be due to any contribution on the part of the plaintiff." [ ]

There is no evidence to suggest that Miller contributed to the injury-causing occurrence. Therefore, the final criterion of the doctrine is met as to Miller's claims against her health care providers.

However, Miller must also demonstrate that her injury would not ordinarily occur in the absence of negligence. Without knowing the professional standard of care for a health care provider placing a Penrose drain during surgery, a layperson would not be able to determine that Miller's injury would not have occurred absent negligence by Ireton. In addition, Ireton did not have exclusive control of the drain following surgery. The drain appeared to be functioning properly while in place, and Ireton was not present when Rockom and Jacoby removed the drain several days later. For these reasons, the doctrine of res ipsa loquitur is not available to impose liability on Ireton.

While the doctrine may be available as to Rockom and Jacoby, there remains a question of fact in this case as to whether these health care providers had exclusive control of the drain. There is a question of fact as to whether exclusive control can be established so as to allow an inference that Rockom and/or Jacoby were liable under the doctrine of res ipsa loquitur for leaving a piece of the drain in Miller's body. This issue should be presented to the fact finder.

Conclusion

The summary dismissal of Miller's claim as to Dr. Ireton is affirmed. The summary dismissal of Miller's claims as to Dr. Jacoby and Northwest Hospital is reversed.

COSTANTINO v. HERZOG

United States Court of Appeals for the Second Circuit, 2000.
203 F.3d 164.

McLAUGHLIN, Circuit Judge:

Background

Dr. David Herzog was the obstetrician who delivered Amanda Costantino. During the delivery, Amanda's shoulder got trapped behind her mother's pubic bone, a condition known as "shoulder dystocia." While attempting to remedy the condition, Dr. Herzog performed: (1) the McRoberts maneuver: pulling Mrs. Costantino's legs toward her head and applying pressure to the area above her pubic bone; (2) the Woods corkscrew: reaching into the womb and rotating baby Amanda to release her trapped shoulder; and (3) the Posterior Arm Sweep: delivering Amanda's free posterior arm to create more space. Ultimately, Dr. Herzog delivered Amanda, but she was born with "Erb's Palsy," an impairment to the nerves running to the arm.

The Costantinos filed a diversity action against Dr. Herzog in the United States District Court for the Eastern District of New York (Gleeson, J.) alleging that by pulling and rotating Amanda's head during the delivery, he had caused her Erb's Palsy. They claimed that Dr. Herzog had deviated from accepted standards of obstetrical practice, and had therefore committed malpractice under governing New York law. The defense denied any malpractice, asserting that Amanda's Erb's Palsy was caused by the normal forces of labor.

The case was tried to a jury. Plaintiffs' first witness was the defendant, Dr. Herzog. Counsel questioned him on an excerpt from a medical treatise edited by Steven G. Gabbe, entitled Obstetrics, that stated: "Once a vaginal delivery has begun, the obstetrician must resist the temptation to rotate the head to a transverse axis." Dr. Herzog acknowledged attempting to rotate Amanda's head, but disagreed with the statement read from the Gabbe treatise.

Plaintiffs' medical expert was Dr. Bernard Nathanson. Among his qualifications, Dr. Nathanson testified that he was a fellow of the American College of Obstetricians and Gynecologists ("ACOG"). ACOG, according to Dr. Nathanson, "is an organization of thirty thousand obstetricians and gynecologists," that "sets up courses for doctors who are in practice so that they will continue to be current with ongoing research." Dr. Nathanson added that ACOG "publishes a great deal of material which serves to contribute to setting a standard of care for obstetricians and gynecologists."

Relying in part on various journals published by ACOG, as well as on the Gabbe treatise, Dr. Nathanson proceeded to testify that it was a departure from the standard of medical care to engage in "any manipulation of the head" during a shoulder dystocia delivery because it does nothing to relieve the trapped shoulder and greatly increases the risk of causing Erb's Palsy.

The defense sought to rebut this theory in several ways. Primarily, the defense relied on another learned treatise—Williams Obstetrics—which stated that "downward traction . . . to the fetal head" was among "the most popular techniques" used to remedy shoulder dystocia. Dr. Nathanson conceded that the Williams treatise was authoritative and that applying traction to the fetal head was indeed the "most popular" treatment technique for shoulder dystocia. He continued, nevertheless, to insist that use of that technique constituted malpractice.

The defense also sought to justify Dr. Herzog's management of Amanda's delivery by introducing a 15-minute videotape from ACOG's audiovisual library, entitled "Shoulder Dystocia." The tape was, according to the defense, "put out by [ACOG] to educate physicians" and portrayed the various techniques recommended to remedy shoulder dystocia.

Both the parties and Judge Gleeson recognized that the ACOG video was hearsay under Federal Rule of Evidence 801. The defense nevertheless sought to introduce it pursuant to the "learned treatise" exception to the hearsay rule set forth in Rule 803(18). Plaintiffs objected, arguing that Rule 803(18) enumerates only "published treatises, periodicals, or pamphlets" as learned treatises, and therefore could not encompass videotapes. Plaintiffs also argued that no foundation had been laid for the video.

After an in camera review of the videotape, Judge Gleeson ruled it admissible. With respect to whether a video could qualify as a learned treatise under Rule 803(18), Judge Gleeson reasoned: "I think . . . focusing on the distinction between . . . something in the form of a periodical or a book, as opposed [to] a videotape is just overly artificial."

As to the foundation, Judge Gleeson found, based on his in camera review, that the ACOG video "was a dissemination to the doctors in the relevant medical community of how they should go about dealing with this problem [of shoulder dystocia]." He also found that it had been "well established" through trial testimony that ACOG was "the source of authoritative information regarding the practices to be used by obstetricians in these circumstances." Included in the trial testimony regarding ACOG and the videotape, were Dr. Nathanson's concessions that he had: (1) viewed the videotape at a staff conference some years ago; and (2) testified in a prior action that he generally accepted "the standards promulgated by ACOG" within the field of obstetrics as "authoritative."

* * *

In its closing credits, the video scrolls across the screen a printed disclaimer, stating:

> This video does not define a standard of care, nor is it intended to dictate an exclusive course of management. It presents recognized techniques of clinical practice for consideration by health care providers for incorporation into their practices.

The closing credits also reveal that the video was awarded the Scientific Program Award at the 1995 Annual Clinical Meeting of ACOG.

* * *

DISCUSSION

I. *The ACOG Video*

The Costantinos argue that because videotapes are not mentioned in Rule 803(18), they can never be learned treatises. Alternatively, they maintain that even if videos can be learned treatises, reversal is still required because Judge Gleeson: (1) erred in admitting the ACOG video without proper foundation; and (2) should have excluded the video as unduly confusing and prejudicial under Rule 403. None of these contentions warrant reversal.

A. *Rule 803(18)*

The primary question presented is whether videotapes can be admitted as learned treatises pursuant to Rule 803(18). We are the first federal Court of Appeals to address this question, though various state courts have considered it under their cognate learned treatise exceptions, and have forged no consensus. * * *

We review Judge Gleeson's legal conclusion that videos can constitute learned treatises de novo. * * *

In its entirety, Rule 803(18) provides:

> The following are not excluded by the hearsay rule, even though the declarant is available as a witness:

> > (18) Learned treatises. To the extent called to the attention of an expert witness upon cross-examination or relied upon by the

expert witness in direct examination, statements contained in published treatises, periodicals, or pamphlets on a subject of history, medicine, or other science or art, established as a reliable authority by the testimony or admission of the witness or by other expert testimony or by judicial notice. If admitted, the statements may be read into evidence but may not be received as exhibits. Fed. R. Evid. 803(18).

The rationale for this exception is self-evident: so long as the authority of a treatise has been sufficiently established, the factfinder should have the benefit of expert learning on a subject, even though it is hearsay. * * *

Emphasizing plain language, the Costantinos argue that videos cannot fall within the scope of Rule 803(18) because unlike "published treatises, periodicals, or pamphlets," they are not specifically listed in the Rule. They rely on Simmons v. Yurchak, 28 Mass.App.Ct. 371, 551 N.E.2d 539 (Mass. App. Ct.), review denied, 407 Mass. 1103, 554 N.E.2d 851 (Mass. 1990), which accepted this contention, and affirmed a trial court's refusal to recognize videotapes as learned treatises under the Massachusetts version of Rule 803(18). According to the Simmons court: "adding videotapes to the list of materials in [the Massachusetts learned treatise exception] would constitute judicial legislation." [ ]

Uttering the dark incantation of "judicial legislation" is to substitute a slogan for an analysis. Indeed, we are exhorted in Rule 102 to interpret the Rules of Evidence to promote the "growth and development of the law ... to the end that the truth may be ascertained." Fed. R. Evid. 102. In this endeavor a certain measure of legislative judgment is required. * * *

In this case, we are compelled to "make law." For we agree with Judge Gleeson that it is just "overly artificial" to say that information that is sufficiently trustworthy to overcome the hearsay bar when presented in a printed learned treatise loses the badge of trustworthiness when presented in a videotape. We see no reason to deprive a jury of authoritative learning simply because it is presented in a visual, rather than printed, format. In this age of visual communication a videotape may often be the most helpful way to illuminate the truth in the spirit of Rule 102. [ ].

In sum, we agree with the Texas Court of Appeals that "videotapes are nothing more than a contemporary variant of a published treatise, periodical or pamphlet." [ ]. Accordingly, we hold that videotapes may be considered learned treatises under Rule 803(18).

* * *

AFFIRMED.

MILLER v. WILLBANKS

Supreme Court of Tennessee, Eastern Section, at Knoxville, 1999.
8 S.W.3d 607.

BARKER, J.

BACKGROUND

On September 19, 1995, Elizabeth Ann Miller gave birth to Heather Nicole Miller at the Morristown–Hamblen Hospital Association ("the Hospital"). Prior to delivery, Mrs. Miller signed a form authorizing Dr. David Willbanks of Hamblen Pediatric Associates, Inc., to provide postnatal examinations and treatment for Heather. The next day, the Hospital discharged Mrs. Miller but kept Heather pursuant to its policy of providing care for 48 hours to infants delivered by caesarean section.

Early September 21, Heather awoke with an elevated body temperature, heart rate, and respiratory rate. A nurse contacted Dr. Willbanks concerning Heather's condition. Dr. Willbanks went to the Hospital, examined Heather, and diagnosed her as suffering from Drug Withdrawal Syndrome (DWS). Dr. Willbanks, though, did not test Heather for the presence of drugs or discuss his diagnosis with Mrs. Miller. By contacting relatives of Mrs. Miller, the Hospital alerted Heather's parents to the infant's condition. After becoming aware of Heather's condition, Wayne Miller, Elizabeth Ann Miller's husband and Heather's father, contacted the Hospital by telephone and spoke with Dr. Willbanks. Dr. Willbanks informed Mr. Miller that Heather was "in distress" and possibly suffering from sepsis, but he would not elaborate in response to questioning by Mr. Miller. Dr. Willbanks also notified Mr. Miller that he would be performing a lumbar puncture on Heather, though he would not explain the purpose for the procedure, indicating only that it was necessary.

Mr. Miller told Dr. Willbanks that he and his wife were going to come immediately to the Hospital, and Dr. Willbanks agreed to wait for them to arrive. The Millers arrived at approximately 4:45 a.m., but Dr. Willbanks was not present and left no message. A nurse directed the Millers to the nursery where they observed Heather lying in a crib with an intravenous needle protruding from her scalp. No medical personnel would answer the Millers' questions concerning Heather's condition, so the Millers waited until approximately 8:30 a.m. for Dr. Willbanks to return.

When Dr. Willbanks finally met with the Millers, he explained that Heather had been acting jittery and crying excessively. He asked Mrs. Miller if she used any drugs during her pregnancy. When Mrs. Miller responded that she had occasionally taken Tylenol, Dr. Willbanks informed her of the importance of answering honestly concerning drug use during pregnancy. Despite Mrs. Miller's denials, Dr. Willbanks said that he did not believe her and that he had frequently seen DWS in infants. Dr. Willbanks stated that he was positive of his diagnosis and that he would continue treating Heather for DWS. Mrs. Miller then agreed to Dr. Willbanks's request that she take a drug test.

Following the meeting between Dr. Willbanks and the Millers, rumors that Heather was a "drug baby" began circulating throughout the Hospital. A Hospital social worker approached the Millers later in the day and questioned them concerning their past drug use, backgrounds, living arrangements, and other children. In addition, Mr. Miller overheard two unidentified people discussing the "drug baby" in the ward. Hospital nurses began treating the Millers rudely, and when Mr. Miller's parents visited the Hospital, they left angry believing Mrs. Miller was responsible for Heather's medical problems.

Throughout the day, the Millers unsuccessfully sought information concerning the drug tests and Heather's condition. At approximately 8:00 p.m., the head nurse finally informed Mr. Miller that the drug tests administered to Mrs. Miller and Heather came back negative at 11:00 a.m. The following day, Dr. Toffoletto, who was an associate of Dr. Willbanks, confirmed the nurse's statement that the drug tests revealed no problems and informed the Millers that the DWS treatments were being continued only as a precaution.

Disregarding the negative drug test results, Dr. Willbanks reported his suspicions concerning Mrs. Miller's alleged drug use to the Grainger County Health Department. Within one week, a social worker and nurse from the Department visited the Millers' home, interviewed the Millers, inspected their living arrangements, and examined Heather—all over Mr. Miller's objections. When the social worker returned less than two weeks later, Mr. Miller reiterated his objections, and the social worker did not visit again.

The Millers sued Dr. Willbanks, Hamblen Pediatric Associates, and the Hospital for the tort of intentional infliction of emotional distress. The defendants then moved for dismissal or summary judgment, which the trial court granted due to the plaintiffs' lack of expert evidence to support their claims of serious mental injury. The Court of Appeals affirmed the decision of the trial court.

We granted the plaintiffs' appeal to decide whether the Court of Appeals erred in holding that expert medical or scientific proof of a serious mental injury was required to support the plaintiffs' claim for the intentional infliction of emotional distress.

DISCUSSION

A. *History of Intentional Infliction of Emotional Distress in Tennessee*

Because our decision is based, in large part, upon the development of the law of mental distress and the erosion of traditional barriers to recovery, we will briefly address the evolution of the law of intentional infliction of emotional distress. At early common law, the right to recover for mental injuries sustained through intentional conduct was afforded little respect. In an influential decision, Lord Wensleydale declared: "Mental pain or anxiety the law cannot value, and does not pretend to redress, when the unlawful act complained of causes that alone." Lynch v. Knight, 9 H.L. Cas. 577, 598 (1861).

However, despite the law's early reluctance to provide a remedy for mental distress, "courts were permitting recovery for emotional injuries alone, frequently by stretching the meaning of traditional tort categories." [ ]. In Tennessee, for example, as early as 1888, courts applied broad interpretations of traditional legal principles to reach a similar result—remedying purely emotional injuries. [ ].

In Knoxville Traction Co. v. Lane, 103 Tenn. 376, 53 S.W. 557 (Tenn. 1899), Maggie Lane sued Knoxville Traction Company for "injuries to [her] feelings and sensibilities" caused by the conduct of an employee of Knoxville Traction. The employee, a motorman, loudly announced that Lane was a "damn good-looking old girl" who he "would like to meet ... when she gets off." [ ]. When Lane rebuffed his advances, the employee made further abusive comments and accused Lane of being "nothing but a whore."[ ]. Finally, after Lane began crying, the employee asserted that Lane "would go out to the lake and throw herself out to the men there." [ ]. Lane sued for $5,000, and a jury returned a verdict of $500 in her favor. [ ].

Knoxville Traction asserted that the suit could not be maintained because it was "based solely upon injury to the feelings of the plaintiff." [ ]. The Court rejected this argument holding that Lane could recover damages for "injuries to her feelings and sensibilities." Id. The Court's decision relied, in part, on the contract of carriage between a common carrier and passenger which includes a duty that the former will protect the latter from insult or injury by its employees or third persons. [ ]. Thus, the Court characterized the gravamen of the action as breach of contract of carriage. [ ]. The Court's conclusion, however, that Knoxville Traction was "liable for the injury and insult willfully inflicted upon Mrs. Lane," [ ], illustrates the attempts of the judiciary to remedy intentional conduct within the narrow confines of then-existing law. See also Hill v. Travelers Ins. Co., 154 Tenn. 295, 294 S.W. 1097 (Tenn. 1927) (concluding plaintiff stated a cause of action for damages from grief, worry, and mental anguish caused by interference with plaintiff's right of possession of deceased spouse's body).

Despite the result in Knoxville Traction and other similar cases, recovery for emotional distress was still limited in that a plaintiff had to fit a claim within a pre-existing legal category or prove an accompanying physical injury. Restrictions on such claims were justified, in part, on grounds that mental injuries were "slight and unimportant" but even when mental injuries were "considerable, they [gave] no right of action, since the law is designed to meet general conditions, and not exceptional cases." [ ]. More significantly, the consequences of mental injuries were characterized as "so elusive in character and the means of testing the truth of the allegations so inadequate" that public policy militated against permitting recovery of damages. [ ]. As early as 1888, this Court conceded that the bases upon which it permitted claims for emotional distress were often no more than legal fictions. [ ]. Nevertheless, Tennessee's common law retained devices including "legal fictions" and requirements of physical injury to distinguish actions based on emotional distress. Consequently, claims for purely emotional injuries that did not fit within traditional causes of action failed. [ ]

[I]n Medlin v. Allied Investment Co., 217 Tenn. 469, 398 S.W.2d 270 (Tenn. 1966), [this court] examined "whether the law recognizes and protects a right to emotional tranquility where recovery is sought for mental or emotional disturbance alone." [ ]. In the context of intentional conduct, the Court concluded that a plaintiff does have a right to emotional tranquility that, if violated, gives rise to an independent cause of action for intentional infliction of emotional distress. [ ]. The Court reached this conclusion by discarding the traditional arguments used to preclude claims for emotional distress.

First, the Court rejected the assertion that emotional injuries were unprovable. It recognized the inherent unfairness in a rule that allowed a plaintiff with a slight physical injury to recover damages for accompanying mental anguish, [ ], while a plaintiff with only a mental injury was left without a remedy. The Medlin Court observed that recovery by a plaintiff falling within the former designation implies that a mental injury may be sufficiently proved to permit an award of damages. [ ]. Indeed, this Court rejected distinctions between mental and physical injury and concluded that "mental suffering . . . is no more difficult to prove and no harder to calculate in terms of money than the physical pain of a broken leg which has never been denied compensation." [ ].

Second, the Court in Medlin dismissed the argument that mental injuries could not be adequately remedied by damages, because they were so intangible and peculiar to a particular individual that they could not be anticipated. [ ]. We acknowledged the view of medical science that emotional distress may well have physical consequences and agreed that such knowledge was possessed by the average person "who understands to some extent that [the consequences of emotional distress] are normal, rather than the unusual result of many types of conduct." [ ]. Thus, this Court "discarded foreseeability as the sole criterion of legal cause." [ ].

Finally, the Court in Medlin addressed concerns that recognizing a cause of action for intentional infliction of emotional distress would lead to a host of trivial claims. The solution to these concerns was found in the requirements of section 46 of the Restatement (Second) of Torts, which provides:

One who by extreme and outrageous conduct intentionally or recklessly causes severe emotional distress to another is subject to liability for such emotional distress, and if bodily harm results from it, for such bodily harm. [ ]

By grounding the cause of action for intentional infliction of emotional distress within the Restatement framework, we limited recovery to those plaintiffs who could satisfy its requirements. In Bain, we had the occasion to clarify the requirements to establish a prima facie case of intentional infliction of emotional distress: (1) the conduct complained of must be intentional or reckless; (2) the conduct must be so outrageous that it is not tolerated by civilized society; and (3) the conduct must result in serious mental injury to the plaintiff. [ ]. It is this third requirement that is the subject of this appeal and to which we now turn our attention.

B. Majority and Minority Approaches to the Necessity of Expert Proof

In the brief history of the tort of intentional infliction of emotional distress, this Court has not examined whether expert testimony is required to establish the existence of a serious mental injury. Other courts, however, that have examined this issue have come to markedly different conclusions.

A minority of jurisdictions requires expert medical or scientific proof of serious mental injury to maintain a claim for intentional infliction of emotional distress.[citations omitted]. These courts reason that expert proof is necessary to prevent the tort from being reduced to a single element of outrageousness, so by requiring expert proof, the elements of outrageous conduct and serious mental injury remain distinct. See Kazatsky [v. King David Mem'l Park, Inc., 527 A.2d 988, 995]. Moreover, courts expressing the minority view contend that because expert proof can be easily obtained, it must be used to prove serious mental injury. [ ]. ("Given the advanced state of medical science, it is unwise and unnecessary to permit recovery . . . without expert medical confirmation that the plaintiff actually suffered the claimed distress."). These courts assert that due to the wide availability of expert proof, plaintiffs will encounter "little difficulty in procuring reliable testimony as to the nature and extent of their injuries." [ ].

A majority of courts that have examined this issue, however, have concluded that expert proof is generally not necessary to establish the existence of a serious mental injury. * * * The flagrant and outrageous nature of the defendant's conduct, according to these courts, adds weight to a plaintiff's claim and affords more assurance that the claim is serious. [citation omitted] Moreover, expert testimony is not essential because other reliable forms of evidence, including physical manifestations of distress and subjective testimony, are available. Courts following the majority approach also contend that expert testimony is normally not necessary because a jury is generally capable of determining whether a claimant has sustained a serious mental injury as a proximate result of the intentional conduct of another person. Additionally, courts expressing the majority view reason that the very nature of the tort of intentional infliction of emotional distress "makes it impossible to quantify damages mainly on expert medical evidence." Chandler [v. Denton, 741 P.2d 855, 867.]

C. Adoption of Majority Approach

We conclude that the majority approach is consistent with our precedents and the underlying policies governing the law of intentional infliction of emotional distress. * * *

We recognize that legitimate concerns of fraudulent and trivial claims are implicated when a plaintiff brings an action for a purely mental injury. Thus, safeguards are needed to ensure the reliability of claims for intentional and negligent infliction of emotional distress. These safeguards, however, differ based on the kind of conduct, rather than the kind of injury, for which a plaintiff seeks a remedy.

With regard to intentional infliction of emotional distress, the added measure of reliability, *i.e.*, the insurance against frivolous claims, is found in the plaintiff's burden to prove that the offending conduct was outrageous. This is an exacting standard requiring the plaintiff to show that the defendant's conduct is "so outrageous in character, and so extreme in degree, as to go beyond all possible bounds of decency and to be regarded as atrocious, and utterly intolerable in a civilized community." Restatement (Second) of Torts § 46 cmt. d (1965). Such conduct is "important evidence that the distress has existed," [ ], and from such conduct, more reliable indicia of a severe mental injury may arise. The outrageous nature of the conduct, therefore, vitiates the need for expert testimony in a claim for intentional infliction of emotional distress. The risk of frivolous litigation, then, is alleviated in claims for intentional infliction of emotional distress by the requirement that a plaintiff prove that the offending conduct was so outrageous that it is not tolerated by a civilized society.

In cases of negligent infliction of emotional distress, however, the conduct giving rise to the tort is not marked by extraordinary or outrageous elements inherent in intentional conduct. Thus, concerns with unwarranted claims are not addressed by the kind of conduct that must be proved to obtain damages for emotional distress. In the absence of any reliable indicia of a severe mental injury suggested by the conduct, some safeguard must be imposed to limit frivolous litigation. Accordingly, when the conduct complained of is negligent rather than intentional, the plaintiff must prove the serious mental injury by expert medical or scientific proof. [ ].

Although we adopt the majority approach and hold that plaintiffs normally will not be required to support their claims of serious mental injury by expert proof in order to recover damages in a suit based upon the intentional infliction of emotional distress, we certainly do not discredit the use of expert testimony at trial. We are fully aware that there will be many cases in which a judge or jury may not appreciate the full extent and disabling effects of a plaintiff's emotional injury without expert evidence. * * *

Our decision today merely recognizes that in most cases other forms of proof may also be used to establish a claim for intentional infliction of emotional distress. Such proof may include a claimant's own testimony, as well as the testimony of other lay witnesses acquainted with the claimant, Physical manifestations of emotional distress may also serve as proof of serious mental injury. Moreover, evidence that a plaintiff has suffered from nightmares, insomnia, and depression or has sought psychiatric treatment may support a claim of a serious mental injury. [citations omitted]. The intensity and duration of the mental distress are also factors that may be considered in determining the severity of the injury.

Such proof, however, is no guarantee that a plaintiff will prevail. The weight, faith, and credibility afforded to any witness's testimony lies in the first instance with the trier of fact who is free to conclude that the subjective testimony of a plaintiff or other lay witnesses is not sufficient to prove a serious mental injury. Thus, although not legally required, "expert testimony may be the most effective method of demonstrating the existence of severe emotional distress." Richardson [ ].

Notes

1) Under what circumstances is lack of due care a matter that can be determined through common knowledge? Do you agree that "reasonable minds can differ" on the issue of whether the absence of insurance coverage is an adequate basis for failing to remove a source of infection?

2) The cost of expert testimony is a major reason that the current medical malpractice system is perceived as unfair. Plaintiffs with actionable claims but without significant damages have difficulty finding attorneys who will handle their cases, much less medical experts whose fees are affordable relative to the expected recovery. As a result plaintiffs often seek less expensive ways of pursuing their cases without expensive experts. *Res ipsa loquitur* and common knowledge doctrine are sometimes utilized.

3) Medical literature is generally sorted into two categories: peer-reviewed and not peer-reviewed, though this distinction is not necessary to the issue of admissibility. If a published treaty is made into a "book on tape" it is easy to see why it is admissible. But if the content were never published, nor peer-reviewed, is it any more reliable than a home video? What about quasi-professional literature available on the internet?

4) Assuming that a lay jury can determine whether plaintiff suffered from intentional infliction of emotional distress, how is it likely to interpret the lack of expert testimony? Is it more likely to assume the task of assessing the weight and credibility of plaintiff's testimony itself, or conclude that the absence of an expert means an expert would have nothing to add? If neither party produces an expert, what does the jury think?

SECTION D. MEDICAL EVIDENCE AND THE JURY

NESTOROWICH v. RICOTTA

Court of Appeals of New York, 2002.
97 N.Y.2d 393, 740 N.Y.S.2d 668, 767 N.E.2d 125.

Ciparick, J.

* * *

I.

In 1994, defendant, Dr. John Ricotta, a vascular surgeon, performed an adrenalectomy on decedent, Walter Nestorowich. This surgery was the culmination of decedent's decade-long bout with renal cell carcinoma. Dr. Joseph Greco, not a party to this action, first diagnosed the cancer in 1983. Shortly thereafter, in an attempt to contain the disease, Greco removed decedent's right kidney and adrenal gland. Unfortunately, the cancer persisted and in 1991, a significant portion of decedent's right lung was removed. The cancer continued to metastasize and in 1993, Greco discovered a large tumor on decedent's left adrenal gland.

Interferon treatment proved unavailing, and the tumor grew to approximately nine inches in length, three times the size of the adrenal gland itself. The growth was, in all respects, extraordinary. Greco recommended surgery to remove the mass, but decedent feared that the operation would result in the loss of his remaining kidney and ultimately force him to undergo dialysis. Nevertheless, decedent agreed that surgery would provide a better chance for survival, and Greco referred decedent to defendant. Defendant met with decedent and his wife, and disclosed the risks inherent in such a procedure. Decedent signed a consent form.

Defendant performed the left adrenalectomy on April 6, 1994 at Millard Fillmore Hospital. A number of factors increased the difficulty of this typically arduous procedure. At the time of the surgery, decedent weighed approximately 300 pounds. His size increased the depth of the surgical cavity, and impaired the doctor's ability to see. The tumor was surrounded by an uncertain number of blood vessels and small arteries, all of which were a potential source of bleeding. Defendant controlled the bleeding by meticulously tying off, or ligating, "bleeders" and vessels as he encountered them. Additionally, the tumor, organs and vessels were encased in layers of muscle and fatty tissue. Ultimately, defendant completed the surgery, removing the tumor in its entirety.

Immediately following the surgery, decedent's urine output was noticeably abnormal. After performing a renal scan, defendant realized that he had inadvertently ligated decedent's renal artery thus preventing blood flow to the kidney. Within hours of the adrenalectomy, defendant rushed decedent back to surgery, located the renal artery and restored blood flow to the kidney. Despite the superficial success of both surgeries, the ligation caused irreparable harm to the plaintiff's remaining kidney.

In 1995, decedent and his spouse commenced this medical malpractice action against defendant and the Hospital. Decedent died the following year of causes unrelated to the surgery * * * At trial plaintiff argued that defendant negligently ligated the renal artery, thereby causing decedent's injury. Plaintiff's expert, Dr. Selwyn Z. Freed, opined that under no circumstances would ligation of the renal artery be considered medically acceptable, and therefore defendant breached his duty of care. Although Freed testified that ligation of smaller vessels may at times be unnecessary, at no point during the trial did plaintiff, or her expert, contest the professional validity of defendant's choice to ligate "bleeders" and arteries in an effort to control bleeding and prevent hemorrhaging. Defendant called Greco and an expert, Dr. Jeffrey L. Kaufman, as witnesses. Both doctors claimed that despite defendant's inadvertent ligation of the renal artery, his conduct was nevertheless within the bounds of acceptable medical practice.

Following an extensive charge conference, and over plaintiff's objection, Supreme Court gave the "error in judgment" charge to the jury. The jury returned a verdict in defendant's favor. Supreme Court denied plaintiff's motion to set aside the verdict and dismissed the complaint. On plaintiff's appeal, the Appellate Division affirmed, concluding that Supreme Court did not err in giving an "error in judgment" charge, and if it did, the error was harmless. * * * We now affirm based on harmless error.

II.

* * *

A doctor is charged with the duty to exercise due care, as measured against the conduct of his or her own peers—the reasonably prudent doctor standard. Implicit within the concept of due care is the principle that doctors must employ their "best judgment in exercising * * * skill and applying [their] knowledge" (*id., citations omitted*). The notion of "best judgment" assures conformance with the prevailing standard of care and accepted medical practice. However, a doctor is not liable in negligence merely because a treatment, which the doctor as a matter of professional judgment elected to pursue, proves ineffective or a diagnosis proves inaccurate. Not every instance of failed treatment or diagnosis may be attributed to a doctor's failure to exercise due care (*see Schrempf v. State of New York*, 66 NY2d 289, 295 [1985]).

The resolution of medical malpractice cases, insofar as a doctor's conduct is measured by an objective reasonably prudent doctor standard, is dependent on the specific facts surrounding each claim. Although the *Pike [v. Honsinger, 155 NY 201 (1898)]* standard is universally applicable to each of these factually diverse situations, the proper evaluation of this standard is sometimes complemented by the application of collateral doctrines, such as the "error in judgment" doctrine. As this Court explained in *Pike*,

"the rule requiring [a doctor] to use his best judgment does not hold him liable for a mere *error of judgment*, provided he does what he thinks is best after careful examination. His implied engagement with his patient does not guarantee a good result, but he promises by implication to use the skill and learning of the average physician, to exercise reasonable care and to exert his *best judgment* in the effort to bring about a good result" [ ] [first emphasis added].

It follows, therefore, that a doctor may be liable only if the doctor's treatment decisions do not reflect his or her own best judgment, or fall short of the generally accepted standard of care [ ].

The Appellate Divisions, as well as certain other jurisdictions, have embraced an "error in judgment" charge [citations omitted]. As it has developed, the charge has been appropriate in instances where parties present evidence of a choice between or among medically acceptable alternatives or diagnoses [ ]. The "error in judgment" charge, as articulated in PJI 2:150, paragraph 5, states: "[a] doctor is not liable for an error in judgment if [the doctor] does what (he, she) decides is best after careful evaluation if it is a judgment that a reasonably prudent doctor could have made under the circumstances" [ ]. Absent a showing that "defendant physician considered and chose among several medically acceptable treatment alternatives" the error in judgment charge has been found inappropriate.

This limited application of the error in judgment charge preserves the established standard of care. Broader application of the charge would transform it from a protection against second-guessing of genuine exercises of professional judgment in treatment or diagnosis into a cloak for professional misfeasance. The doctrine was intended to protect those medical professionals who, in exercising due care, choose from two or more responsible and medically acceptable approaches. A distinction must therefore be made between an "error in judgment" and a doctor's failure to exercise his or her best judgment. Giving the "error in judgment" charge without regard for this distinction would otherwise relieve doctors whose conduct would constitute a breach of duty from liability.

AFFIRMED

MORRA v. HARROP

Supreme Court of Rhode Island, 2002.
791 A.2d 472.

Goldberg, Justice.

FACTS

At the time of his death, plaintiff's father, William Morra (Morra), was a patient of Dr. Harrop's, suffering from bipolar disorder. The evidence disclosed that on May 17, 1993, the patient attempted suicide by an overdose of Tylenol. He was treated for the overdose and subsequently admitted to Butler Hospital (Butler) where, because of the suicide attempt and a recent decampment from another facility, he was placed under close supervision without grounds privileges. The evidence disclosed that during the course of this hospitalization, Morra was restless, became increasingly agitated and threatened suicide during discussions about his potential post-discharge placement. The issue of Morra's living arrangements remained a concern, and Dr. Harrop ordered that he remain under close supervision, with the addition of checks every ten minutes by staff for his continued safety. A discharge meeting with the patient's family and Dr. Harrop was held on May 27, 1993, and, although the question of an acceptable facility was not resolved, Morra's discharge was scheduled for the next day, May 28, 1993. The evidence disclosed that Dr. Harrop then amended his orders, discontinued staff supervision and granted the patient grounds privileges, permitting him to move about the hospital grounds unattended by staff. Doctor Harrop testified that Morra secured grounds privileges at 2:30 p. m. on May 27, 1993, was declared missing at approximately 4 p. m. and that, at approximately 7 p. m., his body was found lying face down in the Seekonk River, near the hospital grounds.

The plaintiff commenced suit against Dr. Harrop, alleging negligent care and treatment of Morra, including the order granting grounds privileges to the patient that, according to the plaintiff, was the proximate cause of his death by suicide. To support her allegation, plaintiff presented the testimony of Dr. Sharp, the associate director for psychiatry inpatient services at Beth Israel Deaconess Medical Center, an expert witness in the field of psychiatry and the treatment of patients hospitalized with suicidal tendencies. Doctor Sharp testified that Morra was admitted to Butler with bipolar disorder, that he was given medications that were inadequate to treat that disorder, that he suffered from suicidal ideation, and had voiced extreme disagreement with the discharge plan. In Dr. Sharp's opinion, on May 27, 1993, at the point that Dr. Harrop authorized grounds privileges, Morra was harboring a suicidal intention and plan. Doctor Sharp concluded that the patient committed suicide by drowning and that, in his opinion, Dr. Harrop's treatment of Morra was negligent and was a deviation from the degree of care and skill that commonly is possessed by other physicians in the field. Specifically, Dr. Sharp testified that given the patient's mental state, the planned discharge to a less secure setting was inappropriate and, in light of the patient's potential for suicide, Dr. Harrop deviated from the standard of care when he approved grounds privileges. In his opinion, Dr. Harrop's failure to recognize that Morra's request for grounds privileges and his sudden upturn in mood could be an indication of intensified suicidal intention and was a deviation from the standard of care.

The issue of causation relative to the manner of death was contested by the defense, and a dispute arose over whether the death was a suicide.

At a hearing outside the presence of the jury, Dr. Sharp excluded as the manner of death homicide, accident, heart failure, seizure, stroke, or any other brain abnormality or disease. He rendered an opinion that the patient committed suicide and testified that he based his opinion as follows:

* * *

"It's my opinion that Mr. Morra died by suicide through drowning; that he had been suicidal throughout his hospitalization and at the point of his requesting grounds privileges. He had a history of serious suicide attempts, including by drowning in the past. That the fact that his body was found in the condition that it was, clothed, face down in the water, the autopsy report supporting death by drowning and not supporting death by homicide or accidental causes, leads me to the conclusion that the only possibility was suicide by drowning." (Emphasis added.)

* * * After plaintiff concluded her case in chief, defendant moved to strike all of Dr. Sharp's testimony on the ground that Dr. Sharp "talked in terms of possibility" and that his testimony lacked a degree of certitude or certainty that "a given state of affairs is a result of a certain cause." Clearly taken by surprise, counsel for the plaintiff argued valiantly that Dr. Sharp's opinion was that suicide was not a mere possibility but was "the only possibility," and further, that Dr. Sharp had excluded all other potential classifications of death. (Emphasis added.) This argument was rejected by the trial justice, who stated, "I don't think I have an alternative but to strike it." The plaintiff's request for a continuance for the "limited purpose of curing that particular language of probability and possibility" was also denied. The trial justice granted the motion to strike Dr. Sharp's testimony and held, "Possibility is not enough in medical negligence cases. There is no room for doubt; there is a term or a concept that's absolutely necessary, and that's probability. There is a term or a concept that is absolutely insufficient, and that's possibility."

The defendant's motion for judgment as a matter of law was immediately granted, thus terminating this case. The plaintiff has appealed.

DISCUSSION

The first issue before us is whether the trial justice erred in striking Sharp's testimony based on his opinion that suicide was "the only possibility" in this case. This question turns on whether Sharp's opinion was expressed with sufficient credibility or validity to assist the fact-finder. The determination of the admissibility of an expert witness's testimony rests within the sound discretion of the trial justice and will not be disturbed on appeal absent an abuse of that discretion. * * * The purpose of expert testimony is to aid in the search for the truth. It need not be conclusive and has no special status in the evidentiary framework of a trial. This Court consistently has held that a jury is free to accept or to reject expert testimony in whole or in part or to accord it what probative value the jury deems appropriate. "Moreover, in the course of expert testimony it is common for the witness, implicitly or explicitly, to exclude conclusions other than the one reached by [the witness]." [ ]. We have never required an expert to "use * * * the talismanic phrase 'strong probability.'" [ ]. This Court clearly has enunciated that the admissibility of expert testimony does not require the use of "magic words" or "precisely constructed talismanic incantations" to achieve its objective. [ ]. "The expert must merely testify to the effect that he reached his conclusion with reasonable medical certainty." [ ]. This standard is equally applicable in negligence cases, including cases in which the alleged tortfeasor is a member of the medical profession. * * *

In the case before us, we are of the opinion that Dr. Sharp's testimony was more than adequate and that the trial justice erred in granting defendant's motion to strike, both on substantive and procedural grounds. In clear and unequivocal language, Dr. Sharp not only classified Morra's death as a suicide, he eliminated homicide, accident and disease. Thus, of the other generally accepted "means or fatal injury that caused a death," Dr. Sharp concluded that suicide was the only possibility. * * * We can hardly envision an expert opinion that is more precise and definite. Dr. Sharp's opinion thus exceeded the term probability and entered the sphere of certainty. There is no stronger way of saying that an event most probably occurred then saying that the event in fact occurred.

Although striking the expert's testimony in its entirety was an abuse of discretion, this error was further compounded by the trial justice's denial of a brief continuance to permit plaintiff to recall Dr. Sharp in an attempt to clarify his testimony and avoid the inevitable Rule 50 judgment.

[Reversed]

Notes

1) Medical practice does not allow a physician to make an "honest mistake" without incurring potential malpractice liability. An honest mistake is nevertheless negligence. The "error in judgment" rule is misleading. A physician who chooses among medically acceptable alternatives under the circumstances does not incur liability if the alternative chosen yields a poor result. "Error in judgment" seems to suggest that having chosen a different alternative would have yielded a better result. This, of course, cannot be known albeit one can always speculate in hindsight. If one alternative is clearly superior to all others, the other alternatives are not medically acceptable (unless, for some reason, the better alternative is unavailable). Indeed, most medical errors, except those that are reckless or intentional, are matters of negligence.

2) Expert witnesses are generally expected to testify that the conclusions they reach carry a "reasonable degree of medical certainty." There is no magic phrase or degree of certainty that allows the testimony to be

considered. On the other hand, mere speculation is unacceptable both as to weight and admissibility. A mere possibility of causal connection, even in the absence of other credible causes, invites the finder of fact to base its decision on evidence that lacks reliability. In the first instance the trial judge determines whether the expert's testimony is stated with a degree of certainty that is sufficient for consideration by the jury.

Chapter 5

CAUSATION, HARMS
AND DAMAGES

INTRODUCTORY NOTE

The practice of personal injury litigation is different from taking courses in law school. In the first-year Torts class, fault is the main concern, followed by causation, with harms and damages a distant last. In personal injury practice, causation and harms and damages take most of attorneys' preparation and trial time, and this is true of all personal injury and wrongful death cases, whether medical liability, auto accident, or product liability. This chapter therefore presents an opportunity for law students to see medical liability cases, a subset of personal injury litigation, as lawyers and trial judges see them.

The jargon that personal injury litigators use is not the same as academic jargon.

The personal injury bar generally lumps causation with negligence as "liability"; harms and quantification are "damages." Trials can be bifurcated, or new trials limited, to liability or damages.

"Specials" are pecuniary elements of damage that are naturally expressed in money, whether out of pocket or future losses, such as lost wages, hospital and medical expenses, and lost earning capacity. "Special damages," on the other hand, are harms that must be alleged specifically if the plaintiff wants to introduce evidence to prove them.

The courts also manipulate the terms "negligence," "causation," "harms," and "damages."

"Contributory negligence" actually operates on causation. If negligence of the plaintiff caused the plaintiff's harm, the plaintiff's negligence is treated as the sole cause, cancelling the plaintiff's whole case.

"Comparative fault" actually operates on the plaintiff's damages. If both plaintiff and defendant were negligent in causing the plaintiff's harms, the plaintiff's damages are reduced to the proportion of the defendant's negligence in the harm-causing event.

"Avoidable consequences," the fancy name for "failure to mitigate damages," also operates on the plaintiff's damages. If the plaintiff's damages include harms that the plaintiff could reasonably have prevented, the defendant should not have to pay for them.

While this field could use some clarification, for the time being, would-be litigators have some learning to do.

There is also interdisciplinary confusion, because lawyers and medical scientists do not see causation, harms, and damages in the same way. Medical negligence was different: in earlier chapters, medical experts gave their opinions on the standards of medical care and whether defendants complied with them, but neither judges nor physicians expected medical practice to be an exact science, and so conflicting opinions on negligence did not threaten cornerstones of either law or medicine.

But both courts and physicians expect that modern medicine will be scientific, and so causation will be a matter of science, and therefore testimony on causation should be "certain." How certain? Scientific theories provide theoretical certainty, but unfortunately for the legal process, a good medical scientist is rarely confident that one event in fact caused another event, let alone that it caused a legal result. Therefore, if certainty were required of scientific testimony as to causation, little expert medical testimony would get to the jury from good scientists.

What happened in courts years ago was the dilution of the test to "reasonable medical certainty." Parsing the phrase, "medical certainty" must be less demanding than "certainty," probably along the lines of the causation that would actuate a medical expert's treatment plan (clinical certainty). "Reasonable medical" certainty must be even less certain than that—less, for example, than presenting the cause of a patient's condition to one's teachers and peers on grand rounds. Under the latest and least demanding test of all, if the expert's qualifications are sufficient, the judge will let the jury hear what the expert says about causation together with whatever uncertainty the expert expresses (including "mere possibilities"), subject to the usual tests of sufficiency and weight.

After the plaintiff's action has satisfied sufficiency requirements for negligence and causation, harms and damages still must be overcome. The recognition of harms and the quantification of damages have a tendency to wash back and forth. If the court refuses to recognize a particular harm, such as fright without impact, the great extent and dazzling clarity of the plaintiff's damages are irrelevant. Likewise a court can refuse to apply unconventional ways of quantifying damages, such as economists' projections, to a conventional harm, which destroys the plaintiff's whole case just as effectively as though no such harm existed.

Finally, lawyers and doctors speak different languages in describing harms and damages, especially nonpecuniary damages. The vocabularies of physicians are full of euphemisms like "discomfort" and "resting quietly." These are not lies; they are ways of reducing emphasis on unwanted symptoms that will go away when the patient gets well.

Physicians therefore resent the way that lawyers dwell on "pain and suffering" as a way of increasing verdicts: there is an element of legal hypocrisy in making money out of other people's pain. Evidently there is not only legal usage but interdisciplinary sympathy to be learned.

SECTION A.   CAUSATION OF HARM BY MEDICAL NEGLIGENCE

LUPINACCI v. MEDICAL CENTER OF DELAWARE

Supreme Court of Delaware, 2002.
805 A.2d 867.

Berger, Justice:

* * *

I.   FACTUAL AND PROCEDURAL BACKGROUND

On October 2, 1995, Maria Lupinacci was injured in an auto accident. She complained of double vision and Dr. David Larned determined that she suffered an "orbital blowout" in her right eye, which occurs when the skull is fractured near the eye orbit. On January 17, 1996, Larned performed two surgeries at the Medical Center of Delaware ("MCD") to correct Lupinacci's condition. He wrote post-operative notes following the first surgery, but not following the second. The notes were relatively general and did not instruct nurses to look for specific symptoms of complications.

Lupinacci stayed in the hospital overnight for observation. At some point in the early evening, a patch or gauze was placed over Lupinacci's right eye, although Larned had not ordered that treatment. Tricia Riedel was the nurse on duty when Lupinacci was brought in from the second surgery at about 7:00 p.m. Lupinacci's pain level at that time was charted at 4 on a scale of 0–10, with 10 being the most severe level of pain * * * . Riedel also testified that, without special orders, she would not contact a surgeon if a patient's pain level was less than 8.

Monica Weir monitored Lupinacci during the 11 p.m.–7 a.m. shift. Although Weir was not familiar with the potential complications of orbital blowout surgery, she was an experienced ophthalmic nurse. According to her notes, Weir checked on Lupinacci just before 1 a.m. on January 18th, and rated Lupinacci's pain as being a "2+" on a 10 point scale. At trial, Weir testified that she examined Lupinacci's eye for bleeding and swelling at that time, but noted no change in Lupinacci's status.

* * * At no point during the night did any nurse call Larned or another doctor to attend to Lupinacci, and the record would support a finding that no nurse checked whether Lupinacci could see out of her surgical eye. When Larned returned the next morning, he noted swelling and bloody discharge, both symptoms of hemorrhaging. He operated immediately, and discovered the presence of a "slow bleed," which had been putting pressure on Lupinacci's right eye throughout the night. The hemorrhage ultimately caused Lupinacci to lose her sight in that eye.

* * *

Larned [testified] that swelling, bleeding, and/or pain are signs of complications that would require his attention. He did not specifically instruct the nurses to look for those symptoms, however, because that is a standard part of a nurse's training. Larned disagreed with Reidel's testimony that she would only call a doctor if the patient's pain were at level 8 or above. Larned said that an increase in pain, even to a level of 5 or 6, would be cause for alarm and should precipitate a call. Larned also testified that, based on Lupinacci's condition when he arrived on the morning after surgery, her eye probably was bruised and swollen a few hours earlier, when Weir did her 4 a.m. and 5 a.m. checks. Such swelling and bruising, according to Larned, should have prompted a call to him.

Lupinacci alleged that Larned was negligent in several respects, including his failure to write specific post-operative orders that would have alerted the nurses to possible complications from the second surgery. Lupinacci also alleged that MCD's nurses negligently failed to provide appropriate care. At trial, after Lupinacci rested her case, Larned moved for judgment as a matter of law. The Superior Court granted Larned's motion, finding that his failure to issue instructions for the nurses was not the proximate cause of Lupinacci's injury because the nurses checked on Lupinacci even without such orders. The jury considered Lupinacci's remaining claims and returned verdicts in favor of MCD and Larned. Lupinacci moved for a new trial pursuant to Superior Court Rule 59, but the Superior Court denied her motion. This appeal followed.

II. Discussion

* * *

Applying this standard, we find that a reasonable jury could have concluded that Larned's failure to issue appropriate instructions was the proximate cause of Lupinacci's injury. Although the nurses knew to watch for swelling, bleeding and/or pain, they were not aware that this type of surgery usually involves minimal pain and should not involve any bleeding. Weir testified that she noticed blood on Lupinacci's eye dressing at 4 a.m., but did not notify Larned because she did not think the bleeding represented a change in Lupinacci's condition * * * Larned [testified] he would have been ''alarmed'' by Lupinacci's condition and would have expected a call.

The issue of proximate cause is generally a question of fact for the jury. This record presents enough evidence for a reasonable jury to conclude that the nurses failed to report symptoms of complications because they used their general training to assess Lupinacci, when they should have received specific instructions from Larned requiring them to report any bleeding, and much lower levels of pain and swelling. Accordingly, the trial court should have denied the motion for judgment as a matter of law.

Lupinacci also argues that the Superior Court abused its discretion in not granting her a new trial against MCD. She contends that no reasonable jury could have found for MCD based on the evidence presented. At trial, Lupinacci offered expert evidence that MCD's nurses breached the standard of care in several respects, including their failure to check Lupinacci's pain level and their failure to chart the results of their periodic patient assessments. MCD offered its own expert testimony that: (i) the standard of care was not as Lupinacci's expert opined, and/or (ii) the nurses met that standard of care. The jury was free to accept the opinion of MCD's expert and reject that of Lupinacci's expert. Accordingly, since there was evidence to support either conclusion, the jury's determination was not against the great weight of the evidence, and the Superior Court did not abuse its discretion in denying Lupinacci a new trial with respect to MCD.

The final issue, on which this Court requested supplemental briefing, is whether MCD should be required to stand trial again when Lupinacci's claim against Larned is retried. In *Chrysler v. Quimby*, this Court held that a partial retrial could be ordered if: "[t]he issue to be retried [is] clearly severable from the other issues; * * * [and] no injustice will result from limiting the issue on retrial."

Courts in other jurisdictions have held that partial retrials are inappropriate where questions of several defendants' liability are intertwined, even if one defendant has obtained a jury verdict in his favor * * *.

We are satisfied that here, as in *Williams [v. Slade, 431 F.2d 605 (5th Cir. 1970)]*, the acts and omissions of Larned and MCD are intertwined. Lupinacci claims that both Larned and the MCD nurses failed to provide adequate post-operative care. According to Lupinacci, Larned should have given specific instructions concerning the circumstances under which he wanted to be called. The nurses, who had no such instructions, should have called Larned to request instructions and, even without instructions, should have monitored Lupinacci more closely. We conclude that, in order to fully appreciate each party's conduct, as well as the potential liability of either party or both, the jury must be allowed to consider the claims against both. . . . [W]e find that the claims are not clearly severable, and a partial retrial may result in an injustice to Lupinacci.

III. Conclusion

REVERSED and REMANDED.

CRAIG v. MURPHREE

United States Court of Appeals for the Tenth Circuit, 2002.
35 Fed. Appx. 765.

LUCERO, Circuit Judges.

* * *

I

Craig, who has an extensive family history of breast cancer and breast lumps, was diagnosed with breast cancer in 1995 after the cancer had spread to her lymph nodes. The cancer developed in the same area that had been needle-biopsied by treating physician Dr. Hope Balluh in 1993 after Dr. Balluh felt a palpable mass there. Dr. Balluh was employed by the federal government at W.W. Hastings Indian Hospital. In 1994, a mammogram showed the presence of several micro-calcifications in that same area, which, according to Craig's experts, were clinically indicative of early cancer and merited further testing and evaluation.

Craig sued the United States for medical malpractice under the Federal Tort Claims Act. At trial, Craig presented expert testimony that Dr. Balluh negligently failed to properly biopsy the breast mass in 1993, negligently relied on a negative needle biopsy, negligently failed to independently view the 1994 mammograms and order further testing based on the presence of micro-calcifications, and negligently failed in 1994 to order further tests to ascertain whether palpable fibrocystic changes in her left breast were malignant.

Craig also stated a claim against Dr. Murphree, a radiologist in private practice, for medical malpractice under state law. Craig alleged that Dr. Murphree negligently misinterpreted the 1994 mammograms as negative for indications of malignancy. Expert testimony supported her claim that Dr. Murphree breached the standard of care by failing to report the micro-calcification changes on the mammogram to Dr. Balluh and by failing to recommend or order further testing that could have conclusively ascertained whether those changes were malignant. Furthermore, Craig presented expert testimony that, but for the failure to timely diagnose and treat the cancer, she would have had a greater than fifty percent chance of a complete cure and that the one-year delay of treatment until after metastasis of the cancer left her with the probability of not surviving more than ten years after its diagnosis.

At trial, the jury was instructed on, and decided only the issue of, Dr. Murphree's negligence, even though it heard almost all the evidence regarding both Dr. Murphree's and Dr. Balluh's alleged negligence. n1 On the issue of Dr. Murphree's negligence, the court instructed the jury [on issues of negligence, direct cause, injury and due care].

* * *

Craig proffered two additional uniform jury instructions on the issues of concurrent causation and joint duty of care. The concurrent causation instruction provided: "There may be more than one direct cause of an injury. When an injury is the result of the combined negligence of two or more persons, the conduct of each person is a direct cause of the injury regardless of the extent to which each contributes to the injury." [ ] The proposed joint duty instruction stated: "Where two or more physicians owe the same duty to a patient, and the acts of each contribute to the same breach of duty, the wrong and injury, if any, to the patient are regarded as the result of joint action of the physicians, and both physicians are liable." [ ] Craig contended that the instructions were factually and legally proper because she had presented evidence that both physicians had a duty to review the 1994 mammogram, identify the visibly suspicious area, and order further testing, making them potentially concurrent tortfeasors under Oklahoma law as to that portion of her claim. [ ] Without the instructions, Craig argued, "the jury [would] be hopelessly confused" because the general direct cause instruction gave insufficient guidance on the issue of causation in the circumstance in which it would be asked to decide only Dr. Murphree's negligence. [ ] According to Craig, the concurrent cause instruction "exactly fit [ ] the facts of this case" (id.) and would help the jury understand that "there may be more than one cause of an injury." (Id. at 41.) Without comment, the court denied Craig's request to submit the two instructions to the jury.

The jury returned a verdict in favor of Dr. Murphree, and six months later, the district court returned a verdict in favor of Dr. Balluh. Craig does not appeal the latter judgment.

II

When a motion for a new trial is predicated, as here, upon a challenge to the jury instructions, we consider the instructions given as a whole. In reviewing the instructions, we consider all the jury heard, and from the standpoint of the jury, decide not whether the charge was faultless in every particular, but whether the jury was misled in any way and whether it had understanding of the issues and its duties to determine these issues.

* * *

We begin with the general principle that a party is entitled to an instruction based on its theory of the case whenever it produces sufficient evidence to support it and submits an instruction that is a correct statement of the law. FDIC v. Schuchmann, 235 F.3d 1217, 1222 (10th Cir. 2000). "It is not error," however, "to refuse to give a requested instruction if the same subject matter is adequately covered in the general instructions." Id. (quotation omitted).

There is no question that the uniform instructions requested by Craig correctly stated Oklahoma tort law. * * * Based on our review of the record, we conclude that Craig presented evidence to support a finding of joint duty and concurrent causation arising from the 1994 examination.

We address Dr. Murphree's contentions that a new trial is not warranted because (1) he and Dr. Balluh acted independently; (2) the jury did not hear all of the evidence relating to and did not decide the issue of Dr. Balluh's alleged negligence; (3) Craig did not appeal the judgment in favor of Dr. Balluh; and (4) he and Dr. Balluh did not owe the "same" duty and thus could not be jointly responsible for Craig's injury.

A

Dr. Murphree's first contention—that the proposed instructions were unwarranted because he and Dr. Balluh acted independently—is without merit. In Radford–Shelton Associates Dental Laboratory v. Saint Francis Hospital, Inc., 569 P.2d 506, 509 (Okla. Ct. App. 1976), the Oklahoma Court of Appeals stated that "concurrent tortfeasors [are] those whose independent, negligent acts combined or concurred at one point in time to injure a third party." Id. (emphasis added).

B

Similarly, the jury's failure to hear the totality of the evidence against Dr. Balluh is not determinative. Juries often determine the negligence of only one alleged tortfeasor (e.g., when other alleged tortfeasors settle before trial). That the jury is not asked to determine the existence or degree of negligence of all tortfeasors does not mean that their actions did not concurrently cause plaintiff's injury.

Although the jury heard all of Craig's evidence regarding Dr. Balluh's alleged negligence, it did not hear all of Dr. Balluh's defense evidence. This circumstance does not detract from the jury's knowledge that Craig alleged that both physicians directly caused her loss of chance of survival by negligently failing to further evaluate the changes evidenced in the mammograms. In light of the evidence presented to the jury and the district court's refusal to instruct on joint duty and concurrent causation, we are not satisfied that the jury understood the issues to be resolved and its duty to resolve them. We are not satisfied that the jury understood that even if Dr. Balluh, as the treating physician and last physician with a duty to view the mammograms and/or to order further testing, breached her duty, Dr. Murphree could still be held liable for any independent failure to properly interpret the mammograms, report changes, and order further testing.

C

We also reject Dr. Murphree's claim that Craig's failure to appeal the judgment in favor of Dr. Balluh forecloses her right to a new trial on the issue of Dr. Murphree's negligence. A conclusion that Dr. Balluh did not breach the standard of care in regard to viewing the mammograms does not mean that Dr. Murphree was not negligent for failing to properly report the micro-calcifications and recommend further evaluations. Dr. Murphree admitted that he did not mention the micro-calcifications on his report, and Dr. Balluh testified that she did not independently notice the micro-calcifications and that Dr. Murphree's report that the mammograms were negative for cancer was reassuring to her. [ ] Dr. Balluh testified that if a radiologist had reported the micro-calcifications, stated that they were possibly new growth, and recommended further evaluation, she would have followed those recommendations. [ ]

Furthermore, the propriety of a jury instruction is determined as of the time the case goes to the jury, not with the hindsight of a later trial court finding that one defendant was not in fact negligent. As the notes to the Uniform Jury Instructions state, the concurrent causes instruction should be used if there is evidence that an injury may have been produced by two or more concurrent causes. In addition to the evidence discussed above, the jury heard expert testimony that, given Craig's history, Dr. Balluh was additionally independently negligent for (1) having failed to order a full biopsy of the mass in 1993 that would have excluded cancer as the cause of the palpable abnormality and (2) having failed to further evaluate a palpable area of fibrosis in the upper left breast quadrant in 1994. [ ] The requested instructions would have allowed the jury to understand that physicians who concurrently provide medical services to a patient have a joint duty to their patients; that there may be more than one direct cause of injury to a patient; and that the jury had a duty to hold Dr. Murphree liable if it found that he was negligent notwithstanding any alleged concurrent negligence of Dr. Balluh. The instructions, as given, did not clarify the confusion created by evidence demonstrating joint duties and concurrent negligence where the jury would be determining the liability of only one physician. The general negligence and direct cause instructions did not inform the jury of the law of joint duty of physicians or of concurrent causes of injury.

D

Finally, we address Dr. Murphree's contention that the joint duty of physicians instruction was inapplicable because he and Dr. Balluh did not have the same duty and thus could not be jointly responsible for Craig's loss of chance. We disagree. The duty that physicians owe to a patient, whether in interpreting a physical examination of the patient or interpreting x-ray reports, is to follow the relevant medical standard of care. [ ] At trial, Craig argued that both physicians concurrently breached their duties to independently notice clinical changes that, given her extensive family history of breast cancer, merited further tests and evaluations. Both Dr. Murphree and Dr. Balluh performed examination and diagnosis techniques intended to discover any early signs of breast cancer. In that regard, the duty they both owed to Craig was the "same"—to properly diagnose her condition. Their continuing duty, whether in interpreting Craig's physical examination or her x-ray reports, was to follow the relevant medical standard of care.

Given the testimony of Craig's experts, the jury could have found that Dr. Murphree breached his standard of care, contributing to Craig's decreased chance of survival. The tendered joint duty of physicians instruction thus would have clarified that Dr. Murphree's negligence, if any, would not be excused by the negligence of Dr. Balluh, if any. Without this instruction, the jury was not fully informed of the law of physicians' joint duties and liabilities.

III

We conclude that the jury was not fully instructed on governing law that "provided [it] with an ample understanding of the issues and the standards applicable." [ ]. We hold that the court abused its discretion in refusing to submit the tendered joint duty and concurrent causes instructions to the jury.

REVERSED and REMANDED for a new trial.

PETERSON v. GRAY

Supreme Court of New Hampshire, 1993.
137 N.H. 374, 628 A.2d 244.

JOHNSON. J

* * *

The plaintiff sought treatment from the defendant, a hand surgeon, because she was experiencing pain in her left hand. The defendant diagnosed arthritis in her carpal metacarpal joint, as well as de Quervain's disease, a type of tendonitis. To relieve the pain caused by the arthritis, the defendant recommended and performed a trapeziectomy— that is, the removal of the trapezium, one of eight bones in the wrist— and filled the space with folded tendons in a procedure known as the "anchovy procedure" because the tendons are folded over like anchovies. Following the operation, another wrist bone, the scaphoid, rotated into the space where the trapezium had been, despite the "anchovy procedure," causing the plaintiff's wrist to collapse and necessitating the fusion of her wrist bones. The plaintiff can now use her left hand only in an "assistive" capacity.

Both parties agree that, during the course of the trapeziectomy, the defendant initially misidentified the scaphoid as the trapezium and mistakenly severed at least three ligaments that connected the scaphoid to two neighboring bones, the lunate and the radius. At trial, the defendant testified that he quickly recognized and repaired his mistake, causing the plaintiff no ill effects. The plaintiff, on the other hand, questioned the effectiveness of the defendant's repair and argued that the error amounted to negligence and proximately caused the collapse of her wrist. The defendant denied the plaintiff's allegations, maintaining that the wrist collapse was an inherent risk of the medically accepted trapeziectomy.

At the close of the evidence, the trial court instructed the jury as to the elements of the plaintiff's case, including proximate cause. The trial court's instruction on proximate cause was particularly important in this case because there was no question that the plaintiff had a pre-existing condition relative to her left wrist. The trial court initially defined proximate cause as follows:

> "An injury or damage is proximately caused by an act or a failure to act whenever you judge from the evidence in the case that the act or

omission probably played a substantial part in bringing about or actually causing the injury, and that the injury or damage was either a direct result or a reasonably probable consequence of the act or omission."

Although the court occasionally spoke of the plaintiff's burden to prove "that the defendant's act or failure to act was a substantial factor in bringing about the alleged injury," the court twice instructed the jury not to award damages to the plaintiff unless she proved that the defendant's actions were "*the* proximate cause" of her injuries. (Emphasis added.) Regarding the plaintiff's pre-existing wrist problems, the trial court stated:

"Should you have occasion to consider the issue of damages in this case, you may not include in the award any amount to cover any physical condition which pre-existed the events complained of. You may only consider those injuries which you find to have been a natural and probable consequence of the defendant's fault, if any."

The plaintiff objected to the court's causation instructions, maintaining that they implied the plaintiff could only recover damages if she proved that the defendant's mistake was the sole cause of her injuries. In response, the trial court gave the following instruction:

"Did the defendant breach the standard of care, and were those injuries—was that breach a substantial cause of the injuries and the damages of which she presently complains, *keep in mind with respect to her prior injuries or the status of her health*. If you find such—for whatever degree you may find the prior condition of her health, while that—they're not a factor in this case; *anyone takes someone as they find them*. So that prior injuries *may or may not* figure in, if you find—if you further first find negligence, *you may find that prior injuries were aggravated by or prior conditions were aggravated by that negligence. That's okay for you to do that*, if you do that—you choose to do that; but you must find, to award a verdict for the plaintiff in this case—you must find that she has met her burden of proof as to the fact that—if you find that fact as to the doctor's negligence, in accordance with that standard of care I gave you, as to the causation and as to the damages."

(Emphasis added.) The plaintiff objected to this statement of the law, too, but the trial court gave no further instructions. The jury returned a verdict for the defendant, and the plaintiff appealed, arguing as she did below that the trial court erroneously instructed the jury on the issues of proximate cause and aggravation of pre-existing conditions.

* * *

Examining the instructions relating to proximate cause first, we note the principle that a defendant's negligence need not be "the sole cause" of a plaintiff's injuries to warrant an award of damages. *See* W. Keeton *et al.*, Prosser and Keeton on the Law of Torts § 41, at 266 (5th ed. 1984). "It is for this reason that instructions to the jury that they must find the defendant's conduct to be 'the sole cause,' or 'the dominant cause,' or 'the proximate cause' of the injury are rightly condemned as misleading error." *Id.* The trial court here twice stated that the plaintiff had to prove the defendant's actions were "*the* proximate cause" of her injuries before she would be entitled to damages. Although the court also used the words "*a* proximate result" and "*a* substantial factor," the court never explained the basic principle that a plaintiff does not have to show that a defendant's negligence was the sole cause of his or her injuries.

We find that the jury could have been misled by these instructions. [ ]. The question of causation was undoubtedly the crucial issue in this case, and no one disputed that the defendant operated on the plaintiff's hand because she had arthritis. In the chain of causation leading to her wrist fusion, the plaintiff's pre-existing arthritis obviously played a major part. But if the jury determined that the plaintiff's arthritis was "*a* proximate cause" of her wrist fusion, then the defendant's actions could not possibly have been "*the* proximate cause." The court's instructions thus encouraged the jury to find for the defendant even if the plaintiff met her burden of proving that his error was a proximate cause of the wrist fusion. As the instructions could have misled the jury into such faulty reasoning, we hold that an injustice was done to the legal rights of the plaintiff, warranting reversal. [ ]

We next turn to the court's instructions regarding aggravation of pre-existing conditions and find that, like the instructions on proximate cause, they did not fairly state the law and could have misled the jury. The court's first instructions on the issue did not define the plaintiff's right to recover for the aggravation of a pre-existing condition at all, [ ] but merely stated that "you may not include in the award any amount to cover any physical condition which pre-existed the events complained of. You may only consider those injuries which you find to have been a natural and probable consequence of the defendant's fault, if any." While correct, this instruction is misleading because it explains only the defendant's half of the aggravation of injury doctrine. [ ].

The court's supplemental instructions, apparently given to meet the plaintiff's objections, appear to have confused the issue further. [ ]. The court told the jury that prior injuries are "not a factor in this case," but then stated that "prior injuries may or may not figure in." The court also admonished the jury to "keep in mind with respect to her prior injuries or the status of her health," but did not explain the effect the prior injuries should have on the jury's determination of liability or damages. Similarly, the court stated, without elaboration, "you may find that ... prior conditions were aggravated by that negligence. That's okay for you to do that.... " Finally, although the jury was informed that "anyone takes someone as they find them," this legal catch phrase for the aggravation of injury doctrine [ ] was never deciphered for the lay jurors.

We conclude that the court did not fairly and adequately explain the law and could have misled the jurors into believing they could withhold recovery for the plaintiff if they found that her present injuries stemmed from a pre-existing condition. As the plaintiff admitted that she sought treatment from the defendant because of a pre-existing condition, the court's instructions on the aggravation of injury doctrine unfairly prejudiced the case against her and thus caused an injustice to her legal rights.

Reversed and remanded.

CHAMBERLAND v. ROSWELL

Court of Appeals of New Mexico, 2001.
130 N.M. 532, 27 P.3d 1019.

BOSSON, Chief Judge.

BACKGROUND

After experiencing abdominal pain for a day, Plaintiff Johnny Chamberland (Johnny) went to the Roswell Osteopathic Clinic (Clinic) on Saturday, October 21, 1995, to see a doctor. Johnny was seen by Dr. Kelley who physically examined him and had a blood test and urinalysis performed. The lab results revealed that Johnny's blood had an elevated white blood cell count indicating the presence of an acute infection. The urinalysis revealed the presence of blood and protein, abnormal conditions for males. Because Johnny did not have any of the classic symptoms of appendicitis, such as tenderness in the abdomen, guarding, decreased bowel sounds, nausea or vomiting, Dr. Kelley concluded that Johnny had a urinary tract infection. He prescribed antibiotics and painkillers to treat the infection, and sent Johnny home. However, Dr. Kelley felt that Johnny needed to be observed closely, and asked him to return to the Clinic to have his blood and urine tested again. A repeat visit with Dr. Kelley followed three days later.

After continuing to experience persistent discomfort, Johnny returned to the Clinic on the following Saturday and was seen by Dr. Fachado. Dr. Fachado had another urinalysis and blood test performed. Although the urinalysis was "completely normal," Johnny's white blood cell count was higher than ever. Dr. Fachado's examination revealed that Johnny's prostate gland was inflamed, and he diagnosed Johnny's condition as prostatitis. Dr. Fachado changed Johnny's prescription to an antibiotic specifically for prostatitis.

Over the next few days Johnny was seen by four other doctors unaffiliated with the Clinic. None of them observed the classic symptoms of appendicitis. Ultimately, Dr. Fachado referred Johnny to Dr. Kiker, a urologist, for a more comprehensive diagnosis. The classic symptoms of appendicitis were observed on October 31, 1995, ten days after Johnny's initial visit to the Clinic, and Johnny was then referred to a surgeon for removal of his appendix. That surgery revealed that Johnny's appendix had already ruptured, creating a large abscess. The abscess was so big that the surgeon opted not to remove what remained of the appendix, choosing instead only to drain the pus. The surgeon drained over 400 cc's of pus from the abscess in Johnny's abdomen.

Johnny and his wife, Laquita, sued Drs. Kelley and Fachado alleging a failure to examine, diagnose, and treat Johnny in a manner conforming to reasonable medical standards. They sued the Clinic alleging inadequate record keeping pertaining to Dr. Kelley's examinations and observations. The Chamberlands alleged that the negligence of all three Defendants caused Johnny's appendicitis to go untreated, which, in turn, caused him to suffer the abscess and other injuries and economic consequences that ultimately resulted.

At trial, the Chamberlands produced expert medical testimony that Johnny likely had appendicitis before he initially visited the Clinic, and his appendix had probably ruptured on the day he arrived there. According to this medical expert, the abscess drained by the surgeon was the direct result of Johnny's ruptured appendix, and it could have been avoided with timely surgery. As it turned out, Johnny did not present earlier with classic appendicitis symptoms because his appendix was retrocecal, meaning that the appendix was pointing towards his back, not his front, as is usually the case.

Notwithstanding the positioning of Johnny's appendix and the absence of classic symptoms, the medical expert testified that if the Clinic's doctors had properly taken Johnny's medical history and performed a physical examination in a manner consistent with reasonable medical standards, Johnny's appendicitis would have been timely diagnosed and removed. The ruptured appendix caused Johnny numerous secondary infections including sepsis and adult respiratory distress, and at least two ileostomys, resulting in pain and suffering plus over $150,000 in medical bills.

Defendants produced expert medical testimony that they were not negligent in examining, diagnosing, and treating Johnny. Specifically, Defendants produced evidence that the appendicitis was not reasonably detectable at the times they examined Johnny and made entries in the medical records because the classic symptoms were absent. According to Defendants' evidence, a reasonably skilled and careful physician could not have determined that Johnny needed surgery until October 31, 1995, when Johnny first exhibited classic appendicitis symptoms.

After all the evidence was presented to the jury, the trial court sent the jury home and heard lengthy legal argument on the jury instructions. Over the Chamberlands' objection, defense counsel requested and received a jury instruction on independent intervening cause.

Soon after the jury had been charged and its deliberations were underway, the jury foreman sent out a note requesting a "definition of the word 'proximate,' either from Black's Law Dictionary or Webster's New Collegiate Dictionary." After the trial court consulted with counsel, the jury was told to refer to the court's instructions to resolve the question. Approximately one-half hour later the jury returned the special verdict form. The jury answered "Yes" to the first question on the special verdict form, "Was any Defendant medically negligent?" In response to the next question, "Was any medical negligence of a Defendant a proximate cause of Johnny Chamberland's injuries and damages?" the jury answered "No."

DISCUSSION

On appeal, the Chamberlands argue that the trial court committed reversible error when it instructed the jury on the issue of independent intervening cause because neither Defendants' evidence nor their legal theory supported the instruction. The Chamberlands rely extensively on Torres, 1999 NMSC 29, 127 N.M. 729, 987 P.2d 386, a Supreme Court opinion issued just twelve days after the trial in this case, that dramatically limits the application of the independent intervening cause instruction under New Mexico tort law. We review jury instructions de novo "to determine whether they correctly state the law and are supported by the evidence introduced at trial." [ ].

At trial, Defendants urged the independent intervening cause instruction on the court over the Chamberlands' objection. Defendants argued that while Johnny was in their care, he only showed the symptoms of a urinary tract infection, not appendicitis. According to Defendants, Johnny's symptoms did not shift to appendicitis until days after Dr. Fachado last saw Johnny and referred him to a specialist. Because the appendicitis was not symptomatic until after Defendants had completed their examinations, Defendants argued that the appendicitis was an intervening cause of Johnny's injuries that arose independently of the care provided by Defendants.

The Chamberlands voiced their disagreement to the court. As they saw it, Defendants were merely arguing lack of causation, not an independent intervening cause, which entitled Defendants to the basic instruction on proximate cause, UJI 13–305 NMRA 2001, unadorned by any reference to independent intervening cause and without a separate instruction on that issue. The Chamberlands failed to persuade the trial court, and the court gave the additional instruction that frames the issue now before us on appeal.

The Uniform Jury Instructions define independent intervening cause as follows: "An independent intervening cause interrupts and turns aside a course of events and produces that which was not foreseeable as a result of an earlier act or omission." [citations omitted]. When supported by evidence, the theory of an independent intervening cause initially appears in the proximate cause instruction, as a cause "which in a natural and continuous sequence [unbroken by an independent intervening cause] produces the injury, and without which the injury would not have occurred." UJI 13–305 (providing for the optional, bracketed language in cases supporting independent intervening cause). The inclusion of independent intervening cause in UJI 13–305 and its accompanying definition in UJI 13–306 "are intended to clarify the meaning of proximate cause in cases in which there is evidence from which reasonable minds could differ in deciding whether an unforeseeable cause has broken the chain of causation." Torres, 1999 NMSC 29, P17, 127 N.M. 729, 987 P.2d 386.

In Torres, our Supreme Court made clear "that the doctrine of independent intervening cause should be carefully applied to avoid conflict with New Mexico's use of several liability." [ ]. The Court concluded that after the adoption of comparative negligence, instruction on the doctrine of independent intervening cause overemphasized the defendant's effort to shift fault away from himself and place it elsewhere. [ ]. The instruction also undermined the goal of simplifying our jury instructions by adding "a complex layer of analysis to the jury's determination of proximate cause." [ ] Because the instruction on independent intervening cause is "sufficiently repetitive of the instruction on proximate cause and . . . apportioning fault," our Supreme Court concluded that the "potential for jury confusion and misdirection outweighs its usefulness " [ ]

We take the Supreme Court's cautionary language to heart. Although the issue before us does not involve comparative fault, as it did in Torres, the potential for juror confusion over independent intervening cause remains very real.[ ]. Even before Torres, the law has consistently limited the independent intervening cause instruction to those instances in which the instruction is properly supported by the evidence and the theory of the defense * * *.

Independent intervening cause is an affirmative defense founded on public policy. That policy recognizes that once a plaintiff establishes negligence and causation in fact, the potential scope of liability could be endless unless courts create reasonable outer limits. [ ] Those limits are phrased in the legal terminology of foreseeability and remoteness. [ ]. These concepts are embodied within the independent intervening cause instruction as a limitation imposed on causation in fact. Thus, the instruction is based on a policy determination that liability should cease at the point where an independent cause intercepts and interrupts the normal progression of causation, because it produces an injury "that which was not foreseeable as a result of an earlier act or omission." UJI 13–306.

The relationship between causation in fact and independent intervening cause is critical to our analysis. To establish liability, there must be a chain of causation initiated by some negligent act or omission of the defendant, which in legal terms is the cause in fact or the "but for" cause of plaintiff's injury. [ ] As the chain of causation progresses in time or place from the negligent act or omission, an unforeseen force may intervene in the sequence of causation to completely disrupt its normal progression, producing unpredictable injuries. The unforeseeable force, be it a force of nature, an intentional tort, or a criminal act, gives rise to an instruction on independent intervening cause which is an affirmative defense that releases the defendant of all liability * * *.

An instruction on independent intervening cause presupposes a defendant's negligence and causation in fact. Without some initial tortious act or omission by a defendant that precipitates the plaintiff's ultimate injury, subsequent causes and their injuries cannot "intervene." * * * If the evidence demonstrates no more than a simple dispute over causation in fact (i.e., whether the defendant's negligence did or did not cause in fact the injuries suffered by the plaintiff), then the issue for the jury is causation alone, not independent intervening cause * * * To our knowledge, no reported New Mexico case has ever authorized the independent intervening cause instruction in the absence of causation in fact.

The present dispute illuminates the distinction between a true independent intervening cause and a mere dispute over causation in fact without an independent intervening cause. In the case before us, only two scenarios were possible in regard to the appendicitis: either it was present at the time Defendants examined Johnny or it was not. If, as the Chamberlands' evidence showed, the appendicitis was present and detectable through the exercise of ordinary care when Defendants examined Johnny, then Defendants were negligent if they failed to exercise reasonable care, and liable for injuries proximately caused if that negligence was a cause in fact of the abscesses and other injuries that followed. On the other hand, as Defendants argued to the jury, if the appendicitis was not reasonably detectable at that point in time (even if it existed in fact), then any negligence in the course of Defendants' examination, record keeping or treatment with respect to Johnny's urinary tract infection, could not have been a cause in fact of Johnny's abscesses and other injuries. According to the undisputed evidence, Johnny's injuries were caused solely by a ruptured appendix and not by any urinary tract infection.

Neither circumstance justifies an independent intervening cause instruction. The dispute gives rise to the standard instruction on proximate cause and no more, because causation in fact is the only issue in dispute other than the quality of Defendants' medical care. Defendants appear to agree that if the jury believed that Johnny had appendicitis when he initially went to the Clinic, then the existence of appendicitis could not be an independent intervening cause of his injuries. * * *

* * *

Having determined that the court erred in giving an instruction unsupported by the evidence, prejudice is presumed. * * *

[Reversed.]

Notes

1) Many of the medical errors that occur are institutional errors: communication gaps between physicians, nurses, technicians, pharmacists and others. In *Lupinacci*, the physician's perception of what the nurse should have known was inconsistent with the nurse's general

training, and specific instructions were not given. The jury is left to sort out the general standard of nursing care and whether specific instructions were required, as well as whether the physician should have known how closely his patient was monitored and at what level of nursing expertise. In hindsight, how could this error have been eliminated? Does the legal result promote the elimination of error in the future?

2) Do concurrent causes produce a legal anomaly? How does a jury sort out liability in matters where there are joint duties and concurrent negligence?

3) *Peterson* highlights the difficulty of issuing jury instructions that adequately distinguish between cause-in-fact, *a* proximate cause, *the* proximate cause, intervening causes and their relationship to the aggravation of pre-existing conditions. Clear jury instructions are essential and their absence can amount to reversible error.

4) *Chamberland* is notable for the jury's dilemma when it is argued that a reasonably competent physician could not have diagnosed a condition as common as appendicitis before rupture, though the plaintiff presented several times with symptoms. Where multiple physicians are involved, the alleged negligence can involve a chain of causation, and the jury is left to sort out cause-in-fact, proximate cause and intervening causes in a matter where the diagnostic science is disputed.

SECTION B. HARMS

ALEXANDER v. SCHEID

Supreme Court of Indiana, 2000.
726 N.E.2d 272.

BOEHM, Justice.

FACTUAL BACKGROUND

In June of 1993, sixty year-old JoAnn Alexanderwas scheduled for hip surgery by Dr. D. Kevin Scheid, an orthopedic surgeon at Orthopaedics Indianapolis, Inc. (Orthopaedics). Scheid ordered a chest x-ray, which was required at his office for patients over the age of sixty to ensure the strength of their lungs to undergo anesthesia. The x-ray was administered on the 24th of that month and revealed a density in the upper right lobe of her right lung. The neuroradiologist generated a report of the x-ray and sent a hard copy of the report to Scheid's office. He also recorded the results of the x-ray into a phone dictating service, which made them available to Scheid's office for approximately four to five days. The report of the results was placed in JoAnn's chart at Scheid's office, but neither Scheid nor his office took any action, despite the fact that the report noted a "density ... in the upper lobe" and concluded that "comparison with old films would be of value."

In the spring of 1994, JoAnn began spitting up blood and went to another doctor. A second chest x-ray revealed a large mass on the upper right lobe of the right lung. In May, after a biopsy, JoAnn was diagnosed with non-small cell lung cancer. Efforts to remove the tumor were not completely successful, and, because the cancer had metastasized to one lymph node in her chest and to the bronchial margin, it was not curable. After JoAnn underwent extensive chemotherapy and radiation treatment, her condition went into remission in approximately October 1994.

* * *

On October 8, 1996, the Alexanders filed an amended complaint * * * alleg[ing] that Scheid and Orthopaedics were negligent in failing to follow up on JoAnn's chest x-ray, and that this negligence resulted in the following harms to JoAnn: (1) "serious and permanent injuries necessitating extensive additional medical care"; (2) an increased risk of harm and decreased chance for long-term survival (later dubbed "loss of chance"), including the loss of "the possibility of successful removal of the tumor"; (3) "the incurrence of substantial medical expenses" and "loss of earning capacity"; and (4) severe emotional distress. In Count II, Jack Alexander alleged loss of consortium. JoAnn asserts that in the months following her first x-ray but preceding her diagnosis with lung cancer her injuries included: (1) deterioration of her overall health, including exhaustion, pneumonia-like symptoms, and feeling "rundown" in general; (2) spitting up blood; (3) an exacerbation of cancer, i.e., an increase in the size of the tumor and metastasis to one lymph node and the bronchial margin, resulting in cancer that is either incurable or at a minimum has a significantly lower probability of being treatable; and (4) damage to healthy lung tissue and lung collapse.

Three doctors were deposed regarding JoAnn's comparative prognoses in June 1993 and May 1994. In capsule form, they presented admissible evidence that (1) JoAnn's cancer was likely in Stage I at the time of the first x-ray but had advanced to Stage IIIa before it was diagnosed; and (2) the probability of her long-term survival was significantly reduced over that period of time. Scheid and Orthopaedics moved for summary judgment, arguing that, in view of JoAnn's remission, JoAnn had suffered no present compensable injury, and therefore, as a matter of law, had no claim. The trial court agreed and the Court of Appeals affirmed, concluding that: (1) Section 323 of the Restatement of Torts does not allow recovery for wrongs that increase the risk of harm unless the harm has come to pass; (2) JoAnn was not presently injured physically; and (3) in the absence of a physical injury, the modified impact rule does not apply to allow JoAnn to recover for negligent infliction of emotional distress.

This case raises four questions. (1) Does Indiana law permit JoAnn to recover for an increased risk of incurring a life shortening disease under the "loss of chance" doctrine or otherwise? (2) If so, what is the appropriate measure of damages? (3) Has JoAnn suffered an impact that would allow her to recover for negligent infliction of emotional distress under the "modified impact rule?" (4) May JoAnn maintain a cause of action for the aggravation to date of her lung cancer?

* * *

I. Decreased Life Expectancy

A. *Issues Raised under the Rubric "Loss of Chance"*

"Loss of chance," also often referred to as "increased risk of harm" is usually traced back to this frequently quoted passage from Hicks v. United States, [368 F.2d 626, 632 (4th Cir. 1966)]:

When a defendant's negligent action or inaction has effectively terminated a person's chance of survival, it does not lie in the defendant's mouth to raise conjectures as to the measure of the chances that he has put beyond the possibility of realization. If there was any substantial possibility of survival and the defendant has destroyed it, he is answerable.

The term "loss of chance" has been applied to a number of related situations. These include: (1) an already ill patient suffers a complete elimination of an insubstantial or substantial probability of recovery from a life-threatening disease or condition; (2) a patient survives, but has suffered a reduced chance for a better result or for complete recovery; and (3) a person incurs an increased risk of future harm, but has no current illness or injury. [ ]. The Alexanders now present the second, which, like the first, typically arises in the context of a claim of negligent health care. The third commonly arises in connection with claims of exposure to toxic substances, where no adverse results have yet emerged.

These cases pose a number of separate but sometimes interrelated issues. First, many courts initially address the issue as one of causation. Mayhue took the view that under traditional medical malpractice theory, when a patient's chance of recovering from a disease is already less than fifty percent, it can never be said that the doctor's malpractice was the proximate cause of the ultimate death. [ ]. Accordingly, recovery under traditional tort standards of causation is barred under those circumstances. This approach views the injury as the ultimate adverse result of the disease, which may be death, but may also be other conditions (paralysis, blindness, etc.).

Just as it is difficult to find causation where the harm is already more than likely to occur, it seems odd to speak of a causal relationship between a defendant's act or omission and an as yet unknown ultimate result. Although an act of malpractice may reduce a patient's chances for survival or for obtaining a better result, this is simply a statistical proposition based on the known experience of a group of persons thought to be similarly situated (in JoAnn's case, persons with four centimeter nodes in the lungs). In any given case, however, the plaintiff's ultimate injury either does or does not occur. Thus, if full recovery is awarded based on an appraisal of causation (or greater than fifty percent probability), the plaintiff who later beats the odds may be overcompensated for an injury that never ultimately emerges. Similarly, the plaintiff who has a less than fifty percent chance, but nonetheless does ultimately bear the full brunt of the disease, may be undercompensated.

One way to deal with this problem is to permit multiple suits as different injuries develop, but that approach has several shortcomings, including the generation of multiple litigation and the attendant costs of that litigation. Delaying suit is another possibility, but that fails altogether to compensate for the very real pain and distress that accompanies an uncertain but probable serious or fatal condition. Delaying suit for medical malpractice in Indiana also has a distinct disadvantage. Given the occurrence-based limitations period for Indiana's medical malpractice claims and our holding that the Indiana Constitution prohibits barring only claims that have accrued but are unknowable, a person in JoAnn's shoes may be forever barred if the claim cannot be presented until the disease recurs.

These factors argue in favor of permitting the Alexanders to bring their claims now. If this is to be done, however, there are further complexities to address. First, there is disagreement as to the elements of recoverable damages. Some courts purporting to address "loss of chance" allow recovery only for medical expenses, lost earnings, or loss of consortium [citations omitted]. Others have explicitly allowed recovery for what the doctrine's name suggests: the loss of the chance itself [citations omitted]. If a lost chance is to be compensable, its valuation also presents issues. Damages may be assessed for the full amount of the injury, if the full extent of the physical injury is already known. * * * Other courts have attempted to assess the damages in proportion to the likelihood that the doctor's negligence caused (or will cause) an injury. * * *

Finally, if damages are awardable for the increased risk of an injury that has not yet occurred, the court faces the difficult task of putting a dollar amount on an as yet unknown loss. The Alexanders' claim here presents that issue as to the ultimate recurrence of the cancer. They also assert current injury in the form of the cancer's metastasizing, and the anxiety generated by the prospect of future recurrence.

* * *

C. "Loss of Chance" as an Independent Injury

Causation and injury are sometimes described together as the collective third element of a medical malpractice claim. See Mayhue, 653 N.E.2d 1384, 1386–87 (reciting that, in order to prevail in a medical malpractice cause of action, a plaintiff must establish: (1) the physician owed a duty to the plaintiff; (2) the physician breached that duty; (3) the breach proximately caused the plaintiff's injuries). Causation and injury are distinct, however, and we are confronted with this distinction here.

We think that loss of chance is better understood as a description of the injury than as either a term for a separate cause of action or a surrogate for the causation element of a negligence claim. If a plaintiff seeks recovery specifically for what the plaintiff alleges the doctor to have caused, i.e., a decrease in the patient's probability of recovery, rather than for the ultimate outcome, causation is no longer debatable.

Rather, the problem becomes one of identification and valuation or quantification of that injury. We view the issue presented by JoAnn's claim as whether a plaintiff may recover for an increased risk of harm, here a decreased life expectancy, caused by a doctor's negligence, before the ultimate consequences are known. Because in this case the ultimate injury is death, the increased risk of that result is a decrease in life expectancy. Although loss of chance could also be applied as a label for this injury, we do not view recognizing this injury as a deviation from traditional tort principles. Rather, in this context it is nothing more than valuation of an item of damages that is routinely valued in other contexts. Scheid and Orthopaedics have conceded, for purposes of summary judgment, that they had a duty toward plaintiff and that they breached that duty. They do not concede that the breach caused a compensable injury, but they have, at this summary judgment stage, not yet contested that their negligence caused JoAnn's chance of long-term survival of cancer to be reduced. * * *

A number of jurisdictions allow recovery for negligence that has "increased the risk of harm," even where the full ramifications of the defendant's actions are not yet known.

* * *

More specifically, many jurisdictions have recognized a decrease in life expectancy as a cognizable injury. * * *

Here, JoAnn has pointed to evidence that would support a finding of both present injury and increased risk of harm. We agree with the authorities that find these sufficient to maintain a cause of action for an increased risk of harm. JoAnn has characterized defendants' actions as having reduced her chance for long-term survival and extinguished the chance for successful removal of her tumor. The doctors testified that JoAnn's chances of complete recovery, sixty to eighty percent in June of 1993, had dropped to a ten to thirty percent chance of surviving five years by May of 1994. JoAnn has suffered physical injuries, including the growth of a cancerous tumor, the destruction of healthy lung tissue, and the collapse of a lung. Scheid and Orthopaedics point to the fact that JoAnn does not ask for past medical expenses or for lost earnings. However, this has no bearing on whether or not she may maintain a separate cause of action for her decreased life expectancy.

In some cases an "intangible" loss may be as great an injury as any that a plaintiff could suffer. JoAnn must live under constant fear that at any time she may suffer a recurrence of her lung cancer. If that occurs, her doctors have testified that she has no chance of survival. This is not too remote or speculative an injury to preclude recovery, and JoAnn should not be forced to wait until she has suffered a relapse to proceed with a cause of action for what is essentially a daily threat of impending death, or to wait until her husband, on her behalf, is left with a wrongful death claim. As already noted, given the occurrence-based statute of limitations for medical malpractice, these future claims may face substantial obstacles. Money is an inadequate substitute for a period of life, but it is the best a legal system can do. The alternative is to let a very real and very serious injury go uncompensated even if due to negligent treatment. Faced with that choice, we hold that JoAnn has stated a viable cause of action and presented evidence sufficient to defeat summary judgment. Specifically, within the parameters set forth here, we hold that JoAnn may maintain a cause of action in negligence for this increased risk of harm, which may be described as a decreased life expectancy or the diminished probability of long-term survival.

Here, we also have an injury that often accompanies a delay in diagnosis—the invasion of healthy tissue by a tumor or other growth. Accordingly, this case does not present the issue whether a plaintiff must have incurred some physical injury as a result of the defendant's negligence in order to recover for an increased risk of harm. Some courts have concluded, particularly in the loss of chance context, that the loss must be "substantial" before it is compensable. We see no obvious method of quantifying that test. Because we measure damages by probabilizing the injury, the likelihood that plaintiffs will bring claims for trivial reductions in chance of recovery seems small. If, in the future, we face a volume of insignificant claims, perhaps such a rule will become necessary. For now, we are content to rely on basic economics to deter resort to the courts to redress remote probabilities or insubstantial diminutions in the likelihood of recovery.

[REVERSED.]

BIRD v. SAENZ

Supreme Court of California, 2002.
28 Cal.4th 910, 123 Cal.Rptr.2d 465, 51 P.3d 324.

WERDEGAR, J

I. Facts and Procedural Background

On [November 30, 1994] plaintiff Janice Bird brought her mother Nita to the hospital to undergo an outpatient surgical procedure. The goal of the procedure was to insert a Port–A–Cath—a venous catheter surgically implanted to facilitate the delivery of chemotherapeutic agents. Nita was undergoing chemotherapy because she had six weeks earlier been diagnosed with metastatic ovarian cancer involving many of her internal organs and lymph nodes. Nita was taken into the operating room about 1:45 or 2:00 p.m. Janice expected the procedure to take about 20 minutes. After an hour had elapsed, Janice asked a hospital volunteer to see why the procedure was taking so long. Over the loudspeaker system, Janice heard the announcement, "thoracic surgeon needed in surgery, stat." Janice assumed the call related to Nita because she believed all other surgeries had been completed. An hour to an hour and a half later, defendant Dr. Eisenkop came to the waiting room to report to Janice. Janice remembers him saying "that they had more trouble inserting the Port–A–Cath than they had anticipated, that when they went to insert it, they thought that they got a bubble in her vein, and they think that she might have had a mild stroke." Janice telephoned her sister, plaintiff Dayle Edgmon, with this news and returned to the waiting room. About 4:30 p.m., someone told Janice that Nita was "sleeping right now" and "should be going up to the fifth floor in about an hour."

Soon thereafter, Janice saw Nita "being rushed down the hallway to the CC—I presume she was going to the CCU [critical care unit]. She was bright blue. The angle of the bed was like this (indicating). Her feet were way up in the air, her head was almost touching the ground, there was all these doctors and nurses around there and they're running down the hallway, down to that end of the hospital.... " The medical personnel rushed Nita into a room and closed the door behind them. Janice, who was in the hallway, asked Dr. Dowds what was happening. Dr. Dowds went to check and returned with this news: "From what I can see," Janice remembers him saying, "I think they nicked an artery or a vein, and it looks like all the blood went into her chest. They're going to have to insert a drainage tube into her chest to drain out the fluid, and they're pumping—they're trying to pump as much fluids and blood into her to keep her alive until the vascular surgeon gets there." Ten or 15 minutes later, Janice saw Dr. Dowds running down the hall with multiple units of blood.

At this point Dayle arrived. Janice told her briefly what was happening. Dr. Dowds then told Dayle what he had already told Janice, namely, that an artery or vein had been nicked and that major surgery would be necessary. Shortly thereafter, Janice and Dayle saw Nita being rushed down the hallway to surgery. In Dayle's words, "All of a sudden I saw, I would say, approximately at least 10 doctors and nurses running down the hall with my mother and I remember her head was towards the floor, her feet were up in the air and she was blue." Janice's description is essentially identical, with the addition that she understood her mother's angle as intended "to keep the blood moving to the heart."

Those are the events on which plaintiffs base their claim for NIED (Negligent Infliction of Emotional Distress). Soon thereafter, emergency surgery stopped Nita's internal bleeding. But plaintiffs do not claim that this subsequent procedure caused them to suffer actionable emotional distress. Nita was discharged from the hospital 33 days later, on January 2, 1995, and resumed chemotherapy the next month.

In pleading their NIED claim, plaintiffs allege they "were all present at the scene of the injury-producing events at issue herein at the time when they occurred" and that they "were all aware that Defendants, and each of them, were causing injury to their mother, Nita Bird." Defendants moved for summary judgment on the ground that the undisputed evidence showed plaintiffs had not been present in the operating room at the time Nita's artery was transected, had not observed the transection, and had learned about it from others only after it had occurred. Plaintiff Kim Moran, moreover, had been out of the state. In support of their motion, defendants cited *Thing v. La Chusa*

(1989) 48 Cal.3d 644, 257 Cal.Rptr. 865, 771 P.2d 814, in which we held "that a plaintiff may recover damages for emotional distress caused by observing the negligently inflicted injury of a third person if, but only if," the plaintiff satisfies three requirements, including the requirement that the plaintiff be "present at the scene of the injury-producing event at the time it occurs and [be] then aware that it is causing injury to the victim." [ ]

* * *

II. DISCUSSION

This case requires us to consider once again the circumstances under which bystanders to an event injuring a third party may sue the allegedly negligent actor for emotional distress. In *Amaya v. Home Ice, Fuel & Supply Co.* (1963) 59 Cal.2d 295, 29 Cal.Rptr. 33, 379 P.2d 513, we declined to recognize such claims, foreseeing if we did a "fantastic realm of infinite liability." [ ] Five years later, in *Dillon v. Legg* (1968) 68 Cal.2d 728, 69 Cal.Rptr. 72, 441 P.2d 912 (*Dillon*), we reversed course. Equating the duty to avoid causing emotional harm to bystanders with the foreseeability they might suffer such harm, we articulated a set of nonexclusive guidelines for assessing foreseeability, and thus duty, on a case-by-case basis. Over the ensuing two decades we, and the lower courts, attempted to apply those guidelines. Looking at that effort in retrospect, however, in *Thing v. La Chusa, supra*, 48 Cal.3d 644 (*Thing*), we discerned that *Dillon* had produced arbitrary and conflicting results and "ever widening circles of liability." [ ] Recognizing this, we did not reverse course yet again, but we did make an important course correction. * * * Specifically, we held "that a plaintiff may recover damages for emotional distress caused by observing the negligently inflicted injury of a third person if, *but only if*, said plaintiff: (1) is closely related to the injury victim; (2) is present at the scene of the injury-producing event at the time it occurs and is then aware that it is causing injury to the victim; and (3) as a result suffers serious emotional distress—a reaction beyond that which would be anticipated in a disinterested witness and which is not an abnormal response to the circumstances." (*Thing*, [ ]) We emphasized the mandatory, exclusive nature of the new requirements by expressly rejecting the suggestion that liability for NIED should be determined under the more general approach. * * *

Applying these requirements to the facts before us in *Thing* [ ], we held that the plaintiff as a matter of law could not state a claim for NIED. The plaintiff mother had been nearby when the defendant's automobile struck and injured her minor child, but the plaintiff had not seen or heard the accident; instead, she became aware of it only when someone told her it had occurred and she rushed to the scene and saw her child lying injured and unconscious on the road. Under these facts, the plaintiff could not satisfy the requirement of having been present at the scene of the injury-producing event at the time it occurred and of having then been aware that it was causing injury to the victim. We reinforced our conclusion by disapproving the suggestion in prior cases that a negligent actor is liable to all those persons "who may have suffered emotional distress on viewing or learning about the injurious *consequences* of his conduct" rather than on viewing the injury-producing *event*, itself. [ ]

Here, only the second *Thing* requirement is at issue. Defendants argue that plaintiffs, who admittedly did not perceive the transection of their mother's artery, were not present at the scene of the injury-producing event at the time it occurred and were not then aware that it was causing injury to the victim.

Certainly defendants are correct that plaintiffs cannot prevail on a claim for NIED based solely on the transection of Nita's artery. The undisputed facts establish that no plaintiff was present in the operating room at the time that event occurred. Indeed, plaintiffs assert that even the defendant physicians, who were present and actively involved in Nita's care, failed to diagnose the transection for some time. Plaintiffs first learned an accident had taken place when they heard that news from a physician and saw some of the injurious consequences. The earlier call for a thoracic surgeon over the hospital's loudspeaker system may seem full of portent in retrospect, but it carried no clear information to a bystander in a waiting room about the progress of a particular surgical procedure. To be sure, *Thing*'s requirement that the plaintiff be contemporaneously *aware* of the injury-producing event has not been interpreted as requiring visual perception of an impact on the victim. A plaintiff may recover based on an event perceived by other senses so long as the event is contemporaneously understood as causing injury to a close relative. [citations omitted] But this slight degree of flexibility in the second *Thing* requirement does not aid plaintiffs here because they had no sensory perception whatsoever of the transection at the time it occurred. Thus, defining the injury-producing event as the transection, plaintiffs' claim falls squarely within the category of cases the second *Thing* requirement was intended to bar.

Conceding the point at least implicitly, plaintiffs seek to redefine the injury-producing event to include something of which they were contemporaneously aware. In their own words, "while Plaintiffs do not dispute that Janice Bird and Dayle Edgmon were not in the operating room at the time Nita Bird's artery was transected, Plaintiffs do contend that Janice Bird and Dayle Edgmon were aware that Nita Bird's artery and/or vein had been injured as a result of Defendants' conduct, that Defendants failed to diagnose that injury and that Defendants failed to treat that injury while it was occurring."

The problem with defining the injury-producing event as defendants' failure to diagnose and treat the damaged artery is that plaintiffs could not meaningfully have perceived any such failure. Except in the most obvious cases, a misdiagnosis is beyond the awareness of lay bystanders. Here, what plaintiffs actually saw and heard was a call for a thoracic surgeon, a report of Nita suffering a possible stroke, Nita in distress being rushed by numerous medical personnel to another room, a report of Nita possibly having suffered a nicked artery or vein, a physician carrying units of blood and, finally, Nita still in distress being rushed to surgery. Even if plaintiffs believed, as they stated in their declarations, that their mother was bleeding to death, they had no reason to know that the care she was receiving to diagnose and correct the cause of the problem was inadequate. While they eventually became aware that one injury-producing event—the transected artery—had occurred, they had no basis for believing that another, subtler event was occurring in its wake.

In other NIED cases decided after *Thing [ ]*, and based on alleged medical negligence, courts have not found a layperson's observation of medical procedures to satisfy the requirement of contemporary awareness of the injury-producing event. This is not to say that a layperson can never perceive medical negligence, or that one who does perceive it cannot assert a valid claim for NIED. To suggest an extreme example, a layperson who watched as a relative's sound limb was amputated by mistake might well have a valid claim for NIED against the surgeon. Such an accident, and its injury-causing effects, would not lie beyond the plaintiff's understanding awareness. But the same cannot be assumed of medical malpractice generally.

* * *

In summary, plaintiffs have not shown they were aware of the transection of Nita's artery at the time it occurred. Nor have they shown they were contemporaneously aware of any error in the subsequent diagnosis and treatment of that injury in the moments they saw their mother rolled through the hall by medical personnel. In view of these undisputed facts, plaintiffs cannot show they were "present at the scene of the injury-producing event at the time it occurred and [were] then aware that it [was] causing injury to the victim." (*Thing [ ]*) Accordingly, the superior court properly granted defendants' motion for summary judgment on plaintiffs' claim for NIED.

Notes

1) Cases alleging "loss of a chance" are among the most difficult matters for assessment of damages. There is disagreement among courts as to the elements of damages that should be recoverable. Some courts have limited damages to out-of-pocket medical expenses, loss of earnings (or earning capacity) and loss of consortium. In cases where the "chance" is unknown, such as exposure to toxic agents with no present compensable injury, the value of the "injury" is particularly difficult to assess. Some courts do award damages for an increased risk of harm when the extent, or even the injury itself, is unknown.

2) In *Verdicchio v. Ricca*, 179 N.J. 1, 843 A.2d 1042 (2004), the New Jersey Supreme Court reversed the finding of the lower court which found that defendant's negligence in failing to detect a malignant tumor

before it metastasized was not a substantial factor in reducing plaintiff's chance of survival. The trial court had granted defendant's motion for judgment notwithstanding the verdict on the basis that plaintiff did not prove when the cancer metastasized, and thus failed to prove that defendant's negligence was a substantial factor in reducing plaintiff's chance of survival. The New Jersey Supreme Court reversed, holding that plaintiff need not quantify the causation element. The Court held that the court's obligation was to apply the "substantial factor" analysis to determine if the defendant's negligence decreased the plaintiff's chance of survival. Plaintiff was not obligated to prove the results of tests that should have been performed, but were not, in order to meet his burden to produce evidence. The jury verdict was reinstated.

3) Negligent and intentional infliction of emotional distress, as a theory of tort recovery, has had an inconsistent course in different jurisdictions. Some refuse to award damages for alleged negligent infliction but will recognize the tort of intentional infliction of emotional distress. Some require as an element of the claim that the plaintiff have suffered some sort of physical impact.

In so-called "bystander" cases, many courts allow recovery to a bystander who observes injury to a third person as a result of negligence, but only under specific circumstances. The alleged bystander must be a close relative; the bystander must actually observe the negligent conduct at the scene of the injury; and the bystander must recognize at the time that the victim is being injured. Some courts limit recovery to those cases in which the bystander suffered serious or out-of-the-ordinary distress.

SECTION C.   DAMAGE DOLLAR AMOUNTS

HACEESA v. UNITED STATES OF AMERICA

United States Court of Appeals for the Tenth Circuit, 2002.
309 F.3d 722.

EBEL, Circuit Judge.

On the evening of Saturday, April 25, 1998, twenty-five year-old Hardy Haceesa walked into a hospital emergency room complaining of a fever, difficult and painful breathing, chest discomfort, and general achiness. He told the nurse he thought his condition could be the result of exposure to mice. Haceesa was sent home that night, diagnosed with bronchitis and told to check back at the local clinic on Monday. By Tuesday evening, he was dead.

Only after his death was Haceesa's disease diagnosed correctly: he died of hantavirus pulmonary syndrome, a rare, deadly disease caused by exposure to airborne particles of the urine of infected mice and characterized in its early stages by flu-like symptoms. Haceesa was a Navajo Indian, and the hospital where he was first seen on April 25—the Northern New Mexico Navajo Hospital in Shiprock, New Mexico—is owned and operated by the Indian Health Service, an agency of the

United States Department of Health and Human Services. As the district court observed, Shiprock Hospital stands "in the geographic center of the world for" hantavirus.

The present suit was brought by Haceesa's widow [ ] alleging medical malpractice in the failure to diagnose Haceesa's hantavirus. * * * After a bench trial in federal district court for the District of New Mexico, the court found the Government liable and awarded the Plaintiffs damages of over $2.1 million. On appeal, the Government no longer disputes its liability, but challenges the damages awarded on three distinct grounds. First, it argues that New Mexico's $600,000 statutory cap on medical malpractice recoveries applies to the Plaintiffs' suit. Second, the Government argues that its liability should be reduced to reflect its comparative negligence relative to a subsequent health care provider that also failed to diagnose Haceesa's hantavirus.

* * *

II. Concurrent/Successive Tortfeasors

During trial, the Government attempted to prove that physicians at San Juan Regional Medical Center (San Juan Regional), where Haceesa visited and was treated on April 27 and 28 (after his visit to Shiprock Hospital on April 25), were negligent in failing to accurately diagnose Haceesa's illness. The Government further argued that damages should be apportioned between it and San Juan Regional. In its post-trial decision, the district court made no factual findings regarding Haceesa's treatment at San Juan Regional, nor did it reach any conclusions regarding San Juan Regional's alleged negligence. Instead, it concluded that "under New Mexico law, ... the negligence of the [Government] was successive, and not concurrent with, any negligence of San Juan Regional Medical Center on April 27th and 28th, 1998," and that, accordingly, the Government was liable for all damages incurred by plaintiffs.

On appeal, the Government contends that the district court erred in labeling it and San Juan Regional as successive rather than concurrent tortfeasors. The Government further argues that the district court should have quantified the fault of the Government relative to that of San Juan Regional and reduced the damages to be paid by the Government. For the reasons outlined below, we agree with the district court that the Government and San Juan Regional were successive tortfeasors, but we reject the district court's conclusion that the Government is responsible for all damages incurred by the plaintiffs.

Joint tortfeasor liability in New Mexico is governed by section 41–3A–1 of the New Mexico Statutes, entitled "Several liability." This provision in effect defines two distinct categories of cases. One category involves cases "where a plaintiff sustains damage as the result of fault of more than one person which can be causally apportioned on the basis that distinct harms were caused to the plaintiff." [ ] As to cases in this category, each tortfeasor "is severally liable only for the distinct harm which that person proximately caused." Id. The other category involves "any cause of action to which the doctrine of comparative fault applies," [ ] which category implicitly consists of all joint tortfeasor cases not covered by § 41–3A–1(D). As to cases in this category, each tortfeasor who establishes that the fault of another is a proximate cause of a plaintiff's injury "shall be liable only for that portion of the total [damages] . . . that is equal to the ratio of such defendant's fault to the total fault attributed to all persons." [ ] These two categories have come to be identified in New Mexico case law respectively as cases involving "successive" tortfeasors and those involving "concurrent" tortfeasors. [citations omitted].

In Lujan [v. Healthsouth Rehab. Corp., 120 N.M. 422, 902 P.2d 1025], the court listed several factors that are relevant in determining whether tortfeasors are successive or concurrent. These factors include:

1) the identity of time and place between the acts of alleged negligence; 2) the nature of the cause of action brought against each defendant; 3) the similarity or differences in the evidence relevant to the causes of action; 4) the nature of the duties allegedly breached by each defendant; and 5) the nature of the harm or damages caused by each defendant. [ ]

Although several factors perhaps could be construed either way, we conclude that the first and fifth factors strongly support the district court's conclusion that the Government and San Juan Regional were successive tortfeasors. It is uncontroverted that the acts of alleged negligence committed by Shiprock Hospital and San Juan Regional occurred days apart from one another and in different locations. In light of the fact that hantavirus is a rapidly progressing disease, and that Haceesa presented to San Juan Regional with more severe symptoms than he did when he visited Shiprock Hospital, we conclude that the alleged negligent acts of Shiprock Hospital and San Juan Regional, though similar in type (i.e., failure to properly diagnose and treat), were distinct.

More importantly, we conclude that the nature of the harm caused by each of the hospitals was different. In Alberts v. Schultz, 1999 NMSC 15, 975 P.2d 1279, 126 N.M. 807 (N.M. 1999), the court recognized the loss-of-chance-of-survival theory. In describing the theory, the court noted that "[a] claim for loss of chance is predicated upon the negligent denial by a healthcare provider of the most effective therapy for a patient's presenting medical problem," and "the negligence may be found in such misconduct as an incorrect diagnosis, the application of inappropriate treatments, or the failure to timely provide the proper treatment." [ ]. The court further noted that "every patient has a certain probability that he or she will recover from the presenting medical problem," and "under the loss-of-chance theory, the health provider's malpractice has obliterated or reduced those odds of recovery that existed before the act of malpractice." [ ]. The court emphasized that "the patient does not allege that the malpractice caused his or her entire injury," but rather claims "that the health care provider's negligence reduced the chance of avoiding the injury actually sustained." [ ]. Consistent with these statements, the court noted: "We see no reason at this time to limit lost-chance claims to those cases in which the chance of a better result has been utterly lost." [ ].

Here, the Government concedes that "Haceesa's [condition] was far more serious when he visited [San Juan Regional] on April 27 and 28, 1998," than when he first visited Shiprock Hospital on April 25, 1998. This admission, in our view, acknowledges that Haceesa had lost a significant chance of survival between his visit to Shiprock Hospital and his subsequent visits to San Juan Regional. Stated differently, we conclude that the Government's failure to properly diagnose and treat Haceesa on April 25 reduced his chance, to some degree, of recovering from his illness, and that San Juan Regional's subsequent failure to properly diagnose and treat Haceesa on April 27 and 28 further reduced his chances, thus resulting in separate and divisible injuries.

The remaining question is whether the Government is responsible for all of the plaintiffs' damages, including those emanating from San Juan Regional's alleged negligent treatment. Plaintiffs assert that the Government was an "original tortfeasor" and thus liable for San Juan Regional's subsequent medical negligence. In support of their assertion, plaintiffs point to the following statement by the court in *Lewis [v. Samson*, 2001 N.M.S.C. 35, 35 P.3d 972 (NM 2001)]: "the original tortfeasor is jointly and severally liable for the entire harm to the plaintiff, including the original injury and any foreseeable enhancement of the injury by medical negligence." [ ].

We reject plaintiffs' arguments. Lewis involved an original tortfeasor who stabbed the plaintiff, and a subsequent tortfeasor who committed medical malpractice while endeavoring to treat the injuries resulting from the original tort. In discussing the liability of the original tortfeasor, the court was careful to emphasize that its discussion was limited to the "narrow class of cases" involving "an initial injury caused by tortious conduct and a subsequent enhancement of the initial injury caused by foreseeable medical negligence occurring during the course of medical treatment for the initial injury." [ ]. Here, in contrast, Haceesa's initial injury was not caused by the Government, but rather by the hantavirus. In other words, the medical negligence allegedly committed by San Juan Regional occurred during an attempt to treat the condition caused by the hantavirus, not during an attempt somehow to treat the injury (loss of chance) caused by the Government's own medical negligence. Thus, Lewis is distinguishable from the instant case, and the district court erred in characterizing the Government as an original tortfeasor responsible for all of plaintiffs' damages. On remand, it will be necessary for the district court to make findings of fact regarding the loss of chance of survival caused by the Government's medical negligence and the amount of damages associated exclusively with that loss of chance.

AFFIRMED IN PART AND REVERSED IN PART

HARDI v. MEZZANOTTE

District of Columbia Court of Appeals, 2003.
818 A.2d 974.

WAGNER, *Chief Judge*:

I.

A. *Factual Background*

According to the evidence, appellee was treated by Dr. John O'Connor in 1990 for diverticulitis, an infectious process affecting the colon. In January and February of 1994, she experienced symptoms which she believed to be a recurrence of that illness. After trying without success to reach Dr. O'Connor, she saw Dr. Hardi, a Board-certified gastroenterologist, on February 3, 1994, and informed him of her suspicions and provided him with a copy of an x-ray report that Dr. O'Connor ordered after he treated her for diverticulitis. The doctor took appellee's history and noted on her chart that Dr. O'Connor had treated her previously with antibiotics for diverticulitis. During his physical examination of appellee, Dr. Hardi felt a mass which he thought to be of gynecological origin. However, he also understood that the mass could be caused by a recurrence of diverticulitis. His medical chart does not show alternate likely causes of appellee's condition or specify diverticulitis as one such cause. Dr. Hardi did not order a CAT–Scan, a test typically ordered when diverticulitis may be present, or initiate a course of antibiotic therapy. He informed appellee that her problems were gynecological in nature and referred her to Dr. Joel Match, a gynecologist, for a work-up with respect to the mass.

On February 8, 1994, Dr. Match saw appellee. He ordered a CA–125 blood test, which he testified is 80% reliable in predicting the existence of gynecological cancer. The test was negative for the disease. The report from the ultrasound examination, which Dr. Match ordered, revealed that there was a mass in the left lower quadrant of appellee's abdomen, but it could not be determined whether it was diverticular or gynecological in origin. Therefore, the radiologist recommended a "close clinical and sonographic follow-up." Notwithstanding the results of the tests, Dr. Match concluded that appellee had ovarian cancer and scheduled a complete hysterectomy (the surgical removal of her uterus, fallopian tubes and ovaries) for March 1994. Dr. Match informed Dr. Hardi of the test results. Although the blood test did not reveal cancer, and the ultrasound exam did not reveal an enlarged uterus, Dr. Hardi "cleared" the performance of gynecological surgery. Dr. Match requested that Dr. Hardi undertake further testing within his specialty in order to rule out the possibility that appellee was suffering from any gastrointestinal diseases.

On February 21, 1994, Dr. Hardi performed a sigmoidoscopy on appellee, which entailed the introduction of an endoscope into her sigmoid colon for purposes of observation. He was unable to complete the procedure after multiple attempts because of an apparent obstruction of the colon caused by the diverticulitis. Appellee's expert witness, Dr. Robert Shapiro, explained that such an obstruction is a "red flag," telling the doctor "there is something wrong with the bowel." Dr. Hardi scheduled a more intrusive procedure, a colonoscopy, performed under general anesthesia, for March 2, 1994. He attempted the procedure multiple times, without success, due to the obstruction, and desisted finally because of "fear of perforation." He ordered Dr. Odenwald, a Sibley Hospital radiologist, to perform a third exploratory procedure, a barium enema of the sigmoid colon, but it could not be completed due to the same obstruction. Dr. Odenwald discussed with Dr. Hardi the possibility that the obstruction resulted from a gastrointestinal disease rather than gynecological cancer.

Immediately following the exploratory procedures on March 2, 1994, appellee's condition deteriorated markedly. These procedures had exerted pressure on her sigmoid colon and caused the spread of her diverticular infection. Appellee was admitted as an emergency patient to Columbia Hospital for Women on March 7, 1994. By then, her diverticular abscess had ruptured, resulting in peritonitis (*i.e.*, infection of the abdomen). Dr. Match ordered a CAT–Scan on March 7, 1994. However, appellee's condition precluded the use of contrast media. Dr. Match also ordered an ultrasound that day, which proved to be non-diagnostic. On March 8, 1994, appellee had surgery which involved removal of her non-cancerous reproductive organs. During surgery, multiple infectious abscesses and pus were encountered. Dr. Hafner, the general surgeon who performed the operation, removed the infectious matter from the patient's abdomen, excised the affected portion of her bowel, and performed a colostomy. After surgery, Dr. Hafner informed appellee's husband that she had diverticulitis, not gynecological cancer. Appellee had a slow recovery due to peritonitis and associated complications, and ultimately, she was required to undergo four additional surgical procedures, involving a "take-down" of her colostomy and the correction of hernias caused by the related weakening of her abdominal wall. These surgical procedures extended into March 1996. Appellee spent a total of eighty-three days as an in-patient at Columbia Hospital for Women and George Washington University Hospital, and a nursing home.

* * *

Appellants argue that the trial court's finding of proximate cause lacks evidentiary support. They contend that: (1) the trial court did not find, to a reasonable degree of medical certainty, that Dr. Hardi's actions were the proximate cause of appellee's injuries; and (2) the evidence was insufficient to establish that his failure to diagnose diverticulitis and prescribe antibiotics caused appellee to have to undergo surgery. Appellants argue that the evidence shows that surgery was medically necessary to remove the mass and that the antibiotic (amoxicillin) prescribed by Dr. Match did not resolve the mass. Appellee contends that the trial court's finding of proximate causation is supported by the record. She contends that the trial court properly found, based upon the evidence, that Dr. Hardi's failure to place diverticulitis at the top of the list proximately resulted in his failure to test properly and promptly and provide treatment which would have resolved the infection and avoided the emergency surgery.

"To establish proximate cause, the plaintiff must present evidence from which a reasonable juror could find that there was a direct and substantial causal relationship between the defendant's breach of the standard of care and the plaintiff's injuries *and* that the injuries were foreseeable." *Psychiatric Inst. of Wash. v. Allen*, 509 A.2d 619, 624 (D.C. 1986) (emphasis in original) [ ]. When the trial court's findings of fact lack evidentiary support, this Court must set aside the ruling. [ ]

The trial court found that there was "little doubt that prompt treatment with antibiotics (intravenously, if necessary) would likely have resolved the infection, thereby obviating the necessity for surgery." This factual finding is supported by the record. Dr. Robert Shapiro, a gastroenterologist, testified that if appropriate antibiotics had been administered, the patient would likely have avoided the March 8, 1994 surgery. He further testified, and the trial court found, that the immediate and direct cause of the "emergency surgery" on March 8th was Dr. Hardi's exploratory procedures several days earlier, which ruptured her diverticular abscess and caused life-threatening peritonitis. According to the evidence, these procedures were contra-indicated, given the patient's condition. There was evidence that the rupture of her diverticular abscess created the necessity for emergency surgery and subsequent medical problems and hospitalizations. Dr. Shapiro testified that appropriate antibiotic therapy should have been started within twenty-four to forty-eight hours of the patient's first visit to Dr. Hardi, and that the sooner started, the better the patient does. He testified that it was his opinion that "more likely than not, if appropriate antibiotics had been administered appellee would have avoided [the March 8th] surgery."

Appellants argue that the trial court observed that whether appellee ultimately would have required surgery was an "open question." A closer reading of the court's Memorandum Opinion, however, shows that the trial court found that there was an "open question" about the "possibility" of an *elective* surgery to address appellee's diverticulitis at some unspecified time in the future. According to Dr. Shapiro's testimony, it was only a possibility that "one might at some time in the future have recommended surgery to prevent further attacks of diverticulitis, but that would be *elective* surgery." (Emphasis added.)

IV.

* * *

B.   Collateral Source Issue

Whether unpaid and "written-off" medical expenses can be recovered by a plaintiff as compensatory damages is an issue of first impression in the District of Columbia. In support of their argument in the trial court, appellants rely here, as they did in the trial court, primarily upon two cases applying Virginia law, *State Farm Mut. Auto Ins. Co. v. Bowers*, 255 Va. 581, 500 S.E.2d 212 (Va. 1998) and *McAmis v. Wallace*, 980 F.Supp. 181, 185 (W.D. Va. 1997). *Bowers* involved a suit by an automobile insurance carrier against its insured for overpayments under a medical payments provision. [citation omitted.] Bowers' policy provided for payment of reasonable and necessary expenses incurred. [ ] The Supreme Court of Virginia, interpreting the language of the policy under the case law of Virginia, concluded that the term "incurred" referred to those amounts that the health care providers accepted as full payment for their services, and not amounts written-off by the providers. [ ]. In *McAmis*, a federal court held that the collateral source rule does not permit a plaintiff to recover medical expenses written-off by her health care providers pursuant to a contract with Medicaid, since she did not incur the written-off amounts. [ ]. The court reasoned that under Virginia law before the collateral source rule applies, the injured party must "establish personal liability, at some time, for that amount." [ ]. Compensatory damages are intended to make a plaintiff whole under Virginia law, and for that to occur, "plaintiff, need only receive the actual costs of medical care borne by Medicaid." [ ] In *McAmis*, the court also rejected plaintiff's argument that she was entitled to recover the write-off as a benefit of paying taxes into the Medicaid system.[ ] In making this ruling, the court recognized that Medicaid benefits do not derive from contract, but are dispersed under a social benefits program. [ ].

Subsequently, the Virginia Supreme Court, distinguishing its earlier holding in *Bowers, supra*, held that the full amount of reasonable medical expenses may be recovered from a tortfeasor without reduction for amounts written-off by health care providers. *See Acuar v. Letourneau*, 260 Va. 180, 531 S.E.2d 316, 321, 323 (Va. 2000). In *Acuar*, the appellant, who admitted liability, sought to exclude from damages medical bills written-off by the injured party's health care providers. [ ]. The court held that the collateral source rule applied and that the amount of damages could not be reduced. [ ]. The court reasoned that:

> the focal point of the collateral source rule is not whether an injured party has "incurred" certain medical expenses. Rather, it is whether a tort victim has received benefits from a collateral source that cannot be used to reduce the amount of damages owed by a tortfeasor. . . .

Those amounts written off are as much of a benefit for which [the injured party] paid consideration as are the actual cash payments made by his health insurance carrier to the health care providers. The portions of medical expenses that health care providers write off constitute "compensation or indemnity received by a tort victim from a source collateral to the tortfeasor."

[ ] The court distinguished *Bowers, supra,* as a case in which it construed the specific terms of an insurance contract and where "neither the tort policy of this Commonwealth nor the collateral source rule was implicated." [ ]

In the case now before the court, the tort policy of the District of Columbia and the collateral source rule are implicated. The trial court was persuaded that the collateral source rule applies, and where the party pays the premium for insurance, she is entitled to the benefit of the bargain contracted for including any reduction in payments that the insurance carrier was able to negotiate. We agree. In reaching this decision, we are persuaded by our own longstanding collateral source doctrine and the sound reasoning of the Virginia Supreme Court in *Acuar.*

Under the collateral source rule, payments to the injured party from a collateral source are not allowed to diminish damages recoverable from the wrongdoer. [citations omitted]. The rule is applicable when either: (1) a payment to the injured party came from a source wholly independent of the tortfeasor, or (2) " 'when the plaintiff may be said to have contracted for the prospect of a double recovery.' " [*District of Columbia v.] Jackson,* 451 A.2d 867, 873 (quoting *Overton v. United States,* 619 F.2d 1299, 1307 (8th Cir. 1980)). A reason for the rule is that a party should receive the benefit of a bargain for which he or she has contracted. [ ]

This case is one in which the payments qualify as a collateral source under both of the above-mentioned criteria. Appellee paid a private carrier to insure her for medical expenses. That contractual arrangement was totally independent of Dr. Hardi. Appellee contracted for them independently of Dr. Hardi, and therefore, Dr. Hardi is not entitled to a credit for those write-offs. [ ]. These amounts are a benefit of appellee's agreement with her health insurance carrier, and constitute a collateral source to the tortfeasor. *Acuar, supra,* 531 A.2d at 322–23 (citation omitted).

Dr. Hardi concedes that appellee is entitled to recover amounts actually paid by her or her insurance carrier, but argues that she should not be able to recover amounts not paid by anyone (*i.e.,* written-off amounts). In support of its argument, Dr. Hardi cites * * * *Moorhead v. Crozer Chester Med. Ctr.,* 564 Pa. 156, 765 A.2d 786 (Pa. 2001). * * * Regardless of any broad language in the opinion in *Moorhead,* that case involved medical services provided by the tortfeasor itself so that an application of the collateral source rule would have required, in effect, double payment. [ ]. In *Moorhead,* the plaintiff sued the medical facility which had treated her for her injuries. [ ]. The medical facility was a voluntary participant in the Medicare program and had a contractual obligation under it to accept a limited amount for its services. [ ]. The court held that "given [the medical facility's] contractual obligations, the trial court did not err in determining that [plaintiff] was limited to recovering . . . the amount that was paid and accepted as payment in full for past medical expenses." [ ]. *Moorhead* is not persuasive because there, it was the tortfeasor who provided medical services at a reduced cost pursuant to its own contract, as opposed to plaintiff's. Since the court allowed plaintiff's damages for the amount actually paid to the medical facility, and the facility itself provided services in the greater amount, it is fair to say that the medical facility actually made plaintiff whole for the full amount of the claimed medical expenses. It was the tortfeasor's contract that accounted for this result, not the plaintiff's, as far as we can tell.

Here, a private insurance carrier paid appellee's medical expenses. That source is wholly independent of appellants. Because any write-offs conferred would have been a by-product of the insurance contract secured by appellee, even those amounts should be counted as damages. [ ] Therefore, because any write-offs enjoyed by appellee were negotiated by her private insurance company, a source independent of appellants, they should be included in her damages. Under the collateral source rule, she is entitled to all benefits resulting from her contract.

MARKLEY v. OAK HEALTH CARE INVESTORS OF COLDWATER

Court of Appeals of Michigan, 2003.
255 Mich.App. 245, 660 N.W.2d 344.

MURPHY, P.J.

In this wrongful death action involving medical malpractice, defendants appeal as of right from a $354,133 judgment entered in favor of plaintiff following a jury trial to determine damages. Defendants maintain that the judgment should have been reduced to reflect plaintiff's earlier settlement with Community Health Center (Community) that was reached in a separate action. In the alternative, defendants argue that the statutory limit on noneconomic damages in a medical malpractice action, MCL 600.1483, should have been applied by the trial court to cap plaintiff's total recovery. * * *

I. UNDERLYING FACTS AND PROCEDURAL HISTORY

The facts of this case are not in dispute * * * In short, plaintiff's decedent was admitted to Community where her eventual misdiagnosis resulted in a large-bowel resection and left-leg amputation in 1994. The decedent's family cared for her immediately after her release from Community, but she was eventually admitted to a nursing home owned and operated by defendant Oak Health Care Investors of Coldwater, Inc. (OHC). While at the nursing home, OHC's nurse practitioner increased the prescribed infusion rate for decedent's intravenous feeding, causing her to go into respiratory distress and, shortly thereafter, die of cardiac arrest.

Plaintiff sued Community, which settled with plaintiff for $460,000; $220,000 of that amount was allocated to "the legal theory arising from the Wrongful Death of [the decedent]" and $240,000 was allocated to "the legal theory arising from the conscious pain and suffering from the injuries to [the decedent] during her lifetime." Before the settlement was reached, plaintiff sued defendants for the same wrongful death in the case at bar. Defendants failed to respond to plaintiff's complaint with an affidavit of meritorious defense as required by MCL 600.2912e, and partial summary disposition was granted to plaintiff * * *. A trial was held solely to determine the amount of damages.

The jury awarded plaintiff $300,000 in total wrongful death damages * * * Defendants had moved to file notice of nonparty fault shortly before trial, and the trial court apparently denied the motion on the basis of defendants' failure to timely file. * * * The jury did not consider the fault of anyone other than defendants.

II. TRIAL COURT'S RULINGS ON LEGAL ISSUES

The trial court found the statutory damage cap [ ] to be unconstitutional as violative of the right to trial by jury. With regard to the requested $220,000 setoff against the $300,000 verdict, the trial court ruled that the amendment of MCL 600.2925d, which until the enactment of 1995 tort reform legislation had expressly allowed a setoff against a judgment predicated on an earlier settlement payment, abrogated any common-law right to a setoff; therefore, defendants were not entitled to any setoff. The trial court ruled that the law now provided for the apportionment of fault; however, this could not form the basis for a reduction in the judgment because defendants failed to timely file notice of nonparty fault, and thus the issue was not before the jury * * *.

IV. ANALYSIS AND HOLDING

Although the parties and the trial court framed the issues, in part, with reference to principles concerning contribution and allocation of fault, the heart of the question that we must answer is whether the common-law rule of setoff survived 1995 tort reform legislation in situations still requiring the application of joint and several liability.

A. Common–Law Rule of Setoff

In Thick v. Lapeer Metal Products, 419 Mich. 342, 348 n.1, 353 N.W.2d 464 (1984), our Supreme Court noted the common-law rule "that where a negligence action is brought against joint tortfeasors, and one alleged tortfeasor agrees to settle his potential liability by paying a lump sum in exchange for a release, and a judgment is subsequently entered against the non-settling tortfeasor, the judgment is reduced *pro tanto* by the settlement amount." [citations omitted].

The common-law rule of setoff is predicated on the principle that a plaintiff is entitled to only one recovery for his injury. * * *

"The American cases offer equitable and convincing reasons for their course, viz.: The liability of tortfeasors for a joint tort is joint and several. The injured party has the right to pursue them jointly or severally at his election, and recover separate judgments; but, the injury being single, he may recover but one compensation. Therefore, he may elect *de melioribus damnis* and issue his execution accordingly, but if he obtains only partial satisfaction he has not precluded himself from proceeding against another co-tortfeasor; his election of the first judgment concluding him only as to the amount he may receive, and whatever has been paid must apply *pro tanto* upon his further recovery."

Assuming here for the moment that defendants are jointly and severally liable for decedent's wrongful death and that the common-law rule of setoff is applicable, it is clear that the $300,000 verdict would be reduced by the $220,000 settlement payment made by Community to plaintiff.

B.   Joint and Several Liability

Under the current statutory scheme, MCL 600.2956 abolished joint liability in most circumstances. However, joint and several liability still exists in medical malpractice cases where the plaintiff is without fault, such as the present case. [ ]

Under established principles of joint and several liability, where the negligence of two or more persons produces a single, indivisible injury, the tortfeasors are jointly and severally liable despite there being no common duty, common design, or concert of action. [ ]. Here, with regard to wrongful death, Community and defendants, through successive negligent acts, produced a single, indivisible injury, i.e., the death of plaintiff's decedent. Although plaintiff filed separate lawsuits, Community and defendants are in theory jointly and severally liable for wrongful death, and we shall treat them as such, otherwise a plaintiff in a similar situation could avoid the effect of our ruling today by simply suing joint tortfeasors in separate actions. We shall effectively treat defendants as if they had been sued jointly with Community by plaintiff in a single action.

C.   Contribution and Allocation of Fault

We find it necessary, in light of some apparent confusion in the trial court, to distinguish setoff from other theories and principles not implicated in the present case. With regard to contribution, the settlement discharged Community from liability to defendants for contribution. [ ]. We are not dealing with contribution because contribution affixes the rights as between joint tortfeasors and not as between one tortfeasor and a plaintiff. MCL 600.2925a. With joint and several liability, each tortfeasor is liable for the full amount of damages. As noted by this Court in Smiley v. Corrigan, 248 Mich.App. 51, 55, 638 N.W.2d 151 (2001):

> As part of its tort reform legislation, the Michigan Legislature abolished joint and several liability and replaced with "fair share liability." The significance of the change is that each tortfeasor will pay only that portion of the total damage award that reflects the tortfeasor's percentage of fault. Accordingly, if the factfinder concludes that a defendant is ten percent at fault for a plaintiff's

injuries and awards the plaintiff $100,000 in damages, the defendant will be responsible only for $10,000, *not the entire damage award, as would have been the case under the former joint and several liability system.* [Emphasis added.]

Defendants are not seeking contribution from Community, but merely a setoff, predicated on the settlement payment, against the $300,000 verdict.

For the same reason, with regard to allocation of fault, even if the jury had been given the opportunity to allocate fault in some degree to Community, it would not have resulted in a reduction of the $300,000 verdict as between defendants and plaintiff because liability is joint and several and plaintiff would have every legal right to recover the full amount from defendants despite the possibility that defendants would pay more than their fair share. Support for this is found in MCL 600.6304(4), wherein it is stated that "except as otherwise provided in subsection (6) [applicable here], a person shall not be required to pay damages in an amount greater than his or her percentage of fault.... " Thus, there would be no basis to reduce the judgment even if defendants jumped through the procedural hoops regarding allocation of fault.

D. MCL 600.2925d

MCL 600.2925d currently provides:

If a release or a covenant not to sue or not to enforce judgment is given in good faith to 1 of 2 or more persons for the same injury or the same wrongful death, both of the following apply:

(a) The release or covenant does not discharge 1 or more of the other persons from liability for the injury or wrongful death unless its terms so provide.

(b) The release or covenant discharges the person to whom it is given from all liability for contribution to any other person for the injury or wrongful death.

Before the 1995 tort reform legislation amended the statute, 1995 PA 161, this same statute included a subsection that provided that a settlement and release "reduces the claim against the other tortfeasors to the extent of any amount stipulated by the release or the covenant or to the extent of the amount of the consideration paid for it, whichever amount is the greater." [ ]. This language, which represented a codification of the common-law rule of setoff was apparently deleted because the tort reform legislation, for the most part, abolished joint and several liability in favor of allocation of fault or several liability. [ ]. There would be no need for a setoff because the tortfeasor-defendant not involved in the settlement would necessarily be responsible for an amount of damages distinct from the settling defendant on the basis of allocation of fault. Therefore, a settlement payment cannot be deemed to constitute a payment toward a loss included in a later damage award entered against the nonsettling tortfeasor. There exists little danger, in cases of several liability, that a plaintiff will receive recovery beyond the actual loss.

We must answer the question whether the amendment of § 2925d revived the common-law rule of setoff in joint and several liability cases, or whether the rule is abolished in its entirety.

E.   Tort Reform Legislation and the Amendment of Section 2925d

There are two competing legal principles at work in trying to resolve whether the amendment of § 2925d abrogated the common-law rule of setoff. First, there is the general rule that "the repeal of a statute revives the common-law rule as it was before the statute was enacted." [ ]. Second, there exists the rule that "where comprehensive legislation prescribes in detail a course of conduct to pursue and the parties and things affected, and designates specific limitations and exceptions, the Legislature will be found to have intended that the statute supersede and replace the common law dealing with the subject matter." [ ] . The comprehensive tort reform legislation, however, simply no longer addressed the issue of setoff in any manner; it is silent. Moreover, the tort reform legislation prescribed in detail a course of conduct regarding allocation of fault and several liability, not joint and several liability. Therefore, joint and several liability principles presumptively remained intact, where, as here, joint and several liability was not abrogated by the Legislature. With tort reform and the switch to several liability, it is logical to conclude that common-law setoff in joint and several liability cases remained the law, where the new legislation was silent, where application of the common-law rule does not conflict with any current statutes concerning tort law, and where a plaintiff is conceivably over-compensated for its injury should the rule not be applied. Considering the general nature and tone of tort reform legislation, we conclude that the Legislature did not intend to allow recovery greater than the actual loss in joint and several liability cases when it deleted the relevant portion of § 2925d, but instead intended that common-law principles limiting a recovery to the actual loss would remain intact.

Here, a jury determined that plaintiff was entitled to $300,000 in total damages for wrongful death; however, plaintiff already received $220,000 for wrongful death. Without reduction of the jury verdict, plaintiff receives $520,000 in compensation for a $300,000 harm. If we were to allow such a recovery, we would defeat the principle underlying common-law setoff, that being that a plaintiff can have but one recovery for an injury. We find that the principle of one recovery and the common-law rule of setoff, in the context of joint and several liability cases, continue to be the law in Michigan.

F.   Cap on Noneconomic Damages in Medical Malpractice Cases

The parties agree that should MCL 600.1483 be applicable, the total amount of damages recoverable by plaintiff could not exceed $328,700. Because defendants are receiving a setoff of $220,000 against the $300,000 verdict, they must only pay $80,000 to plaintiff, plus interest and taxable costs thereon. If the $220,000 settlement payment from the first suit is added to the $80,000 from the second suit, the total amount of noneconomic damages recovered or recoverable by plaintiff is under $328,700; therefore, there is no reason to address the damage cap. Defendants make no argument that the $240,000 settlement payment for conscious pain and suffering should be considered in determining the cap issue, nor that they should receive any setoff for this settlement payment.

[REVERSED]

ZIEBER v. BOGERT

Supreme Court of Pennsylvania, 2001.
565 Pa. 376, 773 A.2d 758.

MR. JUSTICE ZAPPALA

* * *

On June 6, 1992, Robert Zieber experienced severe abdominal pain. His wife, a resident in obstetrics and gynecology, felt what appeared to be a four-centimeter mass in his lower abdomen. Zieber went to the emergency room of Roxborough Memorial Hospital and was examined by Dr. J. Norris Childs. Dr. Childs felt the mass in Zieber's stomach and ordered blood drawn. He later contacted Zieber's primary care physician, Dr. Arthur Bogert, and recommended that he order a C–T scan with intravenous ("IV") contrast, a barium enema and an upper G.I. study.

After examining Zieber on June 11, 1992, Dr. Bogert preliminarily diagnosed him with irritable bowel syndrome. Dr. Bogert ordered the barium enema and the upper G.I. that Dr. Childs had recommended, but did not order the C–T scan. Dr. Bogert later informed Zieber that the studies had confirmed his prior diagnosis of irritable bowel syndrome and that his condition could be managed by adjustments to his diet. Dr. Bogert instructed Zieber to return to his office if severe abdominal pain recurred.

In March of 1993, Zieber experienced flu-like symptoms, including abdominal pain and headache. Due to a switch in health insurance plans, Zieber went to see Dr. Joan Lit, a participating provider of his new plan. Dr. Lit felt the mass in Zieber's lower abdomen and ultimately ordered a C–T scan with IV contrast. The scan revealed a large soft tissue mass, suggesting a lymphoma of the small bowel and numerous enlarged lymph nodes. Exploratory surgery confirmed that Zieber had a large cell lymphoma. The surgery also revealed two masses in his abdomen, one measuring eleven centimeters and the other measuring six centimeters. The larger tumor had invaded the bowel and created an obstruction. Zieber underwent surgical removal of the two masses as well as large sections of his colon and small and large intestines. Aggressive chemotherapy followed, which caused life-threatening side effects. Zieber was thereafter placed on a more conventional regimen and later achieved remission of the disease.

On May 8, 1995, Zieber and his wife (Appellees) filed the instant medical malpractice action against Dr. Bogert et al (Appellants). They sought damages for the past and present injuries associated with the late diagnosis of the lymphoma as well as damages for Zieber's increased risk of recurrence of cancer in the future. Appellees presented the testimony of Dr. Raymond Weiss, who stated that there is a 35% to 50% chance that a patient in complete remission will suffer a relapse within five years after the completion of chemotherapy. Dr. Weiss explained that a patient achieves complete remission when a C–T scan reveals no cancer, although microscopic cancer cells may remain in the patient's body at that time. Zieber testified as to his fear and mental anguish arising from this increased risk. Additionally, the trial court instructed the jury that this was Appellees' "one day in court," and therefore the jury should consider what Zieber's harm might be in the future as a result of what transpired in this case.

At the conclusion of trial, the jury returned a verdict in favor of Appellees, awarding $800,000 to Zieber and $200,000 to his wife on her loss of consortium claim. On appeal, the Superior Court vacated the order of the trial court and remanded for a new trial. It held that the trial court erred in failing to charge the jury on comparative negligence after Dr. Bogert had testified that Zieber refused to undergo the C–T scan. The court, however, upheld the trial court's ruling that evidence of the risk of recurrence of cancer may be considered as part of the jury's assessment of damages. The court distinguished cases precluding recovery for the fear of and/or increased risk of contracting a disease on the ground that Zieber already had an invasive and aggressive form of cancer.

* * * Appellants argue that the Superior Court erroneously relied on Gradel v. Inouye, 491 Pa. 534, 421 A.2d 674 (Pa. 1980), for the proposition that evidence of the recurrence of cancer may be considered by the jury when awarding damages. They contend that this conclusion is inconsistent with our subsequent decision in Simmons v. Pacor, Inc., 543 Pa. 664, 674 A.2d 232 (Pa. 1996), where we rejected claims for increased risk and fear of cancer. Appellants maintain that there is no basis for drawing a distinction between the speculative nature of future damages for the occurrence of cancer versus the *recurrence* of cancer. They urge our Court to apply Simmons to bar Appellees' present "fear" and "risk" claims and allow Appellees to return to court if and when Zieber's disease recurs, when the damages can be more accurately assessed.

We decline Appellants' invitation to extend the rationale of Simmons to cases in which the plaintiff has already contracted cancer and the claims for fear and/or increased risk of recurrence of cancer arise from the metastasis of the disease. The instant case is controlled by our decision in Gradel, where our Court spoke to this very issue.

In Gradel, the plaintiffs filed a medical malpractice action against an orthopedic surgeon who had failed to remove a growing soft-tissue tumor in a young boy's arm. Due to the delay in diagnosis, the tumor invaded the bone and the boy's arm was later amputated above the elbow. Our Court held that in awarding damages, it was proper for the jury to consider medical testimony concerning the boy's increased risk of recurrence of cancer. [ ]. We explained:

As we stated in Boyle v. Pennsylvania Railroad Co. [ ] a doctor properly may be allowed to explain the possible future effects of an injury, and with less definiteness than is required of opinion testimony on causation. Consequently, it was not improper for the jury to consider the possibility of future metastasis in awarding damages. [ ]

Our decision in Simmons did not alter this established rule of law. Simmons was not a medical malpractice law suit, but involved consolidated actions to recover damages for injuries caused by occupational exposure to asbestos. As an element of damages, the plaintiffs sought relief for increased risk and fear of cancer. Unlike the instant case, none of the plaintiffs had contracted mesothelioma or cancer at the time the suits were filed. Instead, they were all diagnosed with asbestos-related pleural thickening, which is the formation of calcified tissue on the membranes surrounding the lungs. Although the condition is detectable by x-ray, it did not cause any lung impairment. The issue for review was whether asymptomatic pleural thickening, i.e., a condition unaccompanied by disabling consequences or physical impairment, is a compensable injury.

We found that it was not a compensable injury giving rise to a cause of action. Our decision was based on the fact that there was no physical injury that necessitated the awarding of damages. Equally significant was the fact that, due to the two-disease rule originally set forth in Marinari v. Asbestos Corporation, Ltd., 417 Pa.Super. 440, 612 A.2d 1021 (Pa. Super. 1992), the plaintiffs were not precluded from subsequently commencing an action for an asbestos related injury when symptoms develop and physiological impairment begins.

We explained that the "two-disease rule" in asbestos exposure cases permitted a plaintiff to commence separate causes of action for separate asbestos related diseases—one cause of action for a nonmalignant asbestos related disease which had become manifest and another cause of action for the subsequent development of a separate malignant disease such as lung cancer or mesothelioma. [ ]. The rule was intended to remedy the inequities that arose in cases involving latent diseases that did not surface until years after the initial exposure. Prior to the adoption of the rule, the cause of action for asbestos exposure accrued at the time the first sign of asbestos-related disease was discovered, when the plaintiff might be unaware of the extent of the resulting harm. Based on the unique construct of these cases, we held that the diagnosis of asymptomatic pleural thickening had no statute of limitations ramifications regarding a claim alleging a nonmalignant physiological impairment.

In a similar vein, we held that because asymptomatic pleural thickening was not a sufficient physical injury, the resultant emotional distress damages were likewise not recoverable. As additional support for our holding, we noted the speculative nature of the damages for fear of cancer. We stated:

> The awarding of such damages would lead to inequitable results since those who never contract cancer would obtain damages even though the disease never came into fruition. The actual compensation due to the plaintiff can be more accurately assessed when the disease has manifested. [ ].

Appellants contend that damages for increased risk and/or fear of *recurrence* of cancer are likewise speculative. As noted, however, this was not the foundation upon which Simmons rested. Rather, the decision was based on the lack of physical injury and the ability of the plaintiffs, pursuant to the two-disease rule, to file a second action if and when the symptoms arise. Neither of these conditions exist in the instant case. Our decision in Simmons expressly recognized that a plaintiff could seek damages for his mental anguish for fear and increased risk of cancer if and when the cancer develops. [ ] Here, Zieber's cancer has developed and he has already suffered its debilitating effects. The requirement of a physical injury has therefore clearly been established. Moreover, Appellees may not commence a second action, if and when the cancer recurs, based upon the same alleged negligence of Dr. Bogert in failing to properly diagnose the condition.

This point is illustrated by the case of Holmes v. Lado, 412 Pa.Super. 218, 602 A.2d 1389 (Pa. Super. 1992), a malpractice action alleging a physician's negligence in failing to timely diagnose breast cancer. In March of 1982, Mrs. Holmes had consulted the defendant-physician concerning lumps in her right breast. Mammograms performed shortly thereafter and again in April of 1985 revealed no malignancy. In August of 1985, Mrs. Holmes was referred to another physician who ordered a biopsy, which revealed stage III breast carcinoma. Mrs. Holmes underwent a mastectomy and received chemotherapy. In November of 1986, a CAT scan revealed metastasis of the cancer to the right frontal and temporal lobes of the brain. Radiation and chemotherapy were unsuccessful and Mrs. Holmes died on March 28, 1987, from metastatic breast carcinoma.

Mr. Holmes filed a survival action in November of 1988. The trial court granted the physician's motion for summary judgment on the ground that the action was barred by the applicable two-year statute of limitations. The Superior Court affirmed, finding that the statute of limitations began to run in August of 1985, when the decedent was informed that a mammogram could not detect cancer and that the only way to do so was to perform a biopsy.

Significant to the instant case, the Superior Court rejected Mr. Holmes's argument that the metastasis, which had been diagnosed within the statute of limitations period, was a new injury for which a separate cause of action could be brought. The court held that the alleged failure to order the diagnostic tests necessary to diagnose the mass as a malignant tumor pertained to the initial cancer and not to the later metastasis.

The logic of allowing one cause of action is sound, considering that the action is based upon the single event of medical negligence. If we were to reject Holmes, as Appellants suggest, a new cause of action purportedly could accrue every time cancer cells lay dormant in the body and subsequently spread to a different organ. Such a rule could conceivably create several causes of action for a misdiagnosed cancer patient where previously there was one. Simply put, the reasons justifying the creation of the separate disease rule are not applicable here, where the plaintiff has already contracted cancer and seeks damages for increased risk of recurrence of the disease.

* * *

In summary, we hold that evidence of the increased risk and/or fear of recurrence of cancer is admissible for the purpose of establishing damages in a medical malpractice case alleging a physician's negligence in failing to properly diagnose the disease. Appellants' concerns regarding the speculative nature of such damages can be presented to the jury during argument, as such challenges go to the weight, rather than the admissibility of the evidence.

AFFIRMED.

FORTE v. CONNERWOOD HEALTHCARE, INC., d/b/a ANDERSON HEALTHCARE CENTER

Supreme Court of Indiana, 2001.
745 N.E.2d 796.

RUCKER, Justice

* * *

FACTS

On October 2, 1995, Jennipher Forte ("Mother") placed her five-year-old developmentally disabled son in the custody of Connerwood Health Care, Inc., a nursing home doing business as Anderson Healthcare Center. n1 According to Mother, over the course of the next several days, the nursing home committed several acts of negligence that led to her son's death on October 9, 1995. Thereafter, on her own behalf and on behalf of her son's estate Mother sued the nursing home along with several members of its medical staff (referred to collectively as "Defendants"). In her initial complaint, Mother sought compensatory damages only. However, alleging that Defendants' negligence was willful and wanton, Mother later amended her complaint to include a claim for punitive damages. After filing their answer, Defendants moved for partial judgment on the pleadings with respect to punitive damages, contending that they are not available under the Child Wrongful Death

Statute. In response, Mother argued that not only was she entitled to recover punitive damages under the statute, but also she was entitled to punitive damages for loss of consortium apart from the statute. The trial court granted Defendants' motion and Mother pursued an interlocutory appeal.

On review, the Court of Appeals agreed that the trial court properly granted Defendants' motion concerning Mother's claim to a statutory right of punitive damages. [ ]. However, the Court of Appeals determined that the allegations in Mother's complaint established facts entitling Mother to punitive damages on another theory—common law loss of services. [ ]. Having previously granted transfer, we affirm the trial court.

DISCUSSION

I. Punitive Damages Under the Child Wrongful Death Statute

Although this Court has never addressed the issue, we agree with the Court of Appeals that punitive damages are not recoverable under the Child Wrongful Death Statute. At common law, there was no liability in tort for killing another because actions for personal injury did not survive the death of the injured party. [citations omitted]. Our legislature first authorized a cause of action for the death of a minor in 1851, the same year Indiana's second constitution was adopted. Since 1851, the statute has been amended several times, the latest of which was in 1998.[3] Until 1987, the changes in the statute from its original enactment were basically those of form. Otherwise the statute remained essentially the same.

Although the predecessor to the 1987 statute contained no provisions concerning damages, case law severely restricted the damages recoverable in such actions to allow recovery only for pecuniary losses sustained by the parents. [ ]. The proper measure of damages for the death of a minor child was determined to be the value of the child's services from the time of death until majority, taken in connection with the child's prospects in life, less the cost of support and maintenance, to which may be added, in a proper case, the expense of care and attention made necessary by the injury, funeral expenses, and medical services. [ ]. As the Court of Appeals observed, "recovery for wrongful death of a child has been restricted to the actual pecuniary loss sustained." Andis v. Hawkins, 489 N.E.2d 78, 83 (Ind. Ct. App. 1986).

With enactment of the 1987 amendment, the legislature set forth the recoverable damages for the first time. Consistent with then existing case authority, the statute excluded any reference to punitive damages.

---

3. The first Child Wrongful Death Act provided:

A father, or in case of his death or desertion of his family, or imprisonment, the mother, may maintain an action for the injury or death of a child; and a guardian for the injury or death of his ward. But when the action is brought by the guardian for an injury to his ward, the damages shall inure to the benefit of his ward. 1852 Ind. Acts vol. 2, pt. 2, ch. 1, art. 2, § 27, p. 56.

The statute has been amended twice since 1987, but the damages portion has remained unchanged.

Concerning the general wrongful death statute, it has been held that because an action for wrongful death did not exist at common law, the statute should be strictly construed against the expansion of liability. [ ]. The same is true for the Child Wrongful Death Statute. "In reviewing such a statute, we presume that the legislature did not intend to make any changes in the common law beyond those declared either in express terms or by unmistakable implication." South Bend Cmty. Schs. v. Widawski, 622 N.E.2d 160, 162 (Ind. 1993).

We acknowledge that for more than a century, Indiana common law has permitted the recovery of punitive damages under appropriate circumstances. [ ]. Thus it may be argued that by enacting the Child Wrongful Death Statute, the legislature did not intend to change the common law with respect to punitive damages. [ ] However, even assuming that punitive damages may have been recoverable at common law, at least since the 1987 amendment, the Child Wrongful Death Statute has contained an exclusive list of damages recoverable by a child's parent or guardian. Absent in the list is any reference to punitive damages. "When certain items or words are specified or enumerated in a statute then, by implication, other items or words not so specified or enumerated are excluded." [ ]. We conclude, therefore, that even if the common law allowed punitive damages in an action for the wrongful death of a child, our legislature has exercised its prerogative to change the common law by "unmistakable implication." [ ] Accordingly, the trial court properly granted Defendants' motion for partial judgment on the pleadings concerning this issue.

* * *

We affirm the judgment of the trial court.

BOCCI v. KEY PHARMACEUTICALS, INC.

Court of Appeals of Oregon, 2003.
189 Ore.App. 349, 76 P.3d 669.*

LANDAU, P. J.

This case is before us for a third time. Defendants Key Pharmaceuticals, Inc., Schering–Plough Corporation, and Schering Corporation (collectively Key), seek a reversal of a punitive damage award entered in 1994 in favor of cross-claim plaintiff Frederick D. Edwards, M.D. (Edwards). For the reasons set forth below, we conclude that Key is entitled to a remittitur of part of the punitive damage award or to a new trial.

The pertinent facts were set forth in this court's original opinions [*Bocci I, (vacated and remanded and Bocci II*).] We summarized those facts in *Bocci II*:

* As Corrected and amended on reconsideration by Bocci, 190 Ore.App. 407, 79 P.3d 908 (Or. Ct. App., Nov. 13, 2003).

"Plaintiff Bocci was a long-time user of defendant Key's prescription asthma medication Theo–Dur, a timed-release theophylline product. In October 1990, Bocci was prescribed the antibiotic ciprofloxacin for a skin rash, but failed to tell the prescribing physician that he was taking Theo–Dur. On October 27, 1990, Bocci went to an urgent care clinic where Edwards worked complaining of nausea, vomiting, and diarrhea. Edwards diagnosed gastroenteritis and sent Bocci home. Edwards did not diagnose theophylline toxicity, because Theo–Dur had been promoted to him as a safe drug, and he did not believe that a patient on a stable dose of the drug could develop a serious toxicity problem. Shortly after Edwards sent him home, Bocci experienced seizures and was admitted to a hospital emergency room. He was treated for theophylline toxicity. He suffered permanent brain damage from the seizures.

"Bocci sued Key and Edwards * * *. Edwards cross-claimed against Key for negligence and fraud on the ground that Key had failed to provide adequate information concerning the potential toxicity of Theo–Dur. The jury returned verdicts in favor of Bocci and Edwards against Key. The jury awarded Bocci more than $5 million in compensatory damages and $35 million in punitive damages. The jury awarded Edwards $500,000 in compensatory damages and $22[.5] million in punitive damages." [ ]

The jury's award was based on a special verdict that included findings that, on Edwards's cross-claims against Key, the latter was negligent and had made fraudulent misrepresentations to Edwards that caused him damage. The jury further found that Key had acted with wanton disregard for the health and safety of others and had knowingly withheld from or misrepresented to the Food and Drug Administration (FDA) or prescribing physicians information known to be material and relevant to theophylline toxicity.

After trial, Key moved for a judgment notwithstanding the verdict or, in the alternative, a new trial or remittitur, making numerous arguments. One of those arguments was that the combined punitive damage awards to Bocci and Edwards were unconstitutionally excessive, in violation of the Due Process Clause of the Fourteenth Amendment to the United States Constitution. As noted in our previous opinion, Key urged the trial court to apply the criteria for examining punitive damage awards set forth in ORS 30.925(2). Key argued that the "imposition in this case of actual damages in the combined amount exceeding $5.5 million by itself serves as a significant and retributive measure" and that the amount of the compensatory damages awarded should be considered in determining excessiveness. In their responses, Edwards and Bocci each presented arguments as to why their respective punitive damage awards were constitutional. In its reply to those arguments, Key posited that the issue was

"whether, *in combination*, they [*i.e.*, the punitive damage awards to Edwards and Bocci] exceed the maximum amount tolerable under the Due Process Clause because *both* awards are premised on the same factual basis and because the jury had before it all of the evidence pertaining to the totality of the wrongful conduct sought to be punished."

(Emphasis added.) The trial court accepted Key's formulation of the issue, applying the criteria set forth in ORS 30.925 to the combined awards to both Edwards and Bocci, but upheld the awards.

Key appealed, arguing, among other things, that the punitive damage award was excessive. Meanwhile, Key settled with Bocci, leaving the challenge as to the award of damages to Edwards only. Key contended that the trial court should have reviewed the punitive damages award to Edwards independently of the award to Bocci. According to Key, an award of $22.5 million in punitive damages is excessive in relation to the $500,000 that the jury awarded Edwards for compensatory damages.

We affirmed the judgment by an equally divided court, with the court dividing on a question unrelated to the punitive damages issue.
* * *

Key petitioned for review. Meanwhile, the Oregon Supreme Court decided *Parrott v. Carr Chevrolet, Inc.*, 331 Ore. 537, 17 P.3d 473 (2001), in which it evaluated a punitive damages award in light of recent pertinent decisions from the United States Supreme Court, in particular, *BMW of North America, Inc. v. Gore*, 517 U.S. 559, 116 S.Ct. 1589, 134 L.Ed.2d 809 (1996). The Oregon Supreme Court remanded this case for reconsideration in light of Parrott. [ ]

In *Bocci II*, we evaluated the punitive damages award in light of *Parrott* and the authorities it discussed. We expressly adopted the concurring opinion in *Bocci I* as to the scope of the question before us. That is, we concluded that, by specifically requesting that the trial court evaluate the punitive damages awards in their entirety, Key waived any argument that the punitive damages should have been evaluated separately. [ ]. We ultimately concluded that, evaluated in their entirety, the punitive damages awards were not excessive. [ ] The Oregon Supreme Court denied review, and Key petitioned for a writ of certiorari.

Meanwhile, the United States Supreme Court once again ventured into the realm of reviewing state court punitive damages awards in *State Farm v. Campbell*, 538 U.S. 408, 123 S.Ct. 1513, 155 L.Ed.2d 585 (2003). In that case, the Court concluded that the Utah Supreme Court had erred in reinstating a verdict for $145 million in punitive damages in a case involving $1 million in compensatory damages. The plaintiff insureds brought an action against the defendant automobile liability insurer for fraud, bad faith failure to settle within policy limits, and intentional infliction of emotional distress. The jury ultimately awarded the plaintiffs $2.6 million in compensatory damages and $145 million in punitive damages. The trial court, however, reduced the damages to $1 million in compensatory and $25 million in punitive damages. The Utah Supreme Court reinstated the original $145 million punitive damages award, relying in significant part on evidence concerning the defendant's national business practices over the preceding 20 years to meet corporate fiscal goals by capping payouts on claims. [ ].

The United States Supreme Court reversed and remanded. In evaluating the punitive damages award, the Court turned to the three-factor test that it had earlier announced in *Gore*, which requires courts to evaluate, *de novo*, punitive damages awards in light of

> "(1) the degree of reprehensibility of the defendant's misconduct; (2) the disparity between the actual or potential harm suffered by the plaintiff and the punitive damages award; and (3) the difference between the punitive damages awarded by the jury and the civil penalties authorized or imposed in comparable cases." *State Farm* [ ].

Applying the "*Gore* guideposts" to the facts of that case, the Court ultimately concluded that a punitive damages award roughly equal to the amount of compensatory damages likely would be justified. In the process, the Court commented that, among other things, the Utah Supreme Court had erred in basing its decision on the defendant's so-called national policies, which the court characterized as "dissimilar acts, independent from the acts upon which liability was premised." [ ] According to the Court, "although evidence of other acts need not be identical to have relevance in the calculation of punitive damages, the Utah court erred here because evidence pertaining to claims that had nothing to do with a third-party lawsuit was introduced at length." [ ]

The United States Supreme Court then acted on Key's petition in this case. It granted the petition, vacated our decision, and remanded to us for reconsideration in light of *State Farm*. The parties submitted briefing to us on the proper application of *State Farm*. In that supplemental briefing, Key argues that either the case should be reversed and remanded for a new trial or the punitive damages remitted to no more than $500,000. Edwards argues that we should simply affirm the existing punitive damages award. For the reasons that follow, we conclude that, in light of *State Farm*, we must remit the award of punitive damages to $3.5 million.

State Farm requires that we evaluate the punitive damages award in light of the three *Gore* guideposts, the first of which is, as we have mentioned, the "degree of reprehensibility of the defendant's conduct." [ ]. As the Court explained in *State Farm*, the relevant factors include whether

> "the harm caused was physical as opposed to economic; the tortious conduct evinced an indifference to or a reckless disregard of the health or safety of others; the target of the conduct had financial vulnerability; the conduct involved repeated actions or was an isolated incident; and the harm was the result of intentional malice, trickery, or deceit, or mere accident." [ ].

Key contends that at least four of the relevant factors are completely absent in this case. According to Key, Edwards suffered no physical or economic injury apart from some "minimal" emotional distress. More-over, it argues, Key's conduct was not a threat to Edwards's health or safety, nor were there repeated instances of reckless or indifferent conduct toward Edwards. At best, Key argues, the jury's verdict may be taken to "imply" that Key had engaged in trickery or deceit. That, says Key, is not enough to support a claim for punitive damages.

Edwards argues that Key has ignored the nature of the jury's verdict and the relevant evidence in this case. He argues that Key's liability was based on persistent and aggressive promotion of Theo–Dur with material misrepresentations as to its safety, which evinced an indifference to and reckless disregard of the health and safety of others. That indifference and reckless behavior, Edwards argues, caused physical and economic harm to both himself and Bocci.

Key insists that Edwards focuses improperly on unrelated acts of misconduct that, under *State Farm*, are irrelevant. In particular, Key argues that, as in *State Farm*, so also in this case, we must reject consideration of its promotional activities outside of Oregon. According to Key, punitive damages may not be awarded by reference to such out-of-state conduct. Similarly, Key argues, under *State Farm*, it is inappropriate to consider the effect of its conduct on anyone other than Edwards, whose award of punitive damages is at issue.

We address, in turn, each of the five factors relevant to the reprehensibility of Key's conduct, beginning with the nature of the harm caused. At the outset, we note that the Court's description of the first factor in *State Farm* does not, by its terms, limit the scope of the evaluation to the single person in favor of whom punitive damages were awarded. In support of its argument to the contrary, Key relies on a reference in the Court's opinion that cautions against consideration of "other parties' hypothetical claims against a defendant under the guise of the reprehensibility analysis." *State Farm* [ ]. The Court's caution was delivered in the context of a discussion of the Utah Supreme Court's consideration of evidence of the defendant insurer's "dissimilar acts" in other cases that "bore no relation" to the harm that the plaintiffs suffered. That is not the case here. There is nothing hypothetical about Bocci's claim against Key or the extensive and permanent brain damage that Key caused him. Moreover, Key's actions with respect to Bocci were not dissimilar at all. They were, in all material respects, the same acts that caused harm to Edwards. In any event, the evidence in this case shows that Key also caused Edwards emotional distress and associated physical harm of more than the "minimal" nature that Key describes.

We turn to whether Key's conduct evinced indifference or reckless disregard "of the health and safety of others." *State Farm*,[ ] Again, Key focuses on whether it disregarded the health and safety of Edwards, when the relevant factor is not so narrowly focused. What is more, Key ignores the jury's findings by clear and convincing evidence that Key acted with wanton disregard for the health and safety of others in knowingly and falsely promoting its product as safe. Key's argument that its out-of-state promotional activities are irrelevant is not well-taken. The Court in *State Farm* said that a jury "may not use evidence of out-of-state conduct to punish a defendant for action that was lawful in the jurisdiction where it occurred." [ ]. It did not say that out-of-state conduct is *per se* irrelevant. To the contrary, it said that "evidence of repeated misconduct of the sort that injured" the plaintiff is entirely relevant. [ ]. In this case, there was evidence that Key engaged in nationwide misconduct in disseminating false and misleading information to the FDA and to physicians about Theo–Dur and that the dissemination of that misleading information led to Bocci's and Edwards's damages. That is not the sort of evidence that *State Farm* suggests is inappropriate to consider in evaluating punitive damages.

The third factor is whether "the target of the conduct had financial vulnerability." [ ]. Neither party addresses that factor.

Next, we consider whether the conduct "involved repeated actions or was an isolated incident." [ ]. As we have noted, there is evidence of Key's continuing misrepresentations concerning the safety of its product.

Finally, we consider whether "the harm was a result of intentional malice, trickery, or deceit, or mere accident." [ ]. Key acknowledges that it may be "implied" from the jury's verdict that trickery or deceit was involved. The jury, in fact, found that Key had knowingly withheld or misrepresented information to the FDA or prescribing physicians concerning theophylline toxicity and the safety of Theo–Dur. In short, contrary to what Key suggests to us, there is substantial evidence of four of the five relevant considerations as to the reprehensibility of its conduct.

We turn, then, to consideration of the second of the *Gore* guideposts, namely, an evaluation of "the ratio between harm, or potential harm, to the plaintiff and the punitive damages award." 123 S.Ct. at 1524. The Court explained that "few awards exceeding a single-digit ratio between punitive and compensatory damages, to a significant degree, will satisfy due process." [ ]. The Court noted that in previous cases it had held that "an award of more than four times the amount of compensatory damages might be close to the line of constitutional impropriety." [ ] It then cited *Gore* for the same proposition, that is, that a 4–to–1 ratio may be close to the limits of constitutionality. [ ]. The Court added, however, that a higher ratio might be appropriate "where a particularly egregious act resulted in only a small amount of economic damages." [ ].

In this case, Key argues that the ratio of $22.5 million in punitive damages to $500,000 in compensatory damages awarded to Edwards is 45 to 1, which it argues is presumptively invalid. Edwards objects to the consideration of punitive and compensatory damages to Edwards independent of the damages awarded to Bocci on the ground that Key waived the argument at trial, as we held in *Bocci II*. Key acknowledges that we held that its argument was waived; it insists that we were wrong in so holding and that, in any event, in light of *State Farm*, we are now required to evaluate the ratio between the harm "to the plaintiff" and the punitive damage award. [ ].

We need not devote too much time to resolving the question whether the relevant ratio of punitive to compensatory damages includes only Edwards's damages as opposed to Edwards's and Bocci's in combination. *Either way*, the ratio exceeds single digits.

As Key correctly notes, the ratio of Edwards's punitive damages ($22.5 million) to his compensatory damages ($500,000) is 45 to 1. That is clearly in excess of the single-digit neighborhood that the Court has suggested lies at the outer edge of constitutionality. The ratio of combined punitive damages ($55.5 million) to combined compensatory damages ($5.5 million) is in excess of 10 to 1. Even that ratio exceeds single digits. Indeed, it exceeds by two and a half times the ratio of 4 to 1 that the Court suggested "might be close to the line of constitutional impropriety." *State Farm* [ ]

The question, then, is whether there are circumstances present in this case that would justify a ratio higher than 4 to 1. As we have noted, the Court suggested that a higher ratio may be appropriate when a "particularly egregious act" resulted in only a small amount of economic damages. *State Farm* [ ]. We would expect, for example, that intentionally malicious conduct that produces only a small amount of compensatory damages would justify a higher ratio.

In this case, there is, as we have noted, evidence of deceitful conduct involving the promotion of a prescription drug as "safe" when it was not, which resulted in misdiagnosis and consequent severe physical injury. It is conduct that is much more reprehensible and blameworthy than an isolated incident or mere accident. Thus, we are willing to approve a ratio in excess of the 4–to–1 ratio that apparently is something of a benchmark for the United States Supreme Court. But, having said that, we must also conclude that Key's conduct does not rise to the level of "particularly egregious," intentionally malicious acts that would justify a ratio in excess of single digits. Under the circumstances of this case, we conclude that the ratio of punitive to compensatory damages is excessive.

The final *Gore* guidepost is the "difference between the punitive damages awarded by the jury and the civil penalties authorized or imposed in comparable cases." *State Farm* [ ]. Key offers no argument regarding that factor. Edwards argues that Key's misconduct in reporting misleading information could have subjected it to criminal prosecution. In *State Farm*, however, the Court cautioned:

"The existence of a criminal penalty does have bearing on the seriousness with which a State views the wrongful action. When used to determine the dollar amount of the award, however, the criminal penalty has less utility. Great care must be taken to avoid use of the civil process to assess criminal penalties that can be imposed only after the heightened protections of a criminal trial have been observed, including, of course, its higher standards of proof. Punitive damages are not a substitute for the criminal process, and the remote possibility of a criminal sanction does not automatically sustain a punitive damages award." [ ].

Taking all relevant considerations into account, we conclude that the punitive damages award to Edwards exceeds the amount tolerable under the Due Process Clause. We conclude that a ratio of punitive to compensatory damages in the amount of 7 to 1 is constitutionally permissible.

Because only the award to Edwards is at issue on appeal, the 7–to–1 ratio must be applied to the compensatory damages awarded to Edwards. *See State Farm* [ ] (the proper measure is the "disparity between the actual or potential harm *suffered by the plaintiff* and the punitive damages award"). Edwards was awarded $500,000 in compensatory damages. An appropriate amount of punitives therefore is seven times that amount, or $3.5 million.

Judgment in favor of Edwards for punitive damages vacated and remanded with instructions to allow defendants' motion for a new trial unless Edwards agrees to remittitur of punitive damages to $3.5 million within 28 days of entry of the appellate judgment; otherwise affirmed.

Notes

1) In *Merced v. Qazi,* 811 So.2d 702 (Fla. App. 2002), plaintiff alleged negligence and vicarious liability against a physician who failed to detect a kidney mass on a CT scan. As a result, plaintiff allegedly suffered a 13–month delay in her cancer treatment, and sought damages for, among other things, increased risk of cancer recurrence and decreased chance of survival. The trial court granted summary judgment for the defendant, but the Florida court of appeal reversed on the basis that these damages were incurred during the 13–month delay in diagnosis. The appeals court affirmed, however, on the denial of plaintiff's claim for damages arising out of failure to remove the malignant tumor for 13 months. Such claim was not an element of damages, but a condition supporting the elements of damages. The court also denied plaintiff's claims for future damages (specifically including the increased risk of recurrent cancer) because there was a lack of evidence to show, to a reasonable degree of medical certainty, that plaintiff's cancer would recur or that her life expectancy would be decreased.

2) The collateral source rule generally provides that evidence of monies paid to a victim through a collateral source (such as insurance) is not admissible to offset the obligation of the tortfeasor to his victim. According to the rule, the prudence of the victim in making collateral provision should not operate as a windfall to the tortfeasor. In *Hardi*, the issue was whether unpaid or "written off" medical expenses enjoyed the same protection from admissibility as collateral sources. The court emphasized that the payment (or write-off) to the plaintiff was from a source entirely independent of the tortfeasor. The court supported the

notion that a party should receive the benefit of a bargain for which he or she alone has contracted.

3) Joint and several liability prevails in most jurisdictions. It provides that defendants who, through successive acts of negligence, produce a single and indivisible injury, become jointly and severally liable to plaintiff regardless of whether they acted in concert. A "set-off" occurs at common law if one of the liable parties negotiates a settlement with the plaintiff, exchanging a sum of money in exchange for a valid release. The plaintiff can still look to the non-settling party for satisfaction of his judgment, but the judgment is "set off," or reduced, by the amount of the settlement.

One alternative to joint and several liability is the "fair share liability" adopted by the Michigan legislature. Under this scheme each tortfeasor pays only (or all of) the percentage of the total damages that is attributed to his portion of the fault.

Medical malpractice reform legislation has altered some of the common law principles applicable to recovery of damages. Joint and several liability, as well as set-off, are among the principles that have been altered by legislation. See *infra,* Chapter 10, for more materials on the role of medical malpractice reform in changing common law tort principles.

4) Punitive damages are appropriate in cases wherein the defendant's actions are so egregious or outrageous as to warrant the imposition of exemplary damages that "punish" defendant's actions. In jurisdictions where there is a statutory cap on malpractice damages, punitive damages are often exempt from the cap. Malpractice carriers may attempt to disclaim liability for punitive damages.

5) *Bocci III* was followed by yet another motion for reconsideration. While denying most issues, the court did correct its figures to indicate that the ratio of combined punitive damages to combined compensatory damages was not, in fact, more than 10–to–1, but instead was 9.4–1. It also noted that damages still exceeded by two times the 4–to–1 ratio that the U.S. Supreme Court in *State Farm v. Campbell* suggested "might be close to the line of constitutional propriety." Further review was denied.

6) In *Markley v. Oak Care Investors of Coldwater, Inc.* the decedent was admitted to Community Health Center of Branch County and would eventually undergo a large bowel resection and leg amputation. She was thereafter admitted to the defendant's nursing home. A nurse increased the plaintiff's intravenous feeding, leading to respiratory distress. The decedent was taken to the hospital where she later died of cardiac arrest and congestive heart failure. The decedent's husband filed suit against both the Health Center and the nursing home. The Health Center settled for $460,000 and assigned to plaintiff all of its rights to pursue the nursing home. Plaintiff thereafter filed suit against the defendant nursing home alleging that, as assignee of the Health Center, he was entitled to common law indemnification from the nursing home for the

amount that the Health Center obtained in the settlement. The trial court granted summary judgment to the plaintiff and awarded $220,000.

The Court of Appeals reversed. It held that because plaintiff alleged that the Health Center's active negligence contributed to the decedent's death, the plaintiff was not entitled to common-law indemnification as the assignee. The appeals court refused to adopt a hard-and-fast rule that would allow initial tortfeasors to obtain common-law indemnification from successive tortfeasors. Instead it held that a "common-law indemnity cannot apply unless the indemnitee is completely devoid of culpability." Thus the appeals court held that common-law indemnification "requires that the person seeking indemnification be completely free from active negligence."

Chapter 6

DEFENDING THE MEDICAL
NEGLIGENCE CASE

INTRODUCTORY NOTE

In defending a medical negligence case, the result desired by the defense is to win quickly, cheaply, and finally. The defendant achieves a good result when, following full trial on the merits, the court enters final judgment for the defendant, but this involves a lot of expensive pleading, discovery, and trial time. An even better result for the defense occurs when it wins the judgment by an early motion, without trial, by invoking an immunity or by establishing an affirmative defense. The defense's best result of all is to forestall the plaintiff's lawyer from commencing the action. One way is to settle the claim; another is to cause the plaintiff's lawyer to fear that, if the plaintiff's case is weak and the defendant prevails, the plaintiff or his/her lawyer might have to pay damages to the defendant.

The defendant invokes an immunity by making a motion equivalent to Fed.R.Civ.P. 12(b)(6), asserting that there is no basis for the court to grant the relief requested. This is a powerful weapon because it takes the defendant completely out of the case, even if the plaintiff states a claim in all other respects. An immunity ought to function early in the proceedings, so the defendant will not have to file an answer or any other motion; however, some immunities may only be established at trial where the parties litigate the defendant's entitlement to claim immunity.

Governmental immunity is in a class by itself. Whatever the justification for governmental immunity, and whatever the extent to which it has been waived by legislation, the courts treat governmental immunity deferentially and waivers of governmental immunity conservatively. Both the United States and state governments and their subdivisions possess governmental immunity, and actions based upon waivers are usually preceded by essential preliminary steps that do not apply to actions against private defendants.

The granting of immunity to a private party calls for a payback in public benefit, as was thought to be the case when the courts gave immunity to private charities. In recent years most courts have decided that the public benefit of charitable immunity is outweighed by the private need for access to compensation for negligent harm, and for the most part, charitable immunity is gone. The recent Massachusetts case, *infra,* is a notable exception. Legislatures also make tradeoffs, whether the issue concerns legislation to create an institutional immunity for the insured employer and its medical employees under a Workers' Compensation Act, or a personal immunity under a Good Samaritan statute for the physician who performs emergency medical services.

An "affirmative defense," the term used by Fed.R.Civ.P. 8(c), operates to destroy a valid claim against a vulnerable and perhaps liable defendant. Affirmative defenses are numerous; this chapter will illustrate only a few of them in the medical negligence context. For example, the plaintiff himself may have been the cause of the harm (contributory negligence or assumption of risk); the plaintiff may have commenced the action too late (statute of limitation); or the plaintiff may already have settled the action (release or satisfaction).

The "countersuit" is an action for damages, based upon a group of rare and disfavored theories of claim such as abuse of process and malicious prosecution: a victorious doctor brings suit against the unsuccessful plaintiff and the plaintiff's lawyer. The countersuit operates not by defending the plaintiff's medical negligence case, but by threatening to make losing it prohibitively expensive. Doctors are more interested than lawyers in the theory and practice of countersuits, and reported cases in which doctors won them are rare. Countersuits are not counterclaims under a rule like Fed.R.Civ.P. 13(a)–(b), because the countersuit does not arise out of the transaction or occurrence (the alleged medical negligence) that is the subject of the plaintiff's action. Furthermore, the joinder of a countersuit with the plaintiff's negligence action, far from being compulsory or permissive or obtainable by consolidation, is not likely to be available at all. For states that have adopted the Fed.R.Civ.P. 11 sanctions procedures for the filing of frivolous pleadings and motions, they may achieve for victorious defendant doctors some of the results sought by countersuits.

SECTION A.   IMMUNITIES

PATTEN v. COMMONWEALTH OF VIRGINIA

Supreme Court of Virginia, 2001.
262 Va. 654, 553 S.E.2d 517.

Thomas E. Patten, III, administrator of the estate of Maura K. Patten (the decedent), filed a motion for judgment against the Commonwealth and certain of its employees alleging, among other things, that based on their negligence, the decedent died while she was a patient at Western State Hospital (Western State). Western State is a residential psychiatric facility operated by the Virginia Department of Mental Health, Mental Retardation and Substance Abuse Services, an agency of the Commonwealth.

* * *

Patten alleged that employees of Western State failed to provide adequate medical treatment to the decedent, which resulted in her death. On the date of her death, the decedent was being held at Western State pursuant to an April 1997 "Certification and Order for Involuntary Admission to a Public or Licensed Private Facility" (the commitment order).

* * *

According to the motion for judgment, the decedent suffered from chronic undifferentiated schizophrenia and had been involuntarily committed to Western State on a continuous basis from February 1991 until her death in July 1997. In addition to schizophrenia, the decedent had a known history of obesity and chronic obstructive pulmonary disease. As a result of changes in the decedent's anti-psychotic medication, she experienced a large increase in weight, which adversely affected her cardiovascular system. In November 1996, a medical evaluation determined that the decedent had an "above average" risk for cardiac disease associated with her use of one of her medications.

The decedent's dosage of this drug was later reduced and an additional drug was added to her daily medications. About a month later, the decedent informed her physicians at Western State that she "did not feel well" when taking her medications.

On July 2, 1997, the decedent called some family members and friends and complained that she "felt like" she was dying. The next day, Margaret Keller, the decedent's sister, called officials at Western State to discuss various concerns regarding the decedent's worsening condition. An employee of Western State indicated that she would request a full medical evaluation of the decedent after the July 4th holiday weekend. The decedent died on July 7, 1997. From July 3, 1997 to July 7, 1997, the only information entered in the decedent's medical chart were notations of medications administered to her. An autopsy report stated that the cause of her death was "coronary insufficiency due to coronary atherosclerosis and cardiomegaly due to hypertension."

In response to Patten's motion for judgment, the Commonwealth filed a plea of sovereign immunity. The Commonwealth relied on Code § 8.01–195.3(4), which provides an exception to the Commonwealth's limited waiver of immunity for tort claims "based upon an act or omission of an officer, agent or employee of any agency of government in the execution of a lawful order of any court." The Commonwealth asserted that the acts alleged in Patten's motion for judgment were taken in the execution of such an order.

The trial court sustained the Commonwealth's plea of sovereign immunity and dismissed Patten's motion for judgment with prejudice. Patten appeals from the trial court's judgment.

Patten argues that the employees of Western State were not acting pursuant to the execution of a lawful court order when they treated the decedent. Patten contends that the commitment order did not require Western State to admit the decedent, and that its only mandate was directed to the sheriff of the City of Staunton. According to Patten, the director of Western State was not ordered to take any action, but had discretion to decide whether to admit the decedent to that facility.

In response, the Commonwealth asserts that this appeal is controlled by our decision in Baumgardner v. Southwestern Virginia Mental Health Institute, 247 Va. 486, 442 S.E.2d 400 (1994), and contends that the acts and omissions of the Western State employees occurred during the execution of a lawful court order. Thus, the Commonwealth asserts that under Code § 8.01–195.3(4), it is immune from liability for the alleged conduct of its employees. We agree with the Commonwealth.

In the absence of express statutory or constitutional provisions waiving the Commonwealth's immunity, the Commonwealth and its agencies are immune from liability for the tortious acts or omissions of their agents and employees. * * *

The present appeal, which requires us to apply the provisions of Code § 8.01–195.3(4), is controlled by our decision in Baumgardner. There, we held that the "court order" exception of Code § 8.01–195.3(4) applied to a wrongful death action against the Commonwealth in which the plaintiff's decedent was admitted to a mental health institute operated by an agency of the Commonwealth. She was placed in "isolation" in a holding cell in the mental health institute and later died from a cardiac arrhythmia. [ ] The plaintiff alleged that the decedent's death was caused by the negligence of certain employees acting within the scope of their employment.

The admission order, issued by a general district court, ordered the director of the mental health institute:

> To detain said patient for a maximum of 48 hours from time of admission to his/her hearing. . . . The [patient] may also be transported to such other facility as may be necessary to obtain emergency medical evaluation or treatment prior to placement in the hospital. The institution and examining physician may provide (only emergency) medical and psychiatric services pursuant to this order. The patient may not be released prior to the expiration of such period except by order of court. Id.

We held that the plain language of Code § 8.01–195.3(4) barred the plaintiff's tort claim because the alleged acts and omissions of the institute's employees occurred in the execution of a lawful court order. [ ]. Under the present facts, we likewise conclude that Patten's motion for judgment is barred under Code § 8.01–195.3(4). The decedent was involuntarily admitted to Western State pursuant to the commitment order, which authorized "the director of Western State" to admit the decedent for the purpose of "involuntary hospitalization and treatment" for a period "not to exceed 180 days."

All the acts or omissions alleged by Patten occurred while the employees of Western State were engaged in the execution of this order for the involuntary hospitalization and treatment of the decedent. The term "court order," within the meaning of Code § 8.01–195.3(4), includes both mandatory and discretionary acts authorized by that order. As we explained in Baumgardner, "Code § 8.01–195.3(4) does not exclude discretionary acts from its scope; instead, it specifically encompasses any claim that is based upon acts or omissions occurring in the execution of a lawful court order." [ ]. Thus, to the extent that Patten's motion for judgment is based on the performance or omission of discretionary acts, those acts are not removed from the scope of Code § 8.01–195.3(4).

We also find no merit in Patten's argument that the commitment order did not require that the director of Western State take any action regarding the decedent. Such a construction would render meaningless the order's language directing the "involuntary hospitalization and treatment [of the decedent] not to exceed 180 days."

Finally, our conclusion that Code § 8.01–195.3(4) bars the present action is not affected by our decision in Whitley v. Commonwealth, 260 Va. 482, 538 S.E.2d 296 (2000). There, we considered whether the "court order" exception in Code § 8.01–195.3(4) barred a wrongful death action against the Commonwealth and certain of its employees based on a claim that the decedent received inadequate medical treatment while incarcerated at a state correctional facility. [ ]. The order at issue directed that the decedent be incarcerated, and did not provide that he be given medical care. [ ]

We held that the employees giving medical care to the decedent were not performing acts "in the execution of a lawful order of any court," as contemplated by Code § 8.01–195.3(4), but merely were providing medical care to the decedent because he was an inmate at the correctional facility. [ ]. Thus, unlike the acts alleged by Patten, the acts alleged in Whitley were outside the scope of the statutory exception.

For these reasons, we will affirm the trial court's judgment.

Affirmed.

KEENE v. BRIGHAM AND WOMEN'S HOSPITAL, INC.

Supreme Judicial Court of Massachusetts, 2003.
439 Mass. 223, 786 N.E.2d 824.

GREANEY, J.

This is a malpractice case in which a baby suffered catastrophic harm within hours of his birth at the defendant hospital. We are asked to decide whether (1) a default judgment on liability was properly entered as a sanction for the defendant's failure to produce in discovery relevant hospital records that it admittedly had lost; (2) damages assessed against the defendant are limited by the $20,000 cap imposed by

G. L. c. 231, § 85K, on damages recoverable from a charitable corporation for a tort committed in the course of the performance of its charitable purpose * * *. A judge in the Superior Court imposed the sanction of default as to liability on the defendant and, as an additional sanction, struck the statutory $20,000 cap on damages (which the parties agree would have applied). * * *

The known facts relevant to the alleged malpractice are as follows. The plaintiff was born at 1:07 A.M. on May 15, 1986, at the defendant hospital. Within the first five hours of life, he experienced some degree of respiratory distress and was sent from the regular care nursery to the special care nursery (also known as the neonatal intensive care unit or NICU) because he was "cyanotic." At 6:25 A.M., blood tests, including a complete blood count and a blood culture, were performed and, immediately thereafter, the plaintiff was sent back to the regular care nursery with a discharge note stating: "routine care in regular nursery"; "watch for [signs and symptoms] of sepsis"; and "hold antibiotics pending CBC results and cultures in 24 [hours], 48 [hours], [and] 72 [hours]." It is not known who received the results of the initial complete blood count (which indicated the presence of Beta–Hemolytic Streptococci Group B) or what actions were, or were not taken, with respect to the plaintiff's condition, because all of the defendant hospital records with respect to his treatment and care between the hours of 6:30 A.M. on May 15, 1986, and 12 A.M. on May 16, 1986, (missing records period) have vanished. The plaintiff's medical records immediately following the missing records period indicate that, by 2:30 A.M., he was suffering septic shock and began having seizures. It was not until this time that antibiotics were ordered and administered. Later testing revealed that the plaintiff had contracted neonatal sepsis and meningitis, resulting in the tragic injuries and situation set forth below.[5]

The plaintiff was discharged from the defendant on June 17, 1986. Existing hospital records for the plaintiff's seven-week hospital stay exceed 470 pages. The only records that cannot be located are those pertinent to the missing record period. Neither party has presented any evidence with respect to who is responsible for this loss or whether the records were intentionally destroyed or negligently or accidentally misplaced.

The timing of the loss, however, is somewhat more certain. On May 1, 1987, following a request by the plaintiff's family for the plaintiff's medical records, the defendant filed a notice of a potential claim with its insurer, Risk Management Foundation (RMF). In response, RMF promptly initiated an investigation into the circumstances of the plaintiff's injury while in the care of the defendant. The plaintiff's medical records, which were requested and received by RMF in the course of its investigation, appear to have been complete at that time. RMF's investigative report, dated August 12, 1987, identified three physicians responsible for the plaintiff's care and stated that "it is questionable whether

---

5. The sepsis and meningitis resulted in profound brain damage to the plaintiff. . . .

or not antibiotics should have been initiated sooner in view of a shift to the left by the complete blood count which would indicate an infection was going on." The report indicated that the plaintiff's mother had received a complete copy of the medical records. It is undisputed, however, that the records received by the plaintiff's family in response to the request that triggered RMF's investigation, did not include the missing records.

On May 12, 1995, the plaintiff, through his parents, commenced this action for medical malpractice, claiming that the defendant had failed properly to diagnose or treat him for the sepsis and meningitis, resulting in serious injury. The defendant asserted, as an affirmative defense, the statutory limitation of damages on a charitable corporation under G. L. c. 231, § 85K. The defendant subsequently provided the plaintiff a set of hospital medical records certified as "a true and complete copy of this hospital's medical record concerning [the plaintiff]."

* * *

At a subsequent deposition, the defendant (through testimony of two medical records department employees) conceded that the plaintiff's medical records with respect to the eighteen-hour period at issue were missing, and admitted that no attempt had been made to identify those doctors and nurses who had treated the plaintiff during the period reflected by the missing records. The deposition was continued (ostensibly to afford the defendant time to make further efforts to locate the missing records). Testimony taken on the continuance date, however, revealed that the records were still missing, and no effort had been made by the defendant to identify further the doctors or nurses who had treated the plaintiff.

On April 12, 1996, plaintiff filed a motion requesting that, as a sanction pursuant to rule 37 (b) (2), the defendant be precluded from introducing in evidence any testimony regarding the treatment provided to the plaintiff during the hours covered by the missing records. The judge (the same judge who had denied the defendant's motion for a protective order) entered a preliminary order for the appearance, in addition to trial counsel, of the chief medical record librarian of the defendant hospital, together with any other medical record librarians who had been involved in the defendant's search for the missing records, at a hearing on the plaintiff's motion on May 3, 1996. On April 30, 1996, the plaintiff filed a supplemental motion for sanctions, seeking entry of default judgment on liability against the defendant and the striking of its affirmative defense asserting the cap set forth in G. L. c. 231, § 85K. The plaintiff also filed an amended complaint, alleging that the defendant's negligent failure to administer antibiotics during the time period covered by the missing records caused the plaintiff to suffer brain damage. The defendant once again asserted, as an affirmative defense, the $20,000 statutory cap on damages.

At the May 3 hearing, the defendant suggested that lost hospital records often were discovered misfiled in records of another patient, and described its efforts to locate the missing records. The defendant indicated, however, that it had not contacted physicians named in the existing records, or the defendant's insurer, RMF, to determine whether other documentation regarding the period covered by the missing files existed.

The judge stated that "the number one [priority was to] use all our efforts to get the entire hospital record" and ordered the defendant to "resurrect the missing pages or, in the alternative, [to determine] what might substitute for those missing pages." The judge instructed the defendant to make contact with (1) any physicians identified in the existing records, to determine whether the physicians possessed any records or information with respect to the period reflected by the missing records; (2) RMF, to determine whether it possessed a file of any statements taken by any persons at the time of its investigation in 1987; and (3) the pediatrician on call in the NICU on May 15, 1986, to determine whether he had any records or knowledge about the missing record period.

On September 17, 1996, a different judge in the Superior Court ordered the defendant, pursuant to rule 37, further to answer the plaintiff's interrogatories with respect to the plaintiff's care during the missing record period. * * * [T]he defendant claimed that it had no information sufficient to respond, because "it had been unable to locate medical records indicating the time at which the results were received or the identity of the person receiving them."

An evidentiary hearing on the plaintiff's motion for sanctions was next conducted. The plaintiff's position was that, without the missing records, the plaintiff had no ability to prove the alleged malpractice nor to determine the identity of the physicians and nurses responsible for the plaintiff's care. The defendant, in turn, contended that it had made every effort to comply with the plaintiff's requests for production of the records and that it had produced the entire record that was available to it. The defendant argued that the plaintiff's claims raised issues of causation that were required to be determined by a fact finder; that circumstances of the case did not justify even the inference of spoliation, much less the "extraordinary" sanction of a default judgment; and that the judge lacked authority to strike the statutory cap on damages.

Subsequently, the judge entered an order allowing the plaintiff's motion. The defendant was defaulted and its defense under G. L. c. 231, § 85K, was struck. In a written memorandum of decision, the judge stated that, although "no evidence has been presented showing wilfulness or bad faith on the part of [the defendant]," the loss of the plaintiff's records nevertheless amounted to "negligence" in view of the statutory duty to keep records imposed on the defendant hospital by G. L. c. 111, § 70. Further, the defendant's failure to maintain the records deprived the plaintiff of "the opportunity to recover from those individuals directly at fault." The judge reasoned that, without the imposed sanctions, the plaintiff "would not be able to prove negligence on the part of the [defendant], and even if [he] could, the damages [he] [has] suffered would greatly exceed the fixed sum [he] would receive. In short, anything less than what [the plaintiff] seeks, by way of sanctions, would effectively deny the plaintiff [ ] [his] day in court.... Allowing [the defendant] the benefit of the statutory cap provided in [G. L.] c. 231, § 85K, when as a result of [its] negligence the plaintiff[ ] [is] left without an adequate remedy is contrary to the principles of fairness, equity and justice." The judge noted that, striking the charitable cap as a sanction was fair, because "the hospital and its doctors are insured by the same entity."

1. We first consider the appropriateness of the default sanction. The parties and the judge considered the situation as one arising under rule 37 (b) (2) (C), which authorizes a judge, when confronted with a party who fails to obey an order to provide or permit discovery, to "make such orders in regard to the failure as are just, and among others ... an order striking out pleadings or parts thereof ... or rendering a judgment by default against the disobedient party." In view of the judge's determination that the defendant was unable (as opposed to unwilling) to produce the documents, this was not correct * * *

* * * [T]he matter should have been disposed of under the doctrine of spoliation, which permits the imposition of sanctions and remedies for the destruction of evidence in civil litigation. The doctrine is based on the premise that a party who has negligently or intentionally lost or destroyed evidence known to be relevant for an upcoming legal proceeding should be held accountable for any unfair prejudice that results. * * *

* * * The defendant's unexplained loss of the plaintiff's medical records during the period when it was statutorily required to maintain them renders the defendant accountable for the resulting prejudice to the plaintiff. In the spoliation context (like in the discovery context) a judge has broad discretion to impose a variety of sanctions against the defendant for the breach of its statutory duty to retain the plaintiff's missing records.

As a general rule, a judge should impose the least severe sanction necessary to remedy the prejudice to the nonspoliating party. See Fletcher v. Dorchester Mut. Ins. Co., supra, (sanction for spoliation should be "addressed to the precise unfairness that would otherwise result"). * * *

This is not a case, however, where it has been established that the defendant's failure to comply was due to no fault of its own.[citations omitted]. As discussed above, the judge properly discerned that the defendant's failure to preserve hospital records as required by law constituted at least negligence. Moreover, unlike an ordinary case of spoliation, the defendant's violation of the statutory mandate that it both keep records and provide them to patients upon request is a violation that itself gives rise to liability as a form of medical malpractice. See G. L. c. 111, § 70E (giving patients the right to inspect and copy their medical records maintained under § 70, and allowing actions under

G. L. c. 231, §§ 60B–60E, if those rights are violated). Finally, the missing records were not simply of potential use to the plaintiff, but formed the critical linchpin of the plaintiff's case.

On this last point, the defendant claims that, because the plaintiff would have been able to establish some proof of his claim without the missing records, the severe sanction of entry of default judgment was both unwarranted and unconstitutional. The judge made every effort to have this case tried on the merits but foresaw no possibility that the missing records could be resurrected. At a hearing on the plaintiff's motion for sanctions held on July 29, 1997, the judge was informed by counsel for the defendant, "We are basically at the end of the line on that issue. All of the cards are on the table and we come before the Court to say we are in an impossible position without those records." In his written memorandum, the judge found that, "from the evidence presented to this court, the records appear to be irreparably lost." Due to the defendant's loss of the plaintiff's medical records for the critical hours during which the alleged malpractice occurred, the plaintiff was left with virtually no evidence that could be presented to a jury concerning his clinical features between the hours of 6:30 A.M. on May 15, 1986, and 12 A.M. on May 16, 1986, or what care had been provided him during that time.

* * *

2. We turn now to the statutory cap on damages imposed by G. L. c. 231, § 85K, concluding that the judge lacked authority to strike the cap as an additional sanction.

General Laws c. 231, § 85K, inserted by St. 1971, c. 785, § 1, provides:

> "It shall not constitute a defense to any cause of action based on tort brought against a corporation . . . that . . . is or at the time the cause of action arose was a charity; provided, that if the tort was committed in the course of any activity carried on to accomplish directly the charitable purposes of such corporation . . . liability in any such cause of action shall not exceed the sum of twenty thousand dollars exclusive of interest and costs. Notwithstanding any other provision of this section, liability of charitable corporations . . . shall not be subject to the limitations set forth in this section if the tort was committed in the course of activities primarily commercial in character even though carried on to obtain revenue to be used for charitable purposes."

The plain text of the statute makes the cap mandatory and contains no language that would warrant its abrogation as a sanction for a violation of the sort that occurred here. Nor does the statutory language, "liability . . . shall not exceed the sum of twenty thousand dollars exclusive of interest and costs," allow an interpretation that negligent conduct on the part of a charitable corporation constitutes a waiver of the mandatory statutory limitation on recovery. The Legislature's purpose behind the charitable cap was "to protect the funds [and other assets] of charitable institutions so they may be devoted to charitable purposes." * * *

Although technically a limitation on liability, the charitable cap set forth in § 85K has been treated as an affirmative defense that must be pleaded under Mass. R. Civ. P. 8 (c), 365 Mass. 749 (1974) (listing specific affirmative defenses, and concluding with the residuary clause "any other matter constituting an avoidance or affirmative defense"). [ ]. Factual matters related to the cap may need to be determined by the fact finder, with the burden on the defendant to prove both that it is a charitable organization and that the tort complained of fell within the range of activities covered by the cap. [ ]. The requirement that it be raised as an affirmative defense in such circumstances prevents unfair surprise, a key focus of the requirement of pleading affirmative defenses, and resulting prejudice to the plaintiff.

The characterization of the cap as an affirmative defense, however, does not change its basic nature as a legislatively mandated limit on the amount of civil damages that can be recovered from a charitable corporation that causes harm by committing a tort in the performance of its charitable purpose, no matter how compelling the circumstances of the injured party. The legislative directive relied on by the plaintiff, providing that, "nothing in [G. L. c. 231, § 85K,] shall be construed to enlarge any protection from tort liability afforded by the common law of the commonwealth prior to the effective date of this act," St. 1971, c. 785, § 2, does not persuade us otherwise. In our view, the directive refers to the requirement that a charitable corporation must be engaged in its charitable purpose to enjoy the benefit of the cap, just as, at common law, the protection of charitable immunity only extended to negligence committed in the course of activities carried on to accomplish charitable activities. The directive provides no basis for striking the charitable cap as a sanction for the loss of relevant evidence in a tort action where, as here, both parties agree that the alleged malpractice occurred when the defendant was performing its charitable activities.

So ordered.

LeMARBE v. WISNESKI

United States Court of Appeals for the Sixth Circuit, 2001.
266 F.3d 429.

KAREN NELSON MOORE, Circuit Judge.

* * *

I. Background

LeMarbe is a state prisoner at the Cotton Correctional Facility in Ionia, Michigan. On July 11, 1996, LeMarbe sought medical treatment for severe abdominal pain at Duane L. Waters Hospital... LeMarbe was treated by a general surgeon named Dr. Wisneski, who discovered during the course of the appointment that LeMarbe suffered from chronic gallstone problems, specifically cholecystitis, and scheduled LeMarbe for surgery to remove his gallbladder.

On July 22, 1996, Dr. Wisneski performed a cholecystectomy or gallbladder removal surgery on LeMarbe * * * On July 24 and 25, 1996, Dr. Wisneski met with LeMarbe for follow-ups to his surgery and noted that LeMarbe was recovering well.

On July 26, 1996, however, LeMarbe's recovery noticeably began to falter, and as a result, Dr. Edgar Eichum, another general surgeon at Duane L. Waters Hospital, ordered lab tests on LeMarbe. On July 29, 1996, Dr. Wisneski reviewed the results of LeMarbe's lab tests and met with LeMarbe. The results of these lab tests indicated that LeMarbe may have had "a bile leak somewhere, or a bile obstruction."

On July 30, 1996, Dr. Wisneski * * * put down a nastrogastric tube to empty [LeMarbe's] stomach," as LeMarbe was suffering from symptoms of nausea and abdominal distention. After unsuccessfully taking other steps to resolve LeMarbe's problems, Dr. Wisneski made a decision to perform exploratory surgery on LeMarbe.

On July 31, 1996, Dr. Wisneski began to conduct an exploratory laparotomy on LeMarbe. Upon entering LeMarbe's abdomen during the laparotomy, Dr. Wisneski encountered approximately five liters of a "muddy yellow-brown odorless fluid." According to Dr. Wisneski, the fluid "looked like ascitic fluid," but "from the color of it [he] thought it was [biliary fluid because] it was lightly tinged yellow and there isn't anything in the abdomen that would give it that color other than bile.". Dr. Wisneski then began to look for the source of the leak. Unable to discover the reasons for the fluid, Dr. Wisneski sought the assistance of Dr. Eichum. Dr. Eichum, however, was also unable to uncover the reason for the fluid. Thereafter, Dr. Wisneski drained the fluid from LeMarbe's abdomen and, although he was concerned about the fluid collecting again in LeMarbe's abdomen, Dr. Wisneski closed LeMarbe's surgical incision and ended the exploratory surgery.

On August 1 and 2, 1996, Dr. Eichum saw LeMarbe again, and according to Dr. Wisneski, LeMarbe's abdomen was not distended at that time. A few days later, on August 5, 1996, Dr. Wisneski saw LeMarbe once more and discharged him the following day. On August 13, 1996, Dr. Wisneski saw LeMarbe again, as LeMarbe's abdomen had become quite distended for a second time. Dr. Wisneski finally referred LeMarbe to a gastroenterologist, Dr. Marlo Hurtado, who saw LeMarbe on August 14, 1996. Thereafter, Dr. Wisneski did not see LeMarbe again.

Dr. Hurtado sent LeMarbe to Foote Hospital on August 16, 1996. On August 20, 1996, Dr. Blaine Tacia performed another exploratory surgery with an intraoperative cholangiogram on LeMarbe. In so doing, Dr. Tacia discovered that LeMarbe's abdomen was distended due to fourteen liters (3 ½ gallons) of bile in the peritoneal cavity in his abdomen. Dr. Tacia commented that the adhesions inside LeMarbe's belly cavity were among the worst he had ever seen and that the accumulation of bile in

LeMarbe's abdomen had caused serious damage to LeMarbe's biliary tract. Dr. Tacia discovered that the leak of fluid was due to a complete transection of LeMarbe's common bile duct and found a clip on that duct, which Dr. Tacia explained was unusual. Dr. Tacia also stated that the transection occurred during one of Dr. Wisneski's surgeries. According to Dr. Tacia, the transection necessitated an immediate repair of the leak, as "there [was] no way for the bile to get down into the bowel." [ ].

Because of the extensive damage in LeMarbe's abdomen, Dr. Tacia then performed a Roux-en-Y choledochojejunostomy on LeMarbe. Despite this surgery, however, LeMarbe still had to undergo several more surgeries at Foote Hospital and at the Detroit Receiving Hospital. In fact, LeMarbe was in and out of hospitals for the two years following his surgery with Dr. Tacia.

As a result of his medical treatment at Duane L. Waters Hospital, LeMarbe filed this lawsuit, alleging a violation of his constitutional right to have his serious medical needs attended to without deliberate indifference. On March 31, 2000, the district court issued an opinion and order accepting the report and recommendation of the magistrate judge to deny Dr. Wisneski's motion for summary judgment, holding that LeMarbe "had presented sufficient facts to rebut Defendant Wisneski's claim that he was not deliberately indifferent to [LeMarbe's] serious medical needs." In so doing, the district court relied heavily on the affidavit of Dr. James Sarnelle, a general surgeon who asserted that LeMarbe's bile leak had to be stopped immediately after its discovery. Dr. Sarnelle explained that any general surgeon would have known, upon discovering five liters of bile in LeMarbe's abdomen on July 31, 1996, that the bile in the abdomen came from a leak, that the bile leak would cause serious, permanent damage to LeMarbe if not stopped, that bile would continue to leak into LeMarbe's abdomen if the bile leak was not stopped, that the bile leak needed to be stopped before LeMarbe's exploratory surgery ended, and that LeMarbe had to be referred immediately to a specialist who could locate and stop the leak if the surgeon was unable to do so himself. Dr. Sarnelle also stated that "the risk of harm to Richard LeMarbe on 7/31/96 was extreme and obvious to anyone with a medical education and to most lay people."

II. ANALYSIS

Dr. Wisneski argues that he is entitled to qualified immunity because he merely exercised his medical judgment in deciding how to treat LeMarbe, and a dispute over the specific method of treatment does not rise to the level of deliberate indifference. "Qualified immunity is 'an entitlement not to stand trial or face the other burdens of litigation.' " [ ]. A government official performing a discretionary function is entitled to qualified immunity from a suit for civil damages unless his actions have violated a clearly established statutory or constitutional right. [ ]. Thus, a plaintiff must prove two factors to show that a government official is not entitled to qualified immunity from his suit: (1) that the facts as alleged by him show a violation of a constitutional right; and (2) that such violated right was clearly established. [ ]

* * *

B.   Qualified Immunity

Upon review of the merits of Dr. Wisneski's appeal, we conclude that the district court did not err in denying Dr. Wisneski's motion for summary judgment based upon qualified immunity. In this case, Le-Marbe has not only alleged facts that would prove a violation of one of his constitutional rights; he has also successfully shown that such right was clearly established. We note that since Dr. Wisneski has stipulated to LeMarbe's version of the facts for purposes of this appeal, we must view "the evidence, all facts, and any inferences that may be drawn from the facts ... in the light most favorable" to LeMarbe. [ ]

1.   Violation Of Constitutional Right

We first conclude that LeMarbe has alleged facts that, when viewed in his favor, would prove a violation of his constitutional right to have his serious medical needs treated without deliberate indifference. Under the Eighth Amendment, a prisoner has a right not to have prison officials act with deliberate indifference to his health and safety. [ ] The Supreme Court has explained that "deliberate indifference describes a state of mind more blameworthy than negligence" and that it entails "something less than acts or omissions for the very purpose of causing harm or with knowledge that harm will result." [ ] Estelle, 429 U.S. at 105 ("An accident, although it may produce added anguish, is not on that basis alone to be characterized as wanton infliction of unnecessary pain."). Consequently, a prison official is only "found liable under the Eighth Amendment for denying an inmate humane conditions of confinement [if] the official knows of and disregards an excessive risk to inmate health or safety." [ ]

In this case, LeMarbe has presented factual evidence, which when viewed in a light most favorable to him, would prove that Dr. Wisneski was aware of facts that supported an inference of a substantial risk of serious harm to LeMarbe and that Dr. Wisneski had both drawn and disregarded that inference when he closed LeMarbe's surgical incision on July 31, 1996, and then failed to take the action that his training indicated was necessary to stop the bile leak in a timely manner. As the Supreme Court explained in Farmer, a prisoner "need not show that [the] prison official acted or failed to act believing that harm actually would befall [the prisoner to prove a violation of his Eighth Amendment right]; it is enough [for the prisoner to show] that the official acted or failed to act despite his knowledge of a substantial risk of serious harm." [ ].

a.   Facts From Which Inference Of Substantial Risk Of Serious Harm Could Be Drawn

First, we conclude that LeMarbe has alleged facts that, when viewed in a light most favorable to him, would show that Dr. Wisneski was aware of facts from which a substantial risk of serious harm could be inferred. These facts are: (1) that Dr. Wisneski encountered five liters of fluid in LeMarbe's stomach on July 31, 1996, and knew that the fluid was bile; (2) that Dr. Wisneski knew that the bile came from a leak; (3) that Dr. Wisneski knew that he had not stopped the bile leak when he closed LeMarbe's surgical incision from the exploratory surgery on July 31, 1996; (4) that Dr. Wisneski made no immediate plans to seek help to stop the bile leak after he sewed LeMarbe back up; and (5) that Dr. Wisneski knew that if the leak were not timely closed, the bile would continue to leak and would cause LeMarbe serious harm.

* * *

* * * In sum, we hold that LeMarbe has successfully alleged facts, which when accepted as true, would prove that Dr. Wisneski was aware of the facts from which a substantial risk of serious harm could be inferred.

b. Drawing The Inference Of Substantial Risk Of Serious Harm And Disregarding It

Second, we conclude that LeMarbe has alleged facts, which when viewed in a light most favorable to him, would show that Dr. Wisneski drew the inference that LeMarbe faced a substantial risk of serious harm from the bile leak in his abdomen and that Dr. Wisneski disregarded such risk when he closed LeMarbe's surgical incision on July 31, 1996, failed to refer LeMarbe immediately to a specialist who could stop the leak, and also failed to inform LeMarbe of the failure to stop the leak so that LeMarbe could take any additional measures necessary to stop the leak in a timely manner, i.e., request medical treatment from a specialist who could stop the leak. Specifically, LeMarbe has provided an affidavit from Dr. Sarnelle, who swore that "anyone with a medical education and [ ] most lay people" who encountered five liters of bile in a patient's abdomen would have known that the bile in LeMarbe's abdomen was due to a leak and that such condition posed a substantial risk of serious harm to LeMarbe if the leak was not closed or stopped before permanent damage occurred.

* * *

The fact that LeMarbe was seen by Dr. Wisneski and other staff after his exploratory surgery on July 31, 1996 does not necessarily immunize Dr. Wisneski from liability for his actions. A government doctor has a duty to do more than simply provide some treatment to a prisoner who has serious medical needs; instead, the doctor must provide medical treatment to the patient without consciously exposing the patient to an excessive risk of serious harm. As the Seventh Circuit recently recognized in Sherrod, "a prisoner is not required to show that he was literally ignored by the staff" to prove an Eighth Amendment violation, only that his serious medical needs were consciously disregarded.... Similarly, the fact that Dr. Wisneski eventually referred LeMarbe to a specialist does not automatically immunize Dr. Wisneski from liability for LeMarbe's intervening injuries. For, as many federal courts have recognized, a deliberately indifferent delay in giving or obtaining treatment may also amount to a violation under the Eighth Amendment. [ ].

In sum, we conclude that, when viewed in a light most favorable to LeMarbe, the facts as alleged and supported by LeMarbe (that Dr. Wisneski knew that the fluid was bile, was aware of the substantial risk of serious harm as explained by Dr. Sarnelle, and failed to seek adequate help to stop the bile leak in a timely manner despite such knowledge) show that Dr. Wisneski clearly acted with a conscious disregard for LeMarbe's health and safety and violated LeMarbe's Eighth Amendment right to have his serious medical needs attended to without deliberate indifference. In other words, we believe that LeMarbe has raised more than just a simple question of whether Dr. Wisneski made the right medical judgment in treating him.

* * *

2.   *Clearly Established Right*

We also conclude that LeMarbe has successfully proven that the allegedly violated right was clearly established. Although a government doctor is entitled to qualified immunity if he has merely made a reasonable mistake in his medical judgment, he is not entitled to such immunity if he correctly perceived all the relevant facts, understood the consequences of such facts, and disregarded those consequences in his treatment of a patient. [ ] As the Supreme Court has repeatedly recognized, a prisoner has a right not to have his serious medical needs disregarded by his doctors. [ ]. Assuming that a jury accepts the facts as alleged by LeMarbe and believes the affidavit of Dr. Sarnelle, in which Dr. Sarnelle claimed that Dr. Wisneski, as a person with a medical education, must have been aware of the risk posed to LeMarbe, then Dr. Wisneski's actions cannot, under all relevant precedents, reasonably be considered to be the result of a mere reasonable mistake or negligence but only the result of a conscious disregard for LeMarbe's health. It is clearly established that, if a doctor knows of a substantial risk of serious harm to a patient and is aware that he must either seek immediate assistance from another doctor to prevent further serious harm or must inform the patient to seek immediate assistance elsewhere, and then fails to do in a timely manner what his training indicates is necessary to prevent such harm, that doctor has treated the patient with deliberate indifference. * * *.

Affirmed.

GRENNAN v. CHILDREN'S HOSPITAL

Court of Appeals of Washington, Division One, 2001.
104 Wash.App. 1016.

KENNEDY, J.

* * *

FACTS

Beginning in 1991, the Grennans actively sought medical attention for developmental delays and neurological abnormalities in their daughter Amanda, who was 2 years old at that time. Amanda was first evaluated by pediatric neurologist Dr. Abern in the Grennans' home state of Illinois. Amanda was subsequently evaluated at several Illinois hospitals by various physicians including Drs. Stack, Plioplyous, Huttenlocher, and Chez. These physicians could not conclusively state whether Amanda's condition was due to autism or epileptic aphasia. Amanda was given various medications to treat seizure activity. A blood test taken by Dr. Huttenlocher in 1993 indicated toxic levels of medication.

In 1994, the Grennans took Amanda to New York University Hospital for evaluation for epilepsy treatment. After diagnosing epilepsy, the New York doctors performed neurosurgery on Amanda, and portions of her brain were removed where abnormalities were detected. Amanda's mother initially noted improvements following surgery, but within several months reported that Amanda's condition had not improved. After seeking further evaluations in Illinois and Michigan, the Grennans were referred to Dr. Ojemann at the University of Washington's neurology department in Seattle.

Dr. Ojemann referred the Grennans to Dr. Donat, the medical director of the pediatric epilepsy surgery program at Children's Hospital in Seattle. In a letter to Dr. Donat, Mrs. Grennan stated that Dr. Abbott of New York University Hospital "understands we are upset that the job was not completed in New York" and that she was "looking for this surgery to be completed." [ ] Dr. Donat noted that doctors at Illinois' Rush Hospital had raised the question of Munchausen's Syndrome by Proxy (MSBP), as those doctors believed Amanda had autism, not epilepsy.

In 1995, Children's Hospital agreed to evaluate Amanda and requested her prior medical records. Dr. Rho of Children's Hospital noted that the Grennans sent an incomplete set of medical records. Dr. Rho requested to speak to Amanda's prior physicians, particularly the surgeons in New York, but this request allegedly was refused by Mrs. Grennan. The Grennans dispute that they were ever asked for any medical records other than those that they provided. After evaluating Amanda, Drs. Donat and Rho found no evidence of epilepsy and concluded that they could not support the Grennans' request for surgery. On April 13, 1995, Drs. Rho and Donat, neuropsychologist Dr. Shurtleff, epilepsy nurse Martin, and hospital social worker Humes met with the Grennans to report that they found no evidence of epilepsy. Humes and Dr. Rho indicated that the Grennans were upset by this report. Mrs. Grennan stated that she remained convinced that Amanda had epilepsy, not autism.

Dr. Rho suspected that Amanda might be a victim of MSBP "[d]ue to the parents' unwillingness to allow contact with her physicians or access to more records, Mrs. Grennan's desire to find a condition responsive to surgery, [and Mrs. Grennan's] absolute rejection of the conclusion that the diagnostic data did not support a diagnosis of [epilepsy.]" Concerned that the Grennans would continue to seek inappropriate surgical intervention for Amanda, Humes referred the case to Children's Hospital's Child Abuse Forum.

The Child Abuse Forum referred the case to Dr. Feldman, a pediatrician who had previously consulted in cases of suspected child abuse. Dr. Feldman reviewed Amanda's records and the Grennans' correspondence with Children's Hospital. He also interviewed the Grennans and discussed the case with Drs. Rho and Donat, who informed him that the Grennans' had refused to allow contact with Amanda's prior physicians. Dr. Feldman recommended a formal referral to CPS, which was made by Humes. CPS contacted the Illinois Department of Child and Family Services (DCFS). Dr. Feldman prepared a child abuse report in which he indicated his suspicion of MSBP. He also indicated that "observation of the spells by both parents and Amanda's very real developmental delays" were factors against a finding of MSBP. Clerk's Papers at 118. He stated that he hoped that the result of the referral would be for DCFS to "secure records, and have a specialist determine which care and how much care was needed."

In Illinois, DCFS filed an action for temporary custody in order to obtain Amanda's complete medical records and to conduct an independent evaluation of her condition. The Illinois court found probable cause of abuse and placed Amanda in the temporary custody of her aunt. After obtaining records and conducting a full evaluation, however, the State of Illinois dismissed the action and returned Amanda to the Grennans' care.

In 1998, the Grennans filed suit against Children's Hospital and Dr. Feldman, alleging negligent diagnosis of MSBP, negligent infliction of emotional distress, and intentional infliction of emotional distress. Children's Hospital and Dr. Feldman moved for summary judgment, claiming immunity from suit under RCW 26.44.060. * * *

* * * Regarding the summary judgment motion, the court ruled that Children's Hospital and Dr. Feldman were immune from suit as a matter of law and dismissed all of the Grennans' claims. This appeal followed.

DISCUSSION

* * *

SUMMARY JUDGMENT ORDER

The trial court dismissed the Grennans' claims after concluding as a matter of law that Respondents met the good faith reporting requirement of RCW 26.44.060 and were thus immune from suit. The Grennans assign error to this ruling.

* * *

RCW 26.44.060(1)(a) states that "any person participating in good faith in the making of a report pursuant to this chapter or testifying as to alleged child abuse or neglect . . . shall in so doing be immune from any liability arising out of such reporting or testifying[.]" RCW 26.44.030 imposes a legal duty to report when a practitioner has "reasonable cause to believe that a child . . . has suffered abuse or neglect[.]" Violation of this reporting requirement is punishable as a gross misdemeanor under RCW 26.44.080.

The one claiming immunity under RCW 26.44.060 has the initial burden of proving that the report was made in good faith. [ ]. However, "there is no legal requirement that information giving rise to a suspicion of child abuse be investigated or verified before it is reported." Id. Whether one negligently suspects abuse and makes a report is irrelevant in determining whether immunity attaches; rather, "the question is whether the reporter acted 'with a reasonable good faith intent, judged in light of all the circumstances then present.' " [ ] Good faith is defined as "a state of mind indicating honesty and lawfulness of purpose." [ ] While the existence of good faith is a question of fact, if reasonable persons could reach but one conclusion from the facts presented, summary judgment is appropriate.

We note at this juncture that the disputed evidence with respect to whether the Grennans did or did not provide all the medical records requested by physicians at Children's Hospital, and did or did not cooperate in allowing those physicians to communicate with Amanda's prior physicians, does not raise a genuine issue of material fact. It is undisputed that Dr. Feldman was told by physicians at Children's Hospital that this was the case, and the material issue here is Dr. Feldman's good faith.

In Miles v. Child Protective Serv. Dep't, Division Two of this court recently held that Dr. Feldman and Children's Hospital, in an unrelated MSBP reporting case, were immune from liability with regard to plaintiffs' claim for negligent diagnosis. [ ]. In determining that Dr. Feldman and Children's Hospital acted in good faith, the Miles court noted that Dr. Feldman acted in conjunction with, and consistently with, physicians from another hospital, a physician in private practice, and all members of the hospital's multidisciplinary team, including physicians, nurses, and social workers.

Similarly, this action arose out of Humes' initial report to CPS and Dr. Feldman's drafting of a child abuse report. To determine whether immunity attaches, we examine whether hospital social worker Humes and consulting physician Dr. Feldman acted in good faith.

Humes

The Grennans brought Amanda to Children's Hospital in order to complete the surgery for epilepsy aphasia that was begun in New York. Drs. Donat and Rho concluded that Amanda was not a candidate for epilepsy surgery. Drs. Donat and Rho suspected MSBP because they found that the Grennans were unwilling to allow contact with Amanda's past physicians or to access her complete records, and it appeared to them that Mrs. Grennan would tailor her presentation of historical data in order to find a condition responsive to surgery. Based on this behavior, Drs. Donat and Rho suspected abuse based on seeking unnecessary medical care. Humes interviewed the Grennans with Drs. Rho and Donat, epilepsy nurse and neuropsychologist, Dr. Shurtleff, and noted that the Grennans appeared upset after being notified that the doctors found no epileptic activity in Amanda. After conferring in a Child Abuse Forum, Humes referred the case to CPS so that CPS could thoroughly investigate before additional medical care was sought.

Dr. Feldman

After suspecting MSBP, Humes referred the case to Dr. Feldman. Dr. Feldman examined Amanda's medical history, as well as the clinical opinions of Drs. Rho, Donat, and Shurtleff. He also met with the Grennans. Based on the information he was given regarding the Grennans' prohibition of communication with prior physicians, the demand for epilepsy surgery, and the tailoring of past medical information, Dr. Feldman agreed in his child abuse report that MSBP was possible. Concerned about the risk to Amanda, Dr. Feldman recommended referral to DCFS in Illinois in order to obtain all medical records and get a comprehensive evaluation of the case. In his report, Dr. Feldman also identified factors that could weigh against a finding of MSBP.

Even when viewed in the light most favorable to the Grennans, no reasonable person could find that Humes or Dr. Feldman acted without good faith. Humes and Dr. Feldman acted in conjunction with and based on clinical information from other clinical staff, such as Drs. Rho and Donat, epilepsy nurse Martin, and Dr. Shurtleff. While the Grennans argue that Dr. Feldman and Children's Hospital had a duty to further investigate the case prior to reporting to CPS, no such duty is imposed upon them by the statute. Whether mistaken or not, Humes and Dr. Feldman were acting to promote the best interests of Amanda. Nor is there any evidence to suggest that Humes or Dr. Feldman were dishonest or acted with any unlawful purpose. Thus, Children's Hospital and Dr. Feldman are immune from liability as a matter of law.

* * *

Affirmed.

Notes

1) The 11th amendment to the U.S. Constitution provides immunity for states from suits by private individuals unless the state consents to such suits. The U.S. Supreme Court held in *Seminole Tribe of Florida v. Florida*, 517 U.S. 44, 116 S.Ct. 1114, 134 L.Ed.2d 252 (1996) that in order for Congress to abrogate a state's sovereign immunity, it must state its intention to do so unequivocally, and act pursuant to constitu-

tional authority. The Supreme Court in *Alden v. Maine*, 527 U.S. 706, 119 S.Ct. 2240, 144 L.Ed.2d 636 (1999) specifically held that states also cannot be sued by private parties in state court for violations of federal law without their consent.

2) Massachusetts is one of only six states that continues to maintain some form of charitable immunity. There was much speculation as to whether the *Keene* decision would result in another state abrogating an outdated principle. However, the Massachusetts court held that doing so was a legislative matter and not one to be implemented by the courts. It also held that abrogating a statutory immunity could not be used as a punitive measure even under circumstances where, arguably, the defendant's negligence in failing to maintain the integrity of its records inured to its own benefit.

3) All states have provisions that certain health care workers are mandatory reporters of child abuse and neglect. This means that a health care worker who has *reasonable cause* to suspect that a child *may have been* abused is obligated to report that suspected abuse to appropriate state authorities. The report only needs to be made in good faith, and need not be investigated by the mandated reporter. This "mandate" is created by professional licensure, and failure to observe this obligation is a violation of the terms of the license. In recognition of the mandated nature of this obligation, reporters are also given immunity (and under some circumstances, anonymity) for their reports unless the report is made in bad faith or with the intent to cause harm.

SECTION B. AFFIRMATIVE DEFENSES

HEIN v. CORNWALL HOSPITAL

Supreme Court of New York, Appellate Division, First Department, 2003.
302 A.D.2d 170, 753 N.Y.S.2d 71.

Sullivan, J.

In this medical malpractice action commenced on January 22, 1999, based on, inter alia, the failure to diagnose and treat timely an obstruction of the bowel, resulting in various corrective surgeries and gastrointestinal injuries, as well as extensive loss of the bowel, plaintiff charges defendants with malpractice committed on July 17, 1996, July 20, 1996, July 20 through July 24, 1996 and July 29, 1996. At issue is the viability of any claim for malpractice committed prior to July 20, 1996, which is, on its face, outside the 2 ½ year statute of limitations [ ]. Rejecting plaintiff's continuous treatment argument, Supreme Court dismissed any such claim as time barred.

On July 16, 1996, at 5:00 A.M., three weeks after his discharge from Memorial Sloan–Kettering Hospital, where he had been treated for testicular cancer over a four-month period in 1996, necessitating two surgical procedures and chemotherapy, plaintiff, then 21 years of age, arrived at the emergency room of defendant Cornwall Hospital, complaining of nausea, vomiting and back and abdominal pain. Doctors

Resch, also a defendant herein, and Madell examined him and prescribed various medications, including Toradol to relieve his pain and Zantac to neutralize any stomach acid. Dr. Resch ordered a blood work-up, a chest X ray and a scan of the spleen. Plaintiff was discharged six hours later without a diagnosis. In the emergency room discharge notice plaintiff was instructed that in the event of a change in condition he was to notify his physician immediately and, in the event he was unable to contact him or her, to call or return to the emergency room.

According to the emergency room record, plaintiff returned to the emergency room at 11:34 P.M. that same day and was seen by Dr. Resch at 12:30 A.M. Dr. Resch prescribed morphine for his pain and conducted urine and blood analyses, which, except for slightly lowered potassium levels, revealed no significant abnormalities. Dr. Resch discharged plaintiff at 4:00 A.M. the next morning, instructing him, as before, to return to the emergency room only if necessary. Later that day, on a referral from his primary care physician, Dr. Wilder, plaintiff saw Dr. Muslim, a gastroenterologist, also a defendant herein, who examined him and arrived at a diagnosis of gastritis brought on by steroids. Dr. Muslim reviewed and confirmed plaintiff's medication regime.

Three days later, on July 20, 1996, plaintiff again experienced abdominal pain and returned to the emergency room at 5:30 A.M., where he was seen by Dr. Resch as well as Dr. Muslim. Plaintiff was given pain medication and discharged when the source of his pain could not be diagnosed. He was again instructed to notify his private physician immediately if he had a change in condition. Later that same day, at the insistence of his father, plaintiff was admitted by Dr. Muslim with a differential diagnosis of "drug dependence versus paraneoplastic syndrome; neuropathy secondary to chemotherapy; anxiety secondary to neoplasm; infectious mononucleosis; viral syndrome; gastritis; etc." Plaintiff was discharged on July 24, 1996 with a diagnosis of "abdominal pain, probably visceral from infectious mono, infection of the capsule of the spleen ... paraneoplastic syndrome, Candida esophagitis, depression," and referred to Dr. Wilder, his primary care physician, and the doctors at Sloan–Kettering. Dr. Muslim noted that he discussed with plaintiff and his family "regarding the lack of the objective findings and disproportionate subjective pain and discomfort." This discussion followed an in-patient referral to Dr. Prabhu, a psychiatrist, who found plaintiff to be "obsessed with his physical condition" and diagnosed him as suffering from a "depressive disorder [secondary] to physical condition."

Plaintiff returned to the emergency room at Cornwall Hospital on July 29, 1996 with the same complaints and was examined by Dr. Resch. Again, a diagnosis could not be made as to the source of his pain. He was referred to Sloan–Kettering, where he was admitted that same day. The next day, July 30, 1996, plaintiff underwent bowel resection at Sloan–Kettering due to a small bowel obstruction and extensive small bowel necrosis/infarction. He later underwent five abdominal surgical procedures, including two laparotomies for treatment of abdominal infections and abscesses.

After joinder of issue, defendants moved for partial summary judgment as to any claim for injuries alleged to have been the result of acts and/or omissions which occurred prior to plaintiff's July 20, 1996 admission to Cornwall Hospital as barred by [New York's] 2 ½ year statute of limitations (CPLR 214–a). In opposition, plaintiff argued the toll of continuous treatment and cross-moved to strike defendants' statute of limitations defense on that ground. Supreme Court rejected plaintiff's continuous treatment argument and granted defendants' motion, relying on language in *Nykorchuck v. Henriques* (78 N.Y.2d 255, 259, 573 N.Y.S.2d 434, 577 N.E.2d 1026) to the effect that the failure to establish a course of treatment is not a course of treatment and holding that "nowhere in the portions of the submitted deposition testimony or in the medical records is there evidence that a plan of treatment was discussed or made." The court noted the absence of the anticipation by both patient and physician of further treatment as manifested by an agreement as to a regularly scheduled appointment in the near future. As noted, the court dismissed any claims based on malpractice that took place prior to July 20, 1996 and denied plaintiff's cross motion. We reverse.

CPLR 214–a, in pertinent part, provides, "An action for medical ... malpractice must be commenced within two years and six months of the act, omission or failure complained of or last treatment where there is continuous treatment for the same illness, injury or condition which gave rise to the said act, omission or failure." Under the continuous treatment doctrine, the statute is tolled until after the plaintiff's last treatment, " 'when the course of treatment which includes the wrongful acts or omissions has run continuously and is related to the same original condition or complaint' " [ ]. Thus, the question for resolution is whether plaintiff's emergency room and office visits of July 16 and July 17, 1996 were part of a course of treatment that may be said to have run continuously.

Supreme Court, in its analysis, quoted *Nykorchuck v. Henriques, supra* [ ], "While the failure to treat a condition may well be negligent, we cannot accept the self-contradictory proposition that the failure to establish a course of treatment is a course of treatment." In the circumstances of this case, this statement is capable of being misleading. As this Court noted in *Williams v. Health Ins. Plan of Greater N.Y.* (220 A.D.2d 343, 633 N.Y.S.2d 22), a case involving a failure to diagnose, "The relevant issue in such a case is not whether there has been a diagnosis, but whether the ongoing treatment is related to the ... condition that gave rise to the lawsuit" [ ]. Throughout the period of July 16, 1996 and through plaintiff's admission to Cornwall Hospital, including the emergency room visits and the office visit to Dr. Muslim, the medical intervention was always for the same reason: plaintiff's severe abdominal pain. The intervention geared to that condition—the repeated administration of medication and testing undertaken to treat and diagnose that symptom—is indeed a course of professional activity deserving of the application of the doctrine of continuous treatment.

This Court has repeatedly ruled that the failure to make the correct diagnosis as to the underlying condition while continuing to treat the symptoms does not mean, for purposes of continuity, that there has not been treatment [ ]. "The fact that the defendants did not initially diagnose plaintiff's [condition] does not detract from the conclusion that defendants treated plaintiff continuously over the relevant time period for symptoms ultimately traceable to the ... condition whose alleged misdiagnosis and alleged mistreatment have given rise to this action." [ ] "Merely because defendants did not diagnose plaintiff's decedent's condition as cancer is not a basis to find that they were not treating him for it if his symptoms were such as to indicate its existence and they nevertheless failed to properly diagnose it."

The medical records in the instant case speak for themselves. They clearly indicate that each of plaintiff's repeated visits—all for abdominal pain, nausea, vomiting and back pain—was for "the same illness, injury or condition" that CPLR 214–a uses as the frame of reference when it specifies the "last treatment" as the accrual date where there is continuous treatment.

Nor, on each occasion that plaintiff sought medical assistance, was it for an examination "undertaken at the request of the patient for the sole purpose of ascertaining the state of the patient's condition," which CPLR 214–a specifically excludes from the term "continuous treatment." Moreover, after the office visit of July 17, 1996 and again after seeing him in the emergency room on July 20, 1996, Dr. Muslim expected to continue to examine and treat plaintiff if the symptoms persisted. Indeed, on his discharge from the emergency room on July 20, 1996, Dr. Muslim instructed plaintiff to call him on "Monday." As the Court of Appeals has held, "Where the physician and patient reasonably intend the patient's uninterrupted reliance upon the physician's observation, directions, concern, and responsibility for overseeing the patient's progress, the requirement for continuous care and treatment for the purpose of the Statute of Limitations is certainly satisfied" [ ].

Defendants' inability, notwithstanding their work-up and prescription of various medications for gastritis, pain, mononucleosis, viral syndrome and depression, to arrive at the correct diagnosis is the very nub of the malpractice claim against them. If the Legislature had intended to shield doctors from malpractice claims for their failure to diagnose and treat symptoms correctly it would not have used the word "omission" in CPLR 214–a. In this regard, the Court of Appeals has set the standard: "Neither individuals suffering from chronic conditions, nor patients being 'monitored' for a specific medical condition to ensure that it improves or at least does not deteriorate (as opposed to a general physical examination), are necessarily outside the doctrine" [ ]. We have considered defendants' other arguments and find that they are without merit.

Accordingly, the order of the Supreme Court, New York County [ ] which granted the motion by defendants [ ] for partial summary judgment and denied plaintiff's cross motion to strike said defendants' affirmative defenses based on statute of limitations, should be reversed * * *.

CARAVAGGIO v. D'AGOSTINI

Supreme court of New Jersey, 2001.
166 N.J. 237, 765 A.2d 182.

LONG, J.

The discovery rule, incorporating as it does a notion of simple justice, has been anything but simple in application, as evidenced by the amount of litigation it has spawned. Decades after its enunciation, lawyers and judges are still grappling with its application. This is another such case.

I

Plaintiff Patricia Caravaggio and her husband were seriously injured in a motorcycle accident on May 23, 1993. Mrs. Caravaggio's specific injury was a segmental fracture of the femur, also called the thighbone. She was taken by ambulance to Morristown Memorial Hospital where the defendant, Dr. Robert D'Agostini, an orthopedic surgeon, performed surgery to repair the bone. Dr. D'Agostini "reamed out" Mrs. Caravaggio's femur bone, inserted a rod manufactured by the Synthes Corporation in the hollow of the bone, and affixed the rod with screws through the bone at both ends to stabilize the fracture.

Mrs. Caravaggio was discharged from the hospital and underwent physical therapy at home, remaining under the care of Dr. D'Agostini who had previously explained to her that she could expect an average healing time of twelve weeks, and that among the complications possible were "infection, blood clots, blood loss or anemia, failure to heal, need for rod removal later, rod breakage." On June 15, 1993, Dr. D'Agostini modified the physical therapy prescription to permit as much weight-bearing on the injured leg as Mrs. Caravaggio could tolerate. On July 13, 1993, Dr. D'Agostini told Mrs. Caravaggio to increase the vigor of her physical therapy, noting that she should continue to use crutches and to bear weight on her injured leg. Two weeks later on July 28, 1993, Mrs. Caravaggio felt a "snap" in her leg while the physical therapist was bending her knee.

Dr. D'Agostini examined Mrs. Caravaggio at his office on August 4, 1993. An x-ray of the leg revealed that the rod had broken through the screw holes. Dr. D'Agostini told Mrs. Caravaggio that he was "very much surprised" that a rod manufactured by Synthes, "probably the best manufacturer of rods in the world", could break in eight weeks.

* * *

Dr. D'Agostini explained to Mrs. Caravaggio that her injuries would now take longer to heal and could require additional surgery to replace the rod. First, however, he recommended bracing and conservative treatment to attempt to avoid additional surgery. Mrs. Caravaggio accepted his recommendation. She continued with follow-up visits, but by September 28, 1993, the doctor determined that her femur would not heal without further surgery.

In early October, Mrs. Caravaggio obtained a second opinion from an orthopedist for insurance purposes. That physician agreed with Dr. D'Agostini's recommendation of surgery and, although he indicated that perhaps Dr. D'Agostini might have chosen a thicker rod to implant, did not suggest directly or obliquely that Mrs. Caravaggio should question the medical care she received from Dr. D'Agostini. Mrs. Caravaggio continued in Dr. D'Agostini's care and he performed the second surgery on October 21, 1993, to replace the broken rod. In that surgery, he "reamed" the femur bone more extensively and inserted a thicker and longer rod.

After the second surgery, Dr. D'Agostini informed Mrs. Caravaggio that there was something wrong with the rod and that she should take it to the lawyer who was representing her in her lawsuit against the operator of the car that struck her. The rod was then sent to the hospital's pathology lab, and at some later date (not determined with specificity in the record) the rod was given to the attorney representing Mrs. Caravaggio in her ongoing auto negligence litigation.

After Mrs. Caravaggio's discharge, in May of 1994, her husband continued to be treated by Dr. D'Agostini well into the fall of 1995, over two and one-half years from the accident. During that period, Mr. and Mrs. Caravaggio both referred family and friends to him.

In the meantime, on July 28, 1994, Mrs. Caravaggio's counsel sent the rod to be analyzed by J. Stephen Duerr, President of Metuchen Analytical. Metallurgic tests revealed that the rod was not defective. The record is unclear exactly when that information was received, although it was certainly after July 1994.

In late 1994 or early 1995, Mrs. Caravaggio met a new attorney who suggested that she might have a medical malpractice claim. She retained that attorney who, in turn, referred her to her present counsel, who filed a complaint on her behalf against Dr. D'Agostini on September 15, 1995.

Dr. D'Agostini moved for summary judgment, arguing that Mrs. Caravaggio's complaint was barred by the expiration of the two year statute of limitations. The trial court ordered a discovery rule hearing as required by Lopez v. Swyer, 62 N.J. 267, 300 A.2d 563 (1973). After the hearing, at which the facts related in this opinion were established and presumably viewed in a light most favorable to Mrs. Caravaggio pursuant to R. 4:46–2(c), the court granted the motion, concluding that Mrs. Caravaggio knew or should have known that she had an actionable claim against Dr. D'Agostini no later than August 4, 1993:

Plaintiff knew she suffered an injury on July 28 or 29, 1993. At that time she believed that the injury was caused by the physical therapist and she expressed that opinion to defendant on August 4, 1993, when she learned that the rod had broken.

* * *

Arguably, defendant's statement may have "lulled" plaintiff into believing that the wrongdoer was neither the physical therapist nor the defendant, because implicit in defendant's statement was an assurance that the physical therapy defendant ordered was actually proper.

Nevertheless, the court concluded that because Mrs. Caravaggio knew she was injured on August 4, 1993, and that "the injury was the product of someone's wrongdoing," summary judgment was appropriate because her cause of action accrued on that date and her complaint was filed two years and fifty-two days later.[1]

The Appellate Division affirmed the trial court's judgment because "the judge's factual findings and conclusions of law [on the statute of limitations issue] are supported by sufficient evidence in the record and the applicable law." * * *

II

N.J.S.A. 2A:14–2 gives a plaintiff a two year period from the accrual of his or her claim in which to file a malpractice action. At common law, there was no limit on the time in which a plaintiff could institute such litigation. [ ]. Since then, statutes of limitations have been adopted regarding all causes of action, in order to "promote repose by giving security and stability to human affairs." [ ]. Their purpose is to penalize dilatoriness and serve as measure of repose. * * * When a plaintiff knows or has reason to know that he has a cause of action against an identifiable defendant and voluntarily sleeps on his rights so long as to permit the customary period of limitations to expire, the pertinent considerations of individual justice as well as the broader considerations of repose, coincide to bar his action. Where, however, the plaintiff does not know or have reason to know that he has a cause of action against an identifiable defendant until after the normal period of limitations has expired, the considerations of individual justice and the considerations of repose are in conflict and other factors may fairly be brought into play.

The latter principle is embodied in the so-called "discovery rule." [ ]. The purpose behind the rule "is to avoid harsh results that otherwise would flow from mechanical application of a statute of limitations." [ ]. Accordingly, the doctrine "postpones the accrual of a cause of action" so long as a party reasonably is unaware either that he has been injured, or that the injury is due to the fault or neglect of an identifiable individual or entity. [ ] Once a person knows or has reason to know of this

---

1. In rendering its opinion, the trial court ventured that Mrs. Caravaggio should have filed a complaint within two years from August 4, 1993, naming fictitious defendants until the identity of the wrongdoer could be established as allowed by R. 4:26–4. R.4:26–4 is entirely irrelevant in these circumstances. . . .

information, his or her claim has accrued since, at that point, he or she is actually or constructively aware "of that state of facts which may equate in law with a cause of action." [ ]

* * *

The question in a discovery rule case is whether the facts presented would alert a reasonable person, exercising ordinary diligence, that he or she was injured due to the fault of another. The standard is basically an objective one—whether plaintiff "knew or should have known" of sufficient facts to start the statute of limitations running. [ ]

That does not mean that the statute of limitations is tolled until a plaintiff has knowledge of a specific basis for legal liability or a provable cause of action. [ ]. It does, however, require knowledge not only of the injury but also that another is at fault. [ ]. Both are critical elements in determining whether the discovery rule applies. For that analysis, it has been held that plaintiffs are to be divided into classes: those who do not know that they have been injured and those who know they have suffered an injury but do not know that it is attributable to the fault of another. [ ]. When a plaintiff's claim falls within the latter class her cause of action does not accrue until she has knowledge of the injury and that such injury is the fault of another.

In many cases, knowledge of fault is acquired simultaneously with knowledge of injury. Fault is apparent, for example, where the wrong tooth is extracted during surgery [ ] or where a foreign object has been left within the body after an operation. See Fernandi, supra, 35 N.J. at 438 (holding that period of limitations on a patient's negligence cause of action began to run when the patient knew or had reason to know about the foreign object left in her body). In other cases, however, a plaintiff may be aware of an injury but not aware that the injury is attributable to the fault of another.

* * *

"A sub-category of the 'knowledge of fault' cases is that in which a plaintiff knows she has been injured and knows the injury was the fault of another, but does not know that an additional party was also responsible for her plight." Martinez v. Cooper Hosp. 163 N.J. 45, 54, 747 A.2d 266 (2000) [ ]. In Martinez, the plaintiff's fiancee, Carl Farrish, was badly beaten in a street fight and died at the hospital shortly thereafter. The plaintiff knew of his injury and that it was the fault of another—the person who administered the beating. Indeed, Farrish's death certificate and accompanying publicity reflected that the death was a homicide. In addition, the physician at the hospital told the plaintiff "they did all they could." [ ]. Because the plaintiff was not present at the hospital, she did not know that, despite the fact that Farrish was in extremis, he waited for many hours before he received any medical treatment. On those facts, we held that the plaintiff "had no reason to suspect malpractice" [ ] until her lawyer was notified, in an anonymous letter, of what occurred at the hospital on the night of the beating. Thus, the complaint filed three and one-half years after Farrish's death, but within two years of the anonymous letter, was timely. In effect, Martinez reaffirmed that a cause of action may accrue against different defendants at different times.

* * *

Two other cases that are instructive are Gallagher v. Burdette–Tomlin Mem'l Hosp. 163 N.J. 38, 747 A.2d 262 (2000), and Mancuso. In Gallagher [ ] we held recently that a plaintiff could invoke the discovery rule long after she sued her surgeon for malpractice when she discovered that her after-care physicians were also at fault. That information was first made known to her during discovery in the case against the surgeon. [ ]. In Mancuso [ ] we held that although the plaintiff pursued a malpractice cause of action against her surgeon, because she did not know or have reason to know that she also had a cause of action against her radiologist until she heard of his alleged malpractice during discovery in the original action, she could invoke the discovery rule to begin an action against him more than two years after his alleged malpractice.

* * *

III

Both the trial court and the Appellate Division ruled the complaint untimely by fifty-two days based on the notion that on August 4, 1993, Mrs. Caravaggio knew or should have known that she was injured and that Dr. D'Agostini bore some responsibility for that injury.

We disagree with that rather expansive view of what a reasonable person would or should have known on August 4, 1993. On that date, Mrs. Caravaggio was told by Dr. D'Agostini that there must have been something "structurally wrong" with the rod and that nothing the physical therapist did, at his behest, could have caused it to snap. It appears that those statements were made in good faith by Dr. D'Agostini who, even at the time of the Lopez hearing on May 22, 1998, and despite the metallurgic analysis, still believed that the Synthes Rod was defective. On August 4,1993, Mrs. Caravaggio had no reason to assume either that he was being untruthful or that he had committed malpractice in the surgery. Indeed, that she did not believe so is underscored by the fact she later underwent further surgery at his hands, that her husband continued in his care, and that both of them referred family and friends to him. It was only when the rod was removed and found not to be defective that Mrs. Caravaggio might possibly have had reason to look elsewhere. The rod removal took place on October 21, 1993, and the complaint against Dr. D'Agostini was filed within two years of that date.

To be sure, Mrs. Caravaggio knew she was injured on August 4, 1993, and, in light of Dr. D'Agostini's statements, had reason to believe that the rod manufacturer was at fault as of that date. That is quite different from knowing or even suspecting Dr. D'Agostini's possible malpractice. Indeed, Mrs. Caravaggio was told, as part of the informed consent ritual at the time of the surgery, that even a procedure performed properly could result in the untoward complication of "rod breakage."

On August 4, 1993, when Mrs. Caravaggio knew the rod had broken, Dr. D'Agostini absolved the physical therapist and, inferentially, himself, indicating that the only thing he could think of was that there was something "structurally wrong" with the rod. Thus, on that date, Mrs. Caravaggio might reasonably have believed either that the rod breakage was just a "complication" of the surgery or that the manufacturer was responsible. She was entirely reasonable in not assuming that Dr. D'Agostini or the therapist were to blame.

Until the rod was removed and analysis revealed that it was not defective, there was no reason for Mrs. Caravaggio to suspect some other cause. Even then, Dr. D'Agostini's negligence was not necessarily implicated. This is not a res ipsa case. Buckelew v. Grossbard, 87 N.J. 512, 525, 435 A.2d 1150 (1981) (confirming use of res ipsa loquitur in medical malpractice cases, such that an inference of defendant's negligence is permitted "where (a) the occurrence itself ordinarily bespeaks negligence; (b) the instrumentality was within the defendant's exclusive control; and (c) there is no indication in the circumstances that the injury was the result of the plaintiff's own voluntary act or neglect." [ ].) As we have noted, Dr. D'Agostini himself acknowledged that he advised Mrs. Caravaggio that rod breakage was a possible complication of properly performed surgery. It thus does not necessarily follow that a reasonable person would have concluded that one of the "universe" of defendants (manufacturer, therapist, physician) had to be responsible.

In Martinez, supra, in a different context, we said:

It is not necessary every time a person dies in a hospital for his or her relatives to immediately suspect malpractice. People die in hospitals in the absence of wrongdoing (for example, those gravely injured in accidents and the infirm elderly). Many times complications arise even if a procedure is performed perfectly. Medicine is not an exact science. [ ]. The rule accepted by the lower courts, that Ms. Martinez was unreasonable because she did not obtain and analyze Farrish's medical records even though she was not suspicious, encourages mistrust and essentially pits patients against their physicians even in cases where there is not even a trace of negligence apparent. [ ]

That language is equally applicable here. Sometimes surgery results in complications, even if all procedures were performed correctly. People have heart attacks under anesthesia, develop blood clots, experience problems with wound healing, reject implants, and suffer failure of mobility after joint replacements. The possibilities, unfortunately, are legion. That is why surgery is always a last resort and why a patient is informed, prior to surgery, that a good result cannot be guaranteed even if the surgery is faultless.

Dr. D'Agostini did not cause Mrs. Caravaggio's original injury. He was retained to bring her back to health. That is what he was trying to do when he implanted the Synthes rod. When it broke and he told Mrs. Caravaggio that there must have been something structurally wrong with the rod, and assured her that the physical therapist could not have done anything to break a non-defective rod, there was no reason whatsoever for her to be suspicious of him. If the rulings of the trial court and the Appellate Division to the contrary were to be approved, it would have the untoward effect of pitting patients against their physicians, at a time at which they have no reason to doubt their physicians, in order not to risk losing their cause of action altogether.

It may be that after discovery and a trial on the merits, a jury will find that Dr. D'Agostini's performance of Mrs. Caravaggio's surgery was deficient. Our inquiry is solely focused on the period of time in 1993 when Mrs. Caravaggio learned the rod had broken. So focused, it is clear that her complaint was timely.

IV

Under presently existing standards governing the discovery rule, Mrs. Caravaggio acted in an objectively reasonable way in this matter, and the facts and circumstances, as known to her on August 4, 1993 did not warrant her concluding that Dr. D'Agostini was guilty of malpractice. She filed suit within two years of the removal of the rod. That was plainly within time.

V

The judgment of the Appellate Division is reversed.

NETT v. BELLUCCI

Supreme Judicial Court of Massachusetts, 2002.
437 Mass. 630, 774 N.E.2d 130.

SOSMAN, J. The United States Court of Appeals for the First Circuit has certified the following questions to this court, pursuant to S.J.C. Rule 1:03, as appearing in 382 Mass. 700 (1981):

"(1) Is the operative date for commencement of an action for purposes of the Massachusetts statutes of repose the date of filing of a motion and supporting memorandum for leave to amend a complaint to add a party (assuming timely service), or is the operative date the date the amended complaint is filed after leave of court is granted, when leave of court is required by the Rules of Civil Procedure to file an amended complaint?

"(2) If the answer to Question No. 1 is that the operative date is the date of filing of the motion for leave to amend, do the policies underlying the statutes of repose require that such filings be in compliance with the local rules of court applicable to the filing of such motions, or do those policies permit the court in its discretion to excuse non-compliance with the local rules?"

[ ] We answer the certified questions as follows: (1) The operative date for commencement of an action for purposes of a statute of repose is

the date of filing of a motion for leave to amend a complaint to add a party; and (2) the policies underlying the statute of repose do not require that the motion for leave to amend comply with the local rules, as long as the motion itself is accepted for filing within the period provided by the statute of repose.

1. Facts. * * * Aaron Nett was born at Milford–Whitinsville Hospital on April 2, 1992, weighing more than eleven pounds. The delivery was complicated because of Aaron's large size, and the infant suffered a nerve injury as a result of those complications. On March 26, 1992, one week prior to Aaron's birth, Dr. Peter Gross had performed and interpreted an ultrasound, estimating the fetal weight at only eight pounds. Dr. Mitchell Bellucci, the obstetrician attending Aaron's delivery, had relied on that ultrasound reading and had therefore not anticipated the complications that ensued during the delivery of a much larger baby.

On April 30, 1996, the plaintiffs filed a complaint against Dr. Bellucci in the United States District Court for the District of Massachusetts, alleging that he had been negligent in the prenatal care and delivery of Aaron. As part of his defense, Dr. Bellucci took the position that he had reasonably relied on the estimated fetal weight provided by the radiologist's ultrasound reading, and that his failure to anticipate delivery of a baby weighing eleven pounds was therefore not negligent.

On June 30, 1998, the plaintiffs served a subpoena duces tecum on the hospital seeking production of the ultrasound films. The hospital told the plaintiffs that the films had been destroyed. At his August 4, 1998, deposition, Dr. Gross testified that his efforts to obtain the ultrasound films had also been unsuccessful, as the hospital had similarly informed him that the films were no longer available. The hospital, responding to a second subpoena duces tecum, finally recovered and produced the ultrasound films on February 4, 1999.

On March 10, 1999, after obtaining an expert's review of the films and an opinion concerning their proper reading, the plaintiffs filed a motion for leave to amend their complaint to add Dr. Gross as a defendant pursuant to Fed. R. Civ. P. 15 (a). The motion and accompanying ten-page memorandum set forth the facts of the case and explained that the plaintiffs had been unable to assert a claim against Dr. Gross at any earlier point due to the hospital's claimed loss of the ultrasound films. * * *

* * *

Dr. Gross filed a motion to dismiss the amended complaint, arguing that the plaintiffs' claims against him were barred by the statutes of repose.[5] [ ] Because he had performed and interpreted the ultrasound on

5. Aaron's cause of action is governed by G. L. c. 231, § 60D, which provides in pertinent part that "any claim by a minor against a health care provider stemming from professional services or health care rendered, whether in contract or tort, based on an alleged act, omission or neglect shall be commenced within three years from the date the cause of action accrues, except that a minor under the full age of six years shall

March 26, 1992, Dr. Gross contended that any amended complaint adding him as a defendant would have had to be filed by March 26, 1999, the expiration of the seven-year repose period provided by the applicable statutes. [ ]. The second motion for leave to amend the complaint, filed on March 29, 1999, and the actual amended complaint, filed on April 26, 1999, both fell beyond that expiration date. The plaintiffs opposed the motion to dismiss, arguing that the repose provisions allowed them until April 2, 1999, Aaron's seventh birthday, to file a complaint against Dr. Gross and that their motion to amend, filed in compliance with local rule 15.1 (b), on March 29, 1999, had "commenced" the action within the repose period.

The Federal District Court initially denied the motion to dismiss. The court determined that the repose period expired on March 26, 1999, rather than April 2, 1999, but excused the violation of local rule 15.1 (b) as harmless error, deemed the motion for leave to amend to have been properly filed on March 10, 1999, and tolled the time that had elapsed between the filing of the first motion for leave to amend and the filing of the amended complaint. On a motion for reconsideration, however, the court reversed itself, concluding that a statute of repose could not be tolled in light of Protective Life Ins. Co. v. Sullivan, 425 Mass. 615, 631 n.19, 682 N.E.2d 624 (1997), and cases cited. Because the plaintiffs had not filed their amended complaint prior to March 26, 1999, the claims against Dr. Gross were dismissed.

On appeal to the United States Court of Appeals for the First Circuit, the plaintiffs were unsuccessful in pressing their theory that the statutes of repose ran from the child's birth date. [ ]. The March 26, 1999, seven-year anniversary of the ultrasound reading was held to be the applicable date for purposes of the statutes of repose, and both the March 29, 1999, motion for leave to amend, and the later April 26, 1999, filing of the complaint, fell outside that repose period. The question, then, was whether the March 10, 1999, filing of a motion for leave to amend qualified as the "commencement" of the action against Dr. Gross for purposes of the statutes of repose. Because the case was a diversity action, State law determined when the action was "commenced" for purposes of statutes of limitations or statutes of repose. [citation omitted]. Finding "no controlling precedent on the question of what constitutes the commencement of an action for the purpose of the Massachusetts statutes of repose," the court certified the two questions now before us. [ ].

2. Commencement of an action. The first certified question asks us to determine, for purposes of our statutes of repose, what step in the proceedings constitutes the commencement of an action against a party who is added by way of amendment to the complaint. Both the statute

have until his ninth birthday in which the action may be commenced, but in no event shall any such action be commenced more than seven years after occurrence of the act or admission which is the alleged cause of the injury upon which such action is based except where the action is based upon the leaving of a foreign object in the body" (emphasis added).

governing medical malpractice tort claims involving minors, G. L. c. 231, § 60D, and the statute governing medical malpractice tort claims generally, G. L. c. 260, § 4, provide that "in no event shall any such action be commenced more than seven years after occurrence of the act or omission which is the alleged cause of the injury upon which such action is based" (emphasis added). Like all statutes of repose, "the effect [of these statutes] is to place an absolute time limit on the liability of those within [their] protection and to abolish a plaintiff's cause of action thereafter, even if the plaintiff's injury does not occur, or is not discovered, until after the statute's time limit has expired."[ ]. Unlike statutes of limitation, statutes of repose may not be "tolled" for any reason, as "tolling" would deprive the defendant of the certainty of the repose deadline and thereby defeat the purpose of a statute of repose. [ ]. The only way to satisfy the "absolute time limit" of a statute of repose is to "commence" the action prior to the expiration of that time limit. * * *

The medical malpractice statutes of repose do not define when an action "commences." Ordinarily, we would look to our rules of civil procedure to determine the date on which an action is "commenced," and, under the straightforward provisions of those rules, we would find that amended pleadings adding or substituting a party, where the claims asserted against the new party arise out of the same conduct, transaction, or occurrence set forth in the original pleading, "relate[ ] back" to the date of the original pleading. [ ] Thus, under the rules, an action against such a party added by amendment is "commenced" on the date that the original complaint was filed.

However, we have already determined that that literal application of the rules would be contrary to the purposes underlying a statute of repose, and have thus, for statute of repose purposes only, rejected the date of commencement that the rules normally prescribe for related claims and parties added by amendment. [ ]. In that case, we held that a plaintiff could not amend a complaint to add an architect and an engineer as defendants after the expiration of the repose period imposed by G. L. c. 260, § 2B—a statute of repose governing torts related to construction projects—even though the original complaint was timely filed. [ ] We fashioned an exception to rule 15 (c), explaining that to allow amended pleadings for claims subject to a statute of repose to relate back to the original pleading "would have the effect of reactivating a cause of action that the Legislature obviously intended to eliminate." [ ] Thus, where the literal application of one of our rules of civil procedure would yield a result contrary to the purposes underlying statutes of repose, we refused to recognize the date of commencement provided by the rules.

Because rule 15 (c) cannot operate in these circumstances to establish the date of commencement as the date of filing of the original complaint, the defendant contends that we should instead apply the literal wording of Mass. R. Civ. P. 3, as amended, 385 Mass. 1215 (1982), which provides in pertinent part that "[a] civil action is commenced by (1) mailing to the clerk of the proper court by certified or registered mail a complaint and an entry fee prescribed by law, or (2) filing such complaint and an entry fee with such clerk." Under the defendant's reading of the rule, the plaintiffs did not "commence[ ]" their action until they filed their amended complaint on April 26, 1999, one month after the expiration of the repose period.

The defendant's argument applies rule 3 to a context it was not meant to govern. Because rule 15 (c) provides its own definition of when an amended complaint "commences" an action, the rule 3 definition of when an action "commences" is not meant to refer to the date of "mailing" or "filing" an amended complaint. Rule 15 (c) was intended to govern actions brought by way of amendment, and rule 3, by its literal wording (with its references to the "entry fee") plainly does not. Thus, rather than apply the literal wording of rule 3 to a situation for which it was not intended or designed, we must determine which step in the process of amending a complaint most resembles the filing of an original complaint, and whether treating that step as the commencement of the action would be consistent with the purposes underlying the statutes of repose. For the following reasons, we conclude that it is the filing of the motion for leave to amend, not the later filing of the amended complaint after that motion is allowed, that best satisfies those criteria.

The original filing of a complaint that "commences" an action under rule 3 is the first document that a plaintiff files in court, comprising the first official step in bringing an action against a defendant. No prior permission of the court is required, and no prior step involving the court need be taken. As such, the plaintiff has unilateral control over when the original complaint is filed, and the plaintiff is responsible for seeing to it that that step "commencing" the action occurs within all applicable statutes of limitation and statutes of repose.

What step in the process of amending a complaint most resembles that first step in the filing of an original action? Beyond the brief period during which a complaint may be amended as of right (see rule 15 [a]), a plaintiff amending a complaint may not do so unilaterally. Court permission is required. Therefore, the first step taken is to request permission from the court by filing a motion. While the plaintiff has unilateral control over when that motion is filed, the plaintiff has no way of controlling or even predicting the time at which any permission to amend will be granted, and thus no ability to control the date on which the amended complaint itself may be filed. It may take only a matter of days before the motion is allowed and the complaint can be filed, but it may be a matter of weeks, or even months, depending on a host of factors, all of which are outside the plaintiff's control. If the statute of repose cannot be satisfied until the later filing of the amended complaint after the motion to amend has been allowed, the repose period will effectively be shortened by some unpredictable amount of time, as a plaintiff would have to file the motion to amend some considerable period in advance of the expiration of the repose period and simply hope that the court's ruling would be sufficiently prompt. It is only that first step, the filing of the motion, that the plaintiff can control. Thus, the filing of the motion is comparable to the original filing of the complaint, both in the sense that each is the first step that a plaintiff takes and the first document that a plaintiff files with the court concerning the action, and in the sense that both the filing of the original complaint and the filing of the motion to amend are steps that remain unilaterally in the plaintiff's control.

It is true that a plaintiff retains the ability to satisfy the statute of repose by filing a separate action against the new defendant, perhaps followed by a motion to consolidate that new action with the previously filed action. [ ]. However, that approach would waste scarce judicial resources and impose pointless litigation costs. Where a defendant would appropriately be added to an action already filed, it creates needless confusion and duplication to force the plaintiff to bring the claim as a separate action, followed by a motion for consolidation, merely to avoid the bar of a statute of repose. Indeed, a plaintiff might well file a motion to amend, wait to see whether the motion would be allowed in time to get the amended complaint filed before the repose period ran out, and, if there were still no ruling from the court as the expiration date drew near, file the separate action and the accompanying motion to consolidate. We fail to see how such duplication of effort and procedural clutter would advance the purposes underlying any statute of repose. See Mauney v. Morris, 316 N.C. 67, 71, 72, 340 S.E.2d 397 (1986) (filing of motion to amend "is sufficient to start the action," noting that that interpretation "promotes judicial economy by avoiding the necessity for separate trials or for plaintiff to file first a separate complaint and then a motion to join the two actions"). Where a more efficient procedural mechanism is already available to bring an additional defendant into an existing action, we should recognize that preferred mechanism as the commencement of the action against the new defendant rather than force the parties and the court to utilize a more cumbersome workaround.

WILLIS v. MULLETT

Supreme Court of Virginia, 2002.
263 Va. 653, 561 S.E.2d 705.

OPINION BY SENIOR JUSTICE HENRY H. WHITING

This appeal involves the constitutionality of a statute that reduces the tolling period provided for infants' tort claims if those claims allege medical malpractice.

I

Code § 8.01–229(A)(2)(a) provides that "if an infant becomes entitled to bring [an] action, the time during which he is within the age of minority shall not be ... counted as any part of the period within which the action must be brought." In 1987, the legislature reduced this tolling period for infants with medical malpractice claims by requiring that any such actions brought on their behalf shall be commenced within two years of the date of the last act or omission giving rise to the cause of action except that if the minor was less than eight years of age at the time of the occurrence of the malpractice, he shall have until his tenth birthday to commence an action. [ ]

II

Taylor R. Willis was 15 years old when Doctors James G. Mullet and Michael A. Sisk, acting for their respective employers, Radiology Associates of Roanoke, P.C., and, Roanoke Neurological Associates, Inc. (collectively the defendants), committed acts of alleged medical malpractice upon him from July 15 to 18, 1995. Over four years later, after he reached his majority, 19–year old Willis filed this medical malpractice action against the defendants.

The defendants filed pleas of the statute of limitations alleging that the medical malpractice statute of limitations for minors required Willis to file this action within two years of July 18, 1995, the date of the final alleged act of malpractice. Willis responded that the statute was unconstitutional and, thus, that he was entitled to the benefit of the general tolling period for infants.

After considering argument on the pleas and memoranda of counsel, which included copies of various study reports of legislative subcommittees, the trial court held that the medical malpractice statute of limitations for minors was constitutional and sustained the defendants' pleas. Willis appeals.

III

Willis challenges the constitutionality of the medical malpractice statute of limitations for minors because it creates a special and reduced tolling period for infants with medical malpractice claims as compared to infants having other tort claims. Willis contends that this distinction violates the equal protection and due process rights guaranteed to him by both the United States Constitution and the Constitution of Virginia and is a "special law" forbidden by Article IV, Section 14 of the Constitution of Virginia.

* * *

* * * Willis argues that since minors have no right to bring actions during their minority, any such actions must be brought in the minor's name by his next friend under the provisions of Code § 8.01–8. Willis notes that if the next friend, negligently or otherwise, fails to file the action within the reduced time required under the medical malpractice statute of limitations for minors, the minor would lose his right to a jury trial. He asserts that this possible loss of a right to a jury trial invalidates the statute.

The possibility that some minors may ultimately see their rights lapse due to the responsible adult's negligence was discussed in a subcommittee report. Report of the Joint Subcommittee Studying the

Liability Insurance Crisis and the Need for Tort Reform, House Doc. No. 12, 1986, at 7. Presumably, this possibility was considered and resolved when the General Assembly weighed the merits of the medical malpractice statute of limitations for minors. [ ] The legislature was thus free to presume that some adult responsible for the minor's welfare, usually a parent, would act diligently and prudently to protect the minor's interests. * * *

The parties agree that if an action is brought by a next friend within the reduced tolling period of the medical malpractice statute of limitations for minors, the minor would have a right to a jury trial on disputed factual claims. Accordingly, the issue is simply one of the validity of the legislative time limitation on Willis's right of action. Such a limitation does not deny a fundamental constitutional right. See Hess v. Snyder Hunt Corp., 240 Va. 49, 53, 392 S.E.2d 817, 820 (1990) (imposition of statute of repose no denial of fundamental constitutional right).

Indeed, because a legislature may abolish "a cause of action, [it] may [also] extinguish a cause of action by the imposition of a statute of limitations" without affecting a fundamental constitutional right. Pulliam v. Coastal Emergency Servs., Inc., 257 Va. 1, 13, 509 S.E.2d 307, 314 (1999) (analogizing imposition of statute of limitations to validate statute imposing medical malpractice cap). Hence, we reject Willis' claim that the medical malpractice statute of limitations for minors effectively denies him the right of a jury trial.

V

Because we conclude that the enactment of the medical malpractice statute of limitations for minors does not involve the denial of Willis's asserted fundamental constitutional right to a jury trial, we apply the so-called "rational basis" test in reviewing its constitutionality under due process, equal protection, and special legislation provisions. Under that test, legislation passes constitutional muster under procedural due process requirements if it "guarantees a litigant the right to reasonable notice and a meaningful opportunity to be heard." [ ]. It also complies with substantive due process requirements "if [it] has a reasonable relation to a proper purpose and is not arbitrary or discriminatory." [ ]

Legislation meets equal protection requirements "if the legislature could reasonably have concluded that the challenged classification would promote a legitimate state purpose." [ ] Further, a statute does not transgress special legislation proscriptions if it bears "a reasonable and substantial relation to the object sought to be accomplished by the legislation." [ ]

In applying the rational basis test, we accord a presumption of constitutionality to the statute, "upholding statutory classifications if they bear some rational relationship to a legitimate legislative interest or purpose." [ ] Also, under this test, if any state of facts reasonably can be conceived that would sustain the necessity for the legislation and the reasonableness of its classifications, that state of facts at the time of the legislative enactment must be assumed. [ ].

VI

Willis's primary contentions are that the medical malpractice statute of limitations for minors violates one or more of the above constitutional provisions because it unreasonably, arbitrarily, and irrationally creates different tolling periods for two classes of infants, those with medical malpractice claims and those with other tort claims, without evidence to justify the distinction. In support, he cites: (1) the evidence presented to the legislative subcommittee of the limited number of claims made by such parties after they had reached their majority; (2) the lack of a study of the effect of a reduction of the tolling period for such claims on medical liability insurance premiums; and (3) the lack of evidence to support the legislature's assertion that medical malpractice claims are much more "complex" than other tort claims, thereby justifying a shortened tolling provision to prevent stale medical malpractice claims by infants.

In response, the defendants note the legislative subcommittee's statement of the background of this and other medical malpractice legislation "to alleviate the 'medical malpractice insurance crisis.' " [ ]

Additionally, they note the following parts of the subcommittee's findings and recommendations:

Insurers find it difficult to adequately assess the risk exposure of health care providers who treat minors because of the long tail on the claim. Under Virginia law, a minor has until his [eighteenth] birthday to file a claim. [ ] It is extremely difficult to document or prove or disprove events which occurred as long as twenty years ago for birth-related injuries. This problem is compounded by the inherent complexity of medical malpractice cases.

Recognizing (i) the particular and severe insurance availability problems facing physicians, (ii) the need of insurers for predictability of risk exposure and (iii) the effect of the provisions tolling the two-year statute of limitations during minority on the availability of insurers to adequately assess their risk of loss, the joint subcommittee recommends that the statute of limitations, as it applies to minors in medical malpractice actions, be modified.... The proposal is based on a similar provision in Indiana law and would require actions by minors who are injured by malpractice while under the age of six to commence the action before reaching age eight. A minor six years of age or older who is injured by medical malpractice would not have the benefit of any tolling provision. The joint subcommittee believes that this proposal will accomplish the goal of relieving the insurance availability crisis while affording reasonable protection to an injured minor.

In the two cases sustaining the constitutional validity of the medical malpractice cap imposed by Code § 8.01–581.15, we said that "the necessity for and the reasonableness of classification are primarily questions for the legislature. If any state of facts can be reasonably conceived ... that would sustain [the classification] that state of facts at the time the law was enacted must be assumed." [ ] Thus, this Court will not "second guess" the legislature's judgment and determine the necessity for and reasonableness of the classification. [ ] Moreover, "a classification will not be ruled unconstitutional merely because it causes some inequality or some discrimination." [ ]

Given these principles and the background of this legislation and applying the rational basis test, we hold that the legislature could reasonably provide different tolling periods and statutes of limitation without violating any of the constitutional provisions relied upon by Willis. Specifically, we cannot say from a due process standpoint that the challenged legislation: (1) does not give prospective litigants reasonable notice and an opportunity to be heard; (2) lacks a reasonable relation to the proper public purposes of "relieving the insurance availability crisis" and eliminating stale medical malpractice claims of infants; or (3) is arbitrary or discriminatory in differentiating between infants with medical malpractice claims and infants with other tort claims. Accordingly, we hold that the medical malpractice statute of limitations for minors does not violate the due process clauses of the United States Constitution or the Constitution of Virginia. [ ]

We also think that the legislature could have concluded that the challenged classification in the medical malpractice statute of limitations for minors would promote the legitimate state purposes of "relieving the insurance availability crisis" and eliminating stale medical malpractice claims of infants. For that reason, the statute passes muster under the Equal Protection Clause of the United States Constitution. [ ]

Finally, with the background of the two subcommittees' reports, we cannot say that the classification resulting from the medical malpractice statute of limitations for minors does not bear a reasonable and substantial relation to public welfare by "relieving the insurance availability crisis." We thus conclude that the statute is not special legislation in violation of Article IV, Section 14 of the Constitution of Virginia * * *.

Affirmed.

VELAZQUEZ v. JIMINEZ

Supreme Court of New Jersey, 2002.
172 N.J. 240, 798 A.2d 51.

LONG, J.

* * *

New Jersey's Good Samaritan Act, N.J.S.A. 2A:62A–1, provides:

Any individual, including a person licensed to practice any method of treatment of human ailments, disease, pain, injury, deformity, mental or physical condition, or licensed to render services ancillary thereto, or any person who is a volunteer member of a duly incorporated first aid and emergency or volunteer ambulance or rescue squad association, who in good faith renders emergency care at the scene of an accident or emergency to the victim or victims thereof, or while transporting the victim or victims thereof to a hospital or other facility where treatment or care is to be rendered, shall not be liable for any civil damages as a result of any acts or omissions by such person in rendering the emergency care.

The issue of first impression presented here is whether that statute can be invoked to immunize a hospital physician who assists a patient at the hospital during a medical emergency.

I

In July 1994, Charmaine and Jose Velazquez (collectively, plaintiffs), individually and as representatives of the estate of their deceased son, Conor, sued St. Peter's Medical Center (Medical Center) and its staff members * * * for damages resulting from their negligence during Conor's delivery.

Before trial, Dr. Jiminez, the Medical Center and the nurses settled with plaintiffs who, in turn, voluntarily dismissed the residents. Dr. Ranzini moved for summary judgment under the Good Samaritan Act [ ]. The trial court denied the motion as a matter of law, holding that the Act does not immunize physicians responding to emergencies within a hospital. Dr. Ranzini went to trial alone.

* * * Mrs. Velazquez was a patient at the Medical Center for the purpose of delivering a baby. Dr. Jiminez was her attending physician. Complications occurred during the delivery because Mrs. Velazquez's baby was suffering from bilateral shoulder dystocia (both of his shoulders were lodged against his mother's pubic bone). After delivering the baby's head, Dr. Jiminez was unable to deliver the rest of the baby's body. She rang for assistance and Dr. Ranzini responded.

Dr. Ranzini had no prior relationship with or connection to Mrs. Velazquez. Dr. Ranzini was an Assistant Professor of Clinical Obstetrics and Gynecology at the University of Medicine and Dentistry of New Jersey (UMDNJ), assigned to the Maternal Fetal Care Unit (MFCU) at the Medical Center. She specializes in maternal fetal medicine and was responsible both for attending to high-risk patients in the MFCU and for supervising resident physicians who cared for their own UMDNJ clinical patients at the Medical Center. Mrs. Velazquez was neither an MFCU nor a clinical patient. Rather, she was the patient of Dr. Jiminez, an attending physician with staff privileges at the Medical Center.

Dr. Ranzini first attempted to complete the delivery vaginally. When those efforts proved unsuccessful, Dr. Ranzini assisted in preparing Mrs. Velazquez and the baby—who was, by virtue of his position, at risk of suffering from hypoxia (a loss of oxygen)—for an emergency Caesarean section. The baby, Conor, ultimately was born severely brain damaged, spent his life in a dependent state and died of pneumonia before reaching his third birthday.

As might be expected in a medical malpractice case, the trial essentially was a battle of experts. Plaintiffs' experts testified that Dr. Ranzini deviated from the standard of care. Dr. Ranzini's experts testified, in essence, that her conduct conformed to all applicable medical standards and that Conor's condition resulted from the negligence of Dr. Jiminez * * *.

The jury returned a verdict in favor of plaintiffs and assigned three percent of the liability to Dr. Ranzini. * * *

* * *

We granted Dr. Ranzini's petition for certification regarding the applicability of the Good Samaritan Act to emergencies involving a patient occurring within a hospital.

II

Dr. Ranzini argues that the Appellate Division erred in concluding that the protections of the Good Samaritan statute stop at the door of the hospital. According to her, the location of an emergency is of no consequence; a physician is immunized so long as he or she acts in the absence of a prior duty to do so. She further contends that the weight of out-of-state authority supports her interpretation, which she claims will encourage physicians to assist in a hospital emergency. Finally, she argues that she had no prior duty to Mrs. Velazquez and thus was entitled to the shield of [the good Samaritan law] as a volunteer.

Plaintiffs counter that Dr. Ranzini's construction of the Act is inconsistent with its plain meaning and legislative purpose. They contend that it would be illogical for the Legislature to have intended the original "scene of an accident or emergency" language to include care rendered in a hospital if, in 1987, it conferred an additional grant of immunity to Good Samaritans while they transport victims from the scene to the hospital. Plaintiffs additionally dispute that most other jurisdictions have immunized physicians in hospitals. Finally, plaintiffs assert that Dr. Ranzini had a pre-existing duty to assist Mrs. Velazquez.

* * *

[The Good Samaritan] sections were directed towards physicians who, by chance and on an irregular basis, come upon or are called to render emergency medical care. Often, under these circumstances, the medical needs of the individual would not be matched by the expertise of the physician and facilities could be severely limited. * * * [ ]

Every scholar who has studied the subject agrees with that circumscribed description of the goals underlying Good Samaritan legislation. Reuter, supra, 20 J. Legal Med. at 189 (noting "the difficulty that confronts the physician who stops at the site of a roadside accident, who can provide little more than first-aid until the EMS team arrives") * * *.

* * *

In sum, Good Samaritan legislation has, at its core, the goal of encouraging the rendering of medical care to those who need it but otherwise might not receive it (ordinarily roadside accident victims), by persons who come upon such victims by chance, without the accoutrements provided in a medical facility, including expertise, assistance, sanitation or equipment.

IV

Currently, eleven jurisdictions unequivocally exclude from statutory immunity emergency care rendered to patients within a hospital or other health care facility * * *.

* * *

Conversely, Good Samaritan statutes in seven jurisdictions immunize emergency care provided in a hospital setting.

* * *

New Jersey is among twenty-nine states whose statutes fall within the third major category and contain general language that does not explicitly address whether in-hospital care can be shielded from liability under a Good Samaritan statute. * * * Pennsylvania's statute is more detailed and provides immunity to any physician or any other practitioner of the healing arts or any registered nurse, licensed by any state, who happens by chance upon the scene of an emergency or who arrives on the scene of an emergency by reason of serving on an emergency call panel or similar committee of a county medical society or who is called to the scene of an emergency by the police or other duly constituted officers of a government unit or who is present when an emergency occurs and who, in good faith, renders emergency care at the scene of the emergency * * * [ ].

To qualify for immunity under Pennsylvania's statute, the Good Samaritan must hold "a reasonable opinion that the immediacy of the situation is such that the rendering of care should not be postponed until the patient is hospitalized." [ ] One statute explicitly extends coverage to emergency care given "wherever required." Okla. Stat. Ann. tit. 76, § 5(a)(1) (West 2002). Others simply immunize "emergency medical or professional assistance to a person in need thereof," Conn. Gen. Stat. § 52–557b(a) (West Supp. 2002) * * *.

Of the twenty-nine states with general statutes like New Jersey's, five have enacted additional specific immunity provisions applicable to emergency obstetrical care. Those statutes include Ariz. Rev. Stat. Ann. § 32–1473 (West Supp. 2001) (applying enhanced "clear and convincing" burden of proof in malpractice actions against health care facility and physicians providing emergency treatment during labor and delivery who have not previously treated patient); Mont. Code Ann. § 27–1–734 (2001) (immunizing hospital, nurse or physician rendering "emergency obstetrical care" to "a patient of a direct-entry midwife in an emergency situation") * * *.

Finally, some general-language jurisdictions (including New Jersey) provide express immunity for medical care rendered while transporting an injured person from "the scene" to a hospital. * * *

* * * In any event, it would be fair to say that there is no universal interpretation of general statutory language among our sister jurisdictions, no roadmap to follow. Thus, to the extent that the parties in this case rely on the weight of out-of-state authority in support of their positions, they have vastly overstated the case.

V

* * *

[I]n enacting our Good Samaritan law, the Legislature was aware that a hospital patient is present in that venue for the very purpose of receiving medical care and is not a person who ordinarily would lack care in the absence of Good Samaritan immunity. Further, physicians in a hospital ordinarily do not come upon a hospital patient "by chance" as would be the case if an accident or emergency occurred on a roadway. Most importantly, our Legislature knew that the fundamental problem facing a Good Samaritan on the street (the ability to do little more than render first aid under less than optimal circumstances) is not present in a fully staffed and equipped facility like a hospital, whose very purpose is "to make available[ ] the human skill and physical material of medical science to the end that the patient's health be restored." Perlmutter v. Beth David Hospital, 308 N.Y. 100, 123 N.E.2d 792, 794 (N.Y. 1954). As Stewart R. Reuter has observed in "Physicians as Good Samaritans," 20 J. Legal Med. 157, 189 (1999):

Physicians who care for patients in hospitals are not volunteers in the sense of the person who by chance comes upon the scene of an accident. Moreover, physicians who provide emergency care in hospitals have at their disposal all the modern diagnostic and therapeutic equipment. Granted, they may not be familiar with the patient's medical history or disease and are at somewhat of a disadvantage when compared with the patient's personal physician. However, this disadvantage does not rise to the level of the difficulty that confronts the physician who stops at the site of a roadside accident, who can provide little more than first-aid until the EMS team arrives. In many cases, the physician or surgeon whose expertise is being requested in a hospital emergency will work with a physician or with hospital personnel who have excellent knowledge of the patient's condition and problems. Even if no other physician is already involved in the emergency, the duration of care provided generally is short—until the hospital's trained Code Blue team arrives.

* * *

Dr. Ranzini's suggestion that she qualifies as a Good Samaritan because she had no prior duty to Mrs. Velazquez misconceives the Good Samaritan Act entirely. Although the absence of a pre-existing duty is one element that volunteers must establish to qualify for Good Samaritan immunity [ ] standing alone it does not satisfy the statute. It is the reduced circumstances in which the volunteer finds himself or herself that the Legislature recognized, and it is the rendering of care in the face of those restrictions that it desired to immunize from suit. Had the Legislature intended to insulate anyone rendering emergency care under any circumstances where no pre-existing duty to render aid exists, it could have done so simply and directly * * *.

* * *

Dr. Ranzini's contention that by not extending Good Samaritan immunity to a hospital we will encourage physicians to simply stand by and allow patients to suffer or die is equally unpersuasive. First, we will not impute such conduct to the highly respected medical profession. Moreover, we note that scholars suggest that physicians' contracts, hospital protocols, ethical rules, regulatory standards and physicians' personal relationships operate to make that potential extremely unrealistic relative to a hospital patient. [ ]. To be sure, the Legislature is free to immunize all persons who render emergency medical treatment without a prior duty to do so, including those who volunteer to act within the walls of a hospital. We tilt neither against nor in favor of such an extension of immunity. We simply are persuaded that the choice is one for the Legislature, and we are unconvinced that the current statute reflects a legislative choice in favor of such immunity.

In sum, Good Samaritan immunity [ ] encompasses only those situations in which a physician (or other volunteer) comes, by chance, upon a victim who requires immediate emergency medical care, at a location compromised by lack of adequate facilities, equipment, expertise, sanitation and staff. A hospital or medical center does not qualify under the terms of the Good Samaritan Act in its present form.

* * *

The narrow holding here does not affect those common law principles that govern the conduct of professionals in a hospital setting. It merely carries out the Legislature's intention to carve out, from the ordinary rules of tort liability, a class of volunteers that ministers to victims suffering through the first critical moments after an unexpected event such as a roadside motor vehicle accident, a dwelling fire, a gas pump explosion, a heart attack, or premature labor in a location at which facilities, staff, equipment, sanitation or expertise are limited.

VII

Because Dr. Ranzini rendered aid to Mrs. Velazquez in a fully equipped and staffed hospital to which Mrs. Velasquez had been admitted for the purpose of receiving medical care, the Good Samaritan Act did not immunize her from suit. When she assisted in Mrs. Velazquez's delivery, our law imposed on her the obligation to do so in accordance with the applicable standard of care. A jury found her to be negligent to a minimal degree. The Appellate Division upheld that judgment and we see no warrant to interfere with it. Thus, we affirm.

Notes

1) Unlike immunities which, when absolute, can operate as a bar to bringing suit, affirmative defenses have to be plead and proved and may be waived if the defendant fails to do so. The statute of limitations is often considered a harsh and unforgiving defense: if plaintiff's lawyer suffers a heart attack on the way to the courthouse and thus does not file the matter on time, the limitations period lapses regardless of the validity of plaintiff's excuse.

2) Unlike matters that involve an "excuse," the discovery rule operates in those cases where the plaintiff, even when exercising due diligence, could not have discovered the cause or effects of plaintiff's tortious conduct. The usual case involves a medical event in which the plaintiff, exercising ordinary diligence, did not know—nor should he have known—of sufficient facts that would lead him to believe that he suffered an actionable injury. It may be that the effects of the medical mishap are latent (e.g. exposure to radiation or a toxic substance) or that the defendant, or his agent, lulled the plaintiff into believing that his symptoms were ordinary and not a consequence of another's fault. However, it is not enough to toll the statute of limitations that plaintiff had general knowledge of an actionable claim but not a specific basis for liability or the ability to prove his claim. It also is not sufficient to toll the limitations period that plaintiff knew he had a claim but could not locate the defendant.

3) Statutes of repose operate, in some respects, as compromise provisions between statutes of limitations (intended to bring closure and finality to stale cases) and the discovery rule (intended to hold open a matter where plaintiff reasonably could not discovered malpractice). They also affect children who, in the absence of statute, generally have until their 18th birthday to begin the running of the limitations period.

4) Whether or not treatment has been "continuous" for statute of limitations purposes has been frequently litigated. In *Sarjoo v. New York City Health and Hospitals Corp.*, 309 A.D.2d 34, 763 N.Y.S.2d 306 (App. Div. 2003) a New York appeals court held that the treatment following a birth injury was not "continuous" and thus did not toll the statute of limitations. There the plaintiff suffered fetal distress during his delivery and, after delivery, was referred for follow up care. Plaintiff's mother, a Guyana citizen, thereafter returned to Guyana. Letters were sent as reminders for follow up care. When plaintiff and his mother returned to the United States for follow up care, they went to another clinic before eventually returning to the defendant. The court held that there was a pattern of interrupted treatment without any clear indication on the part of plaintiff's mother to continue treatment with the defendant. Further, though there was a 10–year tolling provision in the statute of

limitations for infancy, it required leave to file a claim, which plaintiff's mother had not sought.

5) Good Samaritan provisions operate on the principle that a physician has no obligation to treat a patient in the absence of a physician-patient relationship, or some other voluntary or statutory obligation to do so. Nevertheless, to encourage physicians and others to come to the aid of patients outside of the professional setting, Good Samaritan Acts protect those who do so by providing immunity to lawsuits except in egregious situations.

There is inconsistency among jurisdictions as to whether Good Samaritan status applies to a physician in a healthcare setting who helps out under circumstances wherein he or she has no duty to do so. On the one hand, it is argued that extending immunity to the healthcare setting encourages physicians to assist with emergencies not involving their own patients. On the other hand, it is argued that extending the grant of immunity beyond the "scene of the accident" to the hospital and other healthcare facilities could result in healthcare professionals, in the course of their employment, attempting to abdicate their legal responsibility to patients by claiming that they had no duty to a specific patient. In the absurd, healthcare facilities could treat patients using their own staff, only to claim Good Samaritan status when one healthcare worker provides treatment to someone else's patient.

Valazquez highlights the competing policy considerations in those 29 states with Good Samaritan Acts that do not specifically address whether the in-hospital care is intended to be covered under the Act.

SECTION C. COUNTERSUITS

MILLER v. ROSENBERG

Supreme Court of Illinois, 2001.
196 Ill.2d 50, 255 Ill.Dec. 464, 749 N.E.2d 946.

JUSTICE McMORROW delivered the opinion of the court:

BACKGROUND

In November 1988, Elaine Rosenberg filed a medical malpractice lawsuit against Dr. Jerald Miller, a periodontist. Rosenberg, who had been a patient of Dr. Miller between March 1982 and February 1987, claimed in her complaint that, during this time period, Miller negligently failed to detect, diagnose and treat an impacted wisdom tooth in Rosenberg's lower right jaw. According to Rosenberg's complaint, she underwent surgery to extract this tooth in March 1987. Rosenberg alleged that as a direct and proximate cause of Miller's negligence in failing to timely diagnose and treat her lower right wisdom tooth, the tooth became embedded in her jawbone, causing parathesia, or numbness, in her jaw and face. In his answer to Rosenberg's complaint, Miller stated that while Rosenberg was under his care, he referred her to an oral surgeon. Rosenberg, however, failed to follow up on this referral. Miller further alleged that two of Rosenberg's prior treaters had also advised her to undergo an examination by an oral surgeon for the possible extraction of the wisdom tooth.

After the completion of discovery, the circuit court granted summary judgment in favor of Miller. On appeal, the appellate court reversed the grant of summary judgment, and remanded the cause to the circuit court. [ ]. The matter thereafter proceeded to trial. The jury found Miller not liable, and [ ] judgment for Miller was entered on the jury's verdict.

On November 8, 1995, Miller filed a three-count malicious prosecution action against Rosenberg and her attorneys. Only count I of Miller's complaint is at issue in this appeal. Miller alleged that, in commencing and continuing to pursue her medical malpractice lawsuit, Rosenberg acted without probable cause and with malice in several respects. According to Miller, Rosenberg "alleged a lack of knowledge of the presence of an impacted lower right wisdom tooth" while she was his patient, "despite previously being advised of this condition." Further, Miller stated that Rosenberg "failed to properly investigate" both "the facts surrounding her claims of negligence" and "whether the alleged negligence of [Miller] was a cause of her claimed injury." Miller also alleged that Rosenberg had filed and continued to prosecute the medical malpractice lawsuit against him "without probable cause in retribution for perceived incourtesies by [Miller toward Rosenberg]," and that Rosenberg's objective was to "obtain money despite the fact that she knew or should have known that any alleged negligence was not a cause of any alleged injuries." Miller further claimed that, as a direct and proximate result of Rosenberg's lawsuit, he "suffered personal and pecuniary injuries, including but not limited to, mental anguish," experienced "increased anxiety," was forced to incur attorney fees and "expend considerable time and energy in the defense of the underlying action," and was "required to defend his professional reputation and will be required to pay increased premiums for professional liability insurance."

In October 1996, Rosenberg filed a motion to dismiss Miller's malicious prosecution action * * *. Rosenberg alleged that, under Illinois law, in order to validly plead a common law cause of action for malicious prosecution, a plaintiff must claim that he suffered injury or damages over and above the ordinary expense and trouble attendant in defending any civil action. Because Miller had not alleged that he suffered a "special injury" as a result of Rosenberg's lawsuit, Rosenberg argued that Miller had not pled a valid malicious prosecution claim.

In addition, Rosenberg maintained in her motion to dismiss that Miller's complaint could not be saved by section 2–109 of the Code of Civil Procedure * * *:

"In all cases alleging malicious prosecution arising out of proceedings which sought damages for injuries or death by reason of medical[,] hospital[,] or other healing art malpractice, the plaintiff need not plead or prove special injury to sustain his or her cause of action. In all such cases alleging malicious prosecution, no exemplary or punitive damages shall be allowed." [ ]

Rosenberg asserted that the special benefit afforded by section 2–109 to malicious prosecution plaintiffs who also happen to be health care providers violates not only the proscription against special legislation found in article IV, section 13, of the Illinois Constitution of 1970 [ ] but also the guarantee of due process and equal protection contained in article I, section 2 [ ]. Specifically, Rosenberg contended that section 2–109 is unconstitutional because it arbitrarily and irrationally eliminates the common law special injury requirement for this select group of plaintiffs, thereby making it far easier for these plaintiffs to file and proceed with a malicious prosecution claim than it is for other malicious prosecution plaintiffs who must still establish a special injury.

The circuit court denied Rosenberg's motion to dismiss on January 10, 1997. The court found that although section 2–109 confers special privileges upon health care providers who file malicious prosecution actions which arise out of underlying medical malpractice litigation, this special treatment does not violate the Illinois Constitution. The court reasoned that this classification is warranted by the Illinois General Assembly's determination that there existed a medical malpractice crisis at the time section 2–109 was enacted.

On December 9, 1999, the circuit court held a hearing on a motion *in limine* filed by Rosenberg which requested that the court bar Miller in his malicious prosecution action from the recovery of attorney fees he incurred in defending against the underlying malpractice lawsuit. The circuit court agreed with Rosenberg that, pursuant to section 2–622(e) of the Code of Civil Procedure [ ], any claim by Miller to recover attorney fees in connection with the underlying medical malpractice litigation was untimely.

During the hearing on the attorney fee matter, the circuit court judge noted that his previous ruling with respect to the constitutionality of section 2–109 was rendered prior to this court's 1997 decision in *Best v. Taylor Machine Works*, 179 Ill.2d 367, 228 Ill.Dec. 636, 689 N.E.2d 1057 (1997). Because the circuit court judge had "never considered this case in light of the *Best* case," he invited the parties to again submit briefs "to revisit the question of whether or not [section 2–109] is or is not special legislation."

On January 20, 2000, the circuit court declared that section 2–109 violates the Illinois Constitution, specifically, the prohibition against special legislation [ ] and the guarantee of equal protection [ ]. In the course of his ruling, the circuit judge stated:

"In my view, [health care providers] have been singled out without there being a rational basis for singling them out and excluding all of the other individuals who might properly bring a malicious prosecution action. * * * If there was a medical malpractice crisis, that does not permit in my view the adoption of an arbitrary or unrelated means of addressing the problem, and that is what I think has been done in this case, where the health care providers have been allowed to have special advantages in a malicious prosecution [action] that no one else in the state shares. That, in my view, is an arbitrary and unrelated means of addressing the problem of a medical malpractice crisis if one exists. * * * There is nothing inherent in being a health care provider that should give them special rights that nobody in the State of Illinois has."

Miller appealed the circuit court's ruling directly to this court. [ ]

ANALYSIS

* * *

In the matter at bar, Rosenberg urges us to affirm the judgment of the circuit court that the special treatment afforded by section 2–109 to a select group of plaintiffs is unconstitutional. Specifically, section 2–109 relieves health care professionals from the requirement of pleading and proving special injury when those professionals file malicious prosecution suits against unsuccessful medical malpractice plaintiffs. A malicious prosecution action is brought to recover damages suffered by one against whom a suit has been filed maliciously and without probable cause. [ ] Generally, in a complaint for malicious prosecution based upon a prior civil proceeding, the plaintiff must allege that the defendant instituted the underlying suit without probable cause and with malice, that the former action was terminated in the plaintiff's favor, and that as a result of the underlying action the plaintiff suffered a special injury beyond the usual expense, time or annoyance in defending a lawsuit. [ ]. Rosenberg contends that the circuit court correctly ruled that the elimination of special injury as an element of malicious prosecution claims brought by health care professionals arising out of underlying medical malpractice proceedings renders section 2–109 impermissible special legislation and violates the guarantee of equal protection.

Although the prohibition against special legislation and the guarantee of equal protection are not identical, constitutional challenges premised on these provisions are generally judged under the same standards. [Citations omitted]. The parties do not dispute that section 2–109 neither affects a fundamental right nor involves a suspect or quasi-suspect classification. [ ]. Therefore, the appropriate standard for our review of the instant constitutional challenge is the rational basis test. [ ]. Under the rational basis standard, judicial review of a legislative classification is limited and generally deferential. [ ] " 'Under this standard, a court must determine whether the statutory classification is rationally related to a legitimate State interest.' " [ ]. A legislative classification must be upheld if any set of facts can reasonably be conceived which justify distinguishing the class to which the statute applies from the class to which the law is inapplicable. [ ]

Before this court, Rosenberg's constitutional challenge to section 2–109 rests primarily upon her contention that this provision violates our constitution's prohibition against special legislation. [ ]. Indeed, the circuit court's ruling in the instant cause was almost exclusively premised on its finding that section 2–109 constitutes special legislation. We therefore begin our analysis by addressing this claim.

The special legislation clause of the Illinois Constitution provides:

"The General Assembly shall pass no special or local law when a general law is or can be made applicable. Whether a general law is or can be made applicable shall be a matter for judicial determination." [ ]

The special legislation clause "expressly prohibits the General Assembly from conferring a special benefit or exclusive privilege on a person or a group of persons to the exclusion of others similarly situated." [ ]. The purpose of the prohibition against special legislation is to "prevent arbitrary legislative classifications that discriminate in favor of a select group without a sound, reasonable basis." [ ] In determining whether section 2–109 constitutes impermissible special legislation, we must ascertain whether the classification created by that provision is "based upon reasonable differences in kind or situation, and whether the basis for the classifications is sufficiently related to the evil to be obviated by the statute." [ ]

Section 2–109 is one of a number of provisions added to the Code of Civil Procedure in 1985 * * *. By enacting this package of medical malpractice reform legislation, the General Assembly intended to "comprehensively * * * regulate medical malpractice litigation, with a view to reducing the number of such suits and the size of the awards which are given in those in which the plaintiff successfully establishes his claim." [ ]

Shortly after the passage of Public Act 84–7, five provisions of that Act were challenged as unconstitutional in *Bernier v. Burris*, 113 Ill.2d 219, 100 Ill.Dec. 585, 497 N.E.2d 763 (1986). In *Bernier*, this court determined that the establishment of review panels in medical malpractice cases violated provisions in the Illinois Constitution with respect to the source of judicial power and the jurisdiction of the circuit courts [ ]. However, we also held that the remaining four provisions of Public Act 84–7 challenged in *Bernier* were not constitutionally infirm. This court concluded that the periodic payment of certain damages, the modification of the collateral source rule in medical malpractice actions, the elimination of punitive damages in actions for medical malpractice, and a sliding scale of the allowable fees an attorney may charge in representing a medical malpractice plaintiff were all rationally related to the legitimate government interest of "reducing the burdens existing in the health professions as a result of the perceived medical malpractice crisis." [ ]

In his brief to this court, Miller contends that, although section 2–109 was not among the statutory provisions at issue in *Bernier*, the legitimate governmental interests identified in that decision with respect to Public Act 84–7 apply with equal force to section 2–109. Miller asserts that our analysis in *Bernier* therefore leads to the conclusion that the classification in section 2–109 is rationally related to the legitimate legislative goal of remedying the perceived medical malpractice crisis, specifically, that it reduces the burdens against health care professionals and creates a disincentive for the filing of meritless medical malpractice lawsuits.

Rosenberg, echoing the reasoning employed by the circuit court in its ruling, responds that section 2–109 constitutes impermissible special legislation because there is no rational relation between a legitimate state interest and the grant of a special benefit to health care providers who file malicious prosecution actions against unsuccessful medical malpractice litigants. Rosenberg labels as "fallacious" the argument advanced by Miller that section 2–109 bears a rational relation to the perceived medical malpractice crisis. Specifically, Rosenberg contends that in contrast to the statutory provisions of Public Act 84–7 which were upheld in *Bernier* and "were all directly related to the conduct of the medical malpractice litigation itself," section 2–109 "does not apply to medical malpractice litigation in any way during its pendency * * * [and] no rational argument can be made that health care providers deserve greater post-litigation rights when they have allegedly been sued with malice and without probable cause than any other similarly situated civil defendant." Rosenberg therefore concludes that section 2–109 arbitrarily and irrationally eliminates the common law special injury requirement for this select group of malicious prosecution plaintiffs. We reject Rosenberg's arguments.

As stated, it is the burden of the party challenging the validity of a statute to rebut the presumption of constitutionality. [ ]. We hold that Rosenberg has failed to clearly establish that the provisions of section 2–109 violate the proscription against special legislation. Contrary to Rosenberg's assertions that the classification in section 2–109 is irrational and arbitrary, we find that there are discernable, rational reasons why the General Assembly distinguished between health care professionals who file malicious prosecution suits against unsuccessful medical malpractice plaintiffs and all other individuals who may bring a malicious prosecution action. The classification is based upon "a rational difference of situation or condition" between those persons included in the classification and excluded from it [ ], and the classification bears a reasonable relationship to the purposes of the statute.

* * *

This understanding of the purpose of section 2–109 refutes Rosenberg's argument that there is no rational relationship between this statutory provision and the perceived medical malpractice crisis. In enacting section 2–109, the legislature eased the burden of bringing a malicious prosecution action for health care professionals with the specific intent of not only "discouraging" the filing of frivolous medical malpractice lawsuits, but also as a way of "punishing" those plaintiffs who bring baseless medical malpractice claims. The legislature could have reasonably believed that liberalizing the availability of a malicious prosecution action for health care providers is an effective means of curtailing meritless medical malpractice litigation. The possibility of being a defendant in a subsequent malicious prosecution suit where the element of special injury is not required to be pled or established would likely provide a strong incentive to a potential medical malpractice plaintiff to thoroughly investigate the basis of the claim before filing suit. Those potential plaintiffs who conclude that there is probable cause to file a medical malpractice action would have no reason to be discouraged from bringing suit, while those whose claims lack probable cause would be deterred from filing an action.

* * *

As previously discussed, we find that the classification in section 2–109 is reasonably related to a legitimate governmental purpose. It has been amply demonstrated that, in enacting the provisions contained within Public Act 84–7, the legislature intended to remedy what it perceived to be a crisis in medical malpractice litigation. The provisions of section 2–109 are reasonably related to this legitimate public interest by serving as a deterrent against, and punishment for, the filing of frivolous medical malpractice claims. Section 2–109, therefore, is clearly distinguishable from section 2–1117, which appeared to be "designed primarily to confer a benefit on a particular private group without a reasonable basis, rather than to promote the general welfare." [ ]

Circuit court judgment reversed.

MOROWITZ v. MARVEL

District of Columbia Court of Appeals, 1980.
423 A.2d 196.

PRYOR, ASSOCIATE JUDGE.

* * * On or about May 18, 1976, appellants, who are practicing physicians, brought a small claims suit against a patient for monies owing for medical services rendered. On June 23, 1976, counsel retained by the patient asserted a counterclaim alleging medical malpractice and professional negligence in the rendition of the services for which the doctors sought payment. The counterclaim demanded a jury trial and prayed for $30,000 in damages.

A default judgment was entered against the patient in the small claims action. The counterclaim was certified to the Civil Division of the Superior Court and thereafter was withdrawn. This action followed.[1]

It is axiomatic that the American system of jurisprudence favors free access to the courts as a medium of dispute settlement. It is the announced policy of this jurisdiction to allow unfettered access to our courts. In an effort to avoid infringing upon the right of the public to utilize our courts, we are cautious not to adopt rules which will have a

---

1. Editors' Note: The action was brought against the patient's lawyer alone. Hereinafter "appellants" will be replaced by "the doctors," and "appellee" will be replaced by "the lawyer."

chilling and inhibitory effect on would-be litigants of justiciable issues. We are likewise cognizant of our obligations to protect the innocent against frivolous litigation, and to make victims of groundless lawsuits whole where they suffer special injury as the result of the suit. Predictably, our decisions have evolved in response to these competing interests.

In Ammerman v. Newman, 384 A.2d 637 (D.C.1978), this court reviewed the law of this jurisdiction with respect to proceedings asserting malicious prosecution and, aware that the majority of the states have now rejected a special injury requirement, nonetheless opted to affirm our requirement of the same, in the belief that it best promotes this jurisdiction's policy of encouraging free access to the courts.

Thus, we reiterated that to prevail in a claim of malicious prosecution, plaintiff must plead and prove four things: (1) the underlying suit terminated in plaintiff's favor; (2) malice on the part of defendant; (3) lack of probable cause for the underlying suit; and (4) special injury occasioned by plaintiff as the result of the original action.

In the case at bar, the doctors do not allege special injury. The injuries the doctors complain of are those which "might normally be incident to the service of process on anyone involved in a legal suit." Nolan v. Allstate Home Equip. Co., 149 A.2d 426, 430 (D.C.1959). The complaint indicates that the injuries occasioned, if any, are costs incident to any litigation and "professional defamatory-type" damages. Such injury is not actionable in a malicious prosecution claim. See Martin v. Trevino, 578 S.W.2d 763 (Tex.Civ.App.1978), where on similar facts the Texas court found that the injury alleged did not constitute special injury.

We conclude that with respect to the count alleging malicious prosecution, the court did not err in finding that the doctors failed to state a claim upon which relief could be granted.

* * *

The critical concern in abuse of process cases is whether process was used to accomplish an end unintended by law, and whether the suit was instituted to achieve a result not regularly or legally obtainable. "The mere issuance of the process is not actionable, no matter what ulterior motive may have prompted it; the gist of the action lies in the improper use after issuance." Hall v. Hollywood Credit Clothing Co., 147 A.2d 866, 868 (D.C.1959).[2] Thus, in addition to ulterior motive, one must allege and prove that there has been a perversion of the judicial process and achievement of some end not contemplated in the regular prosecution of the charge. Id. * * *

In the instant case, the lawyer merely filed a counterclaim and subsequently withdrew it. Without more, the doctors' proffer, that the

---

2. We are mindful, however, that Super.Ct.Civ.R. 11 mandates that:

The signature of an attorney [on a pleading] constitutes a certificate by him that

he has read the pleading; that to the best of his knowledge, information, and belief there is a good ground to support it; and that it is not interposed for delay.

lawyer filed the counterclaim with the ulterior motive of coercing settlement, is deficient. There is no showing that the process was, in fact, used to accomplish an end not regularly or legally obtainable. * * * Under these circumstances, we cannot find that the trial court erred in dismissing this count of the doctors' amended complaint.

As an alternative ground of recovery, the doctors urge that they have a cause of action against the lawyer for professional negligence. This court has not squarely addressed this issue before, but we are satisfied from a review of the cases in other jurisdictions that such an action cannot lie. Each jurisdiction which has concluded as we do, that a negligence action will not lie by a former defendant against adverse counsel, has done so primarily for the reason that there is an absence of privity of contract between counsel and an opposing party, and for public policy reasons.

Historically, there has been a strict application of the privity of contract rule. Thus, in a landmark case, National Savings Bank v. Ward, 100 U.S. 195, 25 L.Ed. 621 (1879), the Supreme Court held that the doctrine of privity of contract barred suit by a bank against adverse counsel who were professionally negligent in conducting title examinations, despite the fact that the attorneys' neglect clearly occasioned the bank's loss.

Exception was first made to this stringent requirement of privity in cases involving fraud or collusion. Later, courts began relaxing the requirement of privity in cases involving the drafting of wills and the examination of titles.[3] In these instances, the courts relaxed the requirement on the basis that the plaintiffs were direct and intended beneficiaries of the attorney's services. The mere fact that the third party was a foreseeable plaintiff was not, however, sufficient to give rise to a legal duty to the third parties.

In recent years courts which have considered whether a negligence action should lie on facts similar to those before us have overwhelmingly resolved this question in the negative. Decisions in California, Illinois, and New York are illustrative of this view. Unanimously, they have not permitted an adverse party to recover from an opposing counsel on a negligence theory.

California has declined to allow third parties to bring negligence actions against adverse counsel for at least three reasons: (1) an absence of privity of contract; (2) an adverse party is not an intended beneficiary of adverse counsel's services; and (3) policy reasons. Goodman v. Kennedy, 18 Cal.3d 335, 134 Cal.Rptr. 375, 556 P.2d 737 (1976) * * *.

Illinois rejected the notion of a negligence action by third parties against adverse counsel on the grounds that (1) it would be contrary to public policy to impose upon an attorney a duty to an intended defen-

3. Birnbaum, Physicians Counter Attack: Liability of Lawyers for Instituting Unjustified Medical Malpractice Actions, 45 Fordham L.Rev. 1003, 1071–72 (1977). Edi-

tors' Note: See also Annot., Medical Malpractice Countersuits, 84 A.L.R.3d 555 (1978).

dant not to file seemingly frivolous lawsuits; (2) to allow the same would create an "insurmountable conflict of interest between the attorney and client," Berlin v. Nathan, 64 Ill.App.3d 940, 381 N.E.2d 1367, 1376 (1978); and (3) establishment of such a negligence cause of action would inhibit free access to the courts. Pantone v. Demos, 59 Ill.App.3d 328, 375 N.E.2d 480, 485 (1978) * * *.

New York has held fast to the traditional view that since an attorney has no privity of contract with adverse parties in a litigation, absent fraud or collusion, no negligence action will lie. * * * Further, it has declined to permit third parties to bring negligence actions against adverse counsel because it found that "to hold an attorney personally responsible for instituting a frivolous action on behalf of a client would operate to discourage free resort to the courts for the resolution of controversies, contrary to public policy." Drago v. Buonagurio, 89 Misc.2d 171, 391 N.Y.S.2d 61, 63 (Sup.Ct.1977) * * *.

For the reasons enumerated, we are satisfied that an action for professional negligence cannot lie under these circumstances.

Finding no error, we affirm.[4]

Notes

1) Countersuits (also referred to as suits for malicious prosecution or abuse of process) are a powerful, but difficult to sustain, cause of action. A countersuit for malicious prosecution is not an affirmative defense; it presumes that the underlying action is brought to a conclusion. The premise of the countersuit is that defendant not only is free of blame, but the very bringing of the claim is malicious and without foundation. F. R. Civ. P. 11, and its state counterparts, are an alternative to the countersuit. An application under Rule 11 puts plaintiff on notice that defendant intends to allege that the plaintiff's claim is frivolous. If allowed, the court can award costs in a matter that it deems to be frivolous.

2) Even if a defendant physician is able to establish a claim for malicious prosecution, courts require the physician to show "special damages"—harms that go beyond the indignity, loss of time and even increased malpractice insurance premiums caused by being a defendant. The *Miller* court addressed plaintiff's constitutional claims that the "special damages" requirement is an unconstitutional violation of equal protection of the laws as well as due process. Do you find plaintiff's arguments persuasive? Is the legislative purpose sufficient to overcome the constitutional objections?

3) Virtually all states have in a place a mechanism for screening out frivolous medical malpractice actions. See Chapter 10(A), infra. Malprac-

---

4. There are other avenues of redress available to physicians who are the victims of seemingly frivolous medical malpractice actions. If used properly, an administrative proceeding brought by the local bar disci- plinary counsel, based on a violation of professional standards of conduct, can be an effective deterrent to instituting frivolous medical malpractice claims.

tice tribunals and Certificates or Merit are examples. A claim that is brought in bad faith, or might become the subject of a countersuit, is likely to be screened out. Even claims that are screened out, however, might still find their way into the courtroom if, for example, the plaintiff agrees to post bond to cover the court costs of the litigation. Such a case might become the basis for a countersuit.

4) In spite of the interest shown by medical societies in countersuits, cases won on appeal are still very rare. See Bull v. McCuskey, 96 Nev. 706, 615 P.2d 957 (1980). For a good discussion of countersuits and other means of discouraging unfounded medical liability actions, see Blanton v. Morgan, 681 S.W.2d 876 (Tex. App. 1984). Note that a physician's malpractice insurance does not cover the costs of "clearing the physician's good name" by bringing a countersuit.

5) Suppose that a patient is dissatisfied with a physician's treatment and refuses to pay the fee, but declines to bring a malpractice action. What would happen if the physician waited for the limitations period to lapse, and thereafter brought suit against the patient for nonpayment of the fee (under a longer contract statute of limitations)? Though the authors know of no case on point, the alleged medical malpractice might be used as a defense or partial defense to the collection matter (inadequate or badly-performed services.) Might an alternative be that the court that the physician's bringing of the contract action waives his affirmative defense (statute of limitations) to the malpractice action? In the former case, the malpractice is used only as an off-set to the collection action; in the latter the physician might actually open himself up to the malpractice action that he specifically avoided by waiting out the limitations period.

Chapter 7

TREATMENT CONSENT, INFORMATION AND REFUSAL

INTRODUCTORY NOTE

The sections of this chapter all relate to the right of individuals to regulate the medical treatment they receive: whether, how much, from whom, and for what purposes. Patients want to be treated as subjects, not as objects, and the law supports their wishes. A failure to preserve a patient's rights may be regarded legally as negligence or as some other theory of claim.

The technological imperative, that which can be done should be done, has animated great progress in medical science, but treatment that is good for medicine is not necessarily in the best interests of the individual. The concept of individual rights, expressed in various rules of private law considered in this chapter, tries to convert the imperative into the permissive: the physician has the duty to secure the patient's consent to treatment; the patient has the power to refuse treatment, even against medical advice; the patient has the right to be informed of fairly unusual but undesirable outcomes and side-effects of medical and surgical treatment; the patient's consent must be obtained before the patient is enrolled as a subject in biomedical research.

Civil actions for damages are a clumsy and socially expensive way of adjusting the balance between providers and consumers of health care services, but they do get the providers' attention. Litigants and courts have caused hospitals to use consent forms, producing widespread compliance through what lawyers call "general deterrence" and insurance people call "risk-avoidance." Even where legislatures have acted to strengthen patients' powers, the levers of public law have to be applied to individuals through regulatory or adjudicative processes.

Persons of good will in the United States have many legal mechanisms to call upon in reducing confrontations between patients' self-determination and the logic of treatment plans. This is fortunate, because as the means are invented to cope with one problem, another problem arises. For example, the United States has come to require institutional review boards so as to standardize the ways in which people give consent in human experimentation. Yet, states are still experimenting with mechanisms to accommodate the power of families to refuse consent to treatment on behalf of persons in a persistent vegetative state. Even as abortion becomes safer than pregnancy, the political process challenges the access of individuals to abortion as medical treatment. People in the United States expect "the law" to provide access to procedures for deciding individual cases, where no monopoly on rationality is held by political beliefs, individual rights, or scientific capabilities.

One way to challenge the health care provider is through the civil action for the tort of battery. The claim is so easy to plead (an unconsented-to touching), so difficult to defend (justification), and carries such a long train of causation that, as the courts are aware, it is a real menace in the medical context. Consequently, whether by interpretation or statute, the action for failing to obtain informed consent to medical treatment now tends to be treated as a form of negligence; and as close as the concepts of promise and consent may be, the action (and the damages) now lie in tort. Even so, consent is not unlimited, and doctors can be liable for exceeding consent with respect to who treats or what is done.

The states still have not achieved a solid majority position on the place of the patient's testimony: "If only I had known, I would never have consented." The "lay standard" virtually forces the patient to testify (and perhaps lie), and it seems to reward good actors. The "medical standard" seems to place the patient's legal fate in the hands of the doctors, a fundamental contradiction of the principle of individual rights. This is particularly difficult in the context of experimental procedures performed in the name of medical research, where federal law requiring institutional review boards has not preempted civil actions for damages under state law.

Last is the problem of deliberately refused treatment. The medical duty of doctors is to fight morbidity and mortality, but individuals have the right to accept or refuse treatment on the ground that there are living fates worse than death. The legal duty of doctors may be to maximize individual freedom, pressing treatment information upon patients while recognizing their right to reject it, but the doctor's duty to pay money damages for breaching that legal duty is something of a medical paradox.

SECTION A.   TREATMENT WITHOUT CONSENT

MOHR v. WILLIAMS

Supreme Court of Minnesota, 1905.
95 Minn. 261, 104 N.W. 12.

BROWN, J.

Defendant is a physician and surgeon of standing and character, making disorders of the ear a specialty, and having an extensive practice in the city of St. Paul. He was consulted by plaintiff, who complained to him of trouble with her right ear, and, at her request, made an examination of that organ for the purpose of ascertaining its condition. He also at the same time examined her left ear, but, owing to foreign substances therein, was unable to make a full and complete diagnosis at that time. * * * [The plaintiff submitted to general anesthesia on the understanding that the defendant would operate on the diseased right ear. After examining both ears under anesthesia, the defendant decided that the left ear was in worse condition than the right, and so he carefully operated on the left ear only.]

It is claimed by plaintiff that the operation greatly impaired her hearing, seriously injured her person, and, not having been consented to by her, was wrongful and unlawful, constituting an assault and battery; and she brought this action to recover damages therefor.

The trial in the court below resulted in a verdict for plaintiff for $14,322.50. * * * [The trial judge decided that this amount was excessive and ordered a new trial, but he denied the doctor's motion for judgment notwithstanding the verdict. Both parties appealed. The supreme court affirmed the new trial order.]

* * * It cannot be doubted that ordinarily the patient must be consulted, and his consent given, before a physician may operate upon him. * * *

If the physician advises his patient to submit to a particular operation, and the patient weighs the dangers and risks incident to its performance, and finally consents, he thereby, in effect, enters into a contract authorizing his physician to operate to the extent of the consent given, but no further.

It is not, however, contended by defendant that under ordinary circumstances consent is unnecessary, but that, under the particular circumstances of this case, consent was implied; that it was an emergency case, such as to authorize the operation without express consent or permission. * * * But such is not the case at bar. The diseased condition of plaintiff's left ear was not discovered in the course of an operation on the right, which was authorized, but upon an independent examination of that organ, made after the authorized operation was found unnecessary. Nor is the evidence such as to justify the court in holding, as a matter of law, that it was such an affliction as would result immediately in the serious injury of plaintiff, or such an emergency as to justify proceeding without her consent. She had experienced no particular difficulty with that ear, and the questions as to when its diseased condition would become alarming or fatal, and whether there was an immediate necessity for an operation, were, under the evidence, questions of fact for the jury.

* * *

The last contention of defendant is that the act complained of did not amount to an assault and battery. This is based upon the theory that, as plaintiff's left ear was in fact diseased, in a condition dangerous and threatening to her health, the operation was necessary, and, having been skillfully performed at a time when plaintiff had requested a like operation on the other ear, the charge of assault and battery cannot be sustained; that, in view of these conditions, and the claim that there was no negligence on the part of defendant, and an entire absence of any evidence tending to show an evil intent, the court should say, as a matter of law, that no assault and battery was committed, even though she did not consent to the operation. * * * We are unable to reach that conclusion, though the contention is not without merit.

[T]he act of defendant amounted at least to a technical assault and battery. If the operation was performed without plaintiff's consent, and the circumstances were not such as to justify its performance without, it was wrongful; and, if it was wrongful, it was unlawful. [E]very person has a right to complete immunity of his person from physical interference of others, except in so far as contact may be necessary under the general doctrine of privilege; and any unlawful or unauthorized touching of the person of another, except it be in the spirit of pleasantry, constitutes an assault and battery.

In the case at bar, as we have already seen, the question whether defendant's act in performing the operation upon plaintiff was authorized was a question for the jury to determine. If it was unauthorized, then it was, within what we have said, unlawful. It was a violent assault, not a mere pleasantry; and, even though no negligence is shown, it was wrongful and unlawful. The case is unlike a criminal prosecution for assault and battery, for there an unlawful intent must be shown. But that rule does not apply to a civil action, to maintain which it is sufficient to show that the assault complained of was wrongful and unlawful or the result of negligence. * * *

[The supreme court affirmed denial of the doctor's motion for judgment notwithstanding the verdict.]

WALLS v. SHRECK
Supreme Court of Nebraska, 2003.
265 Neb. 683, 658 N.W.2d 686.

Wright, J.

FACTS

As a child, Walls had a condition that caused his left eye to be out of alignment with his right eye. He had surgery on his left eye to correct the condition, but it reoccurred several years later. In March 1999, Walls sought medical treatment from Shreck in North Platte. Shreck is a physician and surgeon licensed under the laws of the State of Nebraska and is a health care provider under the Nebraska Hospital–Medical Liability Act.

Walls met with Shreck and discussed the possibility of strabismus surgery on his left eye to correct the condition. This surgery involves a procedure on the affected eye or on the opposite eye, and the object of the surgery is to bring both eyes into alignment. Walls and Shreck agreed that the best approach to treating Walls was to attempt surgery on the left eye. Shreck testified he told Walls that although the goal was to operate on the left eye, he might have to operate on the right eye instead. Walls testified that he specifically informed Shreck that he did not want surgery performed on his right eye. Shreck admitted that he did not discuss operating on both eyes at the same time.

Prior to surgery, Walls signed an authorization and consent form that included the following language:

a. I hereby authorize Dr. Shreck * * * to perform the following procedure and/or alternative procedure necessary to treat my condition: * * *. Recesion [sic] and Resection of the Left Eye[.]

b. I understand the reason for the procedure is: to straigghten [sic] my left eye to keep it from going to the left[.]

* * *

d. It has been explained to me that conditions may arise during this procedure whereby a different procedure or an additional procedure may need to be performed and I authorize my physician and his assistants to do what they feel is needed and necessary.

During surgery on April 13, 1999, Shreck encountered excessive scar tissue on the muscles of Walls' left eye and elected to adjust the muscles of the right eye instead.

When Walls awoke from the anesthesia, he expressed surprise and anger at the fact that both of his eyes were bandaged. The next day, Walls went to Shreck's office for a followup visit and adjustment of his sutures. Walls questioned Shreck as to the reason he operated on Walls' right eye, and Shreck responded that he had reserved the right to change his mind during surgery.

Walls testified that he would never have entered the hospital if he had known there was a possibility of surgery on his right eye, because he had so many problems with his left eye after the childhood surgery. He said that prior to surgery, he had no problems with his right eye. He also testified that following the April 1999 surgery, he has had daily problems with his right eye.

At trial, Dr. Thomas Roussel provided expert medical testimony on behalf of Walls. Roussel was the only expert witness to testify regarding the standard of care for obtaining informed consent prior to strabismus surgery.

After Walls presented his evidence and rested his case, Shreck moved for a directed verdict and a dismissal. He alleged that Walls had failed to prove a prima facie case. Shreck claimed that there had been no expert testimony that he had failed to obtain Walls' informed consent for the procedure. The trial court concluded that Walls had failed to establish the standard of care required in this situation or that Shreck had violated the standard of care. It sustained Shreck's motion for directed verdict and dismissed the action. Walls timely appealed.

* * *

* * *

A physician's duty to obtain informed consent is measured by the standard of a reasonable medical practitioner under the same or similar circumstances and must be determined by expert medical testimony establishing the prevailing standard and the defendant-practitioner's departure therefrom. [ ]

We review the evidence to determine whether Walls has established by expert testimony (1) the standard of care in North Platte and similar communities for obtaining informed consent prior to performing surgery and (2) whether there was sufficient evidence to establish that Shreck violated such standard of care. * * *

Standard of Care

The Legislature has defined informed consent as follows:

Informed consent shall mean consent to a procedure based on information which would ordinarily be provided to the patient under like circumstances by health care providers engaged in a similar practice in the locality or in similar localities. Failure to obtain informed consent shall include failure to obtain any express or implied consent for any operation, treatment, or procedure in a case in which a reasonably prudent health care provider in the community or similar communities would have obtained an express or implied consent for such operation, treatment, or procedure under similar circumstances. [ ]

Under § 44–2816, there are two parts to the definition of informed consent. The first part refers to the information that is provided to the patient regarding the procedure that is to be performed. Depending on the established standard of care, the information might include a description of what is going to be done, an assessment of the risks involved, and other options that might be considered. The second part refers to the obligation of the health care provider to obtain the patient's express or implied consent to perform any operation, treatment, or procedure.

* * *

Alleged Breach

We next examine whether Walls presented sufficient evidence to establish that Shreck violated the standard of care by operating on Walls' right eye without obtaining informed consent. The trial court concluded that Walls had failed to prove that Shreck had violated the standard of care.

Shreck argues that he obtained informed consent:

> Walls may argue that Dr. Shreck testified that this consent form did not give "permission to do surgery on both eyes." . . . However, this misconstrues Dr. Shreck's testimony. Dr. Shreck opined that he had obtained the patient's informed consent not from the form but from "what we discussed with the patient in the office." . . . The form itself does not operate to give or deny permission for anything. Rather, it is *evidence* of the discussions which occurred and during which informed consent was obtained. [ ]

Shreck therefore asserts that he obtained informed consent to operate on both eyes based on his office discussions with Walls.

In *Robinson v. Bleicher*, 251 Neb. 752, 559 N.W.2d 473 (1997), we held that a physician's duty to obtain informed consent is measured by the standard of a reasonable medical practitioner under the same or similar circumstances and must be determined by expert medical testimony establishing the prevailing standard and the defendant-practitioner's departure therefrom. In deciding whether a patient was properly informed concerning an operation, expert testimony would be required to determine whether the information furnished to the patient was that which would ordinarily be provided to a patient under like circumstances. See *id*. However, whether expressed or implied consent to an operation was obtained does not necessarily require expert testimony. The performance of surgery upon part of a patient's anatomy that the patient has instructed the surgeon not to operate falls within an exception to the requirement of expert testimony on the issue of informed consent.

* * *

Shreck obtained Walls' informed consent to perform surgery on his left eye. However, the issue of whether Shreck obtained Walls' informed consent to perform surgery on the right eye is problematic. Failure to obtain informed consent includes failure to obtain express or implied consent for any operation in which a reasonably prudent health care provider would have obtained such consent. [ ]. Thus, the lack of express or implied consent to operate on a particular part of one's anatomy or a refusal to give express or implied consent to so operate is a failure to obtain informed consent. * * *

The evidence shows that Shreck did not discuss with Walls that surgery might be required on both eyes during the same operation. There is evidence that Walls specifically told Shreck he did not want surgery performed on the right eye. Walls stated that he would never have entered the hospital had he known there was a possibility of surgery on his right eye.

Shreck stated that he was unable to complete the strabismus surgery on Walls' left eye and therefore switched his focus to the right eye and performed the surgery on that eye. When questioned as to the reason for operating on the right eye, Shreck stated that he had reserved the right to change his mind. However, he also stated to Walls' father that he should have done a better job of informing Walls as to the possibility of surgery on the right eye. This evidence creates an inference that Shreck did not obtain informed consent to operate on the right eye.

* * *

Reversed and remanded for further proceedings.

HARRISON v. UNITED STATES OF AMERICA

United States Court of Appeals for the First Circuit, 2002.
284 F.3d 293.

TORRUELLA, Circuit Judge.

I.

* * *

In 1996, Kenyeda Taft ("Ms. Taft") was pregnant with Melvin Harrison, her second child. In March of that year, Ms. Taft, almost four months pregnant, began her prenatal care at the Lynn Community Health Center ("Lynn CHC") with an initial screening visit conducted by a nurse practitioner. During this visit, Ms. Taft provided a medical history, including the fact that her first child, due to her large size of 9 pounds and 3 ounces, suffered an injury during vaginal birth that resulted in Erb's Palsy.

Ms. Taft first met with Dr. Louis Laz ("Dr. Laz"), a Board-certified obstetrician and gynecologist, at the Lynn CHC on April 29, 1996. Ms. Taft informed Dr. Laz that her first child suffers from Erb's Palsy as a result of a shoulder dystocia,[2] due to the baby's large size. At the time, Dr. Laz's general practice with patients who had had a prior large baby was to determine the estimated fetal weight by ultrasound at about 37 weeks' gestation. If the estimated weight was 4500 grams or more, Dr.

---

2. Shoulder dystocia is a complication that can occur during a vaginal birth where the fetus' shoulders impede the fetus' passage through the birth canal after the head has been delivered. Shoulder dystocia can cause Erb's Palsy, although Erb's Palsy can also occur spontaneously.

Laz would offer the patient an elective Cesarean section ("C-section"). If the estimated weight was under this threshold, Dr. Laz would recommend inducing labor at 37 or 38 weeks' gestation.

In addition to her previous large child, Ms. Taft presented with other risk factors that increased the likelihood that her second baby would also be large, and therefore more likely to suffer complications, such as a shoulder dystocia or brachial plexus injury, during a vaginal birth: she was pregnant with her second child, and second children are usually larger than first; the fetus was male, and males are generally larger; Ms. Taft was an obese woman at the time of her pregnancy; Ms. Taft experienced excessive weight gain during the pregnancy; and her prior delivery resulted in an Erb's Palsy injury. While Dr. Laz recognized these risk factors, he considered them to be normal birth risks and therefore did not discuss them with Ms. Taft.

After meeting with Ms. Taft, Dr. Laz obtained the delivery record for Ms. Taft's first child, Keneisha Taft, from Salem Hospital. At trial, Dr. Laz testified that it was his general practice to request the hospital delivery notes for any patient who had a history of delivery complications. The delivery record of Dr. Orkin, the treating obstetrician, indicated that Keneisha's birth occurred "without any complications." Dr. Laz, considering the obstetrician's delivery notes to be the "gold standard of what happened at that delivery," concluded that Ms. Taft did not experience a shoulder dystocia during her first birth. Therefore, Dr. Laz believed that the Erb's Palsy developed spontaneously, rather than as a result of a shoulder dystocia. Although Dr. Laz testified that he would have discussed an elective C-section with a patient where there was documented evidence of a prior shoulder dystocia resulting in an injury, he did not do so in this case, since the delivery notes did not document such complication.

On September 12, 1996, at approximately 37 weeks' gestation, in accordance with Dr. Laz's general practice, Ms. Taft had an ultrasound at Union Hospital to estimate the fetal weight. The ultrasound report estimated the fetal weight to be 3676 grams (a little over 8 pounds). Because the estimated weight was under the 4500 grams threshold, Dr. Laz determined that a vaginal delivery, as opposed to a C-section, was the appropriate mode of childbirth. Dr. Laz recommended to Ms. Taft that labor be induced, but he did not discuss with her either the risks of vaginal birth or the possibility of a C-section.

On September 17, 1996, Ms. Taft, at 37.5 weeks' gestation, was admitted to Beverly Hospital for induction of labor. During labor, the baby's head crowned, but the shoulders did not deliver. Dr. Laz and the delivery team followed standard steps to attempt to resolve the shoulder dystocia. After these steps were unsuccessful, Dr. Laz delivered the posterior (right) arm, which then allowed delivery of the baby at 12:46 a.m. on September 18. The baby, Melvin Harrison, weighed 4508 grams (9 pounds and 15 ounces) at birth and had a weakness of the right arm and hand, which was subsequently diagnosed as Erb's Palsy.

The plaintiff filed suit against Dr. Laz for medical malpractice * * * premised on two grounds of negligence: (1) Dr. Laz's failure to meet the standard of care by not originally offering an elective C-section and by not performing a C-section during labor based on fetal heart monitorings; and (2) Dr. Laz's failure to obtain Ms. Taft's informed consent by not discussing the risks of vaginal birth and disclosing the alternative of a C-section. A bench trial began on December 18, 2000. At the close of the plaintiff's case, the district court granted the United States' motion for judgment as a matter of law on the question of Dr. Laz's compliance with the standard of care during labor.

At the conclusion of the trial, the district court determined that Dr. Laz did not fail to obtain the patient's informed consent and entered judgment for the defendant. The court found that, although the risks of vaginal birth for the baby were "something more than negligible," when these risks were balanced against the risks to the mother from a C-section, "a cesarean section to avoid brachial plexus injury was not a reasonable medical judgment." Therefore, even though the court found that Ms. Taft would have opted for a C-section if informed of the possibility, the court concluded that "Dr. Laz was under no duty to afford [Ms. Taft] the opportunity to have a cesarean section.... "

The plaintiff appeals the court's judgment only on the informed consent claim, arguing that Dr. Laz, because such information was material to her decision to deliver vaginally, did have a duty to inform Ms. Taft of both the risks of vaginal birth and the availability of a C-section as an alternative method of childbirth.

* * *

III.

* * * To recover under a theory of informed consent in Massachusetts, a patient must prove that the physician has a duty to disclose certain information and that a breach of that duty caused the patient's injury. [ ]. To establish a breach of the physician's duty of disclosure, the plaintiff must establish that: (1) a sufficiently close doctor-patient relationship exists; (2) the doctor knows or should know of the information to be disclosed; (3) the information is such that the doctor should reasonably recognize that it is material to the patient's decision; and (4) the doctor fails to disclose this information. [ ] In this case, only the materiality of the information to the patient is contested.[3]

If a duty exists, a physician must disclose "sufficient information to enable the patient to make an informed judgment whether to give or withhold consent to a medical or surgical procedure." Harnish v. Children's Hosp. Med. Ctr., 387 Mass. 152, 439 N.E.2d 240, 242 (Mass. 1982). Failure to do so constitutes medical malpractice. See id.

---

3. Appellee, in its brief, states that the doctor's knowledge of the information is also disputed. However, the doctor's knowledge is not at issue given his and defense counsel's admission at trial that he was aware of Ms. Taft's risk factors for delivering a large child.

There are two primary standards for determining the requisite scope of the physician's disclosure in informed consent cases: "customary practice" and "materiality." [ ]. Many jurisdictions require a physician to disclose whatever information a reasonable physician in similar circumstances would customarily disclose. [ ]. The Commonwealth of Massachusetts, however, has rejected the customary practice standard as providing insufficient protection for the patient's autonomy, which is the very purpose of disclosure. See [ ] Precourt v. Frederick, 395 Mass. 689, 481 N.E.2d 1144, 1149 (Mass. 1985) (balancing patient's right to self-determination and desire to not unduly burden practice of medicine). Instead, Massachusetts has adopted the "materiality" standard, requiring the physician to disclose "information he should reasonably recognize is material to the [patient's] decision." Harnish [ ].

" 'Materiality may be said to be the significance a reasonable person, in what the physician knows or should know is his patient's position, would attach to the disclosed risk or risks in deciding whether to submit or not to submit to surgery or treatment.' " [ ] Material information "may include the nature of the patient's condition, the nature and probability of risks involved, the benefits to be reasonably expected, . . . the likely result of no treatment, and the available alternatives, including their risks and benefits." [ ]

Whether a risk of injury is material to a patient depends upon the severity of the potential injury as well as the probability of its occurrence. [ ] If the likelihood of an injury occurring is negligible, then the risk is not considered material, and the risk is insufficient to trigger the physician's duty to disclose. See Feeley v. Baer, 424 Mass. 875, 679 N.E.2d 180, 182 (Mass. 1997) (holding that physician had no duty to disclose risk of serious infection because plaintiffs failed to prove that there was "more than a negligible risk"); Precourt, 481 N.E.2d at 1148 (noting that a risk of injury "cannot be considered a material factor" if the probability of its occurrence "is so small as to be practically nonexistent"). Similarly, if the severity of the potential injury is "very minor," the risk is immaterial and need not be disclosed. [ ].

In the case at hand, the plaintiff, citing to Feeley, argues that any risk that is more than negligible automatically qualifies as a material factor that must be disclosed. See Feeley, 679 N.E.2d at 182 (stating that "the risk that must exist in order to invoke informed consent principles in this case is a more than negligible risk. . . . "). The defendant, however, challenges the plaintiff's understanding of the Commonwealth's informed consent law. The defendant argues that Feeley and the other Massachusetts informed consent cases indicate that materiality requires more than just non-negligibility. The defendant contends that Feeley stands for the proposition that if a plaintiff can show evidence of only a negligible risk, then there is no duty to disclose, because such a risk is, as a matter of law, not material. See id. [ ] (holding that there was no duty to disclose because plaintiff failed to show "more than a negligible risk").

The district court seemingly adopted the plaintiff's interpretation of the law by stating that "the doctor must inform the patient where there exists more than a negligible risk of one or more serious consequences from the course of treatment that is being undertaken by the doctor." After hearing the evidence, the court found that Dr. Laz was aware of the risk factors for a birth injury and that these risk factors were "something more than negligible." However, the court then weighed the risks to the mother of a C-section, which the court found to be "more than normally associated with the birth of a child," against the risks to the child of a vaginal birth and found "that Dr. Laz was under no duty to afford [Ms. Taft] the opportunity to have a cesarean section and on the particular circumstances of this case a cesarean section to avoid brachial plexus injury was not a reasonable medical judgment."

We believe that the district court erred in its interpretation of Massachusetts law, thereby triggering de novo review of its finding that Dr. Laz owed no duty to disclose the risks and alternative methods of childbirth. [ ] As discussed above, Harnish and Precourt establish materiality as the standard for determining whether a physician has an affirmative duty to disclose. See Harnish, 439 N.E.2d at 243 (noting duty to disclose material information, but that this does not require the disclosure of all risks); Precourt, 481 N.E.2d at 1148–49 (recognizing duty to disclose material information, which does not include "remote risks"). However, Precourt reserved the issue of how to determine when a risk need not be disclosed, except for indicating there is no duty to disclose negligible risks:

> The development of our law concerning the distinction between risks that as a matter of law may be considered remote, and those that may be left to the determination of a fact finder, must await future cases. It is clear, however, that when, as in this case, the evidence does not permit the jury to draw an inference that the physician knew or reasonably should have known that the probability that a particular risk would materialize was other than negligible, the evidence is insufficient to warrant a finding that the physician violated his duty of disclosure. [ ]

Feeley did not change this materiality approach to informed consent. In Feeley, a mother sued for medical malpractice when her child died from streptococcus pneumonia five days after birth. [ ]. The mother alleged that the treating physician, who opted for spontaneous labor (as opposed to inducing labor) after her water broke, failed to disclose any risk of infection from this procedure. [ ]. The Supreme Judicial Court of Massachusetts, citing Harnish and Precourt, undertook a materiality analysis and concluded that "the evidence would not permit a finding that the risk to the child of serious infection was more than negligible." [ ]. Thus, because the severity of the potential injury was minimal, the court concluded that the information was not material, and the doctor, therefore, had no duty to disclose. [ ].

[W]hen the district court's analysis focused on whether the risks were "more than negligible" rather than on materiality, the district court applied the incorrect legal standard. Thus, we vacate the district court's judgment and remand the case to the district court judge to assess the materiality of the risks of vaginal birth to a reasonable person in Ms. Taft's position.

Moreover, the court made a second legal error by balancing the risks to the child from a vaginal birth against the risks to the mother from a C-section and concluding that, because the C-section presented a greater risk and was therefore not medically recommended, the doctor had no duty to disclose the risks of either procedure. The materiality standard for disclosure does not incorporate a balancing test by which the court can weigh the risks of alternate treatments in deciding what information is material to the patient. An obstetrician in the delivery room is in the unique situation of having to take into account the best interests of two individuals, mother and child, in rendering medical care. Cf. Thomas v. Ellis, 329 Mass. 93, 106 N.E.2d 687, 689–90 (Mass. 1952) (holding that evidence could support finding of negligence where doctor's external turning of fetus' position, causing a separated placenta, endangered health of both mother and child). As such, in recommending a course of treatment to his patients, the standard of care may require the doctor to consider the risks to the mother, the risks to the child, and the appropriate balance of these risks.

However, the standard of care that governs a conventional medical malpractice case differs from the materiality standard that governs informed consent cases. See Steinhilber v. McCarthy, 26 F.Supp.2d 265, 272, 274–75 (D. Mass. 1998) (analyzing doctor's negligence under the standard of care of an average member of his profession but his duty to disclose under materiality of the information). Under informed consent law, if a risk to the baby or a risk to the mother is material to the patient-mother's decision, the doctor has a duty to disclose that risk. See Harnish, 439 N.E.2d at 243 (asserting that physician has duty to disclose "all significant information that the physician possesses" that is material to the patient's decision). Once these risks and other material information have been disclosed, it is the patient's prerogative to balance these risks and choose the form of treatment that best meets that patient's needs. See Harnish, 439 N.E.2d at 244 (declaring it is "the patient's right to decide for himself") * * *

* * *

Thus, if, on remand, the district court finds that a risk existed either as to the mother's health or as to the child's health and that such information would have been material to a reasonable patient in Ms. Taft's position, then Dr. Laz had a duty to disclose that risk. Moreover, because there are only two methods of childbirth, if the district court finds the risk of vaginal birth to be material to the patient, then Dr. Laz also had a duty to present the alternative option of a C-section that might minimize such risk, regardless of his medical opinion on the proper course of treatment * * *.

Vacated and remanded for actions consistent with this opinion.

ASHE v. RADIATION ONCOLOGY ASSOCIATES

Supreme Court of Tennessee, Middles Section, at Nashville, 1999.
9 S.W.3d 119.

HOLDER, J.

* * *

BACKGROUND

The plaintiff, Patricia P. Ashe, was diagnosed with breast cancer in 1988. She ultimately underwent a double mastectomy and chemotherapy as treatment for her breast cancer. In 1993, she began experiencing problems with a cough and a fever. She returned to her oncologist, Dr. Michael Kuzu, where she presented symptoms of fever, cough, pain in the abdomen, weight loss, decreased appetite, and irritability. A chest x-ray and a CT scan revealed the presence of a mass in the medial left apex of her left lung.

The record indicates that the lung tumor could possibly have been metastatic cancer from the breast. Ms. Ashe underwent surgery, and the upper portion of her left lung was removed. She underwent chemotherapy and was referred to the defendant, Dr. Steven L. Stroup, for consideration of radiation therapy. Dr. Stroup testified that chemotherapy alone would be indicated if the lung tumor were metastasized breast cancer. He, however, opined that radiation therapy would be indicated if the lung cancer were primary as opposed to secondary cancer.

Dr. Stroup prescribed radiation treatment for Ms. Ashe. She received a daily dose of 200 centigray for twenty-five days. He described the dose as a "midplane dose." Ms. Ashe sustained "radiation myelitis" caused by a permanent radiation injury to her spinal cord. She is now a paraplegic.

Dr. Stroup did not inform Ms. Ashe that the radiation treatment might result in a permanent injury to her spinal cord. According to Dr. Stroup, the risk that she would sustain a spinal cord injury was less than one percent. Mrs. Ashe proffered the testimony of her expert, Dr. Carlos Perez. Dr. Perez opined that the risk of spinal cord injury was one to two percent. Dr. Perez testified that the applicable standard of care required physicians to warn patients about the risk of radiation injury to the spinal cord.

Ms. Ashe filed the present action alleging claims for medical malpractice and lack of informed consent. At trial, she testified that she would not have consented to the radiation therapy had she been informed of the risk of paralysis. Defense counsel on cross-examination pointed out that the plaintiff did equivocate in her deposition on the issue of consent. Her deposition testimony indicated that she did not know what she would have done had she been warned about the risk of spinal cord injury. She then testified on redirect examination as follows:

True, but the risk of being paralyzed and put in a wheelchair for the rest of your life was not one of the items, if there was any discussed, because had he said that within a six-month period—which they said that would be the time frame for it to happen—had he said, 'Patty, if you do this there is a risk that you will be in a wheelchair six months from now,' I would have told him, 'I will take my chances.' I would not have it done.

The trial court found that the plaintiff's trial testimony conflicted with her deposition testimony regarding whether she would have consented to the procedure had she been warned of the risk of spinal cord injury. The trial court, therefore, struck the trial testimony and granted the defendant a directed verdict on the informed consent claim. The plaintiff's malpractice claim went to the jury. The jury was unable to reach a verdict, and a mistrial was declared.

The plaintiff appealed to the Court of Appeals. The Court of Appeals held that as part of the plaintiff's informed consent claim she was required to prove that a reasonable person knowing of the risk for spinal cord injury would have decided not to have had the procedure performed. The Court held that the discrepancy between the trial testimony and deposition testimony went to the issue of credibility and that the trial testimony should not have been stricken. The Court of Appeals reversed the trial court's grant of a directed verdict on the informed consent claim and remanded the case for a new trial.

ANALYSIS

The burden of proof on the standard of care element in medical malpractice informed consent cases is controlled by Tenn. Code Ann. § 29–26–118. Pursuant to § 29–26–118, a plaintiff must prove by expert testimony that the defendant did not supply appropriate information to the patient in obtaining his informed consent to the procedure out of which plaintiff's claim allegedly arose in accordance with the recognized standard of acceptable professional practice in the profession and in the specialty, if any, that the defendant practices in the community in which he practices or in similar communities.

Id. In addition, Tenn. Code Ann. § 29–26–115 requires that the plaintiff prove the recognized standard of acceptable professional practice, that the defendant acted with less than ordinary and reasonable care in accordance with that standard, and that the plaintiff sustained injuries as a result of the defendant's negligent act or omission. Accordingly, the plaintiff in an informed consent medical malpractice case has the burden of proving: (1) what a reasonable medical practitioner in the same or similar community would have disclosed to the patient about the risk posed by the proposed procedure or treatment; and (2) that the defendant departed from the norm. German v. Nichopoulos, 577 S.W.2d 197, 204 (Tenn. Ct. App. 1978).

This Court recently enunciated a distinction between a lack of informed consent case and a pure medical battery case. In Blanchard v. Kellum, 975 S.W.2d 522 (Tenn. 1998), this Court defined a medical battery as a case in which a doctor performs an unauthorized procedure. Id. at 524. A medical battery may typically occur when: (1) a professional performs a procedure that the patient was unaware the doctor was going to perform; or (2) the procedure was performed on a part of the body other than that part explained to the patient (i.e., amputation of the wrong leg). Id. A lack of informed consent claim typically occurs when the patient was aware that the procedure was going to be performed but the patient was unaware of the risk associated with the procedure. Id.

The case now before us is not a medical battery case. Ms. Ashe had authorized the radiation treatment. Ms. Ashe, however, contends that she was not apprised of certain risks inherent in the treatment. Her claim, therefore, is premised on the lack of informed consent.

The issue with which we are now confronted is whether an objective, subjective, or a hybrid subjective/objective test shall be employed when assessing causation in medical malpractice informed consent cases. The issue is one of first impression in Tennessee. The majority of jurisdictions having addressed this issue follow an objective standard. A minority of jurisdictions having addressed the issue follow the subjective approach. One jurisdiction, Hawaii, employed a "modified objective standard" for informed consent cases for approximately ten years. Hawaii has now abandoned the modified approach in favor of the objective standard. We shall now examine the various approaches and the rationales behind these approaches.

Subjective Standard

The plaintiff urges this Court to follow the minority rule or adopt a subjective standard when evaluating causation in an informed consent case. Causation under the subjective standard is established solely by patient testimony. Patients must testify and prove that they would not have consented to the procedures had they been advised of the particular risk in question. [ ] Accordingly, resolution of causation under a subjective standard is premised elusively on the credibility of a patient's testimony.

The subjective standard engages in an abstract analysis. The abstract analysis not only poses a purely hypothetical question but seeks to answer the hypothetical question. One commentator has framed this hypothetical question as follows: "Viewed from the point at which [the patient] had to decide, would the patient have decided differently had he known something he did not know?" [ ]

Proponents of the subjective test argue that a patient should have the right to make medical determinations regardless of whether the determination is rational or reasonable. [ ] Opponents, however, focus on the unfairness of allowing the issue of causation to turn on the credibility of the hindsight of a person seeking recovery after experiencing a most undesirable result. [ ] "Patients cannot divorce their re-created decision process from hindsight." F. Rozovsky, Consent to Treatment, § 1.13.4, 62–63 (1984). Accordingly, the subjective test potentially places the physician in jeopardy of the patient's hindsight and bitterness. [ ]. Moreover, the adoption of a subjective standard could preclude recovery in an informed consent case in which the patient died as a result of an unforewarned collateral consequence. [ ]

Objective Standard

The majority approach or the so-called objective standard emanates from the seminal decision in Canterbury v. Spence, 150 U.S.App.D.C. 263, 464 F.2d 772 (D.C. Cir. 1972). In Canterbury, the court held that causation in informed consent cases is better resolved on an objective basis "in terms of what a prudent person in the patient's position would have decided if suitably informed of all perils bearing significance." [ ]. The objective view recognizes that neither the plaintiff nor the fact-finder can provide a definitive answer as to what the patient would have done had the patient known of the particular risk prior to consenting to the procedure or treatment. [ ]. Accordingly, the patient's testimony is relevant under an objective approach, but the testimony is not controlling. [ ].

Modified Objective Standard

The modified objective standard was first recognized in Leyson v. Steuermann, 5 Haw.App. 504, 705 P.2d 37 (Haw. Ct. App. 1985). In Leyson, the Hawaii Court of Appeals attempted to balance patient's right to self-determination with the concerns espoused in Canterbury of subjecting a physician to a patient's bitterness or hindsight following an undesirable result. The resulting test determined causation "from the viewpoint of the actual patient acting rationally and reasonably." [ ]

Approximately ten years after the inception of the modified approach, the approach was declared to be onerous in application. In Bernard v. Char, 79 Haw. 362, 903 P.2d 667 (Haw. 1995), the Hawaii Supreme Court elaborated that:

In its effort to achieve the desired result of combining the objective and subjective standards, the modified objective standard injects at least one extra level of complexity into the causation analysis. Under the objective standard, the factfinder must suspend his or her own viewpoint and step into the viewpoint of a reasonable person to objectively assess the plaintiff-patient's decision to undergo treatment. Under the subjective standard, the factfinder must simply assess the credibility of the plaintiff-patient when he or she invariably asserts that he or she would have declined treatment with proper disclosure. Under the "modified objective standard," however, the factfinder must first suspend his or her viewpoint, then place himself or herself in the mind of the actual patient, and, then, while maintaining the viewpoint of the actual patient, try to determine what the actual patient would have decided about the proposed medical treatment or procedure, if the actual patient were acting rationally and reasonably. [ ]

Accordingly, the modified approach was abandoned in favor of the objective standard.

Despite being well-intentioned, [it] exacts too much of a cost in the form of added complexity in seeking to solve problems associated with the preexisting objective and subjective standards while at the same time remaining faithful to the laudable purposes behind such standards.

Id. The Court held: (1) that the objective standard provided "a better, simpler, and more equitable analytical process;" and (2) that the objective standard ultimately addressed the concerns which prompted the creation of the modified test.

CONCLUSION

We agree with the majority of jurisdictions having addressed this issue and hold that the objective approach is the better approach. The objective approach circumvents the need to place the fact-finder in a position of deciding whether a speculative and perhaps emotional answer to a purely hypothetical question shall dictate the outcome of the litigation. The objective standard is consistent with the prevailing standard in negligence cases which measures the conduct of the person in question with that of a reasonable person in like circumstances. [ ]. The objective test provides a realistic framework for rational resolution of the issue of causation. We, therefore, believe that causation may best be assessed in informed consent cases by the finder of fact determining how nondisclosure would affect a reasonable person in the plaintiff's position.

We also are of the opinion that the objective test appropriately respects a patient's right to self-determination. The finder of fact may consider and give weight to the patient's testimony as to whether the patient would have consented to the procedure upon full disclosure of the risks. When applying the objective standard, the finder of fact may also take into account the characteristics of the plaintiff including the plaintiff's idiosyncrasies, fears, age, medical condition, and religious beliefs. [ ] Accordingly, the objective standard affords the ease of applying a uniform standard and yet maintains the flexibility of allowing the finder of fact to make appropriate adjustments to accommodate the individual characteristics and idiosyncracies of an individual patient. We, therefore, hold that the standard to be applied in informed consent cases is whether a reasonable person in the patient's position would have consented to the procedure or treatment in question if adequately informed of all significant perils.

In applying the objective standard to the facts of this case, we agree with the Court of Appeals that the jury should not have been precluded from deciding the issue of informed consent. Under the objective analysis, the plaintiff's testimony is only a factor when determining the issue of informed consent. The dispositive issue is not whether Ms. Ashe would herself have chosen a different course of treatment. The issue is whether a reasonable patient in Ms. Ashe's position would have chosen a different course of treatment. The jury, therefore, should have been allowed to decide whether a reasonable person in Ms. Ashe's position would have consented to the radiation therapy had the risk of paralysis been disclosed.

The judgment of the Court of Appeals reversing the trial court is affirmed.

MILLER v. HCA, INC.

Supreme Court of Texas, 2003.
118 S.W.3d 758.

The narrow question we must decide is whether Texas law recognizes a claim by parents for either battery or negligence because their premature infant, born alive but in distress at only twenty-three weeks of gestation, was provided resuscitative medical treatment by physicians at a hospital without parental consent.

I. FACTS

The unfortunate circumstances of this case began in August 1990, when approximately four months before her due date, Karla Miller was admitted to Woman's Hospital of Texas (the "Hospital") in premature labor. An ultrasound revealed that Karla's fetus weighed about 629 grams or 1 ¼ pounds and had a gestational age of approximately twenty-three weeks. Because of the fetus's prematurity, Karla's physicians began administering a drug designed to stop labor.

Karla's physicians subsequently discovered that Karla had an infection that could endanger her life and require them to induce delivery. Dr. Mark Jacobs, Karla's obstetrician, and Dr. Donald Kelley, a neonatologist at the Hospital, informed Karla and her husband, Mark Miller, that if they had to induce delivery, the infant had little chance of being born alive. The physicians also informed the Millers that if the infant was born alive, it would most probably suffer severe impairments, including cerebral palsy, brain hemorrhaging, blindness, lung disease, pulmonary infections, and mental retardation. Mark testified at trial that the physicians told him they had never had such a premature infant live and that anything they did to sustain the infant's life would be guesswork.

After their discussion, Drs. Jacobs and Kelley asked the Millers to decide whether physicians should treat the infant upon birth if they were forced to induce delivery. At approximately noon that day, the Millers informed Drs. Jacob and Kelley that they wanted no heroic measures performed on the infant and they wanted nature to take its course. Mark testified that he understood heroic measures to mean performing resuscitation, chest massage, and using life support machines. Dr. Kelley recorded the Millers' request in Karla's medical notes, and Dr. Jacobs informed the medical staff at the Hospital that no neonatologist would be needed at delivery. Mark then left the Hospital to make funeral arrangements for the infant.

In the meantime, the nursing staff informed other Hospital personnel of Dr. Jacobs' instruction that no neonatologist would be present in the delivery room when the Millers' infant was born. An afternoon of meetings involving Hospital administrators and physicians followed. Between approximately 4:00 p.m. and 4:30 p.m that day, Anna Summerfield, the director of the Hospital's neonatal intensive care unit, and several physicians, including Dr. Jacobs, met with Mark upon his return to the Hospital to further discuss the situation. Mark testified that Ms. Summerfield announced at the meeting that the Hospital had a policy requiring resuscitation of any baby who was born weighing over 500 grams. Although Ms. Summerfield agreed that she said that, the only written Hospital policy produced described the Natural Death Act and did not mention resuscitating infants over 500 grams.

Moreover, the physicians at the meeting testified that they and Hospital administrators agreed only that a neonatologist would be present to evaluate the Millers' infant at birth and decide whether to resuscitate based on the infant's condition at that time. As Dr. Jacobs testified:

What we finally decided that everyone wanted to do was to not make the call prior to the time we actually saw the baby. Deliver the baby, because you see there was this [question] is the baby really 23 weeks, or is the baby further along, how big is the baby, what are we dealing with. We decided to let the neonatologist make the call by looking directly at the baby at birth.

Another physician who attended the meeting agreed, testifying that to deny any attempts at resuscitation without seeing the infant's condition would be inappropriate and below the standard of care.

Although Dr. Eduardo Otero, the neonatologist present in the delivery room when Sidney was born, did not attend that meeting, he confirmed that he needed to actually see Sidney before deciding what treatment, if any, would be appropriate * * *.

Mark testified that, after the meeting, Hospital administrators asked him to sign a consent form allowing resuscitation according to the Hospital's plan, but he refused. Mark further testified that when he asked how he could prevent resuscitation, Hospital administrators told him that he could do so by removing Karla from the Hospital, which was not a viable option given her condition. Dr. Jacobs then noted in Karla's medical charts that a plan for evaluating the infant upon her birth was discussed at that afternoon meeting.

That evening, Karla's condition worsened and her amniotic sac broke. Dr. Jacobs determined that he would have to augment labor so that the infant would be delivered before further complications to Karla's health developed. Dr. Jacobs accordingly stopped administering the drug to Karla that was designed to stop labor, substituting instead a drug designed to augment labor. At 11:30 p.m. that night, Karla delivered a premature female infant weighing 615 grams, which the Millers named Sidney. Sidney's actual gestational age was twenty-three and one-seventh weeks. And she was born alive.

Dr. Otero noted that Sidney had a heart beat, albeit at a rate below that normally found in full-term babies. He further noted that Sidney, although blue in color and limp, gasped for air, spontaneously cried, and grimaced. Dr. Otero also noted that Sidney displayed no dysmorphic features other than being premature. He immediately "bagged" and "intubated" Sidney to oxygenate her blood; he then placed her on ventilation. He explained why:

Because this baby is alive and this is a baby that has a reasonable chance of living. And again, this is a baby that is not necessarily going to have problems later on. There are babies that survive at this gestational age that—with this birth weight, that later on go on and do well.

Neither Karla nor Mark objected at the time to the treatment provided.

Sidney initially responded well to the treatment, as reflected by her Apgar scores. An Apgar score records five different components of a newborn infant: respiratory effort, heart rate, reflex activity, color, and muscle tone. Each component gets a score of zero, one, or two, with a score of two representing the best condition. Sidney's total Apgar score improved from a three at one minute after birth to a six at five minutes after birth. But at some point during the first few days after birth, Sidney suffered a brain hemorrhage—a complication not uncommon in infants born so prematurely.

There was conflicting testimony about whether Sidney's hemorrhage occurred because of the treatment provided or in spite of it. Regardless of the cause, as predicted by Karla's physicians, the hemorrhage caused Sidney to suffer severe physical and mental impairments. At the time of trial, Sidney was seven years old and could not walk, talk, feed herself, or sit up on her own. The evidence demonstrated that Sidney was legally blind, suffered from severe mental retardation, cerebral palsy, seizures, and spastic quadriparesis in her limbs. She could not be toilet-trained and required a shunt in her brain to drain fluids that accumulate there and needed care twenty-four hours a day. The evidence further demonstrated that her circumstances will not change.

The Millers sued HCA, Inc., HCA–Hospital Corporation of America, Hospital Corporation of America, and Columbia/HCA Healthcare Corporation (collectively, "HCA"), and the Hospital, a subsidiary of HCA. They did not sue any physicians, including Dr. Otero, the physician who actually treated Sidney. Instead, the Millers asserted battery and negligence claims only against HCA and the Hospital.

The Millers' claims stemmed from their allegations that despite their instructions to the contrary, the Hospital not only resuscitated Sidney but performed experimental procedures and administered experimental drugs, without which, in all reasonable medical probability, Sidney would not have survived. The Millers also alleged that the Hospital's acts and/or omissions were performed with HCA's full knowledge and consent. Although the Millers did not sue Dr. Otero, they alleged that he and other Hospital personnel were the Hospital's apparent or ostensible agents.

* * *

Though the Hospital was not a party at the trial against HCA, the trial court submitted questions to the jury about the Hospital's conduct. The jury found that the Hospital, without the consent of Karla or Mark Miller, performed resuscitative treatment on Sidney. The jury also found that the Hospital's and HCA's negligence "proximately caused the occurrence in question." The jury concluded that HCA and the Hospital were grossly negligent and that the Hospital acted with malice. The jury also determined that Dr. Otero acted as the Hospital's agent in resuscitating Sidney and that HCA was responsible for the Hospital's conduct under alter ego and single business enterprise theories. The trial court rendered judgment jointly and severally against the HCA defendants on the jury's verdict of $29,400,000 in actual damages for medical expenses, $17,503,066 in prejudgment interest, and $13,500,000 in exemplary damages.

HCA appealed. The court of appeals, with one justice dissenting, reversed and rendered judgment that the Millers take nothing. The court concluded that the Texas Legislature allowed parents to withhold medical treatment, urgently needed or not, for a child whose medical condition is certifiably terminal under the Natural Death Act. But the court held that the Legislature had not extended that right to parents of children with non-terminal impairments, deformities, or disabilities, regardless of their severity.

The court acknowledged that the Natural Death Act did not "impair or supersede any legal right a person may have to withhold or withdraw life-sustaining treatment in a lawful manner." But the court noted that the parties had not cited, and the court did not find, any authority allowing a parent to withhold urgently-needed life-sustaining medical treatment from a non-terminally ill child. Thus, the court concluded that, to the extent an infant's condition is not certified as terminal, a health care provider is under no duty to follow a parent's instruction to withhold urgently-needed life-sustaining medical treatment.

The court noted that when non-urgently-needed or non-life-sustaining medical treatment is proposed for a child, a court order is needed to override a parent's refusal to consent to the treatment because a determination of such issues as the child's safety, welfare, and best interest can vary under differing circumstances and alternatives. But the court held that when the need for life-sustaining medical treatment is or becomes urgent while a non-terminally ill child is under a health care provider's care, and when the child's parents refuse consent to treatment, a court order is unnecessary to override that refusal. According to the court, no legal or factual issue exists to decide about providing such treatment because a court cannot decide between impaired life versus no life at all.

Given this backdrop, the court concluded that the Millers had no right to deny the medical treatment given to Sidney and that no court order was necessary to overcome their refusal to consent. Thus, the court sustained HCA's contentions that it did not owe the Millers a tort duty to: (a) refrain from resuscitating Sidney; (b) have no policy requiring resuscitation of patients like Sidney without consent; and (c) have policies prohibiting resuscitation of patients like Sidney without consent.

The dissenting justice disagreed that no court order was necessary to override the Millers' refusal to consent. According to the dissent, a court must decide the most important issue: What is in the best interest of the child? The dissent concluded that a court decision in favor of resuscitation would afford the physician and the Hospital the consent necessary to treat Sidney. The dissent further concluded that the Natural Death Act was not mandatory and the Millers were not required to seek a directive under the Act.

We granted the Millers' petition for review to consider this important and difficult matter. * * *

II. ANALYSIS

This case requires us to determine the respective roles that parents and healthcare providers play in deciding whether to treat an infant who is born alive but in distress and is so premature that, despite advancements in neonatal intensive care, has a largely uncertain prognosis. Although the parties have cited numerous constitutional provisions, statutes, and cases, we conclude that neither the Texas Legislature nor our case law has addressed this specific situation. We accordingly begin our analysis by focusing on what the existing case law and statutes do address.

Generally speaking, the custody, care, and nurture of an infant resides in the first instance with the parents. As the United States Supreme Court has acknowledged, parents are presumed to be the appropriate decision-makers for their infants:

Our jurisprudence historically has reflected Western civilization concepts of the family as a unit with broad parental authority over minor children. Our cases have consistently followed that course; our constitutional system long ago rejected any notion that a child is "the mere creature of the State" and, on the contrary, asserted that parents generally "have the right, coupled with the high duty, to recognize and prepare [their children] for additional obligations." * * * Surely, this includes a "high duty" to recognize symptoms of illness and to seek and follow medical advice. The law's concept of the family rests on a presumption that parents possess what a child lacks in maturity, experience, and capacity for judgment required for making life's difficult decisions. More important, historically it has recognized that natural bonds of affection lead parents to act in the best interests of their children.

The Texas Legislature has likewise recognized that parents are presumed to be appropriate decision-makers, giving parents the right to consent to their infant's medical care and surgical treatment. A logical corollary of that right, as the court of appeals here recognized, is that parents have the right not to consent to certain medical care for their infant, *i.e.*, parents have the right to refuse certain medical care.

Of course, this broad grant of parental decision-making authority is not without limits. The State's role as *parens patriae* permits it to intercede in parental decision-making under certain circumstances. As the United States Supreme Court has noted:

As persons unable to protect themselves, infants fall under the parens patriae power of the state. In the exercise of this authority, the state not only punishes parents whose conduct has amounted to abuse or neglect of their children but may also supervene parental decisions before they become operative to ensure that the choices made are not so detrimental to a child's interests as to amount to neglect and abuse.

But the Supreme Court has also pointed out:

As long as parents choose from professionally accepted treatment options the choice is rarely reviewed in court and even less frequently supervened. The courts have exercised their authority to appoint a guardian for a child when the parents are not capable of participating in the decisionmaking or when they have made decisions that evidence substantial lack of concern for the child's interests.

The Texas Legislature has acknowledged the limitations on parental decision-making. For example, the Legislature has provided in the Family Code that the rights and duties of parents are subject to modification by court order. And Texas courts have recognized their authority to enter orders, under appropriate circumstances, appointing a temporary managing conservator who may consent to medical treatment refused by a child's parents.

With respect to consent, the requirement that permission be obtained before providing medical treatment is based on the patient's right to receive information adequate for him or her to exercise an informed decision to accept or refuse the treatment. Thus, the general rule in Texas is that a physician who provides treatment without consent commits a battery. But there are exceptions. For example, in *Gravis v. Physicians & Surgeons Hospital*, this Court acknowledged that "consent will be implied where the patient is unconscious or otherwise unable to give express consent and an immediate operation is necessary to preserve life or health." [ ]

In *Moss v. Rishworth*, the court held that a physician commits a "legal wrong" by operating on a minor without parental consent when there is "an absolute necessity for a prompt operation, but not emergent in the sense that death would likely result immediately upon the failure to perform it." But the court in *Moss* expressly noted that "it [was] not contended [there] that any real danger would have resulted to the child had time been taken to consult the parent with reference to the operation." *Moss* therefore implicitly acknowledges that a physician does not commit a legal wrong by operating on a minor without consent when the operation is performed under emergent circumstances—*i.e.*, when death is likely to result immediately upon the failure to perform it.

Moss guides us here. We hold that a physician, who is confronted with emergent circumstances and provides life-sustaining treatment to a minor child, is not liable for not first obtaining consent from the parents. The Millers cite to Texas Family Code [ ] and Texas Revised Civil Statutes [ ] as illustrating that implied consent does not arise from an emergency context when a healthcare provider has actual notice of lack of consent. Because these statutes apply when a parent is not present to consent, the Millers suggest that this must mean that emergency services cannot be provided when the parents refuse consent. But that is not so.

Providing treatment to a child under emergent circumstances does not imply consent to treatment despite actual notice of refusal to consent. Rather, it is an exception to the general rule that a physician commits a battery by providing medical treatment without consent. As such, the exception is narrowly circumscribed and arises only in emergent circumstances when there is no time to consult the parents or seek court intervention if the parents withhold consent before death is likely to result to the child. Though in situations of this character, the physician should attempt to secure parental consent if possible, the physician will not be liable under a battery or negligence theory solely for proceeding with the treatment absent consent.

We recognize that the Restatement (Second) of Torts § 892D provides that an individual is not liable for providing emergency treatment without consent if that individual has no reason to believe that the other, if he or she had the opportunity to consent, would decline. But that requirement is inapplicable here because, as we have discussed, the emergent circumstances exception does not imply consent.

Further, the emergent circumstances exception acknowledges that the harm from failing to treat outweighs any harm threatened by the proposed treatment because the harm from failing to provide life-sustaining treatment under emergent circumstances is death. And as we acknowledged in *Nelson v. Krusen*, albeit in the different context of a wrongful life claim, it is impossible for the courts to calculate the relative benefits of an impaired life versus no life at all.

* * *

III. CONCLUSION

Dr. Otero provided life-sustaining treatment to Sidney under emergent circumstances as a matter of law. Those circumstances provide an exception to the general rule imposing liability on a physician for providing treatment to a minor child without first obtaining parental consent. Therefore, Dr. Otero did not commit a battery. * * *

STRUNK v. STRUNK

Court of Appeals of Kentucky, 1969.
445 S.W.2d 145.

OSBORNE, J.

The specific question involved upon this appeal is: Does a court of equity have the power to permit a kidney to be removed from an incompetent ward of the state upon petition of his committee, who is also his mother, for the purpose of being transplanted into the body of his brother, who is dying of a fatal kidney disease? We are of the opinion it does.

The facts of the case are as follows: Arthur L. Strunk, 54 years of age, and Ava Strunk, 52 years of age, of Williamstown, Kentucky, are the parents of two sons. Tommy Strunk is 28 years of age, married, an employee of the Penn State Railroad and a part-time student at the University of Cincinnati. Tommy is now suffering from chronic glomerulus nephritis, a fatal kidney disease. He is now being kept alive by frequent treatment on an artificial kidney, a procedure which cannot be continued much longer.

Jerry Strunk is 27 years of age, incompetent, and through proper legal proceedings has been committed to the Frankfort State Hospital and School, which is a state institution maintained for the feebleminded. He has an I.Q. of approximately 35, which corresponds with the mental age of approximately six years. He is further handicapped by a speech defect, which makes it difficult for him to communicate with persons who are not well acquainted with him. When it was determined that Tommy, in order to survive, would have to have a kidney the doctors considered the possibility of using a kidney from a cadaver if and when one became available or one from a live donor if this could be made available. The entire family, his mother, father and a number of collateral relatives were tested. Because of incompatibility of blood type or tissue none were medically acceptable as live donors. As a last resort, Jerry was tested and found to be highly acceptable. This immediately presented the legal problem as to what, if anything, could be done by the family, especially the mother and the father to procure a transplant from Jerry to Tommy. * * *

* * *

The Department of Mental Health of this Commonwealth has entered the case as amicus curiae and on the basis of its evaluation of the seriousness of the operation as opposed to the traumatic effect upon Jerry as a result of the loss of Tommy, recommended to the court that Jerry be permitted to undergo the surgery. Its recommendations are as follows:

"It is difficult for the mental defective to establish a firm sense of identity with another person and the acquisition of this necessary identity is dependent upon a person whom one can conveniently accept as a model and who at the same time is sufficiently flexible to allow the defective to detach himself with reassurances of continuity. His need to be social is not so much the necessity of a formal and mechanical contact with other human beings as it is the necessity of a close intimacy with other men, the desirability of a real community of feeling, an urgent need for a unity of understanding. Purely mechanical and formal contact with other men does not offer any treatment for the behavior of a mental defective; only those who are able to communicate intimately are of value to hospital treatment in these cases. And this generally is a member of the family.

"In view of this knowledge, we now have particular interest in this case. Jerry Strunk, a mental defective, has emotions and reactions on a scale comparable to that of normal person. He identifies with his brother Tom; Tom is his model, his tie with his family. Tom's life is vital to the continuity of Jerry's improvement at Frankfort State Hospital and School. The testimony of the hospital representative reflected the importance to Jerry of his visits with his family and the constant inquiries Jerry made about Tom's coming to see him. Jerry is aware he plays a role in the relief of this tension. We the Department of Mental Health must take all possible steps to prevent the occurrence of any guilt feelings Jerry would have if Tom were to die.

* * *

Upon this appeal we are faced with the fact that all members of the immediate family have recommended the transplant. The Department of Mental Health has likewise made its recommendation. The county court has given its approval. The circuit court has found that it would be to the best interest of the ward of the state that the procedure be carried out. Throughout the legal proceedings, Jerry has been represented by a guardian ad litem, who has continually questioned the power of the state to authorize the removal of an organ from the body of an incompetent who is a ward of the state. We are fully cognizant of the fact that the question before us is unique. Insofar as we have been able to learn, no similar set of facts has come before the highest court of any of the states of this nation or the federal courts. * * * "

* * *

The right to act for the incompetent in all cases has become recognized in this country as the doctrine of substituted judgment and is broad enough not only to cover property but also to cover all matters touching on the well-being of the ward. The doctrine has been recognized in American courts since 1844.

"The 'doctrine of substituted judgment,' which apparently found its first expression in the leading English case of Ex parte Whitebread (1816) 2 Meriv 99, 35 Eng Reprint 878 (Ch), supra § 3(a), was amplified in Re Earl of Carysfort (1840) Craig & Ph 76, 41 Eng Reprint 418, where the principle was made to apply to one who was not next of kin of the lunatic but a servant of his who was obliged to retire from his service by reason of age and infirmity. The Lord Chancellor permitted the allowance of an annuity out of the income of the estate of the lunatic earl as a retiring pension to the latter's aged personal servant, although no supporting evidence could be found, the court being 'satisfied that the Earl of Carysfort would have approved if he had been capable of acting himself.' " [ ].

In this state we have delegated substantial powers to committees of persons of unsound minds [ ] and to county courts in their supervision. However, as pointed out in American Jurisprudence, these statutes were not intended to divest the equity courts of their inherent common law powers. * * *

The medical practice of transferring tissue from one part of the human body to another (autografting) and from one human being to another (homografting) is rapidly becoming a common clinical practice. In many cases the transplants take as well where the tissue is dead as when it is alive. This has made practicable the establishment of tissue banks where such material can be stored for future use. Vascularized grafts of lungs, kidneys and hearts are becoming increasingly common. These grafts must be of functioning, living cells with blood vessels remaining anatomically intact. The chance of success in the transfer of these organs is greatly increased when the donor and the donee are genetically related. It is recognized by all legal and medical authorities that several legal problems can arise as a result of the operative techniques of the transplant procedure. [ ]

The renal transplant is becoming the most common of the organ transplants. This is because the normal body has two functioning kidneys, one of which it can reasonably do without, thereby making it possible for one person to donate a kidney to another. Testimony in this record shows that there have been over 2500 kidney transplants performed in the United States up to this date. The process can be effected under present techniques with minimal danger to both the donor and the donee. Doctors Hamburger and Crosneir describe the risk to the donor as follows:

"This discussion is limited to renal transplantation, since it is inconceivable that any vital organ other than the kidney might ever be removed from a healthy living donor for transplantation purposes. The immediate operative risk of unilateral nephrectomy in a healthy subject has been calculated as approximately 0.05 per cent. The long-term risk is more difficult to estimate, since the various types of renal disease do not appear to be more frequent or more severe in individuals with solitary kidneys than in normal subjects.

On the other hand, the development of surgical problems, trauma, or neoplasms, with the possible necessity of nephrectomy, do increase the long-term risks in living donors; the long-term risk, on this basis, has been estimated at 0.07 per cent [ ]. These data must, however, be considered in the light of statistical life expectancy which, in a healthy 35 year old adult, goes from 99.3 per cent to 99.1 per cent during the next five succeeding years; this is an increase in risk equal to that incurred by driving a car for 16 miles every working day [ ] The risks incurred by the donor are therefore very limited, but they are a reality, even if, until now, there have been no reports of complications endangering the life of a donor anywhere in the world. Unfortunately, there is no doubt that, as the number of renal transplants increases, such an incident will inevitably be recorded."

* * * The circuit court having found that the operative procedures in this instance are to the best interest of Jerry Strunk and this finding having been based upon substantial evidence, we are of the opinion the judgment should be affirmed. We do not deem it significant that this case reached the circuit court by way of appeal as opposed to a direct proceeding in that court.

Judgment affirmed.

STEINFELD, Judge (dissenting).

Apparently because of my indelible recollection of a government which, to the everlasting shame of its citizens, embarked on a program of genocide and experimentation with human bodies I have been more troubled in reaching a decision in this case than in any other. My sympathies and emotions are torn between a compassion to aid an ailing young man and a duty to fully protect unfortunate members of society.

The opinion of the majority is predicated upon the authority of an equity court to speak for one who cannot speak for himself. However, it is my opinion that in considering such right in this instance we must first look to the power and authority vested in the committee, the appellee herein. KRS 387.060 and KRS 387.230 do nothing more than give the committee the power to take custody of the incompetent and the possession, care and management of his property. Courts have restricted the activities of the committee to that which is for the best interest of the incompetent. [ ] The authority and duty have been to protect and maintain the ward, to secure that to which he is entitled and preserve that which he has. [ ]

The wishes of the members of the family or the desires of the guardian to be helpful to the apparent objects of the ward's bounty have not been a criterion. "A curator or guardian cannot dispose of his ward's property by donation, even though authorized to do so by the court on advice of a family meeting, unless a gift by the guardian is authorized by statute." [ ]

* * *

The majority opinion is predicated upon the finding of the circuit court that there will be psychological benefits to the ward but points out that the incompetent has the mentality of a six-year-old child. It is common knowledge beyond dispute that the loss of a close relative or a friend to a six-year-old child is not of major impact. Opinions concerning psychological trauma are at best most nebulous. Furthermore, there are no guarantees that the transplant will become a surgical success, it being well known that body rejection of transplanted organs is frequent. The life of the incompetent is not in danger, but the surgical procedure advocated creates some peril.

It is written in Prince v. Massachusetts, 321 U.S. 158, 64 S.Ct. 438, 88 L.Ed. 645 (1944), that "Parents may be free to become martyrs themselves. But it does not follow they are free, in identical circumstances, to make martyrs of their children before they have reached the age of full and legal discretion when they can make that choice for themselves." The ability to fully understand and consent is a prerequisite to the donation of a part of the human body. Cf. Bonner v. Moran, 75 U.S.App.D.C. 156, 126 F.2d 121, 139 A.L.R. 1366 (1941), in which a fifteen-year-old infant's consent to removal of a skin patch for the benefit of another was held legally ineffective.

Unquestionably the attitudes and attempts of the committee and members of the family of the two young men whose critical problems now confront us are commendable, natural and beyond reproach. However, they refer us to nothing indicating that they are privileged to authorize the removal of one of the kidneys of the incompetent for the purpose of donation, and they cite no statutory or other authority vesting such right in the courts. The proof shows that less compatible donors are available and that the kidney of a cadaver could be used, although the odds of operational success are not as great in such case as they would be with the fully compatible donor brother.

I am unwilling to hold that the gates should be open to permit the removal of an organ from an incompetent for transplant, at least until such time as it is conclusively demonstrated that it will be of significant benefit to the incompetent. The evidence here does not rise to that pinnacle. To hold that committees, guardians or courts have such awesome power even in the persuasive case before us, could establish legal precedent, the dire result of which we cannot fathom. Regretfully I must say no.

NEIKIRK and PALMORE, JJ., join with me in this dissent.

Notes

1) Informed consent is determined on the basis of information and consent, not on whether or not a form was signed. A signature on a consent form is evidence of consent, but so is testimony and other admissible evidence. Verbal consent is just as valid, though it may be difficult to prove, and the absence of a consent form under circumstances that one might be expected could create a presumption that consent was

not obtained. What should the law do when a patient signed a form but testifies that he/she was told it was merely a formality and never got the opportunity to read it or have it explained? What if the information on the consent form is different that what the plaintiff testifies he was told? Who has the burden of proof as to inconsistencies?

2) *Harrison* indicates that there are two primary standards for determining the requisite scope of the physician's disclosure: customary practice and materiality. According to customary practice, the physician is obligated to discuss with the patient that information that a reasonable physician under like circumstances would customarily disclose. Massachusetts relies on the higher "materiality" standard: a physician is required to disclose all information that he/she reasonably determines to be material to the patient's informed consent decision: if it is material, it does not matter that the reasonable physician does not ordinarily disclose it. Compare the subjective vs. objective standards discussed in *Ashe*.

3) In *Miller*, the court acknowledged that parents are generally presumed to be appropriate decision makers for their children. It also acknowledged that a physician who administers medical treatment without consent commits a battery. The presence of emergency circumstances offers some protection when the issue concerns life-sustaining treatment to a minor child. The *Miller* court disagreed with plaintiff's argument that no emergency existed because the circumstances that occurred had been discussed ahead of time and the parents had specifically declined "heroic measures". The court held that decisions made before the baby's birth could not have been fully informed until her condition was evaluated, and after birth there was no time to consult the parents and seek consent or challenge the issue in court. Do you agree that this informed consent issue could not have been addressed ahead of time?

SECTION B. REFUSED SERVICES

TRUMAN v. THOMAS

Supreme Court of California, 1980.
27 Cal.3d 285, 165 Cal.Rptr. 308, 611 P.2d 902.

BIRD, CHIEF JUSTICE. * * *

Respondent, Dr. Claude R. Thomas, is a family physician engaged in a general medical practice. He was first contacted in April 1963 by appellants' mother, Rena Truman, in connection with her second pregnancy. He continued to act as the primary physician for Mrs. Truman and her two children until March 1969. During this six-year period, Mrs. Truman not only sought his medical advice, but often discussed personal matters with him.

In April 1969, Mrs. Truman consulted Dr. Casey, a urologist, about a urinary tract infection which had been treated previously by Dr. Thomas. While examining Mrs. Truman, Dr. Casey discovered that she was experiencing heavy vaginal discharges and that her cervix was extremely rough. Mrs. Truman was given a prescription for the infection and advised to see a gynecologist as soon as possible. When Mrs. Truman did not make an appointment with a gynecologist, Dr. Casey made an appointment for her with a Dr. Ritter.

In October 1969, Dr. Ritter discovered that Mrs. Truman's cervix had been largely replaced by a cancerous tumor. Too far advanced to be removed by surgery, the tumor was unsuccessfully treated by other methods. Mrs. Truman died in July 1970 at the age of 30.

Appellants are Rena Truman's two children. They brought this wrongful death action against Dr. Thomas for his failure to perform a pap smear test on their mother. At the trial, expert testimony was presented which indicated that if Mrs. Truman had undergone a pap smear at any time between 1964 and 1969, the cervical tumor probably would have been discovered in time to save her life. There was disputed expert testimony that the standard of medical practice required a physician to explain to women patients that it is important to have a pap smear each year to "pick up early lesions that are treatable rather than having to deal with [more developed] tumor[s] that very often aren't treatable."[1]

Although Dr. Thomas saw Mrs. Truman frequently between 1964 and 1969, he never performed a pap smear test on her. Dr. Thomas testified that he did not "specifically" inform Mrs. Truman of the risk involved in any failure to undergo the pap smear test. Rather,

> I said, "You should have a pap smear." We don't say, "By now it can be Stage Two [in the development of cervical cancer]," or go through all of the different lectures about cancer. I think it is a widely known and generally accepted manner of treatment and I think the patient has a high degree of responsibility. We are not enforcers, we are advisors.

However, Dr. Thomas' medical records contain no reference to any discussion or recommendation that Mrs. Truman undergo a pap smear test.

For the most part, Dr. Thomas was unable to describe specific conversations with Mrs. Truman. For example, he testified that during certain periods

> I saw Rena very frequently, approximately once a week or so, and I am sure my opening remark was, "Rena, you need a pap smear." * * * I am sure we discussed it with her so often that she couldn't [have] fail[ed] to realize that we wanted her to have a complete examination, breast examination, ovaries and pap smear.

---

1. Dr. Thomas conceded at the trial that it is the accepted standard of practice for physicians in his community to recommend that women of child-bearing age undergo a pap smear each year. His records indicate that during the period in which he acted as Mrs. Truman's family physician he performed between 10 and 20 pap smears per month.

Dr. Thomas also testified that on at least two occasions when he performed pelvic examinations of Mrs. Truman, she refused him permission to perform the test, stating she could not afford the cost. Dr. Thomas offered to defer payment, but Mrs. Truman wanted to pay cash.

Appellants argue that the failure to give a pap smear test to Mrs. Truman proximately caused her death. Two instructions requested by appellants described alternative theories under which Dr. Thomas could be held liable for this failure. First, they asked that the jury be instructed that

> It is the duty of a physician to disclose to his patient all relevant information to enable the patient to make an informed decision regarding the submission to or refusal to take a diagnostic test.

> Failure of the physician to disclose to his patient all relevant information including the risks to the patient if the test is refused renders the physician liable for any injury legally resulting from the patient's refusal to take the test if a reasonably prudent person in the patient's position would not have refused the test if she had been adequately informed of all the significant perils.

Second, they requested that the jury be informed that

> [A]s a matter of law * * * a physician who fails to perform a pap smear test on a female patient over the age of 23 and to whom the patient has entrusted her general physical care is liable for injury or death proximately caused by the failure to perform the test.

Both instructions were refused.

The jury rendered a special verdict, finding Dr. Thomas free of any negligence that proximately caused Mrs. Truman's death. This appeal followed.

The central issue for this court is whether Dr. Thomas breached his duty of care to Mrs. Truman when he failed to inform her of the potentially fatal consequences of allowing cervical cancer to develop undetected by a pap smear.

In Cobbs v. Grant, 8 Cal.3d 229, 104 Cal.Rptr. 505, 502 P.2d 1 (1972), this court considered the scope of a physician's duty to disclose medical information to his or her patients in discussing proposed medical procedures. * * *

[T]he court in *Cobbs* stated that a patient must be apprised not only of the "risks inherent in the procedure [prescribed, but also] the risks of a decision not to undergo the treatment, and the probability of a successful outcome of the treatment." 502 P.2d at 10. This rule applies whether the procedure involves treatment or a diagnostic test. On the one hand, a physician recommending a risk-free procedure may safely forego discussion beyond that necessary to conform to competent medical practice and to obtain the patient's consent. * * * If a patient indicates that he or she is going to decline the risk-free test or treatment, then the doctor has the additional duty of advising of all material risks of which a reasonable person would want to be informed before deciding not to undergo the procedure. On the other hand, if the recommended test or treatment is itself risky, then the physician should always explain the potential consequences of declining to follow the recommended course of action.

Nevertheless, Dr. Thomas contends that *Cobbs* does not apply to him because the duty to disclose applies only where the patient consents to the recommended procedure. He argues that since a physician's advice may be presumed to be founded on an expert appraisal of the patient's medical needs, no reasonable patient would fail to undertake further inquiry before rejecting such advice. Therefore, patients who reject their physician's advice should shoulder the burden of inquiry as to the possible consequences of their decision.

This argument is inconsistent with *Cobbs*. The duty to disclose was imposed in *Cobbs* so that patients might meaningfully exercise their right to make decisions about their own bodies. * * * The importance of this right should not be diminished by the manner in which it is exercised. Further, the need for disclosure is not lessened because patients reject a recommended procedure. Such a decision does not alter "what has been termed the 'fiducial qualities' of the physician-patient relationship," since patients who reject a procedure are as unskilled in the medical sciences as those who consent. 502 P.2d at 12. To now hold that patients who reject their physician's advice have the burden of inquiring as to the potential consequences of their decisions would be to contradict *Cobbs*. It must be remembered that Dr. Thomas was not engaged in an arms-length transaction with Mrs. Truman. Clearly, under *Cobbs*, he was obligated to provide her with all the information material to her decision.

Dr. Thomas next contends that, as a matter of law, he had no duty to disclose to Mrs. Truman the risk of failing to undergo a pap smear test because "the danger [is] remote and commonly appreciated to be remote." Ibid. The merit of this contention depends on whether a jury could reasonably find that knowledge of this risk was material to Mrs. Truman's decision.

The record indicates that the pap smear test is an accurate detector of cervical cancer. Although the probability that Mrs. Truman had cervical cancer was low, Dr. Thomas knew that the potential harm of failing to detect the disease at an early stage was death.[2] This situation is not analogous to one which involves, for example, "relatively minor risks inherent in [such] common procedures" as the taking of blood samples. * * * These procedures are not central to the decision to administer or reject the procedure. In contrast, the risk which Mrs. Truman faced from

2. Expert testimony established that if cervical cancer is detected in the early stages of its development, there is a very high probability that the progress of this disease can be permanently arrested.

cervical cancer was not only significant, it was the principal reason why Dr. Thomas recommended that she undergo a pap smear.

Little evidence was introduced on whether this risk was commonly known. Dr. Thomas testified that the risk would be known to a reasonable person. Whether such evidence is sufficient to establish that there was no general duty to disclose this risk to patients is a question of fact for the jury. Moreover, even assuming such disclosure was not generally required, the circumstances in this case may establish that Dr. Thomas did have a duty to inform Mrs. Truman of the risks she was running by not undergoing a pap smear.

Dr. Thomas testified he never specifically informed her of the purpose of a pap smear test. There was no evidence introduced that Mrs. Truman was aware of the serious danger entailed in not undergoing the test. However, there was testimony that Mrs. Truman said she would not undergo the test on certain occasions because of its cost or because "she just didn't feel like it." Under these circumstances, a jury could reasonably conclude that Dr. Thomas had a duty to inform Mrs. Truman of the danger of refusing the test because it was not reasonable for Dr. Thomas to assume that Mrs. Truman appreciated the potentially fatal consequences of her conduct. Accordingly, this court cannot decide as a matter of law that Dr. Thomas owed absolutely no duty to Mrs. Truman to make this important disclosure that affected her life.

* * *

Refusal to give the requested instruction meant that the jury was unable to consider whether Dr. Thomas breached a duty by not disclosing the danger of failing to undergo a pap smear. Since this theory finds support in the record, it was error for the court to refuse to give the requested instruction. * * * If the jury had been given this instruction and had found in favor of the appellants, such a finding would have had support in the record before us. Reversal is therefore required. * * *

CLARK, JUSTICE, dissenting. * * *

The burden of explaining the purposes of a pap smear and the potential risks in failing to submit to one may not appear to be great, but the newly imposed duty upon physicians created by today's majority opinion goes far beyond. The instruction requires disclosure of all "relevant information to enable the patient to make an informed decision regarding the submission to or refusal to take a diagnostic test." In short, it applies not only to pap smears, but to all diagnostic procedures allegedly designed to detect illness which could lead to death or serious complication if not timely treated.

* * *

Few, if any, people in our society are unaware that a general examination is designed to discover serious illness for timely treatment. While a lengthy explanation may result in general examinations for some patients who would otherwise decline or defer them, the onerous duty placed upon doctors by today's decision will result in reduced care for others. Requiring physicians to spend a large portion of their time teaching medical science before practicing it will greatly increase the cost of medical diagnosis—a cost ultimately paid by an unwanting public. Persons desiring treatment for specific complaints will be deterred from seeking medical advice once they realize they will be charged not only for treatment but also for lengthy lectures on the merits of their examination.

The great educational program the majority embark upon, even if justifiable, is a question of public policy for the Legislature to determine: whether the cost warrants the burden, and whether the duty to educate rests with doctors, schools, or health departments. Requiring individual doctors to enlighten the public may be found through legislative hearings to be inefficient, not reaching those who need it most—the ones hesitant to consult doctors.

When a patient chooses a physician, he or she obviously has confidence in the doctor and intends to accept proffered medical advice. When the doctor prescribes diagnostic tests, the patient is aware the tests are intended to discover illness. It is therefore reasonable to assume that a patient who refuses advice is aware of potential risk.

Moreover, the physician-patient relationship is based on trust, and forcing the doctor into a hard sell approach to his services can only jeopardize that relationship.

* * *

Nothing in Cobbs v. Grant, 8 Cal.3d 229, 104 Cal.Rptr. 505, 502 P.2d 1 (1972), warrants imposition of such an onerous duty—to the contrary, that case expressly rejected any such duty. * * *

In *Cobbs,* we expressly circumscribed the duty of the doctor, holding that a "mini-course in medical science is not required," that "there is no physician's duty to discuss the relatively minor risks inherent in common procedures, when it is common knowledge that such risks inherent in the procedure are of very low incidence," that as to common procedures "no warning" is "required as to the remote possibility of death or serious bodily harm," and that recovery would be permitted only if a "prudent person in the patient's position" adequately informed of the perils would have declined treatment. 502 P.2d at 11.

Thus, *Cobbs* is not helpful to the majority because the duty of disclosure in that case was imposed to assure consent to the intrusion would be effective. When no intrusion takes place, no need for consent, effective or otherwise, arises.[3]

3. Like *Cobbs,* all other authority relied on by the majority * * * is concerned with whether consent to therapy was informed and therefore effective. The cases involved situations where there has been an intrusion to the body autonomy and it is claimed the intrusion was consensual. Thus, the question of informed consent is crucial. None involves the situation where the patient has refused the intrusion and thus consent is immaterial.

Furthermore, contrary to the express limitations in *Cobbs,* today's decision requires not only an explanation of the risks of a single procedure but also a "mini-course in medical science," if not a maxi-course. Similarly, because discovery of serious illness in a general examination of an apparently healthy person is remote, the doctor, contrary to *Cobbs,* is now required to disclose remote possibilities of illness. Moreover, the *Cobbs* duty to warn in cases where an adequately informed prudent person would have declined treatment shows a concern for preventing over-selling of services by physicians. By contrast, today's duty appears designed to increase selling of medical services.

* * *

Refusal to give the requested instruction does not warrant reversal. I would affirm the judgment.

RICHARDSON and MANUEL, JJ., concur.

PUBLIC HEALTH TRUST v. WONS

Supreme Court of Florida, 1989.
541 So.2d 96.

KOGAN, JUSTICE. * * *

Norma Wons entered Jackson Memorial Hospital, a medical facility operated by the Public Health Trust of Dade County, with a condition known as dysfunctional uterine bleeding. Doctors informed Mrs. Wons that she would require treatment in the form of a blood transfusion or she would, in all probability, die. Mrs. Wons, a practicing Jehovah's Witness and mother of two minor children, declined the treatment on grounds that it violated her religious principles to receive blood from outside her own body. At the time she refused consent Mrs. Wons was conscious and able to reach an informed decision concerning her treatment.

The Health Trust petitioned the circuit court to force Mrs. Wons to undergo a blood transfusion. At the hearing Mrs. Wons' husband testified that he fully supported his wife's decision to refuse the treatment and that, in the unfortunate event she were to die, their two children would be cared for by Mr. Wons and Mrs. Wons' mother and brothers. Nevertheless, the court granted the petition, ordering the hospital doctors to administer the blood transfusion, which was done while Mrs. Wons was unconscious. The trial judge reasoned that minor children have a right to be reared by two loving parents, a right which overrides the mother's rights of free religious exercise and privacy. Upon regaining consciousness, Mrs. Wons appealed to the third district, which reversed the order. After holding that the case was not moot due to the recurring nature of Mrs. Wons' condition (i.e., it was capable of repetition, yet evading review), the district court held that Mrs. Wons' constitutional rights of religion and privacy could not be overridden by the state's purported interests. [The third district court of appeal certified to the Florida Supreme Court the following question as one of great public importance: "Whether a competent adult has a lawful right to refuse a blood transfusion without which she may well die." Wons v. Public Health Trust, 500 So.2d 679, 680 (Fla.Dist.Ct.App.1987).]

An individual's right to refuse medical treatment must be analyzed in terms of our decision in Satz v. Perlmutter, 379 So.2d 359 (Fla.1980), aff'g 362 So.2d 160 (Fla.Dist.Ct.App.1978). That case, in which this court adopted the fourth district's reasoning in full, established four criteria wherein the right to refuse medical treatment may be overridden by a compelling state interest. These factors are:

(1) Preservation of life,

(2) Protection of innocent third parties,

(3) Prevention of suicide, and

(4) Maintenance of the ethical integrity of the medical profession. 362 So.2d at 162.

It is important to note that these factors are by no means a bright-line test, capable of resolving every dispute regarding the refusal of medical treatment. Rather, they are intended merely as factors to be considered while reaching the difficult decision of when a compelling state interest may override the basic constitutional rights of privacy and religious freedom.

The Health Trust asserts that the children's right to be reared by two loving parents is sufficient to trigger the second compelling state interest in the *Perlmutter* list of criteria. * * * We hold that the state's interest in maintaining a home with two parents for the minor children does not override Mrs. Wons' constitutional rights of privacy and religion.

The Health Trust expressed concern during oral argument that in future cases of this nature, the inconvenience of taking each treatment refusal case to court for an emergency judicial hearing would create problems. The Health Trust complains that this would present too heavy a burden on the hospitals to provide care between court appearances. While we understand the Health Trust's dilemma, these cases demand individual attention. No blanket rule is feasible which could sufficiently cover all occasions in which this situation will arise. Thus, it will be necessary for hospitals that wish to contest a patient's refusal of treatment to commence court proceedings and sustain the heavy burden of proof that the state's interest outweighs the patient's constitutional rights.

[W]e answer the certified question in the affirmative and approve the decision of the district court.

EHRLICH, CHIEF JUSTICE, concurring specially. * * *

* * * Absent evidence that a minor child will be abandoned, the state has no compelling interest sufficient to override the competent patient's right to refuse treatment. Sweeping claims about the need to preserve the lives of parents with minor children have an emotional

appeal that facilely avoids both the constitutionally required scrutiny of the state's authority to act and the search for less restrictive alternatives.

Petitioner conceded below that the other interests enumerated in *Perlmutter* are not implicated in this case. * * * However, analysis of those other interests supports the decision in this case.

Perhaps the most important of the state interests discussed in *Perlmutter* is the interest in the preservation of life. [T]he quality of life for the patient if treatment is administered must be taken into consideration. It does not necessarily follow that where there is a favorable medical prognosis the state's interest automatically overrides the patient's right to refuse treatment. In some circumstances the cost to the individual of the life-prolonging treatment, in economic, emotional, or as in this case, spiritual terms, may be too high. * * * That "cost" must be looked at from the patient's point of view. The dissent assumes that after the blood transfusion Mrs. Wons "could return to a normal life." Is that really the case? Mrs. Wons is a Jehovah's Witness, as are the other members of her family. Receiving a blood transfusion is a serious sin for someone of her faith. After the transfusion she must live with the knowledge of that sin, and, because she has a recurring condition, she must also live with the knowledge that should she again become critically ill, she may again be forced to receive blood. Given the strength of the faith she and her family share, that knowledge must affect not only Mrs. Wons, but her family as well. From her perspective, this situation can hardly be considered "normal." Where a competent adult is involved, the best evidence of how that person views the consequences of accepting medical treatment is that person's own statements and actions. It is not for the court to second guess, or make judgments of, the reasonableness of that view. * * *

The other two state interests discussed in *Perlmutter* are the duty to prevent suicide and the maintenance of the ethical integrity of the medical profession. It is uncontested that this case does not implicate the state's interest in the prevention of suicide. Mrs. Wons does not desire to die. Rather, she has chosen not to live, if to do so would require that she receive blood. Should she die because no blood transfusion is administered, her death would be of natural causes, not suicide. * * *

The preservation of the ethical integrity of the medical profession is, in my view, the least compelling of the state interests involved. * * * Given the fundamental nature of the constitutional rights involved, protection of the ethical integrity of the medical profession alone could never override those rights.

Further, circumstances such as these are clearly distinguishable from the instances cited by the dissent where state interests have been held to override the right to act according to one's religious beliefs. Most, like snake-handling, are prohibitions against taking affirmative religiously grounded action. Only requiring compulsory medical vaccination involves a refusal to act because of religious principles, and there the state interest in preventing the widespread danger to public health is great. * * * Where the religiously grounded "action" the state is attempting to prohibit is a refusal to act rather than affirmative conduct, the state may only interfere where there is a grave and immediate public danger. In re Brown, 478 So.2d 1033, 1037 (Miss. 1985). No affirmative conduct is present in this case. By forcing Mrs. Wons to submit to a blood transfusion forbidden by her religious beliefs, the state compelled rather than prohibited affirmative conduct, and there was no immediate public danger posed by her refusal to consent to the transfusion. Therefore, cases concerning the prohibition of affirmative religiously based conduct are inapposite to this case. * * *

OVERTON, JUSTICE, dissenting.

* * * I find that the majority misapplies our decision in Satz v. Perlmutter, 379 So.2d 359 (Fla.1980). * * *

This court specifically limited *Perlmutter* to its facts * * *. The majority opinion in this case now broadly expands the narrow *Perlmutter* holding and represents a general willingness to uphold the rights of an individual to practice a chosen religion and protect rights of privacy without regard for the effects on innocent third parties, particularly minor children.

I believe the better view has been set forth in Application of the President and Directors of Georgetown College, Inc., 331 F.2d 1000 (D.C. Cir.), cert. denied, 377 U.S. 978, 84 S.Ct. 1883, 12 L.Ed.2d 746 (1964), where the court ordered a blood transfusion to save the life of the mother of a seven-month-old child who had refused the transfusion on religious grounds. The court justified its decision in part on the following reasoning:

The patient, 25 years old, was the mother of a seven-month-old child. *The state, as parens patriae, will not allow a parent to abandon a child, and so it should not allow this most ultimate of voluntary abandonments.* The patient had a responsibility to the community to care for her infant. Thus the people had an interest in preserving the life of this mother. Id. at 1008. (Emphasis added.)

* * *

The majority further fails to recognize the distinction between cases where the prognosis that the patient can be restored to normal life with proper medical procedures is extremely good and cases where the possibility of recovery is slight and the person is diagnosed as terminal. Here, it was unrefuted that, following medical treatment, Wons could return to a normal life, but the majority totally fails to consider this factor in applying *Perlmutter*. The patient in *Perlmutter* was a 73–year–old victim of amyotrophic lateral sclerosis (Lou Gehrig's disease), for which there is no cure, and normal life expectancy, from time of diagnosis, is two years. Mr. Perlmutter was virtually incapable of movement and unable to breathe without a mechanical respirator, and the prognosis of death was within a short time. The majority failed to distinguish the terminal nature of his condition from Mrs. Wons' condition, from which she could completely recover with treatment. This distinction based on prognosis was explained by the New Jersey Supreme Court in In re Quinlan, 70 N.J. 10, 355 A.2d 647, cert. denied, 429 U.S. 922, 97 S.Ct. 319, 50 L.Ed.2d 289 (1976). * * *

The third flaw in the majority's position is that it totally ignores the fourth factor enunciated in *Perlmutter* and necessarily places doctors and emergency medical facilities in an impossible position by leaving unresolved the issue of when and under what circumstances emergency medical personnel should treat patients who have minor children when they seek treatment but refuse blood transfusions. * * * Although the right to religious beliefs is absolute, the manner in which those beliefs are conducted may clearly be restricted by governmental action, motivated by legitimate governmental interests, such as those concerning minor children, instances involving not only blood transfusions but exposure to death from snake-handling, ingestion of poison, use of illegal drugs, and the requirement of medical vaccines. * * * To justify, as a right of the free exercise of religion, a parent's right to abandon a minor child through a death which is totally unnecessary is, in my view, neither a reasonable nor a logical interpretation of the first amendment. James Madison would not believe that his "free exercise" clause could ever be interpreted in this manner.

* * *

CURTIS v. JASKEY

Appellate Court of Illinois, Second District, 2001.
326 Ill.App.3d 90, 259 Ill.Dec. 901, 759 N.E.2d 962.

JUSTICE GROMETER delivered the opinion of the court:

* * *

Plaintiff sought prenatal care from defendant for the first time in May 1996. She saw defendant three additional times in the period between her first visit and the delivery of her child. During the first visit, plaintiff asserts that she informed defendant that he was not to perform an episiotomy during childbirth and that defendant agreed to her request. Plaintiff further asserts that she reminded defendant of this condition during subsequent visits. Defendant disputes that he agreed that an episiotomy would, under no circumstances, be performed. Instead, he contends that he stated he would try to avoid performing one but would have to make the ultimate decision during delivery. Eventually, the decision was made to induce labor. After arriving at the hospital, plaintiff signed a consent form; however, she crossed out the portion of the form indicating that she was consenting to an episiotomy. Additional conflicting evidence concerning whether plaintiff consented to the procedure exists in the record but need not be set forth here. Approximately five hours after arriving at the hospital, plaintiff delivered her child. Plaintiff's labor progressed very quickly. Shortly before delivery, plaintiff's posterior fourchette began to tear. Defendant performed an episiotomy about two minutes prior to the birth.

Dr. Edward Axelrod testified on defendant's behalf in a discovery deposition. Axelrod opined that the circumstances under which defendant performed the episiotomy constituted a medical emergency. Jaskey, in his discovery deposition, also characterized the situation as an emergency. Axelrod added that, given the circumstances, with plaintiff being in the second stage of labor and in pain, it was impractical for Jaskey to obtain consent for the procedure at that time. Both doctors testified regarding the risks an episiotomy is designed to mitigate. The procedure prevents a ragged and uncontrolled tear that can sometimes extend into the vagina. Copious bleeding, the leading cause of maternal death, can result. Compared to a tear, episiotomies are less painful and more cosmetically appealing. They also facilitate healing.

In ruling upon defendant's motion for summary judgment, the trial court first acknowledged that there is no question that plaintiff did not consent to having an episiotomy performed upon her. However, the trial court felt that the real issue in the case was whether an emergency existed and whether obtaining plaintiff's consent was impractical. It answered both questions affirmatively, relying on the testimony of defendant and Axelrod. Accordingly, the trial court granted summary judgment for defendant.

* * *

In the present case, two overriding factual issues are relevant. First, whether plaintiff consented to the episiotomy is hotly disputed. Plaintiff contends that not only did she not consent to the procedure but also she expressly forbade it. As we are required to construe the record liberally in plaintiff's favor, we must accept this contention for the purpose of resolving this appeal. Second, it is undisputed that defendant performed the episiotomy in circumstances that constituted a medical emergency. Defendant and Axelrod both testified to this. * * *

* * *

A corollary to the requirement that a patient's consent must be obtained prior to the performance of a medical procedure is that a patient is entitled to refuse medical treatment. In fact, absent consent, a patient cannot be compelled to submit to a medical procedure even where the patient's life is in jeopardy. In a medical-battery case, a plaintiff may recover by establishing either a total lack of consent to the procedure performed, that the treatment was contrary to the patient's will, or that the treatment was at substantial variance with the consent granted. [Citation omitted] It is unnecessary for a plaintiff to establish hostile intent on the part of the defendant; rather, the gist of an action for battery is the absence of consent on the plaintiff's part.

There are, of course, exceptions to this rule. At issue in this appeal is what is sometimes referred to as the emergency exception. See Longeway, 133 Ill. 2d at 45. This exception provides a defense to physicians who render care in an emergency situation and is reflected in two of Illinois' pattern jury instructions. See Illinois Pattern Jury Instructions, Civil, Nos. 105.06, 105.07 (2000) (hereinafter IPI Civil). The trial court relied on IPI Civil No. 105.07 in reaching its decision. That instruction provides that consent need not be obtained if "an emergency arises and treatment is required in order to protect the patient's health, and it is impossible or impracticable to obtain consent either from the patient or from someone authorized to consent for him." IPI Civil No. 105.07. As noted above, uncontroverted testimony indicates that a medical emergency existed. However, in this case, we are faced with a rather unique circumstance. Defendant argues, and the trial court held, that the existence of an emergency was sufficient to override plaintiff's express refusal to permit defendant to perform an episiotomy upon her. In order to determine if the emergency exception can work such a result, we must examine its nature and basis.

* * *

The Restatement (Second) of the Law of Torts recognizes that the emergency exception is based on implied consent. It provides:

"Conduct that injures another does not make the actor liable to the other, even though the other has not consented to it if

(a) an emergency makes it necessary or apparently necessary, in order to prevent harm to the other, to act before there is opportunity to obtain consent from the other or one empowered to consent for him, and

(b) the actor has no reason to believe that the other, if he had the opportunity to consent, would decline." Restatement (Second) of Torts § 892D (1979).

This section empowers an individual to act where the other is likely to consent, that is, where action is necessary to prevent harm to the other. Subsection (b) provides a limitation. If the individual has reason to believe that the other would not consent, he may not act. Given a belief that the other would not consent, it becomes impossible to imply consent from the circumstances. The first comment to this section confirms this interpretation, stating that the individual is empowered to act "on the assumption that if the other had the opportunity to decide he would certainly consent." Restatement (Second) of Torts § 892D, Comment a at 380 (1979).

Other jurisdictions also base their versions of the emergency exception on implied consent. In Preston v. Hubbell, 87 Cal.App.2d 53, 196 P.2d 113 (1948), a patient sued her dentist, alleging a battery when the dentist repaired her jaw, which had fractured during the removal of an impacted wisdom tooth. The Preston court framed the issue as whether the "plaintiff did not impliedly consent to the performance of such emergency work as became necessary in order to completely repair a condition that developed during the operation." Preston, 87 Cal.App.2d at 57, 196 P.2d at 115. In deciding this case, the court stated:

"It is the general rule that in cases of emergency, or unanticipated conditions where some immediate action is found necessary for the preservation of the life or health of a patient and it is impractical to first obtain consent to the operation or treatment which the surgeon deems to be immediately necessary, the surgeon is justified in extending the operation to remove and overcome such conditions without the express consent of the patient thereto." Preston, 87 Cal.App.2d at 57–58, 196 P.2d at 115.

The court then held that consent "was implied under the circumstances." Preston, 87 Cal.App.2d at 59, 196 P.2d at 117. The Preston court relied, inter alia, on a Nebraska case that stated, "The general rule requires consent of the patient, but consent may be implied from the circumstances and an operation may be demanded by an emergency without consent." McGuire v. Rix, 118 Neb. 434, 440, 225 N.W. 120, 123 (1929) [additional citations omitted.]

Many jurisdictions have articulated a similar basis for the emergency exception. * * *

Thus, it is clear that the emergency exception is based upon the doctrine of implied consent. In ordinary circumstances, when a physician is confronted with a patient who is unable to consent and is in need of prompt medical attention, it is logical to assume that the patient would consent to the procedure and imply the patient's consent from the circumstances. Where, however, a patient has expressly refused to assent to some procedure, implying consent from the circumstances becomes problematic. This proposition is particularly true where the patient is aware of the risks and benefits of a procedure and makes a considered decision to forgo it.

The mere existence of an emergency that places a patient at risk of future harm does not give a physician "a license to force medical treatment and ignore a patient's exercise of the right to refuse medical treatment." Prairie v. University of Chicago Hospitals, 298 Ill.App.3d 316, 325–26, 232 Ill.Dec. 520, 698 N.E.2d 611 (1998). Where a patient expressly refuses medical treatment, or the patient's instructions specifically preclude the treatment rendered, treatment contrary to the patient's will constitutes a battery even when an emergency exists. Anderson v. St. Francis–St. George Hospital, 83 Ohio App.3d 221, 225–26, 614 N.E.2d 841, 844 (1992). * * *

We recognize that unusual circumstances may exist under which an individual's express refusal to allow some sort of treatment may be disregarded. Consent is a question of fact. [ ] It is conceivable that, in some cases, circumstances could change so as to raise a question regarding whether an individual would persist in a refusal. The Leach court provided the following example:

"A terminally ill patient fully advised of an impending crisis might then be able to refuse treatments which would only prolong suffering, while a patient afflicted with a disease which would be terminal in several years and who had generally expressed a desire to die peacefully would not be denied treatment for injuries sustained in an automobile crash. Both doctor and patient would then be protected from statements not made in contemplation of the specific circumstances and the specific medical treatment required." (Emphasis in original.) [ ].

When a patient's refusal is called into doubt by a change in circumstances, like the automobile accident in the Leach court's example, the refusal becomes one factor to consider in deciding the factual question of whether the patient would have consented under the changed circumstances. Similarly, when a refusal is ambiguous, the trier of fact may properly consider whether the patient intended it to apply to a given factual situation. Under appropriate circumstances, then, it is possible to imply consent despite an earlier refusal to assent to a particular procedure. The key consideration here is whether the patient intended the refusal to apply in the circumstances under which the treatment was rendered. If the circumstances under which the procedure was performed were known to the patient, it is likely that the patient intended the refusal to apply.

Accordingly, we hold that, in the face of a clear refusal to submit to a medical procedure, the emergency exception is inapplicable. In the present case, an issue of fact exists as to whether plaintiff expressly forbade defendant to perform an episiotomy. Consequently, the trial court erred in granting summary judgment for defendant.

Reversed and remanded.

IN RE A.C.

District of Columbia Court of Appeals, 1990.
573 A.2d 1235.

TERRY, J.

This case comes before the court for the second time. In *In re A.C.*, 533 A.2d 611 (D.C. 1987), a three-judge motions division denied a motion to stay an order of the trial court which had authorized a hospital to perform a caesarean section on a dying woman in an effort to save the life of her unborn child. The operation was performed, but both the mother and the child died. A few months later, the court ordered the case heard en banc and vacated the opinion of the motions division. [ ]. Although the motions division recognized that, as a practical matter, it "decided the entire matter when [it] denied the stay," [ ], the en banc court has nevertheless heard the full case on the merits.

We are confronted here with two profoundly difficult and complex issues. First, we must determine who has the right to decide the course of medical treatment for a patient who, although near death, is pregnant with a viable fetus. Second, we must establish how that decision should be made if the patient cannot make it for herself—more specifically, how a court should proceed when faced with a pregnant patient, *in extremis*, who is apparently incapable of making an informed decision regarding medical care for herself and her fetus. We hold that in virtually all cases the question of what is to be done is to be decided by the patient—the pregnant woman—on behalf of herself and the fetus. If the patient is incompetent or otherwise unable to give an informed consent to a proposed course of medical treatment, then her decision must be ascertained through the procedure known as substituted judgment. * * *

I

This case came before the trial court when George Washington University Hospital petitioned the emergency judge in chambers for declaratory relief as to how it should treat its patient, A.C., who was close to death from cancer and was twenty-six and one-half weeks pregnant with a viable fetus. After a hearing lasting approximately three hours, which was held at the hospital (though not in A.C.'s room), the court ordered that a caesarean section be performed on A.C. to deliver the fetus. Counsel for A.C. immediately sought a stay in this court, which was unanimously denied by a hastily assembled division of three judges. [ ]. The caesarean was performed, and a baby girl, L.M.C., was delivered. Tragically, the child died within two and one-half hours, and the mother died two days later.

Counsel for A.C. now maintain that A.C. was competent and that she made an informed choice not to have the caesarean performed. Given this view of the facts, they argue that it was error for the trial court to weigh the state's interest in preserving the potential life of a viable fetus against A.C.'s interest in having her decision respected. They argue further that, even if the substituted judgment procedure had been followed, the evidence would necessarily show that A.C. would not have wanted the caesarean section. Under either analysis, according to these arguments, the trial court erred in subordinating A.C.'s right to bodily integrity in favor of the state's interest in potential life. Counsel for the hospital and for L.M.C. contend, on the other hand, that A.C. was incompetent to make her own medical decisions and that, under the substituted judgment procedure, the evidence clearly established that A.C. would have consented to the caesarean. In the alternative, counsel for L.M.C. argues that even if L.M.C.'s interests and those of the state were in conflict with A.C.'s wishes, it was proper for the trial court to balance their interests and resolve the conflict in favor of surgical intervention.

* * *

II

A.C. was first diagnosed as suffering from cancer at the age of thirteen. In the ensuing years she underwent major surgery several times, together with multiple radiation treatments and chemotherapy. A.C. married when she was twenty-seven, during a period of remission, and soon thereafter she became pregnant. She was excited about her pregnancy and very much wanted the child. Because of her medical history, she was referred in her fifteenth week of pregnancy to the high-risk pregnancy clinic at George Washington University Hospital.

On Tuesday, June 9, 1987, when A.C. was approximately twenty-five weeks pregnant, she went to the hospital for a scheduled check-up. Because she was experiencing pain in her back and shortness of breath, an x-ray was taken, revealing an apparently inoperable tumor which nearly filled her right lung. On Thursday, June 11, A.C. was admitted to the hospital as a patient. By Friday her condition had temporarily improved, and when asked if she really wanted to have her baby, she replied that she did.

Over the weekend A.C.'s condition worsened considerably. Accordingly, on Monday, June 15, members of the medical staff treating A.C. assembled, along with her family, in A.C.'s room. The doctors then informed her that her illness was terminal, and A.C. agreed to palliative treatment designed to extend her life until at least her twenty-eighth week of pregnancy. The "potential outcome [for] the fetus," according to the doctors, would be much better at twenty-eight weeks than at twenty-six weeks if it were necessary to "intervene." A.C. knew that the palliative treatment she had chosen presented some increased risk to the fetus, but she opted for this course both to prolong her life for at least another two weeks and to maintain her own comfort. When asked if she still wanted to have the baby, A.C. was somewhat equivocal, saying "something to the effect of 'I don't know, I think so.'" As the day moved toward evening, A.C.'s condition grew still worse, and at about 7:00 or 8:00 p.m. she consented to intubation to facilitate her breathing.

The next morning, June 16, the trial court convened a hearing at the hospital in response to the hospital's request for a declaratory judgment. The court appointed counsel for both A.C. and the fetus, and the District of Columbia was permitted to intervene for the fetus as *parens patriae*. The court heard testimony on the facts as we have summarized them, and further testimony that at twenty-six and a half weeks the fetus was viable, *i.e.*, capable of sustained life outside of the mother, given artificial aid. * * *

* * *

There was no evidence before the court showing that A.C. consented to, or even contemplated, a caesarean section before her twenty-eighth week of pregnancy. There was, in fact, considerable dispute as to whether she would have consented to an immediate caesarean delivery at the time the hearing was held. A.C.'s mother opposed surgical intervention, testifying that A.C. wanted "to live long enough to hold that baby" and that she expected to do so, "even though she knew she was terminal." Dr. Hamner testified that, given A.C.'s medical problems, he did not think she would have chosen to deliver a child with a substantial degree of impairment. Asked whether A.C. had been "confronted with the question of what to do if there were a choice that ultimately had to be made between her own life expectancy and that of her fetus," he replied that the question "was addressed [but] at a later gestational age." * * *

After hearing this testimony and the arguments of counsel, the trial court made oral findings of fact. It found, first, that A.C. would probably die, according to uncontroverted medical testimony, "within the next twenty-four to forty-eight hours"; second, that A.C. was "pregnant with a twenty-six and a half week viable fetus who, based upon uncontroverted medical testimony, has approximately a fifty to sixty percent chance to survive if a caesarean section is performed as soon as possible"; third, that because the fetus was viable, "the state has [an] important and legitimate interest in protecting the potentiality of human life"; and fourth, that there had been some testimony that the operation "may very well hasten the death of [A.C.]," but that there had also been testimony that delay would greatly increase the risk to the fetus and that "the prognosis is not great for the fetus to be delivered post-mortem. . . . " Most significantly, the court found:

> The court is of the view that it does not clearly know what [A.C.'s] present views are with respect to the issue of whether or not the child should live or die. She's presently unconscious. As late as Friday of last week, she wanted the baby to live. As late as yesterday, she did not know for sure.

Having made these findings of fact and conclusions of law * * * the court ordered that a caesarean section be performed to deliver A.C.'s child.

The court's decision was then relayed to A.C., who had regained consciousness. When the hearing reconvened later in the day, Dr. Hamner told the court [that when he told AC of the court's decision, she agreed to the procedure].

When the court suggested moving the hearing to A.C.'s bedside, Dr. Hamner discouraged the court from doing so, but he and Dr. Weingold, together with A.C.'s mother and husband, went to A.C.'s room to confirm her consent to the procedure. What happened then was recounted to the court a few minutes later:

* * *

> DR. WEINGOLD: She does not make sound because of the tube in her windpipe. She nods and she mouths words. One can see what she's saying rather readily. She asked whether she would survive the operation. She asked [Dr.] Hamner if he would perform the operation. He told her he would only perform it if she authorized it but it would be done in any case. She understood that. She then seemed to pause for a few moments and then very clearly mouthed words several times, *I don't want it done. I don't want it done.* Quite clear to me.
>
> I would obviously state the obvious and that is this is an environment in which, from my perspective as a physician, this would not be an informed consent one way or the other. She's under tremen-

dous stress with the family on both sides, but I'm satisfied that I heard clearly what she said.

* * *

Dr. Weingold later qualified his opinion as to A.C.'s ability to give an informed consent, stating that he thought the environment for an informed consent was non-existent because A.C. was in intensive care, flanked by a weeping husband and mother. He added:

> I think she's in contact with reality, clearly understood who Dr. Hamner was. Because of her attachment to him [she] wanted him to perform the surgery. Understood he would not unless she consented and did not consent.

> That is, in my mind, very clear evidence that she is responding, understanding, and is capable of making such decisions.

Dr. Hamner stated that the sedation had "worn off enough for her to wake up to this state" and that "the level of drugs in her body is much different from several hours ago." Consequently, despite A.C.'s continued sedation, Dr. Weingold said that she was "quite reactive," and Dr. Hamner concurred.

After hearing this new evidence, the court found that it was "still not clear what her intent is" and again ordered that a caesarean section be performed. A.C.'s counsel sought a stay in this court, which was denied. *In re A.C.*, 533 A.2d 611, 613 (D.C. 1987). The operation took place, but the baby lived for only a few hours, and A.C. succumbed to cancer two days later.

* * *

IV

* * *

A. *Informed Consent and Bodily Integrity*

* * *

Thus our analysis of this case begins with the tenet common to all medical treatment cases: that any person has the right to make an informed choice, if competent to do so, to accept or forego medical treatment. The doctrine of informed consent, based on this principle and rooted in the concept of bodily integrity, is ingrained in our common law.

* * *

In the same vein, courts do not compel one person to permit a significant intrusion upon his or her bodily integrity for the benefit of another person's health. *See, e.g., Bonner v. Moran*, 75 U.S.App.D.C. 156, 157, 126 F.2d 121, 122 (1941) (parental consent required for skin graft from fifteen-year-old for benefit of cousin who had been severely burned); *McFall v. Shimp*, 10 Pa. D. & C. 3d 90 (Allegheny County Ct.

1978). In *McFall* the court refused to order Shimp to donate bone marrow which was necessary to save the life of his cousin, McFall:

> The common law has consistently held to a rule which provides that one human being is under no legal compulsion to give aid or to take action to save another human being or to rescue. . . . For our law to *compel* defendant to submit to an intrusion of his body would change every concept and principle upon which our society is founded. To do so would defeat the sanctity of the individual, and would impose a rule which would know no limits, and one could not imagine where the line would be drawn.

Even though Shimp's refusal would mean death for McFall, the court would not order Shimp to allow his body to be invaded. It has been suggested that fetal cases are different because a woman who "has chosen to lend her body to bring [a] child into the world" has an enhanced duty to assure the welfare of the fetus, sufficient even to require her to undergo caesarean surgery. [ ]. Surely, however, a fetus cannot have rights in this respect superior to those of a person who has already been born.

* * *

There are two additional arguments against overriding A.C.'s objections to caesarean surgery. First, as the American Public Health Association cogently states in its *amicus curiae* brief:

> Rather than protecting the health of women and children, court-ordered caesareans erode the element of trust that permits a pregnant woman to communicate to her physician—without fear of reprisal—all information relevant to her proper diagnosis and treatment. An even more serious consequence of court-ordered intervention is that it drives women at high risk of complications during pregnancy and childbirth out of the health care system to avoid coerced treatment.

Second, and even more compellingly, any judicial proceeding in a case such as this will ordinarily take place—like the one before us here—under time constraints so pressing that it is difficult or impossible for the mother to communicate adequately with counsel, or for counsel to organize an effective factual and legal presentation in defense of her liberty and privacy interests and bodily integrity. Any intrusion implicating such basic values ought not to be lightly undertaken * * *.

* * *

B. Substituted Judgment

In the previous section we discussed the right of an individual to accept or reject medical treatment. We concluded that if a patient is competent and has made an informed decision regarding the course of her medical treatment, that decision will control in virtually all cases. Sometimes, however, as our analysis presupposes here, a once competent patient will be unable to render an informed decision. In such a case, we hold that the court must make a substituted judgment on behalf of the patient, based on all the evidence. This means that the duty of the court, "as surrogate for the incompetent, is to determine as best it can what choice that individual, if competent, would make with respect to medical procedures." [ ]

Under the substituted judgment procedure, the court as decision-maker must "substitute itself as nearly as may be for the incompetent, and ... act upon the same motives and considerations as would have moved her...." * * *

We have found no reported opinion applying the substituted judgment procedure to the case of an incompetent pregnant patient whose own life may be shortened by a caesarean section, and whose unborn child's chances of survival may hang on the court's decision. Despite this precedential void, we conclude that substituted judgment is the best procedure to follow in such a case because it most clearly respects the right of the patient to bodily integrity. * * *

We begin with the proposition that the substituted judgment inquiry is primarily a subjective one: as nearly as possible, the court must ascertain what the patient would do if competent. [ ] Due process strongly suggests (and may even require) that counsel or a guardian *ad litem* should be appointed for the patient unless the situation is so urgent that there is no time to do so.

Because it is the patient's decisional rights which the substituted judgment inquiry seeks to protect, courts are in accord that the greatest weight should be given to the previously expressed wishes of the patient. This includes prior statements, either written or oral, even though the treatment alternatives at hand may not have been addressed. * * *

Courts in substituted judgment cases have also acknowledged the importance of probing the patient's value system as an aid in discerning what the patient would choose. We agree with this approach. * * *

Although treating physicians may be an invaluable source of such information about a patient, the family will often be the best source. [ ] Family members or other loved ones will usually be in the best position to say what the patient would do if competent. The court should be mindful, however, that while in the majority of cases family members will have the best interests of the patient in mind, sometimes family members will rely on their own judgments or predilections rather than serving as conduits for expressing the patient's wishes. This is why the court should endeavor, whenever possible, to make an in-person appraisal "of the patient's personal desires and ability for rational choice. In this way the court can always know, to the extent possible, that the judgment is that of the individual concerned and not that of those who believe, however well-intentioned, that they speak for the person whose life is in the balance." [ ]

* * *

The Trial Court's Ruling

[T]he court's specific finding before its decision was communicated to A.C. was as follows:

> The court is of the view that it does not clearly know what [A.C.'s] present views are with respect to the issue of whether or not the child should live or die. She's presently unconscious. As late as Friday of last week, she wanted the baby to live. As late as yesterday, she did not know for sure.

The court did not go on, as it should have done, to make a finding as to what A.C. would have chosen to do if she were competent. Instead, the court undertook to balance the state's and L.M.C.'s interests in surgical intervention against A.C.'s perceived interest in not having the caesarean performed.

After A.C. was informed of the court's decision, she consented to the caesarean; moments later, however, she withdrew her consent. The trial court did not then make a finding as to whether A.C. was competent to make the medical decision or whether she had made an informed decision one way or the other. Nor did the court then make a substituted judgment for A.C. Instead, the court said that it was "still not clear what her intent is" and again ordered the caesarean.

It is that order which we must now set aside. What a trial court must do in a case such as this is to determine, if possible, whether the patient is capable of making an informed decision about the course of her medical treatment. If she is, and if she makes such a decision, her wishes will control in virtually all cases. If the court finds that the patient is incapable of making an informed consent (and thus incompetent), then the court must make a substituted judgment. This means that the court must ascertain as best it can what the patient would do if faced with the particular treatment question. Again, in virtually all cases the decision of the patient, albeit discerned through the mechanism of substituted judgment, will control. We do not quite foreclose the possibility that a conflicting state interest may be so compelling that the patient's wishes must yield, but we anticipate that such cases will be extremely rare and truly exceptional. This is not such a case.

Having said that, we go no further. We need not decide whether, or in what circumstances, the state's interests can ever prevail over the interests of a pregnant patient. We emphasize, nevertheless, that it would be an extraordinary case indeed in which a court might ever be justified in overriding the patient's wishes and authorizing a major surgical procedure such as a caesarean section. Throughout this opinion we have stressed that the patient's wishes, once they are ascertained, must be followed in "virtually all cases," [ ], unless there are "truly extraordinary or compelling reasons to override them," [ ]. Indeed, some may doubt that there could ever be a situation extraordinary or compelling enough to justify a massive intrusion into a person's body, such as a caesarean section, against that person's will. Whether such a situation may someday present itself is a question that we need not strive to answer here. * * *

Notes

1) The *Truman* opinions are unsatisfactory as to why Ms. Truman did not want Dr. Thomas to perform a pap smear, or whether she ever had one. From comparison of the vacated court of appeals opinions, 93 Cal.App.3d 304, 155 Cal.Rptr. 752 (1979), with the supreme court opinions, it seems that Dr. Thomas had performed at least two pelvic examinations upon Ms. Truman and that she wanted to pay cash for the pap test (then $6) but didn't have the cash and refused Dr. Thomas's offer of credit. A prudent physician would record such a refusal, but Dr. Thomas offered no such record, and the inference lurks that where a record of an event should have been made but is not produced, the event never took place.

The practical question that split the California supreme court cannot be answered confidently from the data in the opinions. Assuming that Ms. Truman had no strong objection to pelvic examinations, which are quite intrusive, was it fair for the court to demand that Dr. Thomas try harder to persuade her to have the pap smear, which additional intrusion is negligible, but did increase the expense? *Helling v. Carey*, *supra* at Chapter 2 (glaucoma screening) was discussed but firmly rejected by the court of appeals, which also called this an "informed refusal" case, though the dissent disagreed. Might have it been appropriate to remand *Truman* to the trial court for findings as to whether the patient had knowledge when making her informed refusal?

2) The *Wons* opinion follows the trend of judicial opinions with respect to competent adults, though allowing a patient to die for want of a whole blood transfusion is contrary to most physicians' and hospitals' concept of sound medical practice. Whole blood transfusions are indicated today in only a few situations, but where the patient has suffered major blood loss, only whole blood can maintain oxygenation.

For incompetent adults and minors, the trend is not yet clear, and the developments are complicated by such rules as the emancipation of minors and the age of decision making. Jehovah's Witnesses often carry a card expressing their lack of consent to whole blood transfusion, even under emergency circumstances. In some communities there are doctors who will perform elective surgery with minimal blood loss, and arrangements can be made for prior drawing and storage of the patient's own blood in case transfusion is indicated. The health care proxy or durable power of attorney may make it easier to communicate a patient's wishes in case of emergency. When this circumstance arises, the health care provider needs to be ready with procedures that cope with skepticism and contradiction. The Jehovah's Witness usually signs the card when healthy and without specific contemplation of death. Physicians are accustomed to patients who lose their fatalism on the deathbed. What happens when the patient, who carries a card, is then heard to tell the physician "you decide for me?" Allowing such a patient to die is neither good medicine nor good law. Waiting for an appropriate surrogate decision maker is negligence. Often there is less (legal) risk involved in forcibly saving the patients' life, though it is better to respect a patient's wishes as long as they are expressed clearly.

3) *Curtis* involves yet another alleged emergency exception to the need for informed consent. It is not clear that the physician in *Curtis* ever expressly informed the patient of the likelihood of the posterior fourchette tearing and what would be done under those circumstances. Was that discussion warranted in view of plaintiff's alleged adamant objection to an episiotomy? Is it still an emergency when the emergency circumstances are reasonably foreseeable?

4) *In re: A.C.* should be read in conjunction with the cases in Chapter 14, Section A. As a matter purely pertaining to informed consent, it is clear that no consent was present at the time of the operation. Consent might have been given and thereafter revoked; it might have been never legitimately obtained. Consent presumes the patient is competent to give consent. That competence is a legal determination, but more often than not physicians are required to make it.

In Chapter 14, the inquiry will be different. There the court might be asked to determine whether a woman should have the right under certain compelling circumstances to deprive her fetus of a chance of survival when the consequence to the mother in so doing is relatively minimal.

SECTION C.   CONSENT TO RESEARCH

MOORE v. THE REGENTS OF THE UNIVERSITY OF CALIFORNIA

Supreme Court of California, 1990.
51 Cal.3d 120, 271 Cal.Rptr. 146, 793 P.2d 479.

PANELLI, J.

* * *

II. FACTS

* * *

The plaintiff is John Moore (Moore), who underwent treatment for hairy-cell leukemia at the Medical Center of the University of California at Los Angeles (UCLA Medical Center). The five defendants are: (1) Dr. David W. Golde (Golde), a physician who attended Moore at UCLA Medical Center; (2) the Regents of the University of California (Regents), who own and operate the university; (3) Shirley G. Quan, a researcher employed by the Regents; (4) Genetics Institute, Inc. (Genetics Institute); and (5) Sandoz Pharmaceuticals Corporation and related entities (collectively Sandoz).

Moore first visited UCLA Medical Center on October 5, 1976, shortly after he learned that he had hairy-cell leukemia. After hospitalizing Moore and "withdr[awing] extensive amounts of blood, bone marrow aspirate, and other bodily substances," Golde confirmed that diagnosis. At this time all defendants, including Golde, were aware that "certain blood products and blood components were of great value in a number of commercial and scientific efforts" and that access to a patient whose blood contained these substances would provide "competitive, commercial, and scientific advantages."

On October 8, 1976, Golde recommended that Moore's spleen be removed. Golde informed Moore "that he had reason to fear for his life, and that the proposed splenectomy operation . . . was necessary to slow down the progress of his disease." Based upon Golde's representations, Moore signed a written consent form authorizing the splenectomy.

Before the operation, Golde and Quan "formed the intent and made arrangements to obtain portions of [Moore's] spleen following its removal" and to take them to a separate research unit. Golde gave written instructions to this effect on October 18 and 19, 1976. These research activities "were not intended to have . . . any relation to [Moore's] medical . . . care." However, neither Golde nor Quan informed Moore of their plans to conduct this research or requested his permission. Surgeons at UCLA Medical Center, whom the complaint does not name as defendants, removed Moore's spleen on October 20, 1976.

Moore returned to the UCLA Medical Center several times between November 1976 and September 1983. He did so at Golde's direction and based upon representations "that such visits were necessary and required for his health and well-being, and based upon the trust inherent in and by virtue of the physician-patient relationship. . . . " On each of these visits Golde withdrew additional samples of "blood, blood serum, skin, bone marrow aspirate, and sperm." On each occasion Moore travelled to the UCLA Medical Center from his home in Seattle because he had been told that the procedures were to be performed only there and only under Golde's direction.

"In fact, [however,] throughout the period of time that [Moore] was under [Golde's] care and treatment, . . . the defendants were actively involved in a number of activities which they concealed from [Moore]. . . . " Specifically, defendants were conducting research on Moore's cells and planned to "benefit financially and competitively . . . [by exploiting the cells] and [their] exclusive access to [the cells] by virtue of [Golde's] ongoing physician-patient relationship. . . . "

Sometime before August 1979, Golde established a cell line from Moore's T-lymphocytes.[2] On January 30, 1981, the Regents applied for a

---

2. A T-lymphocyte is a type of white blood cell. T-lymphocytes produce lymphokines, or proteins that regulate the immune system. Some lymphokines have potential therapeutic value. If the genetic material responsible for producing a particular lymphokine can be identified, it can sometimes be used to manufacture large quantities of the lymphokine through the techniques of recombinant DNA. * * *

patent on the cell line, listing Golde and Quan as inventors. "[B]y virtue of an established policy ... , [the] Regents, Golde, and Quan would share in any royalties or profits ... arising out of [the] patent." The patent issued on March 20, 1984, naming Golde and Quan as the inventors of the cell line and the Regents as the assignee of the patent. (U.S. Patent No. 4,438,032 (Mar. 20, 1984).)

The Regents' patent also covers various methods for using the cell line to produce lymphokines. Moore admits in his complaint that "the true clinical potential of each of the lymphokines ... [is] difficult to predict, [but] ... competing commercial firms in these relevant fields have published reports in biotechnology industry periodicals predicting a potential market of approximately $3.01 Billion Dollars by the year 1990 for a whole range of [such lymphokines].... "

With the Regents' assistance, Golde negotiated agreements for commercial development of the cell line and products to be derived from it. Under an agreement with Genetics Institute, Golde "became a paid consultant" and "acquired the rights to 75,000 shares of common stock." Genetics Institute also agreed to pay Golde and the Regents "at least $330,000 over three years, including a pro-rata share of [Golde's] salary and fringe benefits, in exchange for ... exclusive access to the materials and research performed" on the cell line and products derived from it. On June 4, 1982, Sandoz "was added to the agreement," and compensation payable to Golde and the Regents was increased by $110,000. "[T]hroughout this period, ... Quan spent as much as 70 [percent] of her time working for [the] Regents on research" related to the cell line.

III. DISCUSSION

A. *Breach of Fiduciary Duty and Lack of Informed Consent*

Moore repeatedly alleges that Golde failed to disclose the extent of his research and economic interests in Moore's cells before obtaining consent to the medical procedures by which the cells were extracted. These allegations, in our view, state a cause of action against Golde for invading a legally protected interest of his patient. This cause of action

---

While the genetic code for lymphokines does not vary from individual to individual, it can nevertheless be quite difficult to locate the gene responsible for a particular lymphokine. Because T-lymphocytes produce many different lymphokines, the relevant gene is often like a needle in a haystack. [ ] Moore's T-lymphocytes were interesting to the defendants because they overproduced certain lymphokines, thus making the corresponding genetic material easier to identify. (In published research papers, defendants and other researchers have shown that the overproduction was caused by a virus, and that normal T-lymphocytes infected by the virus will also overproduce.) [ ]

Cells taken directly from the body (primary cells) are not very useful for these purposes. Primary cells typically reproduce a few times and then die. One can, however, sometimes continue to use cells for an extended period of time by developing them into a "cell line," a culture capable of reproducing indefinitely. This is not, however, always an easy task. "Longterm growth of human cells and tissues is difficult, often an art," and the probability of succeeding with any given cell sample is low, except for a few types of cells not involved in this case. [ ]

can properly be characterized either as the breach of a fiduciary duty to disclose facts material to the patient's consent or, alternatively, as the performance of medical procedures without first having obtained the patient's informed consent.

Our analysis begins with three well-established principles. First, "a person of adult years and in sound mind has the right, in the exercise of control over his own body, to determine whether or not to submit to lawful medical treatment." * * * Second, "the patient's consent to treatment, to be effective, must be an informed consent." * * * Third, in soliciting the patient's consent, a physician has a fiduciary duty to disclose all information material to the patient's decision. [Citations omitted].

These principles lead to the following conclusions: (1) a physician must disclose personal interests unrelated to the patient's health, whether research or economic, that may affect the physician's professional judgment; and (2) a physician's failure to disclose such interests may give rise to a cause of action for performing medical procedures without informed consent or breach of fiduciary duty.

* * *

Indeed, the law already recognizes that a reasonable patient would want to know whether a physician has an economic interest that might affect the physician's professional judgment. As the Court of Appeal has said, "[c]ertainly a sick patient deserves to be free of any reasonable suspicion that his doctor's judgment is influenced by a profit motive." [ ] The desire to protect patients from possible conflicts of interest has also motivated legislative enactments. Among these is Business and Professions Code section 654.2. Under that section, a physician may not charge a patient on behalf of, or refer a patient to, any organization in which the physician has a "significant beneficial interest, unless [the physician] first discloses in writing to the patient, that there is such an interest and advises the patient that the patient may choose any organization for the purposes of obtaining the services ordered or requested by [the physician]." [ ] [referrals to clinical laboratories]. Similarly, under Health and Safety Code section 24173, a physician who plans to conduct a medical experiment on a patient must, among other things, inform the patient of "[t]he name of the sponsor or funding source, if any, ... and the organization, if any, under whose general aegis the experiment is being conducted." [ ]

It is important to note that no law prohibits a physician from conducting research in the same area in which he practices. Progress in medicine often depends upon physicians, such as those practicing at the university hospital where Moore received treatment, who conduct research while caring for their patients.

Yet a physician who treats a patient in whom he also has a research interest has potentially conflicting loyalties. This is because medical treatment decisions are made on the basis of proportionality—weighing the benefits *to the patient* against the risks *to the patient*. As another court has said, "the determination as to whether the burdens of treatment are worth enduring for any individual patient depends upon the facts unique in each case," and "the patient's interests and desires are the key ingredients of the decision-making process." [ ] A physician who adds his own research interests to this balance may be tempted to order a scientifically useful procedure or test that offers marginal, or no, benefits to the patient. n8 The possibility that an interest extraneous to the patient's health has affected the physician's judgment is something that a reasonable patient would want to know in deciding whether to consent to a proposed course of treatment. It is material to the patient's decision and, thus, a prerequisite to informed consent. [ ]

Golde argues that the scientific use of cells that have already been removed cannot possibly affect the patient's medical interests. The argument is correct in one instance but not in another. If a physician has no plans to conduct research on a patient's cells at the time he recommends the medical procedure by which they are taken, then the patient's medical interests have not been impaired. In that instance the argument is correct. On the other hand, a physician who does have a preexisting research interest might, consciously or unconsciously, take that into consideration in recommending the procedure. In that instance the argument is incorrect: the physician's extraneous motivation may affect his judgment and is, thus, material to the patient's consent.

We acknowledge that there is a competing consideration. To require disclosure of research and economic interests may corrupt the patient's own judgment by distracting him from the requirements of his health. But California law does not grant physicians unlimited discretion to decide what to disclose. Instead, "it is the prerogative of the patient, not the physician, to determine for himself the direction in which he believes his interests lie." (*Cobbs* v. *Grant, supra* [ ]) "Unlimited discretion in the physician is irreconcilable with the basic right of the patient to make the ultimate informed decision. . . . " [ ]

Accordingly, we hold that a physician who is seeking a patient's consent for a medical procedure must, in order to satisfy his fiduciary duty and to obtain the patient's informed consent, disclose personal interests unrelated to the patient's health, whether research or economic, that may affect his medical judgment.

1. Dr. Golde

We turn now to the allegations of Moore's third amended complaint to determine whether he has stated such a cause of action. We first discuss the adequacy of Moore's allegations against Golde, based upon the physician's disclosures prior to the splenectomy.

Moore alleges that, prior to the surgical removal of his spleen, Golde "formed the intent and made arrangements to obtain portions of his spleen following its removal from [Moore] in connection with [his] desire to have regular and continuous access to, and possession of, [Moore's] unique and rare Blood and Bodily Substances." Moore was never informed prior to the splenectomy of Golde's "prior formed intent" to obtain a portion of his spleen. In our view, these allegations adequately show that Golde had an undisclosed research interest in Moore's cells at the time he sought Moore's consent to the splenectomy. Accordingly, Moore has stated a cause of action for breach of fiduciary duty, or lack of informed consent, based upon the disclosures accompanying that medical procedure.

We next discuss the adequacy of Golde's alleged disclosures regarding the postoperative takings of blood and other samples. In this context, Moore alleges that Golde "expressly, affirmatively and impliedly represented . . . that these withdrawals of his Blood and Bodily Substances were necessary and required for his health and well-being." However, Moore also alleges that Golde actively concealed his economic interest in Moore's cells during this time period. "[D]uring each of these visits . . . , and even when [Moore] inquired as to whether there was any possible or potential commercial or financial value or significance of his Blood and Bodily Substances, or whether the defendants had discovered anything . . . which was or might be . . . related to any scientific activity resulting in commercial or financial benefits . . . , the defendants repeatedly and affirmatively represented to [Moore] that there was no commercial or financial value to his Blood and Bodily Substances . . . and in fact actively discouraged such inquiries."

Moore admits in his complaint that defendants disclosed they "were engaged in strictly academic and purely scientific medical research. . . . " However, Golde's representation that he had no financial interest in this research became false, based upon the allegations, at least by May 1979, when he "began to investigate and initiate the procedures . . . for [obtaining] a patent" on the cell line developed from Moore's cells.

In these allegations, Moore plainly asserts that Golde concealed an economic interest in the postoperative procedures. Therefore, applying the principles already discussed, the allegations state a cause of action for breach of fiduciary duty or lack of informed consent.

We thus disagree with the superior court's ruling that Moore had not stated a cause of action because essential allegations were lacking. We discuss each such allegation. First, in the superior court's view, Moore needed but failed to allege that defendants knew his cells had potential commercial value *on October 5, 1976* (the time blood tests were first performed at UCLA Medical Center) and had *at that time* already formed the intent to exploit the cells. We agree with the superior court that the absence of such allegations precludes Moore from stating a cause of action based upon the procedures undertaken on October 5, 1976. But, as already discussed, Moore clearly alleges that Golde had developed a research interest in his cells by October 20, 1976, when the splenectomy was performed. Thus, Moore can state a cause of action based upon Golde's alleged failure to disclose that interest before the splenectomy.

The superior court also held that the lack of essential allegations prevented Moore from stating a cause of action based on the splenectomy. According to the superior court, Moore failed to allege that the operation lacked a therapeutic purpose or that the procedure was totally unrelated to therapeutic purposes. In our view, however, neither allegation is essential. Even if the splenectomy had a therapeutic purpose, it does not follow that Golde had no duty to disclose his additional research and economic interests. As we have already discussed, the existence of a motivation for a medical procedure unrelated to the patient's health is a potential conflict of interest and a fact material to the patient's decision.

* * *

Affirmed in part and reversed in part.

GOODMAN v. UNITED STATES OF AMERICA

United States Court of Appeals for the Ninth Circuit, 2002.
298 F.3d 1048.

GOULD, Circuit Judge:

* * *

I.

In 1990, JoAnn Goodman, then a thirty-six year old wife and mother who resided in the eastern part of the State of Washington, was diagnosed with advanced melanoma in her scalp. The cancer was excised, but because of the depth of the tumor, JoAnn Goodman's prognosis was poor. By 1995, the cancer had spread to JoAnn Goodman's liver. Despite extensive chemotherapy, the tumors in JoAnn Goodman's liver did not decrease.

In March of 1995, JoAnn Goodman and her treating physician discussed the possibility that Mrs. Goodman might participate in an experimental clinical study at the National Cancer Institute ("NCI") of the NIH, in Bethesda, Maryland. The study was conceived and directed by the NIH's Dr. Douglas Fraker. This experimental clinical study required patients to undergo a major surgery called isolated liver perfusion ("ILP"). This involved isolating the liver from the rest of the body and then administering increasing doses of a cancer fighting drug, Melphalan, in combination with Tumor Necrosis Factor ("TNF") directly to the tumor. Dr. Fraker wrote the protocol for the ILP and submitted it for review to the Institutional Review Board ("IRB") of the NCI. It received approval from the IRB. The IRB also approved the consent form for patients, such as JoAnn Goodman, who chose to participate in the ILP study.

On April 14, 1995, JoAnn Goodman and her father-in-law traveled from Washington state to Maryland to discuss with NIH doctors whether JoAnn Goodman was eligible to participate in the ILP study. There, they met with Dr. Fraker and Dr. H. Richard Alexander, another doctor involved with the study. JoAnn Goodman discussed the ILP procedure with the NIH doctors. A copy of the consent form was given to her and it was explained.

After her April trip to the NIH, JoAnn Goodman returned home to Washington where she underwent further tests to see if her cancer had spread to other areas. The tests revealed that JoAnn Goodman now had three tumors in her liver. But the cancer had not yet spread to other areas. On June 8, 1995, JoAnn Goodman's treating physician noted in his chart that:

> [JoAnn Goodman] is not able to work, wants to be active, and has a strong personal preference for going ahead with the isolated liver perfusion study. She understands quite well, I think, that it may have only a small chance of helping her, since she has a rapidly growing disease.

Shortly thereafter, JoAnn Goodman returned to the NIH where she was prepared for her ILP surgery.

The day before the surgery, Dr. Alexander discussed with JoAnn Goodman the procedure, the plan for dose escalation, and the experience of the three prior NIH patients who had undergone the ILP procedure at the same dosage levels of the drugs. JoAnn Goodman was, once again, presented with a consent form to participate in the experimental protocol for ILP.[3] JoAnn Goodman signed the form. The next day, she underwent the experimental ILP procedure involving the combined use of Melphalan and TNF. The surgery lasted ten hours.

Tragically, the dosage of Melphalan used during the surgery caused liver toxicity and veno-occlusive disease ("VOD"). VOD is a syndrome where the small blood vessels in the liver are blocked, leading to a lack of circulation and death of the tissue. None of the NIH's prior ILP patients had suffered from VOD. Over the next six weeks, JoAnn Goodman

---

3. This form was identical to the one given to JoAnn Goodman in April during her initial visit to the NIH and it contained the following language:

> Isolated liver perfusion is a major surgical procedure performed in the operating room. During the operation the blood vessels to and from the liver are controlled so that very high concentrations of chemotherapy drugs can be delivered to your liver where the tumor is located. By isolating the liver from the rest of the body large amounts of drug that would be toxic if given by arm vein can be used. The type of drugs used in this study are experimental agents called Tumor Necrosis Factor (TNF) and melphalan.
>
> * * *
>
> Tumor necrosis factor and melphalan have not been used for isolated liver perfusion in patients before. The treatment

you will receive is designed to determine if TNF and melphalan cause side effects when used in isolated liver perfusion and to determine what dose of these drugs can be used safely in this procedure. Your liver tumor might decrease in size in response to the treatment, although the chance of response cannot be predetermined since we have no experience using this type of treatment. Since the treatment drugs are isolated to the liver, this treatment will only effect [sic] tumor in the liver.

> * * *
>
> The side effects of TNF and melphalan in the liver are not completely known but may include liver failure, abnormal blood clotting, or jaundice. The operative procedure itself may cause clotting or blockage of blood vessels to and from the liver leading to liver failure or accumulation of fluid in your abdomen or lower body.

suffered and was given the pain reliever drug, Toradol. JoAnn Goodman died on August 5, 1995.

II.

* * * Paul Goodman, in his individual capacity, filed an administrative claim with the U.S. Department of Health and Human Services ("HHS"), for the wrongful death of his wife [claiming] among other things, that his wife "died of things and/or mistakes while at the NIH where she was receiving treatment." Paul Goodman also [alleged] that the Toradol given to JoAnn Goodman after the ILP surgery "was a mistake and more than likely complicated her condition." Paul Goodman's administrative claim also stated that "things ... were overlooked in the procedure and [JoAnn Goodman] should not have died." In May, 1997, the HHS denied Paul Goodman's claim stating:

> There is no evidence that the death of Mrs. Jo Ann [sic] Goodman was a result of negligence on the part of NIH physicians. Mrs. Goodman underwent an experimental treatment for liver cancer, which involved a risk of death. Mrs. Goodman was well informed of this risk when she gave her consent to undergo the experimental treatment. Her death was the result of a disclosed complication of the treatment rather than any act or omission of NIH physicians.

* * * [Plaintiff thereafter] amend[ed his] complaint and add[ed] a claim for lack of informed consent * * * claiming, *inter alia*, that the NIH doctors failed to warn JoAnn Goodman of the foreseeable risks involved in the ILP surgery and failed to obtain legally effective informed consent.

* * *

IV.

Having addressed the threshold jurisdictional issues, we now address the merits of Paul Goodman's claims that the NIH doctors failed to: (1) inform JoAnn Goodman of the foreseeable risks of the ILP surgery, such as VOD; and (2) obtain a supplemental written consent form in light of the fact that earlier ILP patients had suffered complications from the surgery.

A.

We first address Paul Goodman's argument that NIH doctors failed to warn JoAnn Goodman of the foreseeable risks of ILP surgery, including the possibility that she could suffer VOD. This argument is unpersuasive.

Under Maryland's informed consent doctrine, a physician has a duty "to explain the procedure to the patient and to warn him [or her] of any material risks or dangers inherent in or collateral to the therapy, so as to enable the patient to make an intelligent and informed choice about whether or not to undergo such treatment." [ ] This duty to explain and warn requires the physician to disclose "the nature of the ailment, the nature of the proposed treatment, the probability of success of the contemplated therapy and its alternatives, *and the risk of unfortunate consequences associated with such treatment."* [ ]

Here, the NIH doctors adequately informed JoAnn Goodman of the known material risks associated with the surgery. Furthermore, the record supports the conclusion that the NIH doctors were not, and could not reasonably have been, aware that VOD would occur at the dosage level used in JoAnn Goodman's ILP procedure. As the district court explained after hearing examination of many witnesses, including medical experts, "no expert testimony disputed that position and no other patient in an earlier group participating in [the ILP] study had experienced VOD." It is tragic when death occurs following risky medical procedures based on complications. But in the battle against deadly diseases, progress often will be made only when medical experimentation is permitted. Doctors must give fair warnings of risks that are known or that reasonably should have been known by them. However, here, the NIH doctors were not required to warn JoAnn Goodman, as she embarked bravely on an experimental procedure that might have helped her and others, of an unperceived risk of which they reasonably were not aware.

B.

Next we address Paul Goodman's contention that further supplementation of the written consent form was required. According to Paul Goodman, the written consent form should have incorporated the complications experienced by the three earlier patients at the NIH who underwent the same ILP procedure as JoAnn Goodman. Again, we find this argument unpersuasive. As the district court recognized, "there is no legal requirement that the consent form developed for [the ILP] study must be amended as each group of patients proceeds through the study." To hold that the signed consent form was inadequate would require the NIH to update its already detailed consent form every time a patient experiences any sort of complication from an experimental procedure. The NIH was not required to update the consent form under these circumstances. The consent form and procedures were medically reasonable and legally adequate.

V.

The district court had jurisdiction to decide Paul Goodman's claim. The district court held a full and fair trial on the factual and legal issues pertinent to whether JoAnn Goodman was fairly warned of the risks of the experimental ILP procedure that preceded her tragic death. The factual determinations crediting the NIH doctors' testimony are significant, and such decisions are routinely and properly entrusted to the trier of fact, here the district court, which saw the witnesses who were examined and cross-examined by diligent counsel on both sides. We cannot properly reverse the dispositive factual findings, and we conclude that there was no error in the law applied by the district court. We affirm the decision of the district court denying the claim for lack of informed consent.

AFFIRMED.

Notes

1) In *Moore,* the ex-owner of the spleen that was removed as therapy for leukemia was held to state claims against the surgeon and a number of others for breach of fiduciary duty and lack of informed consent, but not for conversion of property, which might have led to enormous damages for the cell-line that researchers and manufacturers grew out, patented and sold. Ordinarily the removed spleen would have been abandoned by the patient to the hospital which could have used it for research. In *Moore,* however, the surgeon knew that Mr. Moore had rare genetic material and hoped, accurately but secretly, that the spleen would enable the large-scale reproduction of a type of white blood cells. There were three separate opinions, two dissenting in whole or in part as to conversion.

2) In *Goodman,* the plaintiff, diagnosed with an incurable melanoma, agreed to participate in an experimental protocol that required a surgical procedure and a high dose of a cancer-fighting drug used during the surgery. On plaintiff's claim of lack of informed consent, the court found that the form signed by Goodman was ¿¿medically reasonable and legally adequate." In high-risk experimental protocols, what else might the physician have done to ensure that the patient is adequately informed of the risks of the procedure? Are patients whose circumstances are dire considered decisionally impaired, and should there be a special form of consent that applies to patients under these circumstances?

Notes on Liability in Biomedical Research

1. Research Distinguished from Treatment. Traditional medical ethics define medical practice as treatment that is intended to improve illnesses and conditions. The Belmont Report,[1] which is the foundation of U.S. biomedical research ethics, first defines "practice." "[T]he term 'practice' refers to interventions that are designed solely to enhance the well-being of an individual patient or client and that have a reasonable expectation of success." Ethics committees assist physicians in preparing treatment plans. Experience with good medical practice may benefit other patients, but the general benefit is incidental to an individual treatment.

Biomedical research on drugs and devices is different from medical treatment. "[T]he term 'research' designates an activity designed to test an hypothesis, permit conclusions to be drawn, and thereby to develop or contribute to generalizable knowledge (expressed, for example, in theories, principles, and statements of relationships)."[2] As research has become distinct from treatment, good research on humans has been defined in a separate ethical framework that fits human rights into medical science.

1. Ethical Principles and Guidelines for the Protection of Human Subjects of Research (Nat. Comm'n for Protection of Human Subjects of Biomedical and Behavioral Research 1979), 44 Fed.Reg. 23,192 (Apr. 18, 1979).

2. Ibid.

2. Conflicts of Interests and Roles. Conflicts of economic interests in medical practice are managed. For example, the treating physician legitimately expects to be paid for services rendered, while the bill-payer wants to pay as little as possible; the conflict is managed by negotiated payment and reimbursement systems. Non-economic conflicts may not be manageable. The patient who doesn't like the doctor can get another doctor. But physicians are reluctant to treat their children and their close kin, with or without compensation, because this confuses the roles of family and physician, and a physician may avoid the conflict of roles rather than take the risk of failing to manage it.

Physicians have different roles in treatment and research, and the difference affects their professional engagement and detachment. The treating physician is engaged primarily with the patient, and the engagement is more than bedside manner or subservience, it is central to the role. If engagement with the patient calls for unconventional treatment, good medical practice supports the treating physician. If the best interests of the patient call for causing pain, detachment enables the treating physician to order painful treatment.

The medical scientist is engaged primarily with science, and science single-mindedly demands clear hypotheses, rigorous research plans, and clean data. The medical scientist's detachment from the patient is based on the ethics of science, not on the ethics of treatment. Proper professional concern for subjects' rights should not warp the structure or corrupt the outcome of good science.

Another investigator interest has the power to affect research subjects. Performing research benefits the investigator, both through payment from the sponsors of drugs and devices, and through enhanced status for the scientist, especially in the academic medical community. Ethical investigators accept these corollaries as manageable conflicts of interest, not as unacceptable conflicts of roles, but in order to avoid the appearance of exploiting subjects, the process of management needs to be set forth clearly and applied faithfully.

The cases on consent to treatment raised liability questions that are complex and controversial. The cases on medical research are not so numerous; instances of harm from medical research tend to be covered dramatically in the press and then settled quietly without trial. The law is clear that research without consent exposes the investigator to liability, and the experience is clear that the "informed consent form" originated to forestall liability.

3. Research on New Drugs. (a) The Phases of Testing. After laboratory and animal studies demonstrate that a new drug may be beneficial without producing unacceptable side-effects, the sponsor submits the test data and a research plan (protocol) to the U.S. Food and Drug Administration (FDA). If the FDA approves of testing, it issues a numbered investigational drug exemption (IDE), without which the administration of the unapproved drug would be illegal. The medical scientist in charge of a testing program is the "investigator." Some programs use in-patients; others use out-patients. A sponsor may contract-out the design and performance of a testing program. Agents of the sponsor will monitor the investigator's performance.

Phase 1 is the first test on humans. The subjects usually are healthy volunteers who are paid for being "human pincushions," so-called because of the frequent blood-draws to measure the drug in the body. If the normal body responds predictably to the drug, and if the side-effects are acceptable, the tests go on to the next phase.

Phase 2 tests the drug on subjects who have the disease or condition that the drug is supposed to improve. The criteria are "safety" and "efficacy," which means that without doing unacceptable harm, the drug does some good for some subjects.

Phase 3 again tests the drug on subjects who have the disease or condition, this time to measure responses and side-effects for varying doses. Because some subjects respond simply to being tested, the protocol may provide that by chance, part of the subjects will receive "placebo," an inert substance that subjects cannot differentiate from the active drug. This is a "single-blind" study. In a "double-blind" study, the investigator also does not know which subjects receive placebo. Without consent, the blinding would unlawfully mislead subjects. In another type of study design, the test drug is compared with a marketed drug, usually on a blinded basis.

If Phase 3 tests produce results that the sponsor and the FDA regard as favorable, the FDA will approve the marketing of the drug, accompanied by a description of indications and doses (the "package insert") that is addressed to treating physicians who prescribe the new drug. After a new drug is marketed, physicians' use of the drug is within the practice of medicine, which the FDA does not regulate. Physicians may prescribe the drug "off-label"—that is, for conditions and patients not covered by the package insert—harmonizing the risk of medical negligence with the prospect of improved patient care.

(b) The Institutional Review Board (IRB). Institutional review boards (IRBs) are mandated by statute[3] and defined in federal regulations,[4] but the IRB is not a governmental organization, and its members are vulnerable to suit by subjects for the negligent performance of their regulatory duties. A research phase cannot go forward without IRB approval of both the protocol and the informed consent form (ICF).

The core of an IRB is a pool of scientifically qualified persons. A quorum of the IRB must meet on stated occasions. Minutes list the members who attended, summarize the proposals presented, and record the gist and outcome of debate. Most of the members have scientific expertise in the field of the proposed research, and many will be on the same staff as the investigator—hence "institutional." Intermittent IRB membership of most physicians on a medical institution's staff is regarded as a rotating educational requirement that accrues no pay or credit. A person such as a minister of religion, a social worker, or even a lawyer, can be the required "public member," who is not to be a colleague of the medical scientists, and who has informed views on the ethics of human research. The institution's liability insurance should provide first-party coverage to all members of the IRB.

---

3. 42 U.S.C.A. § 289.

4. 21 CFR part 50, Protection of Human Subjects, and 21 CFR part 56, Institutional Review Boards.

"Independent" IRBs developed late in the twentieth century, initially as the response to out-patient research. Independent IRBs are profit-making organizations that advertise familiarity with the IRB process, frequent meetings, large pools of scientific members, and specialized staffs to whom copious paperwork and frequent follow-ups are not a sideline to regular duties. Health care institutions that could have their own IRBs are now saving resources by hiring independent IRBs. The independent IRBs have created their own accrediting agencies that operate outside the government. Liability protection of an independent IRB rests upon the IRB's insurance and its indemnification agreements with sponsors.

(c) What the IRB Does. In reviewing a protocol, the IRB decides whether an informed subject could rationally participate in the research as it is designed. A scientific reviewer should not urge the IRB to disapprove a protocol because the research would better have been designed in a different way, but an IRB should disapprove a protocol whose design would unnecessarily or unreasonably expose subjects to dangers.

In reviewing an ICF, the IRB must find that the ICF expresses the voluntariness of the prospective participant. An investigator may not deploy a human as the *object* of biomedical research, but a human may consent to be the *subject* of biomedical research, provided the consent is "informed." Italicizing "object" and "subject" illustrates the ethical distinction. Research people who use *consent* as a transitive verb, as in "go consent the patient," may reveal unawareness of the ethical distinction.

The preamble to the federal regulations protects voluntariness by stating one principle and one limit.[5]

The principle is that the subject is entitled to due process of medicine: the decision about consent is to be presented under circumstances that provide the "opportunity to consider whether or not to participate and that minimize the possibility of coercion or undue influence," and the subject must understand the language of presentation.

The limit is expressed by the regulation that defines and forbids exculpatory language in an ICF: "language through which the subject or the representative is made to waive or appear to waive any of the subject's legal rights, or releases or appears to release the investigator, the sponsor, the institution or its agents from liability for negligence." Waiver and release may be appropriate in contracts between equals, but they are out of place in an ICF.

The federal regulations prescribe several explanatory components for every ICF: the participation involves research as distinct from treatment; participation has listed risks, discomforts, benefits, and expenses; there may be treatment alternatives; the publication of research results threatens subject confidentiality in ways that treatment does not; and contact names, addresses, and phone numbers for both the IRB and the investigator enable the subject to ask questions. Other components must appear in ICFs where they fit the research.

5.   45 CFR § 46.116 (1988).

The IRB prescribes the interval for review of ongoing research—often six months, sometimes one year. Regular review exposes problems such as failure to enroll any subjects, insufficient records, unreported changes of investigators, and the investigator's desire to terminate the research by simply stopping work.

The IRB process does not always work satisfactorily. If a medical institution's culture trivializes the IRB process as only an impediment to research, the institution can lose its eligibility to conduct research,[6] and investigators can lose FDA permission to test drugs and devices.[7] In recent years FDA audits and institutions' inadequate responses have caused the FDA to shut down research at prominent medical centers. When research resumes, the IRB process must function.

4. Liability: Theories of Claim and Defense. A research subject who suffers harm from causes outside or in excess of consent may sue the persons and organizations involved in the research. The most common theories of claim are listed below, and modern pleading lets the plaintiff join these and other theories in a single complaint.

(a) Battery. The battery claim requires the subject to show an intentional touching (including ingestion and injection) without consent or in excess of consent. Medical expert testimony may be required in order to show the causal connection between touching and harm, but medical expert testimony to show fault is not required because, unlike the claim for negligence, the battery claim has no such element. The investigator will deny the battery, the causation, and the harm, but it is difficult for the investigator to win without trial.

The affirmative defense to battery is consent, by which the defendant asserts that if there was a touching, and if it caused harm, the plaintiff subject consented to the touching and the harm. Consent may vindicate the investigator by summary judgment. While consent may be oral, good research practice calls for a written instrument, the ICF, which seeks to record both the consent and the informational basis for the consent. The ICF has two functions: in law, to record consent as a defense to liability, and in ethics, to inform the research subject.

The plaintiff has a host of arguments to attack the ICF—for example, the foreseeable harm was not listed in the ICF; or owing to age or illness, the subject lacked the mental capacity to give informed consent; or the subject did not understand the long, complicated, jargon-filled ICF and hence did not give the consent was inadequately informed; or the subject revoked consent, perhaps orally.

(b) Fraud. It is easy for an injured subject to assert that the investigator lied, but the law has made it difficult to establish the claim of fraud. Fraud usually arises in the context of a quid-pro-quo agreement, and the intent to defraud has a high burden of persuasion. In the *Moore* case,[8] the court rejected the theory of fraud and selected the

6. 21 CFR § 56.121, Disqualification of an IRB or an Institution.

7. 21 CFR § 312.70, Disqualification of a Clinical Investigator [for misconduct that includes 21 CFR parts 50 and 56].

8. Moore v. Regents of the Univ. of Cal., 51 Cal.3d 120, 271 Cal.Rptr. 146, 793 P.2d 479 (1990).

breach of a fiduciary relationship, where Moore might be able to prove that the investigator breached the duty to disclose.

(c) Negligence. A research subject who suffers injury and sues for negligence can make defendants of everyone in the vicinity—the investigators and their staffs, the investigators' superiors, the sponsors of research, and the IRBs that approve protocols and ICFs—in the hope that in proving themselves out of joinder, some defendants will implicate others. Alleging liability that leads to broad and early joinder is convenient to plaintiffs, but it offends scientists for apparently jumping to a conclusion.

Both the existence of the duty of care and the breach of duty must be established by expert witnesses in biomedical research. Consent is irrelevant; a subject cannot consent to negligence. While the affirmative defenses of contributory negligence and assumption of risk are generally obsolete or inapplicable, the subject's failure to observe or report a side-effect, or the subject's non-compliance with instructions, could constitute comparative fault that reduced the subject's damages.

SECTION D. PATIENT PRIVACY

Note on Medical Information and Federal Privacy Laws

The Health Insurance Portability and Accountability Act of 1996 (HIPAA) is a federal law that was enacted to improve the efficiency and effectiveness of the healthcare system. Recognizing that it is now both possible and efficient to transmit patient medical records using electronic means, the federal government sought to implement safeguards to protect patient privacy while making use of digitized networks. HIPAA's broad goals include (a) guaranteeing health insurance coverage for employees, (b) reducing healthcare fraud and abuse, (c) implementing certain administrative simplifications in health information systems, and (d) protecting individuals' health information from unauthorized access or disclosure. HIPAA has three major sections that relate to privacy, security and transaction code sets, respectively. This note addresses privacy considerations: safeguarding the manner in which health information is gathered, recorded and shared, particularly through the use of electronic means.

HIPAA applies to "covered entities" which are defined as health insurance plans, health care clearinghouses and providers of health care services who maintain patient health information and use electronic means to transmit certain standard transactions. According to Secretary of Health and Human Services Tommy Thompson, HIPAA "protects the confidentiality of Americans' medical records without creating barriers to receiving quality health care. It strikes a common sense balance by providing consumers with personal privacy protections and access to high quality care."

The "common sense balance" is that health care providers must make a good faith effort to advise patients of their privacy rights and their health provider's privacy practices, and to obtain written acknowledgment that patients have been so advised. Once patients are informed and give their consent to providers' privacy practices, HIPAA allows covered entities to use and disclose the patient's protected health information ("PHI") for treatment, payment of claims and healthcare operations without additional specific authorization from each patient.

HIPAA also addresses "incidental uses and disclosures" of PHI that occur as a result of a permitted use (including treatment) and cannot reasonably be prevented. The privacy rule permits such uses and disclosures as long as covered entities develop and implement "minimum necessary" policies and procedures to reasonably safeguard the information from unauthorized disclosure. Covered entities are required to evaluate their routine procedures concerning such practices as securing computers and access to patient information, communicating with patients by mail or telephone, using patient sign-in sheets, leaving patient charts at bedside, addressing patients in waiting rooms, allowing medical personnel access to patient records, etc. In each case a covered entity is required to evaluate its privacy procedures and implement measures intended to reasonably safeguard patient privacy without impeding the routine delivery of health care.

There are certain exceptions to the HIPAA provisions, one of which concerns the manner in which mental health and psychotherapy notes are handled. As to these records, HIPAA requires that patients must give specific authorization for release of that information, and insurance payment or authorization cannot be conditioned upon release of such records. Psychotherapy "process" notes are distinguished from other mental health data such as medication prescriptions, treatment sessions and diagnostic information. Only the former are protected from disclosure without specific patient authorization. HIPAA also limits client access to psychotherapy notes under some narrow circumstances, specifically when access may cause harm to the client or another person.

The implementation of HIPAA has resulted in new rules and procedures that apply to the manner in which confidential patient communications are recorded, stored and disclosed. In some cases HIPAA's minimum federal requirements are less protective of patient privacy than the laws of many states. Under those circumstances the more protective state laws will generally prevail. The privacy rule requirements, which are largely procedural in nature, cannot establish a national privacy standard, but do offer more protection for patients under some circumstances.

SOUTH CAROLINA MEDICAL ASSOCIATION
v. THOMPSON

United States Court of Appeals for the Fourth Circuit, 2003.
327 F.3d 346.

TRAXLER, Circuit Judge:

Appellants, South Carolina Medical Association, Physicians Care Network, and several individual doctors, filed suit seeking to have declared unconstitutional several provisions of the Health Insurance Portability and Accountability Act of 1996 ("HIPAA"), Pub. L. No. 104–191, 110 Stat. 1936 (1996). * * *

I.

Recognizing the importance of protecting the privacy of health information in the midst of the rapid evolution of health information systems, Congress passed HIPAA in August 1996. HIPAA's Administrative Simplification provisions, sections 261 through 264 of the statute, were designed to improve the efficiency and effectiveness of the health care system by facilitating the exchange of information with respect to financial and administrative transactions carried out by health plans, health care clearinghouses, and health care providers who transmit information in connection with such transactions. The preamble to the Administrative Simplification provisions clarifies this goal:

> It is the purpose of this subtitle to improve the Medicare program . . . , the medicaid program . . . , and the efficiency and effectiveness of the health care system, by encouraging the development of a health information system through the establishment of standards and requirements for the electronic transmission of certain health information. [ ]

To this end, Congress instructed the United States Department of Health and Human Services ("HHS") to adopt uniform standards "to enable health information to be exchanged electronically." [ ]. Congress directed HHS to adopt standards for unique identifiers to distinguish individuals, employers, health care plans, and health care providers across the nation * * *.

Within the Administrative Simplification section, Congress included another provision—section 264—outlining a two-step process to address the need to afford certain protections to the privacy of health information maintained under HIPAA. First, section 264(a) directed HHS to submit to Congress within twelve months of HIPAA's enactment "detailed recommendations on standards with respect to the privacy of individually identifiable health information." [ ]. Second, if Congress did not enact further legislation pursuant to these recommendations within thirty-six months of the enactment of HIPAA, HHS was to promulgate final regulations containing such standards. Specifically, section 264(c)(1) provided:

> If legislation governing standards with respect to the privacy of individually identifiable health information transmitted in connection with the transactions described in section 1173(a) of the Social Security Act (as added by section 262) is not enacted by [August 21, 1999], the Secretary of Health and Human Services shall promulgate final regulations containing such standards not later than [February 21, 2000]. Such regulations shall address at least the subjects described in subsection (b).

[ ]. The subjects Congress directed HHS to cover in promulgating privacy regulations included the following: "(1) The rights that an individual who is a subject of individually identifiable health information should have. (2) The procedures that should be established for the exercise of such rights. (3) The uses and disclosures of such information

that should be authorized or required." [ ]. Through individual provisions of HIPAA, Congress outlined whom the regulations were to cover, [ ]; what information was to be covered, [ ] (defining "individually identifiable health information"); what types of transactions were to be covered, [ ]; what penalties would accrue for violations of HIPAA, [ ]; and what time lines and standards would govern compliance with the Act [ ].

Finally, section 264(c)(2) provided that the privacy regulations promulgated by HHS "shall not supercede a contrary provision of State law, if the provision of State law imposes requirements, standards, or implementation specifications that are *more stringent* than the requirements, standards, or implementation specifications imposed under the regulation." [ ]

Pursuant to Congress's mandate, HHS submitted recommendations for protecting the privacy of individually identifiable health information in September 1997. Several detailed and comprehensive medical privacy bills were thereafter introduced; however, Congress did not pass any additional legislation. For its part, HHS followed Congress's directive and drafted regulations that appeared in a November 1999 Notice of Proposed Rulemaking. The proposed regulations drew more than 50,000 comments from affected parties. After several further proposals and amendments were published, HHS promulgated final regulations in February 2001, collectively the "Privacy Rule." Although the effective date of the Privacy Rule was set for April 14, 2001, entities covered by the regulations were given until April 14, 2003, to comply, while some smaller entities were granted an additional year.

Appellants sought declaratory relief from provisions of HIPAA and the accompanying Privacy Rule promulgated by HHS. The district court dismissed the action and this appeal followed. Appellants argue that 1) HIPAA violates the non-delegation doctrine by authorizing HHS to promulgate the regulations at issue in the absence of an intelligible principle from Congress; 2) the Privacy Rule exceeds the scope of authority granted to HHS under HIPAA; and 3) HIPAA's non-preemption of "more stringent" state privacy laws is unconstitutionally vague, in violation of the Due Process Clause of the Fifth Amendment. We address each of these issues in turn.

II.

* * *

Appellants' second argument is that section 264(c) of HIPAA limits HHS to regulating only electronic records transmitted in connection with section 1173(a) of the Social Security Act, [ ] yet HHS impermissibly expanded HIPAA's scope to cover not only electronic transactions, but "every form of information for all Americans held by covered entities." The government responds that neither section 264(c), nor other portions of the Administrative Simplification section to which it refers, limits HHS's authority to regulating purely electronic information. The government also contends that during the rulemaking process

HHS decided that protecting only electronic information would not adequately safeguard patient privacy and that it would be burdensome and ultimately unworkable to distinguish the same information in various stages and formats that could be kept in electronic or nonelectronic form.

The disputed section includes a broad grant of authority from Congress to HHS as to the regulation of medical information. Section 264(c)(1) states in pertinent part as follows:

> If legislation governing standards with respect to the privacy of individually identifiable health information transmitted in connection with the transactions described in section 1173(a) of the Social Security Act (as added by Section 262) is not enacted by [August 21, 1999], the Secretary of Health and Human Services shall promulgate final regulations containing such standards not later than [February 21, 2000].

[ ] In describing what kind of information is to be protected, Congress expressly defined "health information" to include any information, "whether *oral or recorded in any form or medium.*" [ ]. The definition of "individually identifiable health information"—a subset of "health information"—contains no language limiting its reach to electronic media.[2] Thus, the plain language of HIPAA indicates that HHS could reasonably determine that the regulation of individually identifiable health information should include non-electronic forms of that information.

Although appellants argue that the reference in HIPAA § 264(c)(1) to information "transmitted in connection with section 1173(a)" limits the scope of the regulations solely to electronic transactions, another reasonable reading is that section 1173(a) directs HHS to develop "standards for transactions, and data elements for such transactions, to *enable* health information to be exchanged electronically." [ ]. Thus, the focus is on enabling electronic portability, not simply on regulating purely electronic activity. This reading is bolstered by the fact that transactions listed in connection with section 1173(a) are not described in terms that limit their scope to electronic media, but rather include transactions with respect to "enrollment and disenrollment in a health plan," "health care payment and remittance advice," and "health plan premium payments"—terms that do not invite the limitation to a purely electronic scheme. [ ]

2. The phrase "individually identifiable health information" refers to information that:

(B) relates to the past, present, or future physical or mental health or condition of an individual, the provision of health care to an individual, or the past, present, or future payment for the provision of health care to an individual, and

(i) identifies the individual; or

(ii) with respect to which there is a reasonable basis to believe that the information can be used to identify the individual.

42 U.S.C.A. § 1320d–6(b).

The validity of a regulation promulgated by an agency pursuant to a congressional mandate is to be sustained so long as it is "reasonably related to the purposes of the enabling legislation under which it was promulgated." [ ]. Regulating nonelectronic as well as electronic forms of health information effectuates HIPAA's intent to promote the efficient and effective portability of health information and the protection of confidentiality. If coverage were limited to electronic data, there would be perverse incentives for entities covered by the rule to avoid the computerization and portability of any medical records. Such a development would utterly frustrate the purposes of HIPAA. HHS's interpretation of the scope of the grant of authority given by Congress is not inconsistent with the language of the statute and is reasonably related to the larger purposes of HIPAA. The agency reasonably determined that regulating health information in such a way as to foster effective and efficient electronic transmission requires that the rule encompass paper records.

C.

Appellant's final argument is that HIPAA's non-preemption provision, which provides for the preemption of state laws unless they are "more stringent" than HIPAA, is impermissibly vague because it necessarily calls for subjective judgments on the part of health care providers, who face jail or fines for incorrect determinations. Contending that it fails to provide fair notice or minimal guidelines to covered entities and individuals, appellants argue that the statute violates the Due Process Clause of the Fifth Amendment.[3] The Court has stated that "it is a basic principle of due process that an enactment is void for vagueness if its prohibitions are not clearly defined." [ ]. A challenged statutory provision will survive scrutiny "unless it is so unclear with regard to what conduct is prohibited that it may trap the innocent by not providing fair warning, or it is so standardless that it enables arbitrary and discriminatory enforcement." [ ].

The disputed preemption provision is found in section 264(c)(2) and states as follows:

> A regulation promulgated under paragraph (1) shall not supercede a contrary provision of State law, if the provision of State law imposes requirements, standards, or implementation specifications that are *more stringent* than the requirements, standards, or implementation specifications imposed under the regulation.

[ ]. In order to determine what state laws will be preempted under HIPAA, we look to the regulations promulgated pursuant to the non-preemption provision. *See Village of Hoffman Estates v. Flipside, Hoffman Estates, Inc.*, 455 U.S. 489, 504, 102 S.Ct. 1186, 71 L.Ed.2d 362

---

3. The government contends that the vagueness challenge is unripe because "the non-preemption provision has not been applied to plaintiffs in any concrete way that would permit a fair assessment of its clarity in the proper context." [ ]

(1982) (holding that "administrative regulation will often suffice to clarify a standard with an otherwise uncertain scope").

According to the regulations promulgated by HHS, a state law is "more stringent" than HIPAA if it "provides greater privacy protection for the individual who is the subject of the individually identifiable health information." [ ]. To further clarify this standard, the regulation explains that a state law is "more stringent" where it meets one or more of the following criteria: the state law prohibits or restricts a use or a disclosure of information where HIPAA would allow it; the state law provides an individual with "greater rights of access or amendment" to his medical information than provided under HIPAA; the state law provides an individual with a "greater amount of information" about "a use, a disclosure, rights, and remedies"; the state law provides for the retention or reporting of more detailed information or for a longer duration; or the state law "provides greater privacy protection for the individual who is the subject of the individually identifiable health information." [ ]. These criteria will doubtless call for covered entities to make some common sense evaluations and comparisons between state and federal laws, but this does not mean they are either vague or constitutionally infirm. Because the regulations are sufficiently definite to give fair warning as to what will be considered a "more stringent" state privacy law, we affirm the district court's decision on this issue as well.

III.

AFFIRMED

JAFFEE v. REDMOND

Supreme Court of the United States, 1996.
518 U.S. 1, 116 S.Ct. 1923, 135 L.Ed.2d 337.

JUSTICE STEVENS delivered the opinion of the Court.

After a traumatic incident in which she shot and killed a man, a police officer received extensive counseling from a licensed clinical social worker. The question we address is whether statements the officer made to her therapist during the counseling sessions are protected from compelled disclosure in a federal civil action brought by the family of the deceased. Stated otherwise, the question is whether it is appropriate for federal courts to recognize a "psychotherapist privilege" under Rule 501 of the Federal Rules of Evidence.

I

Petitioner is the administrator of the estate of Ricky Allen. Respondents are Mary Lu Redmond, a former police officer, and the Village of Hoffman Estates, Illinois, her employer during the time that she served on the police force. Petitioner commenced this action against respondents after Redmond shot and killed Allen while on patrol duty.

On June 27, 1991, Redmond was the first officer to respond to a "fight in progress" call at an apartment complex. As she arrived at the scene, two of Allen's sisters ran toward her squad car, waving their arms and shouting that there had been a stabbing in one of the apartments. Redmond testified at trial that she relayed this information to her dispatcher and requested an ambulance. She then exited her car and walked toward the apartment building. Before Redmond reached the building, several men ran out, one waving a pipe. When the men ignored her order to get on the ground, Redmond drew her service revolver. Two other men then burst out of the building, one, Ricky Allen, chasing the other. According to Redmond, Allen was brandishing a butcher knife and disregarded her repeated commands to drop the weapon. Redmond shot Allen when she believed he was about to stab the man he was chasing. Allen died at the scene. Redmond testified that before other officers arrived to provide support, "people came pouring out of the buildings," App. 134, and a threatening confrontation between her and the crowd ensued.

Petitioner filed suit in Federal District Court alleging that Redmond had violated Allen's constitutional rights by using excessive force during the encounter at the apartment complex. The complaint sought damages under Rev. Stat. § 1979, 42 U.S.C. § 1983 and the Illinois wrongful death statute [ ]. At trial, petitioner presented testimony from members of Allen's family that conflicted with Redmond's version of the incident in several important respects. They testified, for example, that Redmond drew her gun before exiting her squad car and that Allen was unarmed when he emerged from the apartment building.

During pretrial discovery petitioner learned that after the shooting Redmond had participated in about 50 counseling sessions with Karen Beyer, a clinical social worker licensed by the State of Illinois and employed at that time by the Village of Hoffman Estates. Petitioner sought access to Beyer's notes concerning the sessions for use in cross-examining Redmond. Respondents vigorously resisted the discovery. They asserted that the contents of the conversations between Beyer and Redmond were protected against involuntary disclosure by a psychotherapist-patient privilege. The district judge rejected this argument. Neither Beyer nor Redmond, however, complied with his order to disclose the contents of Beyer's notes. At depositions and on the witness stand both either refused to answer certain questions or professed an inability to recall details of their conversations.

In his instructions at the end of the trial, the judge advised the jury that the refusal to turn over Beyer's notes had no "legal justification" and that the jury could therefore presume that the contents of the notes would have been unfavorable to respondents. The jury awarded petitioner $45,000 on the federal claim and $500,000 on her state-law claim.

The Court of Appeals for the Seventh Circuit reversed and remanded for a new trial. Addressing the issue for the first time, the court concluded that "reason and experience," the touchstones for acceptance of a privilege under Rule 501 of the Federal Rules of Evidence, compelled recognition of a psychotherapist-patient privilege. 5[ ]. "Reason tells us that psychotherapists and patients share a unique relationship, in which the ability to communicate freely without the fear of public disclosure is the key to successful treatment." [ ]. As to experience, the court observed that all 50 States have adopted some form of the psychotherapist-patient privilege. [ ]. The court attached particular significance to the fact that Illinois law expressly extends such a privilege to social workers like Karen Beyer. [ ]. The court also noted that, with one exception, the federal decisions rejecting the privilege were more than five years old and that the "need and demand for counseling services has skyrocketed during the past several years." [ ]

The Court of Appeals qualified its recognition of the privilege by stating that it would not apply if "in the interests of justice, the evidentiary need for the disclosure of the contents of a patient's counseling sessions outweighs that patient's privacy interests." [ ]. Balancing those conflicting interests, the court observed, on the one hand, that the evidentiary need for the contents of the confidential conversations was diminished in this case because there were numerous eyewitnesses to the shooting, and, on the other hand, that Officer Redmond's privacy interests were substantial. [ ] Based on this assessment, the court concluded that the trial court had erred by refusing to afford protection to the confidential communications between Redmond and Beyer.

The United States courts of appeals do not uniformly agree that the federal courts should recognize a psychotherapist privilege under Rule 501. [ ].

II

Rule 501 of the Federal Rules of Evidence authorizes federal courts to define new privileges by interpreting "common law principles ... in the light of reason and experience." * * *

The common-law principles underlying the recognition of testimonial privileges can be stated simply. " 'For more than three centuries it has now been recognized as a fundamental maxim that the public ... has a right to every man's evidence. When we come to examine the various claims of exemption, we start with the primary assumption that there is a general duty to give what testimony one is capable of giving, and that any exemptions which may exist are distinctly exceptional, being so many derogations from a positive general rule.' " *United States* v. *Bryan,* 339 U.S. 323, 331, 94 L.Ed. 884, 70 S.Ct. 724 (1950) (quoting 8 J. Wigmore, Evidence § 2192, p. 64 (3d ed. 1940)). [ ]

Guided by these principles, the question we address today is whether a privilege protecting confidential communications between a psychotherapist and her patient "promotes sufficiently important interests to outweigh the need for probative evidence.... " 445 U.S. at 51. Both "reason and experience" persuade us that it does.

III

Like the spousal and attorney-client privileges, the psychotherapist-patient privilege is "rooted in the imperative need for confidence and trust." [ ] Treatment by a physician for physical ailments can often proceed successfully on the basis of a physical examination, objective information supplied by the patient, and the results of diagnostic tests. Effective psychotherapy, by contrast, depends upon an atmosphere of confidence and trust in which the patient is willing to make a frank and complete disclosure of facts, emotions, memories, and fears. Because of the sensitive nature of the problems for which individuals consult psychotherapists, disclosure of confidential communications made during counseling sessions may cause embarrassment or disgrace. For this reason, the mere possibility of disclosure may impede development of the confidential relationship necessary for successful treatment. As the Judicial Conference Advisory Committee observed in 1972 when it recommended that Congress recognize a psychotherapist privilege as part of the Proposed Federal Rules of Evidence, a psychiatrist's ability to help her patients

> "is completely dependent upon [the patients'] willingness and ability to talk freely. This makes it difficult if not impossible for [a psychiatrist] to function without being able to assure ... patients of confidentiality and, indeed, privileged communication. Where there may be exceptions to this general rule ... , there is wide agreement that confidentiality is a *sine qua non* for successful psychiatric treatment." [ ]

By protecting confidential communications between a psychotherapist and her patient from involuntary disclosure, the proposed privilege thus serves important private interests.

Our cases make clear that an asserted privilege must also "serve public ends." [ ] Thus, the purpose of the attorney-client privilege is to "encourage full and frank communication between attorneys and their clients and thereby promote broader public interests in the observance of law and administration of justice." [ ]. And the spousal privilege, as modified in *Trammel*, is justified because it "furthers the important public interest in marital harmony," [ ] The psychotherapist privilege serves the public interest by facilitating the provision of appropriate treatment for individuals suffering the effects of a mental or emotional problem. The mental health of our citizenry, no less than its physical health, is a public good of transcendent importance.

In contrast to the significant public and private interests supporting recognition of the privilege, the likely evidentiary benefit that would result from the denial of the privilege is modest. If the privilege were rejected, confidential conversations between psychotherapists and their patients would surely be chilled, particularly when it is obvious that the circumstances that give rise to the need for treatment will probably result in litigation. Without a privilege, much of the desirable evidence to which litigants such as petitioner seek access—for example, admissions against interest by a party—is unlikely to come into being. This unspoken "evidence" will therefore serve no greater truth-seeking function than if it had been spoken and privileged.

That it is appropriate for the federal courts to recognize a psychotherapist privilege under Rule 501 is confirmed by the fact that all 50 States and the District of Columbia have enacted into law some form of psychotherapist privilege. We have previously observed that the policy decisions of the States bear on the question whether federal courts should recognize a new privilege or amend the coverage of an existing one. [ ] Because state legislatures are fully aware of the need to protect the integrity of the factfinding functions of their courts, the existence of a consensus among the States indicates that "reason and experience" support recognition of the privilege. In addition, given the importance of the patient's understanding that her communications with her therapist will not be publicly disclosed, any State's promise of confidentiality would have little value if the patient were aware that the privilege would not be honored in a federal court. Denial of the federal privilege therefore would frustrate the purposes of the state legislation that was enacted to foster these confidential communications.

It is of no consequence that recognition of the privilege in the vast majority of States is the product of legislative action rather than judicial decision. Although common-law rulings may once have been the primary source of new developments in federal privilege law, that is no longer the case. In *Funk* v. *United States,* 290 U.S. 371, 78 L.Ed. 369, 54 S.Ct. 212 (1933), we recognized that it is appropriate to treat a consistent body of policy determinations by state legislatures as reflecting both "reason" and "experience." [ ] That rule is properly respectful of the States and at the same time reflects the fact that once a state legislature has enacted a privilege there is no longer an opportunity for common-law creation of the protection. The history of the psychotherapist privilege illustrates the latter point. In 1972 the members of the Judicial Conference Advisory Committee noted that the common law "had indicated a disposition to recognize a psychotherapist-patient privilege when legislatures began moving into the field." Proposed Rules, 56 F.R.D. at 242 [ ]. The present unanimous acceptance of the privilege shows that the state lawmakers moved quickly. That the privilege may have developed faster legislatively than it would have in the courts demonstrates only that the States rapidly recognized the wisdom of the rule as the field of psychotherapy developed.

The uniform judgment of the States is reinforced by the fact that a psychotherapist privilege was among the nine specific privileges recommended by the Advisory Committee in its proposed privilege rules. In *United States* v. *Gillock,* 445 U.S. 360, 367–368, 63 L.Ed. 2d 454, 100 S.Ct. 1185 (1980), our holding that Rule 501 did not include a state legislative privilege relied, in part, on the fact that no such privilege was included in the Advisory Committee's draft. The reasoning in *Gillock* thus supports the opposite conclusion in this case. In rejecting the proposed draft that had specifically identified each privilege rule and substituting the present more open-ended Rule 501, the Senate Judiciary Committee explicitly stated that its action "should not be understood as disapproving any recognition of a psychiatrist-patient ... privilege contained in the [proposed] rules." [ ]

Because we agree with the judgment of the state legislatures and the Advisory Committee that a psychotherapist-patient privilege will serve a "public good transcending the normally predominant principle of utilizing all rational means for ascertaining truth," *Trammel,* 445 U.S. at 50, we hold that confidential communications between a licensed psychotherapist and her patients in the course of diagnosis or treatment are protected from compelled disclosure under Rule 501 of the Federal Rules of Evidence.

IV

All agree that a psychotherapist privilege covers confidential communications made to licensed psychiatrists and psychologists. We have no hesitation in concluding in this case that the federal privilege should also extend to confidential communications made to licensed social workers in the course of psychotherapy. The reasons for recognizing a privilege for treatment by psychiatrists and psychologists apply with equal force to treatment by a clinical social worker such as Karen Beyer. Today, social workers provide a significant amount of mental health treatment. * * * Their clients often include the poor and those of modest means who could not afford the assistance of a psychiatrist or psychologist [ ], but whose counseling sessions serve the same public goals. Perhaps in recognition of these circumstances, the vast majority of States explicitly extend a testimonial privilege to licensed social workers. We therefore agree with the Court of Appeals that "drawing a distinction between the counseling provided by costly psychotherapists and the counseling provided by more readily accessible social workers serves no discernible public purpose." [ ].

* * *

These considerations are all that is necessary for decision of this case. A rule that authorizes the recognition of new privileges on a case-by-case basis makes it appropriate to define the details of new privileges in a like manner. Because this is the first case in which we have recognized a psychotherapist privilege, it is neither necessary nor feasible to delineate its full contours in a way that would "govern all conceivable future questions in this area." [ ].

V

The conversations between Officer Redmond and Karen Beyer and the notes taken during their counseling sessions are protected from compelled disclosure under Rule 501 of the Federal Rules of Evidence. The judgment of the Court of Appeals is affirmed.

DISSENT: JUSTICE SCALIA, with whom THE CHIEF JUSTICE joins as to Part III, dissenting.

The Court has discussed at some length the benefit that will be purchased by creation of the evidentiary privilege in this case: the encouragement of psychoanalytic counseling. It has not mentioned the purchase price: occasional injustice. That is the cost of every rule which excludes reliable and probative evidence—or at least every one categorical enough to achieve its announced policy objective. In the case of some of these rules, such as the one excluding confessions that have not been properly "Mirandized," see *Miranda* v. *Arizona,* 384 U.S. 436, 16 L.Ed.2d 694, 86 S.Ct. 1602 (1966), the victim of the injustice is always the impersonal State or the faceless "public at large." For the rule proposed here, the victim is more likely to be some individual who is prevented from proving a valid claim—or (worse still) prevented from establishing a valid defense. The latter is particularly unpalatable for those who love justice, because it causes the courts of law not merely to let stand a wrong, but to become themselves the instruments of wrong.

* * *

II

* * * Effective psychotherapy undoubtedly is beneficial to individuals with mental problems, and surely serves some larger social interest in maintaining a mentally stable society. But merely mentioning these values does not answer the critical question: are they of such importance, and is the contribution of psychotherapy to them so distinctive, and is the application of normal evidentiary rules so destructive to psychotherapy, as to justify making our federal courts occasional instruments of injustice? On that central question I find the Court's analysis insufficiently convincing to satisfy the high standard we have set for rules that "are in derogation of the search for truth." *Nixon,* 418 U.S. at 710.

When is it, one must wonder, that *the psychotherapist* came to play such an indispensable role in the maintenance of the citizenry's mental health? For most of history, men and women have worked out their difficulties by talking to, *inter alios,* parents, siblings, best friends and bartenders—none of whom was awarded a privilege against testifying in court. Ask the average citizen: Would your mental health be more significantly impaired by preventing you from seeing a psychotherapist, or by preventing you from getting advice from your mom? I have little doubt what the answer would be. Yet there is no mother-child privilege.

How likely is it that a person will be deterred from seeking psychological counseling, or from being completely truthful in the course of such counseling, because of fear of later disclosure in litigation? And even more pertinent to today's decision, to what extent will the evidentiary privilege reduce that deterrent? The Court does not try to answer the first of these questions; and it *cannot possibly have any notion* of what the answer is to the second, since that depends entirely upon the scope of the privilege, which the Court amazingly finds it "neither necessary nor feasible to delineate," [ ]. If, for example, the psychotherapist can give the patient no more assurance than "A court will not be able to make me disclose what you tell me, unless you tell me about a harmful act," I doubt whether there would be much benefit from the privilege at all. That is not a fanciful example, at least with respect to extension of the psychotherapist privilege to social workers. [ ].

Even where it is certain that absence of the psychotherapist privilege will inhibit disclosure of the information, it is not clear to me that that is an unacceptable state of affairs. Let us assume the very worst in the circumstances of the present case: that to be truthful about what was troubling her, the police officer who sought counseling would have to confess that she shot without reason, and wounded an innocent man. If (again to assume the worst) such an act constituted the crime of negligent wounding under Illinois law, the officer would of course have the absolute right not to admit that she shot without reason in criminal court. But I see no reason why she should be enabled *both* not to admit it in criminal court (as a good citizen should), *and* to get the benefits of psychotherapy by admitting it to a therapist who cannot tell anyone else. And even less reason why she should be enabled to *deny* her guilt in the criminal trial—or in a civil trial for negligence—while yet obtaining the benefits of psychotherapy by confessing guilt to a social worker who cannot testify. It seems to me entirely fair to say that if she wishes the benefits of telling the truth she must also accept the adverse consequences. To be sure, in most cases the statements to the psychotherapist will be only marginally relevant, and one of the purposes of the privilege (though not one relied upon by the Court) may be simply to spare patients needless intrusion upon their privacy, and to spare psychotherapists needless expenditure of their time in deposition and trial. But surely this can be achieved by means short of excluding even evidence that is of the most direct and conclusive effect.

The Court confidently asserts that not much truth-finding capacity would be destroyed by the privilege anyway, since "without a privilege, much of the desirable evidence to which litigants such as petitioner seek access ... is unlikely to come into being." [ ]. If that is so, how come psychotherapy got to be a thriving practice before the "psychotherapist privilege" was invented? Were the patients paying money to lie to their analysts all those years? Of course the evidence-generating effect of the privilege (if any) depends entirely upon its scope, which the Court steadfastly declines to consider. And even if one assumes that scope to be the broadest possible, is it really true that most, or even many, of those who seek psychological counseling have the worry of litigation in the back of their minds? I doubt that, and the Court provides no evidence to support it.

* * *

III

Turning from the general question that was not involved in this case to the specific one that is: The Court's conclusion that a social-worker psychotherapeutic privilege deserves recognition is even less persuasive. In approaching this question, the fact that five of the state legislatures that have seen fit to enact "some form" of psychotherapist privilege have elected not to extend *any form* of privilege to social workers, see *ante,* at 15, n. 17, ought to give one pause. So should the fact that the Judicial Conference Advisory Committee was similarly discriminating in its conferral of the proposed Rule 504 privilege, see *supra.* The Court, however, has "no hesitation in concluding ... that the federal privilege should also extend" to social workers, *ante,* at 13—and goes on to prove that by polishing off the reasoned analysis with a topic sentence and two sentences of discussion, as follows (omitting citations and nongermane footnote):

> "The reasons for recognizing a privilege for treatment by psychiatrists and psychologists apply with equal force to treatment by a clinical social worker such as Karen Beyer. Today, social workers provide a significant amount of mental health treatment. Their clients often include the poor and those of modest means who could not afford the assistance of a psychiatrist or psychologist, but whose counseling sessions serve the same public goals." [ ].

So much for the rule that privileges are to be narrowly construed.

Of course this brief analysis—like the earlier, more extensive, discussion of the general psychotherapist privilege—contains no explanation of why the psychotherapy provided by social workers is a public good of such transcendent importance as to be purchased at the price of occasional injustice. Moreover, it considers only the respects in which social workers providing therapeutic services are *similar* to licensed psychiatrists and psychologists; not a word about the respects in which they are different. A licensed psychiatrist or psychologist is an expert in psychotherapy—and that may suffice (though I think it not so clear that this Court should make the judgment) to justify the use of extraordinary means to encourage counseling with him, as opposed to counseling with one's rabbi, minister, family or friends. One must presume that a social worker does *not* bring this greatly heightened degree of skill to bear, which is alone a reason for not encouraging that consultation as generously. Does a social worker bring to bear at least a significantly heightened degree of skill—more than a minister or rabbi, for example? I have no idea, and neither does the Court. The social worker in the present case, Karen Beyer, was a "licensed clinical social worker" in Illinois, App. 18, a job title whose training requirements consist of "master's degree in social work from an approved program," and "3,000 hours of satisfactory, supervised clinical professional experience." [ ] It is not clear that the degree in social work requires *any* training in psychotherapy. The "clinical professional experience" apparently will impart some such training, but only of the vaguest sort, judging from the Illinois Code's definition of "clinical social work practice," viz., "the providing of mental health services for the evaluation, treatment, and prevention of mental and emotional disorders in individuals, families and groups based on knowledge and theory of psychosocial development, behavior, psychopathology, unconscious motivation, interpersonal relationships, and environmental stress." [ ]. But the rule the Court announces today—like the Illinois evidentiary privilege which that rule purports to respect [ ]—is not limited to "licensed clinical social workers," but includes all "licensed social workers." * * *

Another critical distinction between psychiatrists and psychologists, on the one hand, and social workers, on the other, is that the former professionals, in their consultations with patients, *do nothing but psychotherapy*. Social workers, on the other hand, interview people for a multitude of reasons. The Illinois definition of "licensed social worker," for example, is as follows:

> "Licensed social worker" means a person who holds a license authorizing the practice of social work, which includes social services to individuals, groups or communities in any one or more of the fields of social casework, social group work, community organization for social welfare, social work research, social welfare administration or social work education." [ ].

Thus, in applying the "social worker" variant of the "psychotherapist" privilege, it will be necessary to determine whether the information provided to the social worker was provided to him *in his capacity as a psychotherapist*, or in his capacity as an administrator of social welfare, a community organizer, etc. Worse still, if the privilege is to have its desired effect (and is not to mislead the client), it will presumably be necessary for the social caseworker to advise, as the conversation with his welfare client proceeds, which portions are privileged and which are not.

* * *

RUNYON v. SMITH

Supreme Court of New Jersey, 2000.
163 N.J. 439, 749 A.2d 852.

PER CURIAM

This appeal concerns the psychologist-patient privilege.

On January 30, 1995, Diane Runyon sought and obtained a temporary restraining order (TRO) prohibiting her husband, Guy Runyon, from returning to the marital home. Mr. Runyon sought an immediate hearing on January 31, 1995, to contest the issuance of the TRO because he believed Diane Runyon posed a danger to their children. The record is silent as to whether Diane obtained notice of this hearing; she did not appear.

Mr. Runyon called Dr. Maureen Smith, a licensed clinical psychologist, as his first witness. Dr. Smith, who had treated Diane over a five-year period, expressed concern for the welfare and safety of the children. She testified that Diane did not have a history of a good relationship with the children; that Diane had been somewhat of an absentee mother in the past two years; that Diane had been physically and verbally abusive with her oldest son; and that Diane had an obsessive compulsive personality and was involved with a cult-like group. Dr. Smith testified that Mr. Runyon had an excellent relationship with his children and was the primary parent.

A close friend of Diane's also testified, stating that it would be in the best interest of the children to be with their father. Guy Runyon also testified. He confirmed the fact that Diane had used physical violence on their eldest son.

The Family Part judge, finding Dr. Smith's testimony very persuasive, modified the TRO by granting temporary custody of the children to Mr. Runyon.

Subsequent to the January hearing, Dr. Smith submitted to the court a written report dated June 19, 1995, wherein she was critical of Diane Runyon, concluding that it would be a mistake to expose the children to "the ideology of a woman with obvious thought disorders...." This report was relied on to severely restrict Diane's access to her children. Mr. Runyon was awarded custody of the children.

On January 21, 1997, Diane Runyon filed a complaint for monetary damages against Dr. Smith and her employer, Psychological Associates, alleging that Dr. Smith violated the psychologist-patient privilege and the rules and regulations governing psychologists by providing fact and opinion testimony at the January hearing that was based on information learned from counseling sessions with Diane. Further, Diane alleged that Dr. Smith submitted a written report and certification that contained false and inaccurate information.

After filing an answer to the complaint, Dr. Smith and Psychological Associates moved for summary judgment, arguing that the doctor's testimony at the January hearing was necessary to protect the best interests of the children. Diane Runyon filed a cross-motion, arguing that even if Dr. Smith was entitled to breach the privilege, the doctor did not have immunity to make false and inaccurate statements. The court granted partial summary judgment on the issue of piercing the privilege. The court reserved decision on the immunity issue.

In August 1997, Dr. Smith and Psychological Associates filed a second motion for summary judgment, arguing that false and inaccurate testimony by a witness in a judicial proceeding is immunized from liability. The court agreed and dismissed Diane Runyon's remaining claims with prejudice.

Diane Runyon appealed. The Appellate Division reversed the entry of summary judgment in favor of Dr. Smith and remanded for further proceedings. The Appellate Division reasoned that the three-pronged test must be satisfied in order to pierce the psychologist-patient privilege: 1) there must be a legitimate need for the evidence; 2) the evidence must be relevant and material to the issue to be decided; and 3) the information sought cannot be secured from any less intrusive means. The Appellate panel concluded that there was no attempt by the judge to apply this test and that the third prong of the test was not satisfied. More importantly, the panel concluded that there was no reasonable explanation for the submission of the January 19th report. The Appellate Division found that Dr. Smith's testimony at the January hearing and her subsequent report violated the psychologist-patient privilege.

According to the Appellate Division, if a psychologist fails to raise the privilege of the patient and makes disclosure of confidential information without a determination by the court that disclosure is required, the psychologist has breached the duty owed to the patient and the patient has a cause of action against the psychologist for the unauthorized disclosure of confidential information received in the course of treatment.

The Supreme Court granted certification.

PER CURIAM

We affirm the judgment of the Appellate Division substantially for the reasons set forth in its comprehensive opinion. We add these observations to clarify the basis for our disposition and to address the concerns of our dissenting colleagues.

We recognize the dissent's concern about instances in which the psychologist-patient privilege must yield because of "the potential of harm to others." [ ]. In Kinsella v. Kinsella, 150 N.J. 276, 316, 696 A.2d 556 (1997), adverting to that very concern, we observed that "because of the unique nature of custody determinations, the scope of the patient-psychiatrist privilege that may be claimed by parents in relation to custody issues poses more difficult problems that those posed by the scope of the privilege in other situations." We specifically acknowledged in Kinsella that courts in custody disputes "must strike a balance between the need to protect children who are in danger of abuse and neglect from unfit custodians and the compelling policy of facilitating the treatment of parents' psychological or emotional problems." [ ]

We are not prepared on this inadequate record to agree unqualifiedly with the Appellate Division's conclusion that, even absent Dr. Smith's testimony, "there was sufficient evidence from plaintiff's friend and from Mr. Runyon to justify awarding temporary custody of the children to Mr. Runyon." [ ]. We simply cannot assess in hindsight whether the testimony of Mr. Runyon and that of plaintiff's friend provided an adequate basis for the Family Part's temporary custody award. Nevertheless, all parties acknowledge that the Family Part did not conduct the in camera review contemplated by Kinsella [ ] and apparently did not make the appropriate determination on the record that evidence of fitness from other sources was inadequate. We also acknowledge that the hearing in question took place more than two years before Kinsella was decided. However, we cannot turn back the clock and determine now whether adherence to the Kinsella standards and procedures would have permitted the privilege to be pierced. Indisputably, those standards and procedures were not observed. We therefore conclude, as did the Appellate Division [in] Runyon [ ] that "Dr. Smith's testimony at the January hearing and her subsequent report violated the psychologist-patient privilege."

We acknowledge that in certain circumstances a psychologist may have a duty to warn and protect third parties or the patient from imminent, serious physical violence. As part of that duty, the psychologist would be required to disclose confidential information obtained from a patient. [ ]. Nothing in this record demonstrates that the children were exposed to danger of a degree that approached the level of danger that triggers the statutory duty to warn. Moreover, Dr. Smith's testimony occurred about six months after her last session with plaintiff. That six-month interval is itself inconsistent with the statutory standard of "imminent serious physical violence." [ ].

* * *

Affirmed.

FERGUSON v. CITY OF CHARLESTON

[See opinion at p. 745 (Chapter 12 Section C)].

CENTER FOR LEGAL ADVOCACY v. EARNEST

United States Court of Appeals for the Tenth Circuit, 2003.
320 F.3d 1107.

McKAY, Circuit Judge.

This case arose out of the death of a homeless person who died while being treated by the Defendant Hospital. On December 22, 2000, a Mr. Doe apparently fell on a Denver sidewalk and injured his head. He was taken by ambulance to the emergency room at the Hospital where he was admitted and treated for a head laceration and acute alcohol intoxication. The record indicates that as part of his initial treatment he was restrained physically and given Inapsine (a medication used to quiet his behavior). Mr. Doe subsequently experienced respiratory arrest followed by cardiac arrest. He was resuscitated and put on a ventilator and then transferred to the intensive care unit. He remained in the Hospital until he died on December 24, 2000. In January 2001, the Center for Legal Advocacy initiated an investigation into his death.

When the Plaintiff Center for Legal Advocacy undertook to carry out its statutory mandate to "investigate incidents of abuse and neglect of individuals with mental illness and to take appropriate action to protect and advocate the rights of such individuals," it was denied access to certain medical records by the Hospital. [ ] While there were other disputes, the matter ultimately focused on the Hospital's belief that it was required to withhold the records pursuant to the confidentiality provisions of 42 C.F.R. § 2 et seq.

The Center sued to compel access to the information, and the Hospital countersued for a declaratory judgment that it was entitled to enforce the provisions of 42 U.S.C. § 290dd–2(2001) and the accompanying regulations of 42 C.F.R. § 2 *et seq.* As those regulations explain, the confidentiality provisions "cover any information (including information on referral and intake) about alcohol and drug abuse patients obtained by a program (as the terms 'patient' and 'program' are defined in § 2.11) if the program is federally assisted.... " [ ]

The Center filed a motion to dismiss the Hospital's counterclaim pursuant to Rule 12(b)(6), alleging that the Center qualified for a "death investigation" exception to the confidentiality regulations. The Center also requested a preliminary injunction. Both of these motions were denied. After discovery, the Hospital filed a motion for summary judgment on both the complaint and the counterclaim. The Center filed a motion for partial summary judgment on the issue of whether it was the sole arbiter of probable cause, a motion to reconsider the denial of the preliminary injunction, and a motion for judgment on the pleadings pursuant to Rule 12(c). The district court granted the Hospital's motion for summary judgment and denied all of the Center's motions.

The parties agree that if, in the circumstances of this case, the Hospital qualifies as a "program" and Mr. Doe qualifies as a "patient," both as defined in § 2.11, then the Hospital is required to enforce the confidentiality provisions of § 2 *et seq.* Section 2.11 provides:

> *Patient* means any individual who has applied for or been given diagnosis or treatment for alcohol or drug abuse at a federally assisted program....
>
> . . . .
>
> *Program* means:
>
> (a) An individual or entity (other than a general medical care facility) who holds itself out as providing, and provides, alcohol or drug abuse diagnosis, treatment or referral for treatment; or
>
> (b) An identified unit within a general medical facility which holds itself out as providing, and provides, alcohol or drug abuse diagnosis, treatment or referral for treatment; or
>
> (c) Medical personnel or other staff in a general medical care facility whose primary function is the provision of alcohol or drug abuse diagnosis, treatment or referral for treatment and who are identified as such providers.

42 C.F.R. § 2.11.

Because the regulations limit the analysis to specific units within a general medical facility, it is important to distinguish between the Hospital's emergency room and its formal drug and alcohol treatment program known as Denver Cares. Denver Cares is a program which provides treatment for individuals with drug and alcohol abuse problems. Some of the patients treated at Denver Cares are referred from other departments in the Hospital, including the emergency room, and others are sent directly to Denver Cares by the police or other emergency personnel. The parties concede that Denver Cares qualifies as a "program." However, since Mr. Doe was not treated by Denver Cares, we must determine whether the emergency room qualifies as a "program."

In holding that the Hospital's emergency room qualifies as a "program," the district court relied on United States v. Eide, 875 F.2d 1429 (9th Cir. 1989). In Eide, the Ninth Circuit was faced with facts similar to those here and with a prior version of the same confidentiality provisions, including a prior version of the definition of "program" in § 2.11. Applying the then-current regulations to the facts, the Ninth Circuit concluded that, for purposes of the confidentiality provisions, the emergency room at the Veterans Administration Hospital was a "program." [ ]. In reaching this conclusion, the Ninth Circuit explained that "[a] hospital emergency room, while obviously also performing functions unrelated to drug abuse, serves as a vital first link in drug abuse diagnosis, treatment, and referral." [ ].

It is this very language from the Eide opinion that the district court in the instant case relied upon in concluding that the Hospital's emergency room was also a "program." [ ] Applying reasoning similar to the Ninth Circuit's, the district court held that the emergency facility was an alcohol abuse program because (1) patients treated initially in the emergency room were often referred to Denver Cares, (2) the emergency department had access to the records held by Denver Cares, and (3) the emergency facility was closely integrated with Denver Cares and provided initial diagnosis and treatment for eventual patients of Denver Cares. [ ]

Because the Eide court was applying a prior version of the confidentiality regulations, Appellant argues that the district court relied on immaterial facts and overturned law. We review *de novo* a grant of summary judgment, viewing the facts in the light most favorable to the non-moving party. [ ]

In response to the Eide decision, the Substance Abuse and Mental Health Services Administration ("SAMHSA")—the agency charged with promulgating regulations under the confidentiality provisions of the Public Health Services Act [ ]. SAMHSA explained the changes as follows:

> The [Eide] court ruled that the [Veterans Administration Medical Center] was a "person" which is defined at § 2.12 to mean "an individual, * * * Federal, State or local government or any other legal entity," and concluded that "(a) hospital emergency room, while obviously also performing functions unrelated to drug abuse, serves as a vital first link in drug abuse diagnosis, treatment and referral." [ ]

> The Department believes this interpretation too broadly defines the term "program." . . .

> . . . Prior to the 1987 amendments, the regulations applied to any record relating to substance abuse whether the information was

obtained from an emergency room, a general medical unit or a general practitioner so long as there was a Federal nexus. In 1987, however, it was the intent of the Department to limit the applicability of the regulations to specialized programs and personnel.... [ ]

In an effort to realize its stated intent, SAMHSA amended § 2.12(e)(1) to include the following language:

These regulations would not apply, for example, to emergency room personnel who refer a patient to the intensive care unit for an apparent overdose, unless the primary function of such personnel is the provision of alcohol or drug abuse diagnosis, treatment or referral and they are identified as providing such services or the emergency room has promoted itself to the community as a provider of such services.

[ ]. This provision, along with the history of its promulgation, is very instructive. It identifies two grounds on which an emergency room could qualify as a "program": (1) if the primary function of emergency room personnel is the provision of drug and alcohol abuse treatment, or (2) if the emergency room has held itself out to the community as providing such services.

The first possible basis for application of these regulations to the Hospital emergency room requires that the primary function of the emergency room "personnel is the provision of alcohol or drug abuse diagnosis, treatment or referral and they are identified as such." [ ]. The Hospital has provided no evidence, or even assertions, that the emergency room personnel in general, or the personnel who treated Mr. Doe, are identified as primarily providing alcohol and drug abuse treatment.

In fact, there is evidence to the contrary. In his deposition, Dr. Cantrill, the Associate Director of Emergency Medicine at the Hospital, admitted that the emergency room personnel are not identified specifically as licensed alcohol or drug abuse treatment providers or counselors. In another deposition, Dr. Casper, the Director of Behavioral Services at the Hospital, stated that the emergency room was not licensed to provide drug and alcohol treatment and that it primarily provides emergency medical treatment. Finally, Mr. Snyder, the nurse that treated Mr. Doe, also admitted that he was not a provider of alcohol abuse treatment but rather a trauma nurse. Because Appellees have failed to provide any evidence that the primary function of emergency room "personnel is the provision of alcohol or drug abuse diagnosis, treatment or referral" and that "they are identified as such," it is clear that this provision does not render the Hospital a "program" for purposes of the Confidentiality Provisions.

The second potential basis for application of the Confidentiality Provisions to the Hospital emergency room requires that the "the emergency room has promoted itself to the community as a provider of such services." Id. In concluding that the Hospital held out the emergency department as a program, the district court relied on evidence of integration of the emergency room and Denver Cares. Indeed, there is significant evidence of integration. However, these facts are insufficient to prove that the emergency room *holds itself out to the community* as providing drug and alcohol abuse treatment services.

Not only have Appellees failed to provide any evidence that the Hospital has held itself out as such a program, but there is evidence to the contrary. While Dr. Cantrill testified that the emergency department holds itself out as being a fully staffed emergency department and that drug and alcohol abuse often includes medical emergencies, he admitted that the emergency department made no claim that it provided any ongoing care for "the more chronic components of chronic alcohol or chronic drug abuse...." Rec., Vol. II, at 530. Furthermore, Dr. Higgins, a nurse administrator in Behavioral Health Services at the Hospital, admitted in her deposition that the Hospital had never made significant efforts to market the emergency room as part of its drug and alcohol abuse treatment program. Finally, the testimonies of Dr. Casper and Mr. Snyder both point to the fact that neither the emergency room nor its personnel are licensed or identified to the public as part of an alcohol or drug abuse treatment facility.

Having reviewed the record, the opinion of the district court, and the briefs, we conclude that as a matter of law the Hospital's emergency department does not qualify as a "program" within the meaning of Confidentiality Provisions.

REVERSED AND REMANDED.

SACHS v. INNOVATIVE HEALTHCARE, INC.

Court of Appeal of Florida, Third District, 2001.
799 So.2d 355.

RAMIREZ, J.

On Petition for Writ of Certiorari Granted

This is a petition seeking to quash a discovery order which compels the disclosure of the identity of patients' names and addresses. We grant the petition because the discovery order violates the right to privacy of these patients.

Petitioner, Dr. Mark Sachs, is a licensed Florida medical practitioner who specializes in the treatment of HIV infected patients and patients suffering from AIDS. Immunecare is a pharmacy solely owned by Dr. Sachs that purchased pharmaceutical products from Respondent, Innovative Healthcare, Inc., a wholesale distributor of pharmaceutical products. A dispute arose between Immunecare and Innovative over amounts owed for pharmaceutical and infusion products which Immunecare allegedly ordered, received, and failed to pay for. Innovative filed the underlying lawsuit against Immunecare and Dr. Sachs, alleging breach of contract or quantum meruit, tortious interference with a business relationship, defamation, open account, and account stated.

Innovative issued sixteen requests for production and twenty-five interrogatories to Sachs and Immunecare. Immunecare objected to three of the requests for production and three of the interrogatories. The requests for production related to orders for products and supplies, forms of payment used for orders placed and received, and Medicare and Medicaid billing records for products and supplies. The interrogatories sought the names, addresses, and telephone numbers of persons with knowledge of the issues in the lawsuit, the names of patients for which Dr. Sachs and Immunecare transferred services and products to another pharmacy, and the dates and the reasons for such transfers.

Immunecare argues that the discovery requires disclosure of patients' identities and medical conditions which violates the patients' rights to privacy and due process rights, the physician-patient privilege, and the statutory prohibitions against the unauthorized disclosure of information disclosed to a health care practitioner in the course of care and treatment, as well as the disclosure of HIV patients' names and test results. Innovative moved to compel production and Immunecare moved for a protective order.

In its order on Innovative's motion to compel discovery, the trial court overruled each of Immunecare's objections relating to patient-specific information, including patient identity, medical condition, and disclosure of communications in the course of care and treatment. The trial court required Immunecare to answer most of the interrogatories, including the interrogatory involving the disclosure of the names, addresses, and telephone numbers of any patient witnesses relevant to Innovative's claim for defamation. Additionally, the trial court entered an order which required the production of the objected to documents, but allowed redaction of patient-specific information in the documents produced. The trial court stayed its order for thirty days pending review in this Court. We grant the petition for writ of certiorari and quash the order entered below.

Section 456.057(5), Florida Statutes (2000), which concerns ownership and control of patient records, provides:

> ... records may not be furnished to, and the medical condition of a patient may not be discussed with, any person other than the patient or the patient's legal representative or other health care practitioners and providers involved in the care or treatment of the patient, except upon written authorization of the patient.

Subsection (6) of that same statute further provides:

> Except in a medical negligence action or administrative proceeding when a health care practitioner or provider is or reasonably expects to be named as a defendant, information disclosed to a health care practitioner by a patient in the course of the care and treatment of such patient is confidential and may be disclosed only to other health care practitioners and providers involved in the care or treatment of the patient, or if permitted by written authorization

from the patient or compelled by subpoena at a deposition, evidentiary hearing, or trial for which proper notice has been given.

This statute, formerly section 455.241, Florida Statutes (1993), creates a physician-patient privilege, rendering confidential a patient's medical records except in the limited circumstance of a health care provider who reasonably expects to be named as a defendant in a medical negligence action. Acosta v. Richter, 671 So.2d 149, 156 (Fla. 1996).

Section 381.004(3)(e), Florida Statutes (2000), which deals with HIV testing, provides:

> No person who has obtained or has knowledge of a test result pursuant to this section may disclose or be compelled to disclose the identity of any person upon whom a test is performed, or the results of such a test in a manner which permits identification of the subject of the test ... [except under strictly delineated circumstances set forth in this section].

Innovative contends that Immunecare has already violated the claimed privileges by giving Innovative the statutorily protected information at the time in which it placed its orders, or because it had the written consent of the patients to make such disclosures via prescription orders. However, "the nature of the dispute, and the fact that respondent may already have in its records some of this patient information, does not negate the rights of such non-party patients to privacy and confidentiality as to their personal information." [ ]

Even limiting the interrogatories and requests for production to the mere identification of Immunecare patients violates the patients' rights under the privacy statutes, as eighty percent of Dr. Sachs' practice is devoted to treating patients diagnosed with HIV or AIDS. Under these circumstances, the only way to protect the confidentiality of the patients is to protect their identities. Thus, the trial court ignored the essential requirements of the law by entering an order which required the disclosure of the identities of Immunecare patients. On remand, the trial court may fashion an order that provides discovery redacting the identifying information.

Innovative may still be free to obtain this information through other means. In essence, Innovative claims that patients who formerly bought prescription medicine from Innovative began purchasing it elsewhere as a result of Dr. Sachs' allegedly defamatory comments. Innovative's own records should reveal the identity of any patients who stopped buying medicine from it and when they stopped making purchases. Innovative also argued below that it had already received reports from patients about defamatory statements made by Dr. Sachs. Obviously, Innovative is still free to continue to investigate this information in furtherance of its defamation and tortious interference claims.

ESTATE OF BEHRINGER v. MEDICAL CENTER

[See opinion at p. 799 (Chapter 13 Section C)].

SUESBURY v. CACERES

[See opinion at p. 520 (Chapter 9 Section C)].

Notes

1) At issue in *So. Carolina Medical Association* is the constitutionality of the privacy provisions of HIPAA. Plaintiffs specifically contest whether the Department of Health and Human Services (DHHS) was properly authorized to promulgate the HIPAA regulations and the Privacy Rule, as well as the effect of HIPAA in the face of more stringent state laws. This case was filed before the HIPAA privacy rules even took effect (in April, 2003) and was first to challenge the HIPAA regulations. *So. Carolina Medical Association* is expected to herald in a number of challenges to the sweeping provisions of HIPAA, beginning with the question of whether DHHS had adequate constitutional authority to promulgate the regulations at all. The provisions were upheld as to each challenge, but it was only the first case.

2) *Jaffee* reached the Supreme Court around the same time that HIPAA was originally passed, but long before it actually took effect. In between was a lengthy period of proposed regulations and comment. *Jaffee* addresses the discoverability of psychotherapeutic records which petitioner sought to maintain as privileged. While all states have psychotherapist-patient privileges, the federal courts were not obligated to honor them. The Court's decision offers strong support for privacy in the psychotherapist-patient relationship. *Jaffee* did not foreshadow the precise dimensions of the privilege in federal courts, but made it clear that mental health treatment is deserving of special treatment. The HIPAA regulations agree, and psychotherapy notes are afforded special protections: payment for services cannot be predicated upon release of detailed records, and patients must specifically authorize the release of such records at the time that they are sought.

3) *Runyon* makes it clear that a professional who holds a privileged relationship with a fiduciary (such as psychotherapist-patient) cannot voluntarily offer to testify as to privileged materials and, if subpoenaed, is obligated to assert the patient's privilege to allow the court to determine whether there are statutory grounds to pierce the privilege. The court will balance the statutory authority for the privilege with any other provisions for overriding it. These may include, for example, the safety of a child in a child custody matter and the ability of the court to secure the information from a non-privileged source.

As to the psychotherapist's assertion that the information in her testimony was needed to protect a child, all states have mandatory reporting statutes for suspected matters of child abuse. The psychotherapist was obligated to follow the statutory procedure, which generally is to report the matter to the appropriate child protection authority. It is not to violate a privileged communication in court without a judicial determination that a legitimate need overrides the statutory privilege.

4) *Earnest* explores the coverage of the Public Health Services Act, 42 U.S.C. s 290dd–2 (2002), which is a federal law protecting the confidentiality of certain treatment programs for drug and alcohol abuse. The federal statutory provisions override inconsistent state law and ensure the confidentiality of medical records of facilities that qualify under the Act. In this case the court found that an Emergency Room that does not specifically provide drug or alcohol treatment, or hold itself out to the community as providing such, does not qualify under the Act. In fact, however, coverage under the Act is fairly broad as to scope and strict in application so as to encourage individuals to seek drug and alcohol treatment without fear that treatment records will discoverable in future legal actions.

5) *Sachs* raises difficult discovery questions, which are compounded by the particularly confidential nature of the patient files because many are being treated for AIDS. The issue is that certain types of lawsuits cannot proceed unless the petitioner is allowed access to business records containing confidential patient information. When possible, in-camera review or redaction is ordered. Other times, the very information redacted is the information needed to go forward with the suit. Can you think of some creative solutions for balancing the petitioner's need for the information with the rights of "innocent" third party patients whose identities would have to be revealed with no benefit to them? How would the new HIPAA regulations change your response?

Chapter 8

PRODUCT–RELATED MEDICAL LIABILITY

INTRODUCTORY NOTE

As viewed by the law, the physician's professional service consists primarily of advice to patients, the hallmark of the independent contractor, supplemented by personal services. Earlier chapters considered the attribution and allocation of medical liabilities among the providers of health care services.

Health care providers also order for patients, and use in the care of patients, substances and articles that were manufactured by others, such as pharmaceutical drugs, devices, and the tools of diagnosis and care. The product-related responsibilities of health care providers include knowing the appropriate uses and side-effects of drugs and devices, watching for unintended consequences and interactions, warning patients about risks and side-effects, and even keeping track of patients in case new risks turn up in the future. Non-physician bioscientists may be qualified to testify about the use and misuse of health care products.

Because the liabilities of goods-providers are stricter than the liabilities of service-providers, the involvement of health care providers with manufactured goods exposes the providers to theories of liability much stricter than negligence. Where a patient has been injured in the use of a product, the service providers may have to exculpate themselves from responsibility, at the risk of being held liable without proof of fault along with the goods providers.

It is hardly surprising that both providers and manufacturers have sought and are seeking legislative insulation from product-related liability doctrines, whether by statutes declaring that the furnishing of some articles (such as transfused blood) are services rather than sales, or providing outright immunity from liability as the tradeoff for producing beneficial but unavoidably dangerous articles (such as vaccines), or limiting the maximum damages that they and their insurers must pay in medical liability cases.

BRANDT v. BOSTON SCIENTIFIC CORPORATION

Supreme Court of Illinois, 2003.
204 Ill.2d 640, 275 Ill.Dec. 65, 792 N.E.2d 296.

JUSTICE GARMAN delivered the opinion of the court:

* * *

BACKGROUND

Brandt was admitted to the Health Center to receive treatment for urinary incontinence. While there, a ProteGen Sling (sling) was surgically implanted on December 23, 1998. A charge for the sling was included in her bill from the Health Center. In January 1999, the manufacturer of the sling, Boston Scientific Corporation, issued a voluntary recall of the product because the product was causing medical complications in 7% of patients. Brandt suffered serious complications, including pain, infection, bleeding, and erosion of vaginal tissue. In response to these complications, the sling was surgically removed in November 1999.

Brandt filed a six-count complaint in July 2000, alleging negligence, strict liability, and breach of warranty against defendants Boston Scientific Corporation and Sarah Bush Lincoln Health Center. The Health Center filed a motion to dismiss counts IV through VI under section 2–615 of the Code of Civil Procedure (Code) because the Health Center was not a merchant of medical devices and because the transaction between Brandt and the Health Center was predominantly for services instead of goods. * * * The trial court granted the motion to dismiss without prejudice for failure to comply with section 2–622.

Brandt filed a four-count amended complaint in May 2001. The first three counts again were against Boston Scientific Corporation and are not part of this appeal. Count IV alleged a breach of warranty claim against the Health Center; no section 2–622 affidavit was attached. Count IV specifically stated that the Health Center "was engaged in the sale and distribution of medical products, including [the] pubovaginal sling." As for the nature of the transaction, Brandt alleged:

> "Plaintiff, BRENDA BRANDT, purchased a ProteGen Sling catalog no. 820–121, lot. No. 027101, sold and distributed by Defendant, SARAH BUSH LINCOLN HEALTH CENTER, and was implanted with the said product on or about December 23, 1998, at the SARAH BUSH LINCOLN HEALTH CENTER in Mattoon, Illinois."

The Health Center again filed a motion to dismiss under sections 2–615 and 2–619 of the Code, citing the same three arguments it had raised about the original complaint. The trial court dismissed count IV with prejudice for failure to comply with the pleading requirements of section 2–622; the court expressed no opinion regarding the other arguments asserted in the Health Center's motion.

The appellate court found that the trial court erred in holding that count IV alleged a healing art malpractice claim. Thus, section 2–622 did not apply. The appellate court affirmed the dismissal of count IV, however, because it found that the transaction between Brandt and the Health Center was primarily for services rather than goods so that the UCC did not apply. The appellate court acknowledged that *Garcia v. Edgewater Hospital*, 244 Ill.App.3d 894, 184 Ill.Dec. 651, 613 N.E.2d 1243 (1993), reached the opposite conclusion but expressly declined to follow *Garcia*. The appellate court concluded that *Garcia* erroneously relied upon this court's decision in *Cunningham v. MacNeal Memorial Hospital*, 47 Ill.2d 443, 266 N.E.2d 897 (1970), because *Cunningham* had been entirely overruled by subsequent legislation and, further, because *Cunningham* involved a strict liability claim rather than a UCC claim.

Because Brandt prevailed on the section 2–622 issue before the appellate court, she only raises the arguments from the section 2–615 motion to dismiss before this court. She submits that the appellate court erred in finding that her transaction with the Health Center was primarily for services and in asserting that *Cunningham* was no longer good law. We now consider the propriety of the dismissal of the breach of warranty claim against the Health Center.

ANALYSIS

* * *

Article 2 of the UCC imposes the implied warranty of merchantability. [ ]. To succeed on a claim of breach of implied warranty of merchantability, a plaintiff must allege and prove: (1) a sale of goods (2) by a merchant of those goods, and (3) the goods were not of merchantable quality. [ ]. Unless excluded or modified, this warranty is implied in every sale under these conditions. [ ]

Article 2 applies to "transactions in goods." [ ] The UCC defines goods as "all things, including specially manufactured goods, which are movable at the time of identification to the contract for sale." [ ]. Where there is a mixed contract for goods and services, there is a "transaction in goods" only if the contract is predominantly for goods and incidentally for services. [ ]. This analysis is known as the "predominant purpose" test.

The parties here do not dispute that the sling implanted in Brandt satisfies the UCC definition of goods. The parties do dispute, however, whether the exchange between Brandt and the Health Center constituted a transaction in goods; the Health Center argues that it primarily provided medical services rather than goods to Brandt.

In addition, an implied warranty of merchantability applies only to a merchant of goods of the kind involved in the contract. "Merchant" is defined in the UCC as:

"a person who deals in goods of the kind or otherwise by his occupation holds himself out as having knowledge or skill peculiar to the practices or goods involved in the transaction or to whom such knowledge or skill may be attributed by his employment of an agent or broker or other intermediary who by his occupation holds himself out as having such knowledge or skill." [ ].

Section 2–314 provides, "a warranty that the goods shall be merchantable is implied in a contract for their sale if the seller is *a merchant with respect to goods of that kind.*" (Emphasis added.) [ ]. UCC comments explain that this language in section 2–314 requires a merchant to have professional status as to a particular kind of goods, which is narrower than the general definition of merchant found in section 2–104. [ ] The Health Center disputes that it is a merchant of medical devices.

Finally, a plaintiff must show that the goods in question were not of merchantable quality. Merchantable means of a quality commensurate with that generally accepted within the trade under the description of the goods in the contract. [ ]. There is little dispute in this case that the sling was not merchantable. In its notice of voluntary recall of the sling, the manufacturer conceded as much by explaining, "we cannot assure ourselves that the overall experience with ProteGen meets our standards for product performance."

We must determine whether, accepting the truth of the complaint allegations and reasonable inferences, Brandt has stated a cause of action upon which relief may be granted. [ ]. The complaint alleged: (1) Brandt purchased the sling from the Health Center; (2) the sling was implanted in her body at the Health Center; and (3) the Health Center was engaged in the sale of medical products, including slings. Thus, we must determine whether these allegations assert that the transaction between Brandt and the Health Center was predominantly for goods, and if so, that the Health Center can be considered a merchant of slings.

As an initial matter, we address Brandt's contention that such an evaluation is not properly made upon review of a motion to dismiss because we have only the amended complaint and billing statements to consider. Illinois courts on several occasions have evaluated whether a contract involved a transaction in goods or services upon review of dismissal of a UCC claim. *Pitler v. Michael Reese Hospital*, 92 Ill.App.3d 739, 742–43, 47 Ill.Dec. 942, 415 N.E.2d 1255 (1980) (hospital delivery of radiation treatment was predominantly for services, so the breach of warranty claim was properly dismissed) * * *.

In addition, even what ordinarily may be a question of fact becomes a question of law if the factual circumstances are undisputed and no reasonable difference of opinion could arise about the inferences that can be made from those facts. [ ]. The parties do not dispute that Brandt purchased a sling from the Health Center, which was implanted in her body at the Health Center. It is reasonable to infer that Brandt had a medical condition, which was diagnosed and treated through a surgical procedure at the Health Center. According to the billing statement, the hospital clearly provided medical facilities and treatment necessary to enable the implantation of the sling. The purchase of the sling was not an isolated transaction; it is not reasonable to infer that Brandt simply went to the hospital, bought the sling, and left. There is no reasonable dispute about the facts of this case.

Plaintiff asserts that the amended complaint does not allege that the surgeon acted as an employee or agent of the hospital when performing the implantation surgery and that we should not presume as much. Defendant does not dispute the status of the surgeon. The status of the surgeon is not determinative, and we proceed on the assumption that the surgeon was not in any way affiliated with the Health Center because the pleadings do not address the surgeon's status.

Thus, we can analyze, as a matter of law, whether the hospital's sale of the sling and facilitation of its surgical implantation was a transaction in goods under the UCC. There is little Illinois case law evaluating the nature of such a hospital-patient transaction, and other jurisdictions are divided on this issue [ ].

We evaluated a transaction between a hospital and patient in *Cunningham*. Both Brandt and the *Garcia* court rely heavily on *Cunningham* in support of the position that a hospital's provision of a medical device is a sale of goods to which UCC implied warranties apply. In *Cunningham*, however, the plaintiff brought a strict liability claim rather than a UCC claim against a hospital after she contracted hepatitis from a contaminated blood transfusion she received there.[ ]. The defendant, relying on *Perlmutter v. Beth David Hospital*, 308 N.Y. 100, 123 N.E.2d 792 (1954), argued that a blood transfusion is a service rather than a sale of a product so that strict liability could not attach. [ ]. In *Perlmutter*, the Court of Appeals of New York held that the plaintiff could not bring an implied warranty of merchantability claim because a blood transfusion was a service rather than a sale of goods under the New York sales act. *Perlmutter*[ ]. We rejected the *Perlmutter* reasoning. *Cunningham* [ ]. We instead found that the blood transfusion transaction was a sale of a product, and the complaint sufficiently alleged a strict liability claim. [ ]

In response to our holding in *Cunningham*, the General Assembly enacted the Blood and Organ Transaction Liability Act (Act). [ ]. Under this statute, no warranty or strict liability claims can be brought regarding the "procuring, furnishing, donating, processing, distributing or using" human blood products or tissue "for the purpose of injecting, transfusing or transplanting" them into the human body. [ ]. Our appellate court is split in its interpretation of the effect of this legislation. The appellate opinion in this case concluded that the legislature entirely overruled our holding in *Cunningham* through the Act [ ], while *Garcia* found that the legislature foreclosed claims concerning human blood products and tissue but not claims involving drugs, surgical instruments, and other articles usable in the human body [ ]. We note that we applied the rationale of *Cunningham* to the dispensing of birth-control pills subsequently to the enactment of the Act. [ ] In addition, the language of the Act very clearly expresses an intent to address only human blood products and tissue. [ ]. Thus, we find that the Act overruled *Cunningham* only as to human blood products and tissue.

Nonetheless, *Cunningham*, a strict liability case, has limited relevance to the present UCC warranty case. Courts in strict liability cases must find that the defendant sold a product rather than services before imposing liability. [ ] In contrast, under article 2 of the UCC, the transaction between the plaintiff and the defendant must have been *predominantly* for goods rather than services. [ ]. Thus, in *Cunningham*, we were undeterred by the fact that the provision of blood was "an *ancillary* part of the services rendered to that patient" before holding that the blood was a product sold so that the complaint validly alleged a strict liability claim. (Emphasis added.) *Cunningham [ ]*. Thus, the appellate court in *Garcia* incorrectly concluded that *Cunningham* dictated that the predominant purpose test was inapplicable to breach of warranty claims involving transactions between hospitals and patients. *Garcia*[ ].

We also note that the 1970 *Cunningham* case predated application of the predominant purpose test to UCC claims in Illinois. This court did not explicitly endorse application of the predominant purpose test to determine whether there is a transaction in goods under article 2 of the UCC until 2002. *Belleville Toyota* [ ]. The earliest cases applying the test in the lower Illinois courts began to appear in the mid–1970s. * * *

We now apply the predominant purpose test to the facts of this case. Plaintiff's transaction with the Health Center is a mixed contract because the hospital provided both medical services, such as an operating room, and goods, such as the sling, to facilitate treatment of plaintiff's medical condition. Under the predominant purpose test, article 2, and its implied warranties, applies only if a mixed contract is predominantly for goods and only incidentally for services. *Belleville Toyota* [ ]. When evaluating the predominant nature of contracts, Illinois courts have considered contract language in addition to assessing the proportion of goods and services in the contract. [ ].

In this case, Brandt's bill from the Health Center reflects that of the $11,174.50 total charge for her surgery, a charge of $1,659.50, or 14.9%, was for the sling and its surgical kit; a charge of $5,428.50, or 48.6%, was for all movable goods, including pharmaceuticals, medical supplies, and sterile supplies. The remainder of the charges were for various services, including the hospital and operating rooms and various kinds of medical testing and treatment. A charge for the implantation of the sling by the surgeon was not included in the bill. A majority of the charges, 51.4%, were for services rather than goods. Only a small fraction of the total charge was for the sling, the goods at issue in this case. In addition, the bill listed itemized charges under the heading "service description."

There is, however, more to the predominant purpose test than making a simple comparison of money paid for goods and services within a transaction. We must consider the predominate nature of the transaction as a whole. As can be reasonably inferred from the amended complaint, Brandt went to the Health Center for medical treatment for her urinary incontinence, rather than merely to buy a sling as one buys goods from a store. Treatment for her condition involved implantation of the sling. While Brandt clearly purchased these goods from the Health Center, the sling was only potentially useful after its surgical implantation. Even assuming the surgeon was a private physician not affiliated with the Health Center, the Health Center provided services before, during, and after surgery to facilitate implantation of the sling. These services, the medical treatment, were the primary purpose of the transaction between Brandt and the Health Center, and the purchase of sling was incidental to the treatment.

This analysis also has been adopted by the Georgia Court of Appeals when similarly applying a predominant purpose test to determine whether the UCC applies in a breach of warranty claim against a hospital:

> "In this case, McCombs did not go to Southern Regional to purchase a cervical plate but to have her spinal problem surgically repaired. Southern Regional furnished its facility for use *by her surgeon*, and it supplied the requisite underlying support services, including recovery room, laboratory, pharmacy support, and nursing care, to help facilitate the surgery and her recovery from it.

> Thus, the transaction at issue was one involving 'services and labor with an incidental furnishing of equipment and materials.' [Citation omitted.]" (Emphasis added.) [ ].

In fact, the conclusion that the Health Center predominantly provided services in this case is in accord with the national trend on this issue. A majority of foreign jurisdictions hold that a hospital's provision of a defective surgical device is primarily a transaction for services rather than goods so that no implied warranty of merchantability claim is available. * * *

Holding hospitals liable for breach of warranty is not the only legal remedy available to Brandt. She can seek recovery from the manufacturer of the sling. [ ]. In fact, counts I through III of Brandt's amended complaint are directed toward the manufacturer. She also could bring a cause of action against the hospital under a negligence theory. [ ]. Foreclosing a breach of warranty claim under these circumstances does not preclude recovery for Brandt.

CONCLUSION

Because we find that the transaction between Brandt and the Health Center was predominantly a transaction for services, article 2 of the UCC does not apply. Given this holding, we need not evaluate whether the Health Center is a merchant of medical devices. Count IV was properly dismissed from Brandt's amended complaint.

Affirmed.

CRYOLIFE v. SUPERIOR COURT OF SANTA CRUZ COUNTY

Court of Appeal of California, Sixth District, 2003.
110 Cal.App.4th 1145, 2 Cal.Rptr.3d 396.

PREMO, Acting P.J.

* * *

II. FACTUAL AND PROCEDURAL BACKGROUND

A. The First Amended Complaint

According to the allegations of the first amended complaint, this action arises from knee surgery performed on Alan J. Minvielle (Minvielle or plaintiff). The knee surgery involved a surgical graft procedure that utilized an allograft consisting of a patellar tendon obtained from a human cadaver. The allograft was supplied by defendant Cryolife, a tissue bank in the business of harvesting, preserving and distributing products derived from human tissue for medical use. Minvielle's knee pain increased after the surgery, and, two months later, the allograft was removed because it was infected with bacteria.

Cryolife allegedly represented in its marketing and promotional materials that its orthopedic tissue products were safe, sterile and uncontaminated. However, according to plaintiff, the truth was that Cryolife's tissue acquisition and processing methods were inadequate to protect patients from the risk of bacterial infection. Cryolife failed to warn the medical profession of the risk of using Cryolife's products and also failed to establish an adequate system for reporting adverse reactions to its products. Based on these allegations, plaintiff asserted causes of action against Cryolife for negligence, strict liability, fraud, and negligent misrepresentation. He also sought compensatory and punitive damages.

In the strict liability cause of action, plaintiff alleged in more detail that Cryolife's allograft products were not fit for their intended use of implantation in humans and that Cryolife had failed to warn either plaintiff or his health care providers of the risk of using Cryolife's potentially contaminated tissue. Also, plaintiff stated that Cryolife had "procured, harvested, evaluated, preserved, tested, promoted, sold, supplied, distributed and labeled the allograft products that were defective ... [P] [and] knew that its products, and specifically the allograft implanted in Plaintiff's left knee, were to be purchased and used without inspection for defects by Plaintiff." Plaintiff further asserted that Cryolife intentionally and/or in conscious disregard of plaintiff's safety inadequately tested and treated its donor tissue products, misled plaintiff and health care providers regarding the safety of its products, and maliciously denied that an infection could be caused by its products.

B. Cryolife's Demurrers

Cryolife demurred to the causes of action for strict products liability, fraud, and negligent misrepresentation, on the ground that the complaint failed to state sufficient facts for any cause of action. As to the strict products liability cause of action, Cryolife argued that the alleged facts were insufficient because strict products liability does not apply to services, and, as a tissue bank, Cryolife provides a service, not a product. Cryolife relied on Health and Safety Code sections 1635 and 1635.2, which Cryolife asserted showed the Legislature's intent that the collection, processing, storage, and distribution of human tissue for the purpose of transplantation be deemed a service. Cryolife also relied on the decision in *Shepard v. Alexian Brothers Hosp.* (1973) 33 Cal.App.3d 606 [109 Cal.Rptr. 132], which held that strict products liability does not apply to blood banks because the Legislature expressly provided in section 1606 that the processing, distribution and use of blood products is construed to be a service for all purposes. Cryolife argued that the decision in *Shepard v. Alexian Brothers Hosp.* was dispositive of plaintiff's strict liability cause of action, because the public policy rationale favoring an adequate supply of blood over the application of the doctrine of strict liability in tort to the transfusion of blood and blood products applied with equal force to tissue used for tissue transplantation surgeries.

In his opposition to the demurrers, plaintiff responded that the complaint stated sufficient facts for a strict products liability cause of action because it was alleged that Cryolife manufactures tissue products and places them on the market knowing the products may cause serious injury. Plaintiff compared Cryolife's activities to a company that removes, repairs, reconditions, and sells used car parts. As additional support for his contention that Cryolife supplies a product, plaintiff noted that 21 Code of Federal Regulations part 1271.1 et seq., defines human tissue intended for transplantation into another human as a " 'tissue-based product.' "

Plaintiff also disputed Cryolife's contention that section 1635.2 provides tissue banks with statutory immunity from strict products liability. According to plaintiff, the language of section 1635.2 makes clear that the Legislature intended only to make the sales provisions of the Uniform Commercial Code inapplicable to tissue banks. Further, plaintiff argued that Cryolife's reliance upon an analogy between tissue banks and blood banks with respect to statutory immunity was misplaced, because the language of the blood bank statute, section 1606, differs significantly from the language of the tissue bank statute, section 1635.2. Finally, plaintiff argued that the public policy rationale for providing immunity from strict products liability for the lifesaving products of the nonprofit blood industry did not apply to tissue products manufactured for use in elective surgeries by the for-profit tissue bank industry.

* * *

D. The Trial Court's Orders

The trial court overruled Cryolife's demurrers to the causes of action for strict products liability, fraud, and negligent misrepresentation * * *. During the hearing, the trial court indicated that its order overruling the demurrer to the strict liability cause of action was based upon the court's agreement with plaintiff that section 1635.2 does not immunize Cryolife from strict products liability because, unlike section 1606, the blood bank immunity statute, section 1635.2 does not expressly state that tissue banks provide a service "for all purposes."

Cryolife petitioned for extraordinary relief from the trial court's orders and we issued an order to show cause in regard to the order overruling the demurrer to the strict liability cause of action and the order denying the motion to strike. We denied the petition in all other respects. We also issued a temporary stay of trial court proceedings while our writ review was pending.

III.   DISCUSSION

* * *

B.   Strict Products Liability Does Not Apply to Tissue Banks

We first consider the issue of whether the trial court erred in overruling Cryolife's demurrer to the strict liability cause of action. * * *

In the present case, Cryolife contends that the cause of action for strict liability is barred by the defense of a tissue bank's statutory immunity to strict products liability under section 1635.2, despite the allegations in plaintiff's complaint stating that Cryolife manufactures and sells a product. Whether strict products liability applies to a tissue bank that supplied an allegedly defective human tissue for surgical implantation is an issue no California appellate court has considered. In contrast, it is well established that strict products liability does not apply to blood banks or other institutions that provide blood transfusions and blood products. [ ] In enacting section 1606, California, like many other states, enacted a "blood shield law" that provides immunity from strict liability claims.

California's blood shield law, section 1606, provides in pertinent part that "[t]he procurement, processing, distribution, or use of whole blood, plasma, blood products, and blood derivatives for the purpose of injecting or transfusing the same, or any of them, into the human body shall be construed to be, and is declared to be, for all purposes whatsoever, the rendition of a service by each and every person, firm, or corporation participating therein. . . . " The rationale for the blood shield law is that the supplying of blood by a hospital to a patient is "merely incidental" to the services rendered by the hospital. [ ] Also, the public policy in favor of promoting an adequate supply of blood militates against liability in the absence of negligence or intentional misconduct. [ ]

However, plaintiff argues that the Legislature has not enacted a similar shield law for tissue banks, and he emphasizes that the Health and Safety Code provision regarding tissue banks, section 1635.2 is phrased differently than section 1606, the blood shield law. Section

1635.2 provides, "The Legislature hereby declares its intent that the collection, processing, storage, or distribution of tissue for the purpose of transplantation, as regulated by this chapter, shall be deemed a service by those persons engaged in these activities. Therefore, the collection, processing, storage, or distribution of tissue for the purpose of transplantation, as regulated by this chapter, shall not be subject to the requirements of Division 2 [ ] of the Commercial Code."

Plaintiff contends that the omission in section 1635.2 of any language indicating that a tissue bank shall be deemed to provide a service "for all purposes," combined with the reference to the Commercial Code, indicates that the Legislature did not intend to immunize tissue banks from strict products liability and, instead, intended only to prevent application of the Commercial Code provisions for commercial sales. We do not find this argument persuasive, for several reasons.

First, section 1635.2 expressly provides that the collection, processing and storage of human tissue for transplantation "shall be deemed a service." The statute is unequivocal in its plain language, placing no limits on the circumstances in which a tissue bank will be deemed to have provided a service. Accordingly, we must follow the principle of statutory construction that "if statutory language is 'clear and unambiguous there is no need for construction, and courts should not indulge in it.' " [ ] Section 1635.2 clearly and unambiguously provides that tissue banks provide a service for all purposes, despite the omission of the specific phrase "for all purposes" from its language.

Moreover, the inclusion of language pertaining to the Commercial Code does not change the plain meaning of section 1635.2. Rather, the reference to the inapplicability of "Division 2 [ ] of the Commercial Code" further demonstrates the Legislature's intent to categorize a tissue bank regulated under the Health and Safety Code as a service provider. Division 2 of the Commercial Code concerns the sale of goods, including warranties. [ ] "[T]he liability imposed by strict liability in tort and breach of express and implied warranties is virtually the same, i.e., a form of liability without fault." [ ] Therefore, by expressly excluding the application of the sales and warranty provisions of the Commercial Code to "the collection, processing, storage, or distribution of tissue for the purpose of transplantation," [ ] the Legislature implicitly excluded such tissue-related activities from the application of the doctrine of strict liability.

Second, other statutory provisions also demonstrate the Legislature's broad intent that the provision of human tissue not be considered a sale of goods or products. The Uniform Anatomical Gift Act provides, "A person may not knowingly, for valuable consideration, purchase or sell a part for transplantation, therapy, or reconditioning, if removal of the part is intended to occur after the death of the decedent." [ ] However, payment for tissue-related services is allowed, including "the removal, processing, disposal, preservation, quality control, storage, transplantation, or implantation of a part." [ ] The Penal Code also provides that it is unlawful to knowingly sell human tissue (excluding plasma and sperm) for purposes of transplantation. [ ]

Third, we are guided by the analysis of the California Supreme Court in *Murphy v. E.R. Squibb & Sons, Inc.* (1985) 40 Cal.3d 672 [221 Cal.Rptr. 447, 710 P.2d 247], regarding a similar issue. In that case, the issue was whether a pharmacy where an allegedly defective drug was purchased could be held strictly liable for the alleged defects. The court concluded that a pharmacy had statutory immunity from strict liability pursuant to former Business and Professions Code section 4046, which provided that the profession of pharmacy was a "dynamic patient-oriented health service." The California Supreme Court concluded that this statutory provision provided pharmacies with immunity from strict liability similar to the immunity provided by the blood shield law, section 1606, despite the difference in the language of the two statutes.

The court acknowledged that "[i]t is true that section 1606 of the Health and Safety Code provides not only that the distribution and use of blood and blood plasma is a service, but also that they should be deemed not to constitute a sale, whereas [former] section 4046, subdivision (b), does not expressly declare that a sale is not involved in the practice of pharmacy." (*Murphy* [ ]) However, the court determined that when the Legislature enacted former Business and Professions Code section 4046, it must have known that a pharmacist's primary role was to fill prescriptions for medications sold to the public. For that reason, "[t]he Legislature must have intended ... that even though a pharmacist is paid for the medication he dispenses, his conduct in filling a prescription is to be deemed a service, and, like the manufacturer of blood plasma, a pharmacy is immune from strict liability." [ ]

We similarly conclude that, despite the difference in the language of section 1606 and section 1635.2, section 1635.2 provides statutory immunity from strict liability to tissue banks subject to regulation under the Health and Safety Code. When the Legislature enacted section 1635.2 in 1991 as part of a regulatory scheme for tissue banks, it had to know that tissue banks are paid for their activities in connection with providing human cadaver tissue for medical use. By expressly deeming such activities to constitute a service, the Legislature must have intended a tissue bank to be immune from strict liability, just like a pharmacy.

Our conclusion is in accord with other authorities. In *Condos v. Musculoskeletal Transplant Foundation* (D.Utah 2002) 208 F.Supp.2d 1226, 1230, the federal district court ruled for several reasons that donated human bone tissue used to repair the plaintiff's spine was not a product subject to strict products liability. First, the district court determined that no court had applied strict liability to the distribution of human tissue. [ ] Second, the district court found significant Utah's adoption of the Restatement (Third) of Torts, section 19, which states that blood and human tissue are excluded from strict products liability. The district court noted, "This is consistent with a general policy throughout the nation, as observed by the American Law Institute, against applying strict liability to the distribution of human tissue." [ ]

Third, the district court in *Condos v. Musculoskeletal Transplant Foundation* found the intent of the Utah State Legislature that the distribution of human tissue be considered a service was demonstrated by the Legislature's adoption of the Uniform Anatomical Gift Act, which prohibited the sale of human tissue for valuable consideration, as well as the Legislature's enactment of a blood shield law. [ ] The Utah blood shield law recognized that "medical transfusions and transplants are essentially medical services, even though a tangible item is involved in the process." [ ] Accordingly, the district court concluded, "human bone tissue is not a 'product' subject to products liability law, and [the] distribution of human tissue, including reasonable payments for related services, does not constitute a 'sale' for purposes of strict liability." [ ]

Finally, we see no reason that the public policy rationale for exempting blood products from strict liability should not also apply to human tissue products, such as the allograft at issue in the case at bar. This court has previously stated, "In our view there is a legitimate state interest in manufactured blood products. We concur in the perception that 'legislatures have determined that the production and use of human blood *and its derivatives* for therapeutic purposes should be encouraged; and for this purpose those who provide these products, and who are themselves free from fault, should not be required to bear the economic loss which might otherwise be imposed under the rules of strict liability which are applicable to sellers of commercial products generally.' " [ ] The California statutory provisions we have discussed reflect a similar legitimate state interest in human tissue products used for therapeutic purposes.

For these reasons, our de novo review shows that the first amended complaint on its face discloses the defense of statutory immunity under section 1635.2 to the cause of action for strict liability, and we therefore conclude that the trial court erred in overruling Cryolife's demurrer to that cause of action.

* * *

IV. DISPOSITION

Let a peremptory writ of mandate issue directing respondent court to (1) vacate its order overruling Cryolife's demurrer to the cause of action for strict liability and to enter a new order sustaining the demurrer without leave to amend * * *.

TAYLOR v. SMITHKLINE BEECHAM CORPORATION

Supreme Court of Michigan, 2003.
468 Mich. 1, 658 N.W.2d 127.

TAYLOR, J.

* * *

I

Tamara Taylor and Lee Anne Rintz filed a products liability lawsuit in the Wayne Circuit Court against Gate Pharmaceuticals and other manufacturers and distributors of certain prescription diet drugs, seeking damages for injuries resulting from use of the drugs. A similar lawsuit was filed in the Washtenaw Circuit Court by Judith and Kenneth Robards. In each lawsuit, the defendants filed a motion arguing that they were entitled to summary disposition on the basis of MCL 600.2946(5), which limits the liability of drug manufacturers and sellers where the drug at issue was approved for safety and efficacy by the United States Food and Drug Administration and labeled in compliance with FDA standards.

The respective plaintiffs opposed the motions for summary disposition, asserting that the statute was an unconstitutional delegation of legislative power. The Wayne Circuit Court entered an order denying defendants' motion for summary disposition, ruling that the statute was an unconstitutional delegation of legislative power. In contrast, the Washtenaw Circuit Court entered an order granting defendants' summary disposition motion, rejecting the claim that the statute was unconstitutional.

The Court of Appeals granted an application for leave to appeal in each lawsuit and consolidated the appeals. The Court concluded that MCL 600.2946(5) operates as an unconstitutional delegation of legislative authority because it places the FDA in the position of final arbiter with respect to whether a particular drug may form the basis of a products liability action in Michigan. We subsequently granted leave to appeal to defendants.

* * *

III

Before it was amended in 1995, MCL 600.2946(5) provided that evidence showing compliance with governmental or industry standards was admissible in a products liability action in determining if the standard of care had been met. [ ]. The 1995 amendment of the statute went one step further and provided that compliance with federal governmental standards (established by the FDA) is conclusive on the issue of due care for drugs.

MCL 600.2946(5) provides:

In a product liability action against a manufacturer or seller, a product that is a drug is not defective or unreasonably dangerous, and the manufacturer or seller is not liable, if the drug was approved for safety and efficacy by the United States food and drug administration, and the drug and its labeling were in compliance with the United States food and drug administration's approval at the time the drug left the control of the manufacturer or seller. However, this subsection does not apply to a drug that is sold in the United States after the effective date of an order of the United States food and drug administration to remove the drug from the market or to withdraw its approval. This subsection does not apply if the defendant at any time before the event that allegedly caused the injury does any of the following:

(a) Intentionally withholds from or misrepresents to the United States food and drug administration information concerning the drug that is required to be submitted under the federal food, drug, and cosmetic act, [ ] and the drug would not have been approved, or the United States food and drug administration would have withdrawn approval for the drug if the information were accurately submitted.

(b) Makes an illegal payment to an official or employee of the United States food and drug administration for the purpose of securing or maintaining approval of the drug.

Pursuant to this statute, unless the fraud exception in subsection a or the bribery exception contained in subsection b applies (plaintiffs make no such claim here), a manufacturer or seller of a drug that has been approved by the FDA has an absolute defense to a products liability claim if the drug and its labeling were in compliance with the FDA's approval at the time the drug left the control of the manufacturer or seller. Thus, the Legislature has determined that a drug manufacturer or seller that has properly obtained FDA approval of a drug product has acted sufficiently prudently so that no tort liability may lie.

IV

The United States Constitution provides that "all legislative powers herein granted shall be vested in a Congress of the United States. . . . " US Const, art I, § 1. Similarly, the Michigan Constitution provides that "the legislative power of the State of Michigan is vested in a senate and a house of representatives." Const 1963, art 4, § 1. The Michigan Constitution also provides: "The powers of government are divided into three branches: legislative, executive and judicial. No person exercising powers of one branch shall exercise powers properly belonging to another branch except as expressly provided in this constitution." Const 1963, art 3, § 2.

These constitutional provisions have led to the constitutional discipline that is described as the nondelegation doctrine. A simple statement of this doctrine is found in *Field v. Clark*, 143 U.S. 649, 692, 12 S.Ct.

495, 36 L.Ed. 294 (1892), in which the United States Supreme Court explained that "the integrity and maintenance of the system of government ordained by the Constitution" precludes Congress from delegating its legislative power to either the executive branch or the judicial branch. This concept has its roots in the separation of powers principle underlying our tripartite system of government. Yet, the United States Supreme Court, as well as this Court, has also recognized "that the separation of powers principle, and the nondelegation doctrine in particular, do not prevent Congress [or our Legislature] from obtaining the assistance of the coordinate Branches." *Mistretta v. United States*, 488 U.S. 361, 371, 109 S.Ct. 647, 102 L.Ed.2d 714 (1989).

The first category of nondelegation case law involves an assertion that the Congress or a state legislature improperly delegated its legislative power to a federal agency or state agency, respectively.

In the federal courts these improper delegation challenges to the power of federal regulatory agencies have been uniformly unsuccessful since the advent of large regulatory agencies in the 1930s. A recent case, which is representative of the manner in which the federal judiciary has handled these challenges, is *Whitman v. American Trucking Ass'ns*, 531 U.S. 457, 465, 121 S.Ct. 903, 149 L.Ed.2d 1 (2001), in which the United States Supreme Court considered a statute that directed the Environmental Protection Agency to set primary air quality standards "which are requisite to protect the public health" with "an adequate margin of safety." It was argued that this delegation was too vague. It was held, however, that this direction to the EPA was not an improper delegation of legislative authority to the agency because there was within the delegation "intelligible principle."

In Michigan, this Court has considered similar claims regarding statutes where the claims included an allegation of improperly delegating the Legislature's power to a Michigan agency, and we have rejected the claims on a basis similar to the federally developed rationale.

The second category of cases in which there are challenges concerning the delegation of legislative authority involves situations where the Congress, or the Legislature, enacts a statute that might be described as a referral statute in which, depending on a factual development that is outside the control of the legislative body, certain consequences will ensue.

* * *

Michigan's referral statutes are apparently so uncontroversial as to be rarely challenged. This is not surprising when one considers that, for example, any statutory reference to time, weight, age, gender, birth, death, or even print size for legal documents is an exercise of the Legislature referring to findings made by someone other than itself. As is apparent in the case of time this would be the Naval Observatory and when it comes to weights, it would be the National Bureau of Standards. Regarding birth and death, it would be the governmental agencies collecting vital statistics; and, in the case of print size, standards established by consensus in the printing industry. The Legislature can, of course, do such things without fear of running afoul of the nondelegation doctrine because these public or private agency fact findings are considered to be findings of independent significance. That is, there is no improper delegation where the agency or outside body making the finding (such as when it is, say, 7:00 a.m., or when a person was born, or what weight equals a pound, and so forth) is doing it for purposes independent of the particular statute to which it makes reference.

The independently significant standard was described well recently by the New Mexico Supreme Court in *Madrid v. St. Joseph Hosp.*, 1996 NMSC 64, 122 NM 524, 531, 928 P.2d 250 (1996), in which that court stated:

> Where a private organization's standards have significance independent of a legislative enactment, they may be incorporated into a statutory scheme without violating constitutional restrictions on delegation of legislative powers. A private entity's standards cannot be construed as a deliberate law-making act when their development of the standards is guided by objectives unrelated to the statute in which they function.

This concept was also recognized in *Lucas v. Maine Com. of Pharmacy*, 472 A.2d 904, 911 (1984), in which the Maine Supreme Court held that legislative incorporation of a decision by a private entity does not violate the nondelegation doctrine where the decision has aspects of significance beyond the legislature's reliance on it.

The independently significant standard has also been discussed by administrative law scholars. Professor Kenneth C. Davis in 1 Administrative Law (2d ed), § 3.12, p 196, has explained it as follows: "statutes whose operation depends upon private action which is taken for purposes which are independent of the statute." Here in Michigan, Thomas M. Cooley Law School Dean Don LeDuc, in his treatise on Michigan Administrative Law, § 2.25, p 71, has succinctly warned of its limitations and described its operation as follows: "Care must be exercised in distinguishing between statutes which delegate the authority to make the standards to private parties and those which refer to outside standards as the measuring device."

We deal here with the latter type of statute. MCL 600.2946(5) is a statute that refers to factual conclusions of independent significance, i.e., the FDA conclusion regarding the safety and efficacy of a drug, that once made causes, at the Michigan Legislature's direction, Michigan courts to find as a matter of law that the manufacturer or seller acted with due care. The FDA decision is, in Dean LeDuc's formulation, simply a "measuring device."

V

The Court of Appeals in its handling of this matter concluded that MCL 600.2946(5) is an unconstitutional delegation of legislative power because it believed the statute placed "the FDA in the position of final arbiter with respect to whether a particular drug may form the basis of a products liability action in Michigan." [ ]. Yet, this statute only establishes that a determination of independent significance, here the FDA finding that a drug is safe and effective, will be the measure in Michigan of whether the duty of reasonable care has been met by a drug manufacturer or seller in a tort case. While the Court of Appeals recognized that the Legislature can alter the common-law duty of reasonable care in a drug products liability tort case, the panel and the dissent in this Court contend that MCL 600.2946(5) went beyond this and gave the FDA the authority to "make, alter, amend, and repeal laws." [ ]. This is incorrect. The FDA does not decide who may bring a products liability action in Michigan; rather, the FDA, for its own reasons that are independent of Michigan tort law, simply makes a factual finding regarding the safety and efficacy of drugs. It is the Michigan Legislature that has determined the legal consequences that flow from that finding. The Legislature's action in doing so is no different from the Legislature's referring to weights and measures or even dates and times, which are, as discussed above, all findings of independent significance by bodies deemed by the Legislature to be expert. By using such independent determinations as a referent, the Legislature is not delegating how that fact will be used, just as the Congress in 1810 was not delegating the making of rules to France or Great Britain in *Cargo of the Brig Aurora, supra*.

The Court of Appeals acknowledged the independently significant standard, but placed an unjustified limitation on it. The panel correctly stated that, "assimilation of standards adopted for a purpose separate from the incorporating legislation, and having independent significance, presents no problem," but added a condition, which was *"if* the standards are established and essentially unchanging." [ ]. There is no sound legal basis for this limitation. Whether the Legislature's adoption of the actions of an external body as a cause for statutory legal consequences is a delegation of legislative authority cannot rationally depend on a court's perception of the relative permanence of the actions adopted.

The Court of Appeals, in buttressing its holding, relied on language in *Coffman v. State Bd. of Examiners in Optometry*, 331 Mich. 582, 50 N.W.2d 322 (1951), to the effect that the Legislature could not require an applicant for a license to practice optometry to have graduated from an optometry school or college that received a certain rating by the international association of boards of examiners in optometry. This language was dicta because the actual holding in *Coffman* was that the applicant was not entitled to mandamus. As dicta, it is in no sense binding authority.

The Court of Appeals also cited *Colony Town Club v. Michigan Unemployment Compensation Comm.*, 301 Mich. 107, 3 N.W.2d 28 (1942). This case merely rejected a party's *argument* that a decision by the federal government interpreting a federal statute was binding on a substantially similar Michigan statute. In contrast with the argument rejected in *Colony Town Club*, the statute at issue here [ ] neither purports to give the FDA the final say in the interpretation of a state statute nor provides that a Michigan court in applying Michigan law is bound by an interpretation made by a federal agency in interpreting a substantially similar provision of federal law. *Colony Town Club* is thus inapposite.

The Court of Appeals also cited *Dearborn Independent, Inc. v. Dearborn*, 331 Mich. 447, 49 N.W.2d 370 (1951). In *Dearborn*, the Court considered a statute that provided that a newspaper was qualified to publish legal notices if it was admitted by the United States Post Office for transmission of second-class mail. The Court held the statute in violation of the nondelegation doctrine because it "unlawfully attempts to delegate to the United States post-office department the determination of the qualifications of a newspaper to publish legal notices." [ ]. The Court was concerned that the statute made the validity of publication of legal notices dependent on the future as well as present regulations of the United States Post Office. *Id*. To the extent that the post office's decision whether to approve a newspaper for second-class mail is an act of independent significance, which it appears to us to be, *Dearborn Independent* is inconsistent with the independently significant standard. It was, thus, incorrectly decided in light of the law's subsequent development in this area and is overruled.

The Court of Appeals also cited *Radecki v. Director of Worker's Disability Compensation*, 208 Mich.App. 19, 526 N.W.2d 611 (1994). In *Radecki*, the Court considered a state statute that incorporated by reference a federal statute. The Court said that state statutes may incorporate existing federal statutes, but not future legislation. [ ] Utilizing its "no change" argument, the Court of Appeals characterized MCL 600.2946(5) as an impermissible "reference statute" that incorporates future standards promulgated by the FDA. [ ]. We disagree. First, MCL 600.2946(5) is not a "reference statute" as that phrase is used, which is to mean incorporation into Michigan law of a standard from a different jurisdiction as a rule of law to be applied in Michigan courts. Rather, it provides that certain legal consequences flow from factual determinations made by the FDA and is not a delegation. Accordingly, *Radecki*, whatever its merits as law, is not relevant to a consideration of whether MCL 600.2946(5) is an improper delegation of legislative power.

Finally, to deal with the last of the Michigan cases on which the Court of Appeals relied, our analysis is consistent with *Michigan Baptist Homes & Dev. Co. v. Ann Arbor*, 55 Mich.App. 725, 223 N.W.2d 324 (1974). In *Baptist Homes*, a state statute granted a property tax exemption to nonprofit corporations that had obtained financing under § 202 of the National Housing Act [ ]. The plaintiff argued that the Legislature had made the state tax exemption dependent upon action by the Secretary of Housing and Urban Development and that limiting the state statute in this manner was invalid because it was an unconstitutional delegation of power to a federal official to decide who gets the exemption. The Court of Appeals correctly rejected this argument, explaining that the federal official does not make a determination of who shall receive the state exemption. This is because the federal official merely determines which nonprofit corporations are eligible to receive federal financing pursuant to the federal act. This is to be understood, in Dean LeDuc's useful characterization, as an example of the "measuring stick." In our case, also, because the FDA decision is only the measure, i.e., the enabling fact, MCL 600.2946(5) is not an unlawful delegation of legislative authority.

VI

The dissent misunderstands the independently significant standard. What is central to grasping this doctrine is that if the fact or finding to which the Legislature refers has significance independent of a legislative enactment, because the agency or outside body making the finding is doing it for purposes independent from the particular statute that refers to it, then there is no delegation. Whether the fact or finding of independent significance changes thereafter is irrelevant to the question whether there has been an improper delegation.

In sum, MCL 600.2946(5) delegates nothing to the FDA; rather, it uses independently significant decisions of the FDA as a measuring device to set the standard of care for manufacturers and sellers of prescription drugs in Michigan. It represents a legislative determination as a matter of law of when a manufacturer or seller of a prescription drug has acted sufficiently reasonably, solely for the purpose of defining the limits of a cognizable products liability claim under Michigan law. Accordingly, we reverse the judgment of the Court of Appeals that the statute constitutes an improper delegation of legislative power.

FRIEDL v. AIRSOURCE, INC.

Appellate Court of Illinois, First District, Fourth Division, 2001.
323 Ill.App.3d 1039, 257 Ill.Dec. 459, 753 N.E.2d 1085.

JUSTICE BARTH delivered the opinion of the court:

* * *

BACKGROUND

The following is contained in the complaint. Fried suffers from multiple sclerosis. As a result, she is prone to developing sores and lesions on her feet. In an attempt to reduce the pain associated with the lesions, Friedl sought and obtained a prescription from her physician for a portable hyperbaric oxygen chamber. Friedl leased a "Hyper-pulse" intermittent topical oxygen chamber from defendants which delivered it to her home.

Friedl used the machine for several weeks, but the condition of her feet continued to deteriorate. When Friedl complained to defendants, they told her she needed to use the machine for longer periods of time. Friedl continued to use the machine and suffered oxygen burns to her feet as a result. Friedl alleged the oxygen burns were caused by defendants' failure to instruct her properly on the operation of the machine.

Specifically, she alleged that defendants did not instruct her to put water into the machine in order to humidify the oxygen during use, that they did not provide her with the necessary available video and written materials on the machine's use and operation and that the operating instructions they did give her were misleading and insufficient.

Defendants filed a motion to dismiss pursuant to sections 2–615 and 2–619 of the Illinois Code of Civil Procedure (Code). [ ] Defendants section 2–619 motion argued that because the machine was prescribed for Friedl's use by her physician and defendants merely delivered the machine, the learned intermediary doctrine insulated defendants from liability. The trial court dismissed the action against defendants on section 2–619 grounds and this appeal followed.

ANALYSIS

* * *

The learned intermediary doctrine was adopted by our supreme court in Kirk v. Michael Reese Hospital & Medical Center, 117 Ill.2d 507, 111 Ill.Dec. 944, 513 N.E.2d 387 (1987). The Kirk court found that under the learned intermediary doctrine, prescription drug manufacturers' duty to warn of a drug's known dangerous propensities extended only to prescribing doctors. [ ] The doctors, in turn, using their medical judgment, had a duty to convey those warnings to their patients. [ ]. The court recognized that prescription drugs were complex medicines with varied effects and that a physician's selection of a particular drug and drug warnings for a particular patient was an informed one, based on his individual knowledge of the drug's propensities and his patient's susceptibilities. [ ]. Because the physician thus acted as a "learned intermediary" between the manufacturer and the consumer with prescription drugs, a manufacturer had fulfilled its duty to warn if it had informed the physician of the drug's known dangerous effects. [ ]

This court has extended the learned intermediary doctrine set forth in Kirk to pharmacists. Most recently, in Fakhouri v. Taylor, 248 Ill.App.3d 328, 329–30, 187 Ill.Dec. 927, 618 N.E.2d 518 (1993), the plaintiff, as administrator for the decedent's estate, filed a wrongful death action against the defendant pharmacists, alleging the pharmacists should have warned either the decedent or the decedent's doctor that the prescribed dosage of medication exceeded the manufacturer's recommended dosage. The Fakhouri court reviewed with approval our prior decisions in Leesley v. West, 165 Ill.App.3d 135, 116 Ill.Dec. 136, 518 N.E.2d 758 (1988), and in Eldridge v. Eli Lilly & Co., 138 Ill.App.3d 124, 92 Ill.Dec. 740, 485 N.E.2d 551 (1985) which held that like prescription drug manufacturers, pharmacists did not have a duty to warn customers of a drug's potential adverse effects. Fakhouri, 248 Ill.App.3d at 333. In Leesley, the court found that because a prescription drug that has been prescribed by a doctor who has received manufacturer drug warnings is not an unreasonably dangerous product, the learned intermediary doctrine dictated that neither the manufacturer nor the pharmacist was required to provide consumer drug warnings. [ ]. In Eldridge, the court ruled that the selection of a patient's medication required the individualized medical judgment that only the patient's physician possessed and that requiring pharmacists to warn consumers about the dangers of a prescription drug would improperly place the pharmacist in the middle of the doctor-patient relationship. [ ]

The learned intermediary doctrine has been considered by this court in relation to medical device manufacturers. Hansen v. Baxter Healthcare Corp., 309 Ill.App.3d 869, 881, 243 Ill.Dec. 270, 723 N.E.2d 302 (1999), *appeal allowed,* 188 Ill.2d 564, 729 N.E.2d 495 (2000), was a products liability action in which the plaintiff argued the defendant had failed to warn consumers its luer slip connectors used with intravenous tubing could come apart in use. The court explained that in medical device cases, the intended audience for product warnings was not the patients, but the prescribing physicians. [ ] Consequently, as with prescription drugs, medical device manufacturers have a duty to warn physicians of the device's dangerous propensities who then had a duty to convey any relevant warnings to their patients. [ ]. However, since a medical device manufacturer had no duty to warn physicians of a device's dangers if the medical community was already generally aware of those dangers and trial testimony showed the medical community knew the luer slip connectors could separate, the defendant Baxter Healthcare had no duty to warn. * * *

Defendants contended in their motion to dismiss that under the learned intermediary doctrine, they had no duty to warn Friedl of the hyperbaric chamber's dangerous propensities. According to defendants, because they merely delivered the prescription device Friedl's physician had ordered for her, their role was analogous to that of the pharmacist. The trial court's rationale for granting the motion to dismiss is not part of the record before us.

We deem defendants' reliance on the learned intermediary doctrine to be misplaced. Unlike the medical device cases in which the learned intermediary doctrine has previously been considered, suitability of the device as a treatment for a plaintiff's condition is not at issue here. [ ]. The rationale for the development and implementation of the learned intermediary doctrine is not implicated by the complaint. The complaint against the defendants does not suggest that the hyperbaric chamber was wrongly prescribed, taking into consideration the inherently dangerous propensities of the device in conjunction with Friedl's particular susceptibilities. Her complaint does not allege that defendants should have warned her not to use the hyperbaric chamber as prescribed by her physician. [ ]. Nor does it allege defendants failed to warn her of any risks associated with the correct use of the machine as prescribed. [ ]. Instead, Friedl alleged defendants failed to provide her with the basic instructions necessary for the machine's proper operation by failing to tell her the unit needed to be filled with water prior to use in order to humidify the oxygen used in the therapy and by failing to provide her with the necessary available video and written materials illustrating proper operation of the machine. The defendants have not cited, nor has our research discovered, any Illinois case that stands for the proposition that a medical device manufacturer or distributor that provides incomplete operating instructions, resulting in injuries unrelated to whether the device was properly prescribed, is nevertheless immunized from liability by the learned intermediary doctrine. We decline to make such a pronouncement. We hold that the learned intermediary doctrine does not apply to bar actions against distributors of prescribed medical devices for failing to properly instruct the consumer about the device's operation. Accordingly, the trial court erred in dismissing Friedl's action against defendants.

For the reasons set forth, the order of the trial court is reversed and the cause is remanded for further proceedings consistent with this order.

Reversed and remanded.

ANDERSON v. SOMBERG

Supreme Court of New Jersey, 1975.
67 N.J. 291, 338 A.2d 1, cert. denied, 423 U.S.
929, 96 S.Ct. 279, 46 L.Ed.2d 258 (1975).

PASHMAN, JUSTICE.

These negligence-products liability actions had their inception in a surgery performed in 1967 on the premises of defendant St. James Hospital. Plaintiff Henry Anderson was undergoing a laminectomy, a back operation, performed by defendant Dr. Harold Somberg. During the course of the procedure, the tip or cup of an angulated pituitary rongeur, a forceps-like instrument, broke off while the tool was being manipulated in plaintiff's spinal canal. The surgeon attempted to retrieve the metal but was unable to do so. After repeated failure in that attempt, he terminated the operation. The imbedded fragment caused medical complications and further surgical interventions were required. Plaintiff has suffered significant and permanent physical injury proximately caused by the rongeur fragment which lodged in his spine.

Plaintiff sued (1) Dr. Somberg for medical malpractice, alleging that the doctor's negligent action caused the rongeur to break; (2) St. James Hospital, alleging that it negligently furnished Dr. Somberg with a defective surgical instrument; (3) Reinhold–Schumann, Inc., the medical supply distributor which furnished the defective rongeur to the hospital, on a warranty theory, and (4) Lawton Instrument Co. (Lawton), the manufacturer of the rongeur, on a strict liability in tort claim, alleging that the rongeur was a defective product. In short, plaintiff sued all who might have been liable for his injury, absent some alternative explanation such as contributory negligence.

* * *

Defendant Lawton called a metallurgist, John Carroll, as an expert witness. He testified that an examination of the broken rongeur revealed neither structural defect nor faulty workmanship. He said that the examination (conducted at an optical magnification 500 times normal size) revealed a secondary crack near the main crack, but he could not suggest how or when that crack formed. Mr. Carroll offered an opinion as to the cause of the instrument's breaking: the instrument had been strained, he said, probably because of an improper "twisting" of the tool. The strain, however, could have been cumulative, over the course of several operations, and the instrument could conceivably have been cracked when handed to Dr. Somberg and broken in its normal use.

In short, when all the evidence had been presented, no theory for the cause of the rongeur's breaking was within reasonable contemplation save for the possible negligence of Dr. Somberg in using the instrument, or the possibility that the surgeon had been given a defective instrument, which defect would be attributable to a dereliction of duty by the manufacturer, the distributor, the hospital, or all of them.

The case was submitted to a jury on special interrogatories, and the jury returned a finding of no cause as to each defendant. On appeal, the entire appellate panel concurred in an order for a new trial. 134 N.J.Super. 1, 338 A.2d 35 (1973). * * *

The position adopted by the appellate division majority seems to us substantially correct; that is, at the close of all the evidence, it was apparent that at least one of the defendants was liable for plaintiff's injury, because no alternative theory of liability was within reasonable contemplation. Since defendants had engaged in conduct which activated legal obligations by each of them to plaintiff, the jury should have been instructed that the failure of any defendant to prove his nonculpability would trigger liability; and further, that since at least one of the defendants could not sustain his burden of proof, at least one would be liable. A no cause of action verdict against all primary and third-party defendants will be unacceptable and would work a miscarriage of justice sufficient to require a new trial. * * *

In the ordinary case, the law will not assist an innocent plaintiff at the expense of an innocent defendant. However, in the type of case we consider here, where an unconscious or helpless patient suffers an admitted mishap not reasonably foreseeable and unrelated to the scope of the surgery (such as cases where foreign objects are left in the body of the patient), those who had custody of the patient, and who owed him a duty of care as to medical treatment, or not to furnish a defective instrument for use in such treatment, can be called to account for their default. They must prove their nonculpability, or else risk liability for the injuries suffered.

* * *

The rule of evidence we set forth does not represent the doctrine of res ipsa loquitur as it has been traditionally understood. Res ipsa loquitur is ordinarily impressed only where the injury more probably than not has resulted from negligence of the defendant * * *, and defendant was in exclusive control of the instrument. * * * The doctrine has been expanded to include, as in the instant matter, multiple defendants * * *, although even this expansion has been criticized * * *. It has also been expanded to embrace cases where the negligence cause was not the only or most probable theory in the case, but where the alternate theories of liability accounted for the only possible causes of injury. * * * That is the situation in this case, where we find negligence, strict liability in tort, and breach of warranty all advanced as possible theories of liability. In such cases, defendants are required to come forward and give their evidence. The latter development represents a substantial deviation from earlier conceptions of res ipsa loquitur and has more accurately been called "akin to res ipsa loquitur," NOPCO Chem. Div. v. Blaw–Knox Co., 59 N.J. 274, 281 A.2d 793 (1971), or "conditional res ipsa loquitur." Quintal v. Laurel Grove Hosp., 62 Cal.2d 154, 166, 41 Cal.Rptr. 577, 397 P.2d 161 (1965) * * *.

In *NOPCO*, the liability for damages to a delivered product could be attributed with great probability either to the negligence of any one in a series of bailees or the breach of warranty of the seller. The court stated that when several defendants individually owe plaintiff a duty, and all might have caused his loss and have superior knowledge of the occurrence, they all are bound to come forward and give an account of what happened. In that case, the application of res ipsa loquitur was thought to call for an explanatory rather than an exculpatory account, which would be sufficient to meet defendant's burden, according to the traditional rule. * * *

In *NOPCO,* however, plaintiff is still made to bear the burden of proof vis-a-vis each defendant, and it was upon such instruction that the present case was submitted to the jury. We now hold that a mere shift in the burden of going forward, as adopted in *NOPCO,* is insufficient. For this particular type of case, an equitable alignment of duties owed plaintiff requires that not only the burden of going forward shift to defendants, but the actual burden of proof as well. Since at least one primary or third-party defendant must inevitably fail to meet his burden, a verdict must be returned for the plaintiff.

* * *

Further, we note that at the close of all the evidence, no reasonable suggestion had been offered that the occurrence could have arisen because of plaintiff's contributory negligence, or some act of nature; that is, there was no explanation for the occurrence in the case save for negligence or defect on the part of someone connected with the manufacture, handling, or use of the instrument. (Any such proof would be acceptable to negative plaintiff's prima facie case.) Since all parties had been joined who could reasonably have been connected with that negligence or defect, it was clear that one of those parties was liable, and at least one could not succeed in his proofs.

In cases of this type, no defendant will be entitled to prevail on a motion for judgment until all the proofs have been presented to the court and jury. The judge may grant any motion bearing in mind that the plaintiff must recover a verdict against at least one defendant. Inferences and doubts at this stage are resolved in favor of the plaintiff. If only one defendant remains by reason of the court's action, then, in fact, the judge is directing a verdict of liability against that defendant.

* * *

The judgment of the appellate division is hereby affirmed, and the cause remanded for trial upon instructions consonant with this opinion.

JACOBS, J., concurs in the result * * *.

MOUNTAIN, J., dissenting. * * *

[T]he record is replete with testimony that other surgeons—perhaps as many as 20—have used the rongeur during the four years that it has formed part of the surgical equipment of the hospital, and that any one or more of them may perfectly well have been responsible for so injuring the instrument that it came apart while being manipulated in plaintiff's incision; or that it may have been weakened to near breaking point by cumulative misuse, entirely by persons not now before the court. In the face of this uncontroverted proof that the surgical instrument had been used upon approximately 20 earlier occasions and possibly by the same number of different surgeons, in the hands of any of whom it may have been fatally misused, how then can it be said that the wrongdoer is surely in court! There is a far greater likelihood that he is no party to this litigation at all and that his identity will never be established.

* * *

The opinion takes the view that at this point the burden of proof shifted to defendants. This, as is apparently conceded, has not hitherto been the law of this state. * * * Nevertheless this alteration in the law may be entirely reasonable and justified—at least if limited to this kind of medical malpractice case. * * * Thus far, as to the negligence claims, I might be persuaded to agree with the court.

But certainly no farther. At this point the *effect* to be given a shift in the burden of proof becomes the crucial issue. The authorities which have adopted or espoused the view that res ipsa shifts the burden of proof have, as far as I can discover, understood this to mean that upon such a shift taking place, a defendant becomes obliged to offer evidence explaining his own conduct or throwing light upon the circumstances attending plaintiff's injury, which will be of sufficient probative force to establish his lack of fault by a preponderance of the evidence. The fact finder will then be called upon to decide whether the defendant's proofs have met this test or whether they have fallen short.

The view expressed by the court in this case as to the effect of shifting the burden of proof appears to be something quite different. Under this new rule it is no longer enough that a defendant meet the standard described above. His role is no longer simply that of one who may hope to succeed if his proofs justify a verdict. Rather he now finds himself one of a band of persons from among whom one or more *must* be singled out to respond in damages to the plaintiff's claim. He is now a member of a group who must collectively, among themselves, play a game of *sauve qui peut*—and play it for rather high stakes. With all due respect I submit that at this point there has been complete departure from the rule of reason; the argument is now stripped of all rational basis.

* * *

I would vote to reverse the judgment of the appellate division and to reinstate the judgment of the trial court.

CLIFFORD, J., and JUDGE COLLESTER join in this dissenting opinion.[1]

Note on Medical Product Manufacturers' Liability

The manufacturers of prescription drugs, articles, devices, and instruments are liable for personal injuries and death caused by defective and dangerous products. Medical product manufacturers have been in the forefront of developments in the general law of product liability so much so, and producing judicial opinions of such great length, that to treat the liability of medical product manufacturers would call for a chapter as large as any in the casebook. Feeling that law students read these cases in other courses, the editors have devoted this chapter to liabilities of health care providers that arise in connection with medical products.

Here are abstracts of a new, as well as a few older, cases:

Ellis v. C.R. Bard, 311 F.3d 1272 (11th Cir. 2002). An automatic, programmable morphine pump, programmed pursuant to a doctor's orders to regulate the timing of the delivery of the drug, was prescribed for a patient following knee surgery. Although not authorized to allow third persons to activate the pump, a nurse instructed one of the patient's daughters to do so, and she, in turn, instructed another daughter. Both activated the pump, resulting in death of the patient from an overdose of morphine. The manufacturer was sued for failing to include a written warning on the pump indicating the danger of third-party activation. The Eleventh Circuit denied the claim on the basis that the "learned intermediary" rule does not require a manufacturer to warn end-users where only a physician or other health care provider was authorized to activate the pump.

MacDonald v. Ortho Pharmaceutical Corp., 394 Mass. 131, 475 N.E.2d 65, cert. denied, 474 U.S. 920, 106 S.Ct. 250, 88 L.Ed.2d 258 (1985). Where drugs (contraceptive pills) are prescribed to healthy patients who see their physicians only once a year, the manufacturers have the duty under state law to warn patients directly of serious side-effects

---

1. Editors' Note: Three justices joined the plurality opinion, one concurred, and three dissented. The case was retried, and the jury awarded $40,000 to the plaintiff against the manufacturer (which appealed) and the distributor. Accepting the plurality opinion as the law of New Jersey, the appellate division affirmed. 158 N.J.Super. 384, 386 A.2d 413 (1978).

(here stroke). The duty is neither obviated by the physician's role as learned intermediary, under state law, nor preempted by federal regulations that establish the content of manufacturers' brochures that are dispensed to the drug purchasers.

Hymowitz v. Eli Lilly & Co., 73 N.Y.2d 487, 541 N.Y.S.2d 941, 539 N.E.2d 1069, cert. denied 493 U.S. 944, 110 S.Ct. 350, 107 L.Ed.2d 338 (1989). In a DES case, the national market share theory is the appropriate method for determining liability and apportioning damages, but no manufacturer will be liable for damages in excess of its market share. DES cases from other jurisdictions, especially California, e.g., Brown v. Superior Court, 44 Cal.3d 1049, 245 Cal.Rptr. 412, 751 P.2d 470 (1988), are discussed and updated.

In re Richardson–Merrell, Inc., 624 F.Supp. 1212 (S.D.Ohio 1985). Chief Judge Rubin trifurcated the jury trial of an 844–case multi-district proceeding on Benectin birth defect claims. On trial of the first issue, the jury ended the case by finding that the drug did not cause the birth defects. The jury instructions are reprinted in full. Aff'd in this respect, 857 F.2d 290 (6th Cir.1988).

Richardson v. Richardson–Merrell, Inc. In another multi-district Bendectin case tried separately, District Judge Jackson bifurcated the issues and, on the issue of causation, granted judgment for the drug manufacturer notwithstanding the $1.16 million verdict for plaintiffs. 649 F.Supp. 799 (D.D.C.1986). The court of appeals affirmed. 857 F.2d 823 (D.C.Cir.1988).

Senn v. Merrell–Dow Pharmaceuticals, Inc., 305 Or. 256, 751 P.2d 215 (1988). A child received a DPT vaccination in 1977 and developed encephalopathy. Only two manufacturers could have produced the vaccine. The plaintiff argued that they were alternatively liable under Restatement (Second) of Torts § 433B (1965), but in answering questions of Oregon law certified by the Ninth Circuit, the supreme court rejected alternative liability, regardless of the number of defendants.

With respect to legal immunity for manufacturers in order to assure supplies of vaccines, the Swine Flu statute[2] has been followed by the National Childhood Vaccine Injury Act of 1986.[3]

---

2. 42 U.S.C.A. § 247b(k) (repealed; see historical note in U.S.C.A.).

3. 42 U.S.C.A. §§ 300aa–15Faa–33.

Chapter 9

NON–MEDICAL ACTS

INTRODUCTORY NOTE

Health care providers expose themselves to medical liability by performing medical acts, such as negligently diagnosing and treating patients and failing to secure informed consent. Health care providers also incur public liability to strangers and invitees for negligent non-medical acts that arise out of life's general activities, including driving vehicles and maintaining buildings.

Lying between acts of medical negligence and acts of public liability are a miscellaneous group of theories of claim arising from non-medical acts that have their impact upon patients and significant others. Non-medical acts include promising results and methods, making misrepresentations, and otherwise engaging in tortious conduct under theories of claim that the editors call collectively "sue the bastards." The cases here have been selected to illustrate problems that are familiar to physicians in practice; the editors have exercised their policy against including medicolegal horror stories, of which there are many.

None of these theories of claim is used very often. The use of a particular theory testifies to the lawyer's creativity and the client's anger. Usually the theory was employed by the plaintiff's lawyer because the medical negligence claim was not available. The plaintiff usually gave up something of litigation value in order to employ it. Some of the acts alleged are not insurable. It is no accident that many of the cases that follow have not been tried to verdict, but ended at trial by dismissal or summary judgment. By no means do plaintiffs always win, or win much money, on these theories, because they often impute implausible states of mind or intentions to the actor whose non-medical acts allegedly did the harm.

SECTION A. PROMISES AND DAMAGES

SULLIVAN v. O'CONNOR

Supreme Judicial Court of Massachusetts, 1973.
363 Mass. 579, 296 N.E.2d 183, 99 A.L.R.3d 294.[1]

KAPLAN, JUSTICE.

The plaintiff patient, Alice Sullivan, secured a jury verdict of $13,500 against the defendant surgeon, James H. O'Connor, for breach of contract in respect to an operation upon the plaintiff's nose. * * *

[T]he plaintiff alleged that she, as patient, entered into a contract with the defendant, a surgeon, wherein the defendant promised to perform plastic surgery on her nose and thereby to enhance her beauty and improve her appearance; that he performed the surgery but failed to achieve the promised result; rather the result of the surgery was to disfigure and deform her nose, to cause her pain in body and mind, and to subject her to other damage and expense. * * *

* * * The plaintiff was a professional entertainer, and this was known to the defendant. The agreement was as alleged in the declaration. More particularly, judging from exhibits, the plaintiff's nose had been straight, but long and prominent; the defendant undertook by two operations to reduce its prominence and somewhat to shorten it, thus making it more pleasing in relation to the plaintiff's other features. Actually the plaintiff was obliged to undergo three operations, and her appearance was worsened. Her nose now had a concave line to about the midpoint, at which it became bulbous; viewed frontally, the nose from bridge to midpoint was flattened and broadened, and the two sides of the tip had lost symmetry. This configuration evidently could not be improved by further surgery. The plaintiff did not demonstrate, however, that her change of appearance had resulted in loss of employment. Payments by the plaintiff covering the defendant's fee and hospital expenses were stipulated at $622.65.

The judge instructed the jury, first, that the plaintiff was entitled to recover her out-of-pocket expenses incident to the operations. Second, she could recover the damages flowing directly, naturally, proximately, and foreseeably from the defendant's breach of promise. These would comprehend damages for any disfigurement of the plaintiff's nose—that is, any change of appearance for the worse—including the effects of the consciousness of such disfigurement on the plaintiff's mind, and in this connection the jury should consider the nature of the plaintiff's profession. Also consequent upon the defendant's breach, and compensable, were the pain and suffering involved in the third operation, but not in the first two. * * *

---

1. Annot., Measure and Elements of Damages in Action Against Physician for Breach of Contract to Achieve Particular Result or Cure, 99 A.L.R.3d 303 (1980).

By his exceptions the defendant contends that the judge erred in allowing the jury to take into account anything but the plaintiff's out-of-pocket expenses (presumably at the stipulated amount). * * *

It has been suggested on occasion that agreements between patients and physicians by which the physician undertakes to effect a cure or to bring about a given result should be declared unenforceable on grounds of public policy. See Guilmet v. Campbell, 385 Mich. 57, 188 N.W.2d 601, 616 (1971) (dissenting opinion). But there are many decisions recognizing and enforcing such contracts, * * * and the law of Massachusetts has treated them as valid, although we have had no decision meeting head-on the contention that they should be denied legal sanction. * * * These causes of action are, however, considered a little suspect, and thus we find courts straining sometimes to read the pleadings as sounding only in tort for negligence, and not in contract for breach of promise, despite sedulous efforts by the pleaders to pursue the latter theory. See Gault v. Sideman, 42 Ill.App.2d 96, 191 N.E.2d 436 (1963) * * *.

It is not hard to see why the courts should be unenthusiastic or skeptical about the contract theory. Considering the uncertainties of medical science and the variations in the physical and psychological conditions of individual patients, doctors can seldom in good faith promise specific results. Therefore it is unlikely that physicians of even average integrity will in fact make such promises. Statements of opinion by the physician with some optimistic coloring are a different thing, and may indeed have therapeutic value. But patients may transform such statements into firm promises in their own minds, especially when they have been disappointed in the event, and testify in that sense to sympathetic juries.[2] If actions for breach of promise can be readily maintained, doctors, so it is said, will be frightened into practicing "defensive medicine." On the other hand, if these actions were outlawed, leaving only the possibility of suits for malpractice, there is fear that the public might be exposed to the enticements of charlatans, and confidence in the profession might ultimately be shaken. See Miller, The Contractual Liability of Physicians and Surgeons, 1953 Wash.U.L.Q. 413, 416–423. The law has taken the middle of the road position of allowing actions based on alleged contract, but insisting on clear proof.[3] Instructions to the jury may well stress this requirement and point to tests of truth, such as the complexity or difficulty of an operation as bearing on the probability that a given result was promised. * * *

---

2. Judicial skepticism about whether a promise was in fact made derives also from the possibility that the truth has been tortured to give the plaintiff the advantage of the longer period of limitations sometimes available for actions on contract as distinguished from those in tort or for malpractice. See Lillich, The Malpractice Statute of Limitations in New York and Other Jurisdictions, 47 Cornell L.Q. 339 (1962) * * *.

3. Editors' Note: In Sard v. Hardy, 281 Md. 432, 379 A.2d 1014, 1027 (1977), the court wrote,

We * * * adopt the rule that although a patient may recover for breach of an express, pre-operative warranty to effect a particular result, despite the absence of a separate consideration, he may do so only upon proving by clear and convincing evidence that the physician did, in fact, make the alleged warranty.

If an action on the basis of contract is allowed, we have next the question of the measure of damages to be applied where liability is found. Some cases have taken the simple view that the promise by the physician is to be treated like an ordinary commercial promise, and accordingly that the successful plaintiff is entitled to a standard measure of recovery for breach of contract—"compensatory" ("expectancy") damages, an amount intended to put the plaintiff in the position he would be in if the contract had been performed, or, presumably, at the plaintiff's election, "restitution" damages, an amount corresponding to any benefit conferred by the plaintiff upon the defendant in the performance of the contract disrupted by the defendant's breach. See Restatement of Contracts § 329 and comment a, §§ 347, 384(1).

Thus in Hawkins v. McGee, 84 N.H. 114, 146 A. 641 (1929), the defendant doctor was taken to have promised the plaintiff to convert his damaged hand by means of an operation into a good or perfect hand, but the doctor so operated as to damage the hand still further. The court, following the usual expectancy formula, would have asked the jury to estimate and award to the plaintiff the difference between the value of a good or perfect hand, as promised, and the value of the hand after the operation. (The same formula would apply, although the dollar result would be less, if the operation had neither worsened nor improved the condition of the hand.) If the plaintiff had not yet paid the doctor his fee, that amount would be deducted from the recovery. There could be no recovery for the pain and suffering of the operation, since that detriment would have been incurred even if the operation had been successful; one can say that this detriment was not "caused" by the breach. But where the plaintiff by reason of the operation was put to more pain that he would have had to endure, had the doctor performed as promised, he should be compensated for that difference as a proper part of his expectancy recovery. It may be noted that on an alternative count for malpractice the plaintiff in the *Hawkins* case had been nonsuited; but on ordinary principles this could not affect the contract claim, for it is hardly a defense to a breach of contract that the promisor acted innocently and without negligence. The New Hampshire court further refined the *Hawkins* analysis in McQuaid v. Michou, 85 N.H. 299, 157 A. 881 (1932), all in the direction of treating the patient-physician cases on the ordinary footing of expectancy. See McGee v. United States Fidelity & Guar. Co., 53 F.2d 953 (1st Cir.1931) (later development in the *Hawkins* case) * * *.

Other cases, including a number in New York, without distinctly repudiating the *Hawkins* type of analysis, have indicated that a different and generally more lenient measure of damages is to be applied in patient-physician actions based on breach of alleged special agreements to effect a cure, attain a stated result, or employ a given medical method. This measure is expressed in somewhat variant ways, but the substance is that the plaintiff is to recover any expenditures made by him and for other detriment (usually not specifically described in the opinions) following proximately and foreseeably upon the defendant's failure to carry out his promise. Robins v. Finestone, 308 N.Y. 543, 127 N.E.2d 330, 332 (1955) * * *.

This, be it noted, is not a "restitution" measure, for it is not limited to restoration of the benefit conferred on the defendant (the fee paid), but includes other expenditures, for example, amounts paid for medicine and nurses; so also it would seem according to its logic to take in damages for any worsening of the plaintiff's condition due to the breach. Nor is it an "expectancy" measure, for it does not appear to contemplate recovery of the whole difference in value between the condition as promised and the condition actually resulting from the treatment. Rather the tendency of the formulation is to put the plaintiff back in the position he occupied just before the parties entered upon the agreement, to compensate him for the detriments he suffered in reliance upon the agreement. This kind of intermediate pattern of recovery for breach of contract is discussed in the suggestive article by Fuller and Perdue, The Reliance Interest in Contract Damages, 46 Yale L.J. 52, 373 (1936), where the authors show that, although not attaining the currency of the standard measures, a "reliance" measure has for special reasons been applied by the courts in a variety of settings, including noncommercial settings. * * *

The question of recovery on a reliance basis for pain and suffering or mental distress requires further attention. We find expressions in the decisions that pain and suffering (or the like) are simply not compensable in actions for breach of contract. The defendant seemingly espouses this proposition in the present case. True, if the buyer under a contract for the purchase of a lot of merchandise, in suing for the seller's breach, should claim damages for mental anguish caused by his disappointment in the transaction, he would not succeed; he would be told, perhaps, that the asserted psychological injury was not fairly foreseeable by the defendant as a probable consequence of the breach of such a business contract. See Restatement of Contracts § 341, and comment a.

But there is no general rule barring such items of damage in actions for breach of contract. It is all a question of the subject matter and background of the contract, and when the contract calls for an operation on the person of the plaintiff, psychological as well as physical injury may be expected to figure somewhere in the recovery, depending on the particular circumstances. * * *

Again, it is said in a few of the New York cases, concerned with the classification of actions for statute of limitations purposes, that the absence of allegations demanding recovery for pain and suffering is characteristic of a contract claim by a patient against a physician, that such allegations rather belong in a claim for malpractice. * * *. These remarks seem unduly sweeping. Suffering or distress resulting from the breach going beyond that which was envisaged by the treatment as agreed, should be compensable on the same ground as the worsening of the patient's condition because of the breach. Indeed it can be argued that the very suffering or distress "contracted for" that which would have been incurred if the treatment achieved the promised result should also be compensable on the theory underlying the New York cases. For that suffering is "wasted" if the treatment fails. Otherwise stated, compensation for this waste is arguably required in order to complete the restoration of the status quo ante.

In the light of the foregoing discussion, all the defendant's exceptions fail: the plaintiff was not confined to the recovery of her out-of-pocket expenditures; she was entitled to recover also for the worsening of her condition,[4] and for the pain and suffering and mental distress involved in the third operation. These items were compensable on either an expectancy or a reliance view. We might have been required to elect between the two views if the pain and suffering connected with the first two operations contemplated by the agreement, or the whole difference in value between the present and the promised conditions, were being claimed as elements of damage. But the plaintiff waives her possible claim to the former element, and to so much of the latter as represents the difference in value between the promised condition and the condition before the operations.

* * *

Defendant's exceptions overruled.

HANSEN v. VIRGINIA MASON MEDICAL CENTER

Court of Appeals of Washington, Division One, 2002.
113 Wn.App. 199, 53 P.3d 60.

SCHINDLER, J.

* * *

FACTS

Kurt Hansen began experiencing symptoms of neurological dysfunction in the early 1990's. He met with Dr. Lynne Taylor, a neuro-oncologist at Virginia Mason Medical Center, for the first time in March 1993. Hansen had previously seen several physicians, including three neurologists, who had been unable to diagnose his condition.

Dr. Taylor saw Hansen three times between March and June of 1993. During the first visit, Dr. Taylor examined Hansen, reviewed his medical records and concluded it was "most likely" that Hansen suffered from multiple sclerosis. Dr. Taylor recommended further diagnostic tests. Hansen returned again in June to request a letter for his insurance company. Dr. Taylor again performed an examination and concluded that although the "diagnosis is still that of a demyelinating disease" a repeat MRI scan would be helpful. Hansen returned to review the results of the MRI, and Dr. Taylor recommended that he should be seen for a follow-up in six months.

---

4. That condition involves a mental element, and appraisal of it properly called for consideration of the fact that the plaintiff was an entertainer. * * *

Approximately two years later, in September 1995, Hansen returned to see Dr. Taylor. In the intervening period, Hansen had seen other neurologists who had been unable to reach a firm diagnosis of his illness. He saw Dr. Taylor periodically for six months between September 1995 and February 1996. In Dr. Taylor's notes from Hanson's visit in September 1995, she remarked that his condition had significantly deteriorated. Dr. Taylor characterized his illness as "multiple sclerosis with a chronic progressive course". In her notes following an appointment in early January 1996, Dr. Taylor remarked that she had not reached a positive diagnosis, stating: "A bazaar [sic] variety of demyelinating disease is still felt to be possible, though certainly quite atypical." During this six-month period, Hansen underwent further diagnostic testing and Dr. Taylor referred Hansen for an evaluation for a brain biopsy.

During the appointment on January 24, 1996, Dr. Taylor and the Hansens had a conversation which is the subject of this appeal. Kurt Hansen, his spouse Barbara, and their minor son were present. Barbara Hansen testified in her deposition that she was "distraught" during the visit and that she told Dr. Taylor that she was afraid her husband would die within the year. Although she cannot remember the exact wording, she recalls that Dr. Taylor said "he was not terminal within the next year."

Dr. Taylor's chart notes for that day refer to this conversation:

His wife had thought perhaps he was terminal within the next year because of the location of his problems, and I have assured her today this does not seem to be the case.

Taylor later explained:

I assured them that he had no diagnosis of a terminal illness that would lead me to believe that he would die within the next 12 months.

I merely indicated to them that I had not arrived at a diagnosis that would lead me to believe that Mr. Hansen had a condition that would be fatal within the next twelve months. I never used the word 'assurance' or 'promise' or 'guarantee' during this conversation. When offering this opinion about his condition, I was not making any promise to the Hansens.

In March of 1996, another physician performed a brain biopsy at Harborview Medical Center which revealed brainstem encephalitis, an inflammatory process.

From that point, until his death in November of 1996, Hansen was treated by Dr. Alex Spence, a University of Washington neuro-oncologist.

Hansen died on November 10, 1996. The cause of death was determined through an autopsy to be complications arising from pilocytic astrocytoma of the brainstem (a tumor of the brainstem) and a demyelinating viral infection of the brain. None of Hansen's physicians had made this diagnosis.

Hansen's family members sued Virginia Mason and Dr. Taylor. They asserted claims of violation of the Health Care Provider Act for missed diagnosis and breach of promise, negligent infliction of emotional distress, and violation of the Consumer Protection Act.

Both parties moved for summary judgment on the breach of promise RCW 7.70.030(2) cause of action. The Hansens asked the court to rule, as a matter of law, that Dr. Taylor promised the Hansens that Kurt Hansen would not die within the year, that Dr. Taylor breached that promise and the hospital was liable under RCW 7.70.030(2). Virginia Mason and Dr. Taylor (collectively "the hospital") moved for summary judgment to dismiss this cause of action. The trial court granted the Hansens' motion and denied the hospital's motion.

The hospital appealed to this court and we granted discretionary review.

The trial court stayed the litigation pending review.

DISCUSSION

This court reviews a summary judgment order de novo, engaging in the same inquiry as the trial court. Summary judgment is proper if the court, viewing all facts and reasonable inferences in the light most favorable to the non-moving party, finds no genuine issue as to any material fact and the moving party is entitled to judgment as a matter of law.

The Hansens' cause of action is based on RCW 7.70.030 which sets forth the grounds on which a plaintiff may recover for injuries resulting from health care. RCW 7.70.030 provides, in pertinent part:

> No award shall be made in any action or arbitration for damages for injury occurring as the result of health care ... unless the plaintiff establishes one or more of the following propositions:

> * * *

> (2) That a health care provider promised the patient or his representative that the injury suffered would not occur;

The hospital contends that the trial court erred by denying its motion for summary judgment because under either party's version of the facts, the statement made by Dr. Taylor does not constitute a promise within the meaning of RCW 7.70.030(2).

This is a case of first impression. There are no cases interpreting this statutory cause of action in the Health Care Provider Act enacted by the 1975–1976 Legislature. This court reviews the trial court's interpretation of a statute de novo.

The legislative history provides no indication that the Legislature intended to alter the scope of the pre-existing common law cause of action. The only legislative history which specifically relates to the breach of promise claim is that the Legislature considered and eventually rejected a proposal to require that a contract in the health care context be in writing.

The parties agree that the pre-statute common law cause of action was based on contract liability. The parties also agree that the statute codifies the cause of action that existed at common law. The Legislature is presumed to be aware of the common law, and a statute "will not be construed in derogation of the common law unless the legislature has clearly expressed that purpose." Staats v. Brown, 139 Wn.2d 757, 766, 991 P.2d 615 (2000). It is necessary therefore, to examine the nature of the common law cause of action as it existed prior to the enactment of the statute.

The first case to recognize a cause of action was Schuster v. Sutherland, 92 Wash. 135, 136, 158 P. 730 (1916). In this case the Court concluded that a physician entered into a verbal contract in which he "agreed to perform a surgical operation upon the respondent, and contracted, warranted, and promised to remove all gallstones then in the body of the respondent." The Court held that the physician was liable for breach of contract because he did not remove the patient's gallstones. The physician did not challenge the existence of a contract, but disputed the terms of the agreement.

In 1927, the Supreme Court decided Brooks v. Herd, 144 Wash. 173, 257 P. 238 (1927), involving a contract claim against a drugless healer. The Court confirmed that the law was "well-settled that a physician may contract specially to cure and is liable on his contract for failure." [ ]. However, the nature and existence of the contract in Brooks was a question of fact.

In Yeager v. Dunnavan, 26 Wn.2d 559, 174 P.2d 755 (1946) the Court considered a case in which a physician allegedly promised to perform an eye operation which would correct a problem without damaging the patient's health or eyesight. When the patient died due to an allergic reaction to the anesthetic used in the operation, the parents sued for breach of contract. The Supreme Court affirmed the trial court's dismissal of the case reasoning that the "gravamen" of the case was tort rather than contract liability.

In Carney v. Lydon, 36 Wn.2d 878, 220 P.2d 894 (1950), the Court considered a case against another drugless healer who had undertaken to cure a patient's diabetes. On appeal, the Court concluded that the trial court had been correct in ruling, as a matter of law, that there was no breach of contract claim. The Court stated that "[t]he most that could be said on this subject is that [the practitioner] expressed the opinion that his method of treatment was designed to eliminate poison from the body and that should be followed by relief from the disease." [ ].

Finally, in 1958, the Court decided Carpenter v. Moore, a case against a dentist who had agreed to make partial plates for the patient and "expressly guaranteed that all of the work would be done to [the plaintiff's] satisfaction." Carpenter v. Moore, 51 Wn.2d 795, 798, 322 P.2d 125 (1958). The Court held that the evidence was sufficient to support a finding that the dentist had made and breached this contract, but because liability was contractual, the plaintiff could recover only the amount of consideration paid for the dentist's work.

In his opinion concurring in part and dissenting in part, Justice Finley noted that the majority in Carpenter did not mention Yeager in its opinion and that the case was either "in effect overruled" or its authority was "greatly diminished" by Carpenter because Carpenter confirmed that "special contracts by medical practitioners to cure or obtain specific results" are enforceable.

These common law cases demonstrate the existence of a contract cause of action when medical practitioners expressly promise to obtain a specific result or cure though a course of treatment or a procedure. The viability of the contract theory was briefly called into question in Yeager, but subsequently reaffirmed in Carpenter. But the cause of action as it existed was narrow; the health care provider had to expressly and specially contract and guarantee particular results. As indicated by the Court in Carney, the existence of a contract will not be inferred where a practitioner merely offers an opinion regarding the effect of a course of treatment.

Although the Hansens advance the dictionary definition of promise, we conclude that promise is a term of art in contract law. In contract law a promise is a "manifestation of intention to act or refrain from acting in a specified way, so made as to justify a promisee in understanding that a commitment has been made." McCormick v. Lake Washington School Dist., 99 Wn.App. 107, 117, 992 P.2d 511 (1999) (quoting Restatement (Second) of Contracts sec. 2 (1981)). A promise has also been defined as "an undertaking, however expressed, that something shall happen, or that something shall not happen, in the future." Plumbing Shop, Inc. v. Pitts, 67 Wn.2d 514, 517, 408 P.2d 382 (1965). * * *

The statement at issue in this case is related to a diagnosis or prognosis and is not related to a specific undertaking or a specific result or cure through a course of treatment or a procedure. None of the common law cases recognize a claim based on a promise regarding a diagnosis or prognosis. Even in Carney, in which the Court characterized the statement as an "opinion" and not a promise, the provider predicted the result of a particular course of treatment.

The hospital argues that the plaintiffs have not established a claim because they have offered no evidence of mutual assent, consideration, or forbearance. For malpractice and informed consent claims under the Health Care Provider Act, the Legislature enacted additional sections which set forth the required elements of these claims. Presumably, if it had meant to include mutual assent or consideration, the Legislature would have similarly enacted an additional section containing these elements for a cause of action under RCW 7.70.030(2). Moreover, the pre-statute common law cases require only the existence of a promise and breach of that promise and not mutual assent, consideration or forbearance.

The Hansens contend that under any definition of promise, Dr. Taylor's alleged statement is a promise. The Hansens rely on Dr. Taylor's use of the word "assure", in her chart notes. According to Dr. Taylor, when Barbara Hansen asked if her husband was terminal within the next year because of the location of his problems, she "assured" the family that "it did not seem to be the case". Viewing the facts in the light most favorable to the Hansens and assuming Dr. Taylor assured the family that Kurt Hansen was not terminal within the next year, Dr. Taylor did not commit through this assurance or undertake a specific result or cure through a course of treatment or a procedure. An assurance is not an undertaking or commitment to obtain a specific result.

Because we presume that the Legislature intended to codify the common law, we conclude that an enforceable promise under RCW 7.70.030(2) must relate to the provision of specific medical services and the practitioner must expressly undertake or commit to obtain certain results or cure through a procedure or course of treatment. Here, under either version of the facts: whether Dr. Taylor told the family that Kurt Hansen would not die, or whether she assured them that it did not seem to be the case that he would die during the year, there is no evidence of a legally enforceable promise within the meaning of the statute. We reverse the trial court's order granting summary judgment and on remand direct entry of summary judgment in favor of Virginia Mason and Dr. Taylor.

WE CONCUR.

YALE DIAGNOSTIC RADIOLOGY v. FOUNTAIN

Supreme Court of Connecticut, 2004.
267 Conn. 351, 838 A.2d 179.

BORDEN, J. The sole issue in this appeal is whether a medical service provider that has provided emergency medical services to a minor may collect for those services from the minor when the minor's parents refuse or are unable to make payment. * * *

The following facts and procedural history are undisputed. In March, 1996, Fountain was shot in the back of the head at point-blank range by a playmate. As a result of his injuries, including the loss of his right eye, Fountain required extensive lifesaving medical services from a variety of medical services providers, including the plaintiff. The expense of the services rendered by the plaintiff to Fountain totaled $17,694. The plaintiff billed Tucker, who was Fountain's mother, but the bill went unpaid and, in 1999, the plaintiff obtained a collection judgment against her. In January, 2001, however, all of Tucker's debts were discharged pursuant to an order of the Bankruptcy Court for the District of Connecticut. Among the discharged debts was the judgment in favor of the plaintiff against Tucker.

During the time between the rendering of medical services and the bankruptcy filing, Tucker, as Fountain's next friend, initiated a tort action against the boy who had shot him. Among the damages claimed were "substantial sums of money [expended] on medical care and treatment. . . . " A settlement was reached, and funds were placed in the estate established on Fountain's behalf under the supervision of the Probate Court. Tucker was designated the fiduciary of that estate. Neither Fountain nor his estate was involved in Tucker's subsequent bankruptcy proceeding.

Following the discharge of Tucker's debts, the plaintiff moved the Probate Court for payment of the $17,694 from the estate. The Probate Court denied the motion, reasoning that, pursuant to General Statutes § 46b–37 (b), parents are liable for medical services rendered to their minor children, and that a parent's refusal or inability to pay for those services does not render the minor child liable. The Probate Court further ruled that minor children are incapable of entering into a legally binding contract or consenting, in the absence of parental consent, to medical treatment. The Probate Court held, therefore, that the plaintiff was barred from seeking payment from the estate.

The plaintiff appealed from the decision of the Probate Court to the trial court. The trial court sustained the appeal and rendered judgment for the plaintiff, holding that, under Connecticut law, minors are liable for payment for their "necessaries," even though the provider of those necessaries "relies on the parents' credit for payment when [the] injured child lives with his parents. . . . " The trial court reasoned that, although parents are primarily liable, pursuant to § 46b–37 (b) (2), for their child's medical bills, the parents' failure to pay renders the minor secondarily liable. Additionally, the trial court relied on the fact that Fountain had obtained money damages, based in part on the medical services rendered to him by the plaintiff. This appeal followed.

The defendants claim that the trial court improperly determined that a minor may be liable for payment for emergency medical services rendered to him. They further claim that the trial court, in reaching its decision, improperly considered the fact that Fountain had received a settlement, based in part on his medical expenses. We disagree with both of the defendants' claims.

Connecticut has long recognized the common-law rule that a minor child's contracts are voidable. [ ]. Under this rule, a minor may, upon reaching majority, choose either to ratify or to avoid contractual obligations entered into during his minority. [ ] The traditional reasoning behind this rule is based on the well established common-law principles that the law should protect children from the detrimental consequences of their youthful and improvident acts, and that children should be able to emerge into adulthood unencumbered by financial obligations incurred during the course of their minority. [ ]. The rule is further supported by a policy of protecting children from unscrupulous individuals seeking to profit from their youth and inexperience.

The rule that a minor's contracts are voidable, however, is not absolute. An exception to this rule, eponymously known as the doctrine of necessaries, is that a minor may not avoid a contract for goods or services necessary for his health and sustenance. [ ] Such contracts are binding even if entered into during minority, and a minor, upon reaching majority, may not, as a matter of law, disaffirm them.

The parties do not dispute the fact that the medical services rendered to Fountain were necessaries; rather, their dispute centers on whether Connecticut recognizes the doctrine of necessaries. As evidenced by the following history, the doctrine of necessaries has long been a part of Connecticut jurisprudence.

In *Strong v. Foote*, supra, 42 Conn. 205, this court affirmed a judgment in favor of a dentist against a minor for services rendered to the minor, who had an estate and who was an orphan for whom a guardian had been appointed. This court stated: "In suits against minors, instituted by persons who have rendered services or supplied articles to them, the term 'necessaries' is not invariably used in its strictest sense, nor is it limited to that which is requisite to sustain life, but includes whatever is proper and suitable in the case of each individual, having reference to his circumstances and condition in life." [ ] The court further noted that the services were "within the legal limitations of the word 'necessaries,'" and that the plaintiff was not required to inquire as to the minor's guardianship before rendering the services because the services were "necessary to meet an unsupplied want." [ ].

Furthermore, from 1907 to 1959, statutory law regarding minors and the doctrine of necessaries remained unchanged. General Statutes (1958 Rev.) § 42–2 provided: "Capacity to buy and sell is regulated by the general law concerning capacity to contract, and to transfer and acquire property. When necessaries are sold and delivered to an infant, or to a person who by reason of mental incapacity or drunkenness is incompetent to contract, he must pay a reasonable price therefor. Necessaries in this section mean goods suitable to the condition in life of such infant or other person, and to his actual requirements at the time of delivery." Therefore, insofar as it referred to minors, this statute codified the common-law doctrine of necessaries. [ ] We recognize that § 42–2 was repealed in 1959 [ ] when Connecticut adopted the Uniform Commercial Code. That repeal was not intended, however, to eliminate the doctrine because the statute was replaced by General Statutes § 42a–1–103, which contemplated that the Uniform Commercial Code would continue to be supplemented by the general principles of contract law regarding minors.

In light of these precedents, we conclude that Connecticut recognizes the doctrine of necessaries. We further conclude that, pursuant to the doctrine, the defendants are liable for payment to the plaintiff for the services rendered to Fountain.

We have not heretofore articulated the particular legal theory underlying the doctrine of necessaries. We therefore take this occasion to do so, and we conclude that the most apt theory is that of an implied in law contract, also sometimes referred to as a quasi-contract. We further conclude that based on this theory, the defendants are liable.

"In distinction to an implied [in fact] contract, a quasi [or implied in law] contract is not a contract, but an obligation which the law creates out of the circumstances present, even though a party did not assume the obligation.... *It is based on equitable principles* to operate whenever justice requires compensation to be made.... *Brighenti v. New Britain Shirt Corporation*, 167 Conn. 403, 407, 356 A.2d 181 (1974). With no other test than what, under a given set of circumstances, is just or unjust, equitable or inequitable, conscionable or unconscionable, it becomes necessary ... to examine the circumstances and the conduct of the parties and apply this standard. *Cecio Bros., Inc. v. Greenwich*, 156 Conn. 561, 564–65, 244 A.2d 404 (1968)." [ ]

Thus, when a medical service provider renders necessary medical care to an injured minor, two contracts arise: the primary contract between the provider and the minor's parents; and an implied in law contract between the provider and the minor himself. The primary contract between the provider and the parents is based on the parents' duty to pay for their children's necessary expenses, under both common law and statute. Such contracts, where not express, may be implied in fact and generally arise both from the parties' conduct and their reasonable expectations. The primacy of this contract means that the provider of necessaries must make all reasonable efforts to collect from the parents before resorting to the secondary, implied in law contract with the minor.

The secondary implied in law contract between the medical services provider and the minor arises from equitable considerations, including the law's disfavor of unjust enrichment. Therefore, where necessary medical services are rendered to a minor whose parents do not pay for them, equity and justice demand that a secondary implied in law contract arise between the medical services provider and the minor who has received the benefits of those services. These principles compel the conclusion that, in the circumstances of the present case, the defendants are liable to the plaintiff, under the common-law doctrine of necessaries, for the services rendered by the plaintiff to Fountain.

The present case illustrates the inequity that would arise if no implied in law contract arose between Fountain and the plaintiff. Fountain was shot in the head at close range and required emergency medical care. Under such circumstances, a medical services provider cannot stop to consider how the bills will be paid or by whom. Although the plaintiff undoubtedly presumed that Fountain's parent would pay for his care and was obligated to make reasonable efforts to collect from Tucker before seeking payment from Fountain, the direct benefit of the services, nonetheless, was conferred upon Fountain. Having received the benefit of necessary services, Fountain should be liable for payment for those necessaries in the event that his parents do not pay.

Furthermore, in the present case, we note, as did the trial court, that Fountain received, through a settlement with the boy who caused his injuries, funds that were calculated, at least in part, on the costs of the medical services provided to him by the plaintiff in the wake of those injuries. Fountain, through Tucker, brought an action against the tortfeasor and, in his complaint, cited "substantial sums of money [expended] on medical care and treatment. . . . " This fact further supports a determination of an implied in law contract under the circumstances of the case.

The defendants claim, however, that the doctrine of necessaries has been legislatively abrogated by § 46b–37 (b) (2). [ ]. We disagree. Section 46b–37 (b) (2) governs the joint liability of parents for the support and maintenance of their family, and, in doing so, merely codifies the common-law principle, long recognized in Connecticut, that both parents are *primarily* responsible for providing necessary goods and services to their children. [ ] Section 46b–37 (b) (2), however, is silent as to a child's *secondary* liability. That statute neither promotes nor prohibits a determination of secondary liability on the part of a minor when the minor has received emergency medical services and the parents are either unwilling or unable to pay for those services. We, therefore, decline the defendants' invitation to read into § 46b–37 (b) (2), which governs the relationship of parents to one another and to their creditors, any rule regarding the relationship of their minor children to those same creditors. Nothing in either the language or the purpose of § 46b–37 (b) (2) indicates an intent on the part of the legislature to absolve minors of their secondary common-law liability for necessaries.

To the contrary, the purposes behind the statutory rule that parents are primarily liable and the common-law rule, pursuant to the doctrine of necessaries, that a minor is secondarily liable, when read together, serve to encourage payment on contracts for necessaries. Those purposes are (1) to reinforce parents' obligation to support their children, and (2) to provide a mechanism for collection by creditors when, nonetheless, the parents either refuse or are unable to discharge that obligation.

The defendants further contended, at oral argument before this court, that, even if we were to conclude that the doctrine of necessaries is applicable, the defendants are not liable to the plaintiff because there has been no showing that Tucker was unwilling or unable to provide necessaries to Fountain. Specifically, the defendants argue that, because Fountain lived in Tucker's home, it cannot be shown that, as a matter of law, Tucker was unwilling or unable to provide Fountain with necessary medical care. We disagree.

The undisputed facts show that Tucker had four years to pay the plaintiff's bill for the services rendered to Fountain. She did not pay that bill even when the plaintiff pursued a collection action against her. These facts are sufficient to show that Tucker was unwilling or unable to pay for Fountain's necessary medical services.

Furthermore, the premise underlying the legal structure placing primary liability in the parent and secondary liability in the minor, and requiring that the creditor first exhaust reasonable efforts to collect from the parent, is that the creditor has the legal capability, beyond moral suasion, to require the parent to pay. That premise simply disappears when the parent's primary obligation has been erased by an intervening bankruptcy.

This reasoning applies, moreover, whether the minor is living in the parent's home, as was the case here, or elsewhere. The place of the minor's residence is simply irrelevant to the question of whether the creditor has an enforceable claim against the parent. That is because the fact that Tucker may be supplying other necessaries, such as food and shelter, does not undermine the claim that she has not made payment for this necessary medical service, which was already provided by the plaintiff to Fountain.

The judgment is affirmed.

ROBERTS v. WILLIAMSON

Supreme Court of Texas, 2003.
111 S.W.3d 113, 46 Tex.Sup.Ct.J. 944.

Phillips, J.

In these consolidated cases involving two separate appeals in a medical malpractice action, we must decide an issue of first impression: whether Texas recognizes a common law cause of action for a parent's loss of consortium resulting from a non-fatal injury to a child. In addition, we consider whether the court of appeals erred in affirming the trial court's decision * * * in failing to apply prior settlements to reduce the damages award. * * *

I

The day after her birth, Courtnie Williamson began suffering from severe acidosis, a condition with a number of serious complications, including damage to the heart and brain. Dr. Roger Fowler, the attending physician, called Dr. Karen Roberts, the only consulting pediatrician at Laird Memorial Hospital in Kilgore, Texas, and advised her that Courtnie was in respiratory distress. Dr. Roberts arrived from Longview approximately forty-five minutes later and began treating Courtnie. Shortly thereafter, Dr. Roberts and Dr. Fowler placed Courtnie on a pediatric ventilator. The ventilator was not functioning properly, however, and Courtnie did not receive needed oxygen for several minutes.

About one hour after Dr. Roberts' arrival, a colleague suggested that sodium bicarbonate should be administered to counteract Courtnie's worsening acidosis. Two hours later, after consulting with a neonatologist in Shreveport, Dr. Roberts followed this advice, and Courtnie began to improve. Not long thereafter, Courtnie was transported to Schumpert Medical Center in Shreveport. Courtnie now has a permanent shunt implanted in her skull to drain fluids to her abdomen. She suffers from a weakened left side, requires braces to walk, has significant scarring, and is developmentally delayed.

Courtney's parents, Lainie and Casey Williamson, individually and on behalf of their daughter, sued Dr. Roberts, Laird Memorial Hospital, Dr. Mark Miller (the on-call physician), and Dr. Fowler. They contend that the malfunctioning ventilator, the delay in administering sodium bicarbonate, and the failure to immediately transfer Courtnie to a better-equipped hospital, combined to proximately cause Courtnie's injuries. The trial judge appointed a guardian ad litem to represent Courtnie's interests.

The Williamsons' claims against the hospital, Dr. Fowler, and a treating physician who was not named as a defendant were settled for $468,750. The claims against Dr. Roberts and Dr. Miller proceeded to trial. At trial, Dr. Frank McGehee, a board-certified pediatrician, testified that Dr. Roberts was negligent in delaying Courtnie's transfer to a hospital equipped to treat her condition and in failing to administer sodium bicarbonate sooner. Dr. McGehee testified that Dr. Roberts' negligence proximately caused Courtnie to suffer from mental retardation, anti-social behavior, and hemiplegia, a partial paralysis of one side of body caused by an injury to the brain.

* * *

In this Court, Dr. Roberts has filed two separate appeals, complaining about both judgments. We granted both petitions for review and consolidated the two appeals to decide four issues: (1) whether Texas common law recognizes a parent's claim for loss of consortium when a child is seriously, but not fatally, injured; * * * (3) whether a defendant, who is not jointly and severally liable, is entitled to a settlement credit before the application of her percentage of responsibility; * * *.

II

In *Reagan v. Vaughn*, 804 S.W.2d 463, 468, 34 Tex. Sup. Ct. J. 189 (Tex. 1990), we held that a child is entitled to seek damages for loss of consortium when a parent suffers a serious, permanent, and disabling injury. We equated the child's relationship to the parent to that of one spouse to another, a relationship for which we had previously recognized consortium rights. [ ]. We further noted the vulnerable and dependent role of the child in this relationship and the profound harm that might befall a child who has been deprived of a parent's love, care, companionship, and guidance. [ ].

The court of appeals concluded that because of our emphasis in *Reagan* that the parent-child relationship deserved special protection, we must have intended for parents to have consortium rights in the relationship as well. [ ] The court suggests that the parent-child relationship is a reciprocal one, like husband and wife, and that all parties deserve the same protection. [ ] Dr. Roberts counters that *Reagan* does not extend so far, and that the loss to a child caused by a serious injury to the parent is uniquely different from that to a parent of a seriously injured child.

We have not previously considered whether parents have a claim for loss of consortium in non-fatal injury cases, but some courts of appeals have assumed that such a claim is viable. [ ] We recognize the sympathetic and, on the surface, logical appeal to extending consortium rights to parents as well as children. But several states that have recognized a child's right to loss of consortium have denied the parents any reciprocal right, including two of the first states in the nation to recognize the child's right. [ ] [Other] courts have concluded that the child's interest deserves greater protection because of the child's singular emotional dependency on the parents. The Massachusetts Supreme Court explained this distinction in *Norman* [*v. Mass. Bay Transp. Auth.*, 403 Mass. 303, 529 N.E.2d 139, 141–42 (Mass. 1988)] held as follows:

> In the ordinary course of things the dependence of spouses on one another for love and support is found to the same degree in no other relationship except, perhaps, in the relationship of a minor child to his or her parents.

* * *

Although parents customarily *enjoy* the consortium of their children, in the ordinary course of events a parent does not *depend* on a child's companionship, love, support, guidance, and nurture in the same way and to the same degree that a husband depends on his wife, a wife depends on her husband, or a minor or disabled adult child depends on his or her parent. Of course, it is true that such dependency may exist in a particular situation, but it is not intrinsic to the parent-child relationship as is a minor child's dependency on his or her parents and as is each spouse's dependency on the other spouse.*Norman*, 529 N.E.2d at 140–41.

The Wyoming Supreme Court has also rejected a parent's right to consortium damages while recognizing the child's right. Some years after rejecting a parent's claim for consortium in *Gates v. Richardson*, 719 P.2d 193, 201 (Wyo. 1986), the Wyoming Supreme Court concluded that the child's interest in the relationship was so different that it did deserve protection:

> In our society the minor child requires his or her parent's nurturing, guidance, and supervision. The child is uniquely dependent upon the parent for his or her socialization, that maturation process which turns a helpless infant into an independent, productive, responsible human being who has an opportunity to be a valuable, contributing member of our society. Without question, the child's relational interest with the parent is characterized by dependence. In contrast, the parent's relational interest with the child is not. In a real sense, the child is "becoming" and the parent "has become." Thus, the parent's loss of an injured child's consortium is different in kind from the child's loss of an injured parent's consortium. Viewed in this light, our refusal in *Gates* to recognize the parent's claim is inapposite to the legal problem whether we recognize the child's claim.

* * * The Vermont Supreme Court has similarly recognized that the "child is in a uniquely difficult position to make up for the loss of a parent." *Hay v. Med. Ctr. Hosp. of Vt.*, 145 Vt. 533, 496 A.2d 939, 942 (Vt. 1985). It explained:

While "an adult is capable of seeking out new relationships in an attempt to fill in the void of his or her loss, a child may be virtually helpless in seeking out a new adult companion. Therefore, compensation through the courts may be the child's only method of reducing his or her deprivation of the parent's society and companionship." [ ]

We agree with these courts that the parent-child relationship is not reciprocal like husband and wife and that the child is the party to the relationship who needs special protection. We concede that serious injury to a child will have emotional consequences for the parents. Tort law, however, cannot remedy every wrong. Sound public policy requires an end at some point to the consequential damages that flow from a single negligent act. As the New York Court of Appeals has explained: "Every injury has ramifying consequences, like the ripplings of the waters, without end. The problem for the law is to limit the legal consequences of wrongs to a controllable degree." *Tobin v. Grossman*, 24 N.Y.2d 609, 249 N.E.2d 419, 424, 301 N.Y.S.2d 554 (N.Y. 1969). Consequently, the law ordinarily denies recourse to those not directly injured by a negligent act, but whose injury is caused indirectly by the harm to another. There are exceptions to this general rule, including claims for loss of consortium. But all these exceptions have been narrowly cabined. Thus, while we have recognized that spouses and children can recover loss of consortium, we have concluded that siblings and step-parents cannot. [ ]

When recognizing a new cause of action and the accompanying expansion of duty, we must perform something akin to a cost-benefit analysis to assure that this expansion of liability is justified. [ ]. The fundamental purposes of our tort system are to deter wrongful conduct, shift losses to responsible parties, and fairly compensate deserving victims. While the recognition of an additional layer of liability to the parent clearly shifts the loss, it is not at all clear that this additional layer of liability will produce corresponding benefits of deterrence or fair compensation. It is clear, however, that it will foster further uncertainty and widen the divergence in recoveries among similarly situated victims. Courts have generally been willing to tolerate more uncertainty in the calculation of damages when necessary to compensate the primary tort victim. That pain and mental anguish defy objective valuation or that money damages are a poor palliative for catastrophic injury do not justify the denial of a monetary remedy to a victim who has been severely injured. But once courts have fairly compensated the primary victim, they should be more troubled about the difficulties in measuring intangible losses to secondary victims.

The case before us demonstrates the challenges presented to a factfinder when awarding consortium damages. The Williamsons assert that the defendant's negligence caused their daughter to sustain massive brain damage, particularly to the right side of her brain, resulting in permanent and in all likelihood progressive neurological and behavioral problems. They submit that their daughter has and will continue to have difficulty controlling her emotions and will likely suffer from some degree of retardation. Her injuries, however, have not shortened her life expectancy. At the time of trial, the child was three years old. On this evidence, the jury concluded that the value of the "harm to the parent-child relationship" during the first three years of the relationship was $75,000, while future harm to the relationship over several score years was only a dollar. As for the child's personal injury claim, the jury awarded, among other damages, $100,000 for past pain and mental anguish, $35,000 for past physical impairment, $750,000 for future pain and mental anguish, and $300,000 for future physical impairment. The jury apparently concluded that while the child's intangible losses would grow with time, her continuing impairment would have no substantial effect on the parent-child relationship in the future. Another jury after hearing the same evidence might well have reached a very different conclusion.

In *Reagan*, we were willing to let the system sort through these difficulties because of the perceived social importance in protecting the child's interests. Moreover, we concluded that " 'limiting the plaintiffs in the consortium action to the victim's children' " was a rational way to ensure the validity of these intangible losses. *Miles*, 967 S.W.2d at 384 (quoting *Reagan*, 804 S.W.2d at 466). That rationale, however, breaks down when we extend such rights to parents. Because the parent has a less dependent role than that of the child in the relationship, extending consortium rights here could logically lead to the recognition of such rights in other non-dependent relatives or even in close friends, given appropriate facts. [ ] But, like every other jurisdiction, we have already concluded that consortium should not be expanded to this extent. [ ]. We therefore decline to extend a claim for loss of consortium to parents of children who have been seriously injured.

Some may argue that our refusal to extend consortium rights to parents creates a paradox because we permit parents to recover consortium damages in wrongful death cases. [ ]. But there are reasons for distinction. Before abolition of the pecuniary loss rule, the wrongful death of a child did not ordinarily create pecuniary consequences for the negligent tortfeasor because the child was of little monetary value to the family. Abolishing this rule and permitting the "recovery for loss of affection and society in a wrongful death action thus fulfills a deeply felt social belief that a tortfeasor who negligently kills someone should not escape liability completely, no matter how unproductive his victim." *Borer v. Am. Airlines, Inc.*, 19 Cal.3d 441, 138 Cal.Rptr. 302, 563 P.2d 858, 865 (Cal. 1977). But when the child survives, as here, so does the child's own cause of action against the tortfeasor. And if the primary victim of the accident may bring an action, there is no need to recognize actions by other family members to prevent the tortfeasor from escaping liability. Thus, our law is not inconsistent in recognizing certain intangible damages for secondary victims in death actions but not in personal injury actions.

But even if it were an anomaly to do so, we could not unify the rules for recovery of intangible damages in wrongful death and personal injury actions by any decision in this case. All statutory beneficiaries under the Wrongful Death Act are entitled to recover intangible damages not only for loss of companionship but also mental anguish. [ ] These same parties, however, have a much more circumscribed right to recover mental anguish damages when the family member survives. [ ]. Thus, whether or not we were to recognize a right to filial consortium in this case, differences in the award of intangible damages for wrongful death and personal injury would persist. [ ]

We conclude that no compelling social policy impels us to recognize a parent's right to damages for the loss of filial consortium. And, on balance, we believe that the common law is best served by the result we reach here. Accordingly, we disapprove of those cases holding or suggesting to the contrary. [ ]

* * *

IV

Dr. Roberts next asserts that, in calculating the damages against her, the trial court failed properly to apply the $468,750 settlement credit. She maintains that the trial court should have reduced the jury's damage award with this credit before multiplying that number by her proportionate responsibility as found by the jury. In other words, Dr. Roberts contends that the judgment against her should be $369,937.50 (15% x $2,466,250) rather than $440,250. This reduction, she asserts, is required when a defendant timely elects to have a dollar-for-dollar credit. [ ]. We disagree.

The rules of proportionate responsibility and settlement credits are found in Chapter 33 of the Civil Practices and Remedies Code. Pertinent here are sections 33.012 and 33.013, which provide in relevant part:

§ 33.012. Amount of Recovery

(a) . . . the court shall reduce the amount of damages to be recovered by the claimant with respect to a cause of action by a percentage equal to the claimant's percentage of responsibility.

(b) If the claimant has settled with one or more persons, the court shall further reduce the amount of damages to be recovered by the claimant with respect to a cause of action by a credit equal to one of the following . . .

(1) the sum of the dollar amounts of all settlements . . .

§ 33.013. Amount of Liability

(a) Except [when a defendant is jointly and severally liable], a liable defendant is liable to a claimant only for the percentage of damages found by the trier of fact equal to that defendant's percentage of responsibility with respect to the personal injury, property damage, death, or other harm for which the damages are allowed.

TEX. CIV. PRAC. & REM. CODE §§ 33.012(a), (b)(1), 33.013(a). Section 33.012 refers to "the amount of damages to be recovered by the claimant", while section 33.013 refers to the "damages found by the trier of fact." *Id.* The "amount of damages to be recovered by the claimant" under section 33.012 must be reduced by the claimant's proportionate responsibility and by settlements. No corresponding reduction is prescribed under section 33.013 because the "damages found by the trier of fact" are not affected by settlement or the claimant's shared responsibility. Thus, damages under these two sections are the same only when the claimant has not settled and shares no responsibility. And although related, the two sections pose separate inquiries. Section 33.012 controls the claimant's total recovery, while section 33.013 governs the defendant's separate liability.

Under section 33.012, the Williamsons' total recovery, including amounts received in settlement, is limited to $2,935,000, so they can receive no more than $2,466,250 ($2,935,000–$468,750) in satisfaction of this judgment. This limit, however, is independent of section 33.013's limitation on a particular defendant's percentage of responsibility. And section 33.013(a) specifically pertains to defendants who, like Dr. Roberts here, are not jointly and severally liable. That section provides that a severally-liable defendant's monetary liability is calculated by multiplying the damages found by the trier of fact by the defendant's percentage of responsibility. [ ] The trial court did this when it multiplied the jury's damage award by the 15 per cent of proportionate responsibility it assigned to Dr. Roberts. Because Dr. Roberts' liability for $440,250, does not exceed the limit placed on the amount of damages the Williamsons may recovery under section 33.012, no further credit is required.

* * *

We reverse that part of the court of appeals' judgment affirming the award of damages for loss of filial consortium and render judgment that the Williamsons take nothing as to this claim. The judgments of the court of appeals are otherwise affirmed.

SECTION B.   MISREPRESENTATIONS

SIMCUSKI v. SAELI

Court of Appeals of New York, 1978.
44 N.Y.2d 442, 406 N.Y.S.2d 259, 377 N.E.2d 713.

JONES, JUDGE. * * *

On October 19, 1970, Dr. Anthony J. Saeli performed a surgical excision of a node from plaintiff's neck. Plaintiff, Eleanor Simcuski, alleges that during the operation on her neck the surgeon negligently injured a spinal accessory nerve in her neck and also injured branches of her cervical plexus. Following the operation plaintiff told her surgeon that she was experiencing numbness in the right side of her face and neck, and that it was difficult and painful for her to raise her right arm. It is alleged that the physician was aware of the negligent manner in which he had performed the surgery and aware, too, that as a result of his negligence plaintiff had suffered a potentially permanent injury. It is further alleged that the physician willfully, falsely, and fraudulently told plaintiff that her postoperative problems, pain, and difficulties were transient, and that they would disappear if she would continue a regimen of physiotherapy which he had prescribed and which was then being given by Dr. Lane. Plaintiff continued with the physiotherapy prescribed by Dr. Saeli until October 1974. In the meantime she had moved to Syracuse, New York, where she sought further medical advice.

In January 1974 she was first apprised by the Syracuse physician of the true nature of her injury and that it probably had been caused at the time of her surgery. This doctor's diagnosis was substantially confirmed in October 1974 by a professor of medicine, specializing in neurology, at Upstate Medical Center in Syracuse, who also advised that reanastomo sis of the sectioned nerve four years after the surgery would not be a physiologically successful procedure. It is further alleged that Dr. Saeli had intentionally withheld information from plaintiff as to the true nature and source of her injury, in consequence of which she was deprived of the opportunity for cure of her condition.

The present action against Dr. Saeli was commenced in April 1976. Prior to service of an answer, Dr. Saeli moved to dismiss the complaint * * * on the ground that the cause or causes of action alleged were barred by the statute of limitations. Plaintiff cross-moved for leave to amend her complaint specifically to include a cause of action for malpractice. The supreme court denied defendant's motion to dismiss and granted plaintiff leave to amend her complaint as requested. On appeal, the appellate division reversed, granted defendant's motion and dismissed the complaint. * * *

The complaint sufficiently sets forth a cause of action for medical malpractice; the critical issue is whether this cause of action was barred by the then applicable three-year statute of limitations [ ]. Normally the statute would have precluded institution in April 1976 of a claim for damages for malpractice alleged to have occurred in October 1970. This complaint, however, further alleges that defendant intentionally concealed the alleged malpractice from plaintiff and falsely assured her of effective treatment, as a result of which plaintiff did not discover the injury to the nerve until October 1974. In this circumstance principles of equitable estoppel are applicable to relieve plaintiff from the proscriptions of the statute. * * *

It is the rule that a defendant may be estopped to plead the statute of limitations where plaintiff was induced by fraud, misrepresentations or deception to refrain from filing a timely action. [ ] The allegations of her complaint bring this plaintiff within the shelter of this rule. The elements of reliance by plaintiff on the alleged misrepresentations as the cause of her failure sooner to institute the action for malpractice and of justification for such reliance, both necessarily to be established by her, are sufficiently pleaded within the fair intendment of the allegations of this complaint.

* * * The doctrine [of equitable estoppel] has been applied in other states in circumstances which are legally indistinguishable from the present. * * * The quality of the relationship between physician and patient, with confidence normally reposed by the patient in the physician, and the unquestioning reliance which such relationship may be expected to engender in the patient, make application of the doctrine peculiarly appropriate in such cases.

* * * If the conduct relied on (fraud, misrepresentation, or other deception) has ceased to be operational within the otherwise applicable period of limitations (or perhaps within a reasonable time prior to the expiration of such period), many courts have denied application of the doctrine on the ground that the period during which the plaintiff was justifiably lulled into inactivity had expired prior to the termination of the statutory period, and that the plaintiff had thereafter had sufficient time to commence his action prior to the expiration of the period of limitations. * * * That is not the present situation. Plaintiff has alleged that her discovery of the malpractice in this case (the point at which the conduct here relied on ceased to be operational) did not occur until October 1974 (or possibly in January of that year, if inference be drawn from the letter of her Syracuse doctor dated January 9, 1974, submitted in opposition to the motion). Whichever the month of discovery in 1974, the three-year statute of limitations had already expired in October 1973.

Where, as here, the conduct relied on ceases to be operational after the expiration of the period of limitations, two approaches may be discerned in the cases. By one, further delay on the part of the plaintiff in commencing his action may be held to be subject to the counterdefense of laches to be pleaded and proved by the defendant * * *. The preferable analysis, however, holds that due diligence on the part of the plaintiff in bringing his action is an essential element for the applicability of the doctrine of equitable estoppel, to be demonstrated by the plaintiff when he seeks the shelter of the doctrine * * *. Under this approach, which we endorse, the burden is on the plaintiff to establish that the action was brought within a reasonable time after the facts giving rise to the estoppel have ceased to be operational. Whether in any particular instance the plaintiff will have discharged his responsibility of due diligence in this regard must necessarily depend on all the relevant circumstances.

The length of the legislatively prescribed period of limitations is sometimes said to be relevant, and courts have held that in no event will the plaintiff be found to have exercised the required diligence if his action is deferred beyond the date which would be marked by the reapplication of the statutory period, i.e., that the length of the statutory period itself sets an outside limit on what will be regarded as due diligence. * * * In the present case such an outside limit was not exceeded; the action was brought less than three years after discovery in 1974. It is not possible or appropriate, however, on the present motion addressed to the pleading, presenting us as it must with only a skeletal record, to determine whether this plaintiff met her obligation of due diligence when she instituted the present action in April 1976. [I]t cannot now be determined as a matter of law that the reasonable time for bringing the present action had expired prior to its institution in April 1976.

[T]he other cause of action * * * asserts a claim in fraud as an intentional tort. * * *

This is more than another aspect of the malpractice or even another act of alleged negligent malpractice on the part of the treating physician; the complaint alleges an intentional fraud that Dr. Saeli, knowing it to be untrue yet expecting his patient to rely on his advice, advised her that physiotherapy would produce a cure, in consequence of which fraudulent misrepresentation the patient was deprived of the opportunity for cure of the condition initially caused by the doctor's alleged malpractice. If these allegations are proved, they will establish an intentional tort, separate from and subsequent to the malpractice claim. * * * Recovery of damages in such case is governed by the six-year statute of limitations under CPLR 213(8). The application of the three-year statute of limitations is not mandated by the circumstance that the fraud alleged arises as a sequel to an alleged malpractice.[7]

[W]e recognize and approve, but distinguish, cases which hold that, without more, concealment by a physician or failure to disclose his own malpractice does not give rise to a cause of action in fraud or deceit separate and different from the customary malpractice action, thereby entitling the plaintiff to bring his action within the longer period limited for such claims. * * * Such nondisclosure or concealment may affect the damages recoverable, or, conceivably in a proper case in conjunction with other factors, provide a foundation for seeking to invoke the doctrine of equitable estoppel to extend the applicable period of limitations. Standing alone such nondisclosure or concealment will not, however, serve as the basis for a distinct cause of action in fraud.

[A]s in the instance of fraud claims generally, this plaintiff, too, will be required to prove her claim by clear and convincing evidence * * *. If she succeeds in this respect, the available measure of her damages will be that applicable in fraud actions, i.e., damages caused by the fraud, as distinguished in this case from damages occasioned by the alleged malpractice.

---

7. We observe that the alleged tortious conduct in this instance occurred prior to the adoption of CPLR 214–a (L.1975, ch. 109, § 6, eff. July 1, 1975). There is thus no basis here for any assertion that by the enactment of that statute the legislature intended to prescribe a statutory period of limitations with respect to all claims arising out of the physician-patient relationship no matter on what legal theory predicated.

[T]he exposure to liability we here discuss is not based on errors of professional judgment; it is predicated on proof of the commission of an intentional tort, in this instance, fraud. As to that cause of action:

First, it must be established that the physician knew (or demonstrably had reason to know) of the fact of his malpractice and of the injury suffered by his patient in consequence thereof.

Second, it must be established that, knowing it to be false at the time, the physician thereafter made material, factual misrepresentation to the patient with respect to the subject matter of the malpractice and the therapy appropriate to its cure, on which the patient justifiably relied.

Third, all elements of the intentional tort of fraud must be established by clear and convincing evidence. Recognizing, too, the hazards of proliferating litigation of baseless claims, attention is drawn to the requirements of CPLR 3016(b). While, of course, motions to dismiss under CPLR 3211 are properly addressed to the allegations set forth in the complaint, on motions for summary judgment under CPLR 3212 evidentiary proof in admissible form must be tendered in support of all the elements of the alleged cause of action.

Fourth, if there is not an available, efficacious remedy or cure which the plaintiff is diverted from undertaking in consequence of the intentional, fraudulent misrepresentation, as in many instances of medical malpractice there may not be, there will normally be only minimal damages, if any. It will be necessary to demonstrate that the condition caused by the malpractice could have been corrected or alleviated. Thus, in the present case, if it can be shown that at the time of Dr. Saeli's alleged fraudulent misrepresentations it was already too late to undertake a reanastomosis of the severed nerve, this plaintiff will have sustained little or no damages in consequence of the alleged fraud. If only a partial cure were then possible, damages would be assessable on that basis. Recovery would be greatest, of course, if plaintiff were diverted from what could otherwise have been a complete cure.

[T]he present decision is not to be expected to open the proverbial floodgates. On the other hand, in human terms it would be unthinkable today not to hold a professional person liable for knowingly and intentionally misleading his patient in consequence of which, to the physician's foreknowledge, the patient was deprived of an opportunity for escape from a medical predicament which the physician by his own negligence had initially inflicted on his patient. With respect to the application of the doctrine of equitable estoppel to a defense of statute of limitations pleaded in a malpractice action, again we are concerned with an intentional, not merely negligent, wrong—the purposeful concealment and misrepresentation of the fact and consequences of the malpractice. It would not be tolerable to permit a physician by whose fraud, misrepresentation, or deception his patient has been induced to delay filing legal proceedings until after the time limited by statute to reap the benefits of his own misconduct.

[T]he order of the appellate division should be reversed, with costs to abide the event, and the order of the supreme court denying defendant's motion to dismiss reinstated.

COOKE, JUDGE, concurring. * * *

FUCHSBERG, JUDGE,[8] concurring.

Though I wholeheartedly join in the disposition of this case and of the questions necessary to its determination, I find aspects of the majority opinion sufficiently disturbing to compel me to comment.

For one, the court's indorsement of cases which are said to have held that mere "concealment by a physician or failure to disclose his own malpractice" does not toll the statute of limitations is both peripheral and unnecessary to today's decision. Moreover, it suffers from more than the ordinary weakness of dictum. It gratuitously renews the blessing, given at an earlier time and in a different clime, to a proposition whose soundness has, in the intervening years, been the object of widespread and increasing criticism, much of which characterizes willful nondisclosure as "constructive fraud." Morrison v. Acton, 68 Ariz. 27, 198 P.2d 590 (1948); W. Prosser, Torts § 30 at 144 (4th ed. 1971) * * *.

* * *

I also refuse to join in what I regard as the equally unnecessary and, so far as the record reveals, unfounded factual and qualitative assumptions implicit in phrases such as opening the "floodgates," "ballooning malpractice recoveries," and "legitimate concern both from the standpoint of the profession and the public as to the economic import" of malpractice recoveries. Such expressions, which omit the concerns of those injured by medical negligence, are, I respectfully suggest, best avoided. All the more is that so in a situation where, as has been widely reported and openly admitted, large sums have been expended by interested parties to influence public opinion * * *.

HOWARD v. UNIVERSITY OF MEDICINE AND DENTISTRY OF NEW JERSEY

Supreme Court of New Jersey, 2002.
172 N.J. 537, 800 A.2d 73.

LaVECCHIA, J.

In this appeal we consider what causes of action will lie when a plaintiff contends that a physician misrepresented his credentials and experience at the time he obtained the plaintiff's consent to surgery.

I.

Plaintiff, Joseph Howard, came under the care of defendant, Dr. Robert Heary, in February 1997 for neck pain and related complaints.

---

8. Editors' Note: Before he was elected to the New York Court of Appeals in 1975, Judge Jacob D. Fuchsberg had been a prominent plaintiff's lawyer; he was president of the Association of Trial Lawyers of America in 1963–1964.

He had a history of cervical spine disease. Following a car accident in 1991, he was diagnosed with spondyliosis, with spinal cord compression extending from the C3 to C7 cervical discs. According to various doctors who examined him at that time he had severe cervical spinal stenosis, and he was advised to undergo a "decompressive cervical laminectomy because of the extent of his cervical pathology" Although the condition was worsening progressively, at plaintiff decided to forego surgery.

In January 1997, another automobile accident caused plaintiff injuries that included a cerebral concussion, cervical syndrome with bilateral radiculopathies, and low back syndrome with bilateral radiculopathies. Plaintiff sought the care of Dr. Boston Martin, who had treated him after the 1991 accident. Dr. Martin concluded that plaintiff's spinal condition had worsened significantly and recommended that plaintiff be seen at the University of Medicine and Dentistry of New Jersey (UMDNJ) by Dr. Heary, a Professor of Neurosurgery and the Director of UMDNJ's Spine Center of New Jersey.

Dr. Heary had two pre-operative consultations with plaintiff. In the first consultation, Dr. Heary determined that plaintiff needed surgery to correct a cervical myelopathy secondary to cervical stenosis and a significantly large C3–C4 disc herniation. Because of the serious nature of the surgery, Dr. Heary recommended that plaintiff's wife attend a second consultation. The doctor wanted to explain again the risks, benefits, and alternatives to surgery, and to answer any questions concerning the procedure.

Plaintiff returned with his wife for a second consultation, but what transpired is disputed. An Office Note at written by Dr. Heary detailing the contents of the consultation states that "all alternatives have been discussed and patient elects at this time to undergo the surgical procedure, which has been scheduled for March 5, 1997" Dr. Heary asserts that he informed plaintiff and his wife that the surgery entailed significant risks, including the possibility of paralysis. Plaintiffs dispute that they were informed of such risks. Further, they contend that during the consultation plaintiff's wife asked Dr. Heary whether he was Board Certified and that he said he was. Plaintiffs also claim that Dr. Heary told them that he had performed approximately sixty corpectomies in each of the eleven years he had been performing such surgical procedures. According to Mrs. Howard, she was opposed to the surgery and it was only after Dr. Heary's specific claims of skill and experience that she and her husband decided to go ahead with the procedure.

Dr. Heary denies that he represented that he was Board Certified in Neurosurgery.[1] He also denies that he ever claimed to have performed

---

1. Although he was Board Eligible at the time of Mr. Howard's surgery, Dr. Heary did not become Board Certified in Neurosurgery until November 1999. "A physician is considered to be a surgical specialist if the physician: (1) Is certified by an American surgical specialty board approved by the American Board of Medical Specialties; or (2) Has been judged eligible by such a board for its examination by reason of education, training and experience." American College of Surgeons Statements on Principles, Section II.A.

sixty corpectomies per year for the eleven years he had practiced neurosurgery.

Dr. Heary performed the surgical procedure on March 5, 1997, but it was unsuccessful. A malpractice action was filed alleging that Mr. Howard was rendered quadriplegic as a result of Dr. Heary's negligence.

During pretrial discovery, Dr. Heary and Mr. and Mrs. Howard were deposed. Plaintiffs claim that they learned from Dr. Heary's deposition that he had misrepresented his credentials and experience during the pre-surgery consultation. In his deposition Dr. Heary stated that he was not Board Certified at the time of the surgery, and that he had performed approximately a couple dozen corpectomies during his career. Based on that allegedly new information, plaintiffs moved unsuccessfully to amend their original complaint to add a fraud count.

In denying the motion, the trial court reasoned that "the plaintiff can get before the jury everything that is necessary without clouding the issue [with] is there a fraud here against the doctor.... I have to agree with counsel for defendant that that, in essence, is not the nexus of malpractice." The court added that the fraud count would be duplicative, because if it were true that the doctor had misrepresented his credentials and experience plaintiffs still would be required to prove that Dr. Heary deviated from the acceptable standard of care to be entitled to recovery.

On leave to appeal the interlocutory order, the Appellate Division reversed and remanded with direction to the trial court to permit amendment of the complaint to include a "deceit based claim." [ ]. Rejecting the contention that the amended complaint caused undue prejudice to defendant, the Appellate Division held that the denial of the motion for leave to amend did not comport with the interests-of-justice standard. Id. at 38. In respect of the merits of the newly pled claim based on deceit, the panel disagreed that plaintiff would be required to prove negligent performance of the surgery in order to recover damages. Ibid. The Appellate Division likened the claim for fraudulent misrepresentation to a claim for battery, when a doctor, other than the one authorized under principles of informed consent, performs the surgery. [ ]. In such circumstances, proof of negligent performance by the doctor would not be required. [ ].

We granted defendant's motion for leave to appeal * * *.

II.

Presently, a patient has several avenues of relief against a doctor: (1) deviation from the standard of care (medical malpractice); (2) lack of informed consent; and (3) battery. Although each cause of action is based on different theoretical underpinnings, "it is now clear that deviation from the standard of care and failure to obtain informed consent are simply sub-groups of a broad claim of medical negligence." [ ]. The original complaint in this case alleged a standard medical malpractice claim of deviation from the standard of care. Plaintiffs' motion to amend the complaint to add a fraud claim raises the question whether a patient's consent to surgery obtained through alleged misrepresentations about the physician's professional experience and credentials is properly addressed in a claim of lack of informed consent, or battery, or whether it should constitute a separate and distinct claim based on fraud.

* * *

Our common law also authorizes a medical battery cause of action where a doctor performs a surgery without consent, rendering the surgery an unauthorized touching. Perna, supra, 92 N.J. at 460–61. Because battery is an intentional tort, it is reserved for those instances where either the patient consents to one type of operation but the physician performs a substantially different one from that for which authorization was obtained, or where no consent is obtained. Matthies, supra [ ].

In circumstances where the surgery that was performed was authorized with arguably inadequate information, however, an action for negligence is more appropriate. [ ] Battery actions are less readily available in part because of the severity of their consequences. In an action for battery, a patient need not prove that the physician deviated from either the applicable standard for disclosure or the standard for performance of the operation. [ ]. Accordingly, "an operation undertaken without [any] consent (battery) even if perfectly performed with good medical results may entitle a plaintiff to at least nominal and even punitive damages." Whitley–Woodford v. Jones, 253 N.J.Super. 7, 11, 600 A.2d 946 (App. Div. 1992) [ ].

[I]n Perna [v. Pirozzi, 92 N.J. 446, 457 A.2d 431 (1983)] represents the unusual circumstance where the consent granted was vitiated, rendering the circumstances the equivalent of an unauthorized touching—in other words, a battery. In that matter, the defendant urologists were part of a medical group that operated as a self-described "team." [ ]. Their method of operation included a decision made immediately prior to a surgical procedure designating the specific member of the group who was to perform the surgery. Unaware of that practice, the plaintiff entered the hospital on the advice of his family physician for tests and a urological consultation. In the hospital, the plaintiff was examined by one physician member of the practice group who previously had treated the plaintiff for a bladder infection.[ ] The doctor recommended the removal of kidney stones and the plaintiff signed a consent form naming that physician as the surgeon. The operation ultimately was performed by two other physicians from the practice group, both of whom were unaware that only the original doctor's name appeared on the consent form. [ ]. Post-surgical complications developed and the plaintiff became aware of the substitution of doctors. [ ].

Plaintiff sued based on lack of informed consent. [ ]. The court instructed the jury that the plaintiff could recover only if the substitution of surgeons caused his damages. [ ]. The jury found for the defendants, and on appeal the Appellate Division affirmed. [ ] On certification to this Court, the matter was reversed and remanded. 92

N.J. at 465–66. The Court referred to the substitution of surgeons as "ghost surgery" because the doctor to whom informed consent was given was not the surgeon who performed the surgery. In that circumstance, the Court concluded that that surgeon did not have the plaintiff's informed consent. [ ]. Denominating the matter a battery, the Court held that the plaintiff was entitled to "recover for all injuries proximately caused by the mere performance of the operation, whether the result of negligence or not." [ ]. The Court held that if the patient suffers no injuries except those that may be foreseen from the operation, he then is entitled at least to nominal damages and, in an appropriate case, may be entitled to damages for mental anguish resulting from the belated knowledge that the operation was performed by a doctor to whom he had not given consent. [ ].

Thus, although a claim for battery will lie where there has been "ghost surgery" or where no consent has been given for the procedure undertaken, if consent has been given for the procedure only a claim based on lack of informed consent will lie. A claim based on lack of informed consent properly will focus then on the adequacy of the disclosure, its impact on the reasonable patient's assessment of the risks, alternatives, and consequences of the surgery, and the damages caused by the occurrence of the undisclosed risk. [ ]

III.

A.

In finding that a deceit-based claim was appropriate in this matter, the Appellate Division analogized the allegations concerning Dr. Heary's misrepresentations about his credentials and experience to the "ghost surgery" situation discussed in Perna. Howard, supra [ ]. At the outset, we note that this case is not factually analogous to Perna where a different person from the one to whom consent was given actually performed the procedure. [ ] Nor is this a case where someone impersonating a doctor actually touched a patient. See Taylor v. Johnston, 985 P.2d 460, 465 (Alaska 1999) (noting that "battery claim may lie if a person falsely claiming to be a physician touches a patient, even for the purpose of providing medical assistance"). Here, defendant explained the procedure, its risks and benefits, and the alternatives to the surgery. He then performed the procedure; another person did not operate in his stead as in the "ghost surgery" scenario. [ ]. The facts in Perna simply are not helpful here.

Few jurisdictions have confronted the question of what cause of action should lie when a doctor allegedly misrepresents his credentials or experience. Research has revealed only one jurisdiction that has allowed a claim based on lack of informed consent under similar circumstances. See Johnson v. Kokemoor, 199 Wis.2d 615, 545 N.W.2d 495, 498 (Wis. 1996) (analyzing doctor's affirmative misrepresentation as claim for lack of informed consent and finding that reasonable person would have considered information regarding doctor's relative lack of experience in performing surgery to have been material in making intelligent and informed decision). Although some suggest that a claim based in fraud may be appropriate if a doctor actively misrepresents his or her background or credentials, we are aware of no court that has so held. * * *

The thoughtful decision of the Appellate Division notwithstanding, we are not convinced that our common law should be extended to allow a novel fraud or deceit-based cause of action in this doctor-patient context that would admit of the possibility of punitive damages, and that would circumvent the requirements for proof of both causation and damages imposed in a traditional informed consent setting. We are especially reluctant to do so when plaintiff's damages from this alleged "fraud" arise exclusively from the doctor-patient relationship involving plaintiff's corpectomy procedure. See Spinosa, supra [ ] (holding that concealment or failure to disclose doctor's own malpractice does not give rise to claim of fraud or deceit independent of medical malpractice, and noting that intentional tort of fraud actionable " 'only when the alleged fraud occurs separately from and subsequent to the malpractice ... and then only where the fraud claim gives rise to damages separate and distinct from those flowing from the malpractice' "). Accordingly, we hold that a fraud or deceit-based claim is unavailable to address the wrong alleged by plaintiff. We next consider whether a claim based on lack of informed consent is the more appropriate analytical basis for the amendment to the complaint permitted by the Appellate Division.

B.

Our case law never has held that a doctor has a duty to detail his background and experience as part of the required informed consent disclosure; nor are we called on to decide that question here. * * *

Although personal credentials and experience may not be a required part of an informed consent disclosure under the current standard of care required of doctors, the question raised in this appeal is whether significant misrepresentations concerning a physician's qualifications can affect the validity of consent obtained. The answer obviously is that they can.

* * * In Kokemoor, supra, the Supreme Court of Wisconsin reviewed a case in which the plaintiff alleged that her surgeon did not obtain her informed consent to perform a surgical procedure because he had misrepresented his experience in response to a direct question during a pre-operative consultation. [ ] At trial, evidence was introduced suggesting that the type of surgery performed—basilar bifurcation aneurysm—was "among the most difficult in all of neurosurgery" [ ] The court found that evidence of the defendant's lack of experience was relevant to an informed consent claim because "a reasonable person in the plaintiff's position would have considered such information material in making an intelligent and informed decision about the surgery."

* * *

The allegation here is that defendant's misrepresentations concerning his credentials and experience were instrumental in overcoming plaintiff's reluctance to proceed with the surgery. The theory of the claim is not that the misrepresentation induced plaintiff to proceed with unnecessary surgery. * * * Rather, plaintiff essentially contends that he was misled about material * * * information that he required in order to grant an intelligent and informed consent to the performance of the procedure because he did not receive accurate responses to questions concerning defendant's experience in performing corpectomies and whether he was "Board Certified." Plaintiff allegedly was warned of the risk of paralysis from the corpectomy procedure; however, he asserts that if he had known the truth about defendant's qualifications and experience, it would have affected his assessment of the risks of the procedure. Stated differently, defendant's misrepresentations induced plaintiff to consent to a surgical procedure, and its risk of paralysis, that he would not have undergone had he known the truth about defendant's qualifications. Stripped to its essentials, plaintiff's claim is founded on lack of informed consent.

As noted earlier, a patient-specific standard of what is material to a full disclosure does not apply in a claim based on lack of informed consent. Thus, plaintiff's subjective preference for a Board Certified physician, or one who had performed more corpectomies than defendant had performed, is not the actionable standard. Nonetheless, assuming the misrepresentations are proved, if an objectively reasonable person could find that physician experience was material in determining the medical risk of the corpectomy procedure to which plaintiff consented, and if a reasonably prudent person in plaintiff's position informed of the defendant's misrepresentations about his experience would not have consented, then a claim based on lack of informed consent may be maintained.

PETZELT v. TEWES

Court of Appeals of Georgia, First Division, 2003.
260 Ga.App. 802, 581 S.E.2d 345.

RUFFIN, Presiding Judge.

Philip Petzelt sued Patricia Tewes, M.D. and Northside Anesthesiology Consultants, LLC ("Tewes") for compensatory and punitive damages, alleging that Tewes, an anesthesiologist, committed battery, breach of fiduciary duty, and medical malpractice. Petzelt's battery and breach of fiduciary duty claims were based, in part, on his allegation that Tewes had fraudulently obtained his consent to perform certain medical procedures. Tewes moved for partial summary judgment on the latter claims, arguing that there was "no evidence that Dr. Tewes made any false statements to Mr. Petzelt or that she intentionally misled or deceived [him] for the purpose of obtaining his consent." Tewes also sought summary judgment on Petzelt's claim for punitive damages. The trial court granted Tewes' motion, and the remaining claims of malpractice and battery for exceeding the scope of consent were tried by a jury. The jury returned a verdict of $1,500 on Petzelt's battery claim and found for Tewes on Petzelt's medical malpractice claim and his wife's loss of consortium claim. The Petzelts now appeal the trial court's grant of partial summary judgment, and for reasons that follow, we reverse.

Petzelt contends that the trial court erred in granting summary judgment to Dr. Tewes on his claim that she fraudulently obtained his consent to perform the medical procedures by assuring him that his referring orthopedic surgeon, Dr. Edwards, was fully aware of and approved of her treatment plans for him. Petzelt further asserts that the trial court should have allowed his punitive damages claim to go to the jury based on his fraud claim.

* * *

* * * [T]he evidence shows that Dr. Edwards referred Petzelt to Dr. Tewes for treatment of his lower back, specifically for a nerve block to determine whether his pain was caused by a herniated disk. Dr. Tewes performed the procedure, but it did not alleviate Petzelt's pain. Dr. Tewes thus recommended that Petzelt proceed with facet blocks, a different procedure designed to determine whether his pain arose from degeneration in his lumbar facet joints. Petzelt told Dr. Tewes to "discuss [it] with Dr. Edwards and whatever you two decide [he would] be happy to go along with."

When Petzelt returned to Dr. Tewes for the facet blocks, Tewes told him she had been unable to contact Dr. Edwards by telephone, but that she had kept him advised. Petzelt told Dr. Tewes that he was concerned about her not having spoken with Dr. Edwards. According to Petzelt, Tewes "repeated over and over and reassured [him] that she had sent [Dr. Edwards] communications and that [Dr. Edwards] was aware of everything that was being done and that he had been advised. And she said this over and over again to get [Petzelt] to consent to the procedure." Petzelt agreed, and Dr. Tewes then administered three facet blocks on the left side of Petzelt's lower back, which alleviated some of Petzelt's pain.

Dr. Tewes later followed up with Petzelt concerning a continuing treatment plan. Tewes explained to Petzelt that he could undergo another set of facet blocks or he could proceed with a radio frequency denervation, a longer-lasting treatment. Petzelt again told Dr. Tewes to discuss the matter with Dr. Edwards and that he would go along with whatever the two of them decided.

Petzelt subsequently returned to Dr. Tewes for the denervation procedure. Petzelt signed a consent to treatment form, on which the words "facet block/denervation" were circled, and next to that was a handwritten, circled "L." Petzelt testified that Dr. Tewes came into the pre-op room and told him she had not been able to contact Dr. Edwards. Petzelt attempted to call Dr. Edwards himself, but the office had not yet opened and he was unsuccessful. Petzelt testified that Tewes then came back into pre-op and started reassuring me again, over and over again, Mr. Petzelt, you do not need to worry, Dr. Edwards is completely aware of everything that we've done—I have sent him . . . notes on everything that I have done, he is fully aware. Now when someone tells me that, I believe them. And I consented to let her go ahead based on her lies.

According to Dr. Tewes, Petzelt was crying, severely distressed, in severe pain, and wanted to proceed with the denervation.

Dr. Tewes performed the denervation procedures on the left side of three lumbar facet joints, and then began to work on Petzelt's right side. Petzelt instructed her to stop because he only wanted the treatment on his left side, so Tewes stopped, having already performed the procedure in two locations on the right.

Petzelt testified that these procedures gave him no pain relief, but instead exacerbated his pain. He remained bedridden for a week with increasing pain; then his right leg began swelling. After Petzelt developed further complications, he learned that Dr. Edwards was unaware of Dr. Tewes' course of treatment.[4] This lawsuit followed.

As a general rule, if a person consents to undergo a medical procedure, the physician cannot be liable for battery unless the consent was not freely obtained or was obtained by fraud. In a case of fraud, if the physician fails to respond truthfully to a patient's questions about a diagnosis or treatment, the patient's consent may be vitiated.

To establish fraud, a plaintiff must produce evidence showing a "willful misrepresentation of a material fact, made to induce [the plaintiff] to act, upon which [the plaintiff] acts to his injury." Although knowledge that the representation is false is an essential element of fraud, a reckless representation of facts as true when they are not, if intended to deceive, is equivalent to a knowledge of their falsehood *even if the party making the representation does not know that such facts are false.* A misrepresentation is intended to deceive where there is intent that the representation be acted upon by the other party.

And, because fraud is inherently subtle, slight circumstances of fraud may be sufficient to establish a proper case. Proof of fraud is seldom if ever susceptible of direct proof, thus recourse to circumstantial evidence usually is required. Moreover, it is peculiarly the province of the jury to pass on these circumstances showing fraud. Except in plain and indisputable cases, scienter in actions based on fraud is an issue of fact for jury determination.

The evidence in this case is not plain and indisputable. Petzelt claims that Dr. Tewes recklessly misrepresented to him that Dr. Edwards was fully aware of Tewes' treatment plans. Although evidence shows that Dr. Tewes sent Dr. Edwards her treatment notes, this

---

4. It is undisputed that Dr. Tewes never spoke with Dr. Edwards concerning the treatment, and Edwards testified that he never received any treatment notes from Tewes. Although Dr. Edwards' actual testimony apparently is not included in the record, Dr. Tewes acknowledged this testimony in her summary judgment brief.

evidence did not necessarily permit Tewes to assume that Edwards received copies of the notes, that he read the notes, and that he was fully aware of the treatment plans.

As a threshold matter, the evidence that Dr. Tewes sent the notes to Dr. Edwards is not compelling. Specifically, the evidence shows merely that the notes contain the words "cc: Christopher Edwards, MD." Even though this text indicates that Dr. Tewes intended to send a copy of the notes to Dr. Edwards, Tewes testified that she merely dictated the notes and did not personally send them to Edwards. In fact, Dr. Tewes testified that she did not know who was responsible for sending copies to the individuals listed as "cc." Instead, Dr. Tewes merely assumed that the notes were sent to Edwards because it was a policy to "have the medical records office send the records." Even if such evidence would be admissible as habit or routine, considering the lack of any direct evidence that the notes were actually sent, in addition to the evidence that Dr. Edwards never received the notes, a jury could find that the notes were never sent.

Moreover, even if Dr. Tewes reasonably assumed that the notes had been sent, a jury could still find that she was reckless in repeatedly telling Petzelt that Dr. Edwards was *fully aware* of the procedure she was about to perform. Under the circumstances of this case, the implications of Tewes' reassurances, even if well intended, were significant. Petzelt was obviously distressed about the procedure, and he wanted to ensure that Dr. Edwards concurred with Dr. Tewes' suggested treatment. Although Tewes testified in her deposition that "there's no way" she could have known whether Dr. Edwards received the notes, a jury could conclude that her unequivocal reassurances to Petzelt informed him that she knew for a fact that he had not only received them, but also read them. And, considering that the evidence must be viewed in a light most favorable to Petzelt, a jury could infer that Dr. Tewes misrepresented to Petzelt that Dr. Edwards had acquiesced to her treatment plan. That is a reasonable inference if the jurors consider that Dr. Edwards purportedly knew all about Tewes' treatment plan, yet failed to object to the procedure before it was performed.

Under these circumstances, a jury could find that Dr. Tewes pretended to know, as a matter of fact, that Dr. Edwards had seen her notes, that he was fully aware of the proposed treatment, and that he acquiesced in the treatment, when, in fact, Tewes did not actually know any of this to be true and it was not true. And, considering that Tewes made the misrepresentation to Petzelt to quell Petzelt's objections as he waited in pre-op, a jury could also find that Tewes intended to deceive him. Thus, the trial court erred in granting Tewes' motion for summary judgment on Petzelt's claim that his consent was induced by fraud.

2.   Because there is evidence from which a jury could find that Dr. Tewes was culpable of fraud, the trial court also erred in granting her motion for summary judgment on Petzelt's claim for punitive damages.

Judgment reversed. Barnes and Adams, JJ., concur.

Notes

1) New York's liberal interlocutory appeal practice brings up a commonplace procedural maneuver such as that used in *Simcuski*. Before filing a responsive pleading (the answer) the defendant filed a motion to dismiss the complaint because the face of the complaint showed that the statute of limitations had run. The reasoning was that the complaint alleged a date that started the statute running; the clerk's date-stamp stopped the statute and the trial judge should take judicial notice of the length of the statute. The trial judge denied the motion to dismiss; the appellate division reversed, holding that dismissal should not have been granted. The Court of Appeals held the statute, because of fraudulent concealment, did not being to run until late enough to make the filing timely. Alleging a fraud theory permitted another plaintiff to introduce evidence of unnecessary surgery performed on other patients in order to show the doctor's propensity to perform, and the intent to induce the plaintiff to undergo, unnecessary surgery. Under a negligence theory, the report of a quality assurance committee likely would not even have been discoverable.

2) *Howard* is a deceit-based claim masquerading as an issue of informed consent. It raises the issue of whether a significant misrepresentation of the credentials and qualifications of the physician can vitiate informed consent. It is not only the competence of the physician to perform the procedure that it at issue; it is the medical judgment, and the communication of the medical opinion to the plaintiff, regarding whether the procedure was appropriate in the first place. But what if the so-called "reasonable" patient under these circumstances would have opted for the procedure under these circumstances? Does a plaintiff alleging deceit have to prove that, absent the deceit, she would not have opted for the surgery? Is it enough that she might have chosen a physician with better credentials or qualifications?

3) In *Duttry v. Patterson*, 565 Pa. 130, 771 A.2d 1255 (2001), plaintiff consulted with defendant to treat her cancer of the esophagus. Plaintiff inquired of the physician about his expertise in performing the recommended procedure. Plaintiff alleges that the physician told her that he performs this type of procedure approximately once per month. Plaintiff consented to the procedure. Complications arose and the plaintiff was forced to undergo emergency surgery and was left with permanent damage to her lung. Plaintiff alleged, among other things, lack of informed consent, and wanted to introduce evidence that in the five years preceding the surgery, the defendant only performed the procedure 5 times. The trial court refused to allow the evidence on the basis of relevance, and a defendant's verdict was rendered. The Supreme Court reversed, holding that information concerning a physician's qualifications was relevant to plaintiff's claim of lack of informed consent. In order to obtain informed consent, a physician must provide all informa-

tion that a reasonable patient in the plaintiff's situation would consider important including risks, benefits, complications and alternatives. Should competence of the physician be added to the list?

SECTION C.   TORTIOUS CONDUCT

BERTHIAUME v. PRATT

Supreme Judicial Court of Maine, 1976.
365 A.2d 792.

POMEROY, J.

The appellant, as administratrix, based her claim of right to damages on an alleged invasion of her late husband's "right to privacy" and on an alleged assault and battery of him. * * *

The appellee is a physician and surgeon practicing in Waterville, Maine. It was established at trial without contradiction that the deceased, Henry Berthiaume, was suffering from a cancer of his larynx. Appellee, an otolaryngologist, had treated him twice surgically. A laryngectomy was performed; and later, because of a tumor which had appeared in his neck, a radical neck dissection on one side was done. No complaint is made with respect to the surgical interventions.

During the period appellee was serving Mr. Berthiaume as a surgeon, many photographs of Berthiaume had been taken by appellee or under his direction. The jury was told that the sole use to which these photographs were to be put was to make the medical record for the appellee's use. There is nothing in the case to suggest that the photographs were to be shown to students for teaching purposes or were to be used as illustrative photographs in any text books or papers. The only persons to whom the photographs were available were those members of appellee's staff and the appropriate hospital personnel who had duties to perform with respect to medical records.

Although at no time did the appellee receive any written consent for the taking of photographs from Berthiaume or any members of his family, it was appellee's testimony that Berthiaume had always consented to having such photographs made.

At all times material hereto Mr. Berthiaume was the patient of a physician other than appellee. Such other physician had referred the patient to appellee for surgery. On September 2, 1970, appellee saw the patient for the last time for the purpose of treatment or diagnosis. The incident which gave rise to this lawsuit occurred on September 23, 1970.

It was also on that day Mr. Berthiaume died.

Although appellee disputed the evidence appellant produced at trial in many material respects, the jury could have concluded from the evidence that shortly before Mr. Berthiaume died on the 23rd, the appellee and a nurse appeared in his hospital room. In the presence of Mrs. Berthiaume and a visitor of the patient in the next bed, either Dr. Pratt or the nurse, at his direction, raised the dying Mr. Berthiaume's head and placed some blue operating room toweling under his head and beside him on the bed. The appellee testified that this blue toweling was placed there for the purpose of obtaining a color contrast for the photographs which he proposed to take. He then proceeded to take several photographs of Mr. Berthiaume.

The jury could have concluded from the testimony that Mr. Berthiaume protested the taking of pictures by raising a clenched fist and moving his head in an attempt to remove his head from the camera's range. The appellee himself testified that before taking the pictures he had been told by Mrs. Berthiaume when he talked with her in the corridor before entering the room that she "didn't think that Henry wanted his picture taken."

It is the raising of the deceased's head in order to put the operating room towels under and around him that appellant claims was an assault and battery. It is the taking of the pictures of the dying Mr. Berthiaume that appellant claims constituted the actionable invasion of Mr. Berthiaume's right to privacy.

* * *

By our decision in this case we join a majority of the jurisdictions in the country in recognizing a "right to privacy." We also declare it to be the rule in Maine that a violation of this legally protected right is an actionable tort.

Specifically in this case we rule an unauthorized intrusion upon a person's physical and mental solitude or seclusion is a tort for the commission of which money damages may be had.

The law of privacy addresses the invasion of four distinct interests of the individual. Each of the four different interests, taken as a whole, represent an individual's right "to be let alone." These four kinds of invasion are:

(1) intrusion upon the plaintiff's physical and mental solitude or seclusion;

(2) public disclosure of private facts;

(3) publicity which places the plaintiff in a false light in the public eye;

(4) appropriation for the defendant's benefit or advantage of the plaintiff's name or likeness.

As Prosser explains it:

"As it has appeared in the cases thus far decided, it is not one tort, but a complex of four. To date the law of privacy comprises four distinct kinds of invasion of four different interests of the plaintiff, which are tied together by the common name, but otherwise have almost nothing in common except that each represents an interference with the right of the plaintiff 'to be let alone.' " W. Prosser, *Law of Torts*, 804 (4th ed. 1971).

In this case we are concerned only with a claimed intrusion upon the plaintiff's intestate's physical and mental solitude or seclusion. The jury had a right to conclude from the evidence that plaintiff's intestate was dying. It could have concluded he desired not to be photographed in his hospital bed in such condition and that he manifested such desire by his physical motions. The jury should have been instructed, if it found these facts, that the taking of pictures without decedent's consent or over his objection was an invasion of his legally protected right to privacy, which invasion was an actionable tort for which money damages could be recovered.

Instead, a directed verdict for the defendant was entered, obviously premised on the presiding justice's announced incorrect conclusion that the taking of pictures without consent did not constitute an invasion of privacy and the further erroneous conclusion that no tort was committed in the absence of "proof they [the photographs] were published."

Another claimed basis for appellant's assertion that a right to recover damages was demonstrated by the evidence is the allegations in her complaint sounding in the tort of assault and battery. As earlier indicated, the presiding justice announced as his conclusion that consent to a battery is implied from the existence of a physician-patient relationship. While we do not acknowledge the correctness of this pronouncement by the justice presiding because in our view it is so broad as to be inaccurate, even if the statement were true, the action taken by the presiding justice was not legally justified. It was based on a major premise that a physician-patient relationship existed at the time of the actions complained of. The jury had not yet had the opportunity to decide if such a relationship had been established. The evidence in the case at the time of the justice's action clearly established that plaintiff's intestate was under the care of another physician. The patient had been referred to appellee for surgery on two occasions. The only other occasion for direct contact with the patient occurred substantially before the alleged invasion of the right to privacy when appellee examined plaintiff's intestate preliminarily to giving his opinion to the attending physician only as to the advisability of proposed therapy. There is nothing to suggest that the appellee's visit to plaintiff's intestate's room on the day of the alleged invasion of privacy was for any purpose relating to the *treatment* of the patient. Appellee acknowledges that his sole purpose in going to the Berthiaume hospital room and the taking of pictures was to conclude the making of a photographic record to complete appellee's record of the case. From the evidence, then, it is apparent that the jury had a right to conclude that the physician-patient relationship once existing between Dr. Pratt and Henry Berthiaume, the deceased, had terminated.

As to the claimed assault and battery, on the state of the evidence, the jury should have been permitted to consider the evidence and return a verdict in accordance with its fact finding. It should have been instructed that consent to a touching of the body of a patient may be implied from the patient's consent to enter into a physician-patient relationship whenever such touching is reasonably necessary for the diagnosis and treatment of the patient's ailments while the physician-patient relationship continues. Quite obviously also, there would be no actionable assault and battery if the touching was expressly consented to. Absent express consent by the patient or one authorized to give consent on the patient's behalf, or absent consent implied from the circumstances, including the physician-patient relationship, the touching of the patient in the manner described by the evidence in this case would constitute assault and battery if it was part of an undertaking which, in legal effect, was an invasion of plaintiff's intestate's "right to be let alone."

It has been urged upon us that great benefit inures to medical science from the taking and preservation of photographs. The evidence discloses that the appellee had taken photographs at various stages during the course of Berthiaume's fatal illness and had made these photographs a part of appellee's medical record of the case. It is argued that by looking at Berthiaume's photographs appellee would be better able to evaluate and predict the progress of a malignancy of the same type and nature in other patients similarly afflicted. We are urged to declare as a matter of law that it was the physician's right to complete the photographic record by capturing on film Berthiaume's appearance in his final dying hours, even without the patient's consent or over his objections. This we are unwilling to do.

We recognize the benefit to the science of medicine which comes from the making of photographs of the treatment and of medical abnormalities found in patients. However, we agree with the reasoning expressed by Alessandroni, J., sitting in the Court of Common Pleas in Pennsylvania, when in writing of a fact situation almost identical to that now before us, he said in *Clayman v. Bernstein*, 38 Pa.D. & C. 543 (1940):

> "The court recognized that an individual has the right to decide whether that which is his shall be given to the public and not only to restrict and limit but also to withhold absolutely his talents, property, or other subjects of the right of privacy from all dissemination. The facial characteristics or peculiar caste of one's features, whether normal or distorted, belong to the individual and may not be reproduced without his permission. Even the photographer who is authorized to take a portrait is not justified in making or retaining additional copies for himself.

> "A man may object to any invasion, as well as to an unlimited invasion. Widespread distribution of a photograph is not essential nor can it be said that publication in its common usage or in its legal meaning is necessary. It may be conceded that the doctrine of privacy in general is still suffering the pains of its birth and any doctrine in its inception borrows from established precedent. An analogy to the laws of libel, however, is not justified under the circumstances of this case. The author of a libel is the creator and

there can be no offense until the contents are communicated to another. One cannot invade the rights of another merely by expressing his thoughts on paper. Two persons are necessary. One's right of privacy, however, may be invaded by a single human agency. Plaintiff's picture was taken without her authority or consent. Her right to decide whether her facial characteristics should be recorded for another's benefit or by reason of another's capriciousness has been violated. The scope of the authorization defines the extent of the acts necessary to constitute a violation. If plaintiff had consented to have her photograph taken only for defendant's private files certainly he would have no right to exhibit it to others without her permission. Can it be said that his rights are equally extensive when even that limited consent has not been given?''

Because there were unresolved, disputed questions of fact, which, if decided by the factfinder in favor of the plaintiff, would have justified a verdict for the plaintiff, it was reversible error to have directed a verdict for the defendant.

Appeal sustained. New trial ordered.

SUESBURY v. CACERES

District of Columbia Court of Appeals, 2004.
840 A.2d 1285.

STEADMAN, *Associate Judge*:

Ernest C. Suesbury ("Suesbury") was diagnosed with the HIV virus. Cesar A. Caceres, M.D. ("Caceres"), a principal in the medical office of Cesar Caceres, M.D., P.C., was Suesbury's treating physician, and, as such, was privy to Suesbury's HIV status. Suesbury sought treatment from Caceres for unrelated injuries sustained in an automobile accident. Alfred Muller, M.D. ("Muller"), another physician in Caceres' medical office, treated Suesbury during that office visit, in the course of which Suesbury mentioned his HIV condition and a T-cell reading of 700. Suesbury later alleged to Caceres that Muller molested him during this office visit. Following their conversation, Caceres wrote a memorandum to Muller in which he not only discussed Suesbury's allegation, but also indicated that Suesbury was HIV-positive and that Suesbury's T-cell count was 600.

When he learned of this communication by Caceres to Muller, Suesbury filed suit against Caceres and his medical office, claiming breach of the confidential physician-patient relationship and related torts. * * *

I. FACTS

Caceres practices as an internist and maintains a medical office in Washington, D.C. In 1988, Caceres hired Muller, a board certified internist, to work at his medical office. Caceres first examined appellant on January 15, 1988. Suesbury informed Caceres that he was HIV-positive, a fact that was then noted in Suesbury's medical chart. On May

26, 1992, Suesbury returned to Caceres' medical office for an examination and for treatment of injuries suffered during an automobile accident. Because Caceres was unavailable, Muller examined Suesbury. Prior to examining Suesbury, Muller reviewed Suesbury's chart and learned that he suffered from HIV. Suesbury, during his examination, also disclosed to Muller that he was HIV-positive and that his T-cell count was 700.

Suesbury alleged in his complaint that, during this May 26, 1992 examination, Muller sexually molested him. Following that examination, Suesbury, apparently by telephone and in writing, communicated his allegation to Caceres. Caceres indicated that he would investigate the matter and report back to Suesbury. In a memorandum dated September 2, 1992, Caceres told Muller:

> The message attached is from a patient that called to say that he had been massaged and molested sexually during his visit of 5–26.

> I indicated no similar complaint had come thru regarding any other patient seen but would discuss it with you, and call him back. He says he had spoken to a social worker regarding the situation but had decided not to take the matter further. But I was not able to understand fully why he was calling now or whether he wanted some action taken.

> PT HIV status was + in Jan of 88 so I would assume that altho his T 4s are 600 according to his report (NIH) he should be getting to some point at which he will have some difficulty with HIV.

> Please let me know what to tell him regarding his complaint.

On or about February 1, 2001, Suesbury discovered through the media that Muller had been arrested and charged with sexually abusing a 14 year old boy. Suesbury then contacted the Assistant United States Attorney ("AUSA") managing the case against Muller and relayed to her the alleged events of May 26, 1992. As part of the investigation in the on-going criminal case against Muller, the AUSA obtained the September 2, 1992 note from Caceres to Muller, forwarding it to Suesbury.

On May 4, 2001, Suesbury filed suit against Caceres and his medical office, alleging breach of the confidential physician-patient relationship, intentional infliction of emotional distress, invasion of privacy, and negligent hiring and supervision. On June 29, 2001, appellees moved for summary judgment, arguing that no issues were in dispute as to any material fact and that appellees were entitled to judgment on all counts as a matter of law, which the trial court granted.

On appeal, Suesbury challenges the grant of summary judgment insofar as it relates to the claims for breach of the confidential physician-patient relationship and intentional infliction of emotional distress.

II. CONFIDENTIAL PHYSICIAN-PATIENT RELATIONSHIP

The tort of breach of the confidential physician-patient relationship was first recognized in this jurisdiction in the leading case of *Vassiliades v. Garfinckel's, Brooks Bros., Miller & Rhoades, Inc.*, 492 A.2d 580, 591–92 (D.C. 1985). The tort reflects the strong public policy in the District of Columbia to encourage candor by patients and confidentiality by physicians. [ ] To be actionable, a claim for breach of the confidential physician-patient relationship requires the "unconsented, unprivileged disclosure to a third party of nonpublic information that the defendant has learned within a confidential relationship." [ ] The critical question in this appeal, then, is whether Dr. Caceres's disclosure to a fellow physician in his office in the course of dealing with a matter related to the operation of that office was an "unconsented, unprivileged disclosure to a third party." We hold that it was not.

We have not been cited to, nor ourselves found, any case in this jurisdiction, or elsewhere, that squarely addresses the question whether communications between two physicians within the same medical office concerning a patient of that office can constitute a breach of the confidential physician-patient relationship. Cases dealing with invocation of the testimonial privilege, however, support the expectation that there will be interaction among related health care personnel. It is widely acknowledged that the nurse who attends a physician during a consultation or examination, or the technician who makes tests under the doctor's direction, are bound by the privilege. * * *

A similar recognition of the extent and necessity of communication within a professional entity is reflected in available authority relating to the attorney-client privilege as applied to intra-firm communications. [ ] Commentators, similarly, have noted that the privilege should apply to communications between attorneys.

The District of Columbia Rules of Professional Conduct too support the proposition that client information shared among attorneys within a firm is to be expected and remains confidential, an opinion that, in turn, informs our view that communications among physicians in the same medical office enjoy a similar protected status. Rule 1.6, cmt. 10, which concerns the confidentiality of information, states "unless the client otherwise directs, a lawyer may disclose the affairs of the client to partners or associates of the lawyer's firm." Analogously, Rule 1.10, cmt. 6, which discusses imputed disqualification, notes "the rule of imputed disqualification . . . gives effect to the principle of loyalty to the client as it applies to lawyers who practice in a law firm. Such situations can be considered from the premise that a firm of lawyers is essentially one lawyer for purposes of the rules governing loyalty to the client, or from the premise that each lawyer is vicariously bound by the obligation of loyalty owed by each lawyer with whom the lawyer is associated." [P]reserving confidentiality is a question of access to information. . . . A lawyer may have general access to files of all clients of a law firm and may regularly participate in discussions of their affairs; it should be inferred that such a lawyer in fact is privy to all information about all the firm's clients."

We are mindful that the case before us concerns the general duty of a physician to maintain the confidentiality of a patient's medical condition, and not the distinct, albeit related, statutory testimonial privilege, which in general prohibits a physician from testifying as to any confidential information acquired in attending a client in a professional capacity. [ ]. The two are not necessarily co-extensive, since the testimonial privilege of the speaker to remain silent is derivative of the patient's interest while the general confidentiality principle may at times also involve consideration of the propriety of a physician's defensive invocation of a right to communicate free of liability. * * *.

It is true that, in the case before us, the communication was not made in connection with the immediate on-going treatment of a common patient. Nonetheless, the communication was related to and arose as a consequence of such medical treatment and was made in the course of the business of administering the mutual medical practice. Doctors within the same medical office should be allowed to work together with some latitude of freedom of communication not only to treat patients, but also to respond to patient administrative requests and, as here, patient complaints.

Both doctors, moreover, already knew of appellant's HIV-positive status as a result of their treatment of appellant. Appellant argues that Muller was not aware of the NIH report of the decline in appellant's T-cell count from 700 to 600, suggesting a worsening of his condition, and communication of that fact was not directly related to his complaint. We do not think that the content of a communication between two doctors in a common medical practice about a matter involving the operation of that practice should be subjected to such a taxing sentence-by-sentence analysis, especially where the challenged statement is itself medical information acquired as part of the firm's practice. Too exacting an approach, requiring the most guarded attention and analysis of the content of each professional exchange, could well hinder the free flow of information within a given medical practice and work ultimately to the detriment of the medical care of the patients of the firm as a whole. Moreover, when the information relating to a patient's medical record is contained in communications between physicians in the same office relating to that mutual patient, present or past, there can be no doubt that the cloak of confidentiality with respect to that record encompasses both physicians, even when the communication does not directly relate to immediate medical treatment. * * *

In summation, Suesbury was a patient of Caceres' medical office. Muller was a treating physician in that office and had been informed that Suesbury was HIV-positive. Muller normally would be expected to have access to Suesbury's medical information, presumably including the NIH report about Suesbury's T-cell count, at least where he did so for the purposes of treatment, payment, or health care operations. Suesbury complained to Caceres about Muller's actions and, without objection by Suesbury, Caceres said he would investigate. In the course of doing so, he naturally communicated with Muller and, in the process, happened to mention one piece of medical information new to Muller, the decrease in the T-cell count. Caceres' communication related to important practice-related concerns that a patient of the medical practice had voiced. In this setting, the single medical statement of a T-cell count contained in a communication relating to firm operations by one physician to another, made within the bounds of a common professional enterprise and a mutual obligation of confidentiality, simply was not the "unconsented, unprivileged communication with a third party" required to underpin the tort. Suesbury thus failed to establish an essential element of his cause of action in tort for breach of the confidential physician-patient relationship. The trial court correctly granted summary judgment against him on that count, as well as the related count for intentional infliction of emotional distress.

Affirmed.

HARMON v. TEXAS

Court of Appeals of Texas, First District, 2003.
2003 WL 21665488.

MEMORANDUM OPINION

* * *

FACTS

On April 6, 2001, appellant drove a car into a concrete barrier on Memorial Drive in Houston. Another driver, who did not witness the accident, called the police. Houston Police Officer Farias arrived at the scene and noticed that appellant had a strong odor of alcohol on his breath and a sway in his stance. Officer Farias also found two tumblers containing alcohol inside appellant's car. Appellant, who appeared to be injured and was taken to the hospital, was not arrested at that time. After learning that hospital personnel would draw blood from appellant, Officer Farias obtained a grand-jury subpoena requesting appellant's medical records from the hospital. The subpoena stated the following:

Please provide all medical records for Derek Harmon, W/M, DOB 8–5–59, who was treated on 4–6–01 through 4–7–01, [sic] please provide all records reflecting chemical or blood alcohol results. Kindly indicate who drew, transported and tested the blood.

Appellant's medical records showed that he had a blood alcohol content of 0.18.

* * *

EXPECTATION OF PRIVACY

In his first issue, appellant contends that the trial court erred in denying his motion to suppress blood-test results because the State did not meet its burden to prove the reasonableness of the search, because there were defects in the grand-jury subpoena process, and because appellant had a statutory right to privacy under the Health Insurance Portability and Accountability Act of 1996 (HIPAA). Pub. L. No. 104–191, 110 Stat. 1936 (1996).

A. Standing

Appellant first complains that the State failed to meet its burden "to show that the blood test results were obtained pursuant to a recognized exception to the warrant requirement" and because there were defects in the grand-jury subpoena process. The State argues that appellant lacks standing to complain about the manner in which the blood test results were obtained because appellant can have no reasonable expectation of privacy in blood-alcohol test results taken by hospital personnel solely for medical purposes.

To determine whether appellant may complain of the reasonableness of the search, we must determine whether he has established standing. [ ]. An accused has standing to challenge the admission of evidence obtained by a governmental intrusion only if he had "a legitimate expectation of privacy in the place invaded." *Richardson v. State*, 865 S.W.2d 944, 948 (Tex. Crim. App. 1993).

In *State v. Hardy*, the Court of Criminal Appeals held that an accused does not have a legitimate expectation of privacy in medical records containing blood-alcohol test results "taken by hospital personnel solely for medical purposes after a traffic accident." 963 S.W.2d 516, 527 (Tex. Crim. App. 1997). The *Hardy* court based its holding on the determination that the societal interests in safeguarding the privacy of medical records were not sufficiently strong enough to require protection of blood-alcohol test results obtained by medical personnel after traffic accidents.

We addressed complaints in *Garcia v. State* [95 S.W.3d 522 (Tex. App.—Houston) (1st Dist.) 2002] and *Dickerson v. State* [965 S.W.2d 30 (Tex. App.—Houston) (1st Dist.) 1998] that are similar to appellant's complaints. Relying on *Hardy*, we held in both cases that there was "no Fourth Amendment reasonable expectation of privacy . . . that protects the record of blood test results of an injured motorist from being given to law enforcement officers pursuant to a grand jury subpoena." [ ]. We concluded that, because the Fourth Amendment does not confer a reasonable expectation of privacy under these circumstances, an accused does not have standing to assert an unreasonable search or seizure under the Fourth Amendment or to challenge any defects in the grand-jury subpoena process.

Following *Garcia* and *Dickerson*, we hold that appellant does not have standing to challenge either the reasonableness of the search or any defects in the grand-jury subpoena process.

B. HIPAA

Appellant also argues that the grand-jury subpoena under which his medical information was obtained violates HIPAA. [ ].

On August 21, 1996, Congress enacted HIPAA and instructed the Secretary of Health and Human Services to promulgate final regulations containing "standards with respect to the privacy of individually identifiable health information" if Congress failed to enact such privacy standards within 36 months of the enactment of HIPAA. [ ]. On February 13, 2001, the Secretary of Health and Human Services promulgated final regulations imposing the standards, requirements, and implementation specifications under which a health care provider is required to release an individual's health information. [ ].

Even if HIPAA imposed a new statutory right of privacy that trumps the State's power to issue grand-jury subpoenas in a criminal investigation, disclosure of medical records under HIPAA is permissible without an individual's permission when the information is disclosed for law enforcement purposes and is obtained pursuant to a grand-jury subpoena. [ ]

We overrule appellant's first issue.

GRAND–JURY SUBPOENA

In his second issue, appellant contends that the grand-jury subpoena under which his medical information was obtained was overly broad because the subpoena sought all of his medical records made during his hospitalization, rather than the medical records pertaining only to his blood-alcohol tests. Appellant complains that, because the trial court refused to suppress these records, they became "open for full view to prosecutors, grand jurors, courts, and the public."

A two-step inquiry determines whether we address the merits of a claim regarding a trial court's denial of a pretrial motion to suppress evidence prior to a guilty plea. [ ] We first identify the fruits that the trial court refused to suppress. We then determine whether these fruits have "somehow been used" by the State. [ ]. If the fruits have not somehow been used by the State, then we need not address the merits of the claim. In the context of a guilty plea, evidence is used if the evidence could have "contributed in some measure to the State's leverage in the plea bargaining process." [ ]. Evidence is used against a defendant and contributes to the State's leverage if the evidence is inculpatory. [ ].

Appellant, who pleaded guilty to driving while intoxicated, has not identified any information in the remaining portion of his medical records that was inculpatory or that may have contributed in some measure to the State's leverage in the plea-bargain process. Except for appellant's blood-test results, none of the other information in appellant's medical records was discussed at the hearing on appellant's motion to suppress evidence. Because the record does not show that appellant's medical records, other than his blood-test results, contributed to the State's leverage in the plea-bargaining process, we need not address the merits of his claim.

* * *

We affirm the judgment of the trial court.

STRACHAN v. JOHN F. KENNEDY MEM. HOSP.

Supreme Court of New Jersey, 1988.
109 N.J. 523, 538 A.2d 346.

CLIFFORD, J. * * *

At approximately 4:30 p.m. on Friday, April 25, 1980, 20–year–old Jeffrey Strachan shot himself in the head in an apparent suicide attempt. He was rushed to John F. Kennedy Memorial Hospital (the Hospital) * * *. At 5:25 that afternoon Dr. Hummel, the emergency room physician, diagnosed Jeffrey as brain dead. The doctor based his conclusion on several factors, including the absence of spontaneous respiration and reflexive movement, as well as the fact that both pupils were dilated and fixed. Dr. Hummel placed Jeffrey on a respirator.

Examination later that evening by Dr. Cohen, a neurosurgeon and one of the attending physicians, confirmed that Jeffrey was brain dead. The doctor explained that painful reality to plaintiffs and informed them that nothing could be done to restore brain function.

Because the Hospital is actively involved in organ transplants through its affiliate, the Delaware Valley Transplant Program, Dr. Cohen asked plaintiffs to consider donating Jeffrey's organs. He noted on the medical chart that the staff should proceed to "harvest" Jeffrey's organs if the parents gave their permission (the obvious implication being that there was no doubt about Jeffrey's status: he was dead). Because plaintiffs were uncertain about what to do, they deferred a decision and agreed to return in the morning. Jeffrey was then transferred to the intensive care unit, where he was continued on the life support system in order that the organs would remain in a condition for harvesting should the parents' decision be in favor of donation. Jeffrey's parents were allowed to "visit" him in the intensive care unit.

Plaintiffs returned the next morning, Saturday, April 26. They informed a Dr. Pinsler * * * of their decision not to donate any of Jeffrey's organs. They also requested that he be taken off the respirator. Dr. Pinsler advised plaintiffs to "think it over some more." Plaintiffs also discussed their request with Dr. Cohen. When Mr. Strachan asked a nurse when the machine would be turned off, he was informed that the hospital administrator had not given any order for the removal of the machinery, and that the removal could not be effected without such an order.

After speaking with Mr. Strachan that evening Dr. Venkat, also a neurosurgeon and an associate of Dr. Cohen, examined Jeffrey and agreed that the young man was brain dead. He noted plaintiffs' request to turn off the respirator, and indicated on the chart that "as soon as the hospital administrator tells us the procedure, we will do so."

Assistant administrator and nursing director Jeanette Licorice communicated with defendant Augustine R. Pirolli, the hospital administrator, late that same evening. Pirolli in turn called the Hospital's general counsel, Edward Sullivan, for advice. Sullivan suggested that the Hospital obtain plaintiffs' consent for removal of the respirator. He also indicated that the Hospital should run two electroencephalograms (EEGs), twenty-four hours apart, to get a "clear understanding of what the boy's condition is." He suggested to Pirolli that a court order might be obtained as an alternative to a medical decision to turn off the respirator. Another possible solution offered by Sullivan was the convening of a prognosis committee to assist the physicians in the decision to pronounce the patient dead.

The results of the two EEGs confirmed that Jeffrey was indeed brain dead. The Hospital authorities did not convene a prognosis committee. Dr. Weinstein, also a neurosurgeon engaged in practice with Drs. Cohen and Venkat, made an entry on Jeffrey's chart for Monday, April 28, 1980, indicating: "patient officially brain dead and by hospital regulations we may discontinue respiration c̲ [with] family's permission." Plaintiffs signed a release requesting Jeffrey's removal from life-support systems. The release provided:

> We have been advised by the attending physicians of our son, Jeffrey Strachan, that he has been declared "brain dead." It is therefore requested that all life support-life-support-death devices [sic] be discontinued as soon as possible.

> In making this request we are fully aware of our legal responsibilities and further hold harmless John F. Kennedy Memorial Hospital and the attending physicians with regard to discontinuance of life support devices.

At 4:05 p.m., Dr. Weinstein disconnected the respirator. Dr. Santoro pronounced Jeffrey dead and executed a death certificate, after which Jeffrey's body was turned over to his family for burial.

Plaintiffs thereafter instituted this action against the Hospital, administrator Pirolli, the physicians involved, and the Delaware Valley Transplant Program and its representative Stephen Sammut. The action against the physicians, the transplant program, and Sammut was voluntarily dismissed prior to trial, and the case proceeded against the Hospital and administrator Pirolli only.

At the conclusion of trial the court instructed the jury on the bases of liability, including respondeat superior, under which the Hospital would be liable if Pirolli were found liable. The court then submitted the matter to the jury with special interrogatories, including the following:

* * *

2(a) Did the defendant, Augustine R. Pirolli, have a duty to have procedures in place for the removal of Jeffrey Strachan from the life support systems when requested by his parents, and negligently failed to do so, as alleged by the plaintiffs?

2(b) Was this failure a proximate cause of the infliction of additional severe emotional stress upon the plaintiffs?

* * *

4(a) Did the defendant, Augustine R. Pirolli, negligently hold the body of Jeffrey Strachan so as to prevent his proper burial?

4(b) Did this holding result in additional mental distress to the plaintiffs?

The jury responded affirmatively to both parts of questions 2 and 4, and awarded plaintiffs $70,000 each, for total verdicts of $140,000. [A] divided appellate division reversed. 209 N.J.Super. 300, 507 A.2d 718, 58 A.L.R.4th 181[1] (1986).

The foregoing interrogatories, which track the trial court's charge, suggest that there were two separate causes of action, based on separate duties owed by defendants to plaintiffs, on which the jury could make separate determinations: one resting on a duty to have in place procedures for the removal of plaintiffs' son from the life-support system on plaintiffs' request, the other based on a duty to release to the parents their son's dead body. This was error. The circumstances of the case projected but one duty: to act reasonably in honoring the family's legitimate request to turn over their son's body.

* * *

We are disinclined, as a matter of sound public policy, to announce an absolute duty, henceforth to be adhered to by all affected hospitals, to have in place procedures for the removal of a dead body from a life-support mechanism on the request of the next of kin. * * * The imposition of a paperwork duty does little to advance either the mission of health-care providers or the needs of society. If "procedures" are to be viewed as more than mere "paperwork" and considered indispensable in this area—in the nature of a standard that governs the medical community—then those procedures should be designed and imposed by those most directly involved, the physicians and hospitals themselves. That is the business of the medical community itself, not of this court.

That is not to say, however, that the absence of such procedures may not be relevant on the issue of whether these defendants fulfilled the obligation that surely they had: to act reasonably in the face of plaintiffs' request to turn over the body. Plaintiffs produced an expert, Dr. Jerene Robbins, whom the trial court found to be "qualified as a medical doctor, and qualified to give opinions in regard to hospital administration." Dr. Robbins testified that in the circumstances that confronted defendant Pirolli, it was "unthinkable" that there were no forms for the parents to sign to effectuate release of the body, and that if the hospital did not have such forms, then Pirolli "should have on the

---

1. Editors' Note: Annot., Tortious Maintenance or Removal of Life Supports, 58 A.L.R.4th 222 (1987).

instant arranged some kind of writing that he could provide for the hospital in order that releases could be signed." We take the expert's testimony to mean that if a hospital is going to insist on forms and procedures, then it should have them available and in place, or at the least improvise them on the spot, in order to fulfill its underlying obligation to take reasonable steps to release the body to the next of kin.

That there is such an underlying obligation is no longer open to question. For more than half a century this state has recognized a quasi property right in the body of a dead person. * * *

Although the appellate division recognized that cause of action as a quasi property right, the majority held that recovery could not be allowed here because Jeffrey was not legally dead until Monday, April 28, at 4:10 p.m., when he was officially pronounced dead, the respirator was turned off, and the death certificate was signed. 507 A.2d 718 at 725. It was then that Jeffrey's body was turned over to plaintiffs for burial.

Plaintiffs' right of recovery, then, depends on when Jeffrey's death occurred. Jeffrey was pronounced brain dead by the emergency room physician at 5:25 p.m. on Friday. That assessment was confirmed by a neurosurgeon that evening, and again confirmed by other doctors and by the results of additional testing throughout the weekend. The evidence is overwhelming that Jeffrey was deemed brain dead considerably earlier than Monday at 4:10 p.m., when Dr. Santoro pronounced him dead and executed a death certificate. Thus the question comes down to whether our legal definition of death should include brain death.

Traditionally, death was defined as the irreversible cessation of cardiopulmonary function. In re Quinlan, 70 N.J. 10, 355 A.2d 647, 656, cert. denied sub nom. Garger v. New Jersey, 429 U.S. 922, 97 S.Ct. 319, 50 L.Ed.2d 289 (1976). This definition, however, came under attack as failing to reflect advances in medical technology. Because cardiac and respiratory activity can be mechanically maintained for some time, definitions of "death" have increasingly focused on the cessation of brain functions. * * * Once the brain is dead, no technology exists to restore its function.

Technological advances have also made possible the performance of organ transplants on a regular basis. For organs to be preserved for transplant, the donor's cardiopulmonary system must continue functioning until the organs can be removed. Under the traditional definition of death, such a donor would be considered as still alive because the heart continues to beat and the lungs continue to perform the respiratory function. In a very real sense, then, a break from the traditional definition of death is a necessary condition to the existence of transplant programs, for otherwise the organ-removal process might be deemed to have "killed" the donor. * * *

In response to these concerns, many states have adopted new definitions of death, incorporating brain death. The Uniform Determination of Death Act (UDDA) provides:

§ 1. [Determination of Death] An individual who has sustained either (1) irreversible cessation of circulatory and respiratory functions, or (2) irreversible cessation of all functions of the entire brain, including the brain stem, is dead. A determination of death must be made in accordance with accepted medical standards. 12 U.L.A. 236. * * *

By 1985, 13 states and the District of Columbia had adopted the UDDA. [A]t least 30 states have adopted statutory definitions of death that include cessation of brain function. * * *

We therefore conclude that § 1 of the UDDA provides the appropriate legal definition of death. * * * We therefore conclude that there was ample support in the evidence for the jury's conclusion that defendants had "negligently [held] the body of Jeffrey Strachan so as to prevent his proper burial." (Answer to Interrogatory 4(a).)

Our next inquiry is whether the limitations on tort claims for emotional distress bar plaintiffs from recovering for defendant's breach of duty. * * *

The record in this case reveals particularly compelling evidence of distress. Although plaintiffs were told that their son was brain dead and nothing further could be done for him, for three days after requesting that their son be disconnected from the respirator plaintiffs continued to see him lying in bed, with tubes in his body, his eyes taped shut, and foam in his mouth. His body remained warm to the touch. Had Jeffrey's body been removed from the respirator when his parents requested, a scene fraught with grief and heartache would have been avoided, and plaintiffs would have been spared additional suffering.

* * *

Because Jeffrey was no longer alive, defendants breached no duty owed him by their failure to turn off the respirator. Jeffrey suffered no harm as a result of defendants' negligence. Plaintiffs' distress, therefore, was not the result of witnessing another's injury, but rather the result of a breach of duty owed directly to plaintiffs. Perhaps the confusion stems from the fact that the duty owed to plaintiffs related to the handling of Jeffrey's body, but that does not render this a "bystander" case. If, for example, a hospital negligently reported to a patient's parents that the patient's condition was considerably worse than in fact it was, the parents' distress would flow from the breach of a duty owed to them, not one owed to their child. * * *

The requirement of physical injury is grounded on the notion that emotional distress claims are too easily fabricated without such a limitation. Prosser & Keeton on Torts § 54 at 361 (5th ed. 1984). Finding that rationale insufficient to withhold recovery for distress claims that might prove legitimate, an increasing number of courts have abandoned the physical-injury limitation altogether. * * *

We need not decide today whether * * * [under Portee v. Jaffee, 84 N.J. 88, 417 A.2d 521 (1980), the] abandonment of the physical injury requirement for emotional distress claims should extend to all "direct" claims for emotional distress. We need look no further than the long-recognized exception for negligent handling of a corpse [ ] or the especial likelihood that this claim is genuine [ ] to conclude that plaintiffs need not demonstrate any physical manifestations of their emotional distress here. The result at trial was consistent with the stated principles.

* * * Under the circumstances * * * we can have no confidence in the assumption that had the jurors been properly instructed on a single cause of action rather than on two separate and distinct negligence claims, they would have concluded that the total recoverable damages amounted to $70,000. We therefore remand for a retrial on damages only on the claim for failure to have released the dead body.

O'HERN, J., concurring in part, dissenting in part. * * * I would order a retrial on all issues.

Notes

1) *Estate of Berthiaume* was a case of first impression. Clearly the pictures were taken against the patient's will. They were not taken in the name of treatment or research, but rather to record the physician's work. Under those circumstances the estate was held to have stated a claim for invasion of privacy. In the event the purpose of the photographs was found to promote research or treatment, but the patient still objected, would the result have been different? Does a teaching hospital have some sort of implied right of consent under HIPAA? How is that right exercised and revoked?

2) *Suesbury* reaffirms that physicians in the same office can share diagnostic and treatment information with one another without breaching the patient's confidentiality. The written opinion is unclear about the physician's decision to communicate the alleged episode of molestation to the District Attorney. How would you advise the physician? Would you ask your patient for consent before doing so? Should the patient be advised that making a report to the District Attorney may require producing his confidential medical records?

3) *Strachan* presents the liability aspects of a bioethics issue. New medical technology creates new legal problems, although it was difficult for the court to see how the hospital defendant could have failed to provide for those that arose here. In 1980 organ transplantation and life-preserving techniques were well understood, and legal problems had already arisen over keeping donors technically alive pending harvesting of organs. See *Williams v. Hofmann*, 66 Wis.2d 145, 223 N.W.2d 844 (1974). *Strachan* seems to have followed the medical imperative that Jeffrey's organs would be harvested unless his parents were adamant, rather than the legal imperative that the organs would not be harvested unless his parents consented.

SECTION D. INSURANCE DISPUTES

Note on Medical Liability Insurance

1. The Mechanics of Liability Insurance

Accidents will happen, but in insurance language, the word "accident" is too narrow; other potentially compensable events are insurable, and so the preferred one-word insurance term is "incident." If one person sets aside money to pay for future incidents, that is a contingency fund, and the person is a self-insurer. If many persons pay someone else money now in order to be compensated for incidents in the future, the combined fund is insurance as it is commonly understood.[1] If the insuring group consists of dividend- and capital-gain-seeking investors who have no connection with the persons insured, the insurer is a stock insurance company. If a group insures only its own investors, that is mutual insurance, but membership in the group (such as automobile or home owners) may be so broad that the mutuality has little significance to the members.

A medical liability mutual insurance group may be open to all members of a class (such as licensed physicians in a particular state); this is a "reciprocal" insurer. A group of persons having common characteristics and insurance needs, such as obstetricians, can also insure the members of a subgroup as a private voluntary association that has strict membership requirements; the insurance organization then is a "captive" of the members, it may be referred to as a "club," and it has no other insurance functions.

It would be wasteful to bank the whole insurance fund until it is needed, and so some of the money is invested in income-producing assets. Some assets will need to be more liquid than others, because the insured risks are connected with the timing as well as with the amounts of funds needed. For example, at noon today the insurer knows about some incidents that have been reported but have not been evaluated; for them, the insurer sets up a loss reserve that will be easy to write checks on. Some other incidents have undoubtedly been incurred but have not yet been reported; they call for short-term investments. It is possible that very large incidents will happen at unpredictable intervals in the future; against these, insurers buy their own insurance, called reinsurance, so they can more safely put funds into long-term investments.

If the insured incident is harm to the insured person's property or person, that is casualty insurance. The loss may be total or partial; the smaller and rarer the partial losses, the lower are the insurance premiums, and vice versa.[2] If the insured incident is a compensable event such

---

1. While volunteers who donate their services to repair a barn after a storm will accomplish the same result, and while a group of persons could promise one another to pay shares of a future loss, the practice of paying money in advance, so a fund of money will be available when it is needed, underlies the insurance mechanism.

2. While "life" insurance thus looks like casualty insurance, the loss by death is both total and inevitable, and so life insurance is in a class by itself and will receive no further attention.

as negligence that harms the insured's property by making the insured pay damages to another person, that is liability insurance, with the same relationship between losses and premiums.

The two kinds of insurance produce different payouts for a compensable medical incident that causes personal injuries to a patient. If the patient has casualty insurance, it does not matter whether fault caused the accident or not: the insurer will pay (within policy limits) the pecuniary losses of the patient, but it will pay no damages such as pain and suffering. By contrast, if the patient secures a court judgment against a doctor who was at fault in causing the same medical incident, the judgment includes both the patient's economic damages and the patient's non-pecuniary damages, and so liability insurance must cover the whole judgment.

Medical liability insurance is very expensive, because the cost of insuring against the misperformance of services is related to the amount of harm the doctor can do to the patient and others, not to the size of the fee for services. If a doctor charges $100 for one office visit but negligently causes the permanent and total disability of a patient 35 years old who is earning $100,000 a year and has a spouse and three children, the insurer's loss exposure runs into the millions of dollars. While both doctors and insurers worry about the high cost of insurance, their concerns come from different directions.

In spite of the expense of medical liability insurance, few doctors are willing to risk clinical practice without it (also known as "going bare"), and they are all concerned about availability, coverage, and price. If insurance is unavailable, or if coverage is inadequate, or if the price is too high, a doctor may leave the practice of medicine or become an employed doctor or a medical administrator who is insured by the employer.

The insurer is also concerned as a business organization. Its ultimate risk exposure is the loss of profits on operations. Government regulators of insurance companies can force an insurer out of business if it is in danger of being unable to pay claims. People argue about excessive profit rates on liability insurance and how profits are to be calculated, though competition is supposed to hold profits at a sensible level of return on invested capital, but every liability insurance company first has to earn profits on operations. This is not the same as distributable net profits in a profit-making company; it has to do with not spending capital to pay claims, defense costs, and overhead. No insurer, even if it is a not-for-profit membership organization, can run indefinitely at a loss on operations.

Medical liability insurers have difficulty in determining when they have made a profit on operations. The basic unit of the insurer's income is the premium, the basic accounting period is the premium year, and the basic unit of expenditure is the lawsuit. While most businesses know how much money they have made on operations within a few months after the close of each accounting year, this is not true with medical liability insurance. Patients' claims do not have to be filed until the end of the limitation of actions period two or three years later in most states, and with the discovery rule or continuous treatment, perhaps a decade or more. All the while, inflation is running, the interest rate is moving up and down, and juries are awarding larger verdicts.

Setting premiums at a level to assure adequate profit on operations to cover the insurer's risks has enough headaches for three heads:

In order to set premiums, the *actuaries* had to guess how much of the premium revenue received in a given year would be spent in defending and paying claims filed in that year and still being filed well into the next decade. If the actuaries set premiums too low, most insurers cannot go back later and ask for more money from the doctors.[3]

In order to pay dividends, the *accountants* had to guess in a given year how much net profit the insurer had earned in all premium years through the previous year. Deciding when a premium year has closed for accounting purposes is quite arbitrary.

In order to regulate cash flow, the *money managers* had to guess how much of the premium income from each year to set aside to pay claims (the loss reserve, invested in short-term, low-yield assets), how much to invest in long-term, high-yield assets, how much premium income to spend on reinsurance, how the interest cycle is likely to perform, and in a stock company, how much to pay out to investors.

It may be difficult for consumer-oriented people (like law students and doctors) to sympathize with insurance companies, but unless the profitability of medical liability insurance can be assured, the insurance disappears.

2. The Availability of Medical Liability Insurance

A few doctors are unconcerned about the availability of medical liability insurance because they do not carry it.[4] For the rest, the availability of medical liability insurance requires first that an insurer be in business and willing to write a policy. In the 1970s many general insurance companies, which once had considered medical liability so small a part of their general business that they kept no statistics on profitability, decided to drop this "line" completely.[5] In order to preserve

---

3. A few non-profit joint underwriting associations have made their policies assessable. For example, the doctor paid the 2000 premium in 1999, but in 2005 the doctor can be called upon to pay an assessment on the 2000 premium—sometimes as much as the original premium or more.

4. It has been held, however, that a hospital may deny staff privileges to a physician who refuses to carry insurance. Backlund v. Board of Comm'rs, 106 Wash.2d 632, 724 P.2d 981 (1986) (religious motiva-

tion), appeal dismissed for want of a substantial federal question, 481 U.S. 1034, 107 S.Ct. 1968, 95 L.Ed.2d 809 (1987). See Annot., Propriety of Hospital's Conditioning Physician's Staff Privileges on His Carrying Professional Liability or Malpractice Insurance, 7 A.L.R.4th 1238 (1981).

5. In one case the Maryland insurance commissioner tried to force an insurance giant either to keep writing medical liability or to pull out of Maryland altogether, but the Maryland court of appeals held that the availability, many states have authorized the medical professions to set up their own medical liability underwriters, but that does not mean that the doctor-run organization must insure every licensed applicant regardless of claims experience.[6]

Another availability question involves the cost of premiums, because premiums can rise so high as to make insurance effectively unavailable. Here two insurance principles conflict. One principle says that the underwriting classes should be kept broad, so that many doctors will share the costs, the insurers will spread their risks, and overall rates will remain relatively low, even though some doctors will pay too much and others too little. The other principle says that the classes of high-fee, high-risk health care specialists ought to pay more, so as to keep premiums within reach of the class of low-fee, low-risk general practitioners. Evidently there is no single solution to this conflict of principles; the rates and classes change from year to year and from one state to the next.[7]

Finally, availability disappears when the insurer cancels or refuses to renew an individual doctor's insurance. Language in insurance policies tries to preserve the insurer's power to cancel upon proper notice and to refuse to renew without giving reasons, and the courts enforce these provisions if they are clearly written and fairly applied.[8]

It is hard to imagine a place in the United States where medical liability insurance is literally unavailable to doctors with decent claims records. On the other hand, premium costs for high-risk specialties such as obstetrics are causing doctors to change the way they practice, including ceasing to deliver babies. As for individual doctors who claim that medical liability insurance is unavailable to them, uninsurability is a deliberate instrument of health care quality assurance, and a doctor's loss of access to medical practice may be in the best interests of the patient community as well as the insurance industry.[9]

3.   *The Coverage of Medical Liability Insurance Policies*

commissioner had no such power. St. Paul Fire & Marine Ins. Co. v. Insurance Comm'r, 275 Md. 130, 339 A.2d 291 (1975).

6.   A recent case raised but did not dispose of the question. Muhl v. Magan, 313 Md. 462, 545 A.2d 1321 (1988).

7.   It has been held that obstetricians and gynecologists may lawfully agree to pay higher premiums in order to keep their favorite insurer from dropping them all. Sullivan v. Commonwealth Ins. Dep't, 48 Pa.Cmwlth. 11, 408 A.2d 1174 (1979). Some states set a fairly low ceiling on individual coverage, with rates varying according to specialty, then throw all insureds into a common pool for coverage of excess amounts. E.g., Fla.Stat.Ann. § 627.6057 (individual physician coverage), § 766.105 (Patient's Compensation Fund).

8.   E.g., Coira v. Florida Med. Ass'n, Inc., 429 So.2d 23 (Fla.App.1983) (companion cases, one cancellation, one refusal to renew); Pennsylvania Cas. Co. v. Chris Simopoulos, M.D., Ltd., 235 Va. 460, 369 S.E.2d 166 (1988) (declaratory judgment for insurer after claim filed; false answers on application voided the policy). See Annot., Wrongful Cancellation of Medical Malpractice Insurance, 99 A.L.R.3d 469 (1980).

9.   A ten-year study completed in 1987 by the Medical Mutual Liability Insurance Society of Maryland, which insures about 85% of the doctors in Maryland, showed that 5 of 1500 insured doctors accounted for 7.5% of the insurer's payouts, and about 7% of the doctors accounted for about 94% of the payouts. Washington Post, Jan. 11, 1988, at A7.

The medical liability insurance policy today provides two forms of protection to the doctor.[10] First, the insurer promises to pay on behalf of the doctor money owed by the doctor on account of a judgment arising out of an event covered by the insurance contract.[11] Second, the insurer promises to pay for defending the doctor from claims, including attorney, expert witness, and investigation services that arise out of covered events.[12] The duty to defend usually includes the duty to settle within policy limits if good faith indicates settlement and the doctor wants to settle.

Medical liability insurance policies vary in the scope and description of covered events and excluded events. This is not surprising; the insurance policy is a contract, and while in a particular litigation the ambiguities in the language of a particular policy will be construed against the insurer, which drafted the language, over time the bargaining between medical societies and insurers can change the language of policy coverage and exclusions back and forth—for example, the control of settlement.

As for covered events, medical professional services in patient care that cause personal injury, sickness, or death are the object of insurance coverage. Some time ago, policies covered only specified theories of claim and all other theories implicitly were excluded, so the patient's choice of a theory of claim, such as contract, could move the event out of policy coverage that was phrased as "any malpractice, error or mistake."[13] The narrow coverage may have been good law but it was bad for business, and it would have created acute problems with subsequently developed theories of claim such as informed consent and strict liability.

Today, not just the words but the balance of coverage has shifted. Policies cover all broadly enumerated events or incidents or harms, regardless of the theory of claim, using language such as "any claim or claims made against the insured arising out of the performance of professional services"; "an occurrence involving direct patient treatment

10. "Doctor" covers all health care providers: individuals, such as physicians, dentists, and persons for whom they are liable by respondeat superior, and organizations, such as professional associations, partnerships, and corporations. Insurers are careful to require specific insurance for different configurations of business in providing health care. See Miller v. Marrocco, 28 Ohio St.3d 438, 28 Ohio B.R. 489, 504 N.E.2d 67 (1986) (4 to 3) (policy covering medical professional corporation did not cover "employee" doctor-owner).

11. This is liability insurance, not indemnity insurance, because the insurer promises to pay immediately, not after the doctor has already paid. The policy language reads like this: "The insurer will pay on behalf of the insured all sums which the insured shall become legally obligated to pay as damages because of injury to which this policy applies."

12. Some policies spell this out: "The insurer shall have the duty to defend any action against the insured seeking damages because of a professional incident, even if any of the allegations of the action are groundless, false, or fraudulent."

13. For example, the negligence statute of limitations having run, the plaintiff sued a plastic surgeon for breach of a contract to cure, and the court affirmed summary judgment for the insurer. Safian v. Aetna Life Ins. Co., 260 A.D. 765, 24 N.Y.S.2d 92, aff'd, 286 N.Y. 649, 36 N.E.2d 692 (1941). See Annot., Allegations in Third Person's Action Against Insured as Determining Liability Insurer's Duty to Defend, 50 A.L.R.2d 458 (1956) (not confined to medical liability).

provided by the insured;" "damages because of injury arising out of the performance of professional services."[14] Specific exclusions then seek to exclude coverage of particular acts and events, such as indirect and usually pecuniary harms to patients caused by such non-treatment professional activities as reviewing claims. The lists of exclusions, which often exceed a page of insurance policy text, keep growing.

Most of the exclusions today stem from intentional acts of the doctor, not from the theory of the patient's claim. This means that the theories treated earlier in this chapter need to be tested for insurability as well as exclusion. For example, criminal acts of a doctor are not insurable, so they are excluded from coverage regardless of the policy language. Battering patients without justification, and promising methods and cures, are intentional acts; since they lie within the control of the doctor, they do not fit the liability insurance model, and so they are excluded. Some policies exclude intentional acts specifically: "liability arising out of any sexual,[15] fraudulent, criminal or malicious act, or slander, libel, defamation, or malicious prosecution"; "any liability which is assumed under a written or an oral contract or agreement"; "liability for punitive or exemplary damages." Allegations of intentional torts such as defamation may arise out of doctors' "professional committee activities," and a few policies explicitly cover the activities, though they exclude defamation actions arising from "utterances in any publication or electronic medium." Other events are excluded in order to avoid overlapping coverage, such as events covered by workers' compensation and automobile insurance.

LANGLEY v. MUTUAL FIRE, MARINE & INLAND INS. CO.

Supreme Court of Alabama, 1987.
512 So.2d 752.

BEATTY, JUSTICE. * * *

From August 9, 1977, through August 8, 1978, Dr. John Langley's medical malpractice liability insurance carrier was Mutual Fire, Marine and Inland Ins. Co. ("Mutual Fire"). The policy issued to Dr. Langley by Mutual Fire was a "claims-made" insurance policy. The first sentence appearing in Dr. Langley's policy is a statement alerting the insured as to the nature of the "claims-made" type of policy; it provided as follows:

Claims Made Policy: Except to such extent as may be provided otherwise herein, this policy is limited to liability for only those CLAIMS THAT ARE FIRST MADE AGAINST THE INSURED WHILE THE POLICY IS IN FORCE. Please review the policy carefully.

---

14. While the language is quoted from policies in the Editors' possession, the insurers are not identified and omissions are not indicated.

15. E.g., Govar v. Chicago Ins. Co., 879 F.2d 1581 (8th Cir.1989) (exclusion upheld).

See Annot., Coverage and Exclusions of Liability or Indemnity Policy on Physicians, Surgeons, and Other Healers, 33 A.L.R.4th 14 (1984).

Further down on the same page of the policy, under the section entitled "The Coverage," there appears another statement explaining the claims-made character of the policy * * *.

* * * Dr. Langley did not renew his coverage with Mutual Fire, nor did he execute the optional extension of coverage offered by Mutual Fire that would have continued his coverage for three years for claims based on acts or omissions that occurred during the primary term of the Mutual Fire policy. This "optional extension period" is described at length on the second page of Dr. Langley's policy:

4. Optional Extension Period: In the event of the termination of this insurance by reason of non-renewal or cancellation by the Insured, or if the Company shall cancel this policy or terminate it by refusing to renew, then *the Insured upon payment of an additional premium shall have the option to extend this policy, subject otherwise to its terms, limits of coverage, exclusions and conditions, to apply to claims first made against the insured during thirty-six calendar months following immediately upon the effective date of such cancellation or non-renewal, but only for such malpractice committed or alleged to have been committed between the retroactive date and the effective date or such cancellation or termination.* This interval shall be hereinafter referred to as the OPTIONAL EXTENSION PERIOD. (Emphasis added.)

* * *

Following Dr. Langley's non-renewal of his Mutual Fire policy, which was effective on August 9, 1978, he received the following letter from Mutual Fire concerning his option to extend his coverage in accordance with the above-quoted provision of his policy with Mutual Fire:

CERTIFIED MAIL RETURN RECEIPT REQUESTED

August 14, 1978

* * *

OPTION TO EXTEND THE CLAIMS REPORTING PERIOD

Dear Dr. Langley:

We are hereby notifying you of your right in accordance with the terms and conditions of your contract to purchase the Optional Extension Period as defined in your contract under the Section entitled THE COVERAGE.

The premium for the three year Optional Extension Period is $8,833.00, plus any applicable tax.

The right to exercise the Optional Extension Period must be exercised by you in writing no later than forty-five (45) days following August 9, 1978 or ten (10) days from the date of this letter, whichever date is later. Please return your signed and dated response in the business envelope enclosed for your use.

Sincerely,

Carolyn J. Sayre * * *

* * * Dr. Langley did not exercise his option to purchase the extended coverage with Mutual Fire. Instead, on October 20, 1978, Dr. Langley applied for coverage through Wilson & Son, the insurance to be underwritten by St. Paul Fire & Marine Ins. Co. ("St. Paul").

* * *

Dr. Langley continued his malpractice coverage through Wilson & Son until March 24, 1980, when Wilson & Son cancelled the policy for nonpayment of premiums. Dr. Langley also subsequently declined to purchase an optional "Reporting Endorsement" from St. Paul, which would have offered him the same type of benefit as the optional extension of coverage that had been offered Langley by Mutual Fire. Under the terms of the St. Paul policy and the reporting endorsement offered to Dr. Langley by St. Paul, that endorsement would have covered Dr. Langley *on a continuous basis* for injuries or deaths occurring during the policy period (October 24, 1978, through March 24, 1980) without regard to when the claim was made.

In February 1983, a medical malpractice claim was filed against Dr. Langley alleging negligence in the delivery of a child on *July 9, 1978,* which negligence resulted in the severe and permanent brain damage of the child. Dr. Langley first notified Wilson & Son of the claim, but it declined to defend, responding that Mutual Fire was Dr. Landley's insurer on the date of the alleged negligent delivery. Mutual Fire, however, also refused to defend * * *.

In the interest of clarity and convenience, the above narrative of pertinent events is set out below in chronological fashion:

August 9, 1977: Effective date of Dr. Langley's claims-made policy with Mutual Fire.

July 9, 1978: Date of alleged malpractice by Dr. Langley.

August 9, 1978: Mutual Fire policy cancelled (non-renewed).

August 14, 1978: Mutual Fire's letter to Dr. Langley notifying him of his option to purchase extension contract.

October 20, 1978: Date of Dr. Langley's application for coverage through Wilson & Son.

October 24, 1978: Effective date of Dr. Langley's claims-made policy with St. Paul.

March 24, 1982: St. Paul policy cancelled for nonpayment of premiums.

February 1983: Medical malpractice action filed against Dr. Langley for alleged negligence on July 9, 1978.

January 9, 1984: Langley's fraud, negligence, and breach of contract action filed against Mutual Fire, Pharr Hume, and Wilson & Son.

* * * The trial court granted defendants' motions for summary judgment "against plaintiff John Langley on plaintiff's amended complaint." This appeal followed.

Dr. Langley advances two arguments that he contends preclude summary judgment in favor of Mutual Fire.

First, he contends that there is some ambiguity in the wording of the Mutual Fire policy, leaving a question of fact for a jury to resolve. We disagree. The claims-made character of Dr. Langley's Mutual Fire policy is made readily apparent within the policy itself. * * *

[W]e next address Dr. Langley's second contention: that public policy dictates that this claims-made clause be declared null and void, and that, under the circumstances of this case, Mutual Fire should be required to extend coverage. * * *

[U]nder an "occurrence" policy, the time of an "occurrence" of an accident is not the time the wrongful act was committed, but rather it is when the complaining party was actually damaged. * * *

We, therefore, think that in James & Hackworth v. Continental Casualty Co., 522 F.Supp. 785 (N.D.Ala.1980), Judge Grooms correctly concluded that the claims-made type of insurance policy is not void as against the public policy of this state, thereby rejecting the argument that such policies should be treated as occurrence policies * * *.

Dr. Langley, nevertheless, argues in his brief that insurance companies should not be allowed to write contracts in such a manner so as to avoid their obligations, in situations such as the present, by including a phrase in the contract requiring that claims be *presented or made during the policy period* before such claims will be paid or defended. However, Dr. Langley cites no authority consistent with this argument regarding claims-made policies. Indeed, it appears that a decided majority of courts that have considered this argument have gone the other way. See cases discussed at Annot., Event as Occurring Within Period of Coverage of "Occurrence" and "Discovery" or "Claims Made" Liability Policies, 37 A.L.R.4th 382, 457 (1985). In most of those cases where it has been held that coverage should be provided, the decisions are based on the courts' findings that the following policy language is ambiguous because of the words "which may be made": "The company shall indemnify insured against any claim or claims for breach of professional duty *which may be made against them during the policy period."* Ibid. As previously discussed, the policy language in question in this case is not at all like the above language, and is, in fact, quite clear and its meaning readily apparent regarding the claims-made character of the policy.

* * *

Dr. Langley, nevertheless, argues in his brief that none of the options available to him (short of renewing his policy with Mutual Fire) "would have changed the outcome of this case one iota." * * * The reference in this statement is apparently to the fact that the extended endorsement offered by Mutual Fire extended the period for making claims for only up to three years beyond the date the policy was cancelled or nonrenewed, whereas the malpractice claim made against Dr. Langley in this case was filed four and one-half years after the effective date of Dr. Langley's non-renewal of the Mutual Fire policy. * * * We hold, however, that because Dr. Langley elected not to purchase the three-year optional extension of coverage contract, he has no standing to argue that this extension of coverage contract is so inadequate as to make it invalid and violative of public policy. Moreover, Dr. Langley offered no evidence that this optional extension contract would not have been renewed.

If the optional extension contract offered to Dr. Langley by Mutual Fire could have been renewed for additional three-year periods of coverage, Dr. Langley could have so renewed in order to keep his extended coverage in effect long enough for the statute of limitations to run on all potential medical malpractice claims arising from his acts or omissions during the primary policy period, which was August 9, 1977, through August 8, 1978. Under § 6–5–482, Ala.Code, an adult patient/plaintiff has, at the outside, four years "next after the act or omission or failure giving rise to the claim" in which to bring an action thereon. In the case of a minor patient/plaintiff "under four years of age, such minor shall have until his eighth birthday to commence such an action." Thus, Dr. Langley, whose practice included obstetrics, would have needed to extend his coverage period for making claims for at least eight years after the date, within the primary policy term, he last performed medical services injurious to a newborn child. Dr. Langley however, did not even choose to avail himself of the three-year extension contract offered by Mutual Fire, nor has he shown that that contract was nonrenewable. For these reasons, we shall not consider his contentions that the optional extension contract offered him did not afford him any protection whatsoever. We, therefore, hold that summary judgment in favor of Mutual Fire was proper.

[S]ummary judgment in favor of all defendants is * * * affirmed.

BIRTH CENTER v. ST. PAUL COMPANIES

Supreme Court of Pennsylvania, 2001.
567 Pa. 386, 787 A.2d 376.

NEWMAN, J.

FACTUAL AND PROCEDURAL HISTORY

The Underlying Action—Norris v. The Birth Center

This claim arose out of St. Paul's bad faith refusal to engage in settlement negotiations in the underlying action, Norris. In that case, Gerald and Denise Norris ("Parents") filed suit on November 16, 1986 against Birth Center alleging that its negligence during the birth of their daughter Lindsey, caused her to suffer severe physical injury and permanent brain damage. After service of the complaint, The Birth Center turned to St. Paul, its professional liability insurance carrier, for its legal defense. St. Paul hired counsel to defend The Birth Center and undertook an investigation of the Parents' claim.

On August 2, 1991, the Parents proposed, on behalf of Lindsey, to settle the case within the limits of The Birth Center's professional liability insurance policy with St. Paul. The Birth Center notified St. Paul that it was making a firm demand to settle the case within its policy limits. On August 7, 1991, St. Paul refused to settle or to even make an offer of settlement.

During the course of an August 8, 1991 pre-trial conference, the presiding judge recommended settlement of Norris within the limits of The Birth Center's insurance policy. Again, St. Paul refused. At a second pre-trial conference, a second judge assigned to the case also recommended settlement within Birth Center's policy limits. The Birth Center demanded settlement in accordance with the judge's recommendation; but St. Paul refused to negotiate or offer any money.

In January of 1992, St. Paul requested the defense attorneys for The Birth Center and one of the doctors involved in Lindsey's delivery to prepare pre-trial reports for St. Paul's consideration. In her report to St. Paul, defense counsel for The Birth Center stated that The Birth Center had, at best, a fifty-percent chance of successfully defending the lawsuit at trial. Furthermore, she advised that the jury verdict could range from $1,250,000.00 to $1,500,000.00. The doctor's defense counsel advised St. Paul that he believed that The Birth Center had a thirty-five percent chance of winning at trial and predicted a jury verdict of $5,000,000.00 to $6,000,000.00.

On January 27, 1992, the executive director of The Birth Center put St. Paul on written notice of the potential for compensatory damages and expressed her deep concerns regarding the possibility of a verdict in excess of Birth Center's policy limits. She explained that such a verdict would have devastating effects upon The Birth Center and could risk its continued existence. When expressing the same concerns to the St. Paul claims representative assigned to the case, the claims representative informed her that St. Paul tries "all of these bad baby cases, and we're going to trial." [ ].

Before the commencement of the Norris trial, a third judge, who ultimately presided over that trial, held another conference and recommended settlement within The Birth Center's policy limits. St. Paul refused to make any offer whatsoever. Then, on February 12, 1993, the Parents made a high/low offer of settlement, in which St. Paul would pay a non-refundable $300,000.00 amount regardless of the verdict. If, however, the jury returned a verdict in excess of Birth Center's policy limits, the Parents agreed to accept the policy limits as total satisfaction of the verdict. Finally, the settlement offer provided that if the jury returned a verdict lower than The Birth Center's maximum coverage, but higher than the low figure of $300,000.00, then the Parents would accept such verdict as full satisfaction of The Birth Center's liability. St. Paul refused this offer of settlement and made no counter-offer.

On February 16, 1993, the day of trial, a final pre-trial conference took place in the robing room of the trial judge. At this time, the Parents reasserted their high/low offer of settlement. The Birth Center expressed its desire that St. Paul agree to the Parents' proposal; but, a representative of St. Paul, present during the discussion in the robing room, rejected the high/low offer of settlement on the record. Following St. Paul's rejection, the judge stated that he believed that St. Paul's actions were in bad faith and that it was putting its interests ahead of those of its insured. [ ]

The Norris trial ensued. After the start of the trial, but before the jury returned a verdict, the trial judge instructed defense counsel for The Birth Center to contact St. Paul to see if it intended to make any offer of settlement. When counsel returned from her telephone conversation with St. Paul, she stated to those present in the robing room: "They must be crazy. They're not offering a dime. They won't give me authority to offer any money in this case, you know I can't believe it." [ ]

On March 4, 1993, the jury returned a verdict in favor of the Parents for $4,500,000.00, with The Birth Center liable for sixty percent of that amount. The final verdict was molded to include delay damages and interest and totaled $7,196,238. The Birth Center's ultimate liability amounted to $4,317,743.00. St. Paul agreed to indemnify The Birth Center for the entire verdict and the parties settled the case for $5,000,000. Before St. Paul paid the excess verdict, it requested that The Birth Center sign a release in exchange for the payment, but The Birth Center refused to sign the release. St. Paul paid on September 20, 1993.

The Birth Center v. St. Paul—The Bad Faith Action

On June 3, 1994, The Birth Center sued St. Paul, alleging that St. Paul breached its fiduciary duty to The Birth Center, its implied covenant of good faith, and its contract. The Birth Center also claimed that St. Paul's failure to settle Norris within its policy limits constituted negligence, reckless disregard for the rights of Birth Center, willful and wanton behavior and bad faith pursuant to the Bad Faith Statute[ ].

On May 3, 1996, the trial began. The Birth Center claimed that St. Paul's refusal to engage in reasonable settlement negotiations damaged "its business, reputation and credit." After the trial, the jury found, by clear and convincing evidence, that St. Paul acted in bad faith and that its actions were a substantial factor in bringing about harm to The Birth Center totaling, $700,000.00 in compensatory damages. The jury did not award punitive damages.

St. Paul moved for judgment notwithstanding the verdict. On February 7, 1997, the trial court granted St. Paul's motion. The trial court concluded that St. Paul's payment of the excess verdict nullified Birth Center's bad faith claim, that compensatory damages are not available pursuant to 42 Pa. C.S.A. § 8371, and that, because it believed that it had not charged the jury on the breach of contract claim, that The Birth Center could not recover compensatory damages based on that theory.

The trial court denied The Birth Center's motion for reconsideration. On June 10, 1997, the trial court entered judgment in favor of St. Paul.

On appeal, the Superior Court determined that the payment of the excess verdict did not preclude the award of compensatory damages and that the trial court had charged the jury on breach of contract. Therefore, it reversed the decision of the trial court, reinstated the jury award, and remanded the case for a determination of The Birth Center's entitlement to interest, attorney's fees and costs pursuant to 42 Pa. C.S.A. § 8371.

St. Paul appealed the Superior Court's decision to this Court.

Discussion

St. Paul's Arguments in Opposition to the Award of Compensatory Damages

St. Paul sets forth four reasons why it is not liable for Birth Center's compensatory damages. First, it asserts that its payment of the excess verdict barred Birth Center's bad faith claim. St. Paul argues that allowing bad faith claims despite an insurer's "voluntary" excess payment would discourage insurance companies from satisfying future excess verdicts. Second, St. Paul contends that D'Ambrosio v. Pennsylvania National Mut. Ins., 494 Pa. 501, 431 A.2d 966 (Pa. 1981) bars The Birth Center's claim. Third, St. Paul points to 42 Pa.C.S.A. § 8371, which authorizes the award of punitive damages, attorneys fees and costs when an insurer is found to have acted in bad faith, and asserts that because the statute does not mention compensatory damages, none are available. Fourth, St. Paul argues that the trial court did not charge the jury on The Birth Center's breach of contract claim and that, as a result, The Birth Center may not recover compensatory damages based on that claim. In turn, we address and reject St. Paul's arguments.

The Trial Court Charged the Jury on Breach of Contract

Although this is St. Paul's final argument, we address it first because if the trial court did not charge the jury on breach of contract, The Birth Center could only recover compensatory damages from St. Paul if some other theory provided a basis for recovery. As we discuss in this opinion, neither 42 Pa. C.S.A. § 8371 nor any other relevant cause of action provide a basis for recovery. Thus, Birth Center's compensatory damage award depends on whether The Birth Center asserted a contract cause of action and whether the trial court charged the jury regarding that claim.

The Superior Court properly determined that The Birth Center asserted a breach of contract claim. Birth Center's Complaint requests compensatory damages based upon its insurance contract with St. Paul. The Complaint provides:

76. By failing to settle the Norris claim within the limits of the insurance policy of The Birth Center, the Defendants herein breached

their contractual obligations to The Birth Center under said policy of insurance, by failing to protect The Birth Center and their [sic] assets.

77. The Defendants herein, in the performance of the said contract, owed to The Birth Center, a fiduciary duty to act in good faith, and to use due care in representing The Birth Center's interests.

* * *

WHEREFORE, Plaintiff The Birth Center demands judgment against Defendants in an amount in excess of . . . $50,000, plus additional compensatory and/or consequential damages allowed by law, together with interest thereon, Court costs, attorney's fees and such other relief as the Court deems just and proper.

Therefore, it is clear that The Birth Center alleged a claim sounding in contract.

Additionally, the trial court charged the jury with regard to The Birth Center's contract cause of action. The court charged the jurors, inter alia, that if they found that St. Paul breached its contract with The Birth Center, that they were to award compensatory damages if the breach caused the damages, and the damages were reasonably foreseeable at the time the parties entered into the contract and at the time of the breach. Specifically, the trial judge charged, among other things, that:

> where one party to a contract breaches that contract, the other party may recover for those injuries which have been proved to you with reasonable certainty.

* * *

> If you find that defendant St. Paul breached its contract with the Birth Center, you must then decide based on all of the evidence presented what amount of money will compensate the Plaintiff for those injuries, which were a direct and foreseeable result of the breach by St. Paul which the parties could reasonably foresee at the time they made that contract and at the time of the Defendant's breach of the contract.

The jury returned a verdict finding that St. Paul acted in bad faith in its handling of the underlying Norris case, and that the bad faith conduct was a substantial factor in bringing about harm to The Birth Center in the amount of $700,000. The jury verdict sufficiently established that the jury considered the breach of contract claim. The jury found that St. Paul acted in bad faith; St. Paul had a contractual duty to act in good faith; therefore, St. Paul breached its contract.

* * *

A court may not vacate a jury's finding unless "the evidence was such that no two reasonable minds could disagree that the outcome should have been rendered in favor of the movant." Moure, 604 A.2d at 1007 [ ]. While we respect Judge Koudelis' opinion that St. Paul's refusal to engage in settlement negotiations was not in bad faith, the jury was the finder of fact. It found that based upon all of the evidence that The Birth Center proved "by clear and convincing evidence that [St. Paul] acted in bad faith in handling the underlying case of Norris v. The Birth Center." We also note that Judge Clouse, who tried the underlying case, stated, the day of trial, that he believed that St. Paul's settlement posture was in bad faith and inconsistent with its fiduciary duty to the Birth Center. Specifically, Judge Clouse expressed his opinion that:

> there is a clear indication of bad faith here. I think the insurance company is not proceeding in a responsible manner and is not discharging its fiduciary obligation to its insureds in this case ... I think this insurance company has operated in a highly irresponsible manner. I want it clear that they have turned this high/low offer of $300,000.00 down in which [sic] I think is a breach of their fiduciary responsibility to their insureds. And I want that clear on this record.

While Judge Clouse's opinion is arguably irrelevant to the jury's determination that St. Paul acted in bad faith, it is a compelling indication of how a reasonable jury could have come to a similar conclusion that St. Paul acted in bad faith.

While a judge may disagree with a verdict, he or she may not grant a motion for J.N.O.V. simply because he or she would have come to a different conclusion. Indeed, the verdict must stand unless there is no legal basis for it. Without agreeing or disagreeing with Judge Koudelis or Judge Clouse, we view the evidence in the light most favorable to Birth Center, the verdict winner, and give it the benefit of every reasonable inference arising therefrom while rejecting all unfavorable testimony and inferences. From that perspective, we are unable to conclude that no reasonable jury could have found that St. Paul acted in bad faith. Therefore, although, like Judge Koudelis, we may not have reached the same verdict as the jury, there was sufficient evidence to sustain the verdict and a reasonable basis for the jurors to have found, from the evidence that St. Paul acted in bad faith. Consequently, the trial court should not have granted the motion for a directed verdict based on St. Paul's argument that it did not act in bad faith.

* * *

[Pennsylvania law] Does Not Prohibit the Award of Compensatory Damages

In St. Paul's third argument, it incorrectly asserts that compensatory damages may not be awarded when an insurer's bad faith conduct causes the insured to incur actual damages, because the damages are not mentioned in 42 Pa. C.S.A. § 8371. While The Birth Center may not recover compensatory damages based on Section 8371, that Section does not alter The Birth Center's common law contract rights. We begin with the words of the statute. Section 8371 provides:

§ 8371.   Actions on insurance policies

In an action arising under an insurance policy, if the court finds that the insurer has acted in bad faith toward the insured, the court may take all of the following actions:

(1) Award interest on the amount of the claim from the date the claim was made by the insured in an amount equal to the prime rate of interest plus 3%.

(2) Award punitive damages against the insurer.

(3) Assess court costs and attorney fees against the insurer.

42 Pa.C.S.A. § 8371.

The statute does not prohibit the award of compensatory damages. It merely provides an additional remedy and authorizes the award of additional damages. Specifically, the statute authorizes courts, which find that an insurer has acted in bad faith toward its insured, to award punitive damages, attorneys' fees, interest and costs. Id. The statute does not reference the common law, does not explicitly reject it, and the application of the statute is not inconsistent with the common law. Consequently, the common law remedy survives. Metropolitan Property and Liability Insurance Co. v. Insurance Commissioner of Pennsylvania, 525 Pa. 306, 580 A.2d 300 (Pa. 1990). In Metropolitan Property, we rejected an insured's argument that the Unfair Insurance Practices Act abrogated the insurer's contractual, common law right of rescission. We explained that because the statute did not refer to the common law remedy of rescission and its concurrent application was not inconsistent with the statute that the legislature did not intend to preclude the remedy. We determined that:

Under the ... [Statutory Construction Act. 1 Pa. C.S. § 1921 et seq.] an implication alone cannot be interpreted as abrogating existing law. The legislature must affirmatively repeal existing law or specifically preempt accepted common law for prior law to be disregarded.

* * *

[Because 40 P.S. § 1171.5 (the provision at issue in Metropolitan Property)] makes no reference to the common law right to rescission ... such an omission cannot be interpreted as an intention to foreclose such a long-standing right. 525 Pa. at 311.

* * *

Finally, St. Paul's argument that damages not mentioned by Section 8371 are not available is inconsistent with St. Paul's admission that other damages, not listed in Section 8371, remain viable. Notwithstanding that Section 8371 does not provide that courts may require an insurer to pay an excess verdict when it refuses, in bad faith, to settle a case, St. Paul admits, as it must,[16] that such an award is permissible. St. Paul states:

16. An insurer, who acts in bad faith by unreasonably refusing to settle a case, may be liable for the full amount of a verdict notwithstanding that the verdict exceeds

it has long been held in this Commonwealth that when an insurance company fails to settle a third-party claim against its insured, the insurer can be liable for the full amount of any excess verdict, if the decision not to settle was made in bad faith. [St. Paul also admits that] this right has been held to be contractual in nature; it can be enforced by an action in assumpsit; and it is assignable to the injured third party.

St. Paul, thereby, concedes that an insurer who acts in bad faith may be subject to damages other than those set forth in Section 8371. Accordingly, just as courts may require an insurer to pay an excess verdict even though Section 8371 does not mention excess verdict liability, the absence of compensatory damages from Section 8371 does not alter the authority of courts to award compensatory damages.

Requiring insurers, who act in bad faith, to pay excess verdicts protects insured from liability that, absent the insurer's bad faith conduct, the insured would not have incurred. The insured's liability for an excess verdict is a type of compensatory damage for which this court has allowed recovery. Therefore, when an insurer breaches its insurance contract by a bad faith refusal to settle a case, it is appropriate to require it to pay other damages that it knew or should have known the insured would incur because of the bad faith conduct.

The dissent would hold that an insurer's bad faith refusal to settle a claim against its insured does not give rise to a contract cause of action. For the reasons set forth in this opinion, we respectfully disagree. However, we respond to point out that the characterization of the claim by the dissent has no bearing on the outcome of this particular case. Whether Birth Center's cause of action sounds in contract or in tort, the jury found by clear and convincing evidence that St. Paul acted in bad faith and that its actions were a substantial factor in bringing about harm to the Birth Center totaling $700,000.00 in compensatory damages. In appropriate circumstances, compensatory damages are available in both contract and tort causes of action. Indeed, generally, compensatory damages are easier to recover in tort actions than in contract actions. Consequently, in this case, which does not involve a statute of limitations issue, the dissent's assertion that the claim should sound in tort instead of contract is irrelevant.

The only applicable issue raised by the dissent is whether the Bad Faith Statute, 42 Pa.C.S.A. § 8371, bars the recovery of compensatory damages. For the reasons we have discussed, we are not persuaded by the dissent. To the contrary, the provision does not prohibit the award of compensatory damages; it merely provides a basis to award additional damages. The statute does not reference the common law, does not

the insured's policy limits. Cowden, 389 Pa. 459, 134 A.2d 223. In Cowden, we stated that an insurer:

may be liable for the entire amount of a judgment secured by a third party against the insured, regardless of any limitation in the policy, if the insurer's handling of the claim, including a failure to accept a proffered settlement, was done in such a manner as to evidence bad faith on the part of the insurer in the discharge of its contractual duty.

explicitly reject it, and the application of the statute is not inconsistent with the common law. Accordingly, the remedy survives. To hold otherwise as the dissent does would read a statute—that authorizes additional damages—to prohibit the award of compensatory damages, which were already within the power of the courts to award. We cannot countenance such a result because it directly conflicts with the one the legislature intended.

CONCLUSION

Today, we hold that where an insurer acts in bad faith, by unreasonably refusing to settle a claim, it breaches its contractual duty to act in good faith and its fiduciary duty to its insured. Therefore, the insurer is liable for the known and/or foreseeable compensatory damages of its insured that reasonably flow from the insurer's bad faith conduct. Accordingly, we affirm the decision of the Superior Court, reinstate the jury's verdict and remand this case to the trial court for a determination of The Birth Center's entitlement to interest, reasonable attorneys' fees and costs pursuant to 42 Pa.C.S.A. § 8371.

MAZZA v. MEDICAL MUT. INS. CO.

Supreme Court of North Carolina, 1984.
311 N.C. 621, 319 S.E.2d 217.

Plaintiff appellee Jeffrey P. Mazza brought this action which is the subject of this appeal on 8 October 1981 against both defendants, Medical Mutual Insurance Company of North Carolina, hereinafter referred to as Medical Mutual, and Dr. Robert A. Huffaker. Plaintiff sought a determination of whether the Physicians' Liability Insurance Policy, hereinafter referred to as the insurance contract, issued by Medical Mutual to Dr. Huffaker, provides coverage for certain compensatory and punitive damages which were awarded earlier to plaintiff against Dr. Huffaker for medical malpractice.

The facts, as they relate to this case, indicate that on or about 1 May 1976, Medical Mutual issued an insurance contract to Dr. Huffaker. During all times pertinent to the medical malpractice action, the insurance contract was in full force and effect.

On 20 October 1979, plaintiff filed a civil action against defendant in Orange County Superior Court. He alleged that Dr. Huffaker, his attending psychiatrist, had caused him injury and damage in several respects, such as by engaging in sexual intercourse with plaintiff's estranged wife and by abandoning plaintiff in a critical stage of plaintiff's treatment without reasonable notice to him. Plaintiff sought to recover compensatory and punitive damages for criminal conversation, alienation of affections, and medical malpractice arising out of the alleged misconduct of Dr. Huffaker.

At the conclusion of the trial in Orange County, the jury rendered a verdict in favor of plaintiff, awarding him $102,000 in compensatory damages and $500,000 in punitive damages on the medical malpractice count, $50,670 in compensatory damages on the criminal conversation count, and denying him a recovery for alienation of affections. This declaratory judgment action involves only the punitive and compensatory damages awards on the medical malpractice count.

*   *   *

* * * [P]laintiff brought this declaratory judgment action seeking a determination that the insurance contract obligates Medical Mutual to pay on behalf of Dr. Huffaker the actual damages and punitive damages assessed against Dr. Huffaker on the medical malpractice portion of the judgment in the Orange County civil trial. The trial court granted summary judgment in favor of the plaintiff, ruling that the terms of the insurance contract obligate Medical Mutual to pay plaintiff for both the actual damages and the punitive damages awarded on the medical malpractice count.

COPELAND, J.

Medical Mutual maintains that it is not liable for either the punitive damages or the actual damages awarded to plaintiff, and that the trial court committed reversible error in finding it liable. With regard to both the punitive and actual damages, the insurance company proffers similar arguments in support of its contention of non-liability. Defendant first argues that North Carolina's public policy precludes insurance coverage of punitive and compensatory damages caused by intentional misconduct. Second, the terms of the insurance contract did not include coverage for punitive damages.

The provision of the insurance contract which is at issue reads as follows:

I. *Terms*. The Company will pay on behalf of the Insured all sums which the Insured shall become legally obligated to pay as damages because of:

1. *Individual Professional Liability Coverage.*—A. Any claim or claims made against the Insured during the policy period arising out of the performance of professional services rendered or which should have been rendered ... by the Insured ...

According to our interpretation of the insurance contract, the terms provide coverage for actual and punitive damages. Further, this State's public policy does not prohibit insurance coverage of punitive damages nor of actual damages. We shall consider first the contentions of the parties with regard to the punitive damage award.

I.

In making the determination as to punitive damages, we are concerned first with whether public policy prohibits insurance coverage of punitive damages based upon wanton or gross negligence or, as in the present case, medical malpractice, and second, whether the terms of the insurance contract cover punitive damages. There are no North Carolina cases directly on point. Courts in other jurisdictions have considered these questions, and before 1970, it appears that a particular court's decision depended primarily upon which of these two issues the court focused its attention. Our research discloses that courts relying upon the language of the insurance policy generally have decided that punitive damages were recoverable. One of the leading cases reaching this conclusion is *Lazenby v. Universal Underwriters Insurance Co.*, 214 Tenn. 639, 383 S.W.2d 1 (1964). * * *

We believe that the recent trend of those courts considering the public policy question, has been to allow insurance coverage for punitive damages. [ ]. Some [ ] courts have reasoned that public policy is not an issue. Others say that competing public policies outweigh the consideration of punishing the insured by way of punitive damages. [ ]. Additionally, "[w]ith respect to construction of various types of insurance contracts . . . the courts . . . have usually held that coverage of punitive damages was provided when construing policies covering . . . professional . . . entities or their employees. . . . "

Many courts have allowed recovery of punitive damages for willful and wanton negligence because there existed a distinction between negligence and intentional torts. [ ]. This rationale was applied in *Morrell v. Lalonde*, 45 RI 112, 120 A. 435, *error dismissed*, 264 U.S. 572, 68 L.Ed. 855 (1923). That court held that punitive damages were recoverable for medical malpractice under a liability insurance policy.

The main thrust of defendant's argument concerning punitive damages is that allowing insurance coverage for punitive damages is contrary to public policy. Defendant asserts that the "purposes of awarding punitive damages in North Carolina are to punish the wrongdoer individually and to deter the wrongdoer and others from engaging in similar misconduct." Medical Mutual contends that this Court, by allowing insurance coverage for punitive damages, would frustrate the purposes for which punitive damages are awarded.

We know of no public policy of this State that precludes liability insurance coverage for punitive damages in medical malpractice cases. North Carolina General Statute § 58–72 appears to authorize insurers to provide coverage for punitive damages. The modern trend and better reasoned decisions in other jurisdictions are to the effect that it is not against public policy to insure against punitive damages. [ ]

The relief the insurance company now seeks is the development by this Court of a statement of public policy regarding punitive damages stemming from medical malpractice. Defendant bases its argument upon its contention that the act or acts constituting the medical malpractice were intentional. However, the record fails to indicate a specific determination by the jury that the medical malpractice was intentional, as opposed to wanton or gross negligence. We find no merit in defendant's contention that the medical malpractice aspects of this case involved intentional acts by Dr. Huffaker. Medical Mutual argued at trial and in its brief on appeal, that Dr. Huffaker's actions did not constitute medical malpractice since the physician-patient relationship between Dr. Huffaker and the plaintiff no longer existed at the time in question. The trial judge, having determined that there was sufficient evidence of a physician-patient relationship, instructed the jury that the medical malpractice was the negligent care and treatment of a patient by a doctor. The jury returned a verdict in favor of plaintiff based on that charge. Thus, in our opinion, the medical malpractice in the instant case resulted from the attending doctor's negligence in abandoning treatment of the plaintiff and in failing to follow the applicable medical standard of care. However, we emphasize that at this time we neither reach nor decide the question of whether public policy prohibits one from insuring himself from the consequences of his or her intentional tortious acts.

In reviewing the considerations pertaining to public policy in North Carolina, it is important to note that punitive damages are recoverable for injuries other than those intentionally inflicted. This Court has stated that:

> It is generally held that punitive damages are those damages which are given in addition to compensatory damages because of the "wanton, reckless, malicious or oppressive character of the acts complained of."

Oestreicher v. American National Stores, Inc., 290 N.C. 118, 134, 225 S.E.2d 797, 807 (1976). Thus in North Carolina, punitive damages may be awarded in negligence cases for wanton or gross acts.

Since punitive damages are recoverable in North Carolina in cases where intentional injury is not involved, there is a compelling reason that this Court should not create a new public policy prohibiting insurance coverage for punitive damages. The interests of doctors and patients alike can best be served by medical malpractice insurance that protects the doctor and patient, even when the doctor's negligence is wanton or gross. The insurance company in this case would not contend that doctors would be more reckless or would more frequently commit gross negligence simply because they are insured under a professional liability insurance policy that covers punitive damages.

Medical Mutual, in advancing its "public policy" argument, seems to ignore the proposition that the concept of "public policy" involves not one simplistic rule, but various competing doctrines. In this case, the law of contracts and the "public policy" doctrines encompassing that body of law, compete with the defendant's tort related "public policy" argument.

This declaratory judgment action arose out of a contract controversy between Dr. Huffaker and Medical Mutual. The issues before this Court are based on contract, thus, we must consider applicable public policy concerning contract rights. The competing public interests must be carefully balanced. A significant public policy consideration focuses on insurance companies' obligations to honor their contracts. In the present case, Medical Mutual drafted the insurance contract presumably upon the advice of competent counsel, sold the contract, accepted the requisite premiums and tendered protection. Thus under the circumstances, requiring Medical Mutual to honor its obligations would best serve public policy. The right of parties to enter into contracts is a valid and important public interest to consider in balancing the competing interests involved. We should not be quick to invalidate private insurance contracts.

The North Carolina Legislature has not imposed any restrictions or regulations on insurance companies' right to sell liability insurance in this State which covers punitive damages for medical malpractice. [ ].

In addition to the absence of legislative restriction, there is an area of North Carolina case law that supports plaintiff's position in this case. The law and public policy in North Carolina regarding liability for punitive damages under the doctrine of *respondeat superior* is germane to the issue involved in the present case. In our State, a master is liable for punitive damages awarded when the servant or agent causing the injury was acting in the course and scope of the master's business. [ ]. This rule refutes the insurance company's contention that public policy prohibits anyone other than the actual wrongdoer or tortfeasor from paying punitive damages.

Our research reveals a recent case from Michigan involving a similar fact situation and almost identical insurance policy language. In *Vigilant Insurance Company v. Kambly*, 114 Mich.App. 683, 319 N.W.2d 382 (1982), a psychiatrist had induced his patient to engage in sexual relations with him as part of her purported therapy. The insurance company, with whom the doctor had his professional liability coverage, sought to escape payment of the punitive damages awarded claiming that public policy grounds prohibited such coverage. The insurance company contended that the doctor's conduct was intentional and, under Michigan law, felonious, and public policy would therefore preclude the applicability of liability insurance for his protection. It further argued that it was contrary to public policy to permit an insured to profit from his own wrongdoing or to encourage the commission of unlawful acts by relieving the wrongdoer of financial responsibility.

In ruling against the insurance company, the Michigan Supreme Court noted first and foremost that the "insurance policy does not provide exemption for the insurer from liability for judgment arising from injuries sustained as a result of this form of malpractice." [ ]. That court further held that:

> Insurance policies drafted by the insurer must be construed in favor of the insured to uphold coverage. Limitations in the policy must be clearly expressed ... [Citation omitted.] Moreover, the public policy considerations raised by plaintiff which prohibit the insurability of criminal or intentionally tortious conduct are not present here.

With regard to Medical Mutual's argument that there is no contractual liability, we shall utilize a strict contractual analysis focused on the language of the insurance contract to determine whether coverage exists. Medical Mutual Insurance Company contracted to pay on behalf of its insured " ... all sums which the insured shall become legally obligated to pay as damages ... '' We believe that the language used in the present insurance contract is so broad that it must be interpreted to provide coverage for punitive damages for medical malpractice. Many courts have held that the insurer's use of such broad language does include punitive damages. [ ]

Nevertheless, defendant Medical Mutual argues that this policy does not cover punitive damages. It bases this contention upon the policy's definition of damages and one of the stated reasons for punitive damages in North Carolina. The insurance company suggests that this Court isolate one of the stated purposes for punitive damages in North Carolina and construe that together with the definition of ''damages'' in the policy to arrive at a conclusion that the parties in this case did not intend the policy to cover punitive damages relating to professional malpractice. We believe this to be contrary to ordinary common sense and the rules enunciated by our Court in *Grant v. Emmco Insurance Co.*, 295 N.C. 39, 243 S.E.2d 894 (1978) where we stated, speaking through Justice Lake in an unanimous opinion, that:

> ... a contract of insurance should be given that construction which a reasonable person in the position of the insured would have understood it to mean and, if the language used in the policy is reasonably susceptible of different constructions, it must be given the construction most favorable to the insured, since the company prepared the policy and chose the language. (Citations omitted.)

Medical Mutual argues that the term ''damages'' as defined in its insurance contract, includes ''only those damages attributable to a particular injury'' and do not include punitive damages. In looking at the language in the policy, we find the term ''damages'' defined as ''all damages, including damages for death, which are payable because of injury to which this insurance applies.'' In its brief Medical Mutual emphasizes the word ''injury'' and argues that the use of that word in some way excludes punitive damages from the damages covered by the policy. According to Black's Law Dictionary [ ] the word ''injury'' is defined as ''any wrong or damage done to another, either in his person, rights, reputation or property.''

We said in *Jamestown Mutual Insurance Co. v. Nationwide Mutual Insurance Co.*, 266 N.C. 430, 438, 146 S.E.2d 410, 416 (1966), speaking again through Justice Lake:

> In the construction of contracts, even more than in the construction of statutes, words which are used in common, daily, nontechnical speech, should, in the absence of evidence of a contrary intent, be given the meaning which they have for laymen in such daily usage, rather than a restrictive meaning which they may have acquired in legal usage.

We do not believe that an ordinary layman would interpret or understand the insurance policy in this case to mean what Medical Mutual contends. The plain and ordinary meaning of the language used in the policy, particularly from the viewpoint of a layman, covers "all damages" and contains no exclusion for punitive damages.

If any ambiguity exists in the insurance contract, then, the fault lies with the insurance company and not with the insured. Medical Mutual selected and adopted the language and terms used in its policy of insurance and thus placed itself in the position in which it now finds itself. If the insurance company uses "slippery" words in its policy, it is not the function of this Court "to sprinkle sand upon the ice by strict construction" to assist the insurance company. [ ]. We place great emphasis on the fact that there is no specific exclusion in the insurance contract for punitive damages. If the insurance carrier to this insurance contract intended to eliminate coverage for punitive damages it could and should have inserted a single provision stating "this policy does not include recovery for punitive damages."

Furthermore, the fact that a dispute arose as to the interpretation of the insurance contract, which resulted in this lawsuit, makes it apparent that the language of the policy is at best ambiguous. In *Maddox v. Colonial Life and Accident Insurance Co.*, 303 N.C. 648, 650, 280 S.E.2d 907, 908 (1981), we stated that "[a]n ambiguity exists where, in the opinion of the court, the language of the policy is fairly and reasonably susceptible to either of the constructions asserted by the parties." The well established and universal rule is that insurance contracts will be liberally construed in favor of the insured and strictly construed against the insurer, since the insurance company selected the language used in the policy. [ ]. Thus, any ambiguity, with respect to the policy's coverage of punitive damages for medical malpractice, must be resolved in favor of coverage.

In its brief, Medical Mutual relies upon two North Carolina cases [ ] to support its argument that North Carolina case law precludes insurance coverage of punitive damages. A careful examination of the insurance contracts, factual situations, and holdings in [those cases] convinces us that these two cases are clearly distinguishable from the case *sub judice*, and are not any legal precedent upon which to base a decision favorable to the defendant Medical Mutual. In other words, neither *Cavin's* nor *Knight* control in this situation.

We note also that, even if *Cavin's* and *Knight* were not distinguishable from this case, precedents set by the Court of Appeals are not binding on this Court. As we stated in our recent decision of *Northern Nat'l Life Ins. v. Miller Machine Co.*, 311 N.C. 62, 316 S.E.2d 256 (1984), "[i]t is fundamental that the highest court of a jurisdiction may overrule precedents established by decisions of intermediate appellate courts." Nor do we find it determinative that this Court denied a petition for discretionary review in *Knight*, since such a denial does not signify our approval of the Court of Appeals' decision. "It may mean only that no harmful result is likely to arise from the Court of Appeals' opinion."

For the foregoing reasons, we conclude that the terms of the insurance contract in the present case provide coverage for punitive damages, and public policy does not prohibit such coverage.

* * *

Accordingly, we conclude that the trial court properly held that the insurance contract covers the award for punitive damages as well as the award for actual damages. We find no error in the trial court's granting of summary judgment for the plaintiff.

Affirmed.

UPLAND ANESTHESIA MEDICAL GROUP
v. DOCTORS' COMPANY

Court of Appeal of California, Fourth Appellate District, Division Two, 2002.
100 Cal.App.4th 1137, 123 Cal.Rptr.2d 94.

GAUT, J.

1. INTRODUCTION

Upland Anesthesia Medical Group (Upland) appeals from an order of the trial court granting summary adjudication in favor of The Doctors' Company (Doctors), its insurance company. Upland argues it was entitled to a defense in a class action in which it was sued for unfair business practices. The gist of the claims made by the class plaintiffs was that Upland withheld epidural care from indigent women because Medi–Cal would not pay for the procedure.

Doctors relies upon policy exclusion N.12, denying defense or indemnity for an intentional act "even if such activities are related to your rendering or failing to render *professional services*."

We agree Upland was not entitled to an insurance defense or coverage for the class action and affirm the grant of summary adjudication and entry of judgment in favor of Doctors.

2. FACTUAL AND PROCEDURAL BACKGROUND

The complaint filed by Upland against Doctors alleges three causes of action, fraud, breach of contract, and bad faith. All three causes of action are based on Doctors's refusal to defend or indemnify Upland in the class action.

The following facts were undisputed, or not effectively disputed, for purposes of Doctors's motion for summary judgment or, in the alternative, summary adjudication. Beginning in 1993, Upland followed a policy of "notifying Medi–Cal patients that they would need to pay for any epidural anesthesia in advance of presenting for delivery." As a result, two patients, Marilyn House and Christine Reedy, filed medical malpractice complaints against Upland. Doctors defended both those actions and settled them.

Reedy later became the representative plaintiff in the class action against Upland. The class action sought injunctive relief and restitution under the Business and Professions Code section 17200 et seq. and damages for violation of the Consumers Legal Remedies Act [ ]. Upland prevailed in the class action when the court sustained its demurrer without leave to amend. Upland spent approximately $63,000 in legal fees defending the class action.

In its summary judgment motion, Doctors argued there was no coverage for the class action under its insurance policy for public policy reasons and because intentional acts were excluded. The court granted summary adjudication on the breach of contract and bad faith causes of action for those reasons. Upland dismissed its fraud claim and now appeals the judgment in favor of Doctors.

* * *

4. NO DISPUTED MATERIAL FACTS

Upland's first contention on appeal is that a factual question exists about whether Doctors initially provided legal representation to Upland in the class action case and therefore waived any objection to providing coverage. This matter was not presented in Upland's opposing separate statement, although it was argued in supplemental briefing. Some cases have held disputed facts must be presented in the separate statement: "A party waives a new theory on appeal when he fails to include the underlying facts in his separate statement of facts in opposing summary judgment." [*City of San Diego v. Rider* (1996) 47 Cal.App.4th 1473, 1493]. Following those cases would cause us to exclude consideration of whether a Doctors's attorney, Larry Wong, represented Upland in the class action case.

Other cases have emphasized the need to consider all the submitted papers: "The evidence and affidavits of the moving party are construed strictly, while those of the opponent are liberally read." But, even if we consider Upland's evidence concerning whether Wong represented Upland in the class action, we conclude, as argued by Doctors, that Wong's deposition testimony demonstrates he represented Upland in the two medical malpractice actions, not the class action, in which Call, Clayton, & Jensen represented Upland. The only appearances made by Wong in the class action litigation were in connection with the malpractice cases to prevent the doctor-witnesses from being deposed twice. Upland offers a strained misinterpretation of Wong's testimony but not a disputed material fact.

As to the existence of any other disputed facts, in reviewing the separate statements submitted by the parties, we discern no material disputed facts although the parties interpret some of the facts differently. Upland attempts one actual point of disagreement. As an undisputed fact, Doctors states its insurance policy contains the terms of the written contract between Doctors and Upland. In opposition, Upland responds that Doctors promised to defend Upland against any nonmeritorious lawsuits and Doctors gave assurances that its insurance policy would protect Upland against "any liability exposure." Upland asserts those promises and assurances were incorporated into the terms of the insurance policy. As evidence, Upland cites a declaration by an Upland doctor, Dr. Chu, in which he refers to statements made in promotional materials supplied by Doctors. But Upland's disagreement about the scope of the coverage under the insurance contract does not constitute a disputed material fact. Rather Upland is asserting a legal argument about contractual interpretation we will discuss below.

Hence we conclude there are no disputed material facts and analyze the legal correctness of the court's ruling.

5. PUBLIC POLICY

In *Bank of the West v. Superior Court*, [2 Cal.4th 1254, 1267, 10 Cal.Rptr.2d 538, 833 P.2d 545 (1992)] the California Supreme Court held that an insurance policy cannot cover consumer claims for violations of the Unfair Practices Act "to deter future violations of the unfair trade practice statute and to foreclose retention by the violator of its ill-gotten gains."

Upland argues Doctors cannot raise a public policy argument as a reason to deny coverage for the first time in its summary judgment motion. Upland is wrong: "[A]n insurer does not impliedly waive coverage defenses it fails to mention when it denies the claim." [*Waller v. Truck Ins. Exchange, Inc.* 11 Cal.4th 1, 31, 44 Cal.Rptr.2d 370, 900 P.2d 619 (1995)].

* * *

Finally, Upland argues it had an objectively reasonable expectation of coverage that defeats any public policy considerations. It relies on several items of evidence. Upland's Dr. Chu stated in his declaration that he believed Doctors would defend Upland in a class action. His opinion was based on Doctors's promotional materials stating a policy "to defend resolutely all nonmeritorious claims" and a plan to "develop programs that will protect you from today's liability exposures—and tomorrow's."

What Upland fails to do is identify any ambiguity in the subject insurance policy that would allow the court to evaluate Upland's contrary expectations and construe the ambiguity in favor of Upland. Upland's argument about its expectation of coverage fails.

6. INTENTIONAL ACTS EXCLUSION

Upland's last sequence of arguments involves the inapplicability of the policy exclusion for intentional acts. Upland repeats the argument about its expectation of coverage. But, as we have just held, Upland has not successfully shown the policy is ambiguous and therefore subject to judicial interpretation in favor of the insured's objectively reasonable expectation of coverage.

Next Upland mistakenly asserts that the statutory exception against coverage for an insured's willful acts, as provided in Insurance Code section 533, should be used to interpret the meaning of the intentional acts exclusion in the insurance policy. We decline Upland's invitation, unsupported by any authority, to interpret the contract and the statute as equivalent.

Finally, Upland maintains the evidence shows the class action was actually negligence based and therefore subject to coverage. Again, no such evidence was submitted as part of Upland's opposing statement. But we will review it nonetheless.

In the class action, the Los Angeles Superior Court issued a ruling granting a motion to strike the punitive damages claim for failure to comply with Code of Civil Procedure section 425.13, subdivision (a): "The section does not require that there be a cause of action for medical malpractice, it only requires that it 'arise out of the professional negligence of a health care provider . . . . ' Here, that is what is being alleged." Upland points to this ruling as deciding the character of the class action as being one for negligence. We acknowledge Doctors's legitimate complaints about the lack of foundation for this document. But even if the ruling is accepted as genuine, it does not establish that the class action was for negligence.

In the first amended class action, the plaintiffs alleged that Upland "unlawfully, unfairly and fraudulently demanded cash payments from pregnant women, in the throes of childbirth labor, as an additional price for pain-mitigating, epidural anesthesia." The class action further alleges that Upland and other defendants conspired "to disadvantage, damage, defraud and injure Plaintiffs, and to improperly and illegally profit from Plaintiffs' disabled and disadvantaged conditions." The complaint proceeds to describe a scheme of willful misconduct by which Upland and other defendants solicited improper and illegal cash payments for epidural anesthesia, otherwise threatening to deny such relief. * * *

No allegations of negligence—such as duty, breach, and causation—are made. The court ruling on the motion to strike punitive damages in the class action may have determined the allegations demonstrated an injury "directly related to the professional services provided by the health care provider." But that interim ruling on a collateral issue did not convert the class action into a negligence complaint.

Nor are we persuaded by Upland's reliance on a declaration from Scott Leviant, another piece of belated supplemental evidence that was not incorporated into Upland's opposing separate statement. Leviant, an attorney in the class action suit, states in his declaration that the 27–page class action complaint is for negligence because it seeks recovery for "physical, emotional, and economic damages"; because it alleges defendants "knew or should have known that their conduct was directed at profoundly vulnerable disabled persons"; and because the allegations are not expressly limited to intentional acts.

The interpretation of pleadings is a matter of law by the court. We have reviewed the class action complaint and hold it is not for negligence. It alleges a series of intentional acts related to the rendering of or failure to render professional services. The intentional acts exclusion operates to deny insurance coverage to Upland.

DISPOSITION

The judgment is affirmed.

Notes

1) The medical liability insurance policy is a contract, and the medical liability insurer's contractual duty to defend the doctor is defined by the policy language of coverage and exclusions. Most policies promise to defend claims that are "groundless, false or fraudulent." Nowadays the patient does not have to allege a theory of claim, and the facts alleged in a notice-theory complaint may be conclusory and general, and the coverage of medical liability policies extends far beyond negligence; therefore the insurer's duty to defend continues to be broader than its duty to indemnify. Even so, a doctor will occasionally notify the insurer of a claim that the insurer feels no duty to defend, and the insurer will notify the doctor that under the policy, it has no obligation to defend. The doctor may disagree and threaten to sue the insurer for breach of contract.

Whatever the outcome, doctor and insurer are no longer friends but adversaries, and the doctor must retain and pay for a lawyer. How and when is this matter to be decided? The insurer can go ahead and defend the doctor, hoping for a favorable result on the merits, and doubtless insurers have done so, but it is no answer to all cases, because the uncontracted-for costs of a successful defense cannot later be charged back to the doctor.

If the insurer simply refuses to defend, the doctor retains counsel and, after the patient's lawsuit is over, sues the insurer for breaching the policy. This is a bad result in economics because it maximizes transaction costs. It is also risky for the insurer, because the doctor may collect paid-out damages in excess of the policy limits if in bad faith the insurer failed to settle a covered claim within the policy limits.

In years past insurers sometimes tried to perform investigations and even defend at trial under a nonwaiver agreement providing that if the patient won, the insurer would not pay the judgment against the doctor. The nonwaiver agreement was in effect a contract to settle the dispute over contract coverage, because the insurer paid the disputed costs of defense but the doctor accepted the disputed risk of judgment loss.

Insurers also had a much more risky technique, the "reservation of rights" letter, which sought unilaterally to impose the results of the nonwaiver agreement. If the insurer made any substantial defense, the insurer could be found to have assumed inconsistent positions and would be estopped to use the reservation of rights letter.

Nowadays declaratory judgment actions are widely available, enabling the parties to get an early judicial decision on the duty to defend in doubtful cases. The insurer also asks for a stay of the patient's medical liability action against the doctor while the declaratory judgment action over coverage is being litigated, but the patient may want the medical liability action to go forward anyway. While declaratory judgment actions most frequently are brought by insurers, declaratory judgment actions also can be brought by the doctor and by the patient.

2) In *St. Paul Fire & Marine Ins. Co. v. House*, 315 Md. 328, 554 A.2d 404 (1989), Dr. Homer House performed surgery on Shirley J. Platzer's knee October 29, 1984. Part of a needle was removed from the knee November 27, 1984. Ms. Platzer's lawyer wrote Dr. House June 21 and September 16, 1985, asserting a claim and advising Dr. House to consult his insurer, and Ms. Platzer commenced the required malpractice arbitration proceedings on November 15, 1985. Dr. House's claims-made insurance expired January 1, 1986. The arbitration claim was served on Dr. House January 6, 1986, and his insurance agent received it on February 14, 1986, two days after Dr. House mailed it. The insurer declined to defend, resting on this language in its "plain English" policy:

When is a claim made?

A claim is made on the date you first report an incident or injury to us or our agent.

Four judges of the Maryland Court of Appeals thought that "claims made" in plain English could mean "a claim made by the claimant to the doctor" and affirmed declaratory judgment that Dr. House was covered; three judges thought that the policy definition unambiguously required reporting to the agent to make the coverage effective.

Chapter 10

CHANGING THE LITIGATION SYSTEM

INTRODUCTORY NOTE

It was the mid–1970s when it first became widely perceived that the United States litigation system was not handling medical liability claims in a satisfactory manner, and most of the state legislatures enacted either individual statutes, treating one or two perceived problems, or packages that sought to deal with a wide array of problems.[1] The original statutes have been tested by experience and litigation, some have been modified, and further litigation carries forward the testing. Comprehensive packages have been proposed since the late 1980's.[2]

This Note arranges litigation system problems and solutions from various states in the sequence in which litigation progresses. The cases that follow the Note emphasize the challenges to validity of the changes, not the ways in which the statutes operate, though even when a statute has been declared valid, it is fair to ask whether it is a good idea.

---

1. Probably the best known package was California's "MICRA," the Medical Injury Compensation Reform Act of 1975. 1975 Cal.Stat. ch. 1–2, codified in various parts of the California Code of Civil Procedure. Another comprehensive approach was enacted in Indiana. Acts 1975, Pub.L. No. 146, codified as Ind.Code 1976, title 16, art. 9.5; for a survey of causes and a favorable report on experience, see Bowen, Medical Malpractice in Indiana, 11 J.Legis. 15 (1984) (Dr. Bowen was Secretary of Health and Human Services from 1985 to 1989). Some packages were struck down in their entirety, e.g., Wright v. Central Du Page Hosp. Ass'n, 63 Ill.2d 313, 347 N.E.2d 736, 80 A.L.R.3d 566 (1976); Carson v. Maurer, 120 N.H. 925, 424 A.2d 825, 12 A.L.R.4th 1 (1980), but have been replaced with different statutes.

2. See A Proposed Alternative to the Civil Justice System for Resolving Medical Liability Disputes: A Fault–Based, Administrative System (American Medical Association–Specialty Society Medical Liability Project, January 1988) (proposal to replace litigation altogether by a new state administrative agency).

The Model Health Care Provider Liability Reform Act was circulated to state governors in late 1987 by the Secretary of the United States Department of Health and Human Services. The Model Act was prepared by the Secretary's Task Force on Medical Liability and Malpractice; it does not seem to have been published as a government document. A source in HHS said in early 1990 that the Model Act had produced reactions (but no full-scale adoption) in about 15 states.

Claims

The first stage in medical liability litigation is the formulation and filing of the patient's claim against the health care provider. The sheer number of medical liability claims is a significant cost factor in the litigation system, because for every claim, the provider and the insurer incur expenses in setting up files and conducting investigations, no matter what becomes of the claim.

The best way to cut down on claims is to provide safe and successful medical services. Risk management and quality assurance programs in health care institutions seek to prevent medical liability claims.

In spite of preventive measures, claims do arise. Hospital ombudsmen try to reduce confrontations between patients and health care providers, and regardless of blame, patients will accept a lot of bad results if they feel listened-to. Insurers have also experimented with advanced payments to cover patients' out-of-pocket expenses arising from medical incidents that may involve liability, without going through the mechanics of taking a release from liability, but with the hope of keeping claim-creating medical incidents from maturing into litigation.

Incident prevention and claim amelioration can go only so far. It became apparent by the 1970s that lawyer-designed paperwork containing claim-arresting clauses, furnished by providers, and signed by patients in advance of claims, could not prevent future claims: the instruments were adhesive or otherwise contrary to public policy, and the courts refused to enforce them. The entry of some medical liability claims into the litigation system seems therefore to be inevitable, especially under state constitutions that guarantee claimants' access to the courts.

Actions

Once a patient has hired a lawyer to pursue a claim, it is easy for the lawyer to commence an action by filing a complaint in court, but filing the complaint does not establish that the claim has any merit. Doctors describe as "spurious" the complaints that lawyers call "frivolous." Some medical liability complaints are indeed frivolous; others are simply weak. The challenge that these complaints bring to the litigation system is to identify and dispose of, cheaply and quickly, the frivolous actions that should never have been filed and the congenitally weak actions that will never go to trial.

Since 1983, if the plaintiff's attorney files a frivolous complaint in federal court without adequately investigating the patient's angry or greedy assertions, the judge must impose a sanction of one kind or another upon the attorney under Fed.R.Civ.P. 11. Rule 11 is being used a lot in the federal courts, but it is controversial. It remains to be seen whether all states will adopt widely the 1983 sanctions provisions of Rule 11, and if they do, whether the threat of sanctions will shrink the number of medical liability actions that are dismissed on summary judgment for their intrinsic futility.

Some states have raised the threshold to the courthouse door. One technique is to require that the plaintiff's attorney notify the defendant of the intent to sue 90 days before filing the complaint, with the objective of enabling well-informed settlement negotiations to precede filing.[3] Another technique is to require that the plaintiff's lawyer file, along with the complaint, a "certificate of merit" in which the attorney certifies that a medical expert thinks there is a claim, and the expert must also certify to that effect.[4] Without the certificate of merit, the judge will dismiss the complaint, and the certificate of merit therefore may be invalid under a state constitution that provides for access to the courts.

Another way of inducing plaintiffs' attorneys to screen out weak cases before filing the complaint would be to make the ultimately losing plaintiff pay the winning defendant's legal expenses, contrary to the usual "American Rule" under which the parties pay their own lawyers, but this idea has not caught on.[5]

Plaintiffs' lawyers commence some actions as "nuisance" actions, filed on adequate grounds but in the hope of a small settlement rather than full litigation. For each nuisance action, the insurer incurs file-opening expenses, and each settlement shows on the provider's claims record, as well as leaving a permanent scar on the provider's ego. State laws provide for pre-testing the sufficiency of both nuisance and substantial actions by applying either of two basic alternatives to litigation.[6]

Under the first alternative, every medical liability action, before it reaches the courtroom, must detour through a claim-screening system. The states use and misuse various terms, such as "mediation" and "arbitration," but all of the screening systems are designed to pre-test the sufficiency of the evidence supporting the patient's case in chief, the function later performed by a judge on the doctor's motion for summary judgment or directed verdict. The states vary as to what persons comprise the screening panels, what kinds of findings the panels report, and what use can be made in a subsequent trial of the panels' findings, for example, whether the jury can be told about it; but in all of the screening systems, the objective is to force the plaintiff's lawyer to persuade a group of legal and medical experts that substantial evidence is available to litigate negligence, causation, and damages. If the panel finds against

3. E.g., West's Fla.Stat.Ann. § 766–106.

4. E.g., Ill.Rev.Stat. § 2–622; Md.Ann. Code § 3–2A–04(b).

5. Florida tried it. The statute had to be phrased neutrally, so the winner would pay the loser's expenses, West's Fla.Stat.Ann. § 768.56, enacted by L.1980, ch. 80–67, §§ 1, 3, and sometimes the plaintiffs did lose and had to pay; but it soon became apparent that most of the payments were moving from losing defendants to winning plaintiffs, and so the legislature repealed the statute. L.1985, ch. 85–75, § 43. See Spence & Roth, Closing the Courthouse Door: Flor-

ida's Spurious Claims Statute, 10 Stetson L.Rev. 397 (1981).

6. Federal judges have to follow the state law. In Feinstein v. Massachusetts Gen. Hosp., 489 F.Supp. 419 (D.Mass.1979), the district judge referred the claim to a state arbitration panel, which gave the plaintiff an unfavorable report. The plaintiff did not follow subsequent state procedural requirements, so the district judge dismissed the action, and the First Circuit affirmed. 643 F.2d 880 (1981).

the plaintiff, the plaintiff can still go to court, but the plaintiff may have to post a bond for the defendant's legal expenses if the defendant wins. If there is a fatal gap in the plaintiff's case in chief, then the plaintiff's lawyer may withdraw from the case even if the plaintiff wants to fight on. If the plaintiff's case is sound, the defendant's insurer may decide to settle without further litigation. If there is sufficient evidence but genuine controversy, the case may well have to be tried.

The second alternative is to litigate through the out-of-court arbitration process instead of the in-court adjudication process. Three basic formats exist, along with numerous variations, but only where the parties' participation is voluntary can the result be binding.

First, the parties to an *existing dispute* over medical liability may agree to arbitrate it to a binding award. The laws of most states and certainly the federal law encourage the arbitration to proceed to award, and the award can then be entered as a judgment of court. Existing dispute arbitration is not a controversial idea, it rarely produces litigation, and it is being used in medical liability cases.

Second, the provider may supply and the patient may sign a form agreement to arbitrate *future disputes* before any services are performed. When a dispute arises, the enforceability of the agreement is hard to predict, because of the inequality of bargaining positions and the unforeseeability of specific disputes. Some states have enacted statutes that make future disputes arbitration agreements enforceable as long as they meet detailed requirements of language and circumstances.

Third, a state may require parties who want to litigate to enter *compulsory arbitration*. This leads either to a final award, as in existing disputes voluntary arbitration, or to a non-binding result that has some use in subsequent litigation, much like a screening panel report.

In spite of detours on the road to the courthouse, medical liability cases are still litigated, and changes continue to be made in the litigation system itself. Statutes of limitations are a prominent target of change. To the plaintiffs' bar, judicial glosses on the statutes wisely extended the limitation periods in three kinds of cases: where the doctor continued to treat the patient's problem and allayed suspicions about the negligence that caused the problem; where a patient's injuries were undiscoverable until after the statute had run; and where a minor could not sue until reaching majority. To medical liability insurers, these glosses created the "long-tail claims" problem that made it difficult to set premiums. Many legislatures have enacted specialized statutes of limitations that refine statutes of limitations in medical liability actions.

Another problem in litigation has been securing the attendance of treating doctors at trial. Courts, bar associations, and medical societies have created on-call systems to alert doctors when they are about to be needed, instead of keeping them waiting in court for days. But if a busy doctor will not come to court when called, a subpoena will issue, and the judge can then demand obedience regardless of the doctor's inconvenience.[7]

Jury trials pose a number of problems and proposed solutions. For example, evidence can be in hopeless conflict: it may be impossible for the patient to establish satisfactorily that the doctor was negligent, or for the doctor to establish satisfactorily that the patient consented to an unintended consequence. As a matter of social policy rather than truth-finding, the medical liability system lets the jury decide contests over fault, and there is not much that changing the litigation system can do to change the jury system in this respect. As for damages, though, the broader use of special interrogatories can restrain the jury from letting an oversupply of horrible damages overcome weakness in the plaintiff's expert testimony on fault.

For another example, defense-oriented lawyers think that it is in their interests to keep twelve-person juries and unanimous verdicts in medical liability cases, though many states use smaller juries and do not insist upon unanimity.

As the final example, medical scientists think that scientific questions should not be decided by juries. They concede that there is nothing scientific about allocating a dollar value to pain and suffering; the judges have other tools, such as remittitur and new trial, for bringing down extravagant verdicts. But medical scientists are indignant at letting lay juries decide lopsided arguments about medicolegal causation, and they take no comfort from the power of judges to decide that a verdict for a plaintiff is against the clear weight of the evidence. So far, though, no change to the litigation system has tried to cope with this problem; expert juries on scientific questions do not exist, though it is possible that scientific expertise carries more weight before arbitrators than jurors.

Recoveries

Doctors and their insurers have found that they do not necessarily share the payment of large damage verdicts in proportion to their shares of fault. If a jury specifies three doctors' shares of fault in a patient's damages, and if insurance does not cover fully the damage share of Doctor A, the doctrine of several tort liability says that Doctor B or Doctor C or both of them must make up the balance of Doctor A's share of damages. A few states have modified the rule of several liability for medical liability defendants, so no doctor has to pay a share of damages greater than the share of fault.

The aspect of medical liability litigation that gets the most attention is the enormous size of some verdicts. Undoubtedly a multi-million-dollar verdict can have an impact on the insurance premiums paid by insured doctors.[8] Working from the perception that plaintiffs are being

---

7. See In re Tarpley, 293 Ala. 137, 300 So.2d 409 (1974), where the physician narrowly escaped jail for criminal contempt of court.

8. For example, New Jersey had about 20,000 doctors in 1988. 1989 World Almanac 845. In theory, a $2 million case (judgment and defense costs) thus would cost

awarded too much money by judges and juries, state legislatures have enacted three basic methods to reduce recoveries.

The first method is to place a cap on the total amount of the patient's damages, regardless of the type of damages and the number of doctors.

The second method is to place a cap only on the amount of the patient's non-pecuniary damages. Pecuniary damage amounts rest upon documents and financial projections, and they can be reviewed by trial judges for excessiveness. Non-pecuniary damages, usually called "non-economic," are extremely difficult for judges to review at any level, and so some statutes have "capped" non-economic damages at sums in the hundreds of thousands of dollars.[9]

The third method is to reduce the amount of total recovery that will *not* go to the patient. For example, in most cases the patient's lawyer will have contracted with the patient to receive a contingent fee of 30% to 50% that comes out of the patient's recovery, and many states have imposed ceilings or sliding scales on the percentages that the victorious patient's lawyer may recover.

In a few cases, a horribly injured patient will have a short life expectancy but no close and deserving kin, so most of a lump sum payment will go as a windfall to remote recipients, or it may be wasted by the patient or those who were supposed to provide care. Here a few legislatures have sought to guarantee *periodic payments* of funds for care while the patient lives, but to shut off the payments when the patient dies.[10] The concept has its merits, but design and administrability problems have shown up in the small number of cases.

Structured settlements are a familiar mechanism for getting money to patients as long as they need it, but not thereafter. Stretching out the payment of money to patients has two objectives, long-term availability

each doctor $100. However, less dramatic forces also operate on premiums. For example, if only 1% of those doctors (200) had a claim in any one year, and if the insurers spent $10,000 per claim to open files and investigate, the total expense would be $2 million.

9. See Fein v. Permanente Medical Group, 38 Cal.3d 137, 211 Cal.Rptr. 368, 695 P.2d 665, appeal dismissed for want of a substantial federal question, 474 U.S. 892, 106 S.Ct. 214, 88 L.Ed.2d 215 (1985) (Justice White dissented with opinion). The cap is another part of MICRA. It withstood federal constitutional attack in Hoffman v. United States, 767 F.2d 1431 (9th Cir. 1985).

10. See American Bank & Trust Co. v. Community Hosp., 36 Cal.3d 359, 204 Cal. Rptr. 671, 683 P.2d 670, 41 A.L.R.4th 233 (1984) (a MICRA case); the annotation is Validity of State Statute Providing for Periodic Payment of Future Damages in Medical Malpractice Action, 41 A.L.R.4th 275 (1985). The court held that the statute, West's Ann.Cal.Code Civ.P. § 667.7, was constitutional, but three justices dissented in two long opinions that give all the earlier background. In a later case, Kansas declared unconstitutional a second-generation package that included both a damage cap and an annuity provision. Kansas Malpractice Victims Coalition v. Bell, 243 Kan. 333, 757 P.2d 251 (1988); again, there were dissents.

and avoidance of windfalls, that seem to be easier to achieve by contract than by statute.[11]

Many of the forces that push the costs of medical liability claims upward, such as the increasing use of medical care and the expanding expectations for what it can accomplish, are beyond the control of state legislatures and even the Congress of the United States. It seems doubtful that the dollar cost of claims will actually turn downward from any cause, least of all because of changing the litigation system. The rate of increase in medical liability claims costs may be slowed by changing the litigation system, but none of the changes discussed in this chapter have been in place long enough to show this effect clearly.

SECTION A. FORESTALLING CLAIMS

EMORY UNIV. v. PORUBIANSKY

Supreme Court of Georgia, 1981.
248 Ga. 391, 282 S.E.2d 903.

CLARKE, JUSTICE. * * *

Diane Porubiansky became a patient at the Emory University School of Dentistry Clinic in 1976. Prior to treatment she was required to execute an "Information–Consent" form. The clinic * * * offers dental services to the public at fees that, on the average, are less than the average price of those of private practitioners. The form explains that patients are accepted based upon the training needs of the school and that treatment will proceed more slowly than in a private office. There is also a statement that complete dental treatment cannot be assured. The last paragraph of this form provides:

> In consideration of Emory University School of Dentistry perform-
> ing dental treatment, I do hereby expressly waive and relinquish any
> and all claims of every nature I or my minor child or ward may have
> against Emory University, its officers, agents, employees, or stu-
> dents, their successors, assignees, administrators, or executors; and
> further agree to hold them harmless as the result of any claims by
> such minor child or ward, arising out of any dental treatment
> rendered, regardless of its nature or extent.

In April of 1977 Mrs. Porubiansky had an impacted tooth removed by Dr. Haddad, an employee of the dental clinic. She alleged that as a result of negligent treatment her jaw was broken during the surgical procedure and filed suit against Emory University and Dr. Haddad. The defendants denied any negligent treatment and further asserted that the signing of the information-consent form was a complete bar to the action. The trial court granted summary judgment to the defendants based upon the exculpatory clause in the form. The court of appeals held

11. See D. Hindert, J. Dehner & P. Hin-   Payment Judgments (1986).
dert, Structured Settlements and Periodic

the clause in question to be void as against public policy. 156 Ga.App. 602, 275 S.E.2d 163 (1980).

* * * Emory University and Dr. Haddad contend that the form is a valid covenant not to sue which would prohibit recovery for negligent dental treatment. They argue that a doctor and patient may bargain for a shifting of liability without offending any policy of this state, and further contend that the Emory University School of Dentistry occupies a unique position in that it services the public need by training dental professionals and offering dental services to the general public.

We agree that through the dental clinic Emory provides a worthwhile service of lower cost professional care and in the training of dental professionals. We also agree that because the clinic is part of a teaching facility it may require that prospective patients waive the right to insist on complete treatment. However, the attempt to relieve the clinic, its employees and students from the statutory duty of care for licensed professional medical services conflicts with and frustrates the policies of the state as expressed through our General Assembly.

* * * The legislature has established a minimum standard of care for the medical profession. * * * Ga.Code Ann. § 84–924. This standard also governs the duties and responsibilities of a dentist. * * *

We find that it is against the public policy of this state to allow one who procures a license to practice dentistry to relieve himself by contract of the duty to exercise reasonable care. * * *

The status of the Emory University School of Dentistry as primarily a training institution does not allow for an exemption from the duty to exercise reasonable care. The clinic in offering services to the public is engaged in the practice of dentistry. The legislature while allowing such clinics to operate has not exempted them from the standard of care necessary for the protection of the public. * * *

* * * The court of appeals was correct in reversing the summary judgment and allowing Mrs. Porubiansky to proceed on her allegations * * *.

Judgment affirmed.

JORDAN, C.J., and MARSHALL, J., dissent.

ST. GERMAIN v. PFEIFER

Supreme Judicial Court of Massachusetts, 1994.
418 Mass. 511, 637 N.E.2d 848.

ABRAMS, J.

These appeals arise out of a medical malpractice action which the plaintiff, Joseph St. Germain, brought against Drs. Bernard A. Pfeifer, Glen Seidman, Stephen R. Freidberg, and Nurse Kristin Bartelson. Two medical malpractice tribunals convened to evaluate the plaintiff's claims pursuant to G. L. c. 231, § 60B (1992 ed.).[2] The first tribunal, which considered the plaintiff's claim against Nurse Bartelson, among others, determined that the plaintiff's offer of proof with respect to Nurse Bartelson was insufficient to raise a legitimate question of liability appropriate for judicial inquiry. Consequently, in order to proceed with his malpractice claim against Nurse Bartelson, the plaintiff was required to post a bond within thirty days of the docketing of the tribunal's decision. See note 2, supra. The plaintiff did not do so. After the thirty-day period for filing the bond expired, Bartelson made a motion to dismiss the plaintiff's claim based on his failure to post the bond. A Superior Court judge allowed this motion to dismiss and [ ] separate and final judgment was entered dismissing the plaintiff's claims against Bartelson. * * *. The plaintiff appealed.

The second tribunal, which considered the plaintiff's claims against the three defendant doctors, determined that the plaintiff's offers of proof with respect to Drs. Bernard Pfeifer, Glen Seidman, and Stephen Freidberg were insufficient to raise a legitimate question of liability appropriate for judicial inquiry. As with Nurse Bartelson, the plaintiff did not file the required bond with respect to Drs. Pfeifer, Seidman, or Freidberg. However, with respect to these defendant doctors, the plaintiff did file a motion to reduce the bond on the basis of indigency. See note 2, supra. This motion was not acted on by the court either before the expiration of the thirty-day period or at any time thereafter. After the thirty-day period for filing the bond expired, defendants Pfeifer, Seidman, and Freidberg made a motion to dismiss the plaintiff's claim based on his failure to post the bond. A Superior Court judge allowed this motion to dismiss and [ ] separate and final judgment was entered dismissing the plaintiff's claims against these defendants. The plaintiff appealed from the dismissal of his complaint.

In his appeal, the plaintiff contends that the tribunals erred in determining that his offers of proof with respect to Nurse Bartelson and Drs. Pfeifer, Seidman, and Freidberg were insufficient to raise a legitimate question of liability appropriate for judicial inquiry, and that the motion judge erred in dismissing his claims against the defendant

---

2. General Laws c. 231, § 60B (1992 ed.), provides in part: "Every action for malpractice, error or mistake against a provider of health care shall be heard by a tribunal consisting of a single justice of the superior court, a physician licensed to practice medicine in the commonwealth ... and an attorney authorized to practice law in the commonwealth, at which hearing the plaintiff shall present an offer of proof and said tribunal shall determine if the evidence presented if properly substantiated is sufficient to raise a legitimate question of liability appropriate for judicial inquiry.... If a finding is made for the defendant or defendants in the case the plaintiff may pursue the claim through the usual judicial process only upon filing bond in the amount of six thousand dollars in the aggregate secured by cash or its equivalent with the clerk of the court in which the case is pending, payable to the defendant or defendants in the case for costs assessed, including witness and experts fees and attorneys fees if the plaintiff does not prevail in the final judgment. Said single justice may, within his discretion, increase the amount of the bond required to be filed. If said bond is not posted within thirty days of the tribunal's finding the action shall be dismissed. Upon motion filed by the plaintiff, and a determination by the court that the plaintiff is indigent said justice may reduce the amount of the bond but may not eliminate the requirement thereof."

doctors for failure to post the required bond while his motion to reduce the bond was pending. * * *

1. The facts. On August 19, 1988, the plaintiff underwent a mid-lumbar osteotomy performed by Dr. Bernard Pfeifer, an orthopedic surgeon, and Dr. Stephen Freidberg, a neurosurgeon, to alleviate a debilitating spinal deformity. As part of this procedure, fixation hooks and rods were inserted into the plaintiff's spine.

Dr. Pfeifer's postoperative plan was to confine the plaintiff to his hospital bed for the four to five days following the surgery. Contrary to this plan, at 10 A.M. on August 21, 1988, Dr. Glen Seidman, a first-year orthopedic resident ordered that the plaintiff be given a "warm and form lumbar bandage" (a soft orthopedic support) and be moved "out of bed to chair today." Dr. Seidman wrote both of these orders in the "physician orders" section of the plaintiff's chart. However, in the "progress notes" section of the plaintiff's chart, Dr. Seidman only noted his order for the "warm and form bandage."

At approximately noon on August 21, 1988, Dr. Pfeifer acknowledged Dr. Seidman's "progress note" concerning the "warm and form bandage" and added to the note that the plaintiff was to be x-rayed the next day and, "if okay," was to be moved out of bed to a "tilt table." Dr. Pfeifer apparently did not see the order to move the plaintiff which Dr. Seidman entered in the "physician orders" section of the plaintiff's chart. The "physician orders" and "progress notes" sections of the plaintiff's chart were not on the same page.

The orders of both Dr. Seidman and Dr. Pfeifer were noted by the charge nurse, Kristin Bartelson. Pursuant to Dr. Seidman's order, the nurse on duty in the early morning of August 22, 1988, encouraged the plaintiff to get out of bed and walk. As the plaintiff stood up and took a step, he heard a loud snapping noise in his back and fell backward onto the bed screaming in pain. When Dr. Pfeifer arrived shortly thereafter, he yelled at the nurse, "You should never have moved him! Why in hell did you move him!"

As a result of the plaintiff's movement, the hooks and rods which had been inserted in his spine to hold it together "slipped out" of position. The corrective surgery which the plaintiff underwent to reposition this hardware was not successful.

2. The offers of proof. Under G. L. c. 231, § 60B, the medical malpractice tribunal must determine whether the plaintiff's offer of proof presents evidence which, if substantiated, raises a legitimate question of liability for judicial inquiry. See note 2, supra. In order to raise such a question of liability, a medical malpractice plaintiff must show (1) the existence of a doctor or nurse-patient relationship, (2) that the performance of the doctor or nurse did not conform to good medical practice, and (3) that damage resulted therefrom. [ ] In evaluating a plaintiff's offer of proof, the tribunal must apply a standard comparable to that which a trial judge would employ in determining whether to allow a defendant's motion for a directed verdict. [ ] Pursuant to this

standard, a medical malpractice tribunal must conclude that the plaintiff's offer of proof raises a legitimate question of liability appropriate for judicial inquiry if "anywhere in the evidence, from whatever source derived, any combination of circumstances could be found from which a reasonable inference could be drawn in favor of the plaintiff." [ ].

a. Nurse Kristin Bartelson. With respect to his claim against Nurse Kristin Bartelson, the plaintiff presented to the medical malpractice tribunal the affidavit of an expert which stated that "As the R.N. giving written notation to Dr. Seidman's orders, . . . Bartelson owed a duty of care to [the plaintiff] to either carry out the orders or, if not assigned to direct care, to effectively communicate the orders to the assigned care giver. She should have been aware of [the plaintiff's] care plan and should have known of and reported the inconsistent intentions of Dr. Seidman and Dr. Pfeifer regarding [the plaintiff's] movement.... In my opinion, it is reasonably certain that had Kristin Bartelson been aware of [the plaintiff's] care plan, effectively communicated orders to the assigned care givers, and been aware of and reported the inconsistent intentions of Dr. Seidman and Dr. Pfeifer regarding [the plaintiff's] movement, [the plaintiff] would not have suffered the injuries requiring his further surgery."

Because the plaintiff's offer of proof with respect to his claim against Nurse Bartelson contained evidence which, if substantiated, would reasonably support an inference that a nurse-patient relationship existed between Nurse Bartelson and the plaintiff, that Nurse Bartelson's performance did not conform to good medical practice, and that injury to the plaintiff resulted therefrom, the tribunal erred in determining that the plaintiff's offer of proof as to Nurse Bartelson did not raise a legitimate question of liability appropriate for judicial inquiry.

b. Dr. Bernard Pfeifer. With respect to his claim against Dr. Bernard Pfeifer, the plaintiff presented to the tribunal an affidavit from an expert which read as follows:

"DEVIATION FROM THE ACCEPTABLE MEDICAL STANDARDS:

"The records clearly indicate that the intended postoperative plan was not adhered to. Breach of that plan took place on the second postoperative day . . . when Dr. Seidman, on his own volition, gave an order for sitting [the plaintiff] out of bed, having prescribed a soft bandage. By nature, the 'warm and form bandage' has very little immobilizing effect, far less than necessary to protect the internal hardware. Two hours later, Dr. Pfeifer registered a different intent in his progress notes, 'use a tilt table if the x-rays are okay.' However, he did not countermand the sit out of bed order of Dr. Seidman, nor did he document his intent to use the tilt table as an official order.... In my opinion, based on reasonable medical certainty, Dr. Pfeifer failed his duty to communicate clearly his postoperative ambulation plan for the benefit of the staff under his direct control. The outcome of this failure was the unfortunate out of bed order by Dr. Seidman. Although Dr. Pfeifer had a different intent, he failed to countermand Dr. Seidman's order. Additionally, he failed to translate his intent order into an official order for the benefit of the nursing staff. Had he articulated his plan to his Resident, or countermanded Dr. Seidman's order, or placed a clear order for a tilt table, it is more than probable that the resulting injury to [the plaintiff], leading to a second major surgery and ending with permanent neuropathy, would not have happened."

Because the plaintiff's offer of proof with respect to his claim against Dr. Pfeifer contained evidence which, if substantiated, would reasonably support an inference that a doctor-patient relationship existed between Pfeifer and the plaintiff, that Pfeifer's performance did not conform to good medical practice, and that injury to the plaintiff resulted therefrom, the tribunal erred in determining that the plaintiff's offer of proof as to Pfeifer did not raise a legitimate question of liability appropriate for judicial inquiry.

c. Dr. Glen Seidman. With respect to his claim against Dr. Seidman, the plaintiff presented to the tribunal an affidavit from an expert which stated that "Dr. Seidman failed his duty by not knowing, or not inquiring about the intended postoperative plan of the operating surgeon. He took it upon himself to put a sit out of bed order on the second postoperative day, without prior consultation with the operating surgeon, and in breach of the normal acceptable standards.... Had he known or inquired about the operating surgeon's plan, it's more likely than not that his fateful error would have been avoided [and] ... that the sequelae that resulted in the second surgery, ending with permanent nerve damage, would ... have been avoided" (emphasis added).

Dr. Seidman asserts that the plaintiff's offer of proof as to him was insufficient because, in determining that his performance did not conform to good medical practice, the plaintiff's expert did not apply the duty of care applicable to first-year residents. Dr. Seidman offers no support for his position that a first-year resident should be held to a lower standard of care than more senior physicians. While this issue has not yet been addressed in Massachusetts [ ], it has been considered in two other jurisdictions. In Centman v. Cobb, 581 N.E.2d 1286, 1289 (Ind. App. 1991), the Court of Appeals of Indiana held that interns and first-year residents are "practitioners of medicine required to exercise the same standard of care applicable to physicians with unlimited licenses to practice." And in Jenkins v. Clark, 7 Ohio App.3d 93, 101, 454 N.E.2d 541 (1982), the Court of Appeals of Ohio noted that a trial court judge acted properly in instructing that the applicable standard of care in a medical malpractice case involving a first-year resident was "that of reasonably careful physicians[,] ... not that of interns or residents." We agree with these opinions and we decline to apply a lower standard of care to residents from that we apply to other physicians.

Because the plaintiff's offer of proof with respect to his claim against Dr. Seidman contained evidence which, if substantiated, would reasonably support an inference that a doctor-patient relationship existed between Seidman and the plaintiff, that Seidman's performance did not conform to good medical practice, and that injury to the plaintiff resulted therefrom, the tribunal erred in determining that the plaintiff's offer of proof as to Dr. Seidman did not raise a legitimate question of liability appropriate for judicial inquiry.

d. Dr. Stephen Freidberg. With respect to his claim against Dr. Stephen Freidberg, the plaintiff presented to the tribunal an affidavit from an expert which stated that "Dr. Freidberg ... was the surgeon under whose name [the plaintiff] was admitted. He sat with [the plaintiff] on the day of the surgery and 'carefully described the risks and benefits of the surgery to [the plaintiff].' He was the co-surgeon and he himself performed the first half of the surgery. It was his duty to check on [the plaintiff] postoperatively. Instead, [the plaintiff] was seen by Dr. Freidberg's physician's assistant on the first and on the second postoperative days. These physician's assistants clearly did not know what the ambulation plan was. Had Dr. Freidberg made himself available during the fateful postoperative day two, it is more than likely that the appropriate ambulation plan would have been adhered to. It would have been more than likely that the complications resulting from the non protected out of bed activity of [the plaintiff], with the resulting permanent damage, would not have taken place."

In order to raise a legitimate question of liability appropriate for judicial inquiry with respect to his claim against Dr. Freidberg, the plaintiff had to establish that a doctor-patient relationship existed between Dr. Freidberg and himself. The plaintiff's offer of proof did not do this. Immediately after the operation, Dr. Freidberg transferred the plaintiff to the care of Dr. Pfeifer. On the record before us, there is no evidence that Dr. Freidberg attended the plaintiff after the transfer. The plaintiff's expert did not opine that this transfer was improper. Thus, at the time the plaintiff suffered the injury complained of in his complaint, no doctor-patient relationship existed between the plaintiff and Dr. Freidberg. [ ]. Therefore, the medical malpractice tribunal correctly determined that the plaintiff's offer of proof as to Dr. Freidberg was not sufficient to raise a legitimate question of liability appropriate for judicial inquiry.

3. The failure to post a bond. Dr. Freidberg asserts that the plaintiff is foreclosed from proceeding against him on appeal because the plaintiff failed to file a bond within thirty days of the tribunal's determination. We do not agree.

While G. L. c. 231, § 60B, expressly provides a means by which an indigent plaintiff may move to have the amount of the bond reduced, the statute is silent on the question of whether the filing of such a motion will automatically stay the thirty-day deadline for posting the bond. We have not yet addressed this issue.

In determining that the filing of a motion to reduce the bond on the basis of indigency, which the plaintiff submitted with respect to his claim against Dr. Freidberg, did not automatically stay the deadline for posting the bond, the motion judge relied on "the absence of any invitation in the statutory language to allow flexibility in application of the time period." The motion judge's strict interpretation of G. L. c. 231, § 60B, might be true to its provision that "if said bond is not posted within thirty days of the tribunal's finding the action shall be dismissed." However, "time and again, we have stated that we should not accept the literal meaning of the words of a statute without regard for that statute's purpose and history." [ ]

"The statutory provision for reduction of bond is intended to avoid constitutional problems arising from denying to indigents access to the legal system." Denton v. Beth Israel Hosp., 392 Mass. 277, 280, 465 N.E.2d 779 (1984). "The Legislature did not intend that the procedures of § 60B should unreasonably obstruct the prosecution of meritorious malpractice claims. . . . " [ ] Thus, the bond reduction process set forth in G. L. c. 231, § 60B, was intended to alleviate the burden which the statute's bond requirement imposes on indigent plaintiffs.

The burden of acting on a motion to reduce the bond is on the tribunal judge.* * * Once the judge determines that the plaintiff is indigent, he or she must rule on the request to reduce the amount of the bond before the thirty-day period for filing the bond begins to run. Any other result would render the statute's bond reduction provisions for indigents meaningless.

4. Conclusion. We conclude that the medical malpractice tribunals erred in determining that the plaintiff's offers of proof with respect to Nurse Bartelson and Drs. Pfeifer and Seidman were insufficient to raise a legitimate question of liability appropriate for judicial inquiry. We further conclude that the motion judge erred in dismissing the plaintiff's claims against Dr. Freidberg for failure to post the required bond while the plaintiff's motion to reduce the bond was pending. This case is remanded to the Superior Court * * *

NEWELL v. RUIZ

United States Court of Appeals for the Third Circuit, 2002.
286 F.3d 166.

SCIRICA, Circuit Judge.

Romona Newell appeals the dismissal with prejudice of her medical malpractice claim for failure to timely file an Affidavit of Merit in accordance with * * * [the New Jersey Certificate of Merit Statute]. The issue on appeal is whether Newell's compliance with the Certificate of Merit Statute satisfied New Jersey's requirements because her action was transferred from New York to New Jersey.

Newell makes two arguments on appeal—first, that she substantially complied with the Affidavit of Merit Statute; second, that extraordinary circumstances warrant relaxation of the statutory requirements of [the New Jersey statute].

Romona Newell, a New York resident, commenced this medical malpractice action in the United States District Court for the Southern District of New York on March 24, 1999. She alleges Abraham Ruiz, M.D., and the Radiology Professional Association committed malpractice by failing to properly read and interpret her mammograms in June 1997. Newell, who previously had cancer in her right breast, alleges defendants failed to detect abnormal changes in the mammography of her left breast. As a result, she claims a delay in diagnosis and treatment caused the cancer to spread in her left breast and metastasize to other parts of her body. Romona Newell died of cancer in March 2001.

Complying with New York [law] which seeks to weed out frivolous malpractice claims, Newell submitted a "Certificate of Merit," attesting her attorney discussed the case with a physician, who advised there was reason to believe defendants committed malpractice. Dr. Ruiz filed an answer * * *. The Radiology Professional Association filed an answer * * * [and] the case was transferred to the United States District Court for the District of New Jersey.

On January 18, 2000, more than eight months after filing their answers in New York, defendants filed a motion to dismiss Newell's complaint for failure to comply with New Jersey's Affidavit of Merit Statute [ ]. Both the New Jersey and the New York statutes share the same purpose of winnowing out frivolous claims by requiring plaintiffs to make a threshold showing of merit. On February 11, 2000, Newell responded to the defendant's motion and supplied an Affidavit of Merit from a Board Certified Radiologist.[3]

II

A.

N.J. Stat. Ann. § 2A:53A–27 provides:

In any action for damages for personal injuries, wrongful death or property damage resulting from an alleged act of malpractice or negligence by a licensed person in his profession or occupation, the plaintiff shall, within 60 days following the date of filing of the answer to the complaint by the defendant, provide each defendant with an affidavit of an appropriate licensed person that there exists a reasonable probability that the care, skill or knowledge exercised or exhibited in the treatment, practice or work that is the subject of the complaint, fell outside acceptable professional or occupational standards or treatment practices. The court may grant no more than one additional period, not to exceed 60 days, to file the affidavit pursuant to this section, upon a finding of good cause. The person

---

3. The Affidavit declared: "In accordance with good and acceptable medical practice the findings of June 25, 1997 and the changes from the 1995 and the 1996 mammography's [sic] should have been noted in the report. The developing density at 6:00 left breast should have been noted in the report. The reports reviewed indicate that Romona Newell had a history of breast cancer of the right breast. In a woman with a personal history of breast cancer and a change in mammography ... further evaluation was required in accordance with good and accepted medical practice."

executing the affidavit shall be licensed in this or any other state; have particular expertise in the general area or specialty involved in the action, as evidenced by board certification or by devotion of the person's practice substantially to the general area or specialty involved in the action for a period of at least five years. The person shall have no financial interest in the outcome of the case under review, but this prohibition shall not exclude the person from being an expert witness in the case.

When construing a statute, "our 'overriding goal must be to determine the Legislature's intent.' [ ]." * * *

Newell contends she has a meritorious claim and that she substantially complied with New Jersey's Affidavit of Merit Statute. Because the statute does not address its applicability to cases transferred from another jurisdiction, she argues a narrow interpretation would thwart the legislature's intent of barring only frivolous claims.

B.

In several recent decisions, the New Jersey Supreme Court held that if "reasonable effectuation of the statute's purpose has occurred," the Affidavit of Merit Statute does not require strict compliance. * * *. In appropriate cases, "courts invoke the doctrine of substantial compliance to 'avoid technical defeats of valid claims.' " [ ]

The doctrine of substantial compliance requires the defaulting party to show: (1) the lack of prejudice to the defending party; (2) a series of steps taken to comply with the statute involved; (3) a general compliance with the purpose of the statute; (4) a reasonable notice of petitioner's claim; and (5) a reasonable explanation why there was not strict compliance with the statute. Id. This equitable doctrine "requires a fact-sensitive analysis involving the assessment of all the idiosyncratic details of a case to determine whether 'reasonable effectuation of the statute's purpose' has occurred." Galik, 771 A.2d at 1151 [ ].

There is no legal prejudice to the defendants. Newell's complaint, filed in New York federal court on March 24, 1999, was accompanied by a Certificate of Merit attesting to the validity of her claim. * * *

The second and third prongs of the substantial compliance doctrine are related. Newell took steps generally complying with the purpose of New Jersey's Affidavit of Merit Statute. The purpose of [the New Jersey statute] is to "weed out frivolous lawsuits early in the litigation while, at the same time, ensuring that plaintiffs with meritorious claims will have their day in court." [ ]. As noted, New York's [statute] has the same purpose as New Jersey's statute: to "improve the quality of medical malpractice adjudications and deter the commencement of frivolous cases." [ ]

New York's [statute] seeks to achieve this purpose by requiring that a complaint for malpractice actions be accompanied by a certificate, executed by the attorney for the plaintiff, declaring:

The attorney has reviewed the facts of the case and has consulted with at least one physician in medical malpractice actions . . . who is licensed to practice in this state or any other state and who the attorney reasonably believes is knowledgeable in the relevant issues involved in the particular action, and that the attorney has concluded on the basis of such review and consultation that there is a reasonable basis for the commencement of such action.

N.Y. C.P.L.R. § 3012–a.

* * *

Newell has presented a reasonable explanation for her actions. A New York resident, she filed her complaint in New York federal court. At the earliest stages of the litigation, it was reasonable for Newell to believe that New York's Certificate of Merit Statute applied and that by satisfying the statute, she had made a threshold showing her case was meritorious. Furthermore, the New Jersey Affidavit of Merit Statute provides no guidance on the statute's applicability to cases transferred from other jurisdictions, especially when the triggering event, the filing of defendant's Answer, occurs in another state. Even less does the New Jersey statute address a situation in which a substantially similar "merit requirement" has been met at the commencement of suit which best serves its purpose—in the transferor state.

This combination of interlocking factors makes Newell's explanation why there was not strict compliance with the statute reasonable.

* * *

III

Because Newell substantially complied with N.J. Stat. Ann. § 2A:53A–27, the District Court erred in dismissing her claim with prejudice.

We will reverse and remand for proceedings consistent with this opinion.

Notes

1) The effect of the waiver-of-claims or hold-harmless provisions would be to leave the consequences of dental students' negligence on the patients, in return for low-cost services. The *Porubiansky* court was unreceptive to creating a lower standard of care for dental students, though presumably the supervisors and the employer would have been liable for negligent supervision. The patients were in no economic position either to bargain for more rights or to insure themselves. In other cases challenging attempts to secure waivers of claims from patients, the court have given the same response. In *Tunkl v. Regents of the University of California*, 60 Cal.2d 92, 32 Cal.Rptr. 33, 383 P.2d 441 (1963) the court held that a release given to a research hospital was unenforceable.

2) Compare *Porubianski* with the following case, *St. Germain v. Pfeifer*. The defendant alleged that there should be a different standard of medical care applicable to first-year residents than would apply to more senior physicians. The only two courts to confront that argument, *Centman v. Cobb*, 581 N.E.2d 1286, 1289 (Ind. App. 1991) and *Jenkins v. Clark*, 7 Ohio App.3d 93, 101, 454 N.E.2d 541 (1982) were clear that there are not differing standards depending upon one's level of expertise.

3) In its 1985 medical liability package, the Illinois legislature enacted one of the first "certificate of merit" requirements to address the problem of frivolous medical malpractice actions:

Ill.Rev.Stat. Ch. 110. Practice

§ 2–622. Healing Art Malpractice

(a) In any action, whether in tort, contract or otherwise, in which the plaintiff seeks damages for injuries or death by reason of medical, hospital, or other healing art malpractice, the plaintiff's attorney * * * shall file an affidavit, attached to the original and all copies of the complaint, declaring one of the following:

1. That the affiant has consulted and reviewed the facts of the case with a health professional who the affiant reasonably believes is knowledgeable in the relevant issues involved in the particular action and who practices in the same specialty as the defendant if the defendant is a specialist; that the reviewing health professional has determined in a written report, after a review of the medical record and other relevant material involved in the particular action that there is a reasonable and meritorious cause for the filing of such action; and that the affiant has concluded on the basis of the reviewing health professional's review and consultation that there is a reasonable and meritorious cause for filing of such action. * * * A copy of the written report, clearly identifying the plaintiff and the reasons for the reviewing health professional's determination that a reasonable and meritorious cause for the filing of the action exists, must be attached to the affidavit, but information which would identify the reviewing health professional may be deleted from the copy so attached.

* * *

(g) The failure to file a certificate required by this section shall be grounds for dismissal under section 2–619.

After the law was enacted, three districts of the appellate court of Illinois declared it constitutional, but the district that includes Chicago declared that it unconstitutionally delegates the judicial power to persons outside the court system, in violation of the separation of powers clause of Ill.—S.H.A. Const. art. II, § 1, and art. VI, § 1. *DeLuna v. St. Elizabeth's Hosp.*, 184 Ill.App.3d 802, 132 Ill.Dec. 925, 540 N.E.2d 847 (1989). The Illinois experience was instructive to other jurisdictions that have since modeled similar legislation.

SECTION B. LITIGATION ALTERNATIVES AND HURDLES

Note on Agreements to Arbitrate Future Disputes

Most states enforce contract clauses in which the parties agree to arbitrate future disputes, as long as the contracts are otherwise valid. In routine commercial contracts between parties of approximately equal bargaining power, if one party goes to court, the court normally will stay the action and may order arbitration under the contract.

But the forms that patients sign in entering medical service relationships with health care providers are not routine commercial contracts. For example, when a patient goes to a hospital for acute care, and the hospital presents an admitting form that contains a future disputes arbitration clause, and the patient later wants to sue the hospital for medical negligence, the agreement to arbitrate is vulnerable to the charge that the patient never read it or never agreed to it, and so it may be held unenforceable as a contract of adhesion.[1] If arbitration is to function in this context, legislation is the answer, and a few states have enacted this kind of law.[2]

For example, in 1975, the California legislature included in the Medical Injury Compensation Reform Act (MICRA) two statutory texts for health care provider intake forms:

ARBITRATION OF MEDICAL MALPRACTICE
Cal.Code Civ.P. § 1295.

(a) Any contract for medical services which contains a provision for arbitration of any dispute as to professional negligence of a health care provider shall have such provision as the first article of the contract and shall be expressed in the following language:

> It is understood that any dispute as to medical malpractice, that is as to whether any medical services rendered under this contract were unnecessary or unauthorized or were improperly, negligently or incompetently rendered, will be determined by submission to arbitration as provided by California law, and not by a lawsuit or resort to court process except as California law provides for judicial review of arbitration proceedings. Both parties to this contract, by entering into it, are giving up their constitutional right to have any such dispute decided in a court of law before a jury, and instead are accepting the use of arbitration.

1. This was the result in California in a 1976 case testing a form signed in 1971. Wheeler v. St. Joseph Hosp., 63 Cal.App.3d 345, 133 Cal.Rptr. 775, 84 A.L.R.3d 343 (1976) (arbitration ordered and award confirmed; judgment reversed); see Annot., Arbitration of Medical Malpractice Claims, 84 A.L.R.3d 375 (1978).

2. The bulk of decisions nationwide come from California and Michigan. See McKinstry v. Valley Obstetrics–Gynecology Clinic, P.C., 428 Mich. 167, 405 N.W.2d 88 (1987) (validity of arbitration statute upheld with little discussion; text reprinted).

(b) Immediately before the signature line provided for the individual contracting for the medical services must appear the following in at least 10–point bold red type:

NOTICE: BY SIGNING THIS CONTRACT YOU ARE AGREE-ING TO HAVE ANY ISSUE OF MEDICAL MALPRACTICE DE-CIDED BY NEUTRAL ARBITRATION AND YOU ARE GIVING UP YOUR RIGHT TO A JURY OR COURT TRIAL. SEE ARTICLE 1 OF THIS CONTRACT.

(c) Once signed, such a contract governs all subsequent open-book account transactions for medical services for which the contract was signed until or unless rescinded by written notice within 30 days of signature. Written notice of such rescission may be given by a guardian or conservator of the patient if the patient is incapacitated or a minor.

(d) Where the contract is one for medical services to a minor, it shall not be subject to disaffirmance if signed by the minor's parent or legal guardian.

(e) Such a contract is not a contract of adhesion, nor unconscionable nor otherwise improper, where it complies with subdivisions (a), (b) and (c) of this section.

* * *

The California Supreme Court has not passed on the validity of § 1295, but a number of lower court cases have explored the coverage as to claims and persons,[3] and arbitration awards are not always received gladly by the doctors.[4]

MORRIS v. METRIYAKOOL;
JACKSON v. DETROIT MEMORIAL HOSPITAL

Supreme Court of Michigan, 1984.
418 Mich. 423, 344 N.W.2d 736.

KAVANAGH, J.

These cases concern arbitration of medical malpractice claims. The most significant issue presented is whether the [Michigan] malpractice arbitration act [ ] deprives plaintiffs of constitutional rights to an impartial decisionmaker. We hold that it does not.

Plaintiff Diane Jackson was treated in November, 1977, at defendant Detroit Memorial Hospital by defendant Dr. William J. Bloom for a dental malady. At that time, plaintiff agreed to submit to arbitration "any claims or disputes (except for disputes over charges for services

---

3. E.g., Gross v. James A. Recabaren, M.D., Inc., 206 Cal.App.3d 771, 253 Cal. Rptr. 820 (1988) (arbitration agreement held to cover both a series of unrelated procedures performed on the patient and his wife's claim for loss of consortium).

4. See Baker v. Sadick, 162 Cal.App.3d 618, 208 Cal.Rptr. 676 (1984) ($300,000 punitive damages affirmed), hearing denied.

rendered) which may arise in the future out of or in connection with the health care rendered to me * * * by this hospital, its employees and those of its independent staff doctors and consultants who have agreed to arbitrate." In August, 1979, plaintiff brought action for malpractice against defendants in the Wayne Circuit Court. Defendants moved for accelerated judgment, on the basis of the agreement to arbitrate. After a hearing, the court found the act constitutional and, finding no duress, mistake, or incompetency in the execution of the agreement, granted defendants' motion.

The Court of Appeals reversed, holding that [the Michigan law] violates the constitutional guarantee of due process by " 'forcing the litigant to submit his or her claim to a tribunal which is composed in such a way that a high probability exists that such tribunal will be biased against the claimant without mandating the use of an arbitration form explicitly detailing the nature of the panel's makeup' ". [ ] The Court also held that the arbitration agreement is not a contract of adhesion and that, on the present facts, it is not unconscionable. Defendants applied for leave to appeal, and plaintiffs sought leave to cross-appeal, which we granted.

In the second case before us, plaintiff Delores M. Morris was admitted to defendant South Macomb Hospital on November 9, 1976. At the time of her admission, plaintiff executed an agreement similar to the one executed by plaintiff Jackson to arbitrate any claims against defendant hospital and defendant Dr. S. Metriyakool arising out of her treatment for a hysterectomy. Subsequently, plaintiff brought suit against defendants alleging negligence in the surgical procedure, which caused her to develop peritonitis, and negligence in failing to promptly diagnose and treat the condition. Defendants each moved to submit plaintiff's claims to arbitration in accordance with the agreement. The trial court dismissed plaintiff's complaint with prejudice, but without prejudice to her right to file a claim for arbitration.

The Court of Appeals rejected plaintiff's argument that the composition of the arbitration panel was unconstitutionally biased. It also held that the act does not unconstitutionally or unconscionably deprive a patient of a meaningful opportunity to decide whether to relinquish access to a court and a jury trial. The Court further held that the agreement was not a contract of adhesion. Judge Bronson dissented from the holding of constitutionality. We granted plaintiff's application for leave to appeal.

The malpractice arbitration act provides that a patient "may, if offered, execute an agreement to arbitrate a dispute, controversy, or issue arising out of health care or treatment by a health care provider" [ ]or by a hospital.[ ] A patient executing such an agreement with a health-care provider may revoke it within 60 days after execution [ ] or, in the case of a hospital, within 60 days after discharge [ ] options which must be stated in the agreement. All such agreements must provide in 12–point boldface type immediately above the space for the parties' signatures that agreement to arbitrate is not a prerequisite to the receipt of health care. [ ]

For those who have elected arbitration, the act requires a three-member panel composed of an attorney, who shall be chairperson, a physician, preferably from the respondent's medical specialty, and a person who is not a licensee of the health-care profession involved, a lawyer, or a representative of a hospital or an insurance company. [ ] Where the claim is against a hospital only, a hospital administrator may be substituted for the physician. If the claim is against a health-care provider other than a physician, a licensee of the health-care profession involved shall be substituted.

Defendants Detroit Memorial Hospital and Dr. Bloom appeal from the holding that the presence of the medical member unconstitutionally created a biased panel. First, they argue that because the state does not compel arbitration, but only regulates it, state action is not involved.

A basic requirement of due process is a "fair trial in a fair tribunal". [ ] Essential to this notion is a fair and impartial decisionmaker. [ ]. The Due Process Clause, US Const, Am XIV; Const 1963, art 1, § 17, limits state action. [ ]. Private conduct abridging individual rights does not implicate the Due Process Clause unless to some significant extent the state, in any of its manifestations, has been found to have become involved in it [ ] or to have compelled the conduct [ ].

We find it unnecessary, however, to determine here whether the state has significantly involved itself in the challenged action because, even if we were to find so, we have concluded that the composition of the arbitration panel does not offend guarantees of due process.

* * *

In the present case [ ] it has not been demonstrated that the medical members of these panels have a direct pecuniary interest or that their decision may have any substantial effect on the availability of insurance or insurance premiums. We have been shown no grounds sufficient for us to conclude that these decisionmakers will not act with honesty and integrity. We look for a pecuniary interest which creates a probability of unfairness, a risk of actual bias which is too high to be constitutionally tolerable. It has not been shown here.

Plaintiff Jackson also argues that as a class physicians and hospital administrators possess a subliminal bias against patients who claim medical malpractice.

* * *

We do not believe that the medical members of these panels are so identified and aligned with respondents in malpractice cases that they may be expected to favor the respondents. Physicians and other health care professionals are trained in the medical arts and are oath-bound to treat the ill. Hospital administrators are trained in the proper functioning of hospitals. Neither physicians nor hospital administrators have professional interests that are adverse to patients or even malpractice claimants on a consistent, daily basis. Any identity of interest with respondents is not so strong as to create a subliminal bias for one side and against the other.

"All questions of judicial qualification may not involve constitutional validity. Thus matters of kinship, personal bias, state policy, remoteness of interest, would seem generally to be matters merely of legislative discretion." [ ] We are not persuaded that these arbitration panels deprive plaintiffs of fair and impartial decisionmaking.

Plaintiffs next argue that the arbitration agreement waives constitutional rights to a jury trial and access to a court. Because these fundamental rights are waived, they say, the burden should rest with the defendants to show a valid contract, which they can only do by showing that the waiver was made voluntarily, knowingly, and intelligently. The burden of showing a voluntary waiver is not an easy one, argue plaintiffs, because the arbitration agreement was offered at the time of admission to the hospital in an atmosphere infected with implicit coercion. Additionally, plaintiffs argue that a knowing and intelligent waiver will not be easily shown because the defendants are chargeable with constructive fraud. Constructive fraud is said to arise out of the agreement's failure to highlight the fact of waiver, failure to disclose the composition of the arbitration panel (even though this information is contained in an informational booklet accompanying the agreement), and failure to disclose the attitudes of physicians in general, that they and hospital administrators may be biased and the reasonable probability that insurance rates are affected by awards.

* * *

* * * [D]efendants contend that arbitration is a matter of contract and that one who signs a written agreement is presumed to understand it. The act presumes a conforming agreement to be valid [ ]. Therefore, the burden of disproving this arbitration agreement rests with plaintiffs. Moreover, say defendants, the burden of establishing a constitutional violation rests with the party asserting it. The arbitration agreement and informational booklet reasonably indicated that arbitration was an exclusive alternative to trial by jury. Plaintiffs expressly waived their rights to trial by jury. Arbitration is voluntary and not required, which the agreement plainly states in capital letters above the signature. The form of the agreement and the information booklet is strictly controlled [ ] and was approved by the Michigan Commissioner of Insurance.

Plaintiffs, contend defendants, have failed to demonstrate that they were coerced into signing the agreement. Answering the argument of constructive fraud, defendants say that the information booklet given to plaintiffs states that a doctor or hospital administrator serves on the arbitration panel. A chart in the booklet also states that a court case is heard by a judge and jury while an arbitration case is heard by the three-member panel.

We reject plaintiffs' allocation of the burden of proof to defendants. The burden of avoiding these arbitration agreements, as with other contracts, rests with those who would avoid them. The act states that an agreement to arbitrate which includes the statutory provisions shall be presumed valid. [ ]

* * *

Plaintiff Jackson contends that the arbitration agreement is a contract of adhesion, the terms of which exceeded her reasonable expectations. She claims that by not stating explicitly that court access with the right to jury trial was waived, this fact was in effect concealed and hence the contract is unconscionable.

Contracts of adhesion are characterized by standardized forms prepared by one party which are offered for rejection or acceptance without opportunity for bargaining and under the circumstances that the second party cannot obtain the desired product or service except by acquiescing in the form agreement. [ ] Regardless of any possible perception among patients that the provision of optimal medical care is conditioned on their signing the arbitration agreement, we believe that the sixty-day rescission period, of which patients must be informed, fully protects those who sign the agreement. The patients' ability to rescind the agreement after leaving the hospital allows them to obtain the desired service without binding them to its terms. As a result, the agreement cannot be considered a contract of adhesion.

We also reject plaintiff's claim that the arbitration agreement is unconscionable. According to the record before us, the arbitration agreement signed by plaintiff Jackson is six paragraphs long. The first sentence of the first paragraph begins, "I understand that this hospital and I by signing this document agree to arbitrate any claims or disputes". The first two sentences of the second paragraph state:

"I understand that Michigan Law gives me the choice of trial by judge or jury or of arbitration. I understand that arbitration is a procedure by which a panel that is either mutually agreed upon or appointed decides the dispute rather than a judge or jury."

This was not a long contract covering different terms, only one of which, obscured among many paragraphs, concerned arbitration. Arbitration was the essential and singular nature of the agreement. We do not believe that an ordinary person signing this agreement to arbitrate would reasonably expect a jury trial. We also reject plaintiffs' argument that the agreement is unconscionable for failure to highlight these terms. [ ]

Finally, both plaintiffs ask that we find constructive fraud and hold that the agreements are unconscionable because of failure of the contracts to disclose the composition of the panel, the attitudes of physicians, the fact that the medical member of the panel may be intrinsically biased against plaintiffs, and the reasonable probability that malpractice rates are affected by awards in medical malpractice cases.

We decline. We do not believe that the agreements are unconscionable for failing to include plaintiffs' recommendations. Nor do we believe that defendants have breached a legal or equitable duty which has had the effect of deceiving plaintiffs, nor have defendants received an unmerited benefit. [ ]

In *Jackson*, we reverse the finding of unconstitutionality and reinstate the order of the trial court submitting the matter to arbitration.

In *Morris,* we affirm.

BRIARCLIFF NURSING HOME v. TURCOTTE

Supreme Court of Alabama, 2004.
2004 WL 226087.

PER CURIAM.

Briarcliff Nursing Home, Inc., d/b/a Integrated Health Services at Briarcliff, and James Anthony Clements, the defendants in actions pending in the Shelby Circuit Court, appeal the denial of their motions to compel the plaintiffs David Turcotte, executor of the estate of Noella Turcotte, deceased, and Kyra L. Woodman, administratrix of the estate of Sarah Carter, deceased, to arbitrate their wrongful-death claims. The appeals have been consolidated because they raise identical issues. We reverse and remand.

I.

Turcotte and Woodman separately sued Briarcliff and Clements for the alleged wrongful deaths of Noella Turcotte and Sarah Carter while Noella and Sarah were residents at a nursing home owned and operated by Briarcliff. Clements was the administrator of the nursing home at the time of Noella's and Sarah's deaths. (Briarcliff and Clements are hereinafter collectively referred to as "Briarcliff.") Briarcliff moved to compel arbitration on the ground that agents for Noella and Sarah had signed admission contracts that contained an arbitration provision. Turcotte and Woodman opposed the motions to compel arbitration on the grounds that neither of them, in their capacities as executor and administratrix, respectively, of the deceased estates had signed or had otherwise entered into the admission contracts and that the "fiduciary parties" who signed the admission contracts for Noella and Sarah while they were alive could not contractually affect the then nonexistent wrongful-death claims. Turcotte and Woodman also argued that the arbitration provision was a part of a contract of adhesion and was unconscionable.

The arbitration provision in the admission contract reads:

"Pursuant to the Federal Arbitration Act, any action, dispute, claim or controversy of any kind (e.g., whether in contract or in tort, statutory or common law, legal or equitable, or otherwise) now existing or hereafter arising between the parties in any way arising out of, pertaining to or in connection with the provision of health care services, any agreement between the parties, the provision of any other goods or services by the

Health Care Center or other transactions, contracts or agreements of any kind whatsoever, any past, present or future incidents, omissions, acts, errors, practices, or occurrence causing injury to either party whereby the other party or its agents, employees or representatives may be liable, in whole or in part, or any other aspect of the past, present or future relationships between the parties shall be resolved by binding arbitration administered by the National Health Lawyers Association (the 'NHLA').

"THE UNDERSIGNED ACKNOWLEDGE THAT EACH OF THEM HAS READ AND UNDERSTOOD THIS CONTRACT, AND THAT EACH OF THEM VOLUNTARILY CONSENTS TO ALL OF ITS TERMS."

(Boldface type and capitalization original.) The admission contract relating to Noella is signed by David Turcotte in his capacity as "Fiduciary Party," and the admission contract relating to Sarah is signed by Kyra Woodman in her capacities as "Fiduciary Party" and "Attorney–In–Fact under [a] validly executed power of attorney."

The trial court denied Briarcliff's motions to compel arbitration. Briarcliff appeals, arguing that Turcotte and Woodman must arbitrate their wrongful-death claims because Noella and Sarah, through their agents, signed the admission contracts containing the arbitration provision.

II.

The standard of review of a trial court's ruling on a motion to compel arbitration is de novo. [ ].

" 'The party seeking to compel arbitration has the initial burden of proving the existence of a contract calling for arbitration and proving that the contract evidences a transaction substantially affecting interstate commerce. "After a motion to compel arbitration has been made and supported, the burden is on the nonmovant to present evidence that the supposed arbitration agreement is not valid or does not apply to the dispute in question." ' " [ ]

III.

Turcotte and Woodman brought these wrongful-death actions in the names of "the Estate of Noella Turcotte, by and through its Executor David Turcotte" and "the Estate of Sarah Carter by and through its Administratrix, Kyra L. Woodman," respectively. The wrongdoing alleged in both complaints is predicated upon an alleged breach of the duties owed by Briarcliff to Noella and Sarah as residents of the nursing home. Both Noella and Sarah were residents of the nursing home pursuant to the admission contracts, which contained the arbitration provisions. Therefore, Noella's and Sarah's personal representatives are seeking to impose duties that arise from the admission contracts, but they also seek to avoid the arbitration provisions of the same contracts under which they seek recovery.

In SouthTrust Bank, 835 So.2d 990, the underlying dispute involved SouthTrust's negligent cashing of a check on Edwin Edwards's account. Edwards died before the dispute was resolved, and Melody Ford, his daughter, as the administratrix of Edwards's estate, sued SouthTrust alleging that it had negligently cashed the check. She also sued South-Trust in her individual capacity, asserting related claims. The deposit agreement that governed Edwards's account at SouthTrust contained an arbitration provision. On the basis of that provision, SouthTrust moved to compel arbitration; the trial court denied the motion. SouthTrust appealed, and this Court found that "Melody's claim to recover the value of the improperly paid check is subject to arbitration because she is asserting that claim in her role as the administratrix of Edwards's estate." Id. at 994. We further stated:

"We recognize that an administratrix of a decedent's estate stands in the shoes of the decedent. We also recognize that the 'powers [of an executor], in collecting the debts constituting the assets of the estate, are just as broad as those of the deceased.' For the same reason the powers of an executor or an administrator encompasses all of those formerly held by the decedent, those powers must likewise be restricted in the same manner and to the same extent as the powers of the decedent would have been. Thus, where an executor or administrator asserts a claim on behalf of the estate, he or she must also abide by the terms of any valid agreement, including an arbitration agreement, entered into by the decedent."

[ ] Therefore, in this case, Turcotte, as executor of Noella's estate, and Woodman, as administratrix of Sarah's estate, are bound by the arbitration provisions contained in the admission contracts.

Alabama's wrongful-death statute, § 6–5–410(a), Ala. Code 1975, provides:

"(a) A personal representative may commence an action and recover such damages as the jury may assess . . . for the wrongful act, omission, or negligence of any person, persons, or corporation, his or their servants or agents, whereby the death of his testator or intestate was caused, provided the testator or intestate could have commenced an action for such wrongful act, omission, or negligence if it had not caused death."

In the present case, Noella and Sarah could not have commenced an action against Briarcliff for its wrongful acts because they agreed to arbitrate those claims against Briarcliff; therefore, their executor and administratrix, respectively, may not commence such an action.

IV.

We now address Turcotte and Woodman's claims that the arbitration provision was unconscionable. "The burden of proving unconscionability of an arbitration agreement rests with the party challenging the agreement." [ ]. In Vann v. First Community Credit Corp., 834 So.2d 751, 753 (Ala. 2002), this Court stated:

"In determining whether a contract is unconscionable, courts look to four factors: '(1) whether there was an absence of meaningful choice on one party's part, (2) whether the contractual terms are unreasonably favorable to one party, (3) whether there was unequal bargaining power among the parties, and (4) whether there was oppressive, one-sided or patently unfair terms in the contract.' Layne v. Garner, 612 So.2d 404, 408 (Ala. 1992)."

* * *

A.   Terms that are grossly favorable to a party.

Turcotte and Woodman argue that, because the arbitration provision provides that disputes shall be resolved by arbitration administered by the National Health Lawyers Association ("NHLA"), this "dispute resolution procedure is 'unreasonably favorable' to the industry and 'is oppressive, one-sided [and] patently unfair' to the typical, aged nursing home resident." [ ]. Turcotte and Woodman argue that because the NHLA is part of the American Health Lawyers Association ("AHLA"), which, they argue, is a "puppet for the health care and long term care industries" [ ], the industry "further 'stacks the deck' by establishing a system of dispute resolution wherein industry insiders and employers bear sole, non-appealable decision making authority. Such one sided forms of dispute resolution were never envisioned by the drafters of the FAA." [ ] Turcotte and Woodman cite Aetna Life Insurance Co. v. Lavoie, 475 U.S. 813, 824, 89 L.Ed.2d 823, 106 S.Ct. 1580 (1986), holding that constitutional due process entitles parties to unbiased decision-makers. However, Turcotte and Woodman have not established that the NHLA is biased in conducting its arbitration proceedings. Turcotte's and Woodman's only support for this proposition is the "History" of the AHLA provided on its Web site. There is no evidence indicating that the NHLA is biased in its arbitration proceedings, nor is there any other evidence indicating that the terms of the arbitration provision are grossly favorable to either party, or that the admission contract is "oppressive, one-sided and patently unfair." Therefore, we conclude that Turcotte and Woodman have not established that the terms of the arbitration provision grossly favor Briarcliff.

B.   Overwhelming bargaining power.

Turcotte and Woodman argue that Shelby County has only two nursing homes and that, therefore, "there can be no 'meaningful choice' on the part of potential residents"; thus, they argue, "to say that [Briarcliff and the other local nursing home] have unequal bargaining power is therefore an understatement." However, even if there are only two nursing homes in Shelby County, Turcotte and Woodman have not asserted that an elderly person in Shelby County lacks meaningful options to live in a nursing-home in another county or to have in-home care.

Turcotte and Woodman argue that to meet their burden of proof it is not necessary for them to show that the nursing-home market was completely closed. Indeed, in American General Finance, Inc. v. Branch, 793 So.2d at 751, this Court stated that "in order to meet her burden of proof on this issue [overwhelming bargaining power], a consumer need not show that the market was completely closed, only that she was unable to acquire goods or services without considerable expenditure of time and resources." Turcotte and Woodman have not shown that they were "unable to acquire" nursing-home care for Noella and Sarah "without considerable expenditure of time and resources." The only support offered by Turcotte and Woodman for their argument is that, according to the 2000 federal decennial census, Shelby County has 143,293 residents, 8.5% of whom are "persons 65 years old and over." Turcotte and Woodman argue that these figures mean that there are 12,180 elderly persons in Shelby County "fighting to get into two nursing homes with a combined maximum of 361 beds." [ ]. Turcotte and Woodman fail to recognize that not every person 65 years of age and older is in need of or desires nursing-home care. Turcotte and Woodman fail to provide any evidence regarding the actual number of elderly persons seeking to reside in nursing homes in Shelby County.

In Branch, Branch submitted several affidavits from merchants stating that those merchants also required arbitration. In other words, Branch submitted evidence indicating that the service she was seeking was not available unless she agreed to arbitration. In the present case, Turcotte and Woodman have not shown that nursing home care is unavailable without agreeing to arbitration. Therefore, Turcotte and Woodman did not demonstrate "an absence of a meaningful choice," [ ] did Turcotte and Woodman demonstrate that Briarcliff had overwhelming bargaining power.

Because Turcotte and Woodman have not shown that the terms of the arbitration provision grossly favor Briarcliff or that Briarcliff has overwhelming bargaining power, we conclude that Turcotte and Woodman have not met their burden of proof that the arbitration provision is unconscionable.

Turcotte and Woodman argue also that the admission contract is a contract of adhesion. A contract of adhesion is " 'one that is offered on a "take it or leave it" basis to a consumer who has no meaningful choice in the acquisition of the goods or services.' " [ ]. Because Turcotte and Woodman have not demonstrated that Noella and Sarah did not have a "meaningful choice" when deciding on nursing-home care, we conclude that Turcotte and Woodman failed to establish that the contract before us is one of adhesion.

V.

Because Turcotte and Woodman are bound by the admission contracts, we find that the trial court erred in denying Briarcliff's motions to compel arbitration. We also conclude that the arbitration provision is not unconscionable and that the contract containing the arbitration provision is not one of adhesion, and that Briarcliff's activities substantially affect interstate commerce. Therefore, we reverse the trial court's orders denying Briarcliff's motions to compel arbitration and remand the case for further proceedings consistent with this opinion.

REVERSED AND REMANDED.

RAITERI v. NHC HEALTHCARE/KNOXVILLE, INC.

Court of Appeals of Tennessee, at Knoxville, 2003.
2003 WL 23094413.

SUSANO, J.

Lynn Raiteri, as the daughter and next friend of the late Mary Helen Cox ("Mrs. Cox"), sued NHC Healthcare/Knoxville, Inc. ("the defendant"), as well as others for the wrongful death of Mrs. Cox, whose death allegedly resulted from improper care at the defendant's nursing home. We granted the plaintiff's [ ] application for an interlocutory appeal in order to review the trial court's order granting the defendant's motion to compel mediation and arbitration pursuant to the dispute resolution procedures contained in the defendant's nursing home admission agreement. We reverse.

A.

Mrs. Cox, age 77, was admitted to St. Mary's Hospital with chest pains and other symptoms. Her husband, Charles E. Cox ("Mr. Cox"), age 75, anticipated that his wife would receive physical therapy at St. Mary's so she could regain some or all of her mobility; but apparently the hospital was not prepared to render these services to her. Since Mr. Cox was physically unable to lift and otherwise care for his wife at home, he made arrangements to admit her to the defendant's nursing home. On December 20, 2000, Mr. Cox met at the nursing home with the defendant's admissions coordinator. Mrs. Cox was not present at the meeting. The admissions coordinator asked Mr. Cox to sign the nursing home's "Admission and Financial Contract" ("the admission agreement") on his wife's behalf, even though Mrs. Cox had not been diagnosed or adjudicated as mentally incompetent. He complied with her request. It was the intention of the parties that Mrs. Cox would receive physical therapy and vocational rehabilitation services at the nursing home.

Sometime shortly after his wife's admission to the defendant's facility, Mr. Cox also was admitted to the defendant's nursing home. On March 8, 2001, Mr. Cox passed away. Mrs. Cox, while still a resident at the nursing home, died on April 19, 2001. Following her mother's death, the plaintiff filed suit for Mrs. Cox's wrongful death, alleging that the negligence, abuse, neglect, and fraud of the defendant caused her mother's death. In her complaint, the plaintiff seeks compensatory and punitive damages. In response to the complaint, the defendant filed a motion seeking to compel mediation and arbitration.

B.

Before ruling on the defendant's motion, the trial court held an evidentiary hearing. The defendant's admissions coordinator was the only witness for the defendant. She testified that she met with Mr. Cox and that he read and signed the admission agreement as Mrs. Cox's "legal representative." While acknowledging that she handled some 360 admissions a year, she claimed that she remembered that Mr. Cox read the admission agreement. When asked if and how she could remember at the time of the hearing—on September 4, 2002—that Mr. Cox had read the admission agreement some two years earlier, she responded, "I do because all of my admissions read the contract. I see to that."

It is undisputed that Mr. Cox can read. Although the admission agreement specifically defines the term "legal representative" as "anyone authorized by the [patient] to act on the [patient's] behalf," the admissions coordinator admitted that she did not receive any indication from either of the Coxes that Mr. Cox was authorized to sign on Mrs. Cox's behalf. She stated that she did not know if Mr. Cox had his wife's authorization to act on her behalf. She testified that she allowed him to sign the admission agreement simply because he was Mrs. Cox's husband. The admissions coordinator went on to testify that she believed Mrs. Cox was competent when Mr. Cox signed the admission agreement. Despite Mrs. Cox's unquestioned mental capacity, the admissions coordinator did not discuss the admission agreement with her; furthermore, she did not give Mrs. Cox a copy of that document. She stated that she did not know whether Mrs. Cox was ever made aware of the terms and conditions of the admission agreement. Significantly, the admissions coordinator acknowledged that Mrs. Cox "was capable of understanding it," *i.e.* the admission agreement. One of her children described her as "fine mentally" and "very competent."

The admissions coordinator confirmed that Mrs. Cox would not have been admitted if Mr. Cox had refused to sign the admission agreement or had refused to assent to the terms of the dispute resolution procedures in the agreement, which provisions included one waiving Mrs. Cox's right to a jury trial. The admissions coordinator also testified that she informed Mr. Cox of his right to revoke the entire admission agreement within 30 days; however, the witness admitted that Mr. Cox could only revoke the entire agreement, not just the provisions dealing with the dispute resolution procedures. She claimed that she explained the admission agreement to Mr. Cox and encouraged him to ask questions; in response to a question, she stated that she did not tell Mr. Cox that he had the right to consult with an attorney before signing the admission agreement. The admissions coordinator also admitted that she told Mr. Cox that any claim would be settled quickly if it was handled via the dispute resolution procedures in the admission agreement.

At the evidentiary hearing, Mrs. Cox's three children testified for the plaintiff. All three children stated that they believed their mother was fully competent when Mr. Cox signed the admission agreement.

None of Mrs. Cox's three children were aware of any document signed by Mrs. Cox or any other conduct on her part authorizing her husband to act on her behalf or to sign documents for her. The three children agreed that their mother was "sharp" mentally. It is clear from the testimony that the children considered her more mentally competent than her husband.

Contrary to the admissions coordinator's testimony that Mr. Cox was aware of what he was doing, the plaintiff testified that her stepfather "was very upset, very agitated, [and] very confused" after he signed the agreement. The plaintiff also testified that her stepfather told her that his "only choice" was to have his wife admitted to the nursing home because he was physically unable to take care of her. Sandra Nelson, the plaintiff's sister, also testified that she saw Mr. Cox after he signed the admission agreement and that he "was very upset," "distraught," and "was just absolutely bawling." David Cox also spoke to his father that day and confirmed that his father was crying and upset about his inability to care for his wife and the necessity for admitting her to a nursing home.

Ms. Nelson pointed out that she had to admit her stepfather to the nursing home soon after he had signed the admission agreement for his wife. At the time of his admission, he was diagnosed with "pneumonia, malnutrition, dehydration, and [high blood sugar]." Ms. Nelson also met with the admissions coordinator, who told Ms. Nelson that she could legally sign for her stepfather, even though Ms. Nelson did not have explicit authority to do so. Only after Ms. Nelson signed the admission agreement did the admissions coordinator arrange to have powers of attorney executed by the Coxes so Ms. Nelson could act on behalf of her mother and stepfather.

Ms. Nelson testified that, when she commented that reading the admission agreement would take a long time, the admissions coordinator said "That's quite all right. I will explain [the admission agreement] to you." Despite the admissions coordinator's assurances, Ms. Nelson claimed that the admissions coordinator never mentioned mediation or arbitration or pointed out to her that, by signing the document, she was waiving Mr. Cox's right to a jury trial. Instead, Ms. Nelson claimed that the admissions coordinator gave one sentence explanations while quickly flipping through the document.

C.

The admission agreement was admitted into evidence. The dispute resolution procedures read as follows:

DISPUTE RESOLUTION PROCEDURE:

1. Initial Grievance Procedure: The parties agree to follow the Grievance procedure described in the Patient Rights Booklet for any claims or disputes arising out of or in connection with the care rendered to Patient by Center and/or its employees. Patient should know that

Center is prepared to mediate any concerns at any time upon patient request (paragraph 2 below).

2. MEDIATION: In the event there is a dispute and/or disputes arising out of or relating to (i) this contract or the breach thereof or any tort claim; or (ii) whether or not there had been a violation of any right or rights granted under state law, and the parties are unable to resolve such dispute through negotiation, then the parties agree in good faith to attempt to settle the dispute by mediation administered by the Alternative Dispute Resolution Service of the American Health Lawyers Association before resorting to arbitration. The Administrative Fee and mediator's compensation shall be paid by the center.

3. ARBITRATION: Any disputes not settled by mediation within 60 days after a mediator is appointed shall be resolved by binding arbitration administered by the Alternative Dispute Resolution Service of the American Health Lawyers Association, and judgment may be entered in any court having jurisdiction thereof. The arbitrator(s) shall be selected from a panel having experience and knowledge of the health care industry. The same person shall not serve as both the mediator and the arbitrator. The place of arbitration shall be where the Center is located, or, if that is not practical, then as close to the Center as practical. This agreement shall be governed by and interpreted in accordance with the laws of the State. The award shall be made within nine months of the commencement of the arbitration proceedings and the arbitrators shall agree to comply with this schedule before accepting appointment. However, this time limit may be extended by agreement of all the parties or by the arbitrator(s) if it is absolutely necessary, but not to exceed six months. The arbitrator(s) may award compensatory and punitive damages, and with respect to punitive damages arising under State statutes shall comply with the provisions of State statute. By agreeing to arbitration of all disputes, both parties are waiving a jury trial for all contract, tort, statutory and other claims. The award of attorneys' fees and costs of the arbitration shall be determined by the arbitrator(s) in accordance to state law. The Administrative Fee and Arbitrator's compensation shall be paid for by the center.

(Bold print and capitalization in original). Immediately following these provisions is the signature of Mr. Cox dated December 20, 2000.

The admission agreement is eleven pages long. The mediation and arbitration provisions begin at the bottom of page nine and continue on page ten. The dispute resolution procedures are printed in the same color ink, font size, and font type as the rest of the admission agreement. The mediation and arbitration provisions do not include a statement to the patient encouraging him or her to ask questions. However, as in several other areas in the admission agreement, the patient or the patient's legal representative is required to sign immediately following the text, in addition to his or her signature at the end of the document.

The arbitration provisions do not expressly state who is responsible for choosing the arbitrator; instead, the text only states that the "arbitrator(s) shall be selected from a panel having experience and knowledge of the health care industry." The arbitration provisions state that "by agreeing to arbitration of all disputes, *both parties are waiving a jury trial* . . . . " (Emphasis added).

According to the admission agreement, the term "parties" refers to the patient and/or the patient's legal representative and the defendant. As previously noted in this opinion, the term "legal representative" is defined in the admission agreement as "anyone authorized by the [patient] to act on the [patient's] behalf." The dispute resolution procedures do not explain in any detail how mediation or arbitration works; however, the provisions do explain where the process will occur and who will administer it. In the event of mediation or arbitration, the defendant is required to pay the fees associated with the process.

D.

Following the evidentiary hearing, the trial court granted the defendant's motion to compel mediation and arbitration. * * *

The trial court subsequently granted the plaintiff's motion for an interlocutory appeal.

II.

Tennessee has adopted a version of the Uniform Arbitration Act. The Tennessee version provides, in relevant part, that "a provision in a written contract to submit to arbitration any controversy thereafter arising between the parties is valid, enforceable and irrevocable save upon such grounds as exist at law or in equity for the revocation of any contract." [ ].

The Supreme Court in *Buraczynski v. Eyring*, 919 S.W.2d 314 (Tenn. 1996) held that arbitration agreements between physicians and their patients are "not void as against public policy, and are therefore enforceable under the Tennessee Arbitration Act." [ ]. The High Court pointed out that "under the terms of the [Tennessee Arbitration Act], arbitration agreements generally are enforceable unless grounds for their revocation exist in equity or in contract law." [ ]. The court noted a word of caution:

We caution, however, that such agreements may constitute contracts of adhesion which must be closely scrutinized to determine if unconscionable or oppressive terms are imposed upon the patient which prevent enforcement of the agreement.

After determining that no "facial features," in the arbitration agreement under discussion would prevent enforcement, the court stated that this did not end the inquiry. The court explained what it meant by this comment:

We must examine the agreements in question to determine whether they are contracts of adhesion, and if so, whether they contain such unconscionable or oppressive terms as to render them unenforceable.

Alluding to cases from other jurisdictions, the court indicated that it had to decide whether "such [arbitration] agreements are *unenforceable* contracts of adhesion." Quoting directly from Black's Law Dictionary 40 (6th ed. 1990), the Supreme Court defined a contract of adhesion as a standardized contract form offered to consumers of goods and services on essentially a "take it or leave it" basis, without affording the consumer a realistic opportunity to bargain and under such conditions that the consumer cannot obtain the desired product or service except by acquiescing to the form of the contract.

The court noted that the "distinctive feature" of a contract of adhesion "is that the weaker party [*i.e.*, the consumer] has no realistic choice as to its terms." [ ]. The Supreme Court emphasized, however, that a contract of adhesion is not automatically unenforceable. *Eyring.*

The court in *Eyring* concluded that the two identical arbitration agreements before it were contracts of adhesion. It gave its rationale for this conclusion:

The agreements are standardized form contracts prepared by the contracting party with superior knowledge of the subject matter—the rendition of medical services. The agreements, by Eyring's own admission, were offered to the patients on a "take it or leave it" basis. Had these patients refused to sign the agreements, Eyring would not have continued rendering medical care to them. Although the patients could have refused to sign the arbitration agreements and sought out another physician in the area, that action would have terminated the physician-patient relationship (ordinarily one of trust) and interrupted the course of the patient's treatment. To make any choice would be difficult; but to choose not to sign would result in the loss of the desired service—medical treatment from *Eyring.*

The court next turned to the question of whether contracts of adhesion are *enforceable*, stating that enforceability generally depends upon whether the terms of the contract are beyond the reasonable expectations of an ordinary person, or oppressive or unconscionable.

After reviewing cases from other jurisdictions, the court stated that,

in general, courts are reluctant to enforce arbitration agreements between patients and health care providers when the agreements are hidden within other types of contracts and do not afford the patients an opportunity to question the terms or purpose of the agreement. This is so particularly when the agreements require the patient to choose between forever waiving the right to a trial by jury or foregoing necessary medical treatment, and when the agreements give the health care provider an unequal advantage in the arbitration process itself.

The Supreme Court in *Eyring* determined that the agreements before it were enforceable. The High Court reasoned that nothing in the agreements was unconscionable, oppressive, or outside the reasonable expectations of the parties in that case. The court mentioned the following facts as supportive of its conclusion: (1) the agreement was a "separate, one page document[ ] . . . entitled 'Physician–Patient Arbitration Agreement' "; (2) the agreement had an attached "short explanation" that encouraged the patient to ask questions; (3) the physician did not have an unfair advantage in the arbitration procedure; (4) the patient was clearly informed in "ten-point, capital letter red type" that "by signing this contract you are giving up your right to a jury or court trial"; (5) the terms of the agreement are clearly "laid out" and are not buried, including the term that binds the patient's spouse and heirs to the agreement; (6) a patient may revoke the agreement within 30 days and "regain" the right to a trial by jury; and (7) the arbitration agreement "merely [shifts] the disputes to a different forum," rather than limiting liability.

In *Howell v. NHC/Healthcare–Fort Sanders, Inc.*, 109 S.W.3d 731 (Tenn. Ct. App. 2003), we applied the holding in *Eyring* and determined that a mediation and arbitration provision contained in a nursing home's admission agreement was unenforceable. [ ]. The husband in *Howell* executed an admission agreement for his wife before she was admitted to the defendant's nursing home. The wife had to be placed in the nursing home quickly, and the admission agreement had to be executed before she could be admitted. Because the patient's husband could not read, the admissions coordinator undertook to explain the terms of the agreement to him. The estate of the patient subsequently sued the nursing home, claiming abuse and neglect, as well as "infliction of physical suffering and mental anguish." [ ] The nursing home filed a motion to compel mediation and arbitration. *Id.* Before ruling, the trial court conducted an evidentiary hearing where the admissions coordinator, the patient's husband, and the patient's children testified. [ ]

The trial court in *Howell*, which, as previously noted, is the same court as in the instant case, refused to order mediation or arbitration. Its refusal was based upon its determination that the admission agreement was unenforceable because (1) the patient's husband could not read and (2) the admissions coordinator failed to explain that by signing the agreement he was waiving his wife's right to a jury trial. [ ]. We affirmed the trial court in *Howell* because the nursing home "had not demonstrated that the parties bargained over the arbitration terms, or that it [sic] was within the reasonable expectations of an ordinary person." [ ].

We held in *Howell* that the party seeking to enforce an alternative dispute resolution agreement must show that the parties " 'actually' bargained over the arbitration provision or that it was a reasonable term considering the circumstances." [ ].

In *Howell*, we relied upon the following facts in deciding the agreement there was not enforceable: (1) the agreement was eleven pages long and the mediation and arbitration provisions were on page ten; (2) the arbitration and mediation provisions were " 'buried' " in the larger admission agreement, "rather than being a stand-alone document"; (3) the arbitration and mediation provisions were printed in the same font size as the other text in the agreement; (4) "the arbitration paragraph does not adequately explain how the arbitration procedure would work, except as who would administer it"; (5) the patient had to be admitted in a nursing home "expeditiously" and the admission agreement had to be signed first; (6) the admission agreement was presented to the patient's husband on a "take-it-or-leave-it" basis; (7) the patient's husband "had no real bargaining power"; and (8) the patient's husband could not read and the nursing home representative did not "adequately" explain the provision that waived the patient's right to a jury trial. *Id.* at 734–35.

III.

The plaintiff in the instant case makes numerous arguments on appeal. She asserts that the mediation and arbitration language in the instant case is identical to the language that was declared unenforceable in *Howell*. Next, she argues that the mediation and arbitration provisions in this case contain terms that the Supreme Court declared unenforceable in *Eyring*. She further argues that the agreement is not enforceable because Mr. Cox did not have authority to waive any of his wife's rights or bind her to the dispute resolution procedures. She contends that Mr. Cox did not have authority or capacity to consent to arbitration because he did not "knowingly and intelligently" waive his wife's right to a jury trial.

* * *

We hold that the admission agreement in the instant case is a contract of adhesion because the admissions coordinator offered it to Mr. Cox on a take-it-or-leave-it basis, *i.e.*, Mr. Cox had to sign the agreement as written or his wife would not be admitted. [ ] Mr. Cox, as the weaker party, was not afforded an opportunity to bargain over the terms of the agreement. He certainly had no opportunity to bargain over the mediation and arbitration provisions. He was handed a form contract, under, what was for him, very trying circumstances, *i.e.*, his need to quickly find accommodations for his ailing wife. It is clear he had two options: sign the form contract as presented to him by the defendant, thereby clearing the way for his wife's admission to the defendant's facility or refuse to sign the contract and thereafter try to make arrangements for his wife's shelter and related accommodations. This is a classic case of a contract of adhesion.

Following the teachings of *Eyring* and *Howell*, we hold that the mediation and arbitration provisions are unenforceable. In so holding, we rely upon the following facts: unlike *Eyring*, the dispute resolution procedures in this case are a part of an eleven page contract dealing with many issues, including financial arrangements and consent to care, rather than being set forth in a separate stand-alone document; the dispute resolution procedures do not contain any type of "short explanation" encouraging patients to ask questions; essential terms in the mediation and arbitration provisions are "buried" and not clearly "laid out"; there are no provisions addressing how mediation and arbitration work; most significantly, the provision waiving a patient's right to a jury trial is buried—and in no way highlighted—in the third paragraph of the mediation and arbitration provisions; the dispute resolution procedures seem to imply that the defendant alone is responsible for choosing the arbitrator; and, unlike the arbitration agreement in *Eyring*, the dispute resolution procedures before us, including the provision waiving a jury trial, are printed in the same font size, type, and color as the rest of the agreement.

As a stand-alone basis for our decision, we conclude that the evidence before us preponderates against the trial court's implicit decision that Mr. Cox had authority to sign the admission agreement on behalf of his wife. There is absolutely no evidence that he had her express authority to sign for her. We also hold that the defendant cannot rely upon the concept of apparent authority. The evidence reflects that Mrs. Cox had her mental faculties, was "sharper" than her husband, and was otherwise in a position to indicate whether she assented to the terms of these significant contract provisions. The record is also devoid of any exigent circumstances that would clothe Mr. Cox with apparent authority to bind his wife to the admission agreement, particularly the alternative dispute resolution provisions. We certainly find nothing in the record before us, either factually or legally, warranting a holding that Mr. Cox had the right to waive his wife's very valuable constitutional right to a jury trial to adjudicate her rights in this matter. As the admissions coordinator acknowledged, Mrs. Cox "was capable of understanding" the admission agreement. The admissions coordinator did not adequately explain why she did not insist upon Mrs. Cox signing the admission agreement, or, at a minimum, why she did not ask Mrs. Cox to ratify what her husband had purported to do on her behalf.

IV.

In summary, we hold that Mr. Cox did not have the actual or apparent authority to bind Mrs. Cox to the alternative dispute resolution provisions in the admission agreement. Furthermore, these provisions, especially the waiver of the right to a jury trial, are outside the reasonable expectations of a reasonable consumer, and, hence, unenforceable. Following *Eyring* and *Howell*, we hold that the trial court erred when it decreed that the mediation and arbitration terms were enforceable. Therefore, we conclude that the judgment below must be reversed.

Notes

1) In *Imbler v. PacifiCare*, 103 Cal.App.4th 567, 126 Cal.Rptr.2d 715 (2002), a California Appeals Court upheld the trial court's ruling that an Insurer's arbitration provision was not prominently displayed in the enrollment plan. According to the California statute, the arbitration provision had to appear as a "separate article in the agreement" and had to be "prominently displayed on the enrollment form signed by each

subscriber." Finding that the provision was not disclosed in boldface, underlining or italics, the Appeals Court found that it did not comply with the statutory provisions and thus would not be enforced.

2) In *Buckner v. Tamarin,* 98 Cal.App.4th 140, 119 Cal.Rptr.2d 489 (2002) the defendant physician moved to compel arbitration in a wrongful death action that was brought by a deceased patient's three adult daughters. The California Court of Appeal, Second Appellate District, held that the arbitration agreement cannot bind the heirs of a party if they were not parties to the agreement . The court noted that the strong public policy in favor of arbitration does not extend to those who are not parties to the agreement.

3) In *Saint Agnes Medical Center v. PacifiCare of California*, 31 Cal.4th 1187, 8 Cal.Rptr.3d 517, 82 P.3d 727 (2003), a managed care organization filed an action against a health care provider seeking a declaratory judgment that the contract between the parties was void *ab initio*. The health care provider then filed suit against the managed care organization for alleged breach of the agreement. The agreement contained an arbitration clause. The managed care organization sought to compel arbitration under the arbitration provision and the California Arbitration Act. The hospital opposed the petition for arbitration on grounds that the managed care organization waived its right to compel arbitration by asserting that the contract was void *ab initio*. Ultimately reaching the California Supreme Court, the Court noted that there is a strong public policy in favor of arbitration provisions. Accordingly, unless the hospital can show that it was prejudiced by the declaratory judgment action, PacificCare's failure to seek arbitration before filing its claim did not, in and of itself, invalidate the arbitration provision. The Court noted that the determination of prejudice is critical to whether a party will be held to have waived an arbitration provision.

SECTION C.   DAMAGE CAPS

ETHERIDGE v. MEDICAL CENTER HOSPITALS

Supreme Court of Virginia, 1989.
237 Va. 87, 376 S.E.2d 525.

STEPHENSON, JUSTICE. * * *

Louise Etheridge * * * sued Medical Center Hospitals and * * * the estate of Clarence B. Trower, Jr. * * *, alleging that the hospital and Trower were liable, jointly and severally, for damages Richie Lee Wilson sustained as a result of their medical malpractice. Evidence at trial revealed that, prior to her injuries, Wilson, a 35–year–old mother of three children, was a normal, healthy woman. On May 6, 1980, however, Wilson underwent surgery at the hospital to restore a deteriorating jaw bone. The surgery consisted of the removal of five-inch-long portions of two ribs by Trower, a general surgeon, and the grafting of the reshaped rib bone to Wilson's jaw by an oral surgeon. The jury found that both Trower and the hospital were negligent and that their negligence proximately caused Wilson's injuries.

Wilson's injuries are severe and permanent. She is brain damaged with limited memory and intelligence. She is paralyzed on her left side, confined to a wheelchair, and unable to care for herself or her children.

* * *

The jury returned a verdict for $2,750,000 against both defendants. The trial court, applying the recovery limit prescribed in Va.Code Ann. § 8.01–581.15, reduced the verdict to $750,000 and entered judgment in that amount. Wilson appeals.

* * * Section 8.01–581.15, * * * as originally enacted and in effect at all times pertinent to the present case, provided as follows:

> In any verdict returned against a health care provider in an action for malpractice where the act or acts of malpractice occurred on or after April one, nineteen hundred seventy-seven, which is tried by a jury or in any judgment entered against a health care provider in such an action which is tried without a jury, the total amount recoverable for any injury to, or death of, a patient shall not exceed seven hundred fifty thousand dollars.

> It is firmly established that all actions of the General Assembly are presumed to be constitutional. * * * Therefore, the party assailing the legislation has the burden of proving that it is unconstitutional * * *, and if a reasonable doubt exists as to a statute's constitutionality, the doubt must be resolved in favor of its validity * * *.

One of Wilson's primary contentions is that § 8.01–581.15 violates her right under the Virginia Constitution to a trial by jury. * * *

Without question, the jury's fact-finding function extends to the assessment of damages. * * * Once the jury has ascertained the facts and assessed the damages, however, the constitutional mandate is satisfied. * * * Thereafter, it is the duty of the court to apply the law to the facts. * * *

The limitation on medical malpractice recoveries contained in § 8.01–581.15 does nothing more than establish the outer limits of a remedy provided by the General Assembly. A remedy is a matter of law, not a matter of fact. * * * A trial court applies the remedy's limitation only after the jury has fulfilled its fact-finding function. Thus, § 8.01–581.15 does not infringe upon the right to a jury trial because the section does not apply until after a jury has completed its assigned function in the judicial process.

* * *

Wilson also contends that § 8.01–581.15 violates the constitutional guarantee of due process. The due process clauses of the federal and Virginia Constitutions provide that no person shall be deprived of life, liberty, or property without due process of law. U.S. Const. amend. XIV, § 1; Va. Const. art. I, § 11. Both procedural and substantive rights are protected by the due process clauses.

* * * Wilson bases her claim of a due process violation solely upon the irrebuttable presumption rationale. She contends that she has been "deprived of an effective opportunity to be heard, since [§ 8.01–581.15] purports to preordain the result of the hearing." Thus, she asserts, the statute "creates a conclusive presumption that no plaintiff's damages exceed $750,000." * * *

* * * Wilson has not been denied reasonable notice and a meaningful opportunity to be heard. Section 8.01–581.15 has no effect upon Wilson's right to have a jury or court render an individual decision based upon the merits of her case. * * * The section merely affects the parameters of the remedy available to Wilson after the merits of her claim have been decided. We hold, therefore, that Wilson's constitutional guarantee of procedural due process has not been violated.

The effect of § 8.01–581.15 on the remedy available to Wilson likewise is not violative of any substantive due process right. [A] party has no fundamental right to a particular remedy or a full recovery in tort. A statutory limitation on recovery is simply an economic regulation, which is entitled to wide judicial deference. * * * Because § 8.01–581.15 is such a regulation and infringes upon no fundamental right, the section must be upheld if it is reasonably related to a legitimate governmental purpose.

* * * The purpose of § 8.01–581.15—to maintain adequate health care services in this Commonwealth—bears a reasonable relation to the legislative cap—ensuring that health care providers can obtain affordable medical malpractice insurance. We hold, therefore, that substantive due process has not been violated.

Wilson further contends that § 8.01–581.15 violates the doctrine of separation of powers set forth in Article III, § 1 of the Virginia Constitution. That constitutional provision states, inter alia, that "[t]he legislative, executive, and judicial departments shall be separate and distinct, so that none exercise the powers properly belonging to the others." * * *

[W]hether the remedy prescribed in § 8.01–581.15 is viewed as a modification of the common law or as establishing the jurisdiction of the courts in specific cases, clearly it was a proper exercise of legislative power. Indeed, were a court to ignore the legislatively determined remedy and enter an award in excess of the permitted amount, the court would invade the province of the legislature. Accordingly, we hold that § 8.01–581.15 does not violate the separation of powers doctrine.

* * *

Wilson also claims that § 8.01–581.15 violates Article IV, § 14, which provides, in pertinent part, that "[t]he General Assembly shall not enact any local, special, or private law * * * [g]ranting to any private corporation, association, or individual any special or exclusive right, privilege, or immunity." Wilson argues that § 8.01–581.15 "purports to confer special privileges and immunities upon a small segment of the population— physicians and their insurers—while at the same time arbitrarily distinguishing between severely injured victims of medical malpractice and less severely injured malpractice claimants as well as all other tort plaintiffs." We do not agree.

* * *

According the legislation the presumption of validity to which it is entitled, we conclude that the classification is not arbitrary and bears a reasonable and substantial relation to the object sought to be accomplished by the legislation. We further conclude that the legislation applies to all persons belonging to the class without distinction and, therefore, is not special in effect. Accordingly, we hold that § 8.01–581.15 does not violate the prohibition against special legislation.

In Wilson's final constitutional attack upon § 8.01–581.15, she contends that it violates the Equal Protection Clause in the Fourteenth Amendment to the federal Constitution. That clause provides in pertinent part that no state shall "deny to any person * * * the equal protection of the laws." U.S. Const. amend. XIV, § 1.

To withstand an equal protection challenge, a classification that neither infringes upon a fundamental right nor creates a suspect class must satisfy the "rational basis" test. * * *

* * * Section 8.01–581.15 was enacted only after a thorough study had been made of the problem. The General Assembly made specific findings and a legislative judgment as to how the problem could be best addressed. Bearing in mind that the General Assembly is presumed to have acted within its constitutional powers and according its action the presumption of validity to which it is entitled, we cannot say that the means the General Assembly chose to promote a legitimate state purpose are unreasonable or arbitrary. Accordingly, we hold that the classification does not violate the Equal Protection Clause.

* * * Wilson contends that the limit of $750,000 imposed by § 8.01–581.15 "applied as to each health care provider"; therefore, Wilson says she is entitled to recover $1,500,000. * * *

The statute provides that "[i]n any verdict returned against a health care provider in an action for malpractice * * * *the total amount recoverable for any injury to * * * a patient* shall not exceed seven hundred fifty thousand dollars." (Emphasis added.) Wilson's claim was for an indivisible injury * * * caused by the concurring negligence of each defendant. Giving § 8.01–581.15 its plain meaning, we hold that Wilson's damages are limited to a total of $750,000.

[W]e will affirm the trial court's judgment.

RUSSELL, JUSTICE, dissenting. * * *

The General Assembly enacted § 8.01–581.15 with the salutary legislative purpose of providing a remedy for a perceived social problem, the unavailability of medical malpractice insurance at affordable rates. Yet the unintended consequence of the Act was the creation of a class, described as "health care providers," clothed with a special privilege in the courts. Alone among the multitudes of corporations, associations, groups, and individuals who are daily subjected to tort actions in the courts, the members of this privileged elite (and those who insure them) are granted a special immunity from all damages exceeding $750,000 (now $1,000,000). All defendants not falling within the favored class lack that shield and must pay the full amount a jury may decide to award.

The other side of this unhappy equation is that § 8.01–581.15 creates a corresponding disfavored class—those who are so unfortunate as to suffer injury as a result of the negligence of a "health care provider." Their right to recover damages is limited by the Act while those injured by the torts of accountants, airlines, architects, barbers, bandits, banks, bus drivers, cooks, dog owners, engineers, financial advisors, horse trainers, golfers, hotel keepers, inebriates, jailors, kidnappers, lawyers, etc., retain an unlimited right of redress in the courts. This is precisely the kind of economic favoritism at which the special-laws prohibitions were aimed. * * *

It may be argued that the legislature, perceiving a problem, need not attempt its resolution at one stroke, but may move against it piecemeal. Thus, it would be constitutionally permissible to legislate with respect to the "liability crisis" within the field of health care at one session, to turn to the plight of municipalities at the next, and to other professions, businesses, and occupations at another. Fair enough. But the General Assembly enacted the Medical Malpractice Act in 1976, and has made no other discernible approach to the problem as it might affect others subject to the "liability crisis" in the courts during the ensuing twelve years. The special protection granted to the narrowly defined class of "health care providers" stands alone: a unique monument to the effectiveness of a particularly vocal group which sought and found a privileged position in the courts.

* * *

THOMAS, J., and POFF, SENIOR JUSTICE, join in dissent.[1]

PRIMUS v. GALGANO

United States Court of Appeals for the First Circuit, 2003.
329 F.3d 236.

LYNCH, Circuit Judge.

* * *

Sharon Primus, whose husband is in the military, saw a number of physicians at Luke Air Force Base in Arizona between 1989 and 1992 regarding a cyst (or cysts) in her breast.

1. Editors' Note: In Boyd v. Bulala, 877 F.2d 1191 (4th Cir.1989), the court of appeals held that the Virginia cap did not violate the Seventh Amendment right to jury trial or federal separation of powers or due process and equal protection rights. The cap has been raised to $1 million as to claims arising after Oct. 1, 1983. 1983 Va. Acts ch. 496.

On October 18, 1989, Primus saw Dr. Susan Allen, a specialist in family medicine at Luke Air Force Base, for a routine annual examination. Dr. Allen palpated a 2 millimeter lump in Primus's breast. According to Primus's medical records, the lump was located in her left breast; Primus, however, maintains that this is a mistake and that the lump was in her right breast. Dr. Allen ordered a mammogram be performed on Primus the next day. Dr. Allen also referred Primus to Dr. Lawrence Riddles, a surgeon at Luke Air Force Base; Dr. Allen noted in Primus's record that she should be evaluated by a surgeon, and a biopsy should perhaps be performed. Dr. Riddles saw Primus on November 1, 1989. Based on his examination and the mammogram ordered by Dr. Allen, he concluded that there was no evidence of cancer. Dr. Riddles also recommended that Primus return for a follow-up visit in three months' time; Primus did not see Dr. Riddles again, however. Primus did see Dr. Allen in November 1990. At that time, Dr. Allen found no mass in Primus's breast. No biopsy was performed despite Dr. Allen's query.

On July 19, 1991, Primus saw another surgeon at Luke Air Force Base, Dr. Earl Walker. This time, Primus went directly to a surgeon, rather than being referred by a general practitioner. According to Dr. Walker's notes, Primus complained of a month-old cyst in her right breast. Palpation revealed a 4 millimeter cyst in her right breast. Dr. Walker made a preliminary diagnosis of fibrocystic disease, and ordered a mammogram. The mammogram was performed on July 25, 1991, and Primus saw Dr. Walker to discuss it on August 8, 1991. Dr. Walker again diagnosed the lump as fibrocystic disease, noting that it was a 6 millimeter smooth lump. Primus saw Dr. Walker for a third time in January 1992. He noted a 4 to 6 millimeter lump, palpated her lymph nodes, and recommended that she come back in July 1992 for another mammogram. Primus did not have a third mammogram while at Luke Air Force Base.

Primus also saw Dr. Allen for another annual physical examination on December 18, 1991, and complained of a cyst in her right breast. Dr. Allen noted that Primus should follow up with a surgeon, and perhaps a needle aspiration or surgical biopsy could be performed. Again, no biopsy or needle aspiration was performed, nor were such diagnostic procedures ever performed while Primus was in Arizona. Primus also saw a nurse at Luke Air Force Base, Diane Musselwhite, in June 1992. Nurse Musselwhite noted that Primus had a 10 millimeter lump in her breast.

Primus left Arizona in July 1992, and relocated with her family to Massachusetts when her husband was transferred to Hanscom Air Force Base. She became pregnant in August 1992. During Primus's pregnancy, changes in her breast were attributed to normal effects of pregnancy. Primus saw Dr. Martin Gross, an obstetrician, on October 15, 1992. At that time, a hardened area was detected in Primus's right breast. In November 1992, Primus saw Dr. Michael Shaw, a hematologist/oncologist, who recorded that Primus had "normal pregnant breasts." Dr. Gross also did an evaluation of Primus's breasts when he delivered her child in April 1993, and found no mass in her breast.

On October 12, 1993, after the birth of Primus's son, Primus saw Dr. Richard Galgano, a private primary-care physician who saw patients from Hanscom Air Force Base, for a complete medical examination. Galgano palpated a lump and noted in her record a cyst in the outer portion of her right breast. Primus told Galgano that a lump in that breast had been diagnosed as non-cancerous by doctors in Arizona after a 1991 mammogram. She also told him it had not changed in size since then, and that it was not painful. Though he palpated the lump, Galgano did not refer her to a surgeon, nor did he obtain her medical records or perform a work-up.

Primus was diagnosed with breast cancer in 1995. On March 14, 1995, she consulted a general practitioner, Dr. Daniel Melville, who, after palpating a lump in her right breast, immediately arranged for both a mammogram and an ultrasound. Primus had a mammogram, but the ultrasound was not performed at the recommendation of the radiologist, who felt that the mammogram alone clearly indicated the presence of cancer. Dr. Melville called Primus at home the evening of the day she had her mammogram to tell her she needed to see a surgeon as soon as possible. Primus saw the surgeon, Dr. Kevin O'Donnell, the next day, March 29, 1995. Dr. O'Donnell diagnosed breast cancer on the basis of the mammogram and palpation of the lump. He ordered a biopsy on April 11, 1995 to confirm his diagnosis, and then scheduled surgery for Primus shortly thereafter. By that time, the cancer had metastasized into four lymph nodes. The lump was estimated to be 40 millimeters in size, but the final pathology report recorded it as 25 millimeters. She underwent a radical mastectomy on May 12, 1995 that entailed removal of her entire breast and 21 lymph nodes and began chemotherapy in June 1995. After the mastectomy, breast reconstruction was attempted unsuccessfully. At trial, Primus and her husband testified about the pain, suffering, and embarrassment which had resulted from the loss of her right breast, the chemotherapy, and the failed reconstructive surgery.

II.

On March 27, 1998 Primus filed a medical malpractice action in the U.S. District Court in Massachusetts. * * *

The jury returned a verdict for the plaintiff consisting of $500,000 for damages suffered as a result of negligence, and $960,000 for future pain and suffering. Defendant then filed a motion for entry of judgment, styling it as being in accordance with Mass. Gen. Laws Ann. ch. 231, § 60H, and requesting that the district court reduce the verdict to $500,000 as an operation of law. [The] motion [was] denied. Primus v. Galgano, 187 F.Supp.2d 1 (D. Mass. 2002).

The defendant now appeals these rulings, arguing * * * that the verdict must be reduced to $500,000 as an operation of law.

* * *

IV. Mass. Gen. Laws Ann. ch. 231, § 60H

Defendant asks us to reduce the jury's verdict to $500,000 in accordance with Mass. Gen. Laws Ann. ch. 231, § 60H. After the verdict, defendant filed a Motion for Entry of Judgment, arguing that Massachusetts law dictated a cap on pain and suffering damages of $500,000 applicable in this case. The district court denied the motion. [ ]. The district court did not specify under which Federal Rule of Civil Procedure it considered the motion to have been brought. Depending on which rule is considered relevant, our standard of review might well vary. * * *. Whatever the appropriate characterization and standard of review, there was no error here.

Section 60H was enacted in 1986 as part of a series of measures responding to a state crisis in medical insurance and care as a result of malpractice suits. [ ]. The section was intended to limit noneconomic damages, i.e., pain and suffering and other emotional damages, in order to "decrease[ ] expenses and stabilize medical malpractice insurance premiums." Id. Entitled "Limitation of damages for pain and suffering," § 60H provides:

> In any action for malpractice, negligence, error, omission, mistake or the unauthorized rendering of professional services, ... the court shall instruct the jury that in the event they find the defendant liable, they shall not award the plaintiff more than five hundred thousand dollars for pain and suffering, loss of companionship, embarrassment, and other items of general damages unless the jury determines that there is a substantial or permanent loss or impairment of a bodily function or substantial disfigurement, or other special circumstances in the case which warrant a finding that the imposition of such a limitation would deprive the plaintiff of just compensation for the injuries sustained.

Mass. Gen. Laws Ann. ch. 231, § 60H. The cap makes exceptions where there is 1) a substantial or permanent loss of function, 2) a substantial disfigurement, or 3) other special circumstances.

The defendant draws several conclusions from the language of § 60H. First, the defendant argues, because § 60H uses the words "shall instruct," the trial court was mandated to give the instruction, regardless of whether counsel requested it. Second, the defendant reads § 60H as a cap on damages that applies even when the instruction was not given: the trial judge must reduce pain and suffering damages to $500,000 unless one of the exceptions applies. Applying these arguments to the facts of this case, the defendant maintains that the district court made a finding that none of the exceptions were present, and that the cap had to apply as a result. The defendant argues that there was no waiver on his part because of the district court's statement that it doubted that § 60H applied because there was no factual support for a jury finding of permanent disablement. That statement was not, however, a finding that no statutory exception to the cap was met.

The first two conclusions drawn by the defendant are issues of law as to interpretation of § 60H. We reject the defendant's interpretation of § 60H as requiring a reduction in damages regardless of whether the defendant requests an instruction or not. If the defendant wants to take advantage of the protections of § 60H, he must ask for an appropriate instruction. Under Gray v. Genlyte Group, Inc., 289 F.3d 128 (1st Cir. 2002), a defendant who does not request a jury instruction is deemed to have waived it. [ ] There is no basis in the statute for a district court to itself reduce the damages award in the absence of a requested instruction. The statute is phrased in terms of an instruction to the jury.

Here, defendant suggests that his failure to ask for the § 60H instruction is excused by the district court's supposed factual finding. This argument is contradicted, however, by the behavior of defense counsel prior to the delivery of the jury instructions. Defense counsel repeatedly rejected opportunities to request a § 60H instruction, even when the district court essentially invited him to do so. Defense counsel did not request the instructions initially. Then, at a conference to review the instructions, the court itself raised the possibility of delivering a § 60H instruction, but defense counsel did not respond. Finally, after the instructions were delivered but before the jury retired, defense counsel informed the district court that "the defendant is content" with regard to the instructions.

Defense counsel's avoidance of the instructions appears to reflect a strategic decision on the defendant's part not to request the instructions. As affidavits by malpractice lawyers and the district court's own experience attest, judges in malpractice cases under Massachusetts law habitually allow counsel to decide whether to request the § 60H instruction, and defense counsel often opt not to request it, for fear that juries will misinterpret it as a $500,000 floor rather than as a ceiling. [ ]. Defendant cannot, in retrospect, excuse a tactical decision on his part that resulted in the waiver of the instruction in question by the assertion that the trial judge is required to deliver the instruction regardless of the absence of a request for it or that the judge is similarly required to reduce the verdict to the statutory cap even when no instruction regarding the cap has been delivered.

Moreover, as the defendant conceded at oral argument, Primus's radical mastectomy and failed reconstructive surgery did, in fact, amount to a substantial disfigurement, thereby removing her case from the ambit of the § 60H cap. Quite simply, there was no error in the failure to deliver the § 60H instruction.

For these reasons, we leave the amount of the jury's award unchanged. There was no error in the district court's decision not to deliver the § 60H instruction, much less plain error. Nor did the district court misinterpret the statute in refusing to read it as a mandate for an automatic post-verdict reduction in the size of the award, regardless of whether the instruction had been requested or delivered.

V.

The rulings of the district court are affirmed.

ST. MARY'S HOSPITAL v. PHILLIPE

Supreme Court of Florida, 2000.
769 So.2d 961.

PER CURIAM.

We have before us [four cases] which we have consolidated for review. These are medical malpractice wrongful death cases in which the defendants conceded liability. The parties voluntarily chose to use a statutorily created binding arbitration process as an alternative to litigation to provide a faster, more efficient, and less costly means of resolving the issue of damages. Under this process, the parties waived the right to a jury trial and agreed to have the damages restricted in accordance with the statutory process. Following arbitration, the plaintiffs in these cases were awarded various amounts of both economic and noneconomic damages.

* * *

[T]he district court certified the following question:

WHEN THE ALLEGED MEDICAL NEGLIGENCE RESULTS IN THE DEATH OF THE PATIENT, DOES THE CAP ON NON-ECONOMIC DAMAGES OF $250,000 PER INCIDENT IN A VOLUNTARY ARBITRATION UNDER § 766.207 APPLY TO EACH BENEFICIARY UNDER THE WRONGFUL DEATH ACT, OR DOES THE $250,000 CAP APPLY IN THE AGGREGATE TO INCLUDE ALL WRONGFUL DEATH ACT BENEFICIARIES?

[I]n addition * * *, we have been requested to address whether the elements of economic damages awardable in the statutorily created voluntary binding arbitration of a medical malpractice wrongful death claim are controlled by the provisions establishing the arbitration process set forth in the Medical Malpractice Act or by the provisions controlling the elements of damages set forth in the Wrongful Death Act. We have jurisdiction. Art. V, § 3(b)(4), Fla. Const.

FACTS

St. Mary's Hospital, Inc. v. Phillipe

The facts of the first case are as follows. Juslin Phillipe died while giving birth to her daughter, Ecclesianne. Ecclesianne was born severely brain damaged. Charles Phillipe, Juslin's husband and the personal representative of her estate, brought a medical malpractice wrongful death action against St. Mary's Hospital on behalf of himself and the decedent's four surviving children.

The parties in this case chose to proceed under the statutory alternative dispute process for medical malpractice claims [ ]. St. Mary's conceded liability and the case proceeded under that arbitration process on the issue of damages. It is important to note that the independent personal injury action of the brain-damaged child, Ecclesianne, was not part of the arbitration process.

After a hearing, the arbitrators awarded the following damages: $250,000 in noneconomic damages to both Charles, the husband, and Ecclesianne, the daughter; $175,000 in noneconomic damages to each of the remaining children; $2,284,804 to the family in economic damages for loss of services; $943,000 in economic damages for loss of special services to Ecclesianne; $3,398 in funeral expenses; and $510,632 in attorneys' fees. The total amount of the arbitration award was $4,766,834.

St. Mary's appealed the award and filed a motion to stay the award pending review * * *.

* * *

St. Mary's next argued that the arbitrators' total award of noneconomic damages in the amount of $1,025,000 exceeded the $250,000 cap set forth in [the Florida Medical Malpractice Act.] That provision provides that "noneconomic damages shall be limited to a maximum of $250,000 per incident." St. Mary's asserted that the term "per incident" reflected that the limit applies in the aggregate to all claimants, rather than separately to each wrongful death beneficiary. The district court agreed with St. Mary's. The court concluded that the plain language of the statute indicates that "there can be no more than $250,000 in noneconomic damages awarded by the arbitrators [ ] no matter how many different people may have a direct benefit in the award, or the source of their entitlement to share in the award." Accordingly, the district court reversed the arbitration award of noneconomic damages, remanded for the reduction of such damages to $250,000 in the aggregate, and certified the second question for our review.

In its final claim, St. Mary's argued that the award of economic damages for the decedent's loss of earning capacity was improper because such damages are not available under the Wrongful Death Act. The district court disagreed, holding that the elements of economic damages available in a voluntary binding arbitration of a medical malpractice claim are controlled by the Medical Malpractice Act rather than the Wrongful Death Act and that [ ] the Medical Malpractice Act permit the award for loss of earning capacity.

* * *

ISSUE II. MEANING OF THE CLAUSE "NONECONOMIC DAMAGES SHALL BE LIMITED TO A MAXIMUM OF $250,000 PER INCIDENT"

The second issue involves whether the $250,000 "per incident" limitation of noneconomic damages in the arbitration provisions of the Medical Malpractice Act limits the total recovery of all claimants in the aggregate to $250,000 or limits the recovery of each claimant individually to $250,000.

Section 766.207(7)(b) is the provision setting forth the $250,000 noneconomic damages cap. That provision provides:

Noneconomic damages shall be limited to a maximum of $250,000 per incident, and shall be calculated on a percentage basis with respect to capacity to enjoy life, so that a finding that the claimant's injuries resulted in a 50–percent reduction in his or her capacity to enjoy life would warrant an award of not more than $125,000 noneconomic damages.

The claimants argue that the $250,000 per incident cap on noneconomic damages limits the damages per individual claimant. They also assert that the arbitration provisions of the Medical Malpractice Act as interpreted by the district court violate their constitutional rights to equal protection under the law.

St. Mary's contends that section 766.207(7)(b) is clear and unambiguous and that a plain meaning construction of the statute indicates that the Legislature intended to limit noneconomic damages to $250,000 per incident in the aggregate. Additionally, Franzen asserts that the constitutional challenge of the cap on noneconomic damages should not be entertained because this Court has already determined that the Medical Malpractice Act's limitations were constitutional. [ ] For the reasons provided below, we reject [petitioners] arguments.

It is a cardinal rule of statutory construction that a statute must be construed in its entirety and as a whole. [ ] An examination of the entire statute demonstrates that section 766.207(7)(b) is neither clear nor unambiguous.

Section 766.207(7)(b) does state that "noneconomic damages shall be limited to a maximum of $250,000 per incident"; however, within that same provision the statute goes on to describe how these damages shall be calculated, and in so doing refers to "claimant" in the singular. [ ]. Likewise, section 766.207(7)(k) states that:

Any offer by a claimant to arbitrate must be made to each defendant against whom the claimant has made a claim. Any offer by a defendant to arbitrate must be made to each claimant who has joined in the notice of intent to initiate litigation, as provided in s. 766.106. A defendant who rejects a claimant's offer to arbitrate shall be subject to the provisions of s. 766.209(3). A claimant who rejects a defendants offer to arbitrate shall be subject to the provisions of s. 766.209(4).

(Emphasis added.)

For the purposes of this statute, "claimant" is clearly defined as "any person who has a cause of action arising from medical negligence." [ ]

When referring to multiple parties, the statute is also perfectly clear. For example, section 766.207(4), which sets forth the composition of the arbitration panel, states that

In the event of multiple plaintiffs or multiple defendants, the arbitrator selected by the side with multiple parties shall be the choice of those parties. If the multiple parties cannot reach agreement as to their arbitrator, each of the multiple parties shall submit a nominee. . . .

(Emphasis added.)

Furthermore, where the Legislature has intended to limit claimants' damages in the aggregate in other contexts, they have done so explicitly. For example, in section 768.28(5), a provision of Florida's Wrongful Death Act which limits damage claims against the state, the Legislature limited to $200,000 the State's liability for damages arising out of the same incident. Section 768.28(5) states in pertinent part:

Neither the state nor its agencies or subdivisions shall be liable to pay a claim or a judgment by any one person which exceeds the sum of $100,000 or any claim or judgment, or portions thereof, which, when totaled with all other claims or judgments paid by the state or its agencies or subdivision arising out of the same incident or occurrence, exceeds the sum of $200,000.

Therefore, we find that section 766.207(7)(b) is neither clear nor unambiguous. Where there is ambiguity and uncertainty in the words employed in a statute, we must look to the legislative intent for guidance. [ ]

Before the Medical Malpractice Act was implemented, the Legislature established an Academic Task Force for Review of the Insurance and Tort Systems. The Legislature directed the Task Force to study the problems associated with liability insurance. Based upon the Task Force's findings and recommendations, in 1988 the Legislature enacted the Medical Malpractice Act, which contains the voluntary arbitration process at issue in these cases.

In adopting the Act, the Legislature adopted the Task Force's recommendations and findings.

Section 766.201(1) expressly sets forth the Legislature's intent to provide a mechanism for the prompt resolution of medical malpractice claims through mandatory presuit investigation and voluntary binding arbitration of damages. Likewise, section 766.201(2)(b) reveals the Legislature's intent to provide substantial incentives to claimants and defendants to voluntarily submit their cases to binding arbitration. In our opinion in Echarte, we explained the incentives for claimants to voluntarily submit to such a process, stating:

The claimant benefits from the requirement that a defendant quickly determine the merit of any defenses and the extent of its liability. The claimant also saves the costs of attorney and expert witness fees which would be required to prove liability. Further, a claimant who accepts a defendant's offer to have damages determined by an arbitration panel receives the additional benefits of: 1) the relaxed evidentiary standard for arbitration proceedings as set out by section 120.58, Florida Statutes

(1989); 2) joint and several liability of multiple defendants in arbitration; 3) prompt payment of damages after the determination by the arbitration panel; 4) interest penalties against the defendant for failure to promptly pay the arbitration award; and 5) limited appellate review of the arbitration award requiring a showing of "manifest injustice." 618 So.2d at 194.

On the other hand, the most significant incentive for defendants to concede liability and submit the issue of damages to arbitration is the $250,000 cap on noneconomic damages. This limitation provides liability insurers with the ability to improve the predictability of the outcome of claims for the purpose of loss planning in risk assessment for premium purposes.

This predictability can be obtained by interpreting section 766.207(7)(b) so that each claimant is fairly and reasonably compensated for his or her pain and suffering. Such an interpretation would provide increased predictability in the outcome of the claims as the insurers would no longer be contending with the possibility of exorbitant noneconomic damage awards but would have a fixed dollar amount ($250,000), which each claimant's award could not exceed. Moreover, this interpretation does more to promote early resolution of medical negligence claims, as it provides an equitable result which will in turn further encourage claimants to seek resolution through arbitration.

An analysis of the availability of noneconomic damages in other wrongful death contexts demonstrates that our ruling here is consistent with the principles of equity inherent in the distribution of noneconomic damages to survivors. * * *

* * *

These decisions clearly demonstrate that in order for the assessment of a survivor's noneconomic damages to be equitable, each survivor's loss must be independently determined. Moreover, the loss of a survivor is not diminished by the mere fact that there are multiple survivors. Differentiating between a single claimant and multiple claimants bears no rational relationship to the Legislature's stated goal of alleviating the financial crisis in the medical liability insurance industry.

Finally, were we to interpret the noneconomic damages cap to apply to all claimants in the aggregate, we conclude that such an interpretation would create equal protection concerns. * * *

* * *

If we were to accept St. Mary's contention that the Legislature intended to limit noneconomic damages to $250,000 per incident in the aggregate, then the death of a wife who leaves only a surviving spouse to claim the $250,000 is not equal to the death of a wife who leaves a surviving spouse and four minor children, resulting in five claimants to divide $250,000. We fail to see how this classification bears any rational relationship to the Legislature's stated goal of alleviating the financial crisis in the medical liability industry. Such a categorization offends the fundamental notion of equal justice under the law and can only be described as purely arbitrary and unrelated to any state interest. [ ]

Moreover, it is erroneous to claim that this defect can be overcome by the fact that arbitration is voluntary. Arbitration is not voluntary according to section 766.207(7)(k) because "a claimant who rejects a defendant's offer to arbitrate shall be subject to the provisions of section 766.209(4)," which limits the noneconomic damages to be awardable at trial to $350,000. Therefore, instead of five claimants having to divide $250,000 under the arbitration limitations, they are left to divide $350,000, which clearly has no effect on the equal protection concerns.

* * *

ISSUE III. ECONOMIC DAMAGES

The final issue involves the question of whether the elements of economic damages awardable in the voluntary binding arbitration of a medical malpractice wrongful death claim are controlled by the Medical Malpractice Act or the Wrongful Death Act. [Petitioners] argue that when medical negligence results in death, rather than personal injury, the elements of damages recoverable are limited by section 768.21, Florida Statutes (1995), of the Wrongful Death Act. They also contend that the arbitration provisions of the Medical Malpractice Act merely control the amount, rather than the type, of recoverable economic damages. They maintain that the Medical Malpractice Act provides for the full range of economic damages when the parties agree to arbitrate.

* * *

Three provisions of the Medical Malpractice Act discuss economic damages. Section 766.202(3) defines "economic damages" as "including, but not limited to, past and future medical expenses and 80 percent of wage loss and loss of earning capacity." Section 766.207(7)(a) provides that arbitration shall be undertaken with the understanding that "net economic damages shall be awardable, including, but not limited to, past and future medical expenses and 80 percent of wage loss and loss of earning capacity, offset by any collateral source payments." This economic damages provision is replicated under section 766.209, which applies when a claimant rejects an offer to arbitrate.

Unlike the Medical Malpractice Act, the Wrongful Death Act does not provide claimants with such a full range of economic damages. Under section 768.21(1) of the Wrongful Death Act, each survivor may recover the value of lost support and services from the date of the decedent's injury, and under section 768.21(6), the estate may recover the decedent's loss of earnings, loss of prospective net accumulations, and medical and funeral expenses.

We conclude that the arbitration provisions of the Medical Malpractice Act expressly specify the elements of all of the damages available when the parties agree to binding arbitration, regardless of whether the medical malpractice action involves a wrongful death. The plain language of sections 766.202(3) and 766.207(7)(a) indicates that the full range of economic damages is available to claimants as an incentive to forego a jury trial on damages and proceed to arbitration. The legislative intent of the Medical Malpractice Act also indicates that the arbitration provisions were enacted to address soaring noneconomic damage awards, rather than the more predictable economic damage awards. See § 766.201. If the Legislature intended for the Wrongful Death Act to control the elements of damages available in a medical malpractice arbitration, it could have specifically provided for the application of the provisions of that Act in the Medical Malpractice Act. It has not done so.

CONCLUSION

In conclusion, we * * * answer the district court's express certified question by holding that the $250,000 cap on noneconomic damages applies to each claimant individually. [and] reject [petitioner's] contention that the elements of economic damages available in the voluntary binding arbitration process are limited by the Wrongful Death Act.

CHESTER v. DOIG

Supreme Court of Florida, 2003.
842 So.2d 106.

QUINCE, J.

We have for review a decision of the Fifth District Court of Appeal on the following question, which the court certified to be of great public importance:

IS IT APPROPRIATE TO SETOFF AGAINST THE NONECONOMIC DAMAGES PORTION OF AN AWARD AGAINST ONE TORTFEASOR IN AN ARBITRATION OF A MEDICAL MALPRACTICE ACTION THE AMOUNT RECOVERED FROM SETTLEMENT FROM ANOTHER RESPONSIBLE FOR THE SAME INCIDENT CAUSING THE INJURY?

BACKGROUND

Mary Chester (Chester) asserted that her husband died as the result of medical malpractice and blamed both respondent Dr. Doig and Halifax Hospital for his death. Chester settled with Halifax Hospital for $150,000 during presuit proceedings (the settlement award) and then arbitrated with Dr. Doig and recovered $507,321 (the arbitration award). Of the $507,321 recovered from Dr. Doig, $210,321 was designated for economic damages, $250,000 was designated for noneconomic damages, and $47,000 was for attorney's fees. The arbitrators found that Dr. Doig was not entitled to a setoff based on the settlement award. Dr. Doig appealed the arbitrators' finding that he was not entitled to a setoff, and on his second motion for rehearing, the Fifth District reversed the arbitration panel with directions to apply a setoff. [ ]. The issue before this Court is whether the arbitration award should be set off (reduced) by the settlement award.

DISCUSSION

The arbitration provisions of Florida's Medical Malpractice Act allow an arbitration panel to determine damages in a medical malpractice claim once presuit investigation has been completed. [ ]. The arbitration provisions were enacted to provide "substantial incentives for both claimants and defendants to submit their cases to binding arbitration, thus reducing attorneys' fees, litigation costs, and delay." [ ]. In this case, Chester agreed to submit to binding arbitration with Dr. Doig, and under section 766.207(7), the following limitations on damages apply:

(7) Arbitration pursuant to this section shall preclude recourse to any other remedy by the claimant against any participating defendant, and shall be undertaken with the understanding that:

(a) Net economic damages shall be awardable, including, but not limited to, past and future medical expenses and 80 percent of wage loss and loss of earning capacity, offset by any collateral source payments.

(b) Noneconomic damages shall be limited to a maximum of $250,000 per incident, and shall be calculated on a percentage basis with respect to capacity to enjoy life, so that a finding that the claimant's injuries resulted in a 50–percent reduction in his capacity to enjoy life would warrant an award of not more than $125,000 in noneconomic damages.

(c) Damages for future economic losses shall be awarded to be paid by periodic payments pursuant to s. 766.202(8) and shall be offset by future collateral source payments.

(d) Punitive damages shall not be awarded.

. . . .

(h) Each defendant who submits to arbitration under this section shall be jointly and severally liable for all damages assessed pursuant to this section.

[ ]. Chester argues the plain language of [the Florida statute] prohibits a setoff of the settlement award, while Dr. Doig asserts that Florida's setoff statutes require the settlement award be set off against the arbitration award.

The Fifth District concluded that the entire settlement award should be set off against the arbitration award because there was no allocation of fault and Dr. Doig is jointly and severally liable for all noneconomic damages found by the arbitration panel. [ ]. The Fifth District noted that the arbitration panel determined that section 766.207(7) did not specifically permit a setoff for settlements and therefore the panel refused to consider Florida's setoff statutes. [ ] The Fifth District found that in refusing to consider the setoff statutes the arbitration panel ignored the intent of the Legislature to prevent double recovery for the same damages. [ ]. However, we agree with the arbitration panel's approach to the issue in this case for the reasons that follow.

In St. Mary's Hospital, Inc. v. Phillipe, 769 So.2d 961, 972 (Fla. 2000), we were faced with the issue of whether the elements of economic damages awardable in the voluntary binding arbitration of a medical malpractice wrongful death claim were controlled by the Medical Malpractice Act or the Wrongful Death Act. We concluded "that the arbitration provisions of the Medical Malpractice Act expressly specify the elements of all of the damages available when the parties agree to binding arbitration, regardless of whether the medical malpractice action involves a wrongful death." Id. at 973. In other words, "if the Legislature intended for the Wrongful Death Act to control the elements of damages available in a medical malpractice arbitration, it could have specifically provided for the application of that Act in the Medical Malpractice Act." Id. We reach the same conclusion in the instant case with respect to setoff.

Section 766.207(7)(a) provides that net economic damages be offset by any collateral source payments, while section 766.207(7)(c) provides that damages for future economic losses be offset by future collateral source payments. For purposes of the arbitration provisions of the Medical Malpractice Act, collateral sources are defined as follows:

(2) "Collateral sources" means any payments made to the claimant, or made on his or her behalf, by or pursuant to:

(a) The United States Social Security Act; any federal, state, or local income disability act; or any other public programs providing medical expenses, disability payments, or other similar benefits, except as prohibited by federal law.

(b) Any health, sickness, or income disability insurance; automobile accident insurance that provides health benefits or income disability coverage; and any other similar insurance benefits, except life insurance benefits available to the claimant, whether purchased by him or her or provided by others.

(c) Any contract or agreement of any group, organization, partnership, or corporation to provide, pay for, or reimburse the costs of hospital, medical, dental, or other health care services.

(d) Any contractual or voluntary wage continuation plan provided by employers or by any other system intended to provide wages during a period of disability.

[ ]. The plain language of section 766.207(7)(a) and (c) clearly provides that the only setoff available in a medical malpractice arbitration is for collateral sources as defined by section 766.202(2). Because the settlement award in this case does not meet the definition of a collateral source or a collateral source payment, the Fifth District erred in concluding that the settlement award should be set off against the arbitration award. [ ]. If the Legislature intended for Florida's setoff statutes to control the elements of damages available in medical mal-

practice arbitration, it could have specifically provided for the application of those statutes in the Medical Malpractice Act. [ ]. Because the Legislature has not done so, we conclude the arbitration award should not be set off by the settlement award in this case.

We also note, reading further into the statutory scheme, that section 766.208(6), Florida Statutes (1997), provides:

Arbitration to allocate responsibility among multiple defendants.—

* * *

(6) Any defendant paying damages assessed pursuant to this section or s. 766.207 shall have an action for contribution against any nonarbitrating person whose negligence contributed to the injury.

Therefore, because Dr. Doig is paying damages assessed pursuant to section 766.207, he may have an action for contribution against any nonarbitrating party whose negligence contributed to the injury.

CONCLUSION

Based on the foregoing, we conclude that a setoff is not appropriate in this case. We therefore answer the certified question in the negative * * *.

Notes

1) In *Jenkins v. Patel*, 256 Mich.App. 112, 662 N.W.2d 453 (2003), the plaintiff's decedent sued the defendant for alleged negligence leading to death of the decedent after complications of a stroke. A jury awarded $10 million in non-economic damages. The trial court held that Michigan's Wrongful Death Act, and not the medical malpractice statute, applied in this case, and thus there was no cap on damages. The Michigan medical malpractice statute imposes a damages cap for medical malpractice claims. The Michigan Appeals Court affirmed the trial court, holding that the Wrongful Death Act applied to this case and no cap on damages was appropriate. In so holding, the Appeals Court examined the language of the Wrongful Death Act and concluded that the legislative intent of the Wrongful Death Act was for it to apply to medical malpractice actions that resulted in death. Indeed, when the legislature amended its damages cap in the medical malpractice statute, it eliminated reference to death. The court concluded that it was the express intent of the legislature that the Wrongful Death Act would govern medical malpractice actions that resulted in death.

2) Compare the statutory language in Michigan to that of other jurisdictions. In states with both a Wrongful Death Act and a Medical Malpractice Act, the language of the statute will generally make it clear which is intended to apply to medical malpractice that results in death.

3) *Collateral Source Rule:* The general judge-made rule in personal injury litigation is that the plaintiff can "keep" the money that comes in

from accident and disability insurance paid for by the plaintiff; outside sources of funds like insurance are "collateral" to money that the defendant owes to the plaintiff, and so collateral source funds are not deducted from the defendant's judgment. These outside funds indemnify the insured plaintiff for economic damages. It has occurred to persons who are interested in changing the medical liability litigation system that there is an aspect of double recovery where both insurers and the defendant health care provider pay some of the same economic damages, and some states have enacted statutes that try to abolish the overlap.

Two early cases decided the same year tested two collateral source statutes, applying both the federal and state requirements for constitutional validity, and the two courts came out with opposite conclusions on rather different statutes.

In Baker v. Vanderbilt Univ.,[1] the Tennessee statute read as follows:

> Tenn.Code Ann. § 29–26–119. In a malpractice action in which liability is admitted or established, the damages awarded may include (in addition to other elements of damages authorized by law) actual economic losses suffered by the claimant by reason of the personal injury, including, but not limited to cost of reasonable and necessary medical care, rehabilitation services, and custodial care, loss of services and loss of earned income, but only to the extent that such costs are not paid or payable and such losses are not replaced, or indemnified in whole or in part, by insurance provided by an employer either governmental or private, by social security benefits, service benefit programs, unemployment benefits, or any other source except the assets of the claimants or of the members of the claimants' immediate family and insurance purchased in whole or in part, privately and individually.

The federal judge responded to the plaintiffs' challenge on federal equal protection grounds by applying the least-demanding "rational basis" test, finding the statute constitutional as economic and social legislation. He held that the same test also validated the statute under the Tennessee constitution, under the reasoning of a recent Tennessee supreme court decision on another statute in the state's medical liability package.

In Wentling v. Medical Anesthesia Services, P.A.,[2] the Kansas statute read as follows:

> Kan.Stat.Ann. § 60–471(a). In any action for damages for personal injuries or death arising out of the rendering of or the failure to render professional services by any health care provider, evidence of any reimbursement or indemnification received by a party for damages sustained from such injury or death, excluding payments from insurance paid for in whole or in part by such party or his or

---

1.   616 F.Supp. 330 (M.D.Tenn.1985).

2.   237 Kan. 503, 701 P.2d 939 (1985) (5 to 2).

her employer, and services provided by a health maintenance organization to treat any such injury, excluding services paid for in whole or in part by such party or his or her employer, shall be admissible for consideration by the trier of fact * * *. Such evidence shall be accorded such weight as the trier of fact shall choose to ascribe to that evidence in determining the amount of damages to be awarded to such party.

Kansas comprises a single federal district. Two District of Kansas judges in three prior cases had tested this statute, dividing on its validity under the equal protection clauses of the United States and Kansas constitutions. A majority of the Kansas supreme court sided with the reasoning of the federal judge who found the act unconstitutional,[3] illustrating its reasoning in this paragraph.

Assume a married couple is injured in the same catastrophe. They are both treated by the same health care provider with disastrous results. The husband is employed and his employer provides health insurance. The wife is not gainfully employed. In separate actions for similar treatment provided by the same health care provider as a result of the same catastrophe, the fact that the wife's medical expenses were paid by insurance is proper evidence to submit to the jury, but the same evidence as it applies to the husband is not. Such a distinction makes no sense whatsoever.[4]

In 1985 the Kansas legislature repealed § 60–471 and replaced it with a new act.

4) *No–Fault Compensation Programs for Birth–Related Injury*: Legislators, researchers and commentators have criticized the existing medical liability system for years. Some allege that it is unpredictable in assessing liability and inequitable in determining damages. Other criticize its inability to deter negligence. Still others are concerned with its inability to provide fair and timely compensation to its intended recipients. Equally importantly, physicians report that the inefficiency and arbitrariness of the system leaves them feeling vulnerable to liability regardless of the quality of their medical practice. Consequently, sweeping changes are periodically proposed to reform the present system.

The California Medical Injury Compensation Reform Act (MICRA) has been a model for state reform to limit recovery for non-economic damages, encourage arbitration and regulate premiums and attorney's fees. Widespread medical malpractice reform has been proposed on the federal level, but various bills have never made it out of Congress. It has been documented that escalating malpractice premiums are driving physicians out of practice in various locations where annual premiums can exceed $200,000. The system is flawed, but workable solutions have proved elusive.

---

3. Doran v. Priddy, 534 F.Supp. 30 (D.Kan.1981).

4. Wentling v. Medical Anesthesia Services, P.A., 701 P.2d at 950.

No-fault compensation has had some success in New Zealand and Sweden, although it is unclear that either could be a viable model in the United States. While no-fault has been suggested by numerous commentators, no formal full-scale proposal has ever been made. A no-fault compensation scheme was enacted in Florida and Virginia in the 1980's to address the malpractice crisis in obstetrics. Its scope is limited to birth-related neurological injuries. Similar legislation passed in Connecticut in 2004, but was vetoed by Governor Roland who criticized it for failing to include a limitation on non-economic damages.

The Florida Birth–Related Neurologic Injury Compensation Act (NICA) provides compensation regardless of fault when it is determined that there was "injury to the brain or spinal cord of a live infant weighing at least 2500 grams at birth caused by oxygen deprivation or mechanical injury occurring in the course of labor, delivery or resuscitation in the immediate post delivery period in a hospital which renders the infant permanently and substantially mentally and physically impaired." Ch 88–1, Laws of Florida, section 766.302(2). For claims that fall within NICA, the plan is an exclusive remedy for reimbursement, precluding traditional tort claims. Conduct that evidences bad faith or reckless disregard for the welfare of the infant is exempted. Not all providers choose to partcipate, nor is participation mandatory.

A claim for funding is made by filing with the state's Division of Administrative Hearings. Medical documentation is gathered and reviewed, and a decision to accept or deny the claim is made. If funded, compensation includes all medically necessary medical expenses of the infant and up to $100,000 (non-economic damages) payable to the parents or legal guardians. Statutory legal fees are included. The procedures and remedies available are similar in Virginia.

The Florida and Virginia compensation programs represent a possible direction for medical liability reform. It is notable that after nearly 20 years, the reform measure continues to endure. On the other hand, the fact that it has not to spread to other jurisdictions and areas of medicine is also notable. The United States is far from adopting broad-based no-fault medical liability compensation. Even more modest measures of tort reform are slow to emerge.

Chapter 11

ACCESS TO HIGH–QUALITY
HEALTH SERVICES

INTRODUCTORY NOTE

Within the memory of doctors still in practice, family doctors treated their patients in homes and offices, referred them to friendly specialists, and got the patients back again when the specialists were through. Hospitals were hotels where physicians practiced medicine and surgeons practiced surgery. Access to medical services was primarily the private responsibility of medical practitioners, who provided a lot of professional services for reduced fees or for nothing. The quality of doctors' services rested upon the opinions of other doctors, who controlled membership in private organizations such as county medical societies and voluntary hospital staffs. State boards of medical examiners conferred but rarely took away licenses to practice medicine and surgery. "Lay intermediaries" of various kinds paid some of the patients' bills, ran the hospitals, and raised the tax funds for the care of indigents.

Times have changed, mainly in the direction of organized review of patients' care and doctors' performance by organizations that are not controlled by peers whom the doctors know well. Licensure agencies now have disciplinary functions; accreditation of facilities now involves a wide array of medical care activities; certification of specialized knowledge and skills takes up where licensure left off.

Nothing illustrates the changes better than the rise since 1951 of a private accreditation agency, now the Joint Commission on Accreditation of Healthcare Organizations.[1] The Commission is "joint" because it was created by the American College of Surgeons, the American College of Physicians, the American Hospital Association, and (with reluctance) the American Medical Association.

The Joint Commission was and is a not-for-profit corporation rather than a government agency. From its initial concern with hospital facilities and non-physician staffing, the Joint Commission expanded into

---

1. See Jost, The Joint Commission on Accreditation of Hospitals: Private Regulation of Health Care and the Public Interest, 24 B.C.L.Rev. 835 (1983). The commission changed its name slightly in 1988.

medical staff membership and organization, and now it also looks at mechanisms for the prevention of claims, the assessment of patient care outcomes, and the appropriateness of care provided. The expansion of interests has coincided with enlarged public financing for health care services and with the greatly enhanced powers of institutions over the way doctors practice. The Joint Commission performs essential accrediting functions for federal and state funding agencies, and had it not existed already, governments would have had to create it. Its key document, the Accreditation Manual for Hospitals, is the basic checklist for accreditation surveys, but inevitably it also serves as the skeleton for organizing hospitals,[2] and incidentally it is a valuable checklist for attorneys in medical liability practice.

The practice of medicine and surgery today is full of new occupations and organizations, and new terms, acronyms, and abbreviations. For example, the doctor is one of many "health care providers." Three other terms of recent coinage express both the central place of institutions in health care and the ways in which institutions respond to problems of business management in the health care setting. All have implications for medical liability, and all have been impelled to some extent by legal considerations.

First, "risk management," which originated in the insurance context, is intended to prevent legal claims against health care providers, including not only medical liability claims of patients, but also premises liability claims of patients and visitors, and workers' compensation claims of employees. Incident reports are intended to flag dangerous conditions and practices for correction, whether a claim arose or not.

Second, "quality assurance" establishes organizational structures, operational processes, and individual assessments of outcomes that address the patient care delivered by all health care providers: physicians, technicians, nurses, and other physician extenders. The objectives are to set performance standards, to detect persons who do not meet the standards, and to sanction persons who cannot perform satisfactorily.

Third, "utilization review" introduces the concept of managed care, which is intended to reduce the capacity of the patient's attending doctor to order medically unnecessary services (including defensive medicine) or services provided in an overly expensive setting. The primary objective is to hold down costs, but it is accompanied by the risk that economic considerations will reduce the quality and timeliness of clinical judgments.

2. The Manual lists Standards for these units of health care organizations: alcoholism and other drug dependence services, diagnostic radiology services, dietetic services, emergency services, governing body, hospital-sponsored ambulatory care services, infection control, management and administrative services, medical record services, medical staff, nuclear medicine services, nursing services, pathology and medical laboratory services, pharmaceutical services, physical rehabilitation services, plant, technology, and safety management, professional library services, quality assurance, radiation oncology services, respiratory care services, social work services, special care units, surgical and anesthesia services, and utilization review.

The three phrases characterize an entire course that is very timely but quite different from medical liability, the course in health care delivery. This chapter looks at the health care delivery from the viewpoint of medical liability, sampling the liability-producing aspects of contemporary health care delivery systems.

SECTION A.   UTILIZATION REVIEW

CASSIM v. BOWEN

United States Court of Appeals for the Ninth Circuit, 1987.
824 F.2d 791.

SKOPIL, CIRCUIT JUDGE. * * *

M.M. Cassim is a licensed and practicing surgeon in Dallas, Oregon. Forty percent of the income from his practice comes from Medicare patients. In early 1985 the Oregon Medical Professional Review Organization (OMPRO) initiated a routine review of the quality of Cassim's surgical care. OMPRO has a contract with the [United States] Department of Health and Human Services (HHS)[3] to operate as the Medicare peer review organization for the State of Oregon.

After its initial review OMPRO decided to examine all surgery performed by Cassim during a prior six-month period. In April 1985 OMPRO informed Cassim and the hospital where he practiced of its review. OMPRO checked the medical records of 80 of Cassim's patients and identified 13 "gross and flagrant" violations of Cassim's obligation under the Social Security Act to adhere to professionally recognized standards.

In making its investigation, OMPRO did not discuss the cases with Cassim. Nor did it contact any of the patients, the attending nurses, the other physicians involved in the care of the patients, or the hospital's quality assurance committee. Finally, OMPRO did not seek a complete copy of all medical records related to the care of the patients. It lacked some x-rays, scans, and other lab data.

On October 30, 1985, OMPRO informed Cassim of its findings. It listed the patient records it had examined and provided Cassim with its analysis and conclusions. OMPRO gave Cassim 30 days to submit information to "rebut or mitigate" its findings and allowed him to make a "written request to meet with representatives of OMPRO to discuss case specifics." OMPRO warned him that its preliminary recommendation was exclusion from the Medicare program.

Cassim then met with OMPRO's surgical review panel and medical director. OMPRO did not allow Cassim to present witnesses or to confront adverse witnesses. Cassim was, however, represented by counsel. A transcript was made of the meeting. Cassim presented his side of

---

3. Editors' Note: Defendant Otis Bowen was then Secretary of Health & Human Services.

the story and introduced exculpatory documentation, including lab data missing from OMPRO's records. The OMPRO panel questioned him on the techniques he had used in caring for his patients. After the meeting, "based on the additional information * * * [Cassim] provided," OMPRO dropped 5 of the 13 alleged violations.

OMPRO recommended to the Office of Inspector General (OIG) of HHS that Cassim be suspended from the Medicare program for a minimum of one year and informed Cassim of its recommendation. It told him that he had 30 days to submit to OIG "any additional material which affects the recommendation to exclude you from participation in the Medicare program." Cassim, through his attorney, took advantage of this opportunity to defend himself and submitted additional material.

Notwithstanding Cassim's efforts, OIG affirmed OMPRO's findings. * * * It excluded Cassim from Medicare for one year and informed him it would publish "a notice in a local newspaper to advise the community of the effective date, the duration, and the reason for this exclusion." See 42 U.S.C.A. § 1320c–5(b)(2); 42 C.F.R. § 1004.100. Finally, OIG told Cassim of his right to appeal the ruling to an administrative law judge (ALJ). See 42 U.S.C.A. § 1320c–5(b)(4); 42 C.F.R. § 1004.130. Neither the Social Security Act nor its regulations guarantee the timeliness of the hearing on appeal.

Cassim then sought a preliminary injunction in district court. He argued that the Act and its regulations violated due process (1) in not providing for a full-blown pre-exclusion and pre-publication (pre-deprivation) ALJ hearing, and (2) in not guaranteeing the promptness of a post-exclusion and post-publication (post-deprivation) hearing. The district court held that it had jurisdiction over Cassim's action but denied the preliminary injunction. Cassim timely appealed. We granted a stay pending the appeal.

Title 42 U.S.C.A. § 405(g) provides a claimant who has exhausted an agency's administrative process with the right to obtain judicial review. * * *

* * * We conclude that Cassim fulfilled the jurisdictional requirements of § 405(g).

A party seeking a preliminary injunction must fulfill one of two standards * * *. Under the traditional standard, a court may issue preliminary relief if it finds that (1) the moving party will suffer irreparable injury if the relief is denied; (2) the moving party will probably prevail on the merits; (3) the balance of potential harm favors the moving party; and (4) the public interest favors granting relief. * * *. Under the alternative standard, the moving party may meet its burden by demonstrating either (1) a combination of probable success and the possibility of irreparable injury, or (2) that serious questions are raised and the balance of hardships tips sharply in its favor. * * *

The district court held that Cassim failed to satisfy either standard. Under the traditional standard, the court found that Cassim had neither established that he would probably prevail on the merits, nor that the balance of potential harm favored him. Under the alternative standard, it ruled that (1) Cassim raised serious questions, but the balance of hardships did not tip sharply in his favor; and (2) Cassim demonstrated the possibility of irreparable injury, but not the probability of success on the merits.

Cassim challenges the district court's analysis under the alternative standard. * * *

Cassim argues that the district court improperly balanced the hardships. First, he emphasizes that his livelihood, reputation, and professional career will be irreparably harmed. He contends the stigma of exclusion and publication could not be removed even if the ALJ completely exonerated him. Second, he asserts that the district court mistakenly believed he threatened the lives or health of his patients. Instead, he claims, OIG accused him of skillfully performing excessive surgery.

We reject Cassim's argument even though we recognize the possibility of irreparable harm created by the Secretary's sanctions. Cassim is simply mistaken in asserting that HHS did not believe he threatened the health of his patients. OIG charged Cassim with doing unnecessary surgery in eight cases culled from a six-month period. In those eight cases, Cassim's patients ranged in age from 66 to 86. In each case, OIG concluded that Cassim had placed his patients in "high risk" situations or in "imminent danger." The Secretary persuasively argues that unnecessary surgery on elderly patients endangers their health.

Against the harm Cassim might suffer we must balance the harm his patients might suffer. We affirm the district court's finding that the balance of hardships neither tips sharply in Cassim's favor nor favors him. Cassim fails under one prong of the alternative standard.

Under the other prong, he must demonstrate a combination of probable success and the possibility of irreparable injury. Cassim has shown the possibility of irreparable injury. * * *

Cassim alleges that as a matter of due process he is entitled to a full-blown pre-deprivation hearing. He also contends that the Social Security Act and its regulations violate due process because they fail to guarantee the promptness of the post-deprivation hearing. * * * [4]

We assume, arguendo, that Cassim has implicated either a property right or a liberty interest. * * *

Cassim's interests are substantial. * * * On the one hand, only 40% percent of Cassim's income comes from Medicare. * * * Cassim may still treat Medicare patients. If he prevails in his administrative appeal, he must be reimbursed. A successful appeal would also help restore his reputation and practice. The Secretary would have to reinstate Cassim

---

4. As part of his argument on the probability of success on the merits, Cassim asserts that the ALJ will probably reduce or reverse OIG's sanction. This argument misses the point. The "merits" at issue involve the due process claim, not whether OIG properly sanctioned Cassim.

as a Medicare participating physician, 42 C.F.R. § 1004.120(b), and give notice of his reinstatement to the public. 42 C.F.R. § 1001.134(a)(2). On the other hand, even that vindication may not remove all of the stigma associated with the Secretary's sanctions. Some damage might remain. Cassim's patients and members of the public may distrust him.

The Government's interests, however, are compelling. In the judgment of OMPRO and OIG, Cassim performed unnecessary surgery. Such surgery wastes public resources and, even more important, threatens the patient's health. OIG found that Cassim placed his patients in situations with the "potential for * * * harm." In enacting 42 U.S.C.A. § 1320c–5, Congress sought to protect Medicare beneficiaries from questionable medical practices. As an indication of the extent of Congress' concern, if the Secretary fails to act within 120 days of a peer review organization's recommendation, then the physician being investigated is automatically excluded from Medicare. 42 U.S.C.A. § 1320c–5(b)(1). Requiring full-blown pre-deprivation hearings would frustrate Congress' intent and impede the Secretary's ability to act quickly.[5] It would also impose significant administrative costs.

* * * Cassim * * * contends * * * that the statute and its regulations violate due process in failing to guarantee a timely post-deprivation hearing. The Secretary has represented that an ALJ decision could be reached four or five months after Cassim requests a hearing. Cassim does not challenge the constitutionality of the four or five month time period. Instead, he launches a facial attack on the statute and its regulations.

* * * Cassim's suspension from Medicare is for one year. He could receive an ALJ decision four or five months after he requests a hearing. Thus, he will put HHS to its proof before he suffers the full penalty imposed. Cassim may even be able to receive an expedited hearing. Moreover, the ALJ is not authorized to delay issuing an order after a hearing. * * *

* * * We vacate the temporary stay. The district court's denial of the motion for preliminary injunction is affirmed.

WICKLINE v. STATE

California Court of Appeal, 1986.
192 Cal.App.3d 1630, 239 Cal.Rptr. 810, review dismissed.[6]

Rowen, Associate Justice. * * *

[Lois J. Wickline sued the State of California as administrator of the Medi–Cal Act, Cal.Welf. & Inst.Code §§ 14000 et seq., for causing her to be discharged prematurely from a hospital.]

Responding to concerns about the escalating cost of health care, public and private payors have in recent years experimented with a variety of cost containment mechanisms. * * *

---

5. A long-established principle of due process jurisprudence is that Government must sometimes be allowed to act promptly to avoid public harm. * * *

6. Editors' Note: The citation has been simplified, the parties' names have been used throughout, and a few short paragraphs have been run together.

Early cost containment programs utilized the retrospective utilization review process. In that system the third party payor reviewed the patient's chart after the fact to determine whether the treatment provided was medically necessary. If, in the judgment of the utilization reviewer, it was not, the health care provider's claim for payment was denied.

In the cost containment program in issue in this case, prospective utilization review, authority for the rendering of health care services must be obtained before medical care is rendered. * * *

A mistaken conclusion about medical necessity following retrospective review will result in the wrongful withholding of payment. An erroneous decision in a prospective review process, on the other hand, in practical consequences, results in the withholding of necessary care, potentially leading to a patient's permanent disability or death.

* * * In 1976 Mrs. Wickline, a married woman in her mid–40s, with a limited education, was being treated by Dr. Stanley Z. Daniels, a physician engaged in a general family practice, for problems associated with her back and legs. Failing to respond to the physical therapy type of treatment he prescribed, Dr. Daniels had Mrs. Wickline admitted to Van Nuys Community Hospital in October 1976 and brought in another physician, Dr. Gerald E. Polonsky, a specialist in peripheral vascular surgery. * * *

Dr. Polonsky examined Mrs. Wickline and diagnosed her condition as arteriosclerosis obliterans with occlusion of the abdominal aorta, more generally referred to as Leriche's Syndrome. Leriche's Syndrome is a condition caused by the obstruction of the terminal aorta. * * * Dr. Polonsky concluded that it was necessary to remove a part of Mrs. Wickline's artery and insert a synthetic (Teflon) graft in its place. After agreeing to the operation, Mrs. Wickline was discharged home to await approval of her doctor's diagnosis and authorization from Medi–Cal for the recommended surgical procedure and attendant acute care hospitalization. * * * In response to Dr. Daniels' request, Medi–Cal authorized the surgical procedure and ten days of hospitalization for that treatment.

On January 6, 1977, Mrs. Wickline was admitted to Van Nuys by Dr. Daniels. On January 7, 1977, Dr. Polonsky performed a surgical procedure in which a part of Mrs. Wickline's artery was removed and a synthetic artery was inserted to replace it. Dr. Polonsky characterized that procedure as "a very major surgery." [The same day Dr. Polonsky reopened the incision and removed a clot from the graft, and five days later he performed a lumbar sympathectomy in order to stop arterial spasms.]

* * *

Mrs. Wickline was scheduled to be discharged on January 16, 1977, which would mean that she would actually leave the hospital sometime before 1 p.m. on January 17, 1977. On or about January 16, 1977, Dr. Polonsky concluded that "it was medically necessary" that Mrs. Wickline remain in the hospital * * *.

Dr. Polonsky cited many reasons for his feeling that it was medically necessary for Mrs. Wickline to remain in an acute care hospital for an additional eight days, such as the danger of infection and/or clotting. His principal reason, however, was that he felt that he was going to be able to save both of Mrs. Wickline's legs and wanted her to remain in the hospital where he could observe her and be immediately available, along with the hospital staff, to treat her if an emergency should occur.

In order to secure an extension of Mrs. Wickline's hospital stay, it was necessary to complete and present to Medi–Cal a form called "Request for Extension of Stay in Hospital," commonly referred to as * * * [a "180 form"]. * * *

The physician's responsibility in the preparation of the 180 form is to furnish (to the hospital's representative) the patient's diagnosis, significant history, clinical status, and treatment plan in sufficient detail to permit a reasonable, professional evaluation by Medi–Cal's representative, either the "on-site nurse" or/and the Medi–Cal consultant, a doctor employed by the state for just such purpose.

* * *

Doris A. Futerman, a registered nurse, was, at that time, employed by Medi–Cal as a Health Care Service Nurse, commonly referred to as an "on-site nurse." * * * Futerman had the authority, after reviewing a 180 form, to approve the requested extension of time without calling a Medi–Cal consultant. She could not, however, either reject the request outright or authorize a lesser number of days than requested. If, for any reason, she felt she could not approve the extension of time in the hospital as requested, she was required to contact a Medi–Cal consultant and that physician would make the ultimate decision on the request.

Futerman, after reviewing Mrs. Wickline's 180 form, felt that she could not approve the requested eight-day extension of acute care hospitalization. While conceding that the information provided might justify some additional time beyond the scheduled discharge date, nothing in Mrs. Wickline's case, in Futerman's opinion, would have warranted the entire eight additional days requested and, for those reasons, she telephoned the Medi–Cal consultant. She reached Dr. William S. Glassman, one of the Medi–Cal consultants on duty at the time in Medi–Cal's Los Angeles office. The Medi–Cal consultant selection occurred randomly. As was the practice, whichever Medi–Cal consultant was available at the moment took the next call that came into the office.

Dr. Glassman was board certified in general surgery and had practiced in that field until 1975 when he became employed by the Department of Health of the State of California as a Medi–Cal Consultant I. * * *

After speaking with Futerman on the telephone, Dr. Glassman rejected Mrs. Wickline's treating physician's request for an eight-day hospital extension and, instead, authorized an additional four days of hospital stay beyond the originally scheduled discharge date.

* * *

After review of Mrs. Wickline's 180 form, Dr. Glassman testified that the factors that led him to authorize four days, rather than the requested eight days, was that there was no information about the patient's temperature which he, thereupon, assumed was normal; nothing was mentioned about the patient's diet, which he then presumed was not a problem; nor was there any information about Mrs. Wickline's bowel function, which Dr. Glassman then presumed was functioning satisfactorily. Further, the fact that the 180 form noted that Mrs. Wickline was able to ambulate with help and that whirlpool treatments were to begin that day caused Dr. Glassman to presume that the patient was progressing satisfactorily and was not seriously or critically ill.

* * *

Complying with the limited extension of time authorized by Medi–Cal, Mrs. Wickline was discharged from Van Nuys on January 21, 1977. Drs. Polonsky and Daniels each wrote discharge orders. At the time of her discharge, each of Mrs. Wickline's three treating physicians were aware that the Medi–Cal consultant had approved only four of the requested eight-day hospital stay extension. While all three doctors were aware that they could attempt to obtain a further extension of Mrs. Wickline's hospital stay by telephoning the Medi–Cal consultant to request such an extension, none of them did so.

* * *

Dr. Polonsky testified that at the time in issue he felt that Medi–Cal consultants had the state's interest more in mind than the patient's welfare and that that belief influenced his decision not to request a second extension of Mrs. Wickline's hospital stay. In addition, he felt that Medi–Cal had the power to tell him, as a treating doctor, when a patient must be discharged from the hospital. Therefore, while still of the subjective, non-communicated, opinion that Mrs. Wickline was seriously ill and that the danger to her was not over, Dr. Polonsky discharged her from the hospital on January 21, 1977. He testified that had Mrs. Wickline's condition, in his medical judgment, been critical or in a deteriorating condition on January 21, he would have made some effort to keep her in the hospital beyond that day even if denied authority by Medi–Cal and even if he had to pay her hospital bill himself.

* * *

All of the medical witnesses who testified at trial agreed that Dr. Polonsky was acting within the standards of practice of the medical community in discharging Mrs. Wickline on January 21, 1977.

* * *

Mrs. Wickline testified that in the first few days after she arrived home she started feeling pain in her right leg and the leg started to lose color. In the next few days the pain got worse and the right leg took on a whitish, statue-like marble appearance. * * * Thereafter, gradually over the next few days, the Mrs. Wickline's leg "kept getting grayer and then it got bluish." * * * Mrs. Wickline returned to Van Nuys * * * January 30, 1977, nine days after her last discharge therefrom.

* * * Dr. Polonsky concluded that Mrs. Wickline had developed clotting in the right leg, that there was no circulation to that leg, and that she had developed an infection at the graft site.

* * *

Attempts to save Mrs. Wickline's leg through the utilization of anticoagulants, antibiotics, strict bed rest, pain medication and warm water whirlpool baths to the lower extremity proved unsuccessful. On February 8, 1977, Dr. Polonsky amputated Mrs. Wickline's leg below the knee because had he not done so "she would have died." The condition did not, however, heal after the first operation and on February 17, 1977, the doctors went back and amputated Mrs. Wickline's leg above the knee.

Had the eight-day extension requested on Mrs. Wickline's behalf been granted by Medi–Cal, she would have remained in the hospital through the morning hours of January 25, 1977. In Dr. Polonsky's medical opinion, based upon hypothetical questions derived from Mrs. Wickline's recollection of her course subsequent to her discharge from the hospital, had she been at Van Nuys on January 22, 23 or 24, he would have observed her leg change color, would have formed the opinion that she had clotted, and would have taken her back into surgery and reopened the graft to remove the clot again, not an uncommon procedure in this type of case. * * * Dr. Polonsky testified that had Mrs. Wickline developed an infection while she was in the hospital, it could have been controlled with the vigorous use of antibiotics.

In Dr. Polonsky's opinion, to a reasonable medical certainty, had Mrs. Wickline remained in the hospital for the eight additional days, as originally requested by him and her other treating doctors, she would not have suffered the loss of her leg.

* * *

Dr. Polonsky testified that in his medical opinion, the Medi–Cal consultant's rejection of the requested eight-day extension of acute care hospitalization and his authorization of a four-day extension in its place did not conform to the usual medical standards as they existed in 1977. He stated that, in accordance with those standards, a physician would not be permitted to make decisions regarding the care of a patient without either first seeing the patient, reviewing the patient's chart or discussing the patient's condition with her treating physician or physicians.

[The judge entered judgment on the verdict for Mrs. Wickline.]

From the facts thus presented, Medi–Cal takes the position that it was not negligent as a matter of law. Medi–Cal contends that the decision to discharge was made by each of Mrs. Wickline's three doctors, was based upon the prevailing standards of practice, and was justified by her condition at the time of her discharge. It argues that Medi–Cal had no part in Mrs. Wickline's hospital discharge and therefore was not liable, even if the decision to do so was erroneously made by her doctors.

* * *

As to the principal issue before this court, i.e., who bears responsibility for allowing a patient to be discharged from the hospital, her treating physicians or the health care payor, each side's medical expert witnesses agreed that, in accordance with the standards of medical practice as it existed in January 1977, it was for the patient's treating physician to decide the course of treatment that was medically necessary to treat the ailment. It was also that physician's responsibility to determine whether or not acute care hospitalization was required and for how long. Finally, it was agreed that the patient's physician is in a better position than the Medi–Cal consultant to determine the number of days medically necessary for any required hospital care. The decision to discharge is, therefore, the responsibility of the patient's own treating doctor.

Dr. Harry Kaufman [chief consultant at the Los Angeles field office] testified that if, on January 21, the date of Mrs. Wickline's discharge from Van Nuys, any one of her three treating doctors had decided that in his medical judgment it was necessary to keep Mrs. Wickline in the hospital for a longer period of time, they, or any of them, should have filed another request for extension of stay in the hospital, that Medi–Cal would expect those physicians to make such a request if they felt it was indicated, and upon receipt of such a request further consideration of an additional extension of hospital time would have been given.

* * *

The patient who requires treatment and who is harmed when care which should have been provided is not provided should recover for the injuries suffered from all those responsible for the deprivation of such care, including, when appropriate, health care payors. Third party payors of health care services can be held legally accountable when medically inappropriate decisions result from defects in the design or implementation of cost containment mechanisms as, for example, when appeals made on a patient's behalf for medical or hospital care are arbitrarily ignored or unreasonably disregarded or overridden. However, the physician who complies without protest with the limitations imposed by a third party payor, when his medical judgment dictates otherwise, cannot avoid his ultimate responsibility for his patient's care. He cannot point to the health care payor as the liability scapegoat when the consequences of his own determinative medical decisions go sour.

There is little doubt that Dr. Polonsky was intimidated by the Medi–Cal program, but he was not paralyzed by Dr. Glassman's response nor rendered powerless to act appropriately if other action was required under the circumstances. If, in his medical judgment, it was in his patient's best interest that she remain in the acute care hospital setting for an additional four days beyond the extended time period originally authorized by Medi–Cal, Dr. Polonsky should have made some effort to keep Mrs. Wickline there. He himself acknowledged that responsibility to his patient. It was his medical judgment, however, that Mrs. Wickline could be discharged when she was. All Mrs. Wickline's treating physicians concurred and all the doctors who testified at trial, for either Mrs. Wickline or Medi–Cal, agreed that Dr. Polonsky's medical decision to discharge Mrs. Wickline met the standard of care applicable at the time. Medi–Cal was not a party to that medical decision and therefore cannot be held to share in the harm resulting if such decision was negligently made.

In addition thereto, while Medi–Cal played a part in the scenario before us in that it was the resource for the funds to pay for the treatment sought, and its input regarding the nature and length of hospital care to be provided was of paramount importance, Medi–Cal did not override the medical judgment of Mrs. Wickline's treating physicians at the time of her discharge. It was given no opportunity to do so. Therefore, there can be no viable cause of action against it for the consequences of that discharge decision.

* * *

This court appreciates that what is at issue here is the effect of cost containment programs upon the professional judgment of physicians to prescribe hospital treatment for patients requiring the same. While we recognize, realistically, that cost consciousness has become a permanent feature of the health care system, it is essential that cost limitation programs not be permitted to corrupt medical judgment. We have concluded, from the facts in issue here, that in this case it did not.

* * *

The judgment is reversed.

LAZORKO v. PENNSYLVANIA HOSPITAL

United States Court of Appeals for the Third Circuit, 2000.
237 F.3d 242.

ROTH, Circuit Judge:

Patricia Norlie–Lazorko committed suicide in July 1993, allegedly as a consequence of her untreated mental illness. Her husband, Jonathan Lazorko, brought suit in state court against Dr. David Nicklin, Patricia's doctor; University City Family Medicine, Nicklin's employer; Pennsylvania Hospital; the Institute of Pennsylvania; and U.S. Healthcare, Inc., the health maintenance organization (HMO) administering Lazorko's health benefits. After a series of removals of the case to the U.S. District Court and remands to state court, Lazorko appeals the dismissal of his direct claims against U.S. Healthcare * * *.

I. BACKGROUND

Norlie–Lazorko suffered from depression and schizophrenia. In late 1992, she attempted suicide and was hospitalized for six months. She was discharged from the hospital in June 1993 but again began contemplating suicide. Although she asked to be rehospitalized, Dr. Nicklin denied her request. On July 4, 1993, Norlie–Lazorko committed suicide.

Following his wife's death, Jonathan Lazorko, as administrator of her estate, brought suit in Pennsylvania state court. Lazorko alleged as to U.S. Healthcare that under state law it was directly and vicariously liable for his wife's death because the HMO imposed financial disincentives on Dr. Nicklin that discouraged him from recommending her for additional treatment.

Based on this claim, U.S. Healthcare removed the case to federal court * * *

* * *

* * * The court remanded Lazorko's vicarious liability claims against U.S. Healthcare, however, because they alleged medical malpractice, an area of tort law traditionally regulated by the states, which did not implicate the regulation of employer plans and, thus, was outside the scope of ERISA's express preemption.

U.S. Healthcare also moved to sanction Lazorko's attorney, alleging that he had failed to reasonably investigate several of the charges levied against U.S. Healthcare, including the allegations that the company issued sham benefit policies and that it intentionally denied patients treatment so as to maximize profits. The District Court granted U.S. Healthcare's motion in a second June 30, 1998, order, which struck the offending allegations from the complaint and awarded the costs incurred to defend against the challenged allegations.[5] On July 24 and 29, Lazorko appealed both of the June 30 orders. U.S. Healthcare cross-appealed the remand to the state court of the vicarious liability claims against it.

* * *

III. THE DIRECT CLAIMS AGAINST U.S. HEALTHCARE

* * *

Relying on our earlier decision in Dukes v. U.S. Healthcare, Inc., 57 F.3d 350 (3d Cir. 1995), we reasoned that the refusal to offer additional care, whether couched in terms of direct or vicarious liability, could be a question of the quality of care provided. As such, it did not amount to a

---

5. * * * We will affirm the District Court's determination that Lazorko's attorney failed to satisfy the "stop, think, investigate and research" rule before including these paragraphs in his Complaint. * * *

claim that benefits to which the plaintiffs were otherwise entitled had been denied by U.S. Healthcare when administering a plan. Instead, the claim concerned decisions of treatment that were akin to claims for medical malpractice. [ ] We had concluded in Dukes that a claim for vicarious liability against an HMO for a doctor's malpractice fell outside the scope of ERISA's complete preemption clause. In In re U.S. Healthcare, we extended that ruling to encompass claims that an HMO was directly liable for arranging inadequate care. In doing so, we reasoned that financial incentives that discouraged care did not deny plan benefits but instead affected the quality of the care provided. [ ]. Thus, we held that decisions to deny a particular request in the course of providing treatment could be a claim about the quality—and not the quantity—of benefits provided. (In all but the details, Lazorko's claims against U.S. Healthcare fall squarely within this rubric.) On appeal, Lazorko argues that his liability claims amount to ones of quality because U.S. Healthcare implicitly caused Dr. Nicklin to misdiagnose and/or mistreat the severity of Ms. Norlie–Lazorko's illness. Thus, such a claim does not fall within the complete preemption scope of § 502(a)(1)(B).

U.S. Healthcare counters with two basic arguments, neither of which we find persuasive. First, it argues that Dr. Nicklin's refusal to hospitalize Patricia Norlie–Lazorko amounts to a denial of benefits because hospitalization is a benefit under Jonathan Lazorko's HMO plan. We reject this characterization of the claim. Lazorko is not arguing that his plan is supposed to permit hospitalizations for mental illness and that U.S. Healthcare refused his wife's request for guaranteed service. Instead, he is arguing that, when confronted with his wife's requests for additional treatment, Dr. Nicklin, influenced by U.S. Healthcare's financial incentives that penalized a decision to grant additional hospitalizations, made the medical decision not to readmit her to the hospital. Because Lazorko's claim is one concerning the propriety of care rather than the administration of that care, the claim is not completely preempted. In other words, the claim here is that the denial of Norlie–Lazorko's request for hospitalization occurred in the course of a treatment decision, not in the administration of the Lazorkos' plan generally. [ ]

U.S. Healthcare's second contention is that, in light of the recent Supreme Court decision in Pegram v. Herdrich, 530 U.S. 211, 120 S.Ct. 2143, 147 L.Ed.2d 164 (2000), subjecting an HMO to liability is improper because Pegram recognized the centrality of financial incentives to the operation of an HMO. Pegram, however, does not alter our analysis. In evaluating the question of the circumstances under which an HMO owes a fiduciary duty to the members of an ERISA plan, the Pegram court held that mixed eligibility decisions by an HMO (i.e., decisions involving not only the coverage of a particular treatment by the plan but the reasonable medical necessity for the treatment) are not fiduciary decisions under ERISA. The decision in question here, the need to hospitalize Patricia Norlie–Lazorko, appears to be just such a mixed eligibility decision and to the extent that the mixed decision implicates the quality of the care received by Norlie–Lazorko, Pegram does not foreclose the direct claims against U.S. Healthcare.

Before our decision in In re U.S. Healthcare, it was not clear whether the denial of a particular type of benefit, such as hospitalization, fell within § 502(a)(1)(B)'s narrow but exclusive scope. This ambiguity was articulated in Dukes: drawing the line between the denial of benefits under a plan and the provision of substandard care is difficult. [ ]. In ruling on Lazorko's claims here, however, the District Court did not have the benefit of our further analysis in In re Healthcare. We now conclude that Lazorko's claim, as it has been pled, falls on the standard of care, not the denial of benefits, side of the line.

We note, moreover, that since our decision in In re U.S. Healthcare, our district courts have consistently applied its reasoning to determine whether it is the quality of care provided or the denial of a plan benefit that is implicated when treatment is refused.

* * *

Because we conclude that Lazorko's case is not subject to complete preemption, it follows that it was improperly removed from state court. We must therefore vacate the dismissal by the District Court of the direct claims in Count I of the Fourth Amended Complaint and remand those claims to the District Court for remand to state court. When the underlying federal subject matter jurisdiction upon which to remove a case from state court does not exist, the entire case must be remanded. [ ]

On remand, it will be for the state court to further determine whether a § 502 claim of denial of a benefit provided by his plan is lodged in the heart of Lazorko's direct claims in Count I. If such a claim should materialize, that claim will have to be removed once more to federal court. Moreover, on remand the state court will also have the task to determine to what extent, if any, Lazorko's claims against U.S. Healthcare are substantively preempted under § 514. * * *

IV. Conclusion

Because Lazorko requests relief for the consequences of U.S. Healthcare's provision of inadequate services and not for the denial of benefits under his health care plan, Count I of his Complaint was improperly removed to federal court. Consequently, we will vacate the District Court's dismissal of Lazorko's direct claims against U.S. Healthcare and remand Count I to the District Court for remand to the state court for further proceedings. * * *

Notes

1) Utilization review measures the quality of a doctor's services by "professional standards review" for the quality of the decision-making structure, the performance of services and the outcome achieved. It is remote peer review in the sense of "jury of peers" Closer peers may also

review a colleagues' professional behavior—for example, surgery performed mainly for profit is not regarded favorably by a surgeon's peers on the hospital staff or in the county medical society, and these peers have their own ways of expressing disapproval. Utilization reviewers are strangers to the surgeon; they examine medical records rather than witnessing treatment; they are medically trained and supervised, but they are not all doctors.

The underlying objective of utilization review is cost containment; the prevention of malpractice is something of a byproduct. In *Cassim*, retrospective review looked at a number of past cases for patterns of overutilization—other examples might be the long-term use of acute care hospitalization when nursing home care would have sufficed, or ordering inappropriate and expensive tests. The weapon in the arsenal of these retrospective reviewers was relatively blunt: it could prevent future overutilization, but so could the hospital by denying staff privileges to an over-utilizer. See *Cobb County–Kennestone Hospital Authority v. Prince*, 242 Ga. 139, 249 S.E.2d 581 (1978) in which a hospital required its staff neurologists to use the hospital's CAT scanner rather than their own.

Another form of retrospective utilization allows bill-payors to decide whether to pay for services already rendered on a case-by-case basis. Current utilization review works on the extension of services of a patient in current treatment, as occurred in *Wickline*. Preadmission certification occurs before the patient is admitted for future elective treatment. It may be the most effective cost-saver, but it also offers the greatest risk that the doctor's judgment was affected to the patient's detriment by bill-paying considerations. Considering the impact in *Cassim* of the Medicare reimbursement cutoff on the surgeon's livelihood and professional reputation, and since investigations and administrative proceedings take time, the question becomes whether to err on the side of individual reputation or public economy, pending final determination.

Was Dr. Cassim unconstitutionality deprived of his constitutional rights? He had no property interest in participating in the Medicare Program that the court would protect pending final review. As for personal rights, the preliminary injunction standard is designed to test the detriment and likelihood of success on the merits. Since the court did not find that plaintiff's injury was irreparable and that the plaintiff had a substantial probability of success on the merits, the government's interest in the integrity of the utilization review process prevailed over the plaintiff's right to pre-exclusion judicial review.

2) *Wickline* was a case of first impression, though it has not recurred a number of times. The dicta on the possible liability of the utilization reviewers are a real threat. The same court has since criticized *Wickline* and limited other dicta concerning the liability of treating doctors. See *Wilson v. Blue Cross of So. Cal.*, 222 Cal.App.3d 660, 271 Cal.Rptr. 876 (1990).

The treating doctors and the hospital were not parties in *Wickline*. Could the plaintiff have stated a claim against the doctors for negligent prognosis in underestimating the need for longer hospitalization? The facts do not seem to support this theory as it appears that Ms. Wickline was progressing reasonably well. Her thrombus probably developed or became significant after she was discharged. Ms. Wickline had a tenuous causation argument: but for the premature discharge, her condition would have been managed satisfactorily and the amputation would have been avoided. Assuming she was able to overcome that hurdle, was it the doctors or Medi–Cal that caused the amputation?

Assuming that causation could be established, how about a claim against the doctors for refusing to stand up for Ms. Wickline? Medi–Cal had the power only to pay (after authorization) or not to pay (without authorization), but the doctors ordered Ms. Wickline's premature discharge. Only a physician can order the discharge of a patient. If the doctor refuses to do so, the patient is told that he or she may be responsible for the bill unless retrospective utilization review determines that the extra time was necessary. The patient then makes a choice: leave the hospital against medical advice, or risk incurring a large hospital bill. If the patient is unable to pay, the hospital is left with a bad debt. As for the physician who declined to fight harder, including an appeal, if necessary, is there a legitimate concern that providers who frequently seek additional benefits on behalf of their patients will be penalized for failure to observe cost containment?

SECTION B. PEER REVIEW AND STAFF PRIVILEGES

UNIVERSITY HEALTH SERVICES, INC. v. LONG.

Supreme Court of Georgia, 2002.
274 Ga. 829, 561 S.E.2d 77.

Sears, Presiding Justice.

The appellant, University Health Services, Inc. d/b/a University Hospital ("University Hospital"), appeals from an interlocutory injunction prohibiting it from revoking the privileges of the appellee, Dr. Long, an obstetrician and gynecologist at University Hospital, pending a final resolution of Dr. Long's action against the hospital. Because we conclude that the trial court abused its discretion in entering the injunction, we reverse.

Dr. Long has had privileges at University Hospital for approximately 25 years. In the summer of 2000, the hospital instituted administrative proceedings to review the care that Dr. Long had provided to certain patients and to determine whether his clinical privileges should be revoked. After a recommendation was made early in the review process to suspend Dr. Long's privileges, Dr. Long, with the hospital's consent, obtained an interlocutory injunction from the trial court that permitted him to continue practicing until further order of the court. The injunction also provided that the hospital could continue with and complete its administrative review process. After the hospital had completed the review process, the governing body of the hospital revoked Dr. Long's clinical privileges. Because of the initial injunction, the hospital had to petition the trial court to dissolve the injunction to make its revocation of Dr. Long's privileges effective. After the hospital filed its petition to dissolve the injunction, Dr. Long filed an amended complaint asking the trial court, among other things, to continue the interlocutory injunction, reverse the decision of the hospital to revoke his privileges, and rule that the hospital's fair hearing plan violates due process. Ruling in Dr. Long's favor, the trial court declined to dissolve the injunction, and instead continued it in effect until a final resolution of the case. University Hospital has now filed this appeal.

The purpose of an interlocutory injunction is to preserve the status quo pending a final adjudication of the case, and in determining whether to preserve the status quo, a trial court must balance the conveniences of the parties pending the final adjudication, with consideration being given to whether greater harm might come from granting the injunction or denying it. Although a trial court has broad discretion in deciding whether to grant or deny an interlocutory injunction, the trial court's discretion can be ultimately circumscribed by the applicable rules of law.

In balancing the conveniences of the parties in this case, we conclude that the trial court's discretion was fundamentally circumscribed by a rule of law concerning a court's role when reviewing a hospital's revocation of a physician's clinical privileges. In such cases, a court's role " 'is not to substitute [its] judgment for that of the hospital's governing board or to reweigh the evidence regarding the renewal or termination of medical staff privileges.' " Examining the evidence in this case under this standard, we conclude that the only conclusion that can be drawn is that the trial court had to defer to the medical judgment of the hospital governing body that Dr. Long had mismanaged patient care, had exercised poor clinical judgment that had adversely affected patient care, and had deviated from "appropriate clinical practice."

In light of the fact that the trial court and this Court must defer to the governing board regarding Dr. Long's medical skill and judgment, we conclude that the trial court abused its discretion in balancing the conveniences of the parties in Dr. Long's favor. We are mindful of the harm that could arise to Dr. Long from the wrongful suspension of his clinical privileges at University Hospital. However, given that the hospital has found that Dr. Long's care is adversely affecting patients and given that we must, as a matter of law, defer to the hospital's medical judgment in this case, we conclude that that harm to patients outweighs any potential harm to Dr. Long. Accordingly, we conclude that the trial court erred in declining to dissolve the interlocutory injunction.

Judgment reversed. All the Justices concur.

MEYERS v. COLUMBIA/HCA HEALTHCARE

United States Court of Appeals for the Sixth Circuit, 2003.
341 F.3d 461.

CLELAND, District Judge.

Plaintiffs-appellants Dr. Robert Meyers ("Meyers") and his wife, Dr. Mary Meyers, initiated this action against multiple defendants after the Board of Trustees of Logan Memorial Hospital denied Meyers' reappointment to the hospital's medical staff. The district court granted summary judgment in favor of defendants, finding that they were immune under the Health Care Quality Improvement Act ("HCQIA"), 42 U.S.C. § 11101 *et seq.* Defendants moved for an award of costs and attorney's fees under the HCQIA, and the district court denied their motion. Plaintiffs appeal the grant of summary judgment; defendants cross-appeal the denial of costs and fees. We affirm the judgment of the district court on both issues.

I. FACTS

* * * On March 25, 1991, Meyers applied for medical staff privileges at Logan Memorial Hospital, Inc. ("LMH") in Russellville, Kentucky. Shortly thereafter, the Credentials Committee and the Medical Executive Committee ("MEC") approved Meyers for staff privileges. As a result, in September 1991, the LMH Board of Trustees ("Board") approved Meyers for appointment to the medical staff. Pursuant to the LMH Bylaws, all initial appointments to the medical staff were provisional for one year. At the end of that year the physician would be reevaluated to qualify for advancement from associate to active member status.

In the fall of 1992, the Credentials Committee began to evaluate Meyers for his advancement to active staff privileges. On April 12, 1993, the Credentials Committee, which Meyers argues was composed largely of his competitors, voted to deny him staff privileges. In its decision, the committee cited concerns about Meyers' history of moving from hospital to hospital following disputes with hospital staff, his failure to timely and fully disclose disciplinary and corrective action taken against him while working in Virginia, and the quality of his patient care. At this point, pursuant to LMH Bylaws, the Credentials Committee was to notify Meyers of the general nature of its concerns and arrange a meeting with Meyers. The Credentials Committee did, on short notice, invite Meyers to a meeting. According to Fred Mudge, a member of the Board, this invitation did not comply with the Bylaws.

On June 3, 1993, the MEC, half of whose members were also members of the Credentials Committee, voted to accept the Credentials Committee decision and revoke Meyers' staff privileges. Neither of these committees, however, had the power to grant or deny privileges to Meyers. The MEC was to consider the recommendation from the Credentials Committee and make a recommendation to the Board, which had the ultimate authority to grant, deny, or terminate Meyers' privileges.

On January 24, 1994, the Board informed Meyers that it was assuming full responsibility for determining his reappointment and advancement to active staff because of his concerns with the manner in which the peer review process was being handled. Three members of the Board, acting as a Credentials Committee, conducted an independent review. *This committee discussed concerns about Meyers' behavior and inability to get along with others in addition to questions about his surgical technique.* (Emphasis added). The committee gave Meyers the opportunity to put forth additional information, but he maintained that there was none. The committee questioned Meyers about several incident reports concerning disruptive behavior, his history of problems at other hospitals, his failure to timely complete medical records, his hostility towards the operation room staff, reports of breaking the sterile field, and his failure to provide appropriate coverage for patients while he was out of town. Meyers acknowledged that he had a personality problem.

At the same time, the Kentucky Cabinet for Human Resources Drug Control Division was investigating Meyers' prescription practices pursuant to complaints from pharmacists and the Kentucky State Police about the volume of prescriptions he wrote for controlled substances. The investigation concluded that "Meyers may not have used good judgment in prescribing controlled substances to all of his patients." The Kentucky Board of Medical Licensure recommended that Meyers attend a University of Kentucky miniresidency course in prescribing controlled substances.

On March 18, 1994, this three-member committee of the Board voted to deny Meyers' appointment to active staff. The reasons cited for the committee's decision were Meyers' failure to satisfy requirements that he meet LMH's standard of care, abide by the ethics of the profession, work cooperatively with others, and timely complete medical records. The committee outlined Meyers' pattern of disruptive behavior which included, but was not limited to, temper tantrums, repeated refusal to limit elective cases to time periods routinely reserved for him, attempted interference with the right of an attending physician to refer a patient to the surgeon of his choice or to transfer the patient, condescending remarks toward women, refusal to speak to a member of his surgical team during surgical procedures, and several instances of throwing a scalpel during surgery. The committee informed Meyers that "this behavior can have an adverse effect on the quality of patient care by inhibiting the ability of hospital personnel to perform optimally, by making it difficult for the hospital to retain qualified personnel, and by interfering with the judgment of referring physicians." The committee further noted that Meyers' behavior "can also disrupt the efficient operation of the hospital and the smooth operation of the surgical department to the detriment of the medical staff, the hospital, and the community." As for his failure to timely complete medical records, the committee stated that "delinquent medical records can put patients at risk by being inaccurate or incomplete if needed to assist in later diagnosis and treatment of a patient." As for quality of care, the committee noted that Meyers had failed to comply with LMH's policy of obtaining post-operative films and that he had demonstrated repeated instances of violating the sterile field.

At this point, the Board began proceedings under the Medical Staff Bylaws Fair Hearing Plan * * * Meyers was represented by counsel, given the opportunity to present witnesses, affidavits, and other documentary evidence, and given the right to confront, examine, and cross-examine witnesses presented by LMH.

In April 1995, the Fair Hearing Committee issued its report and recommendation that LMH not appoint Meyers to its staff because of his failure to meet LMH's ethical standards and his inability to work cooperatively with others. In May, the Board adopted and affirmed the Fair Hearing Committee's recommendation. The Board informed Meyers of its decision and his right to appeal. Meyers appealed the Board's decision and was again represented by counsel. On August 9, 1995, the Board informed Meyers of its vote to affirm the decision denying clinical privileges to Meyers. This was the Board's final decision and Meyers' privileges were revoked.

II. Procedural History

On August 22, 1995, Meyers brought suit in Kentucky state court (Logan Circuit Court) seeking a restraining order and a temporary and permanent injunction requiring LMH to reinstate his staff privileges and enjoining LMH from making a report to the National Practitioner Data Bank. * * *

* * *

IV. Discussion

A. The district court's grant of summary judgment in favor of Defendants on the basis of HCQIA immunity was proper.

The HCQIA was passed in 1986 to provide for effective peer review and interstate monitoring of incompetent physicians, and to grant qualified immunity from damages for those who participate in peer review activities.[ ] If a "professional review action" satisfies certain reasonableness requirements, then those persons participating in the review "shall not be liable in damages under any law of the United States or of any State . . . with respect to the action." [ ]

Specifically, persons participating in a professional review action are entitled to immunity if the action is taken:

    (1) in the reasonable belief that the action was in furtherance of quality health care;

    (2) after a reasonable effort to obtain the facts of the matter;

(3) after adequate notice and hearing procedures are afforded to the physician involved or after such other procedures as are fair to the physician under the circumstances; and

(4) in the reasonable belief that the action was warranted by the facts known after such reasonable effort to obtain facts and after meeting the requirement of paragraph (3).

[ ] Once the preceding standards are met, the HCQIA offers immunity to:

(A) the professional review body,

(B) any person acting as a member or staff to the body,

(C) any person under a contract or other formal agreement with the body, and

(D) any person who participates with or assists the body with respect to the action.

[ ]

The term "professional review body" includes a "health care entity and the governing body or any committee of a health care entity which conducts professional review activity." [ ]. The district court correctly found that Defendants all fall within the protected categories [ ]. LMH is a health care entity and a professional review body. The individual doctors are covered under (B)–(D) as staff members of LMH, persons under a contract with LMH, or persons who participate with or assist the body with respect to the professional review action.

The HCQIA creates a rebuttable presumption of immunity, forcing the plaintiff to prove that the defendant's actions did not comply with the relevant standards. * * *. As the district court explained, this rebuttable presumption "creates an unusual summary judgment standard" that can be stated as follows: "Might a reasonable jury, viewing the facts in the best light for [the plaintiff], conclude that he has shown, by a preponderance of the evidence, that the defendants' actions are outside the scope of [the standards]. The plaintiff has the burden of overcoming the presumption of immunity by showing that the review process was not reasonable. Meyers argues that Defendants can meet none of the elements for establishing statutory immunity. However, as the district court found, he failed to raise a genuine issue of material fact as to any element. Therefore, we will affirm the grant of summary judgment.

1. The Board's Action Was Taken in the Reasonable Belief that It Was in Furtherance of Quality Health Care

The "reasonable belief" standard of the HCQIA is satisfied if "the reviewers, with the information available to them at the time of the professional review action, would reasonably have concluded that their action would restrict incompetent behavior or would protect patients." *Bryan*, 33 F.3d at 1323 [ ]. It is an objective standard, rather than a subjective good faith requirement. [ ] The Act does not require that the professional review result in actual improvement in the quality of health care, but only that it was undertaken in the reasonable belief that quality health care was being furthered. [ ]

Meyers contends that a reasonable jury could find that this element was not satisfied because: (1) eight members of the medical staff testified on behalf of Meyers and no member testified against him; (2) two independent reviewers gave favorable reviews of Meyers; (3) two psychologists who examined Meyers recommended that he receive his privileges; and (4) although some nurses testified as to disruptive incidents, each of them testified that they could still work with Meyers.

However, the evidence conclusively demonstrates that both the Board's decision and the Fair Hearing Committee's decision were made in the reasonable belief that they were furthering quality health care, and no reasonable jury could find otherwise. Among other evidence, the Fair Hearing Committee heard testimony about twenty-two incident reports involving Meyers which documented loss of temper during surgery, breaking the sterile field, failure to take and document histories before patients were sedated for surgery, and other problems. This evidence was also considered by the Board. The Fair Hearing Committee noted that its decision was based on Meyers' temper tantrums, his use of coercive tactics, delinquent medical records, his inability to work with others, and unethical conduct. As the district court held, these reasons are in furtherance of quality health care, despite the fact that no patients were actually injured. "Quality health care" is not limited to clinical competence, but includes matters of general behavior and ethical conduct. *See Bryan*, 33 F.3d at 1334–35 (finding that the termination of physician's privileges was "taken in reasonable belief that the action was in furtherance of quality health care" where physician had "exhibited a pattern of unprofessional conduct over a period of many years," "was disruptive," and "interfered with the important work of other employees") [ ] Meyers failed to present evidence that the action against him was not taken in the reasonable belief that it furthered quality health care.

2. The Board's Action Was Taken After a Reasonable Effort to Obtain the Facts of the Matter

Similarly, Meyers failed to raise any genuine issue of fact with respect to the second element of HCQIA immunity. The inquiry is whether the "totality of the process" leading up to the professional review action evinced a reasonable effort to obtain the facts of the matter. *Mathews v. Lancaster Gen. Hosp.*, 87 F.3d 624, 637 (3d Cir. 1996). In this case, there was an exhaustive review process. As the district court noted, Meyers was reviewed by both the Credentials Committee and the MEC, as well as by a committee of three Board members who conducted an independent investigation. This three-person committee questioned Meyers and gave him an opportunity to provide them with additional information. It then made a recommendation to the Board, which voted to deny Meyers' appointment to the active staff. Thereafter, the Fair Hearing Committee met on eleven occasions and heard testimony from thirty-five witnesses. Meyers was represented by counsel, given the opportunity to present witnesses, affidavits, and other documentary evidence, and given the right to confront, examine, and cross-examine witnesses presented by LMH. Meyers disputes that a "reasonable inquiry" occurred, but his argument is limited to conclusory statements attacking individual items of evidence considered by the reviewers. He fails, however, to raise a genuine issue to rebut the presumption that the professional review action was taken after a "reasonable effort to obtain the facts."

* * *

4. The Board's Action Was Taken in the Reasonable Belief That the Action Was Warranted by the Facts

The district court also held that no reasonable jury could find that the Board did not take the action in the reasonable belief that it was warranted by the facts. * * * While Meyers challenges certain of the underlying facts upon which Defendants relied, he has not shown that the facts were "so obviously mistaken or inadequate as to make reliance on them unreasonable." *Mathews,* 87 F.3d at 638. Moreover, "a plaintiff's showing 'that [the] doctors reached an incorrect conclusion on a particular medical issue because of a lack of understanding' does not 'meet the burden of contradicting the existence of a reasonable belief that they were furthering health care quality in participating in the peer review process.' " [ ] In view of the Board's well-supported findings that Meyers had failed to meet LMH's ethical standards and that he was unable to work cooperatively with others, there is no genuine issue as to whether the Board's action was taken in the reasonable belief that it was warranted by the facts.

* * *

V. Conclusion

For the foregoing reasons, we affirm the district court's grant of summary judgment and its denial of costs and fees.

ARDISANA v. NORTHWEST COMMUNITY HOSPITAL

Appellate Court of Illinois, First District, First Division, 2003.
342 Ill.App.3d 741, 277 Ill.Dec. 296, 795 N.E.2d 964.

JUSTICE SMITH delivered the opinion of the court:

Defendant Northwest Community Hospital (Northwest) appeals from a circuit court order holding it in contempt for refusing to produce certain documents requested in discovery by plaintiff Richard Ardisana. Northwest contends that the documents in question are protected from discovery under * * * the Medical Studies Act.

Factual Background

The underlying action in this case arises out of medical care provided to plaintiff at Northwest from November 11, 1999, through January 10, 2000. In his second amended complaint, plaintiff alleges in pertinent part that he underwent a surgical procedure at Northwest on November 11, 1999, to remove a growth from his colon. In the days following that surgery, plaintiff developed gastric reflux, vomiting and abdominal bleeding. The vomiting caused wound evisceration, necessitating repair surgery done under general anesthesia on November 16, 1999. Plaintiff aspirated vomit during the latter surgery and subsequently developed aspiration pneumonia.

Plaintiffs complaint further alleges that employees, agents and/or apparent agents of Northwest, including the surgeon (Dr. Robert Aid) and the anesthesiologist for the second surgery (Dr. Subhash Balaney), were negligent in various respects that caused the wound evisceration and the aspiration pneumonia, which in turn led to severe and permanent damage to his lungs.

In the course of discovery, plaintiff filed a supplemental request to produce, asking in part that Northwest produce the following documents:

"Any and all writings, memos or documents pertaining to any conclusions or final recommendations for any peer review process, including the Department of Surgery, pertaining to Richard Ardisana. If any materials are claimed to be privileged, please provide a privilege log identifying the document and its date."

Northwest objected on the ground that the documents it had were privileged pursuant to the Medical Studies Act. The trial court directed Northwest to provide for its *in camera* review a privilege log stating the basis for each claim of privilege, a copy of the documents listed in the log, and a copy of the complaint. Northwest filed the requested documents, as well as the affidavit of its risk manager, Karla Ford, in which it was averred that the documents provided for *in camera* inspection

"were generated in conjunction with investigations by the General Surgery Quality Audit and Anesthesia Quality Improvement Audit Committees. These documents were prepared solely for those two committees and by these committees. The documents referenced in the privilege log under Roman numerals I and II were used exclusively by those committees and were shared with no one outside of those committees. The sole exception is the letter sent to Dr. Balaney, which was sent to him but arose exclusively from the committee's investigation and requested information for the exclusive use of the committee."

The attached privilege log identified two pertinent groups of documents:

1. A quality management worksheet prepared for the surgical quality audit committee, dated February 23, 2000, and minutes of

audit committee meetings held on February 23 and April 19, 2000, at which plaintiffs care was discussed.

2. A quality management worksheet prepared for the anesthesia department quality audit committee dated May 10, 2000; minutes of an audit committee meeting held May 10, 2000, and a letter from the chairman of the audit committee to Dr. Subhash Balaney dated June 5, 2000, requesting certain additional information about plaintiffs care.

Plaintiff did not file a written response to Northwest's objections. The trial court issued a written memorandum decision on June 11, 2002, in which it ruled that all of the material claimed by Northwest to be privileged was discoverable. Specifically, the court held that only material that was generated during the temporal parameters of the peer-review process was privileged and that Northwest had failed to establish when the process in this case commenced and ended. Additionally, the court found that the internal conclusions and recommendations of the committees constituted "results," which are not privileged under the Act.

On June 24, 2002, Northwest filed a motion to reconsider. To that motion were attached two additional affidavits. The first was that of Cynthia Dougherty, R.N., who was director of Northwest's quality measurement and improvement (QMI) department when the medical care at issue was provided. Ms. Dougherty averred that the quality review in this case commenced shortly after plaintiffs discharge and was triggered by the fact that it met established screening criteria set by the departments of surgery and anesthesia. She outlined the reviewing process and the steps taken to ensure that the information generated during the course of that review remained confidential.

The second affidavit was that of Susan Sullivan, another member of the QMI department. Ms. Sullivan was involved with the reviews conducted in this case by both the department of surgery and the department of anesthesia. She averred the department of surgery concluded its review on April 19, 2000, but that, as of the date of her affidavit (June 24, 2002), she was not aware that the department of anesthesia had yet completed its review. Like the affidavit of Ms. Dougherty, Ms. Sullivan's affidavit contained detailed information with respect to the steps taken to preserve the confidentiality of the documents generated during the peer-review process.

Both affiants stated that the documents in question (labeled exhibit E) pertained solely to quality reviews conducted on plaintiffs care and on the care of other patients that the committees reviewed during the same meetings.

On August 12, 2002, the trial court issued its written ruling on Northwest's motion to reconsider. The court ordered that the documents containing references to patients other than plaintiff be redacted because the information was irrelevant. It otherwise denied the motion, however, because the supplemental affidavits could have been submitted prior to the court's initial ruling and because, in the court's view, the added materials still did not specifically identify when the peer-review process began, who started it and when it ended.

Despite the court's ruling, Northwest continued to refuse to produce the disputed documents. On August 22, 2002, the court entered an order, *nunc pro tunc,* in which it held Northwest in contempt, and imposed a fine of $50. This appeal followed.

DISCUSSION

On appeal, Northwest contends that the documents at issue fall squarely within the letter and spirit of the Medical Studies Act and that the circuit court accordingly erred when it ruled that they were not privileged from discovery.

The burden of establishing a privilege under the Medical Studies Act is on the party seeking to invoke it. [ ] * * * However, the question of whether specific materials are part of a medical study or an internal quality control is a factual question within that legal determination, subject to reversal upon review only if it is against the manifest weight of the evidence. [ ]. The Medical Studies Act provides:

> "All information, interviews, reports, statements, memoranda, recommendations, letters of reference or other third party confidential assessments of a health care practitioner's professional competence, or other data of * * * committees of licensed or accredited hospitals or their medical staffs, including Patient Care Audit Committees, Medical Care Evaluation Committees, Utilization Review Committees, Credential Committees and Executive Committees, or their designees (but not the medical records pertaining to the patient), used in the course of internal quality control or of medical study for the purpose of reducing morbidity and mortality, or for improving patient care or increasing organ and tissue donation, shall be privileged, strictly confidential and shall be used only for medical research, * * * the evaluation and improvement of quality care, or granting, limiting or revoking staff privileges or agreements for services * * *." [ ].

The Act further provides that such privileged material "shall not be admissible as evidence, nor discoverable in any action of any kind in any court or before any tribunal, board, agency or person." [ ].

The purpose of the Medical Studies Act is to advance the quality of health care by ensuring that members of the medical profession effectively engage in a peer-review process. [ ]. Absent a confidentiality provision, physicians might be reluctant to engage in strict peer review due to a number of apprehensions: loss of referrals, respect, and friends, possible retaliations, vulnerability to tort actions, and fear of malpractice actions in which the records of the peer-review proceedings might be used. [ ] Thus, the Act protects documents that arise from the workings of a peer-review committee [ ] and that are an integral part but not the result of the peer-review process. [ ].

With the foregoing principles in mind, we examine the trial court's ruling.

A.   *Recommendations vs. Results*

The trial court determined that the "conclusions or final recommendations" of a peer-review committee are the equivalent of discoverable "results." Based on this premise, the court ordered produced pages 1 and 2 of the surgical department quality review, which contain a committee conclusion; page 9 of the minutes of the general surgery QMI conference, which contains two conclusions; the "indication of" conclusions contained in an anesthesia quality management worksheet; and the letter sent by the anesthesia department chair to Dr. Balaney in which additional information for the peer review was sought.

Though the memorandum decision is well-reasoned, we find the trial court's analysis to have been flawed, as it rests on an inaccurate premise. It is true that results of the peer-review process are not privileged; however, the court in its order has purportedly broadened the category of what constitutes "results" beyond the limits we find to be contained in the relevant case law. *Results* of a peer-review committee take the form of ultimate decisions made or actions taken by that committee, or the hospital, and include the revocation, modification or restriction of privileges, letters of resignation or withdrawal, and the revision of rules, regulations, policies and procedures for medical staff. [ ]. The recommendations and internal conclusions of peer-review committees, which may or may not lead to those results, *are not discoverable.* [ ] Indeed, the plain language of the Medical Studies Act provides that "recommendations" used in the course of internal quality control are to receive its protection.

Accordingly, we reverse that portion of the trial court's ruling which provides for the production of any portion of the above-referenced documents, all of which we find to be privileged under the Act in their entirety.

B.   *Temporal Limitations*

The second basis used by the trial court to support its decision is the failure on the part of Northwest to come forward with evidence relating to the start and end dates of the peer-review process.

* * *

* * * [T]he court did find that, even if the materials from the latter two affidavits were considered, Northwest had still failed to establish that the documents at issue were generated while the peer-review process was ongoing, as opposed to before or after the process took place. The court also correctly noted that the Medical Studies Act does not protect against disclosure of information generated before a peer-review process begins or after it ends. [ ]. The burden of establishing the applicability of a privilege under the Act lies with the party who invokes it. [ ]. Claims of privilege may be supported either by submitting the purportedly privileged materials for *in camera* inspection or by submitting affidavits setting forth facts sufficient to establish the applicability of the privilege to the particular documents being withheld. [ ]. In this case, Northwest did both.

We too have examined the disputed documents, which have been supplied under seal. Our examination has revealed that, affidavits and dates notwithstanding, none of the documents are subject to disclosure. This is because each of the documents establishes, by its own content, that it served an integral function in the peer-review information-gathering and decision-making process. [ ]. We agree with Northwest that the minutes from the surgical audit committee and the general surgery QMI committee in which plaintiffs case is discussed self-evidently constitute "investigative and deliberative materials generated by a hospital committee in formulating its recommendations" [ ] and they are therefore privileged under the Act. * * *

As to the quality management/improvement worksheets, it is equally clear from their content that they were authored for the use of a peer-review committee and are thus entitled to protection from disclosure. [ ]

Finally we find that the letter from the anesthesia department chair to Dr. Balaney (the anesthesiologist in plaintiffs second surgery) is, by its own terms, privileged. The letter is a request from the chair, on behalf of the committee, for additional information to be used by the committee in its ongoing investigation. [ ] The fact that the letter was to an individual outside of the committee proper does not compromise its privileged status, since disclosure of information privileged under the Act has no effect on its nondiscoverability. [ ].

Conclusion

For the foregoing reasons, we find that the circuit court abused its discretion in allowing for discovery of the disputed documents. We accordingly reverse * * *

MOORE v. GUNNISON VALLEY HOSPITAL

United States Court of Appeals for the Tenth Circuit, 2002.
310 F.3d 1315.

McKAY, Circuit Judge.

I. Background

As alleged in Appellee's Complaint, he is a physician licensed to practice medicine in Colorado. He joined the medical staff at Gunnison Valley Hospital, a public hospital in the State of Colorado, in June 1995. On March 21, 1998, he was temporarily suspended from practicing medicine at the hospital by an ad hoc committee appointed by certain hospital administrators, including Mr. Austin and Dr. Moloney. The committee members included Dr. Beim, Dr. Long, and Dr. Moloney. The specific reasons for the suspension have not been explained in detail but appear to involve Appellee's mistreatment of a patient at another hospital prior to joining the staff at Gunnison Valley. Five days later, on March 26, 1998, the medical staff at the hospital voted to terminate the summary suspension, and Appellee was allowed to continue working.

On December 22, 1998, Appellee received two formal admonitions by the medical staff of the hospital following a decision by another ad hoc review committee. This second committee was also appointed by Mr. Austin and Dr. Moloney, and it consisted of Dr. McMurren, Dr. Wolkov, and Dr. Long. The admonitions appear to be based upon the same alleged misconduct at issue in the summary suspension.

Prior to both the suspension and the issuance of the admonitions, Appellee was not notified of the existence of the ad hoc committees or the pending investigations, nor was he given an opportunity to appeal or challenge the actions before the admonitions were issued. Appellee was not permitted to appeal the issuance of the admonitions, and he did not appeal the summary suspension before it was terminated.

Appellee brought suit under 42 U.S.C. § 1983 alleging violations of his Fourteenth Amendment right to procedural due process. Appellants moved for dismissal on the ground of absolute immunity, which motion the district court denied. Appellants appeal the denial of absolute immunity.

II. ABSOLUTE IMMUNITY

Appellants were each involved in the peer-review process either as administrators for the hospital or as members of the committees themselves. Appellants assert that Colorado statutes identify the peer-review-committee process as essential to the functioning of the Colorado Board of Medical Examiners and that such statutes authorize the existence and authority of such committees. Based on this premise, Appellants conclude that the peer-review committees should be viewed as extensions of the state medical board and receive the protection of absolute quasi-judicial immunity in connection with the review and discipline of the medical practice.

Appellee counters that the peer-review committees lack certain essential characteristics of a judicial body which is worthy of absolute immunity. In particular, Appellee points to the lack of notice and a hearing, the non-adversarial nature of the process, the absence of any meaningful right to appeal the decisions of the committees, and the lack of oversight by the state medical board.

A. *Immunity Under Cleavinger*

In examining the absolute immunity issue, we follow carefully the test established by the Supreme Court in Cleavinger v. Saxner, 474 U.S. 193, 202, 88 L.Ed.2d 507, 106 S.Ct. 496 (1985) [ ]:

the following factors, among others, [are] characteristic of the judicial process and to be considered in determining absolute as contrasted from qualified immunity: (a) the need to assure that the individual can perform his functions without harassment or intimidation; (b) the presence of safeguards that reduce the need for private damages actions as a means of controlling unconstitutional conduct; (c) insulation from political influence; (d) the importance of precedent; (e) the adversary nature of the process; and (f) the correctability of error on appeal.

Cleavinger, 474 U.S. at 202. These six factors are to be considered in determining whether to grant absolute immunity. With these factors as our guide, we proceed to assess the nature of the peer-review committees at issue in this case.

1. Harassment/Intimidation

The first of these factors is "the need to assure that the individual can perform his functions without harassment or intimidation." Id. The mere existence of this lawsuit warns of the potential harassment members of peer-review committees potentially face. However, it is important to note the potential for harassment in the opposite direction as well. In a situation such as this, and particularly in a small community where there are few members of the relevant profession, there is the potential for peer reviewers to harass other members of their profession by initiating frivolous investigations and disciplinary proceedings. Nevertheless, this factor tends to favor the Appellants in this case.

2. Procedural Safeguards

The second factor we consider is the presence of procedural safeguards that reduce the need for private lawsuits. In analyzing this factor, it is important to consider the appropriate scope of the inquiry. As Appellee alleges, prior to the summary suspension and the issuance of the admonitions, he was afforded no procedural protections. He had no right to a hearing or even to notice of pending action.

While not denying the absence of pre-deprivation protections, Appellants contend that the availability of post-deprivation procedures, as well as review by the state medical board, are adequate. Appellants argue that the summary suspension is a temporary action reserved for emergency situations which only becomes permanent following more substantive proceedings. However, because Appellee has alleged damages from both his temporary suspension and the admonitions, Appellants must show the necessity for this abbreviated emergency process. They fail to identify such emergency circumstances here.

3. Political Influence

The third factor involves the presence of political influence in the decision-making process. Appellants seek the protection of quasi-judicial immunity, and therefore suggest that the peer-review committee was acting as an adjudicatory body. As with any judicial process, independence of the adjudicators is essential. However, this case involves a much higher level of potential political influence. The members of the review committee all work at the same hospital as Appellee and, as peers in a small medical community, are his competitors. Such a situation lacks the kind of independence typical of judicial bodies.

4. Importance of Precedent

The fourth factor emphasizes the importance of precedent. We see two aspects of precedent relevant to this inquiry: internal and external precedent. Regarding internal precedent, there appears to be nothing in the record indicating that Gunnison Valley Hospital was looking to its own prior decisions for guidance or that its decision in this matter would be binding precedent for future actions. There is likewise nothing in the record to indicate that the peer-review committee was relying on any precedent from other hospitals in handling situations of this kind. In the absence of such internal and external precedent, this factor adds little to the analysis.

5. Adversarial Nature

The fifth factor examines the adversarial nature of the process. As discussed above, prior to the issuance of the summary suspension and written admonitions, the process was completely non-adversarial. Without notice of the pending actions, Appellee was unable to challenge those actions before they became effective. Once again, Appellants suggest that Appellee would have had the opportunity for an adversarial process with procedural safeguards had the summary suspension not been terminated. However, this argument ignores the fact that Appellee was adversely affected by the summary suspension and that no process was available following the issuance of the written admonitions.

6. Appealability

The sixth and final factor involves the right of appeal. Appellants point to the procedures under the Bylaws, Rules and Regulations of the Medical Staff of Gunnison Valley Hospital [ ], which are available to any staff member wishing to challenge an adverse action against them. However, while the Bylaws provide a full range of procedural protections, they explicitly deny those procedures for those wishing to challenge the issuance of a letter of admonition. [ ]. The procedures are likewise unavailable to challenge a summary suspension if it has been terminated by the staff. [ ].

Appellants are correct in suggesting that, had the staff failed to terminate the suspension or sought a permanent suspension, Appellee would have had significant procedural protections, including a right to appeal. However, those are not the facts here. Appellee is left with two letters of admonition and a summary suspension on his record with no recourse other than a lawsuit. Appellants' identification of the right to file a lawsuit as a sufficient right of appeal turns the right of appeal on its head. It suggests that the committee should be granted immunity from suit since its procedures do not allow internal appeal but allow the committee to be sued.

Having considered these six Cleavinger factors, we conclude that this peer-review process lacks significant characteristics of a judicial body entitled to judicial immunity. Having rejected the claims focused on the particularities of this peer-review committee, we turn to Appellants' arguments that we should look beyond the specific facts of the case to the more general nature of peer-review committees and their place in the regulation of the medical practice in connection with the state medical board.

B. *Peer–Review Committees as Extensions of the State Medical Board*

Appellants suggest that the district court failed to appreciate the important role of peer-review committees in the regulation and oversight of the practice of medicine in Colorado. In making this argument, Appellants cite a federal and a Colorado statute as examples of the important role of peer review in the regulation of the medical profession. As Appellants concede, however, these statutes do not apply directly in this case as a basis for absolute immunity. Rather, Appellants suggest that these statutory schemes "inform this Court's understanding and analysis of the nature and function of the individual Defendants' role in the professional peer review process at Gunnison Valley Hospital." [ ].

Additionally, Appellants cite several sections of the Colorado Medical Practice Act, [ ], to suggest that the Colorado legislature has extended the authority of the state medical board to include peer-review committees. For example, the Colorado General Assembly recognized

> that the board of medical examiners, while assuming and retaining ultimate authority for licensure and discipline ... cannot practically and economically assume responsibility over every single allegation or instance of purported deviation from the standards of quality for the practice of medicine.... It is therefore the intent of the general assembly that the board of medical examiners utilize and allow professional review committees and governing boards to assist it in meeting its responsibilities under article 36....

Colo. Rev. Stat. Ann. § 12–36.5–103 (2001).

From this statute, Appellants conclude that the peer-review committees are extensions of the state medical board and that they are under the control and authority of that board. The statute clearly expresses the need for peer review and its importance to the regulation of the practice of medicine, as Appellants argue, but we conclude that the statute is insufficient to provide absolute immunity in a federal § 1983 action. [ ]

Likewise, a mere statement by the Colorado legislature that peer-review committees are extensions of the state medical board's authority is insufficient to clothe those committees in the same immunity as the board itself. In order for these committees to be viewed as extensions of the medical board and worthy of similar immunity, the state board must exercise adequate oversight and authority over the peer-review committees. In this case there was no such oversight.

At first blush, the state board appears to claim authority over peer review at the hospital level. However, a more detailed reading of the statute reveals very little control by the state board over peer-review committees. For example, the statute requires that each committee have its own internal procedures and regulations, but it limits oversight by the state board to 1) a requirement that a copy of any recommendations made by a peer-review committee to a hospital governing board be forwarded to the state medical board, and 2) the right of the state medical board to request copies of the records of any peer-review-committee proceeding. [ ]. There is no requirement that the state board actually review the proceedings of any committee or the decision of any hospital governing board. There is likewise no explicit right to appeal to the medical board any decision made by a peer-review committee or governing board.

Without more, this statutory scheme lacks sufficient administrative oversight, control, and authority for peer-review committees to be considered extensions of the state board itself. Consequently, we decline to extend the same immunity enjoyed by the state board to the peer-review committee at Gunnison Valley Hospital.

C. Precedent from Other Circuits

Appellants point to cases from other circuits where peer-review committees were granted absolute immunity, suggesting that these cases are indistinguishable from the present case. While the cases are similar in many respects, each of them involved slightly, yet significantly, different facts.

In Kwoun v. Southeast Missouri Professional Standards Review Organization, 811 F.2d 401 (8th Cir. 1987), the members of the peer-review organization had no authority to impose sanctions or discipline themselves and were subject to the direct supervision of a federal agency, the Department of Health and Human Services. Additionally, the procedure outlined by the federal statute allowed for full administrative review. Id. at 409. Here, there is no mandatory review by the state agency, the discipline is administered at the hospital level, and there is no meaningful right of appeal or review in Appellee's particular circumstances.

* * *

The present case is significantly different than the above cases. There are no significant procedural safeguards. Additionally, these other cases involved direct oversight by a government agency as well as a right to appeal to that agency. Here, there is very minimal and undefined oversight by the state medical board and no explicit right of appeal to that board.

We AFFIRM the district court's denial of absolute immunity.

Notes

1) In *West Virginia ex rel. Charles Town General Hospital v. Sanders,* the plaintiff sought discovery of documents contained in the defen-

dant physician's file concerning his application for staff privileges. She sought to prove that the hospital was negligent in granting the defendant staff privileges, and subsequently renewing them. The West Virginia Supreme Court of Appeals held that documents contained in that file were privileged from disclosure under the state's Peer Review Act. The court held that the application file was protected from discovery to the extent it was "created solely for use by the hospital's credentialing committee in determining whether to issue or renew staff privileges."

2) There have been a number of recent decision addressing physician rights with respect to a hearing concerning suspension or termination of staff privileges. In *Sahlolbei v. Providence Healthcare, Inc.*, 112 Cal.App.4th 1137, 5 Cal.Rptr.3d 598 (2003) a California Appeals Court held that a physician was entitled to a hearing before his privileges were terminated. The hospital provision cited authorized a healthcare provider to immediately suspend a physician when it was necessary to prevent "imminent danger to the health of any individual." Otherwise, the physician was entitled to a pretermination hearing. In this case the hospital voted to deny reappointment of the defendant physician to the medical staff on the basis of alleged improper behavior including derogatory comments and disruptive behavior in his interactions with co-workers. Denial of reappointment effectively terminated his staff privileges. The court discussed the hardship to the physician in having his privileges summarily suspended as well as these the hospital's need to protect patients from poor quality of care. In this case (and under those circumstances) the court held, pursuant to statute, the physician was entitled to a hearing before privileges were terminated.

In contrast, the Fifth Circuit in *Patel v. Midland Memorial Hospital*, 298 F.3d 333 (5th Cir. 2002) held that the hospital did not violate a physician's due process rights when it suspended his staff privileges without prior notice and opportunity to be heard. There the court found that exigent circumstances existed which posed an immediate danger to patient safety. In particular, there was a number of recent deaths and severe complications in the physician's caseload, raising the suspicion that patients were at immediate risk. Although the physician argued that it had not yet been demonstrated that he was *actually* a danger, the suspicion alone, given the particular facts and the reasonable inferences, permitted immediate suspension pending a hearing on the issue.

3) In *Clark v. Columbia/HCA Information Services*, Inc., 117 Nev. 468, 25 P.3d 215 (2001) the Nevada Supreme Court found that the defendant psychiatrist, who had made reports about the Hospital's child psychiatry service to various regulatory agencies, was recommended for termination of staff privileges pursuant to recommendation of the peer review board. Clark sued, alleging that the peer review board was erroneously granted HCQIA immunity. The Nevada Supreme Court noted that "HCQIA grants qualified immunity to peer review participants if the peer review action meets due process requirements and the fairness standards set forth in 42 USC 1112(a), and establishes a rebuttable presumption that peer review action meets these fairness

standards." The Court denied immunity to the defendants on the basis that Clark's actions amounted to good faith reporting of perceived improper conduct. Accordingly, the Court held that Clark overcame the presumption of HCQIA immunity as a matter of law.

4) In *West Virginia ex rel. Charles Town General Hospital v. Sanders*, 210 W.Va. 118, 556 S.E.2d 85 (2001), the defendant physician was sued for alleged negligence in the performance of certain surgical procedures, ultimately requiring the plaintiff to undergo a hysterectomy. The hospital was also named as a defendant in the suit on the basis that it was allegedly negligent in the granting and renewing of staff privileges to the defendant physician. In the course of the proceedings, the plaintiff sought disclosure of documents pertaining to the physician's application for staff privileges at the hospital. The hospital resisted discovery, arguing that the application documents were protected by the state's peer review privilege. The trial court permitted the discovery on the basis that documents generated in the credentialing process were not entitled to the peer review privilege. The appeals court reversed, and was eventually affirmed by the West Virginia Supreme Court. The Court held that the hospital committee that reviews the applications for staff privileges falls within the statutory definition of a "review organization." The Court held that but for the mission of the hospital's review organization that was charged with reviewing applications for staff privileges, the documents never would have come into the possession of the hospital. According to the Court, the documents were generated for the purpose of considering staff privileges that are integral to peer review deliberations, and it would be anomalous to draw a distinction between applications for staff privileges and documents generated for ongoing review.

5) In *Johnson v. Galen Health Care, Inc.*, 39 S.W.3d 828 (Ky. Ct. App. 2001), a Kentucky Appeals court considered whether substantial evidence that a physician did not work well with others was adequate to deny him staff privileges, without evidence that his behavior adversely affected the delivery of health care. The defendant argued that there was a lack of identifiable standards for assessing a physician's ability to work well with others, and its effect on staff privileges. The appeals court rejected the argument that a physician's behavior can be used as a factor in staff privilege decisions only when it is serious enough to affect patient care. Recognizing the subjective nature of the judgment, the appeals court held that due process does not preclude the hospital's use of that criteria in making staff decisions.

6) Finally, in *Sinoff v. Ohio Permanente Medical Group*, 146 Ohio App.3d 732, 767 N.E.2d 1251 (2001) a physician whose staff privileges were terminated brought an action alleging that his due process rights were violated in conducting the termination proceedings. The trial court dismissed his claims. Although the appeals court reversed in part, it held that the Health Care Quality Improvement Act (HCQIA) "does not explicitly or implicitly create a private cause of action for physicians subject to peer review."

SECTION C.   LICENSURE AND PROFESSIONALISM

GILBERT v. MEDICAL ECONOMICS CO.

United States Court of Appeals for the Tenth Circuit, 1981.
665 F.2d 305.

McKay, Circuit Judge.

* * * On April 3, 1978, defendants published in the periodical Medical Economics an article entitled "Who Let This Doctor In The O.R.? The Story Of A Fatal Breakdown In Medical Policing." The article, a copy of which is contained in the record before us, outlines two incidents of alleged medical malpractice in which patients of plaintiff, an anesthesiologist, suffered fatal or severely disabling injuries in the operating room as a result of plaintiff's acts of alleged malpractice. The article indicates that in the case of the disabling injuries, plaintiff's insurer settled the ensuing malpractice action for $900,000. It notes further that in the case of the fatal injury, the patient's family was attempting to reach a settlement. Following a description of these incidents, the article suggests that they occurred because of "a collapse of self-policing by physicians and of disciplinary action by hospitals and regulatory agencies." To show the substantiality of this inadequate policing of medical personnel, the article discusses plaintiff's history of psychiatric and related personal problems. The article suggests (1) that there was a causal relationship between plaintiff's personal problems and the acts of alleged malpractice, (2) that plaintiff's lack of capacity to engage responsibly in the practice of medicine was or should have been known to the policing agents of the medical profession, and (3) that more intensive policing of medical personnel is needed. The article identified plaintiff by name and included her photograph.

On the basis of the pleadings and a copy of the article, the district court held a hearing on cross-motions for summary judgment. Defendants moved for summary judgment on the ground that the article contained only truthful factual statements or opinions relating to newsworthy matters and therefore was protected by the First Amendment. Plaintiff conceded that no issues of fact were involved. She urged summary judgment on the theory that although the general theme of the article was newsworthy and therefore privileged, the defendants nevertheless had tortiously invaded her privacy by including in the article her name, photograph, and certain private facts about her life that were not privileged.

In granting summary judgment for the defendants, the trial court agreed that the general subject of the article was indeed newsworthy insofar as it dealt with the competency of licensed professionals. * * * To question whether defendants should have omitted certain details from this particular article, the court believed, would amount to "editorial second-guessing" rather than legal analysis. The court therefore held that the entire article was protected by the First Amendment.

On appeal, plaintiff's first contention is that defendants tortiously invaded her privacy by publicly disclosing embarrassing private facts about her personal life. Colorado has recognized a common-law right to privacy. * * * Defendants, however, raised the defense of First Amendment privilege, and thus, we must turn to federal substantive law in this diversity case to determine the extent of defendants' federal constitutional defense.

* * *

This privilege is not absolute, however, and as in other areas involving the media, the right of the individual to keep information private must be balanced against the right of the press to disseminate newsworthy information to the public. In attempting to strike an acceptable balance between these competing interests, liability may be imposed for publicizing matters concerning the private life of another "if the matter publicized is of a kind that (a) would be highly offensive to a reasonable person, and (b) is not of legitimate concern to the public." Restatement (Second) of Torts § 652D (1977). As comment h points out, not all matters are of legitimate public interest:

The line is to be drawn when the publicity ceases to be the giving of information to which the public is entitled, and becomes a morbid and sensational prying into private lives for its own sake with which a reasonable member of the public, with decent standards, would say that he had no concern.

Thus, dissemination of non-newsworthy private facts is not protected by the First Amendment.

The privilege does immunize the reporting of private facts, however, when discussed in connection with "matters of the kind customarily regarded as 'news.'" Comment g. Any information disseminated "for purposes of education, amusement or enlightenment, when the public may reasonably be expected to have a legitimate interest in what is published," is also protected by the privilege. Comment j. * * *

Even where certain matters are clearly within the protected sphere of legitimate public interest, some private facts about an individual may lie outside that sphere. * * * Therefore, to properly balance freedom of the press against the right of privacy, every private fact disclosed in an otherwise truthful, newsworthy publication must have some substantial relevance to a matter of legitimate public interest. When these conditions are satisfied, the facts in the publication and inferences reasonably drawn therefrom fall within the ambit of First Amendment protection and are privileged.

* * *

With respect to the publication of plaintiff's photograph and name, we find that these truthful representations are substantially relevant to a newsworthy topic because they strengthen the impact and credibility of the article. They obviate any impression that the problems raised in the article are remote or hypothetical, thus providing an aura of immediacy and even urgency that might not exist had plaintiff's name and photograph been suppressed. Similarly, we find the publication of plaintiff's psychiatric and marital problems to be substantially relevant to the newsworthy topic. While it is true that these subjects would fall outside the First Amendment privilege in the absence of either independent newsworthiness or any substantial nexus with a newsworthy topic, here they are connected to the newsworthy topic by the rational inference that plaintiff's personal problems were the underlying cause of the acts of alleged malpractice.

Plaintiff claims that the drawing of such inferences is not within the protected scope of editorial discretion unless a public tribunal first declares such an inference to be legally established. We conclude, however, that a rule forbidding editors from drawing inferences from truthful newsworthy facts would result in a far too restrictive and wholly unjustifiable construction of the First Amendment privilege. If the press is to have the generous breathing space that courts have accorded it thus far, editors must have freedom to make reasonable judgments and to draw one inference where others also reasonably could be drawn. This is precisely the editorial discretion contemplated by the privilege. Because the inferences of causation drawn in this case are not, as a matter of law, so purely conjectural that no reasonable editor could draw them other than through guesswork and speculation, we hold that defendants did not abuse their editorial discretion in this case.

* * *

Accordingly, the court did not abuse its discretion in finding that defendants are entitled to summary judgment as to every issue in this case.

Affirmed.

COLORADO STATE BOARD OF MEDICAL EXAMINERS v. JOHNSON

Court of Appeals of Colorado, Division Three, 2002.
68 P.3d 500.

DAVIDSON, J.

* * *

Johnson received her medical degree from the American University of the Caribbean (AUC) in Montserrat, West Indies, in 1986, but she received her medical training at other locations. She completed her first two years of coursework at the University of Missouri at Columbia and completed subsequent clinical rotations in the United States in programs approved by the Accreditation Council of Graduate Medical Education (ACGME). She also received more than three years of postgraduate training and board certification in anesthesiology.

In 1999, Johnson applied to the Board for a license to practice medicine in Colorado. Panel A, acting as a subcommittee of the Board, denied the application on the ground that Johnson had not graduated from a[n approved] medical school.

Johnson requested a hearing [ ]. After the hearing, the ALJ's initial decision found, inter alia, that Johnson was "essentially a United States' trained medical professional" and concluded that the Board had abused its discretion and that Johnson should be granted a license.

The Board filed exceptions to the initial decision [ ]. After reviewing the initial decision, another subcommittee of the Board, Panel B, issued its final decision. It rejected some of the ALJ's conclusions and denied Johnson's application, essentially on the ground that her training was not equivalent to that provided by an approved school.

On appeal, Johnson contends that the Board improperly substituted its findings of fact for those of the ALJ, arbitrarily and capriciously denied her application, and violated [the Colorado licensing statute.] We disagree.

Whether Johnson's education, including that at AUC and her post-graduate training, provided qualifications equivalent to those provided by a degree from an approved school is an ultimate conclusion of fact. Accepting the evidentiary findings of the ALJ, the Board was free to reach a different ultimate conclusion, so long as it was supported by the law and substantial evidence in the record and was not arbitrary and capricious.[ ]

In determining whether an administrative agency's decision is arbitrary or capricious, the court must determine whether a reasonable person, considering all of the evidence in the record, would fairly and honestly be compelled to reach a different conclusion. If not, no abuse of discretion has occurred and the agency decision must be upheld. [ ]

We conclude that the Board properly determined that Johnson did not demonstrate that her medical school education was equivalent to that provided by an approved school. Therefore, a reasonable person would not be compelled to reach the conclusion that she was entitled to a medical license [ ] and we must uphold the Board's decision.

I.

We first address the relevant substantive and procedural aspects of the application process for a license to practice medicine in Colorado.

The Board may refuse to license an applicant if it determines that the applicant does not possess the qualifications required by the Medical Practice Act (MPA) [ ]. An application must include "such documents, affidavits, and certificates as are necessary to establish that the applicant possesses the qualifications prescribed by [the MPA]," and the burden of proof is on the applicant. [ ]

One qualification required under the MPA is that the applicant have graduated from "an approved medical college, as defined in section 12–36–108." [which] defines an "approved medical college" as one that meets the educational standards of the liaison committee on medical education (LCME), that has been approved by the LCME, or that has been approved by the Board on its own investigation of the school's educational standards and facilities.

However, § 12–36–107.6(1), captioned "Foreign medical school graduates—degree equivalence," provides a limited exception for foreign medical school graduates:

For graduates of schools other than those approved by the [LCME] ... the board may require three years of postgraduate clinical training approved by the board. An applicant whose foreign medical school is other than as defined in section 12–36–108 shall be eligible for licensure at the discretion of the board if the applicant meets all other requirements for licensure and holds specialty board certification, current at the time of application for licensure, conferred by a regular member board of the American board of medical specialties or the American osteopathic association. The factors to be considered by the board in the exercise of its discretion in determining the qualifications of such applicants shall include the following:

(a) The information available to the board relating to the medical school of the applicant; and

(b) The nature and length of the post-graduate training completed by the applicant.

The Board has adopted a written policy implementing the statutory provisions as they relate to graduates of foreign medical schools. Pursuant to Board Policy 20–5, applicants from foreign medical schools must complete a questionnaire regarding the school's standards and facilities:

If the applicant's answers to the questionnaire are satisfactory and if the Board is not in possession of any derogatory information regarding the medical school, the Board will approve the school for purposes of licensing a specific applicant pursuant to section 12–36–108. If the applicant is Board certified by an ABMS or AOA Specialty Board, approval of the school is not required to license the applicant [ ] If the applicant affirmatively answers all of the questions on the Board's questionnaire regarding the medical school and if there are no other issues (i.e., malpractice history, disciplinary history, etc.) which would require Board review, the application does not need to be forwarded to a Board member for special consideration.

An applicant who is denied a license without a hearing may request a hearing before the agency, conducted pursuant to [ ]. However, such a hearing is not merely a review of the first panel's license denial, but instead requires that findings of fact and conclusions of law be made based on the evidence presented at the hearing. The initial decision rendered pursuant to such a hearing must include "a statement of findings and conclusions upon all the material issues of fact, law, or discretion presented by the record and the appropriate order, sanction, relief, or denial thereof." [ ].

If an appeal to the Board is made by filing exceptions to the initial decision, the Board, acting through the subcommittee that did not originally deny the license, may affirm, set aside, or modify the initial decision consistent with the facts and the law. However, the Board may not set aside the ALJ's findings of evidentiary fact, as distinguished from ultimate conclusions of fact, unless they are contrary to the weight of the evidence. [ ]

Upon review of the Board's action, this court must affirm if it finds no error. However, if the action is arbitrary and capricious, an abuse of discretion, based upon clearly erroneous findings or findings unsupported by substantial evidence, or otherwise contrary to law, this court shall set aside the action. [ ]. The court must view the record as a whole and in the light most favorable to the Board when determining whether the Board's decision is supported by substantial evidence. [ ]

The Board enforces the MPA, with its attendant goals of protecting the public from the "unauthorized, unqualified, and improper practice of the healing arts in this state." [ ]. It is comprised of members with medical degrees and has broad discretion to determine the ultimate fact of whether an applicant is qualified under the MPA. Vesting such discretion in the Board rather than the ALJ promotes uniformity in decision-making. [ ]

II.

Johnson first contends that information about the quality of AUC's medical program may not be considered when assessing her application. Alternatively, she contends that the Board erroneously rejected the ALJ's findings of fact regarding her experience at AUC. We disagree with both contentions.

A.

Johnson contends that the Board's denial of her license based on information about AUC was erroneous because the Board may rely only on the grounds set forth in its notice of denial—here, the nonapproved status of AUC—and approval of her school is unnecessary under § 12–36–107.6 and Board policy because she is board certified. We disagree.

* * *. However, in her answer to the notice of grounds for denial, Johnson raised that section in response to the Board's allegation that AUC was not an approved school. The Board then addressed the requirements of that section at the hearing, relying, inter alia, on information it had on the alleged inadequacy of the AUC program. Because [the] ALJ is required to make findings and conclusions on all material issues presented by the record, the ALJ's initial decision properly considered the information about AUC.

Moreover, § 12–36–107.6 requires the Board to consider the information available to it about the applicant's medical school when exercising its discretion to license board certified graduates of nonapproved medical schools. Johnson's argument to the contrary notwithstanding, the statement in Board Policy 20–5 that approval of the school is not necessary when the applicant is board certified does not indicate that the Board is not to consider information about the applicant's school, but only that the school need not meet the requirements of § 12–36–108.

Section 12–36–107.6 presumes that the applicant has not graduated from an approved medical school and permits the Board to license a board certified applicant, if it determines that the applicant's medical school and postgraduate training are equivalent to training at an approved school and render the applicant "qualified." Thus, the Board did not err in considering information about AUC in determining whether Johnson possessed the qualifications required by the MPA.

B.

Johnson also contends that the Board impermissibly rejected the ALJ's findings of fact regarding certain investigative reports about AUC and her particular AUC experience. We disagree.

1.

In support of a denial of the license application, the Board introduced three reports, based on investigations of AUC made by New York, New Jersey, and California, as negative information available to the Board under § 12–36–107.6(1)(b). The ALJ made the following finding regarding the reports:

The Board possessed old reports from the states of NJ, NY and California in which those states refused to accept students in their respective clinical clerkships. However, the significance of the New York and California reports in this case [was] eradicated by the fact that both of those states granted the Applicant a medical license.

The ALJ concluded that the reports demonstrated only that the investigating states would not accept AUC students into their clinical clerkships, not whether they would license graduates or whether they would accept students who had attended classes at a location other than AUC. The ALJ's ultimate determination, after considering the information available to the Board regarding AUC, was that the information contained in the reports was not a sufficient basis for denying the application and that such a denial would constitute an abuse of discretion.

On review of the initial decision, the Board rejected the ALJ's conclusions and instead concluded that the three reports "provide ample evidence that the AUC ... has an inadequate medical degree program." The Board also concluded that the reports were significant despite their age because their dates corresponded with the period of Johnson's affiliation with AUC; that Johnson's licensure by New York and California did not affect the significance of the reports because the Board operates independently of other state boards and Johnson did not present evidence regarding those states' licensing laws and policies; and that the reports were not limited to the issue of whether students would be accepted into clinical programs, but also included "extensive, relevant information regarding the quality of the admissions process, the faculty, the administration, and the supervision of students such as the Applicant who completed clinical rotations in facilities other than those managed by the AUC."

Johnson characterizes the ALJ's findings regarding the reports as "evidentiary facts" that the Board may not reject unless they are contrary to the weight of the evidence. In contrast, the Board characterizes these findings as "ultimate conclusions of fact," which it may reject and replace as long as its conclusions have a reasonable basis in law. We agree, for the most part, with the Board.

Although the distinction between evidentiary facts and ultimate conclusions of fact is not always clear, evidentiary facts generally include the detailed factual or historical findings on which a legal determination rests. Ultimate conclusions of fact, on the other hand, involve conclusions of law, or at least mixed questions of law and fact, and often settle the rights and liabilities of the parties. [ ]

That New York and California granted Johnson medical licenses is an historical fact. A separate finding of the ALJ reflecting Johnson's licensure in those and other states was not disturbed by the Board. However, the determination whether the significance of the New York and California reports was "eradicated" by Johnson's subsequent licensing in those states depends upon the scope of the investigations and the information contained in the written reports and thus constitutes an ultimate conclusion of fact. We also note that the ALJ made no finding that the New Jersey report was not significant.

To the extent that the dates of the reports are historical facts, the characterization of the reports as "old" includes some connotation as to the effect they should be given on consideration of Johnson's application. However, even if the Board was bound by the finding that the reports were old, such a finding is not necessarily inconsistent with a conclusion that Johnson did not possess the required qualifications. Thus, the Board was free to reach an alternative conclusion as to the content and effect of the reports, so long as the conclusion was supported by the law and the evidence.

2.

Regarding the quality of Johnson's particular medical school training, the ALJ found that Johnson attended the University of Missouri for the first two and one-half years of medical school and then took a leave of absence and that she studied through the AUC for the final two years. The ALJ did not make specific findings regarding the time and place of Johnson's clerkships during her affiliation with AUC, but found that: "Because (1) the Applicant attended a United States college for two of the four years of her medical college education and (2) her medical residency clerkships and medical practice were entirely in the United States, the Applicant is essentially a United States' trained medical professional." The initial decision further stated: "The Applicant's first two years of medical college occurred in the United States. She successfully interned, clerked and worked at several United States hospitals." The ALJ ultimately determined that denying Johnson a license based on an alleged failure to possess the minimum requirements would be arbitrary and capricious.

On review, the Board rejected those portions of the decision regarding Johnson's clerkships and substituted the following:

33. The Applicant's performance during her first two years of medical school at the University of Missouri–Columbia was, in her own words, "sub-optimal" and led to a required leave of absence from which she was never reinstated.

34. The second portion of the Applicant's medical school career occurred through the AUC, which allowed her to arrange her own clinical rotation. The Applicant had no knowledge and presented no evidence regarding the nature of the AUC's supervision of her clinical rotation and the information in the possession of the Board supports the finding that the AUC did not adequately supervise or evaluate those rotations and therefore was not sufficiently accountable for the quality of Applicant's medical school education. This determination is supported by the standards of the [LCME].

The Board rejected the conclusion that Johnson was essentially a United States' trained physician and substituted the conclusion that "when the factors specified in section 12–36–107.6(1) are considered in the context of the record as a whole, the evidence clearly supports the Panel's decision to deny Applicant's application for a license."

"An ALJ's finding of evidentiary fact may not be altered by the Board if supported by the evidence," but the ALJ's conclusions are not binding. [ ]

The ALJ made no specific findings whether AUC adequately supervised Johnson's clinical rotations. However, Johnson contends that the ALJ's findings that she was essentially a United States' trained physician and that she had successfully completed her medical school and postgraduate training constituted findings of evidentiary fact that are inconsistent with a finding that she was not adequately supervised. We do not agree.

The ALJ's findings that Johnson successfully completed clerkships in the United States and was essentially a United States' trained physician contain elements of both evidentiary fact and ultimate fact. That Johnson passed courses and rotations she attended in the United States and graduated from medical school are historical facts that the Board may not, and did not, reject. However, to the extent that the findings that she was "successful" in completing the training and "essentially" a United States' trained physician indicate a conclusion that the training was equivalent to that offered by an approved school in the United States, they are conclusions of ultimate fact, which the Board was free to reject.

Whether AUC's supervision was "adequate" is itself an ultimate fact, determined based on the historical facts regarding the supervision. Johnson had the burden of proving that AUC's supervision of her clinical rotations rendered her education equivalent to that of an approved school or that she had obtained equivalent training in some other manner.

Johnson's argument to the contrary notwithstanding, the Board's determination that AUC did not adequately supervise her clinical rotations is not inconsistent with the ALJ's evidentiary findings and is supported by the record. * * *

While Johnson testified that AUC supervised her clerkships through grading evaluations, that the clerkships were certified by the ACGME, and that she was graded according to the same exam and performance criteria as students from the United States medical schools, she had no knowledge of the existence, or extent, of actual communication between AUC and the clinical programs regarding her performance.

III.

In its order, the Board referred to certain events related to interpersonal problems Johnson displayed in medical school. Information about these and similar problems during her postgraduate training was contained in her license application and referenced during the hearings before the ALJ and arguments presented to Panel B of the Board. Johnson contends that the Board impermissibly relied on this evidence when assessing the qualifications provided by her medical and postgraduate training. We disagree.

Section 12–36–116, C.R.S. 2002, outlines the bases on which the Board may deny a license. The stated grounds are that the applicant fails to possess the qualifications required by the MPA, has engaged in unprofessional conduct, has been disciplined in another state regarding a medical license, or has not actively practiced medicine for the two years next preceding the submission of an application for a license. The absence of interpersonal problems is not one of the qualifications specifically required by the MPA.

However, it does not follow that such problems may not be considered for any purpose. Section 12–36–107.6 states that the factors the Board should consider when assessing the qualifications of a foreign graduate "shall include" information about the school and postgraduate training. This indicates that certain additional information may be considered by the Board when exercising its discretion, so long as it is relevant to a determination of whether the applicant's qualifications are equivalent to a degree from an approved school [ ] whether the applicant has engaged in unprofessional conduct.

Here, the Board cited Johnson's statement in her application explaining that the second two years of her medical education were "better because [she] had performed sub-optimally once before and was determined never to do that again." The Board also noted that she was asked to take a leave of absence from the University of Missouri and failed to return.

Apparently, Johnson was asked to take a leave of absence for a period of one to three years because she was too sensitive to criticism and had issues in handling authority figures. The failure to return was attributed to the fact that, when she decided to return to medical school six years later, the University of Missouri, and all other schools to which she applied in the United States, would not admit her with advanced standing, but instead would require her to repeat the first two years.

* * *

In any event, the Board's order did not explicitly rely on the fact that the leave of absence may have been precipitated by interpersonal problems. While it was not made clear what Johnson meant by performing "sub-optimally," the fact that she was asked to take a leave of absence from the program would seem to fall within any definition.

Further, the Board considered the leave of absence and the failure to return, inter alia, as reflecting poorly on AUC's admissions standards, noting in its exceptions to the initial decision that: "Despite Applicant's admitted 'suboptimal' performance and required leave of absence from the University of Missouri at Columbia medical school, the AUC accepted her on her terms to enter with advanced standing status in 1984." Thus, to the extent that the Board considered the reasons for the leave of absence, it properly viewed these facts as they bore on the quality of AUC and, ultimately, Johnson's qualifications.

In questioning the quality of Johnson's postgraduate training, although it noted that Johnson had completed more than the three years of training required for consideration under § 12–36–107.6, the Board, in its exceptions to the initial decision, pointed to the fact that she had been placed on probation during a portion of her postgraduate training for recurrent interpersonal problems with other hospital personnel. However, the ALJ did not allow testimony on the interpersonal problems, and the probation during postgraduate training was not referenced in the Board's final order.

Thus, regardless of any reliance by the Board on Johnson's interpersonal problems, we conclude that there is sufficient evidence in the record to support the Board's conclusion that Johnson's medical school education and postgraduate training were not equivalent to the training received by a graduate from an approved medical school and did not render her qualified to receive a Colorado license. [ ].

Accordingly, the Board's order denying Johnson's application for a medical license is affirmed.

HASON v. MEDICAL BOARD OF CALIFORNIA

United States Court of Appeals for the Ninth Circuit, 2002.
279 F.3d 1167.

GOODWIN, Circuit Judge:

BACKGROUND

In March of 1995, Michael J. Hason, M. D., applied for a license to practice medicine in the state of California. In April of 1998, the California Medical Board denied, for reasons of mental illness, Dr. Hason's application for a medical license. Dr. Hason subsequently filed a pro se complaint in federal district court alleging violations of his rights under the United States Constitution (brought pursuant to 42 U.S.C. § 1983) and Title II of the ADA, 42 U.S.C. § 12132. The complaint also alleged state law tort claims which are not at issue on this appeal.

Dr. Hason's complaint named as defendants The Medical Board of the State of California ["The Medical Board"], the Department of Consumer Affairs of the State of California and its director, and various other individuals that were either members of or otherwise affiliated with the Medical Board (in both their official and personal capacities). Dr. Hason sought both damages and injunctive relief.

On April 25, 2000, the District Court dismissed Dr. Hason's complaint without prejudice as to the individual defendants in their personal capacities, and with prejudice as to the two named state agencies and the individual defendants in their official capacities. The Report and Recommendation of the United States Magistrate Judge, which was affirmed in its entirety by the District Court, stated three reasons for dismissing Dr. Hason's complaint. First, the Report concluded that Dr. Hason's claims were barred by the Eleventh Amendment. Second, the Report concluded that Dr. Hason failed to state a claim upon which relief could be granted under Title II of the ADA. Third, the Report concluded that Dr. Hason's claims against the individual defendants in their personal capacities should be dismissed for failure to prosecute. [ ]

DISCUSSION

I. Sovereign Immunity

We begin by considering whether the District Court erred in holding that Dr. Hason's claims were barred by the Eleventh Amendment. The Eleventh Amendment prohibits a private party from suing a nonconsenting state or its agencies in federal court. [ ]. The Eleventh Amendment does not, however, prevent a private litigant from suing a state or its agencies in federal court where Congress has abrogated state sovereign immunity acting pursuant to section 5 of the Fourteenth Amendment. We have previously held that in enacting Title II of the ADA Congress validly abrogated state sovereign immunity, and thus states and their agencies may be sued pursuant to Title II. [ ]

Appellees contend, however, that the Supreme Court's recent decision in Garrett overrules both Clark and Dare. In Garrett, the Court held that Congress did not validly abrogate state sovereign immunity in enacting Title I of the ADA. [ ]. The Garrett Court expressly declined to decide whether Congress validly abrogated state sovereign immunity in enacting Title II of the ADA. [ ]. We therefore conclude that Garrett does not overrule either Clark or Dare, and that the Eleventh Amendment does not bar Dr. Hason's Title II claims.

The District Court also erred in its treatment of Dr. Hason's federal civil rights claims, brought pursuant to 42 U.S.C. § 1983, against the various individual state officials. The District Court held that Dr. Hason's section 1983 claims were barred by the Eleventh Amendment. In so holding, the District Court failed to recognize the long-established exception to Eleventh Amendment immunity carved out by Ex Parte Young, 209 U.S. 123, 52 L.Ed. 714, 28 S.Ct. 441 (1908). The Ex Parte Young doctrine provides that the Eleventh Amendment does not bar suits for prospective injunctive relief brought against state officers "in their official capacities, to enjoin an alleged ongoing violation of federal law." [ ]. Dr. Hason's complaint clearly seeks prospective injunctive relief to enjoin the individual defendants' refusal to issue Dr. Hason a medical license. Thus, under the doctrine of Ex Parte Young, Dr. Hason's section 1983 claims seeking prospective injunctive relief from the individual defendants are not barred by the Eleventh Amendment. The District Court erred in concluding otherwise.

II.   Title II of the ADA

We next consider the District Court's dismissal of Dr. Hason's complaint for failure to state a claim for which relief can be granted under Title II of the ADA. Title II of the ADA provides that "no qualified individual with a disability shall, by reason of such disability, be excluded from participation in or be denied the benefits of the services, programs, or activities of a public entity, or be subjected to discrimination by any such entity." [ ]. The District Court dismissed Dr. Hason's complaint based on the magistrate judge's twofold conclusion that (1) the denial of a medical license cannot be challenged under Title II of the ADA because a medical license does not constitute "services, programs, or activities of a public entity" and (2) Dr. Hason is not a "qualified individual with a disability" within the meaning of Title II of the ADA.

With respect to the first of the two above grounds for dismissal, Dr. Hason contends that his complaint properly states a claim because a medical license constitutes "services, programs, or activities of a public entity" under Title II. Dr. Hason argues that the magistrate judge's interpretation of the phrase "services, programs, or activities" to exclude medical licensing is at odds with both the plain language and remedial goals of Title II.

In response, Appellees argue that Title II was not intended to apply to professional licensing. Appellees rely primarily on Zimmerman v. Oregon Department of Justice, 170 F.3d 1169 (9th Cir. 1999). In Zimmerman, the plaintiff brought an action against his employer alleging that the employer's practices discriminated against him in violation of Title II of the ADA. This Court affirmed the district court's holding that Title II of the ADA does not apply to employment. In doing so, we conducted a thorough examination of both the wording of Title II and the structure of the ADA, concluding that Congress intended for Title II to apply only to the "outputs" of a public agency, not to "inputs" such as employment. [ ]

Relying on Zimmerman, Appellees contend that medical licensing does not fall within the scope of Title II because medical licensing is not an "output" of a public agency. According to Appellees, medical licensing is not an" output" because it is a service provided for the benefit of the public at large, not for the benefit of applicants seeking to obtain medical licenses. * * *

We are not persuaded by Appellees' argument. Viewed in the light of the Zimmerman framework, medical licensing is an output of a public agency, not an input such as employment. The act of licensing involves the Medical Board (i.e. a "public agency") providing a license (i.e. providing a "service") to an applicant for a medical license. Although medical licensing does occur within the employment context, medical licensing is not equivalent to employment. The Medical Board does not make employment decisions, and the Board's grant of a license is not tantamount to a promise or guarantee of employment as a physician.

Furthermore, the magistrate judge's narrow construction of the phrase "services, programs, or activities" is at odds with the remedial goals underlying the ADA. * * * Courts must construe the language of the ADA broadly in order to effectively implement the ADA's fundamental purpose of "providing a clear and comprehensive national mandate for the elimination of discrimination against individuals with disabilities." [ ]. In fact, this court has already capitalized upon the opportunity to construe broadly the language of Title II. In Lee v. City of Los Angeles we stated in the Title II context that "the ADA's broad language brings within its scope anything a public entity does." Lee v. City of Los Angeles, 250 F.3d 668, 691 (9th Cir. 2001) [ ]. Medical licensing is without a doubt something that the Medical Board "does." As such, we conclude that medical licensing clearly falls within the scope of Title II.

The second major reason given by the magistrate judge for dismissing Dr. Hason's Title II claims was that Dr. Hason was not a "qualified individual with a disability "within the meaning of Title II of the ADA. Title II defines this requirement as follows:

The term "qualified individual with a disability" means an individual with a disability who, with or without reasonable modifications to rules, policies, or practices, the removal of architectural, communication, or transportation barriers, or the provision of auxiliary aids and services, meets the essential eligibility requirements for the receipt of services or the participation in programs or activities provided by a public entity.

42 U.S.C. § 12131(2).

Dr. Hason argues that the District Court erred in accepting the magistrate judge's conclusion because the question of whether Dr. Hason is a qualified individual with a disability is a factual question that should not be resolved on a 12(b)(6) motion to dismiss. In response, Appellees contend that Dr. Hason is not a "qualified individual with a disability" because Dr. Hason admits in his pleadings that he suffers from a mental disability.

Although at a later stage in the proceedings Appellees might demonstrate that Dr. Hason is not a qualified individual with a disability, they have not yet done so. Appellees are correct that Dr. Hason states in his complaint that he suffers from a mental disability. Dr. Hason's complaint also alleges, however, that by the time of the Medical Board's decision he had received treatment for his disability and was capable of practicing medicine. Accepting these allegations as true and construing them in the light most favorable to Dr. Hason, we conclude that Dr. Hason adequately alleges that he is a qualified individual with a disability. * * *

For the foregoing reasons, we conclude that Dr. Hason states claims for which relief can be granted under Title II of the ADA. The District Court erred in dismissing his complaint pursuant to Rule 12(b)(6).

III.   *Failure to Prosecute*

Dr. Hason next argues that the District Court abused its discretion in dismissing his claims, for failure to prosecute, against the individual defendants in their personal capacities. In recommending that Appellant's suit be dismissed for failure to prosecute, the magistrate judge relied on Federal Rule of Civil Procedure 4(m). Rule 4(m) provides that, if process is not served within 120 days after the filing of the complaint, and the plaintiff cannot show good cause why service was not made within that time, the action is subject to dismissal without prejudice upon the court's own initiative with notice to the plaintiff. The magistrate judge noted that Dr. Hason failed to effectuate service of process on the named individual defendants within 120 days after the filing of his complaint. Dr. Hason also failed to respond to an order to show cause why service had not been made within the 120 day period.

Dr. Hason does not dispute these facts. Rather, he argues that he had determined that the individual defendants were not liable and that he wanted them to be dismissed as defendants. He assumed that he was furthering this goal and helping the court by not responding to the order to show cause. However, when it became clear that the state agencies were going to be dismissed as defendants, Dr. Hason decided that he no longer wanted the individual defendants to be dismissed. Dr. Hason's argument lacks merit, and we conclude that the District Court did not abuse its discretion in dismissing, for failure to prosecute, Dr. Hason's claims against the individual defendants in their personal capacities.

IV. Conclusion

In conclusion, we hold that (1) Dr. Hason's Title II claims are not barred by the Eleventh Amendment; (2) Dr. Hason's section 1983 claims seeking prospective injunctive relief against the individual defendants in their official capacities are not barred by the Eleventh Amendment; (3) Dr. Hason states valid claims under Title II of the ADA; and (4) the District Court did not abuse its discretion in dismissing for failure to prosecute Dr. Hason's claims against the individual defendants in their personal capacities.

REVERSED and REMANDED.

Notes

1) Not all forces that are directed toward improving the quality of medical care emanate from doctors. Was *Medical Economic's* magazine's principal motive in printing its story on Dr. Gilbert to improve the quality of anesthesiology services? Was it to encourage better peer review activities? Was it to persecute Dr. Gilbert? Or, was it primarily just to sell magazines? Under the First Amendment, the publisher's principal motivation matters very little, and doubts about improper motivation (malice) are resolved in favor of the publisher. The court's affirming of summary judgment for the publisher evidences the strength of the First Amendment protection.

Medical Economics, however, is not a case about First Amendment protection for printing false and defamatory assertions about a private figure. The action for invasion of privacy concedes the truth of the publication. The question is how far the First Amendment extends in protecting individuals from exposure by the press of personal or embarrassing private facts that the public has little or no legitimate interest in knowing. The facts were bad enough, but the magazine went on to draw inferences from those facts that ultimately might or might not be warranted. The court says that if the underlying facts are true and newsworthy, then they and whatever plausible inferences can be drawn therefrom can also be reported, regardless of whether the inferences later prove to be fair, let alone true.

2) In *Nguyen v. State of Washington Department of Health*, 144 Wash.2d 516, 29 P.3d 689 (2001) the defendant physician's license was suspended on the basis that his practice of medicine was found to be below acceptable professional standards. The Board agreed to stay the suspension pending supervision. Sometime later amended charges were filed, alleging that he failed to comply with the supervision agreement, and that new charges of unprofessional care had surfaced. Later that year, three charges of sexual misconduct were added. The licensing commission found, by a preponderance of the evidence, that the physician was unfit to practice medicine, and his license was revoked. Al-

though the Appeals Court affirmed, the Supreme Court of Washington reversed. The high court found that, given the subjective nature of some of the judgments needed to reach a conclusion of unfitness to practice medicine, the "preponderance of the evidence" standard was not adequate. Rather, a standard of "clear and convincing evidence" must be met consistent with a three-part test set forth by the U.S. Supreme Court in *Mathews v. Eldridge*, 424 U.S. 319, 96 S.Ct. 893, 47 L.Ed.2d 18 (1976), *supra*. The Court noted that the defendant has both a liberty and a property interest in his medical license, and due process requires the higher standard of proof to reduce the possibility of error.

3) In *Anonymous v. Bureau of Professional Medical Conduct*, 1 A.D.3d 1065, 768 NYS.2d 591 (App. Div. 2003) a general practitioner was brought before the medical disciplinary board on charges that (a) he used a medical procedure without proper certification and (b) he failed to maintain a medical record. After hearing, he was issued a reprimand on the medical record charge only, as the Department of Health (Bureau of Professional Medical Misconduct) failed to prove the former charge. After the reprimand was issued, the DOH entered on its official web site the "Statement of Charges" as well as "Determination and Order" against the petitioner. He objected on the basis that the unproved charges, listed on the, website, would damage his reputation. The trial court dismissed his claim, but the Appellate Division reversed. The appeals court observed that there is a general policy of maintaining the confidentiality of disciplinary proceedings pending resolution for the very purpose of avoiding damage to reputation. For a favorable outcome to be held confidential during the investigation and review process, only to be publicized once a favorable outcome is reached, violates the integrity of the process.

*

Part II

PUBLIC HEALTH

Chapter 12

LEGAL AND ILLEGAL
SUBSTANCES

INTRODUCTORY NOTE

When one thinks about regulation for the benefit of the public health, it is hard not to consider tobacco use first. The morbidity and mortality directly attributable to tobacco products affects millions of people annually. In addition to premature illness and deaths, there is the inescapable exposure to second-hand smoke, nicotine addiction that even the most determined smokers often cannot break and, of course, the millions of children who become unwitting victims by virtue of immaturity and bad luck. Tobacco is truly a public health catastrophe.

Public outrage at the tobacco "problem" is likely tempered by other public health issues that affect "truly" innocent victims—those who had no choice at all in becoming victims. People who are accidentally struck by drunk drivers, poisoned by contaminated products or infected by contagious disease are often outraged that there is not even greater public health activism. People who favor judicial restraint when it comes to individual liberties sometimes want judicial activism when it is they who are the victims.

Drug and alcohol use is a subject that attracts a multitude of opinions. Many believe that drug and alcohol use should be subject to greater regulation. Certainly it is directly related to an enormous amount of public health morbidity and mortality. There is fierce debate about legalization of marijuana, particularly when medicinal use is contemplated. Even those who favor less regulation want recourse through the tort system when it is they who are accidentally injured.

Public health regulation is often regarded as a positivist pursuit, thriving to acquire and apply scientific inquiry for use in the development of sound and fair public health policy. It is governed by ethical inquiry, legal policy and political decision making. It is an imperfect science, and one where legitimate debate is the rule rather than the exception. Public health law attempts to balance ethical values and legal norms, while acknowledging its overriding purpose is to promote and protect the health and well-being of the public.

SECTION A. ALCOHOLIC BEVERAGES

SOUTH DAKOTA v. DOLE

Supreme Court of the United States, 1987.
483 U.S. 203, 107 S.Ct. 2793, 97 L.Ed.2d 171.

CHIEF JUSTICE REHNQUIST delivered the opinion of the Court.

Petitioner South Dakota permits persons 19 years of age or older to purchase beer containing up to 3.2% alcohol. S. D. Codified Laws § 35–6–27 (1986). In 1984 Congress enacted 23 U. S. C. § 158 (1982 ed., Supp. III), which directs the Secretary of Transportation to withhold a percentage of federal highway funds otherwise allocable from States "in which the purchase or public possession . . . of any alcoholic beverage by a person who is less than twenty-one years of age is lawful." The State sued in United States District Court seeking a declaratory judgment that § 158 violates the constitutional limitations on congressional exercise of the spending power and violates the Twenty-first Amendment to the United States Constitution. The District Court rejected the State's claims, and the Court of Appeals for the Eighth Circuit affirmed. 791 F.2d 628 (1986).

In this Court, the parties direct most of their efforts to defining the proper scope of the Twenty-first Amendment. Relying on our statement in *California Retail Liquor Dealers Assn.* v. *Midcal Aluminum, Inc.*, 445 U.S. 97, 110 (1980), that the "Twenty-first Amendment grants the States virtually complete control over whether to permit importation or sale of liquor and how to structure the liquor distribution system," South Dakota asserts that the setting of minimum drinking ages is clearly within the "core powers" reserved to the States under § 2 of the Amendment.[1] [ ]. Section 158, petitioner claims, usurps that core power. The Secretary in response asserts that the Twenty-first Amendment is simply not implicated by § 158; the plain language of § 2 confirms the States' broad power to impose restrictions on the sale and distribution of alcoholic beverages but does not confer on them any power to *permit* sales that Congress seeks to *prohibit*. Brief for Respondent 25–26. That Amendment, under this reasoning, would not prevent Congress from affirmatively enacting a national minimum drinking age more restrictive than that provided by the various state laws; and it would follow *a fortiori* that the indirect inducement involved here is compatible with the Twenty-first Amendment.

These arguments present questions of the meaning of the Twenty-first Amendment, the bounds of which have escaped precise definition. [ ]. Despite the extended treatment of the question by the parties, however, we need not decide in this case whether that Amendment would prohibit an attempt by Congress to legislate directly a national

---

1. Section 2 of the Twenty-first Amendment provides: "The transportation or importation into any State, Territory, or possession of the United States for delivery or use therein of intoxicating liquors, in violation of the laws thereof, is hereby prohibited."

minimum drinking age. Here, Congress has acted indirectly under its spending power to encourage uniformity in the States' drinking ages. As we explain below, we find this legislative effort within constitutional bounds even if Congress may not regulate drinking ages directly.

The Constitution empowers Congress to "lay and collect Taxes, Duties, Imposts, and Excises, to pay the Debts and provide for the common Defence and general Welfare of the United States." Art. I, § 8, cl. 1. Incident to this power, Congress may attach conditions on the receipt of federal funds, and has repeatedly employed the power "to further broad policy objectives by conditioning receipt of federal moneys upon compliance by the recipient with federal statutory and administrative directives." *Fullilove* v. *Klutznick*, 448 U.S. 448, 474 (1980) (opinion of Burger, C. J.) [ ] . The breadth of this power was made clear in *United States* v. *Butler*, 297 U.S. 1, 66 (1936), where the Court, resolving a longstanding debate over the scope of the Spending Clause, determined that "the power of Congress to authorize expenditure of public moneys for public purposes is not limited by the direct grants of legislative power found in the Constitution." Thus, objectives not thought to be within Article I's "enumerated legislative fields," *id.*, at 65, may nevertheless be attained through the use of the spending power and the conditional grant of federal funds.

The spending power is of course not unlimited, *Pennhurst State School and Hospital* v. *Halderman*, 451 U.S. 1, 17, and n. 13 (1981), but is instead subject to several general restrictions articulated in our cases. The first of these limitations is derived from the language of the Constitution itself: the exercise of the spending power must be in pursuit of "the general welfare." See *Helvering* v. *Davis*, 301 U.S. 619, 640–641 (1937); *United States* v. *Butler, supra*, at 65. In considering whether a particular expenditure is intended to serve general public purposes, courts should defer substantially to the judgment of Congress. *Helvering* v. *Davis, supra*, at 640, 645. Second, we have required that if Congress desires to condition the States' receipt of federal funds, it "must do so unambiguously ..., enabl[ing] the States to exercise their choice knowingly, cognizant of the consequences of their participation." *Pennhurst State School and Hospital* v. *Halderman, supra*, at 17. Third, our cases have suggested (without significant elaboration) that conditions on federal grants might be illegitimate if they are unrelated "to the federal interest in particular national projects or programs." *Massachusetts* v. *United States*, 435 U.S. 444, 461 (1978) (plurality opinion). See also *Ivanhoe Irrigation Dist.* v. *McCracken, supra*, at 295, ("The Federal Government may establish and impose reasonable conditions relevant to federal interest in the project and to the over-all objectives thereof"). Finally, we have noted that other constitutional provisions may provide an independent bar to the conditional grant of federal funds. [citations omitted].

South Dakota does not seriously claim that § 158 is inconsistent with any of the first three restrictions mentioned above. We can readily conclude that the provision is designed to serve the general welfare, especially in light of the fact that "the concept of welfare or the opposite is shaped by Congress.... " *Helvering* v. *Davis, supra*, at 645. Congress found that the differing drinking ages in the States created particular incentives for young persons to combine their desire to drink with their ability to drive, and that this interstate problem required a national solution. The means it chose to address this dangerous situation were reasonably calculated to advance the general welfare. The conditions upon which States receive the funds, moreover, could not be more clearly stated by Congress. [ ]. And the State itself, rather than challenging the germaneness of the condition to federal purposes, admits that it "has never contended that the congressional action was ... unrelated to a national concern in the absence of the Twenty-first Amendment." Indeed, the condition imposed by Congress is directly related to one of the main purposes for which highway funds are expended—safe interstate travel. [ ] This goal of the interstate highway system had been frustrated by varying drinking ages among the States. A Presidential commission appointed to study alcohol related accidents and fatalities on the Nation's highways concluded that the lack of uniformity in the States' drinking ages created "an incentive to drink and drive" because "young persons commut[e] to border States where the drinking age is lower." Presidential Commission on Drunk Driving, Final Report 11 (1983). By enacting § 158, Congress conditioned the receipt of federal funds in a way reasonably calculated to address this particular impediment to a purpose for which the funds are expended.

The remaining question about the validity of § 158—and the basic point of disagreement between the parties—is whether the Twenty-first Amendment constitutes an "independent constitutional bar" to the conditional grant of federal funds. *Lawrence County* v. *Lead–Deadwood School Dist., supra*, at 269–270. Petitioner, relying on its view that the Twenty-first Amendment prohibits *direct* regulation of drinking ages by Congress, asserts that "Congress may not use the spending power to regulate that which it is prohibited from regulating directly under the Twenty-first Amendment." B[ ] But our cases show that this "independent constitutional bar" limitation on the spending power is not of the kind petitioner suggests. *United States* v. *Butler, supra*, at 66, for example, established that the constitutional limitations on Congress when exercising its spending power are less exacting than those on its authority to regulate directly.

We have also held that a perceived Tenth Amendment limitation on congressional regulation of state affairs did not comitantly limit the range of conditions legitimately placed on federal grants. In *Oklahoma* v. *Civil Service Comm'n*, 330 U.S. 127 (1947), the Court considered the validity of the Hatch Act insofar as it was applied to political activities of state officials whose employment was financed in whole or in part with federal funds. The State contended that an order under this provision to withhold certain federal funds unless a state official was removed invaded its sovereignty in violation of the Tenth Amendment. Though finding that "the United States is not concerned with, and has no power to regulate, local political activities as such of state officials," the Court nevertheless held that the Federal Government "does have power to fix the terms upon which its money allotments to states shall be disbursed." *Id.*, at 143. The Court found no violation of the State's sovereignty because the State could, and did, adopt "the 'simple expedient' of not yielding to what she urges is federal coercion. The offer of benefits to a state by the United States dependent upon cooperation by the state with federal plans, assumedly for the general welfare, is not unusual." *Id.*, at 143–144 [ ]. See also *Steward Machine Co.* v. *Davis*, 301 U.S., at 595 ("There is only a condition which the state is free at pleasure to disregard or to fulfill"); *Massachusetts* v. *Mellon*, 262 U.S. 447, 482 (1923).

These cases establish that the "independent constitutional bar" limitation on the spending power is not, as petitioner suggests, a prohibition on the indirect achievement of objectives which Congress is not empowered to achieve directly. Instead, we think that the language in our earlier opinions stands for the unexceptionable proposition that the power may not be used to induce the States to engage in activities that would themselves be unconstitutional. Thus, for example, a grant of federal funds conditioned on invidiously discriminatory state action or the infliction of cruel and unusual punishment would be an illegitimate exercise of the Congress' broad spending power. But no such claim can be or is made here. Were South Dakota to succumb to the blandishments offered by Congress and raise its drinking age to 21, the State's action in so doing would not violate the constitutional rights of anyone.

Our decisions have recognized that in some circumstances the financial inducement offered by Congress might be so coercive as to pass the point at which "pressure turns into compulsion." *Steward Machine Co.* v. *Davis, supra*, at 590. Here, however, Congress has directed only that a State desiring to establish a minimum drinking age lower than 21 lose a relatively small percentage of certain federal highway funds. Petitioner contends that the coercive nature of this program is evident from the degree of success it has achieved. We cannot conclude, however, that a conditional grant of federal money of this sort is unconstitutional simply by reason of its success in achieving the congressional objective.

When we consider, for a moment, that all South Dakota would lose if she adheres to her chosen course as to a suitable minimum drinking age is 5% of the funds otherwise obtainable under specified highway grant programs, the argument as to coercion is shown to be more rhetoric than fact. As we said a half century ago in *Steward Machine Co.* v. *Davis*:

"Every rebate from a tax when conditioned upon conduct is in some measure a temptation. But to hold that motive or temptation is equivalent to coercion is to plunge the law in endless difficulties. The outcome of such a doctrine is the acceptance of a philosophical determinism by which choice becomes impossible. Till now the law has been guided by a robust common sense which assumes the freedom of the will as a working hypothesis in the solution of its problems." 301 U.S., at 589–590.

Here Congress has offered relatively mild encouragement to the States to enact higher minimum drinking ages than they would otherwise choose. But the enactment of such laws remains the prerogative of the States not merely in theory but in fact. Even if Congress might lack the power to impose a national minimum drinking age directly, we conclude that encouragement to state action found in § 158 is a valid use of the spending power. Accordingly, the judgment of the Court of Appeals is

Affirmed.

44 LIQUORMART, INC. v. RHODE ISLAND

Supreme Court of the United States, 1996.
517 U.S. 484, 116 S.Ct. 1495, 134 L.Ed.2d 711.

JUSTICE STEVENS announced the judgment of the Court and delivered the opinion of the Court with respect to Parts I, II, VII, and VIII, an opinion with respect to Parts III and V, in which JUSTICE KENNEDY, JUSTICE SOUTER, and JUSTICE GINSBURG join, an opinion with respect to Part VI, in which JUSTICE KENNEDY, JUSTICE THOMAS, and JUSTICE GINSBURG join, and an opinion with respect to Part IV, in which JUSTICE KENNEDY and JUSTICE GINSBURG join.

I

In 1956, the Rhode Island Legislature enacted two separate prohibitions against advertising the retail price of alcoholic beverages. The first applies to vendors licensed in Rhode Island as well as to out-of-state manufacturers, wholesalers, and shippers. It prohibits them from "advertising in any manner whatsoever" the price of any alcoholic beverage offered for sale in the State; the only exception is for price tags or signs displayed with the merchandise within licensed premises and not visible from the street. The second statute applies to the Rhode Island news media. It contains a categorical prohibition against the publication or broadcast of any advertisements—even those referring to sales in other States—that "make reference to the price of any alcoholic beverages."

In two cases decided in 1985, the Rhode Island Supreme Court reviewed the constitutionality of these two statutes. In *S & S Liquor Mart, Inc.* v. *Pastore,* 497 A.2d 729, a liquor retailer located in Westerly, Rhode Island, a town that borders the State of Connecticut, having been advised that his license would be revoked if he advertised his prices in a Connecticut paper, sought to enjoin enforcement of the first statute. Over the dissent of one justice, the court upheld the statute. It concluded that the statute served the substantial state interest in " 'the promotion of temperance.' " *Id.,* at 737. Because the plaintiff failed to prove that the statute did not serve that interest, the court held that he had not carried his burden of establishing a violation of the First Amendment. In

response to the dissent's argument that the court had placed the burden
on the wrong party, the majority reasoned that the Twenty-first Amendment gave the statute " 'an added presumption [of] validity.' " *Id.*, at
732. Although that presumption had not been overcome in that case, the
State Supreme Court assumed that in a future case the record might
"support the proposition that these advertising restrictions do not further temperance objectives." *Id.*, at 734.

In *Rhode Island Liquor Stores Assn.* v. *Evening Call Pub. Co.*, 497
A.2d 331, the plaintiff association sought to enjoin the publisher of the
local newspaper in Woonsocket, Rhode Island, from accepting advertisements disclosing the retail price of alcoholic beverages being sold across
the state line in Millville, Massachusetts. In upholding the injunction,
the State Supreme Court adhered to its reasoning in the *Pastore* case
and rejected the argument that the statute neither "directly advanced"
the state interest in promoting temperance, nor was "more extensive
than necessary to serve that interest" as required by this Court's
decision in *Central Hudson Gas & Elec. Corp.* v. *Public Serv. Comm'n of
N. Y.*, 447 U.S. 557, 563, 65 L.Ed.2d 341, 100 S.Ct. 2343 (1980). It
assumed the existence of other, "perhaps more effective means" of
achieving the State's "goal of temperance," but concluded that it was
"not unreasonable for the State of Rhode Island to believe that price
advertising will result in increased sales of alcoholic beverages generally." *Rhode Island Liquor Stores Assn.* v. *Evening Call Pub. Co.*, 497 A.2d
at 336.

II

Petitioners 44 Liquormart, Inc. (44 Liquormart), and Peoples Super
Liquor Stores, Inc. (Peoples), are licensed retailers of alcoholic beverages.
Petitioner 44 Liquormart operates a store in Rhode Island and petitioner
Peoples operates several stores in Massachusetts that are patronized by
Rhode Island residents. Peoples uses alcohol price advertising extensive-
ly in Massachusetts, where such advertising is permitted, but Rhode
Island newspapers and other media outlets have refused to accept such
ads.

Complaints from competitors about an advertisement placed by 44
Liquormart in a Rhode Island newspaper in 1991 generated enforcement
proceedings that in turn led to the initiation of this litigation. The
advertisement did not state the price of any alcoholic beverages. Indeed,
it noted that "State law prohibits advertising liquor prices." The ad did,
however, state the low prices at which peanuts, potato chips, and
Schweppes mixers were being offered, identify various brands of pack-
aged liquor, and include the word "WOW" in large letters next to
pictures of vodka and rum bottles. Based on the conclusion that the
implied reference to bargain prices for liquor violated the statutory ban
on price advertising, the Rhode Island Liquor Control Administrator
assessed a $400 fine.

After paying the fine, 44 Liquormart, joined by Peoples, filed this action against the administrator in the Federal District Court seeking a declaratory judgment that the two statutes and the administrator's implementing regulations violate the First Amendment and other provisions of federal law. The Rhode Island Liquor Stores Association was allowed to intervene as a defendant and in due course the State of Rhode Island replaced the administrator as the principal defendant. The parties stipulated that the price advertising ban is vigorously enforced, that Rhode Island permits "all advertising of alcoholic beverages excepting references to price outside the licensed premises," and that petitioners' proposed ads do not concern an illegal activity and presumably would not be false or misleading. *44 Liquor Mart, Inc.* v. *Racine*, 829 F.Supp. 543, 545 (RI 1993). The parties disagreed, however, about the impact of the ban on the promotion of temperance in Rhode Island. On that question the District Court heard conflicting expert testimony and reviewed a number of studies.

In his findings of fact, the District Judge first noted that there was a pronounced lack of unanimity among researchers who have studied the impact of advertising on the level of consumption of alcoholic beverages. He referred to a 1985 Federal Trade Commission study that found no evidence that alcohol advertising significantly affects alcohol abuse. Another study indicated that Rhode Island ranks in the upper 30% of States in per capita consumption of alcoholic beverages; alcohol consumption is lower in other States that allow price advertising. After summarizing the testimony of the expert witnesses for both parties, he found "as a fact that Rhode Island's off-premises liquor price advertising ban has no significant impact on levels of alcohol consumption in Rhode Island." *Id.*, at 549.

As a matter of law, he concluded that the price advertising ban was unconstitutional because it did not "directly advance" the State's interest in reducing alcohol consumption and was "more extensive than necessary to serve that interest." *Id.*, at 555. He reasoned that the party seeking to uphold a restriction on commercial speech carries the burden of justifying it and that the Twenty-first Amendment did not shift or diminish that burden. Acknowledging that it might have been reasonable for the state legislature to "assume a correlation between the price advertising ban and reduced consumption," he held that more than a rational basis was required to justify the speech restriction, and that the State had failed to demonstrate a reasonable " 'fit' " between its policy objectives and its chosen means. *Ibid.*

The Court of Appeals reversed. 39 F.3d 5 (CA1 1994). It found "inherent merit" in the State's submission that competitive price advertising would lower prices and that lower prices would produce more sales. *Id.*, at 7. Moreover, it agreed with the reasoning of the Rhode Island Supreme Court that the Twenty-first Amendment gave the statutes an added presumption of validity. *Id.*, at 8. Alternatively, it concluded that reversal was compelled by this Court's summary action in *Queensgate Investment Co.* v. *Liquor Control Comm'n of Ohio*, 459 U.S.

807, 74 L.Ed.2d 45, 103 S.Ct. 31 (1982). See 39 F.3d at 8. In that case the Court dismissed the appeal from a decision of the Ohio Supreme Court upholding a prohibition against off-premises advertising of the prices of alcoholic beverages sold by the drink. [ ].

* * *

III

Advertising has been a part of our culture throughout our history. Even in colonial days, the public relied on "commercial speech" for vital information about the market. Early newspapers displayed advertisements for goods and services on their front pages, and town criers called out prices in public squares. [ ]. Indeed, commercial messages played such a central role in public life prior to the founding that Benjamin Franklin authored his early defense of a free press in support of his decision to print, of all things, an advertisement for voyages to Barbados. Franklin, An Apology for Printers, June 10, 1731, reprinted in 2 Writings of Benjamin Franklin 172 (1907).

In accord with the role that commercial messages have long played, the law has developed to ensure that advertising provides consumers with accurate information about the availability of goods and services. * * *

* * * [O]ur early cases recognized that the State may regulate some types of commercial advertising more freely than other forms of protected speech. Specifically, we explained that the State may require commercial messages to "appear in such a form, or include such additional information, warnings, and disclaimers, as are necessary to prevent its being deceptive," *Virginia Bd. of Pharmacy [n. Virginia Citizens Consumer Council, Inc., 425 U.S. 748, 48 L.Ed.2d 346, 96 S.Ct. 1817 (1976)]* at 772, n. 24. and that it may restrict some forms of aggressive sales practices that have the potential to exert "undue influence" over consumers, see *Bates* v. *State Bar of Ariz.*, 433 U.S. 350, 366, 53 L.Ed.2d 810, 97 S.Ct. 2691 (1977).

Virginia Bd. of Pharmacy attributed the State's authority to impose these regulations in part to certain "commonsense differences" that exist between commercial messages and other types of protected expression. 425 U.S. at 771, n. 24. Our opinion noted that the greater "objectivity" of commercial speech justifies affording the State more freedom to distinguish false commercial advertisements from true ones, *ibid.*, and that the greater "hardiness" of commercial speech, inspired as it is by the profit motive, likely diminishes the chilling effect that may attend its regulation, *ibid.*

Subsequent cases explained that the State's power to regulate commercial transactions justifies its concomitant power to regulate commercial speech that is "linked inextricably" to those transactions. *Friedman* v. *Rogers*, 440 U.S. 1, 10, n. 9, 59 L.Ed.2d 100, 99 S.Ct. 887 (1979); *Ohralik* v. *Ohio State Bar Assn.*, 436 U.S. 447, 456, 56 L.Ed.2d 444, 98

S.Ct. 1912 (1978) (commercial speech "occurs in an area traditionally subject to government regulation"). As one commentator has explained: "The entire commercial speech doctrine, after all, represents an accommodation between the right to speak and hear expression *about* goods and services and the right of government to regulate the sales *of* such goods and services." L. Tribe, American Constitutional Law § 12–15, p. 903 (2d ed. 1988). Nevertheless, as we explained in *Linmark*, the State retains less regulatory authority when its commercial speech restrictions strike at "the substance of the information communicated" rather than the "commercial aspect of [it]—with offerors communicating offers to offerees." 431 U.S. at 96; *Carey* v. *Population Services Int'l*, 431 U.S. at 701, n. 28.

* * *

In reaching its conclusion, the majority explained that although the special nature of commercial speech may require less than strict review of its regulation, special concerns arise from "regulations that entirely suppress commercial speech in order to pursue a nonspeech-related policy." *Id.*, at 566, n. 9. In those circumstances, "a ban on speech could screen from public view the underlying governmental policy." *Ibid.* As a result, the Court concluded that "special care" should attend the review of such blanket bans, and it pointedly remarked that "in recent years this Court has not approved a blanket ban on commercial speech unless the expression itself was flawed in some way, either because it was deceptive or related to unlawful activity." *Ibid.*

IV

As our review of the case law reveals, Rhode Island errs in concluding that *all* commercial speech regulations are subject to a similar form of constitutional review simply because they target a similar category of expression. The mere fact that messages propose commercial transactions does not in and of itself dictate the constitutional analysis that should apply to decisions to suppress them. [ ].

When a State regulates commercial messages to protect consumers from misleading, deceptive, or aggressive sales practices, or requires the disclosure of beneficial consumer information, the purpose of its regulation is consistent with the reasons for according constitutional protection to commercial speech and therefore justifies less than strict review. However, when a State entirely prohibits the dissemination of truthful, nonmisleading commercial messages for reasons unrelated to the preservation of a fair bargaining process, there is far less reason to depart from the rigorous review that the First Amendment generally demands.

Sound reasons justify reviewing the latter type of commercial speech regulation more carefully. Most obviously, complete speech bans, unlike content-neutral restrictions on the time, place, or manner of expression [ ] are particularly dangerous because they all but foreclose alternative means of disseminating certain information.

Our commercial speech cases have recognized the dangers that attend governmental attempts to single out certain messages for suppression. For example, in *Linmark*, 431 U.S. at 92–94, we concluded that a ban on "For Sale" signs was "content based" and failed to leave open "satisfactory" alternative channels of communication; see also *Virginia Bd. of Pharmacy*, 425 U.S. at 771. Moreover, last Term we upheld a 30–day prohibition against a certain form of legal solicitation largely because it left so many channels of communication open to Florida lawyers. *Florida Bar* v. *Went For It, Inc.*, 515 U.S. 618, 633–634, 132 L.Ed.2d 541, 115 S.Ct. 2371 (1995).

The special dangers that attend complete bans on truthful, nonmisleading commercial speech cannot be explained away by appeals to the "commonsense distinctions" that exist between commercial and noncommercial speech. *Virginia Bd. of Pharmacy*, 425 U.S. at 771, n. 24. Regulations that suppress the truth are no less troubling because they target objectively verifiable information, nor are they less effective because they aim at durable messages. As a result, neither the "greater objectivity" nor the "greater hardiness" of truthful, nonmisleading commercial speech justifies reviewing its complete suppression with added deference. *Ibid.*

* * *

Precisely because bans against truthful, nonmisleading commercial speech rarely seek to protect consumers from either deception or over-reaching, they usually rest solely on the offensive assumption that the public will respond "irrationally" to the truth. *Linmark*, 431 U.S. at 96. The First Amendment directs us to be especially skeptical of regulations that seek to keep people in the dark for what the government perceives to be their own good. That teaching applies equally to state attempts to deprive consumers of accurate information about their chosen products * * *.

V

In this case, there is no question that Rhode Island's price advertising ban constitutes a blanket prohibition against truthful, nonmisleading speech about a lawful product. There is also no question that the ban serves an end unrelated to consumer protection. Accordingly, we must review the price advertising ban with "special care," [ ] mindful that speech prohibitions of this type rarely survive constitutional review, *ibid.*

The State argues that the price advertising prohibition should nevertheless be upheld because it directly advances the State's substantial interest in promoting temperance, and because it is no more extensive than necessary. [ ]. Although there is some confusion as to what Rhode Island means by temperance, we assume that the State asserts an interest in reducing alcohol consumption.

In evaluating the ban's effectiveness in advancing the State's interest, we note that a commercial speech regulation "may not be sustained if it provides only ineffective or remote support for the government's purpose." *Id.*, at 564. * * *

* * * Despite the absence of proof on the point, we can even agree with the State's contention that it is reasonable to assume that demand, and hence consumption throughout the market, is somewhat lower whenever a higher, noncompetitive price level prevails. However, without any findings of fact, or indeed any evidentiary support whatsoever, we cannot agree with the assertion that the price advertising ban will significantly advance the State's interest in promoting temperance.

* * *

In addition, as the District Court noted, the State has not identified what price level would lead to a significant reduction in alcohol consumption, nor has it identified the amount that it believes prices would decrease without the ban. *Ibid.* Thus, the State's own showing reveals that any connection between the ban and a significant change in alcohol consumption would be purely fortuitous.

As is evident, any conclusion that elimination of the ban would significantly increase alcohol consumption would require us to engage in the sort of "speculation or conjecture" that is an unacceptable means of demonstrating that a restriction on commercial speech directly advances the State's asserted interest. *Edenfield*, 507 U.S. at 770. Such speculation certainly does not suffice when the State takes aim at accurate commercial information for paternalistic ends.

The State also cannot satisfy the requirement that its restriction on speech be no more extensive than necessary. It is perfectly obvious that alternative forms of regulation that would not involve any restriction on speech would be more likely to achieve the State's goal of promoting temperance. As the State's own expert conceded, higher prices can be maintained either by direct regulation or by increased taxation. 829 F.Supp. at 549. Per capita purchases could be limited as is the case with prescription drugs. Even educational campaigns focused on the problems of excessive, or even moderate, drinking might prove to be more effective.

As a result, even under the less than strict standard that generally applies in commercial speech cases, the State has failed to establish a "reasonable fit" between its abridgment of speech and its temperance goal. *Board of Trustees of State Univ. of N. Y. v. Fox*, 492 U.S. 469, 480, 106 L.Ed.2d 388, 109 S.Ct. 3028 (1989) [ ]. It necessarily follows that the price advertising ban cannot survive the more stringent constitutional review that *Central Hudson* itself concluded was appropriate for the complete suppression of truthful, nonmisleading commercial speech. [ ].

VI

* * *

It is so ordered.

SKINNER v. RAILWAY LABOR EXECUTIVES' ASSOCIATION

Supreme Court of the United States, 1989.
489 U.S. 602, 109 S.Ct. 1402, 103 L.Ed.2d 639.

JUSTICE KENNEDY delivered the opinion of the Court.

The Federal Railroad Safety Act of 1970 authorizes the Secretary of Transportation to "prescribe, as necessary, appropriate rules, regulations, orders, and standards for all areas of railroad safety." 84 Stat. 971, 45 U. S. C. § 431(a). Finding that alcohol and drug abuse by railroad employees poses a serious threat to safety, the Federal Railroad Administration (FRA) has promulgated regulations that mandate blood and urine tests of employees who are involved in certain train accidents. The FRA also has adopted regulations that do not require, but do authorize, railroads to administer breath and urine tests to employees who violate certain safety rules. The question presented by this case is whether these regulations violate the Fourth Amendment.

I

A

The problem of alcohol use on American railroads is as old as the industry itself, and efforts to deter it by carrier rules began at least a century ago. For many years, railroads have prohibited operating employees from possessing alcohol or being intoxicated while on duty and from consuming alcoholic beverages while subject to being called for duty. More recently, these proscriptions have been expanded to forbid possession or use of certain drugs. These restrictions are embodied in "Rule G," an industry-wide operating rule promulgated by the Association of American Railroads, and are enforced, in various formulations, by virtually every railroad in the country. The customary sanction for Rule G violations is dismissal.

In July 1983, the FRA expressed concern that these industry efforts were not adequate to curb alcohol and drug abuse by railroad employees. The FRA pointed to evidence indicating that on-the-job intoxication was a significant problem in the railroad industry. The FRA also found, after a review of accident investigation reports, that from 1972 to 1983 "the nation's railroads experienced at least 21 significant train accidents involving alcohol or drug use as a probable cause or contributing factor," and that these accidents "resulted in 25 fatalities, 61 non-fatal injuries, and property damage estimated at $19 million (approximately $27 million in 1982 dollars)." 48 Fed. Reg. 30726 (1983). The FRA further identified "an additional 17 fatalities to operating employees working on or around rail rolling stock that involved alcohol or drugs as a contributing factor." *Ibid.* In light of these problems, the FRA solicited comments from interested parties on a various regulatory approaches to the problems of alcohol and drug abuse throughout the Nation's railroad system.

Comments submitted in response to this request indicated that railroads were able to detect a relatively small number of Rule G violations, owing, primarily, to their practice of relying on observation by supervisors and co-workers to enforce the rule. 49 Fed. Reg. 24266–24267 (1984). At the same time, "industry participants . . . confirmed that alcohol and drug use [did] occur on the railroads with unacceptable frequency," and available information from all sources "suggest[ed] that the problem includ[ed] 'pockets' of drinking and drug use involving multiple crew members (before and during work), sporadic cases of individuals reporting to work impaired, and repeated drinking and drug use by individual employees who are chemically or psychologically dependent on those substances." *Id.*, at 24253–24254. "Even without the benefit of regular post-accident testing," the FRA "identified 34 fatalities, 66 injuries and over $28 million in property damage (in 1983 dollars) that resulted from the errors of alcohol and drug-impaired employees in 45 train accidents and train incidents during the period 1975 through 1983." *Id.*, at 24254. Some of these accidents resulted in the release of hazardous materials and, in one case, the ensuing pollution required the evacuation of an entire Louisiana community. *Id.*, at 24254, 24259. In view of the obvious safety hazards of drug and alcohol use by railroad employees, the FRA announced in June 1984 its intention to promulgate federal regulations on the subject.

B

* * *

To the extent pertinent here, two subparts of the regulations relate to testing. Subpart C, which is entitled "Post–Accident Toxicological Testing," is mandatory. It provides that railroads "shall take all practicable steps to assure that all covered employees of the railroad directly involved . . . provide blood and urine samples for toxicological testing by FRA," § 219.203(a), upon the occurrence of certain specified events. Toxicological testing is required following a "major train accident," which is defined as any train accident that involves (i) a fatality, (ii) the release of hazardous material accompanied by an evacuation or a reportable injury, or (iii) damage to railroad property of $500,000 or more. § 219.201(a)(1). The railroad has the further duty of collecting blood and urine samples for testing after an "impact accident," which is defined as a collision that results in a reportable injury, or in damage to railroad property of $50,000 or more. § 219.201(a)(2). Finally, the railroad is also obligated to test after "[a]ny train incident that involves a fatality to any on duty railroad employee." § 219.201(a)(3).

After occurrence of an event which activates its duty to test, the railroad must transport all crew members and other covered employees directly involved in the accident or incident to an independent medical facility, where both blood and urine samples must be obtained from each employee. After the samples have been collected, the railroad is required to ship them by prepaid air freight to the FRA laboratory for analysis.

§ 219.205(d). There, the samples are analyzed using "state-of-the-art equipment and techniques" to detect and measure alcohol and drugs. The FRA proposes to place primary reliance on analysis of blood samples, as blood is "the only available body fluid ... that can provide a clear indication not only of the presence of alcohol and drugs but also their current impairment effects." 49 Fed. Reg. 24291 (1984). Urine samples are also necessary, however, because drug traces remain in the urine longer than in blood, and in some cases it will not be possible to transport employees to a medical facility before the time it takes for certain drugs to be eliminated from the bloodstream. In those instances, a "positive urine test, taken with specific information on the pattern of elimination for the particular drug and other information on the behavior of the employee and the circumstances of the accident, may be crucial to the determination of" the cause of an accident. *Ibid.*

The regulations require that the FRA notify employees of the results of the tests and afford them an opportunity to respond in writing before preparation of any final investigative report. [ ]. Employees who refuse to provide required blood or urine samples may not perform covered service for nine months, but they are entitled to a hearing concerning their refusal to take the test. [ ].

Subpart D of the regulations, which is entitled "Authorization to Test for Cause," is permissive. It authorizes railroads to require covered employees to submit to breath or urine tests in certain circumstances not addressed by Subpart C. Breath or urine tests, or both, may be ordered (1) after a reportable accident or incident, where a supervisor has a "reasonable suspicion" that an employee's acts or omissions contributed to the occurrence or severity of the accident or incident, [ ] or (2) in the event of certain specific rule violations, including noncompliance with a signal and excessive speeding, [ ]. A railroad also may require breath tests where a supervisor has a "reasonable suspicion" that an employee is under the influence of alcohol, based upon specific, personal observations concerning the appearance, behavior, speech, or body odors of the employee. [ ]. Where impairment is suspected, a railroad, in addition, may require urine tests, but only if two supervisors make the appropriate determination [ ], and, where the supervisors suspect impairment due to a substance other than alcohol, at least one of those supervisors must have received specialized training in detecting the signs of drug intoxication [ ].

Subpart D further provides that whenever the results of either breath or urine tests are intended for use in a disciplinary proceeding, the employee must be given the opportunity to provide a blood sample for analysis at an independent medical facility. [ ]. If an employee declines to give a blood sample, the railroad may presume impairment
* * *

C

Respondents, the Railway Labor Executives' Association and various of its member labor organizations, brought the instant suit in the United

States District Court for the Northern District of California, seeking to
enjoin the FRA's regulations on various statutory and constitutional
grounds. In a ruling from the bench, the District Court granted summary judgment in petitioners' favor. The court concluded that railroad
employees "have a valid interest in the integrity of their own bodies"
that deserved protection under the Fourth Amendment. [ ]. The court
held, however, that this interest was outweighed by the competing
"public and governmental interest in the ... promotion of ... railway
safety, safety for employees, and safety for the general public that is
involved with the transportation." [ ]. The District Court found respondents' other constitutional and statutory arguments meritless.

A divided panel of the Court of Appeals for the Ninth Circuit
reversed. [ ]. The court held, first, that tests mandated by a railroad in
reliance on the authority conferred by Subpart D involve sufficient
Government action to implicate the Fourth Amendment, and that the
breath, blood, and urine tests contemplated by the FRA regulations are
Fourth Amendment searches. The court also "agreed that the exigencies
of testing for the presence of alcohol and drugs in blood, urine or breath
require prompt action which precludes obtaining a warrant." *Id.*, at 583.
The court further held that "accommodation of railroad employees'
privacy interest with the significant safety concerns of the government
does not require adherence to a probable cause requirement," and,
accordingly, that the legality of the searches contemplated by the FRA
regulations depends on their reasonableness under all the circumstances.
[ ].

The court concluded, however, that particularized suspicion is essential to a finding that toxicological testing of railroad employees is
reasonable. *Ibid.* A requirement of individualized suspicion, the court
stated, would impose "no insuperable burden on the government," [ ]
and would ensure that the tests are confined to the detection of current
impairment, rather than to the discovery of "the metabolites of various
drugs, which are not evidence of current intoxication and may remain in
the body for days or weeks after the ingestion of the drug." *Id.*, at 588–
589. Except for the provisions authorizing breath and urine tests on a
"reasonable suspicion" of drug or alcohol impairment [ ], the FRA
regulations did not require a showing of individualized suspicion, and,
accordingly, the court invalidated them.

* * *

II

The Fourth Amendment provides that "[t]he right of the people to
be secure in their persons, houses, papers, and effects, against unreasonable searches and seizures, shall not be violated...." The Amendment
guarantees the privacy, dignity, and security of persons against certain
arbitrary and invasive acts by officers of the Government or those acting
at their direction. [ ]. Before we consider whether the tests in question
are reasonable under the Fourth Amendment, we must inquire whether

the tests are attributable to the Government or its agents, and whether they amount to searches or seizures. We turn to those matters.

A

Although the Fourth Amendment does not apply to a search or seizure, even an arbitrary one, effected by a private party on his own initiative, the Amendment protects against such intrusions if the private party acted as an instrument or agent of the Government. [ ]. A railroad that complies with the provisions of Subpart C of the regulations does so by compulsion of sovereign authority, and the lawfulness of its acts is controlled by the Fourth Amendment. Petitioners contend, however, that the Fourth Amendment is not implicated by Subpart D of the regulations, as nothing in Subpart D compels any testing by private railroads.

We are unwilling to conclude, in the context of this facial challenge, that breath and urine tests required by private railroads in reliance on Subpart D will not implicate the Fourth Amendment. Whether a private party should be deemed an agent or instrument of the Government for Fourth Amendment purposes necessarily turns on the degree of the Government's participation in the private party's activities[ ]. The fact that the Government has not compelled a private party to perform a search does not, by itself, establish that the search is a private one. Here, specific features of the regulations combine to convince us that the Government did more than adopt a passive position toward the underlying private conduct.

The regulations, including those in Subpart D, pre-empt state laws, rules, or regulations covering the same subject matter [ ], and are intended to supersede "any provision of a collective bargaining agreement, or arbitration award construing such an agreement," [ ]. They also confer upon the FRA the right to receive certain biological samples and test results procured by railroads pursuant to Subpart D. § 219.11(c). In addition, a railroad may not divest itself of, or otherwise compromise by contract, the authority conferred by Subpart D. As the FRA explained, such "authority ... is conferred for the purpose of promoting the public safety, and a railroad may not shackle itself in a way inconsistent with its duty to promote the public safety." [ ]. Nor is a covered employee free to decline his employer's request to submit to breath or urine tests under the conditions set forth in Subpart D. [ ]. An employee who refuses to submit to the tests must be withdrawn from covered service. [ ].

In light of these provisions, we are unwilling to accept petitioners' submission that tests conducted by private railroads in reliance on Subpart D will be primarily the result of private initiative. The Government has removed all legal barriers to the testing authorized by Subpart D, and indeed has made plain not only its strong preference for testing, but also its desire to share the fruits of such intrusions. In addition, it has mandated that the railroads not bargain away the authority to perform tests granted by Subpart D. These are clear indices of the

Government's encouragement, endorsement, and participation, and suffice to implicate the Fourth Amendment.

B

Our precedents teach that where, as here, the Government seeks to obtain physical evidence from a person, the Fourth Amendment may be relevant at several levels. [Citations omitted].

We have long recognized that a "compelled intrusio[n] into the body for blood to be analyzed for alcohol content" must be deemed a Fourth Amendment search. See *Schmerber* v. *California*, 384 U.S. 757, 767–768 (1966). [ ]. In light of our society's concern for the security of one's person [ ], it is obvious that this physical intrusion, penetrating beneath the skin, infringes an expectation of privacy that society is prepared to recognize as reasonable. The ensuing chemical analysis of the sample to obtain physiological data is a further invasion of the tested employee's privacy interests. [ ]. Much the same is true of the breath-testing procedures required under Subpart D of the regulations. * * *

Unlike the blood-testing procedure at issue in *Schmerber*, the procedures prescribed by the FRA regulations for collecting and testing urine samples do not entail a surgical intrusion into the body. It is not disputed, however, that chemical analysis of urine, like that of blood, can reveal a host of private medical facts about an employee, including whether he or she is epileptic, pregnant, or diabetic. Nor can it be disputed that the process of collecting the sample to be tested, which may in some cases involve visual or aural monitoring of the act of urination, itself implicates privacy interests. * * *

III

A

To hold that the Fourth Amendment is applicable to the drug and alcohol testing prescribed by the FRA regulations is only to begin the inquiry into the standards governing such intrusions. [ ]. For the Fourth Amendment does not proscribe all searches and seizures, but only those that are unreasonable. [ ]. What is reasonable, of course, "depends on all of the circumstances surrounding the search or seizure and the nature of the search or seizure itself." *United States* v. *Montoya de Hernandez*, 473 U.S. 531, 537 (1985). Thus, the permissibility of a particular practice "is judged by balancing its intrusion on the individual's Fourth Amendment interests against its promotion of legitimate governmental interests." *Delaware* v. *Prouse*, 440 U.S., at 654 [ ].

In most criminal cases, we strike this balance in favor of the procedures described by the Warrant Clause of the Fourth Amendment. [ ]. Except in certain well-defined circumstances, a search or seizure in such a case is not reasonable unless it is accomplished pursuant to a judicial warrant issued upon probable cause. [ ]. We have recognized exceptions to this rule, however, "when 'special needs, beyond the normal need for law enforcement, make the warrant and probable-cause requirement impracticable.' " *Griffin* v. *Wisconsin,* 483 U.S. 868, 873 (1987), quoting *New Jersey* v. *T. L. O., supra,* at 351 (Blackmun, J., concurring in judgment). When faced with such special needs, we have not hesitated to balance the governmental and privacy interests to assess the practicality of the warrant and probable-cause requirements in the particular context. [ ].

The Government's interest in regulating the conduct of railroad employees to ensure safety, like its supervision of probationers or regulated industries, or its operation of a government office, school, or prison, "likewise presents 'special needs' beyond normal law enforcement that may justify departures from the usual warrant and probable-cause requirements." *Griffin* v. *Wisconsin, supra,* at 873–874. The hours of service employees covered by the FRA regulations include persons engaged in handling orders concerning train movements, operating crews, and those engaged in the maintenance and repair of signal systems. [ ]. It is undisputed that these and other covered employees are engaged in safety-sensitive tasks. The FRA so found, and respondents conceded the point at oral argument. As we have recognized, the whole premise of the Hours of Service Act is that "[t]he length of hours of service has direct relation to the efficiency of the human agencies upon which protection [of] life and property necessarily depends." *Baltimore & Ohio R. Co.* v. *ICC,* 221 U.S. 612, 619 (1911). [ ]

The FRA has prescribed toxicological tests, not to assist in the prosecution of employees, but rather "to prevent accidents and casualties in railroad operations that result from impairment of employees by alcohol or drugs." 49 CFR § 219.1(a) (1987). This governmental interest in ensuring the safety of the traveling public and of the employees themselves plainly justifies prohibiting covered employees from using alcohol or drugs on duty, or while subject to being called for duty. This interest also "require[s] and justif[ies] the exercise of supervision to assure that the restrictions are in fact observed." *Griffin* v. *Wisconsin, supra,* at 875. The question that remains, then, is whether the Government's need to monitor compliance with these restrictions justifies the privacy intrusions at issue absent a warrant or individualized suspicion.

B

An essential purpose of a warrant requirement is to protect privacy interests by assuring citizens subject to a search or seizure that such intrusions are not the random or arbitrary acts of government agents. A warrant assures the citizen that the intrusion is authorized by law, and that it is narrowly limited in its objectives and scope. [ ] A warrant also provides the detached scrutiny of a neutral magistrate, and thus ensures an objective determination whether an intrusion is justified in any given case. See *United States* v. *Chadwick, [433 U.S. 1],* 9. In the present context, however, a warrant would do little to further these aims. Both the circumstances justifying toxicological testing and the permissible limits of such intrusions are defined narrowly and specifically in the regulations that authorize them, and doubtless are well known to covered employees. [ ]. Indeed, in light of the standardized nature of the tests and the minimal discretion vested in those charged with administering the program, there are virtually no facts for a neutral magistrate to evaluate. [ ]

We have recognized, moreover, that the government's interest in dispensing with the warrant requirement is at its strongest when, as here, "the burden of obtaining a warrant is likely to frustrate the governmental purpose behind the search." *Camara* v. *Municipal Court of San Francisco, supra*, at 533. [ ]. As the FRA recognized, alcohol and other drugs are eliminated from the bloodstream at a constant rate [ ], and blood and breath samples taken to measure whether these substances were in the bloodstream when a triggering event occurred must be obtained as soon as possible. [ ]. Although the metabolites of some drugs remain in the urine for longer periods of time and may enable the FRA to estimate whether the employee was impaired by those drugs at the time of a covered accident, incident, or rule violation [ ], the delay necessary to procure a warrant nevertheless may result in the destruction of valuable evidence.

The Government's need to rely on private railroads to set the testing process in motion also indicates that insistence on a warrant requirement would impede the achievement of the Government's objective. * * *

In sum, imposing a warrant requirement in the present context would add little to the assurances of certainty and regularity already afforded by the regulations, while significantly hindering, and in many cases frustrating, the objectives of the Government's testing program. We do not believe that a warrant is essential to render the intrusions here at issue reasonable under the Fourth Amendment.

C

Our cases indicate that even a search that may be performed without a warrant must be based, as a general matter, on probable cause to believe that the person to be searched has violated the law. [ ]. When the balance of interests precludes insistence on a showing of probable cause, we have usually required "some quantum of individualized suspicion" before concluding that a search is reasonable. [ ]. We made it clear, however, that a showing of individualized suspicion is not a constitutional floor, below which a search must be presumed unreasonable. [ ]. In limited circumstances, where the privacy interests implicated by the search are minimal, and where an important governmental interest furthered by the intrusion would be placed in jeopardy by a requirement of individualized suspicion, a search may be reasonable despite the absence of such suspicion. We believe this is true of the intrusions in question here.

* * *

We conclude that the compelling Government interests served by the FRA's regulations would be significantly hindered if railroads were required to point to specific facts giving rise to a reasonable suspicion of impairment before testing a given employee. In view of our conclusion that, on the present record, the toxicological testing contemplated by the regulations is not an undue infringement on the justifiable expectations of privacy of covered employees, the Government's compelling interests outweigh privacy concerns.

IV

The possession of unlawful drugs is a criminal offense that the Government may punish, but it is a separate and far more dangerous wrong to perform certain sensitive tasks while under the influence of those substances. Performing those tasks while impaired by alcohol is, of course, equally dangerous, though consumption of alcohol is legal in most other contexts. The Government may take all necessary and reasonable regulatory steps to prevent or deter that hazardous conduct, and since the gravamen of the evil is performing certain functions while concealing the substance in the body, it may be necessary, as in the case before us, to examine the body or its fluids to accomplish the regulatory purpose. The necessity to perform that regulatory function with respect to railroad employees engaged in safety-sensitive tasks, and the reasonableness of the system for doing so, have been established in this case.

Alcohol and drug tests conducted in reliance on the authority of Subpart D cannot be viewed as private action outside the reach of the Fourth Amendment. Because the testing procedures mandated or authorized by Subparts C and D effect searches of the person, they must meet the Fourth Amendment's reasonableness requirement. In light of the limited discretion exercised by the railroad employers under the regulations, the surpassing safety interests served by toxicological tests in this context, and the diminished expectation of privacy that attaches to information pertaining to the fitness of covered employees, we believe that it is reasonable to conduct such tests in the absence of a warrant or reasonable suspicion that any particular employee may be impaired. We hold that the alcohol and drug tests contemplated by Subparts C and D of the FRA's regulations are reasonable within the meaning of the Fourth Amendment. The judgment of the Court of Appeals is accordingly reversed.

It is so ordered.

SMITH v. MERRITT

Supreme Court of Texas, 1997.
940 S.W.2d 602.

GREGG ABBOTT, J.

The issue in this case is whether a social host can be liable in negligence or negligence per se for injuries resulting from the host's provision of alcohol to a nineteen-year-old guest. Because the Legislature has established a policy against such causes of action, we decline to expand the common law to include those claims. * * *

I

Nineteen-year-old Robert Barbee hosted a party at a lake house owned by his parents, Marita and Bob Barbee, and his grandparents, Margaret and A.P. Merritt. There is no indication that the owners were present or even aware that Barbee hosted this party; however, there is evidence that the owners were aware that Barbee had previously hosted parties at the lake house.

Barbee brought two kegs of beer to the lake house and provided them to the party guests. Nineteen-year-old Robert Hale and eighteen-year-old Colin Smith were two of the guests. After drinking two or three cups of beer, Hale left the party in his car with Smith as a passenger. Soon thereafter, Hale collided head-on with a truck, seriously injuring Smith. Summary judgment evidence showed that Hale may have been driving too fast on the narrow, winding, poorly lit road. A medical report revealed that Hale's blood alcohol concentration was .069 grams per deciliter.

Colin Smith and his father Al Smith sued Robert Barbee and the lake house owners for Colin's injuries. The Smiths alleged that the defendants were negligent and negligent per se for providing Hale with alcohol in violation of liquor control laws and with knowledge that Hale would be driving. The trial court granted the owners' and Robert Barbee's collective motion for summary judgment. The court of appeals affirmed in part, holding that neither Robert Barbee nor the owners owed any common-law duty to the Smiths to prevent Hale from drinking and driving. [ ]. However, the appellate court reversed in part, holding that a fact question existed concerning whether Robert Barbee was negligent per se for violating section 106.06 of the Texas Alcoholic Beverage Code (TABC), which generally prohibits the provision of alcohol to persons under twenty-one. TEX. ALCO. BEV. CODE § 106.06.

The Smiths filed an application for writ of error with this Court, reasserting their claims that the lake house owners and Robert Barbee were liable in negligence and negligence per se. Robert Barbee also filed an application, asserting that the negligence per se cause of action against him under section 106.06 is precluded by Chapter 2 of the TABC, the "Dram Shop Act," which provides the exclusive cause of action for serving alcohol to a person eighteen years of age or older.

II

In determining whether a cause of action in negligence exists, the threshold inquiry is whether the defendants owed the plaintiffs a legal duty. [ ]. Deciding whether to impose a common-law duty involves complex social and economic policy considerations. [ ] This is especially true in deciding whether to impose a duty on a social host because of the competing societal concerns and public policy issues inherent in such a decision. When significant and diverse public policy concerns are implicated, careful consideration should be given to legislative pronouncements reflecting the adoption of a particular public policy. [ ]

Historically, an alcohol provider owed no tort duty to third persons for injuries caused by the provision of alcohol. [ ]. The consumption of alcohol, rather than the provision of it, was considered to be the sole proximate cause of injury to the third person. [ ] In 1987, this Court created a common-law duty owed by commercial providers of alcohol to injured third parties * * *. During the week that opinion was issued, the Texas Legislature superceded the newly recognized common-law duty by amending the TABC to create the Dram Shop Act. [ ].

The purpose of the legislative enactment is clear. Chapter 2 of the TABC is entitled "Civil Liabilities for Serving Beverages." That chapter "provides *the exclusive cause of action for providing an alcoholic beverage to a person 18 years of age or older.*" [ ]. Only "a person who sells or serves an alcoholic beverage under authority of a license or permit issued under the terms of [the TABC] or who otherwise sells an alcoholic beverage to an individual" can be liable under Chapter 2. [ ].

When enacting Chapter 2, the Legislature specifically considered and rejected the inclusion of civil liability for social hosts. [ ]. Early versions of the bill created civil causes of action against both commercial establishments and social hosts. [ ] However, the final version of the bill, and what is currently Chapter 2, creates a statutory cause of action against *commercial* providers only. [ ]. The Legislature demonstrated its intent against the creation of common-law social host liability for serving persons eighteen years of age or older by including language in section 2.03 that liability under Chapter 2 "is in lieu of common law or other statutory law warranties and duties."

This Court has previously deferred to the Legislature on social host liability. In *Graff* [*v. Beard*, 858 S.W.2d 918 (Tex. 1993)] we relied heavily on Chapter 2 of the TABC and its legislative history in declining to create a common-law tort duty for a social host who makes alcohol available to an intoxicated adult guest who will be driving. We decided that, as between social hosts and adult guests, the focus of liability to third parties should remain on the drinker. Absent a special relationship between the social host and the adult guest, the host has neither superior knowledge with which to foresee harm nor a legal right to control the guest. [ ]

Applying our holding in *Graff* and the dictates of TABC Chapter 2, we conclude that the defendants in this case did not owe a common-law tort duty to the Smiths to refrain from providing alcohol to Hale. Our holding does not leave the Smiths without a remedy, however. Nothing in the TABC or the common law prevents the Smiths from asserting a claim against Hale, the individual who made the choice to drink and drive.

III

The Smiths argue that *Graff* is distinguishable from this case because the *Graff* holding concerned *adult* guests of a social host, and the guest in this case, Robert Hale, was a statutory minor according to TABC section 106.01. Section 106.01 provides: "In this code [the TABC], 'minor' means a person under 21 years of age." Section 106.06 establishes a misdemeanor offense (with certain exceptions not applicable here) for anyone who "purchases an alcoholic beverage for or gives or with criminal negligence makes available an alcoholic beverage to a minor." [ ].

Because the guest in this case, Robert Hale, was nineteen and a minor under the TABC, the Smiths urge that two theoretical underpinnings of *Graff*—the inability of social hosts to know the extent of alcohol consumed by their guests and their inability to control their guests' conduct—do not apply. The Smiths contend that social hosts have no need to monitor the alcohol consumption and control the behavior of intoxicated minors because alcohol cannot be legally provided to minors. Because Hale was classified as a "minor" under the Code, the Smiths urge that the reasoning supporting non-liability for a social host who serves alcohol to an intoxicated adult driver is inapplicable.

Robert Hale was an adult at the time of the accident. The fact that he was defined as a minor solely for purposes of TABC section 106.01 is not significant in our negligence analysis.

Since 1973, the age of majority in Texas has been eighteen, except to the extent that there is a conflict with the minimum age provisions of the TABC. [ ]. For purposes other than determining criminal liability under TABC Chapter 106, persons eighteen years of age or older are adults and have the right and corresponding responsibility to make their own choices. [ ] Thus, Hale was an adult for virtually all purposes at the time of this accident. Most importantly, he was an adult for the purpose of being responsible for his own behavior and any civil liability resulting therefrom. [ ] Nineteen-year-old Barbee could not control nineteen-year-old Robert Hale's decision to drive in an inebriated condition. As an adult subject to being sued in his own capacity, Hale's tort duty should not be shifted to the social hosts in this case.

We recognize that section 106.01 does statutorily return persons aged eighteen to twenty to minority status for the purpose of the penal provisions in section 106.06. Nevertheless, the legislative history of Chapter 106 makes clear that the Legislature did not intend for minor status under section 106.01 to alter adult status elsewhere in the TABC or at common law. The Legislature raised the drinking age to twenty-one only for the express purpose of avoiding "the imposition of sanctions against the state and loss of federal highway funds" for failure to comply with a federal highway funding statute. [ ] Moreover, the Legislature expressed a policy preference for lowering the age of majority for alcohol consumption to nineteen by enacting legislation that will cause the age of majority to revert automatically to nineteen if the Attorney General ever certifies that the federal highway funding law is repealed or otherwise unenforceable. [ ] Absent the federal statute related to highway funds, persons aged nineteen and twenty, including Robert Hale, would not be minors under section [ ]. It cannot be fairly reasoned, then, that the Legislature intended persons aged eighteen to twenty to be considered minors for purposes of determining civil liability outside of the Chapter 2 framework.

Moreover, allowing social host liability for merely serving alcohol to a person eighteen or over—as urged by the Smiths—would create the anomalous situation where social hosts could incur civil liability for conduct that the Legislature has expressly stated is insufficient to justify civil liability for commercial providers. Under Chapter 2, commercial providers who serve alcohol to persons aged eighteen to twenty may incur civil liability only if "at the time the provision occurred it was apparent to the provider that the individual being sold, served, or provided with an alcoholic beverage was obviously intoxicated to the extent that he presented a clear danger to himself and others." [ ] Under the Smiths' contention, social hosts may be civilly liable for injuries to third parties merely for the act of furnishing alcohol to a person at least eighteen years of age but under the age of twenty-one, regardless of whether the recipient was "obviously intoxicated." Because commercial providers are much better equipped to determine how much alcohol guests have consumed and when they have approached their limit, it would be odd, indeed, to hold that a statute limiting commercial vendor liability simultaneously allows this Court to create social host liability at a lower standard of culpability.

Considered together, Chapter 2 and Chapter 106 of the TABC reflect the Legislature's deliberate decision not to create a cause of action against social hosts for serving alcohol to persons eighteen years of age and older. We will not circumvent the Legislature's intentions by imposing a duty upon social hosts that the Legislature itself has rejected.

The Smiths also argue that the defendants were negligent per se because they violated section 106.06 of the TABC by providing beer to the nineteen-year-old Robert Hale. The court of appeals allowed the Smiths' cause of action for negligence per se against Barbee, finding that Smith was within both the specific class of persons protected by section 106.06 ("minors" under age twenty-one) and the general class of persons protected by the TABC as a whole (the general public). [ ] We disagree with the court of appeals and hold that section 106.06 of the TABC does not create a negligence per se cause of action when a social host provides alcohol to a person eighteen years of age or older.

Negligence per se is a common-law doctrine in which a duty is imposed based on a standard of conduct created by a penal statute rather than on the reasonably prudent person test used in pure negligence claims. [ ] However, not every penal statute creates an appropriate standard of care for civil liability purposes; therefore, a court is not required to adopt the penal statute's standard. [ ]. In determining whether a penal statute creates an appropriate standard of care, we may consider whether the adoption of such a standard would be inconsistent with legislative intent.

Section 106.06 is located in Title 4 of the TABC, entitled "Regulatory and Penal Provisions," and provides criminal penalties for providing an alcoholic beverage to a person under the age of twenty-one. [ ]. In contrast, Chapter 2 establishes civil liability for serving alcohol. By enacting Chapter 2 separately from Chapter 106, and thereby establishing a bifurcated civil and criminal liability scheme, the Legislature manifested its intent that Chapter 2 should serve as the sole basis of civil liability for serving alcohol to persons aged eighteen to twenty.

We also find significant the Legislature's expressed intention to preclude Chapter 106 from serving as a basis for negligence per se. Section 2.03 clearly states that Chapter 2 "provides the exclusive cause of action for providing an alcoholic beverage to a person 18 years of age or older." [ ] That section further mandates that liability under Chapter 2 "is in lieu of common law or other statutory law warranties and duties of providers of alcoholic beverages." *Id.* Thus, under Chapter 2, civil liability for alcohol providers, as defined in section 2.01, is in lieu of any negligence per se cause of action, even when the provider serves alcohol to a person aged eighteen to twenty.

* * *

We hold that providing alcohol to a person aged eighteen to twenty, in violation of section 106.06 of the TABC, is not sufficient to establish a negligence per se cause of action against a social host. To hold otherwise would ignore the intent and policies of the Legislature.

We affirm the court of appeals' judgment for the defendants on the negligence issue. We reverse in part the judgment of the court of appeals and render judgment that the Smiths take nothing on their negligence per se cause of action.

Notes

1) Under Congress's spending power, it has the ability to attach conditions to the grant of federal funds. In this case, federal highway funds would be withheld from states that allow alcohol to be sold to persons under age 21. So. Dakota chose to allow 19 year olds to purchase 3.2% alcohol beer. Congress's spending power is not, however, unlimited. Can you construct an argument that use of the spending power in this manner is so coercive as to be unconstitutional?

2) The Court in *Liquormart* acknowledged that there is a lack of consensus among researchers as to the impact of advertising on the level of consumption of alcoholic beverages. If such a consensus were available, what impact, if any, would it have on the first amendment argument?

3) In *Skinner*, the Court acknowledged that requiring blood, urine and breath tests is fairly intrusive, but concluded that employees'

privacy interests are outweighed by the government's public health objectives. Suppose that requiring these tests resulted in employees learning sensitive health information about themselves that they would rather not know (or have disseminated to others). As testing becomes more sophisticated, might the *Skinner* balance lean the other way?

4) *Smith v. Merritt* is a "typical" dram shop case that addresses the liability of a social host who serves alcohol to a guest—in that case a minor guest. In *Robinson v. Health Midwest Dev. Group*, 58 S.W.3d 519 (Mo.2001) the Missouri Appeals court considered the liability of a health center whose medical staff allegedly administered an intravenous prescription drug to a patient, known to cause drowsiness and dizziness, and thereafter allowed her to drive home. Plaintiff was seriously injured when the driver crossed the center line of the road and collided head-on with her. Reversing summary judgment for the defendant, the court reasoned that a jury could find that but for the Center's failure to warn its patient not to drive under the influence of the drug, plaintiff would not have been injured. Do dram shop principles apply here? Is *Robinson* better characterized as a medical negligence matter?

SECTION B. TOBACCO AND TOBACCO PRODUCTS

CIPOLLONE v. LIGGETT GROUP, INC.

Supreme Court of the United States, 1992.
505 U.S. 504, 112 S.Ct. 2608, 120 L.Ed.2d 407.

JUSTICE STEVENS delivered the opinion of the Court, except as to Parts V and VI.

"WARNING: THE SURGEON GENERAL HAS DETERMINED THAT CIGARETTE SMOKING IS DANGEROUS TO YOUR HEALTH." A federal statute enacted in 1969 requires that warning (or a variation thereof) to appear in a conspicuous place on every package of cigarettes sold in the United States.[1] The questions presented to us by this case are whether that statute, or its 1965 predecessor which required a less alarming label, pre-empted petitioner's common-law claims against respondent cigarette manufacturers.

Petitioner is the son of Rose Cipollone, who began smoking in 1942 and who died of lung cancer in 1984. He claims that respondents are responsible for Rose Cipollone's death because they breached express warranties contained in their advertising, because they failed to warn consumers about the hazards of smoking, because they fraudulently misrepresented those hazards to consumers, and because they conspired to deprive the public of medical and scientific information about smoking. * * *

---

1. Public Health Cigarette Smoking Act of 1969, Pub. L. 91–222, 84 Stat. 87, as amended, 15 U. S. C. §§ 1331–1340. In 1984, Congress amended the statute to require four more explicit warnings, used on a rotating basis. See Comprehensive Smoking Education Act, Pub. L. 98–474, 98 Stat. 2201. Because petitioner's claims arose before 1984, neither party relies on this later Act.

I

On August 1, 1983, Rose Cipollone and her husband filed a complaint * * * alleg[ing] that Rose Cipollone developed lung cancer because she smoked cigarettes manufactured and sold by the three respondents. After her death in 1984, her husband filed an amended complaint. After trial, he also died; their son, executor of both estates, now maintains this action.

Petitioner's third amended complaint alleges several different bases of recovery, relying on theories of strict liability, negligence, express warranty, and intentional tort. These claims, all based on New Jersey law, divide into five categories. The "design defect claims" allege that respondents' cigarettes were defective because respondents failed to use a safer alternative design for their products and because the social value of their product was outweighed by the dangers it created [ ]. The "failure to warn claims" allege both that the product was "defective as a result of [respondents'] failure to provide adequate warnings of the health consequences of cigarette smoking" [ ] and that respondents "were negligent in the manner [that] they tested, researched, sold, promoted and advertised" their cigarettes [ ]. The "express warranty claims" allege that respondents had "expressly warranted that smoking the cigarettes which they manufactured and sold did not present any significant health consequences" [ ]. The "fraudulent misrepresentation claims" allege that respondents had willfully, "through their advertising, attempted to neutralize the [federally mandated] warning" labels [ ], and that they had possessed, but had "ignored and failed to act upon," medical and scientific data indicating that "cigarettes were hazardous to the health of consumers" [ ]. Finally, the "conspiracy to defraud claims" allege that respondents conspired to deprive the public of such medical and scientific data (*ibid.*).

As one of their defenses, respondents contended that the Federal Cigarette Labeling and Advertising Act, enacted in 1965, and its successor, the Public Health Cigarette Smoking Act of 1969, protected them from any liability based on their conduct after 1965. In a pretrial ruling, the District Court concluded that the federal statutes were intended to establish a uniform warning that would prevail throughout the country and that would protect cigarette manufacturers from being "subjected to varying requirements from state to state," *Cipollone v. Liggett Group, Inc.*, 593 F.Supp. 1146, 1148 (NJ 1984), but that the statutes did not pre-empt common-law actions. *Id.*, at 1153–1170. Accordingly, the court granted a motion to strike the pre-emption defense entirely.

The Court of Appeals accepted an interlocutory appeal pursuant to 28 U. S. C. § 1292(b), and reversed. *Cipollone v. Liggett Group, Inc.*, 789 F.2d 181 (CA 3 1986). The court rejected respondents' contention that the federal Acts expressly pre-empted common-law actions, but accepted their contention that such actions would conflict with federal law. Relying on the statement of purpose in the statutes, the court concluded that Congress' "carefully drawn balance between the purposes of warning the public of the hazards of cigarette smoking and protecting the interests of national economy" would be upset by state-law damages actions based on noncompliance with "warning, advertisement, and promotion obligations other than those prescribed in the [federal] Act." *Id.*, at 187. Accordingly, the court held:

> "The Act pre-empts those state law damages actions relating to smoking and health that challenge either the adequacy of the warning on cigarette packages or the propriety of a party's actions with respect to the advertising and promotion of cigarettes. Where the success of a state law damages claim necessarily depends on the assertion that a party bore the duty to provide a warning to consumers in addition to the warning Congress has required on cigarette packages, such claims are pre-empted as conflicting with the Act." *Ibid.* (footnote omitted).

The court did not, however, identify the specific claims asserted by petitioner that were pre-empted by the Act.

This Court denied a petition for certiorari, 479 U.S. 1043 (1987), and the case returned to the District Court for trial. Complying with the Court of Appeals' mandate, the District Court held that the failure-to-warn, express-warranty, fraudulent-misrepresentation, and conspiracy-to-defraud claims were barred to the extent that they relied on respondents' advertising, promotional, and public relations activities after January 1, 1966 (the effective date of the 1965 Act). 649 F.Supp. 664, 669, 673–675 (NJ 1986). The court also ruled that while the design defect claims were not pre-empted by federal law, those claims were barred on other grounds. *Id.*, at 669–672. Following extensive discovery and a 4–month trial, the jury answered a series of special interrogatories and awarded $400,000 in damages to Rose Cipollone's husband. In brief, it rejected all of the fraudulent-misrepresentation and conspiracy claims, but found that respondent Liggett had breached its duty to warn and its express warranties before 1966. It found, however, that Rose Cipollone had " 'voluntarily and unreasonably encountered a known danger by smoking cigarettes' " and that 80% of the responsibility for her injuries was attributable to her. [ ]. For that reason, no damages were awarded to her estate. However, the jury awarded damages to compensate her husband for losses caused by respondents' breach of express warranty.

On cross-appeals from the final judgment, the Court of Appeals affirmed the District Court's pre-emption rulings but remanded for a new trial on several issues not relevant to our decision. We granted the petition for certiorari to consider the pre-emptive effect of the federal statutes.

II

Although physicians had suspected a link between smoking and illness for centuries, the first medical studies of that connection did not appear until the 1920's. See U.S. Dept. of Health and Human Services, Report of the Surgeon General, Reducing the Health Consequences of

Smoking: 25 Years of Progress 5 (1989). The ensuing decades saw a wide range of epidemiologic and laboratory studies on the health hazards of smoking. Thus, by the time the Surgeon General convened an advisory committee to examine the issue in 1962, there were more than 7,000 publications examining the relationship between smoking and health. *Id.*, at 5–7.

In 1964, the advisory committee issued its report, which stated as its central conclusion: "Cigarette smoking is a health hazard of sufficient importance in the United States to warrant appropriate remedial action." U.S. Dept. of Health, Education, and Welfare, U.S. Surgeon General's Advisory Committee, Smoking and Health 33 (1964). Relying in part on that report, the Federal Trade Commission (FTC), which had long regulated unfair and deceptive advertising practices in the cigarette industry, promulgated a new trade regulation rule. That rule, which was to take effect January 1, 1965, established that it would be a violation of the Federal Trade Commission Act "to fail to disclose, clearly and prominently, in all advertising and on every pack, box, carton, or container [of cigarettes] that cigarette smoking is dangerous to health and may cause death from cancer and other diseases." 29 Fed. Reg. 8325 (1964). Several States also moved to regulate the advertising and labeling of cigarettes. [ ]. Upon a congressional request, the FTC postponed enforcement of its new regulation for six months. In July 1965, Congress enacted the Federal Cigarette Labeling and Advertising Act (1965 Act or Act). The 1965 Act effectively adopted half of the FTC's regulation: the Act mandated warnings on cigarette packages [ ], but barred the requirement of such warnings in cigarette advertising [ ].

Section 2 of the Act declares the statute's two purposes: (1) adequately informing the public that cigarette smoking may be hazardous to health, and (2) protecting the national economy from the burden imposed by diverse, nonuniform, and confusing cigarette labeling and advertising regulations. In furtherance of the first purpose, § 4 of the Act made it unlawful to sell or distribute any cigarettes in the United States unless the package bore a conspicuous label stating: "CAUTION: CIGARETTE SMOKING MAY BE HAZARDOUS TO YOUR HEALTH." In furtherance of the second purpose, § 5, captioned "Preemption," provided in part:

"(a) No statement relating to smoking and health, other than the statement required by section 4 of this Act, shall be required on any cigarette package.

"(b) No statement relating to smoking and health shall be required in the advertising of any cigarettes the packages of which are labeled in conformity with the provisions of this Act."

Although the Act took effect January 1, 1966, § 10 of the Act provided that its provisions affecting the regulation of advertising would terminate on July 1, 1969.

As that termination date approached, federal authorities prepared to issue further regulations on cigarette advertising. The FTC announced

the reinstitution of its 1964 proceedings concerning a warning requirement for cigarette advertisements. [ ] The Federal Communications
Commission (FCC) announced that it would consider "a proposed rule
which would ban the broadcast of cigarette commercials by radio and
television stations." [ ]. State authorities also prepared to take actions
regulating cigarette advertisements.

It was in this context that Congress enacted the Public Health
Cigarette Smoking Act of 1969 (1969 Act or Act), which amended the
1965 Act in several ways. First, the 1969 Act strengthened the warning
label, in part by requiring a statement that cigarette smoking "is
dangerous" rather than that it "may be hazardous." Second, the 1969
Act banned cigarette advertising in "any medium of electronic communication subject to [FCC] jurisdiction." Third, and related, the 1969 Act
modified the pre-emption provision by replacing the original § 5(b) with
a provision that reads:

> "(b) No requirement or prohibition based on smoking and health
> shall be imposed under State law with respect to the advertising or
> promotion of any cigarettes the packages of which are labeled in
> conformity with the provisions of this Act."

Although the Act also directed the FTC not to "take any action
before July 1, 1971, with respect to its pending trade regulation rule
proceeding relating to cigarette advertising," the narrowing of the preemption provision to prohibit only restrictions "imposed under State
law" cleared the way for the FTC to extend the warning-label requirement to print advertisements for cigarettes. The FTC did so in 1972. [ ].

III

* * *

The Court of Appeals was not persuaded that the pre-emption
provision in the 1969 Act encompassed state common-law claims. [ ]. It
was also not persuaded that the labeling obligation imposed by both the
1965 and 1969 Acts revealed a congressional intent to exert exclusive
federal control over every aspect of the relationship between cigarettes
and health. [ ]. Nevertheless, reading the statute as a whole in the light
of the statement of purpose in § 2, and considering the potential
regulatory effect of state common-law actions on the federal interest in
uniformity, the Court of Appeals concluded that Congress had impliedly
pre-empted petitioner's claims challenging the adequacy of the warnings
on labels or in advertising or the propriety of respondents' advertising
and promotional activities. [ ].

In our opinion, the pre-emptive scope of the 1965 Act and the 1969
Act is governed entirely by the express language in § 5 of each Act.
When Congress has considered the issue of pre-emption and has included
in the enacted legislation a provision explicitly addressing that issue, and
when that provision provides a "reliable indicium of congressional intent
with respect to state authority," *Malone v. White Motor Corp.*, 435 U.S.

at 505, "there is no need to infer congressional intent to pre-empt state laws from the substantive provisions" of the legislation. [ ]. Such reasoning is a variant of the familiar principle of *expressio unius est exclusio alterius:* Congress' enactment of a provision defining the pre-emptive reach of a statute implies that matters beyond that reach are not pre-empted. In this case, the other provisions of the 1965 and 1969 Acts offer no cause to look beyond § 5 of each Act. Therefore, we need only identify the domain expressly pre-empted by each of those sections. As the 1965 and 1969 provisions differ substantially, we consider each in turn.

IV

In the 1965 pre-emption provision regarding advertising (§ 5(b)), Congress spoke precisely and narrowly: "No *statement* relating to smoking and health shall be required *in the advertising* of [properly labeled] cigarettes." Section 5(a) used the same phrase ("No *statement* relating to smoking and health") with regard to cigarette labeling. As § 5(a) made clear, that phrase referred to the sort of warning provided for in § 4, which set forth verbatim the warning Congress determined to be appropriate. Thus, on their face, these provisions merely prohibited state and federal rulemaking bodies from mandating particular cautionary statements on cigarette labels [ ] or in cigarette advertisements [ ].

Beyond the precise words of these provisions, this reading is appropriate for several reasons. First, as discussed above, we must construe these provisions in light of the presumption against the pre-emption of state police power regulations. This presumption reinforces the appropriateness of a narrow reading of § 5. Second, the warning required in § 4 does not by its own effect foreclose additional obligations imposed under state law. That Congress requires a particular warning label does not automatically pre-empt a regulatory field. [ ]. Third, there is no general, inherent conflict between federal pre-emption of state warning requirements and the continued vitality of state common-law damages actions. For example, in the Comprehensive Smokeless Tobacco Health Education Act of 1986, n14 Congress expressly pre-empted state or local imposition of a "statement relating to the use of smokeless tobacco products and health" but, at the same time, preserved state-law damages actions based on those products. [ ]. All of these considerations indicate that § 5 is best read as having superseded only positive enactments by legislatures or administrative agencies that mandate particular warning labels.

This reading comports with the 1965 Act's statement of purpose, which expressed an intent to avoid "diverse, nonuniform, and confusing cigarette labeling and advertising *regulations* with respect to any relationship between smoking and health." Read against the backdrop of regulatory activity undertaken by state legislatures and federal agencies in response to the Surgeon General's report, the term "regulation" most naturally refers to positive enactments by those bodies, not to common-law damages actions.

* * *

For these reasons, we conclude that § 5 of the 1965 Act only pre-empted state and federal rulemaking bodies from mandating particular cautionary statements and did not pre-empt state-law damages actions.

V

Compared to its predecessor in the 1965 Act, the plain language of the pre-emption provision in the 1969 Act is much broader. First, the later Act bars not simply "statements" but rather "requirements or prohibitions ... imposed under State law." Second, the later Act reaches beyond statements "in the advertising" to obligations "with respect to the advertising or promotion" of cigarettes.

Notwithstanding these substantial differences in language, both petitioner and respondents contend that the 1969 Act did not materially alter the pre-emptive scope of federal law. n18 Their primary support for this contention is a sentence in a Committee Report which states that the 1969 amendment "clarified" the 1965 version of § 5(b). [ ] We reject the parties' reading as incompatible with the language and origins of the amendments. As we noted in another context, "inferences from legislative history cannot rest on so slender a reed. Moreover, the views of a subsequent Congress form a hazardous basis for inferring the intent of an earlier one." *United States v. Price*, 361 U.S. 304, 313, 4 L.Ed.2d 334, 80 S.Ct. 326 (1960). The 1969 Act worked substantial changes in the law: rewriting the label warning, banning broadcast advertising, and allowing the FTC to regulate print advertising. In the context of such revisions and in light of the substantial changes in wording, we cannot accept the parties' claim that the 1969 Act did not alter the reach of § 5(b).

Petitioner next contends that § 5(b), however broadened by the 1969 Act, does not pre-empt *common-law* actions. He offers two theories for limiting the reach of the amended § 5(b). First, he argues that common-law damages actions do not impose "requirements or prohibitions" and that Congress intended only to trump "state statutes, injunctions, or executive pronouncements." We disagree; such an analysis is at odds both with the plain words of the 1969 Act and with the general understanding of common-law damages actions. The phrase "no requirement or prohibition" sweeps broadly and suggests no distinction between positive enactments and common law; to the contrary, those words easily encompass obligations that take the form of common-law rules. As we noted in another context, "[state] regulation can be as effectively exerted through an award of damages as through some form of preventive relief. The obligation to pay compensation can be, indeed is designed to be, a potent method of governing conduct and controlling policy." *San Diego Building Trades Council v. Garmon*, 359 U.S. 236, 247, 3 L.Ed.2d 775, 79 S.Ct. 773 (1959).

Although portions of the legislative history of the 1969 Act suggest that Congress was primarily concerned with positive enactments by States and localities, see S. Rep. No. 91–566, p. 12, the language of the Act plainly reaches beyond such enactments. "We must give effect to this plain language unless there is good reason to believe Congress intended the language to have some more restrictive meaning." *Shaw v. Delta Air Lines, Inc.*, 463 U.S. 85, 97, 77 L.Ed.2d 490, 103 S.Ct. 2890 (1983). In this case there is no "good reason to believe" that Congress meant less than what it said; indeed, in light of the narrowness of the 1965 Act, there is "good reason to believe" that Congress meant precisely what it said in amending that Act.

* * *

Petitioner's second argument for excluding common-law rules from the reach of § 5(b) hinges on the phrase "imposed under State law." This argument fails as well. At least since *Erie R. Co. v. Tompkins*, 304 U.S. 64, 82 L.Ed. 1188, 58 S.Ct. 817 (1938), we have recognized the phrase "state law" to include common law as well as statutes and regulations. Indeed just last Term, the Court stated that the phrase " 'all other law, including State and municipal law' " "does not admit of [a] distinction ... between positive enactments and common-law rules of liability." *Norfolk & Western R. Co. v. Train Dispatchers*, 499 U.S. 117, 128, 113 L.Ed.2d 95, 111 S.Ct. 1156 (1991). Although the presumption against pre-emption might give good reason to construe the phrase "state law" in a pre-emption provision more narrowly than an identical phrase in another context, in this case such a construction is not appropriate. As explained above, the 1965 version of § 5 was precise and narrow on its face; the obviously broader language of the 1969 version extended that section's pre-emptive reach. Moreover, while the version of the 1969 Act passed by the Senate pre-empted "any State *statute or regulation* with respect to ... advertising or promotion," [ ] the Conference Committee replaced this language with "State *law* with respect to advertising or promotion." In such a situation, § 5(b)'s pre-emption of "state law" cannot fairly be limited to positive enactments.

That the pre-emptive scope of § 5(b) cannot be limited to positive enactments does not mean that that section pre-empts all common-law claims. For example, as respondents concede, § 5(b) does not generally pre-empt "state-law obligations to avoid marketing cigarettes with manufacturing defects or to use a demonstrably safer alternative design for cigarettes." For purposes of § 5(b), the common law is not of a piece.

Nor does the statute indicate that any familiar subdivision of common-law claims is or is not pre-empted. We therefore cannot follow petitioner's passing suggestion that § 5(b) pre-empts liability for omissions but not for acts, or that § 5(b) pre-empts liability for unintentional torts but not for intentional torts. Instead we must fairly but—in light of the strong presumption against pre-emption—narrowly construe the precise language of § 5(b) and we must look to each of petitioner's common-law claims to determine whether it is in fact pre-empted. The central inquiry in each case is straightforward: we ask whether the legal duty that is the predicate of the common-law damages action constitutes a "requirement or prohibition based on smoking and health . . . imposed under State law with respect to . . . advertising or promotion," giving that clause a fair but narrow reading. As discussed below, each phrase within that clause limits the universe of common-law claims pre-empted by the statute.

We consider each category of damages actions in turn. In doing so, we express no opinion on whether these actions are viable claims as a matter of state law; we assume, *arguendo*, that they are.

Failure to Warn

To establish liability for a failure to warn, petitioner must show that "a warning is necessary to make a product . . . reasonably safe, suitable and fit for its intended use," that respondents failed to provide such a warning, and that that failure was a proximate cause of petitioner's injury. [ ]. In this case, petitioner offered two closely related theories concerning the failure to warn: first, that respondents "were negligent in the manner [that] they tested, researched, sold, promoted, and advertised" their cigarettes; and second, that respondents failed to provide "adequate warnings of the health consequences of cigarette smoking." [ ].

Petitioner's claims are pre-empted to the extent that they rely on a state-law "requirement or prohibition . . . with respect to . . . advertising or promotion." Thus, insofar as claims under either failure-to-warn theory require a showing that respondents' post–1969 advertising or promotions should have included additional, or more clearly stated, warnings, those claims are pre-empted. The Act does not, however, pre-empt petitioner's claims that rely solely on respondents' testing or research practices or other actions unrelated to advertising or promotion.

Breach of Express Warranty

Petitioner's claim for breach of an express warranty arises under N. J. Stat. Ann. § 12A:2–313(1)(a) (West 1962), which provides:

> "Any affirmation of fact or promise made by the seller to the buyer which relates to the goods and becomes part of the basis of the bargain creates an express warranty that the goods shall conform to the affirmation or promise."

Petitioner's evidence of an express warranty consists largely of statements made in respondents' advertising. [ ]. Applying the Court of Appeals' ruling that Congress pre-empted "damages actions . . . that challenge . . . the propriety of a party's actions with respect to the advertising and promotion of cigarettes," [ ], the District Court ruled that this claim "inevitably brings into question [respondents'] advertising and promotional activities, and is therefore pre-empted "after 1965. [ ]. As demonstrated above, however, the 1969 Act does not sweep so broadly: The appropriate inquiry is not whether a claim challenges the "propriety" of advertising and promotion, but whether the claim would require the imposition under state law of a requirement or prohibition based on smoking and health with respect to advertising or promotion.

A manufacturer's liability for breach of an express warranty derives from, and is measured by, the terms of that warranty. Accordingly, the "requirements" imposed by an express warranty claim are not "imposed under State law," but rather imposed *by the warrantor*. If, for example, a manufacturer expressly promised to pay a smoker's medical bills if she contracted emphysema, the duty to honor that promise could not fairly be said to be "imposed under state law," but rather is best understood as undertaken by the manufacturer itself. While the general duty not to breach warranties arises under state law, the particular "requirement . . . based on smoking and health . . . with respect to the advertising or promotion [of] cigarettes" in an express warranty claim arises from the manufacturer's statements in its advertisements. In short, a common-law remedy for a contractual commitment voluntarily undertaken should not be regarded as a "requirement . . . *imposed under State law*" within the meaning of § 5(b).

That the terms of the warranty may have been set forth in advertisements rather than in separate documents is irrelevant to the pre-emption issue (though possibly not to the state-law issue of whether the alleged warranty is valid and enforceable) because, although the breach of warranty claim is made "with respect to . . . advertising," it does not rest on a duty imposed under state law. Accordingly, to the extent that petitioner has a viable claim for breach of express warranties made by respondents, that claim is not pre-empted by the 1969 Act.

Fraudulent Misrepresentation

Petitioner alleges two theories of fraudulent misrepresentation. First, petitioner alleges that respondents, through their advertising, neutralized the effect of federally mandated warning labels. Such a claim is predicated on a state-law prohibition against statements in advertising and promotional materials that tend to minimize the health hazards associated with smoking. Such a *prohibition*, however, is merely the converse of a state-law *requirement* that warnings be included in advertising and promotional materials. Section 5(b) of the 1969 Act pre-empts both requirements and prohibitions; it therefore supersedes petitioner's first fraudulent-misrepresentation theory.

* * *

Petitioner's second theory, as construed by the District Court, alleges intentional fraud and misrepresentation both by "false representation of a material fact [and by] concealment of a material fact." [ ] The predicate of this claim is a state-law duty not to make false statements of material fact or to conceal such facts. Our pre-emption analysis requires us to determine whether such a duty is the sort of requirement or prohibition proscribed by § 5(b).

Section 5(b) pre-empts only the imposition of state-law obligations "with respect to the advertising or promotion" of cigarettes. Petitioner's claims that respondents concealed material facts are therefore not pre-empted insofar as those claims rely on a state-law duty to disclose such facts through channels of communication other than advertising or promotion. Thus, for example, if state law obliged respondents to disclose material facts about smoking and health to an administrative agency, § 5(b) would not pre-empt a state-law claim based on a failure to fulfill that obligation.

Moreover, petitioner's fraudulent-misrepresentation claims that do arise with respect to advertising and promotions (most notably claims based on allegedly false statements of material fact made in advertisements) are not pre-empted by § 5(b). Such claims are predicated not on a duty "based on smoking and health" but rather on a more general obligation—the duty not to deceive. This understanding of fraud by intentional misstatement is appropriate for several reasons. First, in the 1969 Act, Congress offered no sign that it wished to insulate cigarette manufacturers from longstanding rules governing fraud. To the contrary, both the 1965 and the 1969 Acts explicitly reserved the FTC's authority to identify and punish deceptive advertising practices—an authority that the FTC had long exercised and continues to exercise. [ ] This indicates that Congress intended the phrase "relating to smoking and health" (which was essentially unchanged by the 1969 Act) to be construed narrowly, so as not to proscribe the regulation of deceptive advertising.

* * *

Conspiracy to Misrepresent or Conceal Material Facts

Petitioner's final claim alleges a conspiracy among respondents to misrepresent or conceal material facts concerning the health hazards of smoking. The predicate duty underlying this claim is a duty not to conspire to commit fraud. For the reasons stated in our analysis of petitioner's intentional fraud claim, this duty is not pre-empted by § 5(b) for it is not a prohibition "based on smoking and health" as that phrase is properly construed. Accordingly, we conclude that the 1969 Act does not pre-empt petitioner's conspiracy claim.

VI

To summarize our holding: The 1965 Act did not pre-empt state-law damages actions; the 1969 Act pre-empts petitioner's claims based on a failure to warn and the neutralization of federally mandated warnings to the extent that those claims rely on omissions or inclusions in respondents' advertising or promotions; the 1969 Act does not pre-empt petitioner's claims based on express warranty, intentional fraud and misrepresentation, or conspiracy.

The judgment of the Court of Appeals is accordingly reversed in part and affirmed in part, and the case is remanded for further proceedings consistent with this opinion.

It is so ordered.

JUSTICE BLACKMUN, with whom JUSTICE KENNEDY and JUSTICE SOUTER join, concurring in part, concurring in the judgment in part, and dissenting in part.

I

The Court today would craft a compromise position concerning the extent to which federal law pre-empts persons injured by cigarette manufacturers' unlawful conduct from bringing state common-law damages claims against those manufacturers. I, however, find the Court's divided holding with respect to the original and amended versions of the federal statute entirely unsatisfactory. Our precedents do not allow us to infer a scope of pre-emption beyond that which clearly is mandated by Congress' language. In my view, *neither* version of the federal legislation at issue here provides the kind of unambiguous evidence of congressional intent necessary to displace state common-law damages claims. I therefore join Parts I, II, III, and IV of the Court's opinion, but dissent from Parts V and VI.

FOOD AND DRUG ADMINISTRATION v. BROWN & WILLIAMSON TOBACCO CORPORATION

Supreme Court of the United States, 2000.
529 U.S. 120, 120 S.Ct. 1291, 146 L.Ed.2d 121.

I

The FDCA grants the FDA, as the designee of the Secretary of Health and Human Services, the authority to regulate, among other items, "drugs" and "devices." See 21 U.S.C. §§ 321(g)–(h), 393 (1994 ed. and Supp. III). The Act defines "drug" to include "articles (other than food) intended to affect the structure or any function of the body." 21 U.S.C. § 321(g)(1)(C). It defines "device," in part, as "an instrument, apparatus, implement, machine, contrivance, ... or other similar or related article, including any component, part, or accessory, which is ... intended to affect the structure or any function of the body." § 321(h). The Act also grants the FDA the authority to regulate so-called "combination products," which "constitute a combination of a drug, device, or biologic product." § 353(g)(1). The FDA has construed this provision as giving it the discretion to regulate combination products as drugs, as devices, or as both. [ ].

On August 11, 1995, the FDA published a proposed rule concerning the sale of cigarettes and smokeless tobacco to children and adolescents. [ ]. The rule, which included several restrictions on the sale, distribution, and advertisement of tobacco products, was designed to reduce the availability and attractiveness of tobacco products to young people. [ ]. A public comment period followed, during which the FDA received over

700,000 submissions, more than "at any other time in its history on any other subject." [ ].

On August 28, 1996, the FDA issued a final rule entitled "Regulations Restricting the Sale and Distribution of Cigarettes and Smokeless Tobacco to Protect Children and Adolescents." [ ]. The FDA determined that nicotine is a "drug" and that cigarettes and smokeless tobacco are "drug delivery devices," and therefore it had jurisdiction under the FDCA to regulate tobacco products as customarily marketed—that is, without manufacturer claims of therapeutic benefit. [ ]. First, the FDA found that tobacco products " 'affect the structure or any function of the body' " because nicotine "has significant pharmacological effects." [ ]. Specifically, nicotine "exerts psychoactive, or mood-altering, effects on the brain" that cause and sustain addiction, have both tranquilizing and stimulating effects, and control weight. [ ]. Second, the FDA determined that these effects were "intended" under the FDCA because they "are so widely known and foreseeable that [they] may be deemed to have been intended by the manufacturers," [ ] consumers use tobacco products "predominantly or nearly exclusively" to obtain these effects, [ ]; and the statements, research, and actions of manufacturers revealed that they "have 'designed' cigarettes to provide pharmacologically active doses of nicotine to consumers," [ ]. Finally, the agency concluded that cigarettes and smokeless tobacco are "combination products" because, in addition to containing nicotine, they include device components that deliver a controlled amount of nicotine to the body [ ].

Having resolved the jurisdictional question, the FDA next explained the policy justifications for its regulations, detailing the deleterious health effects associated with tobacco use. * * *

Based on these findings, the FDA promulgated regulations concerning tobacco products' promotion, labeling, and accessibility to children and adolescents. * * *

The FDA promulgated these regulations pursuant to its authority to regulate "restricted devices." [ ]. The FDA construed § 353(g)(1) as giving it the discretion to regulate "combination products" using the Act's drug authorities, device authorities, or both, depending on "how the public health goals of the act can be best accomplished." [ ]. Given the greater flexibility in the FDCA for the regulation of devices, the FDA determined that "the device authorities provide the most appropriate basis for regulating cigarettes and smokeless tobacco." [ ]. Under 21 U.S.C. § 360j(e), the agency may "require that a device be restricted to sale, distribution, or use ... upon such other conditions as [the FDA] may prescribe in such regulation, if, because of its potentiality for harmful effect or the collateral measures necessary to its use, [the FDA] determines that there cannot otherwise be reasonable assurance of its safety and effectiveness." The FDA reasoned that its regulations fell within the authority granted by § 360j(e) because they related to the sale or distribution of tobacco products and were necessary for providing a reasonable assurance of safety. [ ].

Respondents, a group of tobacco manufacturers, retailers, and advertisers, filed suit in United States District Court for the Middle District of North Carolina challenging the regulations. [ ]. They moved for summary judgment on the grounds that the FDA lacked jurisdiction to regulate tobacco products as customarily marketed, the regulations exceeded the FDA's authority under 21 U.S.C. § 360j(e), and the advertising restrictions violated the First Amendment. [citations omitted] The District Court granted respondents' motion in part and denied it in part. [ ]. The court held that the FDCA authorizes the FDA to regulate tobacco products as customarily marketed and that the FDA's access and labeling regulations are permissible, but it also found that the agency's advertising and promotion restrictions exceed its authority under § 360j(e). [ ]. The court stayed implementation of the regulations it found valid (except the prohibition on the sale of tobacco products to minors) and certified its order for immediate interlocutory appeal. [ ]

The Court of Appeals for the Fourth Circuit reversed, holding that Congress has not granted the FDA jurisdiction to regulate tobacco products. [ ]. Examining the FDCA as a whole, the court concluded that the FDA's regulation of tobacco products would create a number of internal inconsistencies. [ ]. Various provisions of the Act require the agency to determine that any regulated product is "safe" before it can be sold or allowed to remain on the market, yet the FDA found in its rulemaking proceeding that tobacco products are "dangerous" and "unsafe." [ ]. Thus, the FDA would apparently have to ban tobacco products, a result the court found clearly contrary to congressional intent. [ ]. This apparent anomaly, the Court of Appeals concluded, demonstrates that Congress did not intend to give the FDA authority to regulate tobacco. [ ]. The court also found that evidence external to the FDCA confirms this conclusion. Importantly, the FDA consistently stated before 1995 that it lacked jurisdiction over tobacco, and Congress has enacted several tobacco-specific statutes fully cognizant of the FDA's position. [ ]. In fact, the court reasoned, Congress has considered and rejected many bills that would have given the agency such authority. [ ]. This, along with the absence of any intent by the enacting Congress in 938 to subject tobacco products to regulation under the FDCA, demonstrates that Congress intended to withhold such authority from the FDA. [ ]. Having resolved the jurisdictional question against the agency, the Court of Appeals did not address whether the regulations exceed the FDA's authority under 21 U.S.C. § 360j(e) or violate the First Amendment. [ ].

We granted the Government's petition for certiorari [ ], to determine whether the FDA has authority under the FDCA to regulate tobacco products as customarily marketed.

II

The FDA's assertion of jurisdiction to regulate tobacco products is founded on its conclusions that nicotine is a "drug" and that cigarettes and smokeless tobacco are "drug delivery devices." Again, the FDA found that tobacco products are "intended" to deliver the pharmacological effects of satisfying addiction, stimulation and tranquilization, and weight control because those effects are foreseeable to any reasonable manufacturer, consumers use tobacco products to obtain those effects, and tobacco manufacturers have designed their products to produce those effects. [ ]. As an initial matter, respondents take issue with the FDA's reading of "intended," arguing that it is a term of art that refers exclusively to claims made by the manufacturer or vendor about the product. [ ]. That is, a product is not a drug or device under the FDCA unless the manufacturer or vendor makes some express claim concerning the product's therapeutic benefits. [ ]. We need not resolve this question, however, because assuming, *arguendo*, that a product can be "intended to affect the structure or any function of the body" absent claims of therapeutic or medical benefit, the FDA's claim to jurisdiction contravenes the clear intent of Congress.

A threshold issue is the appropriate framework for analyzing the FDA's assertion of authority to regulate tobacco products. Because this case involves an administrative agency's construction of a statute that it administers, our analysis is governed by *Chevron U.S.A. Inc.* v. *Natural Resources Defense Council, Inc.,* 467 U.S. 837, 81 L.Ed.2d 694, 104 S.Ct. 2778 (1984). Under *Chevron,* a reviewing court must first ask "whether Congress has directly spoken to the precise question at issue." *Id.,* at 842. If Congress has done so, the inquiry is at an end; the court "must give effect to the unambiguously expressed intent of Congress." *Id.,* at 843 [ ]. But if Congress has not specifically addressed the question, a reviewing court must respect the agency's construction of the statute so long as it is permissible. [ ]. Such deference is justified because "the responsibilities for assessing the wisdom of such policy choices and resolving the struggle between competing views of the public interest are not judicial ones," *Chevron, supra,* at 866, and because of the agency's greater familiarity with the ever-changing facts and circumstances surrounding the subjects regulated [ ].

* * *

With these principles in mind, we find that Congress has directly spoken to the issue here and precluded the FDA's jurisdiction to regulate tobacco products.

A

* * *

In its rulemaking proceeding, the FDA quite exhaustively documented that "tobacco products are unsafe," "dangerous," and "cause great pain and suffering from illness."[ ]. It found that the consumption of tobacco products "presents extraordinary health risks," and that "tobacco use is the single leading cause of preventable death in the United States." [ ]. It stated that "more than 400,000 people die each year from tobacco-related illnesses, such as cancer, respiratory illnesses, and heart disease, often suffering long and painful deaths," and that "tobacco alone kills more people each year in the United States than acquired immunodeficiency syndrome (AIDS), car accidents, alcohol, homicides, illegal drugs, suicides, and fires, combined." *Ibid.* Indeed, the FDA characterized smoking as "a pediatric disease," [ ], because "one out of every three young people who become regular smokers ... will die prematurely as a result[.]"

These findings logically imply that, if tobacco products were "devices" under the FDCA, the FDA would be required to remove them from the market. Consider, first, the FDCA's provisions concerning the misbranding of drugs or devices. The Act prohibits "the introduction or delivery for introduction into interstate commerce of any food, drug, device, or cosmetic that is adultered or misbranded." [ ]. In light of the FDA's findings, two distinct FDCA provisions would render cigarettes and smokeless tobacco misbranded devices. First, § 352(j) deems a drug or device misbranded "if it is dangerous to health when used in the dosage or manner, or with the frequency or duration prescribed, recommended, or suggested in the labeling thereof." The FDA's findings make clear that tobacco products are "dangerous to health" when used in the manner prescribed. Second, a drug or device is misbranded under the Act "unless its labeling bears ... adequate directions for use ... in such manner and form, as are necessary for the protection of users," except where such directions are "not necessary for the protection of the public health." [ ]. Given the FDA's conclusions concerning the health consequences of tobacco use, there are no directions that could adequately protect consumers. That is, there are no directions that could make tobacco products safe for obtaining their intended effects. Thus, were tobacco products within the FDA's jurisdiction, the Act would deem them misbranded devices that could not be introduced into interstate commerce. Contrary to the dissent's contention, the Act admits no remedial discretion once it is evident that the device is misbranded.

* * *

Congress, however, has foreclosed the removal of tobacco products from the market. A provision of the United States Code currently in force states that "the marketing of tobacco constitutes one of the greatest basic industries of the United States with ramifying activities which directly affect interstate and foreign commerce at every point, and stable conditions therein are necessary to the general welfare." [ ]. More importantly, Congress has directly addressed the problem of tobacco and health through legislation on six occasions since 1965. [ ] When Congress enacted these statutes, the adverse health consequences of tobacco use were well known, as were nicotine's pharmacological effects. * * * Nonetheless, Congress stopped well short of ordering a ban. Instead, it has generally regulated the labeling and advertisement of tobacco products, expressly providing that it is the policy of Congress that "commerce and the national economy may be ... protected to the maximum extent consistent with" consumers "being adequately informed about any adverse health effects." [ ]. Congress' decisions to regulate labeling and advertising and to adopt the express policy of protecting "commerce and the national economy . . . to the maximum extent" reveal its intent that tobacco products remain on the market. Indeed, the collective premise of these statutes is that cigarettes and smokeless tobacco will continue to be sold in the United States. A ban of tobacco products by the FDA would therefore plainly contradict congressional policy.

The FDA apparently recognized this dilemma and concluded, somewhat ironically, that tobacco products are actually "safe" within the meaning of the FDCA. In promulgating its regulations, the agency conceded that "tobacco products are unsafe, as that term is conventionally understood." [ ]. Nonetheless, the FDA reasoned that, in determining whether a device is safe under the Act, it must consider "not only the risks presented by a product but also any of the countervailing effects of use of that product, including the consequences of not permitting the product to be marketed." [ ]. Applying this standard, the FDA found that, because of the high level of addiction among tobacco users, a ban would likely be "dangerous." [ ]. In particular, current tobacco users could suffer from extreme withdrawal, the health care system and available pharmaceuticals might not be able to meet the treatment demands of those suffering from withdrawal, and a black market offering cigarettes even more dangerous than those currently sold legally would likely develop. [ ] The FDA therefore concluded that, "while taking cigarettes and smokeless tobacco off the market could prevent some people from becoming addicted and reduce death and disease for others, the record does not establish that such a ban is the appropriate public health response under the act." [ ].

It may well be, as the FDA asserts, that "these factors must be considered when developing a regulatory scheme that achieves the best public health result for these products." [ ]. But the FDA's judgment that leaving tobacco products on the market "is more effective in achieving public health goals than a ban," *ibid.*, is no substitute for the specific safety determinations required by the FDCA's various operative provisions. Several provisions in the Act require the FDA to determine that the *product itself* is safe as used by consumers. That is, the product's probable therapeutic benefits must outweigh its risk of harm. See *United States* v. *Rutherford,* 442 U.S. at 555 ("The Commissioner generally considers a drug safe when the expected therapeutic gain justifies the risk entailed by its use"). In contrast, the FDA's conception of safety would allow the agency, with respect to each provision of the FDCA that requires the agency to determine a product's "safety" or "dangerousness," to compare the aggregate health effects of alternative administrative actions. This is a qualitatively different inquiry. Thus, although the FDA has concluded that a ban would be "dangerous," it has *not* concluded that tobacco products are "safe" as that term is used throughout the Act.

* * *

The dissent contends that our conclusion means that "the FDCA requires the FDA to ban outright 'dangerous' drugs or devices," *post*, at 14, and that this is a "perverse" reading of the statute, *id.*, at 14, 21. This misunderstands our holding. The FDA, consistent with the FDCA, may clearly regulate many "dangerous" products without banning them. Indeed, virtually every drug or device poses dangers under certain conditions. What the FDA may not do is conclude that a drug or device cannot be used safely for any therapeutic purpose and yet, at the same time, allow that product to remain on the market. Such regulation is incompatible with the FDCA's core objective of ensuring that every drug or device is safe and effective.

Considering the FDCA as a whole, it is clear that Congress intended to exclude tobacco products from the FDA's jurisdiction. A fundamental precept of the FDCA is that any product regulated by the FDA—but not banned—must be safe for its intended use. Various provisions of the Act make clear that this refers to the safety of using the product to obtain its intended effects, not the public health ramifications of alternative administrative actions by the FDA. That is, the FDA must determine that there is a reasonable assurance that the product's therapeutic benefits outweigh the risk of harm to the consumer. According to this standard, the FDA has concluded that, although tobacco products might be effective in delivering certain pharmacological effects, they are "unsafe" and "dangerous" when used for these purposes. Consequently, if tobacco products were within the FDA's jurisdiction, the Act would require the FDA to remove them from the market entirely. But a ban would contradict Congress' clear intent as expressed in its more recent, tobacco-specific legislation. The inescapable conclusion is that there is no room for tobacco products within the FDCA's regulatory scheme. If they cannot be used safely for any therapeutic purpose, and yet they cannot be banned, they simply do not fit.

B

In determining whether Congress has spoken directly to the FDA's authority to regulate tobacco, we must also consider in greater detail the tobacco-specific legislation that Congress has enacted over the past 35 years. At the time a statute is enacted, it may have a range of plausible meanings. Over time, however, subsequent acts can shape or focus those meanings. The "classic judicial task of reconciling many laws enacted over time, and getting them to 'make sense' in combination, necessarily assumes that the implications of a statute may be altered by the implications of a later statute." *United States* v. *Fausto*, 484 U.S. at 453. This is particularly so where the scope of the earlier statute is broad but the subsequent statutes more specifically address the topic at hand. As we recognized recently in *United States* v. *Estate of Romani*, "a specific policy embodied in a later federal statute should control our construction of the [earlier] statute, even though it has not been expressly amended." 523 U.S. at 530–531.

Congress has enacted six separate pieces of legislation since 1965 addressing the problem of tobacco use and human health. See *supra*, at 14. Those statutes, among other things, require that health warnings appear on all packaging and in all print and outdoor advertisements [ ] prohibit the advertisement of tobacco products through "any medium of electronic communication" subject to regulation by the Federal Communications Commission (FCC) [ ]require the Secretary of Health and Human Services (HHS) to report every three years to Congress on research findings concerning "the addictive property of tobacco," [ ] and make States' receipt of certain federal block grants contingent on their making it unlawful "for any manufacturer, retailer, or distributor of tobacco products to sell or distribute any such product to any individual under the age of 18[.]"

In adopting each statute, Congress has acted against the backdrop of the FDA's consistent and repeated statements that it lacked authority under the FDCA to regulate tobacco absent claims of therapeutic benefit by the manufacturer. In fact, on several occasions over this period, and after the health consequences of tobacco use and nicotine's pharmacological effects had become well known, Congress considered and rejected bills that would have granted the FDA such jurisdiction. Under these circumstances, it is evident that Congress' tobacco-specific statutes have effectively ratified the FDA's long-held position that it lacks jurisdiction under the FDCA to regulate tobacco products. Congress has created a distinct regulatory scheme to address the problem of tobacco and health, and that scheme, as presently constructed, precludes any role for the FDA.

On January 11, 1964, the Surgeon General released the report of the Advisory Committee on Smoking and Health. That report documented the deleterious health effects of smoking in great detail * * *

In response to the Surgeon General's report and the FTC's proposed rule, Congress convened hearings to consider legislation addressing "the tobacco problem." 1964 Hearings 1. During those deliberations, FDA representatives testified before Congress that the agency lacked jurisdiction under the FDCA to regulate tobacco products. Surgeon General Terry was asked during hearings in 1964 whether HEW had the "authority to brand or label the packages of cigarettes or to control the advertising there." [ ]. The Surgeon General stated that "we do not have such authority in existing laws governing the ... Food and Drug Administration." [ ] * * *

The FDA's disavowal of jurisdiction was consistent with the position that it had taken since the agency's inception. As the FDA concedes, it never asserted authority to regulate tobacco products as customarily marketed until it promulgated the regulations at issue here. [ ]

* * *

[Finally,] in 1983, Congress again considered legislation on the subject of smoking and health. HHS Assistant Secretary Brandt testified that, in addition to being "a major cause of cancer," smoking is a "major cause of heart disease" and other serious illnesses, and can result in "unfavorable pregnancy outcomes." 1983 House Hearings 19–20. He also stated that it was "well-established that cigarette smoking is a drug dependence, and that smoking is addictive for many people." [ ]. Nonetheless, Assistant Secretary Brandt maintained that "the issue of regulation of tobacco ... is something that Congress has reserved to itself, and we do not within the Department have the authority to regulate nor are we seeking such authority." [ ]. He also testified before the Senate, stating that, despite the evidence of tobacco's health effects and addictiveness, the Department's view was that "Congress has assumed the responsibility of regulating ... cigarettes." Smoking Prevention and Education Act: Hearings on S. 772 before the Senate Committee on Labor and Human Resources, 98th Cong., 1st Sess., 56 (1983) (hereinafter 1983 Senate Hearings).

Against this backdrop, Congress enacted three additional tobacco-specific statutes over the next four years that incrementally expanded its regulatory scheme for tobacco products. In 1983, Congress adopted the Alcohol and Drug Abuse Amendments [ ] (codified at 42 U.S.C. § 290aa et seq.), which require the Secretary of HHS to report to Congress every three years on the "addictive property of tobacco" and to include recommendations for action that the Secretary may deem appropriate. A year later, Congress enacted the Comprehensive Smoking Education Act [ ], which amended the [Federal Cigarette Labeling and Advertising Act (FCLAA)] by again modifying the prescribed warning. Notably, during debate on the Senate floor, Senator Hawkins argued that the Act was necessary in part because "under the Food, Drug and Cosmetic Act, the Congress exempted tobacco products." [ ]. And in 1986, Congress enacted the Comprehensive Smokeless Tobacco Health Education Act of 1986 (CSTHEA) [ ], which essentially extended the regulatory provisions of the FCLAA to smokeless tobacco products. Like the FCLAA, the CSTHEA provided that "no statement relating to the use of smokeless tobacco products and health, other than the statements required by [the Act], shall be required by any Federal agency to appear on any package ... of a smokeless tobacco product." [ ]. Thus, as with cigarettes, Congress reserved for itself an aspect of smokeless tobacco regulation that is particularly important to the FDCA's regulatory scheme.

In 1988, the Surgeon General released a report summarizing the abundant scientific literature demonstrating that "cigarettes and other forms of tobacco are addicting," and that "nicotine is psychoactive" and "causes physical dependence characterized by a withdrawal syndrome that usually accompanies nicotine abstinence." 1988 Surgeon General's Report 14. The report further concluded that the "pharmacologic and behavioral processes that determine tobacco addiction are similar to those that determine addiction to drugs such as heroin and cocaine." [ ]. In the same year, FDA Commissioner Young stated before Congress that "it doesn't look like it is possible to regulate [tobacco] under the Food, Drug and Cosmetic Act even though smoking, I think, has been widely recognized as being harmful to human health." Rural Development, Agriculture, and Related Agencies Appropriations for 1989: Hearings before a Subcommittee of the House Committee on Appropriations, 100th Cong., 2d Sess., 409 (1988). At the same hearing, the FDA's General Counsel testified that "what is fairly important in FDA law is whether a product has a therapeutic purpose," and "cigarettes themselves are not used for a therapeutic purpose as that concept is ordinarily understood." [ ]. Between 1987 and 1989, Congress considered three more bills that would have amended the FDCA to grant the FDA jurisdiction to regulate tobacco products. [ ]. As before, Congress rejected the proposals. In 1992, Congress instead adopted the Alcohol, Drug Abuse, and Mental Health Administration Reorganization Act[ ] (codified at 42 U.S.C. § 300x *et seq.*), which creates incentives for States to regulate the retail sale of tobacco products by making States' receipt of certain block grants contingent on their prohibiting the sale of tobacco products to minors.

Taken together, these actions by Congress over the past 35 years preclude an interpretation of the FDCA that grants the FDA jurisdiction to regulate tobacco products. We do not rely on Congress' failure to act—its consideration and rejection of bills that would have given the FDA this authority—in reaching this conclusion. Indeed, this is not a case of simple inaction by Congress that purportedly represents its acquiescence in an agency's position. To the contrary, Congress has enacted several statutes addressing the particular subject of tobacco and health, creating a distinct regulatory scheme for cigarettes and smokeless tobacco. In doing so, Congress has been aware of tobacco's health hazards and its pharmacological effects. It has also enacted this legislation against the background of the FDA repeatedly and consistently asserting that it lacks jurisdiction under the FDCA to regulate tobacco products as customarily marketed. Further, Congress has persistently acted to preclude a meaningful role for *any* administrative agency in making policy on the subject of tobacco and health. Moreover, the substance of Congress' regulatory scheme is, in an important respect, incompatible with FDA jurisdiction. Although the supervision of product labeling to protect consumer health is a substantial component of the FDA's regulation of drugs and devices[ ], the FCLAA and the CSTHEA explicitly prohibit any federal agency from imposing any health-related labeling requirements on cigarettes or smokeless tobacco products[.]

Under these circumstances, it is clear that Congress' tobacco-specific legislation has effectively ratified the FDA's previous position that it lacks jurisdiction to regulate tobacco. * * *

Although the dissent takes issue with our discussion of the FDA's change in position, *post*, at 26–29, our conclusion does not rely on the fact that the FDA's assertion of jurisdiction represents a sharp break with its prior interpretation of the FDCA. Certainly, an agency's initial interpretation of a statute that it is charged with administering is not "carved in stone." *Chevron*, 467 U.S. at 863 [ ] * * * The consistency of the FDA's prior position is significant in this case for a different reason:

it provides important context to Congress' enactment of its tobacco-specific legislation. When the FDA repeatedly informed Congress that the FDCA does not grant it the authority to regulate tobacco products, its statements were consistent with the agency's unwavering position since its inception, and with the position that its predecessor agency had first taken in 1914. Although not crucial, the consistency of the FDA's prior position bolsters the conclusion that when Congress created a distinct regulatory scheme addressing the subject of tobacco and health, it understood that the FDA is without jurisdiction to regulate tobacco products and ratified that position.

The dissent also argues that the proper inference to be drawn from Congress' tobacco-specific legislation is "critically ambivalent." [ ]. We disagree. In that series of statutes, Congress crafted a specific legislative response to the problem of tobacco and health, and it did so with the understanding, based on repeated assertions by the FDA, that the agency has no authority under the FDCA to regulate tobacco products. Moreover, Congress expressly preempted any other regulation of the labeling of tobacco products concerning their health consequences, even though the oversight of labeling is central to the FDCA's regulatory scheme. And in addressing the subject, Congress consistently evidenced its intent to preclude any federal agency from exercising significant policymaking authority in the area. Under these circumstances, we believe the appropriate inference—that Congress intended to ratify the FDA's prior position that it lacks jurisdiction—is unmistakable.

The dissent alternatively argues that, even if Congress' subsequent tobacco-specific legislation did, in fact, ratify the FDA's position, that position was merely a contingent disavowal of jurisdiction. Specifically, the dissent contends that "the FDA's traditional view was largely premised on a perceived inability to prove the necessary statutory 'intent' requirement." *Post*, at 30. A fair reading of the FDA's representations prior to 1995, however, demonstrates that the agency's position was essentially unconditional. [ ] * * *. To the extent the agency's position could be characterized as equivocal, it was only with respect to the well-established exception of when the manufacturer makes express claims of therapeutic benefit. * * *. Thus, what Congress ratified was the FDA's plain and resolute position that the FDCA gives the agency no authority to regulate tobacco products as customarily marketed.

C

Finally, our inquiry into whether Congress has directly spoken to the precise question at issue is shaped, at least in some measure, by the nature of the question presented. Deference under *Chevron* to an agency's construction of a statute that it administers is premised on the theory that a statute's ambiguity constitutes an implicit delegation from Congress to the agency to fill in the statutory gaps. [ ]. In extraordinary cases, however, there may be reason to hesitate before concluding that Congress has intended such an implicit delegation. * * *

This is hardly an ordinary case. Contrary to its representations to Congress since 1914, the FDA has now asserted jurisdiction to regulate an industry constituting a significant portion of the American economy. In fact, the FDA contends that, were it to determine that tobacco products provide no "reasonable assurance of safety," it would have the authority to ban cigarettes and smokeless tobacco entirely. [ ]. Owing to its unique place in American history and society, tobacco has its own unique political history. Congress, for better or for worse, has created a distinct regulatory scheme for tobacco products, squarely rejected proposals to give the FDA jurisdiction over tobacco, and repeatedly acted to preclude any agency from exercising significant policymaking authority in the area. Given this history and the breadth of the authority that the FDA has asserted, we are obliged to defer not to the agency's expansive construction of the statute, but to Congress' consistent judgment to deny the FDA this power.

* * *

By no means do we question the seriousness of the problem that the FDA has sought to address. The agency has amply demonstrated that tobacco use, particularly among children and adolescents, poses perhaps the single most significant threat to public health in the United States. Nonetheless, no matter how "important, conspicuous, and controversial" the issue, and regardless of how likely the public is to hold the Executive Branch politically accountable [ ], an administrative agency's power to regulate in the public interest must always be grounded in a valid grant of authority from Congress. And " 'in our anxiety to effectuate the congressional purpose of protecting the public, we must take care not to extend the scope of the statute beyond the point where Congress indicated it would stop.' " *United States* v. *Article of Drug ... Bacto–Unidisk,* 394 U.S. 784, 800, 22 L.Ed.2d 726, 89 S.Ct. 1410 (1969) (quoting *62 Cases of Jam* v. *United States,* 340 U.S. 593, 600, 95 L.Ed. 566, 71 S.Ct. 515 (1951)). Reading the FDCA as a whole, as well as in conjunction with Congress' subsequent tobacco-specific legislation, it is plain that Congress has not given the FDA the authority that it seeks to exercise here. For these reasons, the judgment of the Court of Appeals for the Fourth Circuit is affirmed.

It is so ordered.

BOREALI v. AXELROD

Court of Appeals of New York, 1987.
71 N.Y.2d 1, 523 N.Y.S.2d 464, 517 N.E.2d 1350.

OPINION OF THE COURT

* * *

I.

LEGISLATIVE BACKGROUND AND REGULATORY SCHEME

More than two decades ago, the Surgeon General of the United States began warning the American public that tobacco smoking poses a serious health hazard. Within the past five years, there has been mounting evidence that even non-smokers face a risk of lung cancer as a result of their exposure to tobacco smoke in the environment. As a consequence, smoking in the workplace and other indoor settings has become a cause for serious concern among health professionals. [ ]

This growing concern about the deleterious effects of tobacco smoking led our State Legislature to enact a bill in 1975 restricting smoking in certain designated areas, specifically, libraries, museums, theaters and public transportation facilities [ ]. Efforts during the same year to adopt more expansive restrictions on smoking in public places were, however, unsuccessful (*see*, A–4768, introduced Mar. 4, 1975 [Hevesi] [covering school auditoriums, sports arenas, commercial stores and public elevators][further citations omitted]). Subsequent attempts to broaden the coverage of the antismoking statute have similarly failed (*see, e.g.*, A–2746, introduced Feb. 1, 1983 [Grannis, Hevesi, Levy and Bennett] [banning smoking in workplace and other indoor areas open to the public, with certain specifically delineated exceptions]) In fact, it is undisputed that while some 40 bills on the subject have been introduced in the Legislature since 1975, none have passed both houses.

In late 1986 the Public Health Council (PHC) took action of its own. Purportedly acting pursuant to the broad grant of authority contained in its enabling statute [ ], the PHC published proposed rules, held public hearings and, in February of 1987, promulgated the final set of regulations prohibiting smoking in a wide variety of indoor areas that are open to the public, including schools, hospitals, auditoriums, food markets, stores, banks, taxicabs and limousines. Under these rules, restaurants with seating capacities of more than 50 people are required to provide contiguous nonsmoking areas sufficient to meet customer demand. Further, employers are required to provide smoke-free work areas for nonsmoking employees and to keep common areas free of smoke, with certain limited exceptions for cafeterias and lounges. Affected businesses are permitted to prohibit all smoking on the premises if they so choose. Expressly excluded from the regulations' coverage are restaurants with seating capacities of less than 50, conventions, trade shows, bars, private homes, private automobiles, private social functions, hotel and motel rooms and retail tobacco stores. Additional "waivers" of the regulations' restrictions may be obtained from the Commissioner upon a showing of financial hardship [ ]. Implementation of these regulations, which were to become effective May 7, 1987, has been suspended during the pendency of this litigation.

II.

* * *

III.

ANALYSIS

Preliminarily, we stress that this case presents no question concerning the wisdom of the challenged regulations, the propriety of the procedures by which they were adopted or the right of government in general to promulgate restrictions on the use of tobacco in public places. The degree of scientific support for the regulations and their unquestionable value in protecting those who choose not to smoke are, likewise, not pertinent except as background information. Finally, there has been no argument made concerning the personal freedoms of smokers or their "right" to pursue in public a habit that may inflict serious harm on others who must breathe the same air. The only dispute is whether the challenged restrictions were properly adopted by an administrative agency acting under a general grant of authority and in the face of the Legislature's apparent inability to establish its own broad policy on the controversial problem of passive smoking. Accordingly, we address no other issue in this appeal.

A.   The Delegation/Separation of Powers Issue

Section 225 (5) (a) of the Public Health Law authorizes the PHC to "deal with any matters affecting the * * * public health". At the heart of the present case is the question whether this broad grant of authority contravened the oft-recited principle that the legislative branch of government cannot cede its fundamental policy-making responsibility to an administrative agency. As a related matter, we must also inquire whether, assuming the propriety of the Legislature's grant of authority, the agency exceeded the permissible scope of its mandate by using it as a basis for engaging in inherently legislative activities. While the separation of powers doctrine gives the Legislature considerable leeway in delegating its regulatory powers, enactments conferring authority on administrative agencies in broad or general terms must be interpreted in light of the limitations that the Constitution imposes [ ].

However facially broad, a legislative grant of authority must be construed, whenever possible, so that it is no broader than that which the separation of powers doctrine permits [ ]. Even under the broadest and most open-ended of statutory mandates, an administrative agency may not use its authority as a license to correct whatever societal evils it perceives [ ]. Here, we cannot say that the broad enabling statute in issue is itself an unconstitutional delegation of legislative authority. However, we do conclude that the agency stretched that statute beyond its constitutionally valid reach when it used the statute as a basis for drafting a code embodying its own assessment of what public policy ought to be. Our reasons follow.

* * *

The modern view is reflected in this court's statement in *Matter of Levine v. Whalen* (39 NY2d 510, 515 [ ]): "Because of the constitutional provision that '[the] legislative power of this State shall be vested in the Senate and the Assembly' [ ], the Legislature cannot pass on its lawmaking functions to other bodies * * * but there is no constitutional prohibition against the delegation of power, with reasonable safeguards and standards, to an agency or commission to administer the law as enacted by the Legislature". * * *

This does not mean, however, that the regulations at issue here should be deemed valid without further analysis. To the contrary, the courts have previously struck down administrative actions undertaken under otherwise permissible enabling legislation where the challenged action could not have been deemed within that legislation without giving rise to a constitutional separation of powers problem [citations omitted].

A number of coalescing circumstances that are present in this case persuade us that the difficult-to-define line between administrative rule-making and legislative policy-making has been transgressed. While none of these circumstances, standing alone, is sufficient to warrant the conclusion that the PHC has usurped the Legislature's prerogative, all of these circumstances, when viewed in combination, paint a portrait of an agency that has improperly assumed for itself "[the] open-ended discretion to choose ends" (Tribe, op. cit., at 285), which characterizes the elected Legislature's role in our system of government.

First, while generally acting to further the laudable goal of protecting nonsmokers from the harmful effects of "passive smoking," the PHC has, in reality, constructed a regulatory scheme laden with exceptions based solely upon economic and social concerns. The exemptions the PHC has carved out for bars, convention centers, small restaurants, and the like, as well as the provision it has made for "waivers" based on financial hardship, have no foundation in considerations of public health. Rather, they demonstrate the agency's own effort to weigh the goal of promoting health against its social cost and to reach a suitable compromise. Indeed, in its "declaration of findings and intent," the PHC itself asserted: "[Regulations] addressing [this] hazard will cause certain economic dislocations and governmental intrusions which must be justified by the nature and extent of the public health hazard. A balance must be struck between safeguarding citizens from involuntary exposure to secondhand smoke on the one hand, and minimizing governmental intrusion into the affairs of its citizens on the other"[.]

Striking the proper balance among health concerns, cost and privacy interests, however, is a uniquely legislative function. While it is true that many regulatory decisions involve weighing economic and social concerns against the specific values that the regulatory agency is mandated to promote, the agency in this case has not been authorized to structure its decision making in a "cost-benefit" model [ ] and, in fact, has not been given any legislative guidelines at all for determining how the competing concerns of public health and economic cost are to be weighed. Thus, to the extent that the agency has built a regulatory scheme on its own conclusions about the appropriate balance of trade-offs between health and cost to particular industries in the private sector, it was "acting solely on [its] own ideas of sound public policy" and was therefore operating outside of its proper sphere of authority [ ]. This conclusion is particularly compelling here, where the focus is on administratively created exemptions rather than on rules that promote the legislatively expressed goals, since exemptions ordinarily run counter to such goals and, consequently, cannot be justified as simple implementations of legislative values [ ]. In this regard, the regulations at issue here are fundamentally different from those challenged in *Chiropractic Assn. v. Hilleboe* (*supra*, [ ]), where the specific limits on the use of X-ray and fluoroscopic equipment were all promulgated in direct furtherance of the health-related goal of avoiding unnecessary exposure to harmful radiation.

The second, and related, consideration is that in adopting the antismoking regulations challenged here the PHC did not merely fill in the details of broad legislation describing the over-all policies to be implemented. Instead, the PHC wrote on a clean slate, creating its own comprehensive set of rules without benefit of legislative guidance. Viewed in that light, the agency's actions were a far cry from the "interstitial" rule making that typifies administrative regulatory activity [ ].

A third indicator that the PHC exceeded the scope of the authority properly delegated to it by the Legislature is the fact that the agency acted in an area in which the Legislature had repeatedly tried—and failed—to reach agreement in the face of substantial public debate and vigorous lobbying by a variety of interested factions. While we have often been reluctant to ascribe persuasive significance to legislative inaction [citations omitted] our usual hesitancy in this area has no place here. Unlike the cases in which we have been asked to consider the Legislature's failure to act as some indirect proof of its actual intentions [ ], in this case it is appropriate for us to consider the significance of legislative inaction as evidence that the Legislature has so far been unable to reach agreement on the goals and methods that should govern in resolving a society-wide health problem. Here, the repeated failures by the Legislature to arrive at such an agreement do not automatically entitle an administrative agency to take it upon itself to fill the vacuum and impose a solution of its own. Manifestly, it is the province of the people's elected representatives, rather than appointed administrators, to resolve difficult social problems by making choices among competing ends.

Finally, although indoor smoking is unquestionably a health issue, no special expertise or technical competence in the field of health was involved in the development of the antismoking regulations challenged here. Faced with mounting evidence about the hazards to bystanders of indoor smoking, the PHC drafted a simple code describing the locales in which smoking would be prohibited and providing exemptions for various special interest groups. The antismoking regulations at issue here are thus distinguishable from those at issue in *Chiropractic Assn. v. Hilleboe [ ]*, in which we stressed that the PHC's technical competence was necessary to flesh out details of the broadly stated legislative policies embodied in the Public Health Law.

In summary, we conclude that while Public Health Law § 225 (5) (a) is a valid delegation of regulatory authority, it cannot be construed to encompass the policy-making activity at issue here without running afoul of the constitutional separation of powers doctrine. Further, the "separability" provision of the agency's rules [ ] cannot be used to save those rules from the conclusion that, taken as a whole, they are invalid. The PHC's own "Declaration of findings and intent" makes clear that the agency considered the regulatory scheme it adopted to be an integrated code in which the need to protect citizens from "involuntary exposure to secondhand smoke" was delicately balanced against the goal of minimizing "economic dislocations and governmental intrusions" [ ]. It would be pragmatically impossible, as well as jurisprudentially unsound, for us to attempt to identify and excise particular provisions while leaving the remainder of the PHC's antismoking code intact, since the product of such an effort would be a regulatory scheme that neither the Legislature nor the PHC intended.

B. *Preemption and the Legislature's Intentions*

Plaintiffs have also argued that the Legislature "preempted the field" of indoor smoking by enacting Public Health Law article 13–E, which imposes restrictions on smoking in a narrow class of public locations. However, we decline to adopt this contention as an alternative ground for our holding. The preemption doctrine is most often applied where inferior levels of government have attempted to regulate despite pronouncements on the same subject at a higher governmental level [ ]. It has limited utility where, as here, a perceived conflict between legislative policy and administrative action at the same level of government is at issue. In such cases, the salient inquiry is not whether a higher level of government has demonstrated an intention to preclude local regulation in a particular area, but rather whether the legislative branch of government has shown an intent to grant regulatory authority over a specific subject matter to an administrative agency which exists as part of the coequal executive branch [ ]. The inquiry includes an examination of both the scope of the statute authorizing the regulatory activity and the degree to which the administrative rules are either consistent or "out of harmony" with the policies expressed in the statute [ ].

Here, it is apparent that the Legislature has given the PHC a wide field for the exercise of its regulatory authority [ ] and nothing in the Legislature's 1975 adoption of a limited antismoking provision [ ] suggests a legislative intention to narrow the statutory mandate or exclude the area of smoking restrictions. Although the PHC's regulations prohibit smoking in a wider variety of indoor settings than do the Legislature's enactments on the subject, both the regulations and the relevant statutes have a common underlying policy objective—minimizing nonsmokers' exposure to environmental tobacco smoke [ ]. Thus, whether phrased in terms of "preemption" or in terms of consistency with the existing statutory scheme, plaintiffs' arguments concerning the effect of

Public Health Law article 13–E on the PHC's power to regulate public smoking must fail.

IV.

CONCLUSION

Although Public Health Law § 225 (5) (a) confers broad powers on the Public Health Council and there is no indication that the Legislature intended to circumscribe those powers when it enacted a limited antismoking measure of its own [ ], the fundamental constitutional limitations on the respective powers of the legislative and executive branches foreclose a construction of the statute that would include the administrative activity challenged here. In promulgating its antismoking rules, the PHC transgressed the line that separates administrative rule making from legislating and thereby exceeded its statutory powers. Consequently, its actions cannot be upheld.

Accordingly, the order of the Appellate Division should be affirmed.

Bellacosa, J. (dissenting). I would reverse and uphold the Public Health Council (PHC) regulation, adopted to preserve and improve the public health, prohibiting smoking indoors in some public places and in designated portions of workplaces [ ]. This comprehensive plan, based on a thoroughly documented record and a carefully deliberated public procedure, was promulgated to protect innocent bystanders from involuntary exposure to the environmental smoke and others.

The majority accepts the Legislature's delegation of broad authority to the PHC to make regulations concerning a wide range of issues affecting the public health [ ]. They recognize that the legislative delegation may be granted in the most generous terms [ ], that the regulation is in harmony with the statute[ ], and that this court has held the particular delegation under Public Health Law § 225 (4), (5) (a) to be valid [ ]. They even acknowledge that the Legislature did not preempt the field of public smoking or evince an intent to constrict the PHC mandate by enacting its own 1975 narrow smoking ban in Public Health Law article 13–E.

Yet, the majority, wrongly I respectfully submit, concludes that the separation of powers doctrine has been transgressed by the Legislature and by the PHC and, on that basis alone, they uphold the judicial invalidation of the smoking ban regulation.

The statutory authority for protecting the public health was delegated by the Legislature to the PHC 75 years ago in the broadest possible mandate and it has not been withdrawn or narrowed. Indeed, it has been exercised regularly with this court's express approbation [ ]. That power includes adoption and amendment to the Sanitary Code dealing with the root source of authority here—"matters affecting the security of life or health or the preservation and improvement of public health" [ ]. This court, in a definitive ruling, has held that mission, that delegation and its broad implementation, to be constitutionally proper *Chiropractic*

Assn. v. Hilleboe, supra, at 120 [under State Constitution the Legislature properly delegated power to the PHC in Public Health Law § 225].

This antismoking regulation is a fortiori valid compared to the regulation in *Chiropractic Assn. v. Hilleboe (supra)*, which was a restriction on the freedom and access to chiropractic X-ray treatments, protecting patients from their own choices. Inasmuch as the Public Health Council could do that with our approbation, we search in vain for reasons in the majority's decision that the same statutory source of authority cannot protect the public health of innocent, involuntary *third-party victims* from others with this limited regulation.

"[It] is not necessary that the Legislature supply administrative officials with rigid formulas in fields where flexibility in the adaptation of the legislative policy to infinitely variable conditions constitute the very essence of the programs. Rather, the standards prescribed by the Legislature are to be read in light of the conditions in which they are to be applied" [ ].

The Legislature declared its intent that there be a PHC in this State and empowered it to adopt a Sanitary Code for the preservation and improvement of the public health. The Legislature also wisely refrained from enacting a rigid formula for the exercise of the PHC's critical agenda of concerns because that calls for expert attention. That legislative forbearance represents both a sound administrative law principle and, at the threshold, a constitutional one as well [ ]. The Legislature could not have foreseen in 1913 the specific need for PHC regulations in areas of human blood collection, care and storage; X-ray film usage; pesticide labels; drinking water contamination; or a myriad of other public health topics [ ]. It was prescient and sound governance as well to grant flexibility to the objective expert entity so it could in these exceptional instances prescribe demonstrably needed administrative regulation for the public health, free from the sometimes paralyzing polemics associated with the legislative process. Just as many of the other specified categories in the State Sanitary Code have properly been regulated by the PHC, so, too, does the subject of public indoor smoking and its impact on the health and well-being of innocent third-party victims comfortably fall within that identical, broad legislative embrace.

While the court admits the difficulty under the high separation of powers standard of articulating the basis for drawing, and even finding, some line limiting the PHC's conceded exercise of authority, it nevertheless goes ahead and does so. Its line is no line, but rather an arbitrary judgment call of its own. It is this judicial branch intrusion which constitutes the truly egregious separation of powers breach into the exercise of prerogative of the Legislature [ ] and of the executive [ ].

* * *

Notes

1) *Cipollone* raises the issue of the effect as well as the effectiveness of the federal government's required warning on cigarette packaging. The defendant takes the position that having complied with the federal labeling guidelines, it should be shielded from liability based upon common law theories. From a public health point of view, is the warning adequate? Should it be stronger? If tobacco is inherently unsafe, does labeling it as unsafe protect the vendor?

2) Without a direct grant of authority from Congress, the FDA in *FDA v. Brown & Williamson Tobacco Corp.* took the position that it cannot regulate tobacco or tobacco products as drugs or drug-delivery devices. The fact that the FDA had previously declined to assume authority in the tobacco arena was clearly a factor in the Court's decision. At the state level, many states reserve the right to assert authority over drug-like products not regulated by the FDA. For example, Massachusetts, Minnesota and Texas have used state laws to compel the disclosure of tobacco ingredients.

3) Legislatures make governmental policy. To carry out legislative policy in the public health arena, public health agencies are formed. These administrative agencies have only as much authority as is delegated by the legislature. In reviewing the delegation of public health authority, courts often give deference to agency rulings for public health decision making. Nevertheless, separation of powers doctrine requires that the legislature, not the agency, make policy decisions. Was it merely that *Boreali v. Axelrod* was decided in a jurisdiction (New York) where delegation of authority is more restrictive? Since smoking bans in many public places are widespread today, who is responsible for issuing the type of regulation that was struck down in *Boreali*?

SECTION C. LEGAL AND ILLEGAL DRUGS

WHALEN v. ROE

Supreme Court of the United States, 1977.
429 U.S. 589, 97 S.Ct. 869, 51 L.Ed.2d 64.

MR. JUSTICE STEVENS delivered the opinion of the Court.

The constitutional question presented is whether the State of New York may record, in a centralized computer file, the names and addresses of all persons who have obtained, pursuant to a doctor's prescription, certain drugs for which there is both a lawful and an unlawful market.

The District Court enjoined enforcement of the portions of the New York State Controlled Substances Act of 1972 which require such recording on the ground that they violate appellees' constitutionally protected rights of privacy. We noted probable jurisdiction of the appeal by the Commissioner of Health [ ] and now reverse.

Many drugs have both legitimate and illegitimate uses. In response to a concern that such drugs were being diverted into unlawful channels, in 1970 the New York Legislature created a special commission to evaluate the State's drug control laws. The commission found the existing laws deficient in several respects. There was no effective way to prevent the use of stolen or revised prescriptions, to prevent unscrupulous pharmacists from repeatedly refilling prescriptions, to prevent users from obtaining prescriptions from more than one doctor, or to prevent doctors from overprescribing, either by authorizing an excessive amount in one prescription or by giving one patient multiple prescriptions. In drafting new legislation to correct such defects, the commission consulted with enforcement officials in California and Illinois where central reporting systems were being used effectively.

The new New York statute classified potentially harmful drugs in five schedules. Drugs, such as heroin, which are highly abused and have no recognized medical use, are in Schedule I; they cannot be prescribed. Schedules II through V include drugs which have a progressively lower potential for abuse but also have a recognized medical use. Our concern is limited to Schedule II, which includes the most dangerous of the legitimate drugs.

With an exception for emergencies, the Act requires that all prescriptions for Schedule II drugs be prepared by the physician in triplicate on an official form. n9 The completed form identifies the prescribing physician; the dispensing pharmacy; the drug and dosage; and the name, address, and age of the patient. One copy of the form is retained by the physician, the second by the pharmacist, and the third is forwarded to the New York State Department of Health in Albany. A prescription made on an official form may not exceed a 30–day supply, and may not be refilled.

The District Court found that about 100,000 Schedule II prescription forms are delivered to a receiving room at the Department of Health in Albany each month. They are sorted, coded, and logged and then taken to another room where the data on the forms is recorded on magnetic tapes for processing by a computer. Thereafter, the forms are returned to the receiving room to be retained in a vault for a five-year period and then destroyed as required by the statute. The receiving room is surrounded by a locked wire fence and protected by an alarm system. The computer tapes containing the prescription data are kept in a locked cabinet. When the tapes are used, the computer is run "off-line," which means that no terminal outside of the computer room can read or record any information. Public disclosure of the identity of patients is expressly prohibited by the statute and by a Department of Health regulation. Willful violation of these prohibitions is a crime punishable by up to one year in prison and a $2,000 fine. At the time of trial there were 17 Department of Health employees with access to the files; in addition, there were 24 investigators with authority to investigate cases of overdispensing which might be identified by the computer. Twenty months after the effective date of the Act, the computerized data had only been used in two investigations involving alleged overuse by specific patients.

A few days before the Act became effective, this litigation was commenced by a group of patients regularly receiving prescriptions for Schedule II drugs, by doctors who prescribe such drugs, and by two associations of physicians. After various preliminary proceedings, a three-judge District Court conducted a one-day trial. Appellees offered evidence tending to prove that persons in need of treatment with Schedule II drugs will from time to time decline such treatment because of their fear that the misuse of the computerized data will cause them to be stigmatized as "drug addicts."

The District Court held that "the doctor-patient relationship is one of the zones of privacy accorded constitutional protection" and that the patient-identification provisions of the Act invaded this zone with "a needlessly broad sweep," and enjoined enforcement of the provisions of the Act which deal with the reporting of patients' names and addresses.

I

The District Court found that the State had been unable to demonstrate the necessity for the patient-identification requirement on the basis of its experience during the first 20 months of administration of the new statute. There was a time when that alone would have provided a basis for invalidating the statute. *Lochner* v. *New York,* 198 U.S. 45, involved legislation making it a crime for a baker to permit his employees to work more than 60 hours in a week. In an opinion no longer regarded as authoritative, the Court held the statute unconstitutional as "an unreasonable, unnecessary and arbitrary interference with the right of the individual to his personal liberty. . . . " *Id.,* at 56.

The holding in *Lochner* has been implicitly rejected many times. State legislation which has some effect on individual liberty or privacy may not be held unconstitutional simply because a court finds it unnecessary, in whole or in part. For we have frequently recognized that individual States have broad latitude in experimenting with possible solutions to problems of vital local concern.

The New York statute challenged in this case represents a considered attempt to deal with such a problem. It is manifestly the product of an orderly and rational legislative decision. It was recommended by a specially appointed commission which held extensive hearings on the proposed legislation, and drew on experience with similar programs in other States. There surely was nothing unreasonable in the assumption that the patient-identification requirement might aid in the enforcement of laws designed to minimize the misuse of dangerous drugs. For the requirement could reasonably be expected to have a deterrent effect on potential violators as well as to aid in the detection or investigation of specific instances of apparent abuse. At the very least, it would seem clear that the State's vital interest in controlling the distribution of dangerous drugs would support a decision to experiment with new techniques for control. For if an experiment fails—if in this case experience teaches that the patient-identification requirement results in the foolish expenditure of funds to acquire a mountain of useless information—the legislative process remains available to terminate the unwise experiment. It follows that the legislature's enactment of the patient-identification requirement was a reasonable exercise of New York's broad police powers. The District Court's finding that the necessity for the requirement had not been proved is not, therefore, a sufficient reason for holding the statutory requirement unconstitutional.

II

Appellees contend that the statute invades a constitutionally protected "zone of privacy." The cases sometimes characterized as protecting "privacy" have in fact involved at least two different kinds of interests. One is the individual interest in avoiding disclosure of personal matters, and another is the interest in independence in making certain kinds of important decisions. Appellees argue that both of these interests are impaired by this statute. The mere existence in readily available form of the information about patients' use of Schedule II drugs creates a genuine concern that the information will become publicly known and that it will adversely affect their reputations. This concern makes some patients reluctant to use, and some doctors reluctant to prescribe, such drugs even when their use is medically indicated. It follows, they argue, that the making of decisions about matters vital to the care of their health is inevitably affected by the statute. Thus, the statute threatens to impair both their interest in the nondisclosure of private information and also their interest in making important decisions independently.

We are persuaded, however, that the New York program does not, on its face, pose a sufficiently grievous threat to either interest to establish a constitutional violation.

Public disclosure of patient information can come about in three ways. Health Department employees may violate the statute by failing, either deliberately or negligently, to maintain proper security. A patient or a doctor may be accused of a violation and the stored data may be offered in evidence in a judicial proceeding. Or, thirdly, a doctor, a pharmacist, or the patient may voluntarily reveal information on a prescription form.

The third possibility existed under the prior law and is entirely unrelated to the existence of the computerized data bank. Neither of the other two possibilities provides a proper ground for attacking the statute as invalid on its face. There is no support in the record, or in the experience of the two States that New York has emulated, for an assumption that the security provisions of the statute will be administered improperly. And the remote possibility that judicial supervision of the evidentiary use of particular items of stored information will provide inadequate protection against unwarranted disclosures is surely not a sufficient reason for invalidating the entire patient-identification program.

Even without public disclosure, it is, of course, true that private information must be disclosed to the authorized employees of the New York Department of Health. Such disclosures, however, are not significantly different from those that were required under the prior law. Nor are they meaningfully distinguishable from a host of other unpleasant invasions of privacy that are associated with many facets of health care. Unquestionably, some individuals' concern for their own privacy may lead them to avoid or to postpone needed medical attention. Nevertheless, disclosures of private medical information to doctors, to hospital personnel, to insurance companies, and to public health agencies are often an essential part of modern medical practice even when the disclosure may reflect unfavorably on the character of the patient. Requiring such disclosures to representatives of the State having responsibility for the health of the community, does not automatically amount to an impermissible invasion of privacy.

Appellees also argue, however, that even if unwarranted disclosures do not actually occur, the knowledge that the information is readily available in a computerized file creates a genuine concern that causes some persons to decline needed medication. The record supports the conclusion that some use of Schedule II drugs has been discouraged by that concern; it also is clear, however, that about 100,000 prescriptions for such drugs were being filled each month prior to the entry of the District Court's injunction. Clearly, therefore, the statute did not deprive the public of access to the drugs.

Nor can it be said that any individual has been deprived of the right to decide independently, with the advice of his physician, to acquire and to use needed medication. Although the State no doubt could prohibit entirely the use of particular Schedule II drugs, it has not done so. This case is therefore unlike those in which the Court held that a total prohibition of certain conduct was an impermissible deprivation of liberty. Nor does the State require access to these drugs to be conditioned on the consent of any state official or other third party. Within dosage limits which appellees do not challenge, the decision to prescribe, or to use, is left entirely to the physician and the patient.

We hold that neither the immediate nor the threatened impact of the patient-identification requirements in the New York State Controlled Substances Act of 1972 on either the reputation or the independence of patients for whom Schedule II drugs are medically indicated is sufficient to constitute an invasion of any right or liberty protected by the Fourteenth Amendment.

III

The appellee doctors argue separately that the statute impairs their right to practice medicine free of unwarranted state interference. If the doctors' claim has any reference to the impact of the 1972 statute on their own procedures, it is clearly frivolous. For even the prior statute required the doctor to prepare a written prescription identifying the name and address of the patient and the dosage of the prescribed drug. To the extent that their claim has reference to the possibility that the patients' concern about disclosure may induce them to refuse needed medication, the doctors' claim is derivative from, and therefore no stronger than, the patients'. Our rejection of their claim therefore disposes of the doctors' as well.

A final word about issues we have not decided. We are not unaware of the threat to privacy implicit in the accumulation of vast amounts of personal information in computerized data banks or other massive government files. The collection of taxes, the distribution of welfare and social security benefits, the supervision of public health, the direction of our Armed Forces, and the enforcement of the criminal laws all require the orderly preservation of great quantities of information, much of which is personal in character and potentially embarrassing or harmful if disclosed. The right to collect and use such data for public purposes is typically accompanied by a concomitant statutory or regulatory duty to avoid unwarranted disclosures. Recognizing that in some circumstances that duty arguably has its roots in the Constitution, nevertheless New York's statutory scheme, and its implementing administrative procedures, evidence a proper concern with, and protection of, the individual's interest in privacy. We therefore need not, and do not, decide any question which might be presented by the unwarranted disclosure of accumulated private data—whether intentional or unintentional—or by a system that did not contain comparable security provisions. We simply hold that this record does not establish an invasion of any right or liberty protected by the Fourteenth Amendment.

Reversed.

BOARD OF EDUCATION v. EARLS

Supreme Court of the United States, 2002.
536 U.S. 822, 122 S.Ct. 2559, 153 L.Ed.2d 735.

JUSTICE THOMAS delivered the opinion of the Court.

The Student Activities Drug Testing Policy implemented by the Board of Education of Independent School District No. 92 of Pottawatomie County (School District) requires all students who participate in competitive extracurricular activities to submit to drug testing. Because this Policy reasonably serves the School District's important interest in detecting and preventing drug use among its students, we hold that it is constitutional.

I

The city of Tecumseh, Oklahoma, is a rural community located approximately 40 miles southeast of Oklahoma City. The School District administers all Tecumseh public schools. In the fall of 1998, the School District adopted the Student Activities Drug Testing Policy (Policy), which requires all middle and high school students to consent to drug testing in order to participate in any extracurricular activity. In practice, the Policy has been applied only to competitive extracurricular activities sanctioned by the Oklahoma Secondary Schools Activities Association, such as the Academic Team, Future Farmers of America, Future Home-makers of America, band, choir, pom pon, cheerleading, and athletics. Under the Policy, students are required to take a drug test before participating in an extracurricular activity, must submit to random drug testing while participating in that activity, and must agree to be tested at any time upon reasonable suspicion. The urinalysis tests are designed to detect only the use of illegal drugs, including amphetamines, marijua-na, cocaine, opiates, and barbiturates, not medical conditions or the presence of authorized prescription medications.

At the time of their suit, both respondents attended Tecumseh High School. Respondent Lindsay Earls was a member of the show choir, the marching band, the Academic Team, and the National Honor Society. Respondent Daniel James sought to participate in the Academic Team. n1 Together with their parents, Earls and James brought a 42 U.S.C. § 1983 action against the School District, challenging the Policy both on its face and as applied to their participation in extracurricular activities. They alleged that the Policy violates the Fourth Amendment as incorpo-rated by the Fourteenth Amendment and requested injunctive and declarative relief. They also argued that the School District failed to identify a special need for testing students who participate in extracur-ricular activities, and that the "Drug Testing Policy neither addresses a proven problem nor promises to bring any benefit to students or the school." [ ].

Applying the principles articulated in *Vernonia School Dist. 47J* v. *Acton,* 515 U.S. 646, 132 L.Ed.2d 564, 115 S.Ct. 2386 (1995), in which we upheld the suspicionless drug testing of school athletes, the United States District Court for the Western District of Oklahoma rejected respondents' claim that the Policy was unconstitutional and granted summary judgment to the School District. The court noted that "special needs" exist in the public school context and that, although the School District did "not show a drug problem of epidemic proportions," there was a history of drug abuse starting in 1970 that presented "legitimate cause for concern." [ ]. The District Court also held that the Policy was effective because "it can scarcely be disputed that the drug problem among the student body is effectively addressed by making sure that the large number of students participating in competitive, extracurricular activities do not use drugs." [ ].

The United States Court of Appeals for the Tenth Circuit reversed, holding that the Policy violated the Fourth Amendment. The Court of Appeals agreed with the District Court that the Policy must be evaluated in the "unique environment of the school setting," but reached a different conclusion as to the Policy's constitutionality. [ ]. Before imposing a suspicionless drug testing program, the Court of Appeals concluded that a school "must demonstrate that there is some identifi-able drug abuse problem among a sufficient number of those subject to the testing, such that testing that group of students will actually redress its drug problem." [ ]. The Court of Appeals then held that because the School District failed to demonstrate such a problem existed among Tecumseh students participating in competitive extracurricular activities, the Policy was unconstitutional. We granted certiorari [ ] and now reverse.

II

The Fourth Amendment to the United States Constitution protects "the right of the people to be secure in their persons, houses, papers, and effects, against unreasonable searches and seizures." Searches by public school officials, such as the collection of urine samples, implicate Fourth Amendment interests. [ ]. We must therefore review the School District's Policy for "reasonableness," which is the touchstone of the constitutionality of a governmental search.

In the criminal context, reasonableness usually requires a showing of probable cause. [ ]. The probable-cause standard, however, "is peculiarly related to criminal investigations" and may be unsuited to determining the reasonableness of administrative searches where the "Government seeks to *prevent* the development of hazardous conditions." *Treasury Employees* v. *Von Raab,* 489 U.S. 656, 667–668, 103 L.Ed.2d 685, 109 S.Ct. 1384 (1989) [ ]. The Court has also held that a warrant and finding of probable cause are unnecessary in the public school context because such requirements " 'would unduly interfere with the maintenance of the swift and informal disciplinary procedures [that are] needed.' " *Vernonia* [*School Dist. 47J* v. *Acton,* 515 U.S. 646, 653, 132 L.Ed.2d 564, 115 S.Ct. 2386 (1995)], (quoting *T. L. O., supra,* 469 U.S. at 340–41).

Given that the School District's Policy is not in any way related to the conduct of criminal investigations, see Part II–B, *infra,* respondents do not contend that the School District requires probable cause before testing students for drug use. Respondents instead argue that drug testing must be based at least on some level of individualized suspicion. [ ]. It is true that we generally determine the reasonableness of a search by balancing the nature of the intrusion on the individual's privacy against the promotion of legitimate governmental interests. [ ]. But we have long held that "the Fourth Amendment imposes no irreducible requirement of [individualized] suspicion." *United States* v. *Martinez–Fuerte,* 428 U.S. 543, 561, 49 L.Ed.2d 1116, 96 S.Ct. 3074 (1976). "In certain limited circumstances, the Government's need to discover such latent or hidden conditions, or to prevent their development, is sufficiently compelling to justify the intrusion on privacy entailed by conducting such searches without any measure of individualized suspicion." *Von Raab, supra,* 489 U.S. at 668; see also *Skinner, supra,* 489 U.S. at 624. Therefore, in the context of safety and administrative regulations, a search unsupported by probable cause may be reasonable "when 'special needs, beyond the normal need for law enforcement, make the warrant and probable-cause requirement impracticable.' " *Griffin* v. *Wisconsin,* 483 U.S. 868, 873, 97 L.Ed.2d 709, 107 S.Ct. 3164 (1987) [ ].

Significantly, this Court has previously held that "special needs" inhere in the public school context. [ ]. While schoolchildren do not shed their constitutional rights when they enter the schoolhouse [ ], "Fourth Amendment rights ... are different in public schools than elsewhere; the 'reasonableness' inquiry cannot disregard the schools' custodial and tutelary responsibility for children." *Vernonia, supra*, 515 U.S. at 656. In particular, a finding of individualized suspicion may not be necessary when a school conducts drug testing.

In *Vernonia*, this Court held that the suspicionless drug testing of athletes was constitutional. The Court, however, did not simply authorize all school drug testing, but rather conducted a fact-specific balancing of the intrusion on the children's Fourth Amendment rights against the promotion of legitimate governmental interests. [ ]. Applying the principles of *Vernonia* to the somewhat different facts of this case, we conclude that Tecumseh's Policy is also constitutional.

A

We first consider the nature of the privacy interest allegedly compromised by the drug testing. [ ]. As in *Vernonia*, the context of the public school environment serves as the backdrop for the analysis of the privacy interest at stake and the reasonableness of the drug testing policy in general. [ ]. ("Central ... is the fact that the subjects of the Policy are (1) children, who (2) have been committed to the temporary custody of the State as schoolmaster"); [ ] ("The most significant element in this case is the first we discussed: that the Policy was undertaken in furtherance of the government's responsibilities, under a public school system, as guardian and tutor of children entrusted to its care"); [ ] ("When the government acts as guardian and tutor the relevant question is whether the search is one that a reasonable guardian and tutor might undertake").

A student's privacy interest is limited in a public school environment where the State is responsible for maintaining discipline, health, and safety. Schoolchildren are routinely required to submit to physical examinations and vaccinations against disease. See id., at 656. Securing order in the school environment sometimes requires that students be subjected to greater controls than those appropriate for adults. [ ]

Respondents argue that because children participating in nonathletic extracurricular activities are not subject to regular physicals and communal undress, they have a stronger expectation of privacy than the athletes tested in *Vernonia*. [ ]. This distinction, however, was not essential to our decision in *Vernonia*, which depended primarily upon the school's custodial responsibility and authority.

In any event, students who participate in competitive extracurricular activities voluntarily subject themselves to many of the same intrusions on their privacy as do athletes. Some of these clubs and activities require occasional off-campus travel and communal undress. All of them have their own rules and requirements for participating students that do not apply to the student body as a whole. [ ]. For example, each of the competitive extracurricular activities governed by the Policy must abide by the rules of the Oklahoma Secondary Schools Activities Association, and a faculty sponsor monitors the students for compliance with the various rules dictated by the clubs and activities. [ ]. This regulation of extracurricular activities further diminishes the expectation of privacy among schoolchildren. Cf. *Vernonia, supra,* 515 U.S. at 657 ("Somewhat like adults who choose to participate in a closely regulated industry, students who voluntarily participate in school athletics have reason to expect intrusions upon normal rights and privileges, including privacy" (internal quotation marks omitted)). We therefore conclude that the students affected by this Policy have a limited expectation of privacy.

B

Next, we consider the character of the intrusion imposed by the Policy. See *Vernonia,* 515 U.S. at 658. Urination is "an excretory function traditionally shielded by great privacy." *Skinner,* 489 U.S. at 626. But the "degree of intrusion" on one's privacy caused by collecting a urine sample "depends upon the manner in which production of the urine sample is monitored." *Vernonia, supra,* 515 U.S. at 658.

Under the Policy, a faculty monitor waits outside the closed restroom stall for the student to produce a sample and must "listen for the normal sounds of urination in order to guard against tampered specimens and to insure an accurate chain of custody." App. 199. The monitor then pours the sample into two bottles that are sealed and placed into a mailing pouch along with a consent form signed by the student. This procedure is virtually identical to that reviewed in *Vernonia,* except that it additionally protects privacy by allowing male students to produce their samples behind a closed stall. Given that we considered the method of collection in *Vernonia* a "negligible" intrusion, 515 U.S. at 658, the method here is even less problematic.

In addition, the Policy clearly requires that the test results be kept in confidential files separate from a student's other educational records and released to school personnel only on a "need to know" basis. Respondents nonetheless contend that the intrusion on students' privacy is significant because the Policy fails to protect effectively against the disclosure of confidential information and, specifically, that the school "has been careless in protecting that information * * *.

Moreover, the test results are not turned over to any law enforcement authority. Nor do the test results here lead to the imposition of discipline or have any academic consequences. [ ]. Rather, the only consequence of a failed drug test is to limit the student's privilege of participating in extracurricular activities. Indeed, a student may test positive for drugs twice and still be allowed to participate in extracurricular activities. After the first positive test, the school contacts the student's parent or guardian for a meeting. The student may continue to participate in the activity if within five days of the meeting the student shows proof of receiving drug counseling and submits to a second drug test in two weeks. For the second positive test, the student is suspended from participation in all extracurricular activities for 14 days, must complete four hours of substance abuse counseling, and must submit to monthly drug tests. Only after a third positive test will the student be suspended from participating in any extracurricular activity for the remainder of the school year, or 88 school days, whichever is longer. [ ].

Given the minimally intrusive nature of the sample collection and the limited uses to which the test results are put, we conclude that the invasion of students' privacy is not significant.

C

Finally, this Court must consider the nature and immediacy of the government's concerns and the efficacy of the Policy in meeting them. [ ]. This Court has already articulated in detail the importance of the governmental concern in preventing drug use by schoolchildren. [ ]. The drug abuse problem among our Nation's youth has hardly abated since *Vernonia* was decided in 1995. In fact, evidence suggests that it has only grown worse. As in *Vernonia*, "the necessity for the State to act is magnified by the fact that this evil is being visited not just upon individuals at large, but upon children for whom it has undertaken a special responsibility of care and direction." [ ]. The health and safety risks identified in *Vernonia* apply with equal force to Tecumseh's children. Indeed, the nationwide drug epidemic makes the war against drugs a pressing concern in every school.

Additionally, the School District in this case has presented specific evidence of drug use at Tecumseh schools. Teachers testified that they had seen students who appeared to be under the influence of drugs and that they had heard students speaking openly about using drugs. [ ]. A drug dog found marijuana cigarettes near the school parking lot. Police officers once found drugs or drug paraphernalia in a car driven by a Future Farmers of America member. And the school board president reported that people in the community were calling the board to discuss the "drug situation." [ ]. We decline to second-guess the finding of the District Court that "viewing the evidence as a whole, it cannot be reasonably disputed that the [School District] was faced with a 'drug problem' when it adopted the Policy." [ ].

* * *

Furthermore, this Court has not required a particularized or pervasive drug problem before allowing the government to conduct suspicionless drug testing. For instance, in *Von Raab* the Court upheld the drug testing of customs officials on a purely preventive basis, without any documented history of drug use by such officials. [ ] * * *

Respondents also argue that the testing of nonathletes does not implicate any safety concerns, and that safety is a "crucial factor" in applying the special needs framework. [ ]. They contend that there must be "surpassing safety interests," *Skinner, supra,* 489 U.S. at 634, or "extraordinary safety and national security hazards," *Von Raab, supra,* 489 U.S. at 674, in order to override the usual protections of the Fourth Amendment. [ ]. Respondents are correct that safety factors into the special needs analysis, but the safety interest furthered by drug testing is undoubtedly substantial for all children, athletes and nonathletes alike. We know all too well that drug use carries a variety of health risks for children, including death from overdose.

Finally, we find that testing students who participate in extracurricular activities is a reasonably effective means of addressing the School District's legitimate concerns in preventing, deterring, and detecting drug use. While in *Vernonia* there might have been a closer fit between the testing of athletes and the trial court's finding that the drug problem was "fueled by the 'role model' effect of athletes' drug use," such a finding was not essential to the holding. 515 U.S. at 663 [ ]. *Vernonia* did not require the school to test the group of students most likely to use drugs, but rather considered the constitutionality of the program in the context of the public school's custodial responsibilities. Evaluating the Policy in this context, we conclude that the drug testing of Tecumseh students who participate in extracurricular activities effectively serves the School District's interest in protecting the safety and health of its students.

III

Within the limits of the Fourth Amendment, local school boards must assess the desirability of drug testing schoolchildren. In upholding the constitutionality of the Policy, we express no opinion as to its wisdom. Rather, we hold only that Tecumseh's Policy is a reasonable means of furthering the School District's important interest in preventing and deterring drug use among its schoolchildren. Accordingly, we reverse the judgment of the Court of Appeals.

It is so ordered.

REYNOLDS v. McNICHOLS

[See Opinion at page 988].

FERGUSON v. CITY OF CHARLESTON

Supreme Court of the United States, 2001.
532 U.S. 67, 121 S.Ct. 1281, 149 L.Ed.2d 205.

JUSTICE STEVENS delivered the opinion of the Court.

In this case, we must decide whether a state hospital's performance of a diagnostic test to obtain evidence of a patient's criminal conduct for law enforcement purposes is an unreasonable search if the patient has not consented to the procedure. More narrowly, the question is whether the interest in using the threat of criminal sanctions to deter pregnant women from using cocaine can justify a departure from the general rule that an official nonconsensual search is unconstitutional if not authorized by a valid warrant.

I

In the fall of 1988, staff members at the public hospital operated in the city of Charleston by the Medical University of South Carolina (MUSC) became concerned about an apparent increase in the use of cocaine by patients who were receiving prenatal treatment. In response to this perceived increase, as of April 1989, MUSC began to order drug screens to be performed on urine samples from maternity patients who were suspected of using cocaine. If a patient tested positive, she was then referred by MUSC staff to the county substance abuse commission for counseling and treatment. However, despite the referrals, the incidence of cocaine use among the patients at MUSC did not appear to change.

Some four months later, Nurse Shirley Brown, the case manager for the MUSC obstetrics department, heard a news broadcast reporting that the police in Greenville, South Carolina, were arresting pregnant users of cocaine on the theory that such use harmed the fetus and was therefore child abuse. Nurse Brown discussed the story with MUSC's general counsel, Joseph C. Good, Jr., who then contacted Charleston Solicitor Charles Condon in order to offer MUSC's cooperation in prosecuting mothers whose children tested positive for drugs at birth.

After receiving Good's letter, Solicitor Condon took the first steps in developing the policy at issue in this case. * * *

* * * The first section, entitled the "Identification of Drug Abusers," provided that a patient should be tested for cocaine through a urine drug screen if she met one or more of nine criteria.[4] It also stated that a chain of custody should be followed when obtaining and testing urine samples, presumably to make sure that the results could be used in subsequent criminal proceedings. The policy also provided for education and referral to a substance abuse clinic for patients who tested positive. Most important, it added the threat of law enforcement intervention that "provided the necessary 'leverage' to make the policy effective." [ ]. That threat was, as respondents candidly acknowledge, essential to the program's success in getting women into treatment and keeping them there.

The threat of law enforcement involvement was set forth in two protocols, the first dealing with the identification of drug use during pregnancy, and the second with identification of drug use after labor. Under the latter protocol, the police were to be notified without delay and the patient promptly arrested. Under the former, after the initial positive drug test, the police were to be notified (and the patient arrested) only if the patient tested positive for cocaine a second time or if she missed an appointment with a substance abuse counselor. In 1990, however, the policy was modified at the behest of the solicitor's office to

---

4. Section 20–7–490 is contained in the Children's Code and defines "child" as a "person under the age of eighteen" and also defines "abused or neglected child," and "harm."

give the patient who tested positive during labor, like the patient who tested positive during a prenatal care visit, an opportunity to avoid arrest by consenting to substance abuse treatment.

The last six pages of the policy contained forms for the patients to sign, as well as procedures for the police to follow when a patient was arrested. The policy also prescribed in detail the precise offenses with which a woman could be charged, depending on the stage of her pregnancy. If the pregnancy was 27 weeks or less, the patient was to be charged with simple possession. If it was 28 weeks or more, she was to be charged with possession and distribution to a person under the age of 18—in this case, the fetus. If she delivered "while testing positive for illegal drugs," she was also to be charged with unlawful neglect of a child. * * *

II

Petitioners are 10 women who received obstetrical care at MUSC and who were arrested after testing positive for cocaine. Four of them were arrested during the initial implementation of the policy; they were not offered the opportunity to receive drug treatment as an alternative to arrest. The others were arrested after the policy was modified in 1990; they either failed to comply with the terms of the drug treatment program or tested positive for a second time. Respondents include the city of Charleston, law enforcement officials who helped develop and enforce the policy, and representatives of MUSC.

Petitioners' complaint challenged the validity of the policy under various theories, including the claim that warrantless and nonconsensual drug tests conducted for criminal investigatory purposes were unconstitutional searches. Respondents advanced two principal defenses to the constitutional claim: (1) that, as a matter of fact, petitioners had consented to the searches; and (2) that, as a matter of law, the searches were reasonable, even absent consent, because they were justified by special non-law-enforcement purposes. The District Court rejected the second defense because the searches in question "were not done by the medical university for independent purposes. [Instead,] the police came in and there was an agreement reached that the positive screens would be shared with the police." [ ]. Accordingly, the District Court submitted the factual defense to the jury with instructions that required a verdict in favor of petitioners unless the jury found consent. The jury found for respondents.

Petitioners appealed, arguing that the evidence was not sufficient to support the jury's consent finding. The Court of Appeals for the Fourth Circuit affirmed, but without reaching the question of consent. [ ]. Disagreeing with the District Court, the majority of the appellate panel held that the searches were reasonable as a matter of law under our line of cases recognizing that "special needs" may, in certain exceptional circumstances, justify a search policy designed to serve non-law-enforcement ends. On the understanding "that MUSC personnel conducted the urine drug screens for medical purposes wholly independent of an intent to aid law enforcement efforts," id. at 477, the majority applied the balancing test used in *Treasury Employees* v. *Von Raab*, 489 U.S. 656, 103 L.Ed.2d 685, 109 S.Ct. 1384 (1989), and *Vernonia School Dist. 47J v. Acton*, 515 U.S. 646, 132 L.Ed.2d 564, 115 S.Ct. 2386 (1995), and concluded that the interest in curtailing the pregnancy complications and medical costs associated with maternal cocaine use outweighed what the majority termed a minimal intrusion on the privacy of the patients. In dissent, Judge Blake concluded that the "special needs" doctrine should not apply and that the evidence of consent was insufficient to sustain the jury's verdict.[ ]

We granted certiorari [ ], to review the appellate court's holding on the "special needs" issue. Because we do not reach the question of the sufficiency of the evidence with respect to consent, we necessarily assume for purposes of our decision—as did the Court of Appeals—that the searches were conducted without the informed consent of the patients. We conclude that the judgment should be reversed and the case remanded for a decision on the consent issue.

III

Because MUSC is a state hospital, the members of its staff are government actors, subject to the strictures of the Fourth Amendment. [ ]. Moreover, the urine tests conducted by those staff members were indisputably searches within the meaning of the Fourth Amendment. [ ] Neither the District Court nor the Court of Appeals concluded that any of the nine criteria used to identify the women to be searched provided either probable cause to believe that they were using cocaine, or even the basis for a reasonable suspicion of such use. Rather, the District Court and the Court of Appeals viewed the case as one involving MUSC's right to conduct searches without warrants or probable cause. Furthermore, given the posture in which the case comes to us, we must assume for purposes of our decision that the tests were performed without the informed consent of the patients.

Because the hospital seeks to justify its authority to conduct drug tests and to turn the results over to law enforcement agents without the knowledge or consent of the patients, this case differs from the four previous cases in which we have considered whether comparable drug tests "fit within the closely guarded category of constitutionally permissible suspicionless searches." *Chandler v. Miller*, 520 U.S. 305, 309, 137 L.Ed.2d 513, 117 S.Ct. 1295 (1997). In three of those cases, we sustained drug tests for railway employees involved in train accidents, *Skinner v. Railway Labor Executives' Assn.*, 489 U.S. 602, 103 L.Ed.2d 639, 109 S.Ct. 1402 (1989), for United States Customs Service employees seeking promotion to certain sensitive positions, *Treasury Employees v. Von Raab*, 489 U.S. 656, 103 L.Ed.2d 685, 109 S.Ct. 1384 (1989), and for high school students participating in interscholastic sports, *Vernonia School Dist. 47J v. Acton*, 515 U.S. 646, 132 L.Ed.2d 564, 115 S.Ct. 2386 (1995). In the fourth case, we struck down such testing for candidates for designated state offices as unreasonable. *Chandler v. Miller*, 520 U.S. 305, 137 L.Ed.2d 513, 117 S.Ct. 1295 (1997).

In each of those cases, we employed a balancing test that weighed the intrusion on the individual's interest in privacy against the "special needs" that supported the program. As an initial matter, we note that the invasion of privacy in this case is far more substantial than in those cases. In the previous four cases, there was no misunderstanding about the purpose of the test or the potential use of the test results, and there were protections against the dissemination of the results to third parties. The use of an adverse test result to disqualify one from eligibility for a particular benefit, such as a promotion or an opportunity to participate in an extracurricular activity, involves a less serious intrusion on privacy than the unauthorized dissemination of such results to third parties. The reasonable expectation of privacy enjoyed by the typical patient undergoing diagnostic tests in a hospital is that the results of those tests will not be shared with nonmedical personnel without her consent. * * *

The critical difference between those four drug-testing cases and this one, however, lies in the nature of the "special need" asserted as justification for the warrantless searches. In each of those earlier cases, the "special need" that was advanced as a justification for the absence of a warrant or individualized suspicion was one divorced from the State's general interest in law enforcement. This point was emphasized both in the majority opinions sustaining the programs in the first three cases as well as in the dissent in the *Chandler* case. In this case, however, the central and indispensable feature of the policy from its inception was the use of law enforcement to coerce the patients into substance abuse treatment. This fact distinguishes this case from circumstances in which physicians or psychologists, in the course of ordinary medical procedures aimed at helping the patient herself, come across information that under rules of law or ethics is subject to reporting requirements, which no one has challenged here. * * *

While the ultimate goal of the program may well have been to get the women in question into substance abuse treatment and off of drugs, the immediate objective of the searches was to generate evidence *for law enforcement purposes* in order to reach that goal. The threat of law enforcement may ultimately have been intended as a means to an end, but the direct and primary purpose of MUSC's policy was to ensure the use of those means. In our opinion, this distinction is critical. Because law enforcement involvement always serves some broader social purpose or objective, under respondents' view, virtually any nonconsensual suspicionless search could be immunized under the special needs doctrine by defining the search solely in terms of its ultimate, rather than immediate, purpose. Such an approach is inconsistent with the Fourth Amendment. Given the primary purpose of the Charleston program, which was to use the threat of arrest and prosecution in order to force women into treatment, and given the extensive involvement of law enforcement officials at every stage of the policy, this case simply does not fit within the closely guarded category of "special needs."

The fact that positive test results were turned over to the police does not merely provide a basis for distinguishing our prior cases applying the "special needs" balancing approach to the determination of drug use. It also provides an affirmative reason for enforcing the strictures of the Fourth Amendment. While state hospital employees, like other citizens, may have a duty to provide the police with evidence of criminal conduct that they inadvertently acquire in the course of routine treatment, when they undertake to obtain such evidence from their patients *for the specific purpose of incriminating those patients*, they have a special obligation to make sure that the patients are fully informed about their constitutional rights, as standards of knowing waiver require. [ ].

As respondents have repeatedly insisted, their motive was benign rather than punitive. Such a motive, however, cannot justify a departure from Fourth Amendment protections, given the pervasive involvement of law enforcement with the development and application of the MUSC policy. The stark and unique fact that characterizes this case is that Policy M–7 was designed to obtain evidence of criminal conduct by the tested patients that would be turned over to the police and that could be admissible in subsequent criminal prosecutions. While respondents are correct that drug abuse both was and is a serious problem, "the gravity of the threat alone cannot be dispositive of questions concerning what means law enforcement officers may employ to pursue a given purpose." *Indianapolis v. Edmond*, 531 U.S. at—(slip op., at 9–10). The Fourth Amendment's general prohibition against nonconsensual, warrantless, and suspicionless searches necessarily applies to such a policy. [ ].

Accordingly, the judgment of the Court of Appeals is reversed, and the case is remanded for further proceedings consistent with this opinion.

It is so ordered.

JUSTICE SCALIA, with whom THE CHIEF JUSTICE and JUSTICE THOMAS join as to Part II, dissenting.

There is always an unappealing aspect to the use of doctors and nurses, ministers of mercy, to obtain incriminating evidence against the supposed objects of their ministration—although here, it is correctly pointed out, the doctors and nurses were ministering not just to the mothers but also to the children whom their cooperation with the police was meant to protect. But whatever may be the correct social judgment concerning the desirability of what occurred here, that is not the issue in the present case. The Constitution does not resolve all difficult social questions, but leaves the vast majority of them to resolution by debate and the democratic process—which would produce a decision by the citizens of Charleston, through their elected representatives, to forbid or permit the police action at issue here. The question before us is a narrower one: whether, whatever the desirability of this police conduct, it violates the Fourth Amendment's prohibition of unreasonable searches and seizures. In my view, it plainly does not.

I

* * *

It is rudimentary Fourth Amendment law that a search which has been consented to is not unreasonable. There is no contention in the present case that the urine samples were extracted forcibly. The only conceivable bases for saying that they were obtained without consent are the contentions (1) that the consent was coerced by the patients' need for medical treatment, (2) that the consent was uninformed because the patients were not told that the tests would include testing for drugs, and (3) that the consent was uninformed because the patients were not told that the results of the tests would be provided to the police. * * *

* * *

Until today, we have *never* held—or even suggested—that material which a person voluntarily entrusts to someone else cannot be given by that person to the police, and used for whatever evidence it may contain. Without so much as discussing the point, the Court today opens a hole in our Fourth Amendment jurisprudence, the size and shape of which is entirely indeterminate. Today's holding would be remarkable enough if the confidential relationship violated by the police conduct were at least one protected by state law. It would be surprising to learn, for example, that in a State which recognizes a spousal evidentiary privilege the police cannot use evidence obtained from a cooperating husband or wife. But today's holding goes even beyond that, since there does not exist any physician-patient privilege in South Carolina. [ ]. Since the Court declines even to discuss the issue, it leaves law enforcement officials entirely in the dark as to when they can use incriminating evidence obtained from "trusted" sources. * * *

* * *

In sum, I think it clear that the Court's disposition requires the holding that violation of a relationship of trust constitutes a search. The opinion itself implies that in its description of the issue left for the Court of Appeals on remand [ ]: whether "the tests were performed without the *informed* consent of the patients," [ ] (emphasis added)—informed, that is, that the urine would be tested for drugs and that the results would be given to the police. I am happy, of course, to accept the Court's illogical assurance that it intends no such holding, and urge the Court of Appeals on remand to do the same.

STATE v. McKNIGHT

Supreme Court of South Carolina, 2003.
352 S.C. 635, 576 S.E.2d 168.

JUSTICE WALLER, J.

FACTS

On May 15, 1999, McKnight gave birth to a stillborn five-pound baby girl. The baby's gestational age was estimated to be between 34–37 weeks old. An autopsy revealed the presence of benzoylecgonine, a substance which is metabolized by cocaine. The pathologist, Dr. Proctor, testified that the only way for the infant to have the substance present was through cocaine, and that the cocaine had to have come from the mother.[1] Dr. Proctor testified that the baby died one to three days prior to delivery. Dr. Proctor determined the cause of death to be intrauterine fetal demise with mild chorioamnionitis, funisitis[2] and cocaine consumption. He ruled the death a homicide. McKnight was indicted for homicide by child abuse. * * * [T]he jury returned a guilty verdict. McKnight was sentenced to twenty years, suspended to service of twelve years.

ISSUES

1. Did the Court err in refusing to direct a verdict on the grounds that a) there was insufficient evidence of the cause of death, b) there was no evidence of criminal intent, and c) there was no evidence the baby was viable when McKnight ingested cocaine?

2. Did the Court err in refusing to dismiss the homicide by child abuse indictment on the grounds that a) the more specific criminal abortion statute governs, b) the statute does not apply to the facts of this case, and c) the legislature did not intend the statute to apply to fetuses?

3. Does application of the homicide by child abuse statute to McKnight violate her due process right of adequate notice?

4. Does application of the homicide by child abuse statute to McKnight violate her constitutional right to privacy?

5. Did the trial court err in refusing to dismiss the indictment on eighth amendment cruel and unusual punishment grounds?

6. Does application of the homicide by child abuse statute to McKnight violate equal protection?

7. Did the trial court err in refusing to exclude evidence of the results of a urine specimen taken from McKnight shortly after the stillbirth, on grounds that the specimen was obtained in violation of her fourth amendment rights?

* * *

a. Cause of Death

McKnight asserts the state failed to introduce sufficient evidence demonstrating that cocaine caused the stillbirth. We disagree.

Dr. Proctor, who performed the autopsy and who was qualified as an expert in criminal pathology, testified that the only way for the infant to have benzoylecgonine present was through cocaine, and that the cocaine

---

1. He testified that because of the rapid breakdown of pure cocaine, a baby would always have benzoylecgonine in its system, rather than pure cocaine.

2. He testified that chorioamnionitis and funisitis is the medical term given to

the placenta and umbilical cord when they are inflamed, which can be caused by an underlying infection, but that most children with these conditions have live births.

had to have come from the mother. Dr. Proctor determined the cause of death to be intrauterine fetal demise with mild chorioamnionitis, funisitis and cocaine consumption. Dr. Proctor ruled the death a homicide.

Another pathologist, Dr. Woodward, who was qualified as an expert in pediatric pathology testified that the gestational age of the infant was between 35–37 weeks, and that it was viable. He then described how one determines the cause of death of a viable fetus, by looking for abnormalities, placental defects, infections, and the chemical constituency of the child. He explained the effect that cocaine would have on both an adult and a child. He testified that the placenta was the major heart-lung machine while the baby was in utero and that cocaine usage can produce degeneration of the small blood vessels in the placenta. He stated that he found areas of pinkish red degeneration of the blood vessels which were consistent with cocaine exposure. He testified that he did not see any other indications of the cause of death, and found a lack of evidence of other infections, lack of other abnormalities, otherwise normal development of the child, it's size, weight, and lung development. Although Dr. Woodward agreed with Dr. Proctor that chorioamnionitis and mild funisitis were present, he testified that to a reasonable degree of medical certainty, those conditions had not caused the death of the infant. He also opined that neither syphilis, nor placental abruption killed the infant. He concluded that, to a reasonable degree of medical certainty, the cause of death was intrauterine cocaine exposure. Although Woodward could not say the exact mechanism by which the cocaine had killed the infant, he testified the "mechanisms through cardiac function, placental functions, are seen as most probable." On cross-exam, Woodward testified that he believed the death was caused solely by the cocaine effect, and that the drugs could have caused the baby's heart to stop, or to have caused the baby's heart to rise precipitously putting the baby in congestive heart failure. He explained the lack of abnormalities in the heart found by Dr. Proctor's autopsy, stating, "I wouldn't expect to see specific indices in the heart if the heart just stopped or if the heart went into congestive heart failure." Finally, Woodward testified he had seen both children and adults dead with less benzoylecgonine in their systems than McKnight's baby.

Although McKnight's expert, Dr. Conradi, would not testify that cocaine had caused the stillbirth, she did testify that cocaine had been in the baby at one point. She also ruled out the possibility of chorioamnionitis, funisitis or syphilis as the cause of death.

* * *

b. *Criminal Intent*

McKnight next asserts she was entitled to a directed verdict as the state failed to prove she had the requisite criminal intent to commit homicide by child abuse. We disagree.

Under S.C. Code Ann. § 16–3–85(A), a person is guilty of homicide by child abuse if the person "causes the death of a child under the age of eleven while committing child abuse or neglect, and the death occurs under circumstances manifesting an extreme indifference to human life." McKnight claims there is no evidence she acted with extreme indifference to human life as there was no evidence of how likely cocaine is to cause stillbirth, or that she knew the risk that her use of cocaine could result in the stillbirth of her child.

Recently, in State v. Jarrell, 350 S.C. 90, 97, 564 S.E.2d 362, 366 (Ct. App. 2002), the Court of Appeals defined "extreme indifference," as used in the homicide by child abuse statute, stating:

> In this state, indifference in the context of criminal statutes has been compared to the conscious act of disregarding a risk which a person's conduct has created, or a failure to exercise ordinary or due care. [ ]. At least one other jurisdiction with a similar statute has found that "[a] person acts 'under circumstances manifesting extreme indifference to the value of human life' when he engages in deliberate conduct which culminates in the death of some person." Davis v. State, 325 Ark. 96, 925 S.W.2d 768, 773 (1996). Therefore, we ... hold that in the context of homicide by abuse statutes, extreme indifference is a mental state akin to intent characterized by a deliberate act culminating in death.

Similarly, in reckless homicide cases, we have held that reckless disregard for the safety of others signifies an indifference to the consequences of one's acts. It denotes a conscious failure to exercise due care or ordinary care or a conscious indifference to the rights and safety of others or a reckless disregard thereof. [ ].

In Whitner v. State, 328 S.C. 1, 10, 492 S.E.2d 777, 782 (1997), cert. denied 523 U.S. 1145, 140 L.Ed.2d 1104, 118 S.Ct. 1857 (1998), this Court noted that "although the precise effects of maternal crack use during pregnancy are somewhat unclear, it is well documented and within the realm of public knowledge that such use can cause serious harm to the viable unborn child." Given this common knowledge, Whitner was on notice that her conduct in utilizing cocaine during pregnancy constituted child endangerment.[ ] Indeed, more than twelve years ago, Justice Toal wrote:

> The drug "cocaine" has torn at the very fabric of our nation. Families have been ripped apart, minds have been ruined, and lives have been lost. It is common knowledge that the drug is highly addictive and potentially fatal. The addictive nature of the drug, combined with its expense, has caused our prisons to swell with those who have been motivated to support their drug habit through criminal acts. In some areas of the world, entire governments have been undermined by the cocaine industry. [ ]

Here, it is undisputed that McKnight took cocaine on numerous occasions while she was pregnant, that the urine sample taken immediately after she gave birth had very high concentrations of cocaine, and that the baby had benzoylecgonine in its system. The DSS investigator who interviewed McKnight shortly after the birth testified that

McKnight admitted she knew she was pregnant and that she had been using cocaine when she could get it, primarily on weekends. Given the fact that it is public knowledge that usage of cocaine is potentially fatal, we find the fact that McKnight took cocaine knowing she was pregnant was sufficient evidence to submit to the jury on whether she acted with extreme indifference to her child's life. Accordingly, the trial court correctly refused a directed verdict. State v. Pinckney, supra (if the State presents any evidence which reasonably tends to prove defendant's guilt, or from which defendant's guilt could be fairly and logically deduced, case must go to the jury).

* * *

2. Dismissal of Homicide Indictment

McKnight next asserts the trial court erred in refusing to dismiss the homicide by child abuse indictment on the grounds that a) the more specific criminal abortion statute governs, b) the homicide by child abuse statute does not apply to the facts of this case, and c) the legislature did not intend the statute to apply to fetuses. We disagree.

a. Criminal Abortion Statute

Initially, McKnight asserts the criminal abortion statute [ ] is a more specific statute which controls under the circumstances of this case. McKnight did not raise this contention to the trial court. Contrary to the assertions in her reply brief, although McKnight did argue that the statute was inapplicable to the circumstances of this case, at no time did she assert that the criminal abortion statute was the more specific, controlling statute. Accordingly, this issue is unpreserved. State v. Hicks, supra (issue must be raised to and ruled upon by trial court to be preserved for review).

b. Application of Homicide by Abuse Statute in This Case

McKnight next asserts the Legislature did not intend the homicide by child abuse statute apply to the stillbirth of a fetus. We disagree.

McKnight asserts the term "child," as used in the statute, is most naturally read as including only children already born. [ ]. In several cases this Court has specifically held that the Legislature's use of the term "child" includes a viable fetus. [ ] McKnight cites to portions of the statute defining "harm" as relating to corporal punishment and/or abandonment; she asserts this demonstrates that the statute was clearly intended to apply only to children already born. However, [the statute] also defines "harm" as "inflicting or allowing to be inflicted on the child physical injury . . . " and "failing to supply the child with adequate health care . . . " Either of these provisions may clearly be applied to an unborn child. Accordingly, given the language of the statute, and this Court's prior opinions defining a child to include a viable fetus, we find the plain language of the statute does not preclude its application to the present case.

c. Legislative History

McKnight lastly asserts that the legislative history of section 16–3–85 conclusively demonstrates that it does not apply to unborn children. We find this contention unpersuasive.

Section 16–3–85 was amended by 2000 Acts No. 261, § 1. The prior statute read that a person is guilty of homicide by child abuse who "causes the death of a child under the age of eleven while committing child abuse or neglect as defined in Section 20–7–490, and the death occurs under circumstances manifesting an extreme indifference to human life." (Emphasis supplied). The effect of the 2000 amendment was the deletion of the reference to the definitions of "abuse" and "neglect" contained in section 20–7–490, and the addition of subsection (B), defining those terms as follows:

(1) "child abuse or neglect" means an act or omission by any person which causes harm to the child's physical health or welfare;

(2) "harm" to a child's health or welfare occurs when a person:

(a) inflicts or allows to be inflicted upon the child physical injury, including injuries sustained as a result of excessive corporal punishment;

(b) fails to supply the child with adequate food, clothing, shelter, or health care, and the failure to do so causes a physical injury or condition resulting in death; or

(c) abandons the child resulting in the child's death.

There is a presumption that the legislature has knowledge of previous legislation as well as of judicial decisions construing that legislation when later statutes are enacted concerning related subjects. [ ]. The homicide by child abuse statute was amended in May 2000, some three years after this Court, in Whitner, had specifically held that the term "child" includes a viable fetus. The fact that the legislature was well aware of this Court's opinion in Whitner, yet failed to omit "viable fetus" from the statute's applicability, is persuasive evidence that the legislature did not intend to exempt fetuses from the statute's operation. Contrary to McKnight's assertion, we do not find the legislature's decision to define the terms "abuse and neglect" within the confines of [the present statute], deleting the reference to section 20–7–490 of the Children's Code, in any way evinces a retraction from our opinion in Whitner. Although Whitner did examine the policy and purpose of the Children's Code, that discussion was not central to our holding. More fundamentally, Whitner found no basis upon which to grant a viable fetus the status of a "person" for purposes of homicide and wrongful death laws, while denying such status in the context of child abuse. Indeed, if the legislature had intended to remove a fetus from the operation of the statute, it could have plainly said so.

3. DUE PROCESS/NOTICE

McKnight next asserts application of the homicide by child abuse statute to her violates due process; she contends she had no notice the statute could be applied to a woman whose fetus is stillborn. We disagree.

In numerous cases dating since 1960, we have held that a viable fetus is a "person." [ ] In Whitner, supra, we reiterated the fact that a viable fetus is a "child" within the meaning of the child abuse and endangerment statute. Most recently, we held that a viable fetus is both "person" and "child" as used in statutory aggravating circumstances which provide for death penalty eligibility. [ ].

A penal statute offends due process only when it fails to give fair notice of the conduct it proscribes. [ ] The statute must give sufficient notice to enable a reasonable person to comprehend what is prohibited. [ ]. In Whitner, we rejected the claim that application of the child endangerment and neglect statute did not give the defendant fair notice of the conduct proscribed, stating:

The statute forbids any person having legal custody of a child from refusing or neglecting to provide proper care and attention to the child so that the life, health, or comfort of the child is endangered or is likely to be endangered. As we have found above, the plain meaning of "child" as used in this statute includes a viable fetus. Furthermore, it is common knowledge that use of cocaine during pregnancy can harm the viable unborn child. Given these facts, we do not see how Whitner can claim she lacked fair notice that her behavior constituted child endangerment as proscribed in section 20–7–50. Whitner had all the notice the Constitution requires.

Similarly, a person is guilty of homicide by child abuse if the person causes the death of a child under the age of eleven while committing child abuse or neglect, and the death occurs under circumstances manifesting an extreme indifference to human life. Under Whitner, taking cocaine while pregnant constitutes neglect and, as discussed in Issue 1 above, it was a jury question whether McKnight acted with "extreme indifference to human life." Given the ample authority in this state finding a viable fetus to be a person, we find McKnight was on notice that her conduct in ingesting cocaine would be proscribed.

4.   RIGHT TO PRIVACY

McKnight next asserts application of the homicide by child abuse statute to women for conduct during pregnancy violates the constitutional rights of privacy and autonomy.

McKnight asserts several policy reasons why women should not be placed in the position of fearing prosecution for conduct engaged in while pregnant (e.g., choosing abortion over pregnancy, foregoing medical care, etc.). While she raises a number of legitimate concerns, she is in reality attempting to assert the privacy rights of other pregnant women, something she does not have standing to do. Curtis v. State, supra (one cannot obtain a decision as to the invalidity of an act on the ground that it impairs the rights of others).

As to her own right to privacy, this Court specifically rejected the claim that prosecution for abuse and neglect of a viable fetus due to the mother's ingestion of cocaine violates any fundamental right. Whitner, supra. In Whitner we stated,

It strains belief for Whitner to argue that using crack cocaine during pregnancy is encompassed within the constitutionally recognized right of privacy. Use of crack cocaine is illegal, period. No one here argues that laws criminalizing the use of crack cocaine are themselves unconstitutional. If the State wishes to impose additional criminal penalties on pregnant women who engage in this already illegal conduct because of the effect the conduct has on the viable fetus, it may do so. We do not see how the fact of pregnancy elevates the use of crack cocaine to the lofty status of a fundamental right.

Accordingly, we find McKnight's right of privacy was not violated.

5.   EIGHTH AMENDMENT

McKnight next asserts the trial court erred in refusing to dismiss the indictment on Eighth Amendment grounds. We disagree.

The cruel and unusual punishment clause requires the duration of a sentence not be grossly out of proportion with the severity of the crime. [T]his Court reviews three factors in assessing proportionality: (1) the gravity of the offense compared to the harshness of the penalty; (2) sentences imposed on other criminals in the same jurisdiction; and (3) sentences for the same crime in other jurisdictions. [ ]

Here, the gravity of the offense is severe; McKnight is charged with homicide. The sentence for homicide by child abuse [ ] is twenty years to life, and McKnight received a twenty year sentence, suspended upon service of twelve years. The penalty is no harsher than that imposed upon any other individual charged with murder. [ ]

Finally, although other states have not defined a viable fetus as a child for purposes of criminal prosecution of a pregnant mother, other states impose severe sentences on those who are guilty of the murder or neglect of a child. [ ] We find no Eighth Amendment violation.

* * *

McKnight's conviction and sentence are affirmed.

AFFIRMED.

JUSTICE MOORE: I respectfully dissent. Once again, I must part company with the majority for condoning the prosecution of a pregnant woman under a statute that could not have been intended for such a purpose. Our abortion statute [ ] carries a maximum punishment of two years or a $1,000 fine for the intentional killing of a viable fetus by its mother. In penalizing this conduct, the legislature recognized the unique situation of a feticide by the mother. I do not believe the legislature intended to allow the prosecution of a pregnant woman for homicide by child abuse [ ] which provides a disproportionately greater punishment of twenty years to life.

As expressed in my dissent in Whitner v. State [ ] it is for the legislature to determine whether to penalize a pregnant woman's abuse of her own body because of the potential harm to her fetus. It is not the business of this Court to expand the application of a criminal statute to conduct not clearly within its ambit. To the contrary, we are constrained to strictly construe a penal statutes in the defendant's favor. [ ]

Notes

1) Informational privacy is a recurring theme in cases challenging public health regulations. In *Whalen v. Roe*, the issue was whether a state can maintain computerized records (prior to the "computer age" as well as HIPAA) on patients who obtain certain kinds of prescription drugs that are prone to addiction and abuse—when there exists a lawful as well as unlawful market. New York's purpose was primarily one of surveillance to ferret out individuals who obtain multiple prescriptions for the same product. In some cases it was unscrupulous pharmacists who would fill the same prescription multiple times. In holding that the regulation did not unduly infringe on patients' privacy rights the Court specifically declined to address what it might do if there were evidence of "unwarranted disclosure of accumulated private data whether intentional or unintentional" or if there were evidence of security breaches. Would the Court's ruling be different in the 21st century?

2) In *Vernonia School District 47J v. Action*, the Supreme Court held that the suspicionless drug testing of athletes was constitutional. It did not authorize all school drug testing, but instead "conducted a fact-specific balancing of the intrusion on the children's Fourth Amendment rights against the promotion of legitimate governmental interests." As in *Vernonia*, the *Earls* Court declined to comment on the wisdom of drug testing in schools, but only on its constitutionality. Will drug-testing accomplish its intended goal, or will it more likely deter students from participating in extra-curricular activities? Will students who would test negative also be deterred?

3) In *Skinner v. Railway Labor Executives Association* (Section A, *supra*) the Supreme Court articulated a "special needs" doctrine that allows law enforcement to impose departures from usual law enforcement principles when the "special needs of the situation" so dictate. The "special needs" doctrine was considered in *Ferguson v. City of Charleston* where the issue concerned the drug testing of pregnant women. Do you think this was the kind of situation that *Skinner* contemplated as a "special need" of law enforcement?

4) What is the role of a physician who learns or suspects that his pregnant patient is ingesting legal or illegal substances that will have a profound effect on a developing fetus? *McKnight* raises the issue of whether the application of a homicide statute to drug-abusing pregnant women will increase or decrease physicians' willingness to intervene on

behalf of an at-risk fetus. How do you think the South Carolina law will affect pregnant women's willingness to seek medical treatment, or even give birth in a hospital?

Chapter 13

INFECTIOUS DISEASE: PREVENTION AND DETENTION

INTRODUCTORY NOTE

When we think of the protection of individual rights, usually the "protection" required is the rights of the individual as to excessive regulation by the government. Concepts of liberty and privacy and freedom can only be circumscribed by important governmental interests.

In matters of infectious disease, freedom of the individual may mean exposure of other individuals to airborne pathogens and other contagious agents. Public health officials are more likely to view their primary purpose as safeguarding the health of the public, and assume enough flexibility in their authority to accomplish broad-based ends. When the level of constitutional scrutiny employs the "rational relationship" standard, it is difficult to challenge the conclusion that the means used bear a rational relationship to legitimate public health ends.

In part the debate depends upon whether the lawmakers and agency officials formulate public health policy using democratic principles and whether complex policy choices are made only after legitimate scientific inquiry has been made and reviewed. Courts give great deference and wide latitude to legislative agencies to formulate and shape public health policy. If the public is unhappy with the way they carry out their functions, it can register its protests at election time. Meanwhile, the courts are available to hear constitutional challenges and to ensure that public health officials do not overstep their wide bounds.

Jacobson v. Massachusetts is probably the first and, for all intents and purposes, seminal case in public health jurisprudence. It continues to be cited over and over again, for many of the principles enunciated in 1905 remain sound and applicable today.

SECTION A. VACCINATIONS

JACOBSON v. MASSACHUSETTS

Supreme Court of the United States, 1905.
197 U.S. 11, 25 S.Ct. 358, 49 L.Ed. 643.

MR. JUSTICE HARLAN, after making the foregoing statement, delivered the opinion of the court.

[Massachusetts law requires that all individuals be vaccinated against smallpox. Jacobson refused to be vaccinated. Pursuant to Massachusetts law and the regulations of the Board of Health, Jacobson was prosecuted and found guilty. He appealed to the Massachusetts Supreme Judicial Court where his conviction was upheld. Upon further appeal of the United States Supreme Court, Jacobson argued that Massachusetts law requiring compulsory vaccination violated the Preamble to the U.S. Constitution and, as such, would defeat the purposes thereof in derogation of the Preamble.]

The Supreme Judicial Court of Massachusetts said in the present case: "Let us consider the offer of evidence which was made by the defendant Jacobson. * * * Assuming that medical experts could have been found who would have testified in support of [Jacobson's] propositions, and that it had become the duty of the judge, in accordance with the law * * * to instruct the jury as to whether or not the statute is constitutional, he would have been obliged to consider the * * * testimony of experts in connection with the facts that for nearly a century most of the members of the medical profession have regarded vaccination, repeated after intervals, as a preventive of smallpox; that while they have recognized the possibility of injury to an individual from carelessness in the performance of it, or even in a conceivable case without carelessness, they generally have considered the risk of such an injury too small to be seriously weighed as against the benefits coming from the discreet and proper use of the preventive; and that not only the medical profession and the people generally have for a long time entertained these opinions, but legislatures and courts have acted upon them with general unanimity. If the defendant had been permitted to introduce such expert testimony as he had in support of these several propositions, it could not have changed the result. It would not have justified the court in holding that the legislature had transcended its power in enacting this statute on their judgment of what the welfare of the people demands." *Commonwealth* v. *Jacobson*, 183 Massachusetts, 242.

* * *

The authority of the State to enact this statute is to be referred to what is commonly called the police power—a power which the State did not surrender when becoming a member of the Union under the Constitution. Although this court has refrained from any attempt to define the limits of that power, yet it has distinctly recognized the authority of a State to enact quarantine laws and "health laws of every description;"

indeed, all laws that relate to matters completely within its territory and which do not by their necessary operation affect the people of other States. According to settled principles the police power of a State must be held to embrace, at least, such reasonable regulations established directly by legislative enactment as will protect the public health and the public safety.[ ]. It is equally true that the State may invest local bodies called into existence for purposes of local administration with authority in some appropriate way to safeguard the public health and the public safety. The mode or manner in which those results are to be accomplished is within the discretion of the State, subject, of course, so far as Federal power is concerned, only to the condition that no rule prescribed by a State, nor any regulation adopted by a local governmental agency acting under the sanction of state legislation, shall contravene the Constitution of the United States or infringe any right granted or secured by that instrument. A local enactment or regulation, even if based on the acknowledged police power of a State, must always yield in case of conflict with the exercise by the General Government of any power it possesses under the Constitution, or with any right which that instrument gives or secures. [ ].

We come, then, to inquire whether any right given, or secured by the Constitution, is invaded by the statute as interpreted by the state court. The defendant insists that his liberty is invaded when the State subjects him to fine or imprisonment for neglecting or refusing to submit to vaccination; that a compulsory vaccination law is unreasonable, arbitrary and oppressive, and, therefore, hostile to the inherent right of every freeman to care for his own body and health in such way as to him seems best; and that the execution of such a law against one who objects to vaccination, no matter for what reason, is nothing short of an assault upon his person. But the liberty secured by the Constitution of the United States to every person within its jurisdiction does not import an absolute right in each person to be, at all times and in all circumstances, wholly freed from restraint. There are manifold restraints to which every person is necessarily subject for the common good. On any other basis organized society could not exist with safety to its members. Society based on the rule that each one is a law unto himself would soon be confronted with disorder and anarchy. Real liberty for all could not exist under the operation of a principle which recognizes the right of each individual person to use his own, whether in respect of his person or his property, regardless of the injury that may be done to others. This court has more than once recognized it as a fundamental principle that "persons and property are subjected to all kinds of restraints and burdens, in order to secure the general comfort, health, and prosperity of the State; of the perfect right of the legislature to do which no question ever was, or upon acknowledged general principles ever can be made, so far as natural persons are concerned." *Railroad Co.* v. *Husen*, 95 U.S. 465, 471 [additional citations omitted]. In *Crowley* v. *Christensen*, 137 U.S. 86, 89, we said: "The possession and enjoyment of all rights are subject to such reasonable conditions as may be deemed by the governing authority of the country essential to the safety, health, peace, good order and morals of the community. Even liberty itself, the greatest of all rights, is not unrestricted license to act according to one's own will. It is only freedom from restraint under conditions essential to the equal enjoyment of the same right by others. It is then liberty regulated by law." In the constitution of Massachusetts adopted in 1780 it was laid down as a fundamental principle of the social compact that the whole people covenants with each citizen, and each citizen with the whole people, that all shall be governed by certain laws for "the common good," and that government is instituted "for the common good, for the protection, safety, prosperity and happiness of the people, and not for the profit, honor or private interests of any one man, family or class of men." The good and welfare of the Commonwealth, of which the legislature is primarily the judge, is the basis on which the police power rests in Massachusetts. *Commonwealth v. Alger*, 7 Cush. 53, 84.

Applying these principles to the present case, it is to be observed that the legislature of Massachusetts required the inhabitants of a city or town to be vaccinated only when, in the opinion of the Board of Health, that was necessary for the public health or the public safety. The authority to determine for all what ought to be done in such an emergency must have been lodged somewhere or in some body; and surely it was appropriate for the legislature to refer that question, in the first instance, to a Board of Health, composed of persons residing in the locality affected and appointed, presumably, because of their fitness to determine such questions. To invest such a body with authority over such matters was not an unusual nor an unreasonable or arbitrary requirement. Upon the principle of self-defense, of paramount necessity, a community has the right to protect itself against an epidemic of disease which threatens the safety of its members. It is to be observed that when the regulation in question was adopted, smallpox, according to the recitals in the regulation adopted by the Board of Health, was prevalent to some extent in the city of Cambridge and the disease was increasing. If such was the situation—and nothing is asserted or appears in the record to the contrary—if we are to attach any value whatever to the knowledge which, it is safe to affirm, is common to all civilized peoples touching smallpox and the methods most usually employed to eradicate that disease, it cannot be adjudged that the present regulation of the Board of Health was not necessary in order to protect the public health and secure the public safety. Smallpox being prevalent and increasing at Cambridge, the court would usurp the functions of another branch of government if it adjudged, as matter of law, that the mode adopted under the sanction of the State, to protect the people at large, was arbitrary and not justified by the necessities of the case. We say necessities of the case, because it might be that an acknowledged power of a local community to protect itself against an epidemic threatening the safety of all, might be exercised in particular circumstances and in reference to particular persons in such an arbitrary, unreasonable manner, or might go so far beyond what was reasonably required for the safety of the public, as to authorize or compel the courts to interfere for the protection of such persons. [citations omitted]. In *Railroad Company* v. *Husen*, 95 U.S. 465, 471–473, this court recognized the right of a State to pass sanitary laws, laws for the protection of life, liberty, health or property within its limits, laws to prevent persons and animals suffering under contagious or infectious diseases, or convicts, from coming within its borders. But as the laws there involved when beyond the necessity of the case and under the guise of exerting a police power invaded the domain of Federal authority and violated rights secured by the Constitution, this court deemed it to be its duty to hold such laws invalid. If the mode adopted by the Commonwealth of Massachusetts for the protection of its local communities against smallpox proved to be distressing, inconvenient or objectionable to some—if nothing more could be reasonably affirmed of the statute in question—the answer is that it was the duty of the constituted authorities primarily to keep in view the welfare, comfort and safety of the many, and not permit the interests of the many to be subordinated to the wishes or convenience of the few. There is, of course, a sphere within which the individual may assert the supremacy of his own will and rightfully dispute the authority of any human government, especially of any free government existing under a written constitution, to interfere with the exercise of that will. But it is equally true that in every well-ordered society charged with the duty of conserving the safety of its members the rights of the individual in respect of his liberty may at times, under the pressure of great dangers, be subjected to such restraint, to be enforced by reasonable regulations, as the safety of the general public may demand. An American citizen, arriving at an American port on a vessel in which, during the voyage, there had been cases of yellow fever or Asiatic cholera, although apparently free from disease himself, may yet, in some circumstances, be held in quarantine against his will on board of such vessel or in a quarantine station, until it be ascertained by inspection, conducted with due diligence, that the danger of the spread of the disease among the community at large has disappeared. The liberty secured by the Fourteenth Amendment, this court has said, consists, in part, in the right of a person "to live and work where he will," *Allgeyer* v. *Louisiana*, 165 U.S. 578; and yet he may be compelled, by force if need be, against his will and without regard to his personal wishes or his pecuniary interests, or even his religious or political convictions, to take his place in the ranks of the army of his country and risk the chance of being shot down in its defense. It is not, therefore, true that the power of the public to guard itself against imminent danger depends in every case involving the control of one's body upon his willingness to submit to reasonable regulations established by the constituted authorities, under the sanction of the State, for the purpose of protecting the public collectively against such danger.

It is said, however, that the statute, as interpreted by the state court, although making an exception in favor of children certified by a registered physician to be unfit subjects for vaccination, makes no exception in the case of adults in like condition. But this cannot be deemed a denial of the equal protection of the laws to adults; for the statute is applicable equally to all in like condition and there are obviously reasons why regulations may be appropriate for adults which could not be safely applied to persons of tender years.

* * *

Whatever may be thought of the expediency of this statute, it cannot be affirmed to be, beyond question, in palpable conflict with the Constitution. Nor, in view of the methods employed to stamp out the disease of smallpox, can anyone confidently assert that the means prescribed by the State to that end has no real or substantial relation to the protection of the public health and the public safety. Such an assertion would not be consistent with the experience of this and other countries whose authorities have dealt with the disease of smallpox. And the principle of vaccination as a means to prevent the spread of smallpox has been enforced in many States by statutes making the vaccination of children a condition of their right to enter or remain in public schools. [ ]

* * *

The defendant offered to prove that vaccination "quite often" caused serious and permanent injury to the health of the person vaccinated; that the operation "occasionally" resulted in death; that it was "impossible" to tell "in any particular case" what the results of vaccination would be or whether it would injure the health or result in death; that "quite often" one's blood is in a certain condition of impurity when it is not prudent or safe to vaccinate him; that there is no practical test by which to determine "with any degree of certainty" whether one's blood is in such condition of impurity as to render vaccination necessarily unsafe or dangerous; that vaccine matter is "quite often" impure and dangerous to be used, but whether impure or not cannot be ascertained by any known practical test; that the defendant refused to submit to vaccination for the reason that he had, "when a child," been caused great and extreme suffering for a long period by a disease produced by vaccination; and that he had witnessed a similar result of vaccination not only in the case of his son, but in the case of others.

These offers, in effect, invited the court and jury to go over the whole ground gone over by the legislature when it enacted the statute in question. The legislature assumed that some children, by reason of their condition at the time, might not be fit subjects of vaccination; and it is suggested—and we will not say without reason—that such is the case with some adults. But the defendant did not offer to prove that, by reason of his then condition, he was in fact not a fit subject of vaccination at the time he was informed of the requirement of the regulation adopted by the Board of Health. It is entirely consistent with his offer of proof that, after reaching full age he had become, so far as medical skill could discover, and when informed of the regulation of the Board of Health was, a fit subject of vaccination, and that the vaccine matter to be used in his case was such as any medical practitioner of good standing would regard as proper to be used. The matured opinions of medical men everywhere, and the experience of mankind, as all must know, negative the suggestion that it is not possible in any case to determine whether vaccination is safe. Was defendant exempted from the operation of the statute simply because of this dread of the same evil results experienced by him when a child and had observed in the cases of his son and other children? Could he reasonably claim such an exemption because "quite often" or "occasionally" injury had resulted from vaccination, or because it was impossible, in the opinion of some, by any practical test, to determine with absolute certainty whether a particular person could be safely vaccinated?

It seems to the court that an affirmative answer to these questions would practically strip the legislative department of its function to care for the public health and the public safety when endangered by epidemics of disease. Such an answer would mean that compulsory vaccination could not, in any conceivable case, be legally enforced in a community, even at the command of the legislature, however widespread the epidemic of smallpox, and however deep and universal was the belief of the community and of its medical advisers, that a system of general vaccination was vital to the safety of all.

We are not prepared to hold that a minority, residing or remaining in any city or town where smallpox is prevalent, and enjoying the general protection afforded by an organized local government, may thus defy the will of its constituted authorities, acting in good faith for all, under the legislative sanction of the State. * * *

* * *

We now decide only that the statute covers the present case, and that nothing clearly appears that would justify this court in holding it to be unconstitutional and inoperative in its application to the plaintiff in error.

The judgment of the court below must be affirmed.

It is so ordered.

MR. JUSTICE BREWER and MR. JUSTICE PECKHAM dissent.

BROWN v. STONE

Supreme Court of Mississippi, 1979.
378 So.2d 218.

SMITH, J.

This is an appeal by Charles H. Brown, father and next friend of Chad Allan Brown, a six year old boy * * * [seeking] to compel the Board of Trustees of the Houston Municipal Separate School District to admit his son as a student without compliance with the immunization requirements of Mississippi [law].

* * *

The bill recited (a) that six-year old Chad Allan Brown was of sufficient age and residence to qualify for admission to the first grade of the Houston Elementary School, but had not been vaccinated against those diseases specified under [the law], (b) Charles H. Brown, the father, has not permitted his son to be vaccinated because of "strong and sincere religious beliefs actively practiced and followed" by Charles H. Brown, (c) Charles H. Brown is a member of the Church of Christ, a religious body which does not teach against the use of medicines, immunizations or vaccinations prescribed by a physician, (d) Charles H. Brown has sought a religious exemption from vaccination (of his son) but it was denied because the certificate did not comply with [Mississippi law], (e) Charles H. Brown was denied admission to the school because of the failure to be immunized under the provisions of [the law] [which] are invalid "insofar as they force complainants to join a religious organization in order to practice their religious tenants (sic) freely," and the denial of admission of Chad Allan Brown violates complainants' rights protected by the First Amendment to the United States Constitution.

* * *

Appellants concede that mandatory immunization against dangerous diseases, without exemptions based on religious beliefs or convictions, has been held constitutionally valid as a reasonable exercise of police power. *Jacobson v. Commonwealth of Massachusetts*, 197 U.S. 11, 25 S.Ct. 358, 49 L.Ed. 643 (1905); *Zucht v. King*, 260 U.S. 174, 43 S.Ct. 24, 67 L.Ed. 194 (1922). They contend, however, that the provision for religious exemption violates the First Amendment of the United States Constitution protecting the free exercise of religion.

* * *

The fundamental and paramount purpose of the Mississippi Legislature in the enactment of [the Mississippi law] was to afford protection for school children against crippling and deadly diseases by immunization. That this can be done effectively and safely has been incontrovertibly demonstrated over a period of a good many years and is a matter of common knowledge of which this Court takes judicial notice.

If the religious exemption from immunization is to be granted only to members of certain recognized sects or denominations whose doctrines forbid it, and, as contended by appellants, to individuals whose private or personal religious beliefs will not allow them to permit immunization of their children, to this extent the highly desirable and paramount public purpose of the Act, that is, the protection of school children generally comprising the school community, is defeated.

Is it mandated by the First Amendment to the United States Constitution that innocent children, too young to decide for themselves, are to be denied the protection against crippling and death that immunization provides because of a religious belief adhered to by a parent or parents?

In *Wisconsin v. Yoder*, 406 U.S. 205, 92 S.Ct. 1526, 32 L.Ed.2d 15 (1972), the Court dealt with a mandatory school attendance requirement under a Wisconsin statute. Members of the Amish faith refused to comply and were convicted. When the case reached the Wisconsin Supreme Court the convictions were reversed. On certiorari to the United States Supreme Court the action of the Wisconsin Supreme Court was affirmed on the ground that the state's interest in compulsory education was not so compelling that the tenets of the Amish faith should be required to give way.

* * *

The case of *Cude v. State*, 237 Ark. 927, 377 S.W.2d 816 (1964) involved a question closely analogous with that under consideration here. The parents of three school age children refused to permit vaccination of their children as required by statute for school attendance, contending that it was contrary to their religion to do so. Persistent violation of the school attendance law resulted in the conviction of the father. When fined for this breach he continued to refuse to have the children vaccinated so that they could attend school as mandated by statute. The children were placed in custody of the Child Welfare Division and the issue reached the Arkansas Supreme Court. For the purposes of the appeal, the Arkansas Supreme Court assumed that the Cudes held a claimed religious belief in "good faith." In disposing of the case the Court said:

The U.S. Supreme Court said in *Prince v. Commonwealth of Massachusetts*, 321 U.S. 158, 64 S.Ct. 438, 88 L.Ed. 645: "The right to practice religion freely does not include liberty to expose the community or the child to communicable disease or the latter to ill health or death. * * * Parents may be free to become martyrs themselves. But it does not follow they are free, in identical circumstances, to make martyrs of their children before they have reached the age of full and legal discretion when they can make that choice for themselves."

It is a matter of common knowledge that prior to the development of protection against smallpox by vaccination, the disease, on occasion, ran rampant and caused great suffering and sickness throughout the world. According to the great weight of authority, it is within the police power of the State to require that school children be vaccinated against smallpox, and that such requirement does not violate the constitutional rights of anyone, on religious grounds or otherwise. In fact, this principle is so firmly settled that no extensive discussion is required.

* * *

In cases too numerous to mention, it has been held, in effect, that a person's right to exhibit religious freedom ceases where it overlaps and transgresses the rights of others.

* * *

After a thoughtful consideration of the facts and the arguments advanced by appellants, we have concluded that the statute in question, requiring immunization against certain crippling and deadly diseases particularly dangerous to children before they may be admitted to school, serves an overriding and compelling public interest, and that such interest extends to the exclusion of a child until such immunization has been effected, not only as a protection of that child but as a protection of the large number of other children comprising the school community and with whom he will be daily in close contact in the school room. The relationship of parent and child is one in which the law concerns itself more with parental duties than with parental rights. The relationship carries with it a duty resting upon the parent to provide the child with food, clothing and shelter and to protect the child from preventable exposure to danger, disease and immorality. It must not be forgotten that a child is indeed himself an individual, although under certain disabilities until majority, with rights in his own person which must be respected and may be enforced. Where its safety, morals and health are involved, it becomes a legitimate concern of the state.

The protection of the great body of school children attending the public schools in Mississippi against the horrors of crippling and death resulting from poliomyelitis or smallpox or from one of the other diseases against which means of immunization are known and have long been practiced successfully, demand that children who have not been immunized should be excluded from the school community until immunization has been accomplished. That is the obvious overriding and compelling public purpose of [the law]. To the extent that it may conflict with the religious beliefs of a parent, however sincerely entertained, the interests of the school children must prevail. [The law] is a reasonable and constitutional exercise of the police power of the state insofar as it provides for the immunization of children before they are to be permitted to enter school.

The exception, which would provide for the exemption of children of parents whose religious beliefs conflict with the immunization requirements, would discriminate against the great majority of children whose parents have no such religious convictions. To give it effect would result in a violation of the Fourteenth Amendment to the United States Constitution which provides that no state shall make any law denying to any person within its jurisdiction the equal protection of the laws, in that it would require the great body of school children to be vaccinated and at the same time expose them to the hazard of associating in school with children exempted under the religious exemption who had not been immunized as required by the statute.

* * *

We have no difficulty here in deciding that the statute is "complete in itself" without the provision for religious exemption and that it serves a compelling state interest in the protection of school children. Therefore, we hold that the provision providing an exception from the operation of the statute because of religious belief is in violation of the Fourteenth Amendment to the United States Constitution and therefore is void. As the United States Supreme Court said in *In Re Gault*, 387 U.S. 1, 13, 87 S.Ct. 1428, 1436, 18 L.Ed.2d 527 (1967): "Whatever may be their precise impact, neither the Fourteenth Amendment nor the Bill of Rights is for adults alone."

We find that all of the other provisions of the statute are valid and constitutional and embody a reasonable exercise of the police power of the state.

The decree appealed from will, therefore, be affirmed.

LePAGE v. STATE

Supreme Court of Wyoming, 2001.
2001 WY 26, 18 P.3d 1177.

KITE, Justice.

This case raises the fundamental question of whether the language of Wyo. Stat. Ann. § 21–4–309(a) mandates the issuance of an exemption from immunization for schoolchildren upon a written religious objection or whether it permits an inquiry by the Department of Health into the sincerity of the religious beliefs of an applicant. We hold that the Department of Health exceeded its statutory authority by applying the statute inconsistently with its clear and unambiguous language. Our holding is based on the premise that the language of § 21–4–309(a) is mandatory.

ISSUES

Appellant Susan LePage presents the following issue:

> Did the Wyoming Department of Health act arbitrarily and capriciously or otherwise abuse its discretion and legal authority in denying the claimed religious exemption of Appellant?

Appellee State of Wyoming, Department of Health phrases the issues as follows:

> I. Was the Department of Health's final decision to deny the Appellant's request for a religious exemption in accordance with the law?

> II. Was the Department of Health's denial of Appellant's request for a religious exemption constitutional and supported by substantial evidence?

FACTS

On March 25, 1999, Mrs. LePage requested a religious exemption from the hepatitis B vaccination pursuant to § 21–4–309(a) on behalf of her daughter. Mrs. LePage outlined her concerns regarding the hepatitis B vaccination in a four-page letter.[1] The State Health Officer for the

---

1. Mrs. LePage's initial letter began: | We, the parents of ... , are petitioning for religious exemption of the Hepatitis B vaccine. Because of the strong religious

Department of Health delayed a decision pending receipt of further information to assure that faith served as the basis for the request. In particular, the State Health Officer asked Mrs. LePage to define her beliefs as being religious-based and to explain how she acted upon her faith in a consistent manner. Mrs. LePage responded with a second letter, which restated her concerns. On June 10, 1999, Mrs. LePage's request for exemption was denied, and she was informed that, if her daughter was not immunized, she would be unable to attend school.

Mrs. LePage requested a hearing, and the matter was referred to the Office of Administrative Hearings (OAH). A hearing was held on August 5, 1999, at which time Mrs. LePage stated she had recently concluded that all vaccines were not "God's will for our lives." The OAH rendered its decision and determined that Mrs. LePage had failed to provide evidence to justify the religious exemption. The Department of Health issued an amended final decision on September 28, 1999, which specifically found that Mrs. LePage's objection was based on personal, moral, or philosophical beliefs rather than on a principle of religion or a truly held religious conviction. * * *

* * *

DISCUSSION

The United States Supreme Court held in *Jacobson v. Massachusetts*, 197 U.S. 11, 24–25, 25 S.Ct. 358, 49 L.Ed. 643 (1905), that a state has the authority to enact a mandatory immunization program through the exercise of its police power. Moreover, [Wyoming law] grants the Department of Health the power to prescribe rules and regulations for the management and control of communicable diseases.

The question presented in this case requires us to interpret the language of [the statute], which provides for mandatory immunization of Wyoming schoolchildren. That statute provides in pertinent part:

(a) Any person attending, full or part time, any public or private school, kindergarten through twelfth grade, shall within thirty (30) days after the date of school entry, provide to the appropriate school official written documentary proof of immunization.... *Waivers shall be authorized by the state or county health officer upon submission of written evidence of religious objection* or medical contraindication to the administration of any vaccine.

Section 21–4–309(a) (emphasis added). Mrs. LePage asserts the clear language of the exemption statute confirms that the issuance of a religious exemption is not a discretionary function but is a ministerial duty on the part of the Department of Health. Therefore, the Department of Health exceeded its authority by requiring more than an initial

---

beliefs of our family, we do not believe our daughter will engage in behavior that involve[s] exposure to blood or body fluids. We believe that the instituting of mandatory Hepatitis B vaccines is the direct result of our children growing up in a declining moral culture.

written objection which by statute appears to be sufficient to obtain a waiver.

Conversely, the Department of Health argues that Wyoming's immunization waiver allows only for *religious* objections as opposed to personal or philosophical objections. Therefore, the Department of Health must review the asserted objection and determine whether it is based on sincerely held religious beliefs. The Department of Health determined that Mrs. LePage's religious waiver request was based on concerns regarding the health and safety risks of the vaccination as well as the mode of transmission of the hepatitis B virus. According to the Department of Health, Mrs. LePage failed to establish that the requested waiver was based on sincerely held religious beliefs which would entitle her to a waiver.

* * *

The choice of the word "shall" intimates an absence of discretion by the Department of Health and is sufficiently definitive of the mandatory rule intended by the legislature. Similarly, the statutory language lacks any mention of an inquiry by the state into the sincerity of religious beliefs. As a result, the Department of Health exceeded its legislative authority when it conducted a further inquiry into the sincerity of Mrs. LePage's religious beliefs.

When reviewing an administrative agency's decision, this court will consider whether the agency exceeded its statutory authority. [ ]. As a creature of the legislature, an administrative agency has only the powers granted to it by statute * * *. A statute will be strictly construed when determining the authority granted to an agency. * * * [R]easonable doubt of the existence of a power must be resolved against the exercise thereof. * * *. The statute provides mandatory language, and the Department of Health may not circumvent the legislature's clear limitation of its powers or expand its power beyond its statutory authority. There is no justification found within the statute for the Department of Health to institute a religious inquiry. As a result, the decision to do so is not in accordance with the law.

Furthermore, construing the statute as the Department of Health suggests raises questions concerning the extent to which the government should be involved in the religious lives of its citizens. Should an individual be forced to present evidence of his/her religious beliefs to be scrutinized by a governmental employee? If parents have not consistently expressed those religious beliefs over time, should they be denied an exemption? Can parents have beliefs that are both philosophical and religious without disqualifying their exemption request? Should the government require a certain level of sincerity as a benchmark before an exemption can be granted? * * *

We do not believe that the legislature, through its adoption of § 21–4–309(a), anticipated or authorized a broad investigation into an individual's belief system in an effort to discern the merit of a request for exemption. Rather, we construe the statutory language as mandatory and the exemption as self-executing upon submission of a written objection.

In her request for exemption, Mrs. LePage fully complied with both the statutory and the regulatory requirements. However, it should be noted that, in attempting to enforce the immunization for hepatitis B, the Department of Health failed to abide by its own regulations which do not include the hepatitis B vaccination. [ ]. This could be an independent reason for reversing the State Health Officer's conclusion that a religious waiver was necessary for exemption from the hepatitis B vaccination.

We recognize the genuine concern that there could be increased requests for exemption and a potential for improper evasion of immunization. The state certainly has a valid interest in protecting public schoolchildren from unwarranted exposure to infectious diseases. However, we have been presented with no evidence that the number of religious exemption waiver requests are excessive and are confident in our presumption that parents act in the best interest of their children's physical, as well as their spiritual, health. Again, if problems regarding the health of Wyoming's schoolchildren develop because this self-executing statutory exemption is being abused, it is the legislature's responsibility to act within the constraints of the Wyoming and United States Constitutions.

Reversed.

Notes

1) Giving substantial deference to public health policy as determined by the legislature, *Jacobson* sets forth several constitutional standards for limitation on public health authority: (a) *Public health necessity*: the states police powers are only justified if the "necessity of the case" so dictate; (b) *Reasonableness*: the techniques used must be reasonably designed to address the public health threat; (c) *Proportionality*: the regulation cannot impose a burden that is arbitrary or disproportionate to the objective benefit; and (d) *Avoidance of detriment*: the subject of the regulation cannot be exposed to undue risk to his or her own health. It was this last condition that Jacobson argued most vigorously: he believed that the vaccination would cause harm to his own health.

2) *Brown v. Stone* reinforced the holding of *Jacobson*. In *Brown*, the Mississippi court held that a provision for religious objection to a vaccination requirement violated equal protection of the laws. If the vast majority of school children required vaccination, it was unfair to expose them to "the hazard of associating in school with children exempted" from vaccination. In order to succeed on a claim of religious objection, it generally is necessary to argue that the "establishment of religion" clause requires that legislatively-enacted public health regulations include such an exemption.

3) *LePage* held to the contrary. The Court distinguished between a religious objection based upon sincerely held religious beliefs, and a philosophical objection based upon personal belief or morality. Nevertheless, it refused to engage in an inquiry designed to question the sincerity of individual beliefs. The court suggested that if the number of requests became excessive, or if there were indication that people were purposefully evading the operation of the statute, it might find differently. Can you reconcile the holding of the court in *LePage* with that in *Jacobson* and *Brown?*

SECTION B.   QUARANTINE

GREENE v. EDWARDS

Supreme Court of Appeals of West Virginia, 1980.
164 W.Va. 326, 263 S.E.2d 661.

PER CURIAM.

William Arthur Greene, the relator in this original habeas corpus proceeding, is involuntarily confined in Pinecrest Hospital under an order of the Circuit Court of McDowell County entered pursuant to the terms of the West Virginia Tuberculosis Control Act [ ]. He alleges, among other points, that the Tuberculosis Control Act does not afford procedural due process because: (1) it fails to guarantee the alleged tubercular person the right to counsel; (2) it fails to insure that he may cross-examine, confront and present witnesses; and (3) it fails to require that he be committed only upon clear, cogent and convincing proof. We agree.

A petition alleging that Mr. Greene was suffering from active communicable tuberculosis was filed with the Circuit Court of McDowell County on October 3, 1979. After receiving the petition, the court, in accordance with the terms of [the statute and] caused a copy of the petition and a notice of the hearing to be served upon Mr. Greene. The papers served did not notify Mr. Greene that he was entitled to be represented by counsel at the hearing.

After commencement of the October 10, 1979 hearing, the court, upon learning that Mr. Greene was not represented, appointed an attorney for him. The court then, without taking a recess so that the relator and his attorney could consult privately, proceeded to take evidence and to order Mr. Greene's commitment.

W.Va. Code, 26–5A–5, the statute under which the commitment proceedings in this case were conducted, provides in part:

"If such practicing physician, public health officer, or chief medical officer having under observation or care any person who is suffering from tuberculosis in a communicable stage is of the opinion that the environmental conditions of such person are not suitable for proper isolation or control by any type of local quarantine as prescribed by the state health department, and that such person is unable or unwilling to conduct himself and to live in such a manner as not to expose members of his family or household or other persons with whom he may be associated to danger of infection, he shall report the facts to the department of health which shall forthwith investigate or have investigated the circumstances alleged. If it shall find that any such person's physical condition is a health menace to others, the department of health shall petition the circuit court of the county in which such person resides * * * and requesting an order of the court committing such person to one of the state tuberculosis institutions. * * *

It is evident from an examination of this statute that its purpose is to prevent a person suffering from active communicable tuberculosis from becoming a danger to others. A like rationale underlies our statute governing the involuntary commitment of a mentally ill person, *W.Va. Code*, 27–5–4.

In *State ex rel. Hawks v. Lazaro*, W.Va. , 202 S.E.2d 109 (1974), we examined the procedural safeguards which must be extended to persons charged under our statute governing the involuntary hospitalization of the mentally ill. We noted that Article 3, Section 10 of the West Virginia Constitution and the Fifth Amendment to the United States Constitution provide that no person shall be deprived of life, liberty, or property without due process of law * * *.

We concluded that due process required that persons charged under [West Virginia law] must be afforded: (1) an adequate written notice detailing the grounds and underlying facts on which commitment is sought; (2) the right to counsel; (3) the right to be present, cross-examine, confront and present witnesses; (4) the standard of proof to warrant commitment to be by clear, cogent and convincing evidence; and (5) the right to a verbatim transcript of the proceeding for purposes of appeal.

Because the Tuberculosis Control Act and the Act for the Involuntary Hospitalization of the Mentally Ill have like rationales, and because involuntary commitment for having communicable tuberculosis impinges upon the right to "liberty, full and complete liberty" no less than involuntary commitment for being mentally ill, we conclude that the procedural safeguards set forth in *State ex rel. Hawks v. Lazaro, supra*, must, and do, extend to persons charged under [the statute]. Specifically, persons charged under the act must be afforded: (1) an adequate written notice detailing the grounds and underlying facts on which commitment is sought; (2) the right to counsel and, if indigent, the right to appointed counsel; (3) the right to be present, to cross-examine, to confront and to present witnesses; (4) the standard of proof to be by clear, cogent and convincing evidence; and (5) the right to a verbatim transcript of the proceedings for purposes of appeal.

We noted in *State ex rel. Hawks v. Lazaro, supra*, that where counsel is to be appointed in proceedings for the involuntary hospitalization of the mentally ill, the law contemplates representation of the individual by the appointed guardian in the most zealous, adversary fashion consistent with the Code of Professional Responsibility. Since this decision, we have concluded that appointment of counsel immediately prior to a trial in a criminal case is impermissible since it denies the defendant effective assistance of counsel. [ ]. It is obvious that timely appointment and reasonable opportunity for adequate preparation are prerequisites for fulfillment of appointed counsel's constitutionally assigned role in representing persons charged under [the West Virginia statute] with having communicable tuberculosis.

In the case before us, counsel was not appointed for Mr. Greene until after the commencement of the commitment hearing. Under the circumstances, counsel could not have been properly prepared to defend Mr. Greene. For this reason, the relator's writ must be awarded and he must be accorded a new hearing.

* * *

For the reasons stated above, the writ of habeas corpus is awarded, and the relator is ordered discharged, but such discharge is hereby delayed for a period of thirty days during which time the State may entertain further proceedings to be conducted in accordance with the principles expressed herein.

NEW YORK v. ANTOINETTE

Supreme Court of New York, Queens County, 1995.
165 Misc.2d 1014, 630 N.Y.S.2d 1008.

Robert C. McGann, J.

The issue presented at this special proceeding is whether the respondent, a person with active tuberculosis (TB), should be forcibly detained in a hospital setting to allow for the completion of an appropriate regime of medical treatment.

THE LAW

Due to a resurgence of tuberculosis, New York City recently revised the Health Code to permit the detention of individuals infected with TB who have demonstrated an inability to voluntarily comply with appropriate medical treatment. Thus, effective April 29, 1993, New York City Health Code § 11.47 was amended to give the Commissioner of Health the authority to issue an order for the removal or detention in a hospital or other treatment facility of a person who has active tuberculosis. The prerequisite for an order is that there is a substantial likelihood, based on the person's past or present behavior, that the individual cannot be relied upon to participate in or complete an appropriate prescribed course of medication or, if necessary, follow required contagion precautions for tuberculosis. Such behavior may include the refusal or failure to take medication or to complete treatment for tuberculosis, to keep appointments for the treatment of tuberculosis, or a disregard for contagion precautions.

The statute provides certain due process safeguards when detention is ordered. For example, there are requirements for an appraisal of the risk posed to others and a review of less restrictive alternatives which were attempted or considered. Furthermore, there must be a court review within five days at the patient's request, and court review within 60 days and at 90–day intervals thereafter. The detainee also has the right to counsel, to have counsel provided, and to have friends or relatives notified. [ ]

BACKGROUND

The amendment to the Code stems from the recent declaration by the Board of Health acknowledging that the City of New York is in the midst of a tuberculosis crisis characterized by new strains of the disease. In general, tuberculosis is known to be a respiratory illness which is transmitted when airborne TB bacilli are expelled from the lungs of an infectious person and are inhaled by an exposed individual. When the bacilli are transmitted to another, they may either remain inactive or become active. Although most remain in the inactive state, a person in good health exposed to the infection has a 10% lifetime chance of developing active TB. Those with a compromised immune system, however, have a much higher risk of developing the active disease.

It is when the body's immune system fails to hold the organisms in check that they start to multiply resulting in an active case of tuberculosis. The symptoms are persistent cough, loss of appetite, loss of weight, fever, chills and sweats. When the disease initially becomes active, it is often highly infectious, that is, capable of being transmitted to others. A person with infectious TB can normally be rendered noninfectious within days to weeks. Thereafter, the individual must continue to take a full course of medication, generally for six to nine months, to cure the active tuberculosis. If a patient stops taking the appropriate medication before the expiration of these six to nine months, however, that patient will likely become infectious again. Moreover, when the medical regime is interrupted, and the TB resurges in an infectious state, the organisms in the individual's system may eventually mutate and become resistant to the original drugs prescribed. The more times medication is suspended, the more likely is the chance of developing a strain of tuberculosis which is resistant to drugs.

These multidrug resistant strains of TB stay infectious and active over longer periods of time and therefore require long-term treatment with more toxic drugs. By comparison, the standard treatment for nonresistant TB consists of administering two drugs, isoniazid and rifampin, for approximately six months until the patient is cured. The cure rate for those completing this treatment is considered 100%. Multidrug resistant tuberculosis, on the other hand, is resistant to these drugs and to as many as seven other antibiotics. To obtain a cure rate of 60% or less, toxic drugs must be maintained over a minimum period of 18 to 24 months. [ ]. The most critical characteristic of these multidrug resistant strains is that they are capable of being transmitted directly to others during the infectious stage.

Because of an increase in reported incidences of multidrug resistant strains of tuberculosis, the Department of Health issued a resolution proclaiming that the City was in the midst of an epidemic of tuberculosis. The Board recognized that the failure of a tuberculosis patient to complete an effective course of therapy creates the likelihood of relapse and facilitates development of drug resistant strains of the disease. The Board therefore decreed that the refusal or failure of tuberculosis patients, whether or not infectious, to complete a course of antituberculosis therapy creates a significant threat to the public health. Accordingly, the New York City Health Code was amended to allow the Commissioner to issue orders of detention. Where an order is issued, the Commissioner must make an application to the court for enforcement. In the court proceeding, the Commissioner must demonstrate by clear and convincing evidence the particularized circumstances constituting the necessity for the detention.

On March 9, 1995, the Commissioner issued an order of detention for the respondent. At the proceeding held before me for the purpose of enforcing the order, the petitioner relied upon the testimony of Doctor Gabriel Feldman, and numerous hospital records regarding the respondent. The respondent, Ms. R., represented by counsel, testified on her own behalf and called three witnesses in support of her request to be released from detention. Based on the credible and competent evidence, the following facts were adduced.

Findings of Fact

On November 30, 1993 the respondent, a 33–year–old female, was admitted to the Queens Hospital Center with pneumonia under the name of Marie C. exhibiting shortness of breath. A chest x-ray determined that she was suffering from inflammation in the upper right lobe, a classic indicator of tuberculosis. A sputum smear confirmed that she had an active, infectious case of TB. When the patient was interviewed, it was discovered that she had children who lived with her mother. She herself lived with them on occasion but also resided with various friends. She was informed of the consequences of tuberculosis and necessity of completing the appropriate medication to control the disease. Finally, she was recommended by the Department of Health to be a participant in Directly Observed Therapy, a program which involves the Department sending personnel to a patient's residence to observe and verify the patient's compliance with medication treatment. On December 4, however, the respondent left the hospital against medical advice prior to being rendered noninfectious. From December through February of 1994, she could not be contacted through her last known address. Moreover, despite several contacts with the respondent's mother, the mother did not know of her daughter's whereabouts, and was thus unable to provide any help in securing the proper medication for her daughter. In May, after numerous failed attempts at trying to contact the patient, the Department closed her case labeling the file, "Unable to Locate."

On May 31, 1994, the respondent checked into the emergency room at the Queens Hospital Center with breathing difficulties but checked out against medical advice. On June 6, 1994, she was readmitted with fever and chills under the name of Antoinette R. A sputum smear indicated a heavily positive tuberculosis infection. A chest x-ray of the right upper lobe of her lung showed cavitation present, which suggested a worsening of her condition. As a patient, the respondent was informed about tuberculosis pathology and control, she responded to the instructions in an uncooperative manner. In spite of efforts to conceal her identity, it was eventually discovered that the patient, Antoinette R., was the same person who had been unsuccessfully treated under the name of Marie C. She was then issued an order by the Commissioner of Health requiring her detention on June 11, 1994. On July 13, 1994, she was served with a Commissioner's order to participate in Directly Observed Therapy which commenced upon release from the hospital on July 18.

Thereafter, between July 19 and July 31, she kept five of her eight scheduled appointments but kept no appointments after that date. On the occasions of Directly Observed Therapy, the respondent threw out medicine in the presence of the public health advisor assigned to her case. She was subsequently noncompliant and lost to medical followup despite numerous attempts to locate her at shelters and her last known address. Five months after her release from the hospital, her case file was again closed as "Unable to Locate."

On January 31, 1995 the respondent was readmitted to the hospital under the name of Chastity C. Her physical examination indicated a worsening of condition with extensive cavitary infiltrates in the right upper lobe with what appeared to be bronchogenic spread into the right middle and lower lobe on the right and left lungs. These findings were consistent with a reactivation of tuberculosis with bronchogenic spread. A sputum smear was collected which confirmed the diagnosis of infectious tuberculosis. A public health advisor again explained the importance of taking and completing medication and discussed the possibility of participating in Directly Observed Therapy. The respondent agreed to participate and gave her mother's residence as a place of contact but refused to provide a phone contact. On March 8, however, once again it was discovered that the patient was the same person who under different identities refused to participate in out-patient treatment. The order of detention, currently before the court, was subsequently issued on March 9 by the Commissioner of Health. The respondent is presently diagnosed as having active tuberculosis which has been rendered noninfectious. Since it is not of the drug resistant type, the estimated date of completion of treatment is in October 1995, seven months from now.

The mother of the respondent lives in a private home with four of her grandchildren and a newborn great-grandson, the grandchild of the respondent. The mother is willing to take the respondent into her home and provide cooperation should she be released from the hospital. Over the past two months the mother has visited her daughter on several occasions and talked with her over the phone on a daily basis. The mother has noticed a change in attitude in the respondent, that is, she is not as hostile. The mother attributes this change to the respondent's acceptance of religion. The respondent also contends that her attitude has been transformed and credits religion as her motivation. Since being detained at the hospital, she has joined various out-patient programs and attended parenting meetings. A nurses aide and the head nurse, who attend to the medical needs of the respondent, both verify that there has been an improvement in the respondent's demeanor. She is now cooperative while taking her medicines and on occasions has independently approached the nursing staff to request her medicines. Relying on her "change in attitude," the respondent opposes the order of detention and again requests the option of participating in Directly Observed Therapy to be conducted at her mother's place of residence.

CONCLUSION

The petitioner's request for enforcement of the order of the Commissioner is granted. The petitioner has demonstrated through clear and convincing evidence the respondent's inability to comply with a prescribed course of medication in a less restrictive environment. [ ] The respondent has repeatedly sought medical treatment for the infectious stages of the disease and has consistently withdrawn from medical treatment once symptoms abate. She has also exhibited a pattern of behavior which is consistent with one who does not understand the full import of her condition nor the risks she poses to others, both the public and her family. On the contrary, she has repeatedly tried to hide the history of her condition from medical personnel. Although the court is sympathetic to the fact that she has recently undergone an epiphany of sorts, there is nothing in the record which would indicate that once she leaves the controlled setting of the hospital she would have the self-discipline to continue her cooperation. Moreover, her past behavior and lack of compliance with out-patient treatment when her listed residence was her mother's house makes it all the more difficult to have confidence that her mother's good intentions will prevail over the respondent's inclinations to avoid treatments. In any event, the court will reevaluate the progress of the respondent's ability to cooperate in a less restrictive setting during its next review of the order in 90 days.

Accordingly, the respondent shall continue to be detained in a hospital setting until the petitioner or the court determines that the respondent has completed an appropriate course of medication for tuberculosis, or a change in circumstances indicates that the respondent can be relied upon to complete the prescribed course of medication without being in detention. The petitioner is further directed, pursuant to New York City Health Code § 11.47 to apply to the court within 90 days for authorization to continue respondent's detention.

GAMMILL v. UNITED STATES

United States Court of Appeals for the Tenth Circuit, 1984.
727 F.2d 950.

BARRETT, Circuit Judge.

* * *

FACTS

On April 20, 1978, Lauralee Johnson was diagnosed as having infectious hepatitis and gastroenteritis. This diagnosis was made at Fort Carson, Colorado, a United States military installation, by Dr. James Hamilton (Hamilton), a civilian physician employed by the United States.

The next day, Ladonna Gammill, wife of plaintiff Lawrence Gammill, and mother of plaintiff Cynthia Gammill, was told by a member of her church that Mrs. Johnson was ill with hepatitis and there was a need for someone to take care of her two small children, Christie and Stephanie. Mrs. Gammill agreed to baby-sit the children and they were consequently brought to her home for the day. Neither child showed symptoms of serious illness, although Stephanie had diarrhea which required Mrs. Gammill and Cynthia Gammill to change her diapers. When Mr. Gammill came home after work, Mrs. Gammill informed him that Mrs. Johnson had hepatitis. At dinner that evening, Mr. Gammill sat next to Stephanie and assisted in feeding her. The children were returned to the Johnson home later that evening; Mr. Gammill was cautious in not entering their home because he knew hepatitis was contagious.

Seven days later, on April 28, 1978, Mrs. Johnson was informed by the staff at Fort Carson that her daughter, Stephanie, also had hepatitis. Dr. Hamilton had also examined Stephanie, and he recommended that the whole family receive gamma globulin inoculations. Neither Dr. Hamilton, nor the staff at Fort Carson notified the public health authorities of the hepatitis in the Johnson household; such notification is required by Colorado law [and army regulations].

On May 16, 1978, Mr. Gammill was brought home from work because of illness. Some time after May 21st, Dr. Pollard, the Gammill's family physician, tested Mr. Gammill for hepatitis and reported a suspected case of hepatitis to the county health authorities. Mr. Gammill's hepatitis tests were later confirmed and it was also determined that Cynthia Gammill had contracted the disease. As a result of Dr. Pollard's report to the health authorities, five other cases of hepatitis were identified by epidemiological techniques. Mr. Gammill was hospitalized for a time and was ill at home for about five months.

At trial, the Gammill's presented testimony that tended to establish that Stephanie Johnson was the source of infection in the Gammill family, that the Gammills would likely have been contacted by the county health department within twenty-four to seventy-two hours if the department had been properly notified by Dr. Hamilton, and that if the Gammills had been contacted within that time period they would have had several days to receive effective gamma globulin inoculations . [Such inoculations are effective if received within two weeks of exposure to hepatitis.]

FINDINGS AND CONCLUSIONS OF THE DISTRICT COURT

The district court concluded that the Gammills could not recover against the United States pursuant to the Federal Tort Claims Act.[1] [ ]. First, the court found no common-law duty running from the United States to the Gammills that would require the United States to notify the county health department of the hepatitis in the Johnson home. [ ]. To create such a duty would allow liability for nonfeasance on the part of the United States. The court noted that liability for "nonfeasance" was limited to situations where there was a "special relationship" between the parties, and that there was no such relationship in this case. *Id.*

Second, the court found that liability could not be based upon the violation of statute or regulation. The court cited two independent reasons for this: 1) According to Colorado law, no private right of action exists against individuals or entities performing essentially "state services" in accordance with statute; and 2) Colorado courts have held that when a statute provides for criminal punishment, as does C.R.S. § 25–1–649, the intent of the legislature is presumed to be that such punishment is in lieu of all other remedies.

Finally, the district court noted that "no causal connection between the physician's conduct and the resulting injury was established to allow recovery by the plaintiffs." *Id.* at 12. In support of this, the court observed:

> if the physician in this case had notified the appropriate health authorities of the hepatitis in the Johnson family pursuant to the statute, the health officials would have had to investigate the matter, find the Gammills had contact with the Johnson baby for three to four hours before she was diagnosed as having the disease, and seek out and advise the Gammills to receive gamma globulin inoculations. Later the Gammills on their own initiative would have had to actually receive the shots. Note that all this activity would have had to have been accomplished within the relatively short time span of a couple of days, for the plaintiffs were already infected with hepatitis ... seven days before ... the doctor was under the duty to report the diagnosis. *Id.*

---

1. The Federal Tort Claims Act grants jurisdiction to the district courts to hear:

claims against the United States, for money damages, ... for injury or loss of property, or personal injury or death caused by the negligent or wrongful act or omission of any employee of the Gov-

ernment while acting within the scope of his office or employment, under circumstances where the United States, if a private person, would be liable to the claimant in accordance with the law of the place where the act or omission occurred. 28 U.S.C. 1346 (b)(1976).

In addition, the court relied upon testimony that, even if the inoculations were given to the plaintiffs, they still would have become sick with the disease—the inoculation would serve only to lessen the degree of sickness.

I.

In order to recover under the Federal Tort Claims Act, *supra*, a claimant must establish that the United States, acting through its employees, committed a tort as defined by the law of the state where the act or omission occurred. In reviewing the district court's judgment, we must consequently look to the law of Colorado to determine whether the correct law was applied. We are convinced that it was and, therefore, affirm.

STATUTORY CLAIM: First, we note that Colorado courts have been extremely cautious in recognizing private rights of action "implied" by criminal statutes. * * * In the present case, [Colorado law] provides for a criminal fine ranging from five to one-hundred dollars. There is no indication that the legislature also intended to supplement this criminal penalty with a private civil right of action. The Colorado Supreme Court has observed that the creation of such rights "is not a subject in which we should attempt to infer such a legislative intent." *Quintano v. Industrial Commission, supra* 495 P.2d at 1138. * * *

The *type* of statute involved in the present case provides additional support for our conclusion. As the district court pointed out, the purpose of [the law] is "to benefit the public and not any specific individual or even class of persons." *Gammill v. United States, supra* at 7. Colorado courts have long held that such statutes may not be used for the recovery of individual damages because the duty created by them is public, not private; the violation of these statutes is consequently redressed by public, not private, prosecution. * * * [T]he statute simply creates no duty running to specific individuals supporting a private claim of negligence.

COMMON LAW CLAIM: The Gammills also contend that the United States breached a duty owed to them deriving from common law. In support of this, they cite various cases suggesting that the spread of hepatitis to the Gammill family was a foreseeable risk, and that the United States had a duty to disclose this risk to the public via the county health department. After reviewing the cases, however, we are convinced that these arguments are without merit.

* * *

The Gammills contend [ ] that Dr. Hamilton's duty to them arises from his *professional position* and relation to people who contract disease. They argue that, as a physician, Dr. Hamilton owed the public the duty of ordinary care to protect them from the diseases of his patients. * * *

We understand these authorities, however, as expressing a much more limited duty than that urged by the Gammills. A physician may be found liable for failing to warn a patient's *family, treating attendants*, or other *persons likely to be exposed* to the patient, of the nature of the disease and the danger of exposure. [ ]. We note the limited persons to who such a duty is owed, again suggesting the necessity of some special relationship between the physician and those to be warned. It would appear that at the bare minimum the physician must be aware of the specific risks to specific persons before a duty to warn exists. Here, Dr. Hamilton did not know the Gammills; clearly he was unaware of their risk of exposure. Under these circumstances, we agree with the district court that to impose a duty upon Dr. Hamilton to warn the Gammills would constitute an "unreasonable burden" upon physicians.

We hold that the Gammills' claim has no basis in law and, therefore, we need not discuss the remaining issues raised on appeal.

AFFIRMED.

Notes

1) The legislature delegates a substantial amount of power to public health agencies to protect the health and well-being of its citizens. Where, as in *Greene v. Edwards*, there is a significant infringement on individual freedom, the public health regulation has to balance the need for intervention with rights of the individual. Due process requires that the public health regulation be grounded in solid scientific evidence and the individual have adequate procedural due process to assert his objection. Suppose instead of tuberculosis the contagion was SARS. Would be case be handled the same way?

2) *New York v. Antoinette* is another TB case, but the reasonableness of the detention provision was based upon the defendant's efforts to evade public health authorities and refuse alternative outpatient treatment. Assuming the nature of defendant's illness was such that it could be treated in a less restrictive setting, does public health necessity justify detention? Compare *Reynolds v. McNichols*, infra at Chapter 14, in which an admitted prostitute was confined in order to coerce penicillin treatment. Is it a reasonable use of public health authority to compel treatment just for the benefit of the individual? When a small number of other individuals might be at risk? Only when a large number of other individuals might be affected?

3) *Gammill* raises the issue of whether a private right of action exists when a defendant violates a public health reporting requirement and such violation allegedly results in compensable damage. In denying a private right of action, the court held that no such action exists against those performing "state services" pursuant to statute. Furthermore, the Colorado courts have held that a statute that imposes criminal penalties presumes that the intent of the legislature is that the criminal sanctions are an exclusive remedy. And just in case one might argue otherwise, the court noted that it found no causal connection between the physician's

actions and the resulting injury. How do you determine whether a statute intended that its provisions amount to an exclusive remedy? Should the plaintiff in this case have been afforded the opportunity to pursue a private right of action?

SECTION C. HIV AND AIDS

BRAGDON v. ABBOTT

United States Supreme Court, 1998.
524 U.S. 624, 118 S.Ct. 2196, 141 L.Ed.2d 540.

JUSTICE KENNEDY delivered the opinion of the Court.

We address in this case the application of the Americans with Disabilities Act of 1990 (ADA), 104 Stat. 327, 42 U.S.C. § 12101 *et seq.*, to persons infected with the human immunodeficiency virus (HIV). We granted certiorari to review, first, whether HIV infection is a disability under the ADA when the infection has not yet progressed to the so-called symptomatic phase; and, second, whether the Court of Appeals, in affirming a grant of summary judgment, cited sufficient material in the record to determine, as a matter of law, that respondent's infection with HIV posed no direct threat to the health and safety of her treating dentist.

I

Respondent Sidney Abbott has been infected with HIV since 1986. When the incidents we recite occurred, her infection had not manifested its most serious symptoms. On September 16, 1994, she went to the office of petitioner Randon Bragdon in Bangor, Maine, for a dental appointment. She disclosed her HIV infection on the patient registration form. Petitioner completed a dental examination, discovered a cavity, and informed respondent of his policy against filling cavities of HIV-infected patients. He offered to perform the work at a hospital with no added fee for his services, though respondent would be responsible for the cost of using the hospital's facilities. Respondent declined.

Respondent sued petitioner under state law and § 302 of the ADA [ ] alleging discrimination on the basis of her disability. The state law claims are not before us. Section 302 of the ADA provides:

"No individual shall be discriminated against on the basis of disability in the full and equal enjoyment of the goods, services, facilities, privileges, advantages, or accommodations of any place of public accommodation by any person who ... operates a place of public accommodation." [ ]

The term "public accommodation" is defined to include the "professional office of a health care provider." [ ]

A later subsection qualifies the mandate not to discriminate. It provides:

"Nothing in this subchapter shall require an entity to permit an individual to participate in or benefit from the goods, services, facilities, privileges, advantages and accommodations of such entity where such individual poses a direct threat to the health or safety of others." [ ]

* * * [T]he parties filed cross-motions for summary judgment. The District Court ruled in favor of the plaintiffs, holding that respondent's HIV infection satisfied the ADA's definition of disability. [ ]. The court held further that petitioner raised no genuine issue of material fact as to whether respondent's HIV infection would have posed a direct threat to the health or safety of others during the course of a dental treatment. [ ]. The court relied on affidavits submitted by Dr. Donald Wayne Marianos, Director of the Division of Oral Health of the Centers for Disease Control and Prevention (CDC). The Marianos affidavits asserted it is safe for dentists to treat patients infected with HIV in dental offices if the dentist follows the so-called universal precautions described in the Recommended Infection–Control Practices for Dentistry issued by CDC in 1993 [ ].

The Court of Appeals affirmed. It held respondent's HIV infection was a disability under the ADA, even though her infection had not yet progressed to the symptomatic stage. [ ]. The Court of Appeals also agreed that treating the respondent in petitioner's office would not have posed a direct threat to the health and safety of others. [ ]. Unlike the District Court, however, the Court of Appeals declined to rely on the Marianos affidavits. [ ]. Instead the court relied on the 1993 CDC Dentistry Guidelines, as well as the Policy on AIDS, HIV Infection and the Practice of Dentistry, promulgated by the American Dental Association in 1991 (1991 American Dental Association Policy on HIV). [ ].

II

We first review the ruling that respondent's HIV infection constituted a disability under the ADA. The statute defines disability as:

"(A) a physical or mental impairment that substantially limits one or more of the major life activities of such individual;

"(B) a record of such an impairment; or

"(C) being regarded as having such impairment." [ ]

We hold respondent's HIV infection was a disability under subsection (A) of the definitional section of the statute. In light of this conclusion, we need not consider the applicability of subsections (B) or (C).

Our consideration of subsection (A) of the definition proceeds in three steps. First, we consider whether respondent's HIV infection was a physical impairment. Second, we identify the life activity upon which respondent relies (reproduction and child bearing) and determine whether it constitutes a major life activity under the ADA. Third, tying the two statutory phrases together, we ask whether the impairment substantially limited the major life activity. In construing the statute, we are informed by interpretations of parallel definitions in previous statutes and the views of various administrative agencies which have faced this interpretive question.

A

The ADA's definition of disability is drawn almost verbatim from the definition of "handicapped individual" included in the Rehabilitation Act of 1973 [ ] and the definition of "handicap" contained in the Fair Housing Amendments Act of 1988 [ ]. Congress' repetition of a well-established term carries the implication that Congress intended the term to be construed in accordance with pre-existing regulatory interpretations. [ ]In this case, Congress did more than suggest this construction; it adopted a specific statutory provision in the ADA directing as follows:

> "Except as otherwise provided in this chapter, nothing in this chapter shall be construed to apply a lesser standard than the standards applied under title V of the Rehabilitation Act of 1973 (29 U.S.C. 790 et seq.) or the regulations issued by Federal agencies pursuant to such title." 42 U.S.C. § 12201(a).

The directive requires us to construe the ADA to grant at least as much protection as provided by the regulations implementing the Rehabilitation Act.

1

The first step in the inquiry under subsection (A) requires us to determine whether respondent's condition constituted a physical impairment. The Department of Health, Education and Welfare (HEW) issued the first regulations interpreting the Rehabilitation Act in 1977. The regulations are of particular significance because, at the time, HEW was the agency responsible for coordinating the implementation and enforcement of § 504. [ ]. The HEW regulations, which appear without change in the current regulations issued by the Department of Health and Human Services, define "physical or mental impairment" to mean:

> "(A) any physiological disorder or condition, cosmetic disfigurement, or anatomical loss affecting one or more of the following body systems: neurological; musculoskeletal; special sense organs; respiratory, including speech organs; cardiovascular; reproductive, digestive, genito-urinary; hemic and lymphatic; skin; and endocrine; or

> "(B) any mental or psychological disorder, such as mental retardation, organic brain syndrome, emotional or mental illness, and specific learning disabilities." 45 CFR § 84.3(j)(2)(i) (1997).

In issuing these regulations, HEW decided against including a list of disorders constituting physical or mental impairments, out of concern that any specific enumeration might not be comprehensive. [ ]. The commentary accompanying the regulations, however, contains a representative list of disorders and conditions constituting physical impairments, including "such diseases and conditions as orthopedic, visual, speech, and hearing impairments, cerebral palsy, epilepsy, muscular dystrophy, multiple sclerosis, cancer, heart disease, diabetes, mental retardation, emotional illness, and . . . drug addiction and alcoholism.'' *Ibid.*

* * *

HIV infection is not included in the list of specific disorders constituting physical impairments, in part because HIV was not identified as the cause of AIDS until 1983. * * * HIV infection does fall well within the general definition set forth by the regulations, however.

The disease follows a predictable and, as of today, an unalterable course. Once a person is infected with HIV, the virus invades different cells in the blood and in body tissues. Certain white blood cells, known as helper T-lymphocytes or CD4+ cells, are particularly vulnerable to HIV. The virus attaches to the CD4 receptor site of the target cell and fuses its membrane to the cell's membrane. HIV is a retrovirus, which means it uses an enzyme to convert its own genetic material into a form indistinguishable from the genetic material of the target cell. The virus' genetic material migrates to the cell's nucleus and becomes integrated with the cell's chromosomes. Once integrated, the virus can use the cell's own genetic machinery to replicate itself. Additional copies of the virus are released into the body and infect other cells in turn. [Citations omitted]. Although the body does produce antibodies to combat HIV infection, the antibodies are not effective in eliminating the virus. [ ]

The virus eventually kills the infected host cell. CD4+ cells play a critical role in coordinating the body's immune response system, and the decline in their number causes corresponding deterioration of the body's ability to fight infections from many sources. Tracking the infected individual's CD4+ cell count is one of the most accurate measures of the course of the disease. [ ]

The initial stage of HIV infection is known as acute or primary HIV infection. In a typical case, this stage lasts three months. The virus concentrates in the blood. The assault on the immune system is immediate. The victim suffers from a sudden and serious decline in the number of white blood cells. There is no latency period. Mononucleosis-like symptoms often emerge between six days and six weeks after infection, at times accompanied by fever, headache, enlargement of the lymph nodes (lymphadenopathy), muscle pain (myalgia), rash, lethargy, gastrointestinal disorders, and neurological disorders. Usually these symptoms abate within 14 to 21 days. HIV antibodies appear in the bloodstream within 3 weeks; circulating HIV can be detected within 10 weeks. [ ].

After the symptoms associated with the initial stage subside, the disease enters what is referred to sometimes as its asymptomatic phase. The term is a misnomer, in some respects, for clinical features persist throughout, including lymphadenopathy, dermatological disorders, oral lesions, and bacterial infections. Although it varies with each individual, in most instances this stage lasts from 7 to 11 years. The virus now tends to concentrate in the lymph nodes, though low levels of the virus continue to appear in the blood. Cohen & Volberding, AIDS Knowledge 4.1–4, 4.1–8; Saag, AIDS: Etiology 205–206; Strapans & Feinberg, Natural History and Immunopathogenesis of HIV–1 Disease, in Medical Management of AIDS 38. It was once [*636] thought the virus became inactive during this period, but it is now known that the relative lack of symptoms is attributable to the virus' migration from the circulatory system into the lymph nodes. Cohen & Volberding, AIDS Knowledge Base 4.1–4. The migration reduces the viral presence in other parts of the body, with a corresponding diminution in physical manifestations of the disease. The virus, however, thrives in the lymph nodes, which, as a vital point of the body's immune response system, represents an ideal environment for the infection of other CD4+ cells. [ ]

* * *

A person is regarded as having AIDS when his or her CD4+ count drops below 200 cells/mm3 of blood or when CD4+ cells comprise less than 14% of his or her total lymphocytes. * * *

In light of the immediacy with which the virus begins to damage the infected person's white blood cells and the severity of the disease, we hold it is an impairment from the moment of infection. As noted earlier, infection with HIV causes immediate abnormalities in a person's blood, and the infected person's white cell count continues to drop throughout the course of the disease, even when the attack is concentrated in the lymph nodes. In light of these facts, HIV infection must be regarded as a physiological disorder with a constant and detrimental effect on the infected person's hemic and lymphatic systems from the moment of infection. HIV infection satisfies the statutory and regulatory definition of a physical impairment during every stage of the disease.

2

The statute is not operative, and the definition not satisfied, unless the impairment affects a major life activity. Respondent's claim throughout this case has been that the HIV infection placed a substantial limitation on her ability to reproduce and to bear children. [ ]. Given the pervasive, and invariably fatal, course of the disease, its effect on major life activities of many sorts might have been relevant to our inquiry. Respondent and a number of *amici* make arguments about HIV's profound impact on almost every phase of the infected person's life. [ ]. In light of these submissions, it may seem legalistic to circumscribe our discussion to the activity of reproduction. We have little doubt that had different parties brought the suit they would have maintained that an HIV infection imposes substantial limitations on other major life activities.

From the outset, however, the case has been treated as one in which reproduction was the major life activity limited by the impairment. It is our practice to decide cases on the grounds raised and considered in the

Court of Appeals and included in the question on which we granted certiorari. [ ]. We ask, then, whether reproduction is a major life activity.

We have little difficulty concluding that it is. As the Court of Appeals held, "the plain meaning of the word 'major' denotes comparative importance" and "suggests that the touchstone for determining an activity's inclusion under the statutory rubric is its significance." 107 F.3d at 939, 940. Reproduction falls well within the phrase "major life activity." Reproduction and the sexual dynamics surrounding it are central to the life process itself.

While petitioner concedes the importance of reproduction, he claims that Congress intended the ADA only to cover those aspects of a person's life which have a public, economic, or daily character. [ ] The argument founders on the statutory language. Nothing in the definition suggests that activities without a public, economic, or daily dimension may somehow be regarded as so unimportant or insignificant as to fall outside the meaning of the word "major." The breadth of the term confounds the attempt to limit its construction in this manner.

As we have noted, the ADA must be construed to be consistent with regulations issued to implement the Rehabilitation Act. [ ]. Rather than enunciating a general principle for determining what is and is not a major life activity, the Rehabilitation Act regulations instead provide a representative list, defining term to include "functions such as caring for one's self, performing manual tasks, walking, seeing, hearing, speaking, breathing, learning, and working." [ ]. As the use of the term "such as" confirms, the list is illustrative, not exhaustive.

These regulations are contrary to petitioner's attempt to limit the meaning of the term "major" to public activities. The inclusion of activities such as caring for one's self and performing manual tasks belies the suggestion that a task must have a public or economic character in order to be a major life activity for purposes of the ADA. On the contrary, the Rehabilitation Act regulations support the inclusion of reproduction as a major life activity, since reproduction could not be regarded as any less important than working and learning. Petitioner advances no credible basis for confining major life activities to those with a public, economic, or daily aspect. In the absence of any reason to reach a contrary conclusion, we agree with the Court of Appeals' determination that reproduction is a major life activity for the purposes of the ADA.

3

The final element of the disability definition in subsection (A) is whether respondent's physical impairment was a substantial limit on the major life activity she asserts. The Rehabilitation Act regulations provide no additional guidance. [ ]

Our evaluation of the medical evidence leads us to conclude that respondent's infection substantially limited her ability to reproduce in two independent ways. First, a woman infected with HIV who tries to conceive a child imposes on the man a significant risk of becoming infected. The cumulative results of 13 studies collected in a 1994 textbook on AIDS indicates that 20% of male partners of women with HIV became HIV-positive themselves, with a majority of the studies finding a statistically significant risk of infection. [ ]

Second, an infected woman risks infecting her child during gestation and childbirth, *i.e.,* perinatal transmission. Petitioner concedes that women infected with HIV face about a 25% risk of transmitting the virus to their children. [Citations omitted].

Petitioner points to evidence in the record suggesting that antiretroviral therapy can lower the risk of perinatal transmission to about 8%. [ ]. The Solicitor General questions the relevance of the 8% figure, pointing to regulatory language requiring the substantiality of a limitation to be assessed without regard to available mitigating measures. [ ]. We need not resolve this dispute in order to decide this case, however. It cannot be said as a matter of law that an 8% risk of transmitting a dread and fatal disease to one's child does not represent a substantial limitation on reproduction.

The Act addresses substantial limitations on major life activities, not utter inabilities. Conception and childbirth are not impossible for an HIV victim but, without doubt, are dangerous to the public health. This meets the definition of a substantial limitation. The decision to reproduce carries economic and legal consequences as well. There are added costs for antiretroviral therapy, supplemental insurance, and long-term health care for the child who must be examined and, tragic to think, treated for the infection. The laws of some States, moreover, forbid persons infected with HIV from having sex with others, regardless of consent. [ ]

In the end, the disability definition does not turn on personal choice. When significant limitations result from the impairment, the definition is met even if the difficulties are not insurmountable. For the statistical and other reasons we have cited, of course, the limitations on reproduction may be insurmountable here. Testimony from the respondent that her HIV infection controlled her decision not to have a child is unchallenged. [ ] In the context of reviewing summary judgment, we must take it to be true. [ ] We agree with the District Court and the Court of Appeals that no triable issue of fact impedes a ruling on the question of statutory coverage. Respondent's HIV infection is a physical impairment which substantially limits a major life activity, as the ADA defines it. In view of our holding, we need not address the second question presented, *i.e.,* whether HIV infection is a *per se* disability under the ADA.

B

Our holding is confirmed by a consistent course of agency interpretation before and after enactment of the ADA. Every agency to consider the issue under the Rehabilitation Act found statutory coverage for persons with asymptomatic HIV. Responsibility for administering the

Rehabilitation Act was not delegated to a single agency, but we need not pause to inquire whether this causes us to withhold deference to agency interpretations * * *. It is enough to observe that the well-reasoned views of the agencies implementing a statute "constitute a body of experience and informed judgment to which courts and litigants may properly resort for guidance." [ ].

One comprehensive and significant administrative precedent is a 1988 opinion issued by the Office of Legal Counsel of the Department of Justice (OLC) concluding that the Rehabilitation Act "protects symptomatic and asymptomatic HIV-infected individuals against discrimination in any covered program." [ ]. Relying on a letter from Surgeon General C. Everett Koop stating that, "from a purely scientific perspective, persons with HIV are clearly impaired" even during the asymptomatic phase, OLC determined asymptomatic HIV was a physical impairment under the Rehabilitation Act because it constituted a "physiological disorder or condition affecting the hemic and lymphatic systems." [ ]. OLC determined further that asymptomatic HIV imposed a substantial limit on the major life activity of reproduction. The Opinion said:

> "Based on the medical knowledge available to us, we believe that it is reasonable to conclude that the life activity of procreation ... is substantially limited for an asymptomatic HIV-infected individual. In light of the significant risk that the AIDS virus may be transmitted to a baby during pregnancy, HIV-infected individuals cannot, whether they are male or female, engage in the act of procreation with the normal expectation of bringing forth a healthy child." [ ].

* * *

Every court which addressed the issue before the ADA was enacted in July 1990, moreover, concluded that asymptomatic HIV infection satisfied the Rehabilitation Act's definition of a handicap. * * * We are aware of no instance prior to the enactment of the ADA in which a court or agency ruled that HIV infection was not a handicap under the Rehabilitation Act.

* * *

III

The petition for certiorari presented three other questions for review. The questions stated:

> "3. When deciding under title III of the ADA whether a private health care provider must perform invasive procedures on an infectious patient in his office, should courts defer to the health care provider's professional judgment, as long as it is reasonable in light of then-current medical knowledge?

> "4. What is the proper standard of judicial review under title III of the ADA of a private health care provider's judgment that the

performance of certain invasive procedures in his office would pose a direct threat to the health or safety of others?

"5. Did petitioner, Randon Bragdon, D. M. D., raise a genuine issue of fact for trial as to whether he was warranted in his judgment that the performance of certain invasive procedures on a patient in his office would have posed a direct threat to the health or safety of others?"

Of these, we granted certiorari only on question three. The question is phrased in an awkward way, for it conflates two separate inquiries. In asking whether it is appropriate to defer to petitioner's judgment, it assumes that petitioner's assessment of the objective facts was reasonable. The central premise of the question and the assumption on which it is based merit separate consideration.

Again, we begin with the statute. Notwithstanding the protection given respondent by the ADA's definition of disability, petitioner could have refused to treat her if her infectious condition "posed a direct threat to the health or safety of others." [ ] The ADA defines a direct threat to be "a significant risk to the health or safety of others that cannot be eliminated by a modification of policies, practices, or procedures or by the provision of auxiliary aids or services." [ ]. Parallel provisions appear in the employment provisions of Title I. [ ].

The ADA's direct threat provision stems from the recognition in *School Bd. of Nassau Cty.* v. *Arline,* 480 U.S. 273, 287, 94 L.Ed.2d 307, 107 S.Ct. 1123 (1987), of the importance of prohibiting discrimination against individuals with disabilities while protecting others from significant health and safety risks, resulting, for instance, from a contagious disease. In *Arline,* the Court reconciled these objectives by construing the Rehabilitation Act not to require the hiring of a person who posed "a significant risk of communicating an infectious disease to others." [ ]. Congress amended the Rehabilitation Act and the Fair Housing Act to incorporate the language. [ ] It later relied on the same language in enacting the ADA. [ ]. Because few, if any, activities in life are risk free, *Arline* and the ADA do not ask whether a risk exists, but whether it is significant. [ ]

The existence, or nonexistence, of a significant risk must be determined from the standpoint of the person who refuses the treatment or accommodation, and the risk assessment must be based on medical or other objective evidence. [ ]. As a health care professional, petitioner had the duty to assess the risk of infection based on the objective, scientific information available to him and others in his profession. His belief that a significant risk existed, even if maintained in good faith, would not relieve him from liability. To use the words of the question presented, petitioner receives no special deference simply because he is a health care professional. It is true that *Arline* reserved "the question whether courts should also defer to the reasonable medical judgments of private physicians on which an employer has relied." [ ]. At most, this statement reserved the possibility that employers could consult with individual physicians as objective third-party experts. It did not suggest that an individual physician's state of mind could excuse discrimination without regard to the objective reasonableness of his actions.

Our conclusion that courts should assess the objective reasonableness of the views of health care professionals without deferring to their individual judgments does not answer the implicit assumption in the question presented, whether petitioner's actions were reasonable in light of the available medical evidence. In assessing the reasonableness of petitioner's actions, the views of public health authorities, such as the U.S. Public Health Service, CDC, and the National Institutes of Health, are of special weight and authority. [ ]. The views of these organizations are not conclusive, however. A health care professional who disagrees with the prevailing medical consensus may refute it by citing a credible scientific basis for deviating from the accepted norm. [ ].

We have reviewed so much of the record as necessary to illustrate the application of the rule to the facts of this case. For the most part, the Court of Appeals followed the proper standard in evaluating the petitioner's position and conducted a thorough review of the evidence. Its rejection of the District Court's reliance on the Marianos affidavits was a correct application of the principle that petitioner's actions must be evaluated in light of the available, objective evidence. The record did not show that CDC had published the conclusion set out in the affidavits at the time petitioner refused to treat respondent. [ ]

A further illustration of a correct application of the objective standard is the Court of Appeals' refusal to give weight to the petitioner's offer to treat respondent in a hospital. Petitioner testified that he believed hospitals had safety measures, such as air filtration, ultraviolet lights, and respirators, which would reduce the risk of HIV transmission. Petitioner made no showing, however, that any area hospital had these safeguards or even that he had hospital privileges. His expert also admitted the lack of any scientific basis for the conclusion that these measures would lower the risk of transmission. Petitioner failed to present any objective, medical evidence showing that treating respondent in a hospital would be safer or more efficient in preventing HIV transmission than treatment in a well-equipped dental office.

We are concerned, however, that the Court of Appeals might have placed mistaken reliance upon two other sources. In ruling no triable issue of fact existed on this point, the Court of Appeals relied on the 1993 CDC Dentistry Guidelines and the 1991 American Dental Association Policy on HIV. [ ]. This evidence is not definitive. As noted earlier, the CDC Guidelines recommended certain universal precautions which, in CDC's view, "should reduce the risk of disease transmission in the dental environment." [ ] The Court of Appeals determined that, "while the guidelines do not state explicitly that no further risk-reduction measures are desirable or that routine dental care for HIV-positive individuals is safe, those two conclusions seem to be implicit in the guidelines' detailed delineation of procedures for office treatment of

HIV-positive patients." [ ]. In our view, the Guidelines do not necessarily contain implicit assumptions conclusive of the point to be decided. The Guidelines set out CDC's recommendation that the universal precautions are the best way to combat the risk of HIV transmission. They do not assess the level of risk.

Nor can we be certain, on this record, whether the 1991 American Dental Association Policy on HIV carries the weight the Court of Appeals attributed to it. The Policy does provide some evidence of the medical community's objective assessment of the risks posed by treating people infected with HIV in dental offices. It indicates:

"Current scientific and epidemiologic evidence indicates that there is little risk of transmission of infectious diseases through dental treatment if recommended infection control procedures are routinely followed. Patients with HIV infection may be safely treated in private dental offices when appropriate infection control procedures are employed. Such infection control procedures provide protection both for patients and dental personnel."

We note, however, that the Association is a professional organization, which, although a respected source of information on the dental profession, is not a public health authority. It is not clear the extent to which the Policy was based on the Association's assessment of dentists' ethical and professional duties in addition to its scientific assessment of the risk to which the ADA refers. Efforts to clarify dentists' ethical obligations and to encourage dentists to treat patients with HIV infection with compassion may be commendable, but the question under the statute is one of statistical likelihood, not professional responsibility. Without more information on the manner in which the American Dental Association formulated this Policy, we are unable to determine the Policy's value in evaluating whether petitioner's assessment of the risks was reasonable as a matter of law.

The court considered materials submitted by both parties on the cross motions for summary judgment. The petitioner was required to establish that there existed a genuine issue of material fact. Evidence which was merely colorable or not significantly probative would not have been sufficient. [ ].

We acknowledge the presence of other evidence in the record before the Court of Appeals which, subject to further arguments and examination, might support affirmance of the trial court's ruling. For instance, the record contains substantial testimony from numerous health experts indicating that it is safe to treat patients infected with HIV in dental offices. [ ]. We are unable to determine the import of this evidence, however. The record does not disclose whether the expert testimony submitted by respondent turned on evidence available in September 1994. [ ]

There are reasons to doubt whether petitioner advanced evidence sufficient to raise a triable issue of fact on the significance of the risk. Petitioner relied on two principal points: First, he asserted that the use of high-speed drills and surface cooling with water created a risk of airborne HIV transmission. The study on which petitioner relied was inconclusive, however, determining only that "further work is required to determine whether such a risk exists." [ ] Petitioner's expert witness conceded, moreover, that no evidence suggested the spray could transmit HIV. His opinion on airborne risk was based on the absence of contrary evidence, not on positive data. Scientific evidence and expert testimony must have a traceable, analytical basis in objective fact before it may be considered on summary judgment. [ ]

Second, petitioner argues that, as of September 1994, CDC had identified seven dental workers with possible occupational transmission of HIV. [ ] These dental workers were exposed to HIV in the course of their employment, but CDC could not determine whether HIV infection had resulted. It is now known that CDC could not ascertain whether the seven dental workers contracted the disease because they did not present themselves for HIV testing at an appropriate time after their initial exposure.

* * *

We conclude the proper course is to give the Court of Appeals the opportunity to determine whether our analysis of some of the studies cited by the parties would change its conclusion that petitioner presented neither objective evidence nor a triable issue of fact on the question of risk. In remanding the case, we do not foreclose the possibility that the Court of Appeals may reach the same conclusion it did earlier. A remand will permit a full exploration of the issue through the adversary process.

The determination of the Court of Appeals that respondent's HIV infection was a disability under the ADA is affirmed. The judgment is vacated, and the case is remanded for further proceedings consistent with this opinion.

* * *

CHIEF JUSTICE REHNQUIST, with whom JUSTICE SCALIA and JUSTICE THOMAS join, and with whom JUSTICE O'CONNOR joins as to Part II, concurring in the judgment in part and dissenting in part.

I

Is respondent—who has tested positive for the human immunodeficiency virus (HIV) but was asymptomatic at the time she suffered discriminatory treatment—a person with a "disability" as that term is defined in the Americans with Disabilities Act of 1990 (ADA)? The term "disability" is defined in the ADA to include:

"(A) a physical or mental impairment that substantially limits one or more of the major life activities of such individual;

"(B) a record of such an impairment; or

"(C) being regarded as having such an impairment." 42 U.S.C. § 12102(2).

It is important to note that whether respondent has a disability covered by the ADA is an individualized inquiry. The Act could not be clearer on this point: Section 12102(2) states explicitly that the disability determination must be made "with respect to an individual." Were this not sufficiently clear, the Act goes on to provide that the "major life activities" allegedly limited by an impairment must be those "of such individual." [ ].

The individualized nature of the inquiry is particularly important in this case because the District Court disposed of it on summary judgment. Thus all disputed issues of material fact must be resolved against respondent. She contends that her asymptomatic HIV status brings her within the first definition of a "disability." She must therefore demonstrate, *inter alia*, that she was (1) physically or mentally impaired and that such impairment (2) substantially limited (3) one or more of her major life activities.

Petitioner does not dispute that asymptomatic HIV-positive status is a physical impairment. I therefore assume this to be the case, and proceed to the second and third statutory requirements for "disability."

According to the Court, the next question is "whether reproduction is a major life activity." [ ] That, however, is only half of the relevant question. As mentioned above, the ADA's definition of a "disability" requires that the major life activity at issue be one "of such individual." [ ] The Court truncates the question, perhaps because there is not a shred of record evidence indicating that, prior to becoming infected with HIV, respondent's major life activities included reproduction (assuming for the moment that reproduction is a major life activity at all). At most, the record indicates that after learning of her HIV status, respondent, whatever her previous inclination, conclusively decided that she would not have children. There is absolutely no evidence that, absent the HIV, respondent would have had or was even considering having children. Indeed, when asked during her deposition whether her HIV infection had in any way impaired her ability to carry out any of *her* life functions, respondent answered "No." *Ibid.* It is further telling that in the course of her entire brief to this Court, respondent studiously avoids asserting even once that reproduction is a major life activity *to her*. To the contrary, she argues that the "major life activity" inquiry should not turn on a particularized assessment of the circumstances of this or any other case.

But even aside from the facts of this particular case, the Court is simply wrong in concluding as a general matter that reproduction is a "major life activity." Unfortunately, the ADA does not define the phrase "major life activities." But the Act does incorporate by reference a list of such activities contained in regulations issued under the Rehabilitation Act. [ ]. The Court correctly recognizes that this list of major life activities "is illustrative, not exhaustive," but then makes no attempt to demonstrate that reproduction is a major life activity in the same sense that "caring for one's self, performing manual tasks, walking, seeing, hearing, speaking, breathing, learning, and working" are.

Instead, the Court argues that reproduction is a "major" life activity in that it is "central to the life process itself." In support of this reading, the Court focuses on the fact that " 'major' " indicates " 'comparative importance,' " ignoring the alternative definition of "major" as "greater in quantity, number, or extent," *ibid*. It is the latter definition that is most consistent with the ADA's illustrative list of major life activities.

No one can deny that reproductive decisions are important in a person's life. But so are decisions as to who to marry, where to live, and how to earn one's living. Fundamental importance of this sort is not the common thread linking the statute's listed activities. The common thread is rather that the activities are repetitively performed and essential in the day-to-day existence of a normally functioning individual. They are thus quite different from the series of activities leading to the birth of a child.

* * *

But even if I were to assume that reproduction *is* a major life activity of respondent, I do not agree that an asymptomatic HIV infection "substantially limits" that activity. The record before us leaves no doubt that those so infected are still entirely able to engage in sexual intercourse, give birth to a child if they become pregnant, and perform the manual tasks necessary to rear a child to maturity. While individuals infected with HIV may choose not to engage in these activities, there is no support in language, logic, or our case law for the proposition that such voluntary choices constitute a "limit" on one's own life activities.

* * *

ESTATE OF BEHRINGER v. MEDICAL CENTER AT PRINCETON

Superior Court of New Jersey, Law Division, 1991.
249 N.J.Super. 597, 592 A.2d 1251.

Plaintiff, William H. Behringer, was a patient at defendant Medical Center at Princeton (the Medical Center) when on June 17, 1987, he tested positive for the Human Immunodeficiency Virus (HIV), and combined with Pneumocystis Carinii Pneumonia (PCP), was diagnosed as suffering from Acquired Immunodeficiency Syndrome (AIDS). At the time, plaintiff, an otolaryngologist (ENT) and plastic surgeon, was also a member of the staff at the Medical Center. Within hours of his discharge from the Medical Center on June 18, 1987, plaintiff received numerous phone calls from well-wishers indicating a concern for his welfare but also demonstrating an awareness of his illness. Most of these callers were also members of the medical staff at the Medical Center. Other calls were received from friends in the community. Within days, similar calls were received from patients. Within a few weeks of his diagnosis, plaintiff's surgical privileges at the Medical Center were suspended. From the date of his diagnosis until his death on July 2, 1989, plaintiff did not perform any further surgery at the Medical Center, his practice declined and he suffered both emotionally and financially.

Plaintiff brings this action seeking damages for 1) breach of the Medical Center's and named employees' duty to maintain confidentiality of plaintiff's diagnosis and test results, and 2) violation of the New Jersey Law Against Discrimination [ ] as a result of the imposition of conditions on plaintiff's continued performance of surgical procedures at the Medical Center, revocation of plaintiff's surgical privileges and breach of confidentiality. Defendant denies any breach of confidentiality and asserts that any action by the Medical Center was proper and not a violation of [New Jersey law.]

This case raises novel issues of a hospital's obligation to protect the confidentiality of an AIDS diagnosis of a health care worker, as well as a hospital's right to regulate and restrict the surgical activities of an HIV positive doctor. This case addresses the apparent conflict between a doctor's rights under the New Jersey Law Against Discrimination, [ ] and a patient's "right to know" under the doctrine of "informed consent." This case explores the competing interests of a surgeon with AIDS, his patients, the hospital at which he practices and the hospital's medical and dental staff.

* * *

Plaintiff, a Board-certified ENT surgeon, developed a successful practice during his ten years in the Princeton area. His practice extended beyond the limited area of ear, nose and throat surgery and included a practice in facial plastic surgery. He served as an attending physician at the Medical Center since 1979 and performed surgery at the Medical Center since 1981.

In early June 1987, plaintiff felt ill. He complained of various symptoms and treated himself. Acknowledging no improvement, plaintiff consulted with a physician-friend (the treating physician). On June 16, 1987, plaintiff's companion arrived at plaintiff's home and observed that plaintiff was in distress. A call was made to the treating physician, and at approximately 11:00 p.m., plaintiff and his companion proceeded to the Medical Center Emergency Room, where plaintiff was examined initially by a number of residents and, thereafter, by the treating physician. The treating physician advised plaintiff that a pulmonary consultation was necessary, and a pulmonary specialist proceeded to examine plaintiff. A determination was made to perform a bronchoscopy—a diagnostic procedure involving bronchial washings—to establish the existence of PCP, a conclusive indicator of AIDS. The pulmonary consultant assumed that plaintiff, as a physician, knew the implications of PCP and its relationship to AIDS. In addition, the treating physician ordered a blood study including a test to determine whether plaintiff was infected with HIV—the cause of AIDS.

* * *

Conforming to Medical Center policy, plaintiff executed a consent form granting to the pulmonary consultant the general consent to perform a bronchoscopy. * * * Later that day, the pulmonary consultant reported to plaintiff that the results of the tests were positive for PCP, and he concluded that this information was new to plaintiff. Early that evening, the treating physician returned to plaintiff's room, and in the presence of plaintiff's companion, informed plaintiff that the HIV test was positive. Plaintiff was also informed that he had AIDS. Plaintiff's reaction, according to plaintiff's companion, was one of shock and dismay. His emotions ranged from concern about his health to fear of the impact of this information on his practice. Plaintiff's companion described her initial response as "who else knew?" The treating physician responded that he had told his wife; both plaintiff and his companion, close personal friends of both the treating physician and his wife, responded that "they understood."

It was readily apparent to all persons involved at this point that plaintiff's presence in the Medical Center was cause for concern. An infectious disease consultant and staff epidemiologist suggested to plaintiff that he transfer to Lenox Hill Hospital in New York or other available hospitals in the area. After inquiry, it was determined that no other beds were available. This concern for an immediate transfer appeared to be two-fold—to insure the best available treatment for plaintiff (the treating physician suggested that AZT treatment be considered) and to prevent plaintiff's diagnosis from becoming public. It is apparent that all parties involved to this point—plaintiff, the treating physician, the epidemiologist and plaintiff's companion—fully understood the implications of the AIDS diagnosis becoming a matter of public knowledge. A determination was made that plaintiff would leave the hospital and be treated at home.

Plaintiff's concern about public knowledge of the diagnosis was not misplaced. Upon his arrival home, plaintiff and his companion received a series of phone calls. Calls were received from various doctors who practiced at the Medical Center with plaintiff. All doctors, in addition to being professional colleagues, were social friends, but none were involved with the care and treatment of plaintiff. All indicated in various ways that they were aware of the diagnosis. * * *

* * * In July, 1987, plaintiff returned to his office practice. During his short absence from his office and in the ensuing months, calls were received at his practice from doctors and patients alike who indicated an awareness of plaintiff's condition and in many cases, requested transfer of files or indicated no further interest in being treated by plaintiff.

The Medical Center's reaction to plaintiff's condition was swift and initially precise. Upon learning of plaintiff's diagnosis from the Chief of

Nursing, the President of the Medical Center, defendant Dennis Doody (Doody), immediately directed the cancellation of plaintiff's pending surgical cases. This initial decision was made with little information or knowledge of potential transmission of the disease; thereafter, the Chairman of the Department of Surgery, having privately researched the issue, reached a contrary result and urged that plaintiff could resume his surgical practice. The Medical Center procedure for suspending a physician's surgical privileges provides for summary suspension by a vote of the Department chair, President of the Medical Center, President of the Medical and Dental Staff, Chairman of the Board of Trustees, and the physician in charge of the service. While Doody was defeated in a vote for summary suspension, the surgery remained cancelled, and the matter was ultimately brought before the Board of Trustees.

Doody's motivation in seeking the suspension of surgical privileges was described as one of concern for patients but also, and perhaps more important, concern for the Medical Center and its potential liability. Little was known about the dilemma now facing the Medical Center. In any event, plaintiff's surgical privileges were cancelled and would never, during plaintiff's life, be reinstated.

* * *

On June 27, 1988, the Board of Trustees met and, after questions and discussions, adopted the following policy for HIV seropositive health care workers:

POLICY FOR HIV SEROPOSITIVE HEALTH CARE WORKERS

    1. The Medical Center at Princeton Medical and Dental Staff shall continue to care for patients with AIDS without discrimination.

    2. A physician or health care provider with known HIV seropositivity may continue to treat patients at The Medical Center at Princeton, but shall not perform procedures that pose any risk of HIV transmission to the patient.

This policy included a procedure for the recredentialling of physicians. Although the policy was adopted, the Board did not change its prior requirement that a physician obtain written informed consent from the patient prior to the performance of surgical procedures.

Plaintiff's privileges, as a "potential risk," were ultimately suspended under this policy, and no action was taken by him challenging the policy or seeking recredentialling under the policy.

Following his diagnosis of AIDS, plaintiff never again performed surgery at the Medical Center.

* * *

Plaintiff asserts that the Medical Center, Doody and Lee breached a duty of confidentiality in failing to restrict access to plaintiff's medical records, thus causing widespread and improper dissemination of information about plaintiff's medical condition. Plaintiff argues that as a result of this breach of confidentiality, his ability to practice was impaired so significantly that his medical practice was damaged, if not destroyed. Plaintiff's confidentiality-based claims arise out of his status as a patient. While plaintiff was unable to identify specifically the actual sources of the disclosure of his diagnosis, he argues that the Medical Center's failure to implement meaningful restrictions on access to his medical records is sufficient to establish liability. In sum, he urges that the failure of the Medical Center to take reasonable precautions regarding access to his records establishes liability. Defendants argue that any disclosure by its employees or others outside of its control is beyond its responsibility and cannot be the basis of liability.

The physician-patient privilege has a strong tradition in New Jersey. The privilege imposes an obligation on the physician to maintain the confidentiality of a patient's communications. [ ]. This obligation of confidentiality applies to patient records and information and applies not only to physicians but to hospitals as well. [ ]. This duty of confidentiality has been the subject of legislative codification which reflects the public policy of this State. [ ] The patient must be able "to secure medical services without fear of betrayal and unwarranted embarrassing and detrimental disclosure.... " [ ]. The privacy right on which the privilege is based has been held to a level warranting constitutional protection. [ ].

* * *

A physician may not reveal the confidences entrusted to him in the course of medical attendance, or the deficiencies he may observe in the character of patients, unless he is required to do so by law or unless it becomes necessary in order to protect the welfare or the individual or of the community. [American Medical Association, Principles of Medical Ethics, § 9 (1957).] See also Tarasoff v. Regents of Univ. of California, 17 Cal.3d 425, 551 P.2d 334, 131 Cal.Rptr. 14 (1976).

An additional exception to the concept of confidentiality is a physician's or hospital's statutory obligation to report contagious diseases to health authorities. N.J.S.A. 26:4–15 requires that "every physician shall, within 12 hours after his diagnosis that a person is ill or infected with a communicable disease ... report such diagnosis and such related information as may be required by the State Department of Health." N.J.S.A. 26:4–19 similarly requires that the supervisor of a public or private institution report to the local health board any diagnosis of a contagious disease made within the institution. N.J.A.C. 8:57–1.3 sets forth a list of communicable diseases reportable by physicians. The list was amended in 1983, effective March 7, 1982, to require that patients diagnosed with PCP—plaintiff's diagnosed condition—be reported to the New Jersey Department of Health.

Certainly, a most apparent exception to the general rule of confidentiality is the implied right to make available to others involved in the patient's care information necessary to that care. Plaintiff does not argue that the legitimate disclosure of his medical information under this patient care exception is a basis of his cause of action. Both N.J.S.A. 2A:84A–22.2 and the recently enacted provisions of N.J.S.A. 26:5C–8 (which postdate the events in this matter) allow for the dissemination of a patient's records and information

... to qualified personnel involved in the medical education or in the diagnosis and treatment of the person who is the subject of the record. Disclosure is limited to only personnel directly involved in medical education or in the diagnosis and treatment of the person.

It is against this basic policy and statutory framework that the conduct of a hospital dealing with an AIDS patient must be measured.

The present day public perception of AIDS was an important consideration in the adoption and implementation of procedures established by the Department of Health and the Medical Center. The impact of the public perception has been widely recognized.

Individuals infected with HIV, whether HCP [health care professional] or patient, are concerned with maintaining the confidentiality of their health status. HIV infection is associated with sexual practice and drug use, universally regarded as personal and sensitive activities. In addition, the majority of people infected with HIV in the United States are members of groups that are traditionally disfavored. Even before the AIDS epidemic, gays and intravenous (IV) drug users were subject to persistent prejudice and discrimination. AIDS brings with it a special stigma. Attitude surveys show that even though most Americans understand the modes through which HIV is spread, a significant minority still would exclude those who are HIV-positive from schools, public accommodations, and the workplace. Unauthorized disclosure of a person's serologic status can lead to social opprobrium among family and friends, as well as loss of employment, housing 5 and insurance. [ ]

* * *

The Medical Center's disregard for the importance of preserving the confidentiality of plaintiff's patient medical records was evident even before the charting of the HIV test results. A review of plaintiff's hospital chart reveals not only the HIV test results, but the results of the bronchoscopy—PCP—which all concede was a definitive diagnosis of AIDS. While the Medical Center argues that the decision regarding charting is one for the physicians to make, the Medical Center cannot avoid liability on that basis. It is not the charting per se that generates the issue; it is the easy accessibility to the charts and the lack of any meaningful Medical Center policy or procedure to limit access that causes the breach to occur. Where the impact of such accessibility is so clearly foreseeable, it is incumbent on the Medical Center, as the custodian of the charts, to take such reasonable measures as are necessary to insure that confidentiality. Failure to take such steps is negligence. [Citations omitted] The argument that such information may have been transmitted by employees acting beyond the scope of their employment is not persuasive. The requirement of confidentiality is to protect the patient. This was not a patient hospitalized for a trivial or common-place malady. Insuring confidentiality becomes a matter of prime concern. The failure to recognize the potential for employee breach of confidentiality provides no defense.

* * *

Insuring confidentiality even by Medical Center employees required more, in the present case, than simply instructing employees that medical records are confidential. The charts are kept under the control of the Medical Center with full knowledge of the accessibility of such charts to virtually all Medical Center personnel whether authorized or not. Little, if any, action was taken to establish any policy or procedure for dealing with a chart such as plaintiff's.

* * *

Because the stakes are so high in the case of a physician being treated at his own hospital, it is imperative that the hospital take reasonable steps to insure the confidentiality of not only an HIV test result, but a diagnosis which is conclusive of AIDS, such as PCP. These precautions may include a securing of the chart, with access only to those HCWs demonstrating to designated record-keepers a bona-fide need to know, or utilizing sequestration procedures for those portions of the record containing such information. While a designation in a chart of sequestered information such as a diagnosis or test result may lead to speculation or rumor among persons not having access to the charts this speculation is an acceptable cost to prevent free access to a chart where real information improperly disseminated will cause untold harm. This court recognizes that in some circumstances, such as rounds at a teaching hospital, exposure to a patient's records must be greater than to solely physicians or students directly involved in the patient's care. It is incumbent upon the hospital to impress upon these physicians or students the significance of maintaining the confidentiality of patient records.

* * *

This Court holds that the failure of the Medical Center and Lee as Director of the Department of Laboratories, who were together responsible for developing the misstated Informed Consent form, the counselling procedure and implementation of the charting protocol, to take reasonable steps to maintain the confidentiality of plaintiff's medical records, while plaintiff was a patient, was a breach of the Medical Center's duty and obligation to keep such records confidential. The Medical Center is liable for damages caused by this breach.

Plaintiff, as a physician, asserts a cause of action under the New Jersey Law Against Discrimination [ ] based on the [restriction 9 and] ultimate curtailment of plaintiff's surgical privileges at the Medical Center.

New Jersey prohibits unlawful discrimination, or any unlawful employment practice, against a person in a place of public accommodation on the basis that that person is handicapped. [ ] A review of the definitional sections of the LAD bring both the Medical Center and plaintiff within its scope. A hospital such as the Medical Center falls within the definition of a place of public accommodation.

* * *

Courts in other jurisdictions have universally held that AIDS is a handicap within the meaning of laws prohibiting handicap discrimination. Both federal trial 3 and courts of appeal have held AIDS to be a handicap protected under the Vocational Rehabilitation Act of 1973 [ ] which prohibits discrimination against the handicapped by recipients of federal funds. [Citations omitted] Likewise, various state courts have held AIDS to be a qualified handicap under their respective discrimination laws.

* * *

The ultimate resolution reached by the Medical Center restricting invasive procedures where there is "any risk to the patient," coupled with informed consent, implicates serious policy considerations which must be explored. It is axiomatic that physicians performing invasive procedures should not knowingly place a patient at risk because of the physician's physical condition. [ ] The policy adopted by the Medical Center barring "any procedures that pose any risk of virus transmission to the patient" appears to preclude, on its face, the necessity of an informed consent form; if there is "any risk" the procedure cannot be performed. The problem created by the "any risk" standard is best evidenced by the facts of this case. When Doody made his initial decision to cancel plaintiff's scheduled surgical procedures, he did so over the objection of both the President of the Medical and Dental Staff as well as the Chairman of the Department of Surgery. * * *

Reasonable persons professing knowledge of the subject matter may differ as to whether there is "any" risk involved in an invasive surgical procedure by a surgeon carrying a disease that will lead to his death and, if transmitted during the surgical procedure, to the death of the patient. * * *

* * *

Before a physician may perform a surgical or invasive procedure upon a patient, he must obtain the patient's informed consent.

[Informed consent] is essentially a negligence concept, predicated on the duty of a physician to disclose to a patient such information as will enable the patient to make an evaluation of the nature of the treatment and of any attendant substantial risks, as well as of available options in the form of alternative therapies. [Citations omitted].

The physician exposing the patient to a course of treatment has a duty to explain, in terms understandable to the patient, what the physician proposes to do. The purpose of this legal requirement is to protect each person's right to self-determination in matters of medical treatment. See In re Farrell, 108 N.J. 335, 347 (1987). The physician's duty is to explain, in words the patient can understand, that medical information and those risks which are material. Medical information or a risk of a medical procedure is material when a reasonable patient would be likely to attach significance to it in deciding whether or not to submit to the treatment.

Taking into account what the physician knows or should know to be the patient's informational needs, the physician must make reasonable disclosure of the information and those risks which a reasonably prudent patient would consider material or significant in making the decision about what course of treatment, if any, to accept. Such information would generally include a description of the patient's physical condition, the purposes and advantages of the proposed surgery, the material risks of the proposed surgery and the material risks if such surgery is not provided. In addition, the physician should discuss all available options or alternatives and their advantages and risks. [ ]

Plaintiff argues: 1) the risk of transmission of HIV from surgeon to patient is too remote to require informed consent, and 2) the law of informed consent does not require disclosure of the condition of the surgeon.

Both parties focus on the risk of transmission and results therefrom 5 in applying the two standards raised in plaintiff's claim under the LAD. The Jansen standard states that the risk must be one which will create a "reasonable probability of substantial ham," and the Largey standard requires disclosure of a "material risk" or one to which a reasonable patient would likely attach significance in determining whether to proceed with the proposed procedure. It is the court's view that the risk of transmission is not the sole risk involved. The risk of a surgical accident, i.e., a needlestick or scalpel cut, during surgery performed by an HIV-positive surgeon, may subject a previously uninfected patient to months or even years of continual HIV testing. Both of these risks are sufficient to meet the Jansen standard of "probability of harm" and the Largey standard requiring disclosure.

[Defendant] agreed that the statistical risk of transmission from health-care worker to patient is small—less than one-half of one percent. At the time of trial, there were no reported cases of transmission. [ ] But the statistical analysisis flawed. Professor Gostin noted the following:

* * *

Physicians performing seriously invasive procedures, such as surgeons, have a potential to cut or puncture their skin with sharp surgical instruments, needles, or bone fragments. Studies indicate that a surgeon will cut a glove in approximately one out of every four cases, and probably sustain a significant skin cut in one out of every forty cases. Given these data, it has been calculated that the risk of contracting HIV in a single surgical operation on an HIV-infected patient is remote—in the range of 1/130,000 to 1/4,500.

It is impossible accurately to calculate the level 7 of risk of HIV transmission from surgeon to patient. Surgeons who cut or puncture themselves do not necessarily expose the patient to their blood, and even if they do the volume is extremely small. A small inoculum of contaminated blood is unlikely to transmit the virus. This suggests that the risk of infection from surgeon to patient is much lower than in the opposite direction. Nonetheless, the fact that the surgeon is in significant contact with the patient's blood and organs, together with the high rate of torn gloves, makes it reasonable to assume that the risk runs in both directions, as is the case with the hepatitis B virus. The cumulative risk to surgical patients, arguably, is higher. While an HIV-infected patient is likely to have relatively few seriously invasive procedures, the infected surgeon, even if the virus drastically shortens his surgical career, can be expected to perform numerous operations. Assuming that the surgical patient's risk is exceedingly low (1/130,000), the risk that one of his patients will contract HIV becomes more realistic the more operations he performs—1/1,300 (assuming 100 operations) or 1/126 (assuming 500 operations). Patients, of course, 8 cannot expect a wholly risk-free environment in a hospital. But there does come a point where the risk of a detrimental outcome becomes sufficiently real that it is prudent for the profession to establish guidelines.

While the debate will rage long into the future as to the quantifiable risk of HIV transmission from doctor to patient, there is little disagreement that a risk of transmission, however small, does exist. This risk may be reduced by the use of universal precautions, such as double gloving and the use of goggles and other similar devices.

In quantifying the risk, one must consider not only statistical data, but the nature of the procedure being performed. Plaintiff was a surgeon who specialized in surgery performed in the ear and mouth cavities. As Dr. Day indicated, much of plaintiff's surgery involved contact with the mucous membrane 9—an area particularly susceptible to transmission of HIV should the surgeon incur a surgical accident involving the potential for exchange of blood.

* * *

In balancing quantifiable risk with the necessity of informed consent, one must recognize the strong commitment of the New Jersey courts to the concept of a fully informed patient. [ ] Plaintiff argues that the use of the informed consent form is tantamount to a de facto termination of surgical privileges. Plaintiff further urges that patient reaction is likely to be based more on public hysteria than on a studied assessment of the actual risk involved. The answer to these arguments is two-fold. First, it is the duty of the surgeon utilizing the informed consent procedure to explain to the patient the real risk involved. If the patient's fear is without basis, it is likewise the duty of the surgeon to allay that fear. This court recognizes that the burden imposed on 1 the surgeon may not be surmountable absent further education of both the public and the medical community about the realities of HIV and AIDS. Second, the difficulties created by the public reaction to AIDS cannot deprive the patient of making the ultimate decision where the ultimate risk is so significant. The last word has not been spoken on the issue of transmission of HIV and AIDS. Facts accepted at one point in time are no longer accurate as more is learned about this disease and its transmission.

Plaintiff further argues that there is no requirement under the doctrine of informed consent that a surgeon's physical condition be revealed as a risk of the surgery itself. The informed consent cases are not so narrow as to support that argument. In Largey v. Rothman, supra, 110 N.J. at 208, the court spoke of not only an evaluation of the nature of the treatment, but of "any attendant substantial risks." [ ]. As noted earlier, the risks can foreseeably include a needlestick or scalpel cut and, even with universal precautions can result in an exchange of the surgeon's blood.

* * *

The obligation of a surgeon performing invasive procedures, such as plaintiff, to reveal his AIDS condition, is one which requires a weighing of the plaintiff's rights against the patient's rights. New Jersey's strong policy supporting patient rights, weighed against plaintiff's individual right to perform an invasive procedure as a part of the practice of his profession, requires the conclusion that the patient's rights must prevail. At a minimum, the physician must withdraw from performing any invasive procedure which would pose a risk to the patient. Where the ultimate harm is death, even the presence of a low risk of transmission justifies the adoption of a policy which precludes invasive procedures when there is "any" risk of transmission. In the present case, the debate raged as to whether there was "any" risk of transmission, and the informed consent procedure was left in place. If there is to be an ultimate arbiter of whether the patient is to be treated invasively by an AIDS-positive surgeon, the arbiter will be the fully informed patient. The ultimate risk to the patient is so absolute—so devastating—that it is untenable to argue against informed consent combined with a restriction on procedures which present "any risk" to the patient.

In assessing the Medical Center's obligation under the LAD, it is the Court's view that the burden under Jansen has been met, and there was a "reasonable probability of substantial harm" if plaintiff continued to perform invasive procedures. Plaintiff is not entitled to recovery under this statute. The Medical Center acted properly in initially suspending plaintiff's surgical privileges, thereafter imposing a requirement of informed consent and ultimately barring him from performing surgery. These decisions were not made spontaneously or without thought. One need only review the minutes of meeting after meeting where the debate raged and the various competing interests—the Medical and Dental Staff and Board—expressed their views. The seeking of input from medical ethicists and attorneys knowledgeable in this area belies any suggestion of prejudgment or arbitrariness on the part of the Medical Center. The result, while harsh to plaintiff, represents a reasoned and informed response to the problem.

A judgment as to liability is granted in favor of plaintiff against defendant Medical Center and defendant Lee on Counts 1, 2, 3 and 6 of the Complaint. A judgment is entered in favor of defendant Medical Center and defendant Doody as to Counts 4, 5, and 7, no cause for action.

BLANKS v. SOUTHWESTERN BELL COMMUNICATIONS, INC.

United States Court of Appeals for the Fifth Circuit, 2002.
310 F.3d 398.

CLEMENT, Circuit Judge:

Appellant, who is HIV positive, alleges that his former employer, Southwestern Bell ("SWB"), failed to accommodate him as required by the Americans with Disabilities Act of 1990 ("ADA"). 42 U.S.C. § 12101 *et seq*. Appellant further alleges that appellee constructively discharged him from the company. The district court found that, viewing the evidence in the light most favorable to the appellant, there was no triable issue of fact to show: (1) that appellant's HIV status qualified him as disabled under the ADA; (2) that appellee failed to offer appellant reasonable accommodation; or (3) that appellee constructively discharged appellant. Because we conclude Blanks was not a qualified individual with a disability for purposes of the ADA, we affirm.

I. FACTS AND PROCEEDINGS

SWB employed appellant, Albenjamin Blanks ("Blanks"), from 1977 until June 1997. Blanks held several positions in the company, eventually working as a residential customer service representative ("CSR") from 1992 to 1996. In 1996, Blanks took short-term medical disability for depression and work-related stress. While on leave in November 1996, doctors diagnosed Blanks with HIV and he sought treatment for the disease.

Blanks received a medical release to return to work. In granting the release, the doctor recommended that Blanks not work in CSR because dealing with belligerent customers on a daily basis had contributed to his earlier stress and depression. For several months in early 1997, SWB and Blanks attempted to agree upon an appropriate company position. SWB offered Blanks his earlier position as a supplies attendant, but he could not accept the offer because recent hemorrhoid surgery prevented him from doing the required lifting. Blanks requested an internal CSR position, which he thought would be less stressful. SWB denied his request, but eventually offered Blanks a position as a general clerk at a salary approximately $100 less per week than his previous CSR position. Blanks accepted the job and worked for approximately two weeks in

June before submitting a letter of resignation on June 18, 1997, in which he stated that he could not continue to support his family due to the pay cut associated with the clerk position.

Blanks filed a charge of disability discrimination with the Texas Commission on Human Rights ("TCHR") on September 8, 1997. Blanks received his right-to-sue letter and filed suit in the Northern District of Texas. The court granted summary judgment to SWB. In a well-reasoned memorandum opinion by Judge Fitzwater, the court found that Blanks failed to raise a genuine issue of material fact to show: (1) that he qualified for disability status under the ADA; (2) that SWB failed to accommodate him; or (3) that he was constructively discharged.

* * *

III. ANALYSIS

A. *Blanks' Status Under the ADA*

To establish a *prima facie* case for discrimination under the ADA, a plaintiff must be a qualified individual with a disability. *Mason v. United Airlines*, 274 F.3d 314, 316 (5th Cir. 2001). The term "disability" under the ADA means: "(A) a physical impairment that substantially limits one or more of the major life activities of such individual; (B) a record of such an impairment; or (C) being regarded as having such an impairment." 42 U.S.C. § 12102(2).

1. *Actual Disability*

In determining whether an individual's HIV status qualifies as a disability under the first prong, we examine three factors: (1) whether the HIV infection is a physical impairment; (2) whether appellant relies on a particular major life activity under the ADA; and (3) whether the impairment substantially limits the major life activity. [ ]. Major life activities may include "any physiological disorder, or condition, cosmetic disfigurement, or anatomical loss affecting one or more of the following body systems: neurological, musculoskeletal, special sense organs, respiratory (including speech organs), cardiovascular, reproductive, digestive, genito-urinary, hemic and lymphatic, skin, and endocrine." *Sutton v. United Airlines, Inc.*, 527 U.S. 471, 479–80, 119 S.Ct. 2139, 144 L.Ed.2d 450 (1999). The Supreme Court has held that asymptomatic HIV qualifies as a physical impairment from the moment of infection [ ] and that HIV substantially limits the major life activity of reproduction. [ ]. Accordingly, an HIV-positive person who shows that he or she is substantially limited in the major life activity of reproduction is entitled to protection under the ADA. [ ].

Although we consider Blanks physically impaired by his HIV status, *id.* at 637, he fails to cite in his brief or develop in the record how any of his major life activities are impaired. Specifically, Blanks fails to assert that his HIV status substantially impaired his major life activity of reproduction. Blanks testified that after his wife gave birth to their daughter in the early 1990's—long before SWB's alleged discrimination—the couple decided not to have any more children and his wife underwent a procedure to prevent her from having any more children. [ ]. Because Blanks does not want to have any more children, and because he fails to assert any facts to the contrary, he does not raise a triable issue of fact to indicate that his HIV status substantially limited his major life activity of reproduction. [ ].

If an individual is not substantially limited with respect to any other major life activity, the Court may consider whether the individual is substantially limited in the major life activity of working. *Dutcher v. Ingalls Shipbuilding*, 53 F.3d 723, 726 n.10 (5th Cir. 1995). To be substantially limited in the major life activity of working, one must be "significantly restricted in the ability to perform either a class of jobs or a broad range of jobs in various classes as compared to the average person having comparable training, skills and abilities." *Id*. While an individual need not be completely unable to work, one is not substantially limited in working if he or she is unable to perform a single job or a narrow range of jobs. In this case, although Blanks preferred a customer service position, he made it clear in the record that he was willing to do nearly any job that paid the same as the residential CSR position. He maintains that his HIV status only substantially affected his ability to perform his former position as residential CSR. Because Blanks' HIV status only precluded him from performing a single job, he cannot be considered as substantially limited in the major life activity of working. As such, Blanks does not qualify as disabled under the first prong of the ADA.

2. *"Record of" Disability*

The second prong of the ADA entitles a plaintiff to protection if he or she can show that both: (1) the plaintiff has a record or history of impairment; and (2) the impairment limits a major life activity. [ ]. Although an individual may show that he or she has a record of impairment, if he or she fails to show that the impairment is substantially limiting, the individual may not qualify as disabled under this prong. [ ]. While there are sufficient facts to allege that Blanks had a record of impairment, he may not qualify as disabled under the "record of" prong because he failed to raise a genuine issue of fact to show that he was substantially limited in a major life activity.

3. *"Regarded As" Disabled*

An individual may also qualify for protection under the ADA if he or she is "regarded as" disabled by his or her employer. An employee may be "regarded as" disabled if he or she "has an impairment which is not substantially limiting but which the employer perceives as constituting a substantially limiting impairment." [citation omitted] If the employer excludes the impaired employee from a broad range of jobs, the employee is "regarded as" disabled under the ADA. *See id*. at 334. If the employee is merely excluded from a narrow range of jobs, then he or she is not "regarded as" disabled under this prong. *Id*. (asserting that a "broad range" implies more than two job types).

Blanks failed to allege sufficient facts to allow a reasonable trier of fact to conclude that he may have been "regarded as" disabled by SWB. The only proof he puts forth is a statement by a coordinator of his return to work that Blanks "had a permanent disability that would never allow [Blanks] to work as a customer service representative at Southwestern Bell." [ ]. This statement, even when viewed in the light most favorable to Blanks, is not enough for a trier of fact to conclude that Blanks was regarded as disabled under the terms of the ADA. In fact, the coordinator later tried to place Blanks in several alternate positions, thereby making it clear that she did not regard him as unable to perform a broad range of jobs—only the particular job of a customer service representative. [Reference omitted]. Consequently, Blanks also fails the "regarded as" disabled prong of the ADA and is not qualified for protection under the statute.

B. *Blanks' Accommodation and Constructive Discharge Claims*

We conclude that Blanks is not entitled to ADA protection, hence, we need not decide whether SWB failed to reasonably accommodate him or whether SWB constructively discharged him.

IV. Conclusion

Because plaintiff failed to raise a genuine issue of material fact suggesting that he is qualified as disabled under the ADA as a result of his HIV status, we affirm the judgment of the district court.

WADDELL v. VALLEY FORGE DENTAL ASSOCIATES, INC.

United States Court of Appeals for the Eleventh Circuit, 2001.
276 F.3d 1275.

BIRCH, Circuit Judge:

* * * This case requires us to decide whether the district court properly held that Waddell, an HIV-positive dental hygienist, was not otherwise qualified for his employment position because he posed a direct threat to his patients.

I. Background

Waddell, a dental hygienist licensed by the State of Georgia, was employed by Dr. Eugene Witkin from early 1996 until October 1997. In February 1997, Valley Forge took over Witkin's practice. Under this agreement, Witkin and his employees became Valley Forge's employees. Waddell's primary responsibility as a dental hygienist for both Witkin and Valley Forge was the performance of routine prophylaxis, or, in lay terms, the cleaning of teeth.

In September 1997, Dr. Sourignamath Bhat administered a test to Waddell to determine whether he carried the human immunodeficiency virus ("HIV"). Waddell's test results indicated that he was HIV-positive. Bhat telephoned Witkin to inform him of Waddell's test results, and

Witkin in turn alerted Jill Whelchel, a dental hygienist and administrator at Valley Forge, to Waddell's status. Whelchel contacted Jean Welsko in Valley Forge's Human Resources Department and sought advice on how to handle the situation. On Welsko's suggestion, Witkin and Whelchel met with Waddell and put him on paid leave until the three of them could decide what action should be taken. During the next week, Witkin studied his stockpile of dental journals to glean information about the transmission of HIV in the dental context. The Centers for Disease Control and Prevention ("CDC") also was consulted concerning the risk of transmission. Witkin and Whelchel then met with Waddell again and told him that he could no longer treat patients because of his HIV-positive status. They offered Waddell a clerical job at the front desk at roughly half of the salary he had made as a dental hygienist. Waddell took another week off to consider the proposition, and when he ultimately refused to accept the offered job at the offered rate of pay, Valley Forge terminated his employment.

Waddell brought this suit against Valley Forge, seeking relief under the ADA, the Rehabilitation Act, and various Georgia statutory provisions. After conducting discovery, both Waddell and Valley Forge moved for summary judgment. The issues on the ADA claim were limited by the fact that Valley Forge admitted that its decision to remove Waddell from his position as a dental hygienist was based solely on his HIV-positive status. The bulk of the evidence presented in support of the summary judgment motions addressed the question of whether Waddell's HIV-positive status made him a direct threat to dental patients, which would preclude him from demonstrating that he was qualified to perform the duties of a dental hygienist. [ ]. The district court found that Waddell's job entailed "exposure-prone" procedures as that term has been defined by the CDC, and that the necessity of performing the procedures made Waddell a direct threat under the standard we set forth in Onishea v. Hopper, 171 F.3d 1289, 1299 (11th Cir. 1999) (en banc). Consistent with this finding, the district court denied Waddell's motion for summary judgment and instead granted summary judgment in favor of Valley Forge. Waddell appeals the district court's ruling on both summary judgment motions.

II. DISCUSSION

* * *

In order to establish a prima facie case of discrimination under the ADA, Waddell "must demonstrate that [he] (1) is disabled, (2) is a qualified individual, and (3) was subjected to unlawful discrimination because of [his] disability." [ ] As they did in the district court, the parties on appeal focus their arguments on whether Waddell is a qualified individual under [the ADA]. Specifically, the parties debate whether the risk of Waddell transmitting HIV to a patient in the course of treatment poses a direct threat to others in the workplace. [ ]. Waddell carries the burden of establishing that "he was not a direct threat or that reasonable accommodations were available." [ ]. If he cannot meet this burden, he is not a qualified individual and therefore cannot establish a prima facie case of discrimination.

The term "direct threat" is defined as "a significant risk to the health or safety of others that cannot be eliminated by reasonable accommodation." [ ]. Addressing this issue, the Supreme Court explained in School Board of Nassau County v. Arline that "[a] person who poses a significant risk of communicating an infectious disease to others in the workplace will not be otherwise qualified for his or her job if reasonable accommodation will not eliminate that risk." 480 U.S. 273, 287. To determine whether an employee who carries an infectious disease poses a significant risk to others, the Supreme Court has stated that courts should consider several factors, which include:

> [findings of] facts, based on reasonable medical judgments given the state of medical knowledge, about (a) the nature of the risk, (how the disease is transmitted), (b) the duration of the risk (how long is the carrier infectious), (c) the severity of the risk (what is the potential harm to third parties) and (d) the probabilities the disease will be transmitted and will cause varying degrees of harm.

Id. at 288, 107 S.Ct. at 1131 (citation omitted). The Supreme Court also has indicated that an employer in the medical field, "as a health care professional, ... has the duty to assess the risk of infection based on the objective, scientific information available to him and others in his profession," Bragdon, 524 U.S. at 649, 118 S.Ct. at 2210, and that his employment decision concerning an infected employee must be "reasonable in light of the available medical evidence," irrespective of whether his decision was made in good faith. [ ].

We have not had occasion to apply the significant risk analysis enunciated in Arline and Bragdon to a case involving an HIV-positive employee in the medical field, as is the situation here. In Onishea, however, even though the facts did not involve an employee in the medical field, the disability at issue was HIV infection, and in that case we elaborated on the meaning of "significant risk," holding that "when transmitting a disease inevitably entails death, the evidence supports a finding of 'significant risk' if it shows both (1) that a certain event can occur and (2) that according to reliable medical opinion the event can transmit the disease." [ ]. We noted that "when the adverse event is the contraction of a fatal disease, the risk of transmission can be significant even if the probability of transmission is low: death itself makes the risk 'significant.' " [ ]. Moreover, we emphasized that although the "asserted danger of transfer must be rooted in sound medical opinion and not be speculative or fanciful[,] ... this is not a 'somebody has to die first' standard, either: evidence of actual transmission of the fatal disease in the relevant context is not necessary to a finding of significant risk." [ ].

Applying these principles to the case at hand, we conclude that the record establishes that the district court properly granted summary judgment to Valley Forge because an HIV-infected dental hygienist like

Waddell poses a significant risk of HIV transmission to his patients. The district court concluded that Waddell posed a significant risk based on the two-part test we delineated in Onishea [ ]. The court found that a certain event could occur—a dental hygienist like Waddell could cut or prick his finger while performing a procedure in a patient's mouth, and the hygienist's blood then could come into contact with an oral cut or abrasion. The court also found that the procedures used to clean teeth were "exposure-prone" based on the CDC definition of that term, and therefore that reliable medical opinion indicated that if the certain event occurred, Waddell could expose a patient to HIV.

In reaching these conclusions, the district court considered the four factors laid down in Arline, 480 U.S. at 288, 107 S.Ct. at 1131. As to the first factor, the nature of the risk, the district court found that HIV is transmitted when infected blood or other bodily fluids come into contact with the blood, mucous membrane, or other fluids of another person. Neither party on appeal contests this issue, and both parties agree that any risk of HIV transmission in the dental setting would arise from contact between Waddell's blood and an open wound or mucous membrane of a patient.

As to the second factor, the duration of the risk, the court found that HIV infection is indefinite because there is no cure for HIV at this time. Again, both parties agree on this point. As to the third factor, the severity of the risk to third parties, the court found that the potential harm to a person infected is eventual death. Although in this litigation Waddell attempted to downplay the effects of HIV infection on the individual, the court's conclusion on this point appears incontrovertible, especially since Waddell himself admits that there is no current cure for HIV infection. [ ].

At the heart of this case, however, is the district court's analysis of the fourth factor delineated in Arline, the probability of HIV transmission between a dental hygienist and patient. The court noted that because Waddell performed some procedures that entailed the use of sharp instruments, there was a risk that he could cut or prick himself and bleed into an open wound or abrasion in the patient's mouth. Although the court determined that the likelihood of transmission from a healthcare worker to a patient was low, the court found that there was a sound, theoretical possibility that Waddell could transmit HIV to a patient. For this reason, the court concluded that based on our definition of significant risk in Onishea [ ] Waddell posed a direct threat to patients at his workplace and thus was not a qualified individual under the ADA.

Even though Waddell and his experts downplay the procedures Waddell had to perform as a dental hygienist and argue that these procedures are not exposure-prone, we agree with the district court's analysis for several reasons. The uncontroverted evidence establishes that dental cleaning procedures involve the use of sharp objects. In his deposition, Waddell noted that a normal teeth cleaning entailed the performance of "scaling" and "root planing" on the patient. Scaling involves the removal of material from teeth at points above the gumline, and root planing involves the removal of material below the gumline. One of Waddell's medical experts, Dr. Donald Marianos, indicated that scaling involves the use of a sharp instrument. For the root-planing procedure, Waddell stated that he would use "a dental instrument designed with a single blade to cut towards [the] working surface."[ ].

The unrebutted evidence also shows that during routine procedures like scaling and root planing, blood of the patient is commonly present. Waddell, in his own deposition, noted that during the scaling procedure, the patient's blood was present in "most" cases.[ ]. He noted that during the root-planing procedure, "there should always be" blood of the patient present. [ ]. Indeed, in his appellant brief, Waddell acknowledges that "patient bleeding during a routine dental checkup is a common experience." [ ].

The combination of sharp instruments used by the hygienist and a patient's blood commonly being present indicate that the hygienist could cut or prick himself with such an instrument, pierce the skin of his protective glove, and transfer his blood into the patient's mouth, where it would come into contact with an oral cut or abrasion. In fact, the uncontroverted evidence establishes that a dental worker sometimes does stick or cut himself or herself during treatment. For instance, Waddell related that one time when he was performing scaling work on a patient, he turned away from the patient to replace the scaler tip. The scaler tip broke and scratched his skin, and he had to take a break to ensure that the bleeding had stopped and to bandage the site. Valley Forge dental hygienist and administrator, Whelchel, also told in her deposition of an incident that occurred when she was cleaning teeth. She stated that while she was using an instrument on a patient, the tip cut the skin of her finger, which was inside the patient's mouth and near the tongue.

It is true that there is some dispute between the parties as to how often a dental hygienist's fingers are present in a patient's mouth at the same time as sharp instruments. Waddell's own objective medical evidence on this point, however, indicates that a hygienist's fingers are in a patient's mouth along with a sharp instrument at least some of the time. For example, Dr. Marianos, one of Waddell's medical experts, stated that a hygienist's fingers and dental instruments are "rarely," in the patient's mouth at the same time. [ ]. By negative implication, of course, Marianos's statement suggests that at least in some instances, both finger and instrument are in the patient's mouth simultaneously.

In addition, it is important to note that Waddell and his experts in fact acknowledge that there is a possibility of blood-to-blood contact between hygienist and patient, irrespective of precisely how often a hygienist's fingers are in a patient's mouth alongside a sharp instrument. For instance, while Waddell notes in his appellant brief that the exposure of a patient to HIV will not occur during routine procedures, he concedes that "percutaneous ... injuries resulting in blood-to-blood contact theoretically provide opportunities for transmission." [ ]. None of Waddell's medical experts, moreover, appear to dispute that transmission theoretically could happen, even though the risk is small and such an event never before has occurred. This is enough to constitute a significant risk under Onishea, given that HIV has catastrophic effects and is inevitably fatal if transmitted to a patient. * * *

The district court's grant of summary judgment to Valley Forge is consistent with this language because even a small and "theoretically possible method of [HIV] transmission" from Waddell to a patient—a risk that even Waddell's medical experts acknowledge—can create a significant risk under the ADA because transmission, if it occurs, is fatal. [ ].

We also point out that even if there remains some question as to how often Waddell's hand would be in a patient's mouth at the same time as a sharp instrument, Waddell still is unable to refute the assertion that an inadvertent bite or some other accident during a cleaning could lead to the mixture of Waddell's blood with a patient's blood due to an oral cut or abrasion. * * *

In summary, several factors, when taken together, indicate that Waddell poses a significant risk to others in the workplace: the use of sharp instruments by dental hygienists; routine patient bleeding during dental work; the risk that hygienists will be stuck or pricked while using an instrument; the statements of Waddell and medical his experts acknowledging that there is some risk, even if theoretical and small, that blood-to-blood contact between hygienist and patient can occur; and the possibility of an inadvertent bite or other accident during a dental cleaning. These "particularized facts" provide "the best available objective evidence" that Waddell, because he is infected with the fatal, contagious disease of HIV, is a direct threat to his workplace, and therefore not a qualified individual under the ADA. [ ].

III. CONCLUSION

In this appeal, Waddell has argued that the district court erred in denying his motion for summary judgment on his claims under the ADA and the Rehabilitation Act and in granting Valley Forge's summary judgment motion. We have decided that the district court was correct in finding that there was no genuine issue of material fact and that Valley Forge was entitled to judgment as a matter of law on the issue of whether Waddell was a qualified individual. Waddell never controverted the fact that if a certain event occurred—a cut or abrasion to the finger of Waddell while performing dental procedures in a patient's mouth caused by a sharp instrument, an inadvertent bite, or some other accident—there was a specific, theoretically sound possibility of transmission. Because there was such a possibility of transmission, the risk involved, in light of Onishea, was significant due to the fatal nature of HIV. Accordingly, we AFFIRM.

COMMONWEALTH v. SMITH

Appeals Court of Massachusetts, 2003.
58 Mass.App.Ct. 381, 790 N.E.2d 708.

PORADA, J. The defendant appeals from the denial of his motion to withdraw his plea of guilty to an indictment charging him with an assault with intent to commit murder. His sole contention on appeal is that his trial counsel was ineffective in advising him to enter into a stipulation that he is infected with the human immunodeficiency virus (HIV), associated with acquired immune deficiency syndrome (AIDS), as part of a presentment to a grand jury that resulted in the indictment in this case. The defendant argues that this information could not have been obtained without his informed consent based on G. L. c. 111, § 70F, and that, without this information, the grand jury would not have returned the indictment of assault with intent to murder to which he pleaded guilty. We affirm the denial of the motion.

To establish that defense counsel was ineffective, the defendant must show that "there has been serious incompetency, inefficiency, or inattention of counsel * * *—and, if" so, that those shortcomings "deprived the defendant of an otherwise available, substantial ground of defense." [ ]. We are of the opinion that the defendant has failed to meet his burden.

During the course of the grand jury proceeding, the grand jurors heard evidence that the defendant, in his struggle with correction officers, shouted out, "I'm HIV positive.... I'm gonna kill you all.... You're all gonna die.... I have AIDS." The prosecutor then asked the grand jurors if they wished to obtain a court order requiring the defendant to submit to a blood test to determine if the defendant was HIV positive. The grand jurors responded that they did want that information, and a Superior Court judge, finding that the sample would assist the grand jurors in their investigation of certain assaults, ordered the defendant to submit to a blood test to be performed at the State crime laboratory. Defense counsel moved to vacate the court order on the grounds that testing the defendant's blood would not produce relevant evidence and that there were less intrusive methods to obtain such information. Defense counsel referred to G. L. c. 111, § 70F, in his memorandum of law in support of his motion, in which he argued that the statute evinced an intent by the Legislature to keep certain test results confidential, but he did not argue that the statute constituted a bar to obtaining this information without the consent of the defendant. At the hearing on the motion to vacate the order, the defendant agreed to stipulate that he was HIV positive. Another Superior Court judge then vacated the order, and the defendant and his counsel signed a stipulation in which the defendant admitted that he was HIV positive. This stipulation was then presented to the grand jury.

The defendant argues that, if his trial counsel had done adequate research, he would have known that the Commonwealth could not have obtained a test of his blood for HIV without his consent. Without deciding whether the defendant's contention is correct, we nevertheless are of the opinion that counsel's advice was within the range of competence demanded by attorneys in criminal cases.

General Laws c. 111, § 70F, as inserted by St. 1986, c. 241, in pertinent part provides:

"No health care facility, as defined in section seventy E, and no physician or health care provider shall (1) test any person for the presence of the HTLV–III antibody or antigen without first obtaining his written informed consent; (2) disclose the results of such test to any person other than the subject thereof without first obtaining the subject's written informed consent; or (3) identify the subject of such tests to any person without first obtaining the subject's written informed consent."

The statute applies to a health care provider and health care facility as defined in G. L. c. 111, § 1 and § 70E, respectively. Neither the State crime laboratory nor a law enforcement agency is defined as a health care provider or health care facility in the statute. [ ]. Further, at the time the order was issued, there was no case law which had addressed the breadth or scope of this statute, let alone the particular issue raised in this case, and it was well established that, at the request of a grand jury, a court could order a suspect to furnish a sample of his blood for testing if the test would probably produce evidence relevant to the determination of the suspect's guilt. [ ]. Given the language of the statute, the existing case law, and the defendant's admitted disclosure to one of his victims that he had AIDS, we infer that defense counsel justifiably concluded that the Commonwealth would have been able to have the defendant's blood tested for the HIV virus because the evidence would have been relevant to the investigation before the grand jury. Counsel then simply advised the defendant to stipulate to the fact that he was HIV positive to avoid unnecessary medical tests.

The defendant, however, argues that this advice demonstrated serious incompetency, inefficiency, or inattention of counsel. [ ]. To support his argument, the defendant relies on a decision of a single justice of the Supreme Judicial Court in which the single justice ruled that the statute provides an absolute bar to obtaining HIV test results without the subject's consent. Commonwealth vs. Ortiz [ ]. Even if we were to assume that the decision had full precedential value, it is inapplicable to the facts of this case. There, police officers sought disclosure of the defendant's HIV status in order to take appropriate medical steps for their own health. Here, the evidence sought was relevant to prove the crime charged. Additionally, the order of disclosure in the Ortiz matter sought test results that had likely been produced by a health care provider defined in § 70F, whereas in this case, the defendant's blood was to be tested at the State crime laboratory. Further, the decision in the Ortiz matter was issued about twenty months after the stipulation in this case was presented to the grand jury. To the extent that the Ortiz matter in some way relates to defense counsel's competency in this case, the defendant has made no showing that the decision there had been foreshadowed, such that counsel should have anticipated the reasoning therein. [ ].

* * *

Even if we were to assume that defense counsel's advice to the defendant to stipulate to his HIV status fell below that of an ordinary fallible lawyer, which we do not, for the defendant's claim to succeed, he was required to show prejudice. The defendant argues that, but for counsel's advice, he would not have been indicted on two counts of assault with intent to murder because, absent the stipulation, the evidence before the grand jury was insufficient to sustain the charges. We disagree.

* * * The elements of assault with intent to commit murder are assault, the specific intent to kill, and malice. [ ]. In the grand jury proceeding, Nionakis testified that when two other correction officers and he were attempting to move the defendant to a medical cell in the jail, the defendant became abusive and combative. During the struggle, the defendant yelled that he had "HIV" and that "he was going to hurt one of [them]." The defendant then bit Nionakis's forearm and said, "I'm HIV positive. I hope I kill you and your fucking kids." Another correction officer testified that, during the incident, the defendant said, "I'm gonna kill you all.... You're all gonna die.... I have AIDS." The grand jury also heard testimony from a police officer that Dr. Barbara Werner of the department of health had told him that it would be possible for a person infected with the HIV virus to transmit the disease by biting someone, if they broke the skin and their gums contained blood, as in the case of poor gums. Based on the defendant's admission that he had HIV; the absence of any evidence of justification, excuse, or mitigation; and the defendant's statement that he intended to kill Nionakis by infecting him with HIV, coupled with his biting of Nionakis's arm, the jury had sufficient evidence to return an indictment of assault with intent to murder. [ ]. Because an indictment on this charge was inevitable, the defendant cannot claim that he was prejudiced by counsel's advice to stipulate to his HIV status.

Order denying motion to withdraw guilty plea affirmed.

TISCHLER v. DIMENNA

Supreme Court of New York, Westchester County, 1994.
160 Misc.2d 525, 609 N.Y.S.2d 1002.

Lefkowitz, J.

Factual Background

During the period February 1980 until the summer of 1989 plaintiff and Robert Lawson, now deceased, engaged in unprotected sexual intercourse (vaginal, fellatio and cunnilingus). Beginning in the summer of

1989 the parties made sporadic use of condoms. Plaintiff and Mr. Lawson lived together for several years and contemplated marriage.

Plaintiff alleges in her complaint that prior to his death, Robert Lawson contracted "HIV (AIDS) Virus, that eventually caused his death and failed to so advise plaintiff at any time during their relationship". Decedent is survived by a daughter. Plaintiff sues the estate of Robert Lawson for $1,000,000 damages for intentional tort and negligence. Defendant denies the allegations and asserts an affirmative defense of culpable conduct and assumption of risk.

Plaintiff claims that Mr. Lawson became infected with the HIV virus sometime in 1990 as she was told that by Mr. Lawson on his deathbed in December 1991. She stated that Mr. Lawson's best male friend died in 1990 and she believes now that Mr. Lawson and that friend had a homosexual relationship.

As of February 1993 plaintiff has been tested three times for the HIV virus with negative results.

* * *

Phobia Cases

In the landmark decision of the Court of Appeals in *Ferrara v. Galluchio* [ ], the Court sustained a claim of cancer phobia upon a statement by a physician to the patient after a radiation burn that she might contract cancer. The circumstances surrounding the incident—the radiation burn and doctor's advice—provided a "guarantee of genuineness" to the claim [ ].

Nevertheless, the courts of this State have rejected cancer phobia and cancerlike-phobia claims (i.e., asbestosphobia) where there were no chemical manifestations of the disease and no reasonable basis that the disease would develop. Similar judicial reluctance appears in other fear or phobia claim cases. [citations omitted]. The policy reason behind these rulings has less to do with feigned claims; rather, it is the guarantee of trustworthiness of the claim that is lacking, as recovery for damages for the possibility of obtaining a future disease as a result of a *present* physical injury requires medical proof of a reasonable certainty that such developments will occur.

Sexually Transmitted Diseases

Duty of Partners

The law of tortious wrongs, intentional and negligent, recognizes claims for sexually transmitted diseases (STD). [citations omitted]. The usual principles underlying causes of action apply, to wit: defendant must have owed a duty to the plaintiff that was breached and proximately caused the condition complained of. The duty has been found to exist in the relationship between the parties where the defendant knew or should have known that he had a communicable disease. Similar rules apply to AIDS cases. However, in New York for policy reasons against involuntary testing, AIDS is not listed by the State health authorities as a sexually transmittable disease, though it is communicable through sexual contact.

AIDS

Acquired Immune Deficiency Syndrome, for which AIDS is an acronym, is a disease that affects the human immune system by way of a human immunodeficiency virus (HIV). * * * In discussing the qualities, etiology, epidemiology and methodology of AIDS the court is taking judicial notice of those medical facts which are now considered indisputable.

Insofar as relevant to this case the epidemiology of AIDS is communicable through heterosexual contact, oral and vaginal. * * *

There are generally three categories of AIDS: (1) the full blown AIDS disease involving a breakdown of the immunological system; (2) AIDS–Related Complex (ARC) which is a milder form of the disease with some physical symptoms; and (3) asymptomatic with a retrovirus in the system but no abnormal infections. A person in the third category may never develop the disease. The second category is considered a viral precursor to AIDS. A person who tests positive for the HIV virus is called "seropositive".

"Exposure to HIV does not necessarily result in infection. Even a direct exposure through unprotected sex or needle sharing is by no means certain to result in transmission." (AIDS Practice Manual 2–14 [3d ed 1992].)

AIDS Phobia

New York Cases

New York and a minority of jurisdictions have recognized claims for damages for emotional distress caused by exposure to AIDS. Even jurisdictions or cases that deny the claim do so on the usual tort rules of not awarding damages for speculative injuries based on nonexposure to the disease or an unrealistic probability of contracting it from that exposure.

In *Doe v. Doe* (136 Misc.2d 1015 [Sup Ct, Kings County 1987]) in a divorce action the plaintiff wife asserted causes of action for AIDS phobia on the ground that her husband had engaged in homosexual activity. The court rejected application of cancer phobia, zone of danger and lack of physical injury cases that sustained claims for emotional distress, holding that "a specific precipitating incident [on] which ... the alleged emotional distress" arose existed in those cases but was not present here . The causes of action for AIDS phobia were dismissed. Of significance, it was not shown that either party actually had AIDS or the HIV antibody.

In *Hare v. State of New York* (143 Misc.2d 281 [Ct Cl 1989], *affd* 173 A.D.2d 523 [2d Dept 1991], *lv denied* 78 N.Y.2d 859 [1991]) a hospital employee bitten by a prison inmate sued the State for negligence and lack of supervision, claiming AIDS phobia. The plaintiff had tested negative for the AIDS virus three times and there was no proof that the inmate had the virus. The claim for emotional distress caused by the bite was dismissed.

Even where plaintiff can show some exposure the claim has been conditionally dismissed. *(Petri v. Bank of N.Y. Co.,* 153 Misc.2d 426 [Sup Ct, NY County 1992].) In *Petri,* the plaintiff sued his same sex lover, who had been HIV-positive for three years, for having sex during this period with plaintiff without informing plaintiff of the condition. The court observed that a claim in negligence or misrepresentation on these facts was appropriate . However, in dismissing the claim without prejudice to reinstatement if plaintiff developed the HIV antibody the court held "where the plaintiff has only been exposed to possible infection by engaging in ill-defined risky behavior, recovery would be founded upon an uncertainty. Exposure to HIV alone could certainly lead to some fear of AIDS. The courts of this State, though, have been loathe to entertain claims for emotional damage flowing from the possibility of coming down with an illness or disease absent infection or clinical evidence of a related condition sufficient to provide a rational, nonspeculative basis for the fear. Someone who has been exposed to HIV infection but has not come down with it has not suffered a physical injury for which a recovery in damages may be allowed. An HIV-positive person may never develop AIDS and a person who has been exposed to HIV may not become infected with HIV. Plaintiff's claim is therefore too speculative and remote."

Similarly, in *Ordway v. County of Suffolk,* 154 Misc.2d 269, the court granted summary judgment dismissing the claim for AIDS phobia where a physician sued the county for failing to advise him that a prison patient, on whom he operated, had the HIV virus, alleging that he failed to take proper precautions to protect himself. The court noted that there was no precipitating incident that actually exposed plaintiff to the disease.

The only reported decision in New York upholding an AIDS-phobia claim is *Castro v. New York Life Ins. Co.,* 153 Misc.2d 1, where the plaintiff was injured when his thumb was pricked by a hypodermic needle in garbage that he was gathering to dispose. He claimed that he might contract AIDS and the court denied a motion to dismiss. Significantly, plaintiff refused to reveal the results of AIDS tests. In my opinion, while a precipitating incident existed in *Castro* there was no proof of exposure and the case should be limited to its unique facts.

Other Jurisdictions

In *Poole v. Alpha Therapeutic Corp.,* 698 F.Supp. 1367 [ND Ill 1988] plaintiff's husband, a hemophiliac, contracted AIDS from an injection; yet, while acknowledging that plaintiff could be infected through marital sex, the claim for emotional anguish and fear was dismissed. The same result occurred in *Funeral Servs. by Gregory v. Bluefield Community Hosp.,* 186 W.Va. 424, 413 S.E.2d 79, *supra,* where a mortician embalmed a corpse who had AIDS and was not told of the disease until after completion of his services.

In contrast to *Castro v. New York Life Ins. Co.,* 153 Misc.2d 1 is *Burk v. Sage Prods.,* 747 F.Supp. 285, where the plaintiff paramedic injured himself on a needle on a floor of a hospital where AIDS patients resided and sued for his phobia. He tested negative on five occasions, the last test being 13 months after alleged exposure. The court granted summary judgment dismissing the claim holding that the fear of contracting the disease was too speculative. While plaintiff proved a precipitating incident he did not prove exposure. The court commented:

"It is a medically accepted fact, however, that a person who has been infected will *still test positive* [emphasis in original] for the HIV antibody during this latency period when no symptoms are evident, assuming the accuracy of the HIV test. [ ]. It is extremely unlikely that a patient who tests HIV-negative more than six months *after* [emphasis added] a potential exposure will contract the disease as a result of that exposure. * * *

"Although neither party has noted the fact, plaintiff can now be confident, to a high degree of medical certainty, that he will not contract AIDS as a result of the needle-stick injury. The court is reluctant to allow someone to recover for fear of contracting a disease after it has become substantially likely that he will not develop the illness."

Apropos of *Petri v. Bank of N. Y. Co.,* 153 Misc.2d 426, the court in *Lubowitz v. Albert Einstein Med. Ctr.,* 424 Pa.Super. 468, 623 A.2d 3 [1993] granted summary judgment dismissing the claim with leave to sue later if AIDS develops.

A case that sustained an AIDS-phobia claim is *Johnson v. West Va. Univ. Hosps.,* 186 W.Va. 648, 413 S.E.2d 889 [1991] where a police officer was bitten by an HIV infected patient who first bit himself so that he had blood in his mouth at the moment of the second bite. Plaintiff tested negative for HIV but the court sustained a recovery on a jury verdict on the ground of a precipitating event, exposure and reasonable fear.

Two other cases permitted the plaintiff to recover for emotional distress during a "window of anxiety" period where there is proof of a precipitating event and exposure. *Kerins v. Hartley,* 17 Cal.App.4th 713, 729, 21 Cal.Rptr.2d 621, 632, [HIV doctor operated on plaintiff without informing her of his infection; plaintiff tested negative but is emotionally unable to retest]; *Faya v. Almaraz,* 329 Md. 435, 455, 620 A.2d 327, 337. The window of anxiety period limits damages in AIDS-phobia cases to the period that the fear is considered reasonable; that is, generally, the period between when plaintiff learned of the exposure and receipt of HIV-negative results.

Actually, the window of anxiety period should be narrowed to a time measured from discovery of exposure (or when exposure should have been discovered) and viability of the test procedure. On this point one author, James Maroulis, has observed that the person claiming damages for AIDS phobia has a duty to mitigate damages and should be obligated to take the HIV test three months after exposure. [ ]

One court did not even permit recovery for this window period on the reasoning that once the claimant tests negative after six months of alleged exposure, he really was not exposed. *Rossi v. Almaraz,* 59 USLW 2748 [Md Cir Ct 1991] [surgeon who died of AIDS complications in November 1990 had operated on patient in November 1989 when doctor knew he was HIV-positive; patient tested negative in December 1990]. Other jurisdictions have sustained causes of action for AIDS phobia without proof of actual exposure. *Howard v. Alexandria Hosp.,* 245 Va. 346, 429 S.E.2d 22 [1993] [unsterilized surgical instrument used on patient; tests for AIDS negative]; *Marchica v. Long Is. R. R.,* 810 F.Supp. 445 [ED NY 1993] [under Federal Employers' Liability Act a railroad employee pricked by a needle found on employer's property, who tested negative one year after the incident, can sue for AIDS phobia.] * * *

CONCLUSION

Plaintiff has made the requisite showing in opposition to the motion for summary judgment to establish prima facie her claim of emotional distress for the fear of contracting AIDS. The law recognizes that the decedent owed a duty to plaintiff not to intentionally or negligently inflict mental distress. The plaintiff has proven probable exposure to the disease. Whether defendant did knowingly or negligently expose plaintiff are questions for the jury. Similarly, plaintiff's knowledge, actual or constructive, of decedent's condition and his liaison with another man as well as participating in unprotected sexual activity are for the triers of the facts on damages. Additionally, as in other cases where probabilities must be weighed, [ ] the issue of the reasonableness of the plaintiff's fear and for what period of time that fear is compensable are questions for the jury after hearing her testimony and upon a full review of actual medical testimony.

Notes

1) *Bragdon v. Abbott* hinges upon the determination of whether reproduction should be considered a "major life activity" under the Americans' With Disabilities Act. The inquiry includes the question of whether asymptomatic HIV is considered to "substantially limit" reproduction. The division in the Supreme Court opinions is consistent with the debate in the lower courts. Note Rehnquist's opinion (concurring in part and dissenting in part) which raises the additional inquiry of whether reproduction is a "major life activity" that "substantially limits" the plaintiff herself. Also consider the implications of the Supreme Court's determination that reproduction is a major life activity. Must

health insurers provide fertility treatment for those unable to engage in this major life activity? In some states it is already a mandated benefit, but the wisdom of the benefit in an era when nearly 20% of the population is uninsured is the subject of vigorous debate.

2) *Estate of Behringer v. Medical Center* raises issues not only of breach of privacy protections but also informed consent for patients who might be treated by Dr. Behringer subsequent to his diagnosis. Doubtless there are many physicians, as well as non-physicians, who are unaware of their HIV positivity status. No one has heretofore suggested that all physicians who perform invasive procedures must be tested for HIV (and other potentially contagious diseases). Yet once HIV status is known, through chance or design, arguably this becomes a matter of risk that must be communicated to patients in the process of "informed" consent. Will physicians be deterred from undergoing testing? As HIV and AIDS become more treatable, does the physician's HIV status (considering the small likelihood of physician-to-patient transmission) make it a negligible consideration that no longer needs to be communicated in the informed consent process?

3) *Blanks v. Southwestern Bell* examines whether an individual's HIV status qualifies him as "disabled" for purposes of ADA protection. In making that inquiry, the first factor under the ADA concerns whether the plaintiff's alleged disability restricts him from performing a major life activity. Three factors are considered: (1) whether the HIV infection constitutes a physical impairment; (2) whether the individual relies on a particular major life activity; and (3) whether his impairment substantially limits that major life activity. Under the first factor, the court found that appellant failed to prove that he was restricted from performing a major life activity. Under the second factor, to have a "record of disability" under the ADA, plaintiff must show that he or she: (1) has a record or history of impairment; and (2) the impairment limits a major life activity. Although the court found sufficient facts to support that Blanks had a record of impairment, he failed to show that he was substantially limited in a major life activity. Finally, under the third factor, to be "regarded as disabled" plaintiff have "an impairment which is not substantially limiting but which the employer perceives as constituting a substantially limiting impairment." Since the court found that none applied, it did not reach the issue of whether a reasonable accommodation was offered.

4) *Waddell* is another case brought under the ADA. In this case the issue is whether Plaintiff's HIV positivity is an adequate basis to prevent him from undertaking his job functions. In *Waddell*, the District Court relied upon the four factors set forth in *Arline*, 480 U.S. at 288, 107 S.Ct. at 1131. As to the first factor, which examines the nature of the risk, the district court found that HIV transmission could occur in the dental setting if Waddell's blood came into contact with an open wound or mucous membrane of a patient. The second factor is the duration of the risk. The court found that HIV infection was indefinite because there was no cure for HIV. As to the third factor, the severity of the risk, the

court found that the potential harm was eventual death. Finally, the fourth *Arline* factor is the likelihood of HIV transmission between hygienist and patient. On this point, the court found that with the use of sharp instruments, even though the likelihood of transmission from a healthcare worker to a patient was low, there was a "sound, theoretical possibility" that a patient could become infected. Thus Waddell posed a direct threat to patients and was not a qualified individual under the ADA.

5) The major issue in *Commonwealth v. Smith* was whether law enforcement can compel a prisoner to submit to an HIV or AIDS test without his consent. In this case the grand jury concluded that the information would be relevant to its determination of whether there was sufficient information to sustain a criminal indictment. In other cases HIV testing has been requested to determine if a crime victim (such as a rape victim) is at risk for HIV as a result of the crime. No health care institution is permitted to undertake HIV testing without the consent of the patient. In this case, however, the testing would be conducted by the state crime lab, not a health care institution. Under HIPAA, do you think public health necessity would allow law enforcement to compel HIV testing whenever HIV status is relevant to the criminal matter?

6) In *Tischler v. Dimenna* the court addresses "AIDS phobia"—the fear of contracting AIDS even if the plaintiff is currently HIV negative. If there were actual transmission, it would be a different matter and likely governed by the rules that pertain to wrongful transmission of other sexually transmitted diseases. This case, however, is more akin to the "cancer phobia" cases—wrongful exposure to a potential carcinogen that might cause cancer in the future. In those cases in which such a cause of action is recognized, damages include the costs (including emotional) of regular testing, as well as compensation based upon the likelihood the patient will contract the illness. An alternative may be to employ a kind of discovery rule to "wait and see" if the illness develops. In *Tischler*, the likelihood at the time of trial was that plaintiff was not infected, and so damages were sought primarily for the anxiety surrounding months, if not years, of uncertainty.

Chapter 14

PRIVACY, POLICE POWER
AND PROTECTION

INTRODUCTORY NOTE

By the twenty-first century there has been a lengthy history of debate on issues concerning individual rights and the role of the government in imposing restraints on individual liberties in the name of public health. When is judicial activism justified? When is judicial restraint necessary? The first section on family planning provides a sample of cases, but in fact virtually every type of public health regulation can be found in this area.

The second section addresses the role of the government when it comes to the personal choice of life and death. Once again the issue is whether the powers and duties of the government to safeguard the public health are paramount in this area, and whether there should be restraint on the part of the government to allow individuals and their families to promote individual interests in the name of autonomy and privacy.

In the third section domestic violence and abuse often require the state to invoke its police powers to protect and defend its most vulnerable citizens. At the same time, protection of individual rights, specifically those of the victims, requires activism to protect the public's health. There is a constant tug in both directions: individuals want the government to step in when their rights are being violated, and to exercise restraint when their interests are inconsistent with regulation for the benefit of public health.

Finally, in the fourth section there are two types of high-risk activities: those that primarily affect the individuals involved in the activity and those that affect many others as well. Under some circumstances both require protection, either because the activities inevitably draw in other people or because the government in its wisdom believes that it should act on behalf of the individual who fails to act for himself. Arguably prostitution and the diseases that are transmitted only affect willing participants. Arguably other unwitting people, including children, become victims. Arguably prostitution should be ignored, prosecuted or regulated. At the end of the day there is a myriad of judicial decisions and opinions, and just as often there is little consensus.

SECTION A.   FAMILY PLANNING

ROE v. WADE

Supreme Court of the United States, 1973.
410 U.S. 113, 93 S.Ct. 705, 35 L.Ed.2d 147.

MR. JUSTICE BLACKMUN delivered the opinion of the Court.

This Texas federal appeal and its Georgia companion, *Doe* v. *Bolton,* present constitutional challenges to state criminal abortion legislation. * * *

We forthwith acknowledge our awareness of the sensitive and emotional nature of the abortion controversy, of the vigorous opposing views, even among physicians, and of the deep and seemingly absolute convictions that the subject inspires. One's philosophy, one's experiences, one's exposure to the raw edges of human existence, one's religious training, one's attitudes toward life and family and their values, and the moral standards one establishes and seeks to observe, are all likely to influence and to color one's thinking and conclusions about abortion.

In addition, population growth, pollution, poverty, and racial overtones tend to complicate and not to simplify the problem.

Our task, of course, is to resolve the issue by constitutional measurement, free of emotion and of predilection. We seek earnestly to do this, and, because we do, we have inquired into, and in this opinion place some emphasis upon, medical and medical-legal history and what that history reveals about man's attitudes toward the abortion procedure over the centuries. We bear in mind, too, Mr. Justice Holmes' admonition in his now-vindicated dissent in *Lochner* v. *New York*, 198 U.S. 45, 76 (1905):

"[The Constitution] is made for people of fundamentally differing views, and the accident of our finding certain opinions natural and familiar or novel and even shocking ought not to conclude our judgment upon the question whether statutes embodying them conflict with the Constitution of the United States."

I

The Texas statutes that concern us here * * * make it a crime to "procure an abortion," as therein defined, or to attempt one, except with respect to "an abortion procured or attempted by medical advice for the purpose of saving the life of the mother." Similar statutes are in existence in a majority of the States. * * *

Jane Roe, a single woman who was residing in Dallas County, Texas, instituted this federal action in March 1970 against the District Attorney of the county. She sought a declaratory judgment that the Texas criminal abortion statutes were unconstitutional on their face, and an injunction restraining the defendant from enforcing the statutes.

Roe alleged that she was unmarried and pregnant; that she wished to terminate her pregnancy by an abortion "performed by a competent, licensed physician, under safe, clinical conditions"; that she was unable to get a "legal" abortion in Texas because her life did not appear to be threatened by the continuation of her pregnancy; and that she could not afford to travel to another jurisdiction in order to secure a legal abortion under safe conditions. She claimed that the Texas statutes were unconstitutionally vague and that they abridged her right of personal privacy, protected by the First, Fourth, Fifth, Ninth, and Fourteenth Amendments. By an amendment to her complaint Roe purported to sue "on behalf of herself and all other women" similarly situated.

James Hubert Hallford, a licensed physician, sought and was granted leave to intervene in Roe's action. In his complaint he alleged that he had been arrested previously for violations of the Texas abortion statutes and that two such prosecutions were pending against him. He described conditions of patients who came to him seeking abortions, and he claimed that for many cases he, as a physician, was unable to determine whether they fell within or outside the exception recognized * * *.

* * *

The principal thrust of appellant's attack on the Texas statutes is that they improperly invade a right, said to be possessed by the pregnant woman, to choose to terminate her pregnancy. Appellant would discover this right in the concept of personal "liberty" embodied in the Fourteenth Amendment's Due Process Clause; or in personal, marital, familial, and sexual privacy said to be protected by the Bill of Rights or its penumbras, [ ] or among those rights reserved to the people by the Ninth Amendment, [ ]. Before addressing this claim, we feel it desirable briefly to survey, in several aspects, the history of abortion, for such insight as that history may afford us, and then to examine the state purposes and interests behind the criminal abortion laws.

VI

It perhaps is not generally appreciated that the restrictive criminal abortion laws in effect in a majority of States today are of relatively recent vintage. Those laws, generally proscribing abortion or its attempt at any time during pregnancy except when necessary to preserve the pregnant woman's life, are not of ancient or even of common-law origin. Instead, they derive from statutory changes effected, for the most part, in the latter half of the 19th century.

VII

Three reasons have been advanced to explain historically the enactment of criminal abortion laws in the 19th century and to justify their continued existence.

It has been argued occasionally that these laws were the product of a Victorian social concern to discourage illicit sexual conduct. Texas, however, does not advance this justification in the present case, and it appears that no court or commentator has taken the argument seriously. * * *

A second reason is concerned with abortion as a medical procedure. When most criminal abortion laws were first enacted, the procedure was a hazardous one for the woman. This was particularly true prior to the development of antisepsis. * * * Modern medical techniques have altered this situation. Appellants and various *amici* refer to medical data indicating that abortion in early pregnancy, that is, prior to the end of the first trimester, although not without its risk, is now relatively safe. * * *

The third reason is the State's interest—some phrase it in terms of duty—in protecting prenatal life. Some of the argument for this justification rests on the theory that a new human life is present from the moment of conception. The State's interest and general obligation to protect life then extends, it is argued, to prenatal life. Only when the life of the pregnant mother herself is at stake, balanced against the life she carries within her, should the interest of the embryo or fetus not prevail. Logically, of course, a legitimate state interest in this area need not stand or fall on acceptance of the belief that life begins at conception or at some other point prior to live birth. In assessing the State's interest, recognition may be given to the less rigid claim that as long as at least *potential* life is involved, the State may assert interests beyond the protection of the pregnant woman alone.

* * *

It is with these interests, and the weight to be attached to them, that this case is concerned.

VIII

The Constitution does not explicitly mention any right of privacy. In a line of decisions, however * * *, the Court has recognized that a right of personal privacy, or a guarantee of certain areas or zones of privacy, does exist under the Constitution. In varying contexts, the Court or individual Justices have, indeed, found at least the roots of that right in the First Amendment, *Stanley* v. *Georgia*, 394 U.S. 557, 564 (1969); in the Fourth and Fifth Amendments, *Terry* v. *Ohio*, 392 U.S. 1, 8–9 (1968), [ ]; in the penumbras of the Bill of Rights, *Griswold* v. *Connecticut*, 381 U.S., at 484–485; in the Ninth Amendment, *id.*, at 486 (Goldberg, J., concurring); or in the concept of liberty guaranteed by the first section of the Fourteenth Amendment, see *Meyer* v. *Nebraska*, 262 U.S. 390, 399 (1923). These decisions make it clear that only personal rights that can be deemed "fundamental" or "implicit in the concept of ordered liberty,"[ ] are included in this guarantee of personal privacy. They also make it clear that the right has some extension to activities relating to marriage, *Loving* v. *Virginia*, 388 U.S. 1, 12 (1967); procreation, *Skinner*

v. *Oklahoma*, 316 U.S. 535, 541–542 (1942); contraception, *Eisenstadt* v. *Baird*, 405 U.S., at 453–454; *Prince* v. *Massachusetts*, 321 U.S. 158, 166 (1944); and child rearing and education, *Pierce* v. *Society of Sisters*, 268 U.S. 510, 535 (1925).

This right of privacy, whether it be founded in the Fourteenth Amendment's concept of personal liberty and restrictions upon state action, as we feel it is, or, as the District Court determined, in the Ninth Amendment's reservation of rights to the people, is broad enough to encompass a woman's decision whether or not to terminate her pregnancy. The detriment that the State would impose upon the pregnant woman by denying this choice altogether is apparent. Specific and direct harm medically diagnosable even in early pregnancy may be involved. Maternity, or additional offspring, may force upon the woman a distressful life and future. Psychological harm may be imminent. Mental and physical health may be taxed by child care. There is also the distress, for all concerned, associated with the unwanted child, and there is the problem of bringing a child into a family already unable, psychologically and otherwise, to care for it. In other cases, as in this one, the additional difficulties and continuing stigma of unwed motherhood may be involved. All these are factors the woman and her responsible physician necessarily will consider in consultation.

On the basis of elements such as these, appellant and some *amici* argue that the woman's right is absolute and that she is entitled to terminate her pregnancy at whatever time, in whatever way, and for whatever reason she alone chooses. With this we do not agree. * * * As noted above, a State may properly assert important interests in safeguarding health, in maintaining medical standards, and in protecting potential life. At some point in pregnancy, these respective interests become sufficiently compelling to sustain regulation of the factors that govern the abortion decision. The privacy right involved, therefore, cannot be said to be absolute. In fact, it is not clear to us that the claim asserted by some *amici* that one has an unlimited right to do with one's body as one pleases bears a close relationship to the right of privacy previously articulated in the Court's decisions. The Court has refused to recognize an unlimited right of this kind in the past. We, therefore, conclude that the right of personal privacy includes the abortion decision, but that this right is not unqualified and must be considered against important state interests in regulation.

* * *

X

* * *

With respect to the State's important and legitimate interest in the health of the mother, the "compelling" point, in the light of present medical knowledge, is at approximately the end of the first trimester. This is so because of the now-established medical fact [ ] that until the end of the first trimester mortality in abortion may be less than mortality in normal childbirth. It follows that, from and after this point, a State may regulate the abortion procedure to the extent that the regulation reasonably relates to the preservation and protection of maternal health. * * *

This means, on the other hand, that, for the period of pregnancy prior to this "compelling" point, the attending physician, in consultation with his patient, is free to determine, without regulation by the State, that, in his medical judgment, the patient's pregnancy should be terminated. If that decision is reached, the judgment may be effectuated by an abortion free of interference by the State.

With respect to the State's important and legitimate interest in potential life, the "compelling" point is at viability. This is so because the fetus then presumably has the capability of meaningful life outside the mother's womb. State regulation protective of fetal life after viability thus has both logical and biological justifications. If the State is interested in protecting fetal life after viability, it may go so far as to proscribe abortion during that period, except when it is necessary to preserve the life or health of the mother.

XI

To summarize and to repeat:

1.   A state criminal abortion statute of the current Texas type, that excepts from criminality only a *lifesaving* procedure on behalf of the mother, without regard to pregnancy stage and without recognition of the other interests involved, is violative of the Due Process Clause of the Fourteenth Amendment.

(a) For the stage prior to approximately the end of the first trimester, the abortion decision and its effectuation must be left to the medical judgment of the pregnant woman's attending physician.

(b) For the stage subsequent to approximately the end of the first trimester, the State, in promoting its interest in the health of the mother, may, if it chooses, regulate the abortion procedure in ways that are reasonably related to maternal health.

(c) For the stage subsequent to viability, the State in promoting its interest in the potentiality of human life may, if it chooses, regulate, and even proscribe, abortion except where it is necessary, in appropriate medical judgment, for the preservation of the life or health of the mother.

It is so ordered.

* * *

MR. JUSTICE REHNQUIST, dissenting.

* * *

The Court's opinion decides that a State may impose virtually no restriction on the performance of abortions during the first trimester of pregnancy. Our previous decisions indicate that a necessary predicate for such an opinion is a plaintiff who was in her first trimester of pregnancy at some time during the pendency of her lawsuit. * * * Nonetheless, the Court uses her complaint against the Texas statute as a fulcrum for deciding that States may impose virtually no restrictions on medical abortions performed during the *first* trimester of pregnancy. In deciding such a hypothetical lawsuit, the Court departs from the longstanding admonition that it should never "formulate a rule of constitutional law broader than is required by the precise facts to which it is to be applied." [ ]

Even if there were a plaintiff in this case capable of litigating the issue which the Court decides, * * * I have difficulty in concluding, as the Court does, that the right of "privacy" is involved in this case. Texas, by the statute here challenged, bars the performance of a medical abortion by a licensed physician on a plaintiff such as Roe. A transaction resulting in an operation such as this is not "private" in the ordinary usage of that word. Nor is the "privacy" that the Court finds here even a distant relative of the freedom from searches and seizures protected by the Fourth Amendment to the Constitution, which the Court has referred to as embodying a right to privacy. *Katz* v. *United States*, 389 U.S. 347 (1967).

If the Court means by the term "privacy" no more than that the claim of a person to be free from unwanted state regulation of consensual transactions may be a form of "liberty" protected by the Fourteenth Amendment, there is no doubt that similar claims have been upheld in our earlier decisions on the basis of that liberty. * * * [L]iberty is not guaranteed absolutely against deprivation, only against deprivation without due process of law. The test traditionally applied in the area of social and economic legislation is whether or not a law such as that challenged has a rational relation to a valid state objective. [ ]. The Due Process Clause of the Fourteenth Amendment undoubtedly does place a limit, albeit a broad one, on legislative power to enact laws such as this. If the Texas statute were to prohibit an abortion even where the mother's life is in jeopardy, I have little doubt that such a statute would lack a rational relation to a valid state objective * * *. But the Court's sweeping invalidation of any restrictions on abortion during the first trimester is impossible to justify under that standard, and the conscious weighing of competing factors that the Court's opinion apparently substitutes for the established test is far more appropriate to a legislative judgment than to a judicial one.

* * *

The fact that a majority of the States reflecting, after all, the majority sentiment in those States, have had restrictions on abortions for at least a century is a strong indication, it seems to me, that the asserted right to an abortion is not "so rooted in the traditions and conscience of our people as to be ranked as fundamental," *Snyder* v. *Massachusetts*, 291 U.S. 97, 105 (1934). Even today, when society's views on abortion are changing, the very existence of the debate is evidence that the "right" to an abortion is not so universally accepted as the appellant would have us believe.

To reach its result, the Court necessarily has had to find within the scope of the Fourteenth Amendment a right that was apparently completely unknown to the drafters of the Amendment. * * *

PLANNED PARENTHOOD OF SOUTHEAST PENNSYLVANIA v. CASEY

Supreme Court of the United States, 1992.
505 U.S. 833, 112 S.Ct. 2791, 120 L.Ed.2d 674.

JUSTICE O'CONNOR, JUSTICE KENNEDY, and JUSTICE SOUTER announced the judgment of the Court and delivered the opinion of the Court with respect to Parts I, II, III, V–A, V–C, and VI, an opinion with respect to Part V–E, in which JUSTICE STEVENS joins, and an opinion with respect to Parts IV, V–B, and V–D.

I

Liberty finds no refuge in a jurisprudence of doubt. Yet 19 years after our holding that the Constitution protects a woman's right to terminate her pregnancy in its early stages, *Roe v. Wade*, 410 U.S. 113, 35 L.Ed.2d 147, 93 S.Ct. 705 (1973), that definition of liberty is still questioned. * * *

At issue in these cases are five provisions of the Pennsylvania Abortion Control Act of 1982, as amended in 1988 and 1989. * * *. The Act requires that a woman seeking an abortion give her informed consent prior to the abortion procedure, and specifies that she be provided with certain information at least 24 hours before the abortion is performed. [ ] For a minor to obtain an abortion, the Act requires the informed consent of one of her parents, but provides for a judicial bypass option if the minor does not wish to or cannot obtain a parent's consent. [ ]. Another provision of the Act requires that, unless certain exceptions apply, a married woman seeking an abortion must sign a statement indicating that she has notified her husband of her intended abortion. [ ] The Act exempts compliance with these three requirements in the event of a "medical emergency," which is defined in § 3203 of the Act. See [ ]. In addition to the above provisions regulating the performance of abortions, the Act imposes certain reporting requirements on facilities that provide abortion services. [ ].

* * *

After considering the fundamental constitutional questions resolved by *Roe*, principles of institutional integrity, and the rule of *stare decisis*, we are led to conclude this: the essential holding of *Roe v. Wade* should be retained and once again reaffirmed.

It must be stated at the outset and with clarity that *Roe's* essential holding, the holding we reaffirm, has three parts. First is a recognition of the right of the woman to choose to have an abortion before viability and to obtain it without undue interference from the State. Before viability, the State's interests are not strong enough to support a prohibition of abortion or the imposition of a substantial obstacle to the woman's effective right to elect the procedure. Second is a confirmation of the State's power to restrict abortions after fetal viability, if the law contains exceptions for pregnancies which endanger the woman's life or health. And third is the principle that the State has legitimate interests from the outset of the pregnancy in protecting the health of the woman and the life of the fetus that may become a child. These principles do not contradict one another; and we adhere to each.

II

Constitutional protection of the woman's decision to terminate her pregnancy derives from the Due Process Clause of the Fourteenth Amendment. It declares that no State shall "deprive any person of life, liberty, or property, without due process of law." The controlling word in the cases before us is "liberty." Although a literal reading of the Clause might suggest that it governs only the procedures by which a State may deprive persons of liberty, for at least 105 years, since *Mugler v. Kansas*, 123 U.S. 623, 660–661, 31 L.Ed. 205, 8 S.Ct. 273 (1887), the Clause has been understood to contain a substantive component as well, one "barring certain government actions regardless of the fairness of the procedures used to implement them." *Daniels v. Williams*, 474 U.S. 327, 331, 88 L.Ed.2d 662, 106 S.Ct. 662 (1986). * * *

The most familiar of the substantive liberties protected by the Fourteenth Amendment are those recognized by the Bill of Rights. We have held that the Due Process Clause of the Fourteenth Amendment incorporates most of the Bill of Rights against the States. [Citations omitted]. It is tempting, as a means of curbing the discretion of federal judges, to suppose that liberty encompasses no more than those rights already guaranteed to the individual against federal interference by the express provisions of the first eight Amendments to the Constitution. [ ] But of course this Court has never accepted that view.

It is also tempting, for the same reason, to suppose that the Due Process Clause protects only those practices, defined at the most specific level, that were protected against government interference by other rules of law when the Fourteenth Amendment was ratified. [ ]. But such a view would be inconsistent with our law. It is a promise of the Constitution that there is a realm of personal liberty which the government may not enter. We have vindicated this principle before. Marriage is mentioned nowhere in the Bill of Rights and interracial marriage was illegal in most States in the 19th century, but the Court was no doubt correct in finding it to be an aspect of liberty protected against state interference by the substantive component of the Due Process Clause in *Loving v. Virginia*, 388 U.S. 1, 12, 18 L.Ed.2d 1010, 87 S.Ct. 1817 (1967) * * *

The inescapable fact is that adjudication of substantive due process claims may call upon the Court in interpreting the Constitution to exercise that same capacity which by tradition courts always have exercised: reasoned judgment. Its boundaries are not susceptible of expression as a simple rule. That does not mean we are free to invalidate state policy choices with which we disagree; yet neither does it permit us to shrink from the duties of our office.

* * *

Men and women of good conscience can disagree, and we suppose some always shall disagree, about the profound moral and spiritual implications of terminating a pregnancy, even in its earliest stage. Some of us as individuals find abortion offensive to our most basic principles of morality, but that cannot control our decision. Our obligation is to define the liberty of all, not to mandate our own moral code. The underlying constitutional issue is whether the State can resolve these philosophic questions in such a definitive way that a woman lacks all choice in the matter, except perhaps in those rare circumstances in which the pregnancy is itself a danger to her own life or health, or is the result of rape or incest.

* * *

Our law affords constitutional protection to personal decisions relating to marriage, procreation, contraception, family relationships, child rearing, and education. *Carey v. Population Services International*, 431 U.S. at 685. Our cases recognize "the right of the *individual*, married or single, to be free from unwarranted governmental intrusion into matters so fundamentally affecting a person as the decision whether to bear or beget a child." *Eisenstadt v. Baird, supra*, at 453 (emphasis in original). Our precedents "have respected the private realm of family life which the state cannot enter." *Prince v. Massachusetts*, 321 U.S. 158, 166, 88 L.Ed. 645, 64 S.Ct. 438 (1944). These matters, involving the most intimate and personal choices a person may make in a lifetime, choices central to personal dignity and autonomy, are central to the liberty protected by the Fourteenth Amendment. At the heart of liberty is the right to define one's own concept of existence, of meaning, of the universe, and of the mystery of human life. Beliefs about these matters could not define the attributes of personhood were they formed under compulsion of the State.

These considerations begin our analysis of the woman's interest in terminating her pregnancy but cannot end it, for this reason: though the abortion decision may originate within the zone of conscience and belief, it is more than a philosophic exercise. Abortion is a unique act. It is an act fraught with consequences for others: for the woman who must live with the implications of her decision; for the persons who perform and assist in the procedure; for the spouse, family, and society which must confront the knowledge that these procedures exist, procedures some deem nothing short of an act of violence against innocent human life;

and, depending on one's beliefs, for the life or potential life that is aborted. Though abortion is conduct, it does not follow that the State is entitled to proscribe it in all instances. That is because the liberty of the woman is at stake in a sense unique to the human condition and so unique to the law. The mother who carries a child to full term is subject to anxieties, to physical constraints, to pain that only she must bear. That these sacrifices have from the beginning of the human race been endured by woman with a pride that ennobles her in the eyes of others and gives to the infant a bond of love cannot alone be grounds for the State to insist she make the sacrifice. Her suffering is too intimate and personal for the State to insist, without more, upon its own vision of the woman's role, however dominant that vision has been in the course of our history and our culture. The destiny of the woman must be shaped to a large extent on her own conception of her spiritual imperatives and her place in society.

* * *

While we appreciate the weight of the arguments made on behalf of the State in the cases before us, arguments which in their ultimate formulation conclude that *Roe* should be overruled, the reservations any of us may have in reaffirming the central holding of *Roe* are outweighed by the explication of individual liberty we have given combined with the force of *stare decisis*. We turn now to that doctrine.

A

The obligation to follow precedent begins with necessity, and a contrary necessity marks its outer limit. With Cardozo, we recognize that no judicial system could do society's work if it eyed each issue afresh in every case that raised it. * * *

So in this case we may enquire whether *Roe's* central rule has been found unworkable; whether the rule's limitation on state power could be removed without serious inequity to those who have relied upon it or significant damage to the stability of the society governed by it; whether the law's growth in the intervening years has left *Roe's* central rule a doctrinal anachronism discounted by society; and whether *Roe's* premises of fact have so far changed in the ensuing two decades as to render its central holding somehow irrelevant or unjustifiable in dealing with the issue it addressed.

1

Although *Roe* has engendered opposition, it has in no sense proven "unworkable," [ ], representing as it does a simple limitation beyond which a state law is unenforceable. While *Roe* has, of course, required judicial assessment of state laws affecting the exercise of the choice guaranteed against government infringement, and although the need for such review will remain as a consequence of today's decision, the required determinations fall within judicial competence.

* * *

5

The sum of the precedential enquiry to this point shows *Roe's* underpinnings unweakened in any way affecting its central holding. While it has engendered disapproval, it has not been unworkable. An entire generation has come of age free to assume *Roe's* concept of liberty in defining the capacity of women to act in society, and to make reproductive decisions; no erosion of principle going to liberty or personal autonomy has left *Roe's* central holding a doctrinal remnant; *Roe* portends no developments at odds with other precedent for the analysis of personal liberty; and no changes of fact have rendered viability more or less appropriate as the point at which the balance of interests tips. Within the bounds of normal *stare decisis* analysis, then, and subject to the considerations on which it customarily turns, the stronger argument is for affirming *Roe's* central holding, with whatever degree of personal reluctance any of us may have, not for overruling it.

B

In a less significant case, *stare decisis* analysis could, and would, stop at the point we have reached. But the sustained and widespread debate *Roe* has provoked calls for some comparison between that case and others of comparable dimension that have responded to national controversies and taken on the impress of the controversies addressed. Only two such decisional lines from the past century present themselves for examination, and in each instance the result reached by the Court accorded with the principles we apply today.

* * *

The Court's duty in the present cases is clear. In 1973, it confronted the already-divisive issue of governmental power to limit personal choice to undergo abortion, for which it provided a new resolution based on the due process guaranteed by the Fourteenth Amendment. Whether or not a new social consensus is developing on that issue, its divisiveness is no less today than in 1973, and pressure to overrule the decision, like pressure to retain it, has grown only more intense. A decision to overrule *Roe's* essential holding under the existing circumstances would address error, if error there was, at the cost of both profound and unnecessary damage to the Court's legitimacy, and to the Nation's commitment to the rule of law. It is therefore imperative to adhere to the essence of *Roe's* original decision, and we do so today.

IV

From what we have said so far it follows that it is a constitutional liberty of the woman to have some freedom to terminate her pregnancy. We conclude that the basic decision in *Roe* was based on a constitutional analysis which we cannot now repudiate. The woman's liberty is not so unlimited, however, that from the outset the State cannot show its concern for the life of the unborn, and at a later point in fetal development the State's interest in life has sufficient force so that the right of the woman to terminate the pregnancy can be restricted.

That brings us, of course, to the point where much criticism has been directed at *Roe*, a criticism that always inheres when the Court draws a specific rule from what in the Constitution is but a general standard. We conclude, however, that the urgent claims of the woman to retain the ultimate control over her destiny and her body, claims implicit in the meaning of liberty, require us to perform that function. Liberty must not be extinguished for want of a line that is clear. And it falls to us to give some real substance to the woman's liberty to determine whether to carry her pregnancy to full term.

We conclude the line should be drawn at viability, so that before that time the woman has a right to choose to terminate her pregnancy. We adhere to this principle for two reasons. First, as we have said, is the doctrine of *stare decisis*. Any judicial act of line-drawing may seem somewhat arbitrary, but *Roe* was a reasoned statement, elaborated with great care. We have twice reaffirmed it in the face of great opposition.
* * *

The second reason is that the concept of viability, as we noted in *Roe*, is the time at which there is a realistic possibility of maintaining and nourishing a life outside the womb, so that the independent existence of the second life can in reason and all fairness be the object of state protection that now overrides the rights of the woman. * * *

The woman's right to terminate her pregnancy before viability is the most central principle of *Roe v. Wade*. It is a rule of law and a component of liberty we cannot renounce.

On the other side of the equation is the interest of the State in the protection of potential life. The *Roe* Court recognized the State's "important and legitimate interest in protecting the potentiality of human life." *Roe, supra*, at 162. The weight to be given this state interest, not the strength of the woman's interest, was the difficult question faced in *Roe*. We do not need to say whether each of us, had we been Members of the Court when the valuation of the state interest came before it as an original matter, would have concluded, as the *Roe* Court did, that its weight is insufficient to justify a ban on abortions prior to viability even when it is subject to certain exceptions. The matter is not before us in the first instance, and coming as it does after nearly 20 years of litigation in *Roe's* wake we are satisfied that the immediate question is not the soundness of *Roe's* resolution of the issue, but the precedential force that must be accorded to its holding. And we have concluded that the essential holding of *Roe* should be reaffirmed.

Yet it must be remembered that *Roe v. Wade* speaks with clarity in establishing not only the woman's liberty but also the State's "important and legitimate interest in potential life." *Roe, supra*, at 163. That portion of the decision in *Roe* has been given too little acknowledgment and implementation by the Court in its subsequent cases. Those cases decided that any regulation touching upon the abortion decision must survive strict scrutiny, to be sustained only if drawn in narrow terms to further a compelling state interest. [ ]. Not all of the cases decided under that formulation can be reconciled with the holding in *Roe* itself that the State has legitimate interests in the health of the woman and in protecting the potential life within her. In resolving this tension, we choose to rely upon *Roe*, as against the later cases.

Roe established a trimester framework to govern abortion regulations. Under this elaborate but rigid construct, almost no regulation at all is permitted during the first trimester of pregnancy; regulations designed to protect the woman's health, but not to further the State's interest in potential life, are permitted during the second trimester; and during the third trimester, when the fetus is viable, prohibitions are permitted provided the life or health of the mother is not at stake. *Roe, supra*, at 163–166. Most of our cases since *Roe* have involved the application of rules derived from the trimester framework. [ ].

The trimester framework no doubt was erected to ensure that the woman's right to choose not become so subordinate to the State's interest in promoting fetal life that her choice exists in theory but not in fact. We do not agree, however, that the trimester approach is necessary to accomplish this objective. A framework of this rigidity was unnecessary and in its later interpretation sometimes contradicted the State's permissible exercise of its powers.

Though the woman has a right to choose to terminate or continue her pregnancy before viability, it does not at all follow that the State is prohibited from taking steps to ensure that this choice is thoughtful and informed. Even in the earliest stages of pregnancy, the State may enact rules and regulations designed to encourage her to know that there are philosophic and social arguments of great weight that can be brought to bear in favor of continuing the pregnancy to full term and that there are procedures and institutions to allow adoption of unwanted children as well as a certain degree of state assistance if the mother chooses to raise the child herself. " 'The Constitution does not forbid a State or city, pursuant to democratic processes, from expressing a preference for normal childbirth.' " *Webster v. Reproductive Health Services*, 492 U.S. at 511 (opinion of the Court) (quoting *Poelker v. Doe*, 432 U.S. 519, 521, 53 L.Ed.2d 528, 97 S.Ct. 2391 (1977)). It follows that States are free to enact laws to provide a reasonable framework for a woman to make a decision that has such profound and lasting meaning. This, too, we find consistent with *Roe's* central premises, and indeed the inevitable consequence of our holding that the State has an interest in protecting the life of the unborn.

We reject the trimester framework, which we do not consider to be part of the essential holding of *Roe*. [ ]; *id.*, at 529 (O'CONNOR, J., concurring in part and concurring in judgment) (describing the trimester framework as "problematic"). Measures aimed at ensuring that a woman's choice contemplates the consequences for the fetus do not necessarily interfere with the right recognized in *Roe*, although those measures have been found to be inconsistent with the rigid trimester framework announced in that case. A logical reading of the central holding in *Roe* itself, and a necessary reconciliation of the liberty of the woman and the interest of the State in promoting prenatal life, require, in our view, that we abandon the trimester framework as a rigid prohibition on all previability regulation aimed at the protection of fetal life. The trimester framework suffers from these basic flaws: in its formulation it misconceives the nature of the pregnant woman's interest; and in practice it undervalues the State's interest in potential life, as recognized in *Roe*.

* * *

Roe v. Wade was express in its recognition of the State's "important and legitimate interests in preserving and protecting the health of the pregnant woman [and] in protecting the potentiality of human life." 410 U.S. at 162. The trimester framework, however, does not fulfill *Roe's* own promise that the State has an interest in protecting fetal life or potential life. *Roe* began the contradiction by using the trimester frame work to forbid any regulation of abortion designed to advance that interest before viability. [ ]. Before viability, *Roe* and subsequent cases treat all governmental attempts to influence a woman's decision on behalf of the potential life within her as unwarranted. This treatment is, in our judgment, incompatible with the recognition that there is a substantial state interest in potential life throughout pregnancy. [ ] The very notion that the State has a substantial interest in potential life leads to the conclusion that not all regulations must be deemed unwarranted. Not all burdens on the right to decide whether to terminate a pregnancy will be undue. In our view, the undue burden standard is the appropriate means of reconciling the State's interest with the woman's constitutionally protected liberty.

* * *

A finding of an undue burden is a shorthand for the conclusion that a state regulation has the purpose or effect of placing a substantial obstacle in the path of a woman seeking an abortion of a nonviable fetus. A statute with this purpose is invalid because the means chosen by the State to further the interest in potential life must be calculated to inform the woman's free choice, not hinder it. And a statute which, while furthering the interest in potential life or some other valid state interest, has the effect of placing a substantial obstacle in the path of a woman's choice cannot be considered a permissible means of serving its legitimate ends. * * *

Some guiding principles should emerge. What is at stake is the woman's right to make the ultimate decision, not a right to be insulated from all others in doing so. Regulations which do no more than create a structural mechanism by which the State, or the parent or guardian of a minor, may express profound respect for the life of the unborn are permitted, if they are not a substantial obstacle to the woman's exercise of the right to choose.

Even when jurists reason from shared premises, some disagreement is inevitable. [ ] That is to be expected in the application of any legal standard which must accommodate life's complexity. We do not expect it to be otherwise with respect to the undue burden standard. We give this summary:

(a) To protect the central right recognized by *Roe v. Wade* while at the same time accommodating the State's profound interest in potential life, we will employ the undue burden analysis as explained in this opinion. An undue burden exists, and therefore a provision of law is invalid, if its purpose or effect is to place a substantial obstacle in the path of a woman seeking an abortion before the fetus attains viability.

(b) We reject the rigid trimester framework of *Roe v. Wade*. To promote the State's profound interest in potential life, throughout pregnancy the State may take measures to ensure that the woman's choice is informed, and measures designed to advance this interest will not be invalidated as long as their purpose is to persuade the woman to choose childbirth over abortion. These measures must not be an undue burden on the right.

(c) As with any medical procedure, the State may enact regulations to further the health or safety of a woman seeking an abortion. Unnecessary health regulations that have the purpose or effect of presenting a substantial obstacle to a woman seeking an abortion impose an undue burden on the right.

(d) Our adoption of the undue burden analysis does not disturb the central holding of *Roe v. Wade*, and we reaffirm that holding. Regardless of whether exceptions are made for particular circumstances, a State may not prohibit any woman from making the ultimate decision to terminate her pregnancy before viability.

(e) We also reaffirm *Roe's* holding that "subsequent to viability, the State in promoting its interest in the potentiality of human life may, if it chooses, regulate, and even proscribe, abortion except where it is necessary, in appropriate medical judgment, for the preservation of the life or health of the mother." *Roe v. Wade*, 410 U.S. at 164–165.

These principles control our assessment of the Pennsylvania statute, and we now turn to the issue of the validity of its challenged provisions.

V

* * *

Because it is central to the operation of various other requirements, we begin with the statute's definition of medical emergency. Under the statute, a medical emergency is

"that condition which, on the basis of the physician's good faith clinical judgment, so complicates the medical condition of a pregnant woman as to necessitate the immediate abortion of her pregnancy to avert her death or for which a delay will create serious risk of substantial and irreversible impairment of a major bodily function."

18 Pa. Cons. Stat. § 3203 (1990).

Petitioners argue that the definition is too narrow, contending that it forecloses the possibility of an immediate abortion despite some significant health risks. * * *

B

We next consider the informed consent requirement. [ ]. Except in a medical emergency, the statute requires that at least 24 hours before performing an abortion a physician inform the woman of the nature of the procedure, the health risks of the abortion and of childbirth, and the "probable gestational age of the unborn child." The physician or a qualified nonphysician must inform the woman of the availability of printed materials published by the State describing the fetus and providing information about medical assistance for childbirth, information about child support from the father, and a list of agencies which provide adoption and other services as alternatives to abortion. An abortion may not be performed unless the woman certifies in writing that she has been informed of the availability of these printed materials and has been provided them if she chooses to view them.

* * *

To the extent [that prior cases] find a constitutional violation when the government requires, as it does here, the giving of truthful, nonmisleading information about the nature of the procedure, the attendant health risks and those of childbirth, and the "probable gestational age" of the fetus, those cases go too far, are inconsistent with *Roe's* acknowledgment of an important interest in potential life, and are overruled. This is clear even on the very terms of *Akron I* and *Thornburgh*. Those decisions, along with *Danforth*, recognize a substantial government interest justifying a requirement that a woman be apprised of the health risks of abortion and childbirth. [ ] It cannot be questioned that psychological well-being is a facet of health. Nor can it be doubted that most women considering an abortion would deem the impact on the fetus relevant, if not dispositive, to the decision. In attempting to ensure that a woman apprehend the full consequences of her decision, the State furthers the legitimate purpose of reducing the risk that a woman may elect an abortion, only to discover later, with devastating psychological consequences, that her decision was not fully informed. If the information the State requires to be made available to the woman is truthful and not misleading, the requirement may be permissible.

We also see no reason why the State may not require doctors to inform a woman seeking an abortion of the availability of materials relating to the consequences to the fetus, even when those consequences have no direct relation to her health. An example illustrates the point. We would think it constitutional for the State to require that in order for there to be informed consent to a kidney transplant operation the recipient must be supplied with information about risks to the donor as well as risks to himself or herself. A requirement that the physician make available information similar to that mandated by the statute here was described in *Thornburgh* as "an outright attempt to wedge the Commonwealth's message discouraging abortion into the privacy of the informed-consent dialogue between the woman and her physician." 476 U.S. at 762. We conclude, however, that informed choice need not be defined in such narrow terms that all considerations of the effect on the fetus are made irrelevant. As we have made clear, we depart from the holdings of *Akron I* and *Thornburgh* to the extent that we permit a State to further its legitimate goal of protecting the life of the unborn by enacting legislation aimed at ensuring a decision that is mature and informed, even when in so doing the State expresses a preference for childbirth over abortion. In short, requiring that the woman be informed of the availability of information relating to fetal development and the assistance available should she decide to carry the pregnancy to full term is a reasonable measure to ensure an informed choice, one which might cause the woman to choose childbirth over abortion. This requirement cannot be considered a substantial obstacle to obtaining an abortion, and, it follows, there is no undue burden.

* * *

All that is left of petitioners' argument is an asserted First Amendment right of a physician not to provide information about the risks of abortion, and childbirth, in a manner mandated by the State. To be sure, the physician's First Amendment rights not to speak are implicated, [citation omitted], but only as part of the practice of medicine, subject to reasonable licensing and regulation by the State, [ ]. We see no constitutional infirmity in the requirement that the physician provide the information mandated by the State here.

The Pennsylvania statute also requires us to reconsider the holding in *Akron I* that the State may not require that a physician, as opposed to a qualified assistant, provide information relevant to a woman's informed consent. 462 U.S. at 448. Since there is no evidence on this record that requiring a doctor to give the information as provided by the statute would amount in practical terms to a substantial obstacle to a woman seeking an abortion, we conclude that it is not an undue burden. Our cases reflect the fact that the Constitution gives the States broad latitude to decide that particular functions may be performed only by licensed professionals, even if an objective assessment might suggest that those same tasks could be performed by others. [reference omitted]

Our analysis of Pennsylvania's 24–hour waiting period between the provision of the information deemed necessary to informed consent and the performance of an abortion under the undue burden standard requires us to reconsider the premise behind the decision in *Akron I* invalidating a parallel requirement. In *Akron I* we said: "Nor are we convinced that the State's legitimate concern that the woman's decision be informed is reasonably served by requiring a 24–hour delay as a matter of course." 462 U.S. at 450. We consider that conclusion to be wrong. The idea that important decisions will be more informed and deliberate if they follow some period of reflection does not strike us as unreasonable, particularly where the statute directs that important information become part of the background of the decision. * * *.

Whether the mandatory 24–hour waiting period is nonetheless invalid because in practice it is a substantial obstacle to a woman's choice to terminate her pregnancy is a closer question. The findings of fact by the District Court indicate that because of the distances many women must travel to reach an abortion provider, the practical effect will often be a delay of much more than a day because the waiting period requires that a woman seeking an abortion make at least two visits to the doctor. * * *

These findings are troubling in some respects, but they do not demonstrate that the waiting period constitutes an undue burden. We do not doubt that, as the District Court held, the waiting period has the effect of "increasing the cost and risk of delay of abortions," *id.*, at 1378, but the District Court did not conclude that the increased costs and potential delays amount to substantial obstacles. * * *

We are left with the argument that the various aspects of the informed consent requirement are unconstitutional because they place barriers in the way of abortion on demand. Even the broadest reading of *Roe*, however, has not suggested that there is a constitutional right to abortion on demand. [ ] Rather, the right protected by *Roe* is a right to decide to terminate a pregnancy free of undue interference by the State. Because the informed consent requirement facilitates the wise exercise of that right, it cannot be classified as an interference with the right *Roe* protects. The informed consent requirement is not an undue burden on that right.

C

Section 3209 of Pennsylvania's abortion law provides, except in cases of medical emergency, that no physician shall perform an abortion on a married woman without receiving a signed statement from the woman that she has notified her spouse that she is about to undergo an abortion. The woman has the option of providing an alternative signed statement certifying that her husband is not the man who impregnated her; that her husband could not be located; that the pregnancy is the result of spousal sexual assault which she has reported; or that the woman believes that notifying her husband will cause him or someone else to inflict bodily injury upon her. A physician who performs an abortion on a married woman without receiving the appropriate signed statement will have his or her license revoked, and is liable to the husband for damages.

* * *

This information and the District Court's findings reinforce what common sense would suggest. In well-functioning marriages, spouses discuss important intimate decisions such as whether to bear a child. But there are millions of women in this country who are the victims of regular physical and psychological abuse at the hands of their husbands. Should these women become pregnant, they may have very good reasons for not wishing to inform their husbands of their decision to obtain an abortion. Many may have justifiable fears of physical abuse, but may be no less fearful of the consequences of reporting prior abuse to the Commonwealth of Pennsylvania. Many may have a reasonable fear that notifying their husbands will provoke further instances of child abuse; these women are not exempt from § 3209's notification requirement. Many may fear devastating forms of psychological abuse from their husbands, including verbal harassment, threats of future violence, the destruction of possessions, physical confinement to the home, the withdrawal of financial support, or the disclosure of the abortion to family and friends. These methods of psychological abuse may act as even more of a deterrent to notification than the possibility of physical violence, but women who are the victims of the abuse are not exempt from § 3209's notification requirement. And many women who are pregnant as a result of sexual assaults by their husbands will be unable to avail themselves of the exception for spousal sexual assault, § 3209(b)(3), because the exception requires that the woman have notified law enforcement authorities within 90 days of the assault, and her husband will be notified of her report once an investigation begins, § 3128(c). If anything in this field is certain, it is that victims of spousal sexual assault are extremely reluctant to report the abuse to the government; hence, a great many spousal rape victims will not be exempt from the notification requirement imposed by § 3209.

The spousal notification requirement is thus likely to prevent a significant number of women from obtaining an abortion. It does not merely make abortions a little more difficult or expensive to obtain; for many women, it will impose a substantial obstacle. We must not blind ourselves to the fact that the significant number of women who fear for their safety and the safety of their children are likely to be deterred from procuring an abortion as surely as if the Commonwealth had outlawed abortion in all cases.

Respondents attempt to avoid the conclusion that § 3209 is invalid by pointing out that it imposes almost no burden at all for the vast majority of women seeking abortions. They begin by noting that only about 20 percent of the women who obtain abortions are married. They then note that of these women about 95 percent notify their husbands of their own volition. Thus, respondents argue, the effects of § 3209 are felt by only one percent of the women who obtain abortions. Respondents argue that since some of these women will be able to notify their husbands without adverse consequences or will qualify for one of the exceptions, the statute affects fewer than one percent of women seeking abortions. For this reason, it is asserted, the statute cannot be invalid on its face. See Brief for Respondents 83–86. We disagree with respondents' basic method of analysis.

The analysis does not end with the one percent of women upon whom the statute operates; it begins there. Legislation is measured for consistency with the Constitution by its impact on those whose conduct it affects. * * * The proper focus of constitutional inquiry is the group for whom the law is a restriction, not the group for whom the law is irrelevant.

* * *

D

We next consider the parental consent provision. Except in a medical emergency, an unemancipated young woman under 18 may not obtain an abortion unless she and one of her parents (or guardian) provides informed consent as defined above. If neither a parent nor a guardian provides consent, a court may authorize the performance of an abortion upon a determination that the young woman is mature and capable of giving informed consent and has in fact given her informed consent, or that an abortion would be in her best interests.

We have been over most of this ground before. Our cases establish, and we reaffirm today, that a State may require a minor seeking an abortion to obtain the consent of a parent or guardian, provided that there is an adequate judicial bypass procedure. See, *e. g., Akron II*, 497 U.S. at 510–519; *Hodgson*, 497 U.S. at 461 [ ] *Akron I*, 462 U.S. at 440; *Bellotti II*, 443 U.S. at 643–644 (plurality opinion). Under these precedents, in our view, the one-parent consent requirement and judicial bypass procedure are constitutional.

The only argument made by petitioners respecting this provision and to which our prior decisions do not speak is the contention that the parental consent requirement is invalid because it requires informed parental consent. For the most part, petitioners' argument is a reprise of their argument with respect to the informed consent requirement in general, and we reject it for the reasons given above. Indeed, some of the provisions regarding informed consent have particular force with respect to minors: the waiting period, for example, may provide the parent or parents of a pregnant young woman the opportunity to consult with her in private, and to discuss the consequences of her decision in the context of the values and moral or religious principles of their family. [citation omitted].

E

Under the recordkeeping and reporting requirements of the statute, every facility which performs abortions is required to file a report stating its name and address as well as the name and address of any related entity, such as a controlling or subsidiary organization. In the case of state-funded institutions, the information becomes public.

For each abortion performed, a report must be filed identifying: the physician (and the second physician where required); the facility; the referring physician or agency; the woman's age; the number of prior pregnancies and prior abortions she has had; gestational age; the type of abortion procedure; the date of the abortion; whether there were any pre-existing medical conditions which would complicate pregnancy; medical complications with the abortion; where applicable, the basis for the determination that the abortion was medically necessary; the weight of the aborted fetus; and whether the woman was married, and if so, whether notice was provided or the basis for the failure to give notice. Every abortion facility must also file quarterly reports showing the number of abortions performed broken down by trimester. [ ].

[The Court upheld these provisions.]

* * *

VI

Our Constitution is a covenant running from the first generation of Americans to us and then to future generations. It is a coherent succession. Each generation must learn anew that the Constitution's written terms embody ideas and aspirations that must survive more ages than one. We accept our responsibility not to retreat from interpreting the full meaning of the covenant in light of all of our precedents. We invoke it once again to define the freedom guaranteed by the Constitution's own promise, the promise of liberty.

* * *

The judgment * * * is affirmed in part and reversed in part, and the case is remanded for proceedings consistent with this opinion * * *

It is so ordered.

LAMBERT v. WICKLUND

Supreme Court of the United States, 1997.
520 U.S. 292, 117 S.Ct. 1169, 137 L.Ed.2d 464.

Per Curiam.

* * *

In 1995, Montana enacted the Parental Notice of Abortion Act. The Act prohibits a physician from performing an abortion on a minor unless the physician has notified one of the minor's parents or the minor's legal guardian 48 hours in advance. Citation omitted. However, an "unemancipated" minor may petition the state youth court to waive the notification requirement, pursuant to the statute's "judicial bypass" provision. [ ] (quoted in full in an Appendix to this opinion). The provision gives the minor a right to court-appointed counsel, and guarantees expeditious handling of the minor's petition (since the petition is automatically granted if the youth court fails to rule on the petition within 48 hours from the time it is filed). [ ]. The minor's identity remains anonymous, and the proceedings and related documents are kept confidential. [ ].

If the court finds by clear and convincing evidence that *any* of the following three conditions are met, it must grant the petition and waive the notice requirement: (i) the minor is "sufficiently mature to decide whether to have an abortion"; (ii) "there is evidence of a pattern of physical, sexual, or emotional abuse" of the minor by one of her parents, a guardian, or a custodian; or (iii) "the *notification* of a parent or guardian is not in the best interests of the [minor]." [ ] (emphasis added). It is this third condition which is at issue here.

Before the Act's effective date, respondents—several physicians who perform abortions, and other medical personnel—filed a complaint seeking a declaration that the Act was unconstitutional and an order enjoining its enforcement. * * *

In *Bellotti,* we struck down a statute requiring a minor to obtain the *consent* of both parents before having an abortion, subject to a judicial bypass provision, because the judicial bypass provision was too restrictive, unconstitutionally burdening a minor's right to an abortion. 443 U.S. at 647 (plurality opinion); id. at 655–656 (STEVENS, J., concurring in judgment). The Court's principal opinion explained that a constitutional parental consent statute must contain a bypass provision that meets four criteria: (i) allow the minor to bypass the consent requirement if she establishes that she is mature enough and well enough informed to make the abortion decision independently; (ii) allow the minor to bypass the consent requirement if she establishes that the abortion would be in her best interests; (iii) ensure the minor's anonymity; and (iv) provide for expeditious bypass procedures. Id. at 643–644 (plurality opinion). [ ].

In *Akron II,* we upheld a statute requiring a minor to *notify* one parent before having an abortion, subject to a judicial bypass provision. We declined to decide whether a parental notification statute must include some sort of bypass provision to be constitutional. Id. at 510. Instead, we held that this bypass provision satisfied the four *Bellotti* criteria required for bypass provisions in parental *consent* statutes, and that *a fortiori* it satisfied any criteria that might be required for bypass provisions in parental notification statutes. Critically for the case now before us, the judicial bypass provision we examined in *Akron II* was substantively indistinguishable from both the Montana judicial bypass provision at issue here and the Nevada provision at issue in *Glick.* [ ]. The judicial bypass provision in *Akron II* allowed a court to waive the notification requirement if it determined by clear and convincing evidence "that *notice* is not in [the minor's] best interests" (not that *an abortion* is in her best interests). *Ibid.* (emphasis added) [ ]. And we explicitly held that this provision satisfied the second *Bellotti* requirement, that "the procedure must allow the minor to show that, even if she cannot make the abortion decision by herself, 'the desired abortion would be in her best interests.' '' Id. at 511 (quoting *Bellotti, supra,* 443 U.S. at 644).

Despite the fact that *Akron II* involved a parental notification statute, and *Bellotti* involved a parental consent statute; despite the fact that *Akron II* involved a statute virtually identical to the Nevada statute at issue in *Glick*; and despite the fact that *Akron II* explicitly held that the statute met all of the *Bellotti* requirements, the Ninth Circuit in *Glick* struck down Nevada's parental notification statute as inconsistent with *Bellotti*:

"Rather than requiring the reviewing court to consider the minor's 'best interests' generally, the Nevada statute requires the consideration of 'best interests' only with respect to the possible consequences of parental notification. The best interests of a minor female in obtaining an abortion may encompass far more than her interests in not notifying a parent of the abortion decision. Furthermore, in *Bellotti,* the court expressly stated, 'if, *all things considered,* the court determines that an abortion is in the minor's best interests, she is entitled to court authorization without any parental involvement.' *Bellotti,* 443 U.S. at 648 (emphasis added). Therefore, the Nevada statute impermissibly narrows the *Bellotti* 'best interests' criterion, and is unconstitutional." 937 F.2d at 439.

Based entirely on *Glick,* the Ninth Circuit in this case affirmed the District Court's ruling that the Montana statute is unconstitutional, since the statute allows waiver of the notification requirement only if the youth court determines that notification—not the abortion itself—is not in the minor's best interests. [ ].

As should be evident from the foregoing, this decision simply cannot be squared with our decision in *Akron II*. The Ohio parental notification statute at issue there was indistinguishable in any relevant way from the Montana statute at issue here. Both allow for judicial bypass if the minor shows that parental *notification* is not in her best interests. We asked in *Akron II* whether this met the *Bellotti* requirement that the minor be allowed to show that "the desired abortion would be in her best interests." We explicitly held that it did. [ ]. Thus, the Montana statute meets this requirement, too. In concluding otherwise, the Ninth Circuit was mistaken.

Respondents (as did the Ninth Circuit in *Glick*) place great emphasis on our statement in *Akron II,* that "the statute requires the juvenile court to authorize the minor's consent where the court determines that *the abortion* is in the minor's best interest." 497 U.S. at 511 (emphasis added) [ ]. But since we had clearly stated that the statute actually required such authorization only when the court determined that *notification* would not be in the minor's best interests, it is wrong to take our statement to imply that the statute said otherwise. Rather, underlying our statement was an assumption that a judicial bypass procedure requiring a minor to show that *parental notification is not* in her best interests is equivalent to a judicial bypass procedure requiring a minor to show that *abortion without notification is* in her best interests, as the context of the opinion, the statutory language, and the concurring opinion all make clear.

Respondents, echoing the Ninth Circuit in *Glick*, claim that there is a constitutionally significant distinction between requiring a minor to show that parental notification is not in her best interests, and requiring a minor to show that an abortion (without such notification) is in her best interests. [ ]. But the Montana statute draws no such distinction, and respondents cite no Montana state court decision suggesting that the statute permits a court to separate the question whether parental notification is not in a minor's best interest from an inquiry into whether abortion (without notification) is in the minor's best interest. As with the Ohio statute in *Akron II,* the challenge to the Montana statute here is a facial one. Under these circumstances, the Ninth Circuit was incorrect to assume that Montana's statute "narrowed" the *Bellotti* test [ ], as interpreted in *Akron II*.

Because the reasons given by the District Court and the Ninth Circuit for striking down the Act are inconsistent with our precedents, we grant the petition for a writ of certiorari and reverse the judgment of the Ninth Circuit.

It is so ordered.

BABY BOY DOE v. MOTHER DOE

Appellate Court of Illinois, First District, Second Division, 1994.
260 Ill.App.3d 392, 198 Ill.Dec. 267, 632 N.E.2d 326.

Presiding Justice DiVito delivered the opinion of the court:

This case asks whether an Illinois court can balance whatever rights a fetus may have against the rights of a competent woman to refuse medical advice to obtain a cesarean section for the supposed benefit of her fetus. Following the lead of the Illinois Supreme Court in Stallman v. Youngquist (1988), 125 Ill.2d 267, 531 N.E.2d 355, 126 Ill.Dec. 60, we hold that no such balancing should be employed, and that a woman's competent choice to refuse medical treatment as invasive as a cesarean section during pregnancy must be honored, even in circumstances where the choice may be harmful to her fetus.

Both the factual background and the procedural posture of the case are important. "Doe" is a married woman who was expecting her first child. She sought and had been receiving regular prenatal care throughout her pregnancy at St. Joseph's Hospital in Chicago. All parties and the court regarded her as mentally competent.

On November 24, 1993, Dr. James Meserow, a board-certified obstetrician/gynecologist and expert in the field of maternal/fetal medicine who is affiliated with the hospital, examined Doe for the first time. A series of tests he ordered performed on her suggested to Meserow that something was wrong with the placenta, and that the approximately 35–week, viable fetus was receiving insufficient oxygen. Meserow recommended immediate delivery by cesarean section, in his opinion the safest option for the fetus or, in the alternative, by induced labor. Informed of his recommendation, Doe told Meserow that, because of her personal religious beliefs, she would not consent to either procedure. Instead, given her abiding faith in God's healing powers, she chose to await natural childbirth. Her husband agreed with her decision.

Doe was examined by Dr. Meserow again on December 8, and by a Dr. Gautier from the University of Illinois at Chicago on Thursday, December 9. After consulting with Gautier, Meserow concluded that the condition of the fetus had worsened. Meserow advised Doe and her husband that due to the insufficient oxygen flow to the fetus, failure to provide an immediate delivery by cesarean section (Meserow no longer recommended inducement as an option) could result in the child being born dead or severely retarded. Doe reiterated her opposition to a cesarean section, based on her personal religious beliefs.

On December 8, 1993, Dr. Meserow and St. Joseph's Hospital contacted the office of the Cook County State's Attorney. That office filed a petition for adjudication of wardship of the fetus on December 9, seeking to invoke the jurisdiction of the Juvenile Court Act (705 ILCS 405/1–1 et seq. (West 1992)), and asking that the hospital be appointed custodian of the fetus. The juvenile court judge appointed an assistant public defender as counsel for Doe and her husband. The judge, who expressed doubt as to whether the Juvenile Court Act conferred jurisdiction over a fetus in utero, certified the question for immediate appeal to this court * * *.

* * *

During [an] emergency hearing, the assistant state's attorneys asked the court for an order forcing Doe to undergo an immediate cesarean section to deliver the fetus.

* * *

The State called Dr. Meserow as its only witness. Meserow testified that he could not ascertain whether the fetus was already injured, or quantify the degree of risk to the fetus from continuing the pregnancy. He indicated that a fetus has some coping mechanisms to deal with decreased oxygen, and that those mechanisms appeared to be functioning. In his expert opinion, the likelihood of injury to the fetus increased on a daily basis, and the chances that the fetus would survive a natural labor were close to zero. On cross-examination, Meserow further testified about the specific medical procedures involved in a cesarean section, and the serious risks and possible side effects to Doe of such procedures. Although he recommended a cesarean section as the safest mode of delivery for the fetus, Meserow was not advocating that the cesarean section be performed over Doe's objection.

Counsel for Doe and her husband called no witnesses, but entered into a stipulation with the State which was accepted by the court: Doe received the recommendation from the physicians, understood the risks and benefits of the proposed procedures and, in consultation with her husband, decided to await natural childbirth.

* * *

The court made the following conclusions of law in denying the State's request for an injunction:

"1.   The Court has jurisdiction of this matter under its grant of general jurisdiction. The Juvenile Court Act is not applicable. A fetus is not a 'minor' within the meaning of the Act.

2.   In the circumstances of this case, the state has failed to demonstrate that there is statutory or case law to support justifying the intrusive procedure requested herein by way of a court order against a competent person.

3.   The Court denies the State's motion for an injunction.

4.   There is no reason to delay an appeal of this matter and this is a final ruling."

The State and the Public Guardian filed notices of appeal * * *. This court granted the motion for an expedited hearing [ ], heard oral argument from all parties, and in a brief written order affirmed the judgment of the circuit court. In so doing, this court reserved the right to issue an opinion at some future date.

* * * The Public Guardian then applied to the United States Supreme Court for an order remanding the matter to the circuit court of Cook County. That Court, with one justice dissenting, denied the motion [ ]. The Supreme Court subsequently denied certiorari * * *

Doe vaginally delivered an apparently normal and healthy, although somewhat underweight, baby boy on December 29, 1993. The ACLU has since petitioned for the issuance of a written opinion, pointing out that the issue involved is serious and that the situation is likely to arise again, with little time for a circuit court to make an informed judgment. Cognizant of the seriousness of the question presented, and believing that the circuit courts of Illinois require some guidance in this area, this court issues the present opinion.

* * *

Both the State and the Public Guardian argued that the circuit court should have balanced the rights of the unborn but viable fetus which was nearly at full term and which, if the uncontradicted expert testimony of the physicians had been accurate, would have been born dead or severely retarded if Doe delivered vaginally, against the right of the competent woman to choose the type of medical care she deemed appropriate, based in part on personal religious considerations. We hold today that Illinois courts should not engage in such a balancing, and that a woman's competent choice in refusing medical treatment as invasive as a cesarean section during her pregnancy must be honored, even in circumstances where the choice may be harmful to her fetus.

It cannot be doubted that a competent person has the right to refuse medical treatment. The Illinois Supreme Court summed up American attitude and law on this issue very well in In re Estate of Longeway: "No right is more sacred, or is more carefully guarded by the common law, than the right of every individual to the possession and control of [the individual's] own person, free from all restraint or interference of others, unless by clear and unquestionable authority of law." [citations omitted] Thus, "every human being of adult years and sound mind has a right to determine what shall be done with his [or her] own body; and a surgeon who performs an operation without his [or her] patient's consent commits an assault for which he [or she] is liable in damages" [citations omitted].

In Illinois the common law protects the right of a competent individual to refuse medical treatment. [ ]. Moreover, the right "to withhold consent and refuse treatment incorporates all types of medical treatment, including life saving or life sustaining procedures," demonstrating that the right to refuse treatment does not depend upon whether the treatment is perceived as risky or beneficial to the individual.

The United States Supreme Court, in Cruzan v. Director, Missouri Department of Health (1990), 497 U.S. 261, 111 L.Ed.2d 224, 110 S.Ct. 2841, 2851, held that the due process clause of the 14th amendment confers a significant liberty interest in avoiding unwanted medical procedures. Concurring with the majority opinion, Justice O'Connor stated that the liberty guaranteed by the due process clause must protect, if it protects anything, an individual's "deeply personal" decision to reject medical treatment. "Because our notions of liberty are inextricably entwined with our idea of physical freedom and self determination, the Court has often deemed state incursions into the body repugnant to the interests protected by the Due Process Clause." Cruzan, 497 U.S. at 287, 111 L.Ed.2d at 247, 110 S.Ct. at 2856 (O'Connor, J., concurring).

The Illinois Supreme Court has acknowledged that the state right of privacy protects substantive fundamental rights, such as the right to reproductive autonomy. [reference omitted] Further, the court has conceptually linked the right to privacy with the right of bodily integrity. In Stallman v. Youngquist (1988), 125 Ill.2d 267, 275, 531 N.E.2d 355, 360, 126 Ill.Dec. 60, the supreme court refused to recognize a tort action against a mother for unintentional infliction of prenatal injuries because it would subject the woman's every act while pregnant to state scrutiny, thereby intruding upon her rights to privacy and bodily integrity, and her right to control her own life.

Religious liberty, protected by both federal and Illinois constitutions, similarly requires that a competent adult may refuse medical treatment on religious grounds. In In re Estate of Brooks (1965), 32 Ill.2d 361, 205 N.E.2d 435, the Illinois Supreme Court held that an adult may refuse medical treatment on religious grounds even under circumstances where treatment is required to save the patient's life. In that case, an adult

Jehovah's Witness was rendered temporarily incompetent by a life-threatening medical condition. Despite a previously-expressed wish not to be transfused with blood products, a conservator was appointed to consent to transfusions. The State argued that society's interest in preserving life outweighs a patient's right to the free exercise of religion. The Illinois Supreme Court disagreed, out of a recognition that religious liberty and the right to determine one's own destiny are among the rights "most valued by civilized man." [ ] As such, an individual's free exercise of religion may be limited only "where such exercise endangers, clearly and presently, the public health, welfare or morals." [ ] Recognizing that the decision to refuse medical treatment is a matter of individual conscience and not a question of public welfare, the court concluded:

> "Even though we may consider appellant's beliefs unwise, foolish or ridiculous, in the absence of an overriding danger to society we may not permit interference therewith * * * for the sole purpose of compelling her to accept medical treatment forbidden by her religious principles and previously refused by her with full knowledge of the probable consequences." [ ]

The right of a competent adult to refuse medical treatment inconsistent with his or her religious beliefs was reaffirmed in Baumgartner v. First Church of Christ, Scientist (1986), 141 Ill.App.3d 898, 490 N.E.2d 1319, 96 Ill.Dec. 114, cert. denied (1986), 479 U.S. 915, 93 L.Ed.2d 290, 107 S.Ct. 317.

Particularly important to our supreme court's holding in Stallman was the recognition that the relationship between a pregnant woman and a fetus is unique, and

> "unlike the relationship between any other plaintiff and defendant. No other plaintiff depends exclusively on any other defendant for everything necessary for life itself. No other defendant must go through biological changes of the most profound type, possibly at the risk of her own life, in order to bring forth an adversary into the world. It is, after all, the whole life of the pregnant woman which impacts upon the development of the fetus. * * * It is the mother's every waking and sleeping moment which, for better or worse, shapes the prenatal environment which forms the world for the developing fetus. That this is so is not a pregnant woman's fault; it is a fact of life." Stallman, 125 Ill.2d at 278–79.

Appreciating the fact that "the circumstances in which each individual woman brings forth life are as varied as the circumstances of each woman's life," the court strongly suggested that there can be no consistent and objective legal standard by which to judge a woman's actions during pregnancy. Stallman, 125 Ill.2d at 279.

Applied in the context of compelled medical treatment of pregnant women, the rationale of Stallman directs that a woman's right to refuse invasive medical treatment, derived from her rights to privacy, bodily integrity, and religious liberty, is not diminished during pregnancy. The woman retains the same right to refuse invasive treatment, even of lifesaving or other beneficial nature, that she can exercise when she is not pregnant. The potential impact upon the fetus is not legally relevant; to the contrary, the Stallman court explicitly rejected the view that the woman's rights can be subordinated to fetal rights. [ ]

In Illinois a fetus is not treated as only a part of its mother. [ ] It has the legal right to begin life with a sound mind and body, assertable against third parties after it has been born alive. [ ] This right is not assertable against its mother, however, for the unintentional infliction of prenatal injuries. [ ] A woman is under no duty to guarantee the mental and physical health of her child at birth, and thus cannot be compelled to do or not do anything merely for the benefit of her unborn Child. The Public Guardian's argument that this case is distinguishable from Stallman because Doe's actions amounted to intentional infliction of prenatal injuries is not persuasive.

The court of appeals for the District of Columbia has held that a woman's competent choice regarding medical treatment of her pregnancy must be honored, even under circumstances where the choice may be fatal to the fetus. (In re A.C. (D.C. App. 1990), 573 A.2d 1235.) The appellate court, reviewing the case en banc, vacated the lower court's order, which had required a pregnant, dying woman to undergo a cesarean section because the fetus was potentially viable. The lower court, after first ruling that it could not determine the woman's wishes because it questioned her competency, then reached its decision by balancing the fetus's rights against the woman's rights. The appellate court held that the lower court's approach was erroneous. Instead of balancing, the appellate court instructed, the lower court should have ascertained the woman's wishes by means of the doctrine of substituted judgment. The woman's decision, not the fetus's interest, is the only dispositive factor. If the woman is competent and makes an informed decision, that decision will control "in virtually all cases." [ ] While not deciding the question, the court expressed some doubt as to whether there could ever be a situation extraordinary or compelling enough to justify a massive intrusion into a person's body, such as a cesarean section, against that person's will. [ ] The Public Guardian's argument, that this case represents such a situation, is unpersuasive. The In re A.C. court declined to express an opinion with regard to the circumstances, if any, in which lesser invasions (such as a blood transfusion) might be permitted over the woman's refusal. [ ]

Two courts have held otherwise, ordering forced cesarean sections against pregnant women. The Supreme Court of Georgia, in Jefferson v. Griffin Spalding County Hospital Authority (1981), 247 Ga. 86, 274 S.E.2d 457, balanced the rights of the viable fetus against the rights of the mother, and determined that an expectant mother in the last weeks of pregnancy lacks the right of other persons to refuse surgery or other medical treatment if the life of the unborn child is at stake. The Superior Court of the District of Columbia followed the same logic and came to the same conclusion in In re Madyun (D.C. Super. Ct. July 26, 1986), 114 Daily Wash. L. Rptr. 2233.

Those decisions, however, are contrary to the rationale of both Stallman, the controlling law in this jurisdiction, and In re A.C., which hold that the rights of the fetus should not be balanced against the rights of the mother. Additionally, neither the Jefferson nor the Madyun court recognized the constitutional dimension of the woman's right to refuse treatment, or the magnitude of that right. The Supreme Judicial Court of Massachusetts, in Taft v. Taft (1983), 388 Mass. 331, 446 N.E.2d 395, when faced with a similar circumstance, vacated a lower court's order compelling a surgical procedure upon a pregnant woman because the lower court failed to recognize the woman's constitutional right to privacy, and the record did not present circumstances so compelling as to override the right to religious freedom for pregnant Jehovah's Witnesses.

* * *

Federal constitutional principles prohibiting the balancing of fetal rights against maternal health further bolster a woman's right to refuse a cesarean section. In Thornburgh v. American College of Obstetricians and Gynecologists (1986), 476 U.S. 747, 90 L.Ed.2d 779, 106 S.Ct. 2169, the United States Supreme Court struck down a Pennsylvania statute which required that in cases of post-viability abortions, permitted under state law only when necessary to save the woman's life or health, a physician must use the abortion technique providing the best opportunity for the fetus to be aborted alive. The Supreme Court, finding the statute unconstitutional for requiring a "trade-off" between the woman's health and fetal survival, stressed that the woman's health is always the paramount consideration; any degree of increased risk to the woman's health is unacceptable. [ ].

A cesarean section, by its nature, presents some additional risks to the woman's health. When the procedure is recommended solely for the benefit of the fetus, the additional risk is particularly evident. It is impossible to say that compelling a cesarean section upon a pregnant woman does not subject her to additional risks—even the circuit court's findings of fact in this case indicate increased risk to Doe. Under Thornburgh, then, it appears that a forced cesarean section, undertaken for the benefit of the fetus, cannot pass constitutional muster.

Courts in Illinois and elsewhere have consistently refused to force one person to undergo medical procedures for the purpose of benefiting another person—even where the two persons share a blood relationship, and even where the risk to the first person is perceived to be minimal and the benefit to the second person may be great. The Illinois Supreme Court addressed this issue in Curran v. Bosze (1990), 141 Ill.2d 473, 566 N.E.2d 1319, 153 Ill.Dec. 213, where it refused to compel twin minors to donate bone marrow to a half-sibling, despite the fact that the procedures involved would pose little risk to the twins, and the sibling's life depended on the transplant. Nor would the court compel the minors to undergo even a blood test for the purpose of determining whether they would be compatible donors. If a sibling cannot be forced to donate bone marrow to save a sibling's life, if an incompetent brother cannot be forced to donate a kidney to save the life of his dying sister (In re Pescinski (1975), 67 Wis.2d 4, 226 N.W.2d 180), then surely a mother cannot be forced to undergo a cesarean section to benefit her viable fetus.

* * *

Of not insignificant concern in this case is how a forced cesarean section would be carried out. The Public Guardian specifically opposed any effort to use force or other means to compel Doe to have the surgery; the State also opposed the use of force. Thus, we have been asked to issue an order that no one expects to be carried out. This court, as a simple matter of policy, will not enter an order that is not intended to be enforced.

If such an order were to be carried out, what would be the circumstances? The In re A.C. court considered such a question, and concluded that

"Enforcement could be accomplished only through physical force or its equivalent. A.C. would have to be fastened with restraints to the operating table, or perhaps rendered unconscious by forcibly injecting her with an anesthetic, and then subjected to unwanted major surgery. Such actions would surely give one pause in a civilized society, especially when A.C. had done no wrong." In re A.C., 573 A.2d at 1244.

An even more graphic description of what actually happened when a forced cesarean section was carried out may be found in Gallagher, Prenatal Invasions & Interventions: What's Wrong With Fetal Rights, 10 Harvard Women's L.J. 9, 9–10 (1987). We simply cannot envision issuing an order that, if enforced at all, could be enforced only in this fashion.

For all the reasons given above, we affirm the decision of the circuit court.

Affirmed.

Hartman and McCormick, JJ., concur.

WISCONSIN v. KRUZICKI

Supreme Court of Wisconsin, 1997.
209 Wis.2d 112, 561 N.W.2d 729.

ANN WALSH BRADLEY, J. The petitioner, Angela M.W., seeks review of a court of appeals' decision denying her request for either a writ of habeas corpus or a supervisory writ to prohibit the Waukesha County Circuit Court, Kathryn W. Foster, Judge, from continuing to exercise jurisdiction in a CHIPS (child alleged to be in need of protection or services) proceeding. She maintains that the CHIPS statute does not confer jurisdiction over her or her viable fetus. In the alternative, if the CHIPS statute does confer such jurisdiction, the petitioner contends that as applied to her, it violates her equal protection and due process rights.

Because we determine that the legislature did not intend to include a fetus within the Children's Code definition of "child," we reverse the decision of the court of appeals.

Although we visit in the facts of this case the daunting social problem of drug use during pregnancy, the essence of this case is one of statutory construction. The relevant facts are undisputed.

The petitioner was an adult carrying a viable fetus with a projected delivery date of October 4, 1995. Based upon observations made while providing the petitioner with prenatal care, her obstetrician suspected that she was using cocaine or other drugs. Blood tests performed on May 31, June 26, and July 21, 1995, confirmed the obstetrician's suspicion that the petitioner was using cocaine or other drugs.

On July 21, 1995, the obstetrician confronted the petitioner about her drug use and its effect on her viable fetus. The petitioner expressed remorse, but declined the obstetrician's advice to seek treatment. On August 15, 1995, a blood test again confirmed that the petitioner was ingesting cocaine or other drugs. Afterward, the petitioner canceled a scheduled August 28, 1995, appointment, and rescheduled the appointment for September 1, 1995. When she failed to keep the September 1 appointment, her obstetrician reported his concerns to Waukesha County authorities.

On September 5, 1995, the Waukesha County Department of Health and Human Services (the County) filed a "MOTION TO TAKE AN UNBORN CHILD INTO CUSTODY," [ ]. The caption read "In the Matter of: JOHN OR JANE DOE, A 36 Week Old Unborn Child." In its motion, the County requested an order "removing the above-named unborn child from his or her present custody, and placing the unborn child" in protective custody. The motion was supported by the affidavit of the petitioner's obstetrician, which set out the obstetrician's observations and medical opinion that "without intervention forcing [the petitioner] to cease her drug use," her fetus would suffer serious physical harm.

In an order filed on September 6, 1995, the juvenile court directed that:

the [petitioner's] unborn child ... be detained [ ] by the Waukesha County Sheriff's Department and transported to Waukesha Memorial Hospital for inpatient treatment and protection. Such detention will by necessity result in the detention of the unborn child's mother....

Later that same day, before the protective custody order was executed, the petitioner presented herself voluntarily at an inpatient drug treatment facility. As a result, the juvenile court amended its order to provide that detention would be at the inpatient facility. The court further ordered that if the petitioner attempted to leave the inpatient facility or did not participate in the facility's drug treatment program, then both she and the fetus were to be detained and transported to Waukesha Memorial Hospital.

Also on September 6, 1995, the County filed a CHIPS petition in the juvenile court, alleging that the petitioner's viable fetus was in need of protection or services because the petitioner "neglected, refused or [was] unable for reasons other than poverty to provide necessary care, food, clothing, medical or dental care or shelter so as to seriously endanger the physical health of the child [ ]." The County alleged that the petitioner's 36–week–old viable fetus had been exposed to drugs prenatally through the mother's drug use. Instead of a birth date, the petition stated "Due Date 10/4/95." In the space designated for indicating the sex of the subject child, the petition stated "Unknown."

On September 7 and 8, 1995, the juvenile court held detention hearings [ ]. At the first hearing, the petitioner appeared by telephone, but without counsel. At the second hearing, now represented by counsel, she appeared again by telephone, and objected to the juvenile court's exercise of jurisdiction. The juvenile court rejected her jurisdictional challenge, and scheduled a plea hearing on the CHIPS petition for September 13, 1995.

On September 13, 1995, the petitioner commenced an original action in the court of appeals, seeking a writ of habeas corpus, or, in the alternative, a supervisory writ staying all proceedings in the juvenile court and dismissing the CHIPS petition. In support of her request, the petitioner asserted that Chapter 48 does not vest the juvenile court with jurisdiction over her or her viable fetus. Alternatively, if the statute does grant such authority, the petitioner argued that it violates the constitutional guarantees of procedural and substantive due process, as well as equal protection of the laws.

The court of appeals declined to stay the juvenile court proceedings, and issued an order on September 21, 1995, denying both writ petitions. The petitioner gave birth to a baby boy on September 28, 1995. Subsequently, the court of appeals issued an opinion supplementing its earlier order.

A divided court of appeals determined that the juvenile court did not exceed its jurisdiction in this case. [ ] The court reasoned that the United States Supreme Court, the Wisconsin legislature, and this court have each articulated public policy considerations supporting the conclusion that a viable fetus is a "person" within the meaning of the CHIPS statute's definition of "child." The court also held that application of the CHIPS statute to the petitioner did not deprive her of equal protection or due process, since the statute was a properly tailored means of vindicating the State's compelling interest in the health, safety, and welfare of a viable fetus. The petitioner then sought review in this court, raising substantially the same arguments she raised before the court of appeals.

We stress at the outset of our analysis that this case is not about the propriety or morality of the petitioner's conduct. It is also not about her constitutional right to reproductive choice guaranteed under Roe v. Wade, 410 U.S. 113, 35 L.Ed.2d 147, 93 S.Ct. 705 (1973). Rather, this case is one of statutory construction. The issue presented is whether a viable fetus is included in the definition of "child" provided in Wis. Stat. § 48.02(2).

The interpretation of a statute presents a question of law which this court reviews under a de novo standard. [ ]. Our primary purpose when interpreting a statute is to give effect to the legislature's intent. We first look to the language of the statute, and if the language is clear and unambiguous, we define the language of the statute in accordance with its ordinary meaning. If the language of the statute is ambiguous and does not clearly set forth the legislative intent, we will construe the statute so as to ascertain and carry out the legislative intent. In construing an ambiguous statute, we examine the history, context, subject matter, scope, and object of the statute. [ ].

The statutory language at issue confers on the juvenile court "exclusive original jurisdiction over a child alleged to be in need of protection or services which can be ordered by the court. . . . " § 48.13. A "child" is defined in Chapter 48 as "a person who is less than 18 years of age." § 48.02(2). The petitioner contends that the Chapter 48 definition of "child" is clear on its face, and mandates the conclusion that Chapter 48 uses the term "child" to mean a person born alive. In support, she asserts that by having no "age," a fetus cannot be a person who is less than 18 years of age. The petitioner submits that it is therefore unnecessary for this court to construe the statute to determine its meaning. In contrast, the County asserts that courts in this State and other jurisdictions have determined that "child" and "person" are ambiguous terms. As such, the County contends that we are required to look beyond the language of the statute for the meaning of "child."

Statutory language is ambiguous if reasonable minds could differ as to its meaning. [ ]. While the parties' differing interpretations of a statute do not alone create ambiguity, equally sensible interpretations of a term by different authorities are indicative of the term's ability to support more than one meaning. Id.

Case law reveals that different courts have given different meanings to the terms "person" and "child." This court has previously held that a viable fetus is a "person" for purposes of Wisconsin's wrongful death statute. [ ]. On the other hand, the United States Supreme Court has concluded that a fetus is not a "person" under the Fourteenth Amendment to the United States Constitution. Roe v. Wade [ ]. Perhaps most compelling, courts in other states have arrived at different interpretations of statutory language nearly identical to that in § 48.02(2). Compare State v. Gray, 62 Ohio St.3d 514, 584 N.E.2d 710, 713 (Ohio 1992) (holding that a third trimester fetus is not "a child under eighteen years of age," as provided in Ohio's child endangerment statute), with Whitner v. State, No. 24468, 1996 WL 393164, at *3 (S.C. July 15, 1996) (concluding that a viable fetus is a "person under the age of eighteen," pursuant to South Carolina's child abuse and endangerment statute).

Against this backdrop of conflicting authority, we conclude that the term "child" is ambiguous.

In construing the statute, we turn first to the legislative history. Chapter 48 came into existence in 1919 as part of a consolidation and revision of statutory provisions dealing generally with neglected, dependent, or delinquent children. § 2, ch. 614, Laws of 1919. The legislation defined a dependent or neglected child as "any child under the age of sixteen" meeting certain criteria. [ ]. Twenty years later, the definitions were amended to raise the age limit to eighteen years. [ ]. In 1955, the legislature created a separate subsection for definitions, describing a child as "a person under 18 years of age." [ ] In 1977, the legislature created § 48.02(2), which defined a child as a "person who is less than 18 years of age." [ ]. Finally, substantial changes made to Chapter 48 in the last legislative session have left the definition of "child" unaltered for purposes of our analysis. [ ]

In examining the legislative history, we find the drafting files of the more recent amendments to the Code devoid of information which might illuminate our search. We also find no news accounts of debate, dialogue, or even consideration of whether fetus should be included in the definition of "child" in Chapter 48. Furthermore, the parties offer no specific historical references to support their respective positions. The issue of whether the Chapter 48 definition of "child" includes a fetus is one of a controversial and complex nature. One would expect heated dialogue and intense debate if the legislature intended to include fetus within the definition of "child." Yet, we are met with legislative silence.

The dissent maintains that the legislature has impliedly ratified the court of appeals' interpretation of § 48.02(2), because amendments to the Code in the months since the court of appeals' decision have left undisturbed the language at issue. [ ]. However, the very cases relied upon by the dissent demonstrate the fundamental error of applying the doctrine of legislative acquiescence to the present case.

The application of the doctrine of legislative acquiescence is justified when the legislature can be "presumed to know that in absence of its changing the law, the construction put upon it by the courts will remain unchanged." Reiter v. Dyken, 95 Wis.2d 461, 471, 290 N.W.2d 510 (1980) [ ]. Of course, if this court has accepted review of a court of appeals' decision construing a statute, the legislature cannot be presumed to know that the court of appeals' interpretation "will remain unchanged." Our acceptance of review makes clear that the construction given to a statute by the court of appeals is subject to change. Thus, the doctrine presupposes the existence of a decision which, unlike the instant court of appeals' decision, is not subject to further appellate review.

This principle is confirmed by reviewing those cases cited by the dissent in which this court found implied legislative ratification of a prior decision. We observe that in each case, the legislature acquiesced to a prior decision that was either unappealable or no longer subject to review. [ ].

In this case, the petitioner filed a timely petition for review of the court of appeals' decision, and we granted review on January 23, 1996. The purported acts of legislative acquiescence occurred after that date. The dissent fails to explain how the legislature can be presumed to possess advance knowledge that the court of appeals' construction of § 48.02(2) would "remain unchanged" upon review by this court. The obvious answer is that the legislature made the amendments to the Code with full knowledge that the court of appeals' construction of § 48.02(2) was subject to alteration on further review by this court. Thus, there was no unappealable decision to which the legislature could acquiesce.

We turn next to a consideration of context, examining the § 48.02(2) definition of "child" in conjunction with other relevant sections of the Code. When attempting to ascertain the meaning of statutory language, we are obligated to avoid a construction which would result in an absurdity. [ ]. With this in mind, we note that certain relevant sections of the Code would be rendered absurd if "child" is understood to include a viable fetus. For example, in this case, the initial order taking the fetus into custody was issued pursuant to § 48.19(1)(c). That statute allows a child to be taken into custody by judicial order "upon a showing satisfactory to the judge that the welfare of the child demands that the child be immediately removed from his or her present custody." It is obviously inappropriate to apply this language to a viable fetus in utero.

Section § 48.19(2) requires the person taking a child into physical custody to immediately notify the parent by the most practical means. Yet, a pregnant woman would never need notification that her fetus had been taken into "physical custody," for she would already have such notice by virtue of the concomitant circumstance of her own detention.

Section 48.20(2) requires a person taking a child into custody to make every effort to immediately release the child to its parent. This language assumes that the child is at some point removed from the parent. Again, it is axiomatic that a viable fetus in utero cannot be removed from a pregnant woman in the sense conveyed by the statute.

By reading the definition of "child" in context with other relevant sections of Chapter 48, we find a compelling basis for concluding that the legislature intended a "child" to mean a human being born alive. Code provisions dealing with taking a child into custody, providing parental notification, and releasing a child from custody would require absurd results if the § 48.02(2) definition of "child" included a fetus. Each of the provisions addresses a critical juncture in a CHIPS proceeding. Yet, each also anticipates that the "child" can at some point be removed from the presence of the parent. It is manifest that the separation envisioned by the statute cannot be achieved in the context of a pregnant woman and her fetus.

The court of appeals determined, and the County asserts, that some prior decisions of this court support the proposition that a fetus is a child under the Children's Code. For example, the court of appeals analogized the present case to those in which this court has recognized a degree of fetal personhood under tort law. In support of its analogy, the court of appeals cited our holding in Kwaterski that "an eighth-month, viable unborn child, whose later stillbirth is caused by the wrongful act of another, is 'a person' within the meaning of [the wrongful death statute] so as to give rise to a wrongful-death action by the parents of the stillborn infant." Kwaterski, 34 Wis.2d at 15.

The court of appeals also reasoned that because the CHIPS statute is remedial in nature, its use of "person" should be liberally construed to include a fetus so as to effectuate the statute's purpose of protecting children. [ ]t also noted that in the earlier case of Puhl v. Milwaukee Auto Ins. Co., 8 Wis.2d 343, 99 N.W.2d 163 (1959), overruled on other grounds by Stromsted v. St. Michael Hosp., 99 Wis.2d 136, 299 N.W.2d 226 (1980), this court recognized a cause of action of an infant for injuries sustained before birth. In construing "child" to include a fetus, the court of appeals relied heavily on our statement in Puhl that "if the common law has any vitality, ... it should be elastic enough to adapt itself to current medical and scientific truths so as to function as an efficient rule of conduct in our modern, complex society." Id. at 357.

Initially, we note that this court has historically been wary of expanding the scope of the Children's Code by reading into it language not expressly mentioned within the text of Chapter 48. While Chapter 48 is to be liberally construed, § 48.01(2), we will not discern from the statute a legislative intent that is not evident. [ ]. Furthermore, a directive to construe the statute liberally to effectuate its purpose does not give license to liberally expand the definition of "child" to the stages before birth or after the age of 18. The directive is to liberally construe the statute to effectuate its purpose of providing for the care, protection, and development of children. [ ]. The logical extension of the dissent's argument regarding liberal construction would expand the definition of "child" to the moment after conception. No party in this case is advancing such a far-reaching argument. Finally, our decisions placing limited legal duties upon a third person should not be read to confer full legal status upon a fetus. Each must be examined to identify the particular rights and policies underlying the law that is being addressed.

We find the tort law analogy unpersuasive in this context. Instead, we agree with the United States Supreme Court that declaring a fetus a person for purposes of the wrongful death statute does no more than vindicate the interest of parents in the potential life that a fetus represents. [ ] Indeed, we have recognized that until born, a fetus has no cause of action for fetal injury:

Injuries suffered before birth impose a conditional liability on the tortfeasor. This liability becomes unconditional, or complete, upon the birth of the injured separate entity as a legal person. If such personality is not achieved, there would be no liability [to the fetus] because of no damage to a legal person.

Puhl, 8 Wis.2d at 356. For these reasons, we agree with the court of appeals' dissent that our tort law jurisprudence dealing with fetal injury has limited applicability to the present case.

Similarly, we reject the County's argument that the protections accorded fetuses by property law have a bearing on the Children's Code definition of "child." As the dissent below noted, "Property law does not confer the full rights of personhood upon the fetus. Instead, it creates a means of fulfilling the intentions of testators by protecting the right of a fetus to inherit property upon live birth." [ ]. When there is no live birth, there is no inheritance right.

* * *

The court of appeals' reliance on Roe, Kwaterski, [and] Puhl evidences the fundamental error in its analysis. While positing the correct question—whether the legislature intended to include a fetus within the § 48.02(2) definition of "child"—the court of appeals answered a distinctly different one—whether the legislature could, consistent with the United States and Wisconsin Constitutions, have included a fetus within the term "child." Because we conclude that the legislature did not intend to equate a fetus with a child, we do not reach the question answered by the court of appeals.

Finally, the confinement of a pregnant woman for the benefit of her fetus is a decision bristling with important social policy issues. We determine that the legislature is in a better position than the courts to gather, weigh, and reconcile the competing policy proposals addressed to this sensitive area of the law. This court is limited to ruling on the specific issues as developed by the record before it. We base our decisions on the facts as presented by adversarial parties who often narrow the scope of a much larger policy issue.

This court was confronted with a similar dilemma in Eberhardy v. Circuit Court for Wood County, 102 Wis.2d 539, 307 N.W.2d 881 (1981). In Eberhardy, we acknowledged that circuit courts have the subject matter jurisdiction to order the sterilization of the mentally handicapped. However, because the legislature had not yet determined the State's public policy or set guidelines for such sterilization, we directed the courts to refrain from ordering the procedure. This court stated:

This case demonstrates that a court is not an appropriate forum for making policy in such a sensitive area. Moreover, irrespective of how well tried a case may be—and we consider the instant one to have been well presented and carefully considered—there are inherent limitations in the factual posture of any case which make the extrapolation of judicially made policy to an entire area of such a sensitive nature as this risky indeed. The legislature is far better able, by the hearing process, to consider a broad range of possible factual situations. It can marshal informed persons to give an in-depth study to the entire problem and can secure the advice of experts ... to explore the ramifications of the adoption of a general public policy.... Eberhardy, 102 Wis.2d at 570–71.

For similar reasons, we determine that the detention of a pregnant woman for acts harming her fetus is a policy issue best addressed initially by our legislature. * * *

This court in no way condones the conduct of the petitioner. Yet, we are not free to register moral disapproval by rewriting the Children's Code under the guise of statutory construction.

Our search to ascertain and carry out the legislature's intent results in the conclusion that the legislature did not intend to include fetus within the definition of "child." The legislative history sounds in silence. Although the issue of whether to include a fetus within the definition of "child" in Chapter 48 is one of great social, medical, religious, and ethical significance, there is no record of any dialogue or consideration of the issue. A reading of § 48.02(2) in context with other relevant provisions of the Children's Code, supports the conclusion that the legislature intended "child" to mean one born alive. Despite ample opportunity, the legislature has not expressly provided that a fetus is a "child" under the Code. We decline the guardian ad litem's invitation to "take on this burden" to fill the legislative void. Moreover, the sensitive social policy issues raised in this case weigh strongly in favor of refraining from exercising CHIPS jurisdiction over a fetus until the legislature has spoken definitively on the matter.

For the above reasons, we hold that the definition of "child" in § 48.02(2) does not include a viable fetus. Because the court of appeals erroneously held that the § 48.02(2) definition of "child" includes a fetus, we reverse the decision of that court.

N. PATRICK CROOKS, J. (*Dissenting*). I do not join the majority opinion because the majority has not interpreted Wis. Stat. § 48.02(2) (1993–94) in conformity with the express legislative purpose of the Children's Code. I also am not persuaded by the majority's attempt to distinguish the present case from past cases in which this court has indicated that the definitions of "child" and "person" include a viable fetus. Furthermore, I find it significant that although the legislature amended the Children's Code last session, it did not act to alter the court of appeals' interpretation of § 48.02(2) in State ex rel. Angela M.W. v. Kruzicki, [supra]—an interpretation in accord with the one set forth in this dissent.

Wis. Stat. § 48.02(2) defines "child" as "a person who is less than 18 years of age." The majority holds that the legislature did not intend to include a viable fetus within this definition of "child" based on several factors. First, the majority emphasizes the lack of debate and dialogue regarding whether a fetus should be included in the definition of "child" in the legislative history of Chapter 48. [ ]. Second, the majority asserts that certain relevant sections of the Children's Code would be rendered absurd if the definition of "child" includes a viable fetus. Id. at 14–15. Finally, the majority concludes that Kwaterski v. State Farm Mut. Auto. Ins. Co. [supra], in which this court held that the definition of "person" includes a viable fetus, is "unpersuasive in this context." [ ].

A.Z. v. B.Z.

Supreme Judicial Court of Massachusetts, 2000.
431 Mass. 150, 725 N.E.2d 1051.

COWIN, J. We transferred this case to this court on our own motion to consider for the first time the effect of a consent form between a married couple and an in vitro fertilization (IVF) clinic (clinic) concerning disposition of frozen preembryos.[1] B.Z., the former wife (wife) of A.Z. (husband), appeals from a judgment of the Probate and Family Court that included, inter alia, a permanent injunction in favor of the husband, prohibiting the wife from "utilizing" the frozen preembryos held in cryopreservation[3] at the clinic. The probate judge bifurcated the issue concerning the disposition of the frozen preembryos from the then-pending divorce action. The wife appeals only from the issuance of the permanent injunction.

1.   Factual background. We recite the relevant background facts as determined by the probate judge in his detailed findings of fact after a hearing concerning disposition of the preembryos at which both the husband and wife were separately represented by counsel. The probate judge's findings are supplemented by the record where necessary.

a.   History of the couple. The husband and wife were married in 1977. For the first two years of their marriage they resided in Virginia, where they both served in the armed forces. While in Virginia, they encountered their first difficulties conceiving a child and underwent fertility testing. During their stay in Virginia the wife did become pregnant, but she suffered an ectopic pregnancy, as a result of which she miscarried and her left fallopian tube was removed.

In 1980, the husband and wife moved to Maryland where they underwent additional fertility treatment. The treatment lasted one year and did not result in a pregnancy. In 1988, the wife was transferred to Massachusetts and the husband remained in Maryland to continue his schooling. After arriving in Massachusetts, the wife began IVF treatments at an IVF clinic here. At first the husband traveled from Maryland to participate in the treatments. In 1991, he moved to Massachusetts.

Given their medical history, the husband and wife were eligible for two types of fertility procedures: Gamete Inter–Fallopian Transfer (GIFT) and IVF. IVF involves injecting the woman with fertility drugs in order to stimulate production of eggs which can be surgically retrieved or harvested. After the eggs are removed, they are combined in a petri dish with sperm produced by the man, on the same day as the egg removal, in an effort to fertilize the eggs. If fertilization between any of the eggs and

---

1.   We use the term "preembryo" to refer to the four-to-eight cell stage of a developing fertilized egg.

3.   Cryopreservation is the "maintenance of the viability of excised tissues or organs at extremely low temperatures." Stedman's Medical Dictionary 375 (25th ed. 1990).

sperm occurs, preembryos are formed that are held in a petri dish for one or two days until a decision can be made as to which preembryos will be used immediately and which will be frozen and stored by the clinic for later use. Preembryos that are to be utilized immediately are not frozen.

GIFT involves the removal of eggs from the woman that are then transferred simultaneously with the sperm into the fallopian tube where fertilization occurs before the embryo implants in the uterus. The husband and wife initially chose the GIFT procedure because it has a higher success rate than IVF. The GIFT procedure was performed on November 6, 1988. Another ectopic pregnancy resulted and the wife's remaining fallopian tube was removed. Left with no alternatives, the husband and wife turned to the IVF procedure.

They underwent IVF treatment from 1988 through 1991. As a result of the 1991 treatment, the wife conceived and gave birth to twin daughters in 1992. During the 1991 IVF treatment, more preembryos were formed than were necessary for immediate implantation, and two vials of preembryos were frozen for possible future implantation.

In the spring of 1995, before the couple separated, the wife desired more children and had one of the remaining vials of preembryos thawed and one preembryo was implanted. She did so without informing her husband. The husband learned of this when he received a notice from his insurance company regarding the procedure. During this period relations between the husband and wife deteriorated. The wife sought and received a protective order against the husband under C. L. c. 209A. Ultimately, they separated and the husband filed for divorce.

At the time of the divorce, one vial containing four frozen preembryos remained in storage at the clinic. Using one or more of these preembryos, it is possible that the wife could conceive; the likelihood of conception depends, inter alia, on the condition of the preembryos, which cannot be ascertained until the preembryos are thawed. The husband filed a motion to obtain a permanent injunction, prohibiting the wife from "using" the remaining vial of frozen preembryos.

b.   The IVF clinic and the consent forms. In order to participate in fertility treatment, including GIFT and IVF, the clinic required egg and sperm donors (donors) to sign certain consent forms for the relevant procedures. Each time before removal of the eggs from the wife, the clinic required the husband and wife in this case to sign a preprinted consent form concerning ultimate disposition of the frozen preembryos. The wife signed a number of forms on which the husband's signature was not required. The only forms that both the husband and the wife were required to sign were those entitled "Consent Form for Freezing (Cyropreservation) of Embryos" (consent form), one of which is the form at issue here.

Each consent form explains the general nature of the IVF procedure and outlines the freezing process, including the financial cost and the potential benefits and risks of that process. The consent form also requires the donors to decide the disposition of the frozen preembryos on certain listed contingencies: "wife or donor" reaching normal menopause or age forty-five years; preembryos no longer being healthy; "one of us dying;" "should we become separated"; "should we both die." Under each contingency the consent form provides the following as options for disposition of the preembryos: "donated or destroyed—choose one or both." A blank line beneath these choices permits the donors to write in additional alternatives not listed as options on the form, and the form notifies the donors that they may do so. The consent form also informs the donors that they may change their minds as to any disposition, provided that both donors convey that fact in writing to the clinic.

The probate judge noted that the clinic's current GIFT and IVF handbook, which was in evidence, states that the consent forms were "good for one year." There was no evidence whether this one-year limitation was in effect between 1988 and 1991. If a one-year limitation existed at that time, there was no evidence whether the husband and wife were aware of it. We do not attach significance to the provision in the handbook.

c. The execution of the forms. Every time before eggs were retrieved from the wife and combined with sperm from the husband, they each signed a consent form. The husband was present when the first form was completed by the wife in October, 1988. They both signed that consent form after it was finished. The form, as filled out by the wife, stated, inter alia, that if they "should become separated, [they] both agree[d] to have the embryo(s) . . . return[ed] to [the] wife for implant." The husband and wife thereafter underwent six additional egg retrievals for freezing and signed six additional consent forms, one each in June, 1989, and February, 1989, two forms in December, 1989, and one each in August, 1990, and August, 1991. The August, 1991, consent form governs the vial of frozen preembryos now stored at the clinic.

Each time after signing the first consent form in October, 1988, the husband always signed a blank consent form. Sometimes a consent form was signed by the husband while he and his wife were traveling to the IVF clinic; other forms were signed before the two went to the IVF clinic. Each time, after the husband signed the form, the wife filled in the disposition and other information, and then signed the form herself. All the words she wrote in the later forms were substantially similar to the words she inserted in the first October, 1988, form. In each instance the wife specified in the option for "should we become separated," that the preembryos were to be returned to the wife for implantation.

2. The Probate Court's decision. The probate judge concluded that, while donors are generally free to agree as to the ultimate disposition of frozen preembryos, the agreement at issue was unenforceable because of a "change in circumstances" occurring during the four years after the husband and wife signed the last, and governing, consent form in 1991: [11] the birth of the twins as a result of the IVF procedure, the wife's obtaining a protective order against the husband, the husband's filing for a divorce, and the wife's then seeking "to thaw the preembryos for

implantation in the hopes of having additional children." The probate judge concluded that "no agreement should be enforced in equity when intervening events have changed the circumstances such that the agreement which was originally signed did not contemplate the actual situation now facing the parties." In the absence of a binding agreement, the judge determined that the "best solution" was to balance the wife's interest in procreation against the husband's interest in avoiding procreation. Based on his findings, the judge determined that the husband's interest in avoiding procreation outweighed the wife's interest in having additional children and granted the permanent injunction in favor of the husband.

3. Legal background. While IVF has been available for over two decades and has been the focus of much academic commentary, there is little law on the enforceability of agreements concerning the disposition of frozen preembryos. Only three States have enacted legislation addressing the issue. [ ]

Two State courts of last resort, the Supreme Court of Tennessee and the Court of Appeals of New York, have dealt with the enforceability of agreements between donors regarding the disposition of preembryos and have concluded that such agreements should ordinarily be enforced. The Supreme Court of Tennessee, in Davis v. Davis 842 S.W.2d 588 (Tenn. 1992), [ ]considered the issue in a dispute between a husband and his former wife after the two were divorced. The wife sought to donate the preembryos at issue to another couple for implantation. The court stated that agreements between donors regarding disposition of the preembryos "should be presumed valid and should be enforced." 842 S.W.2d at 597. In that case, because there was no agreement between the donors regarding disposition of the preembryos, the court balanced the equitable interests of the two parties and concluded that the husband's interest in avoiding parenthood outweighed the wife's interest in donating the preembryos to another couple for implantation. Id. at 603.

The Court of Appeals of New York, in Kass v. Kass, supra, agreed with the Tennessee court's view that courts should enforce agreements where potential parents provide for the disposition of frozen preembryos. [ ]. The issue arose in that case also in the context of a dispute between a husband and his former wife after divorce. The wife sought custody of the preembryos for implantation. According to the New York court, agreements "should generally be presumed valid and binding, and enforced in any dispute between [the donors]." Id., citing Davis v. Davis, supra at 597. While recognizing that it is difficult for donors to anticipate the future of their relationship, the court concluded that such agreements minimize misunderstanding, maximize procreative liberty, and provide needed certainty to IVF programs. Kass v. Kass, supra. The court determined that the consent form signed by the donors with the IVF clinic unequivocally manifested the donors' mutual intent, and that this intent was further highlighted by the divorce instrument, which was consistent with the consent form and had been signed only months before suit was begun. Id. at 567. Therefore the court enforced the agreement that provided that the frozen preembryos be donated to the IVF clinic. [ ]

4. *Legal analysis.* This is the first reported case involving the disposition of frozen preembryos in which a consent form signed between the donors on the one hand and the clinic on the other provided that, on the donors' separation, the preembryos were to be given to one of the donors for implantation. In view of the purpose of the form (drafted by and to give assistance to the clinic) and the circumstances of execution, we are dubious at best that it represents the intent of the husband and the wife regarding disposition of the preembryos in the case of a dispute between them. In any event, for several independent reasons, we conclude that the form should not be enforced in the circumstances of this case.

First, the consent form's primary purpose is to explain to the donors the benefits and risks of freezing, and to record the donors' desires for disposition of the frozen preembryos at the time the form is executed in order to provide the clinic with guidance if the donors (as a unit) no longer wish to use the frozen preembryos. The form does not state, and the record does not indicate, that the husband and wife intended the consent form to act as a binding agreement between them should they later disagree as to the disposition. Rather, it appears that it was intended only to define the donors' relationship as a unit with the clinic.

Second, the consent form does not contain a duration provision. The wife sought to enforce this particular form four years after it was signed by the husband in significantly changed circumstances and over the husband's objection. In the absence of any evidence that the donors agreed on the time period during which the consent form was to govern their conduct, we cannot assume that the donors intended the consent form to govern the disposition of the frozen preembryos four years after it was executed, especially in light of the fundamental change in their relationship (i.e., divorce).

Third, the form uses the term "should we become separated" in referring to the disposition of the frozen preembryos without defining "become separated." Because this dispute arose in the context of a divorce, we cannot conclude that the consent form was intended to govern in these circumstances. Separation and divorce have distinct legal meanings. Legal changes occur by operation of law when a couple divorces that do not occur when a couple separates. Because divorce legally ends a couple's marriage, we shall not assume, in the absence of any evidence to the contrary, that an agreement on this issue providing for separation was meant to govern in the event of a divorce.

The donors' conduct in connection with the execution of the consent forms also creates doubt whether the consent form at issue here represents the clear intentions of both donors. The probate judge found that, prior to the signing of the first consent form, the wife called the IVF clinic to inquire about the section of the form regarding disposition "upon separation": that section of the preprinted form that asked the donors to specify either "donated" or "destroyed" or "both." A clinic representative told her that "she could cross out any of the language on the form and fill in her own [language] to fit her wishes." Further, although the wife used language in each subsequent form similar to the language used in the first form that she and her husband signed together, the consent form at issue here was signed in blank by the husband, before the wife filled in the language indicating that she would use the preembryos for implantation on separation. We therefore cannot conclude that the consent form represents the true intention of the husband for the disposition of the preembryos.

Finally, the consent form is not a separation agreement that is binding on the couple in a divorce proceeding pursuant to G. L. c. 208, § 34. The consent form does not contain provisions for custody, support, and maintenance, in the event that the wife conceives and gives birth to a child. [ ] In summary, the consent form is legally insufficient in several important respects and does not approach the minimum level of completeness needed to denominate it as an enforceable contract in a dispute between the husband and the wife.

With this said, we conclude that, even had the husband and the wife entered into an unambiguous agreement between themselves regarding the disposition of the frozen preembryos, we would not enforce an agreement that would compel one donor to become a parent against his or her will. As a matter of public policy, we conclude that forced procreation is not an area amenable to judicial enforcement. It is well-established that courts will not enforce contracts that violate public policy. [Citations omitted]. While courts are hesitant to invalidate contracts on these public policy grounds, the public interest in freedom of contract is sometimes outweighed by other public policy considerations; in those cases the contract will not be enforced. [ ]. To determine public policy, we look to the expressions of the Legislature and to those of this court.[ ]

The Legislature has already determined by statute that individuals should not be bound by certain agreements binding them to enter or not enter into familial relationships. In G. L. c. 207, § 47A, the Legislature abolished the cause of action for the breach of a promise to marry. In G. L. c. 210, § 2, the Legislature provided that no mother may agree to surrender her child "sooner than the fourth calendar day after the date of birth of the child to be adopted" regardless of any prior agreement.

Similarly, this court has expressed its hesitancy to become involved in intimate questions inherent in the marriage relationship. Doe v. Doe, 365 Mass. 556, 563, 314 N.E.2d 128 (1974). "Except in cases involving divorce or separation, our law has not in general undertaken to resolve the many delicate questions inherent in the marriage relationship. We would not order either a husband or a wife to do what is necessary to conceive a child or to prevent conception, any more than we would order either party to do what is necessary to make the other happy." Id.

In our decisions, we have also indicated a reluctance to enforce prior agreements that bind individuals to future family relationships. In R. R. v. M. H., 426 Mass. 501, 689 N.E.2d 790 (1998), we held that a surrogacy agreement in which the surrogate mother agreed to give up the child on its birth is unenforceable unless the agreement contained, inter alia, a "reasonable" waiting period during which the mother could change her mind. Id. at 510. In Capazzoli v. Holzwasser, supra, we determined, as an expression of public policy, that a contract requiring an individual to abandon a marriage is unenforceable. And, in the same spirit, we stated in Gleason v. Mann, 312 Mass. 420, 425, 45 N.E.2d 280 (1942), that agreements providing for a general restraint against marriage are unenforceable.

* * *

We derive from existing State laws and judicial precedent a public policy in this Commonwealth that individuals shall not be compelled to enter into intimate family relationships, and that the law shall not be used as a mechanism for forcing such relationships when they are not desired. This policy is grounded in the notion that respect for liberty and privacy requires that individuals be accorded the freedom to decide whether to enter into a family relationship. [ ].

In this case, we are asked to decide whether the law of the Commonwealth may compel an individual to become a parent over his or her contemporaneous objection. The husband signed this consent form in 1991. Enforcing the form against him would require him to become a parent over his present objection to such an undertaking. We decline to do so.

ADOPTION OF GALEN

Supreme Judicial court of Massachusetts, 1997.
425 Mass. 201, 680 N.E.2d 70.

MARSHALL, J. The petitioners, two women whom we shall call Nancy and Laura, challenge an order entered by a judge of the Suffolk Division of the Probate and Family Court Department denying their motion to waive a Department of Social Services (department) home study pursuant to G. L. c. 210, § 5A, in connection with their joint petition to adopt Nancy's biological child, whom we shall call Galen. We remand the case for entry of an order explaining with specificity the reasons for the denial of the motion in light of this opinion or, in the alternative, an order allowing the motion.

1. We summarize the relevant facts as they were presented to the motion judge. At the time they filed their motion (July, 1996), Nancy and Laura had been involved in a relationship with each other for nearly ten years, and had lived together for nine of those years. For some time prior to the birth of Galen, Nancy and Laura planned together for one of them to have a child, and in 1995 Galen was conceived by Nancy through artificial insemination from an anonymous donor from California. Nan-

cy, a respiratory therapist for ten years at a Boston hospital, and Laura, a psychiatric nurse at a different medical institution, jointly own their home and share all their respective financial responsibilities. In July, 1996, Nancy was not working so that she could be at home with Galen, and Laura financially supported both Nancy and Galen. The petitioners share all parenting responsibilities, including all decisions concerning Galen's health, education, and welfare. They intend to continue this arrangement.

Nancy and Laura filed numerous affidavits evidencing that Nancy is a loving and responsible parent and that Laura is equally loving and responsible in her dealings with Galen. In addition to their own affidavits, the petitioners filed affidavits from family members, including affidavits from the mothers of both petitioners (it appears that at least Nancy's father is deceased), brother and sisters, nephews, nieces, and a cousin. The affidavits describe the close bond between Galen and both of the petitioners, and the acceptance of Galen into a warm, welcoming, and loving extended family. There were affidavits filed by friends and colleagues of the petitioners whose observations, in every case based on personal knowledge, describe the stability of the relationship between the petitioners and the stable home environment for Galen. The petitioners also submitted three supportive affidavits from medical professionals, including one from Galen's pediatrician and one from a pediatric nurse who had observed Galen and the two women on numerous occasions.

Recognizing, as we do, that the affidavits were submitted by individuals supportive of the petitioners' wish to adopt Galen, we nevertheless observe that there is no suggestion in any affidavit that hints at any possibility that Galen is being raised in anything but a stable, supportive, and loving home environment, at the center of which are Nancy and Laura, but one that extends broadly to their immediate families, close friends, and colleagues.

2. We consider first the petitioners' claim under G. L. c. 210, § 2A. That section provides that a petition for adoption of a child below the age of fourteen years must be approved in writing by the department, or an agency authorized by it, unless one of four statutory conditions is met. On appeal, the petitioners argue that the decision of the judge ordering the department to undertake a home study implies that unmarried copetitioners must each meet one of the statutory conditions. The judge's order is not entirely clear in this respect, but is at least susceptible to the interpretation suggested by the petitioners. Confusion may have arisen because in Adoption of Tammy, 416 Mass. 205, 213 n.6, 619 N.E.2d 315 (1993), where we concluded that it was permissible for the natural mother and another woman to adopt a child, both women were "blood relatives" of the child because the mother had been artificially inseminated with the sperm from a male relative of the other woman. In that case both petitioners met the requirements of G. L. c. 210, § 2A (B).

In Tammy, we did not mean to suggest that it is a statutory requirement that both petitioners meet one of the conditions of G. L. c.

210, § 2A. See, e.g., Adoption of a Minor (No. 2), 367 Mass. 684, 686–687, 327 N.E.2d 875 (1975), in which the copetitioners were the child's paternal grandmother (a "blood relative") and her husband who did not satisfy any of the statutory conditions. For purposes of G. L. c. 210, § 2A, where a decree of adoption is sought by copetitioners, it is necessary for only one of the petitioners to satisfy one of the conditions specified in G. L. c. 210, § 2A (A)–(D). In this case Nancy satisfies the requirements of § 2A (B); as the natural mother of Galen, she is a "blood relative of the child sought to be adopted." See Curran, petitioner, 314 Mass. 91, 95, 49 N.E.2d 432 (1943) (mother may petition to adopt her own natural child).

3. We turn now to consider the application of G. L. c. 210, § 5A, to this case. That section provides that in every petition for adoption of a child under the age of fourteen years (as Galen is here) the department shall make "appropriate inquiry to determine the condition and antecedents of the child for the purpose of ascertaining whether he is a proper subject for adoption and to determine whether the petitioners and their home are suitable for the proper rearing of the child." The section further provides that within a specified period of time the department shall submit to the court a written report "as will give the court full knowledge as to the desirability of the proposed adoption." The legislation mandates that no decree should be made on a petition for adoption of a child under the age of fourteen years "until such report has been received," but further provides that the court may waive the requirements of a home study "in the case of a petition for the adoption of a child of one of the parties petitioning for said adoption." G. L. c. 210, § 5A, third par. Because Galen is the child of Nancy, one of the parties petitioning for his adoption, the court had the discretion to waive the requirements of a home study by the department.

The petitioners argue that the judge abused her discretion. We are not, on this record, able to ascertain whether the petitioners are correct. In denying the motion to waive the home study, the judge noted that a home study "serves an important purpose" as it "assists the Court in determining whether an adoption should be allowed by providing, through independent child welfare professionals, relevant information about the child, parents and the home." She noted that the "only evidence" was submitted by the petitioners. She gave no further' explanation for her decision.

We recognize, of course, that a home study "serves an important purpose," but a purpose that the Legislature said could be waived where, as here, one of the parties petitioning for adoption is a parent. Similarly, we recognize that the "only evidence" presented to the judge was evidence submitted by the petitioners. That ordinarily would be the case in every instance where a waiver is granted. Similarly, we agree that a judge may be assisted when "relevant" information about the child, parents, and home is provided through independent child welfare professionals, but that information is not available in any case where a waiver is granted. (The fact that an affidavit is submitted by a petitioner does not necessarily mean that it is not "independent").

With respect to the information that the petitioners did submit, there is no basis for the judge to conclude that Galen is not "a proper subject for adoption"; Nancy is his biological mother, and the judge already has ordered that, pursuant to California law, the anonymous sperm donor is not required to be notified. That aspect of the G. L. c. 210, § 5A, home study mandate is satisfied. The only remaining reason for a home study is whether the petitioners and their home are "suitable for the proper rearing" of Galen.

The waiver of the home study permitted by the Legislature in the case of an adoption of a child of one of the parties suggests a legislative acknowledgment that the best interests of the child are usually served in that relationship. This is consistent with other legislative determinations seeking to keep a child with a natural parent. [ ] Second, G. L. c. 210, § 5B, provides that, in making orders for adoption, the judge shall consider "the need of the child for loving and responsible parental care and all factors relevant to the physical, mental and moral health of the child." There were numerous affidavits, including one from the child's pediatrician, based on direct observations of Galen's interaction with both petitioners, that give no cause for concern about the "physical, mental and moral health" of Galen. The affidavits submitted by the petitioners stated unequivocally that they provide loving and responsible care for Galen.

General Laws c. 210, § 6, requires that the petitioners be of "sufficient ability to bring up the child and provide suitable support and education" for him. Both petitioners are educated, professional women, both of whom have been in stable employment situations over extended periods of time. There is nothing in the record to suggest that they have anything but "sufficient ability" and the financial means to care for, support, and educate the child.

The judge's discretion in deciding whether to waive a home study may not be arbitrary or capricious. [ ]. The judge was presented with substantial evidence that the best interests of Galen would be served by allowing the adoption. The fact that the petitioners are both women who are engaged in a long, committed relationship cannot be a bar to adoption. [ ].

* * *

The Attorney General also advises us that, when the department receives a motion to waive a home study, it checks its own records to determine whether it has ever been involved with either of the petitioners or with the child who is the subject of the adoption. If there has been no prior department involvement, and the department does not object to a motion to waive a home study, the court usually grants the motion. There is nothing in the record that establishes on how many occasions the home study is waived. But we see no reason to question the representation made by the Attorney General to this court. Particularly where, as here, a claim has been made that the only reason for ordering a home study is because the petitioners are of the same gender, it is incumbent on the judge to explain the reasons for ordering the home study.

The case is remanded to the Probate Court for entry of an order either explaining with specificity the reasons for the denial of the motion requesting waiver of the home study pursuant to G. L. c. 210, § 5A, or allowing the motion.

So ordered.

DISSENT: O'CONNOR, J. (dissenting, with whom Lynch, J., joins). The first issue raised by the petitioners and dealt with by the court, ante, 425 Mass. 201 at 203, is whether the judge, misinterpreting G. L. c. 210, § 2A, thought that she was required as a matter of law to order a Department of Social Services (department) home study; that is, that she had no discretion to waive a home study. * * *

The record does not demonstrate that the judge abused her discretion by denying the petitioners' motion to waive the home study. The court agrees. Nevertheless, "the case is remanded to the Probate Court for entry of an order either explaining with specificity the reasons for the denial of the motion requesting waiver of the home study pursuant to G. L. c. 210, § 5A, or allowing the motion." [ ]. The court announces three reasons for its order: (1) affidavits and other evidence submitted by the petitioners indicated that the petitioners had "provided loving and responsible care for Galen," [ ], (2) "it is in the best interests of children that there be a speedy resolution of adoption proceedings," [ ]; (3) "a claim has been made that the only reason for ordering a home study is because the petitioners are of the same gender." [ ]

Surely, it is not unusual for petitioners in adoption proceedings to submit evidence favorable to them and to refrain from submitting unfavorable evidence. Perhaps the judge had that in mind when she stated in her order, "However, the homestudy serves an important purpose. It assists the Court in determining whether an adoption should be allowed by providing, through independent child welfare professionals, relevant information about the child, parents and the home. The Child is generally not represented in an adoption proceeding, and the only evidence presented is submitted by petitioners. Home studies may, and have been, ordered to assist the Court even in instances where the Petitioner is a natural parent."

Turning to the court's second reason for its order, I agree that in some situations "it is in the best interests of children that there be a speedy resolution of adoption proceedings." Of course, it is also in the best interests of children involved in such proceedings that the decision to approve or disapprove of the adoption be made by a well-informed judge who has received the input of "independent child welfare professionals." In addition, this is not the type of case in which a child may wait—and wait—for a new and permanent home. In this case the child is not waiting for a new parent and a new home. The child is already united with his mother, having lived with her since birth. Surely, postponement of the adoption decision in this case in order to accommodate a home study neither suggests that the judge is inappropriately biased against the two female petitioners nor indicates that the judge has abused her discretion in any other way. Instead, it suggests that the judge is a conscientious judge who wants to make the right call on the adoption issue with the assistance that a department home study may provide. In my view, remanding this case with an instruction to the judge "either [to] explain [ ] with specificity the reasons for the denial of the motion requesting waiver of the home study pursuant to G. L. c. 210, § 5A, or allowing the motion," [ ] is not called for.

GOODRIDGE v. DEPARTMENT OF PUBLIC HEALTH

Supreme Judicial court of Massachusetts, 2003.
440 Mass. 309, 798 N.E.2d 941.

MARSHALL, C.J.

Marriage is a vital social institution. The exclusive commitment of two individuals to each other nurtures love and mutual support; it brings stability to our society. For those who choose to marry, and for their children, marriage provides an abundance of legal, financial, and social benefits. In return it imposes weighty legal, financial, and social obligations. The question before us is whether, consistent with the Massachusetts Constitution, the Commonwealth may deny the protections, benefits, and obligations conferred by civil marriage to two individuals of the same sex who wish to marry. We conclude that it may not. The Massachusetts Constitution affirms the dignity and equality of all individuals. It forbids the creation of second-class citizens. In reaching our conclusion we have given full deference to the arguments made by the Commonwealth. But it has failed to identify any constitutionally adequate reason for denying civil marriage to same-sex couples.

We are mindful that our decision marks a change in the history of our marriage law. Many people hold deep-seated religious, moral, and ethical convictions that marriage should be limited to the union of one man and one woman, and that homosexual conduct is immoral. Many hold equally strong religious, moral, and ethical convictions that same-sex couples are entitled to be married, and that homosexual persons should be treated no differently than their heterosexual neighbors. Neither view answers the question before us. Our concern is with the Massachusetts Constitution as a charter of governance for every person properly within its reach. "Our obligation is to define the liberty of all, not to mandate our own moral code." Lawrence v. Texas, 156 L.Ed.2d 508, 123 S.Ct. 2472, 2480 (2003), quoting Planned Parenthood of Southeastern Pa. v. Casey, 505 U.S. 833, 850, 120 L.Ed.2d 674, 112 S.Ct. 2791 (1992).

Whether the Commonwealth may use its formidable regulatory authority to bar same-sex couples from civil marriage is a question not previously addressed by a Massachusetts appellate court. It is a question the United States Supreme Court left open as a matter of Federal law in Lawrence, supra at 2484, where it was not an issue. There, the Court affirmed that the core concept of common human dignity protected by the Fourteenth Amendment to the United States Constitution precludes government intrusion into the deeply personal realms of consensual adult expressions of intimacy and one's choice of an intimate partner. The Court also reaffirmed the central role that decisions whether to marry or have children bear in shaping one's identity. Id. at 2481. The Massachusetts Constitution is, if anything, more protective of individual liberty and equality than the Federal Constitution; it may demand broader protection for fundamental rights; and it is less tolerant of government intrusion into the protected spheres of private life.

Barred access to the protections, benefits, and obligations of civil marriage, a person who enters into an intimate, exclusive union with another of the same sex is arbitrarily deprived of membership in one of our community's most rewarding and cherished institutions. That exclusion is incompatible with the constitutional principles of respect for individual autonomy and equality under law.

I

The plaintiffs are fourteen individuals from five Massachusetts counties. [All are in long-term, committed relationships.] The plaintiffs include business executives, lawyers, an investment banker, educators, therapists, and a computer engineer. Many are active in church, community, and school groups. They have employed such legal means as are available to them—for example, joint adoption, powers of attorney, and joint ownership of real property—to secure aspects of their relationships. Each plaintiff attests a desire to marry his or her partner in order to affirm publicly their commitment to each other and to secure the legal protections and benefits afforded to married couples and their children.

The Department of Public Health (department) is charged by statute with safeguarding public health. See G. L. c. 17. Among its responsibilities, the department oversees the registry of vital records and statistics (registry), which "enforces all laws" relative to the issuance of marriage licenses and the keeping of marriage records [ ] and which promulgates policies and procedures for the issuance of marriage licenses by city and town clerks and registers. The registry is headed by a registrar of vital records and statistics (registrar), appointed by the Commissioner of Public Health (commissioner) with the approval of the public health council and supervised by the commissioner.

In March and April, 2001, each of the plaintiff couples attempted to obtain a marriage license from a city or town clerk's office. As required under G. L. c. 207, they completed notices of intention to marry on forms provided by the registry, and presented these forms to a Massachusetts town or city clerk, together with the required health forms and marriage license fees. In each case, the clerk either refused to accept the notice of intention to marry or denied a marriage license to the couple on the ground that Massachusetts does not recognize same-sex marriage. Because obtaining a marriage license is a necessary prerequisite to civil marriage in Massachusetts, denying marriage licenses to the plaintiffs was tantamount to denying them access to civil marriage itself, with its appurtenant social and legal protections, benefits, and obligations.

* * *

II.

* * *

We interpret statutes to carry out the Legislature's intent, determined by the words of a statute interpreted according to "the ordinary and approved usage of the language." Hanlon v. Rollins, 286 Mass. 444, 447, 190 N.E. 606 (1934). The everyday meaning of "marriage" is "the legal union of a man and woman as husband and wife," Black's Law Dictionary 986 (7th ed. 1999), and the plaintiffs do not argue that the term "marriage" has ever had a different meaning under Massachusetts law. * * * This definition of marriage, as both the department and the Superior Court judge point out, derives from the common law. * * * Far from being ambiguous, the undefined word "marriage," as used in G. L. c. 207, confirms the General Court's intent to hew to the term's common-law and quotidian meaning concerning the genders of the marriage partners.

The intended scope of G. L. c. 207 is also evident in its consanguinity provisions. [ ] Sections 1 and 2 of G. L. c. 207 prohibit marriages between a man and certain female relatives and a woman and certain male relatives, but are silent as to the consanguinity of male-male or female-female marriage applicants. [ ] The only reasonable explanation is that the Legislature did not intend that same-sex couples be licensed to marry. We conclude, as did the judge, that G. L. c. 207 may not be construed to permit same-sex couples to marry.

III

A

The larger question is whether, as the department claims, government action that bars same-sex couples from civil marriage constitutes a legitimate exercise of the State's authority to regulate conduct, or whether, as the plaintiffs claim, this categorical marriage exclusion violates the Massachusetts Constitution. We have recognized the longstanding statutory understanding, derived from the common law, that "marriage" means the lawful union of a woman and a man. But that history cannot and does not foreclose the constitutional question.

The plaintiffs' claim that the marriage restriction violates the Massachusetts Constitution can be analyzed in two ways. Does it offend the

Constitution's guarantees of equality before the law? Or do the liberty and due process provisions of the Massachusetts Constitution secure the plaintiffs' right to marry their chosen partner? In matters implicating marriage, family life, and the upbringing of children, the two constitutional concepts frequently overlap, as they do here. See, e.g., M.L.B. v. S.L.J., 519 U.S. 102, 120, 136 L.Ed.2d 473, 117 S.Ct. 555 (1996) (noting convergence of due process and equal protection principles in cases concerning parent-child relationships); Perez v. Sharp, 32 Cal.2d 711, 728, 198 P.2d 17 (1948) (analyzing statutory ban on interracial marriage as equal protection violation concerning regulation of fundamental right). See also Lawrence, supra at 2482 ("Equality of treatment and the due process right to demand respect for conduct protected by the substantive guarantee of liberty are linked in important respects, and a decision on the latter point advances both interests"). [ ] Much of what we say concerning one standard applies to the other.

We begin by considering the nature of civil marriage itself. Simply put, the government creates civil marriage. In Massachusetts, civil marriage is, and since pre-Colonial days has been, precisely what its name implies: a wholly secular institution.[ ] No religious ceremony has ever been required to validate a Massachusetts marriage. In a real sense, there are three partners to every civil marriage: two willing spouses and an approving State. [ ] While only the parties can mutually assent to marriage, the terms of the marriage—who may marry and what obligations, benefits, and liabilities attach to civil marriage—are set by the Commonwealth. Conversely, while only the parties can agree to end the marriage (absent the death of one of them or a marriage void ab initio), the Commonwealth defines the exit terms. [ ].

Civil marriage is created and regulated through exercise of the police power.[ ] "Police power" (now more commonly termed the State's regulatory authority) is an old-fashioned term for the Commonwealth's lawmaking authority, as bounded by the liberty and equality guarantees of the Massachusetts Constitution and its express delegation of power from the people to their government. In broad terms, it is the Legislature's power to enact rules to regulate conduct, to the extent that such laws are "necessary to secure the health, safety, good order, comfort, or general welfare of the community."

Without question, civil marriage enhances the "welfare of the community." It is a "social institution of the highest importance." [Citation omitted]. Civil marriage anchors an ordered society by encouraging stable relationships over transient ones. It is central to the way the Commonwealth identifies individuals, provides for the orderly distribution of property, ensures that children and adults are cared for and supported whenever possible from private rather than public funds, and tracks important epidemiological and demographic data.

Marriage also bestows enormous private and social advantages on those who choose to marry. Civil marriage is at once a deeply personal commitment to another human being and a highly public celebration of the ideals of mutuality, companionship, intimacy, fidelity, and family. "It is an association that promotes a way of life, not causes; a harmony in living, not political faiths; a bilateral loyalty, not commercial or social projects." Griswold v. Connecticut, 381 U.S. 479, 486, 14 L.Ed.2d 510, 85 S.Ct. 1678 (1965). Because it fulfils yearnings for security, safe haven, and connection that express our common humanity, civil marriage is an esteemed institution, and the decision whether and whom to marry is among life's momentous acts of self-definition.

Tangible as well as intangible benefits flow from marriage. The marriage license grants valuable property rights to those who meet the entry requirements, and who agree to what might otherwise be a burdensome degree of government regulation of their activities. [ ]

The benefits accessible only by way of a marriage license are enormous, touching nearly every aspect of life and death. The department states that "hundreds of statutes" are related to marriage and to marital benefits. With no attempt to be comprehensive, we note that some of the statutory benefits conferred by the Legislature on those who enter into civil marriage include, as to property: joint Massachusetts income tax filing [ ]; tenancy by the entirety (a form of ownership that provides certain protections against creditors and allows for the automatic descent of property to the surviving spouse without probate) [ ]; extension of the benefit of the homestead protection (securing up to $300,000 in equity from creditors) to one's spouse and children [ ]; automatic rights to inherit the property of a deceased spouse who does not leave a will [ ] * * *.

Exclusive marital benefits that are not directly tied to property rights include the presumptions of legitimacy and parentage of children born to a married couple [ ]; and evidentiary rights, such as the prohibition against spouses testifying against one another about their private conversations, applicable in both civil and criminal cases . Other statutory benefits of a personal nature available only to married individuals include qualification for bereavement or medical leave to care for individuals related by blood or marriage; an automatic "family member" preference to make medical decisions for an incompetent or disabled spouse who does not have a contrary health care proxy, * * *.

Where a married couple has children, their children are also directly or indirectly, but no less auspiciously, the recipients of the special legal and economic protections obtained by civil marriage. Notwithstanding the Commonwealth's strong public policy to abolish legal distinctions between marital and nonmarital children in providing for the support and care of minors [citation omitted], the fact remains that marital children reap a measure of family stability and economic security based on their parents' legally privileged status that is largely inaccessible, or not as readily accessible, to nonmarital children. Some of these benefits are social, such as the enhanced approval that still attends the status of being a marital child. Others are material, such as the greater ease of access to family-based State and Federal benefits that attend the presumptions of one's parentage.

It is undoubtedly for these concrete reasons, as well as for its intimately personal significance, that civil marriage has long been termed a "civil right." [ ].

Without the right to marry—or more properly, the right to choose to marry—one is excluded from the full range of human experience and denied full protection of the laws for one's "avowed commitment to an intimate and lasting human relationship." [ ]. Because civil marriage is central to the lives of individuals and the welfare of the community, our laws assiduously protect the individual's right to marry against undue government incursion. Laws may not "interfere directly and substantially with the right to marry." [ ].

Unquestionably, the regulatory power of the Commonwealth over civil marriage is broad, as is the Commonwealth's discretion to award public benefits. [ ]. Individuals who have the choice to marry each other and nevertheless choose not to may properly be denied the legal benefits of marriage. [ ]. But that same logic cannot hold for a qualified individual who would marry if she or he only could.

B

For decades, indeed centuries, in much of this country (including Massachusetts) no lawful marriage was possible between white and black Americans. That long history availed not when the Supreme Court of California held in 1948 that a legislative prohibition against interracial marriage violated the due process and equality guarantees of the Fourteenth Amendment [ ], or when, nineteen years later, the United States Supreme Court also held that a statutory bar to interracial marriage violated the Fourteenth Amendment, Loving v. Virginia, 388 U.S. 1, 18 L.Ed.2d 1010, 87 S.Ct. 1817 (1967). As [those cases] make clear, the right to marry means little if it does not include the right to marry the person of one's choice, subject to appropriate government restrictions in the interests of public health, safety, and welfare.

The Massachusetts Constitution protects matters of personal liberty against government incursion as zealously, and often more so, than does the Federal Constitution, even where both Constitutions employ essentially the same language. [ ]. That the Massachusetts Constitution is in some instances more protective of individual liberty interests than is the Federal Constitution is not surprising. Fundamental to the vigor of our Federal system of government is that "state courts are absolutely free to interpret state constitutional provisions to accord greater protection to individual rights than do similar provisions of the United States Constitution." Arizona v. Evans, 514 U.S. 1, 8, 131 L.Ed.2d 34, 115 S.Ct. 1185 (1995).

The individual liberty and equality safeguards of the Massachusetts Constitution protect both "freedom from" unwarranted government intrusion into protected spheres of life and "freedom to" partake in benefits created by the State for the common good. [ ]. Both freedoms are involved here. Whether and whom to marry, how to express sexual intimacy, and whether and how to establish a family—these are among the most basic of every individual's liberty and due process rights. [ ]. And central to personal freedom and security is the assurance that the laws will apply equally to persons in similar situations. "Absolute equality before the law is a fundamental principle of our own Constitution." Opinion of the Justices, 211 Mass. 618, 619, 98 N.E. 337 (1912). The liberty interest in choosing whether and whom to marry would be hollow if the Commonwealth could, without sufficient justification, foreclose an individual from freely choosing the person with whom to share an exclusive commitment in the unique institution of civil marriage.

The Massachusetts Constitution requires, at a minimum, that the exercise of the State's regulatory authority not be "arbitrary or capricious." [ ] Under both the equality and liberty guarantees, regulatory authority must, at very least, serve "a legitimate purpose in a rational way"; a statute must "bear a reasonable relation to a permissible legislative objective." [ ] Any law failing to satisfy the basic standards of rationality is void.

The plaintiffs challenge the marriage statute on both equal protection and due process grounds. With respect to each such claim, we must first determine the appropriate standard of review. Where a statute implicates a fundamental right or uses a suspect classification, we employ "strict judicial scrutiny." [ ]. For all other statutes, we employ the " 'rational basis' test." [ ]. For due process claims, rational basis analysis requires that statutes "bear[ ] a real and substantial relation to the public health, safety, morals, or some other phase of the general welfare." [ ]. For equal protection challenges, the rational basis test requires that "an impartial lawmaker could logically believe that the classification would serve a legitimate public purpose that transcends the harm to the members of the disadvantaged class." [ ]

The department argues that no fundamental right or "suspect" class is at issue here and rational basis is the appropriate standard of review. For the reasons we explain below, we conclude that the marriage ban does not meet the rational basis test for either due process or equal protection. Because the statute does not survive rational basis review, we do not consider the plaintiffs' arguments that this case merits strict judicial scrutiny.

The department posits three legislative rationales for prohibiting same-sex couples from marrying: (1) providing a "favorable setting for procreation"; (2) ensuring the optimal setting for child rearing, which the department defines as "a two-parent family with one parent of each sex"; and (3) preserving scarce State and private financial resources. We consider each in turn.

The judge in the Superior Court endorsed the first rationale, holding that "the state's interest in regulating marriage is based on the traditional concept that marriage's primary purpose is procreation." This is incorrect. Our laws of civil marriage do not privilege procreative heterosexual intercourse between married people above every other form of adult intimacy and every other means of creating a family. General Laws c. 207 contains no requirement that the applicants for a marriage license attest to their ability or intention to conceive children by coitus. Fertility is not a condition of marriage, nor is it grounds for divorce. People who have never consummated their marriage, and never plan to, may be and stay married. [ ] * * * People who cannot stir from their deathbed may marry. [ ]. While it is certainly true that many, perhaps most, married couples have children together (assisted or unassisted), it is the exclusive and permanent commitment of the marriage partners to one another, not the begetting of children, that is the sine qua non of civil marriage.

Moreover, the Commonwealth affirmatively facilitates bringing children into a family regardless of whether the intended parent is married or unmarried, whether the child is adopted or born into a family, whether assistive technology was used to conceive the child, and whether the parent or her partner is heterosexual, homosexual, or bisexual. If procreation were a necessary component of civil marriage, our statutes would draw a tighter circle around the permissible bounds of nonmarital child bearing and the creation of families by noncoital means. The attempt to isolate procreation as "the source of a fundamental right to marry," post at (Cordy, J., dissenting), overlooks the integrated way in which courts have examined the complex and overlapping realms of personal autonomy, marriage, family life, and child rearing. Our jurisprudence recognizes that, in these nuanced and fundamentally private areas of life, such a narrow focus is inappropriate.

The "marriage is procreation" argument singles out the one unbridgeable difference between same-sex and opposite-sex couples, and transforms that difference into the essence of legal marriage. Like "Amendment 2" to the Constitution of Colorado, which effectively denied homosexual persons equality under the law and full access to the political process, the marriage restriction impermissibly "identifies persons by a single trait and then denies them protection across the board." Romer v. Evans, 517 U.S. 620, 633, 134 L.Ed.2d 855, 116 S.Ct. 1620 (1996). In so doing, the State's action confers an official stamp of approval on the destructive stereotype that same-sex relationships are inherently unstable and inferior to opposite-sex relationships and are not worthy of respect.

The department's first stated rationale, equating marriage with unassisted heterosexual procreation, shades imperceptibly into its second: that confining marriage to opposite-sex couples ensures that children are raised in the "optimal" setting. Protecting the welfare of children is a paramount State policy. Restricting marriage to opposite-sex couples, however, cannot plausibly further this policy. "The demographic changes of the past century make it difficult to speak of an average American family. The composition of families varies greatly from household to household." [ ]. Massachusetts has responded supportively to "the changing realities of the American family," [ ] and has moved vigorously to strengthen the modern family in its many variations. * * *

The department has offered no evidence that forbidding marriage to people of the same sex will increase the number of couples choosing to enter into opposite-sex marriages in order to have and raise children. There is thus no rational relationship between the marriage statute and the Commonwealth's proffered goal of protecting the "optimal" child rearing unit. Moreover, the department readily concedes that people in same-sex couples may be "excellent" parents. These couples (including four of the plaintiff couples) have children for the reasons others do—to love them, to care for them, to nurture them. But the task of child rearing for same-sex couples is made infinitely harder by their status as outliers to the marriage laws. While establishing the parentage of children as soon as possible is crucial to the safety and welfare of children, [ ], same-sex couples must undergo the sometimes lengthy and intrusive process of second-parent adoption to establish their joint parentage. While the enhanced income provided by marital benefits is an important source of security and stability for married couples and their children, those benefits are denied to families headed by same-sex couples. [ ] While the laws of divorce provide clear and reasonably predictable guidelines for child support, child custody, and property division on dissolution of a marriage, same-sex couples who dissolve their relationships find themselves and their children in the highly unpredictable terrain of equity jurisdiction. [ ] Given the wide range of public benefits reserved only for married couples, we do not credit the department's contention that the absence of access to civil marriage amounts to little more than an inconvenience to same-sex couples and their children. Excluding same-sex couples from civil marriage will not make children of opposite-sex marriages more secure, but it does prevent children of same-sex couples from enjoying the immeasurable advantages that flow from the assurance of "a stable family structure in which children will be reared, educated, and socialized." [ ]

No one disputes that the plaintiff couples are families, that many are parents, and that the children they are raising, like all children, need and should have the fullest opportunity to grow up in a secure, protected family unit. Similarly, no one disputes that, under the rubric of marriage, the State provides a cornucopia of substantial benefits to married parents and their children. The preferential treatment of civil marriage reflects the Legislature's conclusion that marriage "is the foremost setting for the education and socialization of children" precisely because it "encourages parents to remain committed to each other and to their children as they grow." [ ]

In this case, we are confronted with an entire, sizeable class of parents raising children who have absolutely no access to civil marriage and its protections because they are forbidden from procuring a marriage license. It cannot be rational under our laws, and indeed it is not permitted, to penalize children by depriving them of State benefits because the State disapproves of their parents' sexual orientation.

The third rationale advanced by the department is that limiting marriage to opposite-sex couples furthers the Legislature's interest in conserving scarce State and private financial resources. The marriage restriction is rational, it argues, because the General Court logically could assume that same-sex couples are more financially independent than married couples and thus less needy of public marital benefits, such as tax advantages, or private marital benefits, such as employer-financed health plans that include spouses in their coverage.

An absolute statutory ban on same-sex marriage bears no rational relationship to the goal of economy. First, the department's conclusory generalization—that same-sex couples are less financially dependent on each other than opposite-sex couples—ignores that many same-sex couples, such as many of the plaintiffs in this case, have children and other dependents (here, aged parents) in their care. The department does not contend, nor could it, that these dependents are less needy or deserving than the dependents of married couples. Second, Massachusetts marriage laws do not condition receipt of public and private financial benefits to married individuals on a demonstration of financial dependence on each other; the benefits are available to married couples regardless of whether they mingle their finances or actually depend on each other for support.

The department suggests additional rationales for prohibiting same-sex couples from marrying, which are developed by some amici. It argues that broadening civil marriage to include same-sex couples will trivialize or destroy the institution of marriage as it has historically been fashioned. Certainly our decision today marks a significant change in the definition of marriage as it has been inherited from the common law, and understood by many societies for centuries. But it does not disturb the fundamental value of marriage in our society.

Here, the plaintiffs seek only to be married, not to undermine the institution of civil marriage. They do not want marriage abolished. They do not attack the binary nature of marriage, the consanguinity provisions, or any of the other gate-keeping provisions of the marriage licensing law. Recognizing the right of an individual to marry a person of the same sex will not diminish the validity or dignity of opposite-sex marriage, any more than recognizing the right of an individual to marry a person of a different race devalues the marriage of a person who marries someone of her own race. If anything, extending civil marriage to same-sex couples reinforces the importance of marriage to individuals and communities. That same-sex couples are willing to embrace marriage's solemn obligations of exclusivity, mutual support, and commitment to one another is a testament to the enduring place of marriage in our laws and in the human spirit.

It has been argued that, due to the State's strong interest in the institution of marriage as a stabilizing social structure, only the Legislature can control and define its boundaries. Accordingly, our elected representatives legitimately may choose to exclude same-sex couples from civil marriage in order to assure all citizens of the Commonwealth that (1) the benefits of our marriage laws are available explicitly to create and support a family setting that is, in the Legislature's view, optimal for child rearing, and (2) the State does not endorse gay and lesbian parenthood as the equivalent of being raised by one's married biological parents. These arguments miss the point. The Massachusetts Constitution requires that legislation meet certain criteria and not extend beyond certain limits. It is the function of courts to determine whether these criteria are met and whether these limits are exceeded. In most instances, these limits are defined by whether a rational basis exists to conclude that legislation will bring about a rational result. The Legislature in the first instance, and the courts in the last instance, must ascertain whether such a rational basis exists. To label the court's role as usurping that of the Legislature [ ] is to misunderstand the nature and purpose of judicial review. We owe great deference to the Legislature to decide social and policy issues, but it is the traditional and settled role of courts to decide constitutional issues.

* * *

We also reject the argument suggested by the department, and elaborated by some amici, that expanding the institution of civil marriage in Massachusetts to include same-sex couples will lead to interstate conflict. We would not presume to dictate how another State should respond to today's decision. But neither should considerations of comity prevent us from according Massachusetts residents the full measure of protection available under the Massachusetts Constitution. The genius of our Federal system is that each State's Constitution has vitality specific to its own traditions, and that, subject to the minimum requirements of the Fourteenth Amendment, each State is free to address difficult issues of individual liberty in the manner its own Constitution demands.

Several amici suggest that prohibiting marriage by same-sex couples reflects community consensus that homosexual conduct is immoral. Yet Massachusetts has a strong affirmative policy of preventing discrimination on the basis of sexual orientation. See G. L. c. 151B (employment, housing, credit, services); G. L. c. 265, § 39 (hate crimes); G. L. c. 272, § 98 (public accommodation); G. L. c. 76, § 5 (public education). [ ] The department has had more than ample opportunity to articulate a constitutionally adequate justification for limiting civil marriage to opposite-sex unions. It has failed to do so. The department has offered purported justifications for the civil marriage restriction that are starkly at odds with the comprehensive network of vigorous, gender-neutral laws promoting stable families and the best interests of children. It has failed to identify any relevant characteristic that would justify shutting the door to civil marriage to a person who wishes to marry someone of the same sex.

The marriage ban works a deep and scarring hardship on a very real segment of the community for no rational reason. The absence of any reasonable relationship between, on the one hand, an absolute disqualification of same-sex couples who wish to enter into civil marriage and, on the other, protection of public health, safety, or general welfare, suggests that the marriage restriction is rooted in persistent prejudices against persons who are (or who are believed to be) homosexual. "The Constitution cannot control such prejudices but neither can it tolerate them. Private biases may be outside the reach of the law, but the law cannot, directly or indirectly, give them effect." [ ]. Limiting the protections, benefits, and obligations of civil marriage to opposite-sex couples violates the basic premises of individual liberty and equality under law protected by the Massachusetts Constitution.

IV

We consider next the plaintiffs' request for relief. We preserve as much of the statute as may be preserved in the face of the successful constitutional challenge. * * *

Here, no one argues that striking down the marriage laws is an appropriate form of relief. Eliminating civil marriage would be wholly inconsistent with the Legislature's deep commitment to fostering stable families and would dismantle a vital organizing principle of our society. * * *

We construe civil marriage to mean the voluntary union of two persons as spouses, to the exclusion of all others. This reformulation redresses the plaintiffs' constitutional injury and furthers the aim of marriage to promote stable, exclusive relationships. It advances the two legitimate State interests the department has identified: providing a stable setting for child rearing and conserving State resources. It leaves intact the Legislature's broad discretion to regulate marriage. [ ].

In their complaint the plaintiffs request only a declaration that their exclusion and the exclusion of other qualified same-sex couples from access to civil marriage violates Massachusetts law. We declare that barring an individual from the protections, benefits, and obligations of civil marriage solely because that person would marry a person of the same sex violates the Massachusetts Constitution. We vacate the summary judgment for the department [and] remand this case to the Superior Court for entry of judgment consistent with this opinion. Entry of judgment shall be stayed for 180 days to permit the Legislature to take such action as it may deem appropriate in light of this opinion.

So Ordered.

SPINA, J. (dissenting, with whom Sosman and Cordy, JJ., join). What is at stake in this case is not the unequal treatment of individuals or whether individual rights have been impermissibly burdened, but the power of the Legislature to effectuate social change without interference from the courts, pursuant to art. 30 of the Massachusetts Declaration of Rights. The power to regulate marriage lies with the Legislature, not with the judiciary. [ ]. Today, the court has transformed its role as protector of individual rights into the role of creator of rights, and I respectfully dissent.

1. Equal protection. Although the court did not address the plaintiffs' gender discrimination claim [ ] does not unconstitutionally discriminate on the basis of gender. A claim of gender discrimination will lie where it is shown that differential treatment disadvantages one sex over the other. [ ]. General Laws c. 207 enumerates certain qualifications for obtaining a marriage license. It creates no distinction between the sexes, but applies to men and women in precisely the same way. It does not create any disadvantage identified with gender, as both men and women are similarly limited to marrying a person of the opposite sex. [ ]

Similarly, the marriage statutes do not discriminate on the basis of sexual orientation. As the court correctly recognizes, constitutional protections are extended to individuals, not couples. The marriage statutes do not disqualify individuals on the basis of sexual orientation from entering into marriage. All individuals, with certain exceptions not relevant here, are free to marry. Whether an individual chooses not to marry because of sexual orientation or any other reason should be of no concern to the court.

The court concludes, however, that G. L. c. 207 unconstitutionally discriminates against the individual plaintiffs because it denies them the "right to marry the person of one's choice" where that person is of the same sex. To reach this result the court relies on Loving v. Virginia, [supra], and transforms "choice" into the essential element of the institution of marriage. The Loving case did not use the word "choice" in this manner, and it did not point to the result that the court reaches today. In Loving, the Supreme Court struck down as unconstitutional a statute that prohibited Caucasians from marrying non-Caucasians. It concluded that the statute was intended to preserve white supremacy and invidiously discriminated against non-Caucasians because of their race. The "choice" to which the Supreme Court referred was the "choice to marry," and it concluded that with respect to the institution of marriage, the State had no compelling interest in limiting the choice to marry along racial lines. The Supreme Court did not imply the existence of a right to marry a person of the same sex. * * *

2. Due process. The marriage statutes do not impermissibly burden a right protected by our constitutional guarantee of due process implicit in art. 10 of our Declaration of Rights. There is no restriction on the right of any plaintiff to enter into marriage. Each is free to marry a willing person of the opposite sex. Cf. Zablocki v. Redhail, 434 U.S. 374, 54 L.Ed.2d 618, 98 S.Ct. 673 (1978) (fundamental right to marry impermissibly burdened by statute requiring court approval when subject to child support order).

* * *

Although this court did not state that same-sex marriage is a fundamental right worthy of strict scrutiny protection, it nonetheless deemed it a constitutionally protected right by applying rational basis review. Before applying any level of constitutional analysis there must be a recognized right at stake. Same-sex marriage, or the "right to marry the person of one's choice" as the court today defines that right, does not fall within the fundamental right to marry. Same-sex marriage is not "deeply rooted in this Nation's history," and the court does not suggest that it is. Except for the occasional isolated decision in recent years [ ], same-sex marriage is not a right, fundamental or otherwise, recognized in this country. Just one example of the Legislature's refusal to recognize same-sex marriage can be found in a section of the legislation amending G. L. c. 151B to prohibit discrimination in the workplace on the basis of sexual orientation, which states: "Nothing in this act shall be construed so as to legitimize or validate a 'homosexual marriage'. . . . " St. 1989, c. 516, § 19. In this Commonwealth and in this country, the roots of the institution of marriage are deeply set in history as a civil union between a single man and a single woman. There is no basis for the court to recognize same-sex marriage as a constitutionally protected right.

* * *

Where the application of equal protection principles do not permit rewriting a statute in a manner that preserves the intent of the Legislature, we do not rewrite the statute. * * * We have traditionally and consistently declined to trespass on legislative territory in deference to the time tested wisdom of the separation of powers as expressed in art. [30] of the Declaration of Rights of the Constitution of Massachusetts even when it appeared that a highly desirable and just result might thus be achieved." * * * Principles of equal protection do not permit the marriage statutes to be changed in the manner that we have seen today.

* * *

SOSMAN, J. (dissenting, with whom Spina and Cordy, JJ., join). In applying the rational basis test to any challenged statutory scheme, the issue is not whether the Legislature's rationale behind that scheme is persuasive to us, but only whether it satisfies a minimal threshold of rationality. Today, rather than apply that test, the court announces that, because it is persuaded that there are no differences between same-sex and opposite-sex couples, the Legislature has no rational basis for treating them differently with respect to the granting of marriage licenses. Reduced to its essence, the court's opinion concludes that, because same-sex couples are now raising children, and withholding the benefits of civil marriage from their union makes it harder for them to raise those children, the State must therefore provide the benefits of civil marriage to same-sex couples just as it does to opposite-sex couples. Of course, many people are raising children outside the confines of traditional marriage, and, by definition, those children are being deprived of the various benefits that would flow if they were being raised in a household with married parents. That does not mean that the Legislature must accord the full benefits of marital status on every household raising children. Rather, the Legislature need only have some rational basis for concluding that, at present, those alternate family structures have not yet been conclusively shown to be the equivalent of the marital family structure that has established itself as a successful one over a period of centuries. People are of course at liberty to raise their children in various family structures, as long as they are not literally harming their children by doing so.[ ] That does not mean that the State is required to provide identical forms of encouragement, endorsement, and support to all of the infinite variety of household structures that a free society permits.

Based on our own philosophy of child rearing, and on our observations of the children being raised by same-sex couples to whom we are personally close, we may be of the view that what matters to children is not the gender, or sexual orientation, or even the number of the adults who raise them, but rather whether those adults provide the children with a nurturing, stable, safe, consistent, and supportive environment in which to mature. Same-sex couples can provide their children with the requisite nurturing, stable, safe, consistent, and supportive environment in which to mature, just as opposite-sex couples do. It is therefore understandable that the court might view the traditional definition of marriage as an unnecessary anachronism, rooted in historical prejudices that modern society has in large measure rejected and biological limitations that modern science has overcome.

It is not, however, our assessment that matters. Conspicuously absent from the court's opinion today is any acknowledgment that the attempts at scientific study of the ramifications of raising children in same-sex couple households are themselves in their infancy and have so far produced inconclusive and conflicting results. Notwithstanding our belief that gender and sexual orientation of parents should not matter to the success of the child rearing venture, studies to date reveal that there are still some observable differences between children raised by opposite-sex couples and children raised by same-sex couples. [ ]. Interpretation of the data gathered by those studies then becomes clouded by the personal and political beliefs of the investigators, both as to whether the differences identified are positive or negative, and as to the untested explanations of what might account for those differences. (This is hardly the first time in history that the ostensible steel of the scientific method has melted and buckled under the intense heat of political and religious passions.) Even in the absence of bias or political agenda behind the various studies of children raised by same-sex couples, the most neutral and strict application of scientific principles to this field would be constrained by the limited period of observation that has been available. Gay and lesbian couples living together openly, and official recognition of them as their children's sole parents, comprise a very recent phenomenon, and the recency of that phenomenon has not yet permitted any study of how those children fare as adults and at best minimal study of how they fare during their adolescent years. The Legislature can rationally view the state of the scientific evidence as unsettled on the critical question it now faces: Are families headed by same-sex parents equally successful in rearing children from infancy to adulthood as families headed by parents of opposite sexes? Our belief that children raised by same-sex couples should fare the same as children raised in traditional families is just that: a passionately held but utterly untested belief. The Legislature is not required to share that belief but may, as the creator of the institution of civil marriage, wish to see the proof before making a fundamental alteration to that institution.

* * *

As a matter of social history, today's opinion may represent a great turning point that many will hail as a tremendous step toward a more just society. As a matter of constitutional jurisprudence, however, the case stands as an aberration. To reach the result it does, the court has tortured the rational basis test beyond recognition. I fully appreciate the strength of the temptation to find this particular law unconstitutional— there is much to be said for the argument that excluding gay and lesbian couples from the benefits of civil marriage is cruelly unfair and hopelessly outdated; the inability to marry has a profound impact on the personal lives of committed gay and lesbian couples (and their children) to whom we are personally close (our friends, neighbors, family members, classmates, and co-workers); and our resolution of this issue takes place under the intense glare of national and international publicity. * * * I respectfully dissent.

Notes

1) *Roe v. Wade* is one of the most celebrated and criticized opinions in Supreme Court history. It is celebrated as one of the most significant strides ever taken in favor of women's rights. It is criticized as a travesty of both law and judicial policy making. As a matter of law, the Supreme Court sidestepped substantive due process by making social policy without regard to separation of powers and expanding the Court's role beyond traditional interpretation of the law. Doubtless the framers of the Constitution and particularly the fourteenth amendment did not anticipate the abortion issue or its use as a vehicle of social policy. While there was great concern that *Roe's* interpretation of the fourteenth amendment's right to privacy would be broadly construed in other areas of healthcare, it has not borne out. Even in the abortion context, the Supreme Court subsequently upheld both state Medicaid restrictions and eventually the Hyde Amendment, substantially limiting the use of federal funds for abortion purposes.

2) *Planned Parenthood v. Casey* followed several previous efforts to overturn the *Roe v. Wade* decision, and preserved the basic abortion right by a slim 5–4 margin. The Court did uphold the constitutionality of certain state restrictions as not imposing an "undue burden" on a woman's choice to seek an abortion. These include a waiting period between the time the woman gives her informed consent and the time she obtains her abortion, mandatory information about abortion alternatives, information presented by a physician as a prerequisite to informed consent and certain record keeping and reporting requirements. *Casey* drew the line at the husband notification requirement as it imposed an

"undue burden" on those women whose husbands might put them at risk were notification mandated. Finally, while reaffirming the central holding in *Roe*, *Casey* rejected *Roe v. Wade's* trimester framework, denying that it was an essential holding and declaring it be unworkable. *Casey* declared that the state has a legitimate interest in the health of the woman and the potential life of the unborn fetus throughout pregnancy. Nevertheless, it re-establishes viability as a point where the state interest in the potential life of fetus becomes paramount, and a state law that imposes a substantial obstacle to abortion before that point may be struck down under the "undue burden" analysis.

3) *Baby Boy Doe* is consistent with most case law that addresses the obligation of a woman to undergo an invasive surgical procedure on behalf of her unborn fetus. *Jefferson v. Griffin Spalding County Hospital Authority*, 247 Ga. 86, 274 S.E.2d 457 (1981) is contra, forcing an unwilling mother claiming religious objection to undergo a caesarean section where failure to do so would likely have jeopardized the life of mother and fetus. Other courts have raised the practical dilemma of asking a hospital to physically restrain an unwilling adult to perform a medical procedure that poses some risk to herself. The American Medical Association asserted its objection in *Baby Boy Doe*, and the U.S. Supreme Court refused to intervene. See also *In re Fetus Brown*, 294 Ill.App.3d 159, 228 Ill.Dec. 525, 689 N.E.2d 397 (1997).

4) *Wisconsin v. Kruzicki* questions whether a state can issue an order of protective custody for an unborn fetus whose mother persists in illegal drug use to the detriment of her fetus. Since the fetus is unborn, its mother must also be detained. Prior to *Kruzicki*, virtually no appellate court had upheld the right of a state to take a pregnant woman into custody to promote the well-being of her unborn fetus. The measure had been employed by a number of trial courts, only to be reversed if appeal was taken. In some cases the state purported to rely on its criminal laws for child endangerment or drug-trafficking to impose preventative detention, alleging that illegal drugs were endangering or being supplied to a "minor." See, e.g., *Sheriff, Washoe County v. Encoe*, 110 Nev. 1317, 885 P.2d 596 (1994); *Johnson v. State*, 602 So.2d 1288 (Fla. 1992). Since that time some states have enacted laws to directly address the prenatal substance abuse issue, and avoid distorting other laws clearly not intended for that purpose.

5) *A.Z. v. B.Z.* considers the disposition of frozen preembroyos held in cryopreservation at a fertility clinic. Since more eggs than will ultimately be used are routinely harvested and fertilized in preparation for the *in vitro* process, the disposition of unused preembryos is an important issue. Generally they can be destroyed or donated to other couples at the discretion of the "owners." When the couple disagrees, however, and the record is ambiguous, the court is forced to decide whose interest prevails. The issue is further complicated if one party (usually the woman) wants to implant the embryos and is otherwise unable to produce a child, while the other unwilling party can freely

reproduce. See *Davis v. Davis,* 842 S.W.2d 588 (Tenn. 1992) and *Kass v. Kass,* 235 A.D.2d 150, 663 N.Y.S.2d 581 (App.Div. 1997).

6) *Adoption of Galen* provides a compelling case for looking at the application of the equal protection principles. Were the petitioners not a gay couple, the adoption of Galen, as a biological child of one member of the couple, would not have required a home study. Courts routinely allow new spouses to adopt their mate's child absent an objection of a biological parent or other legitimate reasons to delay the adoption. The petitioners argued, and the court agreed, that declining to waive the requirement of a home study constituted a denial of equal protection of the laws. *Adoption of Galen* would later be cited by the Massachusetts Supreme Judicial Court as an important factor in upholding the constitutionality of gay marriage. See *Goodridge v. Department of Health,* infra. By focusing on the equal protection argument, the Court declined to address the issue that would later become the basis for the vigorous dissent in *Goodridge*: whether to permit gay or lesbian couples to adopt children is a matter that might be entitled to legitimate legislative debate. The dissent discussed the need for "a well-informed judge who has received the input of 'independent child welfare professionals'" but declined to articulate the broader policy issues and precedential value of the decision, instead largely limiting its discussion to the procedural issues.

7) Following the historic 4–3 decision in *Goodridge v. Dept. of Public Health,* the Massachusetts legislature sought an advisory opinion from the Supreme Judicial Court on the issue of whether legislation approving civil unions for gay and lesbian couples, conferring all legal rights but without the status of "marriage", would satisfy the Court's mandate. In another sharply divided 4–3 opinion, the Court declared, in the spirit of *Plessy v. Ferguson* and *Brown v. Board of Education,* "separate is seldom, if ever, equal." The Court went on to state that "[f]or no rational reason the marriage laws of the Commonwealth discriminate against a defined class; no amount of tinkering with language will eradicate that stain ... " A vigorous dissent argued that the two camps were engaged in a battle of semantics, creating "a pitched battle over who gets to use the so-called 'm' word."

In part, the issue over whether gay and couples would be entitled to use the "m" word has to do with the effect of their unions in other states. To date, only Vermont, also by judicial opinion, approved the status of "civil unions" for gay couples, purporting to confer all of the legal rights of marriage, but without marriage status itself. Particularly with passage of the 2003 federal "In Defense of Marriage Act," however, other states are free to choose whether or not to give any legal recognition to Vermont civil unions or Massachusetts marriages.

Will using the "m" word make a difference? In the absence of specific legislation in other states, will a Massachusetts "marriage" of gay or lesbian couples be given full faith and credit around the country? Approximately 40 states adopted the federal "In Defense of Marriage

Act" which limits the definition of "marriage" to the union of one man and one woman. But for those that do not, is "marriage" really "marriage"? The issue is currently being debated in a number of jurisdictions.

A vigorous dissent in *Goodridge* insisted that the issue of whether to recognize gay marriage is one for the legislature and not the court, particularly where a slim 4–3 majority carried the day. Justice Sosman opined that such a decision should be made only after there has been legitimate scientific inquiry regarding the effect of gay marriage on society and a forum for legislative debate. Opponents argued that the exercise of a civil right need not require legislative approval, and the legislature should not be invited to use its process to limit the civil rights of its citizens.

Of course, the undercurrent of the debate has as much to do with the social policy issue of marriage, and whether the history and tradition of marriage embraces same sex couples. The Supreme Judicial Court acknowledged that marriage "bestows enormous private and social advantages" reflecting "a deeply personal commitment ... and [is] a highly public celebration of the ideals of mutuality, security, safe haven and connection that express our common humanity ... " After much impassioned rhetoric on both sides of the issue, and an ongoing, divisive debate, Massachusetts began issuing marriage licenses to gay couples in 2004.

SECTION B.   END OF LIFE

BOWEN v. AMERICAN HOSPITAL ASSOCIATION

Supreme Court of the United States, 1986.
476 U.S. 610, 106 S.Ct. 2101, 90 L.Ed.2d 584.

JUSTICE STEVENS announced the judgment of the Court and delivered an opinion, in which JUSTICE MARSHALL, JUSTICE BLACKMUN, and JUSTICE POWELL join.

This case presents the question whether certain regulations governing the provision of health care to handicapped infants are authorized by § 504 of the Rehabilitation Act of 1973. That section provides, in part:

"No otherwise qualified handicapped individual ... shall, solely by reason of his handicap, be excluded from the participation in, be denied the benefits of, or be subjected to discrimination under any program or activity receiving Federal financial assistance."

I

The American Medical Association, the American Hospital Association, and several other respondents challenge the validity of Final Rules promulgated on January 12, 1984, by the Secretary of the Department of Health and Human Services. These Rules establish "Procedures relating to health care for handicapped infants," and in particular require the posting of informational notices, authorize expedited access to records and expedited compliance actions, and command state child protective services agencies to "prevent instances of unlawful medical neglect of handicapped infants." [ ].

* * *

With respect to the first category, the guidelines do not state that § 504 categorically prohibits a hospital from withholding requested treatment or nourishment "solely on the basis of present or anticipated physical or mental impairments of an infant." [ ]. Rather, the substantive guidelines and two of the illustrative examples recognize that the etiology of and prognosis for particular handicapping conditions may justify "a refusal to treat solely on the basis of those handicapping conditions." [ ] (§ 504 does not require "futile treatment"); [ ] (§ 504 does not require treatment of anencephaly because it would "do no more than temporarily prolong the act of dying"); [ ] (same with severely premature and low birth weight infants). In general, the guidelines seem to make a hospital's liability under § 504 dependent on proof that (1) it refused to provide requested treatment or nourishment solely on the basis of an infant's handicapping condition, and (2) the treatment or nourishment would have been medically beneficial. [ ].

* * *

II

The Final Rules represent the Secretary's ultimate response to an April 9, 1982, incident in which the parents of a Bloomington, Indiana, infant with Down's syndrome and other handicaps refused consent to surgery to remove an esophageal obstruction that prevented oral feeding. On April 10, the hospital initiated judicial proceedings to override the parents' decision, but an Indiana trial court, after holding a hearing the same evening, denied the requested relief. On April 12 the court asked the local Child Protection Committee to review its decision. After conducting its own hearing, the Committee found no reason to disagree with the court's ruling. The infant died six days after its birth.

Citing "heightened public concern" in the aftermath of the Bloomington Baby Doe incident, on May 18, 1982, the director of the Department's Office of Civil Rights, in response to a directive from the President, "[reminded]" health care providers receiving federal financial assistance that newborn infants with handicaps such as Down's syndrome were protected by § 504. [ ]

* * *

On April 6, 1983, respondents American Hospital Association et al. filed a complaint in the Federal District Court for the Southern District of New York seeking a declaration that the Interim Final Rule was invalid and an injunction against its enforcement. Little more than a week later, on April 14, in a similar challenge brought by the American Academy of Pediatrics and other medical institutions, the Federal District Court for the District of Columbia declared the Interim Final Rule "arbitrary and capricious and promulgated in violation of the Administrative Procedure Act." [ ]. The District Judge in that case "[concluded] that haste and inexperience [had] resulted in agency action based on inadequate consideration" of several relevant concerns and, in the alternative, found that the Secretary had improperly failed to solicit public comment before issuing the Rule. [ ].

* * *

IV

The Solicitor General is correct that "handicapped individual" as used in § 504 includes an infant who is born with a congenital defect. If such an infant is "otherwise qualified" for benefits under a program or activity receiving federal financial assistance, § 504 protects him from discrimination "solely by reason of his handicap." It follows, under our decision in *Alexander* v. *Choate*, 469 U.S. 287, 301 (1985), that handicapped infants are entitled to "meaningful access" to medical services provided by hospitals, and that a hospital rule or state policy denying or limiting such access would be subject to challenge under § 504.

However, no such rule or policy is challenged, or indeed has been identified, in this case. Nor does this case, in contrast to the *University Hospital* litigation, involve a claim that any specific individual treatment decision violates § 504. This suit is not an enforcement action, and as a consequence it is not necessary to determine whether § 504 ever applies to individual medical treatment decisions involving handicapped infants. Respondents brought this litigation to challenge the four mandatory components of the Final Rules on their face, and the Court of Appeals' judgment which we review merely affirmed the judgment of the District Court which "declared invalid and enjoined enforcement of [the final] regulations, purportedly promulgated pursuant to section 504 of the Rehabilitation Act of 1973 [ ] The specific question presented by this case, then, is whether the four mandatory provisions of the Final Rules are authorized by § 504.

V

It is an axiom of administrative law that an agency's explanation of the basis for its decision must include a rational connection between the facts found and the choice made. [ ].

Before examining the Secretary's reasons for issuing the Final Rules, it is essential to understand the pre-existing state-law framework governing the provision of medical care to handicapped infants. In broad outline, state law vests decisional responsibility in the parents, in the first instance, subject to review in exceptional cases by the State acting as *parens patriae*. Prior to the regulatory activity culminating in the Final Rules, the Federal Government was not a participant in the process of making treatment decisions for newborn infants. We presume that this general framework was familiar to Congress when it enacted

§ 504. [Reference omitted]. It therefore provides an appropriate background for evaluating the Secretary's action in this case.

The Secretary has identified two possible categories of violations of § 504 as justifications for federal oversight of handicapped infant care. First, he contends that a hospital's refusal to furnish a handicapped infant with medically beneficial treatment "solely by reason of his handicap" constitutes unlawful discrimination. Second, he maintains that a hospital's failure to report cases of suspected medical neglect to a state child protective services agency may also violate the statute. We separately consider these two possible bases for the Final Rules.

VI

In the immediate aftermath of the Bloomington Baby Doe incident, the Secretary apparently proceeded on the assumption that a hospital's statutory duty to provide treatment to handicapped infants was unaffected by the absence of parental consent. [ ]. He has since abandoned that view. Thus, the preamble to the Final Rules correctly states that when "a non-treatment decision, no matter how discriminatory, is made by parents, rather than by the hospital, section 504 does not mandate that the hospital unilaterally overrule the parental decision and provide treatment notwithstanding the lack of consent."[ ]. A hospital's withholding of treatment when no parental consent has been given cannot violate § 504, for without the consent of the parents or a surrogate decisionmaker the infant is neither "otherwise qualified" for treatment nor has he been denied care "solely by reason of his handicap." Indeed, it would almost certainly be a tort as a matter of state law to operate on an infant without parental consent. This analysis makes clear that the Government's heavy reliance on the analogy to race-based refusals which violate § 601 of the Civil Rights Act is misplaced. If, pursuant to its normal practice, a hospital refused to operate on a black child whose parents had withheld their consent to treatment, the hospital's refusal would not be based on the race of the child even if it were assumed that the parents based *their decision* entirely on a mistaken assumption that the race of the child made the operation inappropriate.

Now that the Secretary has acknowledged that a hospital has no statutory treatment obligation in the absence of parental consent, it has become clear that the Final Rules are not needed to prevent hospitals from denying treatment to handicapped infants. * * *

The Secretary's belated recognition of the effect of parental nonconsent is important, because the supposed need for federal monitoring of hospitals' treatment decisions rests *entirely* on instances in which parents have refused their consent. Thus, in the Bloomington, Indiana, case that precipitated the Secretary's enforcement efforts in this area, as well as in the *University Hospital* case that provided the basis for the summary affirmance in the case now before us, the hospital's failure to perform the treatment at issue rested on the lack of parental consent. The Secretary's own summaries of these cases establish beyond doubt that the respective hospitals did not withhold medical care on the basis of handicap and therefore did not violate § 504; as a result, they provide no support for his claim that federal regulation is needed in order to forestall comparable cases in the future.

The Secretary's initial failure to recognize that withholding of consent by *parents* does not equate with discriminatory denial of treatment by *hospitals* likewise undermines the Secretary's findings in the preamble to his proposed rulemaking. In that statement, the Secretary cited four sources in support of the claim that "Section 504 [is] not being uniformly followed." [ ]. None of the cited examples, however, suggests that recipients of federal financial assistance, as opposed to parents, had withheld medical care on the basis of handicap.

* * *

In sum, there is nothing in the administrative record to justify the Secretary's belief that "discriminatory withholding of medical care" in violation of § 504 provides any support for federal regulation: In two of the cases (Robinson, Illinois, and Daytona Beach, Florida), the hospital's refusal was based on the absence of parental consent, but the parents' decision was overridden by state authorities and the operation was performed; in the third case (Colorado Springs, Colorado) it is not clear whether the parents would have given their consent or not, but the corrective surgery was in fact performed.

VII

As a backstop to his manifestly incorrect perception that withholding of treatment in accordance with parental instructions necessitates federal regulation, the Secretary contends that a hospital's failure to report parents' refusals to consent to treatment violates § 504, and that past breaches of this kind justify federal oversight.

By itself, § 504 imposes no duty to report instances of medical neglect—that undertaking derives from state-law reporting obligations or a hospital's own voluntary practice. Although a hospital's selective refusal to report medical neglect of handicapped infants might violate § 504, the Secretary has failed to point to any specific evidence that this has occurred. * * * Even assuming that cases in which parents have withheld consent to treatment for handicapped infants have gone unreported, that fact alone would not prove that the hospitals involved had discriminated on the basis of handicap rather than simply failed entirely to discharge their state-law reporting obligations, if any, a matter which lies wholly outside the nondiscrimination mandate of § 504.

* * *

The particular reporting mechanism chosen by the Secretary—indeed the entire regulatory framework imposed on state child protective services agencies—departs from the nondiscrimination mandate of § 504 in a more fundamental way. The mandatory provisions of the Final Rules omit any direct requirement that hospitals make reports when parents refuse consent to recommended procedures. Instead, the Final Rules command *state agencies* to require such reports, regardless of the state agencies' own reporting requirements (or lack thereof). [ ]. Far from merely preventing state agencies from remaining calculatedly indifferent to handicapped infants while they tend to the needs of the similarly situated nonhandicapped, the Final Rules command state agencies to utilize their "full authority" to "prevent instances of unlawful medical neglect of handicapped infants." [ ]. The Rules effectively make medical neglect of handicapped newborns a state investigative priority, possibly forcing state agencies to shift scarce resources away from other enforcement activities—perhaps even from programs designed to protect handicapped children outside hospitals. The Rules also order state agencies to "[immediately]" review reports from hospitals, [ ], to conduct "on-site [investigations]," *ibid.*, and to take legal action "to compel the provision of necessary nourishment and medical treatment," [ ]—all without any regard to the procedures followed by state agencies in handling complaints filed on behalf of nonhandicapped infants. These operating procedures were imposed over the objection of several state child protective services agencies that the requirement that they turn over reports to HHS "conflicts with the confidentiality requirements of state child abuse and neglect statutes," [ ]—thereby requiring under the guise of nondiscrimination a service which state law denies to the nonhandicapped.

VIII

Section 504 authorizes any head of an Executive Branch agency—regardless of his agency's mission or expertise—to promulgate regulations prohibiting discrimination against the handicapped. [ ] As a result of this rulemaking authority, the Secretary of HHS has "substantial leeway to explore areas in which discrimination against the handicapped [poses] particularly significant problems and to devise regulations to prohibit such discrimination." [citation omitted] .

* * *

This * * * makes irresistible the inference that the Department regards its mission as one principally concerned with the quality of medical care for handicapped infants rather than with the implementation of § 504. We could not quarrel with a decision by the Department to concentrate its finite compliance resources on instances of life-threatening discrimination rather than instances in which merely elective care has been withheld. [ ]. But nothing in the statute authorizes the Secretary to dispense with the law's focus on discrimination and instead to employ federal resources to save the lives of handicapped newborns, without regard to whether they are victims of discrimination by recipients of federal funds or not. Section 504 does not authorize the Secretary to give unsolicited advice either to parents, to hospitals, or to state officials who are faced with difficult treatment decisions concerning handicapped children. We may assume that the "qualified professionals" employed by the Secretary may make valuable contributions in particular cases, but neither that assumption nor the sincere conviction that an immediate "on-site investigation" is "necessary to protect the life or health of a handicapped individual" can enlarge the statutory powers of the Secretary.

The administrative record demonstrates that the Secretary has asserted the authority to conduct on-site investigations, to inspect hospital records, and to participate in the decisional process in emergency cases in which there was no colorable basis for believing that a violation of § 504 had occurred or was about to occur. The District Court and the Court of Appeals correctly held that these investigative actions were not authorized by the statute and that the regulations which purport to authorize a continuation of them are invalid.

The judgment of the Court of Appeals is affirmed.

It is so ordered.

JUSTICE WHITE, with whom JUSTICE BRENNAN joins and with whom JUSTICE O'CONNOR joins as to Parts I, II, IV, and V, dissenting.

Section 504 of the Rehabilitation Act of 1973 forbids discrimination solely on the basis of handicap in programs or activities receiving federal financial assistance. The issue before us is whether the Secretary of Health and Human Services has any authority under the Act to regulate medical treatment decisions concerning handicapped newborn infants. Relying on its prior decision in *United States* v. *University Hospital*, [ ], the Court of Appeals held that the Secretary was without power in this respect and affirmed a decision of the District Court that § 504 does not extend so far and that the Secretary may not regulate such decisions in any manner.

* * *

I

The plurality's initial and fundamental error is its statement that the only question presented here is the specific question whether the four mandatory provisions of the Final Rules issued by the Secretary are authorized by § 504. This conclusion misconstrues the opinion and judgment of the Court of Appeals. The plurality concedes that the District Court's judgment on its face did not stop with enjoining the enforcement of the final regulations. [ ]. In fact, the District Court permanently enjoined the Secretary from implementing the final regulations and also from "continuing or undertaking any other actions to investigate or regulate treatment decisions involving impaired newborn infants taken under authority of Section 504, including pending investigation and other enforcement actions." [ ]. This broad injunction ousted the Secretary from the field entirely and granted the precise relief sought by the complaint, which was filed after [earlier California decision] and which sought to take full advantage of that decision. The Court of Appeals affirmed and in no way modified the injunction that the District Court had entered. In doing so, the Court of Appeals relied on its previous determination in [that opinion] that the Secretary had no statutory authority to regulate medical treatment decisions regarding newborn infants.

It is true that the regulations themselves were invalidated and their enforcement enjoined. This result, however, was directly compelled by the [earlier] conclusion that the Secretary was without power to issue any regulations whatsoever that dealt with infants' medical care, and it did not comprise the whole relief awarded by the District Court and affirmed by the Court of Appeals. I thus see no justification for the plurality's distortion of the Court of Appeals' affirmance of the District Court's all-inclusive injunction, which [ ] now represents the law in the Second Circuit. We should resolve the threshold statutory question that this case clearly pose[s]—namely, whether the Secretary has any authority at all under the Act to regulate medical care decisions with respect to the handicapped newborn.

II

* * * Looking first at the language of the statute, I agree with the Court of Appeals' preliminary conclusion that handicapped newborns are handicapped individuals covered by the Act. There is no reason for importing an age limitation into the statutory definition, and this Court has previously stated that "§ 504 protects handicapped persons of all ages from discrimination in a variety of programs and activities receiving federal financial assistance." [ ] This leaves the critical question whether a handicapped infant can ever be "otherwise qualified" for medical treatment and hence possibly subjected to unlawful discrimination when he or she is denied such treatment.

* * *

Even under the Court of Appeals' interpretation of "otherwise qualified," however, it does not follow that § 504 may never apply to medical treatment decisions for the newborn. An esophageal obstruction, for example, would not be part and parcel of the handicap of a baby suffering from Down's syndrome, and the infant would benefit from and is thus otherwise qualified for having the obstruction removed in spite of the handicap. In this case, the treatment is completely unrelated to the baby's handicapping condition. If an otherwise normal child would be given the identical treatment, so should the handicapped child if discrimination on the basis of the handicap is to be avoided.

* * *

III

The plurality concludes that the four mandatory provisions of the final regulations are invalid because there is no " 'rational connection between the facts found and the choice made.' [ ]. The basis for this conclusion is the plurality's perception that two and only two wholly discrete categories of decisions are the object of the final regulations: (1) decisions made by hospitals to treat or not treat where parental consent has been given and (2) decisions made by hospitals to refer or not to refer a case to the state child protective services agency where parental consent has been withheld. Since the Secretary has not specifically pointed to discriminatory actions that probably resulted from either of these two specific types of decisions, the plurality finds that the Secretary's conclusion that discrimination is occurring is unsupported factually. The plurality's characterization of the Secretary's rationale, however, oversimplifies both the complexity of the situations to which the regulations are addressed and the reasoning of the Secretary.

* * *

IV

My disagreement with the plurality in this case does not end here, however. For even under its chosen rationale, I find its ultimate conclusion dubious. Having assiduously restricted its discussion to the validity of the regulations only, the plurality ends up concluding expansively that not only the regulations but also other investigations taken by the Secretary independent of the regulations are invalid. Thus, the Court apparently enjoins the Secretary's on-site investigations as well as "the regulations which purport to authorize a continuation of them." *Ante*, at 647. And the plurality rests this action on the conclusion that the lower courts "correctly held that these investigative actions were not authorized by the statute." *Ibid*.

* * *

CRUZAN v. DIRECTOR, MISSOURI DEPARTMENT OF HEALTH

Supreme Court of the United States, 1990.
497 U.S. 261, 110 S.Ct. 2841, 111 L.Ed.2d 224.

CHIEF JUSTICE REHNQUIST delivered the opinion of the Court.

Petitioner Nancy Beth Cruzan was rendered incompetent as a result of severe injuries sustained during an automobile accident. Copetitioners Lester and Joyce Cruzan, Nancy's parents and coguardians, sought a court order directing the withdrawal of their daughter's artificial feeding and hydration equipment after it became apparent that she had virtually no chance of recovering her cognitive faculties. The Supreme Court of Missouri held that because there was no clear and convincing evidence of Nancy's desire to have life-sustaining treatment withdrawn under such circumstances, her parents lacked authority to effectuate such a request. [ ]

On the night of January 11, 1983, Nancy Cruzan lost control of her car as she traveled down Elm Road in Jasper County, Missouri. The vehicle overturned, and Cruzan was discovered lying face down in a ditch without detectable respiratory or cardiac function. Paramedics were able to restore her breathing and heartbeat at the accident site, and she was transported to a hospital in an unconscious state. An attending neuro-surgeon diagnosed her as having sustained probable cerebral contusions compounded by significant anoxia (lack of oxygen). The Missouri trial court in this case found that permanent brain damage generally results after 6 minutes in an anoxic state; it was estimated that Cruzan was deprived of oxygen from 12 to 14 minutes. She remained in a coma for approximately three weeks and then progressed to an unconscious state in which she was able to orally ingest some nutrition. In order to ease feeding and further the recovery, surgeons implanted a gastrostomy feeding and hydration tube in Cruzan with the consent of her then husband. Subsequent rehabilitative efforts proved unavailing. She now lies in a Missouri state hospital in what is commonly referred to as a persistent vegetative state: generally, a condition in which a person exhibits motor reflexes but evinces no indications of significant cognitive function. The State of Missouri is bearing the cost of her care.

After it had become apparent that Nancy Cruzan had virtually no chance of regaining her mental faculties, her parents asked hospital employees to terminate the artificial nutrition and hydration procedures. All agree that such a removal would cause her death. The employees refused to honor the request without court approval. The parents then sought and received authorization from the state trial court for termination. The court found that a person in Nancy's condition had a fundamental right under the State and Federal Constitutions to refuse or direct the withdrawal of "death prolonging procedures." [ ]. The court also found that Nancy's "expressed thoughts at age twenty-five in somewhat serious conversation with a housemate friend that if sick or injured she would not wish to continue her life unless she could live at least halfway normally suggests that given her present condition she would not wish to continue on with her nutrition and hydration." *Id.*, at A97–A98.

The Supreme Court of Missouri reversed by a divided vote. * * *

We granted certiorari to consider the question whether Cruzan has a right under the United States Constitution which would require the hospital to withdraw life-sustaining treatment from her under these circumstances.

At common law, even the touching of one person by another without consent and without legal justification was a battery. [citation omitted] Before the turn of the century, this Court observed that "no right is held more sacred, or is more carefully guarded, by the common law, than the right of every individual to the possession and control of his own person, free from all restraint or interference of others, unless by clear and unquestionable authority of law." *Union Pacific R. Co.* v. *Botsford*, 141 U.S. 250, 251, 35 L.Ed. 734, 11 S.Ct. 1000 (1891). This notion of bodily integrity has been embodied in the requirement that informed consent is generally required for medical treatment. Justice Cardozo, while on the

Court of Appeals of New York, aptly described this doctrine: "Every human being of adult years and sound mind has a right to determine what shall be done with his own body; and a surgeon who performs an operation without his patient's consent commits an assault, for which he is liable in damages." [ ]

* * * [T]he common-law doctrine of informed consent is viewed as generally encompassing the right of a competent individual to refuse medical treatment. Beyond that, [ ] cases demonstrate both similarity and diversity in their approaches to decision of what all agree is a perplexing question with unusually strong moral and ethical overtones. State courts have available to them for decision a number of sources—state constitutions, statutes, and common law—which are not available to us. In this Court, the question is simply and starkly whether the United States Constitution prohibits Missouri from choosing the rule of decision which it did. * * *

The Fourteenth Amendment provides that no State shall "deprive any person of life, liberty, or property, without due process of law." The principle that a competent person has a constitutionally protected liberty interest in refusing unwanted medical treatment may be inferred from our prior decisions. In *Jacobson* v. *Massachusetts*, 197 U.S. 11, 24–30, 49 L.Ed. 643, 25 S.Ct. 358 (1905), for instance, the Court balanced an individual's liberty interest in declining an unwanted smallpox vaccine against the State's interest in preventing disease. * * *

But determining that a person has a "liberty interest" under the Due Process Clause does not end the inquiry; "whether respondent's constitutional rights have been violated must be determined by balancing his liberty interests against the relevant state interests." [ ].

Petitioners insist that under the general holdings of our cases, the forced administration of life-sustaining medical treatment, and even of artificially delivered food and water essential to life, would implicate a competent person's liberty interest. Although we think the logic of the cases discussed above would embrace such a liberty interest, the dramatic consequences involved in refusal of such treatment would inform the inquiry as to whether the deprivation of that interest is constitutionally permissible. But for purposes of this case, we assume that the United States Constitution would grant a competent person a constitutionally protected right to refuse lifesaving hydration and nutrition.

Petitioners go on to assert that an incompetent person should possess the same right in this respect as is possessed by a competent person. * * *

The difficulty with petitioners' claim is that in a sense it begs the question: An incompetent person is not able to make an informed and voluntary choice to exercise a hypothetical right to refuse treatment or any other right. Such a "right" must be exercised for her, if at all, by some sort of surrogate. Here, Missouri has in effect recognized that under certain circumstances a surrogate may act for the patient in electing to have hydration and nutrition withdrawn in such a way as to cause death, but it has established a procedural safeguard to assure that the action of the surrogate conforms as best it may to the wishes expressed by the patient while competent. Missouri requires that evidence of the incompetent's wishes as to the withdrawal of treatment be proved by clear and convincing evidence. The question, then, is whether the United States Constitution forbids the establishment of this procedural requirement by the State. We hold that it does not.

Whether or not Missouri's clear and convincing evidence requirement comports with the United States Constitution depends in part on what interests the State may properly seek to protect in this situation. Missouri relies on its interest in the protection and preservation of human life, and there can be no gainsaying this interest. As a general matter, the States—indeed, all civilized nations—demonstrate their commitment to life by treating homicide as a serious crime. Moreover, the majority of States in this country have laws imposing criminal penalties on one who assists another to commit suicide. We do not think a State is required to remain neutral in the face of an informed and voluntary decision by a physically able adult to starve to death.

But in the context presented here, a State has more particular interests at stake. The choice between life and death is a deeply personal decision of obvious and overwhelming finality. We believe Missouri may legitimately seek to safeguard the personal element of this choice through the imposition of heightened evidentiary requirements. It cannot be disputed that the Due Process Clause protects an interest in life as well as an interest in refusing life-sustaining medical treatment. Not all incompetent patients will have loved ones available to serve as surrogate decisionmakers. And even where family members are present, "there will, of course, be some unfortunate situations in which family members will not act to protect a patient." *In re Jobes*, 108 N.J. 394, 419, 529 A.2d 434, 447 (1987). A State is entitled to guard against potential abuses in such situations. Similarly, a State is entitled to consider that a judicial proceeding to make a determination regarding an incompetent's wishes may very well not be an adversarial one, with the added guarantee of accurate factfinding that the adversary process brings with it. [ ] Finally, we think a State may properly decline to make judgments about the "quality" of life that a particular individual may enjoy, and simply assert an unqualified interest in the preservation of human life to be weighed against the constitutionally protected interests of the individual.

In our view, Missouri has permissibly sought to advance these interests through the adoption of a "clear and convincing" standard of proof to govern such proceedings. "The function of a standard of proof, as that concept is embodied in the Due Process Clause and in the realm of factfinding, is to 'instruct the factfinder concerning the degree of confidence our society thinks he should have in the correctness of factual conclusions for a particular type of adjudication.' " * * * Further, this level of proof, "or an even higher one, has traditionally been imposed in cases involving allegations of civil fraud, and in a variety of other kinds of civil cases involving such issues as ... lost wills, oral contracts to make bequests, and the like." *Woodby, supra*, at 285, n.18.

We think it self-evident that the interests at stake in the instant proceedings are more substantial, both on an individual and societal level, than those involved in a run-of-the-mine civil dispute. But not only does the standard of proof reflect the importance of a particular adjudication, it also serves as "a societal judgment about how the risk of error should be distributed between the litigants." *Santosky, supra*, at 755[ ]. The more stringent the burden of proof a party must bear, the more that party bears the risk of an erroneous decision. We believe that Missouri may permissibly place an increased risk of an erroneous decision on those seeking to terminate an incompetent individual's life-sustaining treatment. An erroneous decision not to terminate results in a maintenance of the status quo; the possibility of subsequent developments such as advancements in medical science, the discovery of new evidence regarding the patient's intent, changes in the law, or simply the unexpected death of the patient despite the administration of life-sustaining treatment at least create the potential that a wrong decision will eventually be corrected or its impact mitigated. An erroneous decision to withdraw life-sustaining treatment, however, is not susceptible of correction. In *Santosky*, one of the factors which led the Court to require proof by clear and convincing evidence in a proceeding to terminate parental rights was that a decision in such a case was final and irrevocable. *Santosky, supra*, at 759. The same must surely be said of the decision to discontinue hydration and nutrition of a patient such as Nancy Cruzan, which all agree will result in her death.

It is also worth noting that most, if not all, States simply forbid oral testimony entirely in determining the wishes of parties in transactions which, while important, simply do not have the consequences that a decision to terminate a person's life does. * * *

In sum, we conclude that a State may apply a clear and convincing evidence standard in proceedings where a guardian seeks to discontinue nutrition and hydration of a person diagnosed to be in a persistent vegetative state. We note that many courts which have adopted some sort of substituted judgment procedure in situations like this, whether they limit consideration of evidence to the prior expressed wishes of the incompetent individual, or whether they allow more general proof of what the individual's decision would have been, require a clear and convincing standard of proof for such evidence. [citations omitted]

The Supreme Court of Missouri held that in this case the testimony adduced at trial did not amount to clear and convincing proof of the patient's desire to have hydration and nutrition withdrawn. In so doing, it reversed a decision of the Missouri trial court which had found that the evidence "suggested" Nancy Cruzan would not have desired to continue such measures but which had not adopted the standard of "clear and convincing evidence" enunciated by the Supreme Court. The testimony adduced at trial consisted primarily of Nancy Cruzan's statements made to a housemate about a year before her accident that she would not want to live should she face life as a "vegetable," and other observations to the same effect. The observations did not deal in terms with withdrawal of medical treatment or of hydration and nutrition. We cannot say that the Supreme Court of Missouri committed constitutional error in reaching the conclusion that it did.

* * *

JUSTICE BRENNAN, with whom JUSTICE MARSHALL and JUSTICE BLACKMUN join, dissenting.

A grown woman at the time of the accident, Nancy had previously expressed her wish to forgo continuing medical care under circumstances such as these. Her family and her friends are convinced that this is what she would want. A guardian ad litem appointed by the trial court is also convinced that this is what Nancy would want. [ ] Yet the Missouri Supreme Court, alone among state courts deciding such a question, has determined that an irreversibly vegetative patient will remain a passive prisoner of medical technology—for Nancy, perhaps for the next 30 years. [ ]

Today the Court, while tentatively accepting that there is some degree of constitutionally protected liberty interest in avoiding unwanted medical treatment, including life-sustaining medical treatment such as artificial nutrition and hydration, affirms the decision of the Missouri Supreme Court. The majority opinion, as I read it, would affirm that decision on the ground that a State may require "clear and convincing" evidence of Nancy Cruzan's prior decision to forgo life-sustaining treatment under circumstances such as hers in order to ensure that her actual wishes are honored. [ ]. Because I believe that Nancy Cruzan has a fundamental right to be free of unwanted artificial nutrition and hydration, which right is not outweighed by any interests of the State, and because I find that the improperly biased procedural obstacles imposed by the Missouri Supreme Court impermissibly burden that right, I respectfully dissent. Nancy Cruzan is entitled to choose to die with dignity.

I

A

* * *

The question before this Court is a relatively narrow one: whether the Due Process Clause allows Missouri to require a now-incompetent patient in an irreversible persistent vegetative state to remain on life support absent rigorously clear and convincing evidence that avoiding the treatment represents the patient's prior, express choice. See 497 U.S. at 277–278. If a fundamental right is at issue, Missouri's rule of decision must be scrutinized under the standards this Court has always applied in such circumstances. As we said in *Zablocki* v. *Redhail*, 434 U.S. 374,

388, 54 L.Ed.2d 618, 98 S.Ct. 673 (1978), if a requirement imposed by a State "significantly interferes with the exercise of a fundamental right, it cannot be upheld unless it is supported by sufficiently important state interests and is closely tailored to effectuate only those interests." The Constitution imposes on this Court the obligation to "examine carefully . . . the extent to which [the legitimate government interests advanced] are served by the challenged regulation." [citations omitted]

B

The starting point for our legal analysis must be whether a competent person has a constitutional right to avoid unwanted medical care. Earlier this Term, this Court held that the Due Process Clause of the Fourteenth Amendment confers a significant liberty interest in avoiding unwanted medical treatment. [ ]. Today, the Court concedes that our prior decisions "support the recognition of a general liberty interest in refusing medical treatment." [ ]. The Court, however, avoids discussing either the measure of that liberty interest or its application by assuming, for purposes of this case only, that a competent person has a constitutionally protected liberty interest in being free of unwanted artificial nutrition and hydration.

But if a competent person has a liberty interest to be free of unwanted medical treatment, as both the majority and JUSTICE O'CONNOR concede, it must be fundamental. * * *

The right to be free from medical attention without consent, to determine what shall be done with one's own body, *is* deeply rooted in this Nation's traditions, as the majority acknowledges. [ ]. This right has long been "firmly entrenched in American tort law" and is securely grounded in the earliest common law.

That there may be serious consequences involved in refusal of the medical treatment at issue here does not vitiate the right under our common-law tradition of medical self-determination. It is "a well-established rule of general law . . . that it is the patient, not the physician, who ultimately decides if treatment—any treatment—is to be given at all. * * *

No material distinction can be drawn between the treatment to which Nancy Cruzan continues to be subject—artificial nutrition and hydration—and any other medical treatment. * * *. The artificial delivery of nutrition and hydration is undoubtedly medical treatment. The technique to which Nancy Cruzan is subject—artificial feeding through a gastrostomy tube—involves a tube implanted surgically into her stomach through incisions in her abdominal wall. It may obstruct the intestinal tract, erode and pierce the stomach wall, or cause leakage of the stomach's contents into the abdominal cavity. * * *

Artificial delivery of food and water is regarded as medical treatment by the medical profession and the Federal Government. * * *

The right to be free from unwanted medical attention is a right to evaluate the potential benefit of treatment and its possible consequences according to one's own values and to make a personal decision whether to subject oneself to the intrusion. For a patient like Nancy Cruzan, the sole benefit of medical treatment is being kept metabolically alive. Neither artificial nutrition nor any other form of medical treatment available today can cure or in any way ameliorate her condition. Irreversibly vegetative patients are devoid of thought, emotion, and sensation; they are permanently and completely unconscious. e have been only three even partial recoveries documented in the medical literature.

There are also affirmative reasons why someone like Nancy might choose to forgo artificial nutrition and hydration under these circumstances. Dying is personal. And it is profound. For many, the thought of an ignoble end, steeped in decay, is abhorrent. A quiet, proud death, bodily integrity intact, is a matter of extreme consequence. "In certain, thankfully rare, circumstances the burden of maintaining the corporeal existence degrades the very humanity it was meant to serve." * * *

Such conditions are, for many, humiliating to contemplate, as is visiting a prolonged and anguished vigil on one's parents, spouse, and children. A long, drawn-out death can have a debilitating effect on family members. [ ] For some, the idea of being remembered in their persistent vegetative states rather than as they were before their illness or accident may be very disturbing.

B

* * *

The only state interest asserted here is a general interest in the preservation of life. But the State has no legitimate general interest in someone's life, completely abstracted from the interest of the person living that life, that could outweigh the person's choice to avoid medical treatment. "The regulation of constitutionally protected decisions ... must be predicated on legitimate state concerns *other than* disagreement with the choice the individual has made.... Otherwise, the interest in liberty protected by the Due Process Clause would be a nullity." [ ]. Thus, the State's general interest in life must accede to Nancy Cruzan's particularized and intense interest in self-determination in her choice of medical treatment. There is simply nothing legitimately within the State's purview to be gained by superseding her decision.

Moreover, there may be considerable danger that Missouri's rule of decision would impair rather than serve any interest the State does have in sustaining life. Current medical practice recommends use of heroic measures if there is a scintilla of a chance that the patient will recover, on the assumption that the measures will be discontinued should the patient improve.

III

This is not to say that the State has no legitimate interests to assert here. As the majority recognizes [ ], Missouri has a *parens patriae* interest in providing Nancy Cruzan, now incompetent, with as accurate as possible a determination of how she would exercise her rights under these circumstances. Second, if and when it is determined that Nancy Cruzan would want to continue treatment, the State may legitimately assert an interest in providing that treatment. But *until* Nancy's wishes have been determined, the only state interest that may be asserted is an interest in safeguarding the accuracy of that determination.

Accuracy, therefore, must be our touchstone. Missouri may constitutionally impose only those procedural requirements that serve to enhance the accuracy of a determination of Nancy Cruzan's wishes or are at least consistent with an accurate determination. The Missouri "safeguard" that the Court upholds today does not meet that standard. The determination needed in this context is whether the incompetent person would choose to live in a persistent vegetative state on life support or to avoid this medical treatment. Missouri's rule of decision imposes a markedly asymmetrical evidentiary burden. Only evidence of specific statements of treatment choice made by the patient when competent is admissible to support a finding that the patient, now in a persistent vegetative state, would wish to avoid further medical treatment. Moreover, this evidence must be clear and convincing. No proof is required to support a finding that the incompetent person would wish to continue treatment.

A

The majority offers several justifications for Missouri's heightened evidentiary standard. First, the majority explains that the State may constitutionally adopt this rule to govern determinations of an incompetent's wishes in order to advance the State's substantive interests, including its unqualified interest in the preservation of human life. [ ] Missouri's evidentiary standard, however, cannot rest on the State's own interest in a particular substantive result. To be sure, courts have long erected clear and convincing evidence standards to place the greater risk of erroneous decisions on those bringing disfavored claims. In such cases, however, the choice to discourage certain claims was a legitimate, constitutional policy choice. In contrast, Missouri has no such power to disfavor a choice by Nancy Cruzan to avoid medical treatment, because Missouri has no legitimate interest in providing Nancy with treatment until it is established that this represents her choice. [ ] Just as a State may not override Nancy's choice directly, it may not do so indirectly through the imposition of a procedural rule.

Second, the majority offers two explanations for why Missouri's clear and convincing evidence standard is a means of enhancing accuracy, but neither is persuasive.

Even a later decision to grant him his wish cannot undo the intervening harm. But a later decision is unlikely in any event. "The discovery of new evidence," to which the majority refers, *ibid.*, is more hypothetical than plausible. The majority also misconceives the relevance of the possibility of "advancements in medical science," *ibid.*, by treating it as a reason to force someone to continue medical treatment against his will. The possibility of a medical miracle is indeed part of the calculus, but it is a part of the *patient's* calculus. If current research suggests that some hope for cure or even moderate improvement is possible within the lifespan projected, this is a factor that should be and would be accorded significant weight in assessing what the patient himself would choose.

B

Even more than its heightened evidentiary standard, the Missouri court's categorical exclusion of relevant evidence dispenses with any semblance of accurate factfinding. The court adverted to no evidence supporting its decision, but held that no clear and convincing, inherently reliable evidence had been presented to show that Nancy would want to avoid further treatment. In doing so, the court failed to consider statements Nancy had made to family members and a close friend. The court also failed to consider testimony from Nancy's mother and sister that they were certain that Nancy would want to discontinue artificial nutrition and hydration, even after the court found that Nancy's family was loving and without malignant motive. [ ]. The court also failed to consider the conclusions of the guardian ad litem, appointed by the trial court, that there was clear and convincing evidence that Nancy would want to discontinue medical treatment and that this was in her best interests. [ ]. The court did not specifically define what kind of evidence it would consider clear and convincing, but its general discussion suggests that only a living will or equivalently formal directive from the patient when competent would meet this standard. [ ].

* * *

The testimony of close friends and family members, on the other hand, may often be the best evidence available of what the patient's choice would be. It is they with whom the patient most likely will have discussed such questions and they who know the patient best. "Family members have a unique knowledge of the patient which is vital to any decision on his or her behalf." [ ] The Missouri court's decision to ignore this whole category of testimony is also at odds with the practices of other States.

The Missouri court's disdain for Nancy's statements in serious conversations not long before her accident, for the opinions of Nancy's family and friends as to her values, beliefs and certain choice, and even for the opinion of an outside objective factfinder appointed by the State evinces a disdain for Nancy Cruzan's own right to choose. The rules by which an incompetent person's wishes are determined must represent every effort to determine those wishes. The rule that the Missouri court adopted and that this Court upholds, however, skews the result away from a determination that as accurately as possible reflects the individual's own preferences and beliefs. It is a rule that transforms human beings into passive subjects of medical technology. * * *

C

I do not suggest that States must sit by helplessly if the choices of incompetent patients are in danger of being ignored. [ ]. Even if the Court had ruled that Missouri's rule of decision is unconstitutional, as I believe it should have, States would nevertheless remain free to fashion procedural protections to safeguard the interests of incompetents under these circumstances. The Constitution provides merely a framework here: Protections must be genuinely aimed at ensuring decisions commensurate with the will of the patient, and must be reliable as instruments to that end. Of the many States which have instituted such protections, Missouri is virtually the only one to have fashioned a rule that lessens the likelihood of accurate determinations. In contrast, nothing in the Constitution prevents States from reviewing the advisability of a family decision, by requiring a court proceeding or by appointing an impartial guardian ad litem. * * *

D

Finally, I cannot agree with the majority that where it is not possible to determine what choice an incompetent patient would make, a State's role as *parens patriae* permits the State automatically to make that choice itself. [ ]. Under fair rules of evidence, it is improbable that a court could not determine what the patient's choice would be. Under the rule of decision adopted by Missouri and upheld today by this Court, such occasions might be numerous. But in neither case does it follow that it is constitutionally acceptable for the State invariably to assume the role of deciding for the patient. A State's legitimate interest in safeguarding a patient's choice cannot be furthered by simply appropriating it.

* * *

WASHINGTON v. GLUCKSBERG

Supreme Court of the United States, 1997.
521 U.S. 702, 117 S.Ct. 2258, 138 L.Ed.2d 772 (1997).

CHIEF JUSTICE REHNQUIST delivered the opinion of the Court.

The question presented in this case is whether Washington's prohibition against "causing" or "aiding" a suicide offends the Fourteenth Amendment to the United States Constitution. We hold that it does not.

It has always been a crime to assist a suicide in the State of Washington. * * * Today, Washington law provides: "A person is guilty of promoting a suicide attempt when he knowingly causes or aids another person to attempt suicide." [ ]. "Promoting a suicide attempt" is a felony [ ]. At the same time, Washington's Natural Death Act, enacted in 1979, states that the "withholding or withdrawal of life-sustaining treatment" at a patient's direction "shall not, for any purpose, constitute a suicide." [ ]

Petitioners in this case are the State of Washington and its Attorney General. Respondents Harold Glucksberg, M. D., Abigail Halperin, M. D., Thomas A. Preston, M. D., and Peter Shalit, M. D., are physicians who practice in Washington. These doctors occasionally treat terminally ill, suffering patients, and declare that they would assist these patients in ending their lives if not for Washington's assisted-suicide ban. In January 1994, respondents, along with three gravely ill, pseudonymous plaintiffs who have since died and Compassion in Dying, a nonprofit organization that counsels people considering physician-assisted suicide, sued in the United States District Court, seeking a declaration that the Wash[ington law] is, on its face, unconstitutional.

The plaintiffs asserted "the existence of a liberty interest protected by the Fourteenth Amendment which extends to a personal choice by a mentally competent, terminally ill adult to commit physician-assisted suicide." *Id.*, at 1459. Relying primarily on *Planned Parenthood* v. *Casey*, 505 U.S. 833 (1992), and *Cruzan* v. *Director, Missouri Dept. of Health*, 497 U.S. 261 (1990), the District Court agreed, 850 F.Supp., at 1459–1462, and concluded that Washington's assisted-suicide ban is unconstitutional because it "places an undue burden on the exercise of [that] constitutionally protected liberty interest." *Id.*, at 1465. * * *

A panel of the Court of Appeals for the Ninth Circuit reversed, emphasizing that "in the two hundred and five years of our existence no constitutional right to aid in killing oneself has ever been asserted and upheld by a court of final jurisdiction." *Compassion in Dying* v. *Washington*, 49 F.3d 586, 591 (1995). The Ninth Circuit reheard the case en banc, reversed the panel's decision, and affirmed the District Court. *Compassion in Dying* v. *Washington*, 79 F.3d 790, 798 (1996). Like the District Court, the en banc Court of Appeals emphasized our *Casey* and *Cruzan* decisions. * * *

We begin, as we do in all due-process cases, by examining our Nation's history, legal traditions, and practices. [citations omitted] In almost every State—indeed, in almost every western democracy—it is a crime to assist a suicide. The States' assisted-suicide bans are not innovations. Rather, they are longstanding expressions of the States' commitment to the protection and preservation of all human life. [citations omitted]

More specifically, for over 700 years, the Anglo–American common-law tradition has punished or otherwise disapproved of both suicide and assisting suicide. * * *

Though deeply rooted, the States' assisted-suicide bans have in recent years been reexamined and, generally, reaffirmed. Because of advances in medicine and technology, Americans today are increasingly likely to die in institutions, from chronic illnesses. [ ]. Public concern and democratic action are therefore sharply focused on how best to protect dignity and independence at the end of life, with the result that there have been many significant changes in state laws and in the attitudes these laws reflect. Many States, for example, now permit "living wills," surrogate health-care decisionmaking, and the withdrawal or refusal of life-sustaining medical treatment. [ ] At the same time, however, voters and legislators continue for the most part to reaffirm their States' prohibitions on assisting suicide.

The Washington statute at issue in this case [ ] was enacted in 1975 as part of a revision of that State's criminal code. Four years later, Washington passed its Natural Death Act, which specifically stated that the "withholding or withdrawal of life-sustaining treatment ... shall not, for any purpose, constitute a suicide" and that "nothing in this chapter shall be construed to condone, authorize, or approve mercy killing.... " [citations omitted.] In 1991, Washington voters rejected a ballot initiative which, had it passed, would have permitted a form of physician-assisted suicide. Washington then added a provision to the Natural Death Act expressly excluding physician-assisted suicide. [ ].

California voters rejected an assisted-suicide initiative similar to Washington's in 1993. On the other hand, in 1994, voters in Oregon enacted, also through ballot initiative, that State's "Death With Dignity Act," which legalized physician-assisted suicide for competent, terminally ill adults. Since the Oregon vote, many proposals to legalize assisted-suicide have been and continue to be introduced in the States' legislatures, but none has been enacted. And just last year, Iowa and Rhode Island joined the overwhelming majority of States explicitly prohibiting assisted suicide. [ ] Also, on April 30, 1997, President Clinton signed the Federal Assisted Suicide Funding Restriction Act of 1997, which prohibits the use of federal funds in support of physician-assisted suicide.

Thus, the States are currently engaged in serious, thoughtful examinations of physician-assisted suicide and other similar issues. For example, New York State's Task Force on Life and the Law—an ongoing, blue-ribbon commission composed of doctors, ethicists, lawyers, religious leaders, and interested laymen—was convened in 1984 and commissioned with "a broad mandate to recommend public policy on issues raised by medical advances." [ ] * * *. After studying physician-assisted suicide, however, the Task Force unanimously concluded that "legalizing assisted suicide and euthanasia would pose profound risks to many individuals who are ill and vulnerable.... The potential dangers of this dramatic change in public policy would outweigh any benefit that might be achieved." *Id.*, at 120.

Attitudes toward suicide itself have changed since Bracton, but our laws have consistently condemned, and continue to prohibit, assisting suicide. Despite changes in medical technology and notwithstanding an increased emphasis on the importance of end-of-life decisionmaking, we have not retreated from this prohibition. Against this backdrop of history, tradition, and practice, we now turn to respondents' constitutional claim.

II

The Due Process Clause guarantees more than fair process, and the "liberty" it protects includes more than the absence of physical restraint. [citation omitted] The Clause also provides heightened protection against government interference with certain fundamental rights and liberty interests. [citation omitted] In a long line of cases, we have held that, in addition to the specific freedoms protected by the Bill of Rights, the "liberty" specially protected by the Due Process Clause includes the rights to marry, [ ]; to have children, [ ] to direct the education and upbringing of one's children [ ]; to marital privacy; to use contraception [ ]; to bodily integrity [ ], and to abortion [citations omitted]. We have also assumed, and strongly suggested, that the Due Process Clause protects the traditional right to refuse unwanted lifesaving medical treatment.

But we "have always been reluctant to expand the concept of substantive due process because guideposts for responsible decisionmaking in this unchartered area are scarce and open-ended." [ ]. By extending constitutional protection to an asserted right or liberty interest, we, to a great extent, place the matter outside the arena of public debate and legislative action. We must therefore "exercise the utmost care whenever we are asked to break new ground in this field," *ibid*, lest the liberty protected by the Due Process Clause be subtly transformed into the policy preferences of the members of this Court [ ].

Our established method of substantive-due-process analysis has two primary features: First, we have regularly observed that the Due Process Clause specially protects those fundamental rights and liberties which are, objectively "deeply rooted in this Nation's history and tradition, ..." so rooted in the traditions and conscience of our people as to be ranked as "fundamental", and "implicit in the concept of ordered liberty," such that "neither liberty nor justice would exist if they were sacrificed," [ ]. Second, we have required in substantive-due-process cases a "careful description" of the asserted fundamental liberty interest.

We now inquire whether this asserted right has any place in our Nation's traditions. Here, as discussed above [ ] we are confronted with a consistent and almost universal tradition that has long rejected the asserted right, and continues explicitly to reject it today, even for terminally ill, mentally competent adults. To hold for respondents, we would have to reverse centuries of legal doctrine and practice, and strike down the considered policy choice of almost every State. [ ]

Respondents contend, however, that the liberty interest they assert *is* consistent with this Court's substantive-due-process line of cases, if not with this Nation's history and practice. Pointing to *Casey* and *Cruzan*, respondents read our jurisprudence in this area as reflecting a general tradition of "self-sovereignty," [ ], and as teaching that the "liberty" protected by the Due Process Clause includes "basic and intimate exercises of personal autonomy,"[citations omitted]. According to respondents, our liberty jurisprudence, and the broad, individualistic principles it reflects, protects the "liberty of competent, terminally ill adults to make end-of-life decisions free of undue government interference." [ ]. The question presented in this case, however, is whether the protections of the Due Process Clause include a right to commit suicide with another's assistance. With this "careful description" of respondents' claim in mind, we turn to *Casey* and *Cruzan*.

* * *

Respondents contend that in *Cruzan* we "acknowledged that competent, dying persons have the right to direct the removal of life-sustaining medical treatment and thus hasten death," [ ] and that "the constitutional principle behind recognizing the patient's liberty to direct the withdrawal of artificial life support applies at least as strongly to the choice to hasten impending death by consuming lethal medication[.]". Similarly, the Court of Appeals concluded that "*Cruzan*, by recognizing a liberty interest that includes the refusal of artificial provision of life-sustaining food and water, necessarily recognized a liberty interest in hastening one's own death." [ ].

The right assumed in *Cruzan*, however, was not simply deduced from abstract concepts of personal autonomy. Given the common-law rule that forced medication was a battery, and the long legal tradition protecting the decision to refuse unwanted medical treatment, our assumption was entirely consistent with this Nation's history and constitutional traditions. The decision to commit suicide with the assistance of another may be just as personal and profound as the decision to refuse unwanted medical treatment, but it has never enjoyed similar legal protection. Indeed, the two acts are widely and reasonably regarded as quite distinct. [ ]. In *Cruzan* itself, we recognized that most States outlawed assisted suicide—and even more do today—and we certainly gave no intimation that the right to refuse unwanted medical treatment could be somehow transmuted into a right to assistance in committing suicide. [citation omitted].

Respondents also rely on *Casey*. There, the Court's opinion concluded that "the essential holding of *Roe* v. *Wade* should be retained and once again reaffirmed." *Casey*, 505 U.S. at 846. We held, first, that a woman has a right, before her fetus is viable, to an abortion "without undue interference from the State"; second, that States may restrict post-viability abortions, so long as exceptions are made to protect a woman's life and health; and third, that the State has legitimate interests throughout a pregnancy in protecting the health of the woman and the life of the unborn child. *Ibid*. In reaching this conclusion, the opinion discussed in some detail this Court's substantive-due-process tradition of interpreting the Due Process Clause to protect certain fundamental rights and "personal decisions relating to marriage, procreation, contraception, family relationships, child rearing, and education," and noted that many of those rights and liberties "involve the most intimate and personal choices a person may make in a lifetime." *Id.*, at 851.

"At the heart of liberty is the right to define one's own concept of existence, of meaning, of the universe, and of the mystery of human life. Beliefs about these matters could not define the attributes of personhood were they formed under compulsion of the State." *Casey*, 505 U.S. at 851.

* * * That many of the rights and liberties protected by the Due Process Clause sound in personal autonomy does not warrant the sweeping conclusion that any and all important, intimate, and personal decisions are so protected [citation omitted] and *Casey* did not suggest otherwise.

The history of the law's treatment of assisted suicide in this country has been and continues to be one of the rejection of nearly all efforts to permit it. That being the case, our decisions lead us to conclude that the asserted "right" to assistance in committing suicide is not a fundamental liberty interest protected by the Due Process Clause. The Constitution also requires, however, that Washington's assisted-suicide ban be rationally related to legitimate government interests. [ ] This requirement is unquestionably met here. As the court below recognized, Washington's assisted-suicide ban implicates a number of state interests. [ ]

First, Washington has an "unqualified interest in the preservation of human life." *Cruzan*, 497 U.S. at 282. The State's prohibition on assisted suicide, like all homicide laws, both reflects and advances its commitment to this interest. * * *

Respondents admit that "the State has a real interest in preserving the lives of those who can still contribute to society and enjoy life." [ ] The Court of Appeals also recognized Washington's interest in protecting life, but held that the "weight" of this interest depends on the "medical condition and the wishes of the person whose life is at stake." [ ]. Washington, however, has rejected this sliding-scale approach and, through its assisted-suicide ban, insists that all persons' lives, from beginning to end, regardless of physical or mental condition, are under the full protection of the law. [ ]

Those who attempt suicide—terminally ill or not—often suffer from depression or other mental disorders. New York Task Force 13–22, 126–128 (more than 95% of those who commit suicide had a major psychiatric illness at the time of death; among the terminally ill, uncontrolled pain is a "risk factor" because it contributes to depression.) * * * The New York Task Force, however, expressed its concern that, because depression is difficult to diagnose, physicians and medical professionals often fail to respond adequately to seriously ill patients' needs. [ ]. Thus, legal physician-assisted suicide could make it more difficult for the State to protect depressed or mentally ill persons, or those who are suffering from untreated pain, from suicidal impulses.

The State also has an interest in protecting the integrity and ethics of the medical profession. In contrast to the Court of Appeals' conclusion that "the integrity of the medical profession would [not] be threatened in any way by [physician-assisted suicide]," [ ], the American Medical Association, like many other medical and physicians' groups, has concluded that "physician-assisted suicide is fundamentally incompatible with the physician's role as healer." [citation omitted]. And physician-assisted suicide could, it is argued, undermine the trust that is essential to the doctor-patient relationship by blurring the time-honored line between healing and harming [ ].

Next, the State has an interest in protecting vulnerable groups—including the poor, the elderly, and disabled persons—from abuse, neglect, and mistakes. The Court of Appeals dismissed the State's concern that disadvantaged persons might be pressured into physician-assisted suicide as "ludicrous on its face." [ ] We have recognized, however, the real risk of subtle coercion and undue influence in end-of-life situations. [ ] Similarly, the New York Task Force warned that "legalizing physician-assisted suicide would pose profound risks to many individuals who are ill and vulnerable.... The risk of harm is greatest for the many individuals in our society whose autonomy and well-being are already compromised by poverty, lack of access to good medical care, advanced age, or membership in a stigmatized social group." [ ]

The State's interest here goes beyond protecting the vulnerable from coercion; it extends to protecting disabled and terminally ill people from prejudice, negative and inaccurate stereotypes, and "societal indifference." [ ]. The State's assisted-suicide ban reflects and reinforces its policy that the lives of terminally ill, disabled, and elderly people must be no less valued than the lives of the young and healthy, and that a seriously disabled person's suicidal impulses should be interpreted and treated the same way as anyone else's. [ ]

Finally, the State may fear that permitting assisted suicide will start it down the path to voluntary and perhaps even involuntary euthanasia. The Court of Appeals struck down Washington's assisted-suicide ban only "as applied to competent, terminally ill adults who wish to hasten their deaths by obtaining medication prescribed by their doctors." 79 F.3d, at 838. Washington insists, however, that the impact of the court's decision will not and cannot be so limited. [ ]. If suicide is protected as a matter of constitutional right, it is argued, "every man and woman in the United States must enjoy it." [ ]. The Court of Appeals' decision, and its expansive reasoning, provide ample support for the State's concerns. The court noted, for example, that the "decision of a duly appointed surrogate decision maker is for all legal purposes the decision of the patient himself," that "in some instances, the patient may be unable to self-administer the drugs and ... administration by the physician ... may be the only way the patient may be able to receive them," and that not only physicians, but also family members and loved ones, will inevitably participate in assisting suicide. [citations omitted]. Thus, it turns out that what is couched as a limited right to "physician-assisted suicide" is likely, in effect, a much broader license, which could prove extremely difficult to police and contain. Washington's ban on assisting suicide prevents such erosion.

* * *

We need not weigh exactly the relative strengths of these various interests. They are unquestionably important and legitimate, and Washington's ban on assisted suicide is at least reasonably related to their promotion and protection. We therefore hold that Wash[ington law] does not violate the Fourteenth Amendment, either on its face or "as applied to competent, terminally ill adults who wish to hasten their deaths by obtaining medication prescribed by their doctors." [ ].

Throughout the Nation, Americans are engaged in an earnest and profound debate about the morality, legality, and practicality of physician-assisted suicide. Our holding permits this debate to continue, as it should in a democratic society. The decision of the en banc Court of Appeals is reversed, and the case is remanded for further proceedings consistent with this opinion.

It is so ordered.

JUSTICE O'CONNOR, concurring [joined in part by Justices Ginsburg and Breyer].

Death will be different for each of us. For many, the last days will be spent in physical pain and perhaps the despair that accompanies physical deterioration and a loss of control of basic bodily and mental functions. Some will seek medication to alleviate that pain and other symptoms.

The Court frames the issue in this case as whether the Due Process Clause of the Constitution protects a "right to commit suicide which itself includes a right to assistance in doing so," and concludes that our Nation's history, legal traditions, and practices do not support the existence of such a right. I join the Court's opinions because I agree that there is no generalized right to "commit suicide." But respondents urge us to address the narrower question whether a mentally competent person who is experiencing great suffering has a constitutionally cognizable interest in controlling the circumstances of his or her imminent death. I see no need to reach that question in the context of the facial challenges to the New York and Washington laws at issue here. * * * The parties and *amici* agree that in these States a patient who is suffering from a terminal illness and who is experiencing great pain has no legal barriers to obtaining medication, from qualified physicians, to alleviate that suffering, even to the point of causing unconsciousness and hastening death. [ ] In this light, even assuming that we would recognize such an interest, I agree that the State's interests in protecting those who are not truly competent or facing imminent death, or those whose decisions to hasten death would not truly be voluntary, are sufficiently weighty to justify a prohibition against physician-assisted suicide.

Every one of us at some point may be affected by our own or a family member's terminal illness. There is no reason to think the democratic process will not strike the proper balance between the interests of terminally ill, mentally competent individuals who would seek to end their suffering and the State's interests in protecting those who might seek to end life mistakenly or under pressure. As the Court recognizes, States are presently undertaking extensive and serious evaluation of physician-assisted suicide and other related issues. [ ]. In such circumstances, "the ... challenging task of crafting appropriate procedures for safeguarding ... liberty interests is entrusted to the 'laboratory' of the States ... in the first instance." [ ].

In sum, there is no need to address the question whether suffering patients have a constitutionally cognizable interest in obtaining relief from the suffering that they may experience in the last days of their lives. There is no dispute that dying patients in Washington and New York can obtain palliative care, even when doing so would hasten their deaths. The difficulty in defining terminal illness and the risk that a dying patient's request for assistance in ending his or her life might not be truly voluntary justifies the prohibitions on assisted suicide we uphold here.

JUSTICE STEVENS, concurring in the judgments.

The Court ends its opinion with the important observation that our holding today is fully consistent with a continuation of the vigorous debate about the "morality, legality, and practicality of physician-assisted suicide" in a democratic society. [ ]. I write separately to make it clear that there is also room for further debate about the limits that the Constitution places on the power of the States to punish the practice.

I

The morality, legality, and practicality of capital punishment have been the subject of debate for many years. In 1976, this Court upheld the constitutionality of the practice in cases coming to us from Georgia, Florida, and Texas. In those cases we concluded that a State does have the power to place a lesser value on some lives than on others; there is no absolute requirement that a State treat all human life as having an equal right to preservation. Because the state legislatures had sufficiently narrowed the category of lives that the State could terminate, and had enacted special procedures to ensure that the defendant belonged in that limited category, we concluded that the statutes were not unconstitutional on their face. In later cases coming to us from each of those States, however, we found that some applications of the statutes were unconstitutional.

Today, the Court decides that Washington's statute prohibiting assisted suicide is not invalid "on its face," that is to say, in all or most cases in which it might be applied. That holding, however, does not foreclose the possibility that some applications of the statute might well be invalid.

As originally filed, this case presented a challenge to the Washington statute on its face and as it applied to three terminally ill, mentally competent patients and to four physicians who treat terminally ill patients. After the District Court issued its opinion holding that the statute placed an undue burden on the right to commit physician-assisted suicide, [ ] the three patients died. Although the Court of Appeals considered the constitutionality of the statute "as applied to the prescription of life-ending medication for use by terminally ill, competent adult patients who wish to hasten their deaths," [ ] the court did not have before it any individual plaintiff seeking to hasten her death or any doctor who was threatened with prosecution for assisting in the suicide of a particular patient; its analysis and eventual holding that the statute was unconstitutional was not limited to a particular set of plaintiffs before it.

The appropriate standard to be applied in cases making facial challenges to state statutes has been the subject of debate within this Court. [ ]. Upholding the validity of the federal Bail Reform Act of 1984, the Court stated in *United States* v. *Salerno,* 481 U.S. 739 (1987), that a "facial challenge to a legislative Act is, of course, the most difficult challenge to mount successfully, since the challenger must establish that no set of circumstances exists under which the Act would be valid." *Id.,* at 745. I do not believe the Court has ever actually applied such a strict standard, even in *Salerno* itself, and the Court does not appear to apply *Salerno* here. Nevertheless, the Court does conceive of respondents' claim as a facial challenge—addressing not the application of the statute to a particular set of plaintiffs before it, but the constitutionality of the statute's categorical prohibition against "aiding another person to attempt suicide." [ ] Accordingly, the Court requires the plaintiffs to show that the interest in liberty protected by the Fourteenth Amendment "includes a right to commit suicide which itself includes a right to assistance in doing so." [ ].

History and tradition provide ample support for refusing to recognize an open-ended constitutional right to commit suicide. Much more than the State's paternalistic interest in protecting the individual from the irrevocable consequences of an ill-advised decision motivated by temporary concerns is at stake. * * * Thus, I fully agree with the Court that the "liberty" protected by the Due Process Clause does not include a categorical "right to commit suicide which itself includes a right to assistance in doing so." [ ]

But just as our conclusion that capital punishment is not always unconstitutional did not preclude later decisions holding that it is sometimes impermissibly cruel, so is it equally clear that a decision upholding a general statutory prohibition of assisted suicide does not mean that every possible application of the statute would be valid. A State, like Washington, that has authorized the death penalty and thereby has concluded that the sanctity of human life does not require that it always be preserved, must acknowledge that there are situations in which an interest in hastening death is legitimate. Indeed, not only is that interest sometimes legitimate, I am also convinced that there are times when it is entitled to constitutional protection.

II

In *Cruzan* v. *Director, Mo. Dept. of Health,* 497 U.S. 261 (1990), the Court assumed that the interest in liberty protected by the Fourteenth Amendment encompassed the right of a terminally ill patient to direct the withdrawal of life-sustaining treatment. As the Court correctly observes today, that assumption "was not simply deduced from abstract concepts of personal autonomy." [ ]. Instead, it was supported by the common-law tradition protecting the individual's general right to refuse unwanted medical treatment. *Ibid.* We have recognized, however, that this common-law right to refuse treatment is neither absolute nor always sufficiently weighty to overcome valid countervailing state interests. As Justice Brennan pointed out in his *Cruzan* dissent, we have upheld legislation imposing punishment on persons refusing to be vaccinated [ ], and, as JUSTICE SCALIA pointed out in his concurrence, the State ordinarily has the right to interfere with an attempt to commit suicide by, for example, forcibly placing a bandage on a self-inflicted wound to stop the flow of blood. * * *

Cruzan, however, was not the normal case. Given the irreversible nature of her illness and the progressive character of her suffering, Nancy Cruzan's interest in refusing medical care was incidental to her more basic interest in controlling the manner and timing of her death. In finding that her best interests would be served by cutting off the nourishment that kept her alive, the trial court did more than simply vindicate Cruzan's interest in refusing medical treatment; the court, in essence, authorized affirmative conduct that would hasten her death. When this Court reviewed the case and upheld Missouri's requirement that there be clear and convincing evidence establishing Nancy Cruzan's intent to have life-sustaining nourishment withdrawn, it made two important assumptions: (1) that there was a "liberty interest" in refusing unwanted treatment protected by the Due Process Clause; and (2) that this liberty interest did not "end the inquiry" because it might be outweighed by relevant state interests. [ ]. I agree with both of those assumptions, but I insist that the source of Nancy Cruzan's right to refuse treatment was not just a common-law rule. Rather, this right is an aspect of a far broader and more basic concept of freedom that is even older than the common law. This freedom embraces, not merely a person's right to refuse a particular kind of unwanted treatment, but also her interest in dignity, and in determining the character of the memories that will survive long after her death. In recognizing that the State's interests did not outweigh Nancy Cruzan's liberty interest in refusing medical treatment, *Cruzan* rested not simply on the common-law right to refuse medical treatment, but—at least implicitly—on the even more fundamental right to make this "deeply personal decision."

* * *

The *Cruzan* case demonstrated that some state intrusions on the right to decide how death will be encountered are also intolerable. The now-deceased plaintiffs in this action may in fact have had a liberty interest even stronger than Nancy Cruzan's because, not only were they terminally ill, they were suffering constant and severe pain. Avoiding intolerable pain and the indignity of living one's final days incapacitated and in agony is certainly "at the heart of [the] liberty ... to define one's own concept of existence, of meaning, of the universe, and of the mystery of human life." *Casey,* 505 U.S. at 851.

While I agree with the Court that *Cruzan* does not decide the issue presented by these cases, *Cruzan* did give recognition, not just to vague, unbridled notions of autonomy, but to the more specific interest in making decisions about how to confront an imminent death. Although there is no absolute right to physician-assisted suicide, *Cruzan* makes it clear that some individuals who no longer have the option of deciding whether to live or to die because they are already on the threshold of death have a constitutionally protected interest that may outweigh the State's interest in preserving life at all costs. The liberty interest at stake in a case like this differs from, and is stronger than, both the common-law right to refuse medical treatment and the unbridled interest in deciding whether to live or die. It is an interest in deciding how, rather than whether, a critical threshold shall be crossed.

III

The state interests supporting a general rule banning the practice of physician-assisted suicide do not have the same force in all cases. First and foremost of these interests is the " 'unqualified interest in the preservation of human life,' " [ ] which is equated with " 'the sanctity of life,' " [ ]. That interest not only justifies—it commands—maximum protection of every individual's interest in remaining alive, which in turn commands the same protection for decisions about whether to commence or to terminate life-support systems or to administer pain medication that may hasten death. Properly viewed, however, this interest is not a collective interest that should always outweigh the interests of a person who because of pain, incapacity, or sedation finds her life intolerable, but rather, an aspect of individual freedom.

* * *

The final major interest asserted by the State is its interest in preserving the traditional integrity of the medical profession. The fear is that a rule permitting physicians to assist in suicide is inconsistent with the perception that they serve their patients solely as healers. But for some patients, it would be a physician's refusal to dispense medication to ease their suffering and make their death tolerable and dignified that would be inconsistent with the healing role. * * *

CONSERVATORSHIP OF WENDLAND

Supreme Court of California, 2001.
26 Cal.4th 519, 110 Cal.Rptr.2d 412, 28 P.3d 151.

WERDEGAR, J.

In this case we consider whether a conservator of the person may withhold artificial nutrition and hydration from a conscious conservatee who is not terminally ill, comatose, or in a persistent vegetative state, and who has not left formal instructions for health care or appointed an agent or surrogate for health care decisions. Interpreting Probate Code section 2355 in light of the relevant provisions of the California Constitution, we conclude a conservator may not withhold artificial nutrition and hydration from such a person absent clear and convincing evidence the conservator's decision is in accordance with either the conservatee's own wishes or best interest. * * *

I. FACTS AND PROCEDURAL HISTORY

On September 29, 1993, Robert Wendland rolled his truck at high speed in a solo accident while driving under the influence of alcohol. The accident injured Robert's brain, leaving him conscious yet severely disabled, both mentally and physically, and dependent on artificial nutrition and hydration. Two years later Rose Wendland, Robert's wife and conservator, proposed to direct his physician to remove his feeding tube and allow him to die. Florence Wendland and Rebekah Vinson (respectively Robert's mother and sister) objected to the conservator's decision. This proceeding arose under the provisions of the Probate Code authorizing courts to settle such disputes.

Following the accident, Robert remained in a coma, totally unresponsive, for several months. During this period Rose visited him daily, often with their children, and authorized treatment as necessary to maintain his health.

Robert eventually regained consciousness. His subsequent medical history is described in a comprehensive medical evaluation later submitted to the court. According to the report, Rose "first noticed signs of responsiveness sometime in late 1994 or early 1995 and alerted [Robert's] physicians and nursing staff." Intensive therapy followed. Robert's "cognitive responsiveness was observed to improve over a period of several months such that by late spring of 1995 the family and most of his health care providers agreed that he was inconsistently interacting with his environment. A video recording of [Robert] in July 1995 demonstrated clear, though inconsistent, interaction with his environment in response to simple commands. At his highest level of function between February and July, 1995, Robert was able to do such things as throw and catch a ball, operate an electric wheelchair with assistance, turn pages, draw circles, draw an 'R' and perform two-step commands." For example, "[h]e was able to respond appropriately to the command 'close your eyes and open them when I say the number 3.' . . . He could choose a requested color block out of four color blocks. He could set the right peg in a pegboard. Augmented communication was met with inconsistent success. He remained unable to vocalize. Eye blinking was successfully used as a communication mode for a while, however no consistent method of communication was developed."

Despite improvements made in therapy, Robert remained severely disabled, both mentally and physically. The same medical report summarized his continuing impairments as follows: "severe cognitive impairment that is not possible to fully appreciate due to the concurrent motor and communication impairments ... "; "maladaptive behavior characterized by agitation, aggressiveness and non-compliance"; "severe paralysis on the right and moderate paralysis on the left"; "severely impaired communication, without compensatory augmentative communication system"; "severe swallowing dysfunction, dependent upon non-oral enteric tube feeding for nutrition and hydration"; "incontinence of bowel and bladder"; "moderate spasticity"; "mild to moderate contractures"; "general dysphoria"; "recurrent medical illnesses, including pneumonia, bladder infections, sinusitis"; and "dental issues."

After Robert regained consciousness and while he was undergoing therapy, Rose authorized surgery three times to replace dislodged feeding tubes. When physicians sought her permission a fourth time, she declined. She discussed the decision with her daughters and with Robert's brother Michael, all of whom believed that Robert would not have approved the procedure even if necessary to sustain his life. Rose also discussed the decision with Robert's treating physician, Dr. Kass, other physicians, and the hospital's ombudsman, all of whom apparently supported her decision. Dr. Kass, however, inserted a nasogastric feeding tube to keep Robert alive pending input from the hospital's ethics committee.

Eventually, the 20–member ethics committee unanimously approved Rose's decision. In the course of their deliberations, however, the committee did not speak with Robert's mother or sister. Florence learned, apparently through an anonymous telephone call, that Dr. Kass planned to remove Robert's feeding tube. Florence and Rebekah applied for a temporary restraining order to bar him from so doing, and the court granted the motion ex parte.

Rose immediately thereafter petitioned for appointment as Robert's conservator. In the petition, she asked the court to determine that Robert lacked the capacity to give informed consent for medical treatment and to confirm her authority "to withdraw and/or withhold medical treatment and/or life-sustaining treatment, including, but not limited to, withholding nutrition and hydration." Florence and Rebekah (hereafter sometimes objectors) opposed the petition. After a hearing, the court appointed Rose as conservator but reserved judgment on her request for authority to remove Robert's feeding tube. The court ordered the conservator to continue the current plan of physical therapy for 60 days and then to report back to the court. The court also visited Robert in the hospital.

After the 60–day period elapsed without significant improvement in Robert's condition, the conservator renewed her request for authority to remove his feeding tube. The objectors asked the trial court to appoint independent counsel for the conservatee. The trial court declined, and the Court of Appeal summarily denied the objectors' petition for writ of mandate. We granted review and transferred the case to the Court of

Appeal, which then directed the trial court to appoint counsel. [ ] Appointed counsel, exercising his independent judgment [ ] decided to support the conservator's decision. * * *

* * *

The trial generated the evidence set out above. The testifying physicians agreed that Robert would not likely experience further cognitive recovery. Dr. Kass, Robert's treating physician, testified that, to the highest degree of medical certainty, Robert would never be able to make medical treatment decisions, walk, talk, feed himself, eat, drink, or control his bowel and bladder functions. Robert was able, however, according to Dr. Kass, to express "certain desires. . . . Like if he's getting tired in therapy or if he wants to quit therapy, he's usually very adamant about that. He'll either strike out or he'll refuse to perform the task." Dr. Kobrin, Robert's neurologist, testified that Robert recognized certain caregivers and would allow only specific caregivers to bathe and help him. * * *

* * *

Robert's wife, brother and daughter recounted preaccident statements Robert had made about his attitude towards life-sustaining health care. Robert's wife recounted specific statements on two occasions. The first occasion was Rose's decision whether to turn off a respirator sustaining the life of her father, who was near death from gangrene. Rose recalls Robert saying: "I would never want to live like that, and I wouldn't want my children to see me like that and look at the hurt you're going through as an adult seeing your father like that." On cross-examination, Rose acknowledged Robert said on this occasion that Rose's father "wouldn't want to live like a vegetable" and "wouldn't want to live in a comatose state."

After his father-in-law's death, Robert developed a serious drinking problem. After a particular incident, Rose asked Michael, Robert's brother, to talk to him. When Robert arrived home the next day he was angry to see Michael there, interfering in what he considered a private family matter. Rose remembers Michael telling Robert: "I'm going to get a call from Rosie one day, and you're going to be in a terrible accident." ROBERT REPLIED: "If that ever happened to me, you know what my feelings are. Don't let that happen to me. Just let me go. Leave me alone." Robert's brother Michael testified about the same conversation. Michael told Robert: "[Y]ou're drinking; you're going to get drunk. . . . You're either going to go out and kill yourself or kill someone else, or you're going to end up in the hospital like a vegetable—laying in bed just like a vegetable." Michael remembers Robert saying in response, "Mike, whatever you do[,] don't let that happen. Don't let them do that to me." Robert's daughter Katie remembers him saying on this occasion that "if he could not be a provider for his family, if he could not do all the things that he enjoyed doing, just enjoying the outdoors, just basic things, feeding himself, talking, communicating, if he could not do those things, he would not want to live.''

Based on all the evidence, the court issued a second decision setting out its findings of fact and conclusions of law. Specifically, the court found the conservator "ha[d] not met her duty and burden to show by clear and convincing evidence that conservatee Robert Wendland, who is not in a persistent vegetative state nor suffering from a terminal illness would, under the circumstances, want to die. Conservator has likewise not met her burden of establishing that the withdrawal of artificially delivered nutrition and hydration is commensurate with conservatee's best interests, consistent with California Law as embodied in Barber, [*supra*, 147 Cal.App.3d 1006] and Drabick, supra [200 Cal.App.3d 185].'' Based on these findings, the court granted the objectors' motion for judgment [ ], thus denying the conservator's request for confirmation of her proposal to withdraw treatment. The court also found the conservator had acted in good faith and would be permitted to remain in that office. Nevertheless, the court limited her powers by ordering that she would "have no authority to direct ... [any] health care provider to remove the conservatee's life sustaining medical treatment in the form of withholding nutrition and hydration.'' [ ]

The conservator appealed this decision. The Court of Appeal reversed. In the Court of Appeal's view, "[t]he trial court properly placed the burden of producing evidence on [the conservator] and properly applied a clear and convincing evidence standard. However, the court erred in requiring [the conservator] to prove that [the conservatee], while competent, expressed a desire to die in the circumstances and in substituting its own judgment concerning [the conservatee's] best interests.... '' Instead, the trial court's role was "merely to satisfy itself that the conservator had considered the conservatee's best interests in good faith.... '' This limited judicial role, the Court of Appeal concluded, was mandated by section 2355 [ ]. While acknowledging the trial court had already found the conservator had acted in good faith, the Court of Appeal nevertheless declined to enter judgment for the conservator. Instead, the court remanded to permit the objectors to present any evidence rebutting the conservator's case-in-chief. Finally, recognizing that an amended version of section 2355 [ ] might "be a factor upon remand,'' the court determined the new law did not affect the outcome. We granted review of this decision.

II. Discussion

A. The Relevant Legal Principles

* * *

1. Constitutional and common law principles

One relatively certain principle is that a competent adult has the right to refuse medical treatment, even treatment necessary to sustain life. The Legislature has cited this principle to justify legislation governing medical care decisions [ ], and courts have invoked it as a starting point for analysis, even in cases examining the rights of incompetent persons and the duties of surrogate decision makers [ ]. This case requires us to look beyond the rights of a competent person to the rights of incompetent conservatees and the duties of conservators, but the principle just mentioned is a logical place to begin.

That a competent person has the right to refuse treatment is a statement both of common law and of state constitutional law. * * *

The Courts of Appeal have found another source for the same right in the California Constitution's privacy clause. [ ] The court in *Bartling v. Superior Court* (1984) [ ] held that a competent adult with serious, probably incurable illnesses was entitled to have life-support equipment disconnected over his physicians' objection even though that would hasten his death. "The right of a competent adult patient to refuse medical treatment," the court explained, "has its origins in the constitutional right of privacy. * * *

* * *

Federal law has little to say about the competent person's right to refuse treatment, but what it does say is not to the contrary. The United States Supreme Court spoke provisionally to the point in *Cruzan v. Director, Missouri Dept. of Health* (1990) [ ]. * * * While the case thus did not present the issue, the court nevertheless acknowledged that "a competent person['s] . . . constitutionally protected liberty interest in refusing unwanted medical treatment may be inferred" [ ] from prior decisions holding that state laws requiring persons to submit to involuntary medical procedures must be justified by countervailing state interests. The "logic" of such cases would, the court thought, implicate a competent person's liberty interest in refusing artificially delivered food and water essential to life. [ ] Whether any given state law infringed such a liberty interest, however, would have to be determined by balancing the liberty interest against the relevant state interests, in particular the state's interest in preserving life. [ ]

In view of these authorities, the competent adult's right to refuse medical treatment may be safely considered established, at least in California.

The same right survives incapacity, in a practical sense, if exercised while competent pursuant to a law giving that act lasting validity. For some time, California law has given competent adults the power to leave formal directions for health care in the event they later become incompetent; over time, the Legislature has afforded ever greater scope to that power. * * *

Effective July 1, 2000, the Health Care Decisions Law [ ] gives competent adults extremely broad power to direct all aspects of their health care in the event they become incompetent. The new law, which repeals the former Natural Death Act and amends the durable power of attorney law, draws heavily from the Uniform Health–Care Decisions

Act adopted in 1993 by the National Conference of Commissioners on Uniform State Laws. [ ] Briefly, and as relevant here, the new law permits a competent person to execute an advance directive about "any aspect" of health care. [ ] Among other things, a person may direct that life-sustaining treatment be withheld or withdrawn under conditions specified by the person and not limited to terminal illness, permanent coma, or persistent vegetative state. A competent person may still use a power of attorney for health care to give an agent the power to make health care decisions [ ], but a patient may also orally designate a surrogate to make such decisions by personally informing the patient's supervising health care provider. [ ] Under the new law, agents and surrogates are required to make health care decisions "in accordance with the principal's individual health care instructions, if any, and other wishes to the extent known to the agent." [ ]

All of the laws just mentioned merely give effect to the decision of a competent person, in the form either of instructions for health care or the designation of an agent or surrogate for health care decisions. Such laws may accurately be described, as the Legislature has described them, as a means to respect personal autonomy by giving effect to competent decisions * * *.

In contrast, decisions made by conservators typically derive their authority from a different basis—the *parens patriae* power of the state to protect incompetent persons. Unlike an agent or a surrogate for health care, who is voluntarily appointed by a competent person, a conservator is appointed by the court because the conservatee "has been adjudicated to lack the capacity to make health care decisions." * * *

* * *

2. *Section 2355*

The ultimate focus of our analysis, as mentioned at the outset, must be section 2355, the statute under which the conservator claims the authority to end the conservatee's life. The statute's history indicates that the Law Revision Commission, which drafted the current version, was aware of and intended to incorporate some, but not all, of the *Drabick* [ ] court's construction of the former statute.

As originally enacted in 1979, and at the time the lower courts ruled in this case, section 2355 provided: "If the conservatee has been adjudicated to lack the capacity to give informed consent for medical treatment, the conservator has the exclusive authority to give consent for such medical treatment to be performed on the conservatee as the conservator in good faith based on medical advice determines to be necessary and the conservator may require the conservatee to receive such medical treatment, whether or not the conservatee objects." [ ]

* * *

B.   The Present Case

This background illuminates the parties' arguments, which reduce in essence to this: The conservator has claimed the power under section 2355, as she interprets it, to direct the conservatee's health care providers to cease providing artificial nutrition and hydration. In opposition, the objectors have contended the statute violates the conservatee's rights to privacy and life under the facts of this case if the conservator's interpretation of the statute is correct.

* * *

1.   The primary standard: a decision in accordance with the conservatee's wishes

The conservator asserts she offered sufficient evidence at trial to satisfy the primary statutory standard, which contemplates a decision "in accordance with the conservatee's ... wishes.... " [ ]. The trial court, however, determined the evidence on this point was insufficient. The conservator did "not [meet] her duty and burden," the court expressly found, "to show by clear and convincing evidence that [the] conservatee ... , who is not in a persistent vegetative state nor suffering from a terminal illness would, under the circumstances, want to die." To be sure, the court made this finding under former section 2355 rather than the current version—and not because the former statute expressly called for such a finding but under the belief that case law required it. [ ] But the finding's relevance under the new statute cannot easily be dismissed: The new statute expressly requires the conservator to follow the conservatee's wishes, if known. [ ]

The conservator argues the Legislature understood and intended that the low preponderance of the evidence standard would apply. Certainly this was the Law Revision Commission's understanding. * * *

The objectors, in opposition, argue that section 2355 would be unconstitutional if construed to permit a conservator to end the life of a conscious conservatee based on a finding by the low preponderance of the evidence standard that the latter would not want to live. We see no basis for holding the statute unconstitutional on its face. We do, however, find merit in the objectors' argument. We therefore construe the statute to minimize the possibility of its unconstitutional application by requiring clear and convincing evidence of a conscious conservatee's wish to refuse life-sustaining treatment when the conservator relies on that asserted wish to justify withholding life-sustaining treatment. This construction does not entail a deviation from the language of the statute and constitutes only a partial rejection of the Law Revision Commission's understanding that the preponderance of the evidence standard would apply; we see no constitutional reason to apply the higher evidentiary standard to the majority of health care decisions made by conservators not contemplating a conscious conservatee's death. * * *

* * *

Notwithstanding the foregoing, one must acknowledge that the primary standard for decisionmaking set out in section 2355 does articulate what will in some cases form a constitutional basis for a conservator's decision to end the life of a conscious patient: deference to the patient's own wishes. This standard also appears in the new provisions governing decisions by agents and surrogates designated by competent adults. [ ] As applied in that context, the requirement that decisions be made "in accordance with the principal's individual health care instructions ... and other wishes" merely respects the principal-agent relationship and gives effect to the properly expressed wishes of a competent adult. Because a competent adult may refuse life-sustaining treatment [ ] it follows that an agent properly and voluntarily designated by the principal may refuse treatment on the principal's behalf unless, of course, such authority is revoked. [ ] providing various ways in which the authority of an agent for health care decisions may be revoked or the agent's instructions countermanded].)

The only apparent purpose of requiring conservators to make decisions in accordance with the conservatee's wishes, when those wishes are known, is to enforce the fundamental principle of personal autonomy. The same requirement, as applied to agents and surrogates freely designated by competent persons, enforces the principles of agency. A reasonable person presumably will designate for such purposes only a person in whom the former reposes the highest degree of confidence. A conservator, in contrast, is *not* an agent of the conservatee, and unlike a freely designated agent cannot be presumed to have special knowledge of the conservatee's health care wishes. A person with "sufficient capacity ... to form an intelligent preference" may nominate his or her own conservator [ ], but the nomination is not binding because the appointment remains "solely in the discretion of the court" [ ]. Furthermore, while statutory law gives preference to spouses and other persons related to the conservatee [ ], who might know something of the conservatee's health care preferences, the law also permits the court in its sole discretion to appoint unrelated persons and even public conservators (*ibid.*). While it may be constitutionally permissible to assume that an agent freely designated by a formerly competent person to make all health care decisions, including life-ending ones, will resolve such questions "in accordance with the principal's ... wishes" [ ], one cannot apply the same assumption to conservators and conservatees. For this reason, when the legal premise of a conservator's decision to end a conservatee's life by withholding medical care is that the conservatee would refuse such care, to apply a high standard of proof will help to ensure the reliability of the decision.

The function of a standard of proof is to instruct the fact finder concerning the degree of confidence our society deems necessary in the correctness of factual conclusions for a particular type of adjudication, to allocate the risk of error between the litigants, and to indicate the relative importance attached to the ultimate decision. [ ]. Thus, "the standard of proof may depend upon the 'gravity of the consequences that would result from an erroneous determination of the issue involved.' "[ ] The default standard of proof in civil cases is the preponderance of the evidence. [ ] Nevertheless, courts have applied the clear and convincing evidence standard when necessary to protect important rights.

We applied the clear and convincing evidence standard * * * to ensure that a conservator's decision to authorize sterilization of a developmentally disabled conservatee was truly in the latter's best interests. We have also applied the clear and convincing evidence standard to findings necessary to terminate parental rights [citations omitted] and to findings supporting the discipline of judges [ ]. The Courts of Appeal have required clear and convincing evidence of a person's inability to provide for his or her personal needs as a prerequisite to the appointment of a conservator and of a conservatee's incompetence to accept or reject treatment as a prerequisite to permitting involuntary electroconvulsive therapy [ ]. Similarly, the United States Supreme Court has applied the clear and convincing evidence standard in cases implicating fundamental liberty interests protected by the Fourteenth Amendment, such as proceedings to terminate parental rights [ ], to commit to a mental hospital [ ], and to deport [ ].

In this case, the importance of the ultimate decision and the risk of error are manifest. So too should be the degree of confidence required in the necessary findings of fact. The ultimate decision is whether a conservatee lives or dies, and the risk is that a conservator, claiming statutory authority to end a conscious conservatee's life "in accordance with the conservatee's ... wishes" [ ] by withdrawing artificial nutrition and hydration, will make a decision with which the conservatee subjectively disagrees and which subjects the conservatee to starvation, dehydration and death. This would represent the gravest possible affront to a conservatee's state constitutional right to privacy, in the sense of freedom from unwanted bodily intrusions, and to life. While the practical ability to make autonomous health care decisions does not survive incompetence, the ability to perceive unwanted intrusions may. Certainly it is possible, as the conservator here urges, that an incompetent and uncommunicative but conscious conservatee might perceive the efforts to keep him alive as unwanted intrusion and the withdrawal of those efforts as welcome release. But the decision to treat is reversible. The decision to withdraw treatment is not. The role of a high evidentiary standard in such a case is to adjust the risk of error to favor the less perilous result. The high court has aptly explained the benefits of a high evidentiary standard in a similar context: "An erroneous decision not to terminate results in a maintenance of the status quo; the possibility of subsequent developments such as advancements in medical science, the discovery of new evidence regarding the patient's intent, changes in the law, or simply the unexpected death of the patient despite the administration of life-sustaining treatment at least create the potential that a wrong decision will eventually be corrected or its impact mitigated. An erroneous decision to withdraw life-sustaining treatment, however, is not susceptible of correction." [citations omitted]

In conclusion, to interpret section 2355 to permit a conservator to withdraw artificial nutrition and hydration from a conscious conservatee based on a finding, by a mere preponderance of the evidence, that the conservatee would refuse treatment creates a serious risk that the law will be unconstitutionally applied in some cases, with grave injury to fundamental rights. Under these circumstances, we may properly ask whether the statute may be construed in a way that mitigates the risk. * * *

We base our decision on California law. It is nevertheless worth mentioning that no decision of which we are aware has approved a conservator's or guardian's proposal to withdraw artificial nutrition and hydration from a conscious conservatee or ward.

The highest courts of three other states have spoken to the matter. Of these decisions, *In re Martin*, *supra*, 538 N.W.2d 399, is most like the case before us. Conservatee Michael Martin, like the conservatee here, suffered a head injury in an automobile accident that left him minimally conscious, unable to walk or talk, and dependent on artificial nutrition and hydration. At his highest level of functioning, Michael could move his leg or arm in response to a therapist's request and move his head in response to questions seeking a yes or no answer. On one occasion he indicated "no" in response to the question whether there were ever times when he felt he did not want to go on living; the witnesses, however, disagreed about the consistency and significance of Michael's responses to questions. [ ] The Supreme Court of Michigan, applying that state's common law, did not permit the conservator, Michael's wife, to withdraw artificial nutrition and hydration because clear and convincing evidence did not show he had expressed a desire to refuse such treatment under his present circumstances. The court adopted the clear and convincing standard for essentially the same reasons we do so here, namely, to ensure that a decision to refuse treatment drawing its legal justification from the conservatee's right to make autonomous medical decisions actually enjoys the conservatee's approval [ ], and to impose the risk of an erroneous decision on those seeking to withdraw treatment in view of the decision's grave consequences [ ]. * * *

The Supreme Courts of Wisconsin and New Jersey have also refused permission, under their own states' common law, to withhold artificial nutrition and hydration from incompetent but conscious patients. * * *

* * *

In the case before us, the trial court found that the conservator failed to show "by clear and convincing evidence that conservatee Robert Wendland, who is not in a persistent vegetative state nor suffering from a terminal illness would, under the circumstances, want to die." The conservator does not appear to challenge the trial court's finding on this point; her challenge, rather, is to the trial court's understanding of the law. For these reasons, we need not review the sufficiency of the evidence to support the finding. Nevertheless, given the exceptional circumstances of this case, we note that the finding appears to be correct.

* * *

2. *The best interest standard*

Having rejected the conservator's argument that withdrawing artificial hydration and nutrition would have been "in accordance with the conservatee's . . . wishes" [ ], we must next consider her contention that the same action would have been proper under the fallback best interest standard. Under that standard, "the conservator shall make the decision in accordance with the conservator's determination of the conservatee's best interest. In determining the conservatee's best interest, the conservator shall consider the conservatee's personal values to the extent known to the conservator." [ ] The trial court, as noted, ruled the conservator had the burden of establishing that the withdrawal of artificially delivered nutrition and hydration was in the conservatee's best interest, and had not met that burden.

Here, as before, the conservator argues that the trial court applied too high a standard of proof. This follows, she contends, from section 2355, which gives her as conservator "the *exclusive* authority" to give consent for such medical treatment as she "in good faith based on medical advice determines to be necessary" [ ] * * *. Based on these statements, the conservator argues the trial court has no power other than to verify that she has made the decision for which the Probate Code expressly calls: a "good faith" decision "based on medical advice" and "consider[ing] the conservatee's personal values" whether treatment is "necessary" in the conservatee's "best interest." [ ] The trial court, as noted, rejected the conservator's assessment of the conservatee's best interest but nevertheless found by clear and convincing evidence that she had acted "in good faith, based on medical evidence and after consideration of the conservatee's best interests, including his likely wishes, based on his previous statements." This finding, the conservator concludes, should end the litigation as a matter of law in her favor.

The conservator's understanding of section 2355 is not correct. To be sure, the statute provides that "the conservator shall make the decision in accordance with *the conservator's determination* of the conservatee's best interest." [ ] But the conservator herself concedes the court must be able to review her decision for abuse of discretion. This much, at least, follows from the conservator's status as an officer of the court subject to judicial supervision. While the assessment of a conservatee's best interest belongs in the first instance to the conservator, this does not mean the court must invariably defer to the conservator regardless of the evidence.

In the exceptional case where a conservator proposes to end the life of a conscious but incompetent conservatee, we believe the same factor that principally justifies applying the clear and convincing evidence standard to a determination of the conservatee's wishes also justifies applying that standard to a determination of the conservatee's best interest: The decision threatens the conservatee's fundamental rights to privacy and life. * * *

We need not in this case attempt to define the extreme factual predicates that, if proved by clear and convincing evidence, might support a conservator's decision that withdrawing life support would be in the best interest of a conscious conservatee. Here, the conservator offered no basis for such a finding other than her own subjective judgment that the conservatee did not enjoy a satisfactory quality of life and legally insufficient evidence to the effect that he would have wished to die. On this record, the trial court's decision was correct.

III.   CONCLUSION

For the reasons set out above, we conclude the superior court correctly required the conservator to prove, by clear and convincing evidence, either that the conservatee wished to refuse life-sustaining treatment or that to withhold such treatment would have been in his best interest; lacking such evidence, the superior court correctly denied the conservator's request for permission to withdraw artificial hydration and nutrition. We emphasize, however, that the clear and convincing evidence standard does not apply to the vast majority of health care decisions made by conservators under section 2355. Only the decision to withdraw life-sustaining treatment, because of its effect on a conscious conservatee's fundamental rights, justifies imposing that high standard of proof. Therefore, our decision today affects only a narrow class of persons: conscious conservatees who have not left formal directions for health care and whose conservators propose to withhold life-sustaining treatment for the purpose of causing their conservatees' deaths. Our conclusion does not affect permanently unconscious patients, including those who are comatose or in a persistent vegetative state [ ], persons who have left legally cognizable instructions for health care [ ], persons who have designated agents or other surrogates for health care [ ], or conservatees for whom conservators have made medical decisions other than those intended to bring about the death of a conscious conservatee.

The decision of the Court of Appeal is reversed.

Notes

1) *Bowen v. American Hosp. Ass'n* was decided in the wake of *Baby Boy Doe* wherein the Indiana Supreme Court refused to intervene on behalf of a newborn who was born with Down's Syndrome and a tracheoesophageal fistula. His parents refused to authorize surgery for the latter condition solely on the basis of his Down's Syndrome. Lawyers for the hospital were prepared to appeal to the U.S. Supreme Court, but the baby died in the meantime. Advocates for the developmentally disabled were vocal in their objections. The Department of Health and Human Services, enlisted to correct the injustice, looked to Section 504 of the Rehabilitation Act of 1974, 29 USCA § 794, to prohibit organiza-

tions receiving federal funds from discriminating against handicapped infants. Emergency regulations were authorized by the Secretary of DHHS but were challenged by the American Academy of Pediatrics on procedural grounds. See *AAP v. Heckler*, 561 F.Supp. 395 (1983). Thereafter, the procedural hurdles were cleared and final regulations to the same effect were issued. The final regulations required state child protection agencies to investigate cases of non-treatment of seriously ill newborns. *Bowen* challenged those regulations, and again concluded that the regulations were improperly promulgated. A compromise position was finally reached in what would become the Child Abuse Amendments of 1984. Accordingly, receipt of federal funds thereafter required that states develop procedures for preventing the medical neglect, defined as the "withholding of medically indicated treatment," of handicapped newborns.

2) One option available to the parents following *Cruzan v. Director, Missouri Department of Health* was to move Nancy to a facility in a state that adopted a standard that was less stringent than Missouri's "clear and convincing evidence" standard. Instead, however, the trial court took additional evidence from Nancy's family and friends, sufficient to satisfy the standard, that amply demonstrated she would not want to continue nutrition under these circumstances. The guardians were instructed to discontinued the tube feeding, and Nancy Cruzan died a short time later.

3) The Patient Self–Determination Act was enacted in 1990 as part of a Omnibus Reconciliation Act. This federal statute [42 USCA § 1395cc(a)(1)(f)(1)(A)] applies to hospitals, HMO's, skilled nursing facilities, home health agencies and hospice programs that receive federal funding. The Act requires that patients be provided with written information concerning their rights to accept or refuse medical treatment, and their rights to formulate advance directives in accordance with their state laws. All states make provisions for living wills or health care proxies, and require health care facilities to honor the directives set forth in a properly executed instrument.

4) *Vacco v. Quill*, 521 U.S. 793, 117 S.Ct. 2293, 138 L.Ed.2d 834 (1997), the companion to *Washington v. Glucksberg*, was brought as an equal protection challenge to a New York law that makes it a criminal offense to aid another in the commission of suicide, but allows removal of life support systems. The Supreme Court, in upholding the New York law, held there was a legitimate distinction between competent individuals who are in the latter stages of a terminal illness and hasten their death by removal of life-sustaining equipment, and competent individuals who seek to take their lives with drugs prescribed for that purpose. Implicitly the Court reinforced the idea that there is a difference between allowing a patient to die and helping that patient to die. *Washington v. Glucksberg* [brought in the lower court as *Compassion in Dying*, 850 F.Supp. 1454 (W.D. Wash 1994)] emphasized the need to protect the vulnerable from coercion and the elderly and disabled from a coercive path toward involuntary euthanasia.

5) *Conservatorship of Wendland* raises the next and inevitable question: what to do with patients who lack decisional capacity. Wendland was not unconscious, not terminally ill, not comatose and not in a persistent vegetative state. He also could not speak for himself, and left no instructions by way of advance directives. After three operations to replace a dislodged feeding tube, his wife/conservator eventually recommended in good faith that artificial nutrition and hydration be withheld. A 20–member hospital ethics committee supported the conservator's decision, but had not considered the contrary opinions of Wendland's mother and sister. The trial court denied the conservator's request as it applied the clear-and-convincing-evidence standard and found the evidence lacking. Would the decision have been different if the family was all in agreement?

SECTION C.   DOMESTIC AND SEXUAL VIOLENCE

UNITED STATES v. MORRISON

Supreme Court of the United States, 2000.
529 U.S. 598, 120 S.Ct. 1740, 146 L.Ed.2d 658.

CHIEF JUSTICE REHNQUIST delivered the opinion of the Court.

In these cases we consider the constitutionality of 42 U.S.C. § 13981, which provides a federal civil remedy for the victims of gender-motivated violence. The United States Court of Appeals for the Fourth Circuit, sitting en banc, struck down § 13981 because it concluded that Congress lacked constitutional authority to enact the section's civil remedy. * * *

I

Petitioner Christy Brzonkala enrolled at Virginia Polytechnic Institute (Virginia Tech) in the fall of 1994. In September of that year, Brzonkala met respondents Antonio Morrison and James Crawford, who were both students at Virginia Tech and members of its varsity football team. Brzonkala alleges that, within 30 minutes of meeting Morrison and Crawford, they assaulted and repeatedly raped her. After the attack, Morrison allegedly told Brzonkala, "You better not have any ... diseases." [ ]. In the months following the rape, Morrison also allegedly announced in the dormitory's dining room that he "liked" to get girls drunk and.... ". The omitted portions, quoted verbatim in the briefs on file with this Court, consist of boasting, debased remarks about what Morrison would do to women, vulgar remarks that cannot fail to shock and offend.

Brzonkala alleges that this attack caused her to become severely emotionally disturbed and depressed. She sought assistance from a university psychiatrist, who prescribed antidepressant medication. Shortly after the rape Brzonkala stopped attending classes and withdrew from the university.

In early 1995, Brzonkala filed a complaint against respondents under Virginia Tech's Sexual Assault Policy. During the school-conducted hearing on her complaint, Morrison admitted having sexual contact with her despite the fact that she had twice told him "no." After the hearing, Virginia Tech's Judicial Committee found insufficient evidence to punish Crawford, but found Morrison guilty of sexual assault and sentenced him to immediate suspension for two semesters.

Virginia Tech's dean of students upheld the judicial committee's sentence. However, in July 1995, Virginia Tech informed Brzonkala that Morrison intended to initiate a court challenge to his conviction under the Sexual Assault Policy. University officials told her that a second hearing would be necessary to remedy the school's error in prosecuting her complaint under that policy, which had not been widely circulated to students. The university therefore conducted a second hearing under its Abusive Conduct Policy, which was in force prior to the dissemination of the Sexual Assault Policy. Following this second hearing the Judicial Committee again found Morrison guilty and sentenced him to an identical 2–semester suspension. This time, however, the description of Morrison's offense was, without explanation, changed from "sexual assault" to "using abusive language."

Morrison appealed his second conviction through the university's administrative system. On August 21, 1995, Virginia Tech's senior vice president and provost set aside Morrison's punishment. She concluded that it was " 'excessive when compared with other cases where there has been a finding of violation of the Abusive Conduct Policy,' " [citation omitted]. Virginia Tech did not inform Brzonkala of this decision. After learning from a newspaper that Morrison would be returning to Virginia Tech for the fall 1995 semester, she dropped out of the university.

In December 1995, Brzonkala sued Morrison, Crawford, and Virginia Tech in the United States District Court for the Western District of Virginia. Her complaint alleged that Morrison's and Crawford's attack violated § 13981 and that Virginia Tech's handling of her complaint violated Title IX of the Education Amendments of 1972 [ ]. Morrison and Crawford moved to dismiss this complaint on the grounds that it failed to state a claim and that § 13981's civil remedy is unconstitutional. The United States [ ] intervened to defend § 13981's constitutionality.

* * *

Section 13981 was part of the Violence Against Women Act of 1994, [ ]. It states that "persons within the United States shall have the right to be free from crimes of violence motivated by gender." [ ]. To enforce that right, subsection (c) declares:

> "A person (including a person who acts under color of any statute, ordinance, regulation, custom, or usage of any State) who commits a crime of violence motivated by gender and thus deprives another of the right declared in subsection (b) of this section shall be liable to the party injured, in an action for the recovery of compensatory and

punitive damages, injunctive and declaratory relief, and such other relief as a court may deem appropriate."

Section 13981 defines a "crime" of violence motivated by "gender" as "a crime of violence committed because of gender or on the basis of gender, and due, at least in part, to an animus based on the victim's gender." [ ]. It also provides that the term "crime of violence" includes any

"(A) . . . act or series of acts that would constitute a felony against the person or that would constitute a felony against property if the conduct presents a serious risk of physical injury to another, and that would come within the meaning of State or Federal offenses described in section 16 of Title 18, whether or not those acts have actually resulted in criminal charges, prosecution, or conviction and whether or not those acts were committed in the special maritime, territorial, or prison jurisdiction of the United States; and

"(B) includes an act or series of acts that would constitute a felony described in subparagraph (A) but for the relationship between the person who takes such action and the individual against whom such action is taken." [ ].

Further clarifying the broad scope of § 13981's civil remedy, subsection (e)(2) states that "nothing" in this section requires a prior criminal complaint, prosecution, or conviction to establish the elements of a cause of action under subsection (c) of this section." And subsection (e)(3) provides a § 13981 litigant with a choice of forums: Federal and state courts "shall have concurrent jurisdiction" over complaints brought under the section.

Although the foregoing language of § 13981 covers a wide swath of criminal conduct, Congress placed some limitations on the section's federal civil remedy. Subsection (e)(1) states that "nothing" in this section entitles a person to a cause of action under subsection (c) of this section for random acts of violence unrelated to gender or for acts that cannot be demonstrated, by a preponderance of the evidence, to be motivated by gender." * * *

Every law enacted by Congress must be based on one or more of its powers enumerated in the Constitution. "The powers of the legislature are defined and limited; and that those limits may not be mistaken or forgotten, the constitution is written." *Marbury* v. *Madison*, 5 U.S. 137 [ ]. Congress explicitly identified the sources of federal authority on which it relied in enacting § 13981. It said that a "federal civil rights cause of action" is established "pursuant" to the affirmative power of Congress . . . under section 5 of the Fourteenth Amendment to the Constitution, as well as under section 8 of Article I of the Constitution." [ ] We address Congress' authority to enact this remedy under each of these constitutional provisions in turn.

II

Due respect for the decisions of a coordinate branch of Government demands that we invalidate a congressional enactment only upon a plain showing that Congress has exceeded its constitutional bounds. [ ]. With this presumption of constitutionality in mind, we turn to the question whether § 13981 falls within Congress' power under Article I, § 8, of the Constitution. Brzonkala and the United States rely upon the third clause of the Article, which gives Congress power "to regulate Commerce with foreign Nations, and among the several States, and with the Indian Tribes."

As we discussed at length in *Lopez*, our interpretation of the Commerce Clause has changed as our Nation has developed. [ ]. We need not repeat that detailed review of the Commerce Clause's history here; it suffices to say that, in the years since *NLRB v. Jones & Laughlin Steel Corp.*, [citation omitted], Congress has had considerably greater latitude in regulating conduct and transactions under the Commerce Clause than our previous case law permitted.

Lopez emphasized, however, that even under our modern, expansive interpretation of the Commerce Clause, Congress' regulatory authority is not without effective bounds. *Id.*, at 557. * * * As we observed in *Lopez*, modern Commerce Clause jurisprudence has "identified three broad categories of activity that Congress may regulate under its commerce power." [ ] "Second, Congress is empowered to regulate and protect the instrumentalities of interstate commerce, or persons or things in interstate commerce, even though the threat may come only from intrastate activities." [ ]. "Finally, Congress' commerce authority includes the power to regulate those activities having a substantial relation to interstate commerce, ... *i.e.*, those activities that substantially affect interstate commerce." [ ].

Petitioners do not contend that these cases fall within either of the first two of these categories of Commerce Clause regulation. They seek to sustain § 13981 as a regulation of activity that substantially affects interstate commerce. Given § 13981's focus on gender-motivated violence wherever it occurs (rather than violence directed at the instrumentalities of interstate commerce, interstate markets, or things or persons in interstate commerce), we agree that this is the proper inquiry.

Since *Lopez* most recently canvassed and clarified our case law governing this third category of Commerce Clause regulation, it provides the proper framework for conducting the required analysis of § 13981. In *Lopez*, we held that the Gun–Free School Zones Act of 1990 [ ] which made it a federal crime to knowingly possess a firearm in a school zone, exceeded Congress' authority under the Commerce Clause. [ ]. Several significant considerations contributed to our decision.

First, we observed that § 922(q) was "a criminal statute that by its terms has nothing to do with 'commerce' or any sort of economic enterprise, however broadly one might define those terms." 514 U.S. at 561. Reviewing our case law, we noted that "we have upheld a wide variety of congressional Acts regulating intrastate economic activity where we have concluded that the activity substantially affected interstate commerce." 514 U.S. at 559. Although we cited only a few examples [ ] we stated that the pattern of analysis is clear. [ ]. "Where economic activity substantially affects interstate commerce, legislation regulating that activity will be sustained." 514 U.S. at 560.

Both petitioners and JUSTICE SOUTER's dissent downplay the role that the economic nature of the regulated activity plays in our Commerce Clause analysis. But a fair reading of *Lopez* shows that the noneconomic, criminal nature of the conduct at issue was central to our decision in that case. * * * *Lopez*'s review of Commerce Clause case law demonstrates that in those cases where we have sustained federal regulation of intrastate activity based upon the activity's substantial effects on interstate commerce, the activity in question has been some sort of economic endeavor.

The second consideration that we found important in analyzing § 922(q) was that the statute contained "no express jurisdictional element which might limit its reach to a discrete set of firearm possessions that additionally have an explicit connection with or effect on interstate commerce." *Id.*, at 562. Such a jurisdictional element may establish that the enactment is in pursuance of Congress' regulation of interstate commerce.

Third, we noted that neither § 922(q) " 'nor its legislative history contains express congressional findings regarding the effects upon interstate commerce of gun possession in a school zone.' " [ ]. While "Congress normally is not required to make formal findings as to the substantial burdens that an activity has on interstate commerce," [ ], the existence of such findings may "enable us to evaluate the legislative judgment that the activity in question substantially affects interstate commerce, even though no such substantial effect [is] visible to the naked eye." [ ].

Finally, our decision in *Lopez* rested in part on the fact that the link between gun possession and a substantial effect on interstate commerce was attenuated. [ ]. The United States argued that the possession of guns may lead to violent crime, and that violent crime "can be expected to affect the functioning of the national economy in two ways. First, the costs of violent crime are substantial, and, through the mechanism of insurance, those costs are spread throughout the population. Second, violent crime reduces the willingness of individuals to travel to areas within the country that are perceived to be unsafe." [ ]. The Government also argued that the presence of guns at schools poses a threat to the educational process, which in turn threatens to produce a less efficient and productive workforce, which will negatively affect national productivity and thus interstate commerce.

We rejected these "costs of crime" and "national productivity" arguments because they would permit Congress to "regulate not only all violent crime, but all activities that might lead to violent crime, regardless of how tenuously they relate to interstate commerce." [ ] * * *

With these principles underlying our Commerce Clause jurisprudence as reference points, the proper resolution of the present cases is clear. Gender-motivated crimes of violence are not, in any sense of the phrase, economic activity. While we need not adopt a categorical rule against aggregating the effects of any noneconomic activity in order to decide these cases, thus far in our Nation's history our cases have upheld Commerce Clause regulation of intrastate activity only where that activity is economic in nature. [ ]

Like the Gun–Free School Zones Act at issue in *Lopez*, § 13981 contains no jurisdictional element establishing that the federal cause of action is in pursuance of Congress' power to regulate interstate commerce. Although *Lopez* makes clear that such a jurisdictional element would lend support to the argument that § 13981 is sufficiently tied to interstate commerce, Congress elected to cast § 13981's remedy over a wider, and more purely intrastate, body of violent crime.

In contrast with the lack of congressional findings that we faced in *Lopez*, § 13981 *is* supported by numerous findings regarding the serious impact that gender-motivated violence has on victims and their families. [ ]. But the existence of congressional findings is not sufficient, by itself, to sustain the constitutionality of Commerce Clause legislation. As we stated in *Lopez*, " 'Simply because Congress may conclude that a particular activity substantially affects interstate commerce does not necessarily make it so.' " 514 U.S. at 557 [ ]. Rather, " 'whether particular operations affect interstate commerce sufficiently to come under the constitutional power of Congress to regulate them is ultimately a judicial rather than a legislative question, and can be settled finally only by this Court.' " [ ]

In these cases, Congress' findings are substantially weakened by the fact that they rely so heavily on a method of reasoning that we have already rejected as unworkable if we are to maintain the Constitution's enumeration of powers. Congress found that gender-motivated violence affects interstate commerce

"by deterring potential victims from traveling interstate, from engaging in employment in interstate business, and from transacting with business, and in places involved in interstate commerce; ... by diminishing national productivity, increasing medical and other costs, and decreasing the supply of and the demand for interstate products." [ ].

Given these findings and petitioners' arguments, the concern that we expressed in *Lopez* that Congress might use the Commerce Clause to completely obliterate the Constitution's distinction between national and local authority seems well founded. [ ]. The reasoning that petitioners advance seeks to follow the but-for causal chain from the initial occurrence of violent crime (the suppression of which has always been the prime object of the States' police power) to every attenuated effect upon interstate commerce. If accepted, petitioners' reasoning would allow Congress to regulate any crime as long as the nationwide, aggregated impact of that crime has substantial effects on employment, production, transit, or consumption. Indeed, if Congress may regulate gender-motivated violence, it would be able to regulate murder or any other type of violence since gender-motivated violence, as a subset of all violent crime, is certain to have lesser economic impacts than the larger class of which it is a part.

Petitioners' reasoning, moreover, will not limit Congress to regulating violence but may, as we suggested in *Lopez*, be applied equally as well to family law and other areas of traditional state regulation since the aggregate effect of marriage, divorce, and childrearing on the national economy is undoubtedly significant. Congress may have recognized this specter when it expressly precluded § 13981 from being used in the family law context. [ ]. Under our written Constitution, however, the limitation of congressional authority is not solely a matter of legislative grace. [ ].

We accordingly reject the argument that Congress may regulate noneconomic, violent criminal conduct based solely on that conduct's aggregate effect on interstate commerce. The Constitution requires a distinction between what is truly national and what is truly local. [ ]. In recognizing this fact we preserve one of the few principles that has been consistent since the Clause was adopted. The regulation and punishment of intrastate violence that is not directed at the instrumentalities, channels, or goods involved in interstate commerce has always been the province of the States. [ ]

Because we conclude that the Commerce Clause does not provide Congress with authority to enact § 13981, we address petitioners' alternative argument that the section's civil remedy should be upheld as an exercise of Congress' remedial power under § 5 of the Fourteenth Amendment. As noted above, Congress expressly invoked the Fourteenth Amendment as a source of authority to enact § 13981.

* * *

Petitioners' § 5 argument is founded on an assertion that there is pervasive bias in various state justice systems against victims of gender-motivated violence. This assertion is supported by a voluminous congressional record. Specifically, Congress received evidence that many participants in state justice systems are perpetuating an array of erroneous stereotypes and assumptions. Congress concluded that these discriminatory stereotypes often result in insufficient investigation and prosecution of gender-motivated crime, inappropriate focus on the behavior and credibility of the victims of that crime, and unacceptably lenient punishments for those who are actually convicted of gender-motivated violence. [ ]. Petitioners contend that this bias denies victims of gender-motivated violence the equal protection of the laws and that Congress therefore acted appropriately in enacting a private civil remedy against the perpetrators of gender-motivated violence to both remedy the States' bias and deter future instances of discrimination in the state courts.

As our cases have established, state-sponsored gender discrimination violates equal protection unless it " 'serves "important governmental objectives and ... the discriminatory means employed" are "substantially related to the achievement of those objectives." ' [ ]. However, the language and purpose of the Fourteenth Amendment place certain limitations on the manner in which Congress may attack discriminatory conduct. These limitations are necessary to prevent the Fourteenth Amendment from obliterating the Framers' carefully crafted balance of power between the States and the National Government. [ ] Foremost among these limitations is the time-honored principle that the Fourteenth Amendment, by its very terms, prohibits only state action. The principle has become firmly embedded in our constitutional law that the action inhibited by the first section of the Fourteenth Amendment is only such action as may fairly be said to be that of the States. * * *

* * *

Petitioners contend that two more recent decisions have in effect overruled this longstanding limitation on Congress' § 5 authority. They rely on *United States* v. *Guest*, [ ], for the proposition that the rule laid down in the *Civil Rights Cases* is no longer good law. In *Guest*, the Court reversed the construction of an indictment under 18 U.S.C. § 241, saying in the course of its opinion that "we deal here with issues of statutory construction, not with issues of constitutional power." [ ].

Though these three Justices saw fit to opine on matters not before the Court in *Guest*, the Court had no occasion to revisit the *Civil Rights Cases* and *Harris*, having determined "the indictment [charging private individuals with conspiring to deprive blacks of equal access to state facilities] in fact contained an express allegation of state involvement." [ ]. The Court concluded that the implicit allegation of "active connivance by agents of the State" eliminated any need to decide "the threshold level that state action must attain in order to create rights under the Equal Protection Clause." *Ibid.* All of this Justice Clark explicitly acknowledged.

To accept petitioners' argument, moreover, one must add to the three Justices joining Justice Brennan's reasoned explanation for his belief that the *Civil Rights Cases* were wrongly decided, the three Justices joining Justice Clark's opinion who gave no explanation whatever for their similar view. This is simply not the way that reasoned constitutional adjudication proceeds. We accordingly have no hesitation in saying that it would take more than the naked dicta contained in Justice Clark's opinion, when added to Justice Brennan's opinion, to cast any doubt upon the enduring vitality of the *Civil Rights Cases* and *Harris*.

Petitioners also rely on *District of Columbia* v. *Carter*, 409 U.S. 418, 34 L.Ed.2d 613, 93 S.Ct. 602 (1973). *Carter* was a case addressing the question whether the District of Columbia was a "State" within the meaning of Rev. Stat. § 1979, 42 U.S.C. § 1983—a section which by its terms requires state action before it may be employed. A footnote in that opinion recites the same litany respecting *Guest* that petitioners rely on. This litany is of course entirely dicta, and in any event cannot rise above its source. We believe that the description of the § 5 power contained in the *Civil Rights Cases* is correct:

> "But where a subject has not submitted to the general legislative power of Congress, but is only submitted thereto for the purpose of rendering effective some prohibition against particular state legislation or state action in reference to that subject, the power given is limited by its object, any legislation by Congress in the matter must necessarily be corrective in its character, adapted to counteract and redress the operation of such prohibited state laws or proceedings of state officers." 109 U.S. at 18.

Petitioners alternatively argue that, unlike the situation in the *Civil Rights Cases*, here there has been gender-based disparate treatment by state authorities, whereas in those cases there was no indication of such state action. There is abundant evidence, however, to show that the Congresses that enacted the Civil Rights Acts of 1871 and 1875 had a purpose similar to that of Congress in enacting § 13981: There were state laws on the books bespeaking equality of treatment, but in the administration of these laws there was discrimination against newly freed slaves. The statement of Representative Garfield in the House and that of Senator Sumner in the Senate are representative:

> "The chief complaint is not that the laws of the State are unequal, but that even where the laws are just and equal on their face, yet, by a systematic maladministration of them, or a neglect or refusal to enforce their provisions, a portion of the people are denied equal protection under them." [ ].

> "The Legislature of South Carolina has passed a law giving precisely the rights contained in your 'supplementary civil rights bill.' But such a law remains a dead letter on her statute-books, because the State courts, comprised largely of those whom the Senator wishes to obtain amnesty for, refuse to enforce it." [ ].

But even if that distinction were valid, we do not believe it would save § 13981's civil remedy. For the remedy is simply not "corrective in its character, adapted to counteract and redress the operation of such prohibited state laws or proceedings of state officers." Section 13981 is not aimed at proscribing discrimination by officials which the Fourteenth Amendment might not itself proscribe; it is directed not at any State or state actor, but at individuals who have committed criminal acts motivated by gender bias.

In the present cases, for example, § 13981 visits no consequence whatever on any Virginia public official involved in investigating or prosecuting Brzonkala's assault. The section is, therefore, unlike any of the § 5 remedies that we have previously upheld. For example, in

Katzenbach v. *Morgan* [ ], Congress prohibited New York from imposing literacy tests as a prerequisite for voting because it found that such a requirement disenfranchised thousands of Puerto Rican immigrants who had been educated in the Spanish language of their home territory. That law, which we upheld, was directed at New York officials who administered the State's election law and prohibited them from using a provision of that law. In *South Carolina* v. *Katzenbach* [ ], Congress imposed voting rights requirements on States that, Congress found, had a history of discriminating against blacks in voting. The remedy was also directed at state officials in those States. Similarly, in *Ex parte Virginia*, 100 U.S. 339, 25 L.Ed. 676 (1880), Congress criminally punished state officials who intentionally discriminated in jury selection; again, the remedy was directed to the culpable state official.

Section 13981 is also different from these previously upheld remedies in that it applies uniformly throughout the Nation. Congress' findings indicate that the problem of discrimination against the victims of gender-motivated crimes does not exist in all States, or even most States. By contrast, the § 5 remedy upheld in *Katzenbach* v. *Morgan*, *supra*, was directed only to the State where the evil found by Congress existed, and in *South Carolina* v. *Katzenbach*, *supra*, the remedy was directed only to those States in which Congress found that there had been discrimination.

For these reasons, we conclude that Congress' power under § 5 does not extend to the enactment of § 13981.

IV

Petitioner Brzonkala's complaint alleges that she was the victim of a brutal assault. But Congress' effort in § 13981 to provide a federal civil remedy can be sustained neither under the Commerce Clause nor under § 5 of the Fourteenth Amendment. If the allegations here are true, no civilized system of justice could fail to provide her a remedy for the conduct of respondent Morrison. But under our federal system that remedy must be provided by the Commonwealth of Virginia, and not by the United States. The judgment of the Court of Appeals is

Affirmed.

* * *

JUSTICE BREYER, with whom JUSTICE STEVENS joins, and with whom JUSTICE SOUTER and JUSTICE GINSBURG join as to Part I–A, dissenting.

No one denies the importance of the Constitution's federalist principles. Its state/federal division of authority protects liberty—both by restricting the burdens that government can impose from a distance and by facilitating citizen participation in government that is closer to home. The question is how the judiciary can best implement that original federalist understanding where the Commerce Clause is at issue.

I

The majority holds that the federal commerce power does not extend to such "noneconomic" activities as "noneconomic, violent criminal conduct" that significantly affects interstate commerce only if we "aggregate" the interstate "effects" of individual instances. JUSTICE SOUTER explains why history, precedent, and legal logic militate against the majority's approach. I agree and join his opinion. I add that the majority's holding illustrates the difficulty of finding a workable judicial Commerce Clause touchstone—a set of comprehensible interpretive rules that courts might use to impose some meaningful limit, but not too great a limit, upon the scope of the legislative authority that the Commerce Clause delegates to Congress.

A

Consider the problems. The "economic/noneconomic" distinction is not easy to apply. Does the local street corner mugger engage in "economic" activity or "noneconomic" activity when he mugs for money? [ ] Would evidence that desire for economic domination underlies many brutal crimes against women save the present statute? * * *

The line becomes yet harder to draw given the need for exceptions. The Court itself would permit Congress to aggregate, hence regulate, "noneconomic" activity taking place at economic establishments. [ ]. And it would permit Congress to regulate where that regulation is "an essential part of a larger regulation of economic activity, in which the regulatory scheme could be undercut unless the intrastate activity were regulated." [ ]. Given the former exception, can Congress simply rewrite the present law and limit its application to restaurants, hotels, perhaps universities, and other places of public accommodation? Given the latter exception, can Congress save the present law by including it, or much of it, in a broader "Safe Transport" or "Workplace Safety" act?

More important, why should we give critical constitutional importance to the economic, or noneconomic, nature of an interstate-commerce-affecting *cause*? If chemical emanations through indirect environmental change cause identical, severe commercial harm outside a State, why should it matter whether local factories or home fireplaces release them? The Constitution itself refers only to Congress' power to "regulate Commerce ... among the several States," and to make laws "necessary and proper" to implement that power. [ ]. The language says nothing about either the local nature, or the economic nature, of an interstate-commerce-affecting cause.

This Court has long held that only the interstate commercial effects, not the local nature of the cause, are constitutionally relevant. * * *

Most important, the Court's complex rules seem unlikely to help secure the very object that they seek, namely, the protection of "areas of traditional state regulation" from federal intrusion. The Court's rules, even if broadly interpreted, are underinclusive. The local pickpocket is no less a traditional subject of state regulation than is the local gender-motivated assault. Regardless, the Court reaffirms, as it should, Congress' well-established and frequently exercised power to enact laws that satisfy a commerce-related jurisdictional prerequisite—for example, that some item relevant to the federally regulated activity has at some time crossed a state line. * * *.

And in a world where most everyday products or their component parts cross interstate boundaries, Congress will frequently find it possible to redraft a statute using language that ties the regulation to the interstate movement of some relevant object, thereby regulating local criminal activity or, for that matter, family affairs. [ ]. Although this possibility does not give the Federal Government the power to regulate everything, it means that any substantive limitation will apply randomly in terms of the interests the majority seeks to protect. How much would be gained, for example, were Congress to reenact the present law in the form of "An Act Forbidding Violence Against Women Perpetrated at Public Accommodations or by Those Who Have Moved in, or through the Use of Items that Have Moved in, Interstate Commerce"? Complex Commerce Clause rules creating fine distinctions that achieve only random results do little to further the important federalist interests that called them into being.

The majority, aware of these difficulties, is nonetheless concerned with what it sees as an important contrary consideration. To determine the lawfulness of statutes simply by asking whether Congress could reasonably have found that *aggregated* local instances significantly affect interstate commerce will allow Congress to regulate almost anything. Virtually all local activity, when instances are aggregated, can have "substantial effects on employment, production, transit, or consumption." Hence Congress could "regulate any crime," and perhaps "marriage, divorce, and childrearing" as well, obliterating the "Constitution's distinction between national and local authority." [ ]

This consideration, however, while serious, does not reflect a jurisprudential defect, so much as it reflects a practical reality. We live in a Nation knit together by two centuries of scientific, technological, commercial, and environmental change. Those changes, taken together, mean that virtually every kind of activity, no matter how local, genuinely can affect commerce, or its conditions, outside the State—at least when considered in the aggregate. [ ]. And that fact makes it close to impossible for courts to develop meaningful subject-matter categories that would exclude some kinds of local activities from ordinary Commerce Clause "aggregation" rules without, at the same time, depriving Congress of the power to regulate activities that have a genuine and important effect upon interstate commerce.

Since judges cannot change the world, the "defect" means that, within the bounds of the rational, Congress, not the courts, must remain primarily responsible for striking the appropriate state/federal balance. [ ]

B

I would also note that Congress, when it enacted the statute, followed procedures that help to protect the federalism values at stake. It provided adequate notice to the States of its intent to legislate in an "area of traditional state regulation."[ ]. And in response, attorneys general in the overwhelming majority of States (38) supported congressional legislation, telling Congress that "our experience as Attorneys General strengthens our belief that the problem of violence against women is a national one, requiring federal attention, federal leadership, and federal funds." [ ]

Moreover, as JUSTICE SOUTER has pointed out, Congress compiled a "mountain of data" explicitly documenting the interstate commercial effects of gender-motivated crimes of violence. [ ]. After considering alternatives, it focused the federal law upon documented deficiencies in state legal systems. And it tailored the law to prevent its use in certain areas of traditional state concern, such as divorce, alimony, or child custody [ ] Consequently, the law before us seems to represent an instance, not of state/federal conflict, but of state/federal efforts to cooperate in order to help solve a mutually acknowledged national problem. [ ].

I call attention to the legislative process leading up to enactment of this statute because, as the majority recognizes, *ante*, at 14, it far surpasses that which led to the enactment of the statute we considered in *Lopez*. And even were I to accept *Lopez* as an accurate statement of the law, which I do not, that distinction provides a possible basis for upholding the law here. This Court on occasion has pointed to the importance of procedural limitations in keeping the power of Congress in check. * * *

* * *

I continue to agree with JUSTICE SOUTER that the Court's traditional "rational basis" approach is sufficient. [ ]. But I recognize that the law in this area is unstable and that time and experience may demonstrate both the unworkability of the majority's rules and the superiority of Congress' own procedural approach—in which case the law may evolve towards a rule that, in certain difficult Commerce Clause cases, takes account of the thoroughness with which Congress has considered the federalism issue.

For these reasons, as well as those set forth by JUSTICE SOUTER, this statute falls well within Congress's Commerce Clause authority, and I dissent from the Court's contrary conclusion.

PEOPLE v. HUMPHREY

Supreme Court of California, 1996.
13 Cal.4th 1073, 56 Cal.Rptr.2d 142, 921 P.2d 1.

CHIN, J.

The Legislature has decreed that, when relevant, expert testimony regarding "battered women's syndrome" is generally admissible in a criminal action. [ ] We must determine the purposes for which a jury may consider this evidence when offered to support a claim of self-defense to a murder charge.

I. THE FACTS

A. Prosecution Evidence

During the evening of March 28, 1992, defendant shot and killed Albert Hampton in their Fresno home. Officer Reagan was the first on the scene. A neighbor told Reagan that the couple in the house had been arguing all day. Defendant soon came outside appearing upset and with her hands raised as if surrendering. She told Officer Reagan, "I shot him. That's right, I shot him. I just couldn't take him beating on me no more." She led the officer into the house, showed him a .357 magnum revolver on a table, and said, "There's the gun." Hampton was on the kitchen floor, wounded but alive.

A short time later, defendant told Officer Reagan, "He deserved it. I just couldn't take it anymore. I told him to stop beating on me." "He was beating on me, so I shot him. I told him I'd shoot him if he ever beat on me again." A paramedic heard her say that she wanted to teach Hampton "a lesson." Defendant told another officer at the scene, Officer Terry, "I'm fed up. Yeah, I shot him. I'm just tired of him hitting me. He said, 'You're not going to do nothing about it.' I showed him, didn't I? I shot him good. He won't hit anybody else again. Hit me again; I shoot him again. I don't care if I go to jail. Push come to shove, I guess people gave it to him, and, kept hitting me. I warned him. I warned him not to hit me. He wouldn't listen."

Officer Terry took defendant to the police station, where she told the following story. The day before the shooting, Hampton had been drinking. He hit defendant while they were driving home in their truck and continued hitting her when they arrived. He told her, "I'll kill you," and shot at her. The bullet went through a bedroom window and struck a tree outside. The day of the shooting, Hampton "got drunk," swore at her, and started hitting her again. He walked into the kitchen. Defendant saw the gun in the living room and picked it up. Her jaw hurt, and she was in pain. She pointed the gun at Hampton and said, "You're not going to hit me anymore." Hampton said, "What are you doing?" Believing that Hampton was about to pick something up to hit her with, she shot him. She then put the gun down and went outside to wait for the police.

Hampton later died of a gunshot wound to his chest. The neighbor who spoke with Officer Reagan testified that shortly before the shooting, she heard defendant, but not Hampton, shouting. The evening before, the neighbor had heard a gunshot. Defendant's blood contained no drugs but had a blood-alcohol level of .17 percent. Hampton's blood contained no drugs or alcohol.

B. Defense Evidence

Defendant claimed she shot Hampton in self-defense. To support the claim, the defense presented first expert testimony and then nonexpert testimony, including that of defendant herself.

1. Expert Testimony

Dr. Lee Bowker testified as an expert on battered women's syndrome. The syndrome, he testified, "is not just a psychological construction, but it's a term for a wide variety of controlling mechanisms that the man or it can be a woman, but in general for this syndrome it's a man, uses against the woman, and for the effect that those control mechanisms have."

Dr. Bowker had studied about 1,000 battered women and found them often inaccurately portrayed "as cardboard figures, paper-thin punching bags who merely absorb the violence but didn't do anything about it." He found that battered women often employ strategies to stop the beatings, including hiding, running away, counterviolence, seeking the help of friends and family, going to a shelter, and contacting police. Nevertheless, many battered women remain in the relationship because of lack of money, social isolation, lack of self-confidence, inadequate police response, and a fear (often justified) of reprisals by the batterer. "The battering man will make the battered woman depend on him and generally succeed at least for a time." A battered woman often feels responsible for the abusive relationship, and "she just can't figure out a way to please him better so he'll stop beating her." In sum, "It really is the physical control of the woman through economics and through relative social isolation combined with the psychological techniques that make her so dependent."

Many battered women go from one abusive relationship to another and seek a strong man to protect them from the previous abuser. "[W]ith each successful victimization, the person becomes less able to avoid the next one." The violence can gradually escalate, as the batterer keeps control using ever more severe actions, including rape, torture, violence against the woman's loved ones or pets, and death threats. Battered women sense this escalation. In Dr. Bowker's "experience with battered women who kill in self-defense their abusers, it's always related to their perceived change of what's going on in a relationship. They become very sensitive to what sets off batterers. They watch for this stuff very carefully. . . . Anybody who is abused over a period of time becomes sensitive to the abuser's behavior and when she sees a change acceleration begin in that behavior, it tells them something is going to happen. . . . "

Dr. Bowker interviewed defendant for a full day. He believed she suffered not only from battered women's syndrome, but also from being the child of an alcoholic and an incest victim. He testified that all three of defendant's partners before Hampton were abusive and significantly older than she.

Dr. Bowker described defendant's relationship with Hampton. Hampton was a 49-year-old man who weighed almost twice as much as defendant. The two had a battering relationship that Dr. Bowker characterized as a "traditional cycle of violence." The cycle included phases of tension building, violence, and then forgiveness-seeking in which Hampton would promise not to batter defendant any more and she would believe him. During this period, there would be occasional good times. For example, defendant told Dr. Bowker that Hampton would give her a rose. "That's one of the things that hooks people in. Intermittent reinforcement is the key." But after a while, the violence would begin again. The violence would recur because "basically ... the woman doesn't perfectly obey. That's the bottom line." For example, defendant would talk to another man, or fail to clean house "just so."

The situation worsened over time, especially when Hampton got off parole shortly before his death. He became more physically and emotionally abusive, repeatedly threatened defendant's life, and even shot at her the night before his death. Hampton often allowed defendant to go out, but she was afraid to flee because she felt he would find her as he had in the past. "He enforced her belief that she can never escape him." Dr. Bowker testified that unless her injuries were so severe that "something absolutely had to be treated," he would not expect her to seek medical treatment. "That's the pattern of her life.... "

Dr. Bowker believed defendant's description of her experiences. In his opinion, she suffered from battered women's syndrome in "about as extreme a pattern as you could find."

2. Nonexpert Testimony

Defendant confirmed many of the details of her life and relationship with Hampton underlying Dr. Bowker's opinion. She testified that her father forcefully molested her from the time she was seven years old until she was fifteen. She described her relationship with another abusive man as being like "Nightmare on Elm Street." Regarding Hampton, she testified that they often argued and that he beat her regularly. Both were heavy drinkers. Hampton once threw a can of beer at her face, breaking her nose. Her dental plates hurt because Hampton hit her so often. He often kicked her, but usually hit her in the back of the head because, he told her, it "won't leave bruises." Hampton sometimes threatened to kill her, and often said she "would live to regret it." Matters got worse towards the end.

The evening before the shooting, March 27, 1992, Hampton arrived home "very drunk." He yelled at her and called her names. At one point when she was standing by the bedroom window, he fired his .357 magnum revolver at her. She testified, "He didn't miss me by much either." She was "real scared."

The next day, the two drove into the mountains. They argued, and Hampton continually hit her. While returning, he said that their location would be a good place to kill her because "they wouldn't find [her] for a while." She took it as a joke, although she feared him. When they returned, the arguing continued. He hit her again, then entered the kitchen. He threatened, "This time, bitch, when I shoot at you, I won't miss." He came from the kitchen and reached for the gun on the living room table. She grabbed it first, pointed it at him, and told him "that he wasn't going to hit [her]." She backed Hampton into the kitchen. He was saying something, but she did not know what. He reached for her hand and she shot him. She believed he was reaching for the gun and was going to shoot her.

Several other witnesses testified about defendant's relationship with Hampton, his abusive conduct in general, and his physical abuse of, and threats to, defendant in particular. This testimony generally corroborated defendant's. A neighbor testified that the night before the shooting, she heard a gunshot. The next morning, defendant told the neighbor that Hampton had shot at her, and that she was afraid of him. After the shooting, investigators found a bullet hole through the frame of the bedroom window and a bullet embedded in a tree in line with the window. Another neighbor testified that shortly before hearing the shot that killed Hampton, she heard defendant say, "Stop it, Albert. Stop it."

C. Procedural History

Defendant was charged with murder with personal use of a firearm. At the end of the prosecution's case-in-chief, the court granted defendant's motion under Penal Code section 1118.1 for acquittal of first degree murder.

The court instructed the jury on second degree murder and both voluntary and involuntary manslaughter. It also instructed on self-defense, explaining that an actual and reasonable belief that the killing was necessary was a complete defense; an actual but unreasonable belief was a defense to murder, but not to voluntary manslaughter. In determining reasonableness, the jury was to consider what "would appear to be necessary to a reasonable person in a similar situation and with similar knowledge."

The court also instructed:

"Evidence regarding Battered Women's Syndrome has been introduced in this case. Such evidence, if believed, may be considered by you only for the purpose of determining whether or not the defendant held the necessary subjective honest [belief] which is a requirement for both perfect and imperfect self-defense. However, that same evidence regarding Battered Women's Syndrome may not be considered or used by you in evaluating the objective reasonableness requirement for perfect self-defense.

"Battered Women's Syndrome seeks to describe and explain common reactions of women to that experience. Thus, you may consider the evidence concerning the syndrome and its effects only for the limited purpose of showing, if it does show, that the defendant's reactions, as demonstrated by the evidence, are not inconsistent with her having been physically abused or the beliefs, perceptions, or behavior of victims of domestic violence.''

During deliberations, the jury asked for and received clarification of the terms ''subjectively honest and objectively unreasonable.'' It found defendant guilty of voluntary manslaughter with personal use of a firearm. The court sentenced defendant to prison for eight years, consisting of the lower term of three years for manslaughter, plus the upper term of five years for firearm use. The Court of Appeal remanded for resentencing on the use enhancement, but otherwise affirmed the judgment.

We granted defendant's petition for review.

II. DISCUSSION

* * *

B. Battered Women's Syndrome

Battered women's syndrome ''has been defined as 'a series of common characteristics that appear in women who are abused physically and psychologically over an extended period of time by the dominant male figure in their lives.' (*State v. Kelly* (1984) 97 N.J. 178, 193).

The trial court allowed the jury to consider the battered women's syndrome evidence in deciding whether defendant actually believed she needed to kill in self-defense. The question here is whether the evidence was also relevant on the reasonableness of that belief. Two Court of Appeal decisions have considered the relevance of battered women's syndrome evidence to a claim of self-defense.

People v. Aris, supra, 215 Cal.App.3d at page 1185, applied ''the law of self-defense in the context of a battered woman killing the batterer while he slept after he had beaten the killer and threatened serious bodily injury and death when he awoke.'' There, unlike here, the trial court refused to instruct the jury on perfect self-defense, but it did instruct on imperfect self-defense. The appellate court upheld the refusal, finding that ''defendant presented no substantial evidence that a reasonable person under the same circumstances would have perceived imminent danger and a need to kill in self-defense.'' (*Id.* at p. 1192.) The trial court admitted some evidence of battered women's syndrome, but the defendant argued that it erred ''by excluding expert testimony (1) that defendant was a battered woman based on the expert's psychological evaluation of the defendant and (2) 'explaining how the psychological impact of being a battered woman affected her perception of danger at the time she shot her husband.' '' (*People v. Aris, supra*, 215 Cal.App.3d at p. 1193.)

Although the trial court did not instruct on perfect self-defense, the appellate court first concluded that battered women's syndrome evidence is not relevant to the reasonableness element. ''[T]he questions of the reasonableness of a defendant's belief that self-defense is necessary and of the reasonableness of the actions taken in self-defense do not call for an evaluation of the defendant's subjective *state of mind*, but for an objective evaluation of the defendant's assertedly defensive *acts*. California law expresses the criterion for this evaluation in the objective terms of whether *a reasonable person*, as opposed to the *defendant*, would have believed and acted as the defendant did. We hold that expert testimony about a defendant's state of mind is not relevant to the reasonableness of the defendant's self-defense." (*People v. Aris, supra*, 215 Cal.App.3d at p. 1196, italics in original.)

The court then found the evidence "highly relevant to the first element of self-defense—defendant's actual, subjective perception that she was in danger and that she had to kill her husband to avoid that danger.... The relevance to the defendant's actual perception lies in the opinion's explanation of how such a perception would reasonably follow from the defendant's experience as a battered woman. This relates to the prosecution's argument that such a perception of imminent danger makes no sense when the victim is asleep and a way of escape open and, therefore, she did not actually have that perception." (*People v. Aris, supra*, 215 Cal.App.3d at p. 1197.) The trial court thus erred in not admitting the testimony to show "how the defendant's particular experiences as a battered woman affected her perceptions of danger, its imminence, and what actions were necessary to protect herself." (*Id.* at p. 1198.)

Concerned "that the jury in a particular case may misuse such evidence to establish the reasonableness requirement for perfect self-defense, for which purpose it is irrelevant," the *Aris* court stated that, "upon request whenever the jury is instructed on perfect self-defense, trial courts should instruct that such testimony is relevant only to prove the honest belief requirement for both perfect and imperfect self-defense, not to prove the reasonableness requirement for perfect self-defense." (*People v. Aris, supra*, 215 Cal.App.3d at p. 1199.) The trial court gave such an instruction here, thus creating the issue before us.

In *People v. Day* (1992) 2 Cal.App.4th 405, the defendant moved for a new trial following her conviction of involuntary manslaughter. Supported by an affidavit by Dr. Bowker, she argued that her attorney should have presented evidence of battered women's syndrome to aid her claim of self-defense. Relying on *Aris*, the appellate court first found that the evidence would not have been relevant to show the objective reasonableness of the defendant's actions. [ ] It also found, however, that the evidence would have been admissible to rehabilitate the defendant's credibility as a witness. Finding that counsel's failure to present the evidence was prejudicial, the court reversed the judgment.

The Attorney General argues that *People v. Aris, supra*, 215 Cal. App.3d 1178, and *People v. Day, supra*, 2 Cal.App.4th 405, were correct that evidence of battered women's syndrome is irrelevant to reasonableness. We disagree. Those cases too narrowly interpreted the reasonableness element. *Aris* and *Day* failed to consider that the jury, in determining objective reasonableness, must view the situation from the *defendant's perspective*. Here, for example, Dr. Bowker testified that the violence can escalate and that a battered woman can become increasingly sensitive to the abuser's behavior, testimony relevant to determining whether defendant reasonably believed when she fired the gun that this time the threat to her life was imminent. Indeed, the prosecutor argued that, "from an objective, reasonable man's standard, there was no reason for her to go get that gun. This threat that she says he made was like so many threats before. There was no reason for her to react that way." Dr. Bowker's testimony supplied a response that the jury might not otherwise receive. As violence increases over time, and threats gain credibility, a battered person might become sensitized and thus able reasonably to discern when danger is real and when it is not. "[T]he expert's testimony might also enable the jury to find that the battered [woman] … is particularly able to predict accurately the likely extent of violence in any attack on her. That conclusion could significantly affect the jury's evaluation of the *reasonableness* of defendant's fear for her life." (*State v. Kelly* (1984) 97 N.J. 178)

* * *

Contrary to the Attorney General's argument, we are not changing the standard from objective to subjective, or replacing the reasonable "person" standard with a reasonable "battered woman" standard. Our decision would not, in another context, compel adoption of a " 'reasonable gang member' standard." Evidence Code section 1107 states "a rule of evidence only" and makes "no substantive change." [ ] The jury must consider defendant's situation and knowledge, which makes the evidence relevant, but the ultimate question is whether a reasonable *person*, not a reasonable battered woman, would believe in the need to kill to prevent imminent harm. Moreover, it is the *jury*, not the expert, that determines whether defendant's belief and, ultimately, her actions, were objectively reasonable.

Battered women's syndrome evidence was also relevant to defendant's credibility. It "would have assisted the jury in objectively analyzing [defendant's] claim of self-defense by dispelling many of the commonly held misconceptions about battered women." (*People v. Day*, *supra*, 2 Cal.App.4th at p. 416.) For example, in urging the jury not to believe defendant's testimony that Hampton shot at her the night before the killing, the prosecutor argued that "if this defendant truly believed that [Hampton] had shot at her, on that night, I mean she would have left.... [P] If she really believed that he had tried to shoot her, she would not have stayed." Dr. Bowker's testimony " 'would help dispel the ordinary lay person's perception that a woman in a battering relationship is free to leave at any time. The expert evidence would counter any "common sense" conclusions by the jury that if the beatings were really that bad the woman would have left her husband much earlier. Popular misconceptions about battered women would be put to rest.... ' " (*People v. Day, supra,* 2 Cal.App.4th at p. 417, quoting *State v. Hodges* (1986) 239 Kan. 63) "[I]f the jury had understood [defendant's] conduct in light of [battered women's syndrome] evidence, then the jury may well have concluded her version of the events was sufficiently credible to warrant an acquittal on the facts as she related them." (*People v. Day, supra,* 2 Cal.App.4th at p. 415.)

* * *

We do not hold that Dr. Bowker's entire testimony was relevant to both prongs of perfect self-defense. Just as many types of evidence may be relevant to some disputed issues but not all, some of the expert evidence was no doubt relevant only to the subjective existence of defendant's belief. Evidence merely showing that a person's use of deadly force is scientifically explainable or empirically common does not, in itself, show it was objectively reasonable. To dispel any possible confusion, it might be appropriate for the court, on request, to clarify that, in assessing reasonableness, the question is whether a reasonable person in the defendant's circumstances would have perceived a threat of imminent injury or death, and not whether killing the abuser was reasonable in the sense of being an understandable response to ongoing abuse; and that, therefore, in making that assessment, the jury may not consider evidence merely showing that an abused person's use of force against the abuser is understandable.

We also emphasize that, as with any evidence, the jury may give this testimony whatever weight it deems appropriate in light of the evidence as a whole. The ultimate judgment of reasonableness is solely for the jury. We simply hold that evidence of battered women's syndrome is generally *relevant* to the reasonableness, as well as the subjective existence, of defendant's belief in the need to defend, and, to the extent it is relevant, the jury may *consider* it in deciding both questions. The court's contrary instruction was erroneous. We disapprove of *People v. Aris, supra,* 215 Cal.App.3d 1178, and *People v. Day, supra,* 2 Cal.App.4th 405, to the extent they are inconsistent with this conclusion.

* * *

CUSTODY OF VAUGHN[1]

Supreme Judicial Court of Massachusetts, 1996.
422 Mass. 590, 664 N.E.2d 434.

In 1993, a Probate and Family Court judge awarded primary physical custody of a boy (Vaughn), at the time age eleven years, to his father (Ross). The Appeals Court reversed and remanded the case to the Probate and Family Court for further consideration of evidence regarding domestic violence perpetrated by the child's father against his mother (Leslie) and the effect of the family violence on Vaughn. R.H. v. B.F.[ ]. We granted Ross's application for further appellate review. We

---

1. Fictitious names have been assigned to the principals.

are in agreement with the Appeals Court. We reverse the judgment and remand for further findings consistent with this opinion.

I

Leslie and Ross met in Maine in 1977. Leslie, who was twice divorced, lived with her two children, a girl (Laura) then age nine years and a boy (John) age five years. Leslie worked as a real estate salesperson during the day and as a cocktail waitress at night. The Probate Court judge found that she "has been an abused person. She was abused as a child, she was divorced twice and has endured abuse because of her relationships." Ross, a former marine engineer, was working odd jobs as a carpenter and painter at the time. Shortly after they met, Ross moved into Leslie's home. They have never married. Ross is a big man, six feet five inches tall and weighing some 285 pounds. Leslie is five feet seven inches tall and weighs 150 pounds. The disparity in their size is relevant, because the relationship was fraught with anger and violence from the start. Ross had a terrible temper. The judge found that he "would fly into rages" and strike out at Leslie, once causing her to lose consciousness and requiring her to be sent to the hospital in an ambulance. According to testimony, he inflicted injuries on her on numerous other occasions. Laura and John witnessed a number of these incidents and were terrified of Ross and his rages. The testimony and findings of fact reflected that Ross was also physically and verbally abusive toward them. Both Ross and Leslie drank heavily and used marihuana. Since Leslie joined "Al-Anon" in 1978, her consumption of alcohol has diminished. The testimony is that she drinks mostly on social occasions. Ross has been alcohol free since 1985 and continues to attend Alcoholics Anonymous meetings once a week.

In 1981 the family moved to Nantucket where Leslie obtained a position as a real estate broker. Vaughn was born on July 18, 1982. After the move to Nantucket, Ross began working as a carpenter and caretaker. Leslie was successful at her work and at the time of trial was earning over $100,000 a year. Ross was much less successful financially, although he appeared to have a number of clients with second homes on Nantucket who relied on his services, and at least one of whom established a close friendship with him and Vaughn.

Ross's rages and violence toward Leslie, Laura, and John continued after Vaughn's birth. There was testimony that the police were called on approximately one dozen occasions. Ross's anger and violence, however, did not cease, and he sought psychiatric help. A psychiatrist prescribed Lithium, and there was testimony that when Ross discontinued taking it (on his own) his moods and behavior worsened. Leslie testified that on several occasions she left the house with her children to escape Ross's behavior, that many times Ross also took Vaughn from the house in the course of arguments, and that Ross used the threat of taking Vaughn from his mother as a way of keeping the mother in the relationship. Vaughn was present at many of the episodes of abuse. There was testimony that the father's disposition to use physical force was played out on the boy as well, with cuffing, pushing, knocking, and poking; he also yelled and lost his temper at the boy, as he did at every other member of the household. Laura, who is now a graduate student, further testified that, when she was a teenager, Ross kissed her on the mouth in an inappropriate manner and touched her body in an inappropriate, sexual manner.

The judge also found that Leslie engaged in taunting, provocative, and violent behavior toward Ross. On several occasions she assaulted him in a sexual and humiliating manner. It appears that for some years the parties had not shared a bedroom, and on at least one occasion Leslie without any immediate provocation taunted Ross for his sexual neglect of her. In 1986, on the occasion that received the most attention, she entered Ross's room nude and proceeded to taunt him in the grossest and most explicit terms within the boy's hearing. In 1988, in another similar incident, the judge found that Leslie, "when rejected after demanding sexual favors from [Ross] followed him from the house to the public road. She was naked and directed foul language at him. This too was done in the presence of [Vaughn]."

Until Vaughn was five years old his mother was his primary caretaker. Thereafter Ross undertook more and more responsibilities. Apparently he did the shopping and cooking for the household over the five years immediately prior to trial, and he was greatly occupied with his son's activities. Ross followed his son's progress in school, visited his teachers, attended his sporting events, and joined him in target shooting and other activities. Indeed the evidence suggests that Ross was, if anything, overly involved with his son. He embarrassed his son at times by participating in games with him or cheering with excessive enthusiasm at his team sports, and the two would shower together and would give each other massages. Ross has been very generous to Vaughn—the mother complains overly generous—buying him motorbikes and electronic equipment.

The tension and violence between the parents finally led Leslie, on October 1, 1992, to obtain an order in the District Court pursuant to G. L. c. 209A (1994 ed.), requiring Ross to vacate the couple's home, to surrender custody of the boy to the mother, and to remain away from the home and the mother. The next day Ross commenced this action in the Probate Court to establish paternity (which is not in dispute) and to obtain custody of Vaughn. The parties promptly entered into a temporary agreement providing for joint legal and physical custody, according to which the boy would spend part of each week with each parent. During this arrangement the father bought out the mother's share of the house in which they had been living, and the mother moved into a new home. The parties also agreed that Dr. Michael D. Abruzzese, a clinical psychologist whom they had previously consulted along with the child, should be appointed guardian ad litem to make an evaluation and report regarding custody of the child. On February 21, 1993, Dr. Abruzzese delivered his report, recommending that joint custody be continued but that the boy's primary home during the week be with his father with weekends to be spent with his mother. Thereupon the Probate Court entered a new temporary order maintaining the joint legal custody but giving the father primary physical custody and visitation rights to the mother, substantially in accord with Dr. Abruzzese's recommendations.

* * *

Leslie appealed to the Appeals Court, which reversed the judgment of the Probate Court for errors of law and remanded the case to that court. * * *

II

A

The Appeals Court based its remand to the Probate Court on the failure of that court to make findings regarding the evidence that the father had physically abused the mother throughout the relationship and the effect of this abuse on the child. The Appeals Court gave great weight to this court's Gender Bias Study of the Court System of Massachusetts (1989) and particularly to the recommendation in that study that,

> "The legislature and/or appellate courts should make it clear that abuse of any family member affects other family members and must be considered in determining the best interests of the child in connection with any order concerning custody."

The Appeals Court's remand order is designed to do just that. We endorse the Appeals Court's commitment to the propositions that physical force within the family is both intolerable and too readily tolerated, and that a child who has been either the victim or the spectator of such abuse suffers a distinctly grievous kind of harm. It might be helpful to emphasize how fundamental these propositions are. Quite simply, abuse by a family member inflicted on those who are weaker and less able to defend themselves—almost invariably a child or a woman—is a violation of the most basic human right, the most basic condition of civilized society: the right to live in physical security, free from the fear that brute force will determine the conditions of one's daily life. What our study and the growing movement against family violence and violence against women add to this fundamental insight is that, for those who are its victims, force within the family and in intimate relationships is not less but more of a threat to this basic condition of civilized security, for it destroys the security that all should enjoy in the very place and context which is supposed to be the refuge against the harshness encountered in a world of strangers. Particularly for children the sense that the place which is supposed to be the place of security is the place of greatest danger is the ultimate denial that this is a world of justice and restraint, where people have rights and are entitled to respect. The recent literature also exposes the sham and hypocrisy that condemns violence among strangers and turns a blind eye to it where its manifestations are most corrosive.

* * *

B

The Appeals Court was critical of the Probate Court in a number of related respects. First, the Probate Court judge "failed to make detailed and comprehensive findings of fact on the issues of domestic violence and its effect upon the child as well as upon the father's parenting ability." [ ]. Second, "because [the judge] found the mother and the father to have equally flawed parenting abilities, the relationship between the father and the child and the child's preferences weighed the scales [excessively] in the father's favor." [ ]. And third, the Appeals Court ruled that the Probate Court failed to consider the special risks to the child in awarding custody to a father who had committed acts of violence against the mother. [ ]. An important theme of all these statements was that the Probate Court had failed to give sufficient weight to the effects of domestic violence on women and their children. [ ].

* * * The record leaves no room for doubt that Ross is a man with a poorly controlled temper, who at times threatened and inflicted violence on the mother. He has been a batterer. The Probate Court's findings clearly acknowledge that fact. The judge's findings also acknowledge the intimidation Ross imposed on John and Laura, the two older children in the household who were not Ross's children, and credit the testimony of Leslie's daughter that Ross engaged in conduct to her that can only be described as sexually abusive. * * *

There are two sides to this sad story, and the Probate Court acknowledged both of them. There was testimony, which Leslie sought to put in context but did not deny, that she taunted and struck the father and hurt and humiliated him physically. Some, not all of these incidents might be explained away as defensive or retaliatory. The judge found that: "Neither party exercised such conduct that would make them eligible for any awards or accolades. . . . They both have been physically and emotionally abusive to each other. Their conduct can be described through their profanity, vulgarity, obscenity and nudity."

The mother's expert, Dr. Peter G. Jaffe, who is a specialist in matters relating to family violence and battered women's syndrome, casts all the incidents unfavorable to Leslie as manifestations of that syndrome. Leslie had been abused as a child and in the two marriages that preceded her relationship with Ross. The judge summarized Dr. Jaffe's judgments in his findings of fact, including Dr. Jaffe's statement that children who grow up in abusive households tend to repeat that pattern in their own relationships: "Dr. Jaffe feels that children who are witnesses to violence are also victims of violence. He expressed a concern that if [Vaughn] remained in his father's physical custody, it would reinforce the acceptability of the father's behavior to [Vaughn] which has the potential to make [Vaughn] a batterer himself in the future."

The judge did not, however, make any findings of fact based on Dr. Jaffe's testimony and did not say whether he considered Dr. Jaffe's testimony credible.

Rather the judge seemed moved to give particular weight to the recommendations and testimony of the guardian ad litem, Dr. Abruzzese, and less weight to the analysis and conclusions of Leslie's expert, Dr. Jaffe. Unquestionably Dr. Jaffe has impressive credentials, with very great experience in issues relating to family violence and battered women. But he was also an expert chosen by one of the parties in the context of this litigation.

Dr. Abruzzese, on the other hand, was an impartial witness whom the parties had consulted previously and who had been selected by their mutual agreement to serve as guardian ad litem. * * *

III

We agree with the Appeals Court that the judge below "failed to make detailed and comprehensive findings of fact on the issues of domestic violence and its effect upon the child as well as upon the father's parenting ability." [ ]. The Probate Court failed to consider the special risks to the child in awarding custody to a father who had committed acts of violence against the mother. [ ]. It is well documented that witnessing domestic violence, as well as being one of its victims, has a profound impact on children. There are significant reported psychological problems in children who witness domestic violence, especially during important developmental stages.

Domestic violence is an issue too fundamental and frequently recurring to be dealt with only by implication. The very frequency of domestic violence in disputes about child custody may have the effect of inuring courts to it and thus minimizing its significance. Requiring the courts to make explicit findings about the effect of the violence on the child and the appropriateness of the custody award in light of that effect will serve to keep these matters well in the foreground of the judges' thinking.

The Legislature reached a similar conclusion in respect to shared legal or physical custody. [Massachusetts law] provides that "if, despite the prior or current issuance of a restraining order against one parent . . . the court orders shared legal or physical custody . . . the court shall provide written findings to support such shared custody order." A [restraining] order was outstanding in this case, and the judge made no explicit findings regarding the effect of shared custody on the child. We agree with the Appeals Court that such written findings should also be made attending specifically to the effects of domestic violence on the child and the appropriateness of the joint custody award in light of those effects. [ ]

Accordingly, we remand the case to the Probate Court for such explicit findings * * * on the matters set out above.

So ordered.

CONNECTICUT v. DOE

Supreme Court of the United States, 2003.
538 U.S. 1, 123 S.Ct. 1160, 155 L.Ed.2d 98.

CHIEF JUSTICE REHNQUIST delivered the opinion of the Court.

We granted certiorari to determine whether the United States Court of Appeals for the Second Circuit properly enjoined the public disclosure of Connecticut's sex offender registry. The Court of Appeals concluded that such disclosure both deprived registered sex offenders of a "liberty interest," and violated the Due Process Clause because officials did not afford registrants a predeprivation hearing to determine whether they are likely to be "currently dangerous." [ ]. Connecticut, however, has decided that the registry requirement shall be based on the fact of previous conviction, not the fact of current dangerousness. Indeed, the public registry explicitly states that officials have not determined that any registrant is currently dangerous. We therefore reverse the judgment of the Court of Appeals because due process does not require the opportunity to prove a fact that is not material to the State's statutory scheme.

"Sex offenders are a serious threat in this Nation." *McKune* v. *Lile* [ ] (plurality opinion). "The victims of sex assault are most often juveniles," and "when convicted sex offenders reenter society, they are much more likely than any other type of offender to be re-arrested for a new rape or sex assault." [ ]. Connecticut, like every other State, has responded to these facts by enacting a statute designed to protect its communities from sex offenders and to help apprehend repeat sex offenders. Connecticut's "Megan's Law" applies to all persons convicted of criminal offenses against a minor, violent and nonviolent sexual offenses, and felonies committed for a sexual purpose. Covered offenders must register with the Connecticut Department of Public Safety (DPS) upon their release into the community. Each must provide personal information (including his name, address, photograph, and DNA sample); notify DPS of any change in residence; and periodically submit an updated photograph. The registration requirement runs for 10 years in most cases; those convicted of sexually violent offenses must register for life.[ ].

The statute requires DPS to compile the information gathered from registrants and publicize it. In particular, the law requires DPS to post a sex offender registry on an Internet Website and to make the registry available to the public in certain state offices. [ ]. Whether made available in an office or via the Internet, the registry must be accompanied by the following warning: " 'Any person who uses information in this registry to injure, harass or commit a criminal act against any person included in the registry or any other person is subject to criminal prosecution.' " [ ].

Before the District Court enjoined its operation, the State's Website enabled citizens to obtain the name, address, photograph, and description of any registered sex offender by entering a zip code or town name. The following disclaimer appeared on the first page of the Website:

" 'The registry is based on the legislature's decision to facilitate access to publicly-available information about persons convicted of sexual offenses. [DPS] has not considered or assessed the specific risk of reoffense with regard to any individual prior to his or her inclusion within this registry, and has made no determination that any individual included in the registry is currently dangerous. Individuals included within the registry are included solely by virtue of their conviction record and state law. The main purpose of providing this data on the Internet is to make the information more easily available and accessible, not to warn about any specific individual.' " [ ].

Petitioners include the state agencies and officials charged with compiling the sex offender registry and posting it on the Internet. Respondent Doe is a convicted sex offender who is subject to Connecticut's Megan's Law. He filed this action pursuant to [Connecticut law] on behalf of himself and similarly situated sex offenders, claiming that the law violates, *inter alia*, the Due Process Clause of the Fourteenth Amendment. Specifically, respondent alleged that he is not a " 'dangerous sexual offender,' " and that the Connecticut law "deprives him of a liberty interest—his reputation combined with the alteration of his status under state law—without notice or a meaningful opportunity to be heard." [ ]. The District Court granted summary judgment for respondent on his due process claim. [ ]. The court then certified a class of individuals subject to the Connecticut law, and permanently enjoined the law's public disclosure provisions.

* * * We granted certiorari [ ].

In *Paul* v. *Davis,* 424 U.S. 693 (1976), we held that mere injury to reputation, even if defamatory, does not constitute the deprivation of a liberty interest. Petitioners urge us to reverse the Court of Appeals on the ground that, under *Paul* v. *Davis,* respondent has failed to establish that petitioners have deprived him of a liberty interest. We find it unnecessary to reach this question, however, because even assuming, *arguendo,* that respondent has been deprived of a liberty interest, due process does not entitle him to a hearing to establish a fact that is not material under the Connecticut statute.

In cases such as *Wisconsin* v. *Constantineau,* 400 U.S. 433 (1971), and *Goss* v. *Lopez,* 419 U.S. 565, 42 L.Ed.2d 725, 95 S.Ct. 729 (1975), we held that due process required the government to accord the plaintiff a hearing to prove or disprove a particular fact or set of facts. But in each of these cases, the fact in question was concededly relevant to the inquiry at hand. Here, however, the fact that respondent seeks to prove—that he is not currently dangerous—is of no consequence under Connecticut's Megan's Law. As the DPS Website explains, the law's requirements turn on an offender's conviction alone—a fact that a convicted offender has already had a procedurally safeguarded opportunity to contest. 271 F.3d at 44 (" 'Individuals included within the registry are included *solely* by virtue of their conviction record and state law' " (emphasis added)). No other fact is relevant to the disclosure of registrants' information. [ ]. Indeed, the disclaimer on the Website explicitly states that respondent's alleged nondangerousness simply does not matter. [ ]("'[DPS] has made no determination that any individual included in the registry is currently dangerous' ").

In short, even if respondent could prove that he is not likely to be currently dangerous, Connecticut has decided that the registry information of *all* sex offenders—currently dangerous or not—must be publicly disclosed. Unless respondent can show that that *substantive* rule of law is defective (by conflicting with a provision of the Constitution), any hearing on current dangerousness is a bootless exercise. It may be that respondent's claim is actually a substantive challenge to Connecticut's statute "recast in 'procedural due process' terms." [ ]. Nonetheless, respondent expressly disavows any reliance on the substantive component of the Fourteenth Amendment's protections, Brief for Respondent 44–45, and maintains, as he did below, that his challenge is strictly a procedural one. But States are not barred by principles of *"procedural* due process" from drawing such classifications. [ ]. Such claims "must ultimately be analyzed" in terms of substantive, not procedural, due process. [ ]. Because the question is not properly before us, we express no opinion as to whether Connecticut's Megan's Law violates principles of substantive due process.

Plaintiffs who assert a right to a hearing under the Due Process Clause must show that the facts they seek to establish in that hearing are relevant under the statutory scheme. Respondent cannot make that showing here. The judgment of the Court of Appeals is therefore Reversed.

JUSTICE SCALIA, concurring.

I join the Court's opinion, and add that even if the requirements of Connecticut's sex offender registration law implicate a liberty interest of respondent, the categorical abrogation of that liberty interest by a validly enacted statute suffices to provide all the process that is "due"— just as a state law providing that no one under the age of 16 may operate a motor vehicle suffices to abrogate that liberty interest. Absent a claim (which respondent has not made here) that the liberty interest in question is so fundamental as to implicate so-called "substantive" due process, a properly enacted law can eliminate it. That is ultimately why, as the Court's opinion demonstrates, a convicted sex offender has no more right to additional "process" enabling him to establish that he is not dangerous than (in the analogous case just suggested) a 15–year–old has a right to "process" enabling him to establish that he is a safe driver.

JUSTICE SOUTER, with whom JUSTICE GINSBURG joins, concurring.

I join the Court's opinion and agree with the observation that today's holding does not foreclose a claim that Connecticut's dissemination of registry information is actionable on a substantive due process principle. To the extent that libel might be at least a component of such a claim, our reference to Connecticut's disclaimer, *ante*, at 3, would not stand in the way of a substantive due process plaintiff. I write separately only to note that a substantive due process claim may not be the only one still open to a test by those in the respondents' situation.

Connecticut allows certain sex offenders the possibility of avoiding the registration and reporting obligations of the statute. A court may exempt a convict from registration altogether if his offense was unconsented sexual contact, Conn. Gen. Stat. § 54–251(c) (2001), or sexual intercourse with a minor aged between 13 and 16 while the offender was more than two years older than the minor, provided the offender was under age 19 at the time of the offense, [ ]. A court also has discretion to limit dissemination of an offender's registration information to law enforcement purposes if necessary to protect the identity of a victim who is related to the offender or, in the case of a sexual assault, who is the offender's spouse or cohabitor. [ ]. Whether the decision is to exempt an offender from registration or to restrict publication of registry information, it must rest on a finding that registration or public dissemination is not required for public safety. [ ]. The State thus recognizes that some offenders within the sweep of the publication requirement are not dangerous to others in any way justifying special publicity on the Internet, and the legislative decision to make courts responsible for granting exemptions belies the State's argument that courts are unequipped to separate offenders who warrant special publication from those who do not.

The line drawn by the legislature between offenders who are sensibly considered eligible to seek discretionary relief from the courts and those who are not is, like all legislative choices affecting individual rights, open to challenge under the Equal Protection Clause. [ ]. The refusal to allow even the possibility of relief to, say, a 19–year–old who has consensual intercourse with a minor aged 16 is therefore a reviewable legislative determination. Today's case is no occasion to speak either to the possible merits of such a challenge or the standard of scrutiny that might be in order when considering it. I merely note that the Court's rejection of respondents' procedural due process claim does not immunize publication schemes like Connecticut's from an equal protection challenge.

LESLEY v. DEPARTMENT OF SOCIAL AND HEALTH SERVICES

Court of Appeals of Washington, Division One, 1996.
83 Wn.App. 263, 921 P.2d 1066.

COLEMAN, J.—DSHS caseworker Sally Maurer, suspecting that Diedre and Terell Lesley abused their daughter, removed the child from the parents. Her suspicions proved incorrect, and the Lesleys now contend that Maurer negligently investigated the case and violated their civil rights. Because Maurer may not have followed procedures or acted reasonably, we reverse the summary judgment order for Maurer and the State. The Lesleys also argue that the court erred in holding that Dr. Douglas Lambrecht enjoyed qualified immunity because he was reporting child abuse in good faith. We agree with the trial court and affirm the summary judgment order for the doctor.

* * *

On April 7, 1992, Candyland Day-care workers noticed marks on the lower back and buttocks of Taylor Lesley, the Lesley's 11–month–old African American daughter, when cleaning her backside after severe diarrhea. The workers did not recall seeing the marks previously but noted that they may not be able to see them during normal diaper changes. Day-care manager Shellie Weitz had heard of but never seen Mongolian spots, a birthmark appearing in the vast majority of African American children. Believing that they would be able to determine whether the marks were bruises or birthmarks, she decided to call Child Protective Services.

At around 4 or 4:30 p.m., CPS worker Maurer looked at the marks. The day-care workers told Maurer that they had not seen these marks previously and that the child also had a rash in the vaginal area. Maurer called her supervisor, Sally Scott, who told Maurer to have the police examine the child. Maurer called the police and the child's regular pediatrician, Dr. Arredondo, to determine if the child had any birthmarks and to arrange for an examination. The doctor's office told Maurer that Dr. Arredondo was unavailable and advised her to take Taylor to the emergency room at Valley General Hospital. The police then arrived and examined Taylor. Maurer noted that when the officer pressed on the marks, the child cried "in pain." The officer decided that the child should be taken into protective custody. Maurer told Weitz that she did not have time to talk to the parents. * * *

Maurer took Taylor to Valley General Medical Center's Emergency Room, where two police officers soon arrived. The officers had been dispatched because of the mother's apparently hostile reaction to the news that her daughter had been taken into protective custody. The officers informed Maurer that the parents said the child had normal markings on her backside. Maurer did not then relay this information to Valley General's Dr. Lambrecht, nor did she inform the doctor about Taylor's vaginal rash.

Dr. Lambrecht examined the child, including the vaginal area. He asked Maurer whether Taylor had a history of Mongolian spots. Maurer repeated only what the day-care workers had told her. Dr. Lambrecht called Dr. Arredondo, who was not in her office. Dr. Burkebile, who was on call for Dr. Arredondo, checked Taylor's chart and found no reference to Mongolian spots. Dr. Lambrecht concluded that Taylor did not appear to be sexually assaulted and diagnosed the marks as "contusions to the buttocks and lower back, possible physical child abuse." Dr. Lambrecht advised Maurer to have Dr. Arredondo or an expert at Children's

Hospital or Harborview see Taylor. Maurer did not follow these instructions.

At 7:30 p.m. that day, Maurer brought Taylor to the home of Joanne Maloy, a foster care provider. Maurer told Maloy about the marks and the diaper rash. Maurer called Maloy at least once each day except Sunday and asked her if the marks had changed. Maloy repeatedly told Maurer that the marks had not changed. Maloy stated that Maurer never told her the parents wanted visitation with Taylor over the weekend, which Maloy would have gladly accommodated. Maurer also told Maloy after an interview with the parents that Taylor's mother was "out of control" and "was the one who probably abused the baby[.]"

On or about April 7, Dr. John Neff of Children's Hospital received a call regarding Taylor from a caseworker who stated that she had seen bruises over the child's buttocks. The caseworker asked if the child needed to be seen at Children's Hospital for further confirmation. Dr. Neff asked if photographs had been taken, and the caseworker told him that they had been. Because the caseworker gave him the impression that there were no questions about the diagnosis, Dr. Neff told her that it was not necessary for the child to be seen at Children's Hospital.

On Wednesday, April 8, Maurer and another caseworker interviewed the Lesleys separately and with their attorney, Edna Verzani. Verzani testified that the interviewers were not listening carefully and that she had to correct them several times. Each parent described Taylor's birthmark as a greenish color covering an area of Taylor's lower back and upper buttocks. Diedre Lesley told Maurer that she had similar marks on herself and offered to show her. Maurer declined to look. Maurer asked the parents whether there were any marks on Taylor's lower back. The parents said that there were not. Maurer did not believe that the parent's description adequately described Taylor's marks.

On Thursday, April 9888 [t]he Lesleys observed Taylor's marks and told Maurer that the marks were exactly as they had described. Maurer told them that their description was different. * * *

At a shelter care hearing on Friday, April 10, both parents and Taylor's maternal grandmother, Emma Jane Newell, testified that Taylor had one main birthmark on her backside. Maurer testified that the marks that the parents described were substantially different from the ones she observed. Commissioner Maurice Epstein determined that the child should stay with the foster parent but recommended to return the child as soon as possible if there was strong "or even reasonable evidence that nothing did occur on the part of the parents and that there is no real injury at that time." The commissioner ordered liberal visitation.

* * *

Dr. Neff claimed that on or about April 10, the caseworker again called him and asked what she could do to substantiate bruising. At this time, the caseworker told him that the family said the child had a birthmark. Dr. Neff explained that it was easy to differentiate the two because a bruise would change color or show other signs of resolution.

On Saturday morning, April 11, Maurer told Dr. Lambrecht that the parents claimed the marks were from birth but that they gave a different description in court. She then called Dr. Arredondo, who stated that, based on an emergency room transcription she had received, she could not state whether the marks had changed but that she would examine Taylor. Maurer then called Dr. Neff, who was not on duty, and instead spoke to Dr. Lehman. Dr. Lehman told Maurer to have Dr. Lambrecht recheck the mark to see whether it had changed. Dr. Lehman told her that if Dr. Lambrecht was not convinced, Maurer should bring the child to Children's emergency room, where the doctors would then determine what the marks were.

At about 5:30 p.m. on Saturday, Maurer picked up Taylor to take her to Dr. Lambrecht. * * * Dr. Lambrecht thought that the marks, "if anything," were slightly more grayish. The mark's grayness, the doctor stated, "might weigh slightly more that it was more likely a Mongolian spot than a contusion, but it wouldn't necessarily rule it out." Maurer did not tell Dr. Lambrecht that the foster mother had not noticed any changes in the marks. * * *.

On Monday, April 13, Dr. Kenneth Feldman at Odessa Brown Children's Clinic diagnosed the marks as Mongolian spots and not bruises. He further diagnosed a yeast rash in the genital area and prescribed appropriate treatment. The child was then returned to the Lesleys.

The Lesleys offered the Declaration of Jon Conte, a professor of social work, who found that Maurer investigated in an unreasonable fashion based on biased and partial information. Conte determined that Maurer should have followed Dr. Lambrecht's advice in consulting an expert and that she should have personally notified the parents that the child was being taken into protective custody. Conte found that Maurer made inappropriate remarks to the foster mother indicating her lack of willingness to work in a positive manner and that she inappropriately did not convey complete information to Dr. Lambrecht concerning the marks.

Dr. Abraham B. Bergman, a pediatrician at Harborview Medical Center and the Director of the Child Abuse Consultation Network in Washington, stated that CPS's behavior was outrageous. Additionally, Dr. Feldman stated that Dr. Lambrecht did not make a competent diagnosis following the recognized standards of care required of physicians who examine children for abuse.

The complaint named the caseworkers in their official capacity * * *.

The court granted summary judgment for defendants, finding that because Scott and Maurer's actions were consistent with the statutory framework, they enjoyed qualified immunity for all claims. The court further determined that the State was immune based on the caseworkers' immunity. Additionally, the court granted summary judgment for Dr. Lambrecht based on qualified immunity.

NEGLIGENT INVESTIGATION

We first address the Lesleys' claim that the caseworkers and the State are liable for their negligent investigation into allegations of possible child abuse. The State argues that Washington law does not recognize negligent investigation as an independent cause of action. We thus first address whether Washington recognizes this tort.

In Babcock v. State, [ ] the Supreme Court held that DSHS caseworkers were entitled to qualified, not absolute, immunity for negligent foster care investigation and placement. The alleged negligent investigation occurred when caseworkers placed several young girls with a relative who raped them. [ ]. Defendants attempt to distinguish Babcock, arguing that Babcock involved negligent placement, while this case involves negligent investigation of possible abuse. The Babcock court, however, noted that the gravamen of the complaint was negligent investigation. [ ]. Furthermore, in Dunning v. Pacerelli [ ] the court, rejecting the argument that investigating possible child abuse was distinct from Babcock's foster care placement, explicitly recognized a negligent investigation claim against a DSHS worker. [citations omitted].

* * *

CASEWORKER AND STATE QUALIFIED IMMUNITY

We next address whether Maurer is entitled to qualified immunity as a matter of law. State employees enjoy qualified statutory immunity for reporting child abuse:

> (1)(a) Except as provided in (b) of this subsection, any person participating in good faith in the making of a report pursuant to this chapter or testifying as to alleged child abuse or neglect in a judicial proceeding shall in so doing be immune from any liability arising out of such reporting or testifying under any law of this state or its political subdivisions.

[ ] The burden is on the caseworker to prove that he or she acted in good faith [ ] in reporting the abuse. [ ]. State employees also enjoy qualified common law immunity for investigating child abuse. [ ]. To receive this qualified immunity, the caseworker must (1) carry out a statutory duty, (2) according to procedures dictated by statute or superiors, and (3) act reasonably. [ ]. No issue of fact exists concerning Maurer's initial response to the suspected abuse [ ]. The sole issue is thus whether Maurer is entitled to qualified immunity for her investigation.

The Lesleys claim that Maurer fails to meet Babcock's qualified immunity requirements because she did not follow established procedures. The statute emphasizes the importance of family unity. [ ] ("The bond between a child and his or her parent, custodian, or guardian is of paramount importance, and any intervention into the life of a child is also an intervention into the life of the parent, custodian, or guardian . . . '') * * * The Department of Child and Family Services manual also emphasizes the need for culturally sensitive interviewing techniques and responses that remedy the situation in the shortest reasonable time and prevent or reduce the need for out of home placement. [ ]. Other provisions emphasize expediency. * * *

Here, the Lesley's presented evidence that Maurer removed the child from the day-care without calling the parents. [ ]. Maurer also failed to tell Dr. Lambrecht and the court immediately that the parents said that the marks were Mongolian spots or that the foster mother said that the marks had not changed. [ ]. Additionally, Maurer failed to follow Dr. Lambrecht's advice to take the child to an expert after the doctor expressed reservation about his ability to diagnose the possible child abuse. Such actions may have violated the mandate of speedy family reunification consistent with the child's safety needs. [ ]. Finally, her conversations with Maloy and the Lesleys indicate that Maurer may have lacked cultural sensitivity. * * *

Maurer may have also failed to comply with Babcock's reasonableness requirement. No discovered case has squarely addressed the definition of reasonableness under Babcock. Because reporting decisions must be conducted with reasonable good faith, the investigation following such reporting is also subject to the same standard. The caseworker must act with a reasonable good faith intent, judged in light of all the circumstances then present in conducting an investigation into child abuse. [ ] * * *

Here, whether Maurer acted with reasonable good faith presents issues of fact. [ ] For instance, her delay in resolving the matter, her failure to inform the doctors and the court fully concerning the parents' and foster mother's statements, and her statements to Maloy provide issues of fact concerning her reasonable good faith. We thus find that there are issues of fact concerning reasonableness sufficient to withstand summary judgment.

* * *

DOCTOR QUALIFIED IMMUNITY

We finally consider whether the trial court erred in finding Dr. Lambrecht immune for his actions under [the statute, which] provides immunity to any person participating in good faith in reporting or testifying as to alleged child abuse or neglect in a judicial proceeding. * * *. This statute states that when any practitioner has reasonable cause to believe that a child has suffered abuse or neglect, the practitioner shall ''report'' such incident to the proper law enforcement agencies. [ ]. It also states that any other person who has reasonable cause to believe a child has suffered abuse or neglect may also ''report'' such incident. [ ]. The critical inquiry is whether Dr. Lambrecht was making a report under either [of these provisions,] thus entitling him to qualified immunity.

The Lesleys argue that a "report" refers to an initial report of child abuse before the child has been taken into DSHS custody, and thus, Dr. Lambrecht was not "making a report" as defined by the statute. Dr. Lambrecht claims that the Lesleys' narrow reading defies statutory construction rules. Dr. Lambrecht also argues that if the Legislature intended to Confer immunity only to the first person making the report, it would not have extended immunity to persons testifying.

* * *

While case law is scant, we hold that Dr. Lambrecht is subject to the protections of [the statute]. First, the statute refers to any person making a report, not just the initial reporting person. [The statute] affords immunity for all those testifying concerning abuse. It would thus be nonsensical to provide immunity to the doctor when he testified, but not when he only made a report. Finally, Spurrell indicates that all persons are immune in making reports of child abuse, regardless of whether they were the initial reporter or had increased decision-making responsibility. [ ]

We finally address whether Dr. Lambrecht's actions met [the statute's] "good faith" requirement. To establish good faith, Dr. Lambrecht must have acted with a "reasonable good faith intent, judged in light of all the circumstances then present[.]" [citation omitted]. No evidence indicates that Dr. Lambrecht did not act in reasonable good faith. We thus affirm the summary judgment order for Dr. Lambrecht.

The order of the trial court is affirmed in part and reversed in part.

McKUNE v. LILE

Supreme Court of the United States, 2002.
536 U.S. 24, 122 S.Ct. 2017, 153 L.Ed.2d 47.

JUSTICE KENNEDY announced the judgment of the Court and delivered an opinion, in which THE CHIEF JUSTICE, JUSTICE SCALIA, and JUSTICE THOMAS join.

* * *

I

In 1982, respondent lured a high school student into his car as she was returning home from school. At gunpoint, respondent forced the victim to perform oral sodomy on him and then drove to a field where he raped her. After the sexual assault, the victim went to her school, where, crying and upset, she reported the crime. The police arrested respondent and recovered on his person the weapon he used to facilitate the crime. [ ]. Although respondent maintained that the sexual intercourse was consensual, a jury convicted him of rape, aggravated sodomy, and aggravated kidnapping. Both the Kansas Supreme Court and a Federal District Court concluded that the evidence was sufficient to sustain respondent's conviction on all charges. [ ].

In 1994, a few years before respondent was scheduled to be released, prison officials ordered him to participate in a Sexual Abuse Treatment Program (SATP). As part of the program, participating inmates are required to complete and sign an "Admission of Responsibility" form, in which they discuss and accept responsibility for the crime for which they have been sentenced. Participating inmates also are required to complete a sexual history form, which details all prior sexual activities, regardless of whether such activities constitute uncharged criminal offenses. A polygraph examination is used to verify the accuracy and completeness of the offender's sexual history.

While information obtained from participants advances the SATP's rehabilitative goals, the information is not privileged. Kansas leaves open the possibility that new evidence might be used against sex offenders in future criminal proceedings. In addition, Kansas law requires the SATP staff to report any uncharged sexual offenses involving minors to law enforcement authorities. Although there is no evidence that incriminating information has ever been disclosed under the SATP, the release of information is a possibility.

Department officials informed respondent that if he refused to participate in the SATP, his privilege status would be reduced from Level III to Level I. As part of this reduction, respondent's visitation rights, earnings, work opportunities, ability to send money to family, canteen expenditures, access to a personal television, and other privileges automatically would be curtailed. In addition, respondent would be transferred to a maximum-security unit, where his movement would be more limited, he would be moved from a two-person to a four-person cell, and he would be in a potentially more dangerous environment.

Respondent refused to participate in the SATP on the ground that the required disclosures of his criminal history would violate his Fifth Amendment privilege against self-incrimination. He brought this action under 42 U.S.C. § 1983 against the warden and the secretary of the Department, seeking an injunction to prevent them from withdrawing his prison privileges and transferring him to a different housing unit.

* * *

II

Sex offenders are a serious threat in this Nation. In 1995, an estimated 355,000 rapes and sexual assaults occurred nationwide. * * * As in the present case, the victims of sexual assault are most often juveniles. * * * Nearly 4 in 10 imprisoned violent sex offenders said their victims were 12 or younger.

When convicted sex offenders reenter society, they are much more likely than any other type of offender to be rearrested for a new rape or sexual assault. [citations omitted]. States thus have a vital interest in rehabilitating convicted sex offenders.

Therapists and correctional officers widely agree that clinical rehabilitative programs can enable sex offenders to manage their impulses and in this way reduce recidivism. [citations omitted]. An important component of those rehabilitation programs requires participants to confront their past and accept responsibility for their misconduct.[ ] "Denial is generally regarded as a main impediment to successful therapy," and "therapists depend on offenders' truthful descriptions of events leading to past offences in order to determine which behaviors need to be targeted in therapy." * * *

The critical first step in the Kansas Sexual Abuse Treatment Program (SATP), therefore, is acceptance of responsibility for past offenses. This gives inmates a basis to understand why they are being punished and to identify the traits that cause such a frightening and high risk of recidivism. As part of this first step, Kansas requires each SATP participant to complete an "Admission of Responsibility" form, to fill out a sexual history form discussing their offending behavior, and to discuss their past behavior in individual and group counseling sessions.

The District Court found that the Kansas SATP is a valid "clinical rehabilitative program," supported by a "legitimate penological objective" in rehabilitation. [ ]. The SATP lasts for 18 months and involves substantial daily counseling. It helps inmates address sexual addiction; understand the thoughts, feelings, and behavior dynamics that precede their offenses; and develop relapse prevention skills. Although inmates are assured of a significant level of confidentiality, Kansas does not offer legal immunity from prosecution based on any statements made in the course of the SATP. According to Kansas, however, no inmate has ever been charged or prosecuted for any offense based on information disclosed during treatment. [ ]. There is no contention, then, that the program is a mere subterfuge for the conduct of a criminal investigation.

As the parties explain, Kansas' decision not to offer immunity to every SATP participant serves two legitimate state interests. First, the professionals who design and conduct the program have concluded that for SATP participants to accept full responsibility for their past actions, they must accept the proposition that those actions carry consequences. [ ]. Although no program participant has ever been prosecuted or penalized based on information revealed during the SATP, the potential for additional punishment reinforces the gravity of the participants' offenses and thereby aids in their rehabilitation. If inmates know society will not punish them for their past offenses, they may be left with the false impression that society does not consider those crimes to be serious ones. The practical effect of guaranteed immunity for SATP participants would be to absolve many sex offenders of any and all cost for their earlier crimes. This is the precise opposite of the rehabilitative objective.

Second, while Kansas as a rule does not prosecute inmates based upon information revealed in the course of the program, the State confirms its valid interest in deterrence by keeping open the option to prosecute a particularly dangerous sex offender. [ ]. Kansas is not alone in declining to offer blanket use immunity as a condition of participation in a treatment program. The Federal Bureau of Prisons and other States conduct similar sex offender programs and do not offer immunity to the participants. [ ].

The mere fact that Kansas declines to grant inmates use immunity does not render the SATP invalid. Asking at the outset whether prison administrators can or should offer immunity skips the constitutional inquiry altogether. If the State of Kansas offered immunity, the self-incrimination privilege would not be implicated. * * * So the central question becomes whether the State's program, and the consequences for nonparticipation in it, combine to create a compulsion that encumbers the constitutional right. If there is compulsion, the State cannot continue the program in its present form; and the alternatives, as will be discussed, defeat the program's objectives.

The SATP does not compel prisoners to incriminate themselves in violation of the Constitution. * * * The consequences in question here—a transfer to another prison where television sets are not placed in each inmate's cell, where exercise facilities are not readily available, and where work and wage opportunities are more limited—are not ones that compel a prisoner to speak about his past crimes despite a desire to remain silent. The fact that these consequences are imposed on prisoners, rather than ordinary citizens, moreover, is important in weighing respondent's constitutional claim.

The privilege against self-incrimination does not terminate at the jailhouse door, but the fact of a valid conviction and the ensuing restrictions on liberty are essential to the Fifth Amendment analysis * * * A broad range of choices that might infringe constitutional rights in free society fall within the expected conditions of confinement of those who have suffered a lawful conviction.

The Court has instructed that rehabilitation is a legitimate penological interest that must be weighed against the exercise of an inmate's liberty. * * * Acceptance of responsibility in turn demonstrates that an offender "is ready and willing to admit his crime and to enter the correctional system in a frame of mind that affords hope for success in rehabilitation over a shorter period of time than might otherwise be necessary." *Brady* v. *United States*, [ ].

* * *

For these reasons, the Court in *Sandin* held that challenged prison conditions cannot give rise to a due process violation unless those conditions constitute "atypical and significant hardships on [inmates] in relation to the ordinary incidents of prison life." [ ]. * * * *Sandin* and its counterparts underscore the axiom that a convicted felon's life in prison differs from that of an ordinary citizen. In the context of a legitimate rehabilitation program for prisoners, those same considerations are relevant to our analysis. The compulsion inquiry must consider the significant restraints already inherent in prison life and the State's own vital interests in rehabilitation goals and procedures within the prison system. A prison clinical rehabilitation program, which is acknowledged to bear a rational relation to a legitimate penological objective, does not violate the privilege against self-incrimination if the adverse consequences an inmate faces for not participating are related to the program objectives and do not constitute atypical and significant hardships in relation to the ordinary incidents of prison life.

* * *

In the present case, respondent's decision not to participate in the Kansas SATP did not extend his term of incarceration. Nor did his decision affect his eligibility for good-time credits or parole. [ ]. Respondent instead complains that if he remains silent about his past crimes, he will be transferred from the medium-security unit—where the program is conducted—to a less desirable maximum-security unit.

No one contends, however, that the transfer is intended to punish prisoners for exercising their Fifth Amendment rights. Rather, the limitation on these rights is incidental to Kansas' legitimate penological reason for the transfer: Due to limited space, inmates who do not participate in their respective programs will be moved out of the facility where the programs are held to make room for other inmates. As the Secretary of Corrections has explained, "it makes no sense to have someone who's not participating in a program taking up a bed in a setting where someone else who may be willing to participate in a program could occupy that bed and participate in a program." [ ].

* * *

Respondent also complains that he will be demoted from Level III to Level I status as a result of his decision not to participate. This demotion means the loss of his personal television; less access to prison organizations and the gym area; a reduction in certain pay opportunities and canteen privileges; and restricted visitation rights. [ ]. An essential tool of prison administration, however, is the authority to offer inmates various incentives to behave. The Constitution accords prison officials wide latitude to bestow or revoke these perquisites as they see fit. Accordingly, *Hewitt* v. *Helms* [ ], held that an inmate's transfer to another facility did not in itself implicate a liberty interest, even though that transfer resulted in the loss of "access to vocational, educational, recreational, and rehabilitative programs." * * *

* * *

Determining what constitutes unconstitutional compulsion involves a question of judgment: Courts must decide whether the consequences of an inmate's choice to remain silent are closer to the physical torture against which the Constitution clearly protects or the *de minimis* harms against which it does not. The *Sandin* framework provides a reasonable means of assessing whether the response of prison administrators to correctional and rehabilitative necessities are so out of the ordinary that one could sensibly say they rise to the level of unconstitutional compulsion.

* * *

The Kansas SATP represents a sensible approach to reducing the serious danger that repeat sex offenders pose to many innocent persons, most often children. The State's interest in rehabilitation is undeniable. There is, furthermore, no indication that the SATP is merely an elaborate ruse to skirt the protections of the privilege against compelled self-incrimination. Rather, the program allows prison administrators to provide to those who need treatment the incentive to seek it.

The judgment of the Court of Appeals is reversed, and the case is remanded for further proceedings.

It is so ordered.

* * *

JUSTICE STEVENS, with whom JUSTICE SOUTER, JUSTICE GINSBURG, and JUSTICE BREYER join, dissenting.

No one could possibly disagree with the plurality's statement that "offering inmates minimal incentives to participate [in a rehabilitation program] does not amount to compelled self-incrimination prohibited by the Fifth Amendment." [ ]. The question that this case presents, however, is whether the State may punish an inmate's assertion of his Fifth Amendment privilege with the same mandatory sanction that follows a disciplinary conviction for an offense such as theft, sodomy, riot arson, or assault. Until today the Court has never characterized a threatened harm as "a minimal incentive." Nor have we ever held that a person who has made a valid assertion of the privilege may nevertheless be ordered to incriminate himself and sanctioned for disobeying such an order. This is truly a watershed case.

Based on an ad hoc appraisal of the benefits of obtaining confessions from sex offenders, balanced against the cost of honoring a bedrock constitutional right, the plurality holds that it is permissible to punish the assertion of the privilege with what it views as modest sanctions, provided that those sanctions are not given a "punitive" label. As I shall explain, the sanctions are in fact severe, but even if that were not so, the plurality's policy judgment does not justify the evisceration of a constitutional right. Despite the plurality's meandering attempt to justify its unprecedented departure from a rule of law that has been settled since the days of John Marshall, I respectfully dissent.

I

The text of the Fifth Amendment provides that no person "shall be compelled in any criminal case to be a witness against himself." It is well settled that the prohibition "not only permits a person to refuse to testify against himself at a criminal trial in which he is a defendant, but also 'privileges him not to answer official questions put to him in any other proceeding, civil or criminal, formal or informal, where the answers might incriminate him in future criminal proceedings.' "[ ]. If a person is protected by the privilege, he may "refuse to answer unless and until he is protected at least against the use of his compelled answers and evidence derived therefrom in any subsequent criminal case in which he is a defendant." [ ]. Prison inmates—including sex offenders—do not forfeit the privilege at the jailhouse gate. [ ].

It is undisputed that respondent's statements on the admission of responsibility and sexual history forms could incriminate him in a future prosecution for perjury or any other offense to which he is forced to confess. It is also clear that he invoked his Fifth Amendment right by refusing to participate in the SATP on the ground that he would be required to incriminate himself. Once he asserted that right, the State could have offered respondent immunity from the use of his statements in a subsequent prosecution. Instead, the Kansas Department of Corrections (Department) ordered respondent either to incriminate himself or to lose his medium-security status. In my opinion that order, coupled with the threatened revocation of respondent's Level III privileges, unquestionably violated his Fifth Amendment rights.

Putting to one side the plurality's evaluation of the policy judgments made by Kansas, its central submission is that the threatened withdrawal of respondent's Level III and medium-security status is not sufficiently harmful to qualify as unconstitutional compulsion. In support of this position, neither the plurality nor JUSTICE O'CONNOR cites a single Fifth Amendment case in which a person invoked the privilege and was nevertheless required to answer a potentially incriminating question.

* * *

II

The plurality and JUSTICE O'CONNOR hold that the consequences stemming from respondent's invocation of the privilege are not serious enough to constitute compulsion. The threat of transfer to Level I and a maximum-security unit is not sufficiently coercive in their view—either because the consequence is not really a penalty, just the loss of a benefit, or because it is a penalty, but an insignificant one. I strongly disagree.

It took respondent several years to acquire the status that he occupied in 1994 when he was ordered to participate in the SATP. Because of the nature of his convictions, in 1983 the Department initially placed him in a maximum-security classification. Not until 1989 did the Department change his "security classification to 'medium by exception' because of his good behavior." [ ]. Thus, the sanction at issue threatens to deprive respondent of a status in the prison community that it took him six years to earn and which he had successfully maintained for five more years when he was ordered to incriminate himself. Moreover, abruptly "busting" his custody back to Level I, App. 94, would

impose the same stigma on him as would a disciplinary conviction for any of the most serious offenses described in petitioners' formal statement of Internal Management Policy and Procedure (IMPP). As the District Court found, the sanctions imposed on respondent "mirror the consequences imposed for serious disciplinary infractions." [ ]. This same loss of privileges is considered serious enough by prison authorities that it is used as punishment for theft, drug abuse, assault, and possession of dangerous contraband.

The punitive consequences of the discipline include not only the dignitary and reputational harms flowing from the transfer, but a serious loss of tangible privileges as well. Because he refused to participate in the SATP, respondent's visitation rights will be restricted. He will be able to earn only $0.60 per day, as compared to Level III inmates, who can potentially earn minimum wage. His access to prison organizations and activities will be limited. He will no longer be able to send his family more than $30 per pay period. He will be prohibited from spending more than $20 per payroll period at the canteen, rather than the $140 he could spend at Level III, and he will be restricted in what property he can keep in his cell. [ ] In addition, because he will be transferred to a maximum-security unit, respondent will be forced to share a cell with three other inmates rather than one, and his movement outside the cell will be substantially curtailed. [ ]. The District Court found that the maximum-security unit is "a more dangerous environment occupied by more serious offenders." [ ] Perhaps most importantly, respondent will no longer be able to earn his way back up to Level III status through good behavior during the remainder of his sentence. [ ].

The plurality's glib attempt to characterize these consequences as a loss of potential benefits rather than a penalty is wholly unpersuasive. The threatened transfer to Level I and to a maximum-security unit represents a significant, adverse change from the status quo. Respondent achieved his medium-security status after six years of good behavior and maintained that status during five more years. During that time, an inmate unquestionably develops settled expectations regarding the conditions of his confinement. These conditions then form the baseline against which any change must be measured, and rescinding them now surely constitutes punishment.

* * *

III

The SATP clearly serves legitimate therapeutic purposes. The goal of the program is to rehabilitate sex offenders, and the requirement that participants complete admission of responsibility and sexual history forms may well be an important component of that process. Mental health professionals seem to agree that accepting responsibility for past sexual misconduct is often essential to successful treatment, and that treatment programs can reduce the risk of recidivism by sex offenders. [ ].

The program's laudable goals, however, do not justify reduced constitutional protection for those ordered to participate. "We have already rejected the notion that citizens may be forced to incriminate themselves because it serves a governmental need." [ ] The benefits of obtaining confessions from sex offenders may be substantial, but "claims of overriding interests are not unusual in Fifth Amendment litigation," and until today at least "they have not fared well." [ ]. The State's interests in law enforcement and rehabilitation are present in every criminal case. If those interests were sufficient to justify impinging on prisoners' Fifth Amendment right, inmates would soon have no privilege left to invoke.

Notes

1) After Morrison's challenge to the constitutionality of the Violence Against Women's Act, new civil rights legislation was introduced: The Violence Against Women Civil Rights Restoration Act of 2003. The legislation, still pending, would require, as part of the crime of violence, certain specific instate activities be alleged. For example, an act of violence that interferes with commercial or economic activity of the victim would be covered by the new Act. Are you persuaded by the Court's suggestion that limitations on federal authority require that an act to address gender-based violence be framed as a public rather than private issue?

2) In *Middleton v. McNeil,* ___ U.S. ___, 124 S.Ct. 1830, 158 L.Ed.2d 701 (2004) the U.S. Supreme Court overturned a decision of the Ninth Circuit Court of Appeals granting habeas corpus relief in a case alleging Battered Women's Syndrome as a defense to an act of violence. See *McNeil v. Middleton*, 344 F.3d 988 (9th Cir. 2003). The respondent challenged a jury instruction concerning the need for imminent peril in order to maintain an imperfect self-defense claim. The Supreme Court held that the jury charge correctly stated that respondent's belief that her life was in imminent peril could be an unreasonable belief. "[W]hether one defines imminent peril in terms of an unreasonable belief or instead describes imperfect self-defense as allowing an unreasonable belief in imminent peril, the import of the instruction is the same."

3) *Custody of Vaughn* required the court not only to choose between two imperfect parents to assume custody of their child, but to articulate a standard that courts can rely upon in making these difficult custody determinations. In doing so the court made it clear that domestic violence is harmful to children, not only because they, too, are at increased risk of becoming victims, but because the very witnessing of domestic violence in the home causes emotional harm to children. Accordingly, the directive to any court in the state that determines a child should be placed in the custody of a perpetrator of domestic violence is to articulate clear rationale as to why the placement is nevertheless in the best interest of the child.

4) In many cases child welfare workers are inadequately trained in recognizing child abuse, or are put in positions with decisional authority beyond their expertise. Caseworkers who act reasonably and in good faith are statutorily immune from actions resulting from failures in judgment. However, the immunity is qualified and a caseworker whose actions are unreasonable under the circumstances will not be shielded by the law. To receive qualified immunity, the caseworker must reasonably carry out her duties in accordance with statutory procedures. As to the physician, a mandated reporter who, obligated by statute to report suspected cases of abuse, is generally immune from liability as long as he acts in good faith.

5) *Doe v. Connecticut* raises the difficult question of whether "due process" means that convicted sex offenders, upon completing their sentences and reentering society, have any recourse against a law that allows their names and identities to be posted on the internet so others will be warned. The trial court and Court of Appeals held the Due Process Clause entitles them to a hearing "to determine whether or not they are particularly likely to be currently dangerous before being labeled as such by their inclusion in a publicly disseminated registry." The Supreme Court disagreed, presumably on the basis that the need to protect society outweighed the due process rights of those already convicted.

6) *McKune v. Lile* questions whether the Sexual Abuse Treatment Program (SATP), which allegedly offers incentives to sex offenders for participation in rehabilitation, infringes upon a defendant's right against self-incrimination. SATP requires that inmates take responsibility (i.e. confess) for their sexual offenses, including those not charged, and refuses to confer immunity for disclosures. Should the prisoner agree, the rehabilitation program offers better prison conditions, an opportunity for treatment and some other incentives for participation. While no prisoner has ever been charged with a crime disclosed in this way, the possibility reportedly increases the stakes and improves the effectiveness of the program. That the incentives are coercive is not disputed. The majority finds that the program does not amount to a violation of fifth amendment protections, but a persuasive dissent is also convincing.

SECTION D.   HIGH RISK ACTIVITIES

CITY OF NEW YORK v. NEW SAINT MARK'S BATHS

Supreme Court of New York, Special Term, New York County, 1986.
130 Misc.2d 911, 497 N.Y.S.2d 979.

WALLACH, J.

This action by the health authorities of the City of New York is taken against defendant the New St. Mark's Baths (St. Mark's) as a step to limit the spread of the disease known as AIDS (Acquired Immune Deficiency Syndrome). The parties are in agreement with respect to the deadly character of this disease and the dire threat that its spread, now in epidemic proportions, poses to the health and well-being of the community.

Immediately relevant to this litigation are the scientific facts with respect to AIDS risk groups. During the five years in which the disease has been identified and studied, 73% of AIDS victims have consisted of sexually active homosexual and bisexual men with multiple partners. AIDS is not easily transmittable through casual body contact or transmission through air, water or food. Direct blood-to-blood or semen-to-blood contact is necessary to transmit the virus. Cases of AIDS among homosexual and bisexual males are associated with promiscuous sexual contact, anal intercourse and other sexual practices which may result in semen-to-blood or blood-to-blood contact.

* * *

Prior Proceedings

On October 25, 1985, the State Public Health Council with the approval of the intervening New York State Commissioner of Health, adopted an emergency resolution adding a new regulation to the State Sanitary Code. This added regulation * * * specifically authorized local officials, such as the City plaintiffs (City) here, to close any facilities "in which high risk sexual activity takes place." * * *

* * *

The Public Health Council based this regulation on the Commissioner's "findings" that: "Establishments including certain bars, clubs and bathhouses which are used as places for engaging in high risk sexual activities contribute to the propagation and spread of such AIDS-associated retro-viruses * * * Appropriate public health intervention to discontinue such exposure at such establishments is essential to interrupting the epidemic among the people of the State of New York."

* * * Defendants challenged the State regulation on the grounds that it was an invasion of defendants' patrons' rights to privacy and freedom of association under the United States Constitution.

Nature of the Action

This action is brought pursuant to the Nuisance Abatement Law. Under that law [ ], the City is empowered to enjoin public nuisances * * * as defined in Administrative Code:

"1. By conduct either unlawful in itself or unreasonable under all the circumstances, he knowingly or recklessly creates or maintains a condition which endangers the safety or health of a considerable number of persons; or"

"2. He knowingly conducts or maintains any premises, place or resort where persons gather for purposes of engaging in unlawful conduct."

CONSTITUTIONAL CONSIDERATIONS

The City has submitted ample supporting proof that high risk sexual activity has been taking place at St. Mark's on a continuous and regular basis. Following numerous on-site visits by City inspectors, over 14 separate days, these investigators have submitted affidavits describing 49 acts of high risk sexual activity (consisting of 41 acts of fellatio involving 70 persons and 8 acts of anal intercourse involving 16 persons). This evidence of high risk sexual activity, all occurring either in public areas of St. Mark's or in enclosed cubicles left visible to the observer without intrusion therein, demonstrates the inadequacy of self-regulatory procedures by the St. Mark's attendant staff, and the futility of any less intrusive solution to the problem other than closure.

* * *

To be sure, defendants and the intervening patrons challenge the soundness of the scientific judgments upon which the Health Council regulation is based, citing, *inter alia*, the observation of the City's former Commissioner of Health in a memorandum dated October 22, 1985 that "closure of bathhouses will contribute little if anything to the control of AIDS." (For a vigorous medical opinion to the contrary from a specialist in this field see letter of Stephen S. Calazza, M.D., dated Jan. 24, 1985.) Defendants particularly assail the regulation's inclusion of fellatio as a high risk sexual activity and argue that enforced use of prophylactic sheaths would be a more appropriate regulatory response. They go further and argue that facilities such as St. Mark's, which attempts to educate its patrons with written materials, signed pledges, and posted notices as to the advisability of safe sexual practices, provide a positive force in combatting AIDS, and a valuable communication link between public health authorities and the homosexual community. While these arguments and proposals may have varying degrees of merit, they overlook a fundamental principle of applicable law: "It is not for the courts to determine which scientific view is correct in ruling upon whether the police power has been properly exercised. 'The judicial function is exhausted with the discovery that the relation between means and end is not wholly vain and fanciful, an illusory pretense' [ ].

* * *

Clearly, plaintiff Department of Health had discretion to pursue the remedy of civil injunctive relief. Defendants have no valid due process objection, inasmuch as they have been afforded a complete right to be heard in the course of litigating this application.

Accordingly, defendants' motion to dismiss the complaint is in all respects denied.

REYNOLDS v. McNICHOLS

United States Court of Appeals for the Tenth Circuit, 1973.
488 F.2d 1378.

McWILLIAMS, Circuit Judge.

This is a civil rights case brought by one Roxanne Reynolds under 42 U.S.C. §§ 1983 and 1985 against the City and County of Denver, its Mayor, the Honorable William McNichols, and certain of the city's officials and policemen. The gravamen of the complaint is that several of the constitutional rights of Roxanne Reynolds, hereinafter referred to as the plaintiff, were violated by the city and its officials in their enforcement of Denver's so-called "hold and treat" ordinance. This ordinance, among other things, purports to authorize under prescribed conditions the detention of one reasonably suspected of having a venereal disease, the examination of such person, and the treatment of such disease if it be determined that the person thus detained and examined does in fact have a venereal disease. The ordinance in question, Section 735 of the Revised Municipal Code of the City and County of Denver, is set out as Appendix I to this opinion.

It is the plaintiff's belief that the aforesaid ordinance is unconstitutional on its face, and, alternatively, that it has been unconstitutionally applied as to her. Upon trial to the court, the trial judge concluded that, contrary to the assertions of the plaintiff, the ordinance is constitutional on its face and that it has not been in anywise unconstitutionally applied as to her. Accordingly, the trial court entered judgment in favor of the city and its officials, and the plaintiff now appeals the judgment thus entered. We affirm.

* * *

The plaintiff, a twenty-seven year old female, who described herself as a model and prostitute, moved to Denver in the fall of 1970, and she first came to the attention of the Denver Police Department on November 29, 1970. On this latter date, she was arrested in a hotel room where she was in the company of a male person not her husband. At the trial of the instant civil rights case, the plaintiff testified that on this particular occasion she had agreed to have sexual relations with her male companion for a fee of $100, which fee had been paid. She denied, however, that at the time of her arrest she was in bed, and stated that on the contrary she was fully clothed and having a drink when the officers knocked at the door. So, whether this was a quid pro quo transaction is not disclosed by the record. In any event, the plaintiff was arrested and placed in the city jail and charged with violating city ordinances relating to solicitation and prostitution. In connection with these ordinance violations, the plaintiff was permitted a so-called "deferred prosecution," whereby she was not required to plead either guilty or not guilty, and the charges, after a passage of time, were dismissed. Although the record is not too clear, it appears that while in the city jail, plaintiff was given a blood test and an injection of penicillin and released on bond.

On May 21, 1971, and July 8, 1971, the plaintiff was issued a so-called "walk-in" order by the Denver police after complaints that plaintiff had been soliciting for acts of prostitution at a local Denver hotel bar. On neither of these occasions was the plaintiff placed in jail, but on the contrary she was simply ordered to report to the Department of Health and Hospitals for examination and possible treatment. On the first of these two occasions, the examination revealed that plaintiff had gonorrhea and drugs were administered therefor. On the second of these two occasions, the results of the examination were apparently negative to the end that no treatment was given.

On May 1, 1972, the plaintiff was given another "walk-in" order as she was alighting from her automobile preparatory to entering another Denver motel. On this occasion the plaintiff reported to the Department of Health and Hospitals with her attorney and refused to submit to any examination.

The plaintiff's final contact with the Denver Police Department occurred on June 19, 1972, when she was again arrested in a hotel room with a male person not her husband. On this occasion, according to the plaintiff, she and her male companion were "talking about an act of prostitution," but she added that any agreement had not been finalized. In any event, on this particular occasion plaintiff was again arrested and placed in the city jail, and charged with solicitation and prostitution. Thereafter, she was given the choice of being detained in the jail for forty-eight hours during which period of time she would be examined for venereal disease and treated therefor, if necessary, or simply taking penicillin, without an examination, in which event she would be immediately eligible for release. Plaintiff chose the latter alternative, and was orally given certain drugs, and released from custody. It is on this sequence of events that the plaintiff bases her civil rights action under 42 U.S.C. § 1983 and § 1985, claiming that the city and its officials acting pursuant to Ordinance 735 violated her rights under the Fourth and Fourteenth Amendments. By way of the relief prayed for, she sought monetary damages as well as injunctive relief. Let us now examine the ordinance in question as its various provisions relate to the facts of this case.

The legislative intent behind enactment of Ordinance 735 was to attempt to bring under control, and lessen, the incidence of venereal disease in Denver by determining and treating the source of such infection. The evidence before the trial court showed, incidentally, that the incidence of venereal disease had reached virtually epidemic proportions. To that end, the police were empowered under prescribed conditions to detain in jail certain persons "reasonably suspected" of being infected with a venereal disease, examine them for the presence of a venereal disease, and treat them for the same, if necessary. Such persons thus detained were ineligible for release on bond until the examining process was completed, which, according to the evidence, took forty-eight hours.

As an alternative to detention in jail for examination and treatment, the ordinance also provides that the police may "order in" certain other persons, "reasonably suspected" of having a venereal disease to the Department of Health and Hospitals for examination and treatment of venereal disease on either an in-patient or out-patient basis. As to whether one would be detained in jail for examination and treatment, or simply ordered to report to the Department of Health and Hospitals for examination and treatment, the ordinance further provided that the only persons who could be detained in jail for examination and treatment were those who were "reasonably suspected" of being infected with venereal disease by virtue of the fact that they had been arrested and charged with a violation of certain enumerated offenses * * *

Plaintiff's constitutional argument is summarized as follows: (1) The ordinance authorizes involuntary detention, without bond, involuntary examination and involuntary treatment, all in violation of her Fourth Amendment right to be secure in her person; (2) the ordinance does not spell out adequate guidelines as to the class of persons who can be compelled to submit to examination and treatment; (3) the current practice whereby a person, though initially detained in jail, is nonetheless eligible for immediate release if he or she submits to the injection of penicillin, even though there be no examination to indicate the presence of gonorrhea, results in an unconstitutional coercion of the person thus detained whereby one submits to an invasion of her right to be secure in her person in exchange for immediate release; (4) the injection of penicillin without first determining the presence of gonorrhea is contrary to accepted medical practice; and (5) the ordinance is applied only to females and not to males. In our view, none of these arguments stands up under scrutiny.

The principal thrust of the ordinance is aimed at bringing under control the *source* of communicable venereal disease. To that end, the city authorities are empowered to examine and treat those reasonably suspected of having an infectious venereal disease. It is not illogical or unreasonable, and on the contrary it is reasonable, to suspect that known prostitutes are a prime source of infectious venereal disease. Prostitution and venereal disease are no strangers.

In the instant case, the plaintiff freely admits, and the record amply supports her admission, that for some two and one-half years she was a prostitute operating in the Denver area and the fact that she was a prostitute was known to the local police. And in our view the fact that the plaintiff was a prostitute is of crucial significance. Finally, on at least one occasion, plaintiff was found to be infected with gonorrhea. Let us now examine the authorities.

Involuntary detention, for a limited period of time, of a person reasonably suspected of having a venereal disease for the purpose of permitting an examination of the person thus detained to determine the presence of a venereal disease and providing further for the treatment of such disease, if present, has been upheld by numerous state courts when challenged on a wide variety of constitutional grounds as a valid exercise of the police power designed to protect the public health. * * *

The aforesaid proposition would also appear to be in accord with the rationale of such cases as Jacobson v. Massachusetts, 197 U.S. 11, 49 L.Ed. 643, 25 S.Ct. 358 (1905), and Compagnie Francaise v. State Board of Health, 186 U.S. 380, 46 L.Ed. 1209, 22 S.Ct. 811 (1902), the former being concerned with compulsory smallpox vaccinations and the latter with a statute quarantining persons suspected of having infectious disease and precluding others from entry into the quarantined area. These two cases were concerned with, among other things, the interaction between the police power and the Fourteenth Amendment. Nor in our view is the proposition set forth above foreclosed by Camara v. Municipal Court of the City and County of San Francisco, 387 U.S. 523, 18 L.Ed.2d 930, 87 S.Ct. 1727 (1967). It is true that in *Camara* the Supreme Court struck down on Fourth Amendment grounds a municipal ordinance of San Francisco which authorized under certain conditions a warrantless inspection of an apartment building under the city's housing code. At the same time, however, the Court stated that nothing in the opinion was intended to foreclose "prompt inspections, even without a warrant, that the law has traditionally upheld in emergency situations," and cited with approval both Jacobson v. Massachusetts, *supra*, and Compagnie Francaise v. Board of Health, *supra*.

Under the authorities above cited, we conclude, as did the trial court, that the provisions of Ordinance No. 735 authorizing limited detention in jail without bond for the purpose of examination and treatment for a venereal disease of one reasonably suspected of having a venereal disease by virtue of the fact that she has been arrested and charged with solicitation and prostitution is a valid exercise of the police power. It would seem to follow that the milder provisions of the ordinance providing for a walk-in order of one reasonably suspected of having a venereal disease for the purpose of involuntary examination and treatment are also valid under the police power, and we so hold.

We now turn to the plaintiff's contention that the ordinance has been unconstitutionally applied to her. As above indicated, the evidence was that as a matter of practice a person detained in jail under the provisions of Ordinance 735 was given a choice between staying in jail while the examination was being conducted, or submitting to an immediate injection of penicillin, without examination, in which latter event the person would be eligible for immediate release. According to the record, there was no particular risk involved in the taking of a penicillin shot, nor was there any injurious effect from the injection of one who did not in fact have gonorrhea. On this state of the record, we find no unconstitutional coercion of the plaintiff. The provisions of the ordinance permitting limited detention for involuntary examination and treatment of a venereal disease being in themselves constitutional, the fact that the city provides a less onerous alternative, which the plaintiff in this case elected to follow, does not violate any constitutional right of the plaintiff.

Similarly, the claim that the ordinance was enforced only against females, and not males, is, under the circumstances of this case, insufficient to invoke the equal protection provision of the Fourteenth Amendment. The trial court indicated that it was of the view that the equal protection argument was not properly within the issues raised by the pleadings in the case and accordingly did not consider it. In any event, in our view plaintiff's suggestion that she was unconstitutionally dealt with by the city authorities is under the circumstances unavailing.

In regard to her equal protection argument, the fact that on the two occasions when plaintiff was arrested in a hotel room the plaintiff's customer was not himself arrested and detained for examination is not significant. From the record before us, there is nothing to indicate that plaintiff did in fact have sex relations with either of her male companions, though evidence of solicitation was obvious. Such being the case, there was no reason to examine plaintiff's male companions.

Be that as it may, as above indicated, the ordinance is aimed at the primary source of venereal disease and the plaintiff, being the prostitute, was the potential source, not her would-be customer. Plaintiff's argument in this regard would perhaps carry more weight if she had shown that male prostitutes were dealt with differently than female prostitutes. There is nothing in the record to show that such is the case. In fact, there is nothing in the record to indicate that male prostitution is as yet the vogue in Denver.

Judgment affirmed.

UNITED AUTO WORKERS v. JOHNSON CONTROLS, INC.

Supreme Court of the United States, 1991.
499 U.S. 187, 111 S.Ct. 1196, 113 L.Ed.2d 158.

JUSTICE BLACKMUN delivered the opinion of the Court.

In this case we are concerned with an employer's gender-based fetal-protection policy. May an employer exclude a fertile female employee from certain jobs because of its concern for the health of the fetus the woman might conceive?

I

Respondent Johnson Controls, Inc., manufactures batteries. In the manufacturing process, the element lead is a primary ingredient. Occupational exposure to lead entails health risks, including the risk of harm to any fetus carried by a female employee.

Before the Civil Rights Act of 1964, 78 Stat. 241, became law, Johnson Controls did not employ any woman in a battery-manufacturing job. In June 1977, however, it announced its first official policy concerning its employment of women in lead-exposure work:

"Protection of the health of the unborn child is the immediate and direct responsibility of the prospective parents. While the medical profession and the company can support them in the exercise of this responsibility, it cannot assume it for them without simultaneously infringing their rights as persons.

". . . . Since not all women who can become mothers wish to become mothers (or will become mothers), it would appear to be illegal discrimination to treat all who are capable of pregnancy as though they will become pregnant." [ ]

Consistent with that view, Johnson Controls "stopped short of excluding women capable of bearing children from lead exposure," [ ], but emphasized that a woman who expected to have a child should not choose a job in which she would have such exposure. The company also required a woman who wished to be considered for employment to sign a statement that she had been advised of the risk of having a child while she was exposed to lead. The statement informed the woman that although there was evidence "that women exposed to lead have a higher rate of abortion," this evidence was "not as clear . . . as the relationship between cigarette smoking and cancer," but that it was, "medically speaking, just good sense not to run that risk if you want children and do not want to expose the unborn child to risk, however small. . . . " [ ].

Five years later, in 1982, Johnson Controls shifted from a policy of warning to a policy of exclusion. Between 1979 and 1983, eight employees became pregnant while maintaining blood lead levels in excess of 30 micrograms per deciliter. This appeared to be the critical level noted by the Occupational Safety and Health Administration (OSHA) for a worker who was planning to have a family. The company responded by announcing a broad exclusion of women from jobs that exposed them to lead:

"It is [Johnson Controls'] policy that women who are pregnant or who are capable of bearing children will not be placed into jobs involving lead exposure or which could expose them to lead through the exercise of job bidding, bumping, transfer or promotion rights." [ ]

The policy defined "women . . . capable of bearing children" as "all women except those whose inability to bear children is medically documented." [ ] * * *

In April 1984, petitioners filed * * * a class action challenging Johnson Controls' fetal-protection policy as sex discrimination that violated Title VII of the Civil Rights Act of 1964 [ ]. Among the individual plaintiffs were petitioners Mary Craig, who had chosen to be sterilized in order to avoid losing her job, Elsie Nason, a 50–year–old divorcee, who had suffered a loss in compensation when she was transferred out of a job where she was exposed to lead, and Donald Penney, who had been denied a request for a leave of absence for the purpose of lowering his lead level because he intended to become a father. Upon stipulation of the parties, the District Court certified a class consisting of "all past, present and future production and maintenance employees" in United

Auto Workers bargaining units at nine of Johnson Controls' plants "who have been and continue to be affected by [the employer's] Fetal Protection Policy implemented in 1982." [ ]

The District Court granted summary judgment for defendant-respondent Johnson Controls. * * * The Court of Appeals for the Seventh Circuit, sitting en banc, affirmed the summary judgment by a 7-to-4 vote. [ ] The majority held that the proper standard for evaluating the fetal-protection policy was the defense of business necessity; that Johnson Controls was entitled to summary judgment under that defense; and that even if the proper standard was a BFOQ, Johnson Controls still was entitled to summary judgment.

The Court of Appeals first reviewed fetal-protection opinions from the Eleventh and Fourth Circuits. [ ]. Those opinions established the three-step business necessity inquiry: whether there is a substantial health risk to the fetus; whether transmission of the hazard to the fetus occurs only through women; and whether there is a less discriminatory alternative equally capable of preventing the health hazard to the fetus. The Court of Appeals agreed with the Eleventh and Fourth Circuits that "the components of the business necessity defense the courts of appeals and the EEOC have utilized in fetal protection cases balance the interests of the employer, the employee and the unborn child in a manner consistent with Title VII." [ ]. The court further noted that [ ] the burden of persuasion remained on the plaintiff in challenging a business necessity defense * * *.

* * *

The bias in Johnson Controls' policy is obvious. Fertile men, but not fertile women, are given a choice as to whether they wish to risk their reproductive health for a particular job. Section 703(a) of the Civil Rights Act of 1964, [ ] prohibits sex-based classifications in terms and conditions of employment, in hiring and discharging decisions, and in other employment decisions that adversely affect an employee's status. Respondent's fetal-protection policy explicitly discriminates against women on the basis of their sex. The policy excludes women with childbearing capacity from lead-exposed jobs and so creates a facial classification based on gender. Respondent assumes as much in its brief before this Court.

Nevertheless, the Court of Appeals assumed, as did the two appellate courts that already had confronted the issue, that sex-specific fetal-protection policies do not involve facial discrimination. [ ]. These courts analyzed the policies as though they were facially neutral and had only a discriminatory effect upon the employment opportunities of women. Consequently, the courts looked to see if each employer in question had established that its policy was justified as a business necessity. The business necessity standard is more lenient for the employer than the statutory BFOQ defense. The Court of Appeals here went one step further and invoked the burden-shifting framework set forth in *Wards Cove Packing Co.* v. *Atonio*, 490 U.S. 642 (1989), thus requiring petitioners to bear the burden of persuasion on all questions. The court assumed that because the asserted reason for the sex-based exclusion (protecting women's unconceived offspring) was ostensibly benign, the policy was not sex-based discrimination. That assumption, however, was incorrect.

First, Johnson Controls' policy classifies on the basis of gender and childbearing capacity, rather than fertility alone. Respondent does not seek to protect the unconceived children of all its employees. Despite evidence in the record about the debilitating effect of lead exposure on the male reproductive system, Johnson Controls is concerned only with the harms that may befall the unborn offspring of its female employees. * * *.

Our conclusion is bolstered by the Pregnancy Discrimination Act (PDA), 42 U. S. C. § 2000e(k), in which Congress explicitly provided that, for purposes of Title VII, discrimination " 'on the basis of sex' " includes discrimination "because of or on the basis of pregnancy, childbirth, or related medical conditions." [ ] "The Pregnancy Discrimination Act has now made clear that, for all Title VII purposes, discrimination based on a woman's pregnancy is, on its face, discrimination because of her sex." *Newport News Shipbuilding & Dry Dock Co.* v. *EEOC*, 462 U.S. 669, 684 (1983). In its use of the words "capable of bearing children" in the 1982 policy statement as the criterion for exclusion, Johnson Controls explicitly classifies on the basis of potential for pregnancy. Under the PDA, such a classification must be regarded, for Title VII purposes, in the same light as explicit sex discrimination. Respondent has chosen to treat all its female employees as potentially pregnant; that choice evinces discrimination on the basis of sex.

We concluded above that Johnson Controls' policy is not neutral because it does not apply to the reproductive capacity of the company's male employees in the same way as it applies to that of the females. Moreover, the absence of a malevolent motive does not convert a facially discriminatory policy into a neutral policy with a discriminatory effect. Whether an employment practice involves disparate treatment through explicit facial discrimination does not depend on why the employer discriminates but rather on the explicit terms of the discrimination. * * *

* * *

In sum, Johnson Controls' policy "does not pass the simple test of whether the evidence shows 'treatment of a person in a manner which but for that person's sex would be different.' " *Los Angeles Dept. of Water and Power* v. *Manhart*, 435 U.S. 702, 711 (1978), quoting Developments in the Law, Employment Discrimination and Title VII of the Civil Rights Act of 1964, 84 Harv. L. Rev. 1109, 1170 (1971). We hold that Johnson Controls' fetal-protection policy is sex discrimination forbidden under Title VII unless respondent can establish that sex is a "bona fide occupational qualification."

IV

Under § 703(e)(1) of Title VII, an employer may discriminate on the basis of "religion, sex, or national origin in those certain instances where religion, sex, or national origin is a bona fide occupational qualification reasonably necessary to the normal operation of that particular business or enterprise." 42 U. S. C. § 2000e–2(e)(1). We therefore turn to the question whether Johnson Controls' fetal-protection policy is one of those "certain instances" that come within the BFOQ exception.

* * *

The wording of the BFOQ defense contains several terms of restriction that indicate that the exception reaches only special situations. The statute thus limits the situations in which discrimination is permissible to "certain instances" where sex discrimination is "reasonably necessary" to the "normal operation" of the "particular" business. Each one of these terms—certain, normal, particular—prevents the use of general subjective standards and favors an objective, verifiable requirement. But the most telling term is "occupational"; this indicates that these objective, verifiable requirements must concern job-related skills and aptitudes.

* * *

Our case law, therefore, makes clear that the safety exception is limited to instances in which sex or pregnancy actually interferes with the employee's ability to perform the job. This approach is consistent with the language of the BFOQ provision itself, for it suggests that permissible distinctions based on sex must relate to ability to perform the duties of the job. Johnson Controls suggests, however, that we expand the exception to allow fetal-protection policies that mandate particular standards for pregnant or fertile women. We decline to do so. Such an expansion contradicts not only the language of the BFOQ and the narrowness of its exception, but also the plain language and history of the PDA.

We conclude that the language of both the BFOQ provision and the PDA which amended it, as well as the legislative history and the case law, prohibit an employer from discriminating against a woman because of her capacity to become pregnant unless her reproductive potential prevents her from performing the duties of her job. * * *

* * *

We have no difficulty concluding that Johnson Controls cannot establish a BFOQ. Fertile women, as far as appears in the record, participate in the manufacture of batteries as efficiently as anyone else. Johnson Controls' professed moral and ethical concerns about the welfare of the next generation do not suffice to establish a BFOQ of female sterility. Decisions about the welfare of future children must be left to the parents who conceive, bear, support, and raise them rather than to the employers who hire those parents. Congress has mandated this choice through Title VII, as amended by the PDA. Johnson Controls has attempted to exclude women because of their reproductive capacity. Title VII and the PDA simply do not allow a woman's dismissal because of her failure to submit to sterilization.

* * *

A word about tort liability and the increased cost of fertile women in the workplace is perhaps necessary. One of the dissenting judges in this case expressed concern about an employer's tort liability and concluded that liability for a potential injury to a fetus is a social cost that Title VII does not require a company to ignore. [ ] It is correct to say that Title VII does not prevent the employer from having a conscience. The statute, however, does prevent sex-specific fetal-protection policies. These two aspects of Title VII do not conflict.

More than 40 States currently recognize a right to recover for a prenatal injury based either on negligence or on wrongful death. [ ]. According to Johnson Controls, however, the company complies with the lead standard developed by OSHA and warns its female employees about the damaging effects of lead. It is worth noting that OSHA gave the problem of lead lengthy consideration and concluded that "there is no basis whatsoever for the claim that women of childbearing age should be excluded from the workplace in order to protect the fetus or the course of pregnancy." [ ] Instead, OSHA established a series of mandatory protections which, taken together, "should effectively minimize any risk to the fetus and newborn child." [ ]. Without negligence, it would be difficult for a court to find liability on the part of the employer. If, under general tort principles, Title VII bans sex-specific fetal-protection policies, the employer fully informs the woman of the risk, and the employer has not acted negligently, the basis for holding an employer liable seems remote at best.

* * *

The tort-liability argument reduces to two equally unpersuasive propositions. First, Johnson Controls attempts to solve the problem of reproductive health hazards by resorting to an exclusionary policy. Title VII plainly forbids illegal sex discrimination as a method of diverting attention from an employer's obligation to police the workplace. Second, the spectre of an award of damages reflects a fear that hiring fertile women will cost more. The extra cost of employing members of one sex, however, does not provide an affirmative Title VII defense for a discriminatory refusal to hire members of that gender. [ ] Indeed, in passing the PDA, Congress considered at length the considerable cost of providing equal treatment of pregnancy and related conditions, but made the "decision to forbid special treatment of pregnancy despite the social costs associated therewith." [ ]

We, of course, are not presented with, nor do we decide, a case in which costs would be so prohibitive as to threaten the survival of the employer's business. We merely reiterate our prior holdings that the incremental cost of hiring women cannot justify discriminating against them.

* * *

It is no more appropriate for the courts than it is for individual employers to decide whether a woman's reproductive role is more important to herself and her family than her economic role. Congress has left this choice to the woman as hers to make.

The judgment of the Court of Appeals is reversed[.]

JUSTICE SCALIA, concurring in the judgment.

I generally agree with the Court's analysis, but have some reservations, several of which bear mention.

First, I think it irrelevant that there was "evidence in the record about the debilitating effect of lead exposure on the male reproductive system," [ ]. Even without such evidence, treating women differently "on the basis of pregnancy" constitutes discrimination "on the basis of sex," because Congress has unequivocally said so. Pregnancy Discrimination Act [ ].

Second, the Court points out that "Johnson Controls has shown no factual basis for believing that all or substantially all women would be unable to perform safely ... the duties of the job involved," [ ]. In my view, this is not only "somewhat academic in light of our conclusion that the company may not exclude fertile women at all," it is entirely irrelevant. By reason of the Pregnancy Discrimination Act, it would not matter if all pregnant women placed their children at risk in taking these jobs, just as it does not matter if no men do so. As Judge Easterbrook put it in his dissent below: "Title VII gives parents the power to make occupational decisions affecting their families. A legislative forum is available to those who believe that such decisions should be made elsewhere." [ ]

Third, I am willing to assume, as the Court intimates, that any action required by Title VII cannot give rise to liability under state tort law. That assumption, however, does not answer the question whether an action *is* required by Title VII (including the BFOQ provision) even if it is subject to liability under state tort law. It is perfectly reasonable to believe that Title VII has *accommodated* state tort law through the BFOQ exception. However, all that need be said in the present case is that Johnson has not demonstrated a substantial risk of tort liability—which is alone enough to defeat a tort-based assertion of the BFOQ exception.

Last, the Court goes far afield, it seems to me, in suggesting that increased cost alone—short of "costs ... so prohibitive as to threaten the survival of the employer's business,"—cannot support a BFOQ defense. [N]othing in our prior cases suggests this, and in my view it is wrong. I think, for example, that a shipping company may refuse to hire pregnant women as crew members on long voyages because the on-board facilities for foreseeable emergencies, though quite feasible, would be inordinately expensive. In the present case, however, Johnson has not asserted a cost-based BFOQ.

Notes

1) An earlier New York decision preceding *St. Mark's Bath* laid the foundation for closing establishments that are recognized as having a high and uncontrolled risk of transmitting infectious disease. See *Grossman v. Baumgartner*, 17 N.Y.2d 345, 271 N.Y.S.2d 195, 218 N.E.2d 259 (1966). When the nuisance to be abated has no redeeming social or business value and the activity is "open and notorious" the case is even more compelling. Tattoo parlors and adult bookstores might be similar establishments. If certain legitimate establishments become notorious meeting places for arranging certain types of illegal and unhealthy activities, are they also vulnerable to public health regulation?

2) *Reynolds v. McNichols* provides an old answer to an even older problem. Today it is unclear whether a single injectable dose of penicillin is even sound public health policy. With HIV and AIDS transmission surpassing syphilis as the major public health concerns of prostitution, would the ordinance still be upheld? Does it matter whether reliable treatment is available? Can you think of a more effective way that protection of the public's health can be promoted given the reality of prostitution?

3) Suppose that your goal was to protect women of child-bearing age from being coerced to work at Johnson Controls because there are few jobs in the area that provide the job benefits, stability, etc., of this large battery factory. Suppose these women were being coerced into jeopardizing the well-being of their yet-to-be born children by the economics and other realities of the workplace. Suppose there were credible evidence that the lead affects a woman's reproductive system in ways that make exposure to lead significantly more harmful to women than men. What arguments might you make on their behalf? Can you construct a circumstance in which the science is used to promote public health policy without the discriminatory impact of *Johnson Controls*?

Chapter 15

PUBLIC HEALTH AND SAFETY

INTRODUCTORY NOTE

It is understandable that the federal government would seek to enact federal provisions to protect the health and welfare of all citizens in the United States. Universal issues such as gun control and regulation of safety devices require solutions in every state, and when such matters affect interstate commerce, Congress is entitled to regulate. In the absence of a valid constitutional grant of power, however, protection of health and safety is a state matter, and as sovereign governments, they retain the power granted to them by the tenth amendment: "The powers not delegated to the United States by the Constitution, nor prohibited by it to the States, are reserved to the States, respectively, or to the people."

State police powers safeguard the ability of the state to enact laws and regulations to protect and preserve the health, safety and general welfare of the public. The police power entitles state governments to restrict or regulate private interests such as gun possession, safety standards and devices, quarantine of illness and other harms as long as they do so within the bounds of federal and state constitutional principles.

Of course, there are some public health functions that are legitimately carried out at the federal level. Matters that significantly impact interstate commerce are clear subjects for federal regulation. It is not enough to contend that interstate commerce will be affected, however. In the first two cases that follow, an impact on interstate commerce was alleged, but rejected by the Supreme Court.

The Rehnquist Court of the late twentieth and early twenty-first centuries has been particularly active in the area of public health in contributing to what has become labeled the "new federalism." As a concept of political change, "new federalism" refers to assertion of state power and authority to limit the capacity of the federal government to govern in matters of state authority. This has become particularly contentious in the area of public health where, arguably, more than one level of government has significant interest in matters that affect the well-being of the public.

SECTION A.   FIREARMS

UNITED STATES v. LOPEZ

Supreme Court of the United States, 1995.
514 U.S. 549, 115 S.Ct. 1624, 131 L.Ed.2d 626.

CHIEF JUSTICE REHNQUIST delivered the opinion of the Court.

In the Gun–Free School Zones Act of 1990, Congress made it a federal offense "for any individual knowingly to possess a firearm at a place that the individual knows, or has reasonable cause to believe, is a school zone." 18 U.S.C. § 922 (q)(1)(A) (1988 ed., Supp. V). The Act neither regulates a commercial activity nor contains a requirement that the possession be connected in any way to interstate commerce. We hold that the Act exceeds the authority of Congress "to regulate Commerce ... among the several States.... " U.S. Const., Art. I, § 8, cl. 3.

On March 10, 1992, respondent, who was then a 12th-grade student, arrived at Edison High School in San Antonio, Texas, carrying a concealed .38 caliber handgun and five bullets. Acting upon an anonymous tip, school authorities confronted respondent, who admitted that he was carrying the weapon. He was arrested and charged under Texas law with firearm possession on school premises. [ ]. The next day, the state charges were dismissed after federal agents charged respondent by complaint with violating the Gun–Free School Zones Act of 1990.

A federal grand jury indicted respondent on one count of knowing possession of a firearm at a school zone, in violation of § 922(q). Respondent moved to dismiss his federal indictment on the ground that § 922(q) "is unconstitutional as it is beyond the power of Congress to legislate control over our public schools." The District Court denied the motion, concluding that § 922(q) "is a constitutional exercise of Congress' well-defined power to regulate activities in and affecting commerce, and the 'business' of elementary, middle and high schools ... affects interstate commerce." [ ]. The District Court * * * found him guilty of violating § 922(q), and sentenced him to six months' imprisonment and two years' supervised release.

* * *

The Constitution delegates to Congress the power "to regulate Commerce with foreign Nations, and among the several States, and with the Indian Tribes." Art. I, § 8, cl. 3. The Court, through Chief Justice Marshall, first defined the nature of Congress' commerce power in *Gibbons* v. *Ogden*, 22 U.S. 1, 9 Wheat. 1, 189–190, 6 L.Ed. 23 (1824):

"Commerce, undoubtedly, is traffic, but it is something more: it is intercourse. It describes the commercial intercourse between nations, and parts of nations, in all its branches, and is regulated by prescribing rules for carrying on that intercourse."

The commerce power "is the power to regulate; that is, to prescribe the rule by which commerce is to be governed. This power, like all others vested in congress, is complete in itself, may be exercised to its utmost extent, and acknowledges no limitations, other than are prescribed in the constitution." *Id.*, at 196. The *Gibbons* Court, however, acknowledged that limitations on the commerce power are inherent in the very language of the Commerce Clause.

"It is not intended to say that these words comprehend that commerce, which is completely internal, which is carried on between man and man in a State, or between different parts of the same State, and which does not extend to or affect other States. Such a power would be inconvenient, and is certainly unnecessary.

"Comprehensive as the word 'among' is, it may very properly be restricted to that commerce which concerns more States than one.... The enumeration presupposes something not enumerated; and that something, if we regard the language, or the subject of the sentence, must be the exclusively internal commerce of a State." *Id.*, at 194–195.

For nearly a century thereafter, the Court's Commerce Clause decisions dealt but rarely with the extent of Congress' power, and almost entirely with the Commerce Clause as a limit on state legislation that discriminated against interstate commerce.

In 1887, Congress enacted the Interstate Commerce Act, 24 Stat. 379, and in 1890, Congress enacted the Sherman Antitrust Act, 26 Stat. 209, as amended, 15 U.S.C. § 1 *et seq.* These laws ushered in a new era of federal regulation under the commerce power. When cases involving these laws first reached this Court, we imported from our negative Commerce Clause cases the approach that Congress could not regulate activities such as "production," "manufacturing," and "mining." * * * Simultaneously, however, the Court held that, where the interstate and intrastate aspects of commerce were so mingled together that full regulation of interstate commerce required incidental regulation of intrastate commerce, the Commerce Clause authorized such regulation. [ ].

In *A. L. A. Schechter Poultry Corp.* v. *United States*, 295 U.S. 495, 550, 79 L.Ed. 1570, 55 S.Ct. 837 (1935), the Court struck down regulations that fixed the hours and wages of individuals employed by an intrastate business because the activity being regulated related to interstate commerce only indirectly. In doing so, the Court characterized the distinction between direct and indirect effects of intrastate transactions upon interstate commerce as "a fundamental one, essential to the maintenance of our constitutional system." *Id.*, at 548. Activities that affected interstate commerce directly were within Congress' power; activities that affected interstate commerce indirectly were beyond Congress' reach. *Id.*, at 546. The justification for this formal distinction was rooted in the fear that otherwise "there would be virtually no limit to the federal power and for all practical purposes we should have a completely centralized government." *Id.*, at 548.

Two years later, in the watershed case of *NLRB* v. *Jones & Laughlin Steel Corp.*, 301 U.S. 1, 81 L.Ed. 893, 57 S.Ct. 615 (1937), the Court upheld the National Labor Relations Act against a Commerce Clause challenge, and in the process, departed from the distinction between "direct" and "indirect" effects on interstate commerce. *Id.*, at 36–38 ("The question [of the scope of Congress' power] is necessarily one of degree"). The Court held that intrastate activities that "have such a close and substantial relation to interstate commerce that their control is essential or appropriate to protect that commerce from burdens and obstructions" are within Congress' power to regulate. [ ]

In *United States* v. *Darby*, 312 U.S. 100, 85 L.Ed. 609, 61 S.Ct. 451 (1941), the Court upheld the Fair Labor Standards Act, stating:

> "The power of Congress over interstate commerce is not confined to the regulation of commerce among the states. It extends to those activities intrastate which so affect interstate commerce or the exercise of the power of Congress over it as to make regulation of them appropriate means to the attainment of a legitimate end, the exercise of the granted power of Congress to regulate interstate commerce." *Id.*, at 118.

* * *

But even these modern-era precedents which have expanded congressional power under the Commerce Clause confirm that this power is subject to outer limits. In *Jones & Laughlin Steel*, the Court warned that the scope of the interstate commerce power "must be considered in the light of our dual system of government and may not be extended so as to embrace effects upon interstate commerce so indirect and remote that to embrace them, in view of our complex society, would effectually obliterate the distinction between what is national and what is local and create a completely centralized government." 301 U.S. at 37. * * *

* * *

Consistent with this structure, we have identified three broad categories of activity that Congress may regulate under its commerce power. [ ]. First, Congress may regulate the use of the channels of interstate commerce. See, *e.g., Darby*, 312 U.S. at 114; *Heart of Atlanta Motel, supra*, at 256 (" 'The authority of Congress to keep the channels of interstate commerce free from immoral and injurious uses has been frequently sustained, and is no longer open to question' ") [ ]. Second, Congress is empowered to regulate and protect the instrumentalities of interstate commerce, or persons or things in interstate commerce, even though the threat may come only from intrastate activities. [citations omitted]. Finally, Congress' commerce authority includes the power to regulate those activities having a substantial relation to interstate commerce, *Jones & Laughlin Steel*, 301 U.S. at 37, *i.e.*, those activities that substantially affect interstate commerce [ ].

Within this final category, admittedly, our case law has not been clear whether an activity must "affect" or "substantially affect" interstate commerce in order to be within Congress' power to regulate it under the Commerce Clause. [ ] We conclude, consistent with the great weight of our case law, that the proper test requires an analysis of whether the regulated activity "substantially affects" interstate commerce.

We now turn to consider the power of Congress, in the light of this framework, to enact § 922(q). The first two categories of authority may be quickly disposed of: § 922(q) is not a regulation of the use of the channels of interstate commerce, nor is it an attempt to prohibit the interstate transportation of a commodity through the channels of commerce; nor can § 922(q) be justified as a regulation by which Congress has sought to protect an instrumentality of interstate commerce or a thing in interstate commerce. Thus, if § 922(q) is to be sustained, it must be under the third category as a regulation of an activity that substantially affects interstate commerce.

First, we have upheld a wide variety of congressional Acts regulating intrastate economic activity where we have concluded that the activity substantially affected interstate commerce. * * * Where economic activity substantially affects interstate commerce, legislation regulating that activity will be sustained.

Even *Wickard*, which is perhaps the most far reaching example of Commerce Clause authority over intrastate activity, involved economic activity in a way that the possession of a gun in a school zone does not. Roscoe Filburn operated a small farm in Ohio, on which, in the year involved, he raised 23 acres of wheat. It was his practice to sow winter wheat in the fall, and after harvesting it in July to sell a portion of the crop, to feed part of it to poultry and livestock on the farm, to use some in making flour for home consumption, and to keep the remainder for seeding future crops. The Secretary of Agriculture assessed a penalty against him under the Agricultural Adjustment Act of 1938 because he harvested about 12 acres more wheat than his allotment under the Act permitted. The Act was designed to regulate the volume of wheat moving in interstate and foreign commerce in order to avoid surpluses and shortages, and concomitant fluctuation in wheat prices, which had previously obtained. The Court said, in an opinion sustaining the application of the Act to Filburn's activity:

> "One of the primary purposes of the Act in question was to increase the market price of wheat and to that end to limit the volume thereof that could affect the market. It can hardly be denied that a factor of such volume and variability as home-consumed wheat would have a substantial influence on price and market conditions. This may arise because being in marketable condition such wheat overhangs the market and, if induced by rising prices, tends to flow into the market and check price increases. But if we assume that it is never marketed, it supplies a need of the man who grew it which would otherwise be reflected by purchases in the open market.

Home-grown wheat in this sense competes with wheat in commerce." 317 U.S. at 128.

Section 922(q) is a criminal statute that by its terms has nothing to do with "commerce" or any sort of economic enterprise, however broadly one might define those terms. n3 Section 922(q) is not an essential part of a larger regulation of economic activity, in which the regulatory scheme could be undercut unless the intrastate activity were regulated. It cannot, therefore, be sustained under our cases upholding regulations of activities that arise out of or are connected with a commercial transaction, which viewed in the aggregate, substantially affects interstate commerce.

Second, § 922(q) contains no jurisdictional element which would ensure, through case-by-case inquiry, that the firearm possession in question affects interstate commerce. For example, in *United States* v. *Bass*, 404 U.S. 336, 30 L.Ed.2d 488, 92 S.Ct. 515 (1971), the Court interpreted former 18 U.S.C. § 1202(a), which made it a crime for a felon to "receive, posses[s], or transport in commerce or affecting commerce ... any firearm." [ ]. The Court interpreted the possession component of § 1202(a) to require an additional nexus to interstate commerce both because the statute was ambiguous and because "unless Congress conveys its purpose clearly, it will not be deemed to have significantly changed the federal-state balance." [ ]. The *Bass* Court set aside the conviction because although the Government had demonstrated that Bass had possessed a firearm, it had failed "to show the requisite nexus with interstate commerce." [ ]. The Court thus interpreted the statute to reserve the constitutional question whether Congress could regulate, without more, the "mere possession" of firearms. * * *

Although as part of our independent evaluation of constitutionality under the Commerce Clause we of course consider legislative findings, and indeed even congressional committee findings, regarding effect on interstate commerce [ ], the Government concedes that "neither the statute nor its legislative history contain[s] express congressional findings regarding the effects upon interstate commerce of gun possession in a school zone." [ ]. We agree with the Government that Congress normally is not required to make formal findings as to the substantial burdens that an activity has on interstate commerce. [ ]

* * *

The Government argues that Congress has accumulated institutional expertise regarding the regulation of firearms through previous enactments. [ ]. We agree, however, with the Fifth Circuit that importation of previous findings to justify § 922(q) is especially inappropriate here because the "prior federal enactments or Congressional findings [do not] speak to the subject matter of section 922(q) or its relationship to interstate commerce. Indeed, section 922(q) plows thoroughly new ground and represents a sharp break with the long-standing pattern of federal firearms legislation." 2 F.3d at 1366.

The Government's essential contention, *in fine*, is that we may determine here that § 922(q) is valid because possession of a firearm in a local school zone does indeed substantially affect interstate commerce. [ ]. The Government argues that possession of a firearm in a school zone may result in violent crime and that violent crime can be expected to affect the functioning of the national economy in two ways. First, the costs of violent crime are substantial, and, through the mechanism of insurance, those costs are spread throughout the population. [ ]. Second, violent crime reduces the willingness of individuals to travel to areas within the country that are perceived to be unsafe. [ ]. The Government also argues that the presence of guns in schools poses a substantial threat to the educational process by threatening the learning environment. A handicapped educational process, in turn, will result in a less productive citizenry. That, in turn, would have an adverse effect on the Nation's economic well-being. As a result, the Government argues that Congress could rationally have concluded that § 922(q) substantially affects interstate commerce.

We pause to consider the implications of the Government's arguments. The Government admits, under its "costs of crime" reasoning, that Congress could regulate not only all violent crime, but all activities that might lead to violent crime, regardless of how tenuously they relate to interstate commerce. [ ]. Similarly, under the Government's "national productivity" reasoning, Congress could regulate any activity that it found was related to the economic productivity of individual citizens: family law (including marriage, divorce, and child custody), for example. Under the theories that the Government presents in support of § 922(q), it is difficult to perceive any limitation on federal power, even in areas such as criminal law enforcement or education where States historically have been sovereign. Thus, if we were to accept the Government's arguments, we are hard pressed to posit any activity by an individual that Congress is without power to regulate.

Although JUSTICE BREYER argues that acceptance of the Government's rationales would not authorize a general federal police power, he is unable to identify any activity that the States may regulate but Congress may not. JUSTICE BREYER posits that there might be some limitations on Congress' commerce power, such as family law or certain aspects of education. [ ]. These suggested limitations, when viewed in light of the dissent's expansive analysis, are devoid of substance.

JUSTICE BREYER focuses, for the most part, on the threat that firearm possession in and near schools poses to the educational process and the potential economic consequences flowing from that threat. [ ]. Specifically, the dissent reasons that (1) gun-related violence is a serious problem; (2) that problem, in turn, has an adverse effect on classroom learning; and (3) that adverse effect on classroom learning, in turn, represents a substantial threat to trade and commerce. [ ]. This analysis would be equally applicable, if not more so, to subjects such as family law and direct regulation of education.

For instance, if Congress can, pursuant to its Commerce Clause power, regulate activities that adversely affect the learning environment, then, *a fortiori*, it also can regulate the educational process directly. Congress could determine that a school's curriculum has a "significant" effect on the extent of classroom learning. As a result, Congress could mandate a federal curriculum for local elementary and secondary schools because what is taught in local schools has a significant "effect on classroom learning," cf. *ibid.*, and that, in turn, has a substantial effect on interstate commerce.

JUSTICE BREYER rejects our reading of precedent and argues that "Congress . . . could rationally conclude that schools fall on the commercial side of the line." *Post*, at 629. Again, JUSTICE BREYER's rationale lacks any real limits because, depending on the level of generality, any activity can be looked upon as commercial. Under the dissent's rationale, Congress could just as easily look at child rearing as "falling on the commercial side of the line" because it provides a "valuable service— namely, to equip [children] with the skills they need to survive in life and, more specifically, in the workplace." *Ibid.* We do not doubt that Congress has authority under the Commerce Clause to regulate numerous commercial activities that substantially affect interstate commerce and also affect the educational process. That authority, though broad, does not include the authority to regulate each and every aspect of local schools.

Admittedly, a determination whether an intrastate activity is commercial or noncommercial may in some cases result in legal uncertainty. But, so long as Congress' authority is limited to those powers enumerated in the Constitution, and so long as those enumerated powers are interpreted as having judicially enforceable outer limits, congressional legislation under the Commerce Clause always will engender "legal uncertainty."

* * *

These are not precise formulations, and in the nature of things they cannot be. But we think they point the way to a correct decision of this case. The possession of a gun in a local school zone is in no sense an economic activity that might, through repetition elsewhere, substantially affect any sort of interstate commerce. Respondent was a local student at a local school; there is no indication that he had recently moved in interstate commerce, and there is no requirement that his possession of the firearm have any concrete tie to interstate commerce.

To uphold the Government's contentions here, we would have to pile inference upon inference in a manner that would bid fair to convert congressional authority under the Commerce Clause to a general police power of the sort retained by the States. Admittedly, some of our prior cases have taken long steps down that road, giving great deference to congressional action. [ ] The broad language in these opinions has suggested the possibility of additional expansion, but we decline here to proceed any further. To do so would require us to conclude that the

Constitution's enumeration of powers does not presuppose something not enumerated [ ]and that there never will be a distinction between what is truly national and what is truly local [ ]. This we are unwilling to do.

For the foregoing reasons the judgment of the Court of Appeals is *Affirmed*.

Justice Stevens, dissenting.

* * *

PRINTZ v. UNITED STATES

Supreme Court of the United States, 1997.
521 U.S. 898, 117 S.Ct. 2365, 138 L.Ed.2d 914.

JUSTICE SCALIA delivered the opinion of the Court.

The question presented in these cases is whether certain interim provisions of the Brady Handgun Violence Prevention Act [ ] commanding state and local law enforcement officers to conduct background checks on prospective handgun purchasers and to perform certain related tasks, violate the Constitution.

I

The Gun Control Act of 1968 (GCA), 18 U.S.C. § 921 *et seq.*, establishes a detailed federal scheme governing the distribution of firearms. It prohibits firearms dealers from transferring handguns to any person under 21, not resident in the dealer's State, or prohibited by state or local law from purchasing or possessing firearms, § 922(b). It also forbids possession of a firearm by, and transfer of a firearm to, convicted felons, fugitives from justice, unlawful users of controlled substances, persons adjudicated as mentally defective or committed to mental institutions, aliens unlawfully present in the United States, persons dishonorably discharged from the Armed Forces, persons who have renounced their citizenship, and persons who have been subjected to certain restraining orders or been convicted of a misdemeanor offense involving domestic violence. [ ]

In 1993, Congress amended the GCA by enacting the Brady Act. The Act requires the Attorney General to establish a national instant background check system [ ] and immediately puts in place certain interim provisions until that system becomes operative. Under the interim provisions, a firearms dealer who proposes to transfer a handgun must first: (1) receive from the transferee a statement (the Brady Form), [ ] containing the name, address and date of birth of the proposed transferee along with a sworn statement that the transferee is not among any of the classes of prohibited purchasers, [ ] verify the identity of the transferee by examining an identification document, provide the "chief law enforcement officer" (CLEO) of the transferee's residence with notice of the contents (and a copy) of the Brady Form [ ]. With some exceptions, the dealer must then wait five business days before consummating the sale, unless the CLEO earlier notifies the dealer that he has no reason to believe the transfer would be illegal. [ ].

The Brady Act creates two significant alternatives to the foregoing scheme. A dealer may sell a handgun immediately if the purchaser possesses a state handgun permit issued after a background check [ ] or if state law provides for an instant background check [ ]. In States that have not rendered one of these alternatives applicable to all gun purchasers, CLEOs are required to perform certain duties. When a CLEO receives the required notice of a proposed transfer from the firearms dealer, the CLEO must "make a reasonable effort to ascertain within 5 business days whether receipt or possession would be in violation of the law, including research in whatever State and local recordkeeping systems are available and in a national system designated by the Attorney General." [ ]. The Act does not require the CLEO to take any particular action if he determines that a pending transaction would be unlawful; he may notify the firearms dealer to that effect, but is not required to do so. If, however, the CLEO notifies a gun dealer that a prospective purchaser is ineligible to receive a handgun, he must, upon request, provide the would-be purchaser with a written statement of the reasons for that determination.

[ ]. Moreover, if the CLEO does not discover any basis for objecting to the sale, he must destroy any records in his possession relating to the transfer, including his copy of the Brady Form. [ ]. Under a separate provision of the GCA, any person who "knowingly violates [the section of the GCA amended by the Brady Act] shall be fined under this title, imprisoned for no more than 1 year, or both." [ ].

Petitioners Jay Printz and Richard Mack, the CLEOs for Ravalli County, Montana, and Graham County, Arizona, respectively, filed separate actions challenging the constitutionality of the Brady Act's interim provisions. In each case, the District Court held that the provision requiring CLEOs to perform background checks was unconstitutional, but concluded that that provision was severable from the remainder of the Act, effectively leaving a voluntary background-check system in place. [ ]. A divided panel of the Court of Appeals for the Ninth Circuit reversed, finding none of the Brady Act's interim provisions to be unconstitutional. [ ]. We granted certiorari. [ ].

II

From the description set forth above, it is apparent that the Brady Act purports to direct state law enforcement officers to participate, albeit only temporarily, in the administration of a federally enacted regulatory scheme. Regulated firearms dealers are required to forward Brady Forms not to a federal officer or employee, but to the CLEOs, whose obligation to accept those forms is implicit in the duty imposed upon them to make "reasonable efforts" within five days to determine whether the sales reflected in the forms are lawful. While the CLEOs are subjected to no federal requirement that they prevent the sales determined to be unlawful (it is perhaps assumed that their state-law duties will require prevention or apprehension), they are empowered to grant, in effect, waivers of the federally prescribed 5–day waiting period for handgun purchases by notifying the gun dealers that they have no reason to believe the transactions would be illegal.

The petitioners here object to being pressed into federal service, and contend that congressional action compelling state officers to execute federal laws is unconstitutional.

Because there is no constitutional text speaking to this precise question, the answer to the CLEOs' challenge must be sought in historical understanding and practice, in the structure of the Constitution, and in the jurisprudence of this Court. We treat those three sources, in that order, in this and the next two sections of this opinion.

Petitioners contend that compelled enlistment of state executive officers for the administration of federal programs is, until very recent years at least, unprecedented. The Government contends, to the contrary, that "the earliest Congresses enacted statutes that required the participation of state officials in the implementation of federal laws," * * *

The Government observes that statutes enacted by the first Congresses required state courts to record applications for citizenship * * *

These early laws establish, at most, that the Constitution was originally understood to permit imposition of an obligation on state *judges* to enforce federal prescriptions, insofar as those prescriptions related to matters appropriate for the judicial power.

* * *

* * * [W]e do not think the early statutes imposing obligations on state courts imply a power of Congress to impress the state executive into its service. Indeed, it can be argued that the numerousness of these statutes, contrasted with the utter lack of statutes imposing obligations on the States' executive (notwithstanding the attractiveness of that course to Congress), suggests an assumed *absence* of such power. The only early federal law the Government has brought to our attention that imposed duties on state executive officers is the Extradition Act of 1793, which required the "executive authority" of a State to cause the arrest and delivery of a fugitive from justice upon the request of the executive authority of the State from which the fugitive had fled. [ ]. That was in direct implementation, however, of the Extradition Clause of the Constitution itself [ ].

Not only do the enactments of the early Congresses, as far as we are aware, contain no evidence of an assumption that the Federal Government may command the States' executive power in the absence of a particularized constitutional authorization, they contain some indication of precisely the opposite assumption. On September 23, 1789—the day before its proposal of the Bill of Rights [ ]—the First Congress enacted a law aimed at obtaining state assistance of the most rudimentary and necessary sort for the enforcement of the new Government's laws: the holding of federal prisoners in state jails at federal expense. Significantly, the law issued not a command to the States' executive, but a recommendation to their legislatures. Congress "recommended to the legislatures of the several States to pass laws, making it expressly the duty of the keepers of their goals, to receive and safe keep therein all prisoners committed under the authority of the United States," and offered to pay 50 cents per month for each prisoner. [ ]. Moreover, when Georgia refused to comply with the request, [ ], Congress's only reaction was a law authorizing the marshal in any State that failed to comply with the Recommendation of September 23, 1789, to rent a temporary jail until provision for a permanent one could be made [ ].

* * *

[A] passage of The Federalist reads as follows:

"It merits particular attention . . . , that the laws of the Confederacy as to the *enumerated* and *legitimate* objects of its jurisdiction will become the SUPREME LAW of the land; to the observance of which all officers, legislative, executive, and judicial in each State will be bound by the sanctity of an oath. Thus, the legislatures, courts, and magistrates, of the respective members will be incorporated into the operations of the national government *as far as its just and constitutional authority extends;* and will be rendered auxiliary to the enforcement of its laws." The Federalist No. 27, at 177 (A. Hamilton) (emphasis in original).

The Government does not rely upon this passage, but JUSTICE SOUTER (with whose conclusions on this point the dissent is in agreement [ ]) makes it the very foundation of his position; so we pause to examine it in some detail. JUSTICE SOUTER finds "the natural reading" of the phrases "will be incorporated into the operations of the national government" and "will be rendered auxiliary to the enforcement of its laws" to be that the National Government will have "authority . . . , when exercising an otherwise legitimate power (the commerce power, say), to require state 'auxiliaries' to take appropriate action." [ ]. There are several obstacles to such an interpretation. First, the consequences in question ("incorporated into the operations of the national government" and "rendered auxiliary to the enforcement of its laws") are said in the quoted passage to flow *automatically* from the officers' oath to observe the "the laws of the Confederacy as to the *enumerated* and *legitimate* objects of its jurisdiction." Thus, if the passage means that state officers must take an active role in the implementation of federal law, it means that they must do so without the necessity for a congressional directive that they implement it. But no one has ever thought, and no one asserts in the present litigation, that that is the law. The second problem with JUSTICE SOUTER's reading is that it makes state *legislatures* subject to federal direction. (The passage in question, after all, does not include legislatures merely incidentally, as by referring to "all state officers"; it refers to legislatures *specifically* and *first of all*.)

We have held, however, that state legislatures are *not* subject to federal direction. [ ]

* * *

These problems are avoided, of course, if the calculatedly vague consequences the passage recites—"incorporated into the operations of the national government" and "rendered auxiliary to the enforcement of its laws"—are taken to refer to nothing more (or less) than the duty owed to the National Government, on the part of *all* state officials, to enact, enforce, and interpret state law in such fashion as not to obstruct the operation of federal law, and the attendant reality that all state actions constituting such obstruction, even legislative acts, are *ipso facto* invalid. [ ].

* * *

To complete the historical record, we must note that there is not only an absence of executive-commandeering statutes in the early Congresses, but there is an absence of them in our later history as well, at least until very recent years. * * *

The Government cites the World War I selective draft law that authorized the President "to utilize the service of any or all departments and any or all officers or agents of the United States *and of the several States,* Territories, and the District of Columbia, and subdivisions thereof, in the execution of this Act," and made any person who refused to comply with the President's directions guilty of a misdemeanor. [ ]. However, it is far from clear that the authorization "to utilize the service" of state officers was an authorization to *compel* the service of state officers; and the misdemeanor provision surely applied only to refusal to comply with the President's *authorized* directions, which might not have included directions to officers of States whose governors had not volunteered their services. It is interesting that in implementing the Act President Wilson did not commandeer the services of state officers, but instead requested the assistance of the States' governors * * *

The Government points to a number of federal statutes enacted within the past few decades that require the participation of state or local officials in implementing federal regulatory schemes. Some of these are connected to federal funding measures, and can perhaps be more accurately described as conditions upon the grant of federal funding than as mandates to the States; others, which require only the provision of information to the Federal Government, do not involve the precise issue before us here, which is the forced participation of the States' executive in the actual administration of a federal program. * * *

III

* * *

A

It is incontestible that the Constitution established a system of "dual sovereignty." * * *

The Framers' experience under the Articles of Confederation had persuaded them that using the States as the instruments of federal governance was both ineffectual and provocative of federal-state conflict. [ ]. Preservation of the States as independent political entities being the price of union, and "the practicality of making laws, with coercive sanctions, for the States as political bodies" having been, in Madison's words, "exploded on all hands," [ ] the Framers rejected the concept of a central government that would act upon and through the States, and instead designed a system in which the state and federal governments would exercise concurrent authority over the people—who were, in Hamilton's words, "the only proper objects of government," [ ]. * * *. It suffices to repeat the conclusion: "The Framers explicitly chose a Constitution that confers upon Congress the power to regulate individuals, not States." [ ] The great innovation of this design was that "our citizens would have two political capacities, one state and one federal, each protected from incursion by the other"—"a legal system unprecedented in form and design, establishing two orders of government, each with its own direct relationship, its own privity, its own set of mutual rights and obligations to the people who sustain it and are governed by it." * * *

This separation of the two spheres is one of the Constitution's structural protections of liberty. "Just as the separation and independence of the coordinate branches of the Federal Government serve to prevent the accumulation of excessive power in any one branch, a healthy balance of power between the States and the Federal Government will reduce the risk of tyranny and abuse from either front." *Gregory, supra,* at 458. * * *

* * *

C

The dissent of course resorts to the last, best hope of those who defend *ultra vires* congressional action, the Necessary and Proper Clause. It reasons [ ] that the power to regulate the sale of handguns under the Commerce Clause, coupled with the power to "make all Laws which shall be necessary and proper for carrying into Execution the foregoing Powers," [ ]conclusively establishes the Brady Act's constitutional validity, because the Tenth Amendment imposes no limitations on the exercise of *delegated* powers but merely prohibits the exercise of powers "*not* delegated to the United States." What destroys the dissent's Necessary and Proper Clause argument, however, is not the Tenth Amendment but the Necessary and Proper Clause itself. When a "Law ... for carrying into Execution" the Commerce Clause violates the principle of state sovereignty reflected in the various constitutional provisions we mentioned earlier [ ], it is not a "Law ... *proper* for carrying into Execution the Commerce Clause," and is thus, in the words of The Federalist, "merely [an] act of usurpation" which "deserves to be treated as such." [ ]. We in fact answered the dissent's Necessary and Proper Clause argument in *New York*: "Even where Congress has the authority under the Constitution to pass laws requiring or prohibiting certain acts, it lacks the power directly to compel the States to require or prohibit those acts.... The Commerce Clause, for example, authorizes Congress to regulate interstate commerce directly; it does not authorize Congress to regulate state governments' regulation of interstate commerce." 505 U.S. at 166.

* * *

IV

Finally, and most conclusively in the present litigation, we turn to the prior jurisprudence of this Court. Federal commandeering of state governments is such a novel phenomenon that this Court's first experience with it did not occur until the 1970's, when the Environmental Protection Agency promulgated regulations requiring States to prescribe auto emissions testing, monitoring and retrofit programs, and to designate preferential bus and carpool lanes. The Courts of Appeals for the Fourth and Ninth Circuits invalidated the regulations on statutory grounds in order to avoid what they perceived to be grave constitutional issues, [ ] and the District of Columbia Circuit invalidated the regulations on both constitutional and statutory grounds [ ]. After we granted certiorari to review the statutory and constitutional validity of the regulations, the Government declined even to defend them, and instead rescinded some and conceded the invalidity of those that remained, leading us to vacate the opinions below and remand for consideration of mootness. *EPA* v. *Brown,* 431 U.S. 99, 97 S.Ct. 1635, 52 L.Ed.2d 166 (1977).

Although we had no occasion to pass upon the subject in *Brown,* later opinions of ours have made clear that the Federal Government may not compel the States to implement, by legislation or executive action, federal regulatory programs. * * *

When we were at last confronted squarely with a federal statute that unambiguously required the States to enact or administer a federal regulatory program, our decision should have come as no surprise. At issue in *New York* v. *United States,* 505 U.S. 144, 120 L.Ed.2d 120, 112 S.Ct. 2408 (1992), were the so-called "take title" provisions of the Low-Level Radioactive Waste Policy Amendments Act of 1985, which required States either to enact legislation providing for the disposal of radioactive waste generated within their borders, or to take title to, and possession of the waste—effectively requiring the States either to legislate pursuant to Congress's directions, or to implement an administrative solution. [ ]. We concluded that Congress could constitutionally require the States to do neither. [ ] "The Federal Government," we held, "may not compel the States to enact or administer a federal regulatory program." [ ].

* * *

Finally, the Government puts forward a cluster of arguments that can be grouped under the heading: "The Brady Act serves very important purposes, is most efficiently administered by CLEOs during the interim period, and places a minimal and only temporary burden upon state officers." There is considerable disagreement over the extent of the burden, but we need not pause over that detail. Assuming *all* the mentioned factors were true, they might be relevant if we were evaluating whether the incidental application to the States of a federal law of general applicability excessively interfered with the functioning of state governments. [ ] But where, as here, it is the whole *object* of the law to direct the functioning of the state executive, and hence to compromise the structural framework of dual sovereignty, such a "balancing" analysis is inappropriate. It is the very *principle* of separate state sovereignty that such a law offends, and no comparative assessment of the various interests can overcome that fundamental defect.

* * *

We adhere to that principle today, and conclude categorically [ ]: "The Federal Government may not compel the States to enact or administer a federal regulatory program." *Id.*, at 188. The mandatory obligation imposed on CLEOs to perform background checks on prospective handgun purchasers plainly runs afoul of that rule.

V

What we have said makes it clear enough that the central obligation imposed upon CLEOs by the interim provisions of the Brady Act—the obligation to "make a reasonable effort to ascertain within 5 business days whether receipt or possession [of a handgun] would be in violation of the law, including research in whatever State and local recordkeeping systems are available and in a national system designated by the Attorney General," [ ]—is unconstitutional. Extinguished with it, of course, is the duty implicit in the background-check requirement that the CLEO accept notice of the contents of, and a copy of, the completed Brady Form, which the firearms dealer is required to provide to him [ ].

* * *

We [previously] held that Congress cannot compel the States to enact or enforce a federal regulatory program. Today we hold that Congress cannot circumvent that prohibition by conscripting the State's officers directly. The Federal Government may neither issue directives requiring the States to address particular problems, nor command the States' officers, or those of their political subdivisions, to administer or enforce a federal regulatory program. It matters not whether policymaking is involved, and no case-by-case weighing of the burdens or benefits is necessary; such commands are fundamentally incompatible with our constitutional system of dual sovereignty. Accordingly, the judgment of the Court of Appeals for the Ninth Circuit is reversed.

It is so ordered.

Notes

1) *United States v. Lopez* exemplifies the concept of "new federalism"—the idea that the power of the federal government should be limited in deference to the sovereignty of the states. This is an important concept in public health as the issue frequently arises questioning which government (state of federal) should be responsible for public health regulation. In *Lopez,* Congress took it upon itself to enact the Gun-free Zone Act of 1990 in an effort to prevent firearms in a school zone. Though the government argued that possession of a firearm substantially affects interstate commerce, the Court declined to expand the Commerce Clause in a manner that infringes upon the police powers of the states.

2) *Printz v. United States* is in accord. In this case it is a provision in the Brady Act that purports to regulate background checks and impose other measures with respect to the sale and possession of handguns. The petitioners objected to "being pressed into federal service" and argued that Congress lacked the power to require state officers to enforce a federal program. The Court agreed, and once again deferred to the sovereignty of state courts to regulate the public health.

SECTION B.   SAFETY DEVICES

STATE OF IOWA v. HARTOG

Supreme Court of Iowa, 1989.
440 N.W.2d 852.

LAVORATO, J:

At issue here is whether Iowa's mandatory seat belt law is unconstitutional. The trial court held that it was not. We agree and affirm.

I.   BACKGROUND FACTS AND PROCEEDINGS.

During the early morning hours of November 1, 1987, the defendant, John Hartog, was stopped at a roadblock in Carter Lake, Iowa. The roadblock was jointly conducted by the Iowa State Patrol and local and county law enforcement agencies. An officer checked Hartog's car for safety violations and found none. The officer did, however, issue Hartog a citation for failing to use his seat belt as required by Iowa Code section 321.445(2) (1987). The following month, Hartog was issued another seat belt citation.

Hartog was found guilty on both charges in separate trials before a magistrate. Hartog did not dispute the fact that he had not been wearing his seat belt on either occasion. * * *

On appeal here, Hartog has narrowed his state and federal constitutional challenges to two. First, he asserts that section 321.445(2), the seat belt law, violates his right of privacy as guaranteed by the due process clauses of the fourteenth amendment to the United States Constitution and article I, section 9 of the Iowa Constitution. Second, he contends the seat belt law exceeds the state's police power under the due process clauses of both constitutions.

II. The Seat Belt Law.

Iowa's mandatory seat belt law provides in part:

> The driver and front seat occupants of a type of motor vehicle which is subject to registration in Iowa, except a motorcycle or a motorized bicycle, shall each wear a properly adjusted and fastened safety belt or safety harness any time the vehicle is in forward motion on a street or highway in this state except that a child under six years of age shall be secured [ ].

[The] Iowa Code [ ] exempts the following persons from complying with the seat belt provision: (a) the driver or front seat occupants of a motor vehicle not required to be equipped with safety belts under rules adopted by the state department of transportation; (b) the driver or front seat occupants of a motor vehicle who are actively engaged in work that requires frequent exits from and reentries into the vehicle, provided that the vehicle does not exceed twenty-five miles per hour between stops; (c) rural postal drivers at certain points in their deliveries; (d) passengers on a bus; (e) a person possessing a written certification from a physician that the person is unable to wear a seat belt because of physical or medical reasons; and (f) front seat occupants, except the driver, of an authorized emergency vehicle while such occupants are being transported in an emergency. [ ]. Although not specifically exempted, back seat passengers are not required by [ ] to wear seat belts.

* * *

A violation of section 321.445(2) is subject to a ten-dollar fine but does not subject the violator to the habitual offender provisions of [the] Iowa Code.

Before proceeding to the constitutional issues raised, we wish to emphasize that our task is not to question the wisdom or necessity of this legislation. Rather, our task is to determine whether the legislation passes constitutional muster. [ ].

III. The Right to Privacy.

Hartog first contends that Iowa Code [ ] violates his right to privacy as guaranteed by the due process clauses of the fourteenth amendment to the United States Constitution and article I, section 9 of the Iowa Constitution. In support of his contention, Hartog essentially argues that the statute deprives him of a fundamental right to make a choice pertaining solely to his person and his personal safety. He likens this supposed fundamental right to the fundamental right of a woman to terminate her pregnancy, as recognized in *Roe v. Wade*, 410 U.S. 113, 93 S.Ct. 705, 35 L.Ed.2d 147 (1973).

The due process clause of the fourteenth amendment provides that no state shall "deprive any person of life, liberty, or property, without due process." A similar provision is found in article I, section 9 of the Iowa Constitution: "No person shall be deprived of life, liberty, or property, without due process." The due process clauses of the fourteenth amendment and of article I, section 9 of the Iowa Constitution are limited to state action. [ ]

Judicial review under the federal due process clause of the fourteenth amendment takes two forms: procedural and substantive. Procedural due process review concerns itself only with the fairness of the process by which a governmental entity applies a law to an individual. Substantive due process review, on the other hand, concerns itself only with whether the law is constitutional. [ ]. Here we are concerned with the latter.

In determining whether a law is constitutional, we generally apply a standard of review that requires the law to be rationally related to a legitimate goal of government. [ ]

Our standard of review is more stringent, however, if the law limits a "fundamental" right or liberty under the Constitution. In these circumstances, we are more careful in scrutinizing the underlying factual basis for the law. Our review is thus elevated to the level of "strict scrutiny." [ ].

Under the strict scrutiny standard of review, any law that limits a fundamental right must promote a compelling or overriding interest of government. Otherwise, the law is unconstitutional. [ ]

* * *

The right to privacy in this context simply means the freedom of choice to engage in certain activities. [ ]. The Supreme Court has, however, defined those activities to include only child rearing and education, family relationships, procreation, marriage, contraception, and abortion. [ ]

Moreover, the Court has expressed a resistance to the idea of expanding the right of privacy beyond these activities. *Id.* at 195, 106 S.Ct. at 2846, 92 L.Ed.2d at 148. And, as recently as *Bowers [v. Hardwick* 478 U.S. at 195, 106 S.Ct. at 2846, 92 L.Ed.2d at 148], the Court has specifically refused to do so. * * * *Paris Adult Theatre I v. Slaton*, 413 U.S. 49, 66, 93 S.Ct. 2628, 2640, 37 L.Ed.2d 446, 462 (1973) (right to privacy does not include right of adults to view obscene movies in places of public accommodation). So, while rights of privacy have been found in the shadows of specific constitutional provisions, there will be considerable reluctance to recognize new rights of privacy that stray from those categories already established.

We fail to see how Hartog's claimed right to decide whether to buckle up resembles those liberty interests the Supreme Court has explicitly recognized to be part of the right of privacy implicit in the due process clause of the fourteenth amendment. Granted, Iowa's seat belt law does restrict Hartog's freedom of choice and, in that sense, does affect his interest in liberty. The law, however,

> does not regulate those intimate decisions relating to marriage, procreation, child rearing, education or family that have heretofore been recognized as deserving of heightened constitutional protection.

People v. Kohrig, 113 Ill.2d 384, 395, 498 N.E.2d 1158, 1161, 101 Ill.Dec. 650 (1986) (right of privacy does not include right to choose whether to use seat belts), *appeal dismissed*, 479 U.S. 1073, 107 S.Ct. 1264, 94 L.Ed.2d 126 (1987).

* * *

Moreover, we decline to infer a right of privacy to make such a choice from the words of our own due process clause in article I, section 9 of the Iowa Constitution. We decline to do so for two reasons. First, we have historically held that one's authority to drive on the public highways in Iowa does not rise to the level of a right. *See Gooch v. Iowa Dep't of Transp.*, 398 N.W.2d 845, 847 (Iowa 1987); *Veach v. Iowa Dep't of Transp.*, 374 N.W.2d 248, 249 (Iowa 1985) (operating motor vehicle is a privilege which is not unrestrained; challenged statutes implicated "neither a fundamental right nor a suspect classification"). Such holdings thus belie any notion that one has a fundamental right under our state constitution to decide whether to wear seat belts. One's right to make this decision can surely rise no higher than one's right to drive at all. Second, given the textual similarity between the two due process clauses, we have been inclined in the past to follow Supreme Court interpretations in these circumstances. [ ]. We see no compelling reason to depart from that practice here.

We hold that Iowa's seat belt law does not violate any right to privacy arising out of article I, section 9 of the Iowa Constitution.

Several appellate courts have squarely faced and rejected a right of privacy challenge to a seat belt law. * * *

Finally, legislation requiring motorcycle headgear—legislation conceptually similar to seat belt legislation—has been upheld against right of privacy challenges. [ ]. The rationale for rejecting such challenges is graphically captured by the Nevada supreme court in this oft-quoted passage:

> "There is no place where any such right to be let alone would be less assertable than on a modern highway with cars, trucks, busses, and cycles whizzing by at sixty or seventy miles an hour. When one ventures onto such a highway, he must be expected and required to conform to safety regulations and controls, including some that

would neither have been necessary nor reasonable in the era of horse-drawn vehicles.''

State v. Eighth Judicial Dist. Court, 101 Nev. at 661, 708 P.2d at 1024 (quoting *Bisenius v. Karns*, 42 Wis.2d 42, 55, 165 N.W.2d 377, 384 (1969)). We think the same reasoning applies here.

Hartog raises an additional argument to support his right of privacy contention. He points out that in *Meyer v. Nebraska*, 262 U.S. 390, 399, 43 S.Ct. 625, 626, 67 L.Ed. 1042, 1045 (1923), the Supreme Court recognized that the term ''liberty'' in the due process clause also denotes freedom from bodily restraint. We think the ''bodily restraint'' envisioned by the *Meyer* Court was more akin to incarceration than to the ''restraint'' Hartog is required to fasten in his car.

In summary, because no fundamental right is implicated here, the burden is on Hartog to negate any rational basis for the seat belt law, an issue we next address.

IV. POLICE POWER.

Hartog next contends that the Iowa [law] violates the due process clauses of the federal and Iowa constitutions because the statute lies beyond the reach of the state's police power. In support of this contention, Hartog argues that the purpose of the statute is to protect the individual from his own folly and, consequently, such purpose has no relation to the public health, safety, or welfare. Implicit in Hartog's argument is that the decision whether to wear a seat belt is a personal one affecting him only; therefore, he should be able to make that decision free of state interference.

In determining whether Iowa's mandatory seat belt law is constitutional, our function is not to decide whether the law is desirable or necessary. The issue here is " 'not what the legislature should do but what the legislature can do.' " *Richards*, 743 S.W.2d at 749.

Hartog raises a fundamental issue: whether Iowa's mandatory seat belt law constitutes a valid exercise of the state's police power.

The term ''police power'' refers to the legislature's broad, inherent power to pass laws that promote the public health, safety, and welfare. * * *

The legislature has considerable discretion in determining what constitutes the public health, safety, and welfare. That is why courts grant such legislation a highly deferential standard of review. [ ]. Such laws are thus presumed to be constitutional provided there is some reasonable relation to the public welfare. [ ]. Anyone challenging such laws must overcome this presumption by negating every reasonable basis upon which the laws may be sustained. [ ].

Nevertheless, there are certain parameters to the state's police power. Those parameters were articulated in *Lawton v. Steele*:

[A] large discretion is necessarily vested in the legislature to determine, not only what the interests of the public require, but what measures are necessary for the protection of such interests. To justify the state in thus interposing its authority on behalf of the public, it must appear, first, that the interests of the public generally, as distinguished from those of a particular class, require such interference; and second, that the means are reasonably necessary for the accomplishment of the purpose. . . .

152 U.S. 133, 136–37, 14 S.Ct. 499, 501, 38 L.Ed. 385, 388 (1894) [ ].

One commentator has explained the *Lawton* parameters in the context of a police power challenge to a mandatory seat belt law:

The parameters of the police power are thus defined by a two-part test: first, any law must address a "public" need, as distinguished from a law directed at a particular class of individuals with no impact on the general public and, second, the law's provisions must be reasonably related to the accomplishment of the public purpose. Therefore, in order for a statute to be within the state's police power, its provisions must be reasonably related to the public health, safety, and welfare. This is the benchmark against which the mandatory seat belt law must be measured.

Compton, *Freedom to be Foolish? L.B. 496: The Mandatory Seat Belt Law*, 19 Creighton L. Rev. 743, 750 (1986). We have defined the parameters similarly by requiring the following balancing test: does the collective benefit outweigh the specific restraint? [ ].

With these principles in mind we turn to Hartog's police power challenge.

Concededly, the statute here is designed to protect the driver and front seat passenger from serious injury or death. So there is merit in Hartog's argument that the statute interferes with the individual's choice concerning his or her own safety. The issue immediately narrows to whether the first part of the *Lawton* two-part test is met: does the seat belt law really protect the health, safety, and welfare of the *public* or, as Hartog argues, is the decision whether to wear a seat belt an individual one which affects no one but the individual involved. For reasons that follow we think the public safety and welfare are served by the seat belt statute.

Several courts have rejected the argument Hartog raises, that is, that his unwillingness to use seat belts places only himself at risk. These courts point out that seat belt use enhances a driver's ability to maintain control of the car and avoid injuries not only to the driver but to others. [ ] Similarly, an unrestrained front seat passenger can interfere with the ability of a driver to respond to a collision. [ ]. Several commentators in recent writings have agreed. [ ]

Moreover, studies have shown that such an unrestrained passenger poses danger of injuries to other occupants through direct or indirect body contact brought about by occupant kinetics. For example, instances have occurred in which a person holding a small child has been thrown forcibly against the child, crushing the child to death. * * *

It is readily apparent to us that the legislature could rationally conclude unbelted drivers and passengers endanger the safety of others. [ ] Preventing and reducing resulting injuries seem to us to be valid state interests. [ ].

Although the legislature's failure to require all occupants to use seat belts weakens our conclusion, this failure is not fatal constitutionally. The law

> "need not be in every respect logically consistent with its aims to be constitutional. It is enough that there is an evil at hand for correction, and that it might be thought that the particular legislative measure was a rational way to correct it."

Kohrig, 113 Ill.2d at 402–03, 498 N.E.2d at 1165; *accord Richards*, 743 S.W.2d at 749 (answering argument that seat belt law was inconsistent with aim to reduce injuries and therefore unconstitutional because back seat passengers were not required to wear seat belts).

We think the seat belt law promotes the public interest in another way: reducing the public costs associated with serious injuries and deaths caused by automobile accidents. As one court has pointed out,

> the police power relates not merely to the public health and public physical safety, but also to public financial safety, and ... laws may be passed within the police power to protect the public from financial loss.

Love v. Bell, 171 Colo. 27, 33, 465 P.2d 118, 121 (1970) (holding that a motorcycle headgear statute was constitutional against a police power challenge) * * *.

* * *

Statistics certainly bear out the staggering direct and indirect costs attributable to injuries and deaths from automobile accidents. * * *

Closer to home, Governor Branstad gave similar reasons for signing into law Iowa's mandatory seat belt law:

> In signing Senate File 499, I have carefully considered the concerns of many Iowans who feel this legislation is an unnecessary intrusion by government. I have weighed these objections with the state's responsibility to provide and promote public safety. *I have concluded that the saving of lives, reduction of injuries, and saving of cost related to accidents warrant my signature on this Act.*

* * *

It can scarcely be argued that the Iowa legislature could not have rationally considered the same reasons in passing the statute.

Moreover, we think that

the right to operate a motor vehicle upon a public street or highway is not a natural or unrestrained right, but a privilege which is subject to reasonable regulation under the police power of the state in the interest of the public safety and welfare.

City of Wichita v. White, 205 Kan. 408, 410, 469 P.2d 287, 289 (1970).

* * *

We hold that passage of [the] Iowa Code [statute] was a proper exercise of the state's police power and does not violate the due process provisions of the federal and Iowa constitutions.

V. DISPOSITION.

* * *

Finding no error, we affirm.

BENNING v. VERMONT

Supreme Court of Vermont, 1994.
161 Vt. 472, 641 A.2d 757.

DOOLEY, J. Plaintiffs Joseph C. Benning, the Northeast Kingdom Chapter of Freedom of the Road, and the parent organization Freedom of the Road appeal from a decision of the Caledonia Superior Court dismissing plaintiffs' request for declaratory and injunctive relief from [ ] the motorcycle headgear statute, and a subsequent denial of their motion for reconsideration. We affirm.

In 1989, plaintiff Benning was cited for a violation of [a Vermont law by] operating a motorcycle without wearing approved headgear. However, the Caledonia County State's Attorney dismissed the citation because he found the statute vague and was unable to establish the elements necessary to prosecute the crime. Plaintiffs subsequently filed suit, seeking to have [the law] declared unconstitutional and to have the State enjoined from further enforcement of the statute. Plaintiffs make three arguments based solely on the state constitution: (1) the statute is repugnant to the tenor, spirit and intent of the Vermont Constitution; (2) the statute is void for vagueness; and (3) the statute denies plaintiffs equal protection of the laws. We address each contention in turn.

Section 1256 was enacted in 1968, and states in full:

No person may operate or ride upon a motorcycle upon a highway unless he wears upon his head protective headgear reflectorized in part and of a type approved by the commissioner. The headgear shall be equipped with either a neck or chin strap.

* * *

Within a year of its enactment, the statute came under challenge in State v. Solomon, 128 Vt. 197, 260 A.2d 377 (1969). This decision necessarily informs our current consideration of [the law]. In Solomon, we upheld the validity of [the law] against arguments that the statute exceeded the scope of the state's police power and violated the Due Process Clause of the Fourteenth Amendment to the United States Constitution. This Court concluded then that [the law] was "directly related to highway safety" because an unprotected motorcycle operator could be affected by roadway hazards, temporarily lose control and become a menace to other motorists. [ ] The Court also concluded that "self-injury may be of such a nature to also invoke a general public concern." [ ]. As a result, we held that [the law] "bears a real and substantial relation to the public health and general welfare and it is a valid exercise of the police power." [ ].

In this case, plaintiffs attempt to distinguish their attack on [the law] from Solomon on the grounds that Solomon was decided solely on federal constitutional grounds, whereas they challenge [the law] on state constitutional grounds. Specifically, plaintiffs argue that [the law] violates Chapter I, Articles 1, 9, 11 and 18 of the Vermont Constitution. As we recognized in State v. Kirchoff, 156 Vt. 1, 4, 587 A.2d 988, 991 (1991), "the Vermont Constitution may afford greater protection to individual rights than do the provisions of the federal charter." Plaintiffs argue vigorously that this is a circumstance of greater protection.

Plaintiffs base this argument almost entirely on Chapter I, Article 1 of the Vermont Constitution, which provides:

> That all men are born equally free and independent, and have certain natural, inherent, and unalienable rights, amongst which are the enjoying and defending life and liberty, acquiring, possessing and protecting property, and pursuing and obtaining happiness and safety. . . .

Plaintiffs argue that both safety and liberty are among the "natural, inherent, and unalienable rights" guaranteed by the Article. As to safety, plaintiffs argue that the text gives individuals, not the government, the power to determine what is necessary for personal safety. Plaintiffs claim that they have a liberty interest in operating a motorcycle without a helmet, and since the purpose behind the statute is to protect the safety of the motorcycle operator, it offends their right to determine their own safety needs.

* * *

Given the nature of Article 1, it is not surprising that we can discover no instance where this Court has struck down an act of the Vermont Legislature solely because of a violation of Article 1. The main reason is found in State v. Carruth, 85 Vt. 271, 81 A. 922 (1911), in which the defendant claimed that Article 1 gave him the right to shoot a deer on his land out of season, despite a criminal statute to the contrary. Concerning Article 1, this Court wrote: "Many things contained in the bill of rights found in our State Constitutions 'are not, and from the very nature of the case cannot be, so certain and definite in character as to form rules for judicial decisions; and they are declared rather as guides to the legislative judgment than as marking an absolute limitation of power.' " Id. at 273–74, 81 A. at 923 [ ].

* * * Plaintiffs' right to pursue and obtain safety does not suggest the government is powerless to protect the safety of individuals. Indeed, our recent references to Article 1 suggest that the individual pursues safety through governmental action. [ ] The juxtaposition of safety and happiness is consistent with a general statement of principle rather than an enforceable right. [ ].

* * *

The decisions of other jurisdictions are equally unhelpful to plaintiffs. Plaintiffs cite the single case that has found a motorcycle helmet law unconstitutional, specifically rejecting the Solomon reasoning. [ ]. The vast majority of state courts have adhered to reasoning similar to that of Solomon. [citations omitted].

At the center of plaintiffs' argument is the assertion that Vermont values personal liberty interests so highly that the analysis under the federal constitution or the constitutions of other states is simply inapplicable here. In support of this contention, plaintiffs rely on political theorists, sociological materials and incidents in Vermont's history. Without detailing this argument, we find it unpersuasive not because it overvalues Vermont's devotion to personal liberty and autonomy, but because it undervalues the commitment of other governments to those values. * * *

* * *

For the above reasons, we are not convinced that Article 1 offers plaintiffs any special protections that are applicable to this case. We have also examined Articles 9, 11 and 18 on which plaintiffs place secondary reliance. None of these provisions helps plaintiffs' position.

As a result, we reject the notion that this case can be resolved on the basis of a broad right to be let alone without government interference. We accept the federal analysis of such a claim in the context of a public safety restriction applicable to motorists using public roads. We agree with Justice Powell, recently sitting by designation with the Court of Appeals for the Eleventh Circuit, who stated:

> There is no broad legal or constitutional "right to be let alone" by government. In the complex society in which we live, the action and nonaction of citizens are subject to countless local, state, and federal laws and regulations. Bare invocation of a right to be let alone is an appealing rhetorical device, but it seldom advances legal inquiry, as the "right"—to the extent it exists—has no meaning outside its application to specific activities. The [federal] Constitution does protect citizens from government interference in many areas—speech, religion, the security of the home. But the unconstrained right asserted by appellant has no discernable bounds, and bears

little resemblance to the important but limited privacy rights recognized by our highest Court. Picou, 874 F.2d at 1521.

We are left then with the familiar standard for evaluating police power regulations—essentially, that expressed in Solomon. Plaintiffs urge us to overrule Solomon because it was based on an analysis of the safety risk to other users of the roadway that is incredible. In support of their position, they offered evidence from motorcycle operators that the possibility of an operator losing control of a motorcycle and becoming a menace to others is remote. On the other hand, these operators assert that helmets make a motorcycle operator dangerous. Plaintiffs also emphasize that even supporters of helmet laws agree that their purpose is to protect the motorcycle operator, not other highway users.

We are not willing to abandon the primary rationale of Solomon because of plaintiffs' evidence. The statute is entitled to a presumption of constitutionality. [ ]. Plaintiffs are not entitled to have the courts act as a super-legislature and retry legislative judgments based on evidence presented to the court. [ ] Thus, the question before us is whether the link between safety for highway users and the helmet law is rational, not whether we agree that the statute actually leads to safer highways. [ ]. The Solomon reasoning has been widely adopted in the many courts that have considered the constitutionality of motorcycle helmet laws. [ ]

There are at least two additional reasons why we conclude [the Vermont law] is constitutional. The first is referenced in Solomon. Although plaintiffs argue that the only person affected by the failure to wear a helmet is the operator of the motorcycle, the impact of that decision would be felt well beyond that individual. Such a decision imposes great costs on the public. * * * This rationale is particularly apparent as the nation as a whole, and this state in particular, debate reform of a health care system that has become too costly although many do not have access to it. Whether in taxes or insurance rates, our costs are linked to the actions of others and are driven up when others fail to take preventive steps that would minimize health care consumption. We see no constitutional barrier to legislation that requires preventive measures to minimize health care costs that are inevitably imposed on society.

A second rationale supports this type of a safety requirement on a public highway. Our decisions show that in numerous circumstances the liability for injuries that occur on our public roads may be imposed on the state, or other governmental units, and their employees. [ ]. It is rational for the state to act to minimize the extent of the injuries for which it or other governmental units may be financially responsible. The burden placed on plaintiffs who receive the benefit of the liability system is reasonable.

II.

Plaintiffs next argue that [the Vermont law] is void for vagueness. A criminal statute must "define a criminal offense with sufficient certainty so as to inform a person of ordinary intelligence of conduct which is proscribed, and such that arbitrary and discriminatory enforcement is not encouraged." State v. Cantrell, 151 Vt. 130, 133, 558 A.2d 639, 641 (1989). Lack of statutory clarity offends notions of due process * * *. The test is less strict, however, when, as here, the statute does not threaten to inhibit the exercise of constitutionally protected rights. [ ] Plaintiffs attack the validity of [the Vermont law] on both prongs of the Cantrell vagueness test.

* * *

We find plaintiffs' attack unavailing. It is difficult to see how the statute could be more specific. It clearly proscribes the failure to wear an approved helmet. Plaintiffs' attack is really on the method of administration by the Vermont Commissioner of Motor Vehicles. Specifically, plaintiffs argue that motorcyclists do not have fair warning because "it is virtually impossible for the motorcyclist to find out what headgear is 'approved by the commissioner.'" This in turn, plaintiffs argue, makes it impossible for police to know what is or is not an approved helmet, leading to arbitrary and discriminatory enforcement. * * *

* * * [W]e find that the Commissioner of Motor Vehicles has been sufficiently clear about what headgear is acceptable. By regulation, the Commissioner has provided that a helmet is deemed approved by the Commissioner if it (1) meets the standards set out by the Motorcycle, Scooter, Allied Trades Association; the American Standards Association Inc. Z90.1; or the United States Department of Transportation Federal Motor Vehicle Safety Standards (FMVSS) 218 (49 C.F.R. § 571.218), and (2) an "approval certificate" has been issued for it by the American Association of Motor Vehicle Administrators. [ ]. Contrary to the plaintiffs' position, we construe this regulation to mean that a helmet is approved by the Commissioner if approved by one of the standard-setting organizations pursuant to its regulations. Thus, the dispute here goes to whether operators and law enforcement personnel can determine which helmets have been approved.

The easiest method is labelling. Each set of standards provides for the labelling of an approved helmet. [ ] For example, helmets that have been approved under the FMVSS standard bear the widely recognized United States Department of Transportation (DOT) symbol. The "steel pot" infantry helmet, used as the main example by plaintiffs, lacks the labelling that shows approval.

If labelling does not provide a certain result, motorcyclists may consult the American Association of Motor Vehicle Administrator's list, which is maintained by the Commissioner. The statement accompanying the regulations provides that a certificate of approval for each approved helmet is filed with the Commissioner. The fact that the Commissioner of Motor Vehicles does not maintain a specific state list of approved helmets also does not render the statute or the method of administration infirm.

III.

Finally, plaintiffs argue that [the Vermont law] deprives them of the "equal protection of the laws" guaranteed by Chapter I, Article 7 of the Vermont Constitution. This article of the constitution provides: "That government is, or ought to be, instituted for the common benefit, protection, and security of the people, nation, or community, and not for the particular emolument or advantage of any single man, family, or set of men.... " Plaintiffs make three distinct arguments: (1) motorcyclists are unfairly singled out for treatment different from all other highway users; (2) the statute requires a safety device, the helmet, that lessens some dangers, but increases others; and (3) the statute undermines its public safety purpose by requiring reflectorization without warning of the potential dangers of adhesive application to the helmet.

"Unless a 'fundamental right or suspect class is involved,' a statute comports with Article 7 if it is reasonably related to a legitimate public purpose." State v. George, 157 Vt. 580, 588, 602 A.2d 953, 957 (1991) [ ]. There is no fundamental right here. Therefore, we return to our rational basis analysis. To prevail, one "must show that he was treated differently as a member of one class from treatment of members of another class similarly situated." Id. at 585, 602 A.2d at 956.

These challenges do not require extensive analysis. The requirement that motorcyclists don protective headgear before taking to the public highways is simply a recognition that motorcyclists do not enjoy the physical protection furnished by the body of a car or truck. We conclude that "it is not difficult to discern a rational basis for the legislature's distinction between motorcyclists and ... automobile drivers, whose vehicle affords them substantially more protection than does a motorcycle." Simon, 346 F.Supp. at 279. Similarly, the Legislature can apply the helmet requirement to motorcycles and not to mopeds. A statute need not regulate the whole of a field to pass constitutional muster. [citation omitted]. There is a rational basis for the distinction between motorcyclists and moped riders since the latter travel on average at a lower rate of speed and are forbidden from riding on state highways. [ ]

We have already considered plaintiffs' claim that the statute is flawed because it fails to deal with the dangers of helmet usage. This argument is for the Legislature, not this Court.

Finally, plaintiffs claim that § 1256 undermines its public safety purpose by requiring reflectorization without warning of the potential dangers of adhesive application to the helmet. Based on expert testimony, the trial court found that reflective adhesive tape cannot adversely affect the structural integrity of a motorcycle helmet. Despite the court's additional finding that certain materials should not be used on helmets, the court's determination that reflectorization does not impair a helmet's structural integrity is not clearly erroneous and will not be overturned on appeal.

In summary, we find no reason to overrule Solomon. As a result, we reiterate our conclusion that § 1256 "in no way violates any of the provisions of our state and federal constitutions." Solomon, 128 Vt. at 202, 260 A.2d at 380.

Affirmed.

AIR LINE PILOTS ASSOCIATION v. QUESADA

United State Court of Appeals for the Second Circuit, 1960.
276 F.2d 892.

LUMBARD, J.

On December 1, 1959 the defendant, Elwood R. Quesada, Administrator of the Federal Aviation Agency, promulgated a regulation which provides:

'No individual who has reached his 60th birthday shall be utilized or serve as a pilot on any aircraft while engaged in air carrier operations.'

This regulation took effect on March 15, 1960.

The plaintiffs, thirty-five individual pilots, their collective bargaining representative, Air Line Pilots Association, and its president, brought the suit in January 1960 for a declaratory judgment that the regulation was null and void and for an injunction against its threatened application. The complaint alleged—and the plaintiffs contend on this appeal—that the regulation is invalid because it was issued without the holding of adjudicatory hearings required by the Administrative Procedure Act [ ] and the Federal Aviation Act of 1958 [ ] before an airman's license may be amended, modified, suspended or revoked, and because it was arbitrary, discriminatory and without reasonable relation to the standards [ ]. The plaintiffs also claim that the regulation, by terminating their right to pilot planes in commercial service after age sixty, deprives them of property in their pilots' licenses without due process of law. * * *

The Federal Aviation Act was passed by Congress for the purpose of centralizing in a single authority—indeed, in one administrator—the power to frame rules for the safe and efficient use of the nation's airspace. The Administrator was given the authority, theretofore divided between the Civil Aeronautics Board and the Civil Aeronautics Authority:

* * * To promote safety of flight of civil aircraft in air commerce by prescribing and revising from time to time:

'(5) Reasonable rules and regulations governing, in the interest of safety, the maximum hours or periods of service of airmen, and other employees, of air carriers; * * *

Pursuant to this statutory authority the Administrator and his medical staff in the fall of 1958 began a study concerning the aging process and the diseases and physiological deterioration that accompany it in an effort to determine whether a maximum age should be set for service by commercial pilots. The Administrator took counsel with various experts in aviation medicine and safety and, among other things, determined the practices followed by five foreign air lines with respect to a mandatory retirement age. Finally, in June 1959 the Administrator published a proposed regulation in substance the same as that ultimately prescribed. In accordance with the rule-making requirements of § 4 of the Administrative Procedure Act, 5 U.S.C.A. § 1003, opportunity was afforded for the submission of written data and briefs. About one hundred comments, including those of the plaintiff association, were received. A large majority favored the regulation. No hearing was held since the Administrator determined, as he was entitled to under the rulemaking provisions of the Administrative Procedure Act, that a hearing would not 'serve a useful purpose' and that it was not 'necessary in the public interest.'

* * *

* * * The immediate impetus to the legislation was a series of major air crashes culminating in the midair collision of two large airlines over the Grand Canyon in 1956 with the loss of 128 lives. Congress believed there was a need for a more streamlined and efficient means for safety rule-making in place of the system of divided duties and responsibilities existing under the Civil Aeronautics Act, 49 U.S.C.A. § 401 et seq. * * *

* * *

Plaintiffs assert that the age sixty limitation is arbitrary and discriminatory and without relation to any requirements of safety. For purposes of judicial review, such an argument must mean that the Administrator had no reasonable basis for his exercise of judgment. [ ]. Surely this is not the fact in the case before us as there is considerable support for the Administrator's action. The Administrator found that the number of commercial pilots over sixty years of age has until recent years been very few but is increasing rapidly; that older pilots because of their seniority under collective bargaining agreements often fly the newest, largest, and fastest planes; that available medical studies show that sudden incapacitation due to heart attacks or strokes become more frequent as men approach age sixty and present medical knowledge is such that it is impossible to predict with accuracy those individuals most likely to suffer attacks; that a number of foreign air carriers contacted had mandatory retirement ages of sixty or less; and that numerous aviation safety experts advocated establishing a maximum age of sixty or younger. In spite of these considerations, plaintiffs ask us to weigh other arguments against the establishment of a maximum age and to hold that the Administrator's action was unreasonable. It is not the business of courts to substitute their untutored judgment for the expert knowledge of those who are given authority to implement the general directives of Congress. The Administrator is an expert in his field; this is the very reason he was given the responsibility for the issuance of air safety regulations. We can only ask whether the regulation is reasonable in relation to the standards prescribed in the statute and the facts before the Administrator. Of that there can be no doubt in this case.

Nor is the regulation discriminatory because it applies only to the piloting of commercial aircraft, and does not restrict pilots with respect to other planes. The Administrator did not act unreasonably in placing greater limitations on the certificates of pilots flying planes carrying large numbers of passengers who have no opportunity to select a pilot of their own choice. The Federal Aviation Act contemplates just such distinctions between the regulations governing 'air commerce' and those governing other air transportation.[ ].

The preliminary injunction was properly denied. The order is affirmed.

Notes

1) *Hartog* concerns the constitutionality of Vermont's seat belt laws. After the court rejected Hartog's argument that the seat belt law violated his right to privacy, he next asserted that Vermont's police power did not authorize it to impose criminal laws to regulate seat belt use. "Police power" refers to the state legislature's broad, inherent power to enact laws that promote the public health, safety, and welfare. Considerable discretion is given to the state to determine what constitutes the public health, safety, and welfare. Police power laws generally are presumed to be constitutional as long as there is some rational relationship to protection of the public welfare. In *Hartog*, there was a specific and reasonable relationship between seatbelt use and saving lives in auto accidents. By definition, assertions of the state police power are coercive and paternalistic. Their function is to require people to act to protect their own well-being, as well as others, under circumstances that they otherwise might not do so.

2) *Benning v. Vermont* is another example of governmental paternalism. While required use of motorcycle helmets is controversial in terms of its justification for public health regulation, it is generally upheld by the courts, even when the harm caused is to oneself rather than others. Judicial review under the federal due process clause of the fourteenth amendment can be both substantive and procedural. Procedural due process examines the fairness of the process by which a governmental entity applies a law to an individual. Substantive due process review examines whether the content of the law is fair. In determining whether a law is constitutional, the court generally requires the law to be rationally related to a legitimate governmental goal. Only in matters affecting fundamental rights will courts use the more stringent standard that requires a compelling state interest to be asserted. Most public health regulations are measured using the more lenient ("rational relationship") standard, and seat belt laws are usually found to be reasonably related to a legitimate goal.

3) *Quesada* followed the newly enacted Federal Aviation Act in an effort to increase the safety of air travel. At age sixty, pilots could no longer fly commercial planes carrying large numbers of passengers. Plaintiffs argued that the age limitation was arbitrary and bore no

rational relationship to the actual safety of the public. Using a rational relationship level of due process review, the court disagreed. It held that medical studies show that sudden incapacitation due to heart attack or stroke increases as men (who exclusively served as pilots in the 1950's and 60's) approached age 60. As to the argument that it is discriminatory because it applies only to piloting commercial aircraft, the court noted that commercial passengers have no choice of pilot, and thus are at the mercy of those chosen by the airlines. Further, the court pointed out the Federal Aviation Act's distinction between "air commerce" and "air transportation" and its regulation of the former but not the latter.

SECTION C. PATIENT CARE

UNITED STATES v. OAKLAND CANNABIS BUYERS' COOPERATIVE

Supreme Court of the United States, 2001.
532 U.S. 483, 121 S.Ct. 1711, 149 L.Ed.2d 722.

JUSTICE THOMAS delivered the opinion of the Court.

The Controlled Substances Act, 84 Stat. 1242, 21 U.S.C. § 801 *et seq.*, prohibits the manufacture and distribution of various drugs, including marijuana. In this case, we must decide whether there is a medical necessity exception to these prohibitions. We hold that there is not.

I

In November 1996, California voters enacted an initiative measure entitled the Compassionate Use Act of 1996. Attempting "to ensure that seriously ill Californians have the right to obtain and use marijuana for medical purposes," [ ] the statute creates an exception to California laws prohibiting the possession and cultivation of marijuana. These prohibitions no longer apply to a patient or his primary caregiver who possesses or cultivates marijuana for the patient's medical purposes upon the recommendation or approval of a physician. *Ibid.* In the wake of this voter initiative, several groups organized "medical cannabis dispensaries" to meet the needs of qualified patients. [ ]. Respondent Oakland Cannabis Buyers' Cooperative is one of these groups.

The Cooperative is a not-for-profit organization that operates in downtown Oakland. A physician serves as medical director, and registered nurses staff the Cooperative during business hours. To become a member, a patient must provide a written statement from a treating physician assenting to marijuana therapy and must submit to a screening interview. If accepted as a member, the patient receives an identification card entitling him to obtain marijuana from the Cooperative.

In January 1998, the United States sued the Cooperative and its executive director, respondent Jeffrey Jones (together, the Cooperative), in the United States District Court for the Northern District of California. Seeking to enjoin the Cooperative from distributing and manufacturing marijuana, the United States argued that, whether or not the

Cooperative's activities are legal under California law, they violate federal law. Specifically, the Government argued that the Cooperative violated the Controlled Substances Act's prohibitions on distributing, manufacturing, and possessing with the intent to distribute or manufacture a controlled substance. [ ]. Concluding that the Government had established a probability of success on the merits, the District Court granted a preliminary [ ].

* * *

II

The Controlled Substances Act provides that, "except as authorized by this subchapter, it shall be unlawful for any person knowingly or intentionally . . . to manufacture, distribute, or dispense, or possess with intent to manufacture, distribute, or dispense, a controlled substance." 21 U.S.C. § 841(a)(1). The subchapter, in turn, establishes exceptions. For marijuana (and other drugs that have been classified as "schedule I" controlled substances), there is but one express exception, and it is available only for Government-approved research projects, § 823(f). Not conducting such a project, the Cooperative cannot, and indeed does not, claim this statutory exemption.

The Cooperative contends, however, that notwithstanding the apparently absolute language of § 841(a), the statute is subject to additional, implied exceptions, one of which is medical necessity. According to the Cooperative, because necessity was a defense at common law, medical necessity should be read into the Controlled Substances Act. We disagree.

As an initial matter, we note that it is an open question whether federal courts ever have authority to recognize a necessity defense not provided by statute. A necessity defense "traditionally covered the situation where physical forces beyond the actor's control rendered illegal conduct the lesser of two evils." *United States* v. *Bailey*, 444 U.S. 394, 410, 62 L.Ed.2d 575, 100 S.Ct. 624 (1980). Even at common law, the defense of necessity was somewhat controversial. [ ]. And under our constitutional system, in which federal crimes are defined by statute rather than by common law [ ], it is especially so. As we have stated: "Whether, as a policy matter, an exemption should be created is a question for legislative judgment, not judicial inference." [ ]. Nonetheless, we recognize that this Court has discussed the possibility of a necessity defense without altogether rejecting it. [ ]

We need not decide, however, whether necessity can ever be a defense when the federal statute does not expressly provide for it. In this case, to resolve the question presented, we need only recognize that a medical necessity exception for marijuana is at odds with the terms of the Controlled Substances Act. The statute, to be sure, does not explicitly abrogate the defense. But its provisions leave no doubt that the defense is unavailable.

Under any conception of legal necessity, one principle is clear: The defense cannot succeed when the legislature itself has made a "determination of values." [ ]. In the case of the Controlled Substances Act, the statute reflects a determination that marijuana has no medical benefits worthy of an exception (outside the confines of a Government-approved research project). Whereas some other drugs can be dispensed and prescribed for medical use, [ ] the same is not true for marijuana. Indeed, for purposes of the Controlled Substances Act, marijuana has "no currently accepted medical use" at all.

The structure of the Act supports this conclusion. The statute divides drugs into five schedules, depending in part on whether the particular drug has a currently accepted medical use. The Act then imposes restrictions on the manufacture and distribution of the substance according to the schedule in which it has been placed. Schedule I is the most restrictive schedule. The Attorney General can include a drug in schedule I only if the drug "has no currently accepted medical use in treatment in the United States," "has a high potential for abuse," and has "a lack of accepted safety for use ... under medical supervision." [ ]. Under the statute, the Attorney General could not put marijuana into schedule I if marijuana had any accepted medical use.

The Cooperative points out, however, that the Attorney General did not place marijuana into schedule I. Congress put it there, and Congress was not required to find that a drug lacks an accepted medical use before including the drug in schedule I. We are not persuaded that this distinction has any significance to our inquiry. Under the Cooperative's logic, drugs that Congress places in schedule I could be distributed when medically necessary whereas drugs that the Attorney General places in schedule I could not. Nothing in the statute, however, suggests that there are two tiers of schedule I narcotics, with drugs in one tier more readily available than drugs in the other. On the contrary, the statute consistently treats all schedule I drugs alike. * * * Moreover, the Cooperative offers no convincing explanation for why drugs that Congress placed on schedule I should be subject to fewer controls than the drugs that the Attorney General placed on the schedule. Indeed, the Cooperative argues that, in placing marijuana and other drugs on schedule I, Congress "wished to assert the most restrictive level of controls created by the [Controlled Substances Act]." [ ]. If marijuana should be subject to the most restrictive level of controls, it should not be treated any less restrictively than other schedule I drugs.

The Cooperative further argues that use of schedule I drugs generally—whether placed in schedule I by Congress or the Attorney General—can be medically necessary, notwithstanding that they have "no currently accepted medical use." According to the Cooperative, a drug may not yet have achieved general acceptance as a medical treatment but may nonetheless have medical benefits to a particular patient or class of patients. We decline to parse the statute in this manner. It is clear from the text of the Act that Congress has made a determination that marijuana has no medical benefits worthy of an exception. The statute expressly contemplates that many drugs "have a useful and legitimate medical purpose and are necessary to maintain the health and general welfare of the American people," [ ], but it includes no exception at all for any medical use of marijuana. Unwilling to view this omission as an accident, and unable in any event to override a legislative determination manifest in a statute, we reject the Cooperative's argument.

* * *

For these reasons, we hold that medical necessity is not a defense to manufacturing and distributing marijuana. The Court of Appeals erred when it held that medical necessity is a "legally cognizable defense." * * *.

III

The Cooperative contends that, even if the Controlled Substances Act forecloses the medical necessity defense * * * the District Court had "broad equitable discretion" to tailor the injunctive relief to account for medical necessity, irrespective of whether there is a legal defense of necessity in the statute. [ ]. To sustain the judgment below, the argument goes, we need only reaffirm that federal courts, in the exercise of their equity jurisdiction, have discretion to modify an injunction based upon a weighing of the public interest.

We disagree. Although district courts whose equity powers have been properly invoked indeed have discretion in fashioning injunctive relief (in the absence of a statutory restriction), the Court of Appeals erred concerning the factors that the district courts may consider in exercising such discretion.

* * *

B

But the mere fact that the District Court had discretion does not suggest that the District Court, when evaluating the motion to modify the injunction, could consider any and all factors that might relate to the public interest or the conveniences of the parties, including the medical needs of the Cooperative's patients. On the contrary, a court sitting in equity cannot "ignore the judgment of Congress, deliberately expressed in legislation." [citations omitted]. Courts of equity cannot, in their discretion, reject the balance that Congress has struck in a statute. [ ]. Their choice (unless there is statutory language to the contrary) is simply whether a particular means of enforcing the statute should be chosen over another permissible means; their choice is not whether enforcement is preferable to no enforcement at all. Consequently, when a court of equity exercises its discretion, it may not consider the advantages and disadvantages of nonenforcement of the statute, but only the advantages and disadvantages of "employing the extraordinary remedy of injunction," [ ] over the other available methods of enforcement. * * *

C

In this case, the Court of Appeals erred by considering relevant the evidence that some people have "serious medical conditions for whom the use of cannabis is necessary in order to treat or alleviate those conditions or their symptoms," that these people "will suffer serious harm if they are denied cannabis," and that "there is no legal alternative to cannabis for the effective treatment of their medical conditions." [ ]. As explained above, in the Controlled Substances Act, the balance already has been struck against a medical necessity exception. Because the statutory prohibitions cover even those who have what could be termed a medical necessity, the Act precludes consideration of this evidence. It was thus error for the Court of Appeals to instruct the District Court on remand to consider "the criteria for a medical necessity exemption, and, should it modify the injunction, to set forth those criteria in the modification order." [ ].

* * *

The judgment of the Court of Appeals is reversed, and the case is remanded for further proceedings consistent with this opinion.

It is so ordered.

NATIONAL ASS'N OF PSYCHIATRIC HEALTH SYS. v. SHALALA,

United States District Court for the District of Columbia, 2000.
120 F.Supp.2d 33.

MEMORANDUM OPINION

I. BACKGROUND

Plaintiffs bring this case to challenge the interim final rule promulgated by HHS, which requires a physician or other licensed independent practitioner to evaluate a patient, face-to-face, within one hour after the patient has been placed in restraints or in seclusion. [ ]. This rule will hereafter be referred to as the "one-hour rule."

Plaintiffs are private psychiatric hospitals, and organizations that represent private hospitals, private psychiatric hospitals, and psychiatric units within acute care hospitals. Most of the hospitals represented participate in both the Medicare and Medicaid programs. A few participate in Medicaid but not Medicare.

To participate in Medicare, hospitals must meet certain conditions of participation ("COPs"), which are imposed by statute, regulation, or both. The Medicare statute allows the Secretary to impose additional COPs as necessary to protect the health and safety of Medicare beneficiaries. Hospitals which have received accreditation by a national accreditation body, such as the Joint Commission on Accreditation of Healthcare Organizations ("JCAHO"), are generally deemed to be in compliance with Medicare COPs, except that the Secretary may promulgate standards or requirements higher or more stringent than those prescribed for accreditation by such a national accreditation body. [ ].

The Health Care Financing Administration ("HCFA"), which is the agency within HHS responsible for administering the Medicare statute, assesses hospitals' compliance with Medicare COPs through a survey process generally conducted by state agencies. A hospital which has failed to comply with a COP may continue to participate in Medicare by submitting a plan for achieving compliance within a reasonable amount of time. [ ]. If a hospital fails, within a reasonable period of time, to implement this plan or come in compliance with the COPs, the Secretary may terminate or refuse to renew the hospital's provider agreement for participation in the Medicare program.

By notice in the Federal Register on December 19, 1997, HCFA announced a far-ranging proposed rule to revise many different COPs for hospitals participating in Medicare and Medicaid. Medicare and Medicaid Programs; Hospital Conditions of Participation; Provider Agreements and Supplier Approval [ ] (this notice of proposed rulemaking shall hereafter be referred to as the "NPRM"). Included in this extensive rulemaking was a HCFA proposal to regulate the circumstances under which hospitals may use restraints and seclusion. HCFA did not, in the proposed rule, delineate specific requirements for use of restraints and seclusion, but merely offered general guidelines for such use: that they be used "only when absolutely necessary to prevent immediate injury to the patient or others and when no alternative means are sufficient to accomplish this purpose," and that patients should be released from such restraints or seclusion "as soon as they no longer pose an immediate threat of injury to themselves or others." [ ]

* * *

* * * As to the one-hour rule, the studies and articles document the link between improper use of restraints and injury or death. Injuries include the psychological (aggression, withdrawal, morbidity, loss of self-esteem, etc.) as well as the physical (burns, pressure sores, limb injury, circulatory obstruction, nerve compression, etc.). The record revealed that restraints are a common intervention, estimating that they are applied hundreds of thousands times a day in the United States, but that restraint-related deaths and injuries (estimated at over 100 per year) often go unreported. The comments received in response to the NPRM stressed the need for frequent monitoring and rapid assessment of persons in restraints or seclusion, and stressed that restraints and seclusion should only be used in emergencies. * * *

III. ANALYSIS

* * *

B. *Did Defendant Violate the Notice-and-Comment Requirement of the APA?*

Under the rulemaking provisions of the [Administrative Procedures Act], an agency must provide the public with notice of any proposed rule it wishes to promulgate (through publication in the Federal Register), and must afford the public an opportunity to comment on that proposed rule before it becomes final. 5 U.S.C. § 553(b). The agency, however, is not required to include every possible version of a proposed rule in its notice of proposed rulemaking; instead, the agency may include only a description of the subjects and issues involved. Id. Agencies are also not limited to adopting final rules identical to the proposed rules. [citation omitted]. The relevant inquiry is "whether the notice given affords exposure to diverse public comment, fairness to affected parties, and an opportunity to develop evidence in the record." Id. [ ].

* * *

In the present case, Plaintiffs argue that notice was inadequate because (1) the final rule departed from the JCAHO standards that had been proposed in the NPRM, (2) the JCAHO standard upon which the one-hour rule was based required face-to-face assessment only prior to renewing a restraint order, not subsequent to signing the initial restraint order, and (3) none of the comments in the record suggested or advocated requiring a face-to-face assessment of a patient so shortly after the signing of an initial order of restraint or seclusion by a physician. Plaintiffs argue that the generalized reference to face-to-face assessment in the preamble of the NPRM is insufficient to provide notice of the agency's final rule because it related to the JCAHO standards, which require such an assessment only upon renewal of the restraint order.

Defendant, on the other hand, argues that the mention in the preamble that the Secretary was considering a requirement of a face-to-face assessment was sufficient to put the public on notice that she might adopt such a requirement. Defendant also points out that she can promulgate regulations that are stricter than those required for accreditation by the JCAHO. Finally, Defendant notes that some commentators did comment on the face-to-face assessment requirement, but that in any event, the adequacy of notice cannot be judged by the number and type of comments in response to the NPRM.

This Court finds that the final rule was in fact the logical outgrowth of the proposed rule. Defendant put the commenters on notice that her overriding concern was for the patient's health and safety, that she sought to minimize the use of restraints and seclusion, and she noted that restraints and seclusion have the potential to produce serious psychological and physical harm to the patient. [ ].

Defendant offered a list of prescriptive examples as possible requirements that she might impose on the use of restraints and seclusion, and stated that it was an open question as to whether further, more stringent, requirements should be adopted. Id. One of these examples was the face-to-face evaluation by a physician of a restrained or secluded person prior to the renewal of an order of restraint or seclusion. Id. Further examples of prescriptive requirements being considered included frequent checking of the patient for comfort and safety, frequent documentation of the patient's condition, an outside time limit on orders of restraint or seclusion, requiring physicians to place time limits on such orders (and noting that time-limited orders may be terminated early if the patient demonstrates a change in the behavior that led to being placed in restraints or seclusion), and requiring such orders to be specific as to date, time, reason, and method of restraint or seclusion. Id. It is clear that the Secretary's goals were to ensure that restraints and seclusion not be overused or improperly used, that patients be frequently monitored while in restraints or seclusion, and that patients be removed from them as soon as possible.

The one-hour requirement imposed in the final rule is a logical outgrowth of the proposed rule, as it specifically addressed those goals; an early face-to-face evaluation of a patient placed in restraints or seclusion would ensure that such restraints or seclusion were being properly used, that the patient's health and safety were not being endangered, and that the restraints or seclusion continued to be necessary. The commenters had fair notice that the Secretary wished to address these concerns in her final rule, and their failure to anticipate the exact contours of the Secretary's final rule does not compel the conclusion that the final rule is not a logical outgrowth of the proposed rule. "They cannot now complain because they misread the regulatory waters, incorrectly anticipated how [the agency] would react to their criticisms, and, consequently, submitted comments that left some things unsaid." [ ].

* * *

D. Did Defendants Violate the Regulatory Flexibility Act?

The Regulatory Flexibility Act ("RFA") [ ] requires agencies to assess the negative impact of their rules on small businesses. An agency must perform an initial regulatory flexibility analysis ("IRFA") in its notice of proposed rulemaking [ ], unless the head of the agency certifies that the rule will not "have a significant economic impact on a substantial number of small entities." [ ]. The agency must also perform a final regulatory flexibility analysis ("FRFA") in its final rule * * *.

In the NPRM, the Secretary made a certification of no significant economic impact, and thus did not perform an IRFA. [ ]. Plaintiffs do not challenge this certification, but argue that because the final rule was so dramatically different from the proposed rule, the Secretary was required to perform an adequate FRFA or certify that the rule would have no significant impact. Plaintiffs argue that the Secretary did neither, but instead made the brief, conclusory, and erroneous statement that she did not "anticipate ... a substantial economic impact on most Medicare-participating hospitals." [ ] Plaintiffs specifically argue that the Secretary completely failed to address the second, fourth and fifth components of FRFAs * * *.

The second component of a FRFA requires the agency to summarize the significant issues raised by the public comments in response to the

IRFA, and to summarize the agency's assessment of those issues. [ ]. Plaintiffs argue that Defendant could not have complied with this component, since she never presented the one-hour rule in the NPRM for public comment. Defendant correctly points out that since an IRFA was not needed because she certified that there would be no significant impact to small businesses (a certification which Plaintiffs do not dispute), there were no IRFA-related issues that the Secretary could have discussed in her FRFA.

The fourth component of a FRFA requires the agency to describe what reporting, recordkeeping, or other compliance requirements the rule would likely produce, and to estimate the classes of small entities which will be subject to the requirement and the type of professional skills necessary for preparation of those compliance requirements. [ ] . Plaintiffs argue that the Secretary made no effort whatsoever to comply with this component, and argue that there is nothing in the final rule discussing reporting or recordkeeping requirements, to ensure the rule is complied with. Defendant is again correct in noting that she has complied with this component: as stated in the FRFA, the only new record-keeping requirement imposed by the rule is a telephone call to HCFA regional offices to report deaths from restraint or seclusion. [ ]

The fifth component of a FRFA requires the agency to describe the steps the agency took to minimize the significant economic impact on small businesses, and to include a "statement of the factual, policy, and legal reasons for selecting the alternative adopted in the final rule and why each one of the other significant alternatives to the rule considered by the agency which affect the impact on small entities was rejected."[ ].

As to this requirement, the Secretary's analysis is severely lacking, and the Court cannot find that she has made a "reasonable, good-faith effort to canvass major options and weigh their probable effects." [citation omitted]. The Secretary did not obtain data or analyze available data on the impact of the final rule on small entities, nor did she properly assess the impact the final rule would have on small entities. Plaintiffs point out that in promulgating a restraint and seclusion rule that would apply to nursing homes, the Secretary estimated the economic impact of that rule would be $35 million, but that she performed no such estimate or analysis with respect to this rule. The Secretary also failed to consider other significant alternatives to the rule before settling on the one-hour rule. There is no discussion of what, if any, steps the agency took to minimize the significant economic impact on small businesses. There is no "statement of the factual, policy, and legal reasons for selecting the alternative adopted in the final rule." There is no discussion of what other significant alternatives which affect the impact on small entities were considered (if any in fact were considered), and why those alternatives were rejected. Defendant protests that her FRFA need not exhibit mathematical exactitude, and need take no special form of presentation, as long as each component is covered somewhere in the final rule. The Secretary is not being held to this high a standard. The fact of the matter is that she has totally failed to comply with section (5) of § 604(a) of the FRFA.

E. Should A Permanent Injunction Be Granted?

Plaintiffs ask the Court to permanently enjoin enforcement of the one-hour rule because of Defendant's violation of the RFA. The well-settled requirements for a permanent injunction are adopted from the requirements for a preliminary injunction: [citations omitted] (1) success on the merits; (2) irreparable harm absent the injunction; (3) the balance of hardship tips in favor of the plaintiff if an injunction is not granted; and (4) the public interest lies in granting an injunction.[ ].

It should be noted that although the statute gives the Court the option of deferring enforcement of the Rule against small entities until completion of a compliant FRFA, the statute also permits continued enforcement of the Rule if the Court finds that continued enforcement is in the public interest. [ ]. Consequently, an injunction should issue only if Plaintiffs can show irreparable harm, and that the public interest would best be served by issuance of an injunction.

First, Plaintiffs have failed to show what, if any, irreparable harm would befall them should the Court refuse to enter an injunction. Plaintiffs argue that they will suffer irreparable harm from the enforcement of the rule, because it will allegedly cost them $100 million to come into compliance with this new requirement. Plaintiffs, however, offer no concrete, reliable evidence to support their contentions of irreparable harm. n9

Second, and more importantly, Defendant has clearly established that the public interest would best be served by continued enforcement of the Rule. The Rule was promulgated to protect patients against the unnecessary and excessive use of restraints or seclusion. Delaying enforcement would create the likelihood that injuries or death could result if the restraints or seclusion continued to be used inappropriately, because restraints and seclusion are dangerous interventions. Given the severe psychological and physical injuries that can and do result from inappropriate use of restraints and seclusion, and the fact that many of these injuries go unreported, the public interest lies in continued enforcement of the Rule.

Consequently, the case will be remanded to the agency for completion of a compliant FRFA, without enjoining continued enforcement of the rule while the agency completes a new FRFA.

TELANG v. COMMONWEALTH OF PENNSYLVANIA BUREAU OF PROFESSIONAL AND OCCUPATIONAL AFFAIRS

Supreme Court of Pennsylvania, 2000.
561 Pa. 535, 751 A.2d 1147.

MR. JUSTICE NIGRO

* * *

Frank Wohlsein Telang, M.D. (Telang) was licensed to practice medicine in Pennsylvania and New Jersey until February 1996, when New Jersey's Board of Medicine suspended his New Jersey license pursuant to a finding that Telang sexually abused one of his patients during the course of her treatment. As a result of New Jersey's action, the Pennsylvania Bureau of Professional and Occupational Affairs petitioned the Pennsylvania State Board of Medicine (Medical Board) to suspend Telang's Pennsylvania license, recommending a minimum three-year suspension. Pursuant to § 40(a) of the Medical Practice Act [ ], the Medical Board immediately suspended Telang's license pending a formal hearing, determining that he posed a clear and immediate danger to the public health and safety. An Order to Show Cause was filed by the Commonwealth [ ], charging Telang with one count of violating the Medical Practice Act.[1]

A formal administrative hearing was held on October 28, 1996. At the hearing, Telang, who was present and represented by counsel, admitted that his license had been suspended by New Jersey and that he had been in psychotherapy for his sexual boundaries problem since April 1996. The Hearing Examiner heard testimony from Telang and from his treating psychotherapist, Julian W. Slowinski (Slowinski). At the conclusion of the hearing, the Hearing Examiner ordered that Telang's license be suspended for at least three years, at which point he would be permitted to apply for reinstatement based on his personal rehabilitation and a showing that he did not pose a substantial risk of harm to the health and safety of his patients. [ ].

Telang filed an Application for Review by the Medical Board seeking a lesser sanction. The Medical Board adopted the findings of fact of the Hearing Examiner. On reviewing the sanction imposed, however, the Medical Board found Telang's conduct "a deplorable violation of patient rights and medical ethics," maintaining that "even a single incidence of sexual abuse of a patient warrants a stringent sanction so that the greatest protection to the public available to the Board is afforded and so that integrity of the profession is maintained." [ ]. Determining that suspension was too lenient, the Medical Board revoked Telang's Pennsylvania license. Thereafter Telang requested reconsideration and a hearing on the issue of revocation, which the Medical Board denied.

Telang appealed to the Commonwealth Court, which reversed the order of the Medical Board, finding that the Medical Board violated Telang's constitutional right to procedural due process by *sua sponte* imposing a harsher punishment than that ordered by the Hearing Examiner without giving Telang notice that such a sanction might be contemplated and without affording him an additional opportunity to

---

1. Telang, a neurologist, was treating a patient for muscle spasms in the neck and back when he "removed [her] gown, fondled and massaged her breasts, massaged her vagina, kissed her head and lay on top of her on the examination table . . . moving his body up and down as if in a sexual manner." [ ]. Telang committed the same conduct with the same patient on two occasions, the second having been recorded on videotape by the patient pursuant to police instructions. [ ] * * *

present evidence with regard to a revocation penalty. We disagree and therefore reverse the Commonwealth Court and reinstate the adjudication and order of the Medical Board.

Here, Telang asserts that he has a property interest in his medical license and must therefore, pursuant to the United States Constitution, be afforded procedural due process before that license can be taken away from him. U.S. CONST. amend. XIV, § 1. In order to afford Telang his constitutional rights, the Commonwealth Court determined that Telang was entitled to additional notice specifying that the Medical Board was considering a harsher sanction, and to a second evidentiary hearing in order to present evidence with respect to revocation of his license. We agree that Telang has a property right in his medical license and that he must be afforded procedural due process in adjudicating any administrative charges against him. [ ]. We nonetheless find that he was afforded the full procedural process due him before the Medical Board's sanction was imposed.

Due process requires that a physician be given notice of the charges against him and an opportunity to be heard. [citations omitted]. It is commonly understood that " 'due process,' unlike some legal rules, is not a technical conception with a fixed content unrelated to time, place and circumstances." Mathews v. Eldridge, 424 U.S. 319, 334, 96 S.Ct. 893, 902, 47 L.Ed.2d 18 (1976). In other words, "due process is flexible and calls for such procedural protections as the particular situation demands." Id. [ ].

Mathews presents three distinct factors to consider in examining the adequacy of procedural due process under the Fourteenth Amendment. The first factor looks at the private interest that will be affected by official action. The second assesses the risk of erroneous deprivation of such interest through the procedures actually used and examines the value, if any, of additional or different procedural safeguards. The third examines the government's interest, including any fiscal and administrative burdens that additional or substitute procedural requirements would entail. [ ].

* * *

Here, it is undisputed that Telang has a substantial property interest in his medical license and that the Commonwealth may not deprive him of that license without adequate due process. [ ]. Thus, the parties do not dispute the first factor of Mathews.

The second factor requires that we assess the risk that Telang, without further due process, may have been erroneously deprived of his license. The Commonwealth Court characterizes Telang as "blindsided" by the Medical Board's ruling because he had "no indication at any time before the Board issued its order that it contemplated a harsher sanction." [ ]. We disagree.

* * * Telang was served Notice stating "[a] formal administrative disciplinary action has been filed against you." The first several lines of the document announces, in capital, underlined letters:

YOU MAY LOSE LICENSES, CERTIFICATES, REGISTRATIONS OR PERMITS WHICH MAY BE IMPORTANT TO YOUR PRACTICE OF YOUR PROFESSION, TRADE OR OCCUPATION

Attached to the Notice was the Order to Show Cause, which advised him:

If the Board finds the Factual Allegations to be true and correct, and determines that the [physician] violated the Act, the Board may, in its discretion, impose one or more of the following penalties: The revocation, suspension or other restriction of any licenses, certifications, registrations, permits or other authorizations to practice a profession held by the [physician] in the Commonwealth of Pennsylvania, or the imposition of any other disciplinary or corrective action which the Act authorizes the Board to impose. [ ]

Thus, before appearing before the Hearing Examiner, Telang knew that license revocation was clearly a possibility and that the Medical Board, as the final adjudicator, could impose such a penalty. Furthermore, [ ] the Medical Practice Act, under which Telang was charged, is captioned "Reasons for refusal, revocation, suspension and other corrective actions against a licensee or certificate holder." [ ]. The implication is that for *any* of the infractions listed [ ], the sanctions enumerated were available.

The record of proceedings before the Hearing Examiner belies the Commonwealth Court's finding that Telang was not afforded an opportunity to present evidence or argue against revocation. At the evidentiary hearing, Telang was represented by counsel and testified on his own behalf, admitting that his New Jersey license had been suspended. Telang further admitted his problem with sexual boundaries, acknowledging that he was in therapy because of it. Therefore, the basis on which disciplinary action could be taken was uncontested. Telang also had the opportunity to present witnesses, and chose his treating psychotherapist to testify as an expert witness. With regard to the sanction to be imposed, both Telang and his expert testified as to mitigating factors to be considered. Slowinski recommended that, rather than suspend Telang, he be allowed to continue practicing while undergoing therapy but that he be constantly monitored when seeing patients. In addition, Slowinski recommended regular reporting and patient feedback on Telang. Finding that Slowinski's opinion was based in part on the unverified history from Telang himself that the abuse of record against the New Jersey patient was Telang's only incident of misconduct, the Hearing Examiner decided that constant monitoring was inadequate, and imposed a minimum three-year suspension. Telang appealed to the Medical Board.

The Medical Board determined, as is its prerogative, that additional evidence and argument was unwarranted because there was no factual dispute as to Telang's conduct, and nothing so complex or technical that the collective expertise of the Medical Board could not comprehend. [citations omitted]. Thus, it was the sole task of the Medical Board to determine what sanction, including possible revocation, fit the offense, which the Medical Board had full and final statutory authority to do. [ ]. Based on the record, the Hearing Examiner herself could have properly revoked Telang's license. Simply because the Medical Board, and not the Hearing Examiner, revoked Telang's license does not warrant adding to the procedural due process already afforded Telang by giving him additional notice and a second hearing to argue his fitness to practice. We therefore find that, based on uncontested facts, there was no risk of error in revoking Telang's license without a second notice and hearing. As such, there was nothing that a second notice and/or hearing would remedy.

The third Mathews factor requires an examination of the nature of the government's interest in the matter and an assessment of additional administrative and fiscal burdens, if any, on the government to afford additional or different procedures. Here, the Commonwealth's interest is its obligation to protect the public from medical licensees who sexually assault their patients. In making its ruling, the Medical Board merely assessed the seriousness of Telang's offense differently than the Hearing Examiner did on the same undisputed facts. This is the Medical Board's prerogative. A second hearing would merely reiterate the facts already undisputed, duplicating the function of the Hearing Examiner and needlessly consuming time and resources. [ ] Moreover, at the hearing, Telang availed himself of ample opportunity to present evidence aimed at mitigating any allowable sanctions. Therefore, a second evidentiary hearing nets mere surplusage at the expense of an unwarranted duplication of the Hearing Examiner's efforts. We therefore find that, under a proper three-factor Mathews analysis, Telang was afforded due process rights commensurate with the circumstances of this case.

We therefore conclude that Telang was afforded full procedural due process from the outset, that his Fourteenth Amendment rights were not violated, and that the Commonwealth Court erred in mandating additional notice and a second evidentiary hearing to accommodate new arguments against revocation of Telang's license. We therefore reverse the Commonwealth Court Order and reinstate the Medical Board's Adjudication and Order.

FAIRFAX NURSING HOME v. DEPARTMENT OF HEALTH & HUMAN SERVICES

United States Court of Appeals for the Seventh Circuit, 2002.
300 F.3d 835.

BACKGROUND

A. *Facts*

Fairfax is a skilled nursing facility ("SNF") [ ] participating in Medicare and Medicaid (collectively "Medicare") as a provider. Regulation of SNFs is committed to the Center for Medicare and Medicare Services, formerly known as the Health Care Financing Administration ("HCFA") and to state agencies with whom the Secretary of Health and Human Services has contracted. [ ]. The primary method of regulation is by unannounced surveys of SNFs, conducted in this case by surveyors of the Illinois Department of Public Health ("IDPH"). [ ]. These surveys are conducted at least once every 15 months. [ ]. If the state survey finds violations of Medicare regulations, the state may recommend penalties to CMS. The civil monetary penalty imposed here was based on an IDPH recommendation.

CMS imposed the penalty because of series of failures in Fairfax's care of ventilator-dependent residents. On December 20, 1996, R10, a ventilator-dependent resident at Fairfax, suffered respiratory distress and required emergency care. Respiratory therapists administered oxygen directly to R10, and one therapist turned off R10's ventilator because the alarm was sounding. Once R10 was stabilized, the therapists left, but neglected to turn the ventilator back on. As a result, R10 died. Prompted by this incident, Fairfax began to develop a policy for the care of ventilator-dependent residents. * * * The policy provided that once the resident was stabilized following an episode of respiratory distress:

> the nurse will check the resident & chart Q 15 minutes X 4 (for a total of 1 hr.) encompassing the following: vital signs/respiratory status oxygen stats [saturation] /lung sounds/vent settings /level of consciousness/ odor color and consistency of secretions & comfort level of the resident. [ ]

On March 2, 1997, R126 was observed to have a low oxygen saturation level, an elevated pulse and temperature, and to be breathing rapidly. These signs indicated that the resident was having respiratory difficulties. R126's physician was called; he ordered a chest x-ray and gave several other instructions. However, contrary to Fairfax's policy, R126's medical chart did not reflect whether these orders were carried out. R126 died shortly thereafter.

On March 5, 1997, R127 was found with low oxygen saturation and mottled extremities. Fairfax staff failed to make a complete assessment, took no vital signs, made no follow-up assessments and did not notify a physician. On March 7, R127 was found cyanotic and required five minutes of ambu-bagging. Nurses charted four follow-up notes, but only observed R127's color and oxygen saturation and took no other vital signs. Also on March 7, during the 7 a.m. to 3 p.m. shift, three episodes of respiratory distress were noted, each of which required ambu-bagging. No physician was called. On March 10, R127's skin was observed turning blue, but there was no record of treatment for respiratory distress and no vital signs or assessments were charted. On March 21, R127 had another episode, this time with mottled legs, shaking and a dangerously low oxygen saturation. The physician was present; R127 was ambu-bagged and administered Valium. There was no complete assessment and no follow-up. On March 25, R127 was found to have a severe infection and died on March 27.

On March 23, 1997, R83 was found nonresponsive with low oxygen saturation, low blood pressure, an elevated pulse rate and a low respiratory rate. R83 was ambu-bagged, and the treating physician was called. The first noted follow-up was an hour later and 2–½ hours passed before R83 was monitored again.

On April 2, 1997, a state surveyor observed a Fairfax employee fail to use sterile procedures while performing tracheostomy care on R6 and R11. The same employee also neglected to hyper-oxygenate the residents before or after suctioning the tracheostomy.

On April 3, 1997, R68 became cyanotic, with low oxygen saturation, which required ambu-bagging and an increase in the amount of oxygen given through the ventilator. The records for R68 failed to note R68's vital signs, and the record did not reflect whether R68 oxygen saturation level ever returned to a normal level. On April 4, R68 was not sufficiently stable to permit a routine tracheostomy change.

After a survey on April 8, 1997, IDPH surveyors determined that Fairfax's actions and omissions posed "immediate jeopardy" to the health and safety of its residents. Specifically, Fairfax had violated [the code pertaining to] the special care of ventilator-dependent residents. CMS concurred and notified Fairfax by a letter dated May 7, 1997, that CMS was imposing a CMP of $3,050 per day for a 105–day period, from December 20, 1996, through April 3, 1997, during which Fairfax was not in substantial compliance with HHS regulations governing the care of ventilator-dependent residents. * * *

* * *

II

DISCUSSION

We must now determine whether substantial evidence supports CMS' conclusion that a state of immediate jeopardy prevailed at Fairfax from December 20, 1996, until April 4, 1997.

We first address Fairfax's argument that the ALJ employed the incorrect legal standard. The regulations set up two basic categories of conduct for which CMPs may be imposed. [ ]. The upper range, permitting CMPs of $3,050 per day to $10,000 per day, is reserved for deficiencies that constitute immediate jeopardy to a resident or, under some circumstances, repeated deficiencies. [ ]. By contrast, the lower range of CMPs, which begin at $50 per day and run to $3,000 per day, is reserved for "deficiencies that do not constitute immediate jeopardy, but either caused actual harm or have the potential for causing more than minimal harm." [ ]. "Immediate jeopardy" is defined as "a situation in which the provider's noncompliance with one or more requirements of participation has caused, or is likely to cause, serious injury, harm, impairment, or death to a resident." [ ]

Fairfax emphasizes the ALJ's use of the term "potential" to describe the probability of harm in several of the ALJ's findings. It submits that the ALJ's use of this terminology establishes that the deficiencies in question were deserving of "lower range" penalties. We take each in turn. Finding 1(b):

> Petitioner failed to carry out the treating physician's orders and failed to properly document R126's medical charts. This had the potential for serious injury, harm, impairment, or death to the resident and constitutes immediate jeopardy. [ ]

Fairfax contends that potential for serious harm is insufficient to constitute immediate jeopardy, which requires that the provider's omission be likely to cause serious harm or death. However, in the discussion below this finding, the ALJ found that "Petitioner was woefully inadequate in the treatment and care of R126.... Such conduct caused or was likely to cause serious injury, harm, impairment or death to the resident." [ ]. The ALJ found that "the record presents a picture of a lackadaisical staff, rather than a staff aggressively treating a pneumonia that was further aggravating the resident's already compromised health." [ ]. The ALJ clearly was aware of the proper standard for immediate jeopardy and applied it correctly.

Finding 1(c) addressed Fairfax's failure to monitor R127 after R127's episodes of respiratory distress. The ALJ found that this monitoring failure "had the potential for serious injury, harm, impairment, or death to the resident and constitutes immediate jeopardy." [ ]. Fairfax argues that this is an indication of the ALJ's application of a lower standard than immediate jeopardy as defined in the regulations. Again, the ALJ's discussion of this finding demonstrates that he was well aware of the proper standard and applied it correctly. The ALJ devoted four pages of his opinion to discussing the treatment of R127, and addressed the specific risks posed to the resident by Fairfax's failure to monitor R127 after several respiratory episodes in close succession. He closes his analysis with a finding that the failures of the staff to assess properly and monitor the patient, as well as the failure to call the treating physician, "exposed the resident to risk of serious injury, harm, impairment, or death." [ ].

The other findings of the ALJ that are questioned by Fairfax, when read in context, likewise make clear that the lapses were of a severe nature.

Finding 1(d) discussed Fairfax's failure to monitor R83 and R68, which "had the potential for serious injury, harm, impairment, or death to the resident and constitutes immediate jeopardy." [ ]. In finding 1(e), which addressed Fairfax's failure to ensure that R6 and R11 received proper tracheostomy care, the ALJ concluded that "this had the potential for serious injury, harm, impairment, or death to the residents and constitutes immediate jeopardy." [ ]. Fairfax again cites the ALJ's failure to use the precise terminology [ ] as evidence that he applied the wrong standard. Close attention to the body of the opinion, once again, reveals that the ALJ both understood the term's meaning and applied it correctly.

In finding 1(c), the ALJ had already discussed the risks posed by Fairfax's failure to monitor residents following an episode of respiratory distress, so there was no need to repeat that discussion in finding 1(d), which dealt with the same issue. The ALJ's conclusion with respect to R83 makes manifestly clear that there was no misunderstanding of the applicable standard: "That R83 survived Petitioner's incompetent care and treatment does not excuse the fact that he was placed at risk of serious injury, harm, impairment, or death." [ ]. With respect to R68, the ALJ remarked in a similar vein: "Ms. Daniels testified that it was 'pretty lucky' that nothing serious happened to R68, because, in a matter of minutes, brain damage could be sustained from lack of oxygen. Petitioner's duty to provide appropriate respiratory care to its ventilator-dependent residents cannot be a matter of chance." [ ] (citation omitted). Under finding 1(d), the ALJ did point out Fairfax's violation of its guidelines and its monitoring errors. The conclusion is inescapable that the monitoring failures described in finding 1(d) could lead to the same dire consequences the ALJ chronicled in finding 1(c). The same is true with respect to finding 1(e). In similar language, the ALJ concluded that patients R6 and R11 were "placed at serious risk of injury, harm, impairment or death" from the "deficient tracheostomy" care that they received. [ ].

As the members of the Appellate Division noted, a fair reading of the ALJ's opinion also makes clear that he focused not simply on the situation of each individual patient, but also on the entire state of readiness in the facility during the time in question. Fairly read, his "bottom line" is that a respiratory patient in Fairfax during the time in question was in continuous jeopardy of serious injury or death because of the systemic incapacity of the facility to render the necessary care to sustain life and avoid serious injury. The record is replete with references to the danger of infection to vent-dependent residents living in nursing homes. The death of R10 was the beginning of a series of events that document all too graphically the finding of the ALJ.

Finally, we note that the ALJ carefully and correctly delineated the entire regulatory scheme before he embarked on his analysis of the individual situations of the patients. This manifestation of his understanding of the distinctions that he is now accused of misunderstanding and misapplying supports further the Appellate Division's estimation—and ours—that he both understood the law and properly applied it.

We also believe that the HHS' decision is supported by substantial evidence. The state surveyors documented numerous instances of Fairfax's failure to care adequately for its respirator-dependent residents. The common thread running through most of these omissions is Fairfax's repeated lack of follow-up and monitoring after a resident experienced respiratory distress. Beginning with the death of R10, and continuing throughout the period in question, Fairfax did not ensure that, once a resident had an episode, that resident was examined at regular intervals in the time immediately following the incident. The record firmly supports HHS' determination that a state of immediate jeopardy to resident health existed at Fairfax from December 20, 1996, until April 3, 1997.

CONCLUSION

The Board's decision was supported by substantial evidence and, therefore, it is affirmed.

Notes

1) Nine states currently have "compassionate use" legislation that permits the medical use of marijuana: Alaska, Arizona, California, Colorado, Hawaii, Maine, Nevada, Oregon and Washington. As a drug with palliative properties but also great potential for abuse, it is not surprising that there is substantial controversy surrounding marijuana's medicinal use. *United States v. Oakland Cannabis Buyer's Cooperative* does not answer the question of whether Congress exceeded its power under the commerce clause when it enacted the Controlled Substances Act. Arguably, the Act attempts to regulate the practice of medicine within a state—a regulation that is exclusively the province of the state. The Court's holding is very narrow: medical necessity does not constitute a defense to manufacturing and distributing marijuana. If, as the Dissent suggests, the people of Oakland want to "serve as a laboratory... [for] novel social and scientific experiments," should state or federal law interfere?

2) The so-called "one-hour rule" for checking on patients who are put into restraints is supported by studies and articles that document improper use of restraints and causality for injury or death. Injuries are both psychological (aggression, withdrawal, morbidity, loss of self-esteem) and physical (burns, pressure sores, limb injury, circulatory obstruction, nerve compression). Is the fact that restraints are in common use, reportedly being applied hundreds of thousands of times per day, and that restraint-related deaths and injuries (perhaps more than 100 per year) go unreported an adequate public health concern to justify the regulations in *National Association of Psychiatric Health*?

3) *Telang* is a new twist on an old theme. Petitioner acknowledged sexually abusing patients in the course of his professional practice and that some sanction was appropriate. The scope of the sanction is within the sound discretion of the state Medical Board, unless that Board exceeds its authority. Telang asserts he has a property interest in his medical license that entitles him to procedural due process in the adjudication of any administrative charges against him. His full scope of due process rights were afforded, and thereafter the Medical Board imposed its sanction. Telang preferred a different sanction, namely supervision while he continued to practice. This option was within the

discretion of the Board, but nothing in his claim of property interest entitles him to any particular sanction.

4) *Fairfax Nursing Home v. Department of Health and Human Services* demonstrates the power of the federal government in matters where it is a payor. Fairfax is a skilled nursing facility ("SNF") that participates in the Medicare and Medicaid programs as a provider. SNFs are regulated by the Center for Medicare and Medicare Services (formerly known as the Health Care Financing Administration) and by state agencies by virtue of contracts with the Department of Health and Human Services. Regulation is accomplished primarily by unannounced surveys. Federal regulations provide that such surveys be conducted at least once every 15 months. Penalties are imposed for violations and monetary fines depend upon the severity of the infraction. In the first instance matters are heard by an Administrative Law Judge, and appeal of the findings can be taken in a court of law, as occurred here.

*

Index

References are to Pages

H

HARASSMENT 659, 854

HARMS Chap 5(b), 242–243, 260, 270, 354, 540, 543–544, 986, 989, 1001, 1006

HEALTH CARE QUALITY IMPROVEMENT ACT (HCQIA) 647, 649–651, 663–664

HEALTH INSURANCE PORTABILITY AND ACCOUNTABILITY ACT OF 1996 (HIPAA) 424, 430–435, 454–456, 531–532, 538, 765, 834

HEALTH MAINTENANCE ORGANIZATION (HMO) 142, 144–145, 147, 154, 158, 170–172, 176, 182, 627, 640–642, 946

HEARSAY 6, 225–227

HUMAN RESEARCH 420, 422, 427

I

IMMUNITY 7, 69–72, 112, 120, 134, 136, 299–302, 309, 314–319, 340–345, 359, 446, 457, 465–469, 484, 609, 611, 649–651, 658–664, 676–677, 977, 979–988, 991
Charitable 112, 127, 300, 309, 319
Governmental 299
Qualified 311, 312, 314, 649, 658, 663, 977, 979, 980, 982, 991

IMPACT RULE 58, 59, 60, 61, 62, 260

IMPLIED CONSENT *see also* EMERGENCY 361, 362, 363, 390, 398, 399

INCIDENT REPORT 630, 648, 651

INCOMPETENT PATIENTS 915, 922

INDEMNIFICATION 107, 136, 297, 298, 626

INDEPENDENT CONTRACTOR 113–117, 125–130, 141–142, 171, 176–177, 457

INDIGENT PATIENTS 17, 40

INDIVIDUAL RIGHTS 356–357, 590, 767, 835, 891, 897, 976, 1030

INDIVISIBLE INJURY 280, 297, 610

INFANTS *see* MINORS, and *see* NEWBORNS 137, 228, 334–338, 375, 376–379, 904–911, 946

INFORMED CONSENT 64, 357, 361–373, 385–386, 391, 401, 404–420, 423–429, 485, 494, 513–521, 543, 754, 757, 806–815, 825–826, 833, 842, 851–852, 855, 901, 913–914, 935, 939

INSTITUTIONAL REVIEW BOARD (IRB) 357, 415, 419, 422, 423, 424, 425, 427, 429

INTENTIONAL:
acts exclusion 565, 566, 567
infliction of emotional distress, *see* Emotional distress 79, 83, 160, 229–234, 269, 291, 316, 527, 530

INTERSTATE COMMERCE 594, 598, 725, 950, 9–953, 957–958, 1006–1022

INTERVENING CAUSE 103, 255–259

INVASION OF PRIVACY 62, 75–77, 524, 527, 538, 680, 744, 755

INVOLUNTARY COMMITMENT *see also* INVOLUNTARY ADMISSION, INVOLUNTARY HOSPITALIZATION 96, 782

IRREBUTTABLE PRESUMPTION 609

J

JOINDER 107, 300, 321

JOINT LIABILITY 280, 499
Tortfeasors *see also* Contribution among tortfeasors 279, 280

JOINT COMMISSION ON ACCREDITATION OF HEALTHCARE ORGANIZATIONS (JCAHO) 629, 1042, 1044

JUDGMENT NOTWITHSTANDING THE VERDICT (JNOV) 137, 138, 189, 269, 290, 358, 359, 550

JUDICIAL BYPASS 842, 855–858

JURY TRIAL 190, 278, 335–336, 351, 484, 573, 589–592, 599–606, 608, 611, 616, 622

K

KNOWLEDGE OF FAULT 326

L

LABEL WARNING 716

LACHES 508

LEARNED INTERMEDIARY 47–479, 483–484

LIABILITY INSURANCE 126, 336–337, 346, 539–544, 548–549, 554–560, 567, 619, 620

LIABILITY WITHOUT FAULT *see* STRICT LIABILITY 467

LIBEL *see also* DEFAMATION 525, 544, 976

LIFE–SUPPORT EQUIPMENT 938

†